AF541049

DEVELOPMENT ADMINISTRATION

Potentialities and Prospects

DR. S.L. GOEL

Professor of Public Administration (Retd.),
Panjab University, Chandigarh
Editor, Indian Journal of Public Administration, IIPA, New Delhi
Former Member, UGC, Former Member Distance Education Council
Former Member All India Board of Management, AICTE
Member, Executive Council, IIPA, New Delhi.
Former Vice-President, IIPA, New Delhi.
Emeritus Fellow, University Grants Commission
Former Director, State Bank of India (Local Board) Chandigarh
Former Director, National Horticulture Board, Ministry of Agriculture,
Government of India, New Delhi.

DEEP & DEEP PUBLICATIONS PVT. LTD.

F-159, Rajouri Garden, New Delhi-110027

DEVELOPMENT ADMINISTRATION
Potentialities and Prospects

ISBN 978-81-8450-206-0

Typeset by S.S. COMPOSERS
3190, Mohindra Park, Shakur Basti, Delhi-110034.

Printed in India at MAYUR ENTERPRISES
WZ Plot No. 3, Gujjar Market, Tihar Village, New Delhi-110018.

Published by DEEP & DEEP PUBLICATIONS PVT. LTD.
F-159, Rajouri Garden, New Delhi-110027.
Phones: 25435369, 25440916
E-mail: ddpbooks@yahoo.co.in • ddpubs@gmail.com
Showroom:
2/13, Ansari Road, Daryaganj, New Delhi-110002 • Telefax: 23245122

Contents

Preface

Development is an essential ingredient for socio-economic development of a country especially for people living in developing countries. In addition, development, as stated in Eleventh Five Year Plan must be inclusive, i.e. based on equity and social justice. Public administration is supposed to accelerate the process of development so that people living in poverty, disease unemployment, squalor, etc. can be removed from these irritating situations.

Mohbub ul Haq observes that the basic purpose of development is to enlarge people's choices. In principle, these choices can be infinite and can change over time. People often value achievements that do not show up at all, or not immediately, in income and growth figures; greater access to knowledge, better nutrition and health services, more secure livelihood, security against crime and physical violence, satisfying leisure hours, political and cultural freedoms and sense of participation in community activities. The objective of development is to create an enabling environment for people to enjoy long, healthy and creative lives.

However, our administrative system—a legacy of colonial rule—stands in the way of accelerated socio-economic development, causing stress and strain to our polity which is struggling to march towards socio-economic equity. The emerging challenges of economic globalisation, political decentralisation and social empowerment tend to go along with liberalisation of economy, regionalisation of polity and localisation of society. These factors have had a consistent impact on the role of the administrative systems. There is an all-round agreement now that liberalisation, privatisation and globalisation of economy is here to stay. The responsibility of the public service in the changing circumstances is being concentrated in certain areas and transformed in other areas. The regulatory mechanism during this evolving period requires a high level of professionalism, changed outlook, paradigm shift in policy-making and accuracy and inclusiveness in service delivery.

In order to avoid the problems faced by Public Administration in solving human problems, a new administration known as Development Administration was designed which was supposed to be dynamic, creative, innovative and people's friendly and would solve the ever increasing problems of the people in India. In the words of Donald Stone: "Development Administration is the blending of all the elements and resources (human and physical) … into a concerted effort to achieve agreed-upon goals. It is the continuous cycle of formulating, evaluating and implementing interrelated plans, policies, programs, projects, activities and other measures to reach established development objectives in a scheduled time sequence." However in practice, results are not being achieved. All the countries are engaged in finding problems and their solutions through reforms.

However, Development Administration failed to inject the desired change and promote the welfare of the people. Pt. Jawaharlal Nehru, Former Prime Minister of India's dream of welfare of people could not be achieved which he always cherished. According to him, "Administration is meant to achieve something and not to exist in some kind of Ivory towers following certain rules of procedures and looking Narcissus like. The test of administration is the welfare of the people. Sh. T.N. Chaturvedi, in his editorial to *Fifty Years of Indian Administration: Retrospect and Prospects*, published by IIPA, New Delhi (1998) rightly observed that since the search for good administration—dynamic and sensitive, responsive and responsible, efficient and effective—and, consequently, the need for its restructuring and remodeling—not necessarily its reinventing—is something of a moving equilibrium in human affairs in an unstable and uncertain world. Hence, the paramount need for, and sustained interest in and attention to matters administrative which are dismissed lightly at considerable cost to society later on.

Development Administration in order to be operative needed changes in public administration system currently in force which could not materialize. The objective of good governance is to create an environment so that public servants as well as politicians in government are able to respond to the challenges of governance. Such challenges involve a notion of duty, vocation, and service to the public. Public service as an ideal is and has been the classical view of good governance. How to improve services to citizens by government agencies has been a major cause of concern to governments all over the world. The author emphasizes that unless the reforms address the issue of corruption in the public service, no reform will be hailed as good by the public. Keeping in view the colossal size of the nation's administrative machinery, easy and quick reforms may not be an astute option. One must also keep in mind the constant and ever-growing disruptive impacts of frequent public service reforms and institutional reorganisations. The public service of today requires far-reaching and perhaps unanticipated changes if India is to actualise its great potentialities to be counted among the ranks of great nations. From the ashes of New Public Management, a new phoenix is emerging in the name of Integrated Public Governance (IPG) which is in fact closely related to 'holistic governance'.

Writing Foreword for the Tenth Five Year Plan, 2002-07, the Prime Minister stated that—India can actualise its great potentialities and can be counted among the ranks of great nations—through good governance, creation of a common economic space, removal of the regime of pervasive controls and restrictions towards developing investor-friendly climate, and ensuring accountable institutions and public servants. The essential ingredient for successful transformation depends upon improving the quality of governance, service delivery along with administrative and judicial efficiency. For India to transform itself from an agrarian economy to a modern multi-dimensional economic power-house with supportive administrative infrastructure, necessary reforms in its statecraft are required.[1]

One of the most important Characteristics of Development Administration is the administrative capability which can translate inputs into outputs. Most of the significant recommendations on civil service reforms in the past failed to yield desired result because the mindset of civil servants implementing these recommendations did not change. As a result, most of the civil servants are looked down upon as a predatory group of power brokers. With such an unsavoury public perception, civil servants can hardly be relied upon as trustworthy facilitators in the context of globalisation and liberalisations. The best reform that any Commission can usher will be to make the bureaucracy duty conscious and service-oriented.[2]

1. O.P. Dwivedi, On Administrative Reforms Messages, *IJPA*, July-Sept. 2007, p. 34.
2. P.C. Hota, Administrative Reforms in the era of Liberalization, Globalisation: Need for Change of Mind-set of Civil Servants, *IJPA*, July-Sept., 2007, p. 356.

Good governance is the aim of Development Administration which can if implemented earnestly provide decent services to the people and make development a reality. To quote Second Administrative Reforms Commission: Without good governance, no amount of developmental schemes can bring improvements in the quality of life of the citizens. Good governance has four elements—transparency, accountability, predictability and participation. Transparency refers to availability of information to the general public and clarity about functioning of governmental institutions. Right to information opens up government's records to public scrutiny, thereby arming citizens with a vital tool to inform them about what the government does and how effectively, thus making the government more accountable. Transparency in government organisations makes them function more objectively thereby enhancing predictability. Information about functioning of government also enables citizens to participate in the governance process effectively. In a fundamental sense, right to information is a basic necessity of good governance.

Ajay Banerjee in *The Tribune* dated Feb. 22, 2009 stated that the Comptroller and Auditor General of India commenting on the fiscal ending March 31, 2008, tabled a report in the Rajya Sabha on 21st February, 2009 and showed how a whopping Rs. 1.09 lakh crore were unutilized. In some cases, especially in case of education and minority welfare, the entire allocation, shockingly, were unutilized. Seventeen of the ministries "persistently" returned allocated money without spending. It also raises a question mark over the claims made to have allocated more money for the social sector.

Prime Minister Manmohan Singh in his 15th August 2005 speech from the Red Fort emphasized the need of development administration to promote dynamism in the country. To quote him: "I would like to say that the biggest challenge in running a Government is to ensure that development programmes are implemented in an effective manner. We will ensure that our outlays of expenditure are visible to citizens as outcomes of progress. The Central Government, State Governments and Panchayats have to work together so that the expectations of people are fulfilled. If we have to achieve results, there is need to change the manner in which, government functions. There is no space in our government or in our society for corruption and arbitrary action. We are not prepared to tolerate this at any cost. Government servants must work with a sense of public service and they should be held accountable to the people. Government will have to be made more transparent and accountable. The recently passed Right to Information Act is a landmark step in this direction."

U.C. Agarwal has also highlighted the factors which stand in the way of Development Administration. To quote him: Efficient financial system and its management are vital for the economic development and prosperity of a country. Inspite of huge allocations and a genuine concern for disadvantaged and deprived strata of society the progress of social sector development in India is rather tardy. Besides very large increase in population the single most conspicuous factor for this sluggishness in development is due to inadequacies of implementation and delivery mechanisms. Lack of focussed planning, delays in critical allocations, bureaucratic wrangling and rampant corruption have contributed to failed targets. Yet the strides made in individual sectors have yielded encouraging results.

We cannot assume that the transitions between different stages of development is always so blurred. What is needed is little bit of fine tuning to reflect results of various sectors in nation's Human Development Index. Outlays and outcomes are like optimism and skepticism in development. Characteristically, the hope involves redefinition of past and present in terms of an imagined future. This optimism lies in the fact that an intelligent policy can shape implementation and influence outcomes.

Eleventh Five Year Plan (2007-12) also stresses the role of good governance in making development administration a success. The Eleventh Plan vision of inclusive growth, reducing poverty and bridging the various divides that continue to fragment our society can only be achieved if there is a significant improvement in the quality of governance. There are many different definitions of good governance but it is generally agreed that good governance must be broadly defined to cover all aspects of the interface between individuals and businesses on the one hand and government on the other.

In 2005, the Second Administrative Reforms Commission (ARC) was constituted to prepare a detailed blue print for revamping the public administration system. The First ARC was constituted in 1966 and subsequently several committees and commissions have examined and given recommendations on various aspects of reforming governance. The Second ARC has been given very comprehensive Terms of Reference and it has been asked to suggest measures to achieve a proactive, responsive, accountable, sustainable and efficient administration for the country at all levels of government. The Commission has already submitted Eleven reports on different aspects of administration. It is also working on several other areas including civil service reforms, citizen centric administration, and reorganizing the structure of the government.

The Department of Administrative Reforms and Public Grievances has proposed a framework for good governance in the form of a Code of Governance. The main components of this Code are: (i) improving service delivery; (ii) development of programmes for weaker sections and backward areas; (iii) technology and system improvement; (iv) financial management and budget sanctity; (v) accountability and transparency; (vi) public service morale and anti-corruption; and (vii) incentivizing reforms.

The Tenth Plan drew attention to the implementation of good governance in the following terms: Governance relates to the management of all such processes that, in any society, define the environment which permits and enables individuals to raise their capability levels on the one hand, and provide opportunities to realize their potential and enlarge the set of available choices, on the other. These processes, covering the political, social and economic aspects of life impact every level of human enterprise, be it the individual, the household, the village, the region or the nation. It covers the State, civil society and the market, each of which is critical for sustaining human development. The State is responsible for creating a conducive political, legal and economic environment for building individual capabilities and encouraging private initiative. The market is expected to create opportunities for people. Civil society facilitates the mobilization of public opinion and people's participation in economic, social and political activities.

Development Administration is the essential ingredient for delivering economic development and social upliftment. Administrative culture mediates among individuals, groups and communities that needs to be strengthened if the new millennium is to be made meaningful and socially productive.

Development Administration is dependent mainly on the excellence of human beings in Government and the enlightened citizenry. Development Administration can keep this universe in equilibrium wherein all people can enjoy a decent life, both physical and spiritual. Development Administration must be based on Rule of Law which means that the society must be governed by law or Dharma and not according to the whims and fancies of administrators.

Governance is the manner in which authority, control and power of government is exercised in mobilizing a society's economic and social resources to address the issues of public interest. It is the art of governing, associated with the exercise of authority within specific jurisdiction, and is embedded in the structure of authority. Good governance is epitomized by, among other things, predictable, open and enlightened policy-making. It can be secured by sound, responsive and competent administration, respect to basic human rights and values, strengthened democratic, institutional as well as structural framework to ensure accountability and transparency.

Government, after all, is a tryst with trust, a commitment of the people, for the people, a social contract for the greatest good, the collective conscience of the community. It is not the handiwork of wayward politicians or handmaiden of bureaucrats, or the property of the unscrupulous handfuls who manipulate minority at majority cost; people must have a stake in the government, for people have a stake in their future. Future is the place where all of us will live in the rest of our lives.[3]

The tests of good governance lie in the goals and objectives of a government, in its policies and programmes, in the manner of their execution, in the results achieved and above all, in the general perception of the people about the quality of functioning of its various agencies, their attitudes and behaviour towards the public, their sincerity, honesty and commitment towards public duties. It is also important to see that there is no undue concentration of power.[4]

All the above mentioned functions of Government can only be carried out by well designed theory and practice of Development Administration which would provide the mechanism to attain the welfare of the people. Development administration, in order to be successful should act on the following principles:

(i) Openness in the sense of having wide contact with the people administered;
(ii) A sense of justice, fair play and impartiality in dealing with men and matters;
(iii) Sensitivity and responsiveness to the urges, feelings and aspirations of the common people;
(iv) Securing the honour and dignity of the human being, however humble he or she might be;
(v) Humility and simplicity in the persons manning the administrative machinery and their easy accessibility;
(vi) Creating and sustaining an atmosphere conducive to development and growth and social change; and
(vii) Honesty and integrity in thought and action.

Ethics in development administration is one of the very essential conditions for the stability and development of the country and the well-being of its citizens. History of several countries indicate that serious moral degradation has generated conflicts, miseries and even disintegrations. The civil service conduct rules requires the civil servants to maintain absolute integrity in the discharge of their duties.

To ensure the success of development administration, there is a need to develop good administrative traditions, which may impel civil servants to perform their activities impartially to keep the administration above broad. The civil servants at higher levels of administration must set standards of independence and impartiality through constant practice. Such standards would be imbibed consciously or unconsciously by the personnel at lower echelons in the administration.

---

3. Bata K. Dey, Defining Good Governance, in *IJPA*, July-Sept., 1998, p. 427.
4. U.G. Aggarwal, Good Governance, in *IJPA*, July-Sept. 1998, p. 427.

In this book, "Development Administration: Potentialities and Prospects" the author has covered large number of topics which directly or indirectly impinge on the functioning of Development Administration. The contents reflect the wide coverage in this Book. It is hoped that this book would make a modest contribution to the knowledge and existing literature on this expanding field. Besides, this would help the academicians, national officials, public administrators, research workers and the policy-makers and planners in the proper understanding of the potentialities of Development Administration and its facets. I shall consider my labour well rewarded if the findings of the study are translated to provide decent delivery of development services to the millions of people living in rural areas, urban slums and tribal areas. Development Administration would ensure

(a) Making administration responsive
(b) Making administration citizen-friendly
(c) Making administration transparent
(d) Making administration ethical
(e) Making public services excellent
(f) Making equity and social justice
(g) Making inclusive growth
(h) Making sustainable environment
(i) Making Government machinery development-oriented.

Comments and suggestions from the readers would always be welcome.

Chandigarh S.L. GOEL

CHAPTER

1

Development, Social Development and Social Welfare Administration

The progress and prosperity of a nation is judged from the Socio-Economic status of its population especially of the weaker sections of the society suffering from abject poverty, hunger, disease, unemployment, exploitation, etc. as well as disadvantaged groups like women, children, scheduled castes, tribal people, etc. It is of the prime importance that such segments of the society mostly living in remote, backward, hilly, rural and tribal areas should receive the serious and earnest attention of policy-makers, planners, social welfare administrators, social scientists and academicians, so that the down-trodden section of the society can also live decent life ensured to them by the Constitution of India in 1950 through special provisions in the nature of Fundamental Rights and Directive Principles of the State Policy. This will enable the national endeavour for establishment of a better social order based on Equality, Liberty and Fraternity as mentioned in the Preamble to the Constitution of India and this, in turn, would involve them in the task of national development and modernization.

Swami Ranganathanada observes that this is my interest—to orient the human mind in India in terms of the development of the people of India, for that is what is meant by freedom—freedom to build up this nation. It must become a passion in the minds of people and, particularly, in politics and in administration. We are unhappy and as the years roll by, this human value, this human factor, has been eroded. Everything else is there, power is there, money is there. But the human factor is getting eroded. Naturally the development process becomes arrested and the meaning of freedom becomes absolutely meaningless. After centuries of political subjection, we attained freedom. We have struggled hard to get this freedom. Every leader during the freedom struggle, both political and cultural and spiritual, say, men like Vivekananda or Gandhi, they always emphasized that we need freedom to shape the destiny of all our people. Today we have that opportunity to build up this great nation, this immense manhood and womanhood.[1]

Gone are the days when the wheels of administration were set in motion simply to maintain law and order primarily to safeguard the personal interests of the ruling class. Poverty, backwardness and inequalities are neither regarded as preordained nor as inevitable evil. The process of development is now adopted by the modern states to lift their people from deprivation, disease, disasters and disabilities. The concern for promoting individual happiness and an ardent desire for strengthening community welfare activities through a process of socio-economic development are being considered among the essential characteristics of the modern welfare states.

Mohammad Mohabbat Khan in his article "Development: Meaning, Strategies and Goals" in Rakesh Hooja and K.K. Parnson (eds.) clearly defined that development then can only be understood as a collective process in which the concerns and interests of the entire population is taken into consideration. The fruit of development is shared equitably by all. Fundamentally, development is a process of change which takes place in a society when surrounding social, political, economic and cultural conditions are favourable for such a change. That is why development is defined intra-contactually, that is, in terms of each individual country and according to its own perceived needs, wants and aspirations.

MEANING AND GOALS OF DEVELOPMENT (See Chart 1.1)

The word 'development' is so often used in our daily life that we hardly care to think of its real meaning. The meaning of the term 'develop' is to unfold itself or to grow into a fuller or mature condition, and 'ment' stands for instrument of action, an act or process. In simple words development can be defined as a process of directed change towards some objectives which are accepted as desirable goals. Development implies progressive improvements in the living conditions and quality of life enjoyed by society and shared by its members. It is a continuing process that takes place in all societies.

So development is a multi-dimensional process.[2] It means the continual improvement of the quality of human life.[3] This indicates that development has been conceptualised as a phenomenon of change and growth. It is indeed a dynamic concept.[4]

Development is the centre of politics of all countries, especially in the developing world.[5] It is a universal problem as one American Scholar has observed: "the whole world is caught up in the concept of development—there seems to be no escaping it."[6] It is the issue which has drawn the attention of international community to the twin problems of 'nation-building' and 'socio-economic progress'. International peace and security and international economic and social order will remain insignificant until the problem of 'underdevelopment' and 'mal-development' is solved. The aims and principles of the United Nations will remain only intents if the developing world lags behind the national development. National development is the major goal of countries which have got independent status after World War II. In these countries, national development or modernization is the centre of their politics. The question, 'how to achieve national development is the greatest challenge to the world community today'. Citizens of the developing world are aware of the advancements made in their counterparts. They cannot fail to be impressed by the developed economy and the high level of living in developed countries. Like the developed world, the developing world wants to be modern. There is national resurgence, self-realization and aspiration for self-assertion and rapid socio-economic progress. A new outlook is visible in the developing world. But its major task is the reconstruction of national development. To quote from a United Nations publication: "There is great pressure on Governments to accelerate national development, make use of up-to-date and relevant technological innovations, adopt and facilitate necessary institutional changes, increase national production, make full use of human and their

CHART 1.1

Progressive Improvements of Quality of Life

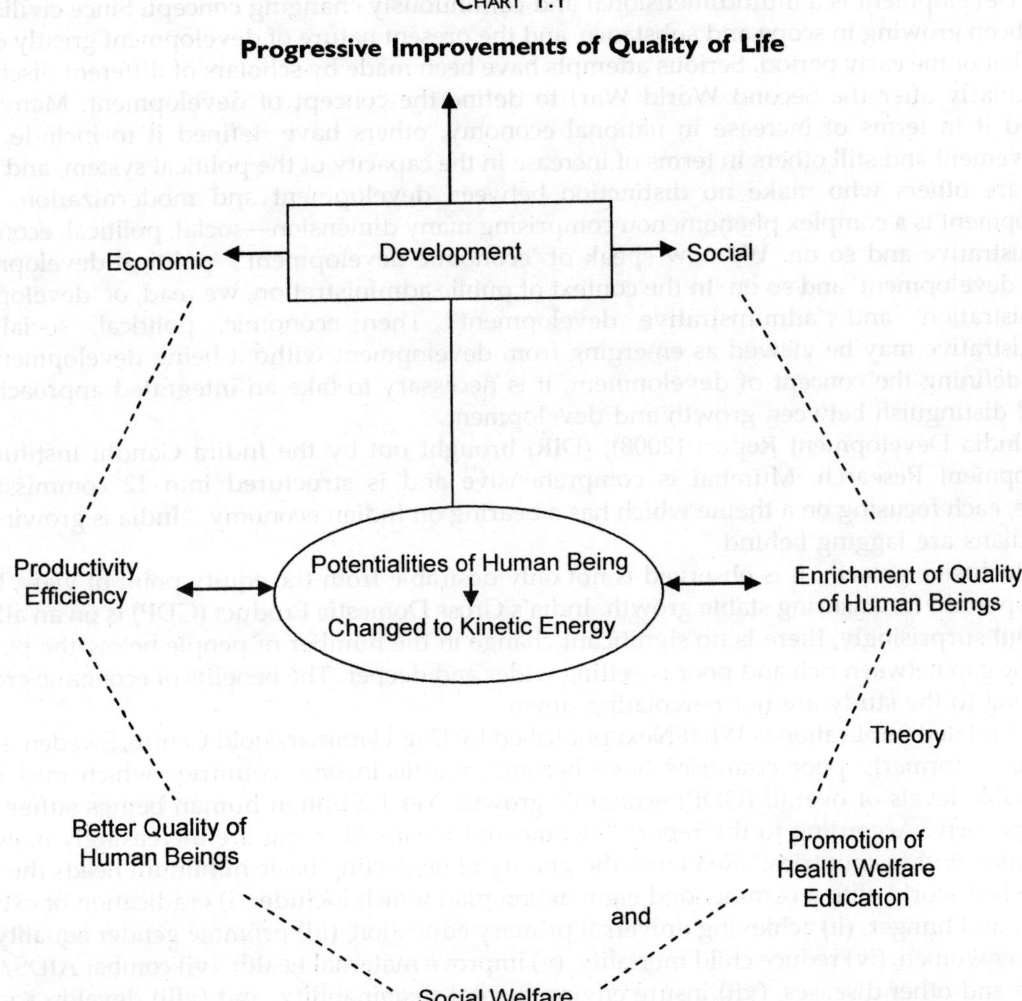

resources, and improve the level of living."[7] The developing world now faces the challenge of accelerating the rate of socio-economic development. Countries of the developing world aspire to modernity.[8] There is high ambition to achieve national development. However, ambition alone does not solve the problem of mal-development and under-development. They have to struggle hard to develop their economy, to sustain improvement in social system and to increase the capacity of the political system with a view to achieving the major goal of national development or modernization.

In other words, it could be said that economic development could be helpful in the process of social development in a vital sense. A.P. Barnabas suggests, "For development to be achieved, there is already a need of establishing a close relations with the people, change cannot be brought about without motivating people and motivation cannot be achieved without establishing personal relations."[9]

Development is a multidimensional and continuously changing concept. Since civilization it has been growing in scope and substance, and the present nature of development greatly differs from that of the early period. Serious attempts have been made by scholars of different disciplines (particularly after the Second World War) to define the concept of development. Many have defined it in terms of increase in national economy, others have defined it to include social improvement and still others in terms of increase in the capacity of the political system, and while there are others who make no distinction between development and modernization. Thus, development is a complex phenomenon comprising many dimension—social, political, economic, administrative and so on. We now speak of 'economic development', 'political development', 'social development' and so on. In the context of public administration, we read, of 'development administration' and 'administrative development'. Then economic, political, social and administrative may be viewed as emerging from development without being development. So, while defining the concept of development, it is necessary to take an integrated approach. We should distinguish between growth and development.

India Development Report (2008), (DIR) brought out by the Indira Gandhi Institute for Development Research, Mumbai is comprehensive and is structured into 12 commissioned articles, each focusing on a theme which has a bearing on Indian economy. "India is growing but the Indians are lagging behind."

Inclusive growth, it is observed is not only desirable from the equity point of view, but is also important for ensuring stable growth. India's Gross Domestic Product (GDP) is on an all time high, but surprisingly, there is no significant change in the number of people below the poverty line. The gap between rich and poor is getting wider and deeper. The benefits of economic growth, according to the study are not percolating down.

A related publication is What Next published by Dag Hammarskjold Centre, Sweden, stated that many formerly poor countries have become middle income countries which may show remarkable levels of overall (GDP) economic growth. Yet 1.2 billion human beings suffer from abject poverty. According to the report "income and means of living are increasingly unevenly distributed within countries." Realizing the gravity of neglecting basic minimum needs the post-globalished world elite recommended eight action plan which include: (i) eradication of extreme poverty and hunger, (ii) achieving universal primary education, (iii) promote gender equality and empower women, (iv) reduce child mortality, (v) improve maternal health, (vi) combat AIDS/HIV, malaria and other diseases, (vii) insure environmental sustainability, and (viii) develop a global partnership for development. According to this report questions about who caused world poverty is never raised by the elite and questions that were central to New International Economic Order of 1980's are not raised. What needs to the understood is that development has two sides. If policy-makers take only the growth path the difficulties in translating growth to development can not be appreciated. A slew of policy options taken to protect the unprotected perhaps may ensure inclusive growth.

The experience of developing countries policy-makers show that their interest in pushing policies aimed at massive increase in economic growth has not been matched by similar efforts at appreciating the role of non-economic factors in development.[10] Eleventh Five Year Plan uses the word Inclusive Growth for Development.

Montek Singh Ahluwalia, Deputy Chairman, Planning Commission observes in his preface to XIth Plan. The Eleventh Plan began in very favourable circumstances with the economy having grown at the rate of 7.7% per year in the Tenth Plan period. However, for too many of our people still lack the basic requirements for a decent living in terms of nutrition standards, access to education and basic health, and also to other public services such as water supply and sewerage. Disadvantaged groups, especially the Scheduled Castes and Scheduled Tribes and the minorities have benefited less than they should have. Regional imbalances have emerged across and even within states.

The Eleventh Plan seeks to remedy these deficiencies by seeking to accelerate the pace of growth while also making it more inclusive. The growth objective is to achieve an average growth rate of 9% per annum for the Plan period. The objective of inclusiveness is reflected in the adoption of 26 other monitorable targets at the national level relating to (i) income and poverty, (ii) education, (iii) health, (iv) women and children, (v) infrastructure, and (vi) environment. Some of these national targets have also been disaggregated into 13 state level targets and it is expected that the state governments design policies and programmes to achieve them.

The strategy for achieving faster growth with greater inclusiveness involves several interrelated components. These are: (i) a continuation of the policies of economic reform which have created a buoyant and competitive private sector capable of benefiting from the opportunities provided by greater integration with the world, (ii) a revival in agricultural growth which is the most important single factor affecting rural prosperity, (iii) improved access to essential services in health and education (including skill development) especially for the poor, which is essential to ensure inclusiveness and also to support rapid growth, (iv) a special thrust on infrastructure development which is a critical area for accelerating growth, (v) environmental sustainability which is becoming increasingly important, (vi) special attention to the needs of disadvantaged groups, and (vii) good governance at all levels, Central, state, and local.

The percentage of the population below the official poverty line has come down from 36% in 1993-94 to 28% in 2004-05. However, not only is this still high, the rate of decline in poverty has not accelerated along with the growth in GDP, and the incidence of poverty among certain marginalized groups, for example the STs, has hardly declined at all. Because population has also grown, the absolute number of poor people has declined only marginally from 320 million in 1993-94 to 302 million in 2004-05. This performance is all the more disappointing since the poverty line on which the estimate of the poor is based is the same as it was in 1973-74 when per capita incomes were much lower. Other indicators of deprivation suggest that the proportion of the population deprived of a minimum level of living is much higher. For example, National Family Health Survey-3 (NFHS-3) shows that almost 46% of the children in the 0 to 3 years' age group suffered from malnutrition in 2005-06, and what is even more disturbing is that the estimate shows almost no decline from the level of 47% reported in 1998 by NFHS-2.

Indicators of human development such as literacy and education, and maternal and infant mortality rates, show steady improvement, but they also suggest that the progress is slow and we continue to lag behind several other Asian countries. While the literacy rate has gone up from 18.3% in 1951 to 64.8% in 2001, the number of illiterate persons still exceeds 304 million, making India the country with the highest number of illiterate persons in the world. Life expectancy at birth has increased from approximately 32 years for both males and females in 1951 to 63.9 years for male and 66.9 years for females in 2001-06. Yet this is well below the life expectancy of around 80 years in industrialized countries and 72 years in China. Although Indian women now have higher life expectancy than Indian men, as is the case of industrialized countries, India also has an adverse sex ratio with only 933 women per 1000 men. More disturbing, the child sex ratio has declined sharply from 962 in 1981 to 927 in 2001. India's maternal and infant mortality rates are much higher than those of countries in East Asia, showing poor access to essential health care services.

Vision for the Eleventh Plan

The central vision of the 11th Plan is to build on our strengths to trigger a development process which ensures broad-based improvement in the quality of life of the people, especially the poor, SCs/STs other backward castes (OBCs), minorities and women. This broad vision of the Eleventh Plan includes several inter-related components; rapid growth that reduces poverty and creates employment opportunities, access to essential services in health and education especially for the poor, equality of opportunity, empowerment through education and skill development, employment opportunities underpinned by the National Rural Employment Guarantee, environmental sustainability, recognition of women's agency and good governance.[11]

According to Esman, development is the rational process of organizing and carrying out prudently conceived and staffed programmes or projects as one would organize and carry out military or engineering operations.[12] To Colm and Geiger, development means change plus growth.[13] Weidner defines it as a "process of growth" in the direction of "nation-building and socio-economic progress."[14] To T.N. Chaturvedi, it is a process which stands for "transformation of society."[15]

Fred W. Riggs defines development in terms of "rising levels of autonomy or discretion (of social systems) in the sense of ability to choose among alternatives, not, of course, in the sense of caution or moderation."[16] He introduces the concept of development "as an increase in the level of discretion of social systems." His definition first stresses the 'growth' made possible by the autonomy of the social systems which (social systems) can transform or reshape the environment. Second, it emphasizes 'performance value' "increasing efficiency, reducing costs, improving the machinery of production of government, of administration."[17] Third, it stresses "the justice values of freedom, independence, equality, change, even revolution."[18] Fourth, it seeks to restructure the social systems. Fifth, it involves levels of diffraction which is a necessary condition for achieving autonomy. Riggs says, "development involves the ability to choose whether or not to increase outputs, whether or not to raise levels of per capita income, or to direct energies to other goals, to the more equitable distribution of what is available, to aesthetic or spiritual values, or the qualitatively different kinds of outputs."[19]

Hahn-Been Lee defines development "as a process of acquiring a sustained growth of a system's capability to cope with new, continuous changes toward the achievement of progressive political, economic and social objectives."[20] Lee sees development as both process and purpose. To Wu "development is a process of societal transformation from a traditional society to a modern society, and such a transformation is also known as modernization."[21]

There has been, in recent years, an intense effort to redefine the concept of development. The strategies assiduously promoted and followed in the three decades after the Second World War are under critical re-examination. Numerous World leaders and others concerned with the welfare of the people and with civilization are striving to bring new concepts and strategies to the fore, and their acceptance and translation into action will require political courage, Optimism and faith in the human race. The index of a society's development should be not merely in terms of the GNP but in terms of opportunities for enhancement of the human potential—genetic, intellectual or other for improving quality of life and satisfaction.

U.C. Agarwal observes, "I would like to say that the biggest challenge in running a Government is to ensure that development programmes are implemented in an effective manner. We will ensure that our outlays of expenditure are visible to citizens as outcomes of progress. The Central Government, State Governments and Panchayats have to work together so that the expectations of people are fulfilled. If we have to achieve results, there is need to change the manner in which, government functions. There is no space in our government or in our society for corruption and arbitrary action. We are not prepared to tolerate this at any cost. Government servants must work with a sense of public service and they should be held accountable to the people. Governments will have to be made more transparent and accountable. The recently passed Right to Information Act is a landmark step in this direction."

Efficient financial system and its management are vital for the economic development and prosperity of a country. Inspite of huge allocations and a genuine concern for disadvantaged and deprived strata of society the progress of social sector development in India is rather tardy. Besides very large increase in population the single most conspicuous factor for this sluggishness in development is due to inadequacies of implementation and delivery mechanisms. Lack of focused planning, delays in critical allocations, bureaucratic wranglings and rampant corruption have contributed to failed targets. Yet the strides made in individual sectors have yielded encouraging results.

We cannot assume that the transitions between different stages of development is always so blurred. What is needed is little bit of fine tuning to reflect results of various sectors in nation's Human Development Index. Outlays and outcomes are like optimism and scepticism in development. Characteristically, the hope involves redefinition of past and present in terms of an imagined future. This optimism lies in the fact that an intelligent policy can shape implementation and influence outcomes.

Truly, "outlays" alone are no guarantee of higher "outcomes." Efficient implementation is very necessary to get the return from every rupee of investment. That was perhaps the intention why the Prime Minister wished to address the collectors directly as they are the king pin for developmental activities in the social sector in the field. Their enthusiasm and commitment are, equally if not more, important than higher budgetary allocations. To convert "outlays" into matching "outcomes" honest, sincere and committed implementation agencies are required. Public administration must aim to provide man-power of the required qualities. No less important, however, is that the political leadership on its part inspires confidence of the persons engaged in implementation of development works so that honest officials need not worry about unfair and false allegations if any made against them by persons with vested interests. Thus in addition to higher "outlays" a host of other factors count no less for obtaining better "outcomes."[22]

The purpose of development is to bring about improvement in the quality of peoples lives by expanding their choices, freedom and dignity. One of the major areas of social development in India is eradication of poverty. Poverty involves much more than restrictions imposed by lack of income. It also entails lack of basic capabilities to lead full, creative, lives. Such deprivations distinguish human poverty from income poverty. Social sector development seeks to address both income as well as human poverty. While economic growth is necessary for increased public spending on social development, it is hardly sufficient. If sufficient investment in social sector is neglected or there is discrimination against the vulnerable sections among population groups, this will weaken the potential benefits that overall economic growth can provide for meeting social development goals. This may lead to what Human Development Reports say 'ruthless growth' - growth does not reach poor people, either because richer households receive most of the increase in income or because governments do not use additional revenue to invest in the social development needs.[23]

The concept of human development introduced by UNDP in the 1990s is now accepted worldwide. 'Building human capabilities is fundamental to expanding choices', 'human development is about creating an environment in which people can develop their full potential and lead productive, creative lives in accordance with their needs and interests' (UNDP HDR 2001). The three main components of human development as discussed above, are, longevity or the capacity to live a long and healthy life; education the ability to read, write and acquire knowledge and skills; and command over economic resources sufficient to provide a decent standard of living. Once these capacities are assured, then other opportunities in life will follow. Other important prerequisites are political freedom and guaranteed human rights, which include promotion of economic and gender equity, as well as social and cultural rights, especially those pertaining to education, healthcare, food, water, shelter, environment, culture, etc. It is recognised that public policies should be centred around people's choices and their capabilities and the policy thrust should be to combat illiteracy, poverty, unemployment, disease, save the lives of mothers and children, and address the inequities caused by gender and caste.

Though there is a broad consensus now about the three core dimensions of human development, i.e. health, education and income, measuring achievements in these three critical areas poses certain methodological issues.

As stated in Dag Hammarskjold Report, entitled "What Now", the goal of development is to ensure. (See Chart 1.2)

"Development of every man and woman ... and not just the growth of things, which are merely means 'for' development geared to the satisfaction of needs beginning with the basic need of the poor ... "and for development to ensure the humanisation of man by the satisfaction of his needs for expression, creativity, conviviality, and for deciding his own destiny."

Development is a process of growth in the direction of modernity, especially towards nation-building and socio-economic progress. It has been stressed that "development is the rational process of organising and carrying out prudently conceived and staffed programmes or projects as one would organize and carry out military or engineering operations."[24] Development has been defined in the same Report, "What Now", published by the Dag Hammarskold Foundation, Uppasala, Sweden. It states:

"Development is a whole; it is an integral, value loaded, cultural process, it encompasses the natural environment, social relations, education, production, consumption and well-being .... Development is endogenous; it brings from the heart of each society which relies first on its own strength and resources and defines in sovereignty the vision of its future, cooperating with societies sharing its problems and aspirations."

Rajiv Gandhi, former Prime Minister of India, has rightly remarked that "Development is not about factories, dams and roads. Development is basically about people. The goal is people's material, cultural and spiritual fulfilment. The human factor, the human context is of supreme values."[25] It is for this reason that in the Seventh Five Year Plan, Government of India has provided proportionately larger allocation for human resources development.

Policies and programmes in the field of education, culture, health, housing, nutrition, welfare of women and youth, uplift of Scheduled Castes and Scheduled Tribes and other weaker sections of the society are aimed at creating a stronger and more cohesive national community. All must have access to the benefit of modern knowledge. At the same time the heritage, the poise and strength of our inner spirit must be preserved.[26]

It may be added here that development administration is an action and goal-orientedprocess. It is a coordinated effort encompassing a very wide range of activities directed to ameliorate the lot of millions of unfortunate; less privileged people leading a life of deprivations and dejection. The essence of development administration is holistic change undertaken through integrated, organised and properly directed governmental action. The development

CHART 1.2

Progressive Improvements of Quality of Life

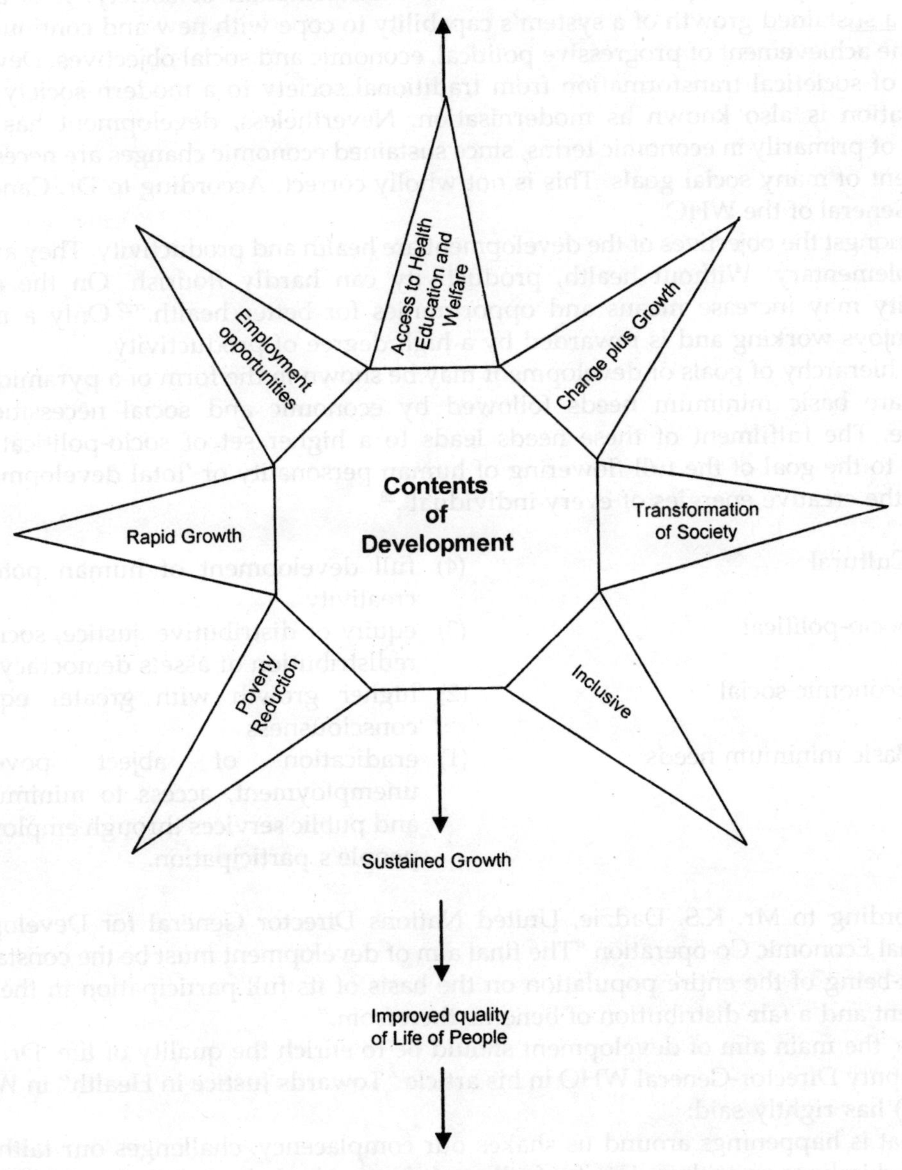

administration, therefore, centres around the word's "Change" and "Operation Problems." Change includes both social and economic. Most of the countries in Asia, Africa and Latin America are labelled as developing countries or poor countries or less developed countries or emerging nations or third world and likewise, because they are relatively young because they are engaged in the development tasks of nation-building and socio-economic progress because their per capita national income is less, because they are technologically less advanced and finally they are socially backward.

That is why development is regarded as transformation of society. It is a process of acquiring a sustained growth of a system's capability to cope with new and continuous changes towards the achievement of progressive political, economic and social objectives. Development is a process of societical transformation from traditional society to a modern society and such a transformation is also known as modernisation. Nevertheless, development has often been conceived of primarily in economic terms, since sustained economic changes are necessary for the achievement of many social goals. This is not wholly correct. According to Dr. Candua, former Director-General of the WHO:

"Amongst the objectives of the development are health and productivity. They are reciprocal and complementary. Without health, productivity can hardly flourish. On the other hand, productivity may increase means and opportunities for better health."[27] Only a man who is healthy, enjoys working and is rewarded by a high degree of productivity.

The hierarchy of goals of development may be shown in the form of a pyramid wherein at the base are basic minimum needs followed by economic and social necessities for bare subsistence. The fulfilment of these needs leads to a higher set of socio-political needs and ultimately to the goal of the full flowering of human personality or 'total development and the release of the creative energies of every individual'.[28]

(4) Cultural	(4) full development of human potentials and creativity
(3) Socio-political	(3) equity of distributive: justice, social equality, redistribution of assets democracy
(2) Economic-social	(2) higher growth with greater equity, mass consciousness
(1) Basic minimum needs	(1) eradication of abject poverty and unemployment, access to minimum income and public services through employment with people's participation.

According to Mr. K.S. Dadzie, United Nations Director General for Development and International Economic Co-operation "The final aim of development must be the constant increase of the well-being of the entire population on the basis of its full participation in the process of development and a fair distribution of benefits therefrom."

Thus, the main aim of development should be to enrich the quality of life. Dr. T. Adeoya Lambo, Deputy Director-General WHO in his article "Towards Justice in Health" in *World Health* (July, 1979) has rightly said:

"What is happenings around us shakes our complacency, challenges our faith in human progress and imbues us with an intense feeling of shame, doubt and guilt. In a world where the gigantic scientific and phenomenal technological achievements command our administration and almost fetish acceptance, we are witnessing an intolerable degradation of man. Our pride, in belonging to a generation that for the first time since the genesis of man has set foot on another planet cannot, however disguise the aweful truth that it may be easier to travel to moon than to erase from the surface of the earth, the image of inevitable poverty, human exploitation, injustice and the degradation of human welfare.

Our first concern is to redefine the whole purpose of development. This should not be to develop things but to develop man. Any process of growth that does not lead to human fulfilment or, even worse, that inhibits it, is a travesty of the idea of development.

According to Prof. Peter Drucker, "Development is largely a matter of the dynamics of individuals and of a local community. These can be supplied only by generating local, responsible initiative and multiplying human energies.[29]

ASPECT OF DEVELOPMENT

In fact there are three aspects of development—economic, political and social. It is very difficult to isolate one from the other. Economic development in terms of an increase in national income per capita is no longer regarded as the only development objective. The same is true of the other two aspects.

Perspectives of Economic Development

Economic development—a high growth rate of the national product is a means to an end,, i.e., it cannot in itself be—the ultimate objective—the final goal of a dynamic' society. Economic growth is never more than the method of obtaining the means through which a nation plans to achieve some form of social progress or social change. Developing nations have become increasingly conscious of the social aspects of economic planning. It is now generally realised that economic growth should be a means towards the eradication of hunger, illiteracy, disease, and reduction of existing social and economic inequalities. The consequences of growth without development are too painful to be ignored.[30] The correlation between economic growth and social development has tended to be low in the Asian, African and Latin American countries. In a recent study,[31] this relationship has been critically examined. For this purpose, the authors devised a method of measuring development which combines social, economic and political factors. They, then studied the relationship between this measure and the per capita GNP—a usually accepted economic growth index among 74 developing countries. They found that per capita GNP is responsible only for about half of the variation in the indicators of meaningful development, bearing out the conclusion that economic growth has often failed to be really reflected in socio-economic development. The late Max Milikan had said,

> "There is a growing recognition that economic growth alone will not automatically bring with it all the virtues of modernization."[32]

In other words, there is a realization that development is a social as well as an economic process. Because of this intimate relationship, it is very difficult to isolate social development from the economic context.

"If this interrelationship is not taken into account material advances may be accompanied by loss of social cohesion, impurity, delinquency, mental stress and other social ills. In fact, the trend is now for economic planning to give way to the socio-economic planning that involves for the social goals, with economic development as means rather than an end."[33]

Many writers have defined economic development in a broader sense. Myrdal has defined it as nothing less than the "upward movement of the entire social system."[34] Or it may be interpreted as the attainment of ideals of modernisation. Such as rise in productivity, industrialization, social and economic equalisation, development of modern knowledge, improved—institutions and attitudes, and a rationally coordinated system of policy measures that may on the one hand remove the host of undesirable conditions in the social system that have perpetuated a state of underdevelopment while on the other promote better nourishment, better health, better education, better living, conditions, etc.[35] After over a quarter of a century's experience and experiments with economic growth models based on western models, we find that this model stands as the 'God that failed'. Nobel Laureate, Jan Tinbergen has rightly said:

> "The poor countries should reject the aim of imtiating western patterns of life. Development is not linear process, and the aim of development is not to 'catch up' economically, socially, politically or culturally. Many aspects of western life have become wasteful and senseless and do not contribute—to people's real happiness. For poor nations to attempt to imitate the rich may only mean that they trade one set of problems for another and in doing so discard or destroy much that is valuable in terms of their human resources and values."[36]

Thus began in the early seventies a search for another development (social development). To quote Mr. Mahbub Aly Haq:

> "We are taught to take care of our GNP, since this would take care of poverty. Let us revise this and take care first of poverty itself since GNP can take care of itself, for it is only a convenient summation, and not a motivation for human effort."[37]

Perspectives of Social Development

Social development is a broad concept encompassing improvement in the social status of the people. Social development lays stress on provision of health services education, housing. cultural amenities, protection of children, a change in the status of women, regulation of labour and improved status for workers and reduction of disease, poverty and other social illness.

It is now widely acknowledged that conventional measures of well-being such as per capita gross domestic product or consumption expenditure or poverty ratios do not capture the broader aspects of human capability. Important as it is, high economic growth does not automatically translate into betterment of the lives of all people, especially if the benefits of that growth are not accessible to large sections of the population. The experiences of certain countries and states in India reveal that despite significant achievements in economic development, the proportion of people below the poverty line can actually increase, instead of dwindling as envisaged, or there might only be a small modicum of improvement in their status.

Harsh Mander in his article, "The Silent tragedy of hunger" in *The Hindu*, dated April 5, 2009 clearly mentioned that Development administration in order to be successful has to tackle a large number of problems.

Government programmes are woefully inadequate to address destitution; in fact, they tend to be blind to or in denial of the fact that large numbers of people lack even the elementary means and power to survive with dignity. It is stressed that this is a duty of the State, not to the dead but to the precariously living. It requires public vigilance about individuals, communities and several categories living with starvation and absolute hunger. It requires the State to act, not after there is an emergency like a drought or flood, not even after people die of starvation, but proactively, before people slip into destitution and fail to access, in an assured and reliable manner, with dignity, the nutritious and culturally appropriate food they require to lead healthy lives.

Gandhi offered us a "talisman" to use in moments of doubts and confusion. He asked us to recall the face of the poorest, most defenceless, most powerless man we have encountered (Today he would have recognized that she would probably have been a woman!) We must ask ourselves whether what we are attempting has meaning for this person; does it touch her life with dignity and worth? Does it augment her power and self-reliance? If it does, it must surely be the right thing to do. It is this talisman that we need to hold up to public policy in the glittering world of vast reservoirs of darkness today.

According to T.K.N. Unnithan, "Social development may be seen as a process of ushering in a new order of existence. The quality of life and the quality of social relations which exist would indicate the level of the order of existence."[38]

ECAFE meeting of the Working Party on Social Development held at Bangkok redefines the social development as:

> "the greater capacity of the social system, social structure, institutions and policy to utilize resources to generate favourable changes in levels of living interpreted in the broad sense as related to accepted social values and a better distribution of income, wealth and opportunities."[39]

This is a comprehensive definition given by ECAFE (now ESCAP) in terms of the capacity of the social system to bring about favourable changes in the levels of living.

Social development is more concerned with the investment in human beings. A unit of investment in education, health, social welfare, etc., is, in the ultimate analysis, as productive as a unit of investment in agriculture, industry or trade. Research undertaken at the United Nations Research Institute for Social Development (UNRISD) in Geneva has indicated that developing countries which have relatively high scores on social indicators, also tend to have high growth rates. Therefore, we must take a comprehensive view of development. Such a view of the development process would enable the planners to estimate realistically the social and economic changes and to accelerate those already taking place. Planning for 'people' must replace merely planning for aggregate production growth. According to Dr. Salima Omer, Associate Professor, University of Nebraska, USA, social development is a "process that aims at the total development of people ... social development is inter-sectoral, inter-regional and inter-disciplinary and visualises institutional and structural reforms to provide greater social justice."[40]

It has been realised increasingly over the years that social development is necessary not only to provide opportunities to individuals for self-development but also as a vital contribution to economic development. The distinction between social and economic development is no longer tenable. Economic development is necessary to achieve most social goals and social development which is in turn necessary to achieve most economic goals. The purpose of development is to permit people to lead economically productive and socially satisfying lives.

The emphasis of the strategy of UN Second Development Decade (1971-80) as well, is on growth with social justice, removal of poverty and substantial rise in the level of employment. This strategy is fully based on the idea of total development, i.e., combining the social and economic development. To quote the strategy:

> "As the ultimate purpose of development is to provide increasing opportunities to all people for a better life, it is essential to bring about a more equitable distribution of income and wealth for promoting both social justice and efficiency of production, to raise

substantially the level of employment, to achieve greater degree of income security, to expand improved facilities for education, health, nutrition, housing and social welfare, and to safeguard the environment. Thus quantitative and structural changes in the society must go hand in hand with rapid economic growth, and existing disparities—regional, sectoral and social-should be substantially reduced."[41]

Dr. Mahler has very succinctly remarked in this connection:

"Economic growth, without being specifically attuned to human needs and human realizations, is not worth very much. Once more you hear everywhere people speaking about nuclear energy, oil energy solar energy, wind energy and everybody seems to be overlooking the fact that without human energy, there would be no kind of progress either socially or economically."[42]

Recently, four Asian scholars viewed development in terms of fundamental humanistic values rather than in narrow techno-economic terms. They mentioned five core principles "which stand inseparably together."[43]

(1) Man as the end of development—which is therefore, to be judged by what it does to him.
(2) Delineation of man, in the sense that he feels at home with the process of development in which he becomes the subject as well as the object.
(3) Development of collective personality of man in which he finds his richest experience.
(4) Participation as the true form of democracy.
(5) Self-reliance as the expression of man's faith in his own abilities.

Thus we see that social development deals with the society and human resources, whereas economic development deals with economy and material resources. Social justice and human welfare are the key objectives of social development. Social development is considered as the development of society.[44] Society is not just an assembly of people; it is a manifestation of human craving for reaching out to others. It is a web of human relations, conceiving Society in this manner. Social development may be defined as development of the society from a less human to a more human state of affairs. Social development comprises of four components, viz., material and social well-being of man; enlargement of human consciousness as reflected in the rise of a multinational human self; growth of humanitarian concern, i.e. concern for others; and strengthening of the sense of community life.[45] Political development has been interpreted in several senses. We shall like to interpret it here as enhancement of the capability of a political system to satisfy the primary needs and aspirations of its members in regard to their physical protection, physical and social well-being and harmony as well as enjoyment of civil and political rights.

The economic development, political development and social developments are complimentary. Their interactions constitute the national advancement (Refer Chart 1.3).

SOCIAL DEVELOPMENT IN INDIA (See Chart 1.3)

The term 'social development' was separated from 'economic development' in 1950s by the united nations in their report on the world social situation, giving an impression that the

CHART 1.3

Social Development Model at a Glance

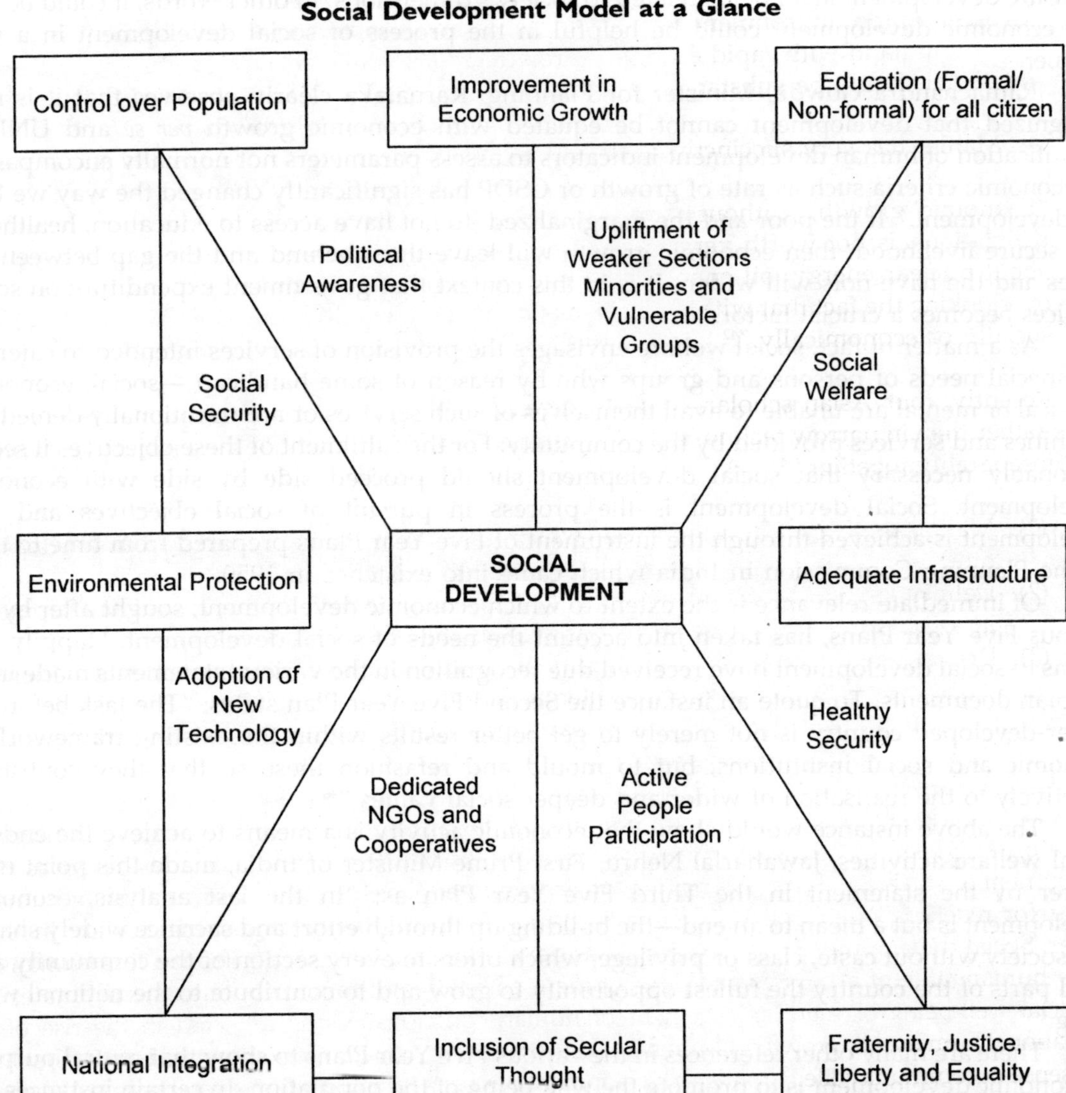

Source: P.C. Sikligar, Social Development: A Profile, in *IJPA*, April-June 1998, p. 182.

human factors, like cultural dimension, value, social security, social justice, social welfare, social service, social policy, social work, political orientation, environmental issues, etc., were neglected since time immemorial in the framework of economic development. Earlier, social development was perceived as economic growth. Later on global economists also realised development and realised that social development was much vaster than economic development. Keeping in mind the human orientations, they accepted that the entire economic development could not become social development but it could only be a part of social development. In the process of development they emphasised that social development is more than economic development and the necessity to ensure development in all fields related to society's dimensions. In other words, it could be said that economic development could be helpful in the process of social development in a vital manner.

Ramachandra Gowda, Minister for Planning, Karnataka clearly observes that it is now recognized that development cannot be equated with economic growth *per se* and UNDP's identification of human development indicators to assess parameters not normally encompassed by economic criteria such as rate of growth or GSDP has significantly changed the way we look at "development." If the poor and the marginalized do not have access to education, healthcare and secure livelihood, then economic growth will leave them behind and the gap between the haves and the have-nots will widen. It is in this context that government expenditure on social services becomes a crucial factor.

As a matter of fact, social welfare envisages the provision of services intended to cater for the special needs of persons and groups who by reason of some handicap —social, economic, physical or mental are unable to avail themselves of such services or are traditionally denied the amenities and services provided by the community. For the fulfilment of these objectives it seems reasonably necessary that social development should proceed side by side with economic development. Social development is the process in pursuit of social objectives and this development is achieved through the instrument of Five Year Plans prepared from time to time by the Planning Commission in India which came into existence in 1950.

Of immediate relevance is the extent to which economic development, sought after by the various Five Year Plans, has taken into account the needs of social development. Happily, the claims of social development have received due recognition in the various statements made in all the plan documents. To quote an instance the Second Five Year Plan states: "The task before an under-developed country is not merely to get better results within the existing framework of economic and social institutions, but to mould and refashion these so that they contribute effectively to the realisation of wider and deeper social values."[46]

The above instance would show that economic activity is a means to achieve the ends of social welfare activities. Jawaharlal Nehru, First Prime Minister of India, made this point even clearer by the statement in the Third Five Year Plan as: "In the last analysis, economic development is but a mean to an end—the building up through effort and sacrifice widely shared of a society without caste, class or privilege, which offers to every section of the community and to all parts of the country the fullest opportunity to grow and to contribute to the national well-being."[47]

There are many other references in the various Five Year Plans to show that central purpose of economic development is to promote the well-being of the population. In certain instances the references in the plan documents have gone even further. They have recognised that expenditure incurred on schemes like child development is in fact an investment. The following statement in the introduction of the First Plan will prove this: it is obvious that no plan can succeed unless it 'invests' in the improvement of the human material.

Furthermore, and quite correctly, the First Plan document has conceded that the increase of output in various forms such as industry, agriculture, commerce and the like, ultimately depends upon the quality of man produced through a planned process. The axiom that a better man resulting from the provision of better health; education and training is an asset for higher output is admitted in the Plan literature in the words: 'Even from the point of view of increasing production, social services like education; technical training and health bring many significant returns."[48]

Notwithstanding these statements of wisdom and balanced judgement, when it actually came to making provision for social developments, it appears that it was the economic view, that prevailed.

The result was that instead of social development being inter-locked with economic development to produce an organic plan, there was differentiation between the 'core' sectors and the 'fringe' items. This plural approach seems to have caused a setback to the programme of social development.

Economic growth and social development are complementary processes. Economic prosperity is the foundation on which the structure of social development could be built. Social development can come only through national will, sustained hard work, purposeful planning and faithful planning and faithful implementation. The objective of social welfare is to promote the social betterment of a class or group of people who are defined as disadvantaged, handicapped, or deprived. Such persons face a set of common problems arising form the nature of the trait or quality which sets them apart form the rest of society. Programmes of social welfare are then planned to meet these needs. Since the first five-year plan the scope of social welfare has undergone a continuous change. While social welfare services during the first four five-years plans were mainly confined to the provision of relief to the handicapped and under-privileged sections of society, the fifth plan strategy has laid greater emphasis on the developmental programmes of social welfare, integration between social and economic aspects of planning for the weaker sections, and extension of the basic health, nutrition, child care and functional literacy services. The sixth plan seeks to sustain these priorities including women's education.

Quite often the concepts of social administration, social welfare administration and social service administration are used inter-changeably to denote the organisation and management of welfare programmes for the disadvantaged groups. Social service organizations are differentiated from other economic organizations by two fundamental characteristics: (a) their input of raw material are people with specific problems, and their production output are human beings processed or improved in a predetermined manner, and (b) their basic objective is that of 'service', that is, to maintain and improve the general social health and well-being of the people (Hasenfled and English, 1974). Examples of such organizations are: Day-care centres, special schools, rehabilitation agencies, mental asylums, borstal and certified institutions, socio-economic units, after-care homes and a plethora of non-institutional programmes. The ever escalating tensions and social dysfunctionalities have resulted in the vast proliferation of social service organizations. This indispensability of social organizations in contemporary society is due to the vital functions they perform, both at the societal level and the individual level.

Productivity is defined as a mathematical relationship between inputs and outputs. It means to produce more and more from less and less inputs. Productivity in social welfare administration denotes an interrelationship between the inputs of money, materials, manpower and management style, and the efficiency and effectiveness of service outcomes at local, regional and national levels. The measurement of these galaxy of variables is indeed a formidable problem and the available research on this subject is almost nil in the Indian context. There should be a sincere endeavour in every social service enterprise in the country to produce services at an economical cost. One can maximize efficiency and effectiveness and thereby increase productivity and it is here that the vital human factor comes into play. The substance of this proposition is the creation of an understanding that the employees and employers in social service agencies on the one hand and the agencies and the beneficiaries on the other are in pursuit of a common goal and a common objective and the ultimate objective, in a limited sense, is the functional efficiency of he enterprise and in a broader sense the well-being of the disadvantaged communities. Productivity in social administration is influenced by a number of factors either directly or indirectly. Among these factors are: capital, training and health of welfare functionaries, the state of technology, style of management, organisational climate, social attitude to work and welfare, and attitude towards change and innovation. Organisational structures have seldom been examined in social administration to examine why they actually discourage productivity. Similarly the base of capital formation has been a cause of concern in social welfare.[49]

The fact that such an approach is unwise and detrimental to the ultimate aims was brought out in the following words by Jawaharlal Nehru when he addressed the Planning Commission Seminar on Social Welfare in Developing Economy in September, 1963: "I was little surprised because it appeared to draw a distinction between social welfare and development economy almost as thought if social welfare was not specially tagged on to a developing economy, it would not be there. What is the object of economic development? Obviously, it is social welfare, not merely in the restricted sense in which the expression is used by social workers, but in the wider sense of maximizing the welfare of all persons in society, whether handicapped or normal. This is first objective of any civilized state; and it is the first objective of our programme of economic development."

The first Prime Minister of free India, therefore, urged that schemes for social development and economic development should run parallel to each other but that unlike all parallel lines, they should ultimately meet each other. It may, however, be made clear here that our aim through the present book, is not at all of determining processes of social planning or the inter-action of social and economic growth but simply of pointing out the incongruities between the two, i.e. economic and social development. These observations may be treated as the indicators that in most modern communities, social security is an inevitable commitment of economic development. Any advancement towards the achievements of complete social security measures can be determined largely by the availability of economic resources and other factors. Since the economic resources of developing countries like India are meager; we cannot for the present think of having a complete social security in India. The immediate need seems to be aiming at providing welfare services for groups that need them the most. This leads us to the inevitability of the organisation of social welfare services in a planned way.

Karnataka Human Development Report, 2005-06: Financing human development is a very critical aspect of ensuring that public policies become concrete realities and that the poor and other vulnerable sub-populations are supported by the state, enabling them to become empowered beings capable of realising their inherent potential in a participatory and democratic context. As the UNDP Human Development Report (1991) noted, the best strategy for human development is to ensure, through strong policies, generation and better distribution of primary incomes. In addition, government services in social infrastructure (schools, health clinics, nutrition and food subsidies) as well as physical infrastructure (roads, electricity and housing) can help the poor bridge the gap caused by paucity of incomes. However, despite sound intentions, governments do not always provide adequately for the social sectors. And, sometimes, when budgets are adequate, they may not target the core sectors of human development (e.g. primary healthcare, elementary education) and focus, instead, on other areas.

Indian states have a dominant role in the provision of social services such as education, healthcare, housing, social welfare, water supply and sanitation. State governments incur over 85 per cent of the expenditure on these services. Therefore, deterioration in states' finances and undue pressure to compress their expenditures as part of a fiscal adjustment strategy reduces the fiscal space available to state governments. Unfortunately, the constituency demanding a larger allocation to social sector expenditures is not strong, although there is now a ground-well building up at the grassroots, consequent upon the devolution of political and executive powers to local bodies, which have begun to demand improved services. Currently, however, the expenditure compression at the state level impacts adversely the resources allocated to these sectors, notwithstanding their high social value and productivity. This environment of fiscal constraint has shaped the trends in human development spending in the last decade.

In this context the concept of institutional building for social development assumes a key role not from a narrow perception of elite-orientedcivil service procedures but as a critical element in national development by taking contingence of the emerging forces from among those who have so far been denied the access to education, health, housing, nutrition and other essentials of life. Such an approach would require a shift from organisations based on the system maintenance approach to a net work of institution built upon the criteria of objectivity, rationality, effectiveness and efficiency to serve the social needs of the people.

It may be useful to conclude with the remarks that the process of development is holistic in nature encompassing political, social, economic, cultural and also environmental processes of change.

SOCIAL POLICY (See Chart 1.4)

One of the major objectives of social development is to improve the well-being of the people. It is generally measured by the provision of social welfare services and the living levels. So in order to achieve this social welfare objective, it is necessary to attend to a wide variety of problems that the new industrialising countries are facing. These problems have been enlisted in Encyclopedia of Social Work in India. These are as follows:

(1) Problems generated because of lack of industrial or economic development:
  (a) Poverty.
  (b) Ill-health.
  (c) Ignorance.
(2) Problems born out of industrialization and urbanization:
  (a) Bad housing, overcrowding and mushroom growth of slums.
  (b) Family change, family breakdown, widowhood, orphanhood, old age, etc.
  (c) Juvenile delinquency, crime and social defence.
  (d) Psychological strains and breakdowns.
(3) Problems which crop up because of value change and readjustment of interests;
  (a) The traditionally underprivileged groups and communities.
  (b) The lower status of women.
(4) Problems resulting from political reorganization:
  (a) Political minorities.
  (b) Refugees.
(5) Problems of individual handicaps:
  (a) The physically handicapped, blind, deaf, victims of accidents, prolonged illness, etc.
  (b) The mentally deranged, the backward and retarded.
  (c) The mentally ill.

CHART 1.4

Major Objectives of Social Development

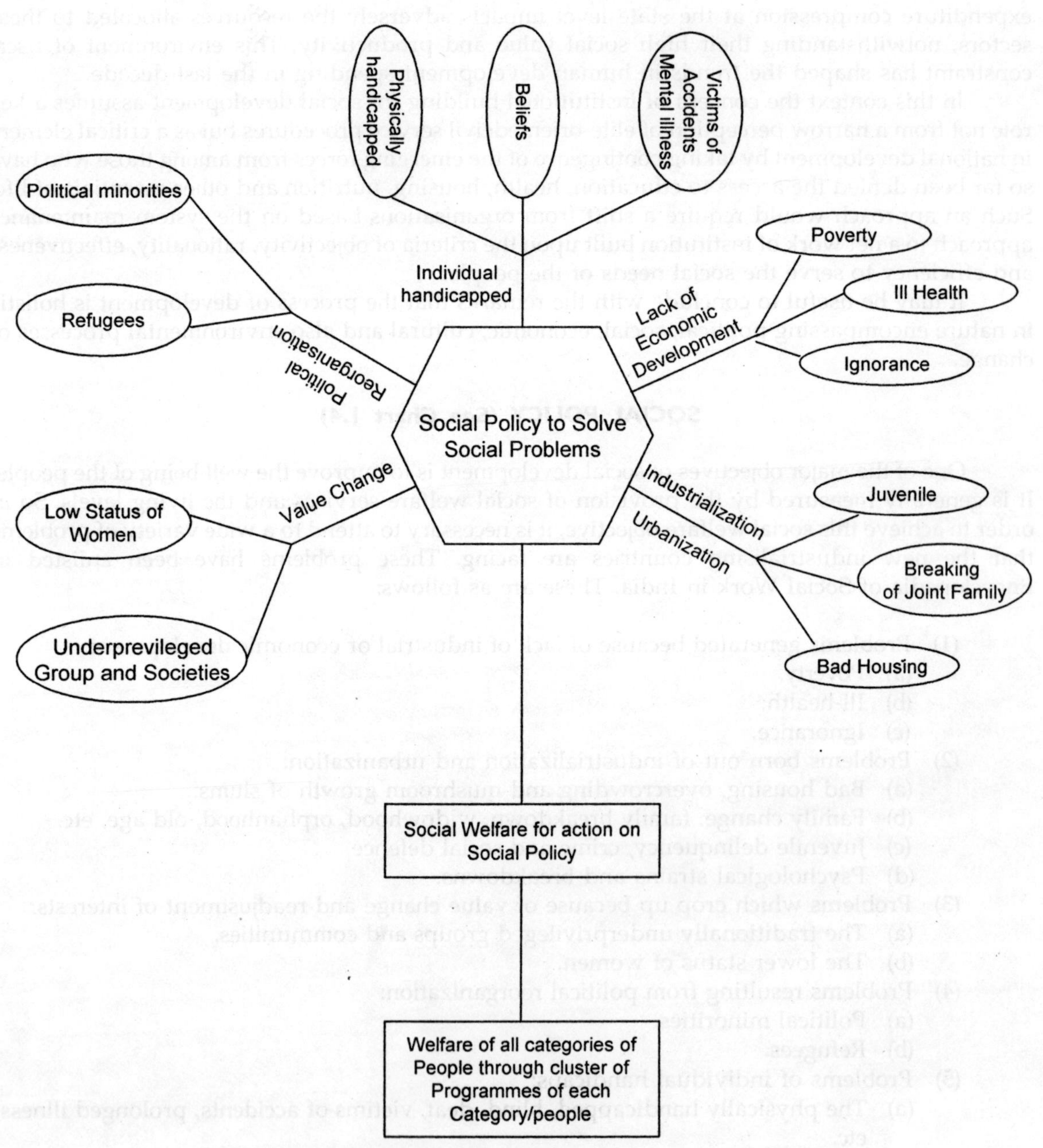

The social development of services is to be improved, recognised and strengthened in these areas.

In order to tackle these existing and emerging problems, we must have a social policy. Policy is vital to the task of planning a course of action. Marshall Dimock defines it as, "the consciously acknowledged rules of conduct that guide administrative decisions."[50]

A policy can be a verbal, written or implied basic guide to action. It is essential in administration as it gives a concrete shape to the political and social objectives which the government lays down in the form of laws, resolutions and policy statements. Social policy deals with the objectives to be implemented to secure and improve the welfare of the population. According to Beales, "Social policy is a collective term for the public process through which we attack insecurity and correct the weak tendencies of our capitalist inheritance."[51]

Titmus refers to acts of government deliberately designed and taken to improve the welfare of the civil population as the main area of social policy.[52] There is no single pattern of social policy but a complex phenomenon varying in character of importance. According to Tarlok Singh, the tasks which social policy should accomplish can be viewed from three angles. First, it can be looked at in terms of programmes and measures directed towards expansion of social services and their qualitative improvement, welfare and development of the weaker and more vulnerable sections of the population, social reform, and social change. Second, social policy may be seen in terms of different sections of the population. A third approach to social policy may be in relation to section of the population whose special development needs must become a matter of social concern to the community as a whole .... Its ultimate purpose is to achieve integration between diverse elements and a sense of common citizenship and common values.[53]

This means that social policy is understood by many writers overseas as well as here in India in terms of continual improvement of the quality of social life and human relations. In India, there have been demands for a statement of social policy on the analogy of industrial and scientific policies.[54] Statement of policies, it is believed, would set the framework and provide the guidelines for the public as well as for the legislators and administrators. So far there has not been any response to these demands from Government, either at the Centre or in any State.[55] However, a widespread opinion prevails that the social objectives as expressed in the Directive Principles of State Policy in the Constitution of India and in Five Year Plan documents clearly serve the purpose of the statement of social policy.[56] Nevertheless, an understanding of the concept in more specific pattern of the elements of social policy could enable administrators to develop a critical awareness as a prelude to constructive action in any spheres of developmental activity in which they are currently engaged.[57] With regard to social planning, a well defined social policy is also required because social development is not the sole responsibility of the State. The community at large has to be awakened and prepared to shoulder the burden. There are multiple of official agencies engaged in process of community action in the field of social development but the role of Non-Governmental Organisations (NGOs) can't be overlooked. The NGOs are not only to be encouraged and supported to take up the reins of development administration but these have to be guided and helped to initiate social action in challenging setting without overlapping and duplication of official effort. With the declaration of a social policy not only the roles and functions of NGOs (voluntary organisation) and Government would be clearly defined but the areas of actions would also be identified for more concerned and determined social action.

Madison has observed that social planning is thought of as an institutionalized process to achieve a more rational use of resources. It emphasizes ways of reaching goals for specific functional activities or sectors. To be effective, it must be intimately connected with the society's practical policies and its governmental machinery and as the implementor of social policy it should be purposeful and yet flexible.[58] India began the process of planned development nearly Fifty-nine years ago with the formulation of the First Five Year Plan in April 1951. The primary objective of planning was that of initiating a process of development which could raise the standard by providing new opportunities to the people for a richer and satisfying life. The extent to which this purpose was translated into specific objectives, however, varied from Plan to Plan. Broadly, the basic objectives of planning in India have been removal of poverty, the building of a modern society making maximum use of science and technology and attainment of self-reliance.[59] In one way or the other these objectives reflect the needs of various section of the population and are representative of a national interpretation of the aims of planning.[60] Within this broad framework of objectives, planning for promoting social justice can be termed as social planning.[61]

SOCIAL WELFARE

The concept of social welfare essentially is a dynamic process. The meaning of social welfare is a matter of interpretation in context with the particular situation of the existing forces which determine the very equilibrium in the society and give every shape to it. These forces nonetheless dynamic in themselves, may be coined as social, economic, cultural; religious and political climate of that particular country. The scope of social welfare, as such varies from time to time and from country to country.

The whole corpus of remedial services for the destitute, the deprived; the handicapped and mal-adjusted individuals form the core of social sector. Social welfare is, therefore, not to be conceived only in the traditional sense of providing *post mortem* or ameliorative services. Experiences have shown that it constitutes curative and preventive services also. It can contribute to a change and adjustment of social institutions to the creation of the required infrastructure of community services and can enable people to accept and provide social change for over all development.[62]

Another view point is the emphasis on providing composite and comprehensive integrated service for each group-children, women and the handicapped. But a poor underdeveloped country cannot in early stages of economic development really afford such redistributive measures which in the advanced countries are known under the label of 'social security'.[63]

The whole concept of social welfare may be grouped into two areas of study: (a) social problems, and (b) the ways in which society responds to these problems. Social problems are problems which effect not just the individual but the society also in which he lives. These problems arise from individual human needs which are common to all members of the society. Some needs are more conceptional and sophisticated like the need for dignity and status; some are powerful and intangible like the need for love and affection. These common human needs are largely met by personal and family action. When these needs are not met by the individual and the family, they give rise to problems which society as a whole increasingly tries to tackle. These social problems are poverty, housing problems, unemployment, crime, sex, loneliness among the aged and infirm and child neglect, etc. As the problems are varied, it is not possible to give a once for all agreed definition for social problems or to make a list of them.[64]

The second area is the ways in which society organises itself to meet the needs and cope with the problems. This is related to the need of a 'social policy' and it involves an understanding of development of social problems; of the legislations which make it explicit of the government machinery and administrative procedures concerned with social provisions, of role of voluntary action, the recruitment and expertise, and the problems of finances, etc.

Harold has defined Social Welfare "as those formally organised and socially sponsored Institutions, Agencies and Programmes which function to maintain or improve the economic condition, health or inter-personal competence of some part or whole population.[65] Social Welfare in its broader connotations is understood to imply total reordering of socio-economic relations in the context of rapid development in science, technology, communication and experience or expectations.

However, one of the widely accepted definition of social welfare in the developed countries is read as: "It is the organised system of social welfare institutions designed to aid disadvantaged individuals and groups to attain satisfying standards of life and health. It aims at personal and social relationship which permits individuals to develop their full capacities and the promotion of their well-being in harmony with the needs of the community."[66]

One can observe that the above definitions of social welfare are forming apart: One view is taking into the fields of social welfare, the entire area of human resources development including what are known as social services. It would only be another step forward to make social welfare co-terminus with social development which may be taken to include not only development of social services but every thing also that helps to the transformation of attitudes, values, etc. And between social development and social change the only distinction seems to be that while the former is brought about, the latter just occurs but even this may be only verbal because the social scientists are to discuss problems of planning for social change and 'direct social change'.[67]

Broadly speaking in India the concept of social welfare has been evolved out of the phrases most frequently heard here and outside like "mutual help", "Religious duty." Deeds to ensure spiritual salvation "Charity", "Philanthrophy", "Alms Giving", "Poor Relief", "Benevolence" and "Social Reform."

Social Welfare in the words of Dr. D. Paul Chawdhry can be compared to "Automobile Engineering which restores defective individual and brings them to road."[68]

Social Welfare, an organized activity is of a very recent origin. Started as essentially a voluntary effort on the part of individuals or groups of individuals, we now have sufficiently large and complex organizations in the field of social welfare. These organizations are not different from what—T. Parsons calls a broad type of collectivity which has assumed a particularly important place in modern industrial society—the type to which the term 'bureaucracy' is most often applied (1965,16). It would suffice here to note that organizations, whether bureaucratic or non-bureaucratic, are social units (or human groupings) deliberately constructed or reconstructed to seek specific goals (Etzioni, 1972, 3). Having specific goals and striving to attain the same are, therefore, important characteristics of any organisation.

Social welfare effort has always been in the nature of a spontaneous response on the part of some individuals and groups to situations of need in their community (Gore, 1965,138). This effort has often led to the form action of organizations with some goals. The goal may be as simple as to provide protection and care to the orphan child or as difficult as to treat and change the behaviour of the delinquent child. It may be as crucial as to spread the ideal of small family and bring down the rate of birth or to try for the upliftment of the weaker sections and welfare and rehabilitation of the handicapped persons. Thus we have orphanages, correctional welfare institutions, family welfare and family planning organizations, women's councils and organizations for backward classes' welfare, and so on. Besides these organisations, there are government departments formulating and implementing welfare policies in all major areas of social welfare.

The basic question, however, is whether these organizations succeed reasonably in achieving their goals. There can be no dispute over the fact that on the whole the achievement of welfare efforts are far from being satisfactory.

There can be two solutions to this state of affairs: (1) To effect necessary change in the structure of social welfare organisation—right from a smallest agency to government department dealing with the administration of social welfare policy—to suit the need for attainment of their goals. (2) The social welfare organizations should adopt a strategy or strategies most suitable for the attainment of their proposed goals.

The first alternative is not to be ruled out. In fact there has been a distinctive shift in thinking about organizations and approach to build them since 1983, when the finding of Roethlisberger and Dickons study were published (Duby,1973, 180). The shift is from the classical to the "Human Relations or community participation" and more recently to the structural approach to build (social welfare) organizations. Such a change, however, requires a long-term endeavour. Again, whatever approach we adopt in building social welfare organizations, the need to adopt or evolve a scientific strategy for the attainment of the organisational goals still remains.[69]

Briefly stated, social welfare may be defined as the organised provision of resources and services for the society to deal with social problems. These services may be provided by the state or voluntary organization with a view to correct the conditions of the people affected by problems as well as to protect others who are likely to be effected in the future.

Nature and Scope

In a developing society, the role of social welfare in ensuring growth with social justice needs no emphasis. But the determining of the nature and scope of social welfare however, is also by no means an easy task. There is considerable ambiguity in the meanings of the various terms used in the literature on welfare. A variety of terms such as 'social development programmes', 'social programmes', 'social measures', 'social action', 'social services', 'social welfare', etc., are used. The aim of these various terms is however, the total well-being of the community. The two terms that is social services and social welfare services are generally considered as synonymous by layman, but are different. In India these two terms have been understood in two different connotations. Social services are those which are required on a very extensive scale by all sections of population. They seek to meet the primary needs of the people and include services for health, education, housing, nutrition and water-supply. They aim at developing the quality of human life. Social welfare services on the other hand are those which are required for the vulnerable sections of the society and include services for the handicapped and traditionally under-privileged groups.[70]

In the past welfare services were restricted to remedial and curative aspects only. As the concept of the welfare is a dynamic one, social welfare process is considered as an integral part of the developmental process. Now, it is not viewed as charity but an investment in the development of the potentialities of the physically and socially handicapped, as well as of women and children from backward, rural, urban and tribal areas. Social Welfare not only covers the curative and rehabilitative services but also preventive and developmental programmes, enabling the individual and groups to become self-reliant and overcome their own constraints.[71]

Social welfare, as an integral part of national development, has its foundation in the Indian Constitution. It provides guidelines and directions to welfare endeavours.[72] In its broader aspects, to implement the provisions in the Constitutions and to achieve the national goal of providing social and economic justice to citizens, a planned programme for the economic and social development was launched in 1951. In the First Five Year Plan (1951-56) social welfare efforts were at a low key. In the subsequent plans greater emphasis was laid on social welfare programmes.

The scope and content of social welfare services at any point of time would obviously be determined by the national perception of the social issues and the capacity to cope with them. If social welfare is viewed in terms of providing only rehabilitative and curative services the clientele would not be expected to be very large. But when the aim is to provide promotional and preventive services besides rehabilitative services, the scope and coverage of social welfare would be expected to be wide. When the aim is also improvement of social relations, the scope of social welfare would be still wider. Social welfare is thus a dynamic concept and a widening process.[73]

Social welfare includes cluster of programmes and schemes as given below[74]:

(a) Programmes for women,
(b) Programmes for children,
(c) Composite programmes for women and children,
(d) Schemes for maladjusted groups,
(e) Programmes for physically handicapped persons,
(f) Social legislation, and
(g) Programmes for SC/ST, etc.

The programmes listed above are being managed partly by Central Government and partly by State governments. Both the governments are implementing the programmes partly through official agencies and partly through voluntary organizations whose numbers have been growing in recent years. This has led to administrative changes and expansion as well as institutional building in the non-official field.

Programmes of labour welfare, family welfare, community development and housing are not included under social welfare and for purposes of Five Year Plan formulation even the welfare of backward classes including Scheduled Castes, Schedules Tribes and denotified tribes, is treated as a separate part of general social welfare.[75] The plan documents have also stressed that the voluntary organisation has to be strengthened and the State's help to act as a catalytic agent.

The concept of social welfare, however, would have to be enlarged and would have to be considered as an organised function, designed to enable families, groups and communities to cope with social problems arising out of changing social conditions particularly in regard to the structure of family as a unit.

SOCIAL WELFARE ADMINISTRATION

While discussing social welfare administration, D.V. Kulkarni described it as the administration of the social welfare programmes. He further stated that administration of social services and social welfare programmes legitimately should fall in the sub-area of social administration. Social Administration is, therefore, concerned with an ill-defined but recognisable territory— the development of collective action for the advancement of social welfare. The job is to identify and clarify problems with this territory—to throw light upon them, drawing light from any discipline that appears to be relevant and to contribute where possible to solution of these problems. This is precisely what was and is needed to be done but appears to have not received adequate attention. In India one of the subject to be investigated therefore is the suitability or otherwise of the present administrative apparatus for the goal to be realised through social services and welfare services.[76]

It is admitted in the western model of welfare states also that of he many aspects of social welfare practices, the least developed, conceptually, is administration. The literature is sparse, and the research embryonic. There is little that one can identify as useful theory or even as thoughtful theoretical perspective. In India, literature on the subject of social welfare administration is comparatively new and requires to be explored more and more. Social welfare administration, it is hoped, will emerge as a popular discipline and a unique profession in due course of time as people become aware and convinced of its validity and utility.[77]

The success of social welfare ultimately depends upon the adequacy of the administrative apparatus prevailing in the country. People have new aspirations and urges. These have to be adequately met by the administration. The guiding principle of any good system of administration is the fellow feeling, belongingness and total well-being of the citizens for whom it exists. Many people are not satisfied with current state of affairs with the social welfare administration as well as social welfare organisations and point it as highly unresponsive to the well-being of the people. Such label reflects both in degree of substance and a degree of exaggeration. A concerted drive and a vigorous action however, is needed at various joints, though that does not mean, that all is bad. Despite constraints and stresses and inadequacies, the system of the social welfare organisations is working. What is required is avoidance of frictions and clear understanding of the situation and issues involved. This has to be viewed in relation to environmental context which for the present seems to have not been viewed. It is our duty to provide the requisite frame-work within which the administration can function with sufficient confidence, responsibility and initiative. Politics and Bureaucracy have to go for a change. No one would be suspectible for any change in any direction. In order to strengthen the apparatus and making it action-oriented. The cracks in the walls do suggest weaknesses which lie deeper in the structure and the time has come to reflect calmly so that administrative structure does not find itself clogged and pulled back from within. Further to say that despite the new responsibility and functions assigned to social welfare field attention has to be given by the organisation to bring changes within the administrative set-up keeping in view people's needs and aspirations on the top.

Social policy seeks to bring change through social action. According to Elizabeth Wickneden:

> "Social action is a term commonly applied to that aspect of organised social welfare activity directed towards shaping, modifying, or maintaining the social institutions and policies that collectively constitute the social environment. Social action is concerned with the better adjustment of the social environment ... to meet organised needs of individuals and to facilitate those social relationships and adjustment necessary to its own best functioning."

Social administration is an instrument of bringing social action through implementation of social policy. Social policy must be studied in the socio-economic perspective of the country which is undergoing a constant change. Social administration in this sense is a process of bringing community welfare through social change and the implementation of social policy decisions for the total welfare of the community. It "encompasses every act, every technique and every consideration in the process necessary to transforming social policy into social service." Narrowly defined, social administration "is the study of development, structure and practices of the social services."[78]

A comprehensive definition of Social Welfare Administration, however, is given in the curriculum study of the American Council of Social Work Education as follows: "Social Welfare Administration is the process of transforming community resources into a programme of community service, in accordance with goals, policies and standards which have been agreed by those involved in the enterprise. It is creative in that it structures roles and relationships in such a way as to alter and enhance the total product. It involves the problem-solving process of study, diagnosis and treatment (solution or action and evaluation of results).[79]

Broadly defined, it is an attempt to apply the social sciences to the analysis and solution of a changing range of social problems. According to K.M. Slack:

"Social administration is not one more social science with its own theory and body of knowledge. It makes use of the findings of any of the social sciences which are relevant to its sphere, which includes ... the solving of social problems, the implementation of social policy and the promotion of social welfare. It may focus attention on one area or synthesize various areas of knowledge of social institutions and human behaviour and thereby increase understanding. But its distinctive character is that it combines and benefits from any of the conclusions of the social sciences which assist it and uses them as tools in the performance of the functions which are its particular concern."[80]

To quote Forder:

"Social administration is concerned with the study of the welfare system, and particularly the government-sponsored social services."[81]

Social development policy, complementary to economic and political development policies, aims at provision of opportunities to individuals, families and groups for their self and social development. Social administration finds the means of delivering services and goods to persons and families for availing such opportunities. It also tries to provide assistance and services to the socially and physically handicapped or vulnerable sections of people for ameliorating their disabilities and enabling them to stand on their own legs as far as possible. This part of social development administration is also termed as social administration.

This tradition tends to emphasise three characteristics of social administration which are as follows:

(a) Social administration is not a distinct discipline but a multi-disciplinary field of study;
(b) Social administration's field of study is essentially statutory welfare provision; and
(c) Statutory welfare provision aims at meeting individual needs—there is thus a distinction drawn between 'personal' social services and public services that benefit the 'community' at large in an indiscriminate way.[82]

Social administration may be understood as that part of administration which provides and operates services leading to removal of prevailing disabilities and to the creation of opportunities for the well-being of individuals and families in the community.[83]

Social administration in its broader sense thus refers also to regulatory, development and welfare administration but in its narrower sense, it refers to two aspects only: administration of social legislation to either one or to both. This statement does not clarify what is meant by social administration, like Chinese ethics, it may be a combination of Social and Administration. But if we seek to find its meaning by relating it to social legislation, we must define the content of the latter. That task is not easy either because some writers confine the term social legislation to matters affecting labour, especially social-security and labour welfare. But other writers extend it to include laws relating to family relations and social pathological problems like crime, drink, prostitution, etc.[84]

If we understand social administration as the administration of social agencies, we have to define the content of the term "Social agencies." These agencies are generally understood to include those which are helping the human beings or which seek to promote the welfare of society. Here too the problem of what to include and what to exclude is not clear. It may, therefore, be said that the term social administration by itself does not exclude or include any subject. We may attempt to limit our field to certain acknowledged fields of activity such as: (i) community services; (ii) social security; and (iii) social welfare. This may include the administrative aspects of social reform legislation. These are distinguished from the regulatory and economic aspects of public administration and are styled as subject-matters of social administration.[85]

So far no attempt has been made to evolve management strategies for social welfare organizations. Each welfare agency develops its own approach for its functioning. This is mainly influenced by the individual who controls the organizations. It is no accident that MBO was first applied in the industrial and business field, for, they have a large history and more sophisticated organizations than what we find in the field of social welfare. However, MBO approach is likely to be most useful in this field, for the following reasons:

1. It will help he social welfare organizations to constantly review their objectives and modify their functioning accordingly.
2. It will help integrate work activity with the organisational objective, thus making it possible to scrutinize activities in terms of organisational goals.
3. It will help social welfare organizations to systematically plan their activities which will ensure judicial use of time by the personnel engaged.
4. It will help in improving motivation of the personnel. The specific goals associated with MBO can serve as incentives even though there may not be material reward.
5. It helps making better use of human resources.
6. It will help in reducing role conflict and role ambiguity which result in lower job satisfaction, decreased confidence in the organisation and higher level of tension. (Role conflict results when an individual in a job is subjected to conflicting demands placed upon him by two or more people. Role ambiguity refers to uncertainty about the way one's work is evaluated.)
7. It helps in the identification of problems which are because of frequent reviews.
8. It helps in achieving clarity of goals at all levels.[86]

Scope of Social Administration

Social administration implements, social legislation, aims at private philanthropy and religious charities into the dynamics of services and benefits for humanity or it is an art of implementing social policy into social action. Titmus has given a comprehensive definition relating to the scope of social administration. According to him:

"Social administration may broadly be defined as the study of social services whose object is the improvement of conditions of life of the individual in the settling of family and group relations. It is concerned with the historical development of these services, both statutory and voluntary, with the moral values implicit in social action, with the roles and functions of the services, with their economic aspects and with the part they play in meeting certain needs in the social process. On the one hand, then we are interested in the machinery of administration which organises and dispenses various forms of social assistance, on the other, in the lives, and needs, and the mutual relations of these members of the community for whom the services are provided by reason of their belonging to that community.[87]

Quite often the concepts of social administration, social welfare administration and social service administration are used inter-changeably to denote the organization and management of welfare programmes for the disadvantaged groups. Social service organizations are differentiated from other economic organisations by two fundamental characteristics: (a) their input of raw material are people with specific problems, and their production output are human beings processed or improved in a predetermined manner, and (b) their basic objective is that of 'service', that is, to maintain and improve the general social health and well-being of the people (Hasenfeld and English, 1974). Examples of such organisations are: Day-care centres, special schools, rehabilitation agencies, mental asylums, borstal and certified institutions, socio-economic units, after-care homes and a plethora of non-institutional programmes. The ever escalating tensions and social dysfunctionalities have resulted in the vast proliferation of social service organisations. This indispensability of social organisations in contemporary society is due to the vital functions they perform, both at the societal level and the individual level.

Productivity is defined as a mathematical relationship between inputs and outputs. It means to produce more and more from less and less inputs. Productivity in social welfare administration denotes an interrelationship between the inputs of money, materials, manpower and management style, and the efficiency and effectiveness of service outcomes at local, regional and national levels. The measurement of these galaxy of variables is indeed a formidable problem and the available research on this subject is almost nil in the Indian context. There should be a sincere endeavour in every social service enterprise in the country to produce services at an economical cost. One can maximize efficiency and effectiveness and thereby increase productivity and it is here that the vital human factor comes into play. The substance of this proposition is the creation of an understanding that the employees and employers in social service agencies on the one hand and the agencies and the beneficiaries on the other are in pursuit of a common goal and a common objective and the ultimate objective, in a limited sense, is the functional efficiency of the enterprise and in a broader sense the well-being of the disadvantaged communities. Productivity in social administration is influenced by a number of factors either directly or indirectly. Among these factors are: capital, training and health of welfare functionaries, the state of technology, style of management, organisational climate, social attitude to work and welfare, and attitude towards change and innovation. Organisational structures have seldom been examined in social administration to examine why they actually discourage productivity. Similarly, the base of capital formation has been a cause of concern in social welfare.[88]

If we analyse this definition and others, we can say that the following areas constitute the scope of social administration:

(a) Nature, purpose and scope of social services.
(b) Evolution of social services in the context of the needs of the society.

(c) Sources of financing these services.
(d) The content and method of social services programmes.
(e) Legislation and standard setting.
(f) Agencies international, national, local, voluntary-interested in social welfare.
(g) Planning, organising, staffing, directing, coordination, reporting and budgeting of these services.
(h) Citizen's participation in these programmes.
(i) Aspects of social services—health, education, social welfare, etc.
(j) Social policy and social action.

The aim of any state is to provide good life to the people. The well-being of the community is becoming increasingly dependent on efficient governmental management, i.e. public administration rather than on the separate efforts of individuals. If public administration fails the whole structure of modern society and civilisation would collapse like a house of cards. "There is no subject", says Charles Beard, "more important than this subject of administration. The future of civilised government, and even I think of civilisation itself leads upon our ability to develop a science and a philosophy and a practice of administration competent to discharge the functions of civilised society."[89] The success of 'social welfare' ultimately depends on the adequacy of the administrative apparatus prevailing in a country. The administrative set-up must respond to the social milieu and to the ideas, beliefs, expectations and values of the people. Prof. V. Jagannathan is of the view that there are three broad principles which are essential for the success of Social Welfare Administration to support socio-economic change guided by social justice; utmost decentralisation in administration appropriate to the different levels in government; unification in planning for welfare and allied subjects and services of personnel policies, programmes and administrative procedures to facilitate efficient flow of services to the people.

In conclusion, to improve the productivity in social welfare administration, the following measures are necessary: (a) provision of infrastructural facilities, (b) improvement of working conditions, (c) upgrading of skills of workers and training of people, (d) improvement of health and nutrition as well as living conditions, (e) adoption and adaptation of new technologies, (f) expansion of research and development facilities, (g) strengthening of planning, implementation and monitoring procedures in social welfare, (h) effecting saving through reduction of wasteful expenditure, (i) better quality control, (j) design of systematic information system with reliable and measurable indicators of performance, and finally (k) creation of productivity consciousness among the administrators, the agencies and the citizens.

The blazing advances recorded in science, technology and management hold out promises and hopes for solving the challenging problems of social welfare administration. However, the adaptation and adoption of these discoveries to social administrations is beset with problems. The contribution of the International Labour Organisation to these efforts is praiseworthy. The national productivity council should act as a resource centre for dissemination of knowledge about productivity in social administration through research and development and publications. Research should be geared to the task of working out productivity strategy for achieving plan objectives. Suitable methodologies have to be generated for measurement of productivity and for constructing appropriate indices. Operational models of service delivery for optimal productivity have to be designed in social welfare. No doubt, the tasks are formidable and time-consuming.[90]

SOCIAL SERVICES ADMINISTRATION

Significance and Meaning

The social services play a very important role in a modern society. These ultimately help in the socio-economic development of the country. Prof. Donnison remarks:

> "They are not an unproductive frill tagged into the economy as a charitable after-thought. They are an integral and (in one form or other) a necessary part of our economic and social structure—a form of collective provision required to meet the needs of an expanding society."[91] These services lay the foundation of the social development which affect the economic development.

The term 'Social Services' cannot be defined in a way that is universally acceptable. The United Nations' group of experts which prepared a report on the Development of National Social Service programmes defined the term in a narrow sense. This group gave the following definition:

> "Social service is ... an organised activity that aims at helping towards a mutual adjustment of individuals and then social-development. This objective is achieved through the use of techniques and methods designed to enable individuals, groups and communities to meet their needs and solve their problems of adjustment to a changing pattern of society, and through co-operative action to improve economic and social conditions."[92]

According to this group, the activities which can be included are as follows:

(1) Community services, including community planning; the organisation of local voluntary services and village or area councils of social services; the extension of organised social services to rural areas; the organisation of citizens' committees for social action, and of community and family centres.

(2) Services for families and individuals, including family counselling, family life education, family-budgeting, child and youth welfare services, day-care services, and care services for the aged; also social services to deal with persons in economic difficulties, including emergency relief, material assistance to persons in continuing need, and supplementary feeding scheme.

(3) Services for groups, including information, education, clubs, day camps, and other organised leisured activities for different age groups.

(4) Services for individuals and groups with special needs, including children deprived of a normal home life; the socially, physically and mentally handicapped; the sick and those suffering from other problems of health, including mental health; the chronically ill and disabled, the socially maladjusted, including juvenile delinquents and adult offenders, migrants, refugees and minority or other groups in the population having special needs.

In addition, the group listed the activities undertaken within the framework of related services, i.e., medical social work, mental health or psychiatric social work, social work in family planning, rehabilitation of the handicapped, school social work, social work in the armed forces, industrial social work, social work in vocational guidance and placement, court social work, the treatment of offenders through preventive services; social work in penal institutions, aftercare and parole, social work in housing projects, social work in social security agencies, and social work in community development programmes.[93]

Social services are those services which help in the enhancement of the personal welfare of individual citizens in the community. According to S.L.M. Eyden,

> "Social services is a social institution which has been developed to meet personal needs of individual members of society not adequately or effectively met either by the individual form his own or his family's resources or by commercial or industrial concern."[94]

In a broader sense, social services include programmes encompassing education, health, social security, the construction of adequate housing, the provisions of employment and a fair wage. In other words, it includes all measures designed to satisfy man's material, social and spiritual needs to the fullest possible extent.

There is no consensus of opinion regarding the definition and scope of social services. Indeed, it is difficult to define it precisely. These different interpretations of the term 'Social Services' determine the varying national approaches and differences in points of view in theory and practice with respect to social service programmes. Whether the basic approach adopted in a particular country refers to one or another definition will obviously have a bearing on the organisation and administration of social services in that country.

CONCLUSION AND RECOMMENDATIONS

The present crises in the field of social welfare administration *vis-a-vis* social welfare organisations can be attributed partly due to external factors and pressure groups. Besides the organisational effectiveness of the social welfare organizations—the foremost concern of the administration has greatly been influenced by the managerial capabilities, the knowledge, the skills, the motivation, and productivity of men who are working within the organisation. Another concern has been that the manager of social welfare organisations have not been motivated to secure, develop and utilise human resources effectively for accomplishment of organisational goals and to develop flexibility of systems of matching the objectives with the objectives of social development. That is why, in order to mitigate the lacunae the new managerial revolution has to take a system's view of management in which the sole perspective of the organisational setting is to be taken into consideration. The individual sub-systems have to be together, checked and operated so as to achieve the goals of the system in a most efficient manner. The intention is to provide decision-makers with full, accurate and meaningful summary of information relevant to clearly defined issues and, alternatives through a well-built management information system. The execution of welfare programmes by the social welfare organizaions being of technical nature, there is no way out but to adopt a system's view of management and administration. Hence to make the social welfare organisations more efficient and effective, sound organisation base for these is necessary. As presently, gaps are there. These have to be bridged.

In a system's view as outlined above, the performance of organisation depends upon the cooperation, coordination and support of many. When any lapse on the part of the social welfare organisation is detected, lest it should undermine the whole system it is necessary to let the social welfare organisation know as what is being thought of its performance based upon results racked up in the attainment of specific tasks and targets. The weakness and strength has to be clearly analysed. The supervising executive can reasonably discuss concrete situations with the subordinates. Such an appraisal is worth consideration and applicability of Management by Objectives approach provides several important advantages. The organisational effectiveness of the social welfare organisation cannot be achieved unless each head of the branch or division finds out the unproductive and time consuming activities so that effective time management can be done. Time management plays an important role in planning and executing welfare programme for social development.

In social welfare organisations as the number of beneficiaries involved run into lakhs, organisational planning has to be systematic and continuous. The resources and capacities of the organisation has to be analysed for fulfilling the desired roles. A well planned strategy has to be designed which matches with the future environmental opportunities, desired social economic roles, values and aspirations. Efforts have also to be made to provide a broad-based framework to help maximum number of beneficiaries to participate in the planning process. Planning for social development has to provide leadership and staff development.

The following facts and suggestions may be taken into consideration while administering the social programmes:

1. Need of Clearly Spelling out the Objectives of Social Welfare Services

The objectives of social welfare services must be spelt out in clear terms. Besides, social welfare services must be linked with broader objectives of social policy and socio-economic development to achieve an integrated National Social Welfare Service Programme.

Social welfare service programmes should be closely coordinated with economic development to achieve an integrated national social service programme. Adequate coordination is required among all the governmental bodies concerned with social welfare services and related social programmes, such as education, health, housing, justice and labour at the central level and all other levels of government, among the central authorities responsible for social welfare services and their field offices or the responsible agencies at subordinate levels of government; among governmental, semi-governmental and non-governmental organisations. The planning and coordinating machinery may also facilitate communication and the continuous exchange of general and specific information, as well as ensure effective collaboration at the operational level. According to J.F. Bulsara:

> "Social and economic development are complementary and social services and social welfare are essential for a balanced and healthy growth of the society, whether it be technologically advanced or economically under-developed. Social welfare services contribute substantially to economic productivity by creating amongst the people a healthy psychological atmosphere and a sense of belonging in being cared for thorough an appropriate provision of badly needed social and welfare services."[95]

In developing countries, the objectives of social welfare services are not spelt out clearly. This results in low priority being given to these services in these countries.

2. Need of the Development of Scientific Social Planning

All-round social planning should be based on scientifically collected and pertinent factual data. Such planning is not being done in the developing world because of the non-availability of reliable data of right quantity and quality. In the absence of such data, it becomes difficult to convince the planners resulting in the poor allocations to social welfare services.

3. Need of Active Participation of the Beneficiaries

We should encourage the active participation of citizens in the planning and implementation of social welfare programmes. Public cooperation is an active and living element in a dynamic democracy. The resources in the developing world are limited and we can serve more people in an efficient manner through their active involvement.

4. Need of Decentralisation to Ensure Speedy and Efficient Implementation

Responsibility for the administration of social services should be decentralised to a great extent to ensure close relationship with the beneficiaries and communities to be served. This would also help in getting the feedback from the people which would be useful in the planning and evaluation of social welfare programmes. Besides, we must provide the services in the rural areas, urban slums .and tribal areas.

Special efforts may be made to extend social welfare services to neglected rural areas on an adequate basis, taking into account the particular needs of rural areas. These services must be provided in these areas according to the needs of the areas.

5. Need of Developing Technical Standards

Technical standards for social welfare service programmes may be evolved with the help of institutions engaged in the education and training of social workers. These standards may be adapted according to different situations to ensure implementation of the overall social policy. Technical standards has to be simple and clear so that they are really understandable to all concerned with social welfare programmes and activities and to the general public.

6. Strengthening of Voluntary Organizations

In many countries, voluntary organisations have traditionally played and continue to play an important role in providing social welfare services, Governments should encourage and assist such organisations by providing finances, technical consultation and supervision to help them maintain standards .and improve their effectiveness. The care may be taken that the voluntary organisations may not be reduced to bureaucratic organisations.

7. Need of Developing Administrative Competence in the Field of Social Welfare Services

There is a need to make selections on the basis of administrative ability and technical qualifications in the field of social welfare services, so that qualified and talented personnel are attracted to join this sector.

8. Well-defined Procedures to Assess the Functioning of Social Welfare Services

Clearly defined administrative procedures has to be developed for handling all complaints regarding the functioning of social welfare service activities. This procedure should be simple and intelligible so that beneficiaries and general public can make use of it. This will help to assess the impact of these services on the people.

Good relationship with the general public are of importance to the development and administration of social welfare programmes. Suitable provisions should therefore be made for public relations activities to be carried out by the bodies responsible for social welfare programmes. Such activities should be designed to provide interpretation and wider understanding of the programmes, stimulate interest and support of social welfare and development and to create a favourable climate of public opinion. The public relations activities relevant to social welfare programmes should be coordinated and conducted in close cooperation with those of such other central or local authorities responsible for general public relations activities of the government on an overall basis.

India today is at the cross-roads. We are in a curious predicament. The obverse of the coin is bright, the reverse grim. We are heirs to a glorious civilization whose mighty stream has been flowing uninterruptedly down the millennia, enriching and ennobling all on its path. Fifty-nine years back we have also recovered our political independence from the largest empire the world has seen, and that without firing a single shot—something unique in history. Yet chaos stalks the land. Things are falling apart. Values cherished over the centuries are getting eroded. In a country of rich natural resources the poverty of the masses is abysmal. The haves exploit the have-nots in a hundred ingenious ways. Women and the weaker sections of society reel under injustice and handicaps. Corruption is rampant. Mindless violence maims and destroys the precious lives of the innocent. The sensitive citizen finds himself asking, 'Whither India?'

Notes and References

1. Swami Ranganathanada, "Democratic Administration in the light of Practical Vendanta" 2003, p. 112.
2. T.N. Chaturvedi, "Development: The Dynamics Thorns and Thistles", in Dynamics of Development: An International Perspective (ed.) S.K. Sharma, New Delhi, Concept Publications Company, 1978, Vol. II, pp. 693-709. Also S.P. Aiyer, Liberalism and Welfare State, in Perspective on the Welfare State (ed.) S.P. Aiyer, Bombay Manaktala, pp. 67-68.
3. Edward, W. Weidner, "The Goals, Strategy and Environment of Development", in Dynamics of Development: An International Perspective (ed.) S.K. Sharma, *ibid.*, Vol. II, pp. 31-46.
4. Norman, D. Palmer, "Development: The Need for an Effective Dialgouge", in Dynamics of Development: An International Perspective (ed.) S.K. Sharma, *ibid.*, Vol. II, pp. 95-101.
5. Most countries of Asia, Africa and Latin America are labelled as 'developing countries', or 'poor countries' or 'less developed countries' or 'emerging nations', or 'third world' and likewise, because they are relatively young, because they are confronted with similar development problems, because they are engaged in the development tasks of 'nation-building' and 'socio-economic progress', because their national income per capita is less, because they are technologically less advanced and finally they are socially backward.
6. Eva T.H. Brann, "The Conditions of Exchange", in International Educational and Cultural Exchange, Vol. XX (Spring 1977), p. 4.
7. Development Administration: Current Approaches and Trends in Public Administration for National Development (U.N. Publication, Sales No. E. 76. II. H. 1), p. 9.
8. Edward Shils, "Political Development in the: New States" (The Hague, Mounton, 1962), p. 10.
9. P.C. Sikligar, "Social Development: A Profile", *IJPA*, April-June 1998, Vol. XLIV, No.2, p. 176.
10. Ramabrahman and Soumendra Mohanty, "Growth *versus* Development: Caution to Policy-Makers and Effective Policy-making", *IJPA*, April-June, 2008, Vol. LIV, No. 2, pp. 369-72.
11. GOI, Planning Commission, XI Plan, Vol. I, pp. 1-2.
12. Milton J. Esman, "The Politics of Development Administration" In Montgomery and Siffin (eds.), Approaches to Development: Politics Administration and Change (New York, McGraw Hill, 1966), p. 95.
13. Gerhard Colm and Theodore Geiger, "Country Programming as a Guide to Development", in Development of the Emerging Countries: An Agenda for Research (Washington, Brookings Institution, 1962), p. 47.
14. Edward W. Weidner, "The Elements of Development Administration", in Weidner (ed.), Development Administration in Asia (Durham, N.C., Duke University Press, 1970; p. 8.
15. T.N. Chaturvedi, Development: The Dynamics Thorns and Thistles", in Sudesh Kumar Sharma (ed.), Dynamics of Development: An International Perspective (Delhi, Concept, 1978), Vol. 2, p. 693.
16. Fred W. Riggs, "The Idea of Development Administration," in Edward W. Weidner (ed.), *op. cit.*, p. 27.
17. *Ibid.*, p. 71.
18. *Ibid.*

19. *Ibid.*, p. 72.
20. Hann-Been Lee, "The Role of the Higher Civil Service Under Rapid Social and Political Change", in Weidner (ed.) *op. cit.*, p. 108 .
21. Chi-Yuen Wu, "The Nature of Modern Development: Challenge of Underdevelopment and Mal-development", in Sharma (ed.), *op. cit.*, Vol. 1, p. 2.
22. U.C. Aggarwal, "Social Sector Development: Outlays *vs.* Outcomes—An overview, *IJPA*, July-Sept., 2005, Vol. LI, No. 3, pp. 315, 322.
23. J.C. Mohanty, Social Sector Crossroads, *IJPA*, July-Sept., 2005, Vol. LI, No. 3, p. 532.
24. Milton J. Esman, "The Politics of Development Administration", in Montgomery and Siffin, (eds.), Approaches to Department Politics, Administration and Change (New York, McGraw-Hill, 1965), p. 9.
25. Seventh Five Year Plan (1985-90), Government of India, New Delhi. Planning Commission, 1985; Vol. 1, Foreword.
26. *Ibid*.
27. Message from Dr. M.G. Candua, Director General of the WHO in the *World Health*, March 1969, p. 5.
28. R.C. Malhotra, "An Alternative Strategy for Self-sustained Development with Focus on Participation by the Poor at the Local Level", paper presented to Consultative Meeting on- Alternate Strategy for Development with Focus on Local-level Planning and Development (from 31 Oct. to 4 Nov., 1978)—UN, Asian and Pacific Development Institute, Bangkok, April 1979, p. 5.
29. Peter F. Drucker, "Economic Development and Human Talents", American Review, January, 1970, p. 27, Vol. XIV, No. 2, put by USIS, New Delhi.
30. Salvatore Schiavo-campo and Hans W. Sorger, Perspectives of Economic Development (Houghton Mifflin Co., Boston, 1970).
31. Irma Adelman and Cynbla T. Morris, Society, Politics and Economic Development, John, Hoptrus Press, 1967.
32. Max Milikan, "A Strategy for Development" Vni Centre for Social and Economic Information, Executive Briefing, New York, 1970.
33. WHO, Public Health Papers, "Inter-relationship between Health Programmes and Socio-economic Development", 49, Geneva, 1973, p. 32.
34. Gunnar Myrdal, Asian Drama: An Enquiry into the Poverty of National, New York. Herwords-worth, Penguin, 1968, p. 1869.
35. C.B. Black, The Dynamics of Modernization, New York, 1966, pp. 55-60.
36. Jan Tinbergen. Reshaping the International Order: A Report of the Club of Rome, New York, B.P. Datton and Co., Inc., 1976, Chapter 5, pp. 61-64.
37. Mahbub-ul-Haq, The Poverty Curtain, p. 48.
38. T.K.N. Unnithan, "Development Processes in any Under-development Country (India) In Carle, C. Zimmerman and Richard B. Damon (ed.), Sociology, of Underdevelopment, Jaipur, Rawat, 1976 (Asian ed.), p. 402.
39. ECAFE, Seminar on Meeting of the Working Party on Social Development, (Bangkok, 8-15. December, 1970).
40. UN, Asian and Pacific Development Institute, Proceedings of a Consultative Meeting, Bangkok, April 1979. p. 11.
41. UN General Assembly Resolution, 24th October, 1973, para 83.
42. Text of Address of Dr. H. Mahler, Director General, WHO—WHO Regional Committee for South-East Asia, Thirtieth Session, Bangkok, Thailand, 2-8 Aug., 1977. published in Final Report and Minutes of the Meeting of the Thirtieth Session, WHO, New Delhi, Sept., 1977, p. 64.
43. Wahidul Haque. Niranjan Mehta, Anjsur Rahmam and Poona Wignaraja, "Towards a Theory of Rural Development", Development dialogue, 1977: 2 Dag Hammarskjold Foundation. Uppasala, Sweden in P.B. Desai, Planning in India (1951-78), Vikas Publishing House, Ghaziabad (UP), 1979, p. 158.
44. Shankar Pathak, Social Welfare: An Evolutionary and Development Perspects, New Delhi: MacMillan India Limited, 1981, pp. 153-55.
45. V. Jagannadham, "Administration and Social Development", *The Indian Journal of Public Administration*, Vol. XXIV, No. 3, July-Sept. 1980. pp. 528-34, Also Utpal K. Banerjee, "Social Communication and Social Indicators", *The Indian Journal of Public Administration*, Vol. XXVI, No. 2, April-June, 1981, pp. 263-300.

46. Second Five Year Plan, Government of India, New Delhi, Planning Commission, 1956.
47. Third Five Year Plan, Government of India, New Delhi, Planning Commission, 1961.
48. First Five Year Plan, Government of India, New Delhi. Planning Commission, 1957.
49. Mukkavilli Seetharam, "Productivity in Social Welfare Administration", *IJPA*, July-Sept. 1982, Vol. XXXVII, No. 3, pp. 665-66.
50. M. Dimock, and Dimock, Public Administration, New York, Holt, 1964, p. 82.
51. H.C. Beales, The Making of Social Policy, OUP, 1594, L.T. Hobhous Memorial Trust Lecture No. 15.
52. *Ibid.*, p. 77.
53. Tarlok Singh, "Social Policy", in Encyclopedia of Social Work in India, Government of India, New Delhi, Vol. II, pp. 287-93.
54. P.D. Kulkarni, "Social Policy in India", Bombay, Tata Institute of Social Sciences, 1965, pp. 7-8, India International Centre, 1964, The Need for a Social Policy Resolution.
55. Incidentally, no State Government seems to have so far come forward with a Statement of Policy on the subject.
56. V.M. Kulkarni, Essays in Social Administration, Delhi: Research Publications in Social Sciences, 1972, pp. 9-10.
57. K.D. Gangrade, "Development of Social Policy in India: A Critical Review", Talk delivered on April 24, 1976, in the Department of Public Admn., P.U. under the auspices of the Regional Branch of Indian Institute of public Admn., Chandigarh (an unpublished document).
58. Bernice Q. Madison, "The Meaning of Social Policy, The Comparative Dimensions in Social Welfare", London: Groom Helm Ltd., 1980. pp. 63-64.
59. Planning Commission, Seventh Five Year Plan (1985-90), New Delhi, Government of India, Planning Commission, 1985, Vol. I, Preface.
60. *Ibid.*
61. K.D. Gangrade and M.V. Sastri, "Social Planning as an Alternative Strategy of Growth", in Dynamics of Development: An International Perspective, Vol. II, *op. cit.*, pp. 511-18.
62. Indian National Committee Report on New Strategies for Social Development, Role of Social Welfare, XV International Conference on Social Welfare, Manila, The Philippines, 6th-12th September, 1970, New Delhi, Department of Social Welfare, pp. 2-3.
63. Gunnar Myrdal, "Economic Theory and Under-Developed Regional, Gerald Duckworth and Company Ltd., London, 1957, p. 82,
64. M.S. Gore, "Social Work and Social Work Education", Asia Publishing House, Bombay, 1964, p. 5. Also Hobman Daisy, L., "The Welfare State", Murry, London, 1953, p. 23.
65. Harold Wilensky and Charles N. Lebeaux, "Industrial Society and Social Welfare", Russel Sage Foundation, New York, 1958, p. 17.
66. R.M. Titmus, "Commitment to Welfare", Georgic Alien and Unwin Ltd., London, 1968, pp. 16-18. Also Philip Klim, "Discussion on Social Work." The International Encyclopaedia of Social Services. 1934, Vol. 14, p. 165,
67. Brown Moreal, "Introduction to Social Administration in Britain", Hutchenson University Library, London, 1971, pp. 11-17. Also Philip Klim, "Discussion on Social Work", The International Encyclopaedia of Social Services, 1934, Vol. 14, p. 165.
68 D.P. Chowdhry, "Some Random Thoughts on Social Welfare" in *Indian Journal of Social Work*, June 1951, 117.
69. N.K. Dave, "MBO for Social Welfare Organizations: An Approach and a Philosophy", *IJPA*, July-Sept. 1982, Vol. XXVIII, No. 3, pp. 552-53.
70. D.V. Kulkarni, "Social Administration "in Public Welfare Agencies", in Encyclopaedia of Social Work in India, Planning Commission, New Delhi, Government of India, The Publication Division, 1968, Vol. II, pp. 232~34. Also Shankar Pathak, "Social Welfare Health and Family Planning in India", New Delhi: Marwah Publications, 1978, pp. 7-8.
71. Sixth Five Year Plan (1980-85), New Delhi, Government of India Press, The Planning Commission, 1981, pp. 420-38.
72. Constitution of India.
73. M.S. Gore, "Social Work and the Eradication of Poverty", in Dynamics of Development: An International Prospective, (ed.), S.K. Sharma, *op. cit.*, Vol. II, pp. 531-38.

74. Government of India, India 1985, New Delhi: Ministry of Information and Broadcasting, Publication Division, December 1982.
75. Sixth Five Year Plan, *op. cit.* pp. 430-38.
76. V.M. Kulkarni, "Essays in Social Administration", *op. cit.*, pp. 9-10.
77. S.L. Kaushik and Pardeep Sachdeva, "Social Welfare Administration as a Discipline and a Profession, Perspectives and Prospects", *IJPA*, Jan-March 1992, Vol. XXXVII, No. 1, p. 63.
78. D.V. Donnison, "The Teaching of Social Administration", *The British Journal of Sociology*, Vol. III, 3 Sept. 1961.
79. S.L. Kaushik and Pradeep Sachdeva, "Social Welfare Administration as a Discipline and a Profession: Perspectives and Prospects", *IJPA*, Jan.-March 1992, Vol. XXXVII, No. 1, p. 51.
80. K.M. Slack, Social Administration and the Citizen, London, 1966, p. 29.
81. Forder, Concepts in Social Administration, London, 1974, p. 1.
82. India International Centre, Proceedings of the Seminar on Social Administration in Developing Countries (March 16-21) 1964, held at New Delhi, the India International Centre, New Delhi, p. 27.
83. John Carrier and Ian Kendall, "Social Administration as Social Science", in Foundations of Social Administration, (ed.) by Helmuth Neisler, London, 1977, pp. 25-26.
84. Jagannadham, "A Note on the Status of Social Administration in relation to Public Administration", Proceedings of the Seminar on Social Administration in Developing Countries, March 16-21, 1964, New Delhi, India International Centre, n.d., p. 108
85. *Ibid*.
86. N.K. Dave, "MBO for Social Welfare Organizations: An Approach and a Philosophy", *IJPA*, July-Sept. 1982, Vol. XXVIII, No. 3, p. 562.
87. Richard, M. Titmus, Essays on the Welfare State, London, 1958, pp. 14-15.
88. Mukkavilli Seetharam, "Productivity in Social Welfare Administration", *IJPA*, July-Sept., 1982, Vol. XXVIII, No. 3, pp. 665-66.
89. A. Lepowsky, "The Art and Science of Organisation and Management", Administration, New York, Knopp, 1952, p. 17.
90. Mukkavilli Seetharam, "Productivity in Social Welfare Administration", *IJPA*, July-Sept. 1982, Vol. XXVIII, No. 3, p. 673.
91. D.V. Donnison, Inaugural Lecture—"The Development of Social Administration", 1962.
92. United Nations Publications, Sales No. 60, IV, I, para 6.
93. United Nations Publications, Sales No. 60, IV, 1, para 42.
94. J.L.M. Eyden, "Social Services in Modern State", Case Conference, Feb. 1955.
95. J.F. Bulsara, "Social Planning in India" in Encyclopaedia of Social Work in India, Vol. 11, p. 285.

CHAPTER 2

Sustainable Development

(See Chart 2.1)

Sustainability means meeting the needs of present generation without compromising the abilities and opportunities of future generation. It thus, implies both inter-generational and intra-generational equity. Sustainability is an important dimension of human development. Human development is a process of enlarging people's choices. But such enhancement must be for both present and future generations without sacrificing one for the other. Thus, sustainable development is a technique of eating the portion of bread and butter by the present generation in such a way that it must last long so as to enable the future generations to enjoy over it.[1]

The concept of sustainable development encompasses economic, ecological and social parameters. The economic approach focuses on generating maximum income/economic growth while maintaining the stock of assets or capital. The ecological view stresses the stability of biological and physical systems and their protection and management for posterity. The social concept is people-oriented and seeks to maintain the stability of social and cultural systems leading to human capital formation. Correspondingly, sustainable development has economic growth, human development and resource management as its central goals.

In the opinion of Gilbert and Braat (1991) sustainable development, can be described as a "pattern of social and structural transformation which optimises the economic and social benefits available in the present without jeopardising the likely potential for similar benefits on the future". Furthermore, Gladwin, Kennelly and Krause (1995) have examined the concept as "a process of achieving human development—in an inclusive, connected, equitable, prudent and secure manner.

O.P. Dwivedi in his article, "India in a Globalized World: Transforming Bureaucracy for the Well-being and Prosperity of All" in the *IJPA*, Oct.-Dec. 2007, Vol. LIII, No. 4 quoted that Robert Prescott-Allen published a report, "The Well-being of Nation: A Country-by-country Index of Quality of Life and the Environment", with the central argument that a society or a nation can be well and sustainable provided both its people and the ecosystem are healthy. His contention

CHART 2.1

Use of Resources for Present Generation

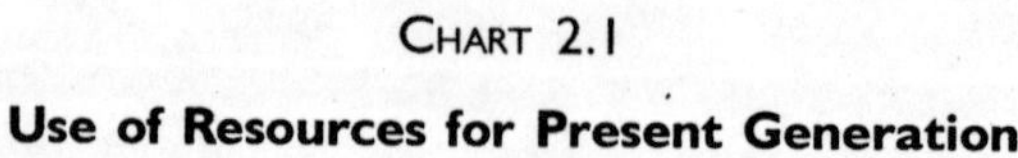

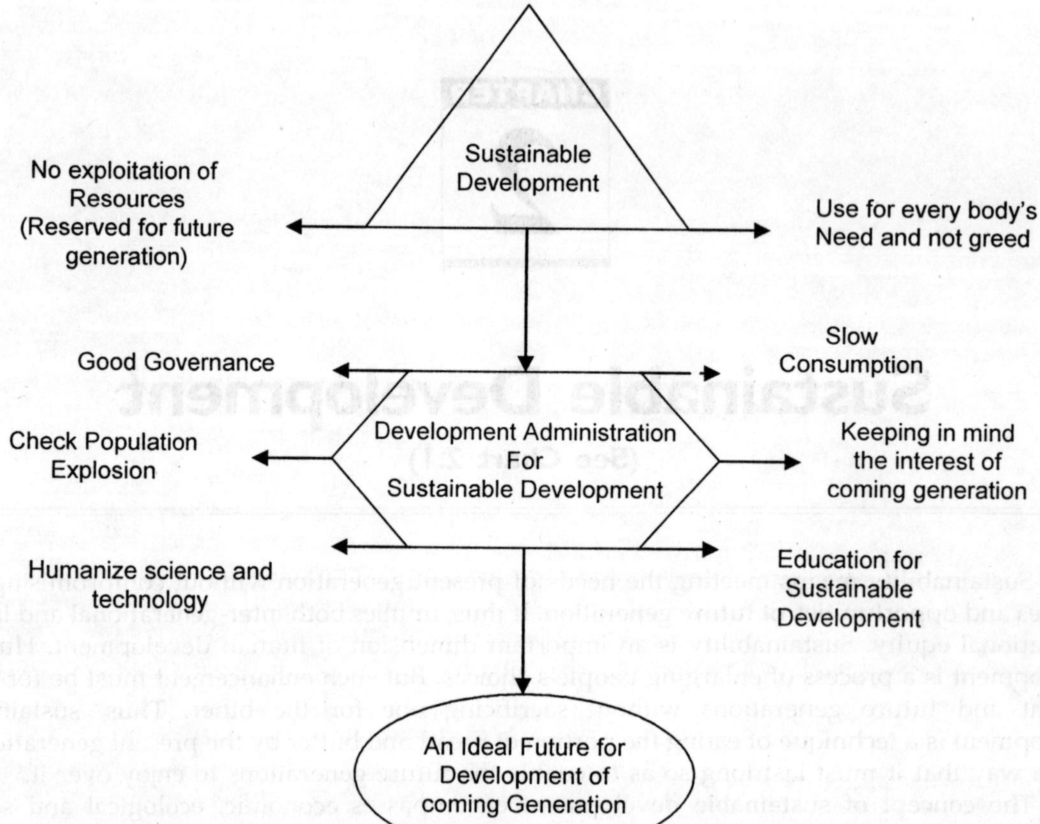

is that human well-being and the health of the ecosystem are closely linked because the ecosystem surrounds people much in the same manner "as the white of an egg surrounds and supports the yolk." WCD denotes sustainable development as "a process of change in which the exploitation of resources, the direction of investments, the orientation of technological development and institutional change are made consistent with future as well as present needs."[2]

The need of 21st Century for sustainable development is to stop the mad game of antagonizing nature and to befriend it once again. Here alone lies the sure path to progress and prosperity. For this purpose we shall have to humanize science and technology and make humanities scientific. Education for sustainable development is therefore the call of the day and sooner we realize it the better it is for our survival and quality of life.

Any holistic model of sustainable development should take into account the three-fold transformation of human individual, human society and the cosmos. This should be the end-all and be-all of all planning and strategies of development at the global level. Then only it can be a total development which can be really sustainable and enduring.[3]

Unbridled economic growth and population explosion in some parts of the globe coupled with speedy industrialization and rapid consumption of additional man-made and natural resources are raising questions in regard to a sustainable future. Planning a sustainable future, on the other hand, is also becoming increasingly difficult in view of unprecedented rates of population growth specially in the developing world, over the last century. All these factors have created new imbalances and vulnerabilities which threaten future sustainability.

From times immemorial, our seers and guides, have made our society believe that the man only needs three basic things to tread on the path of human-graphics in ones life. They had been also guiding us to observe penance and perseverance in all spheres of our activities.

The three basics, they had enumerated as "Horne, Hearth and Helmet." No doubt, all these three are subject to their maintenance, through money and money only. For the achievement of this motive, they had also given us a set pattern of human endeavours, fixed, in certain parameters, and had advised the human race not to contravene those parameters, otherwise the man would suffer from the mental as well as physical disorders.[3A]

Now with the passage of time, the old perceptions have been rendered totally redundant by the man-made short-cuts and selfish tendencies, and a sort of rat-race is going on, on all sides of the world, in which the only object of life seems to be collection of money. With the new innovations, the new trade laws have come up in national and international arena and to opt these practices has (to some extent) become a necessity. The moral content of our culture and traditions has now taken a back seat, and the driving force is the unethical and unprincipled tendencies, which are sprouting and multiplying everyday, in these fast changing conditions.[4]

The Earth Summit 1992 is widely regarded as being one of the most important events of the century to address issues of global environmental degradation, inequalities between nations and possible strategies to protect the future of life on earth. Agenda 21, which emanated from the earth summit, effects a global consensus and political commitment at the highest level on development and environment cooperation. It provides a framework for governments in their endeavour to seek a balance between population and pathways of development. It strives to formulate plans of action that meet the needs of people while providing for the ecological security of natural systems.

The main policies and programmes contained in Agenda 21 provide a major re-affirmation of a number of traditional values inherent in the Indian culture. It is also in conformity with all those values that are enshrined in the Indian constitution. The notion of sustainable developments is not a new one. The history of the country is replete with innumerable initiatives undertaken by people that demonstrate not just concern for environment, but also the awareness of the need to balance it with livelihood resources. This 'tradition' of care, conservation and preservation of environmental resources is also reflected in the spirit of the constitution of India, which has acted as the guiding inspiration of the nation now for over half a century. The strength of the Indian Constitution lies in the fact that it does not advocate any new or imported principles, instead it builds on the deep-rooted and therefore, resilient, practices of sustainable development that have evolved over time in the country.

Thus, the congruity of Agenda 21's objectives of sustainable development with India's own traditional values provided renewed thrust several initiatives in the country. It also provided new direction in sectors that have emerged as areas of global concern.

From the beginning of time people have heard the still small voice of obligation and brotherhood. When they have listened society has worked. Why they have refused to listen, society has broken.[5]

The Stockholm Declaration (1972) on the human environment, said to be the

"Magnacharta" on human environment proclaimed: "The natural resources of the earth, including air, water, land, flora and fauna are especially representative samples of natural eco-system, must be safeguarded for the benefit of present and future generation through careful planning and management, as appropriate. The state should take all possible steps to prevent pollution of seas by substances that are liable to create hazards to human health, to harm living sources and marine life, to damage amenities or to interfere with other legitimate uses of the seas. The man and his environment must be spared against the nuclear weapons and all other means of mass destruction.[6]

The continuing multiplication of want associated with the spread of materialistic philosophy of life has brought the world to the brink of a major disaster. This is reflected in the ecological crisis, the ramifications of which is becoming clearer. Natural resources are being depleted at a faster rate. An economy based on the foundation of endless wants would therefore not last long. It is in this context, that Gandhian doctrine of want limitation (which should be better understood as want regulation or moderation) becomes extremely significant for the survival of mankind.

Environmental concern arises essentially on two grounds. First, a reckless use of resources to maximize short-run gain can lead to depletion which would adversely affect development in future, which may not be a very distant future. It is not in the interests of sustainable development. Second is that one does not have to wait for future generations to feel the adverse impact on environment. Livelihoods are lost, sources of drinking water are made unusable, and victims are subjected to agonising misery (sometimes irreversible) due to negative externalities (environment) of so-called development projects. While a few already better of sections may become still better-off, many others become worse-off. The former cannot offset the latter's effect.

Rapidly growing population, urbanization, changing agricultural, industrial and water resource management, increasing use of pesticides and fossil fuels have all resulted in a perceptible deterioration in the quality of environment and attendant adverse health consequences. Environment pollution due to developmental activities are increasingly becoming the focus of concern. The interactive interdependence of health, environment and sustainable development was accepted as the fulcrum of action under Agenda 21 at the Earth Summit in Brazil in 1992. In the case of India, against an economic growth of 163 percent in the past 20 years, the pollution load has increased by more than 475 percent. During the period from 1975 to 1995 industrial pollution grew by 247 percent, whereas the vehicular pollution load shot up phenomenally by 650 percent. Environmental health in its broader perspective would have to address the detection, prevention and management of:

(i) Existing deficiencies or excesses of certain elements in natural environment;
(ii) Macro-environmental contamination of air, land, water and food; and
(iii) Disaster management.

This ordering of priorities has brought our civilization to the brink of ruin. We know we must find a way out, a way back to values and priorities that represent the real, whole nature of man. But all the ways that were once intended to help us from our authentic well-being and our authentic responsibility are themselves deeply stained by the money question.

K. Ramamurthy in his Article, "Environment and Development" some issues in G.S. Monga rightly states: "Excessive technological growth has created an environment in which life has become physically and mentally unhealthy. Polluted air, irritating noise, traffic congestion, chemical containments, radiation hazards and many other sources of physical and psychological stress have become part of everyday life for most of us. These manifold health hazards are not just incidental by products of technological progress, they are integral features of an economic system obsessed with growth and expansion, continuing to intensify its high technology in an attempt to increase productivity." This passage from best seller, "The Turning Point by Fritijo Capra" admirably sums up the effects of so-called 'development' of the Western countries. Development without regard for ethics and environment has produced many harmful effects. The last hundred years have seen whole families of previously unknown diseases: new infections, genetic disorders that frustrate any attempts at prevention, endocrine disorders, allergies, toxic diseases, including the 'radiation and toxic allergic sickness gaining momentum with the growing mass of synthetic materials totally alien to natural human environment; the notorious AIDS is but the latest addition to the list. Further, the development has the effect of making the developed countries richer and developing countries poorer, besides the mindless exploitation of valuable natural resources.[7]

India has over a billion people spread across 3.28 million sq. km. of land and associated water resources, surviving on an astonishing range of biodiversity and other natural resources. Policy-makers struggle with the choice of pathways to development in a country that presents a spectrum of lifestyles that ranges from the very rich, comparable with those of the most developed countries, to those that are among the poorest. The complex poverty issues in the country force a large number of persons to remain at low levels of resource consumption.

Despite the seemingly desperate race by people of all classes to use all means available to exploit resources, there are still institutions of management that advocate caution. Over hundreds of years the people of India have evolved refined mechanisms of conservation and prudent utilization of their livelihood resources. Many of these have survived the test of time; others that have not, have given way to newer and more opposite institutional arrangements.

The question is how can the available land/water mass (2.5% of the world) sustainably provide for a rapidly increasing population (16% of the world)? The positive answer to the question requires the most unprecedented mobilization of people's minds, ideas, institutions and resources to come up with a socially just and environmentally sustainable blueprint for survival.

More than 165 countries that subscribe to Agenda 21, have over the last decade adopted varied and innovative means of interpreting and implementing Agenda 21, suitable to their respective contexts. The Indian context presents a unique mosaic of biological, anthropic, cultural, physiographic and climatic diversity, with a population as diverse as its geography. Approximately one-fourth of them live in extreme poverty and amongst them are included the tribal people. One-fourth of world's tribal people are habitants of India.

The last decade witnessed a heightened awareness of the detrimental environmental impacts associated with high industrial growth and economic progress. There was also a growing appreciation of the fact that sustainable development cannot be achieved in a climate where socio-economic development and environment planning are pursued as independent activities. This environmental concern is reflected in the various measures as are mentioned below:

- Developing a set of standards for regulating emissions and effluents from polluting industries.
- Periodic monitoring of the status of polluting industries. This resulted in a significant increase in the number of units that installed pollution control equipments.
- Seeking to control the discharge of effluents into water bodies by identifying the 851

grossly polluting industries and directing them to install effluent treatment systems or face closure. This resulted in 829 out of the 851 industries adopting effluent treatment plants. The remaining plants were forced to close down.

- Setting up of Common Effluent Treatment Plants (CETP) for Small Scale Industry (SSI) clusters.
- Preparing Zoning Atlas to help locate industries in areas where minimum environmental damage can take place.
- Encouraging research and development of clean technologies for use in various types of industries.
- Introducing and actively encouraging industry to adopt internationally accepted environmental management systems like ISO 14001 (launched in 1996).

The greed for exploitation of natural resources by people has led to different types of disasters—earthquake, floods, pollution, violence, accidents, etc. The frequency of disasters is on the increase. If the peeple do not use the resources in a balanced way, there is going to be disasters and disasters at a very fast rate. The only answer to prevent disasters is prevention through sustainable development.

The fact that India is the second most populous country that survives on just 2.4% of world's landmass, creates its own population resource tension. Combined with the colonial legacy of systems that sub-served the exploitative objectives of the then colonial administration, was made the task of change that much more difficult. Thus, despite the creation of an enabling framework for sustainable development, India continues to face enormous challenges in search of options for development that are environmentally sound and suitable to its specific social conditions.

Understandably, one billion strong populace has an immense impact on the total volume and quality of resources. The heterogeneous demands emanating from diverse set of claimants, ranging from subsistence goods to seeking support for opulent life styles put pressure on the forest cover and water resources and its contribution to environmental pollution is enormous.

FOREST COVER

Forests constitute an important component of livelihood resource, especially for the tribal people and those living in the forest fringes estimated to be around 100 million people. The forests also provide environmental benefits such as watershed protection, prevention of soil and water run-off, ground water recharge, purification of air and water by acting as a sink for green house gases like carbon dioxide, conservation of genetic resources and bio-diversity, recreational services and aesthetic value.

However, in India less than 1/5th of the total land area is under forest cover and has remained so for nearly two decades. While the dense forest cover over the same period has stabilized to around 37 million hectares, approximately 25 million hectares are open forests. Since open forests have a canopy cover of less than 40%, it affects the quality of ecosystem services and the quality of life of some of the poorest people in the country, who derive their sustenance from that resource.

Water Resources

Of the total estimated 432 cubic Km. of replenishable ground water resources, nearly 92%

are estimated to be utilizable. So far however, India has been able to exploit only 32% of the same. The total river water resources have been estimated at around 1953 cubic Km. Despite the estimated quantity of available water, it is predicted that the country's total water resources in the year 2050 will barely be able to match the country's total water requirements. This underscores the urgent need to develop an integrated approach to the development and management of water resources in the country. In addition, maintaining a balance between the availability and requirements across basins, regions and between sections of the population adds another dimension to the challenge.

The other important issue is the deteriorating quality of our water resources. The task of continually monitoring the water quality standards of the nation's aquatic resources is the mandate of the Central Pollution Control Board (CPCB) in collaboration with the State Pollution Control Boards. The monitoring results indicate that organic and bacterial contaminations are the predominant sources of pollution in the water resources of the country. The unmitigated release of untreated municipal sewage into the rivers and river systems of the country is reducing the level of dissolved oxygen required to support aquatic life. As a result, the pollution levels in terms of Biological Oxygen Demand (BOD) are increasingly leading to the destruction of aquatic life. Chemical effluents released into the water are also similarly having a detrimental effect on the quality of the aquatic resources of the country.

Environmental Health Risks

Environmental health risk emanate from a combination of complex factors. Poverty, among others, is perhaps the most crucial that puts populations at risk. Other factors include access to safe drinking water and sanitation in rural and urban area, air quality (especially in urban areas), indoor air pollution (especially in poor rural and urban households), solid waste management and agro-industrial pollution.

The current environmental and development trends in the world are clear indication that the world is far from attaining the objectives enshrined in Agenda 21. Some will question even the rate of progress, which has been rather slow and uneven. One part of the reason of the unsatisfactory progress can be traced to the global system of location of resources and unredeemed promises while the other part remains the responsibility of national governments.

Empowering people to nurture these resources for sustainable livelihoods will remain a cornerstone of our policies. However, the full empowerment of people to undertake this responsibility is as yet an unfinished task. There is a tremendous scope in the country for improving the technological inputs for urban waste management and institutionalization of responsible social practices that will facilitate an efficient and environmentally safe method of disposal of waste of all kinds. Science and technology will play an important role in improving access to drinking water, sanitation, improvement of health as also in development of technologies that provide clean energy, efficient transportation and safe industries. Harnessing of India's scientific and technological pre-process to set increasingly higher environmental standards and their strict adherence through robust institutions is a potential that remains to be exploited fully. By setting specific sectoral targets India is attempting to accelerate the process of realizing that potential. [8]

In the 21st century the Deep Ecologists begin to feel a sense of oneness with nature and as a part of natural order of life, the very same philosophy our ancestors practiced, propagated and insisted to adopt to maintain peace on the planet. They had respect for nature, which is the fastest, cleanest and most refined level of inter-species communication and communication.

It would be unrealistic, however, to suppose that the damage that has been done, and still continues to be done, can be arrested and undone in the short-term. Rather, long-term global policies must be envisaged and if they are to be successful, they will require changes in our perceptions of man in nature. If our global physical environment is not to be further degraded, we must change our conceptual environment, our ways of thinking and behaving. Perhaps the worst environment pollution is pollution of the mind, and the greatest need is for well thought out principles of environment ethics.

All spheres of human conduct, private and public, are subject to ethical principles or rules. When governments or other corporate bodies despoil the environment in the name of development or political dominance or national security, when governments adopt *laissez faire* policies that permit the exploitation of nature for narrow, short-term gains, they contravene the basic ethical principle of the greatest good for the greatest number of people.

In reviewing all these environmental effects of water, earth and air and their possible dangers, we should not however reach too gloomy a conclusion. A comforting finding, which may be extended to many other aspects, is the recent discovery that fish caught in the last century and preserved in museums have been found to have similar mercury levels as those found in fish today. And after all, the human race with its great adaptability has survived the innumerable disasters and environmental hazards it has encountered for several million years. Modern is replacing old ones, and there is no reason to doubt that man's ingenuity and intelligence will prevail as far as environment problems are concerned.

Carl Sagan in his magnificent, awe inspiring work Cosmos has described human predicament and dilemmas that surround us in the most thought provoking manner. The earth is a lovely and more or less placid place. Things change, but slowly. We can lead a full life and never personally encounter a natural disaster more violent than a storm. And so we become complacent, relaxed, unconcerned. But in the history of Nature, the record is clear. World have been devastated. Even we humans have achieved the dubious technical distinction of being able to make our own disasters, planets where the records of the past have been preserved there is abundant evidence of major catastrophes. It is all a matter of time scale. An event that would be unthinkable in a hundred years may be inevitable in a hundred million.

The greed, lust and material urges in modern times have led to the exploitation of the mother earth ignoring all the valuable principles enshrined in Ancient Sanskrit Literature leading to disastrous results, earthquake, cyclone, floods, deforestation, etc. The mother earth has been plundered and has become unsafe place to live. This is the result of our own actions. What is required is to make use of earth only to meet the needs so that earth and human beings can live in perfect harmony.

Our lovely blue planet, the earth, is the only home we know. Venus is too hot. Mars is too cold. But the earth is just right, a heaven for humans. After all, we evolved here. But our congenial climate may be unstable. Is there any danger of driving the environment of the earth towards the planetary Hell of Venus or the global ice age of Mars? The simple answer is that nobody knows. The study of the global climate, the comparison of the earth with other worlds, are subjects in their earliest stage of development. They are fields that are poorly and grudgingly funded. In our ignorance, we continue to push and pull to pollute the atmosphere and brighten the land, obvious to the fact that the long-term consequences are largely unknown.

A few million years ago, when human beings first evolved on Earth, it was already a middle aged world, 4.6 billion years along from the catastrophes and impetuosities of its youth. But we humans now represent a new and perhaps decisive factor. Our intelligence and our technology have given us the power of affecting the climate. How will we use this power? Are we willing to tolerate ignorance and complacency in matters that affect the entire human family? Do we value short-term advantages above the welfare of the Earth? Or will we think on longer time scales, with concern for our children and our grand children, to understand and protect the complex life-support system of our planet. The earth is a tiny and fragile world. It needs to be cherished.

Bearer of all things, hoard of treasures rare, sustaining, Mother Earth. What of thee I dig out, let that quickly grow over. Let me not hurt thy vitals, or the heart.

—*Atharva Veda*

Mother Earth! Sacred are the hills, snowing mountains, and deep forests, be kind to us and bestow upon us happiness. May you continue supporting people of all races and nations."

—*Atharva Veda*

In India, it is the constitutional obligation of the State to protect and improve the environment and to safeguard the natural resources like the forest and wildlife of the country. It is also one of the fundamental duties of every citizen under the Constitution of India to protect and improve the natural environment including forests, lakes, rivers and wildlife and to show compassion for living creatures. The conjoint consideration of both the duty of citizens and the obligation of the State in the light of the provisions of Article 21 of our constitution, any destructive disturbance of the environment and ecology that affects the guaranteed fundamental right to life and personal liberty either directly or indirectly is forbidden.

The lessons to be learnt in environmental protection may be identified and crystallized as under:

(a) the state is a trustee of all such natural resources as seashores, running waters, airs, forests, and ecologically fragile lands that are by reason of their very intrinsic value and character meant for the enjoyment of all.

(b) As a trustee, the state is under an affirmative duty to preserve and protect the natural resources, which are the peoples' common heritage.

(c) The natural resources meant for public use cannot be allowed to be converted by the state into private ownership or commercial interests.

(d) As a part of planning and allocation of natural resources, if the State may have to approve their appropriation, the same has to be consistent with the purposes of public trust. If allocated, the State is empowered to rescind the allocation, if there occurred harm to public interest uses despite the anticipation of that harm.

The public trust doctrine expounded in the context of preservation and protection of environment and ecology is essentially and truly global in character, environmental degradation knows no barrier drawn by man. This doctrine, therefore, needs to be perceived and practiced from that perspective. In the Indian jurisprudential thought, this is the perspective which is so eloquently expressed by our sages when they ordain us to treat all the inhabitants of this earth as members of one big family and direct that all human activities must be anchored in the welfare of all the raison de etre of our social existence.[9]

Notwithstanding the significant progress in the areas of poverty eradication, improvement of literacy rates and health standards, etc. and the emergence of an enabling framework for sustainable development, India continues to face enormous challenges in achieving sustainable development. There still remains a disparity between India and the rest of the world on various social development indicators. India has been as a challenge to reduce the poverty ratio, ensure attendance of children in schools, reduce gender gaps in literacy and age rates by 50%, reduce population growth, attain atleast 75% literacy, reduce infant mortality to 45 per 1000 live births, reduce maternal mortality rate to 2 per 1000 live births, increase forest cover to 25% provide sustained access to drinking water in rural areas and to clean up major stretches of polluted rivers.

The levels of poverty and its inter-regional and inter-class variations remain a major challenge. Poverty alleviation will continue to be high on India's agenda and its commitment to bringing it down to below two-digit figure by 2015. Strong pressure of population has an immense impact on the total volume and quality of resources on one hand and on the food security and environmental health on the other.

Empowering people to nurture these resources for sustainable livelihoods will remain a cornerstone of our policies. However, the full empowerment of people to undertake this responsibility is as yet an unfinished task. There is a tremendous scope in the country for improving the technological inputs for urban waste management and institutionalization of responsible social practices that will facilitate an efficient and environmentally safe method of disposal of waste of all kinds. Science and technology will play an important role in improving access to drinking water, sanitation, improvement of health as also in development of technologies that provide clean energy, efficient transportation and safe industries. Harnessing of India's scientific and technological prowess to set increasingly higher environmental standards and their strict adherence through robust institutions is a potential that remains to be exploited fully. By setting specific sectoral targets, India is attempting to accelerate the process of realizing that potential.[10]

It is realized that industrialization is essential if an economy is to develop. But the transformation of natural resources for industrialization is accompanied by serious environmental degradation. When this transformation of nature by man, instead of showing a symbiotic relationship between man and nature, shows a man centric effort to conquer nature and ultimately overpower it, the economy that is aimed to be built by man to protect himself and prosper, is itself stressed. This gives the background of one's understanding on industrial ecology. If mankind is to live over generations, the eco-system, which feeds them, has to be sustained and there comes the question of controlling man's exercise of power over nature.[11]

Most of the environmental problems of the present day are essentially man-made. The role of man is therefore important because it is his attitude and values which shape the environment. In developed countries mad race after materialism puts too much pressure on environment. The materialistic attitude of man multiplies the human needs and ultimately leads towards resources exploitation, without considering the future consequential disharmony with the environment. Man has to evolve a balanced way of thinking, acting and feeling towards the environment. So human ethics, attitude, values, decision-making analysis of ecological, economic, social and technical aspects come under the scope of environmental education.[12]

Education, including formal education, public awareness and training should be recognized as a process by which human beings and societies can reach their fullest potential. Education is critical for promoting sustainable development and improving the capacity of the people to address environment and development issues. While basic education provides the underpinning for any environmental and development education, the latter needs to be incorporated as an essential part of learning. Both formal and non-formal education are indispensable to changing people's attitudes so that they have the capacity to assess and address their sustainable development concerns. It is also critical for achieving environmental and ethical awareness, values and attitudes, skills and behaviour consisted with sustainable development and for effective public participation in decision-making. To be effective, environment and development education should deal with the dynamics of both the physical/biological and socio-economic environment and human (which may include spiritual) development, should be integrated in all disciplines, and should employ formal and non-formal methods and effective means of communication. Sanskrit literature is full of techniques, methods, rationale and philosophy of saving human beings from the horrible impact of environment pollution. What is required is to educate the people in advanced and developing countries to stop exploiting nature for making palatial buildings, huge industries, nuclear plants, etc. All this is possible if we develop virtuous people as defined in Gita, Vedas, and other ancient Sanskrit scriptures.

Dr. S. Radhakrishnan in his book, "Recovery of Faith" rightly suggests about the present environment. To quote: Man's memory makes him aware of the age of his race so that now as two thousand years ago or four thousand years ago he feels that he is living in a terminal period.

But formerly when civilizations were destroyed in one or more continents, in other regions they survived and the accumulated knowledge of the past enabled our brethren to save the future of the race. The Egyptian, the Greek and the Graeco-Roman civilizations belonged to small parts of the world, areas which did not comprise the whole of mankind. The forces of modern civilization are world-wide. Again, when other civilizations collapsed the attack came mainly from without; today, the menace is from within. The world is undergoing changes so vast that they are hardly comparable to the changes which occurred in the past. The contemporary situation is pregnant with great possibilities, immense dangers or immeasurable rewards. It may be end or a new beginning. The human race may end by destroying itself or its spiritual vitality may revive and a new age may dawn when this earth will become a real home for humanity. The contemporary mind is vacillating between vague apocalyptic fears and deep mystical yearnings.[13]

With all the resources at our command, with all the gifts with which we have been endowed, with all the powers that we have developed, we are unable to live in peace and safety. We have grown in knowledge and intelligence but not in wisdom and virtue. For lack of the latter, things are interlocked in perpetual strife. No center holds the world together. Religion has been the discipline hitherto used for fostering wisdom and virtue. But the drift from religious belief has gone much too far and the margin of safety has become dangerously small. The social pathos of the age is exploited by countless individuals in different parts of the world who pose as leaders and proclaim their foolishness as wisdom. We are sowing grain and weeds at random. To assume that we are helpless creatures caught in the current which is sweeping us into the final abyss is to embrace a philosophy of despair, of nihilism. We can swim against the current and even change its direction.[11]

The mind of man today both in developed and developing countries, more in developed countries, is prone to limitless desires in all areas whether industrialization, mining, construction activities, means of conveyance and communication, resulting into exploitation of environment beyond its capacity leading into frequent calamities in the form of earthquakes, floods, cyclones, health hazards, etc. All these make the life of the people poor, nasty and restless. Every nation must create a culture of service and not accumulation as it can induce positive vibrations in the environment.

Hindu Philosophy advises equanimity under all circumstances. It says, man should try to remain calm in face of both pleasure and pain, success and failure. Whatever may happen he should remain unperturbed. But is it possible? According to Hinduism, it is possible if man can rid his mind of desires. Desirelessness is considered an ideal state of mind. To attain this state he has to practice discrimination. Most of the time he craves for ephemeral things; instead, he should struggle to get things that last long. What are those things. In one word, perfection.

There is no short cut to perfection. One has to struggle hard for it. Hinduism does not believe in any miracle except the miracle of hard work. To be at peace with himself, man has to have this perfection.[15]

Disasters of all types, e.g. earthquakes, floods, accidents, cloud bursts, cyclones, etc. have been occurring since time immemorial and causing great disturbances in the environment. However, their frequency, magnitude and area have increased many times in all parts of the world, in recent times. While natural disasters cannot be controlled with the available advanced knowledge of science and technology, many other disasters are the result of wrong developments or planning in all spheres, be it construction of dams, roads, buildings, factories or industries. We are in a great hurry to accelerate the process of development. But with what result and at what cost? We must also be aware of the greater disaster series awaiting us like AIDS, corruption, frauds, cheating, etc. What has been the result of all these disasters? These have resulted in loss *of* life, half dead living persons, hunger, poverty, unemployment, disease, etc. There are the scars on the face of humanity in this age of nuclear science and information technology. With all these problems environment leads to pollution.

Dr. T. Adeoya Lambo has aptly said that, "What is happening around us shakes our complacency, challenges our faith in human progress and imbues us with an intense feeling of shame, doubt and guilt. In a world, where the gigantic scientific and phenomenal technological achievements command our admiration and almost fetish acceptance, we are witnessing an intolerable degradation of man. Our pride in belonging to a generation that for the first time since the genesis of man has set foot on another planet cannot, however, disguise the awful truth that it may be easier to travel to the moon than to erase from the surface of the earth, the image of inevitable poverty, human exploitation, injustice and the degradation of human welfare. First concern is to redefine the whole purpose of development. This should not to develop things but to development.[16]

The past decade has witnessed an extraordinary increase in the number and extent of natural disasters because of increasing environmental pollution. As Kofi Annan, Secretary General of the United Nations, points out, "The facts are startling. The costs of weather-related disasters in 1998 exceeded the costs of all such disasters in the decade of the 1980s. In the Caribbean, the hurricanes designated George and Mitch, killed more than 13,000 people, with Mitch being the deadliest Atlantic storm in 200 years. Major floods hit India, Nepal, Bangladesh and much of East Asia with thousands killed. Two-thirds of Bangladesh was inundated for months, leaving millions homeless. There were three times as many great natural hazards in the 1990s as in the 1960s, while disaster costs increased more than nine-fold in the same period."

Dr. R.R. Mukherjee in his Presidential address, delivered at Haridwar to the participants of All India Oriental Conference, has rightly elaborated the fact that Indian thought speaks of three types of work in the service of man and society; the first, the physical one, that removes the physical want of the man and saves his physical life; the second, intellectual one, that eradicates illiteracy and increases work-efficiency; and the third, the spiritual one, that imparts spiritual knowledge and is ranked as the highest in the scale of value. It has been now accepted by all social scientists that the modern man's greatest challenge is presented by inner impoverishment in the context of external achievements and inner insecurity in the face of external insecurity. The only solution of this is the gift of spiritual knowledge, so nicely reflected by Indian mind in all its literary creations beginning from the Upanisads down to the great poets of the classical age. Swami Vivekananda has given a magnificent formula of this principle in the following words: "The miseries of the world cannot be cured by physical help only. Until man's nature changes, these physical needs will always arise and miseries will always be felt, and no amount of physical help will cure them completely. Ignorance is the mother of the evil and of the misery we see. Let man have light, let them be pure and spiritually strong and educated; then alone will misery cease in the world."[17]

Conservation of natural resources in India, be it land, forests, mountains, or marine ecosystems, is linked to the conservation of livelihoods resources of at least 62% of the current working population and resources for the welfare of the future generations. Indian agriculture is the largest private sector enterprise in the country that contributes about 26% of Gross Domestic Product (GDP) and provides food to one billion people. Of the total workforce of India, 58.4% are either cultivators or agricultural labourers. An additional 4.07% of the workforce is engaged in household industries, which are largely based on utilisation of natural resources and their produce. Similarly, approximately 20 million households derive a significant part of their livelihood from forests and another 5.96 million from fishing in fresh waters and marine areas. Animal husbandry is a secondary occupation for most cultivators, agricultural labourers and main occupation for transhumant pastoralists and landless including women. Conservation of natural resources is therefore essential for sustainability of livelihoods of two-thirds of the nation besides contributing to environmental sustainability.

CONCLUSION

UN Secretary General in 2004 Report on Implementation of the Millennium Declaration EMBARGO 2004 states that even regions that have made significant progress towards achieving many other goals, such as parts of Asia, tend to have a poorer record on environmental issues. Protected areas have increased in all regions, but there has been a loss of forest cover in some parts of the world, notably those with tropical forests. Energy use and per capita carbon dioxide emissions have increased in developing countries but fell in the economies in transition with the decline in industrial production in the 1990s. The use of ozone depleting chlorfluoro carbons has been almost eliminated globally.

Progress in the implementation of the global conventions has been mixed. The Kyotol[18] Protocol to the United Nations Framework Convention on Climate Change[19] has been ratified by 120 countries, but it requires ratification by either the Russian Federation or the United States in order to come into force. The United Nations Convention to combat Desertification in Countries Experiencing Serious Drought and/or Desertification, particularly in Africa[20] was adopted in 1994 and entered into force in 1996, but a lack of financial resources has limited its implementation. More encouragingly, there has been progress towards the full implementation of the Convention on Biological Diversity,[21] with the adoption of measurable indicators and specific goals to reduce the current rate of biodiversity loss by 2010, and the entry into force of the Cartagena Protocol on Biosafety[22] in September 2003. On the question of deforestation and forest degradation, nine international processes involving 150 countries that encompass 85 percent of the world's forests have made progress in developing criteria and indicators for sustainable forest management. The Second World Conference on Disaster Reduction, held in Kobe, Japan, in January 2005, tried to help intensely cooperation to reduce the number and effects of natural and man-made disasters, particularly through the International Strategy for Disaster Reduction.

The greed for exploitation of natural resources of people has led to different types of disasters—earthquake, pollution, violence, accidents, etc. The frequency of disasters is on the increase. If the people do not use the resources in a balanced way, there is going to be disasters and disasters at a very fast rate. The only answer to prevent disasters is prevention through sustainable development.

Notes and References

1. Baidyanath Prasad Singh, Environment and Sustainable Development: A Suitable Strategy Needed for their striking balance, p. 72.
2. IWCD, 1987, p. 9.
3. S.R. Bhati, Welfare State in Indian Classics in M.M. Shankhdher and Sharda Jain (Eds.) Social Security, Welfare and Polity, New Delhi, Deep and Deep, 2004, pp. 309-10

3A. UN: World Summit For Social Development, New York, August, 1995, p. v.

4. Gurcharan Singh, "Pollution to Purity of Environment", Deep & Deep Publications, New Delhi, 2000, p. 4.
5. Mathur (ed.) ETMG, p. 632.
6. *Ibid.*, p. 4.
7. K. Ramamurthy, Environment and Development Ed. G.S. Monga, Deep and Deep, pp. 74-75.
8. "Empowering People for Sustainable Development", GOI, Ministry of Environment and Forest, 2002.
9. M.K. Gandhi, *Hind Swami*, *op. cit.*, pp. 61-62.
10. Empowering people for Sustainable Development, Ministry of Environment and Forests, 2002, p. 54.
11. S.S. Narata Roa and Pratibha Narata, Industrialization and Environment: Agenda for the 21st Century, Editors S. Radha, Amar Singh, Sankhayan, 2002, p. 124.
12. Maba Kumar Patnaik and P. Sasi Bhushan Rao, Environment Education for 21st Century in Environment Management and Audit, P. Sasi Bhushan Rao and P. Mohana Rao, Deep and Deep, New Delhi, 2000, p. 206.
13. Agenda 21, UNCED, Rio-de Janerio, Brazil, pp. 3-14, 1992, Chapter 36.
14. S. Radhakrishnan, Recovery of Faith: An Orient Paperback, New Delhi, 1967, pp. 9-10.
15. Swami Lokeswarananda: Practical Spirituality, the Ramakrishna Mission Institute of Culture, Calcutta, 1995, p. 6.
16. Dr. T. Adeoya Lambo, Towards Justice in Health in *World Health*, July 1979.
17. J. Mishra, Address of the General President, 38th Session, All India Orient Conference, January 28-30, 1997, Jadavpur University, Calcutta, 1997, pp. iv-v.
18. FCCC/CP/1997, 17, Add. I, Decision, 1/CP 3. Annex.
19. United Nations, Treaty Series, Vol. 1771, No. 30822.
20. *Ibid.*, Vol. 1954, No. 33480.
21. *Ibid.*, Vol. 1760, No. 30619.
22. See UNEP/CBD-/ExCOP/1/1 and Corr. 1, Part two, Annex.

CHAPTER

3

Development Administration

Need

The success or failure of development administration depends upon the executive branch of Government which must show enthusiasm, creativity and excellence in development administration. Creativity and steadfastness—Will Power are the two aspects of mind which come under this head of personality development at mental level. It has been well recognized that creativity is the core of Development Administration.

'Will Power' is an essential requirement for all persons to accomplish any development work, however insignificant or great the task be. There is a fine Sloka in Niti Satakam describing three types of people:

Prarabhayate na vighna bhayena nicaih
Prarabhya vighna vihatah viramanti madhyah
Muhurmuhurapi pratihanyamanah
Prarabdhamuttamajanah na parityajanti

(Niti Satakam)

Fearing possible obstacles and difficulties, the lowest do not start the work at all. Having come to face with obstacles one after another the middle type leave the work uncompleted. But best are they who reach out to completion of the task inspite of all odds and obstacles torturing and crushing them all through. We need such people to carry out development administration activities. They are called leaders. Leaders, according to Shri APJ Abdul Kalam possess the following qualities which help them in making development administration a success.

- Leader must have a vision
- Leader must have perseverance to realize the vision
- Leader must be able to travel into an explored path
- Leader must know how to manage a success and failure

- Leader must have courage to take decisions
- Leader should have mobility in management
- Leader should be transparent in every action
- Leader must work with integrity and succeed with integrity

But the problems that confront us today are not problems to be tackled by a small minority of dedicated people, that creative minority we always had in India. But the problems are so complex, multifarious, and urgent that we need to have this spirit of vision and dedication more widely diffused in the various sections of our population, and more especially, in that branch of our population known as the administrative branch, both at the centre and in the states. I have always felt that, ever since we became free, the greatest responsibility for national welfare rests upon our administration. Just as, in the field of health, the doctor does the operation, but it is the nurse who, through her devoted and efficient care in the light of the doctor's directions, brings the patient back to health, so it is with respect to the health of the nation. Between the two branches of politics and administration, the latter is more responsible for the achievement of the direction with energy and dedication. Hence the importance of all our training programmes for our administrators. Such training programmes are meant not only to impart and acquire the technical know-how of the subject, but also to impart and acquire a sense of national vision, a spirit of national dedication.

This is very relevant today when we are engaged in transforming our erstwhile police state of the period of alien rule into a welfare state of the era of freedom. There is need for our administrators, from the highest to the most ordinary cadre, to be constantly impressed with the fact that their country is engaged today in a mighty task of peaceful social reconstruction and transformation of revolutionary dimensions, in response to the centuries-long suppressed urges and aspirations of our people.

It is in this context that the problems of administrative efficiency in our newly established democracy become urgent. That efficiency is to be measured by only one test, namely, its dynamic responsiveness to the national urges. This is achieved only by the administrative personnel, representing a cross-section of the national intelligentsia, getting trained in imaginative sympathy and national dedication. It is self-centredness and lack of concern for others that lead to corruption; and that evil is already afflicting man and society alike in India. We are not required to forego all concern for ourselves and become ascetics. We are only called upon to put this concern for ourselves in the context of a larger concern for others. This changes the whole aspect of our life and work. This is called enlightened self-interest in political philosophy. It is self-interest, but with a touch of spiritual enlightenment, resulting in the recognition of mutuality, inter-dependence and the spirit of service, as the truth of all healthy social processes.

Free India seeks to be a welfare state. There is one definition of a welfare state in our classical Sanskrit literature. It is given by Kalidasa in his Raghuvamsa. Describing the greatness of king Dilipa to whose dynasty sir Rama belonged, Kalidasa says:

Prajanam eva bhutyartham SA tabhyo balimagrahit;
Sahasragunamutsrastum adatte hi rasam ravih-

'It was only for the welfare of the people that he (king Dilipa) took taxes from them, just like the sun, which takes moisture from the earth only to return it thousand fold in the form of beneficent rain.'

That is a welfare state in which the state returns to the people hundred rupees for every rupee taken from them through taxation, direct and indirect. Our fourth five-year plan has allocated a target of twenty-five thousand crores of rupees for investment in development. In a true welfare state, that amount should rise to at least a hundred thousand crores in benefit when it reaches the people. What makes this possible? Only this administrative efficiency, proceeding from the competence, social awareness, and character of the administrators.[1] .

In any developmental and welfare administration, that is the only right attitude. The administration takes money from the people as taxes, only to restore it back in hundred fold and in thousand fold measure to the people as welfare measures. How is the administration able to perform this miracle? Because the men who handle that money have that yoga-bala, energy of yoga, within them; they have imaginative sympathy; they have efficiency; they have dedication; they are always conscious that they are basically citizens of free India, who are called upon to perform a tremendous national function and mission. That attitude achieves a revolutionary miracle within them; they become dynamic persons instead of remaining static individuals.

Genesis

Development administration emerged in the beginning of 1960's about the time when public administration had reached its zenith.[2] But since the mid-1960s, the label development administration has acquired a growing popularity in developing countries, although it is not entirely clear what that label means.[3] One source of this trend is of the view that it is new name given by the scholars of public administration, especially American to the developing countries so that through this the Governments of these countries could carry out development programmes and projects. As one article indicates: "The emerging problem is how to combine skills which exist in these (developing) countries and bring them to bear more effectively in action progmmmes which will accelerate economic growth, expand social well-being, and improve public services. This is the essence of development administraticn.[4] In the developing countries of Asia, Africa and Latin America, the need of development administration has been well recognized as a means of implementing policies and plans directed towards nation-building and socio-economic progress.[5] The basic assumption towards 'development administration' is the "focus of attention on the building and improving of a public administration system as part of the total effort of national development."[6]

MEANING OF DEVELOPMENT ADMINISTRATION

With a view to carrying out development goals and activities the mechanism in the name of 'development administration' has been given the prominence. To study development administration, it is necessary to have some sort of working definition of the subject. A number of scholars of public administration and related disciplines have attempted to define the concept development administration.

According to Edward W. Weidner, "development administration is concerned with maximizing innovation for development."[7] He defines innovation for development as "the process of planned or intended change in the direction of modernity or nation-building and socio-economic change. [8] In the same voice, John Montgomery defines the development administration as, "carrying out planned change in the economy in agriculture or industry or the capital infrastructure supporting either of these, and to a lesser extent, in the social service of the state (especially education and public health).[9]

To Inayatullah development administration is "the complex of organisational arrangements for the achievement of action through public authority in pursuance of (i) socio-economic goals, and (ii) nation-building. It presupposes policies, plans and programmes with a distinct development bias as well as a bureaucracy which consciously and continually seeks to modernize to meet the demands of planned change.[10]

T.N. Chturvedi in his editorial remarks: A single comprehensive theory of development does not exist. The contemporary theoretical approaches to development are: (1) pluralistic, recognising many pathways to development, and (2) less Western in their cultural assumptions. Key elements in contemporary development approaches, reflected in the thinking of Rogers,[11] Korten[12] and Klaus,[13] Bjur Bryant and White,[14] include: (1) greater equality in distribution of development benefits, (2) popular participation, knowledge-sharing, and empowerment to facilitate self-development efforts by individuals, groups, and communities, (3) self-reliance and independence in development, emphasizing the potential of local resources, (4) limiting growth of population[15], and (5) integration of "appropriate" technology with "big" modern technologies in order to facilitate development.[16]

FROM PRODUCTION-CENTRED APPROACH TO A PEOPLE-CENTRED APPROACH

Another trend in contemporary development administration theorising is a shift from a production-centred to a people-centred approach to development. The production-centred development approach emphasises production of goods and services to maximise returns on investment.[17] This approach stresses: (1) industry over agriculture, (2) urban development over rural development, (3) utilisation of capital resources over human resources, (4) exploiting the environment for short-term gains over sustained harnessing of natural resources, and (5) establishing large-scale industries over small-scale industries.[18] Such a development approach neglects the basic needs of the rural poor in Third World countries, and promotes socio-economic inequality.

In the people-centred approach to development, the needs of the people take precedence over the needs of the production system. This approach views an individual not as a subject but as an actor, who defines the goals, controls the resources, and directs the processes affecting his/her life.[19] The central themes of people-centred development are: (1) empowerment of people, and (2) development of an administrative process which responds to the needs of the people.[20]

Key elements in people-centred development are: (1) human growth and well-being, (2) equality, (3) self-reliance, (4) participation, and (5) sustainability. Sustainability is a measure of lasting quality in a development programme. A development programme can be sustained by: (1) creating a felt need among beneficiaries about the efficacy of the programme, (2) developing institutions which continually adapt,[21] (3) providing elites and community groups.[22]

Development continues to be a matter of concern both at the conceptual level and at the implementation level. Attempt to evolve a comprehensive and convincing definition of development administration have failed mainly due to a persistent inadequacy of comprehension about the ever-expanding role of administration in the wide growth of complexities and subtleties of related specialization and the marsh of multidisciplinary intricacies in the midst of changing political and systemic realities. In such a situation, familiarity with trends and developments in the process of theory building in the field of development administration doubtlessly facilitates a better understanding of public administration.

Fred W. Riggs defines development administration as "organized efforts to carry out programmes or projects thought by those involved to serve developmental objectives.[23] Further placing an emphasis on administration of development and development of administration, Riggs observes that "development administration refers not only to a government's efforts to carry out programmes designed to reshape its physical, human, and cultural environment, but also to the struggle to enlarge a government's capacity to engage in such programmes.[24]

Going through the various definitions, it is found that the primary objective of development administration is to strengthen the administrative machinery which would bring about socio-politico-economic development. In brief development administration is the direction of nation-building and socio-economic progress through an administrative organization. It is, through public as well as non-public organizations and their proper management that a developing country can carry development policy measures for the realization of national goals.

In the words of Donald Stone: Development Administration is the blending of all the elements and resources (human and physical)....into a concerted effort to achieve agreed upon goals. It is the continuous cycle of formulating, evaluating and implementing interrelated plans, policies, programs, projects, activities and other measures to reach established development objectives in a scheduled time sequence.

Development administration was supposed to be based on a professionally-oriented, technically competent, politically and ideologically neutral bureaucratic machinery. It was to retool the foreign aid (both in the form of funds received and ideas suggested) and also to act as a main instrument for nation-building by transforming the inputs received into development outputs. The ostensible output was modernisation, preceded by institution-building and adaptation of the indigenous bureaucratic machinery to undertake developmental tasks. Thus, the developmental bureaucracy, as a spearhead of modernisation, was seen more as an adapter than as an innovator.

Development administration, sired by the West, assumed many Western values, including separation of politics from administration. It was thought that management of public service would be done largely by administrators, ably assisted by economic plans formulated to achieve national goals. Consequently, there was no place for political influence in the administration of development. However, as the Iran experience and similar instances elsewhere proved, politics could not be kept separate from economic planning, management of resources and government administration. Either the administrative system responded to political demands or politicians simply bypassed the established administrative apparatus and created their own network to accomplish their objectives. This created confusion and delays which were blamed on the inability of leaders and administrators to run a smooth machinery. Public sector management then became a source of economic ills, administrative mismanagement and political blundering. Separation of politics from administration remained artificially embedded in the parlance of theory and practice of development administration, while political factors dominated economic, social and administrative concerns. This realization is yet to be acknowledged by many scholars, practitioners and international aid personnel.[25]

It may be added here that development administration is an action and goal-orientedprocess. It is a coordinated effort encompassing a very wide range of activities directed to ameliorate the lot of millions of unfortunate; less privileged people leading a life of deprivations and dejection. The essence of development administration is holistic change undertaken through integrated, organised and properly directed governmental action. The development administration, therefore, centres around the words "Change" and "Operation Problems." Change includes both social and economic. Most of the countries in Asia, Africa and Latin America are labelled as developing countries or poor countries or less developed countries or emerging nations or third world and likewise, because they are relatively young because they are engaged in the development tasks of nation-building and socio-economic progress because their per capita national income is less, because they are technologically less advanced and finally they are socially backward.

Development Administration, according to the author means "the delivery of services relating to health, education, social welfare to enhance the competence and capability of people especially the people who are below the poverty line and disadvantaged groups e.g. scheduled castes, scheduled tribes, women, old people and children, other backward classes, minority, handicapped persons as well as to create conditions for development through making the society free from terrorism and violence. All methods, techniques and activities carried out to promote human development on a sustainable basis fall under the purview of development administration. Such administration requires innovation, creativity, motivation, change of mindset of the persons, dedication, perseverance, determination and commitment, engaged in development administration. Development administration with all the above mentioned elements can promote a social structure where growth with justice and equity would prevail and promote socio-economic development and better quality of life. In recent times substantial part of resources are being diverted to combat terrorism law and order and violence. Development administration can achieve its goal provided terrorism, and violence are also tackled side by side and never allow it to nurture out of proportion. The development administration can grow perfectly on a sub-stratum which has been tackling violence and terrorism as a zero tolerance act and dealt with strength and resolve. All these would require active participation of people, administrative ethics, dynamic political leadership and an effective administrative system. (See Chart 3.1)

NATURE OF DEVELOPMENT ADMINISTRATION (See Chart 3.2)

The concept of development administration has two major facets. One facet of it refers to 'development of administration'. By this we mean to develop administration. It involves strengthening and improving administrative capabilities as a means for achieving development goals. The other facet of it is 'administration of development'. According to this interpretation, we expect development administration (administrative organization) to act as an instrument in the implementation of development programmes, projects and policies. This may involve raising the standards of education, transforming social systems, improving public health, raising national income, stabilizing political system, conserving national resources, improving communication system, constructing dams, power plants and undertaking many other developmental tasks of national importance.

Development of administration and administration of development are thus two facets of the concept of 'development administration'. These are two sides of one coin in this context, Fred W. Riggs very aptly remarks: "The reciprocal relatedness of these two sides involves a chicken and egg type of causation. Administration cannot normally be improved very much without changes in the environmental constraints (the infrastructure) that hamper its effectiveness; and the environment itself cannot be changed unless the administration of developmental programmes is strengthened.[26] Unless the administrative effectiveness of government is increased, the developmental objectives which a developing country may aspire for fulfilment cannot be realised.

Thus the subject of development administration covers both the development of administration (measures to increase the administrative capabilities) and administration of development (administration as a mechanism of national development).

CHART 3.1

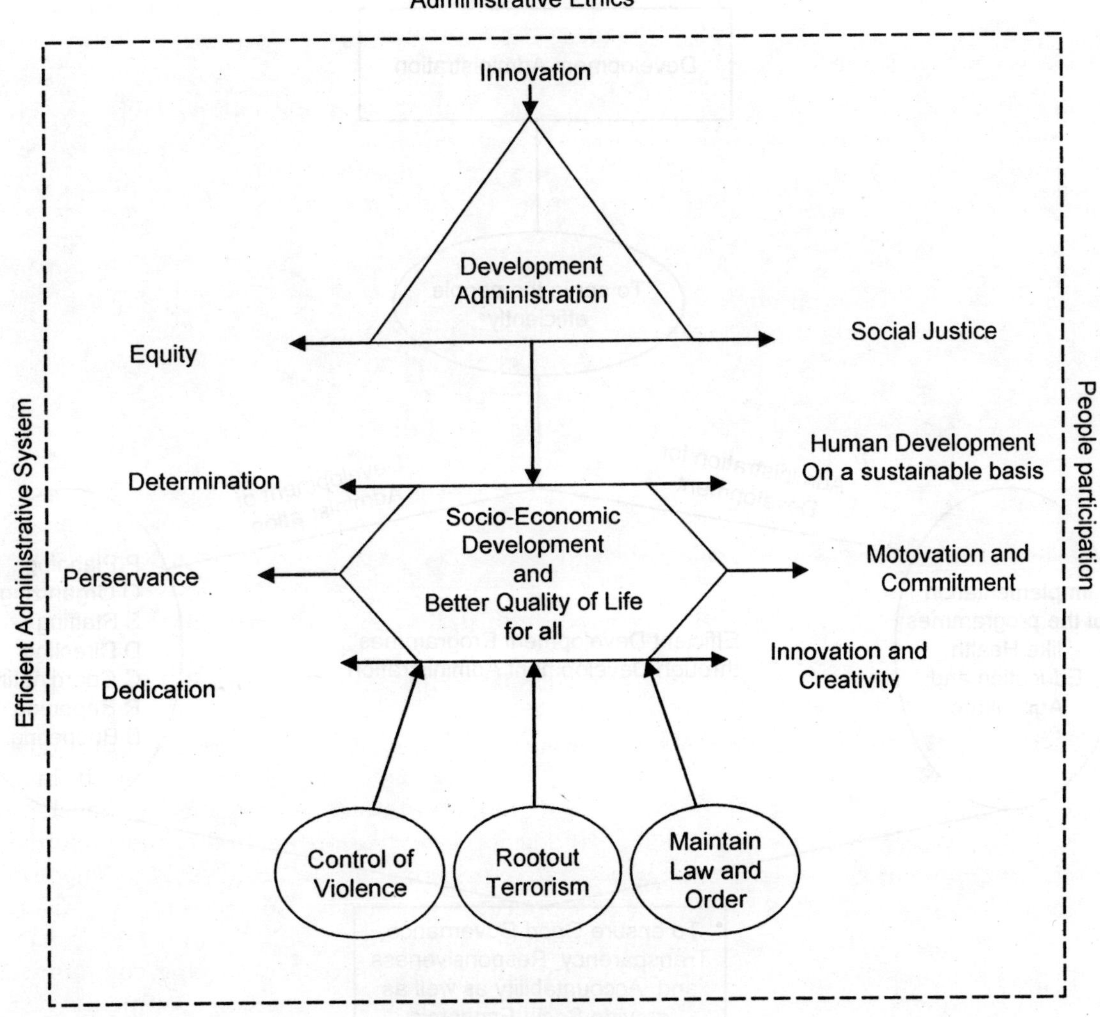

SCOPE AND FUNCTIONS OF DEVELOPMENT ADMINISTRATION (See Chart 3.2)

The scope and functions of development administration vary among developing countries depending upon their economic and political systems. Nevertheless, there is a convergence of experience about the increasing role of the Government in managing national development. This puts development administration as the process of carrying out development programmes and projects in the direction of nation-building and socio-economic progress through public organizations. Thus, the principal function of development administration is to carry out development programmes and projects attuned to the developmental objective of nation-building

CHART 3.2

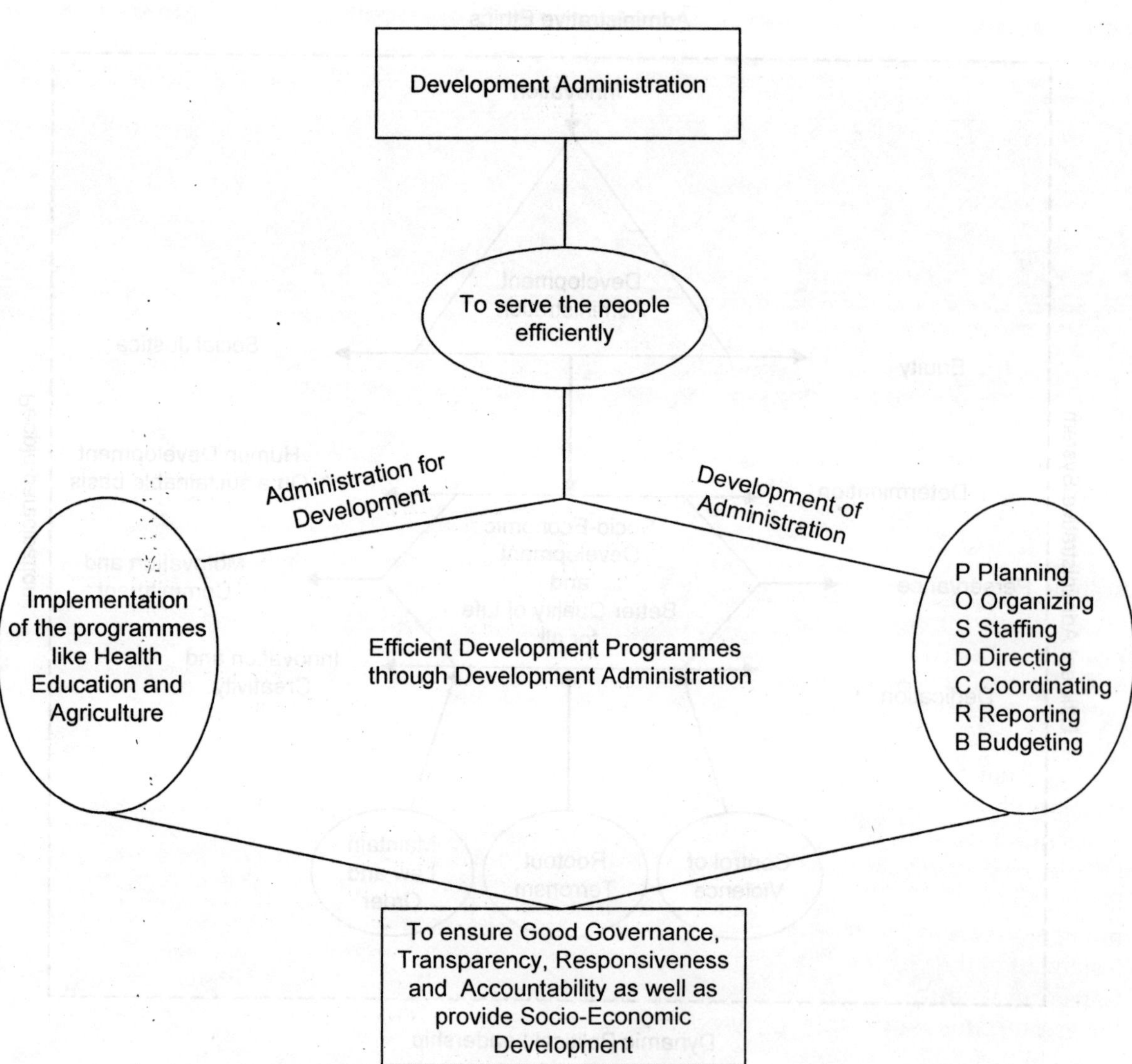

and socio-economic progress and to strengthen the government's capacity to engage in such programmes and projects.

J.N. Khosla divides the functions of development administration into the following six categories:

"1. Formulation of. development goals and policies:
2. Programme formulation and programme/project management;
3. Reorganization of administrative structures and procedures;

4. Evaluation of results;
5. People's participation in the development effort; and
6. Promotion growth of social and political infrastructure."[27]

We may, however, broadly divide the functions of development administration into two categories:

1. Functions concerned with development of administration, and
2. Functions concerned with administration of development.

I. Development of Administration

Money is dead, until man imparts life to it. Men with energy and vision bring more and more out of a given amount of money than men without it. That is the only way to achieve a welfare society; a high level of social welfare in a community of men reflects a high level of ethical awareness, human concern, and practical efficiency among its members. The ratio of administrative work and character-efficiency to social welfare is well revealed in Kalidasa's verse, in his raghuvamsam, describing briefly the welfare state achieved by the kings of the Raghu dynasty, to which belonged Sri Rama.

In any developmental and welfare administration, that is the only right attitude. The administration takes money from the people as taxes, only to restore it back in hundred-fold and in thousand-fold measure to the people as welfare measures. How is the administration able to perform this miracle? Because the men who handle that money have that yoga-bala, energy of yoga, within them; they have imaginative sympathy; they have efficiency; they have dedication, they are always conscious that they are basically citizens of free India, who are called upon to perform a tremendous national function and mission. That attitude achieves a revolutionary miracle within them; they become dynamic persons instead of remaining static individuals.

That the philosophy of administration as taught in the Gita, combining the energy of vision with the energy of action, and imparting to man the double energy resource of character-efficiency and work-efficiency, the heroism of saintliness with the heroism of manliness, can lead people, any people, to all-round greatness, is the grand testament affirmed by the Gita itself in its luminous last verse. Our national politics and administration can do nothing more inspiring and momentous today, as much internationally as nationally, than begin to check and verify that great testament in the vast modern anthropological development laboratory of our ancient country, and transform its dubious distinction of being the largest democracy into the luminous one of being the greatest democracy.[28]

In this sphere, development administration is concerned with increasing and improving the capabilities of the administrative system. Clearly if the developmental goals are to be carried out successfully with efficiency and effectiveness, there is the concomitant need of increasing the capacity of those involved in developmental tasks. Apparently development administration has to perform the functions of improving the education of, and imparting, training to the personnel engaged in developmental goals. Although, policy-making, planning and budgeting are advisory functions of development administration, yet they constitute a significant part of efforts to enhance administrative capacity for development. Administrative capability also involves the use of modern management techniques and other ways and means to identify individual objectives with developmental goals. Thus improving and enhancing the administrative capabilities are directly related to achieving developmental goals. Katz say, "Administrative capability for development involves the ability to mobilize, allocate and combine the actions that are technically needed to achieve development objectives."[29]

As rightly pointed out by the Prime Minister Manmohan Singh in his recent joint address to the US Congress, "The real test of a democracy is not in what is said in the constitution but in how it functions on the ground..."[30]

David Shand points out the tests for efficient development ideals of the Welfare State viz. progress, prosperity and protection to the common man, can be secured only through impartial, honest and efficient development administration. In the words of Prof. Charles Bernard, "The future of civilized government and even, I think of civilization itself rests upon our ability to develop a science, philosophy and a practice of administration, competent to discharge the functions of civilized society." Thus, there is a need that Public Administration must be modernized, i.e. recreated, renewed and revitalized to produce the pre-designed changes and output necessary to provide goods and services to the people at the minimum cost. This needs a different trend and magnitude of Administrative Management, culture and capability. We are living in a period of momentous changes, which have far-reaching Implications for not only the world-at-large, but specifically for the developing countries.

We need to take care of the following aspects through development administration to promote administrative reforms:

1. A closer focus on results in terms of efficiency and effectiveness, and service quality;
2. The replacement of highly centralised hierarchical organisational structures with decentralised management environments, where decisions on resource allocation and service delivery are taken closer to the point of delivery, and which provide scope for feedback from clients and other interest groups;
3. Flexibility to explore alternatives to direct public provision, which might provide more cost-effective policy outcomes;
4. New personnel management policies to provide greater flexibility in the deployment of staff (e.g., through multi-skilling);
5. The use of mechanisms to improve performance such as performance contracting and the creation of competitive market environment within and among public sector organisations;
6. Incentives to improve performance (or at least removing disincentives) through enabling organisations to retain a portion of savings from improved performance;
7. The strengthening of strategic capacities at the centre to "steer" government to respond to external changes and diverse interests quickly, flexibly and at least cost; and
8. Greater accountability and transparency through requirements to report on results.[31]

Dr. K. Kasturirangan, Chairman, Indian Space Research Organisation/Secretary, Department of Space, Government of India, has rightly said that "There are no short cuts or magic in the nation-building task. We have to learn to work effectively in a network, extending mutual faith and goodwill and achieve excellence as a team. In the knowledge-based society of the future, success comes to those who can organize networks of multi-function and multi-disciplinary systems which can deliver complex products or services, with increasing efficiency and productivity."[32]

Keith Henderson and O.P. Dwivedi in his article "Administered Development: The Fifth Decade-1990" in *IJPA*, 1992 defined that given the acute shortage of qualified human resources to manage the public service, innovations often originated with expatriates and foreign experts, or were simply cosmetic structural changes that brought no real alternation in the *status quo*. Also, over-planning and over-administration tended to have the same nefarious results (or lack of results) as lack of planning and under-administration. Confronted with an ineffectual developmental bureaucracy, the Western solution was more administrative development. Technical solutions about means were more palatable than much-needed substantive political decisions to bring about real socio-economic change.

2. Administration of Development

The second category of development administration is the administration of development which is further simplistically meant as administering development. This is identified with organisational developments-government departments, public enterprises, regulatory agencies, public corporations, cooperative institutions, etc. The government machinery is responsible for achieving the broader socio-economic and political goals. Let us mention some of the functions of administration of development:

- to promote the welfare of the people by securing and protecting a social order in which justice—social, economic and political—shall inform all institutions of national life;
- to frame and adopt certain principles of policy towards securing right, of men and women equally to an adequate means of livelihood;
- equitable distribution of material resources to sub-serve the common good;
- deconcentration of wealth and means of production;
- equal pay for equal work;
- opportunities and facilities to children to develop in conditions of freedom and dignity, and protection of childhood and youth against exploitation and moral and material abandonment;
- right to work, to education and to public assistance in cases of unemployment, old age, sickness and disablement;
- participation of workers in the management of undertakings, organisations in any industry;
- free and compulsory education for all children until they complete the age of 14 years;
- uniform civil code throughout the territory of India;
- educational and economic interests of weaker sections of society, in particular the scheduled castes and tribes and their protection from social injustice and all forces of exploitation;
- organisation and establishment of Village Panchayats to function as units of self-government; and
- protection and improvement of environment, forests and wild life.

Prime Minister Manmohan Singh in his foreward to the Eleventh Plan outlines the new priorities for the public sector. These relate to reviving dynamism in agriculture and building the necessary supportive infrastructure in rural areas, expanding access to health and education, especially in rural areas, undertaking programmes for improving living conditions for the weaker sections and for improving their access to economic opportunity. It also includes a major thrust for infrastructure development in general, which is a critical constraint on our development.

Improved performance in agriculture is necessary if our growth is to be inclusive. The

Eleventh Plan adopts a multi-pronged approach towards this end. It provides for a major expansion in the programmes for irrigation and water management. The Rashtriya Krishi Vikas Yojana (RKVY) has been launched to assist the States in development and implementation of district level agricultural plans, based on local agro-climatic conditions. As a step towards food security, which has assumed special relevance in view of recent international developments, the National Food Security Mission aims at increasing cereal and pulses production by 20 million tons over a five year period.

In health, the Plan aims at providing improved broad based health care in rural areas through the National Rural Health Mission. The Rashtriya Swasthya Bima Yojana will provide the much needed insurance cover against illness. the population below the poverty line. Our initiatives in implementing a nationwide mid-day meals scheme in schools and improving the implementation of the ICDS will also improve the health and nutrition status of our children.

To summarize development administration has two main functions; one relates to realizing development goals and objectives, the other to improving and enhancing capabilities of those involved in development, goals and objectives. For example, one of the goals of administration is to provide decent health care to all and for achieving this goal, there is need of efficient and effective health administration. Both are essential and complimentary. We cannot achieve the goals of development activities without the interlinking both of them.

DEVELOPMENT ADMINISTRATION AND PUBLIC ADMINISTRATION (See Chart 3.3)

The expansion of the study of public administration towards, "development administration' is simply that something is more needed. The concept of development administration is a widely recognized concept these days and it has significantly stimulated the interest of scholars, not only of public administration but also of social sciences. It is being attended to heavily in the developing countries with a view to orienting it to development aspects (programmes and projects, related to socio-politico-economic progress) of administration. It does not imply that development administration is subservient to public administration. Development administration is as much important as the 'public administration' is the former refers to organized efforts to carry out development-oriented goals, the latter to the general or regulatory administration of the government. To quote Shou-Sheng Hsueh, "development administration" is essentially a public administration to maintain the general activity of the government as a going concern. On the other hand, development administration, as the expression implies, lays emphasis on that role of public administration which is to develop the activity of the government, especially in the economic and political and social fields."[33] Thus Hsueh does not draw a clear line between the developmental and the general activities of the administration.

The conventional public administration is concerned with maintenance, of law and order, collection of revenue and application of rules, policies, etc. But it differs from development administration in its objective and scope. First, development administration is a goal-orientedadministration which is geared to the objectives of nation-building and socio-economic progress. Second, it lays emphasis on increasing the administrative capacity for development and second as "development of administration". Thus development administration has a wide scope of activities than the one public administration has. Katz observes: "No longer is it limited to the maintenance of law and order, the provision of some limited public services, and the collection of taxes; rather it is specifically involved in the mobilization of resources and their allocation to a great variety of development activities, on a massive scale."[34]

CHART 3.3

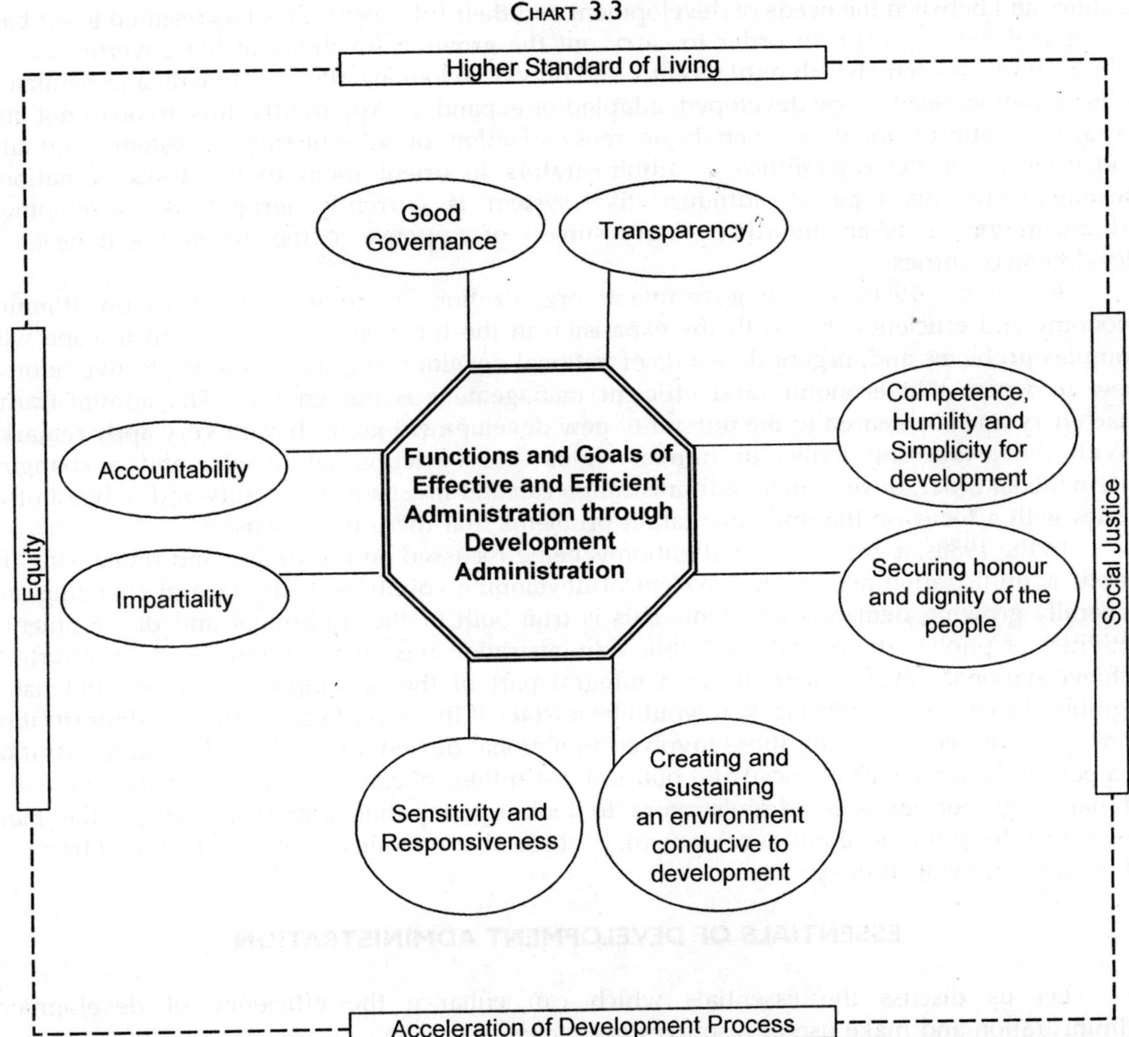

It follows from Katz's views that development administration is charged with the increasing responsibility of carrying out planned change in the economic, social and political fields. However, while making a distinction between development administration and public administration, their respective importance should not be lost sight of. Tarlok Singh in the context of development administration in India, agrees: "The character of the prevailing structure of general administration has a decisive influence on the strength and weakness of development administration. This is because of links which subsist between general and development administration."[35] The objective of development administration is the attainment of development goals. If is the word 'development' that is important that draws a line of demarcation between the two—public administration and development administration.

Since the Second World War the functions of the government have increased in size and number. But with this, serious imbalance has emerged between the hopes of the people and realities and between the needs of development and their fulfilment. This has resulted in set-back of national development. In order to carry out the growing functions of the government, the administrative system, which until recently had only been looking after the general and regulatory administration, needs to be developed, adapted or expanded. Apparently, this involves not only expansion, improvement or even basic reorganization of administrative systems, but also enhancement of the capabilities of administrators to orient them to the tasks of national development. This type of administrative system is currently termed as 'development administration'. It is an 'interdisciplinary subject of response to the development needs of developing countries.

Before the 1960s in the government organizations there was emphasis on attaining economy and efficiency, but with the expansion in the functions of government to cope with complex problems and, urgent demands of national development, many administrative reforms now recognize that economic and efficient management is not enough. The administrative machinery must be geared to the pursuit of new development goals. Bryant very aptly remarks: "With the awakening issues of human rights and basic human needs, and a changing international order, development administration can and must address equity and redistributive issues with a focus on the implementation problems that these issues raise."

In the 1980s, a great deal of attention is being focussed on improving and revitalising the public administration and finance system of developing countries in the face of changing and generally growing demands on them. This is true both of the traditional and developmental activities of public administration. Public administration has an important assets in efforts to achieve national development. It is an integral part of the development process and has a significant role to play in this task. It would be mistake if the importance of public administration were not fully recognized by those involved in national development. As public administration is a part of the large web of social and political institutions of country, it is important on the part of nation authorities and administrators to look upon public administration as the main instrument for bringing about development, be it social, economic or political. It should be a part of the development strategy.

ESSENTIALS OF DEVELOPMENT ADMINISTRATION

Let us discuss the essentials which can enhance the efficiency of development administration and make use of resources optimally.

1. Economy

Economy is minimizing the cost of resources used for an activity, having regard to the appropriate quality. Economy issues focus on the cost of the inputs and processes as well as curtail wasteful expenditure which has been occurring in India in both union and state governments, need be checked and curbed so that more benefits can accrue to poor people and not be diverted to rich people through corruption. Economy occurs where equal-quality resources are acquired at lower prices, i.e., spending less. Judging economy in itself implies forming an opinion on the resources (human, financial and material) deployed. The central question is to access whether given the context—resources have been acquired, upheld and used economically.

A. Ranghchari, "Austerity in government, yet another routine exercise" in *The Hindu*, Dec. 29, 2008 observes in the wake of the latest concern of the Reserve Bank of India Governor over the fiscal situation and inflation, the Prime Minister has called for cuts in expenditure by different ministries. This is a welcome development. Fiscal correctives to fight inflation have so far been confined to tax reductions. It is now recognised that cutting down unproductive expenditure to tackle the budget deficit is also a necessary anti-inflationary fiscal measure.

In the context of the current austerity it will be useful to know the specific results of such reviews and the actual budgetary savings effected. It should be clearly understood as to what the government should do and pay for, what it should pay for but not do and what it should neither do nor pay for issuing austerity circulars will not automatically lead to meaningful expenditure reviews targeting specific non priority, unproductive and inefficient items. This exercise cannot be left to the ministries. The Finance Ministry may also not be able to initiate and follow up such a systematic review; over the years, delegation of powers and the system of integrated financial advisers in spending ministries may also have eroded its special expertise in expenditure management. The PMO may be entrusted with this work. Periodic progress reports may help the public to follow the outcome of this effort. In many cases, reports of commissions and task forces are already available identifying the problems and offering solutions.

2. Efficiency

Efficiency is the relationship between the output, in terms of goods, services, other results and the resources used to produce them. Efficiency exists where the use of financial, human, physical and information resources is such that output is maximized with any given set of resource inputs, or input is minimised for any given quantity and quality of output, i.e., spending well.

The main question related to efficiency is whether the resources have been put to optimal or satisfactory use or whether the same or similar results in terms of quality turn-around time could have been achieved with fewer resources. The question refers the relationship between the quality and quantity of goods and services yielded and cost of resources used to produce them, in order to achieve the results. A finding on efficiency can be formulated by means of a comparison with activities, with other periods or with a standard, which the entity has explicitly adopted. Sometimes, standards such as best practices are applicable. Assessments on efficiency might also be based on conditions that are not related to specific standards, i.e. where matters are so complex that there are no standards. In such cases assessments must be based on the best available information and arguments and in compliance with the analysis carried out in the administration.

3. Effectiveness

Effectiveness is the extent to which objectives are achieved and the relationship between the intended impact and the actual impact of an activity. Effectiveness address the issue of whether the programme/activity has achieved its objectives, i.e. spending wisely. When focusing on effectiveness, it is important to distinguish between immediate outputs or products and the ultimate impacts or outcomes. Effectiveness achieved, for instance, where, there is improved achievement of a programme objective. Outcomes are important to the effectiveness of programmes/activities but may be more difficult to measure and assess than the inputs and outputs. Outcomes will often be influenced by external factors and may require long-term rather than short-term assessment.

Effectiveness is essentially a goal-attainment concept. It is concerned with the relationship between the objectives set-up, outputs provided and objectives met. Some of the questions to ask in effectiveness are. Are the objectives of the policy being met by the means employed, outputs provided and impacts observed? Are the means employed and the results achieved consistent with the objectives of the policy and perhaps the most difficult are the impacts really the results of the policy rather than other circumstances? The last one may be difficult to establish in most cases and will call for a cautious approach.

4. Equity and Ethics

Equity in the context of programme management relates to fairness and impartiality in use of public funds. Ethics in managing public affairs enjoins the qualities of honesty and integrity in personal conduct and devotion to the duty as manager of public funds. The ethics in management of public funds and affairs enjoins the qualities of honesty and integrity in personal conduct and devotion to the duty as the managers. The ethical issues should be viewed distinctly from the efficiency concept, which is concerned with use of human, financial and other resources to maximise the output. For example, inability of the management to apply the resources for the objective for which these are provided addresses the efficiency parameter, whereas intentional unauthorized siphoning of resources for other purpose or negligent/incorrect performance information may relate to ethical integrity.

Through Total Quality Management, Governments can measure the existing methods of resource utilization. Questions about the efficiency in utilizing resources, the levels of wastage and the knowledge of costs of governance may be addressed. Through active and continuous brainstorming, ideas may be generated, which identify waste and lead to steps to eliminate waste. Costs of activities may be scrutinized closely and may be reduced. Performance standards can be drawn up, attained and further improved. Customer satisfaction may be more difficult to measure but the positive impact on the economy is measurable and can be used as a proxy parameter. TQM practices can be invoked either on a small scale within departments and organisations or on a large scale at the national level.

5. Outcome Evaluation

(a) Process evaluation: assess the extent to which a programme is operating as intended typically, it is concerned with the programme activities, conformance to statutory regulatory requirements, programme design and professional standards or expectations. (b) Outcome evaluation: assesses the extent to which a programme achieves its outcome-oriented objectives. It focuses on outputs and outcomes (including unintended effects) in order to judge programme effectiveness, but it may also assess programme processes in order to understand how outcomes are produced. Deputy Chairman Planning Commission in his preface to XIth plan stresses that the challenges before the Eleventh Plan is to improve upon this growth performance and also ensure greater sustainability and inclusiveness so that the development process being unleashed has the widest possible spread of benefits. In the search for inclusion, the Plan pays special attention to the needs of the weaker sections including the Scheduled Castes, Scheduled Tribes, OBCs, and minorities. The objectives of the plan cannot have meaning if they are not translated into a visible flow of benefits to these groups.

6. Impact Evaluation

Assesses the net effect of a programme by comparing programmme outcomes with an estimate of what would have happened in the absence of program. This form of evaluation is employed when external factors are known that influence the programme's outcomes, in order to isolate the programme's contributions to the achievement of its objectives.

7. Social Cost and Social Benefit

Socially profitable projects are those projects where discounted social benefits are greater than discounted social costs. Beyond rationalizing the structure of the public sector there is a need to improve public management systems to make public programs more efficient and accountable. Involving civil society in planning, monitoring, and evaluating public programs and policies is also crucial to ensure steady progress towards a fully responsive and accountable state.

This would be possible only if—

- Public administrations implement policies efficiently and are accountable and responsive to users, corruption and harassment are curbed, and the power of the state is used to redistribute resources for actions benefiting poor people.
- Legal systems promote legal equity and are accessible to poor people.
- Central and local governments create decentralized mechanisms for broad participation in the delivery of public services and minimize the scope for capture by local elites.
- Governments generate political support for public action against poverty by creating a climate favourable to pro-poor actions and coalitions, facilitating the growth of poor people's associations, and increasing the political capacity of poor people.
- Political regimes honour the rule of law, allow the expression of political voice, and encourage the participation of poor people in political processes.

Any strategy to overcome these inequalities will undoubtedly want to accord highest priority to overall poverty alleviation broad-based social and economic development.

8. Helpful in Crisis Administration

Development administration must handle crisis efficiently and quickly to avoid any risk. There are problems of crisis as development administration is to deal with challenging activities.

John P. Kotter, in his article, "A Sense of Urgency" in *Economic Times* dated 2.1.2009 observes: ALWAYS think of crises as potential opportunities, and not only dreadful problems that automatically must be delegated to the damage control specialists. A crisis can be your friends. Never forget that crises do not automatically reduce complacency. If not monitored and handled well, burning platforms can be disastrous, leading to fear, anger, blame, and the energetic yet dysfunctional behaviour associated with false urgency. To use a crisis to reduce complacency, make sure it is visible, unambiguous, related to real business problems, and significant enough that it cannot be solved with small, simple actions.

Fight the impulse to minimize or hide bad news. To use a crisis to reduce complacency, be exceptionally proactive in assessing how people will react, in developing specific plans for action, and in implementing the plans swiftly. Plans and actions should always focus on others' hearts an much or more than their minds. Behaving with passion, conviction, optimism, urgency, and a steely determination will trump an analytically brilliant memo every time. If urgency is low, never patiently wait for a crisis to solve your problems. Act with urgency every day. Certainly we need to be prudent. But in a more rapidly changing world, finding opportunities in crises probably reduces your overall risk.

9. Unity of People

While implementing Development progrmmes, there are bound to be reactions from certain quarters which can be a source of terrorism, fundamentalism, etc. Development administration in such situations must take the support of the people to fight such forces.

Nilotpal Basu, "Different Hues" in *Deccan Herold*, Dec. 25, 2008 observes: There is no way for an isolationist solution. Security systems, appropriate laws in place in themselves cannot bring salvation. Unless people can be united with a purpose, both within and across the region, the forces of terrorism cannot be contained. In that battle, communalism, fundamentalism and the imperialist presence and their unilateralism are all challenges that have to be resisted by galvanizing our popular unity. Knee jerk reactions and unthinking fit of mad rage could create more problems than provide solutions.

10. Knowledge of Human Rights

Development Administration is to ensure that all people enjoy human rights which are the essential ingredients for development. This may require energy and enthusiasm among development administrators. Daisaku Ikeda in his article, "Revisiting the Spirit of Human Rights" in *Decan Herald* dated Dec. 25, 2008 observes that however, the reality of today is that people in many places around the world are deprived of their basic human rights and freedoms and struggle under the heel of oppression. In addition to armed conflicts in various regions, extreme poverty, and shortages of food, drinking water, and medical supplies claim nearly 24,000 lives every day.

What is important now is to heighten people's awareness of human rights, to return once more to the spirit in which the UDHR was created and ensure that people around the world deepen their commitment to bringing human rights to life.

The core of the UDHR consists of "first-generation human rights"—which are essentially related to civil and political rights, and "second-generation human rights"—economic and social rights. Since the UDHR was promulgated, and with the achievement of independence by countries in Africa and Asia in the second half of the 20th century, increasing attention has been given to "third-generation human rights"—the so called "solidarity rights", which include the right to development, to a safe and healthy environment, to peace, and to access humanity's common heritage.

Contributing to others, working for the sake of others, is not a matter of duty. It is not simply a matter of morality. It is the highest pinnacle of our lives as humans. As can be strongly affirmed by mothers around the world who cherish life, to be able to contribute to the happiness of others is, indeed, a human right.

11. Welfare of People

The Yardstick for the success of development administration is the welfare of the people. Pt. Jawaharlal Nehru has rightly said that administration is meant to achieve something and not to exist in some kind of Ivory towers following certain rules of procedures and looking. Narcisseus like the test of administration is the welfare of people. Prime Minister Manmohan Singh said in *The Hindu*, Dec. 20, 2008 "We also need to be alive to the need for providing access to quality education to the poor and the disadvantaged," "to become partners in the process of transformation of India into a knowledge society."

We have walked the pragmatic middle path, and will continue to do so. We must walk on two legs."

For a poor country like India, pursuing development and welfare of the people in the framework of a liberal democracy was not a easy journey. "Many nations stared this journey with us and drifted away. Some chose not to walk this path, others were denied that opportunity," he said. In this dimension, India's achievement had global relevance even today.

12. Professional Integrity

Development administration cannot be successful merely by talking and gossping as words written or spoken are of no use unless put to action. It can achieve its goal only through planning unless put to action. It can achieve its goal only through professionals who believe and practice integrity, action, skills and job satisfaction. Nitya Sai Soumya in his article, "Do not indulge in gossip" in *The Hindu*, Dec. 24, 2008 clearly defined that trust is very important to lead a successful professional life and gossip just damages that. Our friends can desert us or turn into enemies, the employer can hesitate to assign important assignments and increase vigilance on us. There are many cases where frivolous gossip has led to deep investigations causing many in the line to lose their jobs! Though gossip can bring in short-term benefits, it will slowly become a habit and affect our future career.

Difficult times do tempt us to resort to unsavoury actions or shortcuts. But firmly believing that nothing except our skills, professionalism and integrity can contribute to success will help us resist such temptations!

13. Assess Performance

Development administration should make use of Management by objectives to achieve socio-economic development. According to George Odiorne, "MBO (Management By Objectives) is a system wherein the superior and the subordinate managers of an organization jointly define its common goals, define each individual's major areas of responsibility in terms of the result expected of him and use these measures as guides for operating the unit and assessing the contribution of each of its members.[36] (See Chart 3.4)

INGREDIENTS OF MBO

We mention here some essential ingredients required for the success of MBO:

(a) Active participation and involvement of the subordinates in planning, implementation and evaluation.
(b) Emphasis on team spirit and team approach.
(c) Open Communication among the members of the Organization irrespective of their status.
(d) Increased skill in Inter-personal communication.
(e) Personal Counseling and guidance.

Hema Gopalakrishna in his articles, "Performance must be critic to fix blames of erring workers" in *The Hindu*, Dec. 24, 2008 observes that some employees find it easy to shift the blame because of the management's failure to properly monitor employee output. Also there is no clear definition of performance expectations from employees. Individual performance tends to get over-shadowed by team goals and there is no clear definition of individual accountability. The management fails to take an objective of real perspective of performance or people issues when a crisis happens, this allows employees to find a scapegoat.

CHART 3.4

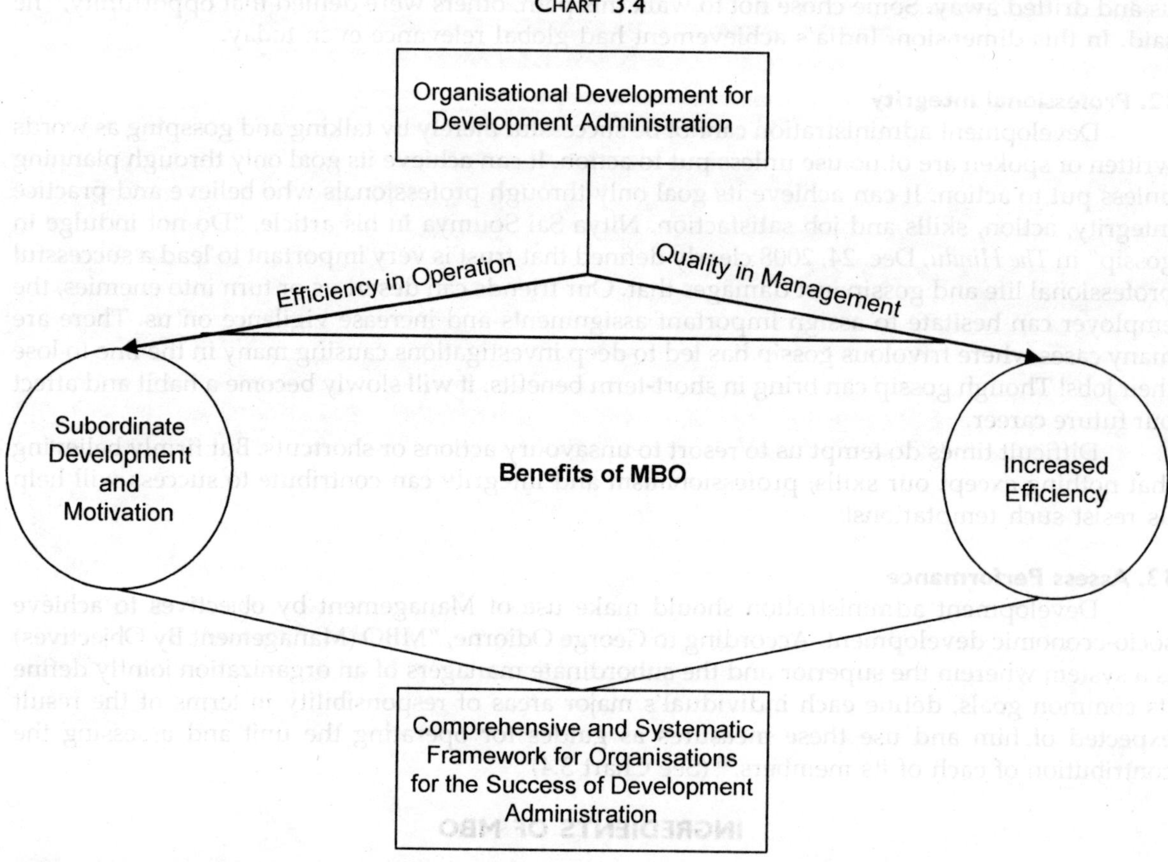

On the contrary when problems crop up, the management should look into the history, background and context of the situation to get a complete picture. Individual roles and responsibilities must be clearly specified so that employees cannot shift the blame. They should invest on building mutual trust and respect among employees to prevent such incidents. There should be fair play and justice when dealing with a problem.

Shifting the blame creates an unhealthy work environment where people are interested in only saving their skin rather than put in their best efforts at work. Openness and clear lines of communication can prevent this.

14. Benefits to Poor People

Development administration must pay more attention to the poor to ensure social justice but in practice we find that poor are neglected and there is more fear of their neglect in the present economic crisis.

Amartya Sen observed (reported by Shyam Ranganathan) that growth in India being maintained at high levels over the last few years did not directly benefit the poor. Only a part of the wealth actually flowed back to them, and this too mainly because of increased revenue collection. Even the current global slowdown would also cause only an indirect problem to the poor due to reduced State spending on many essential services.[37]

15. Glaring Inequalities

There were also glaring inequalities in the coverage provided to events affecting the rich and the coverage to the more chronic and continuous problems faced by the poor, and this had to be addressed to reduce poverty, Dr. Sen said.

Many projects in India were not able to attain their objectives due to focus on the "neeti" type of argument, with the phrase "I did my (best {within the rules)" sufficing to explain away failure. What was required to eliminate the inequities in the Indian system was to focus on working towards achieving specific goals within the pragmatic "nyaya" framework.

Efficient civil services: Development administration depends upon civil servants who are to implement development programmes honestly and sincerely. P.P. Rao, "Public Service Commissions—Look for persons of merit and integrity in *The Tribune*, 5 January, 2009 observes in Subhash Chander's case, the Punjab and Haryana High Court lamented "that the dream of the founding fathers, in creating the State Public Service Commissions as the bulwarks of our Constitution to ensure the independence, integrity and apolitical nature of the Civil Service and to effectuate the constitutional guarantee of equality of opportunity in matters of public employment, now stands wholly soured."

It is equally essential to streamline public services at all levels, if need be, by amending Article 311 of the Constitution. In addition to attractive voluntary retirement schemes, a provision for premature retirement of undesirable public servants on payment of some compensation could be a feasible alternative for getting rid of them quickly, instead of initiation of time-consuming criminal prosecutions or disciplinary proceedings. Speed is the essence of any cleansing operations.

16. Need of a New Outlook

Development administration needs a new mind, a new type of attitude, that is suffused with human values. You are not dealing with a table or a chair, but with a human being. He or she has problems. You are there to solve them. That chair of authority on which you sit is not a chair of comfort. It is a chair with a heavy human responsibility on your head. Rise to the level of the responsibility that chair signifies. Our mental awareness must rise to that level.

Raveen Thukral, "Unending Police excesses" in Chandigarh *Tribune* dated Jan. 5, 2009 observed. It is sad that the Indian police has become notorious for use of brute physical power instead of taking recourse to highly refined scientific techniques of investigations. Raw power has substituted professionalism and disturbingly it's not only the undereducated constabulary or those who have risen from the lower ranks but also IAS and IPS officers who show little regard for law.

And what is disheartening is that there are no safeguards for the citizens against such humiliation. There is no fair, just and transparent inquiry mechanism if such allegations are made and since judicial probes cannot be conducted in every case, one have to rely on departmental inquires. But then what can be a justification of an inquiry by a senior fellow colleague or a magistrate who is part of the same system?

Courts are perhaps the only recourse but the judicial process is unfortunately so lengthy and costly that it acts as a deterrent and usually victims learn to live with such humiliations rather than getting into the legal maze. So one can only again wish that our police force attains that humane face and this uniformed arrogance ends. She further adds (*Tribune*, Feb. 2005) that In the interest of the speedier justice, the three wings of constitutional governance have to work in tandem—the legislature by enacting appropriate laws, the executive by honesty doing its jobs of investigation and prosecution and the judiciary , in this context, by gearing up to devote more judge-hours to contribute to the pace and quantum of justice delivery.

PROBLEMS OF DEVELOPMENT ADMINISTRATION

1. Lack of Persons with Desired Qualifications to Implement Development Programmes

Personnel engaged for development administration are the same persons dealing with routine administration. For development administration we must strive to find out administrators possessing the following qualifications: competence, missionary-zeal, the capacity to motivate other people, the capacity to communicate with others, the ability to get along with colleagues and the people, culture adaptability, the capability to organize and manage the capacity to inspire confidence in others, patience and dignity. Besides, they must have faith in the ideal of their work, be willing to accept hardships and prepare to work in a spirit of service. Their ambition and enthusians should not be dampened by local conditions which may not provide them with the necessary facilities. Unfortunately, the sense of dedication has been the crassest causality of the prevailing atmosphere of cynicism bred by increasing propensity towards expediency.

2. Lack of Emphasis on Implementation of Development Administration Programmes through Hardwork rather than being Engaged Merely on Paper Planning

Words, written or spoken, are of no use unless put into actions. The emphasis should be more on performance rather than paper planning. Khalil Gibran has rightly said that "Believing is a fine thing, but placing those beliefs into execution is a test of strength. Many are those who talk like the roar of the sea, but their lives are shallow and stagnant, like the rotting marshes. Many are those who lift their heads above the mountain tops, but their spirit remain dormant to the obscurity of the carverns."

Thus, the future of this budding developing democracy depends upon the attitudes of its political and administrative elite. There is no substitute for hardwork which would be reflected in better life of the people. Nevertheless, without a concerted attempt to make the administration much more action-oriented than at present, these may not yield enough results.

Kaibara Ekken, the Japanese sage has nicely put it as: If by study, enquiry or thought, we have learned the truth, we should then put it into practice in both our speech and action. Let what we say be true and what we do discreet. Regulate the emotions, and suppress anger and selfish desires. Shake off evil and cling to good. Discovering our faults, let us not hesitate to correct them. Towards others let us be considerate. All this is the way of true action—without putting what we have learned into practice, it bears no fruit.

3. Lack of Sincere and Earnest attempt by Civil Services to make Development Administration Programmes Successful

All the persons engaged in development administration programmes are not sincere and enthusiastic Robert M. Hutchines states quoted in M.R. Pinto, Values in Public Services, (*IJPA*, January-March, 1989.) "Thus, all organizations can function and achieve excellence provided all its members strive to pursue the goals of the organization earnestly, sincerely, whole-heartedly and with dedication."

Our thought is the seed which determines the fruit of our action. If the seed is good, then the flowers and fruits which come from the seed must be good and must prove beneficial to ourselves and others. But if we plant in our hearts a poisonous seed, it will harm not only ourselves but all who come in contact with us. Human life is a great responsibility. Only a thoughtless man will say: I cannot help what happens, I am not responsible. We are constantly influencing ourselves and our fellow-beings by what we think, because our thought shapes our inner nature and we radiate consciously or unconsciously what we are. Let us be wakeful then. Let us be thoughtful in whatever we do. Let us be faithful to our true self; for all blessings must come to us, if we prove ourselves true to our higher nature.

4. Corrupt Practices among Political and Administrative Personnel engaged in Development Administration Programmes which Erode the Credibility of Development Administration

The country is passing through a terrible crisis these days. The aggravation of material greed has, as a reaction, set ablaze the fire of corruption at all levels. Through the dominant influence of the present material civilization, and the ideal of enjoyment fostered by it, even the basic framework and moral fibre of the country has been affected by an internal demoralization. The heart trembles at the sight of the moral degradation practised today in the field of public administration. There is no limit to the fraud and hypocrisy that are being practised in the name of politics.

Most of the problems in Public Administration are emanating from political corruption and interference. The credibility gap between the political and administrative leadership is on the increase. Most of the commissions, committees and the daily press have been emphasizing the gravity of the situation. No organization can progress until and unless its political leaders are above board. One of the founding fathers of the Indian Constitution, Mr. H.V. Kamath regrets that the total devaluation of moral values and ethical ideals in public life and administration today has given rise to the present day rat race for position, power and pelf by any means, more by crook than by hook. What can be done to ensure confidence of the staff and the people in the integrity of the political elite? The answer is plain and simple, i.e., the political elite must demonstrate integrity and instill faith among their subordinates about their fairness and impartiality. Faith is a contagious disease and once it is developed, it would bend the various levels of the administration into a cohesive structure

5. Beneficiaries not Involved in the Formulation and Implementation of Development Projects

The success or failure of the projects ultimately depends upon the acceptance of these projects by the people. If the people are not taken into confidence during the formulation and implementation of development projects, these would be less successful. People's participation would provide extra energy to ensure the success of the projects. Most of the beneficiaries contacted by the writer were of the view that they are not treated as equal partners in the process of formulation and implementation of development projects. The failure of the scheme is because of the absence of identification of the people with the programmes. It is essential for the experts in the developing countries to motivate and encourage the people to participate in the formulation and implementation of projects. Although people's participation in affairs governing their lives dates back to the beginning of human society, the concept has taken a new dimension as societies have grown in size and complexity. This is partly because the management has become more and more of a specialized enterprise, an area for technocrats and trained general administrators and political leaders. Although they officially advocate and preach people's involvement, in practice, they bring them into picture only after the major decisions have been taken. Hence, they often leave the ordinary citizens to follow their pre-determined paths. Peter Berger agrees with this contention when he says that "the overwhelming majority of these people have little or no opportunity to influence policy, and their perspectives on the situation are systematically ignored by almost all theorists. For them the problem of development is one of the everyday life."[38]

Local communities are treated as passive participants in improvement and betterment of their lives. Most of the project personnel working in the villages return to the cities after their duty hours. The villagers cannot make their views known to them in cities. The result is lack of communication among them. When the project fails, it is intentionally ascribed to the obstinacy, fatalism, illiteracy or apparent irritationality of the poor people. The potential for community involvement has been seriously under estimated. We must encourage people's participation through all methods to promote development administration.

6. Absence of Satisfactory Monitoring System to Measure the Regulated Performance during Implementation of Development Administration Programme

Most of the projects are never completed within the budgeted resources and fixed time schedules. It has become a normal feature to extend the life of the project resulting in the wastage of huge financial resources. It clearly indicates the weakness of controlling mechanism and lack of development administration. Project control is the managerial function that helps the managers to keep the project functioning as scheduled. It is possible only if the realistic advance targets of output are fixed before implementation. This is not being done as is evident from the perusal of most of the projects studied. Monitoring, if properly designed, can help the managers in keeping the process of implementation as scheduled. The project performance is compared at different intervals of time with the controlled indicators. Whenever deviations are located, causes of deviations are examined, solutions are found to correct the deviations.

7. Lack of Clarification of Authority, Responsibility and Relationships on Development Administration Activities

In the developing world, the persons responsible for implementation of development administration programmes do not work as a team, as there is no clarification of authority, responsibility and relationships amongst them, i.e., the roles of various participants are not often mutually understood. This results in friction among these persons. Most of the time of these persons is spent in their mutual disputes. It becomes very difficult for them to devote their whole attention to the project.

8. Lack of Emotional Intelligence in Implementing Development Administration Programmes

HRD should pay more attention to the development of emotional intelligence. Dr. Rakesh Sinha, Mind Management Therepist, in his article, "Express Your Emotions" has rightly said that Emotions are complex and can be difficult to manage. Actions that spring from the emotional mind carry a particularly strong sense of certainty that cannot be justified or explained by the rational mind.

In organisations, human resources are considered as the greatest assets. It is, thus, pertinent for organisations to understand the role of Emotional Intelligence (EI) in enhancing the productivity of its human resources to achieve overall success. A large number of surveys have shown that emotions of the employees play a significant role in determining their output. In fact, critical consequences have been observed in those organisations where the EI of its people is low. HRD should focus on enhancing the EI of the oragnisation to ensure development.

9. Lack of Excellent Leadership essential for Development Administration

Peter Drucker defined it as the lifting of man's visions to higher sights, the raising of man's performance to higher standard, the building of man's personality beyond its moral limitations. According to Chester I Bernard, "It refers to quality of the behaviour of the individual whereby they guide people on their activities in organized efforts." According to G.R. Terry, "leadership is the activity of influencing people to strive willingly for group objectivity."

The leader of the participative or helping style wants his staff to participate in setting objectives for their work. He uses them for decisions, team planning and the team cooperation in getting work done. Consequently the staff take responsibility for the work and are committed to the work.

The participative leader trusts his staff's abilities. He listens to their opinions and encourages them to contribute their ideas as to how to provide better services. He always help them improve their skills. He gives them more responsibility as their skills improve. He spends much of his time with his staff. He works with them to solve problems in the community. Leadership trait mostly include the following for making development administration a success.

- Intelligence
- Emotional stability
- Energy and enthusiasm
- Accommodation and adaptability
- Human engineering
- Co-existence with subordinates
- Objectivity
- Willingness to make personal sacrifices to assist subordinates
- Develops team spirit

10. Lack of Creativity among Development Administration

To see work as a potential for creating joy and to experience the happiness of creating something totally new. It is immensely satisfying to do work, which contributes to the lives of others and creates radical transformation in the quality of life of those around us. Creative work, which creates a new form, which is original, is very satisfying. Work which is without an effect, or which can be done equally well by anyone else, never inspire us. We all like to give our special touch to whatever we do. This creates an interesting paradox; whether our responses influence the quality of work or does work influence the quality of our responses? The answer is to go beyond the dichotomy. Creativity is the answer which can create genuine atmosphere for development administration.

11. Lack of use of IT for e-Governance for Development Administration

IT increases knowledge and knowledge is power. It can easily travel across the world enlightening the lives of the people everywhere. E-governance is really e-nabled government, effective government and excellent government e-government is government any time any where.

Prosperity through IT is at our door step. We must open the door fully and not keep it shut. E-governance is the future of development administration and we must go in first to make the future bright. In the context of development administration, IT has to be used as an "enabling technology" to achieve the broader goal of good governance. But to have an idea of how to go about it, let us take a look at the following agenda items of good governance to promote Development Administration.

Enhancing effective and efficient development administration;
Improving quality of life of citizens;
Establishing legitimacy and credibility of development institutions;
Making development administration responsive, citizen friendly, and citizen caring;
Ensuring accountability of development services;
Securing freedom of information and expression;
Reducing cost of governance as resources are limited for development administration;
Making every development related department result-oriented;
Improving quality of public services;
Improving productivity of employees engaged in development;
Removal of arbitrariness in exercise of authority; and
Use of IT-based services to de-mystify procedures and improve the citizen government interface.

CONCLUSION (See Chart 3.5)

It may be added here that development administration is an action and goal-oriented process. It is a coordinated effort encompassing a very wide range of activities directed to ameliorate the lot of millions of unfortunate; less privileged people leading a life of deprivations and dejection. The essence of development administration is holistic change undertaken through integrated, organised and properly directed governmental action. The development administration, therefore, centres around the words "Change" and "Operation Problems." Change includes both social and economic. Most of the countries in Asia, Africa and Latin America are labelled as developing countries or poor countries or less developed countries or emerging nations or third world and likewise, because they are relatively young because they are engaged in the development tasks of nation-building and socio-economic progress because their per capita national income is less, because they are technologically less advanced and finally they are socially backward.

Development administration could not achieve much in developing countries. It has become a fashion to name Development administration to old administrative structures, without introducing changes. The same personnel with the old administrative apparatus are implementing development programmes with utter failures, resulting in the wastage of human, material and financial resources. These remarks have been based upon a number of evaluation studies conducted by the author.

It may be mentioned here that all the Five Year Plans, including the Tenth Plan, and statements of top leaders are emphatic on the role of Development administration to promote social change and development, as well as provide special care to the unprivileged and underprivileged sections of the society. However, India is still lagging behind in developing its own administrative system based upon its needs. As discussed earlier, even our ancient literature mentions about social values of public administration. Kautilya, in his Arthasastra, has also emphasized the welfare of the people as the most important function of the King.

Reorganization of development administrative structures and procedures are essential to weed out impediments through innovation. Administrative innovation is the *sine qua non* for development administration and good governance. The organisational reforms in India have thus tended to exist mainly in form rather than in real substance—leaving little impact on the efficiency of the system. We cannot have effective administration without a close fit between policy

CHART 3.5

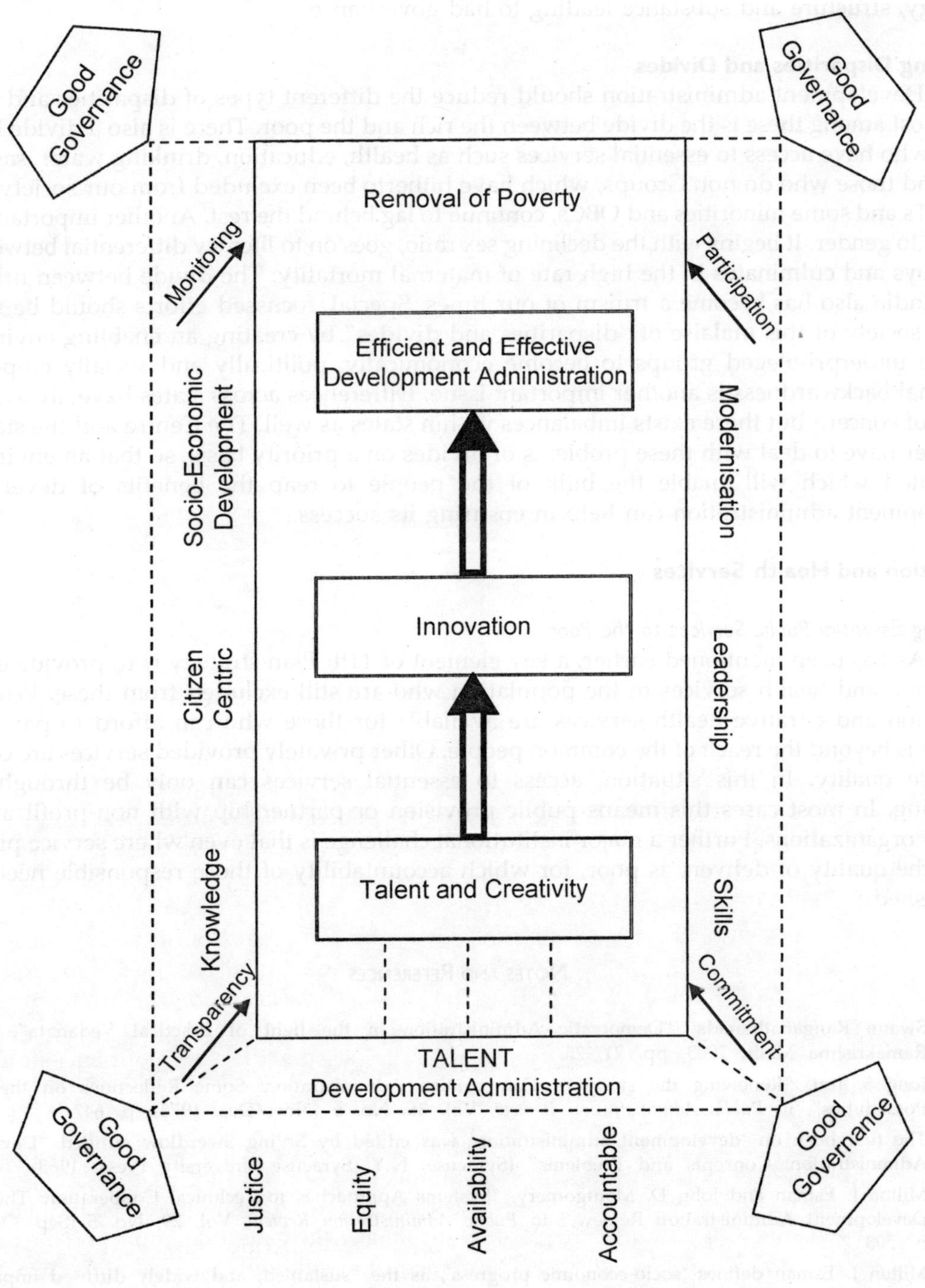
Good Governance
Good Governace
Removal of Poverty
Monitoring
Participation
Efficient and Effective Development Administration
Socio-Economic Development
Modernisation
Innovation
Citizen Centric
Leadership
Talent and Creativity
Knowledge
Skills
Transparency
Commitment
TALENT
Development Administration
Good Governance
Good Governance
Justice
Equity
Availability
Accountable

objectives, organisational design, operational procedure and personnel motivation. What has been lacking in India's administrative reforms in the past four decades is the congruence between strategy, structure and substance leading to bad governance.

Bridging Disparities and Divides

Development administration should reduce the different types of disparities and divides. Foremost among these is the divide between the rich and the poor. There is also a divide between those who have access to essential services such as health, education, drinking water, sanitation, etc., and those who do not. Groups, which have hitherto been excluded from our society such as SCs, STs and some minorities and OBCs, continue to lag behind the rest. Another important divide relates to gender. It begins with the declining sex ratio, goes on to literacy differential between girls and boys and culminates in the high rate of maternal mortality. The divide between urban and rural India also has become a truism of our times. Special, focussed efforts should be made to purge society of this malaise of "disparities and divides" by creating an enabling environment for the underprivileged groups to become economically, politically and socially empowered. Regional backwardness is another important issue. Differences across states have always been a cause of concern but there exists imbalances within states as well. The Centre and the states will together have to deal with these problems of divides on a priority basis, so that an environment is created which will enable the bulk of the people to reap the benefits of development. Development administration can help in ensuring its success.

Education and Health Services

Providing Essential Public Services to the Poor

As has been mentioned earlier, a key element of 11th Plan strategy is to provide essential education and health services to the population who are still excluded from these. While both education and curative health services are available for those who can afford to pay, quality service is beyond the reach of the common people. Other privately provided services are of highly variable quality. In this situation, access to essential services can only be through public financing. In most cases this means public provision or partnership with non-profit and civil society organizations. Further a major institutional challenge is that even where service providers exist, the quality of delivery is poor, for which accountability of those responsible needs to be established.

Notes and References

1. Swami Ranganathanada, "Democratic Administration in the light of Practical Vedanata", Chennai, Ramakrishna Math, 2003, pp. 21, 25.
2. Jong S. Jun, "Renewing the study of Comparative Administration: Some Reflections on the Current Possibilities", in *Public Administration Review*, Vol. 36, No. 6 (Nov./Dec. 1976), p. 647.
3. The first bock on 'development administration' was edited by Srving Swerdlow entitled "Development Administration: Concepts and Problems" (Syracuse, N.Y. Syracuse University Press, 1963).
4. Milton J. Esman and John D. Montgomery, "Systems Approaches to Technical Cooperation: The Role of Development Administration Review," in *Public Administration Review*, Vol. 29, No. 5 (Sep. Oct. 1969), p. 508.
5. Milton J. Esman defines 'socio-economic progress', as the "sustained, and widely diffused improvement in material and social welfare", and 'nation-building' as "the deliberate fashioning of an integrated

political community with in fixed geographic boundaries in which the nation-state is the prominent political institution." See Montgomery and Siffin (eds.), Approaches to Development: Politics, Administration and Change (New York, McGraw Hill, 1966), pp. 59-60.

6. Development Administration: Current Approaches and Trends in Public Administration for National Development (United Nation Publication Sales No. E. 76, II. H.I.), p. 3.
7. Edward W. Weidner. "Development and Innovational Roles, in Weidner (cd.), *op. cit.*, p. 399.
8. *Ibid.*
9. John Montgomery, "A Royal Invitation: Variations on Three Classic Themes," in Montgomery and William Siffin (eds.), Approaches to Development: Politics, Administration and Change (New York), McGraw-Hill,. 1966), 259.
10. Inayatullah, "Local Administration in a Developing Country—The Pakistan Case", in Weidner (ed.), *op. cit.*, p. 278.
11. Everett M. Rogers, "Communication and Development, the Passing of Dominant Paradigm, *op. cit.*
12. Donald, C. Korten and Rudi Klans (eds.), People Centred Development: Contribution Towards Theory and Planning Framework, Hartford, C.T. Kumarian Press, 1984.
13. Welsley Bjur and A. Zomorrodian, "Towards Indigen.... Theories Administration, Los Angles, School of Public Administration, University of Southern California, 1986.
14. C. Byrant and Louise White, Managing Development in Third World Boulder Westview Press, 1988.
15. Stockwell and Lin Law.
16. E.F. Schumacher, Small is Beautiful, Economics and its people mattered, New York, Harper and Rood, 1973.

(Footnotes 11-16 are quoted in T.N. Chaturvedi, Editorial *IJPA*, Oct.-Dec. 1989, pp. 846-48.

17. David C. Korten and George Camer, Planning Framework For People Centred Development in David C. Kotren and Rudi Klow (eds.) People Centred Development, Contributions Towards Theory and Planning Framework.
18. *Ibid.*
19. *Ibid.*
20. Peter L. Berger and Richard Neuhans, "To Improve People", in David C. Korten and Rudi Klaus (eds.).
21. Wesley Bjur, Towards a Theory of Optimal Institutionalization, Los Angles, Schools of Public Administration, University of Southern California, 1977.

(Footnotes 17-21 quoted in Arvind Singhal, "Evolution of Development and Development Administration Theory", *IJPA*, Oct.-Dec., 1989, Vol. XXXV, No. 4, pp. 847-48.

22. Louise G. White, Creating Opportunities for Change, Boulder Co. Lyme-Rienw, 1987.
23. Riggs, "The Context of Development Administration", in Riggs (ed.), Frontiers of Development Administration, *op. cit.*, p. 73.
24. *Ibid.*, p. 75.
25. O.P. Dwivedi, "Development Administration: An Overview" Fifty Years of Indian Administration—Retrospect and Prospects, ed. T.N. Chaturvedi, 1998, pp. 49, 51, 60.
26. *Ibid.*, p. 75.
27. J.N. Khosla, "Research in Development Administration" in Pai Panandikar (ed.), *op. cit.*, pp. 219-20.
28. Swami Ranganathanna, Democratic Administration in the Light of Practical Vedanta, 2002, p. 71.
29. Saul M. Katz, "A Methodological Note on Appraising Administrative Capability for Development", in Appraising Administrative capability for Development (United Nations Publication, Sales No. E. 69, 11, H. 2), pp. 99-100.
30. *Deccan Chronicle*, 21 July, 2005, p. 8.
31. David Shad, New Public Management Challenges and Issues in an Interntional perspective, in *IJPA*, July-Sept., 1998, pp. 717-18.
32. AIU, *University News*, New Delhi, Aug. 21, 2000.

33. Shou-Sheng Hsueh, "Technical Co-operation in Development Administration in South and South-East Asia", in Edward W. Weidner (ed.), Development Administration in Asia (Durham, NC: Duke University Press, 1970), p. 340.
34. Saul M. Katz, "Exploring a Systems Approach to Development Administration in F.W. Riggs (ed.). Frontiers of Development Administration (Durham, Ne, Duke University Press, 1970), p. 120.
35. Tarlok Singh, "Administration for Development," in V.A. Pai Panandikar (ed.) Development Administration in India (New Delhi, Macmillan, 1974).
36. George S. Odorie, Practice of Management, 1954, pp. 135-36.
37. *The Hindu*, Dec. 24, 2008.
38. Peter Berger: Pyramids of Sacrifice, Political Ethics and Social Change, (Garden City, N.Y., Anchor Books, 1976), p. 6.

CHAPTER

4

Public Administration in Developed and Developing Countries

Public administration is the heart of development. As early as 1950, the Secretary-General of the United Nations pointed out: "Any systematic effort towards economic development must be preceded by, or coupled with efforts, to make more effective the functioning of governmental machinery."[1] Administration is essential both for developed and developing countries. No system of Government can survive without a good system of administration. It can be found in the poetic couplet: For forms of government, let fools contest, whatever administered best, is the best. Dr. Rajendra Prasad said at the concluding session of the Constituent Assembly: Whatever the Constitution may or may not provide, the welfare of the country will depend upon the way in which the country is administered. That will depend upon the men who administer it. It required men of strong character, men of vision, men who will not sacrifice the interests of the country at large for the sake of smaller groups and areas, and who rise above the prejudices which are born of these differences.[2]

"Good Public Administration," writes Leif H. Share, Director of the Government Institution of Organization and Management, Oslo, Norway, "could serve as a major instrument for promoting economic and social development and for introducing needed advances in science and technology; but major reforms in the organizations and operations of government and in the knowledge, skills and attitudes of public employees at all levels were often necessary for it to do so; deficiencies in administration had been a major reason for past failures in the implementation of national development plans."[3]

Paul Appleby's observations are worth our quotation:

"A clearer understanding of the present reality with respect to policy-making and administration is needed by many political scientists and by many students and practitioners of public administration. It is needed by newspaper correspondents who

CHART 4.1

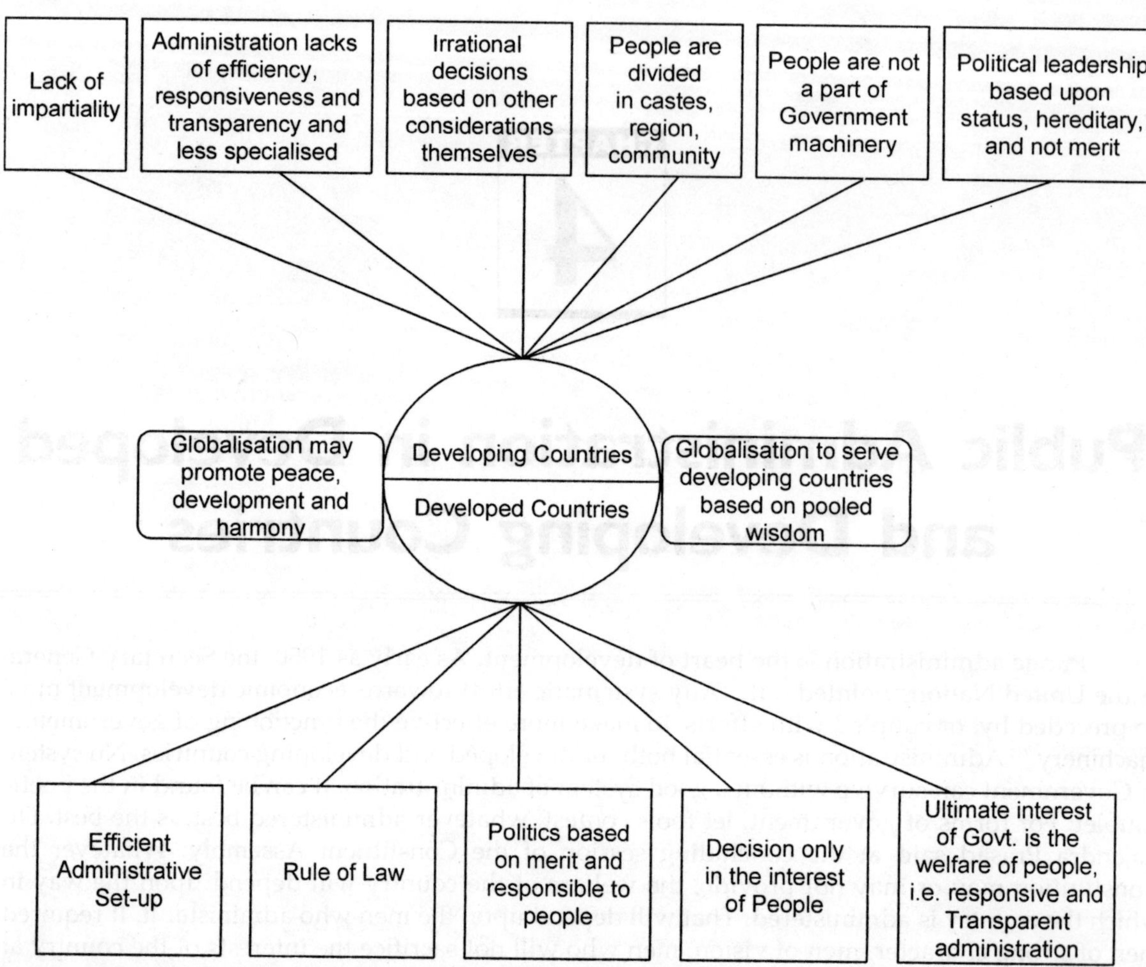

report on 'bureaucracy' and government in general. It is badly needed by members of congress suffering from a sense of inadequacy before extravagant popular expectations that congress will function as the policy-making branch, and that individual members of congress will be able to control specific administrative actions. They need better to understand their own actual practice, and to make it more consciously and thoughtfully a movement of role upward in levels of importance. Most of all, a clearer understanding is needed by citizens, confused by the complexity of government in complex society, they need to know how to make democratic, citizen concerns central to that government."[4]

S.R. Chirmade in his article, 'Administrative Preconditions for Nation Building' in *IJPA*, April and June 1988, has rightly said that "the worldwide commitment of new nations and low-income countries to achieve, virtually within a short span of time, higher levels of economic and social development has given a new dimension to traditional concepts of public administration. The formulation and implementation of strategies and programmes for the modernization of a nation, without doubt, present the greatest single challenge to public administration. Public administration is the process by which objectives are defined, plans and policies formulated, institutions created and managed, human energies mobilised, resources utilized and changes effected."

Public administration, through social and economic changes, has to attempt societal transformation either through direct involvement or through the regulation of other instruments of development. So public administration has to serve the process of the transformation of the society in both developed and developing countries.

"To meet even a part of its growing responsibilities the modern service state must develop the administrative capacity to implement its programmes of economic and social progress. Public administration is the machinery used by the service state to place itself in a position to make plans and programmes that can carry out the plans and programmes it has made."[5]

Burke rightly remarked: "Without proper management your commonwealth is no better than a scheme on paper and not a living, active, effective constitution. Administration is there-under all situations. There would be no existence without administration."

Dimock says: "It does not take much thought to realize that popular government can only be made competent enough through proper administration to survive the complexities and confusion of a technological civilization."

Alexander Pope rightly observes: "For the forms of government let fools context; whatever is administered best, is best."

Paul Pegeon observes: "Public administration ensures the continuance of the existing order with a minimum of effort and risk. Its fundamental aim is to carry on rather than to venture along new and untried paths. Administrators are, therefore, the stabilizers of society and guardians of tradition."

A.D. Gorewala remarks: "In a democracy there can be no successful planning without a clear, efficient and impartial administrtion."

According to one school, development exists in societies:

1. that have relatively equal distributions of benefits;
2. that utilize modern technology;
3. that assign rewards according to personal achievement and not according to family, caste or tribal background;
4. that use specialisits in economic and governmental roles, instead of generalists who must provide leadership in a full range of activities; and
5. that have governmental units that can adjust to social or economic change and acquire new capabilities to meet new demands."[6]

Riggs interprets development in terms of differentiation of structures. According to him, "The phenomenon of development involves a gradual separation of institutionally distinct spheres, the differentiation of separate structure for the wide variety of functions that must be performed in any society.[7]

Let us now examine separately the role of public administration in developing and developed countries.

SIGNIFICANCE OF PUBLIC ADMINISTRATION IN DEVELOPING COUNTRIES

According to First Five Year Plan, "An underdeveloped economy is characterized by the existence in greater or less degrees of unutilized, or under-utilized manpower on the one hand and of unexploited natural resources on the other. This state of affairs may be due to stagnancy of techniques or the certain inhibiting socio-economic factors which prevent the more dynamic forces in economy from asserting themselves.[8]

There is no doubt that the distinction between underdeveloped and developed countries is rather loose and also arbitrary to a certain extent. The United Nations group of experts states, "We have had some difficulty in interpreting the term 'underdeveloped countries'. We use it to mean countries in which per capita real income is low when compared with the per capita real incomes of the United States of America, Canada, Australia and Western Europe. In this sense, an adequate synonym would be poor countries."

The term 'underdeveloped countries' is relative. In general, those countries which have real per capita income less than a quarter of the per capita income of the United States, are underdeveloped countries. More recently, instead of referring to these economies as underdeveloped, the UN publications prefer to describe them as 'developing economies'. The term 'developing economies' signifies that though still underdeveloped, the process of development has been initiated in these countries. Thus, we have 'developing economies' and 'developed economies'.

The World Bank in its *World Development Report* (2005) classified the various countries on the basis of Gross National Income (GNI) per capita.

Developing countries are divided into: (a) Low income countries with 2005 GNI per capita of $ 906 and below; and Middle income countries with GNI per capita ranging between $ 906 and $ 1I,1I5. As against them, the High Income Countries which are mostly members of the Organisation for Economic Co-operation and Development (OECD) and some others have GNI per capita of $ 11,116 or more.

Two sub-categories of middle income countries are lower-middle income with per capita income in the range of $ 906 to $ 3,595 and upper middle income countries with per capita income of $ 3,596 to $ 1I,1I5.

From the data given in Table 4.1, it may be noted that in 2006 low income countries comprise nearly 36.9 per cent of the world population (2,403 million), but account for only 2.7 per cent of total world GNI. The middle income countries, which are less developed than the highly developed countries, but comparatively speaking, more developed than the low income countries comprise 47 per cent of world population but account for 19.4 per cent of world GNI. Taking these two groups which are popularly described as developing economies, it may be stated that they comprise about 84 per cent of the world population but account for about 23 per cent of the world GNI. Most countries of Asia, Africa, Latin America and some countries of Europe are included in them.

As against them, High Income economies which comprise only about 16 per cent of world population account for 77 per cent of world GNI. In other words, bulk of the poor people reside in the low income and middle income developing countries. They, to quote A.K. Caimcross, constitute the slums of the world economy.

India with its population of 1,110 million in 2006 and with its per capita income of $ 820 is among the poorest of the economies of the world. It had a share of 17.0 per cent in world population, but accounts for only 1.9 per cent of World GNI on exchange rate basis.

TABLE 4.1

Distribution of World Population and World GNI among Various Groups of Countries (2006)

Country/Group	*Population*		*GNI Exchange Rate basis*		*GNI PPP basis*		*Per Capita GNI*	
	Million	*%*	*Billion $*	*%*	*Billion US$*	*%*	*Exchange rate basis $*	*PPP basis US$*
1. Low income	2403	36.9	1562	3.2	6485	9.7	650	2698
2. Middle Income	3086	47.3	9415	19.4	24613	36.7	3051	7976
(A) Lower Middle Income	2276	34.9	4625	9.5	15850	23.6	2037	7020
(B) Upper Middle Income	810	12.4	4790	9.9	8763	13.1	5913	10817
3. High Income	1029	15.8	37529	77.4	35692	53.6	36487	34701
4. World	6518	100.0	48482	100.0	66596	100.0	7439	10218
China	1312	20.1	2642	5.4	10153	15.1	2010	820
India	1110	17.0	906	1.9	4217	6.3	7740	3800

Source: World Bank, World Bank Report, 2008.

Let us mention the important features of Development of Indian Economy:

India is an under developed country though a developing economy.

(1) Low per capita income and low rate of economic growth and high proportion of below the poverty line.

(2) Low level of productive efficiency due to poor health resulting from low nutritions and malnutrition.

(3) Population pressure absorbs the benefits of development.

(4) Unemployment, illiteracy and disease burden.

(5) Low output of agriculture and other sectors of economy. Eleventh Five Year Plan observes that: The percentage of the population below the official poverty line has come down from 36% in 1993-94 to 28% in 2004-05. However, not only is this still high, the rate of decline in poverty has not accelerated along with the growth in GDP, and the incidence of poverty among certain marginalized groups, for example the STs, has hardly declined at all. Because population has also grown, the absolute number of poor people has declined only marginally from 320 million in 1993-94 to 302 million in 2004-05. This performance is all the more disappointing since the poverty line on which the estimate of the poor is based is the same as it was in 1973-74 when per capita incomes were much lower. Other indicators of deprivation suggest that the proportion of the population deprived of a minimum level of living is much higher. For example, National Family Health Survey-3 (NFHS-3) shows that almost 46% of the children in the 0 to 3 years' age group suffered from malnutrition in 2005-06, and what is even more disturbing is that the estimate shows almost no decline from the level of 47% reported in 1998 by NFHS-2.

Indicators of human development such as literacy and education, and maternal and infant mortality rates, show steady improvement, but they also suggest that the progress is slow and we continue to lag behind several other Asian countries. While the literacy rate has gone up from 18.3% in 1951 to 64.8% in 2001, the number of illiterate persons still exceeds 304 million, making India the country with the highest number of illiterate persons in the world. Life expectancy at birth has increased from approximately 32 years for both males and females in 1951 to 63.9 years for males and 66.9 years for females in 2001-06. Yet this is well below the life expectancy of around 80 years in industrialized countries and 72 years in China. Although Indian women now have higher life expectancy than Indian men, as is the case in industrialized countries, India also has an adverse sex ratio with only 933 women per 1000 men. More disturbing, the child sex ratio (ages 0-6) has declined sharply from 962 in 1981 to 927 in 2001. India's maternal and infant mortality rates are much higher than those of countries in East Asia, showing poor access to essential health care services.

The central vision of the Eleventh Plan is to build on our strengths to trigger a development process which ensures broad-based improvement in the quality of life of the people, especially the poor, SCs/STs, other backward castes (OBCs), minorities and women. The National Development Council (NDC), in approving the Approach to the Eleventh Plan, endorsed a target of 9% GDP growth for the country as a whole. This growth is to be achieved in an environment in which the economy is much more integrated into the global economy, an integration that has yielded many benefits but also poses many challenges. If this is achieved, it would mean that per capita GDP would grow at about 7.6% per year to double in less than ten years. However, the target is not just faster growth but also inclusive growth, that is, a growth process which yields broad-based benefits and ensures equality of opportunity for all.

This broad vision of the Eleventh Plan includes several inter-related components: rapid growth that reduces poverty and creates employment opportunities, access to essential services in health and education especially for the poor, equality of opportunity, empowerment through education and skill development, employment opportunities underpinned by the National Rural Employment Guarantee, environmental sustainability, recognition of women's agency and good governance.

The persistence of poverty on the scale at which it still exists is not acceptable. A decisive reduction in poverty and an expansion in economic opportunities for all sections of the population should therefore be a crucial element of the vision for the Eleventh Plan. Rapid growth of the economy is an essential requirement to achieve this outcome since it is an instrument for achieving a steady increase in employment and incomes for large numbers of our people.

Growth in the Eleventh Plan should be better balanced to rapidly create jobs in the industrial and services sectors. This is necessary if a significant portion of the labour force is to shift out of agriculture, where it is currently engaged in low productivity employment, into a non-agricultural activity that can provide higher real incomes per head. This must be accompanied by efforts to improve the income-earning opportunities of those who remain in agriculture by raising land productivity. This process would also lead to higher farm incomes and a rise in real wages of agricultural labour whose bargaining power will improve as surplus labour is shifted out of this sector.

Rapid growth in the economy at large, and especially in the employment generating sectors such as medium and small industry and services, needs to be supplemented by targeted livelihood support programmes aimed at increasing productivity and incomes of the poor in several low income occupations which will continue as important sources of employment for quite some time.

Special programmes aimed at target groups such as small and micro-enterprises, weavers, artisans, craftsmen, etc. will therefore remain important in the Eleventh Plan period. Considerable experience has been gained over the years in the management of these programmes. This experience must be brought to bear in redesigning the programmes in the Eleventh Plan to make them more effective in achieving their stated objectives.[9]

Developing countries are characterised by low GNP low per capita income widespread poverty, scarcity of capital, rapid population growth and high dependency-burdens, low level of productivity, technological backwardness, high level of unemployment and underdevelopment, greater income inequalities, wide gap between urban and rural development, a negative balance of trade and a non or semi-industrial agrarian economy mal-distribution of wealth and poor quality of human capital.

Developing Countries (with GNP per capita income of $ 580 and below) constituted 57 per cent of the world population accounting for only 5 per cent of the total world GNP. As compared to it, the developed economies with per capita income of $ 18~330 constituted 16 per cent of the world population and accounted for 73 per cent of world GNP. Such a situation is politically unstable, morally untenable and psychologically unsound. According to Prof. Jacob Viner, a developing country is one "which has good potential prospects for using more capital, or more labour, or more available natural resources, or all of these, to support its present population on a higher level of living."[10] Gunnar Myrdal has termed the developing countries as "soft states."[11]

Coupled with these economic features, developing countries are run through traditional administration, based on outdated processes and procedures, corrupt practices, and ill-equipped politico-administrative leadership. Henderson and Dwivedi in their brilliant article, 'Administered Development: The Fifth Decade—1990's',[12] have warned the developing countries of poor performance if they do not improve their administrative system.

To quote them: "The emergent administrative system tended to be imitative and ritualistic. Generally practices, styles and structures of administration unrelated to local traditions, needs and realities succeeded in reproducing the symbolism, but not the substance of a British, French or American bureaucracy. Administrative reforms when and if attempted, tended to have the long-run consequence of strengthening the old framework. The developing nations have a vital stake in orderly functioning of their administrative systems. The time has come for them to opt for accelerated development so as to catch the progress thwarted by their creation of a thicket of rules regulations/permits, and the like, in the past. The 21st century will test their capability if they are able to mobilise their financial and human resources. They can ill afford another decade of stagnation or arrest of growth; and further, they should know that economic prosperity is not the monopoly of the West alone; anyone can aspire and achieve that but not by remaining a passerby." The role of public administration in developing countries can be summed up as under:

DEVELOPMENT OF SOCIAL COHESION THROUGH SOCIAL VALUES

Developing countries are entrenched in heterogeneity based on caste, religion, area, etc. For example, in India, even after more than six decades of independence, we still find the existence of explicit manifestation of hostile heterogeneity which is detrimental to development. Huge resources are wasted in solving unproductive problems. Public administration should generate social change to inject modernisation. According to Jawaharlal Nehru, "Political integration has already taken place to some extent but what I am after is something much deeper than that, viz., an emotional integration of the Indian people so that we might be welded into one, and made into one strong national unit, maintaining at the same title all our wonderful diversity .

Sardar Patel rightly said, "What we have is not Swaraj but only freedom from foreign rule. The people have still to win internal Swaraj, abolish distinctions of caste and creed, banish unsociability, improve the lot of hungry masses, and live as one joint family—in short, to create a new way of life and bring about a change of heart and a change of outlook."

Public administration in these countries, through impartial and honest administration, needs to create social cohesion where social upheavals may not germinate. This should be the first priority. The calamities resulting from social upheavals like Ayodhya issue may be more serious for the country than the World Wars.

GENERATION OF SOCIO-ECONOMIC DEVELOPMENT

The widespread poverty and the depressed standards of living among such large number of people pose a very serious threat to peace as well as socio-economic development. The reason for poverty and misery in the developing countries is not essentially the lack of potentialities or resources, human or material, but under-utilisation of these resources. Today, developing countries are not utilizing more than 15 per cent of the potential capacity of their human resources owing to inadequate expertise and deficient system of public administration.

Creating Conditions for the Absorption of Science and Technology

During the last few decades, phenomenal changes are taking place at a fast rate in the field of science and technology as well as in external environment. These changes have their impact on public administration also, which, today, has to shoulder multifarious tasks designed to fulfil the rising aspirations of the people. In the words of Prof. Waldo, public administration is "a part of the cultural complex, and it not only is acted upon, it acts." It is a great creative force. The technology scene seems to be exploding, and the result, instead of the desired improvement in productivity; seems to be confusion what they are too often not prepared for are the overwhelming managerial problems involved in the implementation of these technologies. There is an urgent need to re-orient (improve) the systems of public administration to cope with changes in technology and social behaviour and maximize opportunities for raising productivity, and thus the standard of living of the people.

Improving Administrative System—Good Governance

Ideals of the welfare state—progress, prosperity and protection to the common man can be secured only by impartial, honest and efficient administration. In the words of Prof. Charles Beard, "the future of civilised government, and even I think of civilization itself, rests upon our ability to develop a science, a philosophy and practice of administration competent to discharge the functions of civilized society." Thus, there is a need that public administration must be modernized, i.e., recreated, renewed and revitalized to produce the predesigned changes and output necessary to provide goods and services to the people at the minimum cost. This needs a different trend and magnitude of administrative, culture and capability.

IMPROVING ADMINISTRATIVE CAPABILITY AND CAPACITY

The administrative capability of a government and the manner in which the development programmes are likely to be carried out are intimately related. On the other hand, administrative inadequacies in a national government have a retarding influence on economic and social development. These deficiencies prevent the vast flood of money, talent and material from achieving their objectives.

ENLISTING THE SUPPORT OF THE PEOPLE

Public administration in developing countries has not been able to involve the people in the process of development in spite of the creations of many institutions like Panchayati Raj system and thus these countries are not utilising the unlimited potential power in them. All the plans and programmes are based on the premises that people's support would be forthcoming but in practice, administration makes no realistic effort. Hiroshi Nakajima, Director General of World Health Organisation, has rightly said that we must learn to harness the energy, wisdom and will of the people we serve.[13]

Thus, the significance of people's participation in public administration in developing countries is tremendous as it is the main instrument of development.

Strengthening of Law and Order Machinery to Ensure Safety of the People

Economic development in the developing countries is not possible without ensuring a good law and order system in which people feel safe and free. Law and order in the developing countries is still considered primitive and an arm of the ruling party in power. People have lost their faith in the impartiality and true role of law and order machinery. Developing countries must ensure a good law and order machinery which can create conditions for development and modernisation.

Removal of Corruption

Corruption in developing countries has become cancerous. In the nation's highest places, daily cases of corrupt practices are reported involving huge amounts. Most of the activities are carried out not on merit but other considerations. It is high time that corrupt practices are eliminated so that all attend to their work sincerely, honestly and with dedication.

Incompetence of Bureaucracy

Ferrel Heady identified the major characteristics of national bureaucracies in the developing countries. These are:

(1) The basic pattern of administration is imitative rather than indigenous;
(2) The bureaucracies are deficient in skilled manpower necessary for developmental programmes;
(3) These bureaucracies emphasize orientations that are other than production-oriented, i.e. they work for the realization of goals other than the achievement of programme objectives;
(4) Widespread discrepancy between form and reality;
(5) Operational autonomy: These features combine and militate against bureaucratic legitimacy, efficiency and political responsiveness. Such bureaucracies tend to be very hierarchical and dominated by a group which is culturally and socially unrepresentative of the population at large.

The Eleventh Plan vision of inclusive growth, reducing poverty and bridging the various divides that continue to fragment our society can only be achieved if there is a significant improvement in the quality of governance. There are many different definitions of good governance but it is generally agreed that good governance must be broadly defined to cover all aspects of the interface between individuals and businesses on the one hand and government on the other.

Achieving a successful outcome in all these dimensions is not easy, and the effects of initiatives taken today will take time to manifest themselves. Nor is it easy to measure the extent of progress achieved. It is also important to recognize that perceptions are important and perceptions of the state of governance depend upon the expectations of the people. These expectations are rising as indeed they should, and from this perspective, we need to recognize that while increased concern about inadequacies of governance may not reflect an absolute deterioration in the quality of governance, they do point to rising demands that need to be met.

The Tenth Plan drew attention to the implementation of good governance in the following terms:

> "Governance relates to the management of all such processes that, in any society, define the environment which permits and enables individuals to raise their capability levels on the one hand, and provide opportunities to realize their potential and enlarge the set of available choices, on the other. These processes, covering the political, social and economic aspects of life impact every level of human enterprise, be it the individual, the household, the village, the region or the nation. It covers the State, civil society and the market, each of which is critical for sustaining human development. The State is responsible for creating a conducive political, legal and economic environment for building individual capabilities and encouraging private initiative. The market is expected to create opportunities for people. Civil society facilitates the mobilization of public opinion and people's participation in economic, social and political activities."

In our situation, good governance should cover the following distinct dimensions:

- As a democratic country, a central feature of good governance is the constitutionally protected right to elect government at various levels in a fair manner, with effective participation by all sections of the population. This is a basic requirement for the legitimacy of the government and its responsibility to the electorate.
- The government at all levels must be accountable and transparent. Closely related to accountability is the need to eliminate corruption, which *is widely* seen as a major deficiency in governance. Transparency is also critical, both to ensure accountability, and also to enable genuine participation.
- The government must be effective and efficient in delivering social and economic public services, which are its primary responsibilities. This requires constant monitoring and attention to the design of our programmes. In our situation, where the responsibility for delivery of key services such as primary education and health is at the local level, this calls for special attention to ensuring the effectiveness and efficiency of local governments.
- Governments at lower levels can only function efficiently if they are empowered to do so. This is particularly relevant for the PRIs, which currently suffer from inadequate devolution of funds as well as functionaries to carry out the functions constitutionally assigned to them.

- An overarching requirement is that the rule of law must be firmly established. This is relevant not only for relations between the government and individuals enabling individuals to demand their rights but also for relations between individuals or businesses. A modern economic society depends upon increasingly complex interactions among private entities and these interactions can be efficiently performed only if legal rights are clear and legal remedies for enforcing these rights are swift.
- Finally, the entire system must function in a manner which is seen to be fair and inclusive. This is a perceptional issue but it is real nonetheless. Disadvantaged groups, especially the SCs, STs, minorities and others, must feel they have an equal stake and should perceive an adequate flow of benefits to ensure the legitimacy of the State.[14]

SIGNIFICANCE IN DEVELOPED COUNTRIES

Public administration is equally important, rather more important, in developed countries as well. Public administration in developed countries has to ensure the maintenance of development as well as accelerate development from their point of view.

Developed countries are facing new challenges like environmental pollution, economic strains visible through unemployment and low growth rates, growing violence, less capacity to provide technical assistance as compared to the demand from developing countries, adjustment of the administrative system with the fast changes in science and technology, maintenance of good relationship among the developed world, preservation of their hold on developing world, and so on. All these challenges require a system of public administration which is engaged constantly to take care of the existing, potential and future problems as well as concentrate on keeping its health fit and fine.

Ferrel Heady outlines the following characteristics of bureaucracy in these countries:

(1) The public Service is large-scale, complex and instrumental, i.e. its mission is understood to be that of carrying out the policies of the political decision-making.
(2) The Bureaucracy exhibits a sense of professionalization in the sense of identification with the public service as a profession, and in the sense of belonging to a narrow field of professional or technical specialization within the service.
(3) The bureaucracy is highly specialized and reflects in its ranks most of the professional and occupational categories found in the society.
(4) The role of bureaucracy in the political process is fairly clear and the line of demarcation between the bureaucracy and other political institutions is generally definite and accepted. This is duc to the fact that the political system as a whole is relatively stable and mature and the bureaucracy is more fully developed.
(5) The bureaucracy is subject to effective policy control by other functionally specific political institutions.

Public administration in the developed countries has the following important role to play. President Roosevelt has rightly said that poverty any where is a danger to prosperity. So, the developed world should help the developing countries.

William Jefferson Clinton in his statement in *The Tribune*, January 14, 2002 rightly observes that the great question of this new century is whether the age of interdependence is going to be good or bad for humanity. The answer depends upon whether we in the wealthy nations spread the benefits and reduce the burdens of the modern world, or whether the poor nations enact the changes necessary to make progress possible, and on whether we all can develop a level of consciousness high enough to understand our obligation and responsibilities to each other.

We cannot make it if the poor of the world are led by people like Osama Bin Laden who believe they can find their redemption in our destruction. And we cannot make it if the wealthy are led by those who cater to shortsighted selfishness and advance the illusion that we can forever claim for ourselves what we deny to others. We are all going to have to change.

It thus seems fundamental to me that we cannot have a global trading system without a global economic policy, a global health care policy, a global education policy, a global environment policy and a global security policy.

In effect, we have to create more opportunity for those left behind by progress, thus reducing the pool of potential terrorists by increasing the number of potential partners. To make new partners, the wealthy world has to accept its obligation to promote more economic opportunity and help reduce poverty.

Regulating the Private Sector to Promote Accelerated Development

Public Administration in advanced countries has to develop the administrative machinery to regulate the development through private sector so that it may fall in line with the total development and may benefit the citizens. We generally listen about market economy model of development in advanced countries but it is absurd to think that it is totally free of control. In USA, there are well established inter-state regulatory commissions.

Public administration exercises this regulatory role to such an extent that private sector cannot deviate from the policies of the Government. In developed countries, public administration through 'management by exception' gets better results through the regulation of the private sector than entering in the field directly. In this way, the private sector is held in high esteem by the citizens in the context of services provided by it. We may make use of such devices in India.

Refinements of the Instruments of Public Administration to Promote Efficient Services

People in developed countries are highly sensitive of their rights. Being educated, they exert pressure on the machinery of Government to get their due status. Public administration has to refine its procedures and methods to provide best services to the people and remove all irritants. People in these countries are treated as human beings and not like beasts, as is the case in developing countries.

Public administration has to make the administrative system citizen-oriented. Since the demands of the citizens are likely to increase, therefore, public administration in developed countries has to keep its administrative apparatus frictionless and efficient.

Maintenance of Reputation, Image and Goodwill of the Country

Public administration in developed countries is keen to maintain its reputation, image and goodwill so that people from developing countries can be attracted for political, economic and social relations. It has been seen that persons from developing countries in high offices and wealthy people would prefer to get treatment in foreign health institutes even if that very facility is available in the country. Similarly, people from developing countries would prefer to get education in foreign educational institutions because of their higher standard of education and educational administration.

Constant Engagements on Administrative Improvements and Reforms

Public Administration in developed countries is keen to keep its machinery well lubricated. In some of these countries, it is statutory to get the administrative system analysed after a period of three years. The result of all this is that their administrative system is well designed and result-oriented. They have rather followed the definition given by Jawaharlal Nehru, the late Prime Minister of India, "Administrative is meant to achieve something and not to exist in some kind of ivory tower following certain rules of procedure and looking Narcissus like—the test of administration is the welfare of the people."

Highly specialized to Discharge Complicated and Complex Functions

Public administration is keen to achieve more and more specialization Highly Specialized to Discharge complicated and complex functions. Public Administration is keen to deal with the tasks of development. Take the case of any field of development—health, education, industry, etc., and we would find the latest technology being put in use and prompt change in administrative system installed to suit scientific and technological developments.

PUBLIC ADMINISTRATION THROUGH ENVIRONMENTAL ADMINISTRATION AND MANAGEMENT ENGAGED IN CONTROLLING HORRIFIC ENVIRONMENTAL DEGRADATION

Environmental problems, a by-product of development, are causing anxiety and worry more to the developed world. The UN Secretary-General's report on problems of environment sounds a pessimistic note. To quote, "If current trends continue, the future of life on earth could be endangered and, thus, it is urgent to focus world attention on these problems which threaten humanity in an environment that permits the highest realization of human values."[15] Public administration in developed countries needs to attend to this problem on priority basis. Environment needs no passport. Hence, public administration has not to keep a watch not only on its immediate environment but also on the totality of environment based on good management information system.

Incidentally, public administration in developed countries may help the developing world so that environmental problems in these countries may not affect the quality of life in the developed world.

Public Administration to Check Crime

Public administration needs to devise ways and means to control increasing violence, and social problems like rape, drug addictions, AIDS, etc. Public administration in the developed world is facing the problem of increasing violence born out of affluence. Connected with it are the social problems of rape, drug addiction, AIDS, etc. Public administration needs to face these problems through new approaches to law and order and social welfare administration. These aspects of public administration are more important as the acceleration in economic development is dependent upon them. Besides, the main aim of administration, i.e., to provide means to the populace to lead a good life, may not be possible without tackling these problems.

We can thus conclude by saying that public administration in developed countries is of great significance to maintain and accelerate the process of development and to keep in check its negative effects. It may be kept in mind that the more a country is developed, the more efficient system of public administration is required. Thus, the significance of public administration is more in developed countries as compared to the developing. It would be correct to say that development is linked directly to a good system of public administration and vice-versa. Advanced countries, as already said cannot survive till the developing countries are also able to get food, clothing, shelter, etc. There cannot be two worlds on this earth—affluent and poor. Therefore, it is the duty of developed countries to help developing countries in their efforts for socio-economic development.

Recent meltdown of economy in developed countries has revealed the failure of administration in developed countries.

Globalization

The difference between developed and developing countries are fading away under the impact of globalization. Globalisation is a multi-dimensional set of economic, political, and cultural conditions constructed in the context of technological change and discursive narrative of power and knowledge. It spans the increasing internationalisation of production, political struggles over the conditions for living in a world where social life is increasingly constructed by a hybridised blend of local and global forces, and changing forms of local and global culture. In a concise definition, which emphasises the common paradigms of globalisation, Thomas Friedman says, "it is the integration of trade, finance and information that is creating a single global market and culture." Thus, globalisation is a highly differentiated phenomenon involving domains of activity and interaction as diverse as the political, military, economic, cultural, migratory and environmental. The concept of globalisation spans separate yet overlapping, of which each involves different patterns of relations and activities. Ultimately, however, it is spearheaded by multinational financial and industrial conglomerates. The widely discussed globalisation phenomenon fundamentally results from the globalization of economic life, seen as unfettered capitalism, and driven by market expansion.

Globalisation is strongly affecting internal governance, but it is far from making the nation-state obsolete as being claimed by some political and administrative scholars and practitioners. The existence of "useful inefficiencies" and the persistence of national political traditions and cultures means that the state will remain the basic institution of governance well into the 21st Century. But domestic polities will be under pressure from the erosion of economic inefficiency, tensions around the redistribution and inequality that accompany economic globalisation, and the increasing roles of transnational and third sector actors. But, overall, in the present scenario, globalisation is irreversible and unstoppable. Almost all the countries of the world, willingly or unwillingly, have already accepted it and others may have to accept it. However, it is mostly agreed that globalization should be introduced with humane face for the benefit for the poor and the needy. This era of globalization is opening plethora of opportunities for millions of people around the world. Increased trade, new technologies, foreign investments, expanding media and internet connection are trigering economic growth and human advancement.[16]

O.P. Dwivedi favours that India way of doing things. Perhaps a hybrid system might appear with good values being used from both the local customs and the global system. Still the biggest challenge to India is how to transform its large human resources into a great economic and knowledge force by upgrading their skills. Finally, in addition to reforming its own system, India needs to solidify and extend regional economic cooperation with Pakistan, Bangladesh, Nepal and Sri Lanka. Good neighbours and cordial relationship with them, make a country stronger and free from cross-broader problems.[17]

CONCLUSION

In the new Era of Globalization liberalization and privatization (GLP) we expected that the developing countries would get support from developed world to make this world a small village inhabitated by healthy and creative people to support sustainable development based on equity and social justice. However, we are experiencing tough times in the form of economic meltdown with inherent dangers of economic recession or depression. There is a need to sort out the problems of globalization which may not worsen the situation. We must achieve through globalization welfare of all as stated in India vedantic Benediction, i.e. 'Welfare of All'.

Notes and References

1. Official Records of the ECOSOC, (Fl1708) Agenda item 10, p. 3.
2. Quoted in Khanna, R.R.: Making of India's Constitution, Lucknow, Eastern Book Company, 1981, p. VI.
3. UN Document: Staff, M/56, New York, 1971, p. 39.
4. Peter Self, Administrative Theories and Politics, George Allen and Unwin Ltd., London, 1972, p. 12.
5. A handbook of Public Administration, 1961, ed., p. 1.
6. Ira Sharkansky: Public Administration Policy-making in Government Agencies, Rand, Chicago, 1978, p. 30.
7. Fred W. Riggs: Bureacrats and Political Developoment: A Paradoxical view: in Joseph La Palombara (ed.); Bureaucracy and Political Development; Princeton University Press, Princeton; 1963; p. 122.
8. Ruddar Datt and K.P.M. Sundharam, Indian Economy, New Delhi, S. Chand & Company, 2008, pp. 3-4.
9. GOI, Planning Commission, Eleventh Five Year Plan, Vol. I, pp. 1-2.
10. Viner Jacob, 'The Economics of Development', in Approaches to Under-development, 1985 (eds.), R.N. Aggarwal and S.P. Singh, Oxford University Press, p. 17.
11. Myrdal, Gunnar, The Challenge of World Poverty, pp. 208-52
12. Henderson, Keith M. and Dwivedi O.P., Administered Development: The Fifth Decade, 1992, pp. 1-16.
13. W.H.O.: *World Health*, May-June, 1992, p. 3.
14. GOI, Planning Commission, Eleventh Five Year Plan, Vol. I, pp. 1-2.
15. Thant, U., Quoted in Challan, M.C. and Grants (Eds.) Protecting Our Environment (New York, 1970), p. 206.
16. Furquan Ahmad and Akhtar Ali, "Globalization, Governance and the State", *IJPA*, Vol. LIV, No. 2, April-June, 2008, pp. 366-67.
17. O.P. Dwivedi, India in a Globalized World: Transforming Bureaucracy for the Well-Being and Prosperity of All, in *IJPA*, Oct.-Dec. 2007.

APPENDIX 4.1

Selected Indicators of the Indian Economy

S. No.	1951-52	1970-71	1990-91	2000-01	2006-07
1. GDP at factor cost (Rs. Crores) at 1999-00 prices	2,23899	4,70,254	10,67,494	18,41,755	28,45,155*
2. Per capita NNP (Rs.) at 1999-00 prices	5,708	8.091	11,535,	16,172	22,553*
3. Index of Industrial Production (Base 1993-94)	7.9	28.1	9.16	162.6	247.1
4. Index of Agricultural production (Base: 3 year ending 1981-82)	46.2	85.9 148.4165.7		197.1	
5. Gross domestic capital formation (as per cent of GDP	8.7	15.4	36.3	24.0	35.9**
6. Cross domestic saving (as percent of GDP)	8.9	14.6	23.1	23.4	34.8**
7. Foodgrains (Million tones)	50.9	108.4	176.4	169.8	216.1
8. Finished steel (Million tones)	1.04	4.64	13.53	30.3	50.1
9. Cement (Million tones)	2.7	14.3	48.8	97.6	154.7
10. Coal and Lignite (Million tones)	32.3	76.3	225.5	332.6	462.0
11. Crude Oil (Million tones)	0.3	6.8	33.0	32.4	34.0
12. Electricity generated (Utilities only)	5.1	55.8	264.3	499.5	662.0
13. Wholesale price index (Base 1993-94)	6.8	14.3	72.7	155.7	06.6
14. Consumer price Index (Base 1982)	17	38	193	444	125*
15. Foreign Exchange reserves (US $ million)	1,914	2.584	2236,	39.554	191,924
16. Exports (Rs. Crores)	606	1.535	32,553	203,571	571,779
17. Imports (Rs. Crores)	608	1,634	43,198	230,873	740,506
18. Population (Millions)	361.1	548.2	486.3	1,019	1,112
19. Birth Rate (per 1000)	39.9	36.9	29.5	25.4	23.5,
20. Death Rate (per 1000)	27.4	14.9	9.8	8.4	7.5
21. Life expectancy at birth (in year)	32.1	45.6	58.7	65.3	63.9
a. Male	32.4	46.4	59.0	63.9	63.9
b. Female	31.7	44.7	58.7	66.9	66.9
22. Literary rate (per cent)	18.3	34.5	52.2	64.8	65.4+
a. Male (percent)	27.3	46.0	64.1	75.3	75.8+
b. Female	8.9	22.0	39.3	53.7	54.2+
23. Registered Medical Practitioners (RMP)	61.8	151.1	—	575.6	—
24. RMP (per 10,000 population)	1.7	2.8	4.7	5.6	—
25. Beds all types per 10,000	3.2	6.4	9.5	9.5	—

* Provisional Estimates

** Quick Estimates

Source: Government of India, Economic Survey (2007-08).

CHAPTER

5

UN System and Development

Pt. Jawaharlal Nehru emphasized the need of true Internationalism in his various writings. He wrote, "Walls are dangerous companions. They may occasionally protect from outside evil and keep out an unwelcome intruder. But they also make you a prisoner and a slave, and you purchase your so called purity and immunity at the cost of freedom. And the most terrible of walls are the walls that grow up in the mind which prevent you from discarding an evil tradition simply because it is old, and from accepting a new thought because it is novel. The ancient saints of India and the leaders of India have always exhibited their interest and faith in Internationalism. Mahatma Gandhi has rightly said that there is no limit to extending our services to our neighbours across state made frontiers. God never made these frontiers even at the eve of India's Independence. Pt. Nehru said that "It is fitting that at this solemn moment we take a pledge of dedication to the service of India and her people and to the still larger cause of humanity."

The United Nations system evolved in response to meet the multi-faceted needs of the people of the world is a dynamic, growing and pioneering international system. The evolution of the system can be seen in the way its underlying concepts have changed since the late 1940's. For a number of years after the Second World War the agencies were primarily serving as clearing houses of information. They organised international cooperation, harmonized policy, promoted research and set standards in their respective fields. As the development needs of countries in Africa, Asia and Latin America came increasingly to the fore, however, the "operational" aspects of their work increased. It was realised that the huge gap between the affluent nations and a much larger number of non-affluent nations generates a sense of international misunderstandings, jealousies and tensions. Such a state of affairs cannot be conducive to good and peaceful relations among the nations of the world.

The potential benefits inherent in the UN system can reach the millions of the people around the world provided the UN System is administered and managed efficiently. The efficiency of the system in turn depends upon the capability, intelligence, experience, motivation, ethics, ethos, responsiveness and responsibility of the staff engaged in them.

In the post-war period, a very significant development has been the establishment of a

CHART 5.1

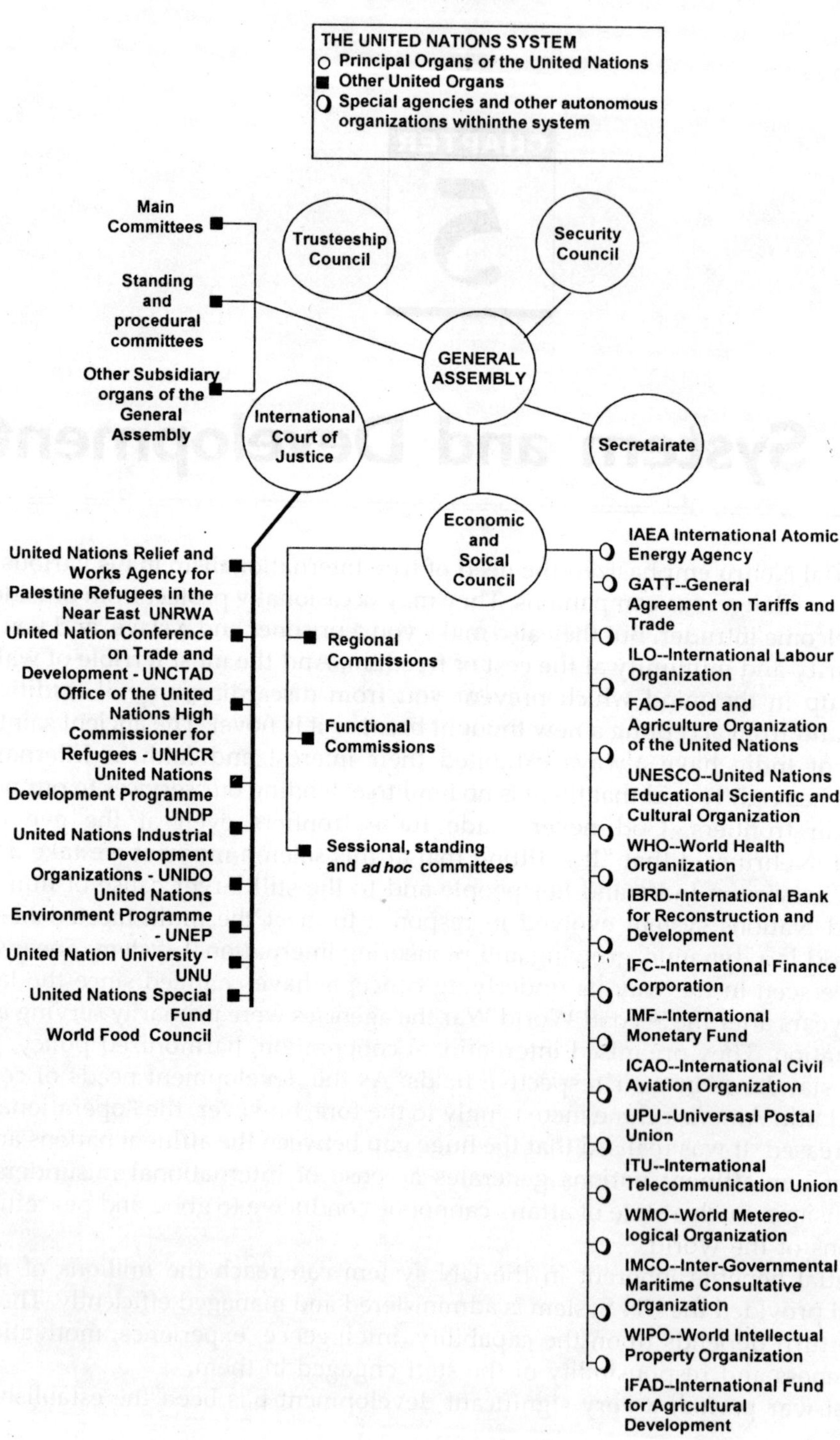
THE UNITED NATIONS SYSTEM
Principal Organs of the United Nations
Other United Organs
Special agencies and other autonomous organizations withinthe system
Main Committees
Standing and procedural committees
Other Subsidiary organs of the General Assembly
Trusteeship Council
Security Council
GENERAL ASSEMBLY
International Court of Justice
Secretairate
Economic and Soical Council
United Nations Relief and Works Agency for Palestine Refugees in the Near East UNRWA
United Nation Conference on Trade and Development - UNCTAD
Office of the United Nations High Commissioner for Refugees - UNHCR
United Nations Development Programme UNDP
United Nations Industrial Development Organizations - UNIDO
United Nations Environment Programme - UNEP
United Nation University - UNU
United Nations Special Fund
World Food Council
Regional Commissions
Functional Commissions
Sessional, standing and ad hoc committees
IAEA International Atomic Energy Agency
GATT--General Agreement on Tariffs and Trade
ILO--International Labour Organization
FAO--Food and Agriculture Organization of the United Nations
UNESCO--United Nations Educational Scientific and Cultural Organization
WHO--World Health Organiization
IBRD--International Bank for Reconstruction and Development
IFC--International Finance Corporation
IMF--International Monetary Fund
ICAO--International Civil Aviation Organization
UPU--Universasl Postal Union
ITU--International Telecommunication Union
WMO--World Metereo-logical Organization
IMCO--Inter-Governmental Maritime Consultative Organization
WIPO--World Intellectual Property Organization
IFAD--International Fund for Agricultural Development

pivotal international organisation concerned with the problems of world peace and human welfare. This organisation is commonly known as United Nations. Since its birth, it has been playing an increasingly vital role in easing the world tensions and conflicts which can erupt into a world conflagration as well as in alleviating the widespread hunger, poverty, ignorance, want, disease and allied problems. This organisation has been supplemented by the establishment of closely allied specialised agencies which deal with each of these stupendous problems more specifically.

When the UN Charter was being framed, attention was initially focused on the problems of peace and security in the world. But at the instance of the USA, at the Yalta Conference, it was decided to create an Economic and Social Council as an integral part of the new international organisation (UN) to deal with the rapidly emerging economic and social problems. The ECOSOC is to study the problems of human and social well-being as well as to formulate appropriate policies and direct their implementation in this connection. The UN system is thus founded upon the sound idea that no peace can be stable unless it is based upon nations whose citizens are substantially free from distress, privation and frustration. The realisation that removal of poverty and improvement of economic conditions all around would be potent factors for peace prompted the expansion of the UN system. The United Nations Development System comprises the UN itself, five regional economic commissions and 20 other major programmes and organs. Besides, there are 17 separate inter-governmental specialised agencies.

The question arises as to how the UN System can translate its aims and objectives enshrined in the UN Charter and the constitutions of the Specialised Agencies to promote peace and human welfares. That is possible only if the UN System is administered and managed efficiently as well as the genuine cooperation of the Member-states is ensured. Organizations are not mere structures but are action systems, and the success and failure of any organization is to be measured in terms of this action system. An action system is a structured device in which resources are mobilized and transformed by the use of certain skills and technology to produce pre-designed output.

THE ESTABLISHMENT OF THE UNITED NATIONS

The quest for peace and security through international organizations did not end with the coming of the Second World War. On the contrary, statesmen, scholars and many men and women everywhere were firm in their determination that the lessons learnt during the twenty years of the League be put to use to set-up a new international institution. For more than three years, the United Nations was taking shape in rudimentary form, first in the minds of the planners, then in the declaration of various states and finally in the conferences at Dumbarton Oaks, Yalta, and San Francisco. It was finally completed and ratified in 1945 at the San Francisco Conference on Oct. 24, 1945.

Objectives of the UN

The preamble to the United Nations Charter expresses the ideals and the common aims of all the people whose governments joined together to form the United Nations. The following are the objectives of the United Nations:

- To save succeeding generations from the scourge of war which twice in our life time has brought untold sorrow to mankind;

- To reaffirm faith in fundamental human rights, in the dignity and worth of the human person, in the equal rights of men and women of nations large and small;
- To establish conditions under which justice and respect for the obligations arising from treaties and other sources of international law can be maintained; and
- To promote social progress and better standards of life in larger freedom.

AND for these Ends:

- To practise tolerance and live together in peace with one another as good neighbours;
- To unite our strength to maintain international peace and security;
- To ensure by the acceptance of principles and the institution of methods, that armed force shall not be used, save in the common interest, and
- To employ international machinery for the promotion of the economic and social advancement of all peoples.

The objectives of the UN are clearly laid down in Article 1 of the UN Charter. According to this Article, the purposes of the United Nations are:

1. To maintain international peace and security, and to that end, to take effective collective measures for the prevention and removal of threats to the peace and for the suppression of acts of aggression or other threats to breach of the peace and bring about by peaceful means and in conformity with the principles of justice and international law, adjustment or settlement of international disputes or situations which might lead to a breach of the peace;
2. To develop friendly relations among nations based on respect for the principle of equal rights and self-determination of peoples, and to take other appropriate measures to strengthen universal peace;
3. To achieve international co-operation in solving international problems of an economic, social, cultural or humanitarian character, and in promoting and encouraging respect for human rights and for fundamental freedom for all without distinction as to race, sex, language or religion; and
4. To be a centre for harmonizing the actions of nations in the attainment of these common ends.

Principles

The UN acts in accordance with the following principles: (Article 2)

1. It is based on the sovereign equality of all its members;
2. All members are to fulfil in good faith their charter obligations;
3. They are to settle their international disputes by peaceful means and without endangering peace, security and justice;
4. They are to refrain in their inter national relations from the threat or use of force against other states;
5. They are to give the United Nations every assistance to any action it takes in accordance with the charter and shall not assist states against which the United Nations is taking preventive or enforcement action;

6. The United Nations shall ensure that states which are not members act in accordance with these principles in so far as is necessary for the maintenance of international peace and security; and
7. Nothing in the charter is to authorize the United Nations to intervene in matters which are essentially within the domestic jurisdiction of any state.

ORGANIZATION OF THE UNITED NATIONS

There are six principal organs of the UN through which it achieves its purpose. These are:

I. The General Assembly

A ponderous and complicated organism, the General Assembly is the central focus of the multifold activities of the organization. The General Assembly is composed of all member-states numbering 192 as on 30th September, 2008. It is the main deliberative organ of the United Nations, and has the right to discuss and make recommendations on all matters within the scope of the charter. The General Assembly deals with its work through six main committees on which all members are represented. They are:

First Committee (Political and Security, including the Regulation of Armaments)
Special Political Committee (Shares the Work of the First Committee)
Second Committee (Economic and Financial)
Third Committee (Social, Humanitarian and Cultural)
Fourth Committee (Trusteeship, including Non-self Governing Territories)
Fifth Committee (Administrative and Budgetary)
Sixth Committee (Legal).

In addition, the General Assembly meets frequently during a session to supervise the smooth running of the Assembly's work. It is composed of the President and 17 Vice-Presidents of the Assembly and the Chairmen of the seven main committees.

The General Assembly's regular session begins each year on the third Tuesday in September and continues until mid-December. All decisions on important questions are taken by a two-thirds majority of those present and voting; decisions regarding less important questions may be taken by a simple majority of votes.

The General Assembly performs the following functions:

1. To consider and make recommendations on the principles of international co-operation in the maintenance of peace and security, including the principles governing disarmament and the regulation of armaments;
2. To discuss any problem affecting peace and security and, except where a dispute or situation is currently being discussed by the Security Council, to make recommendations on it;
3. To discuss and with the same exception, to make recommendations on any question within the scope of the charter or affecting the powers and functions of any Organ of the United Nations;
4. To initiate studies and make recommendations to promote international political co-operation, the development of international law and its codification, the realization of

human rights and fundamental freedoms for all, the international collaboration in economic, social, cultural, educational and health fields;
5. To receive and consider reports from the Security Council and other Organs of the UN;
6. To make recommendations for the peaceful settlement of any situation regardless of origin which might impair friendly relations among nations;
7. To supervise, through the trusteeship council, the execution of the Trusteeship agreements for all areas not designated as strategic;
8. To elect the non-permanent members of the Security Council, the members of Economic and Social Council and those members of the Trusteeship Council which are elected, to take part with the Security Council in the election of Judges of the International Court of Justice; and on the recommendations of the Security Council, to appoint the Secretary General; and
9. To consider and approve the budget of the UN to apportion the contributions among members and to examine the budgets of specialized agencies.

Under the 'Uniting for Peace' resolution adopted by the General Assembly in November, 1950, the Assembly may take action if the Security Council, because of the lack of unanimity of its permanent members, fails to act in a case where there appears to be a threat to the peace or act of aggression. The Assembly is empowered for collective measures-including, in the case of a breach of the peace or act of aggression, the use of armed force when necessary to maintain or restore international peace and security. If the Assembly is not in session, it may meet in an emergency special session within 24 hours of a request for such a session by the Security Council, on the vote of any nine of its members, or by a majority of the members of the United Nations. The passing of the Uniting for Peace Resolution, in the words of Hoffman, "meant a drastic *de facto* revision of the Charter, and which appeared to reopen the road to collective security."

While the assembly is empowered to make only non-binding recommendations to states on international issues within its competence, it has, nonetheless, initiated actions—political, economic, humanitarian, social and legal—which have affected the lives of millions of people throughout the world. The landmark Millennium Declaration, adopted in 2000 and the 2005. World Summit Outcome Document reflect the commitment of Member States to reach specific goals to attain peace, security and disarmament along with development and poverty eradication; safeguard human rights and promote the rule of law; protect our common environment; meet the special needs of Africa; and strengthen the United Nations.

Each member State in the Assembly has one vote. Votes taken on designated important issues, such as recommendations on peace and security and the election of Security Council members, require a two-thirds majority of Member States, but other questions are decided by simple majority.

In recent years, a special effort has been made to achieve consensus on issues, rather than deciding by a formal vote, thus strengthening support for the Assembly's decisions. The President, after have consulted and reached agreement with delegations, can propose that a resolution be adopted without a vote.

The framers of the Charter at San Francisco envisaged a sort of equilibrium between the functions of the General Assembly and those of the Security Council. Sixty-four years of practice reveals a situation entirely different from the one just posed. The Council was started as the leading organ for political action but a reverse trend which began in 1948 led to a gradual decline in its importance. Before the middle of 1948, the Council was called upon to consider more political issues than the Assembly. But since that time more questions have been submitted to the Assembly and there has been a considerable decrease in the number of Council sessions. Many reasons are responsible for it. The decline of the Security Council and the consequent rise of the Assembly to the role of the pre-eminent Organ of the United Nations is probably the most striking constitutional change that has been experienced by the organization.

2. Security Council

The organ which has the primary responsibility for maintaining peace and security is the Security Council. It has 15 members. Five of these—China, France, the Russia, the United Kingdom and the United States—are permanent members. The other ten are elected by the General Assembly for a term of two years.

Each member of the Council has one vote. Decisions on matter for procedure are made by an affirmative vote of at least 9 of the 15 members. Decisions of substantive matters also require 9 votes including the concurring votes of all five permanent members. This is the role of great power unanimity, often referred to as the 'Veto'. All five permanent members have exercised the veto right at one time or another. If a permanent member does not support a decision but has no desire to block it through a veto, it may abstain; as abstention is not regarded as a veto.

The following are its Functions and Powers:

1. To maintain international peace and security in accordance with the purposes and principles of the United Nations;
2. To investigate any dispute or situation which might lead to international friction;
3. To recommend methods of adjusting such disputes or the terms of settlement;
4. To formulate plans for establishment of a system to regulate armaments;
5. To determine the existence of a threat to the peace or act of aggression and to recommend what action should be taken;
6. To call on members to apply economic sanctions and other measures not involving the use of force in order to prevent or stop aggression;
7. To take military action against an aggressor;
8. To recommend the admission of new members and the terms on which states may become parties to the statute of the International Court of Justice;
9. To exercise the Trusteeship functions of the United Nations in 'strategic areas';
10. To recommend to the General Assembly the appointment of the Secretary-General and together with the General Assembly, to elect the Judges of the International Court of Justice; and
11. To submit annual and special reports to the General Assembly.

Also, under Articles 5 and 6 of the Charter, a member-state against when preventive or enforcement action has been taken by the Security Council may be suspended from the exercise of the rights and privileges of membership of the General Assembly upon recommendation of the Council. A member-state which has persistently violated the principles contained in the Charter may be expelled from the organization by the General Assembly upon the recommendation of the Council.

The Security Council acts on behalf of all members of the UN under Article 25 of the Charter; all members "agree to accept and carry out" its decisions. Under Article 43, they undertake to make available to the Security Council "armed forces, assistance and facilities" necessary for the maintenance of international peace and security. The Security Council is so organized as to be able to function continuously, and a representative of each of its members must be present at all times at UN headquarters. The Council may meet elsewhere than at the Headquarters if it considers this advisable.

A state which is a member of the UN but not of the Security Council may take part in its discussions when the Council considers that the country's interests are specially affected. Both members and non-members are invited to take part in the Council's discussions, when they are parties to the disputes. In the case of a non-member the Council lays down the conditions under which it may participate.

3. The Economic and Social Council

The Economic and Social Council under the authority of the General Assembly is the organ which co-ordinates the economic and social work of the United Nations and the specialized agencies and institutions—known as the "United Nations Family" of organizations. It consists of 54 members, elected for three years terms by the General Assembly.

The Economic and Social Council provides multilateral technical assistance. When the UN Charter was being framed, attention was initially focussed on the problems of peace and security in the world. But at the instance of the USA, at the Yalta Conference, it was decided to create an Economic and Social Council as an integral part of the new international organization (UN) to deal with the rapidly emerging economic and social problems.[1] The ECOSOC is to study the problems of human and social well-being as well as to formulate appropriate policies and direct their implementation in this connection. The UN system is thus founded upon the sound idea that no peace can be stable unless it is based upon nations whose citizens are substantially free from distress, privation and frustration.[2] To quote the UN ex-Secretary-General U Thant:

"I cannot help feeling that too much attention has been given in the past to the military, ideological and political factors which tend to divide the world into various groups and interest blocs. The time has come for us to direct our attention more to the economic and social structure of society and particularly to the disparity in the wealth of nations which is one of the root causes of political tension. It is possible, within the United Nations system, to stress the common responsibility of nations, rich and poor, in the economic and social fields, and to organize North-South as well as East-West co-operative for the promotion of human welfare."[3]

The less developed world constitutes 66 per cent of the wolld population while in terms of Gross National Product (GNP), it constitutes only 12.5 per cent.[4] The developing world shares only one-sixth of income, one-third food production and less than one-tenth of its industrial output.[5] The position has become worse since this publication.

The widespread poverty and the depressed standards of living among such large numbers of people pose a very serious threat to peace as well as human creativeness. Moreover, the gap between the affluent nations and a much larger number of non-affluent or backward nations generates a sense of international misunderstandings, jealousies and tensions. Such a state of affairs cannot be conducive to good and peaceful relations among the nations of the world. "The problem of mass poverty and the need for redoubled co-operative efforts to come to grip with it", was the main thrust of a message from ex-Secretary-General, Kurt Waldheim to the thirty-third session of the ESCAP which opened in Bangkok on 20th April, 1977. In any inter-dependent world, the idea of what U Thant described as "prosperous provincialism" was dangerous for world order.[6]

Mr. Kurt Waldheim, ex-Secretary-General stated that "the majority of nations and peoples are affected in varying degrees by acute problems of instability, poverty and economic weakness, often exacerbated by political and economic developments elsewhere in the world. While aspirations of their people are high, economic dependence or instability shackles many of them to an economic system which no longer meets the requirements of an independent world of free nations. For many of them their first generation of independence has coincided with the challenge of coming to terms with a new world, a world in a state of revolutionary technological change. Thus the general longing for peace and equity is shadowed by a widespread unease and lack of confidence in the future."[7]

The reason for poverty and misery in the developing countries is not essentially the Jack of potentialities or resources human or material but under-utilization of these resources. Today, developing countries are not utilizing more than 15 per cent of the potential capacity of human beings due to inadequate expertise and resources at their disposal.[8] The main aim of technical assistance is to promote economic and social development in under-developed countries. It seeks to achieve this objective through international transfer of scientific knowledge and technology, demonstration of improved techniques by international experts, training of local personnel in the use of these techniques, build-up of essential training institutions and assistance in the dissemination of these techniques. It may also include financial assistance for rapid industrial development. In a report submitted to the Governing Council, Paul G. Hoffman, an ex-Administrator of the UN Development Programme, said:

"External assistance has a limited but a vital role to play. It will help break the vicious cycle due to the fact that poverty breeds poverty and poverty of opportunity perpetuates it. Poor nations, like poor people, are caught up in the day-to-day fight for survival. Forced to live a hand-to-mouth existence, they cannot put enough to invest adequately in their own future, poor because they cannot develop their own resources and unable to develop their resources because they are poor."[9]

Aid can be provided either through bilateral or multilateral sources. Multilateral aid has several advantages over bilateral aid. The aid through the former is normally untied. It is more acceptable politically to the recipients and, to a large extent, it takes national politics out of foreign assistance that often complicates bilateral operations. The multilateral medium tends to eliminate the donor's political and strategic objectives from the aid given and directs it more specifically to the recipient's economic and social objectives. In other words, these channels are governed more by technical than by political considerations. Moreover, the recipients as well as the donors share in controlling these multilateral agencies on an equal footing. It provides access to resources of all member-states on a virtually world-wide basis and a multilateral opening for co-operation among developed and developing countries on a basis of equality. Mr. Ronald Robinson, who edited the papers submitted to the Overseas Studies Committee, has commented:

"The International aid-giving authorities are thus peculiarly well placed to arbitrate fairly between individual donors and recipients to exert powerful admonitory pressure upon them to adopt sound economic policies and observe good standards of performance and to co-ordinate their individual activities into comprehensive operations for international, regional and national economic co-operation."[10]

While discussing the comparative merits and demerits of the two types of assistance, it would not be proper to describe the problem as one of bilateral *versus* multilateral aid. For one thing, the freedom of choice between the two the marginal so long as taxpayers in donor countries vote for bilateral and not for multilateral assistance; for another, their roles are inter-changeable.

To quote U. Thant:

"In this field, the resources available so far to the United Nations have been small, almost marginal, in relation to the resources which have been expended by Governments on a bilateral basis. I believe, however, that the United Nations and its family of agencies provide a unique opportunity for organizing global attack on the common problems of mankind. In this way the UN can also help prevent the world from becoming frozen into antagonistic interest blocs."[11]

The Council makes recommendations and initiates activities relating to problems of development, world trade, industrialization, natural resources, human rights, the status of women, population, social welfare, science and technology, prevention of crime, human rights and many other economic and social questions. The Council has 54 members. Eighteen members are elected each year by the General Assembly for a three year term of office. Voting in the ECOSOC is by simple majority; each member has one vote.

Its functions are:

1. To be responsible, under the authority of the General Assembly, for the economic and social activities of the UN;
2. To make or initiate studies, reports and recommendations of international economic, social, cultural, educational, health and related matters;
3. To promote respect for and observance of, human rights and fundamental freedom for all;
4. To call international conferences and prepare draft conventions for submission to the General Assembly on matters within its competence;
5. To negotiate agreements with the specialized agencies, defining their relationship with the United Nations;
6. To co-ordinate the activities of the specialized agencies by means of consultations with them and recommendations to them, and by means of recommendations to the General Assembly and the members of the United Nations;
7. To perform services approved by the Assembly, for members of the United Nations, and request, for the specialized agencies; and
8. To consult with non-governmental organizations concerned with matters with which the Council deals.

Subsidiary Bodies

The ECOSOC generally holds two-month long sessions each year, meeting in New York and Geneva. Throughout the year, however, there are meetings of the Council's standing committees, commissions and other bodies at the headquarters or in other locations. There are Standing Committees on Non-governmental Organizations, Negotiations with Inter-governmental Agencies; Housing, Building and Planning; Programme and Co-ordination; Natural Resources; Science and Technology for Development; Review and Appraisal; Development Planning; and Crime Prevention and Control. The functional commissions are: Commission on Human Rights; Commission on the Status of Women; Commission on Narcotic Drugs; and the Social Commission. Also under the Council's authority are regional economic commissions whose aim is to assist in the economic and social development of their respective regions and to strengthen economic relations of the countries in each region, both among themselves and with other countries of the world. These include the economic commissions for Africa (based in Addis Ababa), economic and social commission for Asia and the Pacific (Bangkok), economic commission for Europe (Geneva), economic commission for Latin America (Santiago) and economic commission for Western Asia (Beirut). They all deal directly with their member-governments though they report their activities to ECOSOC. This has inevitably created a further problem of co-ordination.

The ECOSOC has been carrying on a multiplicity of functions. Its most important role has been in making the world conscious of the socio-economic problems faced by the member-states and the remedies to overcome them. Its contribution lies not in "the information assembled but in the collective self-consciousness bred in its assembling."[12]

4. The Trusteeship Council

The Trusteeship Council was assigned under the Charter to supervise the administrations of trust territories which were placed under the International Trusteeship System. It consists of five permanent members. The major goals of the system were to promote the advancement of the inhabitants of the territories and their progressive development towards self-government and independence. By 1982 all but one of the Trust Territories had attained independence, or had chosen to join other independent states. Only the Trust Territory of Islands, designated a strategic area, remains under Trusteeship system.

5. The International Court of Justice

The International Court of Justice whose seat is at The Hague is the principal judicial body of the United Nations. Its statute is an integral part of the United Nations Charter. It consists of 15 Judges, known as the 'members' of the Court. They are elected by the General Assembly and the Security Council, voting independently. The Judges are chosen on the basis of their qualifications, not on the basis of their nationality. Care is taken, however to see that the principal legal systems of the world are represented in the Court. No two Judges can be nationals of the same state. The Judge serve for a term of nine years and may be re-elected.

The jurisdiction of the Court covers all questions which the states refer to it, and all matters provided for in the United Nations charter or in treaties or conventions in force. States may bind themselves in advance to accept the jurisdiction of the Court in special cases either by signing a treaty or convention which provides for reference to the Court or by making a special declaration to this effect. Such declaration accepting compulsory jurisdiction may exclude certain classes of cases.

6. The Secretariat

By the Charter of the United Nations, the Secretariat has been established as one of the six principal organs of the United Nations. The Secretariat services the organs of the United Nations and administers the programmes and policies laid down by them. At its head is the Secretary-General, who is appointed by the General Assembly on the recommendation of the Security Council. The Secretary-General occupies a key position in the UN System. Dag Hammarskjold described this office as a "one man executive" in his address at Chicago in May, 1960. In article 97 of the UN Charter, the Secretary General has been designated as the "Chief Administrative Officer" of the Organization. Article 97 is followed by Articles 98 and 99. In Article 98 it is provided not only that the Secretary-General "shall act in that capacity" in meetings of the organs, but that he "shall perform such other functions as are entrusted by these organs." Article 99 provides political powers to the Secretary-General as he "may bring to the attention of the Security

Council any matter which in his opinion may threaten the maintenance of international peace and security." Legal scholars are of the view that Article 99 also empowers the Secretary-General a broad discretion to conduct inquiries and to engage in informal diplomatic activity in regard to matters which are of grave danger to international peace and security.

The emergence of the Secretary-General as the 'key figure' in UN crisis diplomacy is one of the most important and controversial developments in the history of the UN. He has become the central figure in almost all the UN's peace-keeping operations. A large number of factors have been responsible for this development:

(a) Growth in the UN membership.
(b) Multiplication of administrative, technical and diplomatic responsibilities.
(c) Failure of the Security Council to make Chapter VII of the Charter Operative.
(d) Rivalries and Deadlocks in the Security Council and the General Assembly.

While answering questions in a press conference held on 12th September, 1979, at UN headquarters, Mr. Kurt Waldheim, UN ex-Secretary-General also confirmed the above contention. He said, "It is evident that the Secretary-General is in a unique position to be helpful in difficult situations. It so happens that from time to time other UN organs are not able to do so because there is a division. In such situations it is the duty of the Secretary-General to look into the situation and see what he personally can do in order to contribute to a solution of the problem. I tell you in all frankness that I have firmly decided to continue this policy as I did at the Geneva Conference on the Humanitarian Situation in Indo-China."

But there are limits to the duties and responsibilities that the Secretary-General can be expected to assume or that are beyond his effective powers and influence. His political position is not sufficiently strong to permit him to oppose a major power. However, the Secretary-General's actual influence on a given situation is bound to be determined largely by his intelligent and skilful use of methods that are essentially diplomatic in nature.

At the Sixty-sixth Annual Meeting (April 27-29, 1972) of the American Society of International Law on a panel of discussions on "A more powerful Secretary-General for the UN", there was agreement that a private diplomatic role as opposed to a more public role for the Secretary-General is desirable.[13]

SPECIALIZED AGENCIES

Article 57 of the UN Charter lays down that specialized agencies having wide international responsibilities as defined in their basic instruments, in economic, social, cultural, educational, health and related fields, should be brought in relationship with the UN as envisaged in Art. 63. Close contact is maintained, however, between an agency and the UN through an agreement negotiated by the Economic and Social Council.[14] The same Article stipulates three criteria on the fulfilment of which alone can an organ be recognized as a specialized agency. First, the organization has to be established by an inter-governmental agreement, which means that the basic instrument requires ratification or acceptance in accordance with the constitution of the state concerned. Second, the organ should have international responsibilities. This excludes organizations of a purely regional character and those having limited membership. Third, the agency has to be brought into close relationship with the UN through specific accords and agreements.[15]

Much of the UN work aimed at improving the economic and social conditions of the people of the world is carried out by specialized inter-governmental agencies. Each specialized agency is autonomous in respect of its membership, constitution, structure, budget and appointment of officials, etc. Broadly, each agency has the same general organisational structure: an assembly or conference composed of all members as the policy-making organ, an executive council, Board or committees having executive or supervisory duties, a Director or a Secretary-General or a Director-General. Each has its own Secretariat which is independently recruited.

While the specialized agencies have some common features, there are significant differences as well. Some of the agencies are new, some are old and some are still in the making. For example, the International Tele-Communication Union (ITU) was established in 1932; the Universal Postal Union (UPU) in 1875 and the International Labour Organization (ILO) in 1919. Thus two of them, the ITU and the UPU, antedated the League of Nations. After the outbreak of World War II, various conferences established 14 additional agencies, making a total of seventeen.

The functions of some of the agencies like the UPU, the ITU and the WMO are of a regulatory nature and their activities are mostly directed from the headquarters. In contrast, each of the agencies like the ILO, the WHO, the FAO, the UNESCO and the IMCO has developmental functions, comprising educational, technical, research and advisory assistance in regard to its substantive field of activity, i.e., Health, Education, Food, Labour Welfare, etc.

There are also differences in structure and membership. Admission of non-members of the United Nations is usually accompanied by a two-thirds vote of the Assembly. On the other hand, admission of such members to the WHO is permitted by a simple majority vote of the Health Assembly. The various organs generally comprise representatives of governments. In the case of the WHO's Executive Board, however, members are selected on the basis of their technical competence in the field of health. Ordinarily, each member has one vote in the policy-making body, but with respect to the Banks and the Fund the number of votes cast by each member is in proportion to its monetary contribution. The ILO has a novel system of representation and voting. Each member-state selects four delegates, two of whom represent the Government, one labour and the other the employers. Since each delegate casts one vote, sometimes the voting of a country's delegation is split. There are wide divergences among the agencies in general field of administration and in policy-making.

Almost every aspect of economic and social development is covered by this complex institutional framework. Under the United Nations Charter, responsibility for the overall co-ordination of the policies and the activities of the United Nations and the specialized agencies is vested in the General Assembly and under its authority, the Economic and Social Council, Relationship Agreements have been concluded on the basis of the provisions of the Charter between the United Nations and the various autonomous agencies; though most of the agreements are quite similar, those with IBRD and IMF, because of the nature of these organizations, are in several respects looser. On this constitutional basis, and with the help of the Administrative Committee on Co-ordination (ACC) which brings together under the Chairmanship of the Secretary-General, the executive heads of the specialized agencies, IAEA and the major United Nations units, it has proved possible over the years to form a meaningful "United Nations System."

Besides the UN and its agencies, there are various organs of the UN which help in the promotion of peace and human welfare. We can divide these organs into two categories:

- Organs responsible for the promotion of peace.
- Organs responsible for the promotion of Socio-Economic Development.

DEVELOPMENT AND WORKING OF THE UN SYSTEM

Since its inception, the UN System has developed both in magnitude as well as in direction. It has often been torn and jarred by events, but the marks it bears are those of a vital participant in the hurly-burly of international life. This expansion can be anlaysis quantitatively by comparing personnel and budgets. Another important development in the direction of internationalism has been the greater geographical dispersion of the UN activities. Today, the UN experts are serving in every corners of the world. They are helping the national administrations in their tasks of national development. Thus, we have passed through an unprecedented change since the United Nations was established at San Francisco in 1945, and the United Nations itself, reflecting these new priorities and concerns of mankind, has changed greatly. Indeed its strength has emerged from its capacity to adapt itself to new circumstances and to respond effectively to the many problems which the world faces.

Under the United Nations, international organization has reached "an unparalleled comprehensiveness and integration." Its present membership approaches universality, crossing all geographical, political and ideological lines. The United Nations provides the most extensive framework yet achieved for joint action on international problems. Secretary-General Dag Hammarskjold described the United Nations as "an institutional system of co-existence."

Most of the work of the United Nations measured in terms of money and personnel involved goes into the varied programmes aimed at achieving a better life for all peoples of the world. Since the first tentative steps in its early years, the organization has greatly expanded its activities in the economic and social fields. In the first Development Decade, many developing countries achieved progress in terms of the rate of increase in GNP, but gains were offset by growing population pattern and heavy burdens of debts. There was no world plan or 'strategy' on the measures required to reach the broadly stated goals. The need for such a strategy was recognized before the first Decade ended and intensive work over a period of years led to agreement on the International Development Strategy for the Second United Nations Development Decade. In December, 1980, the thirty-fifth Session of the General Assembly proclaimed the Third United Nations Development Decade, starting on January 1, 1981. Fourth Development Decade is in operation with more priorities. Besides, the UN is also paying attention to other human rights questions, such as the abolition of slavery, servitude, forced labour, the elimination of religious intolerance, etc.

In more than six and a half decades of its existence, the UN has been called upon to prevent a dangerous situation from escalating into war, to persuade opposing parties to use the conference table rather than resort to arms, and to help restore peace or at least halt the fighting when conflicts occur. Despite frustration and setbacks, the Organization has steadily developed its capacity as a peace-keeping and peace-making organization. No one doubts that the current problems of the UN peace-keeping operations are great. Its present authority is limited and in one sense is even uncertain. Nevertheless, the UN has provided a forum where member-states can come together, discuss and voice a common desire for peace and justice. It is evident that in this nuclear age, machinery like UN peace-keeping is indispensable for human survival.[16]

Mr. Kurt Waldheim says that the future of the UN depends on the answers to the following questions:

> "Can the sovereign nations of our interdependent world, in the new circumstances in which we live, reach a sufficient consensus and generate the necessary collective will to

give real and lasting effect to the original idea of the United Nations as an effective instrument for keeping the peace? Can they develop the capacity of the organization for dealing with global problems which now face all nations and which can certainly not be dealt with in isolation or by one nation or groups of nations alone"?[17]

The answers to these questions have been given by the Secretary-General in his I976 annual report. He says that the institution which the world desperately needs is a full-fledged instrument of co-operation with sufficient international solidarity and prestige not to be ignored in dangerous times or thrown off balance by sudden controversies and confrontations.[18]

He further suggests that "the United Nations is unique in providing a place where national interests can be articulated, group interests identified and global interests distilled and worked for. If national and group interests can inter-act in the United Nations within the third dimension of global priorities and with a determination to get real results, it should be possible to move forward steadily on many of the great issues where we now seem to be calmed. There is nothing basically wrong with the existing international mechanism except the apparent inability of Governments to use it to its full potential. For that to happen, we need to develop a confidence in, and a vision of, the future which is not incessantly clouded or neutralized by narrow aims or temporary setbacks. With confidence and vision the United Nations is capable of becoming a decisive instrument in human development "[19] We can be optimistic about its future role. The UN has demonstrated that it can sometimes play a significant and unique role in the strengthening of international peace and security. During the last three and a half decades, the organization has developed a system for the promotion of peace. The wealth of experience has enabled it to respond rapidly when the need for peace-keeping arises. Mr. Kurt Waldheim strikes a note of optimism in his annual report about the role of UN. He says, "All around we hear talk of frustration and despair echoed throughout the world by the media. Every now and then, however, we receive striking proof of the validity of the Charter concept of inter-national order and of the necessity and usefulness—sometimes in the darkest hours—of the United Nations. It is on these positive developments that we should strive to build the future order, which will also be the future United Nations."[20] However, the former Secretary-General, Mr. Javier Perez De Cuellar, in his annual report 1982, strikes a pessimistic note when he says, "I believe that we are at present embarked on an exceedingly dangerous course, one symptom of which is the crisis in the multilateral approach in international affairs and the concomitant erosion of the authority and status of world and, regional inter-governmental institutions. Such a trend must be reversed before once again we bring upon ourselves a global catastrophe and find ourselves without institutions effective enough to prevent it." He further says: "We take the United Nations seriously when we desperately need it. I would urge that we also seriously consider the practical ways in which it should develop its capacity and be used as an essential institution in a stormy and uncertain world."

The United Nations Millennium Development Goals aim at: (i) eradication of extreme poverty and hunger, (ii) achievement of universal primary education, (iii) promoting gender equality, (iv) reduction in child mortality, (v) improvement ofmaternal heatlh, (vi) combating HIV/AIDS, Malaria and other diseases, (vii) ensuring environment sustainability, and (viii) developing global partnership for development, including partnership with private sector and civil society in technological development. And India has pledged to achieve these goals by 2015.

CONCLUSION

UN System has been taking initiative in all the fundamental issues e.g. Violence against Women, Children Rights, Human Rights, Population Control, Welfare of Aged, Helping the disabled, promoting development, helping the developing countries, etc. The main focus of UN has been:

(a) Eradication of poverty
(b) Enrichment of Human beings
(c) Enhanced Status of women
(d) Practice of Human Rights
(e) Decent life of all people
(f) Pooled Wisdom
(g) Promotion of Health, education and welfare
(h) Controlling disasters
(i) Mentenance of Peace.

No one can make an acceptable prediction for the future World organization. What is reasonable to predict is that the UN will continue and become more effective with time. Its present political weakness may be partly offset by its economic efforts and the member nations may sometimes decide to entrust it with the necessary powers to keep the world in order.

However, in recent times, funds at the disposal of UN systems are shrinking and because of the recent economic crisis, developing countries are facing great hardships in promoting development. It is hoped that under the dynamic leadership of Honourable Obama, new President of USA, there will be resurge in development as he in his first speech after assuming the office of President of USA, remarked that USA would support development for USA and other countries.

NOTES AND REFERENCES

1. E. Stettinius, The Yalta Conference, p. 25.
2. Norman Hill, International Organization, New York, 1952, p. 48.
3. U. Thant, Toward World Peace, Thomas Yoseloff, New York, 1964. p. 124.
4. Lester B. Pearson, Partners in Development, London, 1969. p. 24.
5. Irwin Isenberg, The Developing Nations: Poverty and Progress, New York, H.W. Wilson, 1969, p. 13.
6. UN Annual Report of ESCAP (7 April, 1974-7 March, 1975) N.Y., 1975, p. 45.
7. UN Chronicle, Vol. XVI. July-October, 1979, p. 6.
8. 12th Session of the UNDP Governing Council, 7-23 June, 1971, pp. 112-14 (UNDP.E/5043, Rev. I).
9. *Ibid.*
10. Ronald Robinson, International Co-operation in Aid (Ed.) Cambridge . University Overseas Studies Committee, Sept., 1966, p. 30.
11. U. Thant. Towards World Peace, Thomas Yoseloff, New York, 1964, p. 124.
12. Nicholas, *op. cit.,* p. 13.
13. A.J.LL., Vol. 66, No. 4, Sept., 1972 (Supplement) pp. 78-79.
14. UN Charter, Art. 63.
15. Robert E. Ascher, *et. al.* The United Nations and Promotions of the General Welfare, Washington, D.C., 1957, p. 64.

16. Francis P. India and U.N.: Peace-keeping Operation, New Delhi, p. 19.
17. UN: Introduction to the Report of the Secretary-General on the Work of the Organization, New York, 1975, p. 4.
18. UN: Introduction to the Report of the Secretary-General on the Work of the Organization, New York, 1976, pp. 25-26.
19. UN: *UN Chronicle*, Vol. XVI, July-Oct., 1979, p. 85.
20. UN: General Assembly, Official Records: Twenty-third Session, New York, 1978 (Supplement) No. 1 (A/83/1), p. 10.

CHAPTER

6

Role of Bureaucracy in Development

With the initiation of national plans for development, the administrative machinery has increased in size and complexity. Old government organisations have expanded, numerous new administrative agencies have been added, with the result that the number of personnel in government has multiplied both in size and magnitude and the cost of administration has greatly gone up.

There has, however, been a sharp deterioration of administrative output all round, delays have been built into normalcies and administrative failures are openly admitted in the evaluation reports of the plan, projects and schemes.

The quality of personnel, level of efficiency, motivation and enthusiasm have not been maintained at a high level. Complaints by the citizens regarding inefficiency and lack of devotion to duty on the part of government employees have become quite articulate, and many people are even losing confidence in the existing administrative system thereby widening the credibility gap. The image of Indian Public Administration is that it is slow in action, lacking in initiative, flexibility, adaptability and often rude in dealing with the public. It is characterised by existence of problems over long periods of time, dilatory paper work, rigid procedures, tight administrative controls and other symptoms of ineffective performance.

During the last fifty years, the country has taken up vast developmental responsibilities, but it has not been able to modernise administrative tools, techniques, organisation structure and staffing patterns to the requirements of development. Besides, no substantial efforts seem to have been made to professionalise the services to achieve a high level of competence and capability in them.

A developing economy needs high level technical manpower as urgently as it needs capital. A crucial factor in improving the coverage and quality of services is the availability of adequate number of personnel with task-oriented training. Among the three components required for developmental tasks-men, money and material (M3), it is more the men (or the human element) duly qualified, than any other factor which determines the quality and quantity of the performance and output. After all, even the contribution of money and material to performance depends substantially upon their manipulation by the men in an organization. Human resources are critical for the success of any social activity. (See Chart 6.1)

CHART 6.1

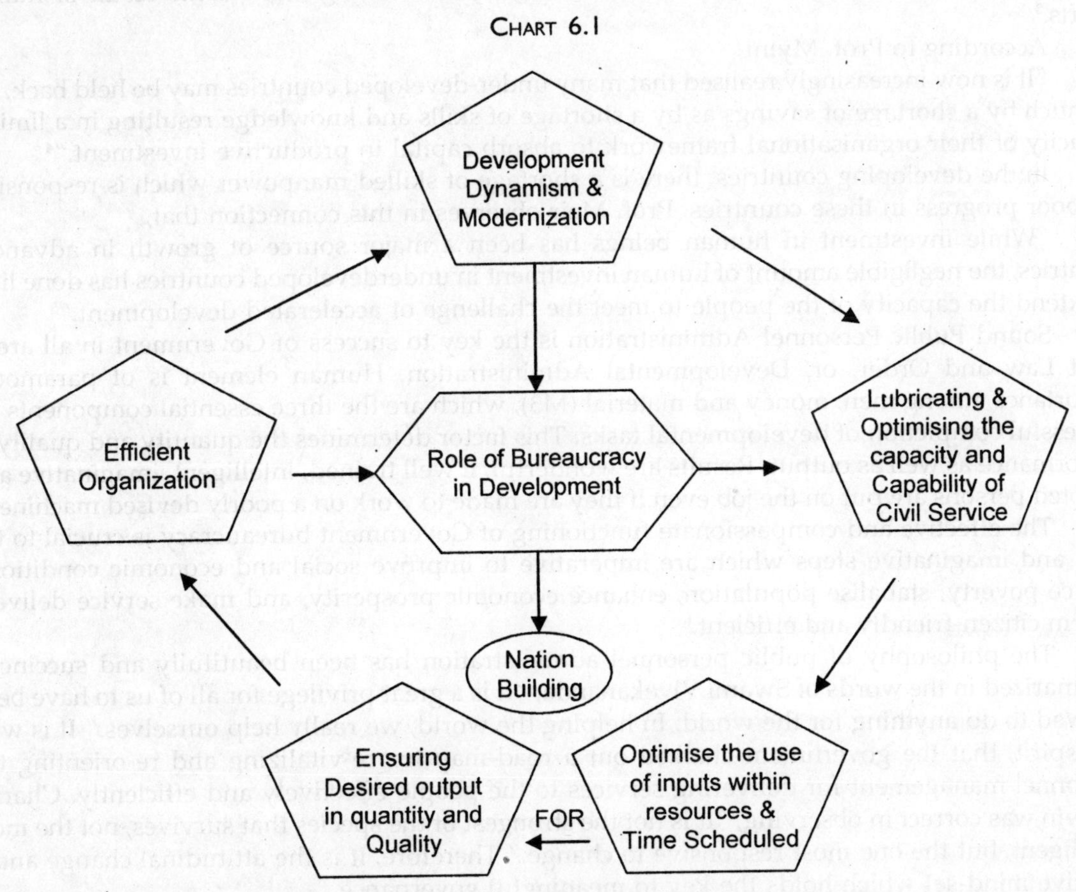

Dr. C.D. Deshmukh has rightly said that, "Good management provides the surplus which on investment nourish the processes of industrialisation and modernisation of society. Good administration furnishes the infrastructure of services which secure the order, stability and social development. Carefully recruited and periodically trained or re-trained top-personnel is needed for both spheres of operation. How to regulate the affairs of the nation so as to maximise the efficiency of both is the supreme challenge to political leadership. Only by meeting it successfully can a democratic polity survive in the not-too-long-run."[1]

Development is not a mechanical process. It is a human enterprise and its success will depend ultimately on the skill, the quality and motivation of the persons associated with it. Human rather than capital is the key to development. According to Prof. Merle Fainsod: "Improvements in the effectiveness of development administration depends on the quality and training of public servants who man it and on a social and political environment which liberates their energies. Structural adjustments can work no developmental miracles where administrative manpower is inadequate or the will to develop is lacking. The secret of development is not concealed in the interstices of governmental or administrative structure. Development takes place where skill is supported by commitment and the human material resources exist to translate dreams into actualities."[2] Professor Lewis has rightly said that growth is the result of human efforts.[3]

According to Prof. Myint,

"It is now increasingly realised that many under-developed countries may be held back, not so much by a shortage of savings as by a shortage of skills and knowledge resulting in a limited capacity of their organisational framework to absorb capital in productive investment."[4]

In the developing countries, there is a shortage of skilled manpower which is responsible for poor progress in these countries. Prof. Meir observes in this connection that,

"While investment in human beings has been a major source of growth in advanced countries, the negligible amount of human investment in underdeveloped countries has done little to extend the capacity of the people to meet the challenge of accelerated development."[5]

Sound Public Personnel Administration is the key to success of Government in all areas, be it Law and Order, or, Developmental Administration. Human element is of paramount importance among men, money and material (M3), which are the three essential components for successful completion of developmental tasks. This factor determines the quantity and quality of performance as well as output. Results are wonderful, if well trained, intelligent, imaginative and devoted persons are put on the job even if they are made to work on a poorly devised machinery.

The effective and compassionate functioning of Government bureaucracy is crucial to the bold and imaginative steps which are imperative to improve social and economic conditions, reduce poverty, stabalise population, enhance economic prosperity, and make service delivery system citizen-friendly and efficient.[6]

The philosophy of public personnel administration has been beautifully and succinctly summarized in the words of Swami Vivekananda, "It is a great privilege for all of us to have been allowed to do anything for the world. In helping the world, we really help ourselves." It is with this spirit, that the government chalked out a road-map for re-vitalizing and re-orienting the personnel management for delivering services to the people effectively and efficiently. Charles Darwin was correct in observing, "It is not the strongest of the species that survives, not the most intelligent, but the one most responsive to change.". Therefore, it is the attitudinal change and a positive mind-set which holds the key to meaningful governance.

In "A Handbook of Public Administration: Current Concept and Practice with special reference to Developing Countries" it is observed that "Trained and competent persons are required to deal with such difficult and highly specialized matters as economic and social fact finding and analysis, financial management, bridge and dam construction industrial development, administration of housing, social welfare, health, education or agriculture. A career service based on merit and fitness lies at the heart of modern public administration."

It has now been proved, country after country that an honest, professionally sound, contended Bureaucracy is a critical element of any program ... It is thus of utmost importance that the best brains in the country are attracted to the Public services. They should hot only be motivated to enter the services but also serve in a professional and dedicated manner. This necessitates a careful handling of all the major parameters from their induction to retention. (Central Fifth Pay Commission).

M. Veerappa Moily, Chairman Second Administration Reforms Commission, in its Tenth Report mentioned that Rapid and fundamental changes are taking place in the political, economic and technological fields. These call for major changes in the civil service. Far-reaching changes in the global economy have made it necessary to build a competent, well-functioning civil service. As a result of recent changes induced by globalisation, countries are competing internationally not only in the market place but also on the quality of their governance structures. The changed policy of deregulation, liberalisation and competition has suggested a new role for the civil service, emphasising the strategic management of the economy in less prescriptive and more market-driven approaches. The changes in the economic structure raise new demands related to control and accountability of the civil service as well as new definitions of professional obligations. In addition, the role and importance of civil society organisation and of the private sector in the Indian economy and the society in general have increased substantially over the years. As a result, it is important for the civil servants to see the private sector and civil society organisations as partners in the process of economic and social development of the country.

As instruments of public service, civil servants have to be ready for change. The common experience, however, is that they resist changes as they are wedded to their privileges and prospects and thereby, have become ends in themselves. In the political field, the 73rd and 74th Amendments to the Constitution have brought about major changes. Rural and urban local governments have been enabled to become institutions of self-government. In order to make it meaningful, the existing system of administration of departments and the District Collectorate has to undergo fundamental changes. This has not happened to the extent envisioned. One of the principal reasons is the marked reluctance on the part of the civil service to accept the changes in control and accountability as well as the altered roles and responsibilities. This is because of the fact that most of the civil servants have been socialised to act in a manner that accentuates command and control methods rather than respond to people's needs and aspirations.

Bureaucracy is the purest form of rational-legal authority. It runs routine business with technical means and professional skills, with its stability, discipline, precision and reliability, it increases calculability and rationality. It hinder irrational decisions. It is mechanism for achieving the goal laid down by those who control it. Its parts are interchangeable. It can be easily re-organised to attain the same or different goals.

Today we often think of bureaucracies as vast, impersonal organizations that put impersonal efficiency ahead of human needs. We should be careful, though, not to apply our negative connotations of the word bureaucracy to the term as Weber used it. Like the scientific management theorists, Weber sought to improve the performance of socially important organizations by making their operations predictable and productive. Although we now value innovation and flexibility as much as efficiency and predictability, Weber's model of bureaucratic management clearly advanced the formation of huge corporations such as ford. Bureaucracy was a particular pattern of relationships for which Weber saw great promise.

Early managers and management writers sought the "one best way" a set of principles for creating an organisational structure that would work well in all situations. Max Weber, Frederick Taylor, and Henri Fayol were major contributors to the so-called classical approach to organisational design. They believed that the most efficient and effective organizations had a hierarchical structure in which members of the organization were guided in their actions by a sense of duty to the organization and by a set of rational rules and regulations. When fully developed, according to Weber, such organizations were characterized by specialization of tasks, appointment by merit, provision of career opportunities for members, routinization of activities, and a rational, impersonal organisational climate. Weber called this a bureaucracy.

Weber praised bureaucracy for its establishment of rules for decision-making, its clear chain of command, and its promotion of people on the basis of ability and experience rather than favoritism or whim. He also admired the bureaucracy's clear specification of authority and responsibility, which he believed made it easier to evaluate and reward performance. He and other classical writers, alongwith their contemporaries in management, lived in a time when this approach to organisational design had precedent in government civil services. The term bureaucracy has not always carried the modern negative connotation—a framework for slow, inefficient, unimaginative organisational activity.

Personnel administration is now recognized as a well-established academic discipline. Most of the universities in India and abroad are today engaged in the teaching and research in personnel administration. Personnel move the administrative machinery, that is why it has been rightly said that human beings rather than capital are the key to development. The quality of the institutions run by the government would be dependent to a great extent upon the quality of the employees engaged in their operation. Personnel in an organization are an independent variable in the sense that even the contribution of money and material to performance depends substantially upon their manipulation by men in an organization.

Manpower utilization is concerned with the efficient use of the existing manpower resources. At present, we have large number of personnel in various organizations without much work for them, resulting in useless expenditure and indiscipline. (See Chart 6.2)

There are two methods for assessing manpower utilization. The first one is the manning ratio which is based on the relationship between the number of the personnel employed in an organization and a specified measures of productivity. The second method is work study.

While the personnel administrator's set of beliefs and premises may be either obvious to him or below his level of awareness, he does in fact function on the basis of some theory. It would be worthwhile if there is a rationale that determines his view of how work is to be done and how people relate to one another in the work situation. Whether this theory is acquired by conscious study, by induction, from experience, or simply by unconscious absorption from the Organisational setting in which the administrator works, it shapes the decisions and actions that constitute visible administrative practice. Thus, it is important for personnel administrators to undergo courses in personnel administration to keep themselves abreast of the theory and practice of the subject. Refresher courses should be given to those administrators who have been earlier trained so that knowledge of the latest advanced techniques can be imparted to them. Waldo concedes that "Public Administration presently is given responsibility beyond its knowledge and power, beyond the authority it can command and the virtue it can summon." Therefore, the personnel departments should have professionally qualified and experienced personnel to ensure optimum use of the capability of personnel.

There is a great need to enhance the Administrative capability of public services, so .that they can achieve the objectives of the Government in the shortest time possible. Administrative capability is an important means of converting or processing programme inputs into outputs such as goods and services. Kantz says: "Administrative Capability for development involves the ability to mobilize, allocate and combine the actions that are technically needed to achieve development objective."[7] It is felt that the scope of experimentation is a costly and slow process. As such, we need to learn from the experience of others and use their results to help achieve our goals. In this context, Ernest Dale and L.C. Machelon observe that, "Today's Managers lives in a world of rapid change, yet, the rate of change is likely to increase in the years ahead. Unless he can keep up with this change, he is likely to find himself obsolete—perhaps unpromotable or

CHART 6.2

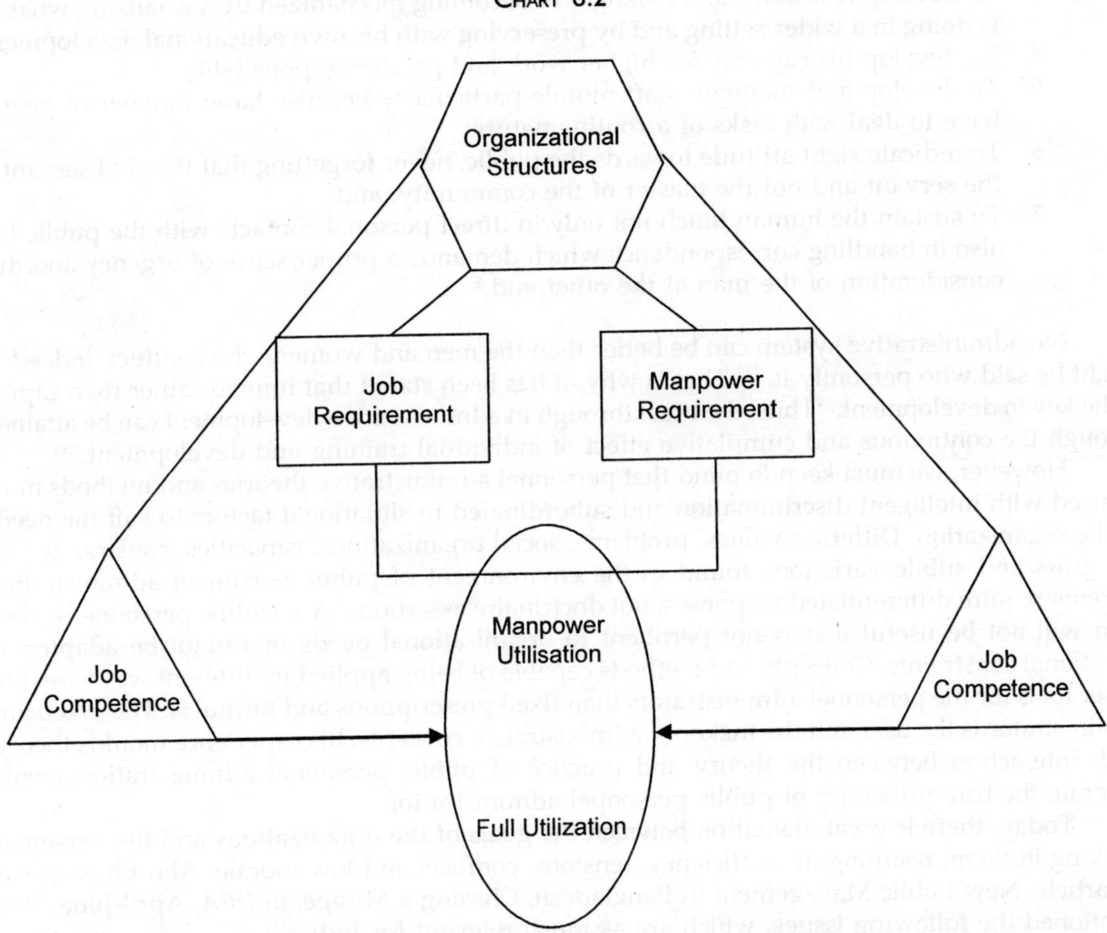

even unemployable."[8] Despite all the efforts of governments through their internal resources, despite the spectacular scientific and technical progress, despite the efforts of the governments through external resources, through bilateral and multi-lateral agencies, the poverty is still a naked fact, which is forcing millions of people to lead a very poor life with poor standards of living. In the words of Joseph Klatzmann, Professor at the National Institute of Agronomy in Paris: "It is really easier to go and collect pebbles from the surface of the moon than to feed the hungry masses of Bombay and Calcutta." In order to overcome these grave problems, it is necessary that the capacities and capabilities of existing systems should be upgraded and their human resources optimized so that they will be self-sufficient technically, financially and institutionally.

Krishna Mohan Mathur in his Article on Human Resources Development in Administration, in *The Indian Journal of Public Administration*, April-June 1987, Vol. XXXIII, No. 2, pp. 213-12; has mentioned the following objectives:

1. To equip the civil servant with precision and clarity in transaction of business;
2. To attune the civil servant to new tasks which he will be called upon to perform in a changing world;

3. To develop resistance to the danger of becoming mechanized by Visualizing what he is doing in a wider setting and by preserving with his own educational development;
4. To develop his capacity for higher work and greater responsibility;
5. To develop and maintain staff morale particularly because large number of people have to deal with tasks of a routine nature;
6. To indicate right attitude towards the public, never forgetting that the civil servant is the servant and not the master of the community; and
7. To sustain the human touch not only in direct personal contacts with the public but also in handling correspondence which demands a proper sense of urgency and due consideration of the man at the other end.[9]

No administrative system can be better than the men and women who conduct; indeed, it might be said who personify it."[10] That is why, it has been stated that human rather than capital is the key to development. "Thus, the breakthrough in administrative development can be attained through the continuous and cumulative effect of individual training and development."[11]

However, we must keep in mind that personnel administrative theories and methods must be used with intelligent discrimination and subordinated to situational factors to suit the needs of the organization. Differing values, problems, social organizations, capacities, constraints—all the gross and subtle variations found in the environment of public personnel administration systems-require differentiated responses, not doctrinaire assertions. A scientific personnel system plan will not be useful if it is not pertinent to organisational needs or cannot be adapted to situational constraints. Concepts and methods capable of being applied in different ways are thus better tools for the personnel administrators than fixed prescriptions and formulas. The practicing administrator is the user and the maker of administrative concepts, his experience moulds theory. Such interaction between the theory and practice of public personnel administration would generate the true principles of public personnel administration.

Today, there is great alienation between the goals of the organizations and the personnel working in them, resulting in inefficiency, tensions, conflicts and low morale. Abu Eli Sarber in his article, New Public Management in Bangladesh, Chasing a Mirage, in *IJPA*, April-June, 2001 mentioned the following issues, which are as much relevant for India:

- Lowlevels of efficiency, effectiveness, accountability, transparency and dynamism.
- Culture of secrecy in public service; high degree of centralization in decision-making.
- Weak instruments of control and accountability; low level of compensation.
- Over-sized organizations and over-staffing.
- Inefficient public employment system; inter-cadre rivalry; lack of favorable conditions for women; lack of linkage between rewards and performance.
- Mounting corrupt practices by public officials caused by the poor remuneration of public officials and their concomitant low self-motivation.
- Weak enforcement of laws and regulations.
- Wastages in public offices caused by unscientific management of human resources and wasteful management of public properties.
- Politicization of service delivery systems.
- The supremacy of the executive.

Personnel in any organization have abundant potential, energy and capacity. Why then is the management ineffective in utilizing this energy? Since the 1960s many Committees and Commissions appointed at the Union and State levels either to advise exclusively on Personnel Administration in totality or segments of Personnel Administration have mentioned that the Personnel System needs overhauling to cope with the existing and changing functions of the Government. Such thinking is visible not only in the developing countries but also in the developed countries.

Asstt. Editor V. Eshwar Anand in his article "Civil Services: The Blunted Edge" in *Sunday Tribune* dated January 25, 2009 observed that The Second Administrative Reforms Commission, in its tenth report under the title, "Refurbishing of Personnel, Administration: Scaling New Heights, has recommended wide-ranging reforms to make the administrative system responsive. A significant recommendations of the Commission is the need to weed out the deadwood after periodic review of the civil servants performance Few can differ with this view. Job security and time-scale promotions have made our bureaucrats too lethargic. The present system is such that even a non-performing bureaucrat automatically gets promoted to the next higher ranks and pay oblivious of its deleterious impact on the administrative system and the quality of governance.

It proposed two intensive reviews, one after 14 years and another after 20 years. While in the first, the officer will be apprised of his strengths and shortcomings for future advancement, in the second review, his "fitness" for further continuation in service will be assessed.

However, the training modules are too generic and do not inculcate greater domain knowledge in civil servants. The Commission wants suitable measures to be put in place for mandatory training of officers periodically at all levels—senior, middle and lower in addition to the induction stage—in view of the rapidly changing environment and the increasing demand for improved governance. The quality of training, too, should improve It should seek to impart officers the functional knowledge, skills and aptitude necessary for performing their assigned jobs diligently. At the cutting edge level, the focus should be citizen-centric and service-oriented.

The need of the hour is not to protect corrupt, inefficient and non-performing officers but strive for an honest, effective and result-oriented administration at the Centre and in the states.

In New Zealand, reforms were initiated by the Government elected in mid-1984. Their key concepts were transparency and consistency. A study of the reforms program in New Zealand shows that three aspects have been extremely successful. Transparency in the activities and processes of the State, liberation of managers from central input controls, and the new financial management and accounting systems are revolutionizing the way in which departments and officials work. New Zealand's economy has recovered, its audit rating has inched upwards, inflation has been reduced to less than two percent and employment has been growing steadily. The 1993 World Competitiveness Report ranked New Zealand as first in quality of government and as second on business community optimism.

In February 1991, the Prime Minister of Malaysia unveiled his Vision 2020, which declares the National aspiration to attain a fully industrialized and developed nation status, within the next three decades. This vision can be achieved only if there is an excellent Public Service to meet the challenges of rapid development in a constantly changing environment. The Public Service has identified seven fundamental values which are deemed necessary for this purpose. These are quality, productivity, innovativeness, discipline, integrity, accountability and professionalism.

The starting point for the Government of Canada's journey on the road to administrative reform is the process entitled "Public Service 2000." This was mainly the effort of the federal public service itself. Although it had political interest and support, it was not closely directed and actively managed by the politicians. Thus, it does not bear the imprint of a particular political agenda as in some other countries.

Public Service 2000 chalked out some key themes. For example, the public service should strive to provide a high quality service and increased client satisfaction. The Public Service must become more engaged, more open, more visible and more consultative. Public Service managers must create organizations in which people are valued for their skill, dedication, energy and loyalty. Public Service must invest more heavily in the development of its people. It must reduce the burden of internal controls so that intelligent, well-motivated managers have greater latitude to improve service quality and client satisfaction.

Most of the thought revolves revision of the basic concepts of personnel policy modernization of administrative recruitment methods, modification of the need of personnel policy, practices, reform of the structure and emoluments of the staff, greater delegation of authority and responsibility in selected areas of Personnel Management from the office of Personnel to other departments and offices and structural changes in that office. There is also a lack of clearly defined administrative norms, which need examination, review and analysis. There have been a large number of such commissions of inquiry into public service in both development and developing countries.

There is a need to change mind-set of civil services, without which no reforms can take place. B.G. Deshmukh, in his article, "Indian Bureaucrat-Facing its future", in *IJPA*, Jan.-March, 1998 talks about this issue as follows: "One of the crucial change, that should be made by the civil servants itself is the change in the mind-set. One can understand as to why the civil service finds it difficult to change its mind-set but the real reason behind this is its sense of insecurity in facing the future. And it is this aspect which is the most critical item before the civil service. It was created by colonial administration but it really became omni-potent and omni-present during a socialist era after independence. Since, the whole world is undergoing a transition. Indian civil service cannot remain aloof, otherwise there is every danger of the people forcing it to change. Any resistance on the part of the civil service would only damage it."

D.M. Nanjundappa in his article, "Management by Values" in *University News*, November 5-11, 2001 rightly stresses that work in life becomes worship, if it is in the service of the nation, poor, hungry and the helpless and not for self. The Vedantic human orientation finds an inspiring expression that inevitably raises the quality of life. To quote Swami Vivekanand observation, "This life is short, the vanities of the world are transient; but they alone live who live for others. The rest are more dead than alive."

We have taken pains "in analyzing the totality of the personnel system not only in terms of its core functions but also other factors—political, administrative, informal, and financial which directly or indirectly interact with the personnel system. It is because of this complexity, that the field of Personnel Administration reform is becoming challenging. A.B. Villanueva, Professor of Political Science, Western illinois University, USA, in his Article, "Political Changes and Value Conflicts in American Civil Service Reform" in *IJPA*, Oct.-Dec., 1991, has rightly said that, of the many complex phenomena in American politics, perhaps the most problematic is that of civil service reform. John Halligan, Professor at the University of Canberra, Australia, rightly comments that the "Australian Public Service now lacks some of the special qualities which most clearly differentiated the Public Service career in the past." Many experts have also indicated that the civil services in developed and developing countries have lost their traditional social purpose because the people and politicians have now started preferring the role of private enterprise to ensure economy and efficiency. We have examined all these questions and suggested remedies to reassure the credibility of public service.

Presently, the procedures involving personnel management in government are kept so much in wraps that even government servants themselves are not aware of them. Many of these activities like policy of transfers and postings, procedure for empanelment and even the list of persons who have made it to a panel remains a closely guarded secret. Transparency in dealing with matters relating to appointments, promotions, placements and personnel management is essential. We recommend that clearly defined criteria for all matters concerning promotions, transfers, appointments, etc. of government employees should be laid down. When a panel is drawn up, it should be published so that everyone knows where he stands. Apart from reducing frustration amongst government employees, this will obviate the need for fighting service-related cases in the courts.

NEED OF BUREAUCRATIC REFORMS

Development of public administration in that manner should be accompanied by initiating administrative reforms on a large scale in a "case-by-case" approach, applying the following administrative principles:[12]

- Administrative action should be user-oriented,
- Expertise and authority should rest with those who are closer to the customers or users,
- Competition between services should be allowed and institutionalized, and
- Internal organisational re-adaptation measures should be followed by a managerial approach through efficient use of financial and personnel resources.

To realize these principles in everyday life of public administration, management analysis of the government organization and that of public enterprises becomes necessary. As a part of serious efforts to upgrade governance and to reform bureaucratic authorities, the modern state has to simplify the organisational structures and administrative procedures, and prepare job profiles of the personnel.

Vincent Ostrom observes, "When the central problem in Public Administration is viewed as the provision of public goods and services, alternative forms may be available for the performance of those functions apart from an extension and perfection of bureaucratic structures. Bureaucratic structures are necessary but not sufficient structures for a productive and responsive public service economy. He thus opts for the public choice theory in which the individual is the unit of analysis and methods which are effective in economies are adopted.

The challenge before the leaders and administrators of developing nations is as to how to achieve sustainable development and yet provide basic human needs (the provision of food, appropriate habitat, health and education), as well as social justice, removal of poverty and self-reliance with very limited resources. They will have to be more self-reliant in the 21st Century, as they cannot expect the same level of development aid, since the attention of the West is turning more towards helping Eastern Europe. So they must consider being self-reliant and using their own resources among and between themselves much more than they have done so far. For this, they will require a cadre of professionally trained and dedicated administrators, as well as moral and just politicians who can stand against the forces of corrupt politics and unscrupulous commercial and business interests. Specially, development administrators have an obligation to serve the public in a manner, which strengthens the integrity and process of governance. Such is the challenge and duty for the leaders and administrators of developing nations in the 21st century.[13]

The Governments, both at the Center and the State, share the concern for ensuring responsive, accountable, transparent, decentralized and people-friendly administration at all levels. There is, however, considerable frustration and dissatisfaction amongst the people, especially the weaker sections of society, about the apathy, irresponsiveness and lack of accountability of public servants, even as the expenditure on staff continues to increase. There is increasing anxiety about growing instances of corruption and criminalisation in public life and administration. The people, particularly the vulnerable groups, are also greatly concerned about the deterioration in the performance of agencies concerned with law and order and the investigation of offences. Their faith in the registration of offences, their timely investigation and the delivery of prompt justice has been eroded.

Time has come for a strong message to be conveyed that administration is for the people and not for the public servants themselves. There has to be a change of attitudes and public servants should realize that efficiency will be measured not in terms of what the services purport to offer, but in terms of public satisfaction. Simultaneously, there should be a drive towards cleansing of the services and codification of the ethics, value system and the interface with the politicians.

The civil services in India have played a significant, indeed a critical, role in maintaining the integrity of the country and in bringing about major developments in post-independent India. However, in recent times, the services have been facing a grave crisis of identity and role definition. People now believe that public services are meant to benefit government servants and politicians and not the public. The emphasis here is on all public services, which subsume all technical, professional, law enforcement and administrative personnel. Though issues relating to efficiency and effectiveness of the administrative machinery have been discussed from time to time, the reforms initiated have only dealt with minor procedural changes, without really addressing the issue of improvement in the quality of services.

The crisis in administration calls for a redefinition of the role of government and its function and its real focus is to serve the public effectively, as much as to ensure efficient and cost-effective administration. Accountability, transparency and cleansing public service are all inter-connected issues for ensuring a clean and responsive administration. It is necessary to converge the efforts of various public agencies for delivery of basic services in rural and urban areas and for one-step and single window dealings with the public. This calls for steps to reorganize work procedures, for delegation down the line and an effective management information system, accessible to all. Simultaneous steps to address the right-sizing of public services, value for money on public expenditure, restoring effective audit, monitoring and evaluation, good financial management systems, etc. are needed.

The State Government could consider .an urgent review of the system of redressal of public grievances at the State, District, city, block and village levels, and devise mechanisms for their sensitive and prompt redressal, and ensure regular independent review of these systems. Steps could be taken to fix responsibility in each office for dealing with grievances, for attitudinal orientation of officials at all levels, and for continuous monitoring of the redressal system. This could be integrated with the overall package of measures for responsive administration. The State Government could consider setting up independent watchdog committees at the district and city levels to report to high-powered cells in the State Government on the functioning of the local grievance redressal systems, as well as cases of negligence and delay.

All employees in public services should promote and exhibit public and private conduct in keeping with the appropriate behaviour and standards of excellence and integrity. They should support the juniors in the latter's efforts to resist wrong or illegal directives and in abiding by the Code of Ethics. At the same time, they should reward good work and punish any dereliction of duty or obligations, based on objective and transparent criteria.[14]

All the functions performed by the civil services must be oriented to rebuild the country, transform its economy, instill in people an ambition for higher standards of life and arouse in them the will and determination to work for such standards. The ambition of the greatest man of our times, Mahatma Gandhi, was to wipe out every tear from every eye. The work of the civil service will not be complete until this noble objective is achieved. In a broader sense, the Government, through its civil servants, should ensure happiness to the people, as embodied in the following in Sruti:

> "All human beings may enjoy happiness and bliss. All should be free from troubles. All should promote the welfare of others. No one should suffer from any visible cause which can be prevented by human efforts."

In a nutshell, we may keep the following commandments in mind:

- Timely, prompt service
- Minimum red tape and forms to fill
- Courteous Behaviour
- Minimum waiting time
- Good Ethical Values
- Minimum visits to multiple offices and Minimization of arbitrariness
- Prompt information on delays, waiting times, etc. Prompt information on status of application
- Prompt disposal of cases

These are standards, which service firms too expect their staff to maintain so that they have satisfied customers. It would not be wrong to predict that governments, which strive to attain higher and higher standards in the above expectations, will be rated higher by the public with consequent benefits to the government of the day. These small acts would enhance the prestige and dignity of Government.

Y.K. Alagh, in an Article, "Civil Service Perspectives" in *Platinum Jubilee Souvenir* (1926-2001) of Union Public Service Commission has observed:

Perspectives for the civil service need to be placed in the context of the broader changes taking place in the country. The kind of issue we are discussing, in fact, the issue of human resource development, is one of the few decision-making contexts, which require a genuinely long-term perspective. A civil servant, once inducted and trained, will have an effective working life of over three decades. This in turn implies that when a decision to hire a permanent civil servant is made, the characteristics being searched for and the attributes to be nurtured in terms of training or incentives decided, implicit judgements are being made of society's requirements of civil services support over a long-term frame. It is, therefore, useful to set out this perspective, to the extent possible in precise terms. It would be naive to assert that the future can be precisely spelt out. However, broad tendencies can be outlined in terms of an outline perspective with a greater degree of precision in the immediate and intermediate time horizon, but also setting borders within which developments may be expected to take place in the long-term.

O.P. Dwivedi, an eminent scholar, suggests the need of moral base for the Government to save the country from further degradation. To quote him, "No country is immune from the moral disarray which we have seen recently. Even in the People's Republic of China, which was hailed as a paragon of public virtue and morality by some cases of public service unethical activities and corruption have been reported. In many nations, a widespread sense of moral disarray exists, neither industrial nor Third World countries are exempt from this disarray. Everywhere, instances are on the rise detailing the collapse of standard and quality of service. This has contributed to the public cynicism; but at the same time, public is clamouring for a new set of bases for public morality and decent moral standards. Because, if we don't wish to be swallowed by the sea of amorality and self-centered hedonism, there will have to be some agreement (or consensus) about the behaviour of individuals, particularly those holding public offices."[15]

The vacuum created because of traditional and 'old-fashioned' values drawn from religious sources and based on common sense being discarded in favour of materialism and selfish individualism, clearly points to the need for a code of ethics. As a matter of fact, no specific standards were left sacred against which the conduct of public officials (as well as business people) could be measured. And as clergy and religious leaders were told to keep out of the state affairs, the protective layer of public morality was left exposed to the onslaught of corruption, dishonesty, sleaziness, deception and selfish individualism. That protective layer in the body politic is needed back. For no nation or a society, irrespective of its political and religious orientation, can live in a moral vacuum. There have to be some articles of faith (drawn from the societal culture, traditions, and religions) governing our lives, which must be resurrected and strengthened.

Moral values, in simple terms, are the values that tell us what is the right, proper and acceptable way of behaving. Moral values are indispensable for good governance. An efficient and technologically sound administrative machinery, unless it stands on high moral pedestal, does not serve the public, but it services a self-perpetuating and exploitative system.

Unfortunately, the Indian Government sector cannot boast of high moral standards. Superior courts have made highly critical comments on the conduct of bureaucrats, and the media is full of reports of high-handedness, corruption and other forms of inappropriate conduct of the bureaucrats. Honest and upright civil servants themselves are concerned about the low morality of the bureaucracy and have been voicing concern at various fora.

Second Administrative Reforms Commission suggested the following Code of Ethics: which should be included in the Code of Ethics for civil servants:

(i) *Integrity*: Civil servants should be guided solely by public interest in their official decision-making and not by any financial or other consideration either in respect of themselves, their families or their friends.

(ii) *Impartiality*: Civil servants in carrying out their official work, including functions like procurement, recruitment, delivery of services etc, should take decisions based on merit and free from any partisan consideration.

(iii) *Commitment to public service*: Civil servants should deliver services in a fair, effective, impartial and courteous manner.

(iv) *Open accountability*: Civil servants are accountable for their decisions and actions and should be willing to subject themselves to appropriate scrutiny for this purpose.

(v) *Devotion to duty*: Civil servants should maintain absolute and unstinting devotion towards their duties and responsibilities at all times.

(vi) *Exemplary behaviour*: Civil servants should treat all members of the public with respect and courtesy and at all times should behave in a manner that upholds the rich traditions of the civil services.

UNDERSTAND RELIGIOUS FOUNDATIONS OF ADMINISTRATIVE CULTURE (ETHICS)

We already know that one cannot legislate honesty, and good behaviour; these have to come from within. For, that, one has to look to our religions where such attributes are considered sacred. But, one does not acquire such attributes by thinking alone; these have to be drilled in the thinking process of the officials. But that could be possible if their moral consciousness is raised so that they are able to fight against the forces of corruption, favoritism, and malpractice. Otherwise, they will continue to be adrift in the sea of amoralism, of which the prevailing administrative culture has come to symbolise. It is to prevent further decay that they ought to think in terms of drawing on their priceless spiritual and cultural heritage. Thus, there is a need within the secular domain of the administrative culture to seek the spiritual guidance. Only by demonstrating high standards of personal integrity, fairness, justice, and by regarding their work as Dharma, public officials may be able to arrest those insidious forces which have penetrated the foundation as well as the structure of India's administration. Such is the requisite of a moral government.[16]

The Scriptures of many world religions contain pearls of wisdom about how one should behave in the public office; of what is expected of those who govern people. When scriptures were written, the world was ruled by kings; hence advice is rendered for the king and his servants. Hindu religion is no exception to this pattern; except that unlike some other religions, edicts and codes are not handed down by the rulers. The religious foundation of the duties and conduct of public officials as described in some scriptures of *the Hindu* religion is examined here. Let us begin by quoting Krishna in Gita:[17]

> One ought to understand what is duty
> and what is forbidden in the regulations laid down by the scriptures (Shastras).
> Knowing such rules and regulations, one
> should behave accordingly.
>
> (Gita, Chapter XVI, Verse 24)

> Lord Krishna further says:
> O Partha ! that understanding by
> which one knows what ought to be done
> and what ought not to be done,
> what is to be feared and what is not,
> what is obligatory and what is permitted,
> leads to the righteous path.

That righteous path in Hindu religion is called Dharma. How does one know the righteous path for specific functions or duties, Hindu scriptures (Shastras) provide guidelines. These guidelines or rules of Dharma have been prescribed by great many seers, each according to his or her wisdom.

SIGNIFICANCE OF PERSONNEL MANAGEMENT

The quality of the institutions run by Government would be dependent to a great extent upon the quality of the employees engaged in their operation. Personnel move the administrative machinery. To quote Mrs. Indira Gandhi: "If Government has to do more for the people, its employees must play a more dynamic and more creative role as the instrument for implementing government policies and programmes."[18] Thus, the progress of development would also depend upon the role of personnel in an organization.

Ferrel Heady says, "The importance of administration is almost universally recognized amongst commentators on development. Visually an effective bureaucracy is coupled with a vigorous maximizing elite as a prerequisite for progress."[19] Among the three components required for developmental tasks-men, money and material (M3),—it is more the men (or the human element) rather than any other factor, which determines the quantity and quality of the performance and output. After all, even the contribution of money and material to performance depends substantially upon their manipulation by the men in an organization. Walter R. Sharp has aptly remarked, "Good administration is a composite of effective organization, adequate material facilities and qualified personnel ...Even poorly devised machinery may be made to work if it is manned with well-trained, intelligent, imaginative and devoted staff. On the other hand, the best planned organization may produce unsatisfactory results if it is operated by mediocre or disgruntled people."[20]

Personnel constitute an integral part of the organization. It is with their requisite skills, aptitude, integrity and organizing capacity that they can build the image of their organizations as effective institutions in the nation-building process. Dr. Rajendra Prasad rightly remarked at the concluding session of the Constituent Assembly: "Whatever the Constitution may or may not provide, the welfare of the country will depend upon the way in which the country is administered. That will depend upon the men who administer it. It requires men of strong character, men of vision, men who will not sacrifice the interests of the country at large, for the sake of smaller groups and areas and who rise above the prejudices, which are born of these differences."[21]

There is a general tendency in the organizations to lay emphasis on materials and financial management to the utter neglect of the personnel. What are the consequences? It is observed that the process of development takes longer and sometimes even fails. Why? The main reason for this is that we are not attending to the administration of personnel earnestly and forget that they are the real agents of development and ultimately the beneficiaries of the process of development. If the personnel are properly selected and given the job of their choice, the organization is sure to produce excellent results, else they would become a liability on the organization.

Public morality has touched a new low. Accepted norms have collapsed all round. Appearances were once sought to be maintained, at least outwardly. Even the pretence is now shed. Conscience is no longer troubled in doing something wrong. There is no sense of shame in being found out. Lies are told brazenly and hawked as truth even in the country's highest temple of democracy. Good administration is provided by the virtue, public spirit, honor and sense of justice of its civil servants. Administration stinks when the courageous among its civil servants are banished from the mainstream because they dare to be honest and the profligates are rewarded because they flatter the power brokers only to betray the people.

Civil Service Reforms

Eleventh Five years Plans asserts that a serious effort will have to be made to protect honest civil servants. Protecting the public services from political interference and abuse of power on the part of politicians will involve: (i) enforcement of objective and transparent criteria and procedures for appointments and promotions; (ii) definite tenure for civil servants holding senior positions. The abridgement of tenure through transfers should be for objective reasons to be recorded in writing; (iii) Public Service Commissions/Administrative Tribunals should have a role in monitoring tenure, transfers and promotions; (iv) no civil servant should be suspended without the prior concurrence of the Public Service Commission; (v) rules of business in government should be strictly enforced, particularly the recording of reasoned orders in writing; and (vi) protection for civil servants who expose corrupt practices.

An important question today is developing a climate of probity in public life. Codes of ethics, therefore, need to be developed for civil servants and other public functionaries. A number of countries, like the UK and Spain, have developed their code of ethics. The ARC has made extensive recommendations on these issues.

Some of the values which a civil servant could be mandated, to follow are objectivity, integrity, neutrality, dedication to public service, transparency, exemplary conduct, accessibility and efficiency.

These values have also been studied in the context of developing an Act for the Civil Services. Some principles which they should observe in their functioning are:

- Allegiance to the various ideals—enshrined in the preamble to the Constitution;
- Apolitical functioning;
- Good governance for the betterment of the people to be the primary goal of civil service;
- Duty to act objectively and impartially;
- Accountability and transparency in decision-making;
- Maintenance of the highest ethical standards; and
- Ensuring economy and avoidance of wastage in expenditure.

Asst. Editor V. Eshwar Anand in his article, Civil Services: The blunted edge" in *the Sunday Tribune*, dated 25 Jan., 2009 observed that The Second Administrative Reforms Commission, in its tenth report under the title, Refurbishing of Personnel Administration, Scaling New Heights, has recommended wide-ranging reforms to make the administrative system responsive. A significant recommendation of the Commission is the need to weed out the deadwood after periodic review of the civil servants' performance. Few can differ with this view. Job security and time-scale promotions have made our bureaucrats too lethargic. The present system is such that even a non-performing bureaucrat automatically gets promoted to the next higher rank and pay oblivious of its deleterious impact on the administrative system and the quality of governance.

However, the training modules are too generic and do not inculcate greater domain knowledge in civil servants. The Commission wants suitable measures to be put in place for mandatory training of officers periodically at all levels—senior, middle and lower in addition to the induction stage—in view of the rapidly changing environment and the increasing demand for improved governance. The quality of training, too, should improve. It should seek to impart officers the functional knowledge, skills and aptitude necessary for performing their assigned jobs diligently. At the cutting edge level, the focus should be citizen-centric and service-oriented.

The need of the hour is not to protect corrupt, inefficient and non-performing officers but strive for an honest, effective and result-oriented administration at the Centre and in the States.

The fact that India is the second most populous country that survives on just 2.4% of world's landmass, creates its own population resource tension. Combined with the colonial legacy of systems that sub-served the exploitative objectives of the then colonial administration, has made the task of change much more difficult. Thus, despite the creation of an enabling framework for sustainable development, India continues to face enormous challenges in search of options for development that are environmentally sound and suitable to its specific social conditions through good governance.

Combating poverty and its eventual eradication has been the central theme of all the major policies and programmes of the Government of India since Independence: In the decades of the 90's, the focused intervention of the Government on various social development sectors bore fruit. At the beginning of the 90's, an estimated 320 million people, or 36% of the total population, were below the poverty line. However, by the end of the decade, India succeeded in bringing down the number of people living below the poverty line by 18.75% to 260 million. In absolute numbers, a huge 60 million people were brought above the poverty line in 10 year's time. Despite the impressive statistics, the nation is aware that the absolute number of people still living below the poverty line is huge. The proportions of poor people in rural and urban areas are 27% and 23.62% respectively.

The Government of India, both at the Centre and the states, share the concern for ensuring responsive, accountable, transparent, decentralized and people-friendly administration at all levels. There is, however, considerable frustration and dissatisfaction amongst the people, especially the weaker sections of society, about the apathy, irresponsiveness and lack of accountability of public servants, even as the expenditure on staff continues to increase. There is increasing anxiety about growing instances of corruption and criminalisation in public life and administration. The people, particularly the vulnerable groups, are also greatly concerned about the deterioration in the performance of agencies concerned with law and order and the investigation of offences and social welfare. Their faith in the registration of offences, their timely investigation and the delivery of prompt justice has been eroded .

L.M. Singhvi rightly stresses that a process of enlightened, well-informed and rational reform in public administration is thus necessitated, not merely for the sake of cosmetic window-dressing but for securing greater functional efficiency and recognizing and rewarding real merit, honesty and probity and taking effective measures to curtail, correct, discipline and punish the inept, the dishonest and the self-serving public-servants. Reforms have also to be aimed at accelerating the development for resolving the problems and redressing the grievances of the public in a just and fair manner and for creating a responsible and responsive system of public administration in the hope of maximizing public satisfaction."

Swami Ranganathananda, Former President of Swami Rama Krishana Mission has beautifully described this. To quote him:

> "It is in this context that the problems of administrative efficiency in our newly established democracy become urgent. That efficiency is to be measured by only one test, namely, its dynamic responsiveness to the national urges. This is achieved only by the administrative personnel, representing a cross-section of the national intelligentsia, getting trained in imaginative sympathy and national dedication. It is self-centredness and lack of concern for others that lead to corruption; and that evil is already afflicting man and society alike

in India. We are not required to forego all concern for ourselves and become ascetics. We are only called upon to put this concern for ourselves in the context of a larger concern for others. This changes the whole aspect of our life and work. This is called enlightened self-interest in political philosophy. It is self-interest, but with a touch of spiritual enlightenment, resulting in the recognition of mutuality, inter-dependence and the spirit of service, as the truth of all healthy social processes."

We are now experimenting on human welfare, human development, in our country. We had never done it before on the colossal scale that we are doing today. We had the necessary philosophy and ideas; but the implementation was arrested in later centuries. Therefore, the stress today should be on practical implementation, faster and still faster, and watching a new India, healthy and strong, rising on the horizon. This should be the great watchword of all administration in the Centre and the States, down to the Zilla Parishad and Gram Panchayat institutions, in our country.

Second Administrative Reforms has recommended the following to make Civil Service Efficient:

Setting Right the Asymmetry of Power

It was noted that there is an imbalance in the exercise of power in governance. Often systemic rigidities, needless complexities and over-centralization make public servants ineffective and helpless in achieving positive outcomes. On the other hand, negative power of abuse of authority through flagrant violation of law, petty tyranny and nuisance value is virtually unchecked. This situation is further aggravated by the asymmetry of power in our society. The 'privileged' government position gives even the lower government functionaries, enormous power over most of the citizens given the abject poverty, illiteracy and a lingering feudal culture. This needs to be set right in any effort towards public services reforms.

Insulating Civil Servants from undue Political Interference

In a democracy, the civil service has to be answerable to the elected government. There is criticism, however, that increasingly partisan intervention and cynicism are undermining the Rule of Law, distorting incentives and condoning corruption. This is adversely affecting the morale of public servants. The relationship between the political executive and the civil services needs to be transformed on the basis of mutual understanding, respect and recognition of each other's distinct roles and responsibilities.

Professionalisation with Stability of Tenure and Competition

There is need to recognize the complex challenges of modern administration in various spheres of activities. Meeting such challenges require domain expertise and long experience in the sectors concerned. There is also need to foster excellence in the public system. Existing procedures and practices do not adequately help in developing domain expertise, nor do they help in utilizing the available domain expertise.

Citizen-centric Administration

The fact that the functioning of the civil services has an impact on the quality of governance and thus on the well-being of the citizen and the welfare of the community as a whole is often forgotten. The perception of the civil services today is of a vast impersonal organization without commitment to human needs and values. It is necessary to redress the situation particularly in this era of participative democracy by making the governance apparatus an instrument of service to the people.

Accountability

There is a general feeling that existing mechanisms of accountability are inadequate. On the one hand, there are alibis for non-performance and on the other, competence and integrity are not adequately recognized or rewarded. Therefore, innovative and effective mechanisms need to be put in place to protect public money, guarantee intended outcomes and enforce accountability.

Outcome-orientation

Monitoring in government is primarily through measurement of expenditure against outlays and at best through defined outputs. Clearly, there is need to move towards measurement of outcomes. A change in this direction has already started with the initial outcome budgeting exercises. In order to engineer this shift to outcomes, major changes in attitudes, monitoring and evaluation systems, incentives and accountability measures are necessary.

Promoting Public Service Values and Ethics

Apart from the traditional civil service values of efficiency, integrity, accountability and patriotism, it is necessary for civil servants to inculcate and adopt ethical and moral values including probity in public life, respect for human rights and compassion for the downtrodden and commitment to their welfare.

CONCLUSION

The civil services in India have played a significant, indeed a critical, role in maintaining the integrity of the country and in bringing about major developments in post-independent . India. However, in recent times, the services have been facing a grave crisis of identity and role definition. People now believe that public services are meant to benefit government servants and politicians not the public. The emphasis here is on all public services, which subsume all technical, professional, law enforcement and administrative personnel. Though issues relating to efficiency and effectiveness of the administrative machinery have been discussed from time to time, the reforms initiated have only dealt with minor procedural changes, without really addressing the issue of improvement in the quality of services.[22] The inherent and external factors lmpinging on civil service can be handled through career development programmes. There is a need to induce positive values to create vitality and customer focus in bureaucracy. Introduction of efficiency models as in UK, would promote merit-based promotion scenario, change work ethics and eliminate redundant. activities and processes. Successive centralisation of resources and responsibility to lower levels of government would result in flexibility of services to meet local demands and increase local accountability. Suitable training interventions would ensure adequacy to skills to cope up with challenges both present and future. The organisation could thus become an asset, which strives for excellence of its members as well as the department.

The greatest efficiency and productivity will flow from the efforts of those who find satisfaction in their work and conditions of services, who sense an awareness of usefulness of their function, who feel encouraged to move ahead and to meet new challenges who perceive their working environment as one in which high standards of performance are maintained and rewarded and not one in which indolence and incompetence can be ignored or even protected and rewarded. Motivation can do miracle as a motivated worker can achieve more than an expert with no motivation. Managers must, therefore, devote considerable time and effort in planning for and achieving high levels of motivation and morale. In such a situation, we would achieve goal congruence, i.e., identity between the individual goals and the organisational goals.

SUGGESTION

- It has now been proved in country after country that an honest, professionally sound, contented bureaucracy is a critical element of any programme of economic resurgence.[23]
- The entire machinery of government has got to be reinvented. This is a mammoth task.[24]
- There has to be delayering in order to reduce levels and (help) level-jumping in order to reduce delays.[25]
- A shift has to be made towards accountability in the positive sense wherein a greater emphasis will be laid on achieving the end result rather than a mere adherence to rules and procedures.[26]
- In this country, the work of the government is shrouded in mystery and the Official Secrets Act gives furtiveness a legal sanction. What is required is a Right to Information Act, under which citizens have a right to find out exactly what is going on, at least immediately after a decision is taken. Transparency also means that all decisions are reasoned ones and contain an innate justifying logic.[27]
- Any premature transfer before completion of the prescribed tenure should be based on sound administrative grounds which should be spelt out in the transfer order itself. The transfer order must, therefore, contain detailed reasons for the transfer.[28]
- In order to ensure transparency in reporting and to serve the intended objective of providing a feedback to employees to improve their performance, partial openness may be desirable. For this purpose, the final grading of employees, as recorded in the confidential reports, should be conveyed to them.[29]
- Performance appraisal is another area of reform. If we develop better methods of appraisal, which are linked to actual performance in quantitative and qualitative terms, and link promotion and other incentives to such objective appraisal, we would be creating best motivation for higher productivity.[30]
- At the very least, the citizen is entitled to a good explanation or an apology. In many cases, he should have the right to demand redressal and compensation. This would also the coverage of all governmental services under the Consumer Protection Act. [31]
- Wherever discretionary powers have to exist, these should be exercised by a group of officials with disparate backgrounds. In such cases, there should always be a recorded decision giving full justification for the stand taken. These groups should never be headed by ministers.[32]

Certain selected extracts from Report of the Fifth Central Pay Commission, Government of India, New Delhi, January 1997, on "Public Services Management", i.e. " ... General Policy which Government ought to pursue in the area of Civil Service Reform[33] ... " which have been neglected are cited above. These recommendations on Public Services Management have, by and large, not even been considered either by the Central Government or any of the State Governments. Had these recommendations of the Fifth Central Pay Commission Report been also implemented by the Government of India and the State Governments, the face of bureaucracy in India would have changed.

Notes and References

1. C.D. Deshmukh, Management Administration, New Trends, Department of Personnel, Government of India, Abstract No. 17.
2. Merle Fainsod in Irving in Swerdlow (ed.) Development Administration: Concepts and problems, Syracuse, 1963, p. 23.
3. W.A. Lewis, *op. cit.*, p. 23.
4. H. Myint, *op. cit.*, p. 173.
5. Gerald, M. Meier, *op. cit.*, p. 599.
6. OP. Dwivedi, India is a Globalized World: Transforming Bureaucracy the well-being and Prosperity of all ", *IJPA*, Oct.-Dec., 2007, p. 717.
7. M. Kantz, Saul: Methodological notes on appraising administrative Capability for Development, UN Publication (Salés No. E-69-II-4.2) p. 8
8. Ernest Dale and L.D. Michelon, "Modern Management Techniques", Pengium Books, 1974, p. 9.
9. Asheton Committee Report on Training of Civil Servants, 1944, Quoted in Training of Civil Servants in the United Kingdon, Training Monograph, No. 12, Training Division, 1972, p. 1
10. UN: Standards and Techniques of Public Administrations, New York, 1951, pp. 20-54.
11. Habib Mohammad Zafarullah, "Perspective in Administrative Training", The Dacca University Studies, Vol. XXXVI, Part A, June 1977, p. 106.
12. OCED, Public Management Development: Update, 1992, Paris, OCED, 1992; and A Peter Aucoin, "Administrative Reform in Public Management: Paradigms, Principles, Paradoxes and Pendulums", *Governance*, Vol. 3, 1990, pp.115-37
13. O.P. Dwivedi, Development Administration: An Overview, in *IJPA*, July-Sept. 1997, pp. 321-22.
14. Action Plan for an Effective and Responsive Government Document prepared by Administrative Reforms, Public Grievance, Ministry of Personal Public Grievances, New Delhi, GOI.
15. O.P. Dwivedi, Administrative Theology, *IJPA*, July-Sept. 1990, pp. 418-19.
16. N.R. Ranganathan, A Charter of Ethics, Reading Material for Trainees (Some abstracts)
17. O.P. Dwivedi, Administrative Theology in *IJPA*, July-Sept., 1990, pp. 408-09.
18. Presidential Address by Mrs. Indian Gandhi delivered on October 22, 1971, at the Annual Meeting of IIPA, New Delhi.
19. Ferrel Heady, Public Administrative: A Comparative Perspective Second Edition, Revised and Expanded, New York, Marcel Dekker, Inc., N.Y. 1979, p. 270.
20. Walter R. Sharp: Field Administrative in the United Nations System, London, 1961, p. 19.
21. Quoted in H.R. Khanna: Making of India's Constitution, Lucknow, Eastern Book Company, 1981, p. vi.
22. India, Report of the Fifth Central Pay Commission, New Delhi, GOI, January, 1997, Vol. I, pp. 102-103 # 5.21
23. *Ibid.*, Vol. I, p. 127 # 9.1.
24. *Ibid.*, Vol. III, p. 2056, # 6.
25. *Ibid.*, Vol. I, p. 145, # 11.23.
26. *Ibid.*, Vol. III, p. 2056, # 7.
27. *Ibid.*, Vol. I, p. 217, # 25.9.
28. *Ibid.*, Vol. I, p. 185, 21.14.
29. *Ibid.*, Vol. I, p. 144, # 11.14.
30. *Ibid.*, Vol. I, p. 2111, # 24.12 (g).
31. *Ibid.*, Vol. I p. 152 # 13.9.
32. *Ibid.*, Vol. I, p. 83, # 2.2.
33. Ministry of Personnel, Public Grievances, New Delhi, (Document for an Effective and Responsive Government), 1997.

    Quoted in Suresh Chander Jain, Mobing Indian Bureaucracy Responsible, Accountable and Result-oriented, in *IJPA*, April-June, 2000, pp. 264-65.

CHAPTER

7

Public Policy: Formulation and Implementation

PART A

"It is hard enough to design public policies and programs that look good on paper. It is harder still to formulate them in words and slogans that resonate pleasingly in the ears of political leaders and the constituencies to which they are responsive. And it is excruciatingly hard to implement them in a way that pleases anyone at all, including the supposed beneficiaries or clients."

—*Eugene Bardach*

In the realm of public policy-making, modern public administration recognizes involvement of both political and administrative components. As Carl Friedrick observes:

Public policy, to put it flatly, is a continuous process, the formation of which is inseparable from its execution. Politics and administration play a continuous role in both formation and execution though there is a probably more politics in the formation of policy, and more administration in the execution of it. Insofar as particular individuals or groups are gaining or losing power or control in a given area, there is politics; insofar as officials act or propose action in the name of public interest, there is administration.[1]

The first and foremost essential ingredient of the process of development is to formulate policy in all areas, like industrial policy, monetary policy, food policy, Health Policy, Education Policy, etc. Policy formulation is both a science and an art and if rightly used, can help us in making most of the problems solved.

Policies may be thought of as the main system, which provides the framework for the accomplishment of intended objectives. Formulation of policies involves making explicit the various assumptions regarding the basic premises, needs and the priorities and allocating the

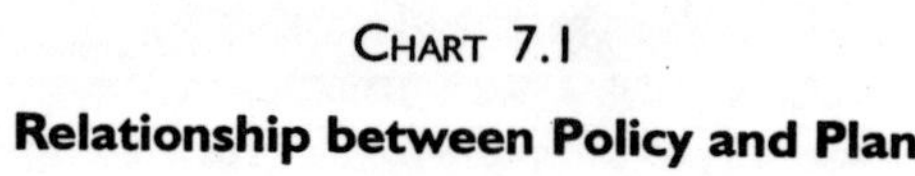

CHART 7.1

Relationship between Policy and Plan

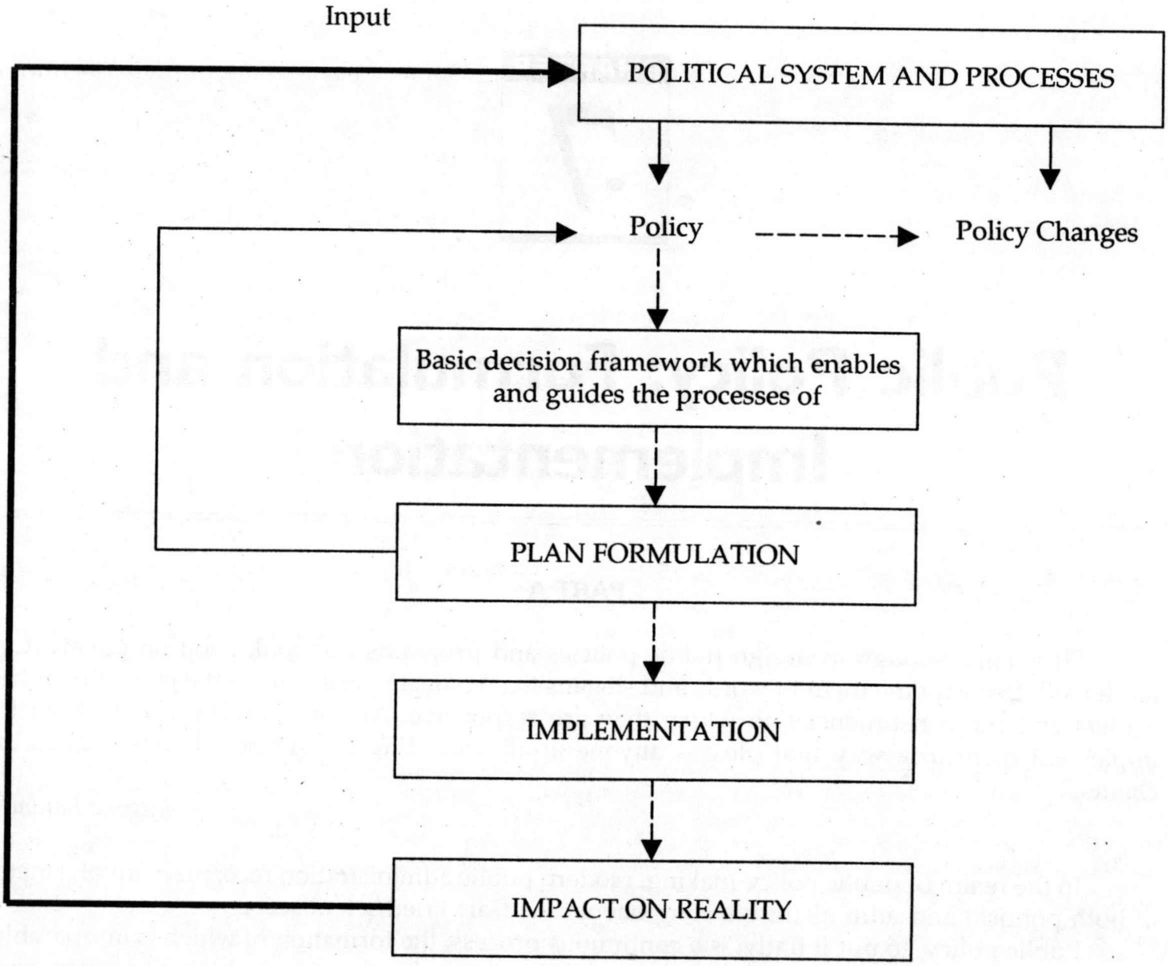

Source: *WHO Chronics*, Vol. 31, No. 11.

finances accordingly. Besides, policies are intended to spell out the parameters in the context of which organization's decisions are to be made. Policy gives a concrete shape to the political and social objectives, which the government lays down in the form of laws, rules, regulations, etc. Davis states:

"A policy is basically a statement either expressed or implied of those principles and rules that are set-up by executive leadership as guides and constraints for the organization's thought and action. Its principal purpose is to enable executive leadership to relate properly the organization's work to its objectives."

Policies may be looked upon as general guides to action. The politics set the overall boundaries for action by individuals or groups in an organisational setting and indicate the framework within which executives may take decisions for the performance of organisational action. According to Ishwar Dayal: "Policy prescribes the aims, the objectives, the targets that would be used to achieve the objectives. Operationally, the policy statement, in this sense, must specify the expected results, the measures for achieving them and mechanism or method with which the results are expected to be achieved .... Policy formulation refers to that aspect of administration which is concerned with defining the objective and determining the choice of action."[2]

The public policies may be written or unwritten, explicit or implicit. Important policies of the government are often clearly expressed in a written form. Generally Public policies are formally adopted by the government authorities. However, there are public policies embodied only in a set of practices, conventions and precedents. According to Koontz and O'Donnell, written policy is preferable, as:

"It builds on proved decisions of the past conserving executive energy for new decisions: it creates an atmosphere in which individual actions may be taken with confidence; it speeds administration by reducing repetition to routine; it supports consistency of endeavour across a large group through the years; it stabilizes the enterprise; it frees the top management so that more creative considerations can be given to the problem of today and the new programme of tomorrow."

Public policy management in India is in the stage of infancy. The ongoing process of the integration of the Indian society is providing a rigour to the art and science of public policy management in India.[3] A sound public policy management is expected to contribute to both the country's political stability and its efforts to bring about the much desired socio-economic transformation.[4]

RELATIONSHIPS BETWEEN POLICY-MAKING AND PLANNING

Planning and policy-making are interrelated. Policy determines the principle for action and planning provides the instrument for the application of policy and review. Policy decisions are needed in the planning process and in defining its goals and limitations (Chart 7.1). Koontz and O'Donnell have rightly said that "the more strategies and policies are carefully developed and dearly understood, the more consistent and effective will be the framework of plans." Therefore, planners who ignore policy only jeopardize the good results of their endeavour. On the other hand, planning process has various possible feedback effects on policy. For example:

(a) It requires explicit policy statements, thus bringing certain subjects to the political arena,
(b) It should reflect the rationale of the policies, show how they can be implemented, and indicate their financial and other implications,
(c) It provides the policy-makers with instruments for dialogue-co-ordination, mobilization of resources; and continuity of action, and
(d) Its impact on the national situation and influence future policy-making.[5]

RELATIONSHIP BETWEEN POLICY-MAKING AND DECISION-MAKING

Decision-making is an important constituent of the process of policy-making and planning as the decisions weave individual choices into a web of relationships, which constitute the policy.

Policies delimit an area within which a decision is to be made and assure that the decision will be consistent with and contribute to the objectives. Policies may be regarded as a means of encouraging discretion and initiative but within limits. Policies are general statements or understandings which guide or channel thinking and action in decision-making. According to Herbert A. Simon, decision-making comprises of three principal phases: finding occasions for making a decision, finding possible courses of action; and choosing among courses of action. The first phase has been described as intelligence activity, the second phase as design activity, and the third phase as choice activity. This analysis of the process of decision-making has special reference for the policy-makers and planners in the government as they are to ensure that the policies based on such decisions must not only be correct and just; the same must also appear to be correct and just to the people at large.

PARAMETERS OF POLICY-MAKING

Policy-making must be done to suit the legal, social, economic and political framework prevailing in a country. Policy-making must be in consonance with the constitutional system and structure of the government and administrative apparatus. Besides, policy-making to be effective must be broadly acceptable to the people as we know that ultimate sovereignty rests with the people. Effective policy formulation can help organizations to respond to and react to the changes in the environment-establish environment linkages. Linkages are points of interactions with the environment. These can be classified into four categories-enabling, functional, normative and diffused linkages. Enabling linkages ensure and protect the organisational authority to operate its access to resource and its power to achieve results. Since political constraints are neither permanent nor inseparable, there is urgency in adopting policies designed to optimize the positive contributions of political support as well as minimize and mitigate the harmful effects of partisan interferences. The job of functional linkages is to link the policies with the task environment, i.e., help in achieving cooperation and coordination among allied agencies. Diffused linkages ensure that the policies must reach the beneficiaries through mass media and personal contact. The art of developing common understanding among people through policies is vital to bring about changes of attitudes and behaviour through users' participation. Normative linkages attempt to fit the policies into the value system. Besides, the policies must try to change the norms with the cooperation of the people to induce socio-economic changes. (Chart 7.2)

According to Christopher Pollit and others, the following are essential characteristics of Public Policy:

1. Policies are process of decision-making and activity. They customarily involve a series of decisions taken over an extended period of time—an exercise of power and rationality.
2. The process of decision-making takes place mainly though not exclusively, within a framework of prescribed organisational roles. In the case of public policy, these roles are those constituting a series of formal institutions with special legal characteristics. They are the institutions of the state.
3. Policies commonly involve exchanges of information resources, discussions, bargaining, etc., without and within the state agencies, with a variety of 'external' interest groups. The content, closeness and timing of these interactions is an important subject for empirical investigation.

CHART 7.2

Model of the Political System

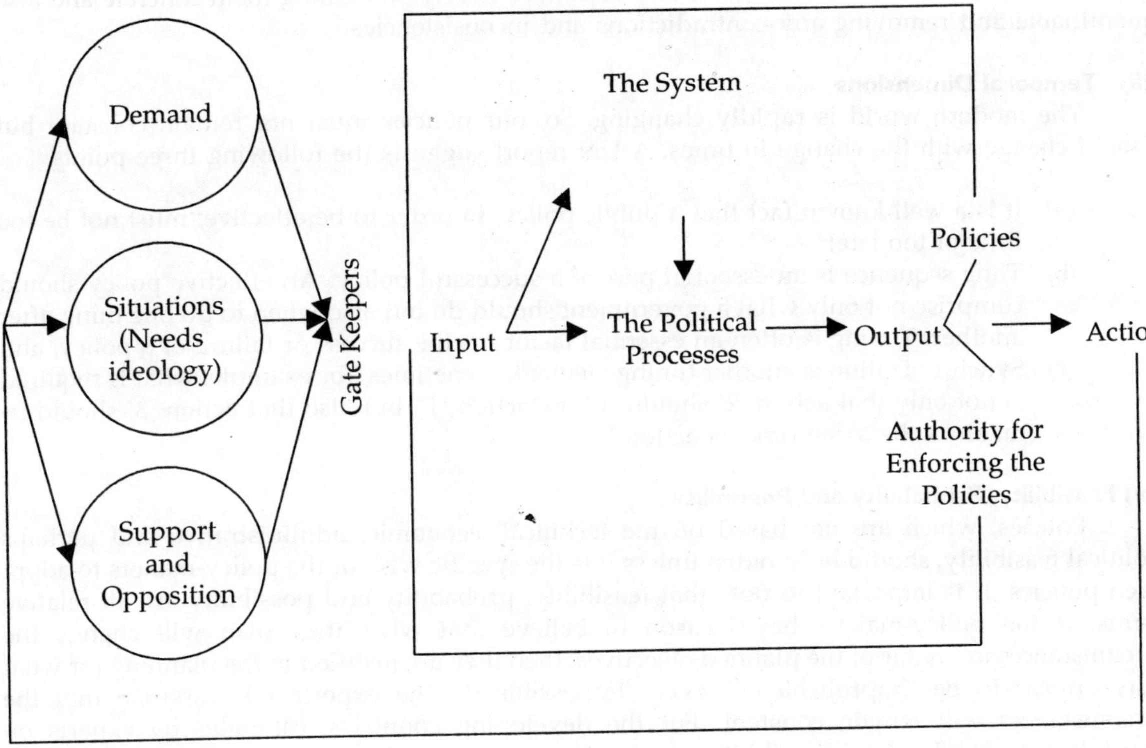

Source: WHO 77674.

4. Not all decisions are part of 'Policy' but only those which are of a strategic (in the military sense) or guideline nature.
5. Policy is directed at the increasing probability of occurrence of desired stakes of the world in the future.
6. The state institutions, which claim responsibility for public policies, almost invariably legitimatize their activities by claiming that their policies are in general public interest rather than favouring any group, section or individual.

SUGGESTIONS TO IMPROVE POLICY-MAKING

If order to frame policies to achieve productivity, efficiency, profitability effectiveness, and relevance, it is necessary to keep the following important facts in mind.

(i) Policies should be made in Consonance with the Objectives

By goal or objective is meant the end towards which action is directed. Since a policy is a guidance for action, it is reasonable to expect that a policy indicates the direction towards which action is guided, either explicitly or implicitly. For this reason, students of policy sciences often define public policies as a programme of goals and objectives

(ii) Absence of Contradictions and Inconsistencies

It is necessary for public administrators to help in making policies purposeful and goal-oriented and to assist in defining goals and objectives clearly, in making them concrete and also quantifiable and removing any contradictions and inconsistencies.

(iii) Temporal Dimensions

The modern world is rapidly changing. So, our policies must not remain constant but should change with the change in times. A UN report suggests the following three points:

(a) It is a well known fact that a public policy, in order to be effective, must not be too little or too late;
(b) Time sequence is an essential part of a successful policy. An effective policy should comprise not only what a government should do but also when to do one thing after another. Timing is often an essential factor for the success or failure of a policy; and
(c) Synchronization is another timing element. Sometimes, for example, what is required is not only that action '2' should follow action '1', but also that action '3' should be taken at the same time as action '1'.[6]

(iv) Feasibility, Probability and Possibility

Policies, which are not based on the technical, economic, administrative and perhaps political feasibility, should be avoided unless it is the specific wish of the policy-makers to adopt such policies. It is important to note that feasibility, probability and possibility are all relative terms. If the policy-makers have reason to believe that what they plan will change the circumstances in favour of the planned objectives, then they are justified in the planning for what may appear to be 'Improbable' or even 'Impossible' to the experts who assume that the circumstances will remain constant. For the developing countries, estimates by experts on feasibility, probability, and possibility are often poorly informed guess work, in part owing to a lack of sufficient or decisive evidence and in part owing to a high degree of uncertainty. A United Nations document warning against 'paper planning' and blind commitments to the 'blatantly impossible states' that:

> "From the previous extremes of seeking the impossible, the planners may go for in emphasizing the possible that they will think mainly of short-run feasibility. In this effort, they will often be encouraged by economists who have become accustomed to fighting utopia, with myopia, that is with 'hard nosed' calculations of small benefits that might be obtained quickly. The result can easily be that instead of planning for the impossible, they will focus upon most possible and feasible of all, namely, the inevitable. This is the fallacy of epiphenomenal planning. Here, the main advantage is that the planners can take credit for any major progress that might have taken place."[7]

(v) Relevant Forecasts and Projections

Forecasting and projection are important for public policy-making mainly for two reasons. First, as just indicated, policy is a guidance for action that lies necessarily in the future, therefore, no rational approach to policy-making is possible without some basis for making assumptions about the future. Forecasting and projection can assist policy-makers, in this respect. Secondly, public policies should be used, if at all possible, to avoid crisis rather than to meet crisis situations. Unless a government is capable of making useful forecasts and projections, it is not in a position to avoid crisis and may have to devote most of its resources to crisis management. At the same time, a government which is under constant pressure from immediate crisis may not be able to devote its attention and resources to the future in order to prevent the recurrence of crisis. This is a vicious circle which a government should break, and it can succeed in doing so only by assigning suitable priority to forecasting the future.

(vi) Appropriate Administrative Machinery

Within the central policy cluster, there should also be special arrangement for ensuring that appropriate administrative machinery is established for:

(a) Policy and plan implementation,
(b) Reporting and feedback,
(c) Evaluation and control, and
(d) The adjustment and revision of policies, plans and programmes.

This would ensure effective relationship between policy formulation and policy implementation.[8]

(vii) Understanding the Implications of Policy

Policies must be explained, interpreted and taught to all members of the organization. What people do not understand, they cannot use correctly and are likely to distrust. Therefore, there is a need to explain it to all persons to whom it applies.

(viii) Environmental Considerations

Policy is based on actual information or factual data which can be collected from a number of sources by applying different methods. But, before the data can be changed into a policy, many factors have to be taken into consideration, e.g. policies must be made in accordance with the provisions of the constitution and the laws enacted by the legislature; these must also be made in accordance with the social, political, cultural, economic and ethical environment prevailing in the country; these must also be linked with the agencies interested in the same policy to have maximum utility and effectiveness; these must also be made in accordance with the opinion of the public, otherwise they (the people) would not cooperate with the government in their execution.

POLICY-MAKING IN NEW MILLENNIUM

Policy-making is getting complicated, as the number of variables impinging on Policy-making is becoming increasingly complex. This can be attributed to an increase in the magnitude and direction of various impinging factors. Besides, globalisation, privatization and competitiveness have made policy-making more difficult. How can we cope with this complex situation? How can we make a reliable policy? The answer is to make use of information technology the way the business is being done by organisations.

Modern technology has the potentiality to make available to the policy-makers the knowledge in a comprehensive and intelligent manner. With the proliferation of information technology and electronic access to information, the availability and accessibility of information has undergone profound change. E-mail, inter-net, world wide web (www) and easy access to remote data base, we now have new opportunities to find information at a press of the computer key. The administrators can make use of this rich data in policy formulation.

While modern technology opens the doors, it does not compel us to enter. We have to use various technologies, keeping in view availability, accessibility, acceptability, validity, quality, specificity and sensitivity. There is a lot of potentiality in new technology for policy-makers.

Let us illustrate, the policy-making in health. A new discipline "Health Telematics" has emerged based on modern information technology.

Dr. Prakrom Vuthipongse, Permanent Secretary, Ministry of Public Health, Thailand in the Inter-country Workshop on Tele Medicine for Health Development in 21st century from 30th March-3 April 1998 at Bangkok said that as a decision-maker he was aware of the advancement in today's technology, especially in its applications which will help to bring better quality of health care to people in remote and rural areas in cost effective manner. He also said that the initiation of Tele Medicine in the Ministry of Public Health has emerged from the fact that, in remote and rural areas, there has been mal-distribution of medical specialties, resulting in poor health care services. He expected the workshop to come up with fruitful recommendations on regional and national plans of action as well as on inter-country cooperation. Health Telematics is defined as a composite term for health-related activities, services and systems carried out over a distance by means of information and communications technologies for the purpose of global health promotion, disease control and health care, as well as education, management and research for health.

The policies for developing the Health Telematics infrastructure can be categorized as under:

(a) *Technological policies*: Deal with the definition of technological standards for hardware, software, management and communications.
(b) *Resources policies*: Address the issues of human and material resources.
(c) *Financial policies*: Identify the sources of finance.

Health Telematics raises certain ethical issues, such as the acceptability of transmitting personal information across cultural boundaries; young doctors setting professionally affected, and the confidentiality of the relationship between the patient and the treating doctor. Full cooperation of the medical and paramedical staff involved, as well as patients is essential. Even in the most advanced form, Health Telematics might not provide a blanket solution for each situation. There would be cases where human intervention is needed. It also raises concern on widening the gap between the poor and the privileged.

The following services are likely to be provided through the Tele Medicine system:

- Medical consultation
- Tele radiology
- Tele cardiology
- Tele pathology
- Distance learning
- Administrative meetings
- Voice and data network
- Internet
- Local call system among the project sites.

Machiavelli said in a famous remark—"There is nothing more difficult to take in hand, more perilous to conduct, more uncertain in its success than to take the lead in the introduction of a new order of things."

However, we must keep in mind the limitations of modern technology. Modern technology can provide us tool—but we must have the expertise to make use of these tools. Human mind still remains the super computer to control all these tools. R.P. Sapru rightly stresses that processing of information has two components-one that involves merely the communications of verbal, visual or printed facts, and the second that involves evaluation of the information. Distortions can be introduced at one or both these stages. The quality of information needs to be judged on the basis of the degree of distortions introduced at different stages. In the case of the human mind, such a system of quality control has proved elusive so far even though the need is obvious and pressing. Policy-making is a continues process and not a one time activity.[9]

Beneath the drafting of all constitutions is the. awareness. that change is the law of nature, and as in any other sphere of life, so in the affairs of the state, things cannot remain stationary. It is not given to anyone, however gifted he may be, to foresee the shape of things as they will be after some years, much less after some decades. No constitutional expert, no political philosopher, no man in active public life can pierce through the visage of time and lift the veil of the future to know beforehand the problems which are going to beset the nation and prescribe solution of those problems.[10]

Prof. R.B. Jain feels that Perhaps it would be worthwhile for universities and professional institutions around the country to organise special seminars and conferences in which ministers, legislators, civil servants and scholars could get get-together to discuss current policy and administrative problems. Imparting knowledge to public policy-making should be made an essential part of such exercises. One cannot help noting that despite the growth of centres of advanced studies in different disciplines, there are hardly any institutions devoted to public policy research and study like the Centre for Policy Research and the Institute of Defence Analysis, New Delhi. And whatever knowledge is imparted in professional institutions is woeful inadequate. This discipline has yet to find its place in university curriculae. Besides strengthening existing institutions, additional centres to provide policy knowledge to the civil servants and conduct research may have to be established to meet growing needs.

It would also be necessary to instal a system of constant evaluation and analysis of public policies, which would require continuous feedback from the actors in the field to those at headquarters, and *vice versa.* Above all, it would be of crucial importance to build an effective information system in each government and public organisation to provide the basic data and infrastructure for policy development and implementation. Unfortunately, at this juncture, there is little evidence to indicate that the administrative system is moving from its position of *ad hocism* to maturity, stability and dynamism in the crucial areas of public policy processes.[11]

PART B

POLICY IMPLEMENTATION

Policy implementation would be more crucial than formulation of policy, as the outcome of policy would be dependent purely on its effective implementation. The modern advancement of information technology has been of a great help to policy-makers, but the art and science of policy implementation has not really progressed. We have formulated excellent education policy, health policy, population policy, industrial policy, but the desired outcome of these policies is nowhere near expectation. Why? Because we are not attending seriously to the meticulous designing of policy implementation contours. An added factor is the human factor upon whose will and determination would depend the outcome of policy implementation. Renis Likert has beautifully brought forth this point. To quote him:

> "The performance and output of any enterprise depend entirely upon the quality of the human organization and its capacity to function as a tightly knit, highly motivated, technically competent entity, i.e., as a highly effective interaction-influence system. High productivity, high quality products, high earnings, and successful use of research and development are not accomplished by impersonal equipment or computers. These goals are achieved by human beings. Successful of organizations are those making the best use of competent personnel to perform efficiently all the tasks required by the enterprise."[12]

Richard Elmore has identified four distinct institutional models, which describe alternative approaches of implementation process:

- The "System management model" views implementation as an ordered and goal directed activity;
- The "bureaucratic process model" views implementation as a mere routine process of continuing direction;
- The "organisational development model" views implementation as participatory process in which implementers shape policies and claim them as their own; and
- The "conflicting and bargaining model" views implementation as a conflict and bargaining process. This model is based on the principle of circularity.[13]

Policy should not remain only on the paper, without yielding any results, or subjected to inappropriate implementation. What can be done to ensure that policy implementation is as per the requirements of policy decisions? How can we check this perpetual tendency of neglecting implementation and not bothering about policy issues. The following suggestions would go a long way in making policy implementation a success.

1. Symphony between Policy Formulation and Policy Implementation: Create Mutual Appreciation and Understanding

At present, persons engaged in policy formulation remain in ivory towers, and consider themselves as a highly superior lot. They never wish to be associated with the ground reality, resulting in the failure of the policy at the implementation level. There is a need for joint efforts of persons engaged in policy formulation as well as policy implementation. To quote S.N. Sadasivan:

> "Policy as a rule is the product of extensive study and intensive analysis of available data and information and therefore, it is apparently believed to be a superior function confined to the top echelons of administration. The execution of policy demands at times, greater imagination, resourcefulness, alertness, perseverance, diligence and sagacity than at the formulation stage. By force of tradition and administrative practice, the making of policy however, continues to remain in a separate province and the skill and knowledge necessary for it are still believed to be a distinct or superior quality."[14]

Thus, in order to reduce/prevent dichotomy between policy-making and implement, a participatory model of leadership should be adopted.

2. Policy Implementation Guided by Extraneous Considerations and Pressures: Designing Appropriate Technology

At times, the policy implementation is carried out as per the wishes of funding agencies like world bank, USAID, etc., who are not aware of the local administrative and cultural ethos. The consultants employed by them are also urban-based, whereas most projects are implemented in the rural areas. Thus inherent issues regarding administrative bottlenecks, strengthening of delivery system, etc. are not addressed, decreasing the effectiveness of policy implementation. For example, World Bank has financed a project of Rs. 3000 crores for six states of India to improve their Secondary Health Care system. The implementation of the policy leaves much to be desired as huge amount is being spent on overheads and non-essential items. Hence, the desired results of implementation are not forthcoming. The need of the hour is therefore adaptation of new technology/techniques and its adaptation to local needs rather than direct emulation/replication.

3. Unsuitable Organisational Structure: Analyse Dynamic Relationships between Authority and Responsibility

Policies are implemented through the administrative machinery, which may not be suitable or equipped for the purpose. For example, Education Policy is to be implemented through University Grants Commission (UGC), for higher Education. However, UGC has no statutory control over the Universities. So far, UGC has not been able to ensure 180 working days and the presence of teachers for 40 hours a week, even after 22 years of the enactment of Education Policy. Therefore, we must select the right Organisation for policy-making and equip it with necessary authority to discharge its functions.

Besides, the structure of the organization plays an important role in determining as to how the policy will be carried out. It could be an important asset as well as a potential liability. On one hand it may provide continuity and stability to the implementation process and on the other, it can produce rigidities, inertia and distortions in realizing the policy goals.

4. Bias in Favour of Influential People: Ensure Equitable Benefits

Henry W. Ehrmann rightly observes that the larger the policy-making function of the bureaucracy, the more intensely the groups turn to it for protection.[15]

Similarly Nicos P. Mouzelis observes that indeed individuals and groups have differential control over decision and policy-making as well as differential access to organisational resources. The distribution of control over resources, the behaviour of others and formation of interest groups-competing with each other in their attempt to preserve or change in their favour the above distribution, are crucial clues for understanding organisational reality.[16] The attempt should be made to reduce power distance by decentralizing the authority and responsibility. The governmental functionaries are closer to those who can establish direct rapport with the decision-makers than to those who are poor, ignorant and remotely situated. The social distance and social linkage between the government and the governed in rural India is determined by caste and class status of the governed. The blood and flesh of governmental accountability is provided by social status of the clients of public agencies. Pai Panandiker reports, "a large number of small cultivators in sample in both the districts felt that the first preference of the visiting officials in meeting the people was for big cultivators and the second preference for local leaders and influential persons."

There is a need to devise appropriate mechanisms to empower the poor so that they can become the real beneficiaries of public policy. The wide gap between the rich and poor needs to be seriously plugged through decentralized governance.

5. Lack of Accountability: Fix Responsibility

To quote Royal Commission on Financial Management—"Accountability relies on a system of connecting links—a two-way circuit involving a flow of information that is relevant and timely, not only for managers but for those who must scrutinize the decisions and deeds of managers. We gauge its presence when we observe that a certain 'discipline' has been imposed from those who are assigned roles and duties in the system. Thus, the likelihood that agreed goals and objectives will be attained, is enhanced."[17]

However, due to a variety of reasons like hierarchical stratification of organizations, delays in decision-making, emphasis on procedure rather than end result conflicting demands of various pressure groups, etc., the accountability in implementation is not ensured. The organizations need to fix responsibility in advance and fix time frames for the managers in charge for ensuring timely and successful implementation of policies.

6. Redundancy of Implementing Agencies: Revitalise and Restructure Organisations

A large number of institutions created for implementation of various policy measures are either non-functional or defunct, yet incur loss on account of infrastructure maintenance and salary of personnel working there. Thus, the intended objectives of the policy remain unfulfilled. Most Public sector undertakings, cooperative institutions and welfare corporations, etc. fall in this category. The government needs to take a hard look at these institutions and force them to adopt innovative approaches.

7. Complexity and Jargon in Policy-making: Demstify and Simplify

Most often, policy-makers are experts in the theoretical and conceptual aspects of the subject dealt with. They tend to idealise the policy and set-up lofty objectives, which are difficult to attain. The policy statements are often fraught with technical jargons and complex conceptualization without elaboration of its presumptions, thus making its comprehension difficult for the implementers.

8. Multiplicity of Implementing Agencies: Ensure Coordination Mechanism

The goals envisaged in the policy decisions may have to be executed through more than one agency, e.g. removal of poverty in rural and urban areas are entrusted to separate implementing agencies. This causes duplication of efforts/resources and sometimes conflicts and contradictions in approach. Hence, the policy decision should detail the set of processes required to execute the policy so that synergies are exploited through appropriate selection of agencies for implementation.

In the realm of public policy-making, modern public administration recognizes involvement of both political and administrative components. As Carl Friedrick observes:

Public Policy, to put it flatly, is a continuous process, the formation of which is inseparable from its execution. Politics and administration play a continuous role in both formation and execution• though there is probably more politics in the formation of policy, and more administration in the execution of it. Insofar as particular individuals or groups are gaining or losing power or control in a given area, there is politics; insofar as officials act or proposes action in the name of public interest, there is administration.

Perhaps it would be worthwhile for universities and professional institutions around the country to organise special seminars and conferences in which ministers, legislators, civil servants and scholars could get get-together to discuss current policy and administrative problems. Imparting knowledge to public policy-making should be made an essential part of such exercises. One cannot help noting that despite the growth of centres of advanced studies in different disciplines, there are hardly any institutions devoted to public policy research and study like the Centre for Policy Research and the Institute of Defence Analysis, New Delhi. And whatever knowledge is imparted in professional institutions is woefully inadequate. This discipline has yet to find its place in university curriculae. Besides strengthening existing institutions, additional centres to provide policy knowledge to the civil servants and conduct research may have to be established to meet growing needs.

It would also be necessary to instal a system of constant evaluation and analysis of public policies, which would require continuous feedback from the actors in the field to those at headquarters, and *vice versa*. Above all, it would be of crucial importance to build an effective information system in each government and public organisation to provide the basic data and infrastructure for policy development and implementation. Unfortunately, at this juncture, there is little evidence to indicate that the administrative system is moving from its position of ad hocism to maturity, stability and dynamism in the crucial areas of public policy processes.[18]

CONCLUSION

It is high time that the Union and State Governments should attend seriously to the process and mechanism of implementation, so that development does not merely remain on paper and instead be visible through a perceptible change in the standard of living of the people, especially the disadvantaged sections of the society.

While examining policy implementation in the public sector, we have seen that existence of an implementation gap between policy formulation and implementation causes unsuccessful implementation of policy.

We have also seen availability of different types of approaches to policy implementation from which public sector can choose. The ultimate choice, however, should not be hasty emulation of other successful models. An intelligent and informed choice surely depends on suitability of such an approach to the unique circumstances, needs and objectives of each public sector enterprise. Such an approach, however, should aim at substantially improving the implementation of policy decisions, especially in the areas of timing, cost, acceptance of risk, cost effectiveness of information, etc. Such improvements may be forthcoming if implementation is considered early in the policy-making process rather than after the exercise of choice.[19]

NOTES AND REFERENCES

1. Carl J. Friedrich, "Public Policy and the Nature of Administrative Responsibility" in Carl J. Friedrich and E.S. Mason (eds.) Public Policy, Cambridge, Mass, Harvard University Press, 1940, reproduced in Françis E. Rourke (ed) Bureaucratic Power in National Politics, Baston, Little Brown, p. 318.
2. Ishwar Dayal, Organization for Public Policy in Government. A paper submitted to the Seventeenth Conference of the Indian Institute of Public Administration, Oct. 30, 1973.
3. Q.U. Khan, "A Model of Public Policy Implementation Process", *Indian Journal of Public Administration*, Vol. 33, No. 1, January-March 1987, pp. 31-39.
4. K.D. Madan, K. Dinesh, Ashok Pradhan and C. Chandra Sekharan, Policy-making in Government, New Delhi, Publication Division, 1982, pp. 1-11.

5. WHO, *WHO Chronicle*, November 1977, pp. 441-48.
6. Quoted in Waldo, Ideas and Issues in Public Administration, p. 71.
7. UN, the Administration of Economic Development Planning, Principles and Fallacies (ST/TAD/M/32), Paras 44 and 45.
8. UN, Administration of National Development Planning: Report of a meeting experts (5T/TAD/M/27).
9. R.P. Sapru, Coping with an Information overload, *The Daily Tribune*, 27th March, 2000.
10. Justice, H.R. Khanna, Sardar Patel Memorial Lecture, 1977.
11. R.B. Jain., Fifty Years, p. 101.
12. Renis Likert, The Human Organisation: Its Management and Values, New York, Mc-Graw Hill, 1967, International Student Edition, Kogakusha Company, Tokyo, p. 134.
13. Q.N. Khan, A Model of Public Policy Implementation Process, in *IJPA*, Jan.-March, 1987, p. 354.
14. S.N. Sadasivan, Bynamics of Public Policy in *IJPA*, Oct.-Dec. 1985, p. 1204.
15. Henry, W. Ehrmann, "French Bureaucracy and Organised Interests" in Robert T. Golembiewski, *et. al.* (eds.) Public Administration: Readings in Institutions, Processes, Behaviour, Chicago, Ran Mcnally, 1966, p. 124.
16. Micos, P. Mouzells, Organisation and Bureaucracy: An Analysis of Modern Theories, London, Routledge and Kegan Paul, 1967, p. 158.
17. In March, 1979, Royal Commission on Financial Management an Accountability (also known as Lambert Commission) submitted its final report to Government of Canada. This important report, published by Ministry of Supply and Services, Government of Canada, Ottawa, made several important recommendations, and observations on the subject. However, keeping in view the interest our readers may have in these recommendations, we are publishing here the summary of recommendations along with the introduction part of the report.
18. Carl J. Friedrich, "Public Policy and the Nature of Administrative Responsibility", in Carl J. Friedrich and E.S. Mason (ed.), Public Policy, Cambridge, Mass., Harvard University Press, 1940, reproduced in Francis E. Rourke (ed.) Bureaucratic Power in National Politics, Boston, Little Brown, p. 318.
19. Joseph Kasongo, Policy Implementation in Public Sector in *IJPA*, January to March, 1999, p. 5.

CHAPTER

8

Organisation for Development Planning at Centre, State and District Level

The subject of planning is of crucial importance in Public Administration. The reason is very simple: one must plan one's act, and then act one's plan. Planning means drawing up of a plan for future course of action. To plan means to formulate a programme of action. Planning is an inherent part of individual and of co-operative or collective endeavour. Every aspect of governmental action is to be planned-objectives, policies, organisation, finances, work methods, incentive system and public relations. In the words of Pfiffner, it is "a rational process characteristic of all human behaviour."[1] Planning is of particular significance to an under-developed country where a lot has to be achieved with limited resources and within a restricted time. Thus, in our country and, in all other countries with developing economies, planning is perhaps the best way to pull up the economy to a self-sustaining and self-generating stage. It has been rightly said that "all organisations must plan if they are to achieve their ends."[2]

MEANING

"To plan is to produce a scheme for future action, to bring about specified results, at specified cost, in a specified period of time. It is a deliberate attempt to influence, exploit, bring about; and control the nature, direction, extent, speed and effects of change. It may even attempt deliberately to create change. It is a carefully controlled and co-ordinated activity."

Terry defines: "planning is the selecting and relating of facts and the making and using assumptions regarding the future in the visualisation and formulation of proposed activities believed necessary to achieve the desired results."

According to Peter Drucker, "Planning is the continuous process of making present knowledge of their futurity, organising systematically the efforts needed to carry out these decisions, and measuring the results of these decisions against the expectation. through organized, systematic feedback."[3] Simon, Smithburg and Thompson define it as "that activity that concerns itself with proposals for the future, with the evaluation of alternative proposals, and with the methods by which these proposals may be achieved."[4] In short, the planning is the process of organizing efforts for the achievement of defined objectives and goals.

According to a United Nations Publication—planning for Economic Developments is "Planning is an invaluable aid to policy. In providing for explicit analysis and evaluation to the realistic alternatives that confront individual countries and in setting forth the applications of the alternative policies, planning greatly assists the process of decision-making. It is in this pragmatic spirit that numerous developing countries as well as more advanced economies have employed Planning, as a tool for achieving their national economic goals." In this way, planning implies utilisation of resources to fulfil long-term objectives set by a country and involves state participation also. The whole complex ideology of planning in all its manifestations, rightly observes Gunnar Myrdal, is thus essential Myrdal, is thus essentially rationalist in approach and interventionist in conclusion.

From the above discussion, it can rightly be inferred that planning is a way of life. It is both a necessity and a reality all over the globe. It is a means to achieve socio-political, economic and cultural growth by organising and utilizing the resources to maximum extent.

It must be remembered that planning is (i) a continuous process, (ii) rational, conscious and deliberate, (iii) a dynamic and not static process, (iv) flexible, and (v) a comprehensive and integrative process.

TYPES OF PLANNING

We can discuss various types of planning under the following headings:

1. Project Planning

Project planning, refers to planning of a certain project. It has a special relevance in underdeveloped countries where a few projects may be so urgent and pressing that top priority may be given to them.

2. Sectoral Planning

Sectoral planning, apparently, is related with sectoral development. Since in developing countries, all sectors cannot and need not grow simultaneously, pick and choose may be necessary and desirable.

3. Target Plannmg

The economic plans of some countries clearly state quantitative production targets like that of food, coal, iron and steel, fertilizers and so on. These plans also state investment in different sectors, technical assistance, balance of payments position, food and manpower and many other things over a period of time.

4. Authoritarian Planning

Authoritarian planning, refers to that type of planning where market forces are isolated or completely neutralized. The term 'controlling plan' is also used for this type of planning. As

Professor Arthur Lewis observes that plans made by communist countries are documents of authorization. They tell each industrial unit what it must produce and how much it timely invest. They have to be followed and achieved. This is one type of planning. Let us here add that the ultimate aim of this type of planning is also rapid, economic development of the economy, and some of the socialist countries have remarkably succeeded in attaining higher rates of growth and they challenge comparison with top capitalist countries.

5. Perspective and Short-term Planning

In a planned economy, we project a perspective for development over a period of time, say ten years, or twenty years. It is called perspective planning. When planning is limited only for a short and a fixed period, it may be called short-term planning. A long-term programme is broken into different plans for smaller periods. A perspective plan will determine the strategy of the short-term plans, will determine the objective and strategy of the perspective plan.

6. Centralised and Decentralised Planning

In the case of centralised planning, main economic decisions are taken by the top leaders at the Centre. The decisions are taken regarding production investment, rate of interest price, wages and other details. All coordinations and adjustments are made at the centre. In decentralised planning, decisions are taken by the central authority and also by public and private enterprises. Central authority generally fixes total amount of investment, prices and rate of interest. The enterprises decide the nature and amount of production, pattern of investment, on the basis of prices and interest. In Socialist countries planning is of centralised type and capitalist countries planning is that of decentralized type.

7. Corrective and Development Planning

There is a basic difference between these two types. The difference is on account of the nature of the economies. In a developed, free enterprise economy, the planning aims to eliminate the evils of unrestricted to ensure a steady rate of growth. In underdeveloped countries, primary objective is to accelerate the rate of growth. It can be said that in the former case, the use of planning is for corrective purpose to maintain a steady rate of growth, and in the latter case, it is essentially for development purposes. We can call them corrective and development planning respectively.

SOME IMPLICATIONS OF DEVELOPMENT PLANNING

When development planning is carried on successfully, it involves many implications. Some of which are as follows: "First, it greatly increases the load on social and administrative institutions. Development planning being the instrument of growth and change" is expected to make a great contribution to national progress by effecting social and administrative tasks. Second, development planning is concerned with the organization of planning system itself which, in turn, suggests that politico-socio-economic structure of the country should be taken into account to meet the needs of its users. Third, development planning stresses the need of having large-scale organization through "networks and complexes" so that objectives of nation are realized. Fourth, development planning requires the availability of sufficient data so that decision-making process in the planning does not suffer. Fifth, it further requires that institutional arrangement for policy analysis should be strengthened so that planning system become more effective. Sixth, it calls for continuing changes in the capabilities of administrative systems in the light of the goals and strategies of the development plans being finalised. In the last it may be stated that successful practice of development planning requires not only sufficient resources at its disposal and adequate administrative capability but also strong political support and popular participation.

FEATURES OF A DEVELOPMENT PLAN

A development plan may contain any or all of the following features:

(i) a survey of the current economic situation;
(ii) proposals for improving the institutional framework of economic activity;
(iii) a list of proposed government expenditures;
(iv) a review of major industries;
(v) a set of targets for the private sector; and
(vi) a macro-economic projection for the whole economy.[5]

Planning Process

Planning process is definitely a complicated, comprehensive and time consuming process. It involves mainly three stages: Formulation. Implementation and Evaluation. Here an attempt is made to discuss in brief the existing machinery for the planning process.

(i) Formulation of Plans

The national plan evolves gradually in a series of following six stages:

(a) General Approach

The first stage is the consideration of the general approach to the formulation of the Five Year Plan. This begins about three years in advance of the commencement of the Plan and involves an examination of the state of the economy, identification of its social, economic and institutional weakness, an appraisal of past trends in production and rate of growth in relation to the long-term view of the progress of the economy An attempt is made also to suggest the: directions in which, during the period of the Plan, imbalances must be corrected or more intensive efforts ensured. Preliminary conclusion on these and related aspects are submitted by the Planning Commission to the Cabinet at the Centre and the National Development Council. The first phase of deliberations leads to preliminary indications about the rate of growth to be assumed for the next plan and the objectives and considerations which should receive special emphasis.

(b) Setting-up of Working Groups and Panels

The second stage consists. in studies, not yet in too great detail which are intended to lead to the consideration of what may be described as the draft of a Memorandum on the physical content or the Five Year Plan. The inter-relationships and the broader dimensions of the Plan are studied within the Planning Commission. While these studies proceed, the Planning Commission constitutes a series of working groups, composed of its own specialists and those of the Ministries concerned at the Centre. The groups review the performance of the economy in their respective fields, assess progress in achieving the policy objectives outlined in the current and preceding plans, and point out deficiencies which may have been observed. As the working groups at the Centre begin their work. State Governments are also advised to constitute similar working groups of their own. The Planning Commission also constitutes Panels, composed of leading experts and workers drawn mainly from outside the Government to advise on the broader aspects of policy and approach towards the formulation of the Plan; in their respective fields for example Panel of Economists, Panel of Scientists and Panels for agriculture, land reform, education, health, housing and social welfare, etc.

(c) Preparation of a Draft Memoranda

In the third stage, on the basis of preliminary studies under taken by the various groups and, to the extent available, the preliminary suggestions of Panels, the Planning Commission gathers the main features of the Plan under formulation, including the principal magnitudes, into a Draft Memorandum. This document also presents the principal issues requiring consideration at the highest policy level and draws attention to the directions in which the effort envisaged in the proposals is likely to fall short of the requirements of the economy and should be further augmented. The document is submitted to the Central Cabinet, where it is discussed in detail, each Ministry being deeply concerned with the adequacy of proposals in its respective field, and is then placed before the National Development Council. At this stage the regional breakup of the various proposals is not furnished, one of the main aims being to provide a considered basis for the formulation of State plans.

(d) Revised Draft Memorandum of the NDC Comments

The fourth stage culminates in the preparation of the Draft Plan where the comments made by the NDC on the document are taken care of. An opportunity is also taken by the Planning Commission, to confer on some of the major issues involved with representatives of the main political parties in Parliament.

The Draft Plan is considered as an elaboration of the earlier document. It is intended to give more content to the plans envisaged for different sectors and to bring out the main issues of policy and objectives and the approach which is proposed to be adopted.

(e) Discussion of Draft Plan

During the course of the fifth stage, the draft plan is commented upon by the various Ministries and the State Governments and is considered in the Central Cabinet before being submitted to the National Development Council. With the approval of the Council, the Draft Plan is published as a document for the widest public discussion and consideration. The Draft Plan is also debated by the Parliament first in a general way for a few days at a time, and then in greater detail through a series of Parliamentary Committees.

Simultaneously the Planning Commission, in association with the Ministries at the Centre holds detailed discussions regarding the plans of individual States. The discussions are held both at the expert level and at the political level, the final conclusions being reached in consultation with the Chief Ministers of individual States. These conclusions are regarded as understandings between the Planning Commission and the States for the size and composition of each State's Plan and the main targets and programmes to be fulfilled.

(f) Preparation of a Final Plan

At the last stage, the Commission on the basis of detailed discussions held with the states and comments received from different sources submits a fresh Memo to the Central Cabinet and the National Development Council in which it brings together the principal features of the plan, the *policy* directions to be stressed and the issues which may require further consideration before the Report on the Plan is drawn up. The conclusions reached on this Memorandum become the basis of the final Report on the Five Year Plan. This detailed report, outlining the objectives, policies, programmes and projects in the Plan, is again commented upon in draft by the Ministries at the Centre and by the State Governments and is finally submitted to the Cabinet and the National Development Council. With the approval of the Council, the Report is published and presented to Parliament, usually by the Prime Minister. After discussions, Parliament accords its general approval to the Plan and gives a call to the nation for its implementation, and for the achievement of the objectives and targets embodied in it.

A candid review of the planning experience of four-and-a-half decades reveals the broad limitations of the "top down" or "trickle down" approaches to development. To improve the effectiveness of the various programmes which help the poorest of the poor, the institutions of plan administration must be reoriented to capture and internalize the aspirations of the common man and suitably modify to them keeping in view the resource availability and the state of technology. The 73rd and 74th Constitutional Amendments will pave the way for the flourishing of the PRIs and Ninth Plan must hasten the process of giving "power to the people."

The state governments are further required to endow the panchayats with necessary power and authority to enable them to function as institutions of self- government with the responsibility of preparing plans for economic development and social justice, and implementing them. In the Ninth Plan, it is expected that 29 subjects identified in the eleventh schedule would be transferred to the PRIs. Correspondingly, transfer of resources would have to be effected. In addition to the grants out of the consolidated fund of the states and allocations received from central government for implementation of centrally-sponsored schemes, the panchayats would have to be given revenue-raising power of their own. By and large, gram panchayats have relied largely on the grants of the states as they have had very limited revenue-raising powers.[6]

(ii) Implementation of Plans

After the plan has been given the approval by the Parliament, the implementation stage of the planning begins. This stage is of crucial importance as it involves several executing agencies. The Central, State and local Ministries have the primary responsibility of implementing the national plans. The Planning Commission at the Centre and State Planning Boards at the State levels have no executive responsibility. Their functions are advisory in character. The Commission/Boards have, however advisers on programme/project administration who tour the States and assess the progress on a continuing basis and suggest steps which help in the implementation of plans. At the central level, the planning commission is assisted by two organizations-Committee on the Plan Projects and the Programme Evaluation Organization for the implementation and evaluation of the plan projects and programmes.

In the planning process, implementation stage has been the subject of heavy criticism. This is the weaker link in the chain of the entire planning process. Plan documents have stressed the importance of strengthening the implementation machinery so that the plan projects and programmes are executed timely and efficiently. Implementation needs to be supported by adequate monitoring and current and post-evaluation of major programmes so that lessons of experience enable improvements in the design of programmes themselves.

A close examination of the planning process at the implementation stage reveals several weaknesses. Some of them are: lack of competent and qualified staff, inadequate and ineffective supervision, poor willingness on taking on responsibility, lack of people participation, poor communication and information network, insufficient coordination at various levels. Deficiencies in implementation may also be due to "inadequate planning of projects at the initial stage causing slippages in schedule, cost over-runs and poor performance."[7]

(iii) Evaluation of Plans

Each plan needs to be evaluated to determine its progress and regress. The Planning Commission/State Planning Boards have the evaluation responsibility. They appraise from time to time the progress achieved in the execution of each stage of the plan and recommend the adjustment of policy and measures that such appraisal might show to be necessary. The Commission/Boards make the evaluation results: (i) through monthly/quarterly/annual reports obtained from the Central Ministries and the State Governments; (ii) through its advisers on programme administration who tour the States; and (iii) through its Programme Evaluation Organization.

Adequate organization and systems at present do not exist for monitoring and evaluation of plan projects and programmes at different levels. At the Central level, monitoring systems. have been established in respect of major projects in certain key sectors, but there are very few monitoring systems at the State level.

The implementation of the plan both by the State Government, as well as the Central Ministries would not be effectively monitored with a view to ensuring that for each scheme various targets relating to time and cost, production of goods and services, social and economic benefits relating to the individual projects in the industrial, agricultural, education, irrigation, family planning, health or any other sector of the economy are realized.

FUNCTIONS OF DEVELOPMENT PLANNING AGENCIES

Most economies, particularly the developing, have a development plan extending from one year to ten years. Each development plan has different goals and strategies to achieve within the socio-politico-economic structure of the concerned country. There is always great variation in the degree of details of the plan and also on going levels of administrative capabilities. The principal functions of the development planning agencies are: 1. formulation of development plans, and 2. the control of their execution, appraisal and the provision of advice to the executive bodies on policy questions arising in the process of formulation and implementation. But it is difficult to carry out successfully this complex task when the Government of most developing countries have defects such as the following:

"(a) At the time at which they came into being as sovereign entities, there was in many of them only one, a hundred or, at the most, a couple of hundred graduates (and worse still in the wrong specialization), and the mass of the population is still plagued by illiteracy;

(b) Their economies are at an early stage of development, lopsided and grossly subject to the vagaries of nature and to externally induced fluctuations, both of which are unpredictable and uncontrollable;

(c) The public administration that they have inherited and since improved (or only patched up) leaves much to be desired with respect to organization, staffing and efficiency; and

(d) The information required (on the operation of economy and society at large) is all but non-existent, incomplete when available and often unreliable.[8]

However, the main elements of planning process consists in the evaluation of possibilities and objectives, the formulation of plans and policies for their realization, the preparation of specific programmes of action, the execution of plans and their periodic review and adjustment. The nature of the machinery established to perform these planning functions varies considerably from country to country, reflecting such factors as the importance of the role assigned to planning, the stage of development, the nature of the political and economic system and the existing structure of government."[9] Development planning is not a fairy expected to achieve everything by a wave of its magic wand. It is an organisational activity concerned with giving rise to better and more efficient performance. But if the development planning is improperly organized and staffed, there is every possibility that over-all, government administration may fail in its implementation. Nevertheless, emphasising the fact that development planning is essentially an essential and pivotal means of guiding and accelerating economic and social development in developing countries. "It would seem that whatever the scope and particular nature of a socio-economic activity, its 'planning' would invariably mean an organized and ordered effort, exhausting *itself* only in the totality of a given set of actions."[10] The Seminar on Organisation and Administration of Development planning Agencies: held at Kiev, Ukrainian Soviet Socialist Republic from 16 to 25 October 1972, listed the following interlocked actions to be obtained by the development planning agencies:

(a) Position assessment;
(b) Analysis of issues and causes;
(c) Assessment of resources;
(d) Consideration of the outcome of alternative resource allocation;
(e) Identification of policy instruments; .
(f) Determination of priorities and objectives;
(g) Plan and policy formulation; and
(h) Implementation follow-up (including the identification of corrective measures).

These are the interlinked functions which are performed by a development planning agency. Further, development planning agency is required to confine its advice to development aspects, wholly for the sake of trying to ensure consistency and to maintain its technical character without losing its grasp of practical implications.

Similarly the First Session of the Conference of Asian Economic Planners held in New Delhi, from 26 September to 3 October 1961, agreed that the planning agency should act as an advisory body functioning within the structure of the government, and that it should perform the following functions:

"(a) to assess natural, human and capital resources;
(b) to formulate plans of economic development—long-term medium term and annual;
(c) to report on the progress of the plan and the development of the economy from time to time and to undertake evaluation of the working of the plan;
(d) to suggest the nature of the machinery needed for securing the implementation of different aspects of the plan; and
(e) to indicate factors which may tend to retard economic development and make such recommendations as may be necessary for the successful execution of the plan."[11]

PLANNING MACHINERY

Planning machinery at the national and state levels consists of a net work of agencies and institutions which are concerned with the various aspects of the planning process—plan formulations; plan implementations, plan appraisal and evaluation, plan financing, etc. Thus viewed, planning machinery at the various levels include the following:

1. National Development Council.
2. Planning Commission.
3. Planning Ministry and other Ministries.
4. Parliament and its Consultative Committees.
5. State Planning Department and Planning Board, and other Government Departments, and
6. District and Block Level Planning Boards.

We shall now discuss in brief about the organization, structure, functions and critical appraisal of the actual performance of some of the important organs at various levels.

I. NATIONAL DEVELOPMENT COUNCIL

This is the highest body so far as policy matters on planning are concerned. The Council was set-up in the year 1952. The NDC is an important organisation, whose main functions are as follows:

To evaluate the implementation of National Planning form time to time, to examine the social and economic policies that influence the economic development, to give suggestions in order to achieve the determined goal in National Plan and to achieve maximum co-operation measures for the development of under-developed and backward classes and also to mobilise resources for National Development, to study the Plan prepared by the Planning Commission and after mutual discussions give it the final shape. It is only after its ratification that the format of the Plan is published.[12]

It comprises of Prime Minister as the Chairman and the Chief Ministers of State Governments as members while the members of Planning Commission are its *ex-officio* members, Several Ministers of the Central Government are also invited by the Chairman to attend the meetings as non-members, in order to put forward their viewpoint on matters within their respective ministerial jurisdiction. The Council may set-up a committee for various subjects or fields on planning. The main functions of the Council may be summarised as:

(a) To formulate and prescribe guidelines for the preparation of the National Plan as well as to suggest ways and means for mobilisation of resources for the Plan.
(b) To discuss and scrutinise the Draft National Plan as prepared by the Planning Commission.
(c) To examine policy questions arising in regard to the Plan.
(d) To review relevant questions relating to the implementation of the plan.

The decisions of the National Development Council along with the Draft National Plan are sent to the cabinets and legislatures of all the governments in the country for discussion. These high powered organs of the government have thus the final voice in regard to the nature and scope of plan as well as for the strategy and resources for its implementation.

In recent years, the N.D.C. has ceased to be the embodiment of the national consensus on development planning and the highest economic and social policy-making body in the system of federal polity. Its sessions, often called fitfully and after prolonged intervals to suit personal and political conveniences of the Central leadership, are reduced, to a ritual for the leaders to secure one-sided publicity.[13]

The walk-out by the Chief Ministers of four states from meeting of the council (July 1984), the counter reaction of the Prime-Minister in throwing out the officials, and adoption of a resolution condemning the C.M.'s action, are the indicators of tragic events in the annals of NDC's meeting. Incidentally, the Council was to consider and approve the paper on approach to the 7th Five' Year Plan to be launched from the year 1985. This meeting of the Council, by some Journalist, has been regarded as a special session of celebration by the Power-political establishment on taking, clearly and decisively—the road to non-planning.[14] Let the good sense prevail so that the council can prove to be an asset to give national backing and authority to the planning process and the planning machinery .

2. PLANNING COMMISSION

India has perhaps the largest tradition of planning in any non-socialist country. The nearest parallel to it in Western Europe is the French System of Planning. The main difference, however, is that, India has a federal structure of government and the achievement of socialistic pattern of society is her avowed objective.

The Government of India set-up the Planning Commission in March 1950 to undertake planning for economic and social development. It was established by a cabinet resolution and not by a law in Parliament. It was assigned an advisory function rather than the executive responsibility. Thus it may be pointed out that the Central Planning Commission is not a statutory body like the Finance commission but an advisory body.

When established in March 1950, the Planning Commission was assigned the following functions:

(1) To make an assessment of the material, capital and human resources of the country, including technical personnel and investigate the possibilities of augmenting such of these resources as are found to be deficient in relation to the nation's requirements.

(2) To formulate a plan for the most effective and balanced utilisation of the country's resources.

(3) To define the stages in which the plan should be carried out and to propose allocation of resources for the completion of each stage on a determination of priorities.

(4) To indicate the factors which tend to retard economic development and to determine the conditions which, in view or the current social and political situation, should be established for the successful execution of the plan.

(5) To determine the nature of the machinery necessary for securing the successful implementation of each stage of the plan in all its aspects.

(6) To appraise-from time to time the progress achieved in the execution of the plan stage by stage and recommend adjustments in policy measures that such appraisal may show to be necessary.

(7) To make such interim or ancillary recommendations as appear to the Planning Commission to be appropriate either for facilitating the discharge of the duties

assigned to it or on consideration of the prevailing economic conditions, current policies and monetary and development programmes, on an examination of such specific problems as may be referred to it for advice by the Central or State Governments.

The Commission is assigned to play an important and curative role in economic and social development. The Commission provides a significant link to ensure uniform sectoral and spatial plan. Although it is a body with the responsibility of formulating plans, evaluating the process and making recommendations on socio-economic goals and development policies, it is not responsible for the execution of plans.

With regard to structure, the Commission is headed by the Prime Minister as its Chairman who presides over all the meetings of the Commission. The Deputy Chairman of the Commission acts as the technical and administrative head of the Commission. He is appointed by the Union Cabinet for fixed term. He enjoys the status of a Cabinet rank minister despite the fact that he may not be a member of Parliament or the Cabinet. He attends all the cabinet meeting but is not entitled to vote. He is responsible for the preparation and submission of the draft plan to the Government for its approval. The composition of the Central Planning Commission vary from time to time. The composition in 2008 is as follows. (See Chart 8.1)

CHART 8.I

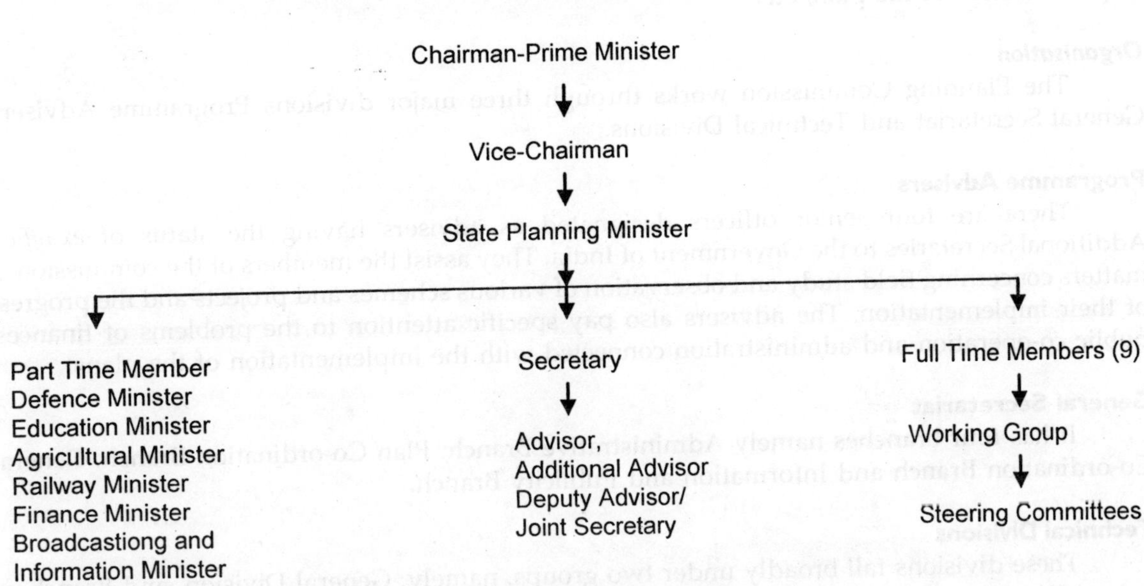

Chairman-Prime Minister

↓

Vice-Chairman

↓

State Planning Minister

Part Time Member	Secretary	Full Time Members (9)
Defence Minister Education Minister Agricultural Minister Railway Minister Finance Minister Broadcastiong and Information Minister	↓ Advisor, Additional Advisor Deputy Advisor/ Joint Secretary	↓ Working Group ↓ Steering Committees

In this regard an ex-official of the Planning Commission writes: "All the members of the Commission work as a body, but for convenience each member has charge of one or more subjects and directs the study of programmes in these spheres. The Deputy Chairman is primarily concerned with matters of general coordination and administration. The Minister of Planning bas been allocated, certain subjects like any other member, but he is also responsible for the Commission as a whole to Parliament and the Central Cabinet. Important, proposals that have financial implications and which might have repercussions on the economic policy are referred to member (finance) in addition to cases submitted to him as a member of the Commission. All cases involving policy are submitted for Consideration at one of the meetings of the Commission. The cases to be considered by the Planning Commission as a whole include recommendations in regard to the formulation and the progress of the five year and annual plans, adjustments in the plans, matters involving departure from the plan, policies, advice to the central ministry in a matter to be placed before the cabinet, important cases involving agreement with a central ministry of a state government or difference of opinion between two members of the Commission, and any policy between two members of the Commission, and any policy matter relating to internal organisation and methods of work"[15]

"The Commission bas been established as a multi-member body but as usual single administrative department. The very composition of the Commission ensures effective liason with government. Though the Commission is a staff agency to advise government. Government in itself is represented on the body of the Commission."[16]

"In some way the Central Planning Commission is a unique institution and in the sphere of Governmental organisation there has hardly been any recent development comparable, in its practical importance or in its general significance from the point of view of the 'Science of Public Administration', to the growth of the Planning Commission. It is the chief staff agency—the nerve centre of national thinking—on matters of planning and development. It has, from time to time, also undertaken some line functions newly emerging from national planning e.g., general direction and supervision community projects, enlistment of public cooperation in the implementation of the plan, etc."[17]

Organisation

The Planning Commission works through three major divisions Programme Advisers, General Secretariat and Technical Divisions.

Programme Advisers

There are four senior officers designated as advisers having the status of *ex-officio* Additional Secretaries to the Government of India. They assist the members of the commission in matters concerning field study and observation of various schemes and projects and the progress of their implementation. The advisers also pay specific attention to the problems of finances, public co-operation and administration connected with the implementation of the plans.

General Secretariat

It has four branches namely Administrative Branch, Plan Co-ordination Branch, General Co-ordination Branch and Information and Publicity Branch.

Technical Divisions

These divisions fall broadly under two groups, namely, General Division, and Branch or Subject Divisions. The General Divisions, are concerned with the problem of overall economic and social planning, each examining some specific aspects of these problems. The Subject Divisions, on the other hand deal with specific sectors of the economy like land and Irrigation and Power, Food and Agriculture, Education, Housing, etc. The Technical Divisions are responsible for scrutinizing and analysing various schemes and projects to be incorporated in the plan; conducting technical studies and research regarding plan projects and programmes, preparing study material and reports on the plan, etc. The heads of these Divisions are generally subject-specialists designated as Chiefs or Directors who are assisted by Deputy and Assistant Chiefs and some research staff.

There is also a Programme Evaluation Organisation (set-up in 1952) which scientifically evaluates the results achieved in terms of the objectives and targets of various sector plans, state plans, programme and projects which together comprise the National Development Plan.

Prime Minister is the Chairman of Planning Commission assisted by Deputy Chairman and Ministers of State Planning and Parliamentary affairs. In addition there are 9 full time members. On the administrative side, there is a Secretary, 5 Principal Advisors, 2 Senior Consultants, One Chairman of Special Task Force on Bihar, 23 Additional Secretaries/Special Advisors/Joint Secretary, 16 Joint Advisors/Special Consultants/Consultant/42 Directors, 41 Deputy Secretary/ Dy. Adivsors/Joint Directors. There are 31 Divisions detailed as below:

Divisons' Name

1. Agriculture Division (Agri.)
2. Backward Class & Tribal Development Division (BC)
3. Communication and Information Division (C & I)
4. Development Policy Division (DP)
5. Education Division (Edu.)
6. Environment and Forest Division (E & F)
7. Financial Resources Division (FR)
8. Health, Nutrition and Family Welfare Division
9. Housing, Urban Development and Water Division (HUD &W)
10. Industry and Minerals Division (M & M)
11. International Economic Division (IE)
12. Infrastructure Division (Infra)
13. Labour, Employment and Manpower Division (LEM)
14. Multi-Level Planning Division (MLP)
15. Organization and Method and Coordination Division
16. Perspective Planning Division (PP)
17. Plan Coordination Division (PC)
18. Power and Energy Division (PE)
19. Programme Evaluation Organization (PEQ)
20. Project Appraisal and Management Division (PAMD)
21. Programme Outcome and Response Monitoring Division
22. Rural Development Division (RD)
23. Science and Technology Division (S & T)
24. Social Justice & Women's Empowerment Division (SJ & WE)
25. Socio-Economic Research Division (SER)
26. State Plans Division (SP)
27. Transport Division (Trspt.)
28. Village and Small Enterprises Division (VSE)
29. Water Resources and Water Supply Division (WR &WS)
30. Administration and Services Division
31. Other Units:
    (a) Border Area Development Programme
    (b) Western Ghat Development Programme

3. PLANNING COMMISSION: *vis-à-vis* FIVE YEAR PLANS

Since 1950, the Planning Commission has formulated/launched eleven Five Year Plans as a blue print of total national effort. The plan documents have been laying stress on Agricultural production, industrial production, socialistic pattern of society, growth with justice, 'Garibi Hatao', self-reliance, etc. It is in tune with achieving: these objectives, that targets for various ministries are fixed and massive outlays are allocated in consultation with the Commission. To make the point more clear, let us look at the role of cooperative sector in achieving the objectives enshrined in the constitution, the plan documents and the various policy documents. It is now even accepted by all concerned that there is no other instrument as potentially powerful and full of social purpose as the cooperative organisations. These organisations have turned out to be one of the principal structural mechanisms to attain the objectives based on cardinal principle of initiative and freedom.

It is in this context that Planning Commission has played a pivotal role in formulation of Five Year Plans for the cooperative sector. This shows the intensity of the arduous and complex nature of role being played by the Commission.

Formulation of the 11th Five Year Plan

The 11th Five Year Plan to be launched from 2007. In his forward to XIth Five Year Plan Prime Minister observed India's commitment to planned economic development which is a reflection of our society's determination to improve the economic conditions of our people and an affirmation of the role of the government in bringing about this outcome through a variety of social, economic, and institutional means. The Eleventh Five Year Plan, which was approved by the National Development Council on 19th December 2007 reaffirms this commitment. It provides a comprehensive strategy for inclusive development, building on the growing strength of the economy, while also addressing weaknesses that have surfaced.

The strength of the economy is evident from the remarkable transition to a high growth path, which has been achieved in recent years. The Tenth Plan period (2002-03 to 2006-07) began modestly, but then saw the economy accelerating steadily to achieve an average growth rate of 7.7%, for the Plan period as a whole, which is the highest ever achieved in any Plan period. In the last four years the growth rate has averaged 8.9% making India one of the fastest growing economies in the world. The transition to high growth is an impressive achievement, but we must not forget that growth is not the only measure of development. Our ultimate objective is to achieve broad-based improvement in the living standards of all our people. Rapid growth is essential for this outcome because it provides the basis for expanding incomes and employment and also provides the resources needed to finance programmes for social uplift. However, it is not by itself sufficient. We also need to ensure that growth is widely spread so that its benefits, in terms of income and employment, are adequately shared by the poor and weaker sections of our society, especially the Scheduled Castes (SCs) and the Scheduled Tribes (STs), Other Backward Classes (OBCs) and minorities. For this to happen, the growth must be inclusive in the broadest sense. It must occur not just in our major cities but also in our villages and small towns. It must be spread across all states and not just limited to some. It must generate sufficient volumes of high quality employment to provide the means for uplift of large numbers of our population from the low income low quality occupations in which too many of them have been traditionally locked.

Deputy Chairman in his preface mentioned that the Eleventh Plan began in very favourable circumstances with the economy having grown at the rate of 7.7% per year in the Tenth Plan period. However, far too many of our people still lack the basic requirements for a decent living in terms of nutrition standards, access to education and basic health, and also to other public services such as water supply and sewerage. Disadvantaged groups, especially the Scheduled Castes and Scheduled Tribes and the minorities have benefited less than they should have. Regional imbalances have emerged across and even within states.

The Eleventh Plan seeks to remedy these deficiencies by seeking to accelerate the pace of growth while also making it more inclusive. The growth objective is to achieve an average growth rate of 9% per annum for the Plan period. The objective of inclusiveness is reflected in the adoption of 26 other monitorable targets at the national level relating to (i) income and poverty, (ii) education, (iii) health, (iv) women and children, (v) infrastructure, and (vi) environment. Some of these national targets have also been disaggregated into 13 state level targets and it is expected that the state governments design policies and programmes to achieve them.

The strategy for achieving faster growth with greater inclusiveness involves several interrelated components. These are: (i) a continuation of the policies of economic reform which have created a buoyant and competitive private sector capable of benefiting from the opportunities provided by greater integration with the world, (ii) a revival in agricultural growth which is the most important single factor affecting rural prosperity, (iii) improved access to essential services in health and education (including skill development) especially for the poor, which is essential to ensure inclusiveness and also to support rapid growth, (iv) a special thrust on infrastructure development which is a critical area for the accelerating growth, (v) environmental sustainability which is becoming increasingly important, (vi) special attention to the needs of disadvantaged groups, and (vii) good governance at all levels, Central, State and local.

Role of Planning Commission

Over the years, the role of the Planning Commission has been commented upon from three angles:

(1) It functions as a super cabinet,
(2) It is ineffective as its advice is not always accepted,
(3) It has no responsibility in the execution of plans.

V.T. Krishnamachari who was one time a member and Deputy Chairman of the Planning Commission observed:

"These comments appear to be based on a mis-apprehension of the role of planning body in a parliamentary democracy. It might, therefore, be useful to stress the more important aspects of the position the Planning. Commission occupies *vis-a-vis* the union and state governments. When a plan is under preparation the strategy of the plan, the financial resources for it, the broad pattern and inter-sector allocations are settled by the cabinet and National Development Council at a number of meetings. On the basis of proposals worked out by the Planning Commission in close consultation with the union ministries and state government and the other bodies mentioned within this framework, allocations are made by the Planning Commission according to priorities after consultations with ministries and state governments which extend over several weeks. In fixing priorities the Planning Commission examines projects and programmes in the perspective of the economy as a whole. In the nature of things, these allocations, which inevitably mean reduction of the demands of ministries and state government have to be accepted as the best possible in the circumstances. To this extent the Planning Commission and the governments are supplementary. The Planning Commission viewing the question in the context of the economy as a whole and not being saddled with everyday problems of administration can give useful assistance to ministries in the formulation of projects and policies."[18]

There is however, some truth in levelling the allegations against the functioning of Planning Commission. Firstly, there is a wide gap between the promise of planning and its implementation. This is evident right from the sixties. After the plan holiday for 3 years, none of the plans has covered its full tenure. The 4th Plan, 5th Plan, and the 6th Plan (launched both by Janata Government and Congress Party) had its premature death. Whenever, the mid-term appraisal of these plans was made, tall claims were made that corrective measures would be taken in the next plans. The .above statement amply demonstrates that plans no longer evoke popular confidence or expectations.

Immediately after independence India tackled her economic problems through mixed economy model of Nehruvian socialism by creating state owned enterprises in power, steel, fertilizers, chemicals, mines and other key sectors of economy. The government also took upon itself the task of social development by making substantial investments in education, health, irrigation, drinking water, transport and communications. Various Five Year Plans made huge allocations for poverty alleviation programmes. But the tardy pace of results inspite of all the efforts and money spent is the direct consequences of corruption, waste and negligence on the part of implementing agencies.[19]

Secondly, the Commission has ceased to be an expert body in planned economic development. Instead, it has turned into merely one more department of the Union Government and confines its activities in arm twisting the State Governments at the behest of the Central Government.

Thirdly, it was during the tenure of our first Prime Minister, Sh. Jawahar Lal Nehru that the commission had acquired the status of a super cabinet, but, after him its position underwent a significant change. In the subsequent years, it has been named as a Committee of the Cabinet for two obvious reasons, i.e., proliferation of the vested interests and induction of generalists into the leading position. It is however, very recently that the Commission has started in the process of rebuilding its professional expertise and shedding the political power establishment.

Fourthly, the Commission is not at all responsible for the effective execution of the plans, i.e. two different agencies are concerned with formulation and implementation of plans without any cohesive coordination and cooperation between the two.

Lastly, it is seen that the political will to implement the development plans is generally found lacking and the plans have been treated as "sophisticated election manifesto" to satisfy the intelligent and vocal sections.

Like 'development' 'social development' too has several connotations and is often used very broadly to refer to improvements in human well-being. It is also used to refer to development that is not strictly economic or market driven. It includes improvements in the quantity and equality of public social services, such as education, health, sanitation, access to clean water and other goods and services that are to be provided to all people by public institutions.

But "Social Development" in the Indian context implies poverty alleviation and reduction in income inequalities. The Indian plans, however, have not paid the required attention to these objectives. India still has the largest number of illiterate people in the world. In terms of quality of life of the people, India is among the few lowest ranking countries in the world.

The problems of distorted development are not far to seek in India where the chasm between the rich and the poor has grown too wide. India has followed an economic growth model, which has tended to exacerbate inequities. The benefits of development have been captured by the privileged few, both in rural and urban areas. The government has been too slow to recognize equity as an explicit objective of policy action owing to the politically charged nature of the issue. Under the impact of Structural Adjustment Programmmes, economic reforms of the past few years have exacted huge social costs. To make things worse, adjustment policies are being implemented without sufficient sensitivity to social consequences. The retreat of the state from discharging its social obligations has complicated the already complex issues of overall development. The centrality of human person in development has taken a backseat in the free interplay of market forces. The IMF and World Bank 'conditionalities' or structural adjustment policies have sharply reduced government intervention in the economy, curtailed social expenditures and limited social planning. As a result, the social initiatives, which were adopted earlier, have been impeded and, in some cases, discontinued. Though there has been progress in the social and economic areas of the country during the last five and a half decades, but it cannot be considered satisfactory.

In India the real problem is that people's participation in policy formation and policy implementation is either absent or is kept to the bare minimum. Too often the blue print approach predominates. Planning is based on quantitative data and cast into a rigid time schedule. Targets are determined from the outset and are expressed numerically. Planning is often followed by large scale project implementation. People's participation in both policy formation and policy implementation is necessary. Schemes should be prepared at grassroots level and be approved by higher authorities and by the Planning Commission.

Empowering the institutions of local self governments may be useful in this regard. Non-Government Organisations (NGOs) will also be of much use. Governments lack resources and knowledge of he different parts of the country. People of different areas know their problems better. So, NGOs, run by honest and dedicated persons, can do much with the help of local people. NGOs can ensure participation of the local people in the programmes for their development. NGOs can also generate resources from within the local people.

People's participation is necessary also for making the political leadership and bureaucrats responsive and work empathetically. In this way, the situation may change and social sector development be a reality.[20]

A candid review of the planning experience of four-and-a-half decades reveals the broad limitations of the "top down" or "trickle down" approaches to development. To improve the effectiveness of the various programmers which help the poorest of the poor, the institutions of plan administration must be reoriented to capture and internalise the aspirations of the common man and suitably modify them keeping in view the resource availability and the state of technology. The 73rd and 74thc constitutional amendments will pave the way for the flourishing of the PRIs and ninth plan must hasten the process of giving "power to the people."

4. PARLIAMENTARY CONSULTATIVE COMMITTEE ON PLANNING

Besides the N.D.C. and the Planning Commission at the centre, it has been the practice to constitute 'Parliamentary Consultative Committee on Planning'. It facilitates, deeper probe into the various issues involved in plan formulation. As Parliamentary time is very limited, this committee, consisting of a few members of Parliament both from the ruling party and the opposition parties, goes into annual progress reports on plan performance in detail and make necessary recommendations. The Committee holds meetings and discussions periodically and reviews critically its progress in formulation and implementation. For instance, the Union Minister for irrigation recently addressing a meeting of the Consultative Committee attached to his ministry observed that in the 7th Plan, emphasis would be on completing the irrigation projects which could yield full or partial benefits. He added that there was no possibility of undertaking any new major projects.[21]

5. PLANNING MACHINERY (STATE LEVEL)

Planning machinery at the state level consists of (i) Planning Department, (ii) State Planning Board together with its specialized working groups, (iii) Ministries of the State Government, and (iv) State Legislature.

(i) State Planning Board

At the State level there is a planning machinery called as State Planning Board. This Board is an apex-body for the formulation, review and evaluation of the various plan programme/ schemes. The organisation of the Planning Board in most of the states is more or less the same. The main functions of the State Planning Boards recommended by the Administrative Reforms Commission are as follows:

(i) To make an assessment of the state resources and formulate plans for the most effective and balanced utilization of those resources;

(ii) To determine plan priorities of the State within the framework of the priorities of the National Plan;

(iii) To assist district authorities in formulating their development plans within the spheres in which such planning is considered useful and feasible and to coordinate these plans with the State Plan;

(iv) To identify factors which tend to retard economic and social development of the State and determine conditions to be established for successful execution of the plans; and

(v) To review the progress of implementation of the Plan programmes and recommend such adjustments in policies and measures as the review may indicate.

The State Planning Board is generally headed by the Chief Minister as its Chairman while the Planning and Finance Minister is the Deputy Chairman of the Board. The Board has Chief Secretary, Financial Commissioner (Development), Finance Secretary, Secretary (Irrigation and Power) and Principal Secretary to the Chief Minister as ex-officio Members. Besides there are 4 to 10 non-official part-time members (in the case of Punjab, there are 10 members) representing different fields of specialization. The Secretary Planning is the Member Secretary of the Board. Besides the House keeping Division, the staff working in the Planning Board has been divided into several Divisions. In the case of Punjab there are 14 Divisions for dealing with different subjects, namely: 1. Plan Coordination, 2. Economic, 3. Local Plan, 4. Agriculture and Rural Development, 5. Employment and Man-Power, 6. Irrigation. Drainage and Flood Control, 7. Energy, 8. Trade and Transport 9. Industry and Mineral, 10. Housing and Urban Development, 11. Special Backward Area, 12. Social Services, 13. Monitoring and Evaluation, and 14. Special Component Plan Division.[22]

Experience has shown that Plans at the State level are formulated in the light of main guidelines received from the Planning Commission and the general directives of the Council of

CHART 8.2

Planning Process

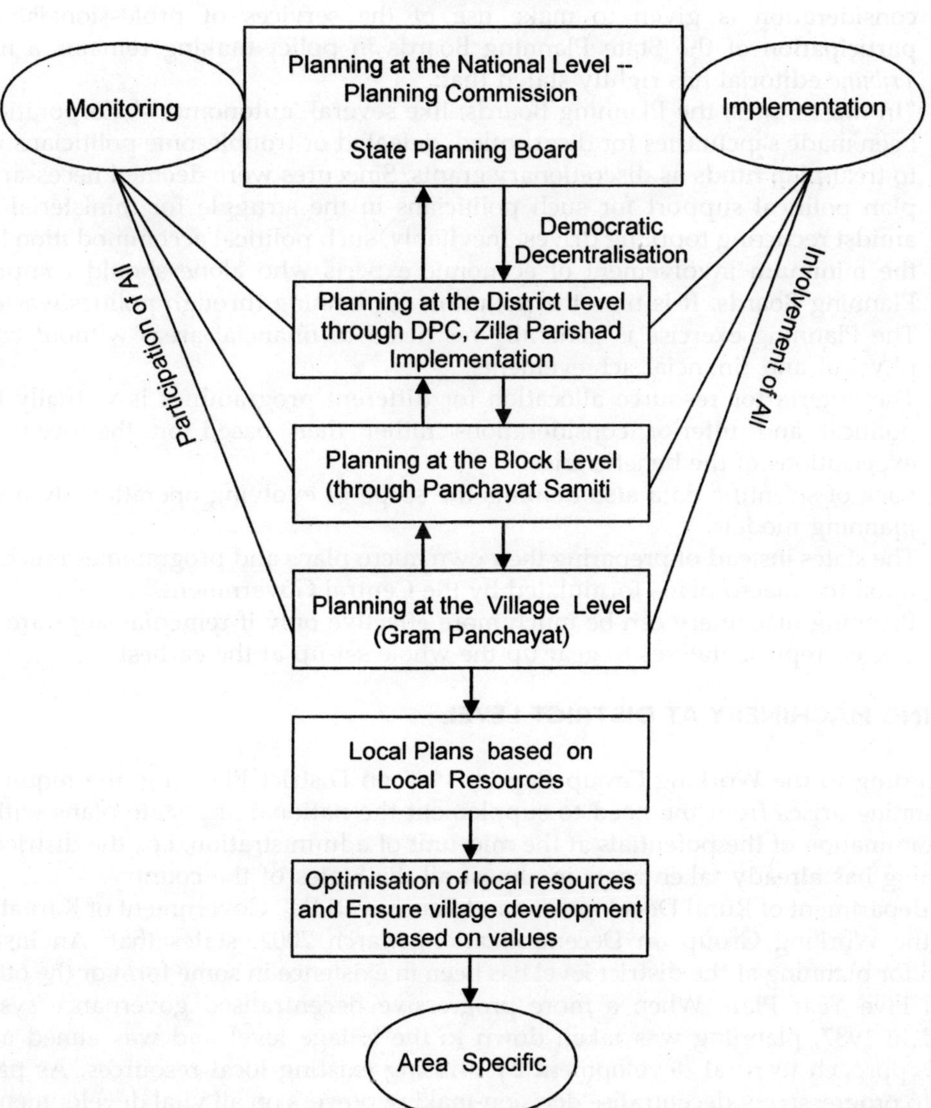

Ministers of the State. The plan prepared by the Board/Department is submitted first to the Council of Ministers of the State and then to the State Development Board or Planning Advisory, committee and finally to the State Legislature.

State Planning Machinery at Work

It has been generally observed that inspite of introduction of the concept of decentralized planning on democratic basis, it has remained more or less apparent than real on account of following factors:

1. The Planning Department generally consists of administrators and not much consideration is given to make use of the services of professionals. As such, participation of the State Planning Boards in policy-making remains a myth. *The Tribune* editorial has rightly stated that:
"In most States, the Planning Boards; like several 'autonomous' Corporations, have been made sanctuaries for disgruntled, defeated or troublesome politicians who tend to treat plan funds as discretionary grants. Sinecures were deemed necessary to treat plan political support for such politicians in the struggle for ministerial survival, amidst recurring toppling drives. Inevitably, such political accommodation has led to the minimum involvement of economic experts who alone should comprise State Planning Boards. It is time the pollution of planning through politics was ended."[23]
2. The Planning exercise is generally restricted to financial areas without correlating physical and financial achievements.
3. The criteria for resource allocation for different programmes is virtually based on political and ulterior considerations rather than based on the needs, desires, expectations of the beneficiaries.
4. Lack of scientific data also delimits the scope of evolving operationally meaningful planning models.
5. The states instead of preparing their own micro plans and programmes much depends upon the macro plans formulated by the Central Government.
6. Planning machinery can be much more effective only if remedial steps are taken by elected representatives to gear up the whole set-up at the earliest.

6. PLANNING MACHINERY AT DISTRICT LEVEL

According to the Working Group Report, 1984 on District Planning, the requirement of district planning arises from the need to supplement the national and state plans with a more detailed examination of the potentials at the mid-unit of administration, i.e., the district. District level planning has already taken roots in almost all the States of the country.

The department of Rural Development and Panchayati Raj, Government of Karnataka in its report of the Working Group on Decentralization, March 2002, states that: An institutional mechanism for planning at the district level has been in existence in some form or the other, since the Fourth Five Year Plan. When a more progressive decentralised governance system was established in 1987, planning was taken down to the village level and was aimed at a more integrated approach to rural development by utilising existing local resources. As part of the initiatives to progressively decentralise decision-making powers on all vital development matters affecting people's life, the planning process was also to be strengthened as an instrument to translate this objective into reality.

However, the efficacy of institutional mechanisms for decentralised planning have been seriously eroded by several distortions that have taken away most of the decentralised nature of planning. Some of these distortions are elaborated below:

(a) Lower levels of the PR system have neither been provided with the machinery nor capacity needed for undertaking meaningful planning.

(b) While the modalities of the planning process were established in 1986 and plan sizes were fixed in 1987-88 by identifying sectors and reserving allocations to them, in practice allocations to each sector have been made depending on the state's resource position and plan size.

(c) The criteria suggested by the State Finance Commission for devolution of funds are not being followed by the Government. There is a difference between precept and practice when providing untied funds to PRIs.

(d) The planning process as implemented does not stir meaningful debate at the PRI level. There is often no rationale for separation of schemes into 'District Sector' and 'State Sector Schemes'; except the perceived convenience of Officialdom.

(e) The Planning process at taluk and village levels is of poor quality and neither does, or is permitted to reflect peoples' aspirations.

(f) Integration of Grama and Taluk Panchayat plans into the District plan tends to be mere summation, and not a synergistic integration.

DEVELOPMENT ACTIVITIES ENTRUSTED TO THE PRIs

The Eleventh Schedule to the Constitution of India contains an impressive list of development activities which could be entrusted to PRIs. These could be broadly categorised into following:

(i) Programmes for Productive Activities

Agriculture, animal husbandry, poultry, fishery, small scale industries including food processing, cottage industries, fuel, and fodder and Irrigation.

(ii) Land Development Programmes

Land reforms, soil conservation, minor irrigation, water management and watershed development, wasteland development, social forestry and grazing lands.

(iii) Education and Cultural Activities

Primary schools, adult education, technical education and libraries.

(iv) Social Welfare

Welfare of the women and child development, family welfare, care of disabled and mentally retarded.

(v) Provisions of Civic Amenities

Drinking water, rural electrification, non-conventional sources of energy, rural roads, bridges, culverts, water-ways, sanitation, rural housing and health.

(vi) Poverty alleviation and allied programmes for social and economic upliftment of weaker sections.

(vii) Maintenance of community assets and public distribution system.

(viii) Organisation and control of rural markets and village fairs.

ROLE OF PANCHAYAT RAJ INSTITUTIONS IN PLANNING

If the main responsibility of development planning at the district or block level is left to the bureaucratic hierarchy under the control of the ministry at the centre/state level, democratic decentralisation will remain an empty slogan. It must. be conceded that our commitment to democratic decentralisation implies progressive devolution of decision-making on all vital matters affecting people's life, to their elected representatives under the Panchayat Raj system. Besides, there is no doubt that active involvement of the Panchayat Raj institutions in the planning process will provide a better climate for peoples participation in the implementation of the plan, a condition crucial to its success.

The Constitution has enjoined upon the State Governments to endow the Panchayats with the powers and authority so as to enable them to function as institutions of self-governance. Panchayats should be responsible for preparing plans for economic development and social justice and implementing schemes relating thereto. To ensure that decentralised planning for development becomes the direct responsibility of the local bodies in India, Article 243 has been introduced in the Constitution of India, establishing a District Planning Committee in every district "to consolidate the plans prepared by the Panchayats and the Municipalities in the district and to prepare a draft development plan for the district as a whole."

Decentralised planning has been conceived as the most desirable system to promote the expression of the citizens' views in shaping official policy. It has two important elements: (i) it encompasses the developmental needs at the level of micro-unit, be it the area of a Gram Panchayat or a cluster of villages; and (ii) it is based on the felt needs of the people. However, felt needs of the people cannot be elicited unless they participate in plan formulation and implementation at grass-roots level. Accordingly, the Panchayats have been given mandatory responsibilities to plan and implement schemes for economic development and social justice in the Panchayati Raj System. In the given scenario, a Gram Panchayat has to necessarily develop the capacity to prepare plan for the development of its area and such plan is to be based on the felt needs of the people. The basic planning unit, as conceived under the 73rd Amendment Act, has always to be a Gram Panchayat. The socio-economic activities which can be planned and executed at the Gram Panchayat and Intermediate Panchayat level can be divided into four categories as under:

1. Development of natural resources such as land, soil, forest pastures, water resources and the steps necessary for increasing production of agriculture, horticulture, livestock, fuel, fodder and timber, and raw material for small and cottage industries.
2. Development and maintenance of physical infrastructure such as drinking water, roads, street lights, sanitary drains, latrines, building of schools, dispensaries, community hall, market complex, common working place, place of weekly market haat/shandy, etc.
3. Programmes for poverty alleviation and social justice covering below poverty line families, SCs, STs, women and children, handicapped, old-age, etc.
4. Development of adequate, timely and quality services such as education and medical facilities, public distribution system, power supply, drinking water supply and other social services.

The basic objective of the planning at Gram Panchayat is to identify the felt needs and aspirations of the people, which are to be jointly shouldered by the people's representatives and Panchayats. Such process of planning is expected to be useful in identifying the local problems and local resources, ascertaining the growth potential of the Panchayat in the light of their resources, structuring not only in choosing schemes from shelf of projects but properly sequencing them in such a way that forward and backward linkages are established. The inputs required for planning are to be collected primarily from the people themselves in the Gram Sabha Meetings.

Decentralised planning process begins at the Gram Panchayat level and all items which can be taken up by the Gram Panchayat within its jurisdiction form part of the Gram Panchayat plan. All other items which cover more than one Gram Panchayat form part of the plan of the Intermediate Panchayat. The Gram Panchayat plan is prepared in two stages:

(i) Preparation of Resource Inventory; and
(ii) Formulation of Gram Panchayat Plan.

The details of the tasks to be carried out in these stages are given below:

(i) Preparation of Resource Inventory

Each Gram Panchayat prepares Gram Panchayat Resource Inventory listing information regarding all items under the four categories as mentioned above and also village population, number of households/families below poverty line (BPL) landless, small and marginal farmers, artisans, old-age, handicapped, annual deaths/births and the list of programmes implemented/being implemented at Gram Panchayat levels, beneficiaries assisted under various programmes, etc. Information on all the above items is consolidated into a Gram Panchayat Resource Inventory. The information available in the Resource Inventory makes it easy to identify the developmental schemes needed for the Gram Panchayat.

(ii) Formulation of Gram Panchayat Plan

The projects/schemes identified on the basis of the Gram Panchayat Resource Inventory is classified as follows:

(i) List out the projects which can be implemented by the Gram Panchayat with its own resources and voluntary manpower;
(ii) List out the projects which can be implemented by the Gram Panchayat for which funds are provided through different schemes/programmes fully or where a certain percentage is to be contributed by the Gram Panchayat;
(iii) List out the projects which can not be planned and executed by the Gram Panchayat and need help of the government machinery/line departments; and
(iv) List out the projects which are essential for the Gram Panchayat, but the coverage of the project goes beyond the jurisdiction of the Gram Panchayat, and can be planned and executed by the block/district level Panchayats. Again, after finalising the list of works/projects as per the above categorisation, it should be put before the Gram Sabha for further scrutiny as well as to ascertain the following:
   (a) Whether the project identified for the Gram Panchayat are relevant and related to their needs?
   (b) Since all the projects/schemes can not be taken up in the same year and at the same time, these should be prioritised according to the urgency and importance.

(c) The proposed projects need to be matched with sources of funds under various programmes and Sectoral departments, own resources of Gram Panchayat and possible public contribution in kind and labour.

(d) Identify the BPL families, old-age, handicapped, etc. and prepare a list of beneficiaries under various poverty alleviation programmes, and place this list before the Gram Sabha for approval/recommendation.

After consultation with Gram Sabha, an Annual Action Plan and a Five Year Plan is prepared in the following manner:

(i) To classify the projects/schemes which can be completed within a year, two years and more than two years.

(ii) On the basis of the availability of funds flow pattern under various programmes and the duration/cost of the projects to phase them into Annual Action Plan.

The Gram Sabha Meetings are vital for the identification of beneficiaries and for knowing the felt needs for preparing the plan. It has been reported at various forums that the level of participation in the Gram Sabha is very low in several States. As Gram Sabha Meetings are not held regularly, much of the planning is done by the officials. This has deprived PRIs of the benefit of assessing the perceptions of the people and translating their desires into more articulated programmes under decentralised planning. It is, therefore, necessary that the institution of Gram Sabha is made functional so that the concept of decentralised planning could be operationalised effectively.

In most of the States, a three-tier system of local governance is in vogue. Since the Gram Panchayats cover a small area and population in most States, the Panchayats at the middle level will also have to be activated, so as to become effective planning bodies at that level. They have to consolidate the demands of the lower level Panchayats and bring them into the planning frame. A strong training component has to be introduced at the district and State levels, if the people are to prepare plan for the projects/schemes in a meaningful way.

PROVISIONS OF KARNATAKA PANCHAYAT RAJ ACT, 1993

The areas for district planning have been identified by the Act of 1993. The District Sector Schemes are brought under the purview of the ZP and these schemes are further classified as GP Schemes, TP Schemes and ZP Schemes. Section 58, Schedule I, of the Act enlists the general functions of the GP. The Act further provides for the aggregation of GP Plans with the plan prepared by the Taluka Panchayat. Section 309 of the Act provides for the aggregation of TP and GP plans with the annual plan of the ZP, thus providing for an over-all plan for the district. The devolution of financial powers for the implementation of these programmes at TP level is also taking shape. These plans from below are expected to be the building blocks for the State Plan. This in turn is expected to bring a practical rapport between the local area plans and the State level sectoral initiatives aimed at strengthening the economy of the State as a whole. For effectively implementing the process of decentralised planning under ZP set-up there is a need for high degree of co-ordination, consultation, guidance, interaction and resolution of conflicts at different tiers, viz. GP, TP, ZP and State Levels.

Lumpsum Allocation

Prior to the Panchayat Raj Act, 1983, state government used to prescribe sector and scheme-wise allocations. The actual process of thinking on local level planning and translating the ideas into concrete developmental programmes was initiated when the Government decided to assign a free outlay in the form of lumpsum allocation for ZPs for formulating their developmental plan, as per the Act of 1983. This lumpsum allocation includes not only outlay from state plan schemes but also the outlay from centrally-sponsored and central sector plan formulation has to be done against lumpsum allocation indicated to the ZPs, TPs and GPs based on the functions assigned to them. Based on the plans formulated by ZPs for this outlay and approval by the Government, the budgeting is done, major head of accountwise in the budget documents of the state government. As long as there is conformity between the lower tiers of government and the state government as regards the priorities for such schemes, there may not be any problem. But conflicts arise if their perspectives for certain schemes differ. In order to avoid any such possible conflicts, it is necessary to earmark outlays for some of these important schemes, which the state government thinks, need to be implemented. Thus, Planning department indicates this, while indicating lumpsum allocation for plan formulation.

Calendar for Planning

Under the existing planning process, a calendar for planning is fixed and followed strictly to formulate the state's plan by incorporating ZP's plans. Hence, the Government has decided to adopt the following calendar for planning.[24]

15th July	Adopting the tentative size for the state's Annual Plan of the next year.
25th July	Government in the planning department to indicate to ZPs the financial ceiling within which their annual plan should be formulated for the next year.
15 August	GPs to send their plan proposals to ZPs.
20th September	ZPs to build the GPs proposals into the district plant upto the Government in the planning department and concerned head of the department at the state.
28th Sept.	Discussion with the ZPs on their draft district plan by the planning department for achieving consistency and interaction of district sector with state sector schemes/plans.
10th Nov.	Government/State Heads of Departments to consolidate these proposals and build them into the state's draft plan and send the same of the Planning Commission.
15th January	Approval of the Planning Commission to the State's plan.
25th Feb.	Finalising the state's plan budget in the light of Planning Commission's approval to the state plan and finalizing the district plans to ZPs.
1st week of March	Presentation of the State's budget to the legislature along with the link documents giving scheme-wise, sector-wise and ZP-wise outlays.

Planning by ZP

Zilla Panchayat provides a necessary link for funding, policy-making, guiding, monitoring and evaluating the entire process. The finance and planning committee of the ZP is vested with overall powers for deciding the sectoral outlays of the annual plan, compiling the micro-level plans originating from the GPs, co-ordinating and monitoring its implementation at various levels. Administratively, the planning wing is headed by the Chief Planning Officer (CPO), who is on deputation from the planning and statistics department. He is assisted by 3 junior colleagues from the same department, in following areas:

(1) Manpower and regional planning,
(2) Credit-based planning, and
(3) Monitoring and evaluation.

These officials guide and assist the ZP sub-committee chairman and members in plan formulation. The sub-committee meetings are attended by the heads of the line departments. The state-planning department indicates the tentative allocations from the centre and the state sector plans for the year. The planning sub-committee of the ZP works out the bifurcation of these funds among district, taluka and GPs as per the schemes that are entrusted to each level by the Act.

Planning at the Intermediate Level, i.e. Taluka/Block

The necessity of interdependence among GPs for socio-economic infrastructure and transfer of technology generates the need for a Taluka level institution, which helps to reduce the inter-GP disparities, through the balancing exercise during allocation of funds at its disposal.

Out of the ZP funds, devolution to TPs and GPs is done through GADGIL formula, wherein, criteria for distribution of Plan funds to GPs and TPs is as follows:

60% weightage is given to the population,
15% weightage is given to the area,
15% weightage is given to the dry land area, and
10% weightage is given to the Agricultural populations.

According to the TP Adhyakshas who were interviewed about the Seventy-third which Amendment enables the States to assign many more functions to this level of Panchayats. However, the intermediate level of Panchayats has, by and large, remained ineffective in the scheme of democratic decentralisation practiced in different States so far. One reason is the lack of clarity on the part of the states in this regard. Another reason has been that the geographical jurisdiction of this level of Panchayats is loosely coterminous with that of a member of the State Legislative Assembly. So, the MLAs are not enthusiastic to have a parallel centre of power.

Karnataka has posted an Executive Officer (EO) of the level of Assistant Commissioner for each of the Intermediate Panchayats. The BDO works under the EO and is particularly responsible for monitoring poverty alleviation programmes in the taluka. Thus, TPs can play a valuable role in organising inter-GP co-ordination in formulation of developmental plans such that the overhead costs could be substantially reduced. Lastly, the TP would be able to consolidate relevant issues through such interactions and help the ZP in formulating the overall development plan for the district. In summation one would visualize the District Panchayat, performing monitoring and advising and implementation by GPs.

PLANNING AT THE VILLAGE LEVEL

The role of GP becomes extremely crucial, in planning for basic needs of the people and also for optimal exploitation of all the available resources of the village. Presently, the GPs are directly planning for the Employment generation programmes. They also plan for the amount collected by way of local cess and taxes. However, the role of GP in preparing and implementing developmental schemes need not be confined to poverty alleviation, etc. Even for implementing schemes transferred to ZPs and TPs, involvement of GPs is essential, e.g., while construction and maintenance of minor irrigation tanks vests with ZP, the task of distribution of the water from such tanks would be more appropriately handled by the GPs. For this reason, it is advisable to take the GPs into confidence while planning for such an irrigation work and also keep the latter involved during execution of the same. Similarly, development of fisheries in smaller irrigation tanks should be assigned to GPs. These examples show the need for devolving the planning activities to GPs from the Panchayats at higher levels for effective implementation and monitoring of development programmes for an area.

Multiplicity of Planning Agencies in the District

Other than the Zilla Panchayat Annual Plan, there are a large number of schemes directly monitored by the state headquarters. These programmes even tend to cater to sectors extending across the district boundaries, e.g., the border area or the watershed development programmes or, those requiring specialised technical interventions like Power Projects, Major Irrigation Works, etc. The multiplicity of agencies involved in planning and implementing development programmes for an area, is an issue of concern. Every implementing agency has become an independent planning agency also for example in Dakshin Kannada district, the following agencies are engaged in preparing development plans:

1. The Zilla Panchayat, with an Annual Plan budget of Rs. 45 crore and a Non-Plan budget of Rs. 70 crore takes care of rural developmental in the district.
2. For removing intra-regional disparities, the Malnad Area Development Board (MADB), is working to bring the area at par with the rest of the State in terms of development indicators. Its budget for the district is Rs. 10 crore.
3. The Border Areas Development Programme (BADP) meant to fill-up the critical infrastructure gaps in bordering talukas and the Ashraya Housing Scheme for the houseless poor families is being implemented by the District Collectors. The annual budget is Rs. 10 crore.
4. The Dry Land Development Board (DLDB), to promote and undertake the dry land development techniques in selected watershed areas, has a budget of about Rs. 1 crore. It is monitored from State Level.
5. Government Agencies, such as the Karnataka Electricity Board (KEB), Karnataka Scheduled Castes and Scheduled Tribes Development Corporation, Karnataka Women's Development Corporation, etc., focus on specialised sectors of development all over the state and yearly budget is Rs. one crore approximately for this district.
6. Departments of the State Government other than the above mentioned agencies such as horticulture, agriculture, fisheries public works, irrigation, etc. plan almost parallel to the departments in the Zilla Panchayats, totalling Rs. 100 crore for the district.

7. District Level Bankers' Committee prepares a credit plan for about 250 crore for the District.

Thus, apart from 115 crore budget of DKZP, the district gets around Rs. 400 crore for its development through t.he above mentioned half a dozen agencies. All these agencies are engaged in planning and developing almost the same region. There are standing instructions from the government to the effect that these agencies should consult each other, while preparing their annual developmental plans. However, these instructions are not supported by institutional networking and they also lack any statutory base, which results in:

(I) Duplication of Efforts

One finds the departments of agriculture, horticulture, sericulture, or SC/ST Corporation, etc. approaching the same beneficiary with conflicting assurances and various scheme assistance for his betterment through their respective programmes. As a result, some people are confused while a few others manage to corner benefits from all sides.

(2) Regional Disparities

Inequitable attention is being. accorded to different micro-regions of micro-demographic groups. Some areas get attended to by all the agencies, whereas some other are omitted by all, e.g., too remote village is never, visited by the extension/supervisory officials and even the Village level functionaries stationed there, are seldom to be found.

(3) Rural-Urban Dichotomy

Existing scheme of development planning keeps the urban and rural areas quite isolated from each other, although the two have been influencing each other in an ever-increasing manner and degree.

(4) Planning Agencies doing the Job of Financing

In fact, no single agency focuses solely on the planning for the region. Technical agencies mentioned above are involved in planning, executing and to a great extent, monitoring their own programmes. The net effect is that the expenditure gets priority at the cost of the planning and monitoring functions. This leads to a system of planning where the 'ongoing works' overshadow the perspective need-based planning for the area.

DISTRICT PLANNING COMMITTEES

It is in this context that the provision of the Constitution relating to the District Planning Committees (DPCs) deserves to be examined. As per Article 243ZD of the Constitution, inserted through the Seventy-fourth Amendment, it is mandatory for the States to constitute the DPCs in every district to consolidate the plans prepared by the Panchayats and the Municipalities in the district and to prepare a draft development plan for the district as a whole. The concept of District Planning Committee offers a fresh hope. The DPC is a body, which will engage in monitoring. It is not expected to execute any plan or projects by itself. It would be able to view the strength and weaknesses of the district and gauge the opportunities and threats surrounding the developmental scenario of the district in an objective fashion.

The DPC has the potential of bringing on one platform all the developmental agencies operating in the district and encouraging them to listen to each other for the purposes of identifying the developmental potential and the strategy for the district. This would obviously call for an appropriate composition of the DPC, which would also need a solid database and trained manpower to prepare an objective and realistic developmental plan for the district. While most of the states have not constituted DPCs, those who have constituted them, have done it only partially in areas which are politically convenient.

Role of Voluntary Agencies

We may now discuss the role of voluntary agencies and professional institutes in the preparation of plans. The rationale of entrusting the task of preparing micro-level plans in consultation with voluntary agencies is that they have a dedicated band of workers, well acquainted with the felt needs and aspirations in the area of operation and as such would be in a better position to enlist people's co-operation in the implementation of development programmes. The voluntary agencies will have to depend on the district administrative machinery for all their data requirements, acquaintance with the on-going programmes, and a host of practical and technical inputs needed for the preparation of the plan. There is ample evidence to show that the Government machinery does not take blindly to this sort of arrangement.

Planning at all levels involves a lot of technical expertise, which is quite distinct from what a subject matter specialist would possess in his own discipline. There are quite a few institutes with proven ability to prepare area development plans. The Planning Commission may compile a list of such institutes with relevant details and make it available to the State Governments/ districts. With all their shortcomings, the district officials know the ground, the operational problems, why and how work -gets done or hindered. Hence, sooner than later, the official machinery of the Government must develop the technical competence for the preparation of the plans and progressively reduce their dependence on outside agencies.

CONCLUSION

We have examined the process of planning in DKZP. Although the financial constraint has been a major cause of lack of interest in the planning process and resorting to first come first serve basis for allocation of funds within the annual plan, yet the new leadership emerging within the PRIs is amenable to the conceived benefits of such a scientific and systematic means of rural development. This is indeed a very healthy trend, which augurs well for the success of these institutions. We suggest here below some of the existing lacunae in this regard.

I. Lack of Training and Motivation of Persons Associated with the Plan Formulation

Most of the persons associated with the plan formulation for Panchayat Raj system in DKZP have neither the requisite skill nor the necessary aptitude to formulate a realistic plan, in consonance with the goals of rural development. The training efforts should cover various line organisations, as well as the elected members of the PRIs. It is not correct to say that the latter are not interested or not capable of understanding the nuances of micro-planning. It should be the constant effort of the planners and administrators to transfer the technology of planning from the portals of research institutions to the field functionaries and elected members of the PRIs.

2. Lack of Adequate and Reliable Information Required for Planning

In the absence of proper statistics, district plans are built on a weak base. DKZP has not developed an adequate management information system, through which realistic information can be collected. Efforts should be made to collect data through properly designed sample surveys, especially those designed for obtaining specific information. The district statistical officer of district is very poorly equipped in terms of manpower/equipment to carry out the above task.

3. Beneficiaries not Involved in the Formulation and Implementation of Plans

People's participation provides extra energy for the success of the plan. Although district officials advocate and preach people's involvement, in practice they bring them into picture only after the major decisions have been made. People should form an integral part of the planning process. There is also a need to set-up effective citizens' bureau like Citizen Advice Bureau (CAB) in the UK where expert services may be made available to the citizens to ensure effective collaboration between the citizens and Governments at all levels.

4. Poor Linkages among Allied Projects at Planning Stage

In DKZP, a number of programmes are being Implemented to Improve the standard of living of the people. Most of the programmes are complementary and supplementary. Poor co-ordination among various departments at the district level results in poor linkages. For example, a project for Agriculture development to grow more food can be gainfully linked with the health project on nutrition. Similarly, population control has many dimensions and needs the co-operation of many agencies. Thus, there is a need for developing an integrated approach.

5. Planning not Based on Population Needs

Planning should be based on the felt needs of the population due to various strings in the form of centralised scheme/budget controls. A population base, in contrast to an institutional base, is absolutely necessary for objective planning.

6. Lack of Competence and Interest of Elected Representatives in Planning

The ultimate decision of planning rests with the elected representatives. They must have proper perception of the problems of the area. They may also be apprised without any fear by the bureaucracy and the technocrats, based on their administrative and technical knowledge. The political elite need to .have an over-all perspective of their political consIderations to be reflected in the plan at the time of its formulation.

7. Absence of Balance between Need, Resources and Use Pertaining to an Area

The allocation, organisation and evaluation of human, technological, financial and physical resources are the principal functions of planning. There are number of ways in which comparable data on perceived need, resources and use can be combined so as to advance our understanding of their relationships. For this purpose, geographically defined areas can be divided in relation to whether they are above or below the medians for appropriate measure of need, use and resources, provided these are defined uniformly for all the project areas and based on comparable data. Chart 8.3 shows a model in which areas can be assigned to one of the 8 cells on the basis of their relative balance of need, resources and use.

The assignment depends on the finding for each area being above or below the median level of need, resources, or use for all areas in the set. In this model, for example, a relatively high level of resources and a relatively high rate of use in the presence of a relatively high rate of perceived need is defined as balance (TYPE A). Conversely, a relatively low level of resource allocation, in conjunction with relatively low use in the presence of low need, is also regarded as constituting balance (TYPE H). A cybernetic model like this would not allow the investment in costly resources to continue longer than is justified by the perceived needs of the population.

8. Importance of the Quantum and Direction of Economic Investment

The quality, nature and direction of ZP's plan efforts at the field level are primarily aimed at making the budget provision in financial terms and corresponding physical targets. The focus should however be on economic investments leading to raising of production/productivity levels to depress poverty levels. Therefore, the results that emerge, should be quantifiable and should bear a favourable cost benefit relationship.

The district plan tends to cover all the sectors and hence gets diluted in terms of its priorities and objectives, e.g., the agriculture and related primary sector contributes nearly 1/3rd of the State's GDP, yet the direct investment effort in this sector at the level of ZPs, is only 5%, to meet the cost of extension services in Agriculture, Horticulture, Fisheries, Animal Husbandry, dairy and forestry and for a few subsidy-linked schemes. Similarly, the irrigation potential and its use being low, the plans for tapping additional surface water to irrigate all dry lands through watershed technology for storing the available flowing water at the present levels of investment would take at least 50 years to be achieved.

9. Lack of Planning Focus on the Poorest of the Poor

In order to make any meaningful impact on poverty, action plans have to be driven with the visionary approach to push the poorest of the poor up from the very bottom, applying the pressure at the very base of poverty. Decentralisation is canvassed as a thrust for poverty eradication at micro-level.

Although political and other interests in poverty removal and decentralised planning may be plentiful, there are lacunae in the policy thrust, as there is insufficient recognition of the need to let the poor and the weak decide what they want and how their lot can be ameliorated. At present, their participation is sought, but only in moulds of the planner's choosing, through organisational instruments such as schemes and programmes, which treat them as no more than "receiving mechanisms" rather than as people with traditional wisdom, values and skills. This gap must go.

10. Lack of Integration between National and Local Planning

ZP functionaries mentioned that the percentage of totally uncommitted funds given to the ZPs in 1988-89 carne to about 14 percent. The untied allocation given to ZPs is not expected to go beyond 30 percent of the total plan outlay. Good local-level planning, dovetailed into national level planning, will give depth and wholeness to the national plan.

11. Lack of Recognition of the Need for Open-ended Funding for Micro-level Programmes

Micro-level poverty alleviation programmes should be given open-ended funding. That is, the local-level executives should be handed bags of gold without labels to be used as they and the target peoples' representatives in mutual consultation, deem fit. What would then result is decentralisation based on lumpsum budgets, inter-sectoral choice availability and divergence of planning activity across plan units. The arrangement would imply self-monitoring by these agents. The motto would be that virtue is its own reward and the invisible hand of group interest acts as the co-ordinator.[25]

CHART 8.3

High	Type–A Balanced Appropriate allocation of resources	Type–B Compensatory high productivity of resources	Type–E Unbalanced overuse of resources	Type–F Unbalanced high productivity of resources
Low	Type–C Unbalanced Under use of investment resources	Type–D Unbalanced under use in resources	Type–G Unbalanced over investment in resources	Type–H Balanced appropriate allocation of resources

Note: Needs, resources and use may be defined by any appropriate measure as long as they are uniform over all the areas being considered.

Source: WHO, Public Health Papers, 1967, p. 80.

12. Absence of Result-oriented Monitoring System

At present, the functionaries of GP are over-burdened with the progress reporting formats to be regularly submitted to higher level tiers, in terms of physical and financial targets achieved. However, in a decentralised set-up, reporting of progress and checking of result should be largely by word of mouth and visual inspection. Information systems, which do not move from bottom up, have to be envisaged. At least, the success stories of one area can become known in other areas.

13. Need for Autonomy with Accountability

PRIs require functional and administrative autonomy to prove their worth. The functional autonomy would be based on the following principles:[26]

1. The Principle of Efficiency

A function, which could be done better at a particular level, should be done at that level and not at any other level.

2. The Principle of Complimentarily

Allocation of functions for various levels should be complementary to each other. They must not be competitive or overlapping.

3. The Principle of Clarity

The line of command and control should be clear, certain and predictable so that the autonomy of the tier, other things being equal, is always respected.

4. Agency Functions should not Dominate

If PRIs continue to function as agents of the state and Union Government, they could never become instruments of self-government.

14. Enforcing Financial Discipline while Planning

There is a widespread view that PRIs tend to be profligate in their spending and such assessments are not wide-off the mark. PRIs routinely take up works that are much more than the allocations made to them. Works are often included in the action plan with only a token allocation made for them or without any funds allocation at all, under pressure from elected representatives and local contractors. This is especially true with respect to road works and buildings. It is not as if given the level of funds that are actually available for works, what they suggest cannot be completed within the annual plan period—elected members are often not as interested in completion of their work, but in the fact that a commitment towards inclusion is made in the plan, through a 'token provision' of funds. Once a work is included in the action plan, there is always the possibility that pressure can be mounted to grab payments by diversion of funds later on. Such a situation arises basically from the fact that the planning process has itself deteriorated into a 'spoils sharing' system under which elected representative vie for inclusion of 'their' schemes and works. Quite often, we have seen the phenomenon of an outgoing PRI making huge commitments towards new works, so that the new body is burdened down by the need to provide funds for spill over works. This problem has snow balled and brought a bad name to the entire concept of decentralization planning. The concept has now been subverted into a "grab what you can when it lasts" exercise, done by PRI members beyond closed doors.

The result of such lack in planning discipline is two-fold. First, it reinforces the belief of the State Government that PRIs are irresponsible spenders and second, if such plans are indeed approved, it spreads funds too thin, becomes counter productive and results in time and cost overruns. Another possibility of lack of financial discipline is that the PRIs could easily change their budget time and time again through simple resolutions. This could affect financial discipline and hamper effective downward monitoring by the people.

The State must empower and facilitate District Panchayat, Intermediate Level Panchayat and Gram Panchayat to prepare their Annual Action Plan. It must be ensured that the District Planning Committees should prepare composite District Plan after taking into account, Annual Action Plans prepared by the Panchayats at all the three tiers.

Notes and References

1. Pfiffner and Presthus: Public Administration, p. 83.
2. *Ibid.*
3. Drucker, Peter F.: Long Range Planning ... Challenge to Management Science, in *Management Science*, April, 1959, p. 233.
4. Simon, B.A., Smithburg, D.W., and Thompson V.A.: Public Administration.
5. Sixth Five Year Plan (1980-85), p. 89.
6. Madhu Dandavate, "Ethos of Planning and Plan Administration in India", *IJPA*, Oct.-Dec. 1997, Vol. XLIII, No. 4, pp. 871.
7. W. Arthur Lewis, "Development Planning: The Essentials of Economic Policy" (London, George Allen, 1966), p. 23.
8. Proceedings of Inter-regional Seminar in Organisation and Administration of Development Planning Agencies (U.N., Sales No. E. 74. 11, H. 2) Vol. I, p. 118.
9. Planning for Economic. Development: Report of the Secretary General (U.N. Publication, Sales No. 64. II. B. 3), 84.
10. Proceedings of Interregional Seminar, *op. cit.*, p. 119.
11. Economic Bulletin for Asia and the Far East, Vol. XII, No. 3, (U.N., December 1961), p. 79.

12. Ahmad Shamshad and M.D. Nafees Ahmad, "Planning Commission: Fifty-Five years of Planned Development and Social Sector", *IJPA*, July-Sept., 2005, Vol. LI, No. 3, p. 469.
13. *The Tribune*, July 17, 1984.
14. *The Tribune*, July 24, 1984.
15. P.P. Agarwal, "The Planning Commission," in *the Indian Journal of Public Administration*, October-December 1957, p. 332.
16. *Ibid*.
17. *Ibid*.
18. V.T. Krishnamachari, "Fundamentals of Planning in India", Orient Longman.
19. Madan Gopal Sinha, "An Analysis of the Social Sector Development in India", *IJPA*, July-Setp. 2005, Vol. LI, No. 3, p. 510.
20. Madan Gopal Sharma, "An Analysis of the Social Sector Development in India", *IJPA*, July-Sept., 2005, Vol. LI, No. 3, p. 515.
21. *The Tribune* (August 18, 1984).
22. Administrative Reforms Commission, *op. cit.*, p. 47.
23. *The Tribune*, Chandiarh, 1 August, 1979.
24. K.P. Trivedi, "A Study of Official-non-official relations at Block Level of Panchayat Raj in U.P.", *Political Scientist*, Vol. 5, 1968-69, p. 108.
25. A. Krishnaswamy Aiyanagar, "Relationship between officials and Elected Representatives in Panchayat Raj Institutions", in R.N. Haldipur and V.R.K. Parmahamsa (ed.), Local Government Institutions in Rural India, Hyderabad, NIRD, 1979, p. 272.
26. William F. Ogburn, and Meyer, F. Nimkoff, A Hand Book of Sociology, New Delhi, Eurosia, 1979, p. 87.

CHAPTER

9

Development Project Management: Formulation, Implementation and Evaluation

As stated in Ninth Five Year Plan, "For the realisation of the intended Plan objectives, the quality of design and effectiveness of implementation of the Plan programmes are as important as the availability of resources. Past experience has shown that many development projects and programmes, having laudable objectives, have failed to deliver the result because of the inadequacies in design and implementation. Time and cost overruns have been widespread and substantial in public sector infrastructure and investment projects.

According to the PMBOK Guide, 3rd Edition, Chapter 3 there are five project management process groups used to manage a project—initiating processes, planning processes, executing processes, controlling processes, and closing processes. They can be viewed as shown in Chart 9.1.

These processes are followed from the very beginning of a project until it is closed out. But more than that, these processes are used for each phase within the project as well. The team initiates a phase, plans how to accomplish the work, executes and controls the work, and finally closes out the phase and moves into the next phase. These processes are not performed in isolation. They interact with each other a shown in Chart 9.1.

Project management includes identifying requirements; establishing clear and achievable objectives; balancing demands for quality, scope, time, and cost; and adapting the specifications, plans and approach to the needs and concerns of various stakeholders. But this is just one aspect of what is taken to call the project a success.

Projects are usually performed by a team rather than by just one person, so a major component of being a successful project manager is managing people to achieve the project goals. Many new project managers mistakenly think that project management is just another task to be done on top of developing the product.

CHART 9.1

The Five Project Management Process

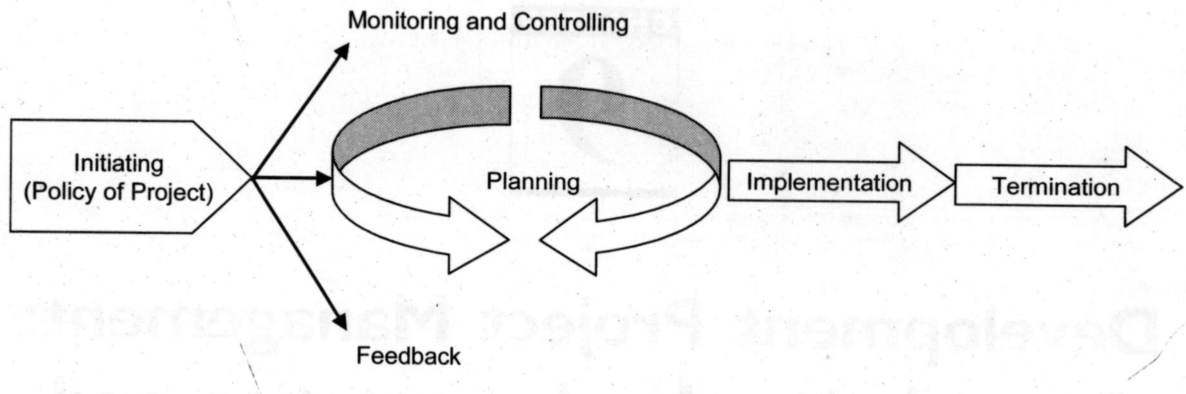

DEFINITION OF A PROGRAMME

Webster's Seventh New Collegiate Dictionary defines 'Programme' as "a brief outlines of the order to be pursued or the subjects embraced." In one of the United Nations Publications, Professor Egbert de Vries takes the programme to mean "a form of organized social activity with a specific objective, limited in space and time. It often consists of an interrelated group of 'projects' and usually is limited to one or more organizations and activities."[1] For example, in the field of health programme is considered to be "Changes in the output of the health system such as the provision of medical care, environmental health and other health services—are considered as operating services of a programme."[2]

DEFINITION OF A PROJECT

As stated in a UN publication entitled 'Manual of Economic Development Projects', project is defined as "the compilation of data which will enable an appraisal to be made of the economic advantages and disadvantages attendant upon the allocation of country's resources to the production of specific goods and services."[3] As such project means the specifications and accomplishments, within a given period, of related set of activities that will result in a measurable change in any system's capacity to improve the status of the community directly or indirectly. Besides, the projects are "a link in the process of successive approximations involved in the technique of programming and an important element in the flexibility and continuous services of the programme."[4]

From these definitions, we can locate the characteristics which are common to all projects. A project aims at specific goals and purposes. Secondly, it is a time bound activity. Thirdly, it requires co-operation and co-ordination with other projects to achieve the goals of plan.

A project may be small or wide; limited or comprehensive in nature and scope. It may be set-up with purely indigenous resources or with the help of bilateral agencies or with the help of multi-lateral technical assistance. The term 'Project' is used in the following discussion as a generic concept. No attempt is made to classify the project into different categories or to state the unique administrative requirements of different types of projects. The emphasis is on the common administrative elements of projects, irrespective of their size, sector or substance. These administrative elements should *mutatis mutandis,* apply to all projects. We shall now discuss the various stages involved in the project management.

Project management is the application of skills both professional and administrative knowledge, and abilities to change input into output. The components that lead to successful projects are technical knowledge, general management abilities, project management skills, and availability of inputs in time. The project manager must have competence of the technical aspects of the project. The project manager also needs some capability in the area of general management, including skills in budgeting, analysis, planning and coordinating. Finally, the project manager must apply project management skills, tools and techniques to make the projects a success. (See Chart 9.2)

CHART 9.2

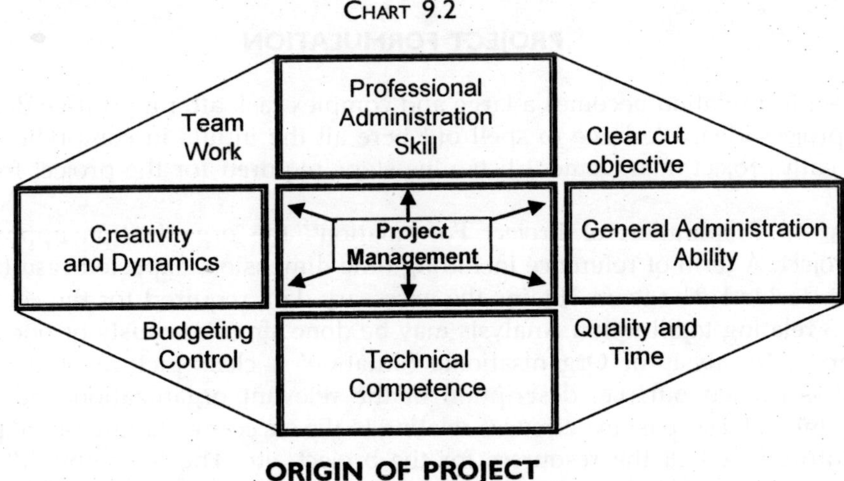

ORIGIN OF PROJECT

Projects usually do not emerge themselves. The motivation and decision to set-up a project mostly emerge within the existing organizations at various levels. Sometimes, bilateral and multilateral agencies promote the organization to set-up a project. The impetus to set-up a project can come from the political parties, pressure groups, interest groups, or can emerge from the researches, evaluations or studies conducted by the Universities/Training Institutions. Before the project may take birth, it is necessary to ensure that the project is:

(a) according to the socio economic policy of the country,
(b) According to the priority needs of the people,
(c) Linked properly with the objectives and goals of planning,
(d) Fitted into the overall economic and social development of the country,
(e) Properly linked with projects in the allied area, and
(f) Able to achieve useful and permanent results.

Besides, there must be sufficient administrative capability and financial resources to continue the programme after the termination of the project. All these factors are very important in order to conceive a sound project. Lack of well conceived projects retards the implementation of development projects.

J.M. Kitchlu while outlining the phases of life cycle of a project says, "The need for carrying out detailed planning is being increasingly recognized but there is still cases where projects are being approved without essential steps regarding all stages of preparation and scrutiny being undertaken in the pre construction stage. This has resulted in the formulation of incompletely conceived plans and estimates and thus had led to unsound decisions on project size, scope, location and product-mix."[5] The effective project choice would enhance the value of plans as well. As started in a UN publication, "The availability of well conceived projects and the institution of work on their formulation, simultaneously with the institution of the formulation of plans will improve their implementability. By the time a plan is finalized and improved enough implementability. By the time a plan is finalized and improved enough projects should be available to go in the implementation phase."[6]

PROJECT FORMULATION

Project formulation becomes a large and complex task after a positive decision has been taken on a project idea. We have to spell out here all the inputs in comprehensive form. The manual of heath project management lists nine steps required for the project formulation (See Chart 9.3).

In step 1, 'Preparation of Project Formulation', the organization appoints a team to formulate project. A term of reference including time dimension, expected results, resource and problems are decided. The team obtains the necessary data required for the concerned project. Steps 2 and 3 relating to Situation Analysis may be done simultaneously or one after the other.

In step 2, 'Analysis of Organisational Situation' a clear picture of the organisational environment is carried out, i.e. description of the relevant organization and agencies; their decision-making process, past experiences relating to the success or failure of the project, need of current or future levels of the resources for the project, etc. The team should concentrate on producing reasonable and information summaries.

In step 3, 'Analysing the Socio-economic and Demographic Situation,' the present and future analysis is done of the socio-economic situation and the demographic situation.

In step 4, 'Analysis and Projection of the Problem,' we define the problems and projection of the future situation which is worked out on the assumption that existing trends continue without change in the relevant systems and their policies.

In step 5, 'Getting the Objectives and Targets,' entails a statement of the problem-reduction to be achieved through the project and translating them into the kind and magnitude of services (operational targets that would have to be provided at various future times in order to reach the objectives).

In step 6, 'Identification of Potential Obstacles', an attempt is made to predict the potential obstacles that might stand in the way of reaching the operational targets established in step 5.

In step 7, 'Design of Strategies,' the key sub-steps involved are the establishment of explicit criteria for strategy design, the selection of flexible strategies, the assessment of their implications in costs and requirements, and revision of the targets and strategies under consideration in the light of the assessment.

In step 8, 'Planning the Project,' the team decides design of efficient performance. The thinking of the team shifts here from 'what is to be developed' to how is it to be developed.

CHART 9.3

Steps in Project Formulation

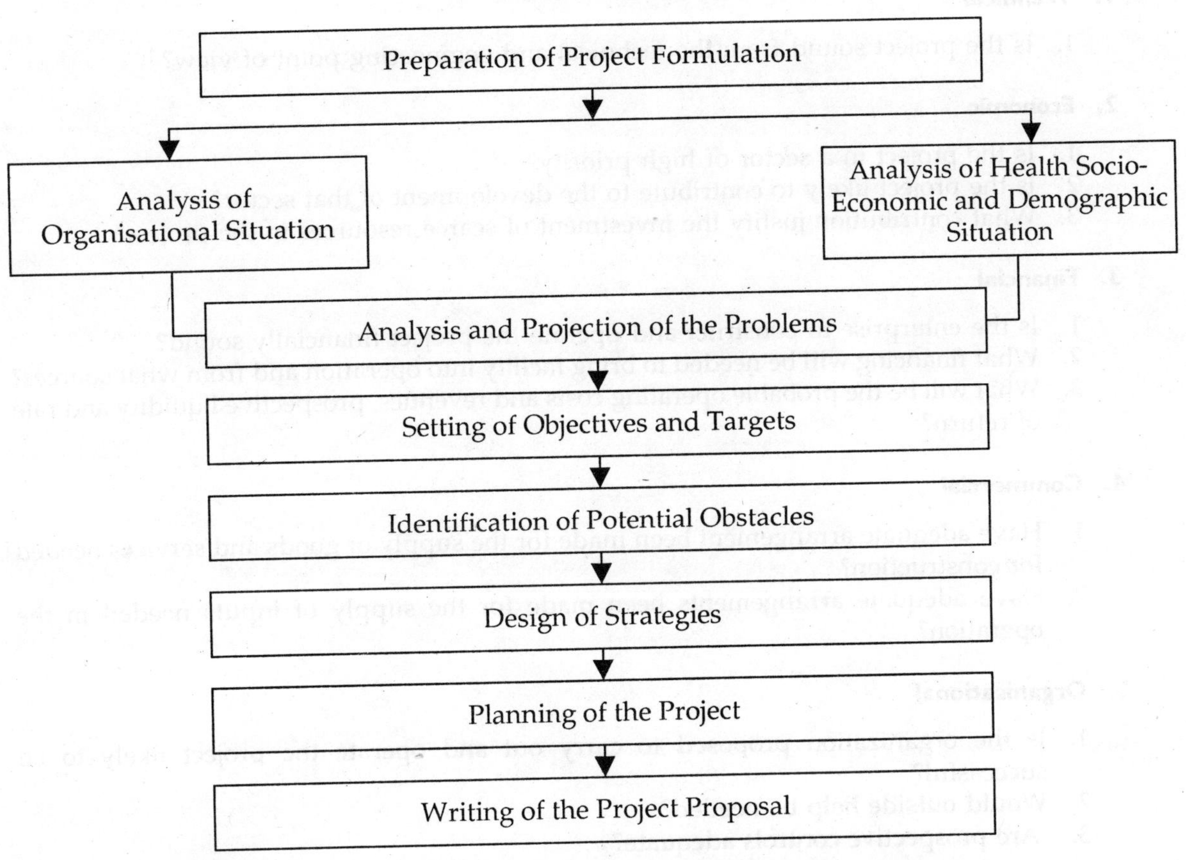

Source: WHO 76550.

In the final step 9, 'Writing the Project Proposal,' the products of earlier steps are re-examined, synthesized, and documented in the form of a project proposal.

In this whole process, the details would differ from country to country.

(1) In situations where such planning has not taken place, the formulation procedures provides useful guidance and support to such planning as part of project formulation.

(2) In situations in which such higher level planning has taken place, the analytical and general design steps would be considerably shortened and made more specific in content than the procedures now indicate."[7]

After the project has been formulated, there is a need to examine its soundless. J.P. Gupta says that in the appraisal of a project, following questions need to be answered; [8] (See Chart 9.4)

Project planning has to be more scientific and approval procedure more realistic to ensure that avoidable time and cost overruns are much less frequent. The approval procedure should be

Aspects	Basic question

1. Technical

1. Is the project sound from the technical and engineering point of view?

2. Economic

1. Is the project in a sector of high priority?
2. Is the project likely to contribute to the development of that sector?
3. What contribution justify the investment of scarce resources in the project?

3. Financial

1. Is the enterprise to construct and operate the project financially sound?
2. What financing will be needed to bring facility into operation and from what sources?
3. What will be the probable operating costs and revenues, prospective liquidity and rate of return?

4. Commercial

1. Have adequate arrangement been made for the supply of goods and services needed for construction?
2. Have adequate arrangements been made for the supply of inputs needed in the operation?

5. Organisational

1. Is the organization proposed to carry out and operate the project likely to be successful?
2. Would outside help be needed?
3. Are prospective controls adequate?

6. Managerial

1. What is the quality of the proposed management? It is likely to be adequate to ensure performance not inferior to that to be expected from the appraisal?

7. Social

1. What are the changes caused by the project in the behavioural pattern and the attitude in the population?
2. What are the attitudes of the population towards the projects?
3. Does the project require specific element of social change?

8. Environmental

1. Does the project cause pollution?
2. Does the project disturb the equilibrium of ecology?
3. Does the project fit into the environment?

linked with early completion of incomplete projects and sustainability of project output. Because of the unrealistic approval procedure, many of the projects are delayed. At the other extreme, less stringent approval procedures encourage a tendency to get too many projects cleared without the requisite financial resources in sight. There is, thus, a need for striking a balance between these extremes. It is important to ensure that rigour in appraisal and planning does not itself become a cause of delay because of repetitive and multi-level examination of technical and economic data. Strict time-tables need to be laid down for completion of the approval processes and preliminary work. Similarly, strict financial procedures should be formulted for eliminating projects, which do not have financial backing.

The lessons learnt from the experience of executing thousands of development schemes during the last fifty years can be briefly summarised as follows:

- There is inadequate analysis of available information during programme formulations. This happens primarily, because there is no established mechanism through which the programme agencies can have ready access to the relevant information regarding the target groups/areas or the findings of evaluation studies. As a result, avoidable errors at the planning stage creep in. For example, in a programme designed for the empowerment of rural women, the basic and well-known fact that most rural women, in India are illiterate was not explicitly considered while formulating the operational rules and designing the delivery system.
- The operational cost of some programmes tends to be abnormally high, partly because of redundant and ineffective administration and partly due to other inadequacies in planning and implementation.
- The general approach in implementation is "top-down" and "target-oriented." Some physical and financial targets are sought to be achieved in most programmes. However, evaluation studies by the Planning Commission reveal that the fulfilment of these targets does not necessarily ensure that the programme objectives are being met. In many anti-poverty programmes though the targeted number of families/ beneficiaries/districts/villages have been covered and the alloted money spent, such programmes have failed in making the desired impact on the well-being of the beneficiaries. The implementing agencies are often more concerned with the mere fulfilment of targets assigned to them than with the actual flow of benefits to the targets groups.
- Formulation of a multiplicity of programmes in an area of social concern without any specific thrusts can lead to several problems. Available resources are spread too thinly across a large number of projects leading to sub-optimal projects outcome.
- For some programmes separate implementing agencies are created, whereas these are actually implemented by the existing line departments, who work independently for different components of a programme. This results in lack of focus on target groups, wastage of resources and lack of coordination among the line departments. The creation of such agencies without the necessary institutional changes makes them redundant and affects the implementation and operation of programmes.
- Lack of accountability of the implementing agencies either to the Government or to the people has been the single major cause for diversion of funds in development programmes.

Several social sector programmes are formulated without addressing the question of sustainability of benefits. The most distressing part of financing of the development projects and programmes under the Five Year Plan regime has been the failure to ensure timely and adequate flow of funds to the implementing agencies.

The essential ingredients of people's participation for self-development, as revealed in the success stories, are assessment of local resources and local level planning, sensitizing people and building local organisations for collective actions and an umbrella support mechanism to facilitate people's development actions. If these processes and mechanisms are to be multiplied on a wider scale, these will have to be institutionalized. The multiplication process requires a major political commitment by the State to provide the necessary political space and a policy framework for a sensitive support mechanism. This will call for, among other things, simplification of ground rules that would facilitate participation of grassroots level organisations in the development process, bringing about flexibility and dynamism among the providers of public services, and orienting the judicial system for speedy disposal of disputes and sensitive to the needs of the disadvantaged people.

PROJECT IMPLEMENTATION

Proper implementation of the programme is vital and great attention and energy are required to ensure this. In this context, India's Planning Commission said: "The success of the Third Plan will rest very largely on the efficiency with which it is implemented."[9] The purpose of implementation is to ensure that the project activities have been completed on schedule and within budget, and that there are favourable conditions to maintain the desired changes generated by the project after the project as such is terminated. Project implementation steps are repetitive ones and each project manager will have to adopt the procedures to his own situation depending upon the nature of the project and the organisational structures. The stages of implementation has been discussed in the 'Health Project Management Manual' which are described below (see Chart 9.4)

1. Initiating the project

Obtaining approval for the project proposal, appointing the project manager, preparing the interim budget and beginning the recruitment of other project staff.

2. Specifying and Scheduling the Work

Projecting the details of work and deciding what tasks are to be done by whom and when.

3. Clarifying Authority, Responsibility and Relationships

Obtaining agreement as to who is responsible for ensuring that the work gets done, distributing decision-making authority among the project team and the existing organisational units, and establishing formal lines of communication.

4. Obtaining Resources

Obtaining the funds, manpower, supplies and equipment necessary for doing the project activities.

CHART 9.4

Steps in Project Management

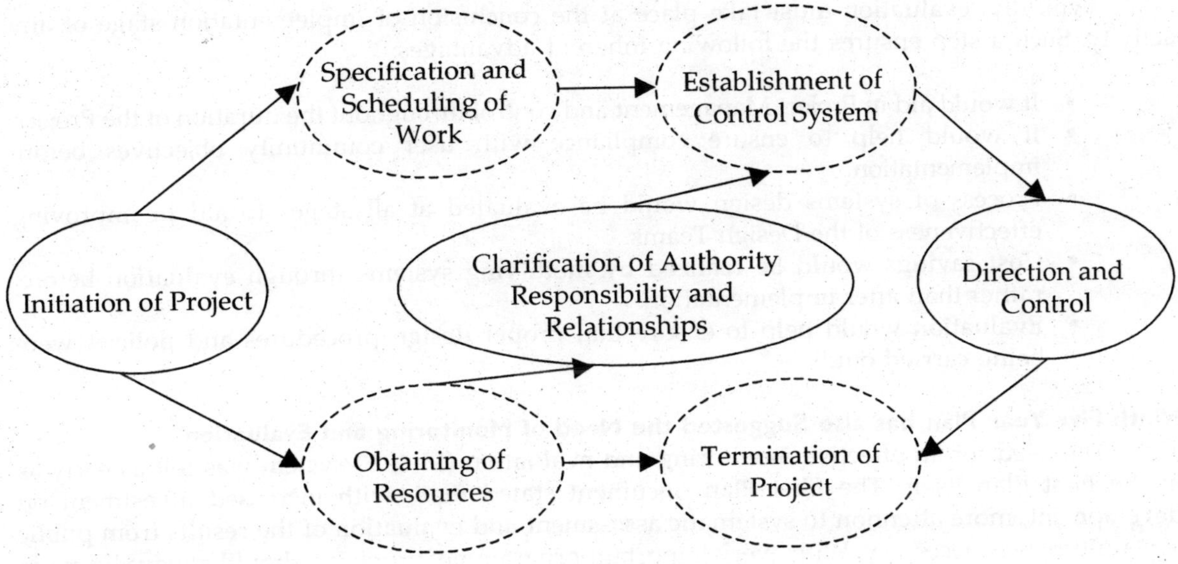

Specification and Scheduling of Work → Establishment of Control System

Initiation of Project → Specification and Scheduling of Work

Initiation of Project → Obtaining of Resources

Obtaining of Resources → Clarification of Authority Responsibility and Relationships

Clarification of Authority Responsibility and Relationships → Establishment of Control System

Establishment of Control System → Direction and Control

Obtaining of Resources → Termination of Project

Direction and Control → Termination of Project

Source: WHO 70549.

5. Establishing the Control System

Determining what information is necessary for project control, identifying sources of such information and setting up reporting systems for the project.

6. Directing and Controlling

Motivating project staff, executing project activities, obtaining information for control and taking corrective action as necessary.

7. Terminating the Project

Handing over responsibilities to existing staff and preparing the final report.

The implementation machinery can resort to modern methods of management to achieve desired results.

EVALUATION OF PROJECTS

All development projects undertaken need to be evaluated for the results they have achieved or failed to achieve. Careful evaluation is the backbone of all projects. It is indispensable as a guarantee of effective use of resources and of accountability for their use. Evaluation of results achieved in a project is required in order to benefit fully from the experience. Evaluation would be futile unless it is carried out on a systematic and co-ordinated fashion with clearly defined objectives and consistent procedures applied by the competent evaluators. Barnabas contends that "to be most effective, evaluation must not be made merely of physical achievements but also of the cost of such achievements."[10]

Evaluation can be effective only if we have well designed format to secure timely, regular and dependable information on the performance of projects. Ninth Five Year Plan has also suggested the need of monitoring and Evaluation.

Typically, evaluation must take place at the conclusion of implementation stage of any activity. Such a step ensures the following inherent advantages:

- It would aid in Project Management and control throughout the duration of the Project.
- It would help to ensure compliance with user community objectives before implementation.
- Process of systems design would be evaluated at all stages to aid in improving effectiveness of the Design Teams.
- Cost savings would be realized by modifying systems through evaluation before, rather than after implementation.
- Evaluation would help to ensure that proper design procedures and policies were being carried out.[11]

Ninth Five Year Plan has also Suggested the Need of Monitoring and Evaluation

The need for an effective monitoring and evaluation (M & E) system was felt as early as in the First Plan itself. The First Plan document stated that "with increased investment on development, more attention to systematic assessment and evaluation of the results from public expenditure was necessary. With every important programme, provision should always be made for the assessment of results. Inspite of considerable development in economic and social sciences, our knowledge of human motivation and social processes is but limited. We cannot always say for certain that a given set of causes will produce a particular, clearly definable, set of results and none other." The Second Plan document emphasized the need for a strong. M & E system building up a strong development administration, training and personnel, informing and educating the public and organizing a sound system of planning based as much on the participation of the people at each level as on the best technical, economic and statistical information available. As a review of the past Plan performance revealed gaps in achievement in various areas of development, the need for a strong M & E system only got reinforced in subsequent Plan documents.

Over time and elaborate monitoring and evaluation mechanism has been built for efficient development administration and a large number of institutions for training in public administration at the Centre and State level have been created. While the M & E system has proved its utility in development administration, it is not as effective as it should be. The scope and nature of development programmes have been undergoing changes and the interaction between a programme and its environment is becoming increasingly complex. The government now operates under increasing financial and competitive pressures. The M & E system has not shown the necessary dynamism to cope with these changes and complexities. The Working Group on Monitoring and Information System of the Seventh Five Year Plan identified the following programs:

- Ineffectiveness in identifying/reducing likely delays and problems.
- Large data gaps, delays in data generation and transmission, inadequate data Analysis, feedback not reaching proper users.
- Inadequate information on interlinked projects.

- Information difficult to retrieve in the absence of data bank.
- Information not reflecting the true picture.
- More emphasis on reporting than on action.
- Inadequate use of monitored information in decision-making.

CRITICAL APPRAISAL

Based upon the studies of a number of projects, we would examine the problems which need solution to ensure the efficient functioning of the project. Let us mention here the problems and their possible solutions.

1. Lack of Training and Motivation on the Part of Persons Associated with the Project Formulation

Most of the persons associated with the project formulation have neither the requisite skill nor the necessary aptitude to formulate the project in consonance with the goals of the project. In developing countries, people are appointed in the project formulation team on the basis of their status and not on the basis of their capability and interest. Besides, it is understood in these countries that any general administrator can be fit enough to formulate a project. This assumption in this age of specialization and sophistication does not hold good. Project formulation is an art which must be learnt. Secondly, it requires hard work and motivation. Even the best trained persons are of no use if they do not posses high morale—a socio-psychological situation in which men and women voluntarily work on a chosen filed because of their intellectual satisfaction. The trained person with high morale can be very successful in the management of projects. It has been rightly mentioned that, "Project formulation can be characterized in two words—hard work. The fact that a logical sequence of steps is outlined, some which utilized techniques of system analysis and modern management, should not mislead the reader into thinking that this is a quick and easy method for producing bullet proof proposals. A good deal of information must be reviewed, structured and manipulated. A great deal of thinking must be done by intelligent, experienced and practical people for this.

Before implementing the project it would be better to arrange a workshop to provide training for the persons responsible for this task. In such a workshop, potential difficulties may be analysed and solutions may be found to solve such difficulties. The workshop should not be converted into a class room situation, but should encourage active participation so that the participants get sufficient training and motivation to handle the project efficiently.

2. Linkages with the Allied Projects Missing

In particular geographical or functional area, a number of projects are being implemented to improve the standard of living of the people. Most of the projects are complementary and supplementary. Because of the poor coordination among the various departments, at the state level, the projects are implemented in the area without developing linkages with each other. For example, a project for the agriculture development to grow more food can be beautifully linked with health projects on nutrition. Population control has many dimensions and needs the co-operation of many agencies. Thus, there is a need of area planning and developing an integrated area approach where different projects may develop linkages to have optimum benefit.

3. Project Implementations team not clear about Project Objectives

In most of the developing countries, there is a dichotomy between the personnel responsible for the formulation and the personnel responsible for the implementation of projects. The latter are not clear about the implications of the projects. Because of lack of identify, they develop low morale resulting into the poor management. It was mentioned by a number of persons working on some project without proper briefing about the project and its rationale in the total system. Besides, the supervisors, at the head quarters, never guide them about their role in the projects." Furthermore, the persons are transferred during the operation of the project resulting into the induction of new untrained persons. There has been hardly any project where the persons appointed in the beginning of the project implementation continue till the termination of the project. Thus, there is a great need of the involvement of the persons associated with the implementation of the projects at some stage of the formulation and appraise them of full, implications of the project. Besides, they must be briefed properly and recurrent guidance may be provided to keep them rightly informed. This will develop a good rapport between the formulators and implementers of the projects.

4. Projects under the Centrally Sponsored Schemes are not Adapted but Adopted

There are a large number of projects which are sponsored by the Union Government (India). States get 100 per cent re-imbursement on such schemes. The schemes designed by the Union Government cannot suit all the areas equally. The administrative machinery and inputs of the projects must be designed by the State Governments according to the ecological conditions existing in that area. For example, the family planning projects must be adjusted according to the needs of the area. What is happening is that the structure devised by the Union Government for the implementation of projects is adopted by the State Government. This becomes the main cause of the failure of a number of projects.

5. Beneficiaries not involved in the Formulation and Implementation of Projects

The success or failure of the projects ultimately depends upon the acceptance of these projects by the people. If the people are not taken into confidence during the formulation and implementation of projects, these would be less successful. People's participation would provide extra nuclear energy to the success of the projects. Most of the beneficiaries contacted by the writer were of the view that they are not treated as equal partners in the process of formulation and implementation of projects. The failure of the scheme is because of the absence of identification of the people with the programmes. It is essential for the experts in the developing countries to motivate and encourage the people to participate in the formulation and implementation of projects. Although people's participation in affairs governing their lives dates back to the beginning of human society, the concept has taken a new dimension as societies have grown in size and complexity. This is partly because the management has become more and more a specialized enterprise, an area for technocrats and trained general administrators and political leaders. Although they officially advocate and preach people's involvement, in practice, they bring them to picture only after the major decisions have been made. Hence, they often leave the ordinary citizens to follow their pre-determined paths. Peter Berger agrees with this contention when he says that "the overwhelming majority of these people have little or no opportunity to influence policy, and their perspectives on the situation are systematically ignored by almost all theorists. For them the problem of development is one of the everyday life."[12]

Local communities are treated as passive participants in improvement and bettering of their lives. Most of the project personnel working in the villages return to the cities after their duty hours. The villagers cannot make their views known to them in cities. The result is lack of communication among them. When the project fails, it is intentionally ascribed to the obstinacy, fatalism, illiteracy or apparent irritationality of the poor people. The potential for community involvement has been seriously under-estimated. We must encourage people's participation through all methods to promote development.

6. Absence of any Satisfactory Monitoring System to Measure the Regulated Performance during Implementation

Most of the projects are never completed within the budgeted resources and fixed time schedules. It has become a normal feature to extend the life of the project resulting in the wastage of huge financial resources. It clearly indicates the weakness of controlling mechanism. Project control is the managerial function that helps the managers to keep the project functioning as scheduled. It is possible only if the realistic advance targets of output are fixed before implementation. This is not being done as is evident from the perusal of the most of the projects studied. Monitoring if properly designed can help the managers in keeping the process of implementation as scheduled. The project performance is compared at different intervals of time with the control indicators. Whenever deviations are located, causes of deviations are examined, solutions are found to correct the deviations.

Seventh Five Year Plan has suggested the following essentials of monitoring:

Essentials of Monitoring

- The primary responsibility of monitoring lies with the agency entrusted with the execution of programme/project.
- The monitoring responsibility cannot be entrusted to a single individual. It must be a group effort.
- Monitoring should not be construed as a mistrust or a direct interference in the functioning of an organisation.
- Monitoring team should have the motto of furnishing fearless, honest and business like reports.
- Monitoring to be effective and a dynamic force pre-supposes a firm commitment, involvement and team spirit from all concerned.
- Monitoring and scheduling being inter-dependent should have a close rapport with each other.
- In relatively small projects, it would be advisable if both these functions are performed by one body known as scheduler or monitor.
- The scope of monitoring need not be confined to top management. Instead, information in a filtered form may flow from the field to the highest authorities pinpointing critical areas at the appropriate levels.
- Monitoring team should be manned by those who are talented, trained and have the aptitude in the art of monitoring. Suitable environment also needs to be created so that the personnel get job satisfaction and their future is not at stake.
- The time interval of measuring progress should be in direct proportion (appropriate) to the phenomenon being studied.
- Information reports may be made available to those who can really facilitate in influencing a timely action on them.

- In the case of monitoring of complex projects, renowned Project Management Companies may be engaged who have vast experience of project execution and also keep a band of specialists from all disciplines with them. The Seventh Plan document has also stressed the need for developing management consultancy to play its role in quick and economical execution of projects.[13]

7. Lack of Proper Follow-up after the Termination of the Project

It has been observed generally that the programmes are generally shelved on one pretext or the other after the termination of the project. There is a great fan fare when the project is set-up but it would be of no use if the projects do not continue and change into permanent ongoing programmes. There is a great need to improve the capability, ethos, perception and attitudes of the political elite so that they can take correct decision in the ultimate interest of the people. Gabriel A. Almond defines political development as "the acquisition of new capability, in the sense of a specialized role structure and differentiated orientations which together give a political system of possibility of responding efficiently and more or less autonomously to a new range of problems."[14]

Thus, "a political system is said to be developing when there is an increase in its ability to sustain successfully and continuously new types of special goals and creation of new types of organization."[15]

8. Project not Dovetailed with National Policies and Plans

Projects are not the outcome of plans and policies resulting in the poor impact on the total development. Projects must emerge from the policies and plans for greater coherence and effectiveness. There must be effective linkages among projects, plans and policies.

9. Unscientific Manpower Planning: Insufficient Utilization of Project Personnel

The success of the project depends upon the quality and quantity of personnel associated with it. it was observed that in many projects, the projects personnel have their utilization time as low as 20 per cent. This is highly serious as the resources are being consumed by the establishment rather than invested in the welfare of the people. Because of the absence of manpower planning, personnel of the project utilize very little time. People in the area remarked about the workers appointed to motivate people to adopt family planning norm: "They are not available at all. They rarely devote any time for this work. They remain away from their work." It is essential to see through proper manpower planning that only needed persons are appointed and they are utilized to increase in the over all cost productivity, efficiency and effectiveness. The projects should be so administered as to lead to overall improvement in its performance.

10. Lack of Clarification of Authority, Responsibility and Relationships

In the developing word, the persons responsible for implementation of the project do not work as a team as there is no clarification of authority, responsibility and relationships amongst them, i.e, the roles of the various participants are not often mutually understood. This results into friction among these persons. Most of the time of these persons are spent in their mutual disputes. It becomes very difficult for them to devote their whole attention to the project.

11. Irregular Supply of Inputs of Right Quality Impede the Smooth Progress of the Project

After the project is formulated, the project manager must ensure the availability of necessary inputs. It has been generally observed that the projects are delayed because of the absence of timely availability of all the inputs simultaneously. In one of the projects, the health personnel had no work to do because of the non-availability of vaccine. Obtaining resources is a process that takes place periodically throughout the life of the project. It was revealed that failure to obtain resources simultaneously in time is the most common cause of delay in implementation. The project manager must begin the process of procuring resources immediately after the formulation stage. Sometimes, the process may be started quite early if the resources are scarce and not easily available. The absence of the one resource would inflate the cost of the project as the other resources would remain idle. The project manager must take the following steps:

(a) Working with the relative administrative units in preparing a time table of administrative steps to be taken to obtain the planned resources.
(b) Monitoring this time table to ensure that the administrative steps are being completed in time.
(c) Taking corrective action as and when necessary.[16]

Inspite of all these precautions, there is possibility of not reaching the resources in time. What can be done under such critical situation? Most of the experts indicated that the whole project staff remains idle for months toghether. This is very serious in big projects.

It is suggested that project officers may be delegated powers of purchase the inputs locally or employ persons, if not available from the agency as planned. This would keep the schedule of the project.

12. No Lessons Learnt from the Past Implementation Experience

It was a great surprise to learn that there are no records of past experiences in relation to project implementation. One can always learn from the mistakes of others. Some of the project personnel remarked that "they do not know anything about the difficulties encountered by the project personnel and the causes of the failures of the project undertaken earlier." It is beneficial to examine how major projects have been managed in the past. It would also be better to identify those approaches which have been most successful. We can keep a record of good and bad points of the past projects and this cumulative experience may be passed on to the present project managers. In this way, many of the difficulties likely to be encountered would vanish.

Frank A. Wilson in his article, "Planning for Project Management" in the *journal of Administration Overseas* (July 1979) has rightly mentioned that, "Disappointing and inefficient project performance is a fact of life ... *Ex-post* evaluation of existing projects can be the means by which we can systematically seek to analyse the potential for improving project management. Evaluation studies give the opportunity for developing a greater understanding of the way projects are managed and implemented."

13. Faulty and Cumbersome Administrative Procedures

Whenever a project is formulated, we do not pay much attention to the problems of communication, coordination, headquarter-field relationship, supervision, etc. The purpose of these procedures is to help in the smooth functioning of the project. Without proper procedures developed most of the project personnel remain engrossed in preparing unnecessary reports. These procedures should be clarified in the initial stages of project management, so that no confusion arises later on. If there are already set procedures in a particular organization, these may be adopted otherwise new procedures may be adopted and made known to the project personnel. It must be clear that administrative procedures are an aid to help the efficient functioning of the project. The meticulous application of these procedures may result into red tapism and inefficiency.

14. No Correlations between Need, Resources and Use

To quote WHO; The allocation, organization and evaluation of human, technological, financial and physical resources are the principal functions of planning. There are a number of ways in which comparable data on perceived need, resources and use can be combined so as to advance our understanding of their relationships. For this purpose, geographically defined areas can be divided in relation to whether they are above or below the medians for appropriate measures of need, use and resources, provided these are defined uniformly for all the project areas and based on comparable data.

Table 9.1 shows a model in which areas can be assigned to one of 8 cells on the basis of their relative balance of need, resources, and use. The assignment depends on the findings for each area being above or below the median level of need, resources, or use for all areas in the set. In this model, for example, a relatively high level resources and a relatively high rate of use in the presence of a relatively high rate of perceived need is defined as balance (Type A). Here, the population's perceived need is reflected in a supply of appropriate combination and in levels of use that indicate neither excess capacity of, nor unmet demand for, a particular resource category. Conversely, a relatively low level of use in the presence of low need, is also regarded as constituting balance (Type H).

A cybernetic model like this would not allow the investment in costly resources to continue longer than is justified by the perceived needs of the population, because the information made available to decision-makers would show them that the use of the services or the application of

TABLE 9.1

Model of Relationships between Need, Resources and Use

Use	*High Need*		*Low Need*	
	High Resources	*Low Resources*	*High Resources*	*Low Resources*
High	Type–A Balanced Appropriate allocation of resources	Type–B Compensatory high productivity of resources	Type–E Unbalanced overuse of resources	Type–F Unbalanced high productivity of resources
Low	Type–C Unbalanced Under use of resources	Type–D Unbalanced underinvestment in resources	Type–G Unbalanced over investments in resources	Type–H Balanced appropriate resources

Source: World Health Organisation: Manual on Project Management.

resources has become excessive in relationship to perceived need. Ninth Five Year Plan has also indicated the following issues:

A recent review of the 187 Central sector projects, each costing more than Rs.100 crore, by the Department of Programme Implementation (DPI) showed that, as on February, 1997 as many as 118 projects were running behind schedule and the time overrun varied from one month to 200 months. A study of a few major projects indicated that the cost overrun, for reasons other than inflation and changes in the duty/exchange rate regimes, ranged from 40% to 75% of the original estimates. Past experience reveals that the factors responsible for time and cost overruns are:

- Poor project formulation due to inadequate field investigation, lack of adequate data, inadequate analysis of environmental and rehabilitation implications, changes in prices and exchange rate regimes, etc.
- Delays in clearance from various regulatory agencies, in land acquisition and in procurement of materials. Such delays are primarily due to poor coordination and project planning, as these problems are not explicitly considered or taken into account at the planning stage.
- Change in design or scope of projects midway through execution.
- Inability of the project management to take prompt decisions on various aspects of these projects even when the objective circumstances warrant such decisions.
- Management problems such as personnel, labour and contractor disputes, mis-match of equipments, etc.
- Inadequate and untimely release of funds.
- Unforeseeable factors such as adverse geo-mining conditions and natural calamities.

We can improve the management of projects if we keep these difficulties or problems or obstacles in mind and try to reduce them to negligible proportions. Besides, there is a need of training project personnel in the art of project management.

SUGGESTIONS

Recent Development: Eleventh Five Year Plan, Vol. III suggests the following:

(A) Need of Innovations

The National Knowledge Commission, set-up by the Planning Commission, has highlighted the following aspects in its national survey on innovation:

- Innovation intensity (i.e., the percentage of revenue from products/service less than three years old) has increased for large firms and SMEs, with the SMEs registering a greater increase in innovation than large firms.
- About 7.3% of the large firms have achieved breakthrough in innovation while 76.4% have introduced incremental innovation.
- Internal processes for innovation such as maintaining a specific innovation department, allocating funds, rewarding innovative employees, maintaining physical locations for innovations, and constituting cross functional teams are all important factors which encourage firms to become more innovative.
- Firms with more patent filings and use of IPR consultants are more innovative.

- Firms partnering with government agencies, collaborating with universities and R&D labs also tend to be innovative.

However, the most important barrier to innovation is skill shortage and a lack of effective collaboration with the R&D institutions. NDC has recommended that there is a need for systematic reforms of the higher education system, including skill-based marketable vocational education in India which would facilitate the development of the required intellectual capital as well as enable more effective collaboration between industry, educational institutions, and the government. Apart from this, it is necessary to encourage innovation through fiscal incentives on a continuing basis.

(B) Appraisals of Autonomous Institutions in Industry Sector

Over the past Plans a number of autonomous institutions were set-up to support the industry to meet various needs, such as technology transfer, skill development, and introduction of advanced technology. These institutions were designed to function in close coordination with industry and the governing bodies included all stakeholders. Some industry associations set-up such institutes on their own initiative with initial government support. Some institutes such as the Central Pulp and Paper Research Institute (CPPRI) and Institute of Pesticides Formulation Technology (IPFT) were set-up with assistance from international organizations such as United Nations Industrial Development Organization (UNIDO). Institutes such as the National Test House (NTH) have the backing of statutes for some of the activities although they work on a commercial basis also.

The emphasis in the Eleventh Plan would continue to promote self-sufficiency in these institutions so that they can operate on a self-sustaining basis without the requirement of budgetary support. The government support will be limited to one time grants for the creation of new facilities, with recurring expenses being met from the revenues generated by them.

Autonomous Institutions in Industrial Sector

- Quality Council of India (OCI).
- Central Manufacturing Technology Institute (CMTI), Bangalore.
- National Council for Cement and Building Materials.
- Indian Rubber Manufacturers Research Association (IRMRA).
- NID.
- National Productivity Council.
- Central Institute of Plastic Engineering and Technology (CIPET).
- National Institute of Pharmaceutical Education and Research (NIPER) and IPFT.
- Six Textiles Research Associations *(TRAs).*
- WIFTH.
- Bureau of Indian Standards (BIS).
- NTH.
- Automotive Research Association of India (ARAI), Pune.
- NATRIP.
- Fluid Control Research Institute (FCRI).
- National Ship Design and Research Centre, Visakhapatnam.
- Biju Patnaik National Steel Institute.
- National Institute of Secondary Steel Technology.

(C) Area Development for Industry

Since the beginning of planned development, a policy has been followed for the development of industrial areas and industrial estates within such areas to facilitate the establishment of small and medium industrial units. Initiative has also been taken for improving the infrastructure of existing clusters outside of such areas. At the end of the Tenth Five Year Plan there were a multiplicity of schemes of cluster and area development established for the creation or upgradation of infrastructure.

(D) Intellectual Property Rights (IPRS)

Recognizing the importance of the IPRs as a means for fostering innovation and contributing to enhanced economic growth and competitiveness, India has adopted a four-pronged strategy to strengthen, etc. IPR regime; (i) to meet international obligations, (ii) to safeguard national interests (iii) to modernize the IPR administration, and (iv) to create awareness regarding IPRs.

The legislative and administrative initiatives taken during the last few years have had a very positive impact on the creation and securing of IP in India during the Tenth Five Year Plan period. Patent filing which was a mere 11466 in 2002-03 has gone up by two and a half times to 28882 in 2006-07. The patents granted also registered a five fold growth from 1379 to 7559 during the same period. The number of trade marks registered increased phenomenally from 11190 in 2002-03 to 109391 in 2006-07.[17]

Notes and References

1. Bilbert de Veries, "Programme Formulation and Implementation, in Administration of Development Programme and Projects, p. 25.
2. WHO: Technical Report Series, 596, p. 51
3. UN: Manual on Economic Development Projects (UN Publications Sales No. 58 II G.5), p. xiii.
4. *Ibid.*, p. 5.
5. J.M. Kitchlu, "Project Management" in V.A. Pai Panandiker (ed.)," Development Administration in India, Delhi, Macmilan, 1974, pp. 83-84.
6. UN: Administration of Development Programmes and Projects: Some Major Issues Continued, (UN Publication, Sales No. E-71-11 H.47), p. 75.
7. WHO: Technical Report Series, 596, p. 54.
8. J.P. Gupta, Priorities of Programme Planning and Implementation, (Mimeographed).
9. G.O.I.: Third Five Plan (Draft), 1960, p. 58.
10. A.P. Barnabas, "Reporting Appraisal and Evaluation in Development Administration" in V.A. Paipanandiker, ed., Development Administration in India, Delhi, Macmillan Company, 1974, pp. 219-20.
11. Gary/Green and Robert T. Kein, "After Implementation, What's Next? Evaluation" *Journal of Systems Management*, Vol. 34, No. 9, Issue No. 269, Sept. 1983, Association for Systems Management, Cleveland, Chill).
12. Peter Berger, Pyramids of sacrifice: Political ethics and social change (Garden City, New York, Anchor Books, 1976), p. 6.
13. GOI, Seventh Five Year Plan, Planning Commission, New Delhi, 1985, p. 413.
14. Gabriel, A. Almond, "Political System and Political Change" in *American Behavioural Scientist*, Vol. VI, June 1963, p. 8.
15. Alfred Diamant, "Political Development: Approaches to Theory and Strategy", in *Montgomery and Siffin*, eds., "Approaches to Development: Politics, Administration and Change' (New York, McGraw Hill, 1966), pp. 25-26.
16. WHO: Health Project Management, p. 228.
17. GOI, Planning Commission, Eleventh Five Year Plan, Vol. III, 2007-12, New Delhi, pp. 152-61.

CHAPTER

10

Administrative Capability

There are no two opinions that the success or failure of the national development depends much upon the administrative capability of a country at all levels. This is one of the most scarce resource particularly in a developing country. As such, the policy-makers and decision-makers have not only to be extra cautions to make use of this rare resource to the optimum but to create and develop a conducive environment where it can grow. (See Chart 10.1) Administrative Capability is an action-oriented system to achieve objectives of development administrations.

The administrative capability of a government and the manner in which the development programmes are likely to be carried out are intimately related. As early as 1950, the Secretary General of the United Nations pointed out that, "Any systematic effort towards economic development must be preceded by or coupled with efforts to make more effective the functioning of governmental machinery."[1] In this connection, J.I. Iboko has remarked: "It is accepted that inability to manage efficiently or utilize effectively the available and potential resources is the common ill of less developed countries. It follows that the successful development demands a sound programme for managerial improvement."[2]

Of late a great deal of stress is being placed upon the performance or administrative capability. As we are dealing with development administration in this book, it is assumed that development is the major goal of the Country. It is therefore performance for development or administrative capability for development which can make development successful. Any appraisal of performance or administrative capability must be therefore relevant to development goal. No organization which has an important role to play in the development process can be effective unless its components are capable. As pointed out by the Interplan study:

"Administration defined as the guidance or managing of organizations and systems of organizations—is a major factor in development process at all levels: national, regional, local and producing unit. Indeed, even in the private sector where enterprises are vitally affected by government programmes, no developmental programme in any field can be successful without administrative capability in the public sector."[3]

Andrew Mariados Packajraj in his article, "Administration that Delights the People" in

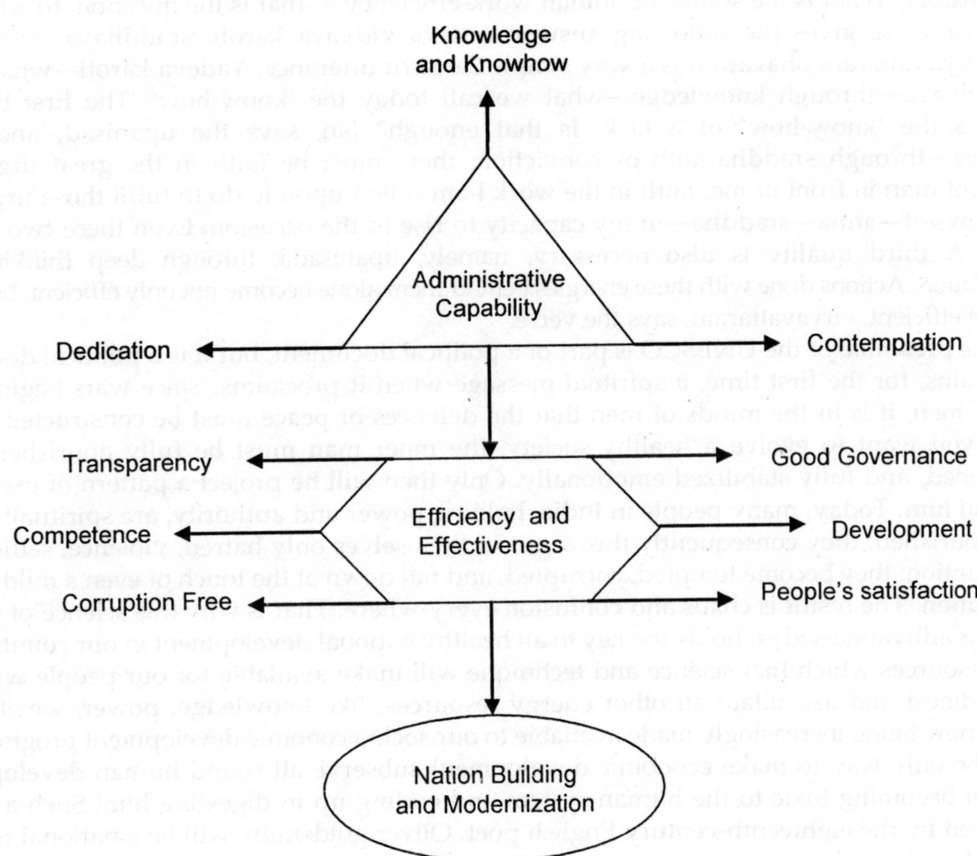

MIG, July to Sept. 2000, rightly mentioned that people in India now expect the Government of India to PERFORM. They are disenchanted with hollow promises, speeches, rhetorics and eloquent repertories. They don't just desire effective and responsive governments but they demand a Government that meets their aspirations. It is for the Government to be effective and responsive in their own interest, otherwise they will be thrown out for falling short of people's expectations.

The three most vital players in the arena are the Elected Ruling Government, the Appointed Administrative Machinery and the Demanding Public. While the ultimate responsibility and answerability/accountability rests with the first component, the actual job of delivering results rests on the administrative machinery. It is, in the ultimate analysis a joint team effort of the three but any weak link can jeopardize the outcome and efforts of any other.

It is this human transformation in the art and science of administrative capability that must come to all in our administration, and also to all men and women in our various professions. We have a great message on this subject in a verse of one of our Upanishads, namely, the chandogya upanisad, only next in importance and size to the greatest among all the upanisads, the brhadaranyaka upanisad. These are between three thousand and four thousand years old.

What inspiring and profound ideas come out of this great literature of so ancient a period of human history! What is the source of human work-efficiency?—that is the question, to which the chandogya verse gives the following answer Yadeva vidyaya karoti, sraddhaya, upanisada, tadeva viryavattaram bhavati. It is a very simple Sanskrit utterance. Yadeva karoti—whatever is done; vidyaya—through knowledge—what we call today the 'know-how'. The first thing to acquire is the 'know-how' of a task. Is that enough? No, says the upanisad, and adds: sraddhaya—through sraddha-faith or conviction; there must be faith in the great urges and longings of man in front of me, faith in the work I am called upon to do to fulfil those urges and faith in myself—atma—sraddha—in my capacity to rise to the occasion. Even these two are not enough. A third quality is also necessary, namely, upanisada, through deep thinking and contemplation. Actions done with these energies behind them alone become not only efficient, but more and more efficient, viryavattaram, says the verse.

The preamble of the UNESCO is part of a political document; but it is a political document that contains, for the first time, a spiritual message when it proclaims. Since wars begin in the minds of men, it is in the minds of men that the defences of peace must be constructed.

If you want to evolve a healthy society, the inner man must be fully nourished, fully strengthened, and fully stabilized emotionally. Only then will he project a pattern of excellence all around him. Today, many people in India, holding power and authority, are spiritually weak and ill-nourished; they consequently throw out of themselves only hatred, violence, selfishness, and corruption: they become tempted, corrupted, and fall down at the touch of even a mild breeze of temptation. The result is chaos and confusion every-where. That is why this science of man in depth, this adhyatma-vidya, holds the key to all healthy national development in our country. The energy resources which that science and technique will make available for our people will help them to digest and assimilate all other energy resources, like knowledge, power, wealth, and position, now being increasingly made available to our socio-economic development programmes. That is the only way to make economic development subserve all round human development, instead of becoming toxic to the human system and ending up in digesting him! Such a result, as observed by the eighteenth-century English poet, Oliver goldsmith, will be a national tragedy for us today:

> Ill fares the land, to hastening ills a prey,
> Where wealth accumulates and men decay!

We have to ask: why should men decay when wealth accumulates? And the clear answer comes: because wealth digests spiritually weak man instead of man digesting wealth; and that latter digestion is a spiritual digestion similar to man's physical body digesting the food indigested and gaining growth and strength thereby. This is the finest and sweetest fruit of all true education-savidya ya vimuktaye-that is knowledge which liberates, which gives freedom; and freedom is a spiritual value. And our nation will be marching in the direction of true human progress, says Vedanta, when millions of our people will experience this value of spiritual freedom in this very life and not as a post-mortem promise.[4] Thus administrative capability must possess strength among administrators.

Newman has identified 5 characteristic of Administrative capability:

1. *Saturation*: To be familiar with the problem..
2. *Deliberation*: To consider alternative solutions and to rearrange them.

3. *Incubation*: To let the sub-conscious mind work on the problem.
4. *Illustration*: To get a new idea and sensing that it may work.
5. *Accommodation*: To work out the new ideas so that it is a practical solution to the problem.[5]

Hicks gives the following types of creativity in sound decision-making:

1. *Innovative*: Creativity to think totally new ideas.
2. *Synthesis*: Creativity to absorb, combine and use ideas from different sources and making it new.
3. *Extension*: Creativity to use old or new ideas
4. *Duplication*: Creativity to use the other's successful ideas.[6]

In the economic and social development of a country and even in the total transformation of a society, administrative capability has much, to contribute. It is becoming not only a crucial but also a major factor in the success or failure of development efforts. With the significant increase in the complexity and magnitude of government functions, after the Second World War, the need for administrative capability has been felt much greater to solve complex operational problems and to aid in the implementation of development plans, programmes and projects. The increase in the level of knowledge and skills in the appraisal of administrative capability is, therefore, important, especially for countries which aspire for modernity.[7] To quote from a United Nations Publication: "Sound appraisal of administrative capability is essential for sound development planning; and administrative planning and the growth of administrative capability are essential for implementation of development plans."[8] That is why; national leaders, administrators, managers, and other technicians in recent years have felt the need to "evaluate and improve the administrative capabilities so that the intended results are realized. It has been emphasized that "Public administration must be recreated, renewed, revitalized to produce the changes and achievements in the transformation of societies. This necessitates a different kind and magnitude of administrative capability."[9] (See Chart 10.2)

Administrative capability simply stated is the capacity of the .administrative arm to achieve the desired objectives. Katz says: "administrative capability for development involves the ability to mobilize, allocate and combine the actions that are technically needed to achieve development objectives."[10] To him technical needs that are needed are five in groups: skilled manpower; financing, logistics of supplies and information; individual and group participation, and legitimated power to enforce decisions. A publication of the United Nations defines administrative capability as the management capacity of government or of the public sector as a whole, to the administrative capability of specific organizations, or sets of organizations, or to the administrative feasibility of specific development projects or programmes. In any of these three categories, administrative capacity is a major and crucial factor in the success or failure of development efforts."[11] In the context of administrative capacity for development, we may refer to it as the ability or capacity of the administrative system to achieve development objectives. Administrative capability among civil servants in India must be provided to ensure a successful change from colonial rule to democracy and development.

The Indian model of development through democracy was not only a historically dictated one but also it was consciously and deliberately sought by Pandit Nehru, one of the staunchest democrats and the architect of modern India. Democracy becomes both the means and one of the

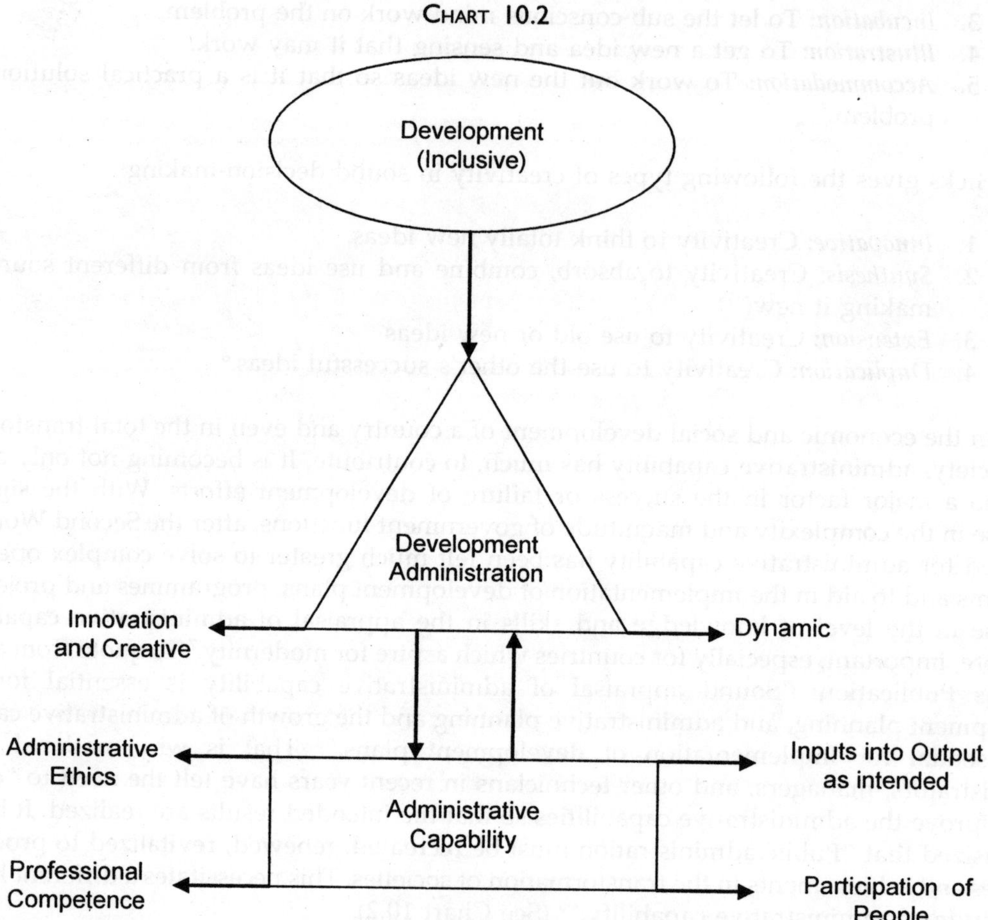

goals of development in Nehru's perspective. To quote him:

> ...the whole structure of Government in India has changed from rather an autocratic structure to a democratic structure- a structure which was based on some outside authority to a structure which is based on an authority not only within the country but ultimately responsible to the people of the country. That is a basic change. Together with that, other changes have come. That is to say, the State has become a dynamic State—not a static State... (in which) Services (administrators) have to adapt themselves to the changes....have to adopt methods to the changed conditions of work and the changed objectives of work.[12]

The Constitution of India and the policies of the government cast a heavy responsibility on the shoulders of the administrator/civil servants as the principal agents of social change and economic development in the country. The then Prime Minister Nehru, called upon the members of the Services—civil, military or police—to change their old attitudes and develop new attitudes, i.e. one of active cooperation with the public, of active service to the public and the public side also has the attitude of welcoming that cooperation and giving their cooperation too.[13] Nehru gave a clarion call that "the Services must gradually cease to think of themselves as some select coterie apart from the rest of the people. They must think of themselves as part of the people of India cooperating in this great adventure of building up India."[14] Nehru reminded members of the civil service that the great task of execution of India's development plans called for "a more progressive and realistic attitude", "faith in India's future, a genuine belief in the value of national objectives and a determination to go ahead, and, willingness and capacity to work."[15] Above all, the members of the bureaucracy must understand that "it is their duty to work for the unity of India, to break down barriers which come in the way of the unity of India and always be a crusader in that behalf."[16]

What was the British period administration? What is the post-independence administration? One was law and order administration. The other is developmental administration. How to develop this country? How to develop our people? That is why administration proliferated in various directions with all our five-year plans and so many other things but that was only in number. The quality did not keep pace with the number. Human motivation became eroded little by little. When the community development projects were inaugurated, the minister concerned Mr. S.K. Dey (who was my close friend), the secretary of the department at that time, as well as myself used to discuss in Ramakrishna mission, new Delhi, about the projects. We were all enthusiastic. It was a wonderful thing. But the whole thing fizzled out in no time. It became dead, dull administration. This is the greatest misfortune of our people who, after centuries of political subjection, misfortune of our people who, after centuries of political subjection, got freedom, but didn't know how to use that freedom, did not know how to squeeze it to the fullest advantage of the nation. This is something amazing. What has happened to us? We have first class brains; there is no want of intellect in this country. Various other qualities are there but one quality is missing—the concern for others. That is what is lacking throughout the nation.[17] For enhancing administrative capability, there is a need of political support and extensive and intensive training to civil servants.

In this context, Joseph La Palombara suggests two highly generalized strategies, namely, political support and education, which can lead to increased administrative capacity. Unless the administrators secure the support of political leadership, little can be done to increase or improve administrative capacity. La Palombara writes, "where upper-level bureaucrats are not also the central political leaders of the society, it is doubtful (although not impossible) that they will develop the attributes of guardians. In any case, effecting administrative change in such situations absolutely requires that such a goal be accorded high priority by the political leadership."[18] Proper education and good training also greatly improve the skill of administrators. La Palombara writes, "No broad-gauged educational strategy to improve administrative capacity in the developing areas is likely to be successful unless administration is seen for what it always is and must be an integral part of all public policy-making and execution, no matter how technical or esoteric, involving a set of skills in human organization and behaviour without which policy implementation is at best, haphazard and at worst, chaotic and clamorous failure."[19]

Personnel in the organization need to be developed to achieve the objectives of the organization and to develop a sense of responsibility towards these objectives. The objectives of the organization require a change in the personality of administrator. His skills and knowledge on the job can be enhanced by imparting training extensively in the respective fields.[20]

Like economic planning or health planning, a government should also focus its adequate attention on administrative planning strategy. Its emphasis should be on investing in administrative capacity. Its objective should be to aid the chief executive and heads of departments and other agencies in their development planning, programme budgeting and execution. Since the factor of administrative capability is involved to the entire process of formulating, executing and evaluating development programmes and plans, it is good to institutionalize administrative reforms units. Which should receive continuous support at all levels.[21] The primary function of these units is to develop effective organization, administrative or management system. Secondly administrative planning strategy should be charged with the duty of pre-service and in-service training programmes and to produce persons with the needed capabilities and motivations.

World Bank's reform programme to improve administrative capability and its impact.

The World Bank has tried to introduce rationalist reforms in bureaucracies in the third world countries which comprises the following:

- Installing in civil services personnel information and management systems which are more tightly linked to payrolls, and including clear and appropriate career development schemes;
- Staff audits to determine what personnel is on hand;
- Improved training systems;
- Revision, usually meaning simplification, of legal framework governing the civil service; and
- Getting the right people into administration, partly by stronger incentives to attract and retain them, partly by changing objectives and procedures in an effort to make the work situation more challenging and rewarding.

However, these measures suffer from contextlessness. Measures such as performance pay, greater bureaucratic accountability or decentralisation have been ineffective because these reform measures largely discount the influence of various contextual factors, such as inter-class and inter-group conflicts, expansive bureaucratic power, and unequal access to bureaucratic decisions.[22]

No effort to improve administrative capability by developing countries themselves. In developing countries, the tolerance of misadministration is high and there is a "paralysis of national will" to change the existing bureaucratic system. No exogenously induced reform is likely to succeed unless there is a strong social movement from within seeking the change.

Unless there are simultaneous and corresponding changes in social, political and economic spheres, third world bureaucracies will resist any move to change the *status quo*. In fact, several countries have attempted to reform the system through a series of administrative reform commissions but since they were mainly composed of senior bureaucrats, and 'political will' for such a reform has been markedly lacking there has been little success in inducing rationality into the system.[23]

Administrative capability need to acquire reinvention of administrative system to promote development.

Public administration as a systematic developing body of knowledge did not exist until Woodrow Wilson invented it in the year 1887. We reinvented public administration in the form of new public administration in the early second half of the 20th century to achieve objectives of social justice, equity, relevance and socio-economic progress. The last exercise in reinvention, attempted in 1990s—called new public management which is also known as entrepreneurial government—aims at efficiency, economy and effectiveness. Although all areas of government are undergoing a process of dramatic change, yet the outdated objectives, norms and roles, and traditional theories and classical approaches to public administration are still very much in evidence. New theories, concepts, and methods are warranted to meet the demands of growth, complexity and change.[24]

As per K.V.V. Subramanian, sitting on the threshold of the 21st century, it is time for soul searching. A proper understanding of the evils bedeviling the system alone can set in place correctives for the future. Some of the major afflictions identified by him are:

1. chronic and almost incurable delays at all levels;
2. equally chronic habit of evading decision-making;
3. non-availability or inaccessibility of officials at all levels to individual citizen;
4. singular lack of courtesy, consideration and concern to the grievances of individual citizens or groups;
5. lack of a humane approach to the visitor in any government office;
6. time-consuming meetings and discussions with ministers and high officials which are mostly unproductive and which eat into administrative time;
7. spectacular schemes from political leadership which are mostly populist and fail to touch the grassroots;
8. failure and indifference of officials to bend their energies to issues affecting common man;
9. failure of system of inspection and controls which are time-honored tools of gauging the work and efficiency at all levels; and
10. consequently, corruption in the form of 'speed money' for getting irregular things done.[25]

The most important solution to these problems would be in ensuring and developing administrative capability. Administrative capability involves a multi-dimensional approach to promote development and lay the foundation of development administration.

Public administration today has broken away from its stereotype image of a rigid conservative, inept and impersonal entity and the administrator has assumed the new image of a humane, innovative and responsive being. In this context, he has acquired a multiplicity of roles and responsibilities as follows which are ingredients of administrative capabilitiy.

1. crusading reformer intent on transforming some aspect of community life according to preconceived notions of the ideal society:
2. proactive policy formulator, ready with possible strategies to meet the unknown;
3. social change-agent, ready to accept new ideals and to push others into accepting them also;
4. crisis manager, slow to burn out but quick to react and brilliant at immediate improvisation;
5. dynamic programme manager. Able to show new courses and adapts on-going arrangements;
6. humanitarian employer. Treating staff with respect and meeting out even-handed justice;
7. political campaigner, responsive to public needs and champion of public causes;
8. competent administrator, ensuring effective performance with minimum political embarrassment;

9. interest broker. Choosing among competing interests and reconciling all parties to the outcome;
10. public relations expert, adept at building up support, showing his area to advantage;
11. speedy decision-maker, oriented to assume responsibility and clear instructions;
12. constructive thinker, not easily lead astray by others who would want to make up his mind for him; and
13. optimistic leader, not easily discouraged in adversity, but able to command attention and stimulate subordinates.[26]

Contents of Administrative capability in 21st century: public administration of the 21st century should gear itself to human development, economy, performance-orientation, empowerment of the people, adhocracy, technocracy, cultural-specificity and women-oriented structures and should have the lofty objectives of human rights, empowerment, gender-equity, care for non-humans and concern for future generations.

The onus rests on public administration to reconcile and direct the advances in science and technology, benefit from information revolution, computerization and automation to speed up human development. The human dimension is likely to emerge as the most crucial factor in the 21st century with a strong case for redesigning and remoulding the civil services into a human development service to enable public-administration to be truly an instrument of human development.[27]

Administrative capability can inspire moral values in administration which is sine-qua non for development administration. A moral public servant, to be specific, is not simply one who obeys the laws and behaves within the confines of bureaucratic values, but also one who strives for a moral government. Such is the duty for those who wish to be involved in the difficult and complex world of statecraft. This is the essence and basis of a moral state. Only by demonstrating the highest standards of personal integrity, honesty, fairness, justice, and by considering their work as vocation, can public officials inspire public confidence and trust, the true hall marks of a moral government. Administrative theology, then can act as a source of strength for them, for the statecraft, and for society at large.[28]

MEASURING ADMINISTRATIVE CAPABILITY

Like economic development, in terms of an increase in gross national product per capita, is it possible to measure administrative capability? It is said administrative capability can also be measured.[29]

It is in terms of performance that the administrative capability can be appraised. Norman Uphoff suggests four kinds of 'performance', namely, Efficiency (organization), Effectiveness (Linkages), Innovation (Planning) and Efficacy (feed-back).[30] According to him these performances relate to the process of transforming inputs into outcomes. He says, "Efficiency relates to the conversion of inputs into outputs, with special attention to how the inputs are used. Effectiveness relates to the production of outputs which are intended to yield certain desired outcomes. Innovation can relate to the whole process, but its key function is to get more outputs that achieve desired outcomes. Efficacy deals with their achievement but in extra bureaucratic ways, especially involving inputs from the public so that the outputs of administration indeed 'match' with public needs."[31]

As already said in an organization, it is the personnel input that matters very much for the output. Basically, an organization constitutes administrative machinery which is designed to achieve specific goals with the help of management technology. A person in an organisation cannot perform the functions assigned to him well without adequate physical inputs—office, pen, paper, telephone, etc. Thus, in an organization the personnel input as well as the physical input are important valuables that determine the performance. According to the Classical School of Public Administration, performance means "efficiency." Frederick Taylor, Henri Fayol, Max Weber Luther Gulick and Lyndall Urwick concentrated their attention on 'Productivity' or 'Efficiency'. The idea of efficiency and productivity provided a unifying theme in the work of these pioneers.[32] These increase when the output is higher than input. This output may be in the form of profitability or efficiency. Thus 'profitability' may be expressed in terms of monetary terms, 'productivity' in terms of contribution of labour and capital to produce goods and services, and 'efficiency' in terms of technical efficiency in the sense of increase in output. As such the classical, approach defined performance of an administrative system as the ratio of output to input (0/1) Max. Weber emphasised the use of 'formal bureaucratic organization' for increasing efficiency. He hailed bureaucracy as capable of attaining the highest degree of efficiency and formally the most rational known means of carrying out imperative control over human beings."[33]

In brief the classical school of public administration wanted to achieve efficiency through a formal organization. The task of public administration was to improve and raise performance, expressed in terms of efficiency to the highest level.

After the Second World War, many nations emerged as independent countries and it became necessary that development of these countries popularly known as developing countries, should be carried out by the Governments. Development or modernization became the goal of the Governments of developing countries. Since the Government and its administrative arm play a key role in affecting national development.[34] There is therefore a strong need for improving the, capabilities of those upon whom depends, the performance of the country. Thus the scope of public administration has widened to include development administration as well. The administrative arm of the government is, presently, not only concerned with the implementation of policies and decisions but it is also associated with policy-making. Its active role in planning and programming is called for. Hence the issue of administrative capability becomes a very important one.

ASSESSMENT OF ADMINISTRATIVE CAPABILITY OF INDIAN ADMINISTRATION

The last 50 years since Independence are marked by the continuous down-hill journey of Indian bureaucracy. Time and again, questions have been raised about the imperviousness, wooden-headedness, obstructiveness, rigidity, and rule and procedure-bound attitude of the bureaucracy. Only the context has changed in which these harsh but often well-deserved judgments have been passed. Initially, it was in the context of lack of enthusiasm of the bureaucracy for implementation of various development scheme and programmes, Jawaharlal Nehru the First Prime Minister of India, was often despondent and lamented about the "bureaucratic jungle." Currently, the onslaught is in the context of bureaucracy's opposition to the economic liberalization and globalization policies being pursued since 1991. It is also often alleged that the bureaucracy is opposed to decentralization of powers and functions as envisaged earlier in the Panchayat Raj and, more recently, in the 73rd and 74th Amendments to the Constitution. Thus, Indian bureaucracy is perceived as incapable of giving its best in any situation in which it is asked to function.[35]

It is of much importance to appraise performance as a whole taking into consideration the organisational objectives and the administrative efforts involved in achieving those objectives. Performance thus in a broad sense constitutes the following aspects:

1. Inputs in the form of human and material resources (Money Costs).
2. Methods (Management Technology) involved in mobilizing and utilizing inputs to produce outputs.
3. Outputs in the form of goals and services produced (e.g., number of candidates conducted for interview, or number of cases handled) which can be measured in terms of quantity and quality.
4. Beneficial and harmful effects of both inputs and outputs in terms of cost-benefit analysis (e.g., ecological, political, economic, social or other factors).
5. Outcomes (outputs/inputs) may be expressed in terms of profitability.

Thus, in the appraisal of performance as a whole, these five indicators may take the form of an appraisal of administrative capability of an administrative system. Administrative capability can be appraised when the administrative system is actually performing well in the sense of achieving intended results effectively and efficiently. The administrative capability includes the capacity to deal with the complex tasks of the organization including decision-making, planning, programming, projecting coordinating, budgeting, executing, supervising, directing and controlling. A few measures have been taken to establish and maintain transactional linkages with organizations so that the objectives are achieved. To bring about measures, "many countries recognize the desirability of promoting feedback, cross, fertilization and mutual reinforcement of ideas and improvements among central public administration institutions and processes and their sectoral and programme counterparts. Unless those in general public administration improvement activities are able to receive information on management problems in different sectors and programmes, and in turn disseminate ideas and improvement, their contribution to administration for development is likely to remain limited."[36]

Again the administrative capability of an organisational unit includes its ability to perform the tasks under contextual environment (for example environment may be affected by natural calamity, war and instability, adverse political change or the like). In such a case the development administrator needs to have a thorough knowledge not only of the administrative unit in which he works but also of the inter-acting units—local, regional, national and international. In addition he must have knowledge about the socio-economy state of the country, its transport and communication system, its development of modern technologies and its relations with major countries in matters of trade and finance.

As far as the structure of an organization affecting the performance is concerned, it is composed of human as well as physical resources. An analysis of these resources is important in any appraisal of performance or administrative capability. People constitute the principal resources of an organisational unit. Such questions as the quantity and quality of people, their roles in terms of job descriptions, their training qualifications and their participation in policy-making and planning which affect the performance of an administrative system or unit are very important. Questions relating to physical resources, such as office equipment supplies, telephones, and tools of communication, transport, housing and office space, have far-reaching effects on the performance. of an administrative system. The administrative capability of an organization particularly in a developing one is very much constrained by the physical resources which it possesses or lacks.

Again the division of labour or differentiation (specific functions by specific unit) in an organisational unit is the key to the performance or to the administrative capability. In this connection, the internal relation between various component parts of an organization' Constitute a key factor in the system of division of labour or differentiation. It is the internal relations which coordinate various activities of components, solve their problems and assure quick action.

In the nation-building and socio-economic development of a 'Country, the strengthening of the central government for expediting the political, economic and social change is essential in most cases. However, at a certain stage, there is a complexity of development functions. The central government in such a case must take steps to decentralize the authority and delegate authority to lower levels of government—State and local—and the autonomous bodies like the Public Enterprise, Corporation, Board, etc. In fact, the ability to, delegate authority with confidence and without losing control constitutes an important factor in the development of administrative capability. In the administrative development there is also a felt need to have the reorganization or reconstruction of existing organizations, abolition of ineffective units and building of new institutions. Stone calls for "revamping administrative structures, process and managerial practices and a large amount of pre-service and in-service training, with both concentrated on development administration for total social benefit.[37]

Emphasis has also been stressed on the missing components. which can seriously impair the administrative capability of an organisational unit. It is important to point out that no organization can be completely self-sufficient. It has to depend upon other organizations for providing missing components-units responsible for the making of major development policies, planning, budgeting and finance, and evaluation and control. Effective administrative management of an organisational unit calls for a combination of dynamic policy and programme leadership and competent managerial direction with a professional man who plans, directs and improves the work of the unit.

OBSTACLES IN THE WAY OF ADMINISTRATIVE CAPABILITY

In the context of developing countries like ours, there are a large number of factors which come in the way of enhancing administrative capability for development programmes. Some of the factors are listed below:

1. *Lack of clarity of objectives*: Sometimes objectives of organizations are not clear. They can be unknown, undefined or abstract. They can be ideal and beyond man's achievement. Again there may be contradiction between policies and objectives. Administrative objectives may conflict, societal objectives. This affects administrative capability.
2. *Difficult to evaluate social cost and social benefit*: There is difficulty in evaluating the performance of an organization. The main problem is how to determine quantitatively social cost and social benefit.
3. *Difficult to identify task environment and contextual environment*: Environmental effect on the working and function of administrative complex organizations is very difficult to determine. Both the environments, i.e. task environment and contextual environment affect the performance and thus administrative capability.
4. *Lack of definite structure*: Obstructive structure of the organization is another drawback of good performance. There is little doubt that bureaucratic organization develop a tendency towards centralization and rigidity and demand conformity from their members.

5. *Lack of effective management system*: Lack of effective management system is another problem. According to Luther Gullick, the true goals of management are to make the conduct of affair technically sound, politically responsible, publicly acceptable, professionally approved and socially constructive. Tasks of management which need attention are: Policy formulation, Decision-making, Planning, Co-ordination Communication, Delegation, Supervision and Public Relations. Attention must be paid to all of them.
6. *Administrative procedures outdated*: Administrative methods, procedures, collection of data, system of feed back, etc., has a bearing on administrative capability which are outdated.
7. *Lack of administrative capability in personal*: Personal working in the organizations are not properly recruited, trained and motivated.
8. *Integrity missing*: Lack of integrity among the members of the staff.
9. *Lack of leadership*: Lack of administrative leadership is another problem which hampers administrative efficiency.

Swami Ranganathananda spells out as how we have stopped using our administrative capability to develop the country. To quote him: I wish to draw your attention to the deficiencies that have crept into our national life ever since that blessed occasion of our achievement of political independence on 15th august 1947. The whole nation was in ecstasy on that day when, after centuries of political subjection and immobilization, we became free; we got the power to shape our destiny in our own way. That really was an occasion for national rejoicing, behind which were the wide-spread heavenly attitudes of renunciation and service, tyaga and seva, of the decades-long freedom struggle. But, as I often refer to in my speeches to various gatherings all over India, what was a heaven on the first day of independence began to be converted into more and more of a hell from the very next day onwards. We allowed, day by day, in the post-freedom years, all sorts of negative and self-centred attitudes and actions, and fissiparous tendencies, to invade our hearts and our public life. We steadily forgot the message of tyaga and seva and started creating a hell out of that heaven, with the result that today, after 39 years of freedom, we are confronted with staggering problems of mass poverty, illiteracy, corruption, all sorts of social malpractices, and much callousness and human unconcern in the administration.

What is India today? A bit of a hell. We cannot trust each other; politics, administration, and many among the citizens, are corrupt; we cannot work together; we have lost the national vision and fallen under the tyranny of regional and caste loyalties. We more often pull each other down; we quarrel and fight on petty matters, like linguistic, regional, and water-resources-sharing issues; we resort to violence at the slightest provocation. How can we have human resource development in such a situation? Something has gone wrong somewhere during the last few decades. The spirit that animated the nation during the political struggle for freedom is not animating it today. That spirit should have, on the other hand, animated the people of an undeveloped nation like ours ten-fold in our post-freedom period, in order to make that freedom meaningful to the millions of our weaker sections. That did not happen; and that has been our post-freedom tragedy.

These are beautiful ideas arising from the philosophy of Bhagvad Gita instead of nurturing ourselves with these inspiring ideas and striving hard to bring light and life to the millions of our people sunk in poverty, ignorance, and exploitation, many in our administration allowed themselves to become reduced, in these momentous post-freedom years, to 'clods of ailments and grievances ever complaining that the world (and the government) does not devote itself to making them happy.' To quote the pungent words of Bernard Shaw.

What do our officers and clerks generally discuss when they meet together in tea clubs, in secretariat, rooms, or elsewhere, all over India? Mostly three 'momentous' P's, namely pay, prospect, and promotion! Nothing about the country and the mountainous problems of their own people and what their role is in solving them! This is the normal pattern all over India and in all its diverse offices.

If there are exceptions, it is because these few have been touched by the inspiration of this higher national vision and ideology. And the small minority of the inspired keeps the nation going. The nation needs the services of more and more of such people to solve its pressing human problems. We have to generate that human-motivation energy-resource, in order to bring out the maximum benefits from the money resources provided in our five-year plans.[38]

SOME SUGGESTIONS TO IMPROVE ADMINISTRATIVE CAPABILITY

I. Need of Implementation of Reforms

It has been the endeavour of our Government to ensure that the above obstacles do not stand in any way in the effective and efficient implementation of the socio-economic and developmental plans launched from time to time. It was for this specific reason that in 1966, Government of India set-up a high level Administrative Reforms Commission to look into the various aspects of the administrative system and suggest ways and means to bring about substantial improvements in the administrative capability and integrity. The Commission laboured 4-5 years and submitted 20 reports to the government, each dealing with the critical examination of an aspect of administrative capability and integrity. Some of the relevant recommendations of the Commission on organisational structure, the personnel, the processes and the procedures are the following:

1. A more rational distribution of work among the departments and ministries as well as among the executive agencies attached to them.
2. Strengthening and extending the existing arrangements for co-ordination within the increasing and rapidly growing administrative agencies which comprise the administrative system at the federal level and similarly at the state level.
3. Reduction in the number of administrative agencies and their personnel by a rigorous rationalisation of administrative functions and operations.
4. Strengthening the top policy-making level within the administrative system by re-organising the cabinet as well as by strengthening the staff agency within a department so that the minister and the departmental secretary can get adequate information and assistance for policy-making.
5. Integration of the field agencies with secretariat department in order to avoid delays by cutting down the duplication of administrative work.
6. Reducing the hierarchical levels for the consideration of an administrative proposal or a case in a government department so that unnecessary delays and expenditure can be cut down.
7. Delegating administrative authority within the department for speedier disposal of work.
8. Improving personnel management through more effective recruitment, employee development programme, improvement of promotional opportunities, rationalisation

of pay structures and scientific appraisal of the result achieved by civil servants individually.

9. Fixation of definite responsibility for achieving results by an agency and carefully evaluating the actual performance.
10. Redress of citizens' grievances by improving machinery as well as by the appointments of new high level functionaries similar to Ombudsman to be called Lok Pal and Lok Ayukta.

Most of these recommendations have been accepted by the government and implemented. As a result of these measures, some change has been made in the administrative capability and integrity. (See chapter on Administrative Reforms for the Role of Second Administrative Reforms Commission which has submitted by now 10 Reports).

More recently, the one man Economic Administration Reforms Commission (headed by Mr. L.K. Jha) has suggested far-reaching recommendations to tone up the administrative affairs, which if implemented in the right earnestness, would have a lasting impact in improving administrative capability—a scarce resource.

Thus, no development programme or project can be carried out successfully in an organisational unit or system without the sufficient growth of administrative capability. The basic requirement is, therefore, to attach as much importance to measures to create increase and preserve administrative capabilities for formulating and implementing programmes and projects attuned to socio-economic progress and nation-building as is devoted to mobilizing scarce resources for formulating and implementing plans and projects. It is, important always to bear in mind that this scarce resource should not be diverted to unnecessary tasks.

2. Promoting Good Governance for Administrative Capability

The answers to the long-standing ills and deficiencies of civil services will have to be basic and sweeping. Any patchwork of temporary remedies will not serve the purpose. It is often forgotten that good governance is basic to any other reforms and changes in society. Everything else can be purchased for a price but not people-friendly, socially conscious and clean administration deeply committed not to any political ideology but to the basic values of Rule of Law, respect for secularism, human rights and the welfare of weaker sections of society. This is the charter for the civil services. Looking to the present state of affairs, it sounds utopian but, if it is to be translated in reality, it will require both administrative and political will. Unfortunately, both are missing in this quest for good governance. The bureaucracy is, therefore, at cross-roads. The road it takes will make all the difference to where India finds itself in the 21st Century. It is a travesty that no one has time to pause and ponder on these vital issues.[39]

3. Administrative Capability needs Changing Mind-set of Civil Servants

One of the crucial change, that should be made by the civil servants itself is the change in the mind-set. This is very important since, even if everything else as mentioned above is achieved, the civil service would still not deliver the goods if it harbours the same old mind-set, arrogantly assuming that it knows the best and it alone can execute. This is why even though the process of liberalization might be implemented, though with hiccups, the process of de-regulation had not taken off. The civil service still thinks that it should not give up its authority and discretion and it must be added here itself that this is also a very critical area which breeds corruption. The civil service should, therefore, not resist taking away its discretion or having in position very strict and also very transparent parameters within which such a discretion can be exercised at all. for this purpose, various rules and regulations should be modified or even dismantled. In any case, many of them are archaic ones, for example telecommunications scene today is based on the Indian Telegraph Act of the last century. Same is the case with many industrial Acts. To give an example; a factory inspector once issued a notice to a factory owner that it is not enough that there is a water cooler on the premises, but there has to be an earthen pot full of water for drinking purpose as the latter is prescribed under the rules.

One can understand as to why the civil service finds it difficult to change its mind-set but the real reason behind this is its sense of insecurity in facing the future. And it is this aspect which is the most critical item before the civil service. It was created by colonial administration but it really became omni-potent and omni-present during a socialist era after independence. But the whole world is undergoing a transition and Indian civil service cannot remain aloof, otherwise there is every danger of the people forcing it to change. Any resistance on the part of the civil service would only damage it.[40]

4. Creating an Atmosphere of Creativity

Bindu Sridhar in an article, "A culture that stresses on team spirit fosters creativity" dated Dec. 24, 2008 in *The Hindu* observes that to develop a company culture that believes in making creativity happen, encourage interaction, feedback and exchange of ideas. The knowledge, intelligence and skills of your employees are just as valuable for the business as any other asset So make an effort to exploit it to the maximum. One way of doing this is to set-up a system to consistently gather, record and explore the potential of suggestions made by employees usually have some of the best ideas about improving their job and the organisation as a whole.

5. Promoting Motivation

Keep your people motivated. Creativity tends to happen in fits and starts and it is easy to get dejected when efforts don't bear fruit immediately. As a manager, it is important to hang in there with your team through tough times, contributing ideas, suggestions and pepping up morale when the chips are down.

6. Foster Team Work, Foster Collaboration, not Competition

It is a myth that competition will motivate creativity. In fact, it may have the opposite effect. When the creative process is made competitive by using incentives like money, fear or deadlines, it puts undue pressure on the employees. It may even tempt them to guard their turf and hold on to their ideas and knowledge. On the other hand, a culture that stresses on group work and team spirit will motivate employees to share ideas freely and positively influence organisational culture in the long-run.

7. Create Diversity

Create diversity. Diversity in thought processes, opinions, skills and even solutions, makes for more creativity and innovation. Allow employees to feel a sense of ownership and purpose towards their jobs and the organisation. Introduce an element of fun and excitement into the process and be generous with praise and recognitions. Get people from different background to participate in the creative process. Sometimes even people completely unconnected to the process may have a valuable contribution to make. Believe it or not, even Albert Einstein discussed some of his famous theories with his wife and benefited from her advice!

8. Encourage Versatility

There can be more than one way of doing things. Just because something has been done in particular way for long, it does not automatically mean that other options need not be explored. Inquisitiveness, playfulness and exploration in the creative process will yield the best ideas.

9. Need of Creativity

It is important to remember that creativity is not the prerogative of a chosen few. Almost everybody, irrespective of age, education or the type of work is capable of exhibiting creativity in your organization. The right working conditions and settings can spur creativity and innovation in your waiting for? Come and harness creative power of your employees to save money, improve productivity and motivate your people.

CONCLUSION

Administrative Capability for developmental administration needs a new mind, a new type of attitude that is suffused with human values. You are not dealing with a table or a chair, but with a human being. He or she has problems. You are there to solve them. That chair of authority on which you sit is not a chair of comfort. It is a chair with a heavy human responsibility on your head. Rise to the level of the responsibility that chair signifies. Our mental awareness must rise to that level.

Our people are hungering for development. Government servants are the instruments of that developmental administration. These instruments must become more humanised, more concerned with human development. Then something great will happen. Things will march faster, faster. Whatever achievements we have made so far have not been due to steady purposeful progress, but are the product of our mostly wobbly movements. Some good has come, but the real progress will come when this human value becomes embedded in every part of the administration so that his or her work becomes dynamic. Everything will become dynamic and the tendency to corruption and value erosion will become correspondingly less. Take away the human value element, corruption and evil must fill the administration and public life. Put human value within and to that extent they will be reduced thereby. We have increased evils in society only because we took away the one central inspiring principle, 'the concern for the next individual'.

Our men and women have not become humanized. He or she is not a free citizen of India, but only a job-hunter, and job-holder. We have yet to develop the attitude that this is my country and these are my fellow citizens. If this attitude is not there, all this money will be simply waste, the fruits of the crores become very much reduced by the time it reaches the people concerned. It is here that human values come in to correct the situation.

The qualities required for Administrative Capability require that there must be an earnest and concerted effort by all the staff to put an end to all these serious evils in our administration; this can be achieved, and can be achieved only, by developing enlightened citizenship awareness, with its concomitant virtues of self-discipline, punctuality, work-efficiency, talking less and working more, dedication to human service and welfare, imaginative sympathy, and impersonal loyalty to our democratic state and its noble constitution.

This imaginative sympathy helps to bring about a change of perspective in you, when you move from your chair in your home to the chair in the municipal corporation office. That office chair is connected with, and involved in, the happiness or misery of thousands of people; by imaginative sympathy, you galvanize that chair with human motivations and you become an instrument 'to wipe the widow's tear or stop the orphan's wails', in the words of Vivekananda, or to wipe the tear from the eye of the poorest and humblest, in the words of Gandhiji. This is the true joy of human life; the sooner our people realize that the so-called high life is but an empty life—in spite of its glitter, of plenty of ill-gotten money in the pocket and giving or participating in parties in high hotels—the better for them and for the nation.

Administrative capability can be a reality, when we substitute a dynamic spirituality for that piety-fringed worldliness, and a deep social concern in place of our bundle of negative virtues and self-centred socio-political attitudes, we develop the capacity for impersonal sympathy, the sympathy of a wide ranging and sustained quality. This is imaginative sympathy. It is not tied down to a concrete suffering in front, nor does it end up by the tossing of a coin to the sufferer. Imaginative sympathy proceeds from a deeper source in the human personality; it proceeds from its spiritual dimension from which dynamic ethical and social values proceed.

This is the personality of the citizen. Such citizens alone are the guarantee of social health and social progress. And when administrators are recruited from a social milieu which consists of a general body of such citizens, the administration becomes responsive to social urges and needs. The difference between a police state and a state aiming to be a welfare state lies in this social responsiveness of the latter. And this is the product of that spiritual growth of the members of the administration, yielding a precious capacity for impersonal sympathy, for imaginative sympathy. The secretariat and other institutional offices of the state are far away from the actual scenes of human life with its urges and privations. Yet the administrator, through his imaginative sympathy, recognizes, and responds to that faraway social situation. With his imaginative sympathy, he sees the file in front of him stirring into life and whispering words of human urges and aspirations. Every citizen needs to develop this rare capacity, but the administrator and the politician need it more. Without it, they both, singly or in combination, can turn a nation into a mess of problems; with it, they can lift a nation from the mess of problems to the sun-lit heights of cheer and hope.[41]

Notes and References

1 U.N.: Official Records of the Economic and Social Council (E/1708), Agenda Item 10.

2 J.I. Iboko, "Developing the Administration in a Developing Country" in *International Review of Administrative Sciences*, Vol. XXXVIII, No. 2, 1972, p. 293.

3. United Nations, "Appraising Administrative Capability for Development (Inter plan) (U.N. Publication, Sales No. E-69. II H. 2), p. 5.

4. Swami Ranganathananda, "Democratic Administration in the light of Practical Vedanta", 2003, p. 111-112.

5. Newman William H. and Others, The process of Management (Englewood Cliffs, N.Y., Prentice Hall, 1967, pp. 338-45.

6. Hicks Herbert G. "The Management of Organization (NY, McGraw Hill, 1967), pp. 169-71.

7. Fred W. Riggs, "The Context of Development Administration" in Riggs (ed.), Frontiers of. Development Administration (Durham, N.C., Duke University Press, 1970), p. 73.

8. Appraising Administrative Capability for Development (U.N. Publication, Sales No. 69, II, H. 2), preface.

9. Public Administration in the Second United Nations Development Decade: Report of the Second Meeting of Experts, 16-26 January, 1971 (U.N. Publication, Sales No. E. 71, n. H. 3), p. 4.

10. Saul M. Katz, "A Methodological Note on Appraising Administrative Capability for Development", in Appraising Administrative Capability for Development, *op. cit.*, pp. 99-100.

11. Development Administration: Current Approaches and Trends in Public Administration for National Development (U.N. Publication, Sales No. E. 76. II. H.I.), p. 32.

12. Jawaharlal Nehru, "A World to the Services" delivered on Dec. 9, 1955 to an audience of the Public Servants, Jawaharlal Nehru and Public Administration, New Delhi, IIPA, 1975, p. 43.
13. *Ibid.*, p. 45.
14. *Ibid.*, p. 47.
15. *Ibid.*, p. 40.
16. Anand Sarup and Sulabha Brahma, Planning for the Millions, New Delhi, Wilsey Eastern, 1990, pp. 43-44.
17. Swami Ranganathananda, Democratic Administration in the light of Practical Vedanta, 2003, p. 116.
18. Joseph La Palomhara, "Alternative Strategies for Developing Administrative Capabilities Emerging Nations" in Riggs (ed.), *op. cit.*, p. 193.
19. *Ibid.*, p. 204.
20. Administrative Reforms Commission, "Report On Personnel Administration" (New Delhi, Government of India, 1969), p. 62.
21. For example at the Ministry of Home, Government of India, there is the Department of Personnel and Administrative Reforms which has one objective of bringing about reforms in the administration not only at the Centre but also to some extent, at the States.
22. Gerald E. Caiden, Administrative Reforms, London, Aldine, 1969.
23. Anuradha Balram, Examining Substitution of Weberian Model in *IJPA*, April-June, 2000, p. 156.
24. Solfi Ali and Anita Rao, Reinvesting Public Administration for 21st Century, in *IJPA*, April-June, 2000, p. 119.
25. *Ibid.*, pp. 176-77.
26. A David Osbore and Tech Grabbler, Reinventing Government How the Entrepreneurial Spirit is Transforming the Public Sector, Wesler, 1992.
27. Sofi Ali and Anita Rao, Reinventing Public Administration for 21st Century, in *IJPA*, April-June 2000, pp. 169, 177, 188.
28. O.P. Dwivedi, "Moral Dimensions of Statecraft: A Plea for an Administrative Theology, *IJPA*, Oct.-Dec. 1988, Vol. XXXIV, No. 4, p. 1127.
29. Norman Uphoff, "An Analytical Model of Process and Performance for Development Indicators of Administrative Capability", in *Philippine Journal of Public Administration*, Vol. XVII, No.3, (July 1973), pp. 372-79.
30. *Ibid.*, pp. 373-74.
31. *Ibid.*, p. 374.
32. Betram M. Gross, "The Managing of Organization" (London, Free Press of Glencoe, 1964), Vol. I, pp. 119-148.
33. A.M. Henderson and T. Parsons (trs), "From Max Weber: The Theory of Social and Economic Organization (London, Free Press, 1947), p. 337.
34. R.K. Sapru, "Development and Development Administration", Chandigarh, Mohindra, (1977), p. 178.
35. Madhav Godbole, "Bureaucracy at Cross-Roads", Fifty Years of Indian Administration—Retrospect and Prospects, ed. T.N. Chaturvedi, 1998, p. 300.
36. Public Administration and Finance for Development (U.N. Publication, Sales No. E. 75. II. H. 2), pp. 57-58.
37. Donald C. Stone, "Removing Administrative and Planning constraints to Development", in *Journal of Administrative Overseas*, Vol. XII, No. I (January 1973), p. 12.
38. Swami Ranganathananda, Democratic Administration in the Light of Practical Vedanta, 2003, pp. 178-179.
39. Madhav Godbole, "Bureaucracy at Cross-Road, Fifty years of Indian Administration—Retrospect and Prospects", ed. T.N. Chaturvedi, 1998, pp. 305-06.
40. B.G. Deshmukh, "Indian Bureaucracy—Facing the Future", Fifty years of Indian Administration—Retrospect and Prospects, ed. T.N. Chaturvedi, 1998, pp. 558, 567-68.
41. Swami Ranganathananda, *op. cit.*, pp. 123-24, 162, 244.

CHAPTER 11

Public Enterprises: Objectives and Forms

After the turn of the century, specially after 1914, growth in the public sector of economy, relative to the private sector have occurred in all countries. In the developing countries, however, this growth has been tremendous. The public sector in this category of countries has occupied a more important position than that in the developed countries of Western Europe and North America. In the developing countries increasing intervention by the State Governments in economic and social field has been a marked feature. Today there is hardly any sphere of human activity which is not the exercise of the regulatory function of the State Government. The *laissez-faire* policy has been replaced by welfare policy and the government is now looked upon as an agency of social and economic control. But State control varies from country to country depending upon social, economic and political system the country has. In this context it is worth while to quote observations made by a veteran, late Sh. T.T. Krishnamachari. He rightly said, "The public and private sector has to be integrated together. The Government's object is not to build a monolithic state of socialism but to make people as partners in a common enterprise."

Thus on a general understanding, a public enterprise can be termed as under:[1]

> "An enterprise is public when the state on any other national, regional or local authority holds at least 51% of its capital; it is under state control and reports to the state; and its objectives are of a public or multi-dimensional nature. This multi-dimensional aspect presupposes financial investments, marketing of products and services, financial returns, a system of business accounts and a social return which the enterprise must account for."

Among other organizations such as government departments, regulatory agencies, and adhoc organizations available to government for development efforts, public enterprises constitute the most significant form. They are becoming an important instrument in the socio-economic development of the country. In countries, particularly developing, in which economic growth is the major goal, they have acquired relatively a great importance. Hanson says, 'Whatever the ultimate perspective may be, the country anxious to develop economically has no alternative but to use public enterprise on a considerable scale, at the very least in order to get things going."[2] Before we go ahead with our discussion on public enterprises, it is good to know what we understand by it. The term 'public enterprise' is generally used to denote an undertaking in which the Government has a larger interest of ownership and management. According to President Roosevalt, any Business organisation clothed with power of government, can be called as a public enterprise. A very comprehensive definition has been given in a recent United Nations publication. It is referred to as "economic undertaking, especially industrial, agricultural or commercial concerns, which are owned (wholly or in part) and controlled by the State. It includes those 'mixed enterprises' which are controlled by the State. A mixed enterprise is one jointly owned by the State and by private persons. If the State contributes over half of its capital, it automatically has a controlling interest. In some cases, the State even has control over a mixed enterprise for which it provides less than half of its capital."[3]

After 1947, the Industrial Policy Resolutions of 1948 and 1956 envisaged a mixed type of economy and emphasized the need for a planned development of the country. It was realised that goal of socialistic pattern of society could be achieved only by starting large scale public utility services in public sector. Besides other industries which are essential and require investment on a scale which only the state in the present circumstances could provide, have also to be in Public Sector. For this in 1954, a National Industrial Corporation was set-up with a view to achieving a balanced growth of Public and Private Sector.

Today role of public sector has been undergoing a tremendous change. This sector covers a wide range of activities from manufacturing and trade to promotional and financial institutions. The pattern of investment in Five Year Plans has further strengthened its role in national development.

S.S. Khera has used this term to mean "the industrial, commercial and economic activities carried on by the central government or by a state government or jointly by the Central government, and a State government, and in each case either solely or in association with private enterprise, so long as it is managed by a self-contained management."[4]

REASONS FOR PUBLIC ENTERPRISE GROWTH

Before we discuss reasons for the growth of public enterprises, it may be mentioned at the outset that factors responsible for setting up of public enterprises in the economies (developed, developing, under-developed) differ from one country to another, depending basically on its economic, political and social system. In a system of private enterprise (a country like U.S.A.) there is hardly any public enterprise except where certain services such as the postal services, production of military weapons, Public utilities, especially at the local level, are major concerns of the government; there public enterprises are sometimes found preferable. Countries which have a mixed form of socialism, for instance England, nationalisation has been given prominence means to acquire socialist character in policy matters. In centrally planned economy or socialist countries, such as the erstwhile U.S.S.R., public enterprise has become public property. In many countries, such as India, Sri Lanka, Thailand, a system of mixed economy has been adopted where the enterprise is owned both by the State and the private persons. In a mixed economy like ours, the government has been prompted to set-up public enterprises on account of the following practical considerations:

Firstly, the developing countries tend to be very anxious about their planned economic development. The Govt.'s participation in public enterprises through Industrial Policy Resolutions is a direct outcome of planned economy. It is now generally admitted world-over that Japan which was hard-hit in the 2nd World War is one of most prosperous countries of the world due to adopting a planned economy strategy.

Secondly, it has been the considered view of all concerned that private sector generally shirks in running and managing such industries which demand huge investments partly for want of resources available and partly such enterprises having a long-term planning may not yield the expected returns. As such, the state has to enter in such areas so that it can vouch safe the interests of the general public. For instance, the state could achieve the results from Hindustan Steels after a gap of more than a decade for which it had to invest more than Rs. 700 crores.

Thirdly, the modern welfare Government with its arduous and enoromous responsibility cannot meet the desires, needs, and expectations of the public at large by medium of taxation alone. Setting up of Public Enterprises not only supplements the financial resources of the state, but also helps in removing mal-distribution of wealth, reducing gap between haves and have not and avoiding concentration of wealth in a few hands. Thus, public enterprises are one of the instruments of achieving the ideals of Socialistic Pattern of Society.

Fourthly, state has to guard the consumer's interest which is possible only if it can undertake public utility services like electricity, transport, etc. on its own. Otherwise, there is every likelihood that the consumers would be subject to exploitation by the vested interests on all fronts.

Fifthly, it is the bounden duty of the state to compete with the monopolistic attitude adopted by the private trade in matters of pricing policy. Whereas, the private trade is always keen to maximise profits, the state has to fix the pricing policy in such a manner that it may yield marginal profit, no profit no loss, or even subsidise the losses. In such an eventuality, the state has to resort to public enterprises. For instance, the Government has been subsidizing a crores of rupees to the Food Corporation of India for handling the foodgrains business with the sole idea that the weakest section of the society may not fall prey to the vagaries of private trade for the basic necessities of life, i.e., food.

Sixthly, in the developing countries, unemployment an off-shoot of population explosion, has been the bane of planning. Every year, millions of people are registered on the rolls of the Employment Exchanges inspite of the various employment generation programmes launched by the Government. The opening of more and more public-enterprises by the state, opens new occasions for absorbing unemployed ones, and thereby restrict the alarming increase of unemployment to a certain extent. Besides, the public enterprises tend to become pace-setters as Model Employers. This in turn gives rise to more benefits, perks and service conditions for the personnel *vis-a-vis* the private sector.

Seventhly, there are always certain strategic and public utility services like defence, railways, posts and telegraphs which cannot be left at the hands of private sector. Such services have inevitably to be managed by the state itself. Hence, these factors as well necessitate the government ownership in public enterprises.

Eighthly, the state cannot leave the natural resources an asset of any governmental system under the control of private people. These resources being limited in nature, have to be best exploited in the most economic manner for the welfare of the community as a whole. As such, public enterprises alone can best manage and control of natural resources to their optimum. This was one of the reasons that the British Government nationalised her coal industry.

Lastly, enforcement of' national policies and programmes in tune with the objectives enshrined in the Constitution, Five Year Plan documents, policy resolutions, also necessitate opening of public enterprises. For example, the Banks as well as the transportation system have been nationalized in our country purely to execute the policies set forth by our political executives.

A U.N. expert in development administration has advanced the following pragmatic reasons which lead a Government to expand public enterprises: (a) national defence, war and related activities which the Government does not feel desirable to leave in private hands; (b) lack of appropriate private enterprises for certain purposes, (e.g. agricultural credit). (c) the inability of private interests to develop certain lines of production, (e.g. in manufacturing industry); (d) the need for certain forms of government assistance to private undertakings. e.g., marketing and production of certain kinds of goods); (e) a desire to impose a more rational organization on specific sectors of the economy (e.g., in public utilities); (f) a desire to establish 'model' productive units (e.g., in agricultural processing); and (g) the fact that certain economic undertakings have traditionally been public enterprises (e.g., ports). Closely related to (b) and (c) is the strong-desire of the governments of many developing countries to accelerate economic growth, to speed up the process of diversification through new enterprises (where the economy heavily depends on the export of a small number of primary products), to achieve greater self-sufficiency and self-reliance and or to reduce the excessive influence of enterprises owned by foreigners/or by unpopular minority groups, and the incapability of private enterprises to achieve these objectives."[5]

From the social view point, Glentworth says that there is a social dimension to the motives, for creating public enterprises in developing countries. By this he meant a desire to create opportunities for the citizenry, to gain experience and reasonably secure places in the country,"[6] Haldipur also says, "Only public sector undertakings have the risk-taking to take on less or the un-profitable projects viz. those with long gestation period and those employing less advanced technology for social reasons (increased employment)."[7]

In brief the expansion of public enterprises is basically development-oriented as they are generally considered the main instrument in the Implementation of national development plans.[8] They play an important role not only in the growth of the 'gross national product', but also in the promotion of social justice. Development of power transport and communication, post office, public housing, etc., the advancement of technology, the training of technical personnel and the furthering of technological progress, production and sale of services and goods, securing social equity such as equitable distribution of income, preventing monopolistic profit by the private sector and ensuring utilization of human and other resources are now the concerns of public enterprises.

INSTRUMENT OF ECONOMIC DEVELOPMENT

Needless to emphasize that the public enterprises in the developing countries have become almost instruments for the socio-economic development. Since the Government has a majority interest of ownership, public enterprise has been regarded as an institutional form of economic organization to achieve certain economic and social objectives. Some of the objectives which a developing country may declare either statutorily or through governmental statements are:[9]

(1) to achieve economic justice by controlling and regulating the principal means of production;
(2) to prevent the accumulation of wealth;
(3) to increase the productive investment and to promote industrial activity;

(4) to promote the establishment of certain import-substituting and export-promoting activities in the country;
(5) to avail of foreign aid and co-operation prospects from foreign countries;
(6) to generate surplus resources for future development and growth;
(7) to shift the commercial and industrial activities from the hands of capitalists or private concerns to the public sector themselves;
(8) to promote balanced regional development;
(9) to utilize the human and material resources in a better way; and
(10) to promote savings by generating resources through appropriate public enterprises prices.

The Annual Survey of Public Enterprises in so many words has specifically laid down multiple objective to be achieved by the public enterprises namely:

- to help in the rapid economic growth and industrialization of the country and create the necessary infrastructure for economic development;
- to earn return on investment and thus generate resources for development;
- to promote re-distribution of income and wealth;
- to create employment opportunities;
- to promote balanced regional development;
- to assist the development of small scale and ancillary industries; and
- to promote import substitution, save and earn foreign exchange for the economy.[10]

According to S.S. Khere, "by state undertakings is meant the industrial, commercial and economic activity carried on by the central government or a state government or jointly by the Central government or a state government and is each case either solely or in association with private enterprises."

To achieve the above cited economic objectives which have been pronounced in the National Plans or Development Plans public enterprises have been mainly operated. The government has assumed the responsibility for the development programmes of national or state importance which otherwise cannot be accomplished without the help of public enterprises. Thus, it may be summed up that, public enterprises in the developing countries have been playing an instrumental role in the field of socio-economic activity.

RAPID EXPANSION OF PUBLIC SECTOR DESPITE POOR PERFORMANCE

In India, like in most developing countries, 60s and 70s were characterised by interventions by the State in the market place and the public sector seems to have grown at a rapid pace. The almost euphoric expansion of Public Sector in India in this period led even to interventions in areas which were not at all strategic, like hotels and manufacture of consumer goods, like scooters, soft drinks, bread, etc.

Even though the Indian public sector attracted the best human resource in brains, talents and skills, the problem of poor performance, lack of competitiveness and low productivity was entirely due to management control structure characterised by multiple principles and multiple goals, which forced them into a bureaucratic rather than commercial mode of behaviour characteristic of which was lack of autonomy and accountability. Therefore, there was need on the part of government for both the strategies, i.e. (i) of being able to let go, and (ii) to fashion an administrative interface between itself and the enterprise that optimised their commercial performance by tackling the problems highlighted above. The new policy package, which emerged in 1991 out of the unique Taxonomic Examination and Performance Contracting System, effectively addressed these issues and requirements by focusing on a dual strategy, and, therefore, could be termed as being both flexible and comprehensive.

Elements of New Economic Policy Affecting PSEs

The pre-1991 policy, which was unidimensional and status quoits, failed to deliver either adequate growth or allocative justice. What it delivered in plenty was inefficiency, red-tape and corruption. The post-1991 thrust was on greater efficiency, productivity and competitiveness in order to plug into the global market. This required a policy which was multi-dimensional and permitted options to either retain or let go investments.

The seven new elements of the policy were restructuring of: (a) policy environment, (b) portfolio of investments, (c) equity or ownership pattern, (d) boards of PSUs, (e) quality of interface between the government and the boards, (j) sickness in PSUs, and (g) safety net for workers. It is worthwhile noticing that not only issues of investment policy were tackled but also issues of corporate governance of PSUs in order to improve performance and, at the same time, dealing with sickness and poor performance by exercising all available options rather than carrying failures indefinitely for want of options.

It is unfortunate that such a comprehensive policy, on whose each element some steps were initiated, the people at large generally tended to consider it as a policy of disinvestment for covering the yawning fiscal deficit and nothing more. And once a misplaced criticism of the actual operation of disinvestment was started, reinforced by the mindset of the old policy whose life span had not ended, progress on all elements of the policy slowed down to a virtual halt. Even the disinvestment operation failed because, except for the year 1991-92, the budgetary targets were never met. The appointment of a Disinvestment Commission by the United Front government does not carry with it any conviction about a move forward in the direction of public sector reform since this Commission has no viable charter. The disinvestment process remains in doldrums.[11]

The New Public Sector Policy

As a part of the statement of Industrial Policy, a statement of Public Sector Policy was announced by the Government of India on July 24, 1991. The policy attempts at improving the portfolio and performance of PSUs. The statement contains the following decisions:

1. Portfolio of public sector investments will be reviewed with a view to focus the public sector on strategic, high-tech and essential infrastructure. Whereas some reservation for the public sector is being retained, there would be no bar for area of exclusivity to be opened up to the private sector selectively. Similarly, the public sector will also be allowed entry in areas not reserved for it.
2. Public enterprises which are chronically sick and unlikely to be turned around will, for the formulation of revival/rehabilitation schemes, be referred to the Board for Industrial and Financial Reconstruction (BIER.), or other similar high-level institutions created for the purpose. A social security mechanism will be created to protect the interests of workers likely to be affected by such rehabilitation packages.
3. In order to raise resources and encourage wider public participation, a part of the

government's share-holding in the public sector would be offered to mutual funds, financial institutions, general public and workers.

4 Boards of public sector companies could be made more professional and given greater powers.

5. There will be a greater thrust on performance improvement through the Memoranda of Understanding (MOU) system through which managements would be granted greater autonomy and held accountable. Technical expertise on the part of the Government would be upgraded to make the MOU negotiations and implementation more effective.

6. To facilitate a fuller discussion on performance, the MOU signed between Government and the public enterprises would be placed in Parliament. While focussing on major management issues, this would also help place matters on day-to-day operations of public enterprises in their correct perspective.

It is clear that during the last 50 years, public sector units has registered a growth in jurisdiction, volume of investment and activities. The performance of public enterprises, which at times was dismal, has improved to some extent. Large number of contributions have been made by the public enterprises in the past. Even after liberalisation, the public sector will play an important role in the economic development of our country. What is required is to have a supporting role from the private enterprises. Instead of privatisation of the public sector units, one can argue that there is a need to bring in private culture of management in the PSUs. Efficiency is not the function of ownership, but of management. In case, we are able to provide the real operational autonomy, reduce the bureaucratic way of functioning, bring about modern techniques of management, reduce considerably the size of manpower and bring about effective accountability, the public sector would still occupy commanding heights and play a significant role in the economic development with social justice in India.[12]

Forms of Organization

The forms of organization of public enterprises in India have been undergoing change right since their inception. To begin with, before independence and to some extent even after independence, departmental form of organization was adopted. During 1960's statutory public corporations found favour with the government as a result of which all public enterprises set-up during this period were in the form of public corporations. 1970 onwards, the government company form replaced public corporations and even at present different types of government companies are floated when ever any new public enterprise has to be started. This is only a rough compartmentalization of different forms of organization just to indicate the popular trends of organization during different periods.

There are mainly three forms of organization found for the successful conduct of an enterprise. These are: Government Department, Joint Stock Company (Government Company), and the Public Corporation. In addition to these, there is the another from known as Development Corporation.

Departments

The Departments are the oldest and largest division of the administrative structure. These are major units of an organization. It is the traditional pattern of administrative organization. The Departmental form of organization is also known as the Integrated system of organization. Under this system the agencies performing common services are grouped into various Departments and the departments are linked together and placed under the authority of the Chief Executive directly. In India, we have the Defence Department, Railway Department, Education Department, Foreign Affairs Department, Home Affairs Department, etc.

A system of administration where authority is vested in a number of simplification agencies or commissions is known as independent or uncorrelated or disintegrated system. In this system all these commissions or agencies are not lined together. Each service is treated as an independent unit having little or no direct relation with other services. The American system is called the independent, disintegrated or unrelated one.

The integrated system is generally favoured because it leads to simplification of Government activities and helps in smooth passage of legislative as well as democratic control over the administration. There is no question regarding the conflict of jurisdiction, overlapping of the functions in this type of organisation. On the other hand, it enables coordination by the chief executive.

The departmental form of organisation is generally based on the formula devised by Luthur Gulick-4 Ps, i.e. Purpose, Process, Persons and Place. The purpose or objective common to all departments is the starting point. The process stands for specialised skill aspect of the organisation. The Persons or things refers to the beneficiaries or clients being served by the organisation. Lastly, area or place refers to the geographical coverage of the organisation. Of all the principles, the basis 'purpose' which is directly related to organisaitonal output, is considered as the most important one. Since the purpose or function of an organization is in direct proportion to its objectives, it is here that political factors play a vital role in determining and designing the number of ministries and their structure. Peter Self has rightly observed, "any principle of functional allocation must be squared with requirements of political management."[13]

Some of the distinct features of a Departmental form of organisation are as follows:

(1) These organisations are fully owned by the Government
(2) These do not have any legal personality of their own, i.e. sovereign immunity of the state.
(3) These are created for regulating activities of the Government.
(4) These are mostly the money spending agencies.
(5) These are financed by annual appropriations and are not self-sufficient in themselves.
(6) These are subject to strict accounting and audit controls.
(7) The employees working in these organisations are civil servants.
(8) These organisations do not enjoy much freedom and flexibility in their operations.
(9) These organisations are solely responsible for their acts of commission and commissions to their political executive, i.e. the minister.

The above features clearly reveal that Departmental form of organisations are suitable only for those spheres and activities which affect the entire community or are of strategic importance so as to keep a direct control on their working.

The departmental enterprise is found to be inadequate as its rules do not give it too much autonomy. It is subject to executive and legislative interventions. These rules hinder the smooth working of the enterprise. For example, in the field of transport, it was observed that "general trend is away from departmental undertakings and towards the increased use of semi-autonomous or independent agencies, public corporations and government companies."[14]

One of the U.N. Seminars in 1959 pointed out the biggest disadvantages against this form of organisation is its bureaucratic control, inflexibility and red-tappism. Despite these severe criticisms, there is an ample evidence of the efficient functioning of Railways and Post and Telegraphs in Germany and England respectively, as the Departmental form of organisation.

Government Companies (Joint Stock Companies)

The word 'Company' has no strictly technical meaning. In the terms of the Companies Act, a Company means company formed and registered under the Companies Act (1956). In common law a company is a "Legal person" or "legal entity" separate from and capable of surviving beyond the lives of its members. But the Company is not merely a legal institution. It is a combined political, social, economic and legal institution. Thus the term company has been variously described. It is a means of co-operation in the conduct of an enterprise. It is an intricate centralized, economic administrative structure run by professional managers who hire capital from the investors.

Recognising the vital role that the Government companies were to play in the country's economy in the future years. Section 617 of the Company Act reads that:

> "For the purpose of this Act, Government company means any company in which not less than fifty-one percent of the paid up share capital is held by the Central Government or by any State Government or Governments or partly, by the Central Government and partly by one or more State Governments and includes a company which is the subsidiary of a company as thus defined."

A Government company is generally set-up for profit-making business. It facilitates, the management to take timely and quick decisions without much outside interference and execute them without observing strictly, the due procedures, etc. Besides unlike the Departmental or Public Corporation type, it is easier to form a company under the Act.

S.S. Khera enumerates a number of reasons for the setting up of Government Companies. These are:

(1) It provides for a good deal of flexibility and freedom of action in management. In certain specific ways it releases, the management from the trammels of prescribed governmental procedures.

(2) It is a good thing, for a public undertaking doing business to constitute itself into and be seen to be, a separate commercial entity.

(3) The Company being a separate commercial entity, it enables and stimulates the management itself and those whom the management of the company has to deal with, to adopt and adhere to sound commercial practices.

(4) The Company form provides for the association of non-officials with the managerial function and responsibility.

(5) The Company form enables legally very large formal delegations of function and assignment of resources.

A Government Company has a number of salient features, namely:

(a) It has most of the features of a private limited company;

(b) The whole of the capital stock or 51 per cent or over of it is owned by the Government;
(c) All the directors or a majority of them are appointed by the Government depending upon the extent to which private capital is;
(d) It is a body Corporate created under a general law, i.e. the Companies Act;
(e) It can sue and be sued, enter into contract and acquire property in its own name;
(f) Unlike the Public Corporation, it is, created by an executive decision of the Government without Parliament's specific approval having been obtained and its Articles of Association though conforming to an Act, are drawn up and are revisable by Government;
(g) Its funds are obtained from Government and in some cases from private share-holders and through, revenues derived from the sale of its goods and services;
(h) It is generally exempt from the personnel, budget, accounting and audit laws and procedures applicable to Governments; and
(i) Its employees excluding the deputationist are not civil servants.

A cursory look at the above features clearly reveals that a Government company has an important characteristic of flexibility and autonomy in its functioning. That is why in most of the countries like ours, the company form of organisation has received the attention of policy-makers and decision-makers *vis-a-vis* the departmental and public corporation type of organisation. This form of organisation is also a good device to serve and attract foreign capital. Even the parliamentary committees, (Estimates Committee of Lok Sabha) have justified the formation of Government Companies especially under the following circumstances:

(i) When the Government may have to take over an existing enterprise in an emergency;
(ii) Where the state wishes to launch an enterprise in association with private capital; or
(iii) Where Government wishes to start enterprise with a view of eventually transferring it to private management.

From the above discussion, one should not conclude that company form of organisation is the best one. It has its own weaknesses as well. The practice of setting up of Government companies has received a lot of criticisms on account of a number of reasons.

Firstly, it evades constitutional responsibility because it is responsible to executive and not to the democratic constituted legislature.

Secondly, the laws regulating the commercial companies generally become a mere fiction since all or most of the functions normally vested in the share-holders and in the management are reserved to the Government by the Statute Setting up the Company.

Thirdly, in state owned companies like Hindustan Steel or H.M.T. the whole investment has been made by the government and as such question of the participation of private party does not arise. In this context, one of the Comptroller and Auditor General of India had rightly remarked that company form of organisation is a fraud both on the Company Act and the Constitution of India.

Inspite of the severe attack against this form of organization, the critics have largely favoured for setting up of more and more Government Companies. To quote Sh. A.D. Gorwala, Company forms organization is most suitable for manufacturing enterprises because it is more flexible.

Public Corporation

In the words of President Franklin D. Roosevelt in connection with the Tenneesee Valley Authority (TVA) of the United States, Public Corporation may be defined as "an autonomous commercial organization established at government insistence outside the framework of government departments and company legislation."[15]

Prof. M.E. Dimock, defines "Public Corporation as a public owned enterprise that has been chartered under federal, state or local law for a particular business or financial purpose." According to Prof. J.M. Pfifiner "A Corporation is a body framed for the purpose of enabling a number of persons to act as single person."

According to Earnest Devies, "Public corporation is a corporate body, created by public authority, with defined powers and functions and financially independent. It is administered by a board appointed by public authority, to which it is answerable." A public corporation may also be defined as a "legal entity created by the government but exterior to the government organization, hence financially independent, for carrying specific activities prescribed in the law creating it."[16] In simple words, it is a corporate body created by Legislature with defined powers and functions, and financially independent having a clearcut jurisdiction over a particular type of commercial activity.

FEATURES OF PUBLIC CORPORATION

A Public Corporation has be following principal features:

(1) A Public Corporation comes into existence as a result of an Act passed by the legislature of the country. It differs from a departmentally run enterprises or a government Company which are created by the executive without any special legislation. The Act creating the Public Corporation also defines its aims and objects, powers and duties, immunities, the form of management and relationship with established departments and ministries.

(2) It is a legal person capable of suing and being sued, entering into contracts, acquiring and owning property in its own name, Corporations conducting business in their own name have been generally given greater freedom in making contracts and acquiring and disposing of property than ordinary government departments.

(3) It is wholly owned by the state. For example, the Damodai Valley Corporation Act provides that the three participating governments, the Government of India, Bihar and West Bengal, have to provide the entire capital required by the Corporation for the completion of the projects undertaken by it, in proportions specified for the various kinds of projects in the Act."

(4) Except for appropriations to provide capital or to cover losses, a Public Corporation is usually independently financed. It obtained its funds from borrowing, either from the treasury or the public and from revenues derived from the sale of goods and services. It is authorized to use and reuse its revenues.

(5) It is generally exempted from most regulatory and prohibitory statues applicable to expenditure of public funds. No hard and fast rules bind them in the matter of making contracts of buying and selling works, etc., e.g. tenders may not be called if better terms are obtainable by direct negotiation. Thus, a great deal of flexibility and discretion is left for the management in the matter of procedure.

(6) It is ordinarily not subject to the budget, accounting and audit laws and procedures applicable to government departments. For example, Section of the Air Corporation Act, 1952 provides that the two Corporations are required to maintain proper accounts. Their audit is to be done by the Comptroller and Auditor General of India or any other person appointed by him. However, the accounts and audit both are of a commercial nature.

(7) Excluding the officers taken from Government departments on deputation, the employees of Public Corporation are not civil servants and are not governed by government regulations in respect of conditions of service rules. Promotion is by merit rather than by seniority. Personnel can be terminated easily if they are incompetent.

(8) Corporations are more free from the control of the Legislature.

W. Friedman has listed the following features of public corporations:

(i) They are normally created by the state (exceptionally) or by the charter.
(ii) They have no shares or shareholders, either private or public.
(iii) The responsibility of the corporations is to administer representing the Government and through him to parliament.
(iv) Administration is in the hands of broad appointed by the minister. Neither the board nor its employees are civil servants.
(v) Their capital is provided by fixed interest-bearing stock guaranteed by the treasury;
(vi) They have the legal status of a corporate body with independent legal personality; and
(vii) They have independent accounting and auditing and some form of public control which varies from corporation to corporation.[17]

W.A. Robson states, "The public corporation is in my judgement by far the best organ so far devised in this or any other country for administrating nationalized industries or undertakings. Allowing for some teething troubles which are still not entirely cured, the public corporations which we have evolved is an outstanding contribution to public administration in a new and vitally important sphere."[18]

An analysis of the above features gives an ample evidence that Public Corporation acts as an independent unit. It reconciles the cardinal principle of reconciling autonomy with the legislature from pressure of work.

It takes the purely business services of the government outside the arena of politics. It relieves the Corporations of the unnecessary administrative, accounting, auditing procedures. Estimating the values of this form of Organisation the American's President Committee on Administrative Management had said in 1932, "Its peculiar value lies in freedom of operation, flexibility, business efficiency and opportunity for experimentation." In the words of Morrison, "we are seeking a combination of public ownership, public accountability and business management for public ends."

Thus this form of organization has come to be regarded as the best form for carrying out the functions of public enterprise. W.A. Robson states, "The public corporation is in my judgement by far the best organ so far devised in this or any other country for administering nationalized industries or undertakings. Allowing for some teething troubles which are still not entirely cured, the public corporations which we have evolved is an outstanding contribution to public administration in a new and vitally important sphere."[19]

The Administrative Reforms Commission has also favoured for setting up of Public Corporations due to its inherent advantages. To quote the Commission, the form of public corporation is the one that is best suited for commercial and industrial undertakings in the Public Sector. To conclude with W.A. Robson, Public Corporations have very adequately and successfully replaced private sector and have ensured that national wealth will be utilised for development purposes.

Inspite of the arguments advanced for the public corporations, these organisations have to face heavy odds in its functioning and the same would be explained in details in the later section. It would be suffice here to quote observations of Glentworth. He says that the laws governing public corporations are currently inadequate and are undervalued as a tool in achieving the right balance between control and autonomy.[20]

Since the debate for selection of a particular pattern of an undertaking is not yet settled finally in view of the experiments going on in different countries with different forms, we can sum up our discussion on the best form of public enterprises with a U.N. Publication. According to the publication, "Discussion about the relative advantages and disadvantages of these three forms of organization continues unabated. Whereas there is still some doubt as to suitability of the company as a means of combining operational freedom with public control, there is general agreement that, other things being equal, both the company and the corporation are superior to the department. Such agreement, however, may not mean very much, as inter-country comparisons are difficult to make."[21]

Notes and References

1. Dietrich-Carsten Burning, "Public Enterprises in France and Germany", *State Enterprises*, Vol. II, No. 2 (New Delhi, Standing Conference of Public Enterprises, April-June 1983), p. 147.
2. A.H. Hanson, "Public Enterprise and Economic Development", 2nd ed. (London, Routledge & Kegan Paul, 1972), p. 23.
3. Development Administration; Current Approaches and Trends in Public Administration for National Development (United Nations Publication, Sales No. E. 76 II,. H.I), p. 66.
4. S.S. Khera, "Government in Business" (New Delhi, National, 1977), p. 64
5. *Ibid.*, p. 167.
6. Garth Glentworth, "Public Enterprises in Developing Countries: Some Suggestions on Creation, Organization and Control", in *Journal of Administration Overseas*, Vol. XII, No. 3 (July 1973), p. 191.
7. R.N. Haldipur, "Improving Performance of State Level Public Sector Undertaking", in Sudesh Kumar Sharma (ed.), Dynamics of Development: An International Perspective (Delhi, Concept, 1978), Vol. 2, p. 356.
8. Measures of Improving performance of Public Enterprises in Developing Countries (U.N. Publication, Sales No. E. 70. II. H.I), p. 1.
9. These objectives have been directly or indirectly emphasized in the national plans of the developing countries.
10. Public Enterprizes Survey, 1983-84, Vol. I, B.P.E., Ministry of Finance, Delhi, 1985, p. 1
11. Suresh Kumar, "Public Sector in Independent India", Fifty Years of Indian Administration—Retrospective and Prospects, edited, T.N. Chaturvedi, IIPA, 1998, pp. 353-54.
12. O.P. Minocha, "Public Sector in India: From Commanding Heights to the Present Status", Fifty Years of Indian Administration—Retrospective and Prospects, edited, T.N. Chaturvedi, IIPA, 1998, p. 364.
13. Peter Self, Administrative Theories and Politics, George Allen, London, 1972, p. 58.
14. Institution Building for Transport Development in Developing Countries (United Nations Publications, Sales No. E.71, VIII, 1), p. 20.

15. Organization, Management and Supervision of Public Enterprises in developing countries (United Nations Publications, Sales No. E. 74, II, H4), p. 63.
16. Gupta, K.R. Issues in Public Enterprises, New Delhi, 1975, p. 25.
17. W. Friendmann Ed. The Public Corporation, Toranto, 1954, p. 135.
18. W.A. Robson, "Nationalized Industry and Public Ownership" (London, Allen and Unwin, 1960), p. 493.
19. *Ibid*.
20. Glenthworth, *op. cit.*, p. 205.
21. A.H. Hanson, Organization and Administration of Public Enterprises, Report of a Preliminary Study (U.N. Publication, Sales No. E. 68, II, H.I.), Para 58.

CHAPTER 12

Growth and Performance of Public Enterprises

Public Enterprises have grown fast both in magnitude and direction. They were supposed to usher an era of development wherein all people can enjoy a decent life. Let us discuss the developments of Public enterprises. (See Chart 12.1)

Hanson says, "Whatever the ultimate perspective may be, the country anxious to develop economically has no alternative but to use public enterprise on a considerable scale, at the very least in order to get things going."[1]

A UN Publication mentions the following reasons for adoption of Public enterprises:

"(a) national defence, war and related activities which the Government does not feel desirable to leave in private hands;
(b) a lack of appropriate private enterprises for certain purposes (e.g., agricultural credit);
(c) the inability of private interests to develop certain lines of production (e.g. in manufacturing industry);
(d) the need for certain forms of government assistance to private undertakings (e.g., marketing and production of certain kinds of goods);
(e) a desire to impose a more rational organization on specific sectors of the economy (e.g., in public utilities);
(f) a desire to establish 'model' productive units (e.g., in agricultural processing); and
(g) the fact that certain economic undertakings have traditionally been public enterprises (e.g., ports). Closely related to (b) and (c) is the strong desire of the Governments of many developing countries to accelerate economic growth, to speed up the process of diversification through new enterprises (where the economy heavily depends on the export of a small number of primary products), to achieve greater self-sufficiency or self-reliance and/or to reduce the excessive influence of enterprises owned by foreigners or by unpopular minority groups, and the incapability of private enterprises to achieve these objectives."[2]

CHART 12.1

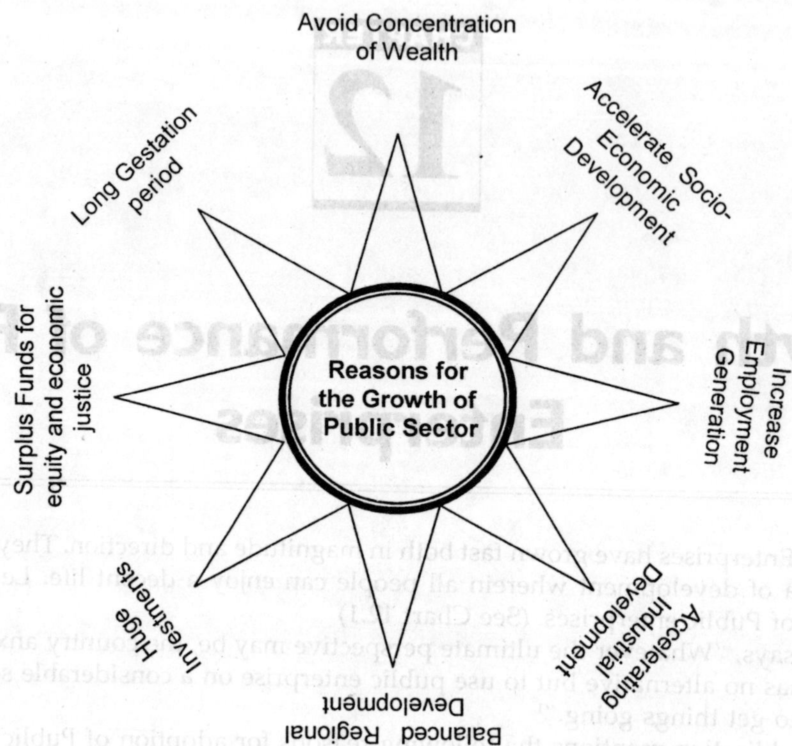

MAIN DEVELOPMENTS

1. Expansion of Public Enterprises

Ever since the planned era, there has been a rapid increase in the public sector investments. It has not only widened the scope for increasing employment and industrial products, but has also laid greater stress on social and economic welfare activities. (Refer Table 12.1)

On the eve of the First Five Year Plan there were 5 CPSEs with a total (Financial) investment of Rs. 29 crore. Both the number of enterprises and the investment in CPSEs recorded an overwhelming increase over the years, especially so after the Second Five Year Plan. As on 31st March 2007, there were a total of 247 CPSEs (Excluding 7 insurance companies) out of which 217 enterprises were in operation and 30 enterprises were under construction.

2. Investments

Investments have increased from 249855 crores to 665124 crores between 1977-78 to 2006-07. Net profit has increased from 31119 crore to 77702 crores between 2002-03 to 2006-07. However it is still very low.

TABLE 12.1

Macro View of Central Public Sector Enterprises

(Rs. in crore)

	1997-98	*1998-99*	*1999-00*	*2000-01*	*2001-02*	*2002-03*	*2003-04*	*2004-05*	*2005-06*	*2006-07*
No. of operating enterprises	236	235	232	234	231	226	230	227	226	217
Capital employed	249855	265093	302947	331372	389934	417160	452336	504407	585484	665124
Turnover	276002	310179	389199	458237	478731	572833	630704	744307	837295	964410
Net Worth	134443	148064	160674	171406	225472	241846	291828	341595	397275	452995
Profit before Dep., Iot., Tax & EP (PBDITEP)	53062	56495	62212	69287	89550	101691	127320	142554	150262	178083
Depreciation	15856	16768	19942	20520	26360	28247	31251	33147	34848	33138
DRE/Prel. Exps. Written Off	-	-	-	-	-	-	-	-	-	-
Profit before Int., Tax & EP (PBITEP)	37206	9727	42270	48767	63190	72539	95039	108420	114422	139102
Interest	17990	20025	20233	23800	24957	23921	23835	22869	23708	27069
Profit before Tax & EP (PBTEP)	19216	19702	22037	24967	38233	48618	71144	85550	90714	112033
Tax Provisions	5634	6499	7706	9314	12255	17499	22134	21662	24370	34330
Net Profit before EP	-	-	-	-	-	31119	49010	63889	66344	77702
Net Extra Ordi. Items and Prior Period Adj.	-	-	-	-	-	-1225	-3933	-1075	-3192	-3847
Net Profit	13582	13203	14331	15653	25978	32334	52985	64964	69536	81550
Profit of Profit-making CPSEs	20279	22508	24633	28494	36432	43316	61606	74432	76382	89773
Loss of Loss increasing CPSEs	6697	9305	10302	12841	10454	10972	8522	9003	6845	8223
Profit-making CPSEs (No.)	134	126	126	123	120	119	139	143	160	156
Less incurring CPSEs (No.)	100	107	105	110	109	105	89	73	63	89
CPSEs Making no profit/no loss	2	2	1	1	2	2	2	-	1	1

(Contd.)

	1997-98	1998-99	1999-00	2000-01	2001-02	2002-03	2003-04	2004-05	2005-06	2006-07
Opersating CPSEs not furnished information (No.)	-	-	-	-	-	-	-	-	2	1
Dividend	3609	4932	5455	8260	8068	13769	15288	20718	22886	26805
Dividend Tax	464	537	790	842	8	1193	1961	2852	3215	4105
Retained Profit	9509	7734	8086	6551	17902	17382	35835	41394	43435	50640
Dividend Payout Ratio	36.6	37.4	38.1	52.8	31.06	42.57	26.80	3189	32.91	33.28

Source: Public Enterprise Survey, 2001-07, Annual Report on the Macro Views of Central Public Sector Enterprises.

Top Ten Enterprises in Terms of Gross Block/Investment

Total real investment/'gross block' in top ten enterprises accounted for 73.76 percent of the total investment equal to Rs. 577501.36 crores as on 31.3.2007. ONGC Limited, BSNL and NTPC are the top three CPSEs in terms of real investment. As a category, the oil CPSEs have the lion's share in (real) investment.

TABLE 12.2

Top Ten Enterprises in Terms of Real Investment/Gross Block during 2006-07

S.No.	*Name of the Enterprises*	*Investment in terms of Gross Block*	*Share of Total real (%) investment*
1.	Oil & Natural Gas Corporation Ltd.	129984	16.60
2.	Bharat Sanchar Nigam Ltd.	123851	15.82
3.	NPTC Ltd.	74406	9.50
4.	Indian Oil Corporation Ltd.	63625	8.13
5.	Power Grid Corporation of India Ltd.	47895	6.12
6.	Steel Authority of India Ltd.	32385	4.14
7.	Nuclear Power Corpn. of India Ltd.	32611	4.16
8.	National Hydroelectric Power Corpn. Ltd.	27456	3.51
9.	Bharat Petroleum Corpn. Ltd.	21162	2.70
10.	Hindustan Petroleum Corpn. Ltd.	24136	3.08
	Total Top Ten	577501	73.76
	Total Gross Block:	782992	100.00

Source: Public Enterprises Survey, 2006-07, Vol. I, p. 5.

3. Top Ten Profit and Loss Making CPSEs

Table below provide the list of the top ten profit-making and top ten loss-making CPSEs, ONGC Ltd. BSNL an IOC Ltd. Ranked first, second and third amongst the profit-making CPSEs, which coincides with the cognate group-wise performance as discussed in the paragraph above. Equally significant to note is that these ten companies accounted for 62.76 percent of the total profits of all profit-making CPSEs. Amongst the loss making companies , the fertilizer companies led the rest. The total net loss of these ten CPSEs amounted to Rs. 6223 crore during 2006-07 which is as high as 75.48% of the total net loss of loss-making enterprises. This includes accounting losses of closed/non-operating CPSEs as well.

TABLE 12.3

Top Ten Profit Making CPSEs

S.No.	*Name of the CPSEs*	*Net Profit 2006-07*	*%age share*
1.	Oil & Natural Gas Corporation Ltd.	15642.92	17.42
2.	Bharat Sanchar Nigam Ltd.	7805.87	8.70
3.	Indian Oil Corporation Ltd.	7499.47	8.35
4.	National Thermal Power Corporation Ltd.	6864.71	7.65
5.	Steel Authority of India Ltd.	6205.29	6.91
6.	Coal India Ltd.	2822.81	3.14
7.	Bharat Heavy Electricals Ltd.	2414.70	2.69
8.	GAIL (INDIA) Ltd.	2386.87	2.66
9.	National Aluminium Company Ltd.	2381.38	2.65
10.	National Mineral Development Corpn. Ltd.	2320.21	2.58
	Total	56341.03	62.76

Source: Ibid.

TABLE 12.4

Top Ten Loss Making CPSEs

S.No.	Name of the CPSEs	Net Loss 2006-07	%age share
1.	Fertilizer Corp. of India Ltd.	(-)1432.59	17.42
2.	Hindustan Fertilizer Corpn. Ltd.	(-)1065.14	12.95
3.	National Jute Manufacturers Corpn. Ltd.	(-)794.49	9.66
4.	Hindustan Photofilms Manu. Co Ltd.	(-)653.06	7.94
5.	National Textile Corpn. Ltd.	(-)535.80	6.52
6.	Air India Ltd.	(-)447.93	5.54
7.	ITI Ltd.	(-)405.26	4.93
8.	Indian Drugs and Pharmaceuticals Ltd.	(-)351.16	4.27
9.	Hindustan Cables Ltd.	(-)310.58	3.78
10.	Indian Airlines Ltd.	(-)240.29	2.92
	Total	6236.40	75.84

Source: Ibid.

4. Contribution to the Central Exchequer

CPSEs contribute to the Central Exchequer by way of dividend payment, interest on government loans and taxes and duties. Taxes and duties constituted the largest component of this contribution (85.92%) followed by dividend payment (12.74%) and interests (1.34%). While the share of taxes and duties and interest has gone up, the share of dividend has come down in this contribution; although, in absolute terms all the three components have shown increase during 2006-07 over 2005-06 in table below:

TABLE 12.5

Contribution to the Central Exchequer

Particulars	*2006-07*	*2005-06*	*2004-05*
I. On Investment by CPSEs			
1. Dividend	18825.68	15200.85	1522.85
2. Interest	1975.08	138.22	731.67
Total (I)	20800.76	15339.07	15934.52
II. Taxes and Duties (Central)			
1. Excise Duty	24026.92	53278.48	44262.34
2. Customs Duty	11048.26	8601.18	10431.95
3. Corporate Tax	31997.93	26046.69	23613.61
4. Dividend Tax	383.12	3242.94	2742.48
5. Sales Tax	2817.25	5026.70	4487.80
6. Other Duties and Taxes	16654.04	13920.87	9132.97
Total (II)	126927.54	110116.86	94671.15
Grand Total (I & II)		125455.93	110603.67

Source: Ibid.

5. Disinvestment

Disinvestment of Government equity in CPSEs began in 1991-92. Till 1999-2000, disinvestment was primarily through sale of minority shares in small lots. From 1999-2000 till 2003-04, the emphasis of disinvestment changed in favour of strategic sale. At present, the emphasis is to list large, profitable CPSEs on domestic stock exchanges and to selectively sell small portions of equity in listed, profitable CPSEs (other than the Navratnas). The proceeds from disinvestment from April 1999 to November 2005 amounted to Rs. 47,671.62 cores.

6. Board structure of Public Enterprises

The Department of Public Enterprises (DPE) formulates policy guidelines on the Board structure of Central Public Sector Enterprsies (CPSEs) and advises on the shape and size of their organisational structure. CPSEs are categorized into four Schedules namely "A", "B", "C", "D", based on various quantitative, qualitative and other factors. The pay scales of Chief Executives and full time Functional Directors in CPSEs are determined as per the schedule of the concerned enterprise.

Proposals received from the administrative Ministries/Departments for categorization/upgradation of PSEs are examined in DPE in consultation with PESB. During 2006-07, DPE considered 14 proposals relating to categorization of PSEs in appropriate schedules. As a result, 2 CPSEs were categorized in appropriate schedules, 6 CPSEs were upgraded to higher schedule, one CMD was granted personal upgradation and 2 new posts of Functional Directors were created.

As on 31.3.2007, there were 247 CPSEs of which 54 are in Schedule "A", 77 are in Schedule "B" and 48 are Schedule "C" and 6 are in Schedule "D". The rest 62 are covered under the uncategorized category. The details of the Board level posts (who time) in the categorize CPSEs

TABLE 12.6

Position of Board Level Executives

	Chief Executive		Whole time Director	
	2006	*2007*	*2006*	*2007*
Schedule A	52	54	-	-
Schedule B	87	77	194	201
Schedule C	87	77	194	201
Schedule D	07	06	68	67
Total	200	185	471	449

Source: Ibid.

7. Professionalisation of Boards

In pursuance of the public sector policy being followed since 1991 several measures have been taken by the Department of Public Enterprises to professionalize the Boards of public enterprises. The guidelines issued in 1992 provide that outside professionals should be inducted on the Boards of CPSEs in the form of part-time non-official Directors and that the number of such Directors should be at least 1/3rd of the actual strength of the Board. In the case of listed CPSEs headed by executive Chairman, the number of non-official Directors (Independent Directors) should be at least half the strength of the Board. The guidelines also provide that the number of Government Directors on the Boards should be not more than one-sixth of the actual strength of the Board subject to a maximum of two. Apart from this, there should be some functional Directors on each Board whose number should not exceed 50% of the actual strength of the Board.

8. Employment

The public enterprises have been responsible to generate vast employment opportunities to tackle the severe problems of unemployment and under-employment.

As on 31.3.2007 the 247 CPSEs employed over 16.74 lakh people (excluding casual workers). Nearly one-fourth of the manpower comprises managerial and supervisory cadres. The CPSEs have thus a highly skilled workforce, which is the basic strength of CPSEs. The CPSEs in turn, provide lifetime employment of their employees. The CPSEs however, operate under dynamic market conditions. While some CPSEs may face shortage of people, the others may have excess of manpower. The Government, therefore, initiated a voluntary Retirement Scheme to help these enterprises to shed excess manpower.

TABLE 12.7

Employment and Average Annual Emoluments

Year	*No. of Employees (in lakh)*	*Average annual per capita emoluments*	*% increase in average annual emoluments*
2001-02	19.92	193554	(-)11.89
2002-03	18.66	225986	16.76
2003-04	17.62	248481	9.95
2004-05	17.00	286112	15.14
2005-06	16.49	248123	(-)6.95
2006-07	16.14	325738	14.65

Source: Ibid.

The basic parameters of the model Voluntary Retirement Scheme (VRS) which were notified by the Government vide Deptt. of Public Enterprises OM dated 5.10.1988 and 6.1.89 were in force since 1988 till April, 2000. Government have improved upon the said scheme and introduced new schemes of VRS on 5.5.2000 and again on 6.11.2001. As per the available information, about 5.87 lakh employees opted for Voluntary Retirement Scheme till 31.3.2007

A good many CPSEs, today, are faced with a high rate of 'attrition' as employees are leaving to join other organizations on account of higher salaries being offered elsewhere. The total number of employees in CPSE that was 16.49 lakhs in 2005-06 came down further to 16.14 in 2006-07.

9. Memorandum of Understanding

The Memorandum of Understanding (MoU), as applicable to public sector enterprises, is a negotiated document between the government and the management of the enterprises specifying clearly the objectives of the agreement and the obligations of both the parties. The main purpose of the MoU system is to ensure a level playing field to the public sector enterprises *vis-à-vis* the private corporate sector.

MoU is aimed at providing greater autonomy to public sector enterprises *vis-à-vis* the control of the government. The 'management' of the enterprise is, nevertheless, made accountable to the government through promise for performance or 'performance contract'. The government, nevertheless, continues to have control over these enterprises through setting targets in the beginning of the year and by 'performance evaluation' at the end of the year.

Performance evaluation is done based on the comparison between the actual achievements and the annual targets agreed upon between the government and the CPSE. The targets constitute of both financial and non-financial parameters with different weights assigned to the different parameters. In order to distinguish 'excellent' from 'poor', moreover, performance during the year is measured on a 5-point scale.

Table below 12.8 provides a summary of the performance of MoUs signing CPSEs as reflected in their MoU rating during the last five years:

TABLE 12.8

Performance Rating of CPSEs

Rating	*2002-03*	*2003-04*	*2004-05*	*2005-06*	*2006-07*
Excellent	46	54	45	44	45
Very Good	21	21	31	36	31
Good	12	10	12	14	12
Fair	16	11	10	08	06
Poor	02	00	01	00	00
Total	97	96	99	102	94

Source: Ibid.

10. Corporate Taxes

The CPSEs constitute a very important segment of the corporate sector in India. Its share in the total corporate taxes stood at around 26 per cent. In terms of 'gross block', the investment in all CPSEs grew by 9.49 per cent during 2006-07 (over 2005-06). Both the 'power' and 'mining' (including oil exploration) sectors saw high growth in investment of 13.9 per cent and 10.72 per cent respectively. This was followed by investment in the manufacturing CPSEs that grew by 8.05 per cent. In terms of sources of investment, the share of Central Government that was 37.78 per cent in 2004-05 declined to 35.81 per cent in 2006-07. The share of financial institutions (and others), on the other hand, went up from 39.89 per cent in 2004-05 to 45.56 per cent in 2006-07. This only exhibits the greater confidence of the banks in CPSEs. A significant portion of investment is being made also from internal resources. The 'reserves and surplus' alone, out of the internal resources of all the CPSEs put together, stood at Rs. 416494.25 crore in 2006-07.[1]

According to Annual Report, 2007-08, Ministry of Heavy Industries and Public Enterprises, GOI as on 31.3.2007, there were 247 Central Public Sector Enterprises (CPSEs) out of which 217 were in operation and 30 were under construction, having a financial investment of Rs. 421089 crore. Of the 217 operating CPSEs, 156 CPSEs earned a profit of Rs. 89773 crore and 58 CPSEs incurred a loss of Rs. 8223 crore, the net profit of all operating CPSEs taken together was Rs. 81550 crore.

CRITICAL APPRAISAL

Public enterprises are not running as expected, as many of them have become sick units. It has been rightly stated in *Economic Times*.

Over the years, the public enterprises have lost much of its 'Charm in the context of economic structure' and overall planning of the country. This question has already taxed the brains of administrators, political executives, academicians, professionals and the like engaged in this field. Suggestions have been made from various quarters for an appropriate policy framework and simplified procedures not only for future investment decisions but also for the closure of non-viable public undertakings.[2] (See Chart 12.2)

One of the Economic Surveys his rightly depicted the success story of public enterprises. It has stated: "The performance of public enterprises last year gives room for doubt about their ability to fulfil all the expectations held about them. Similarly, ever-rising non-developmental expenditures on account of interest, subsidies, defence expenditure, etc., seem to make it difficult to meet the saving target. The brunt of resource mobilisation therefore, has to fall on additional taxation."[3] (Chart 12.2)

CHART 12.2

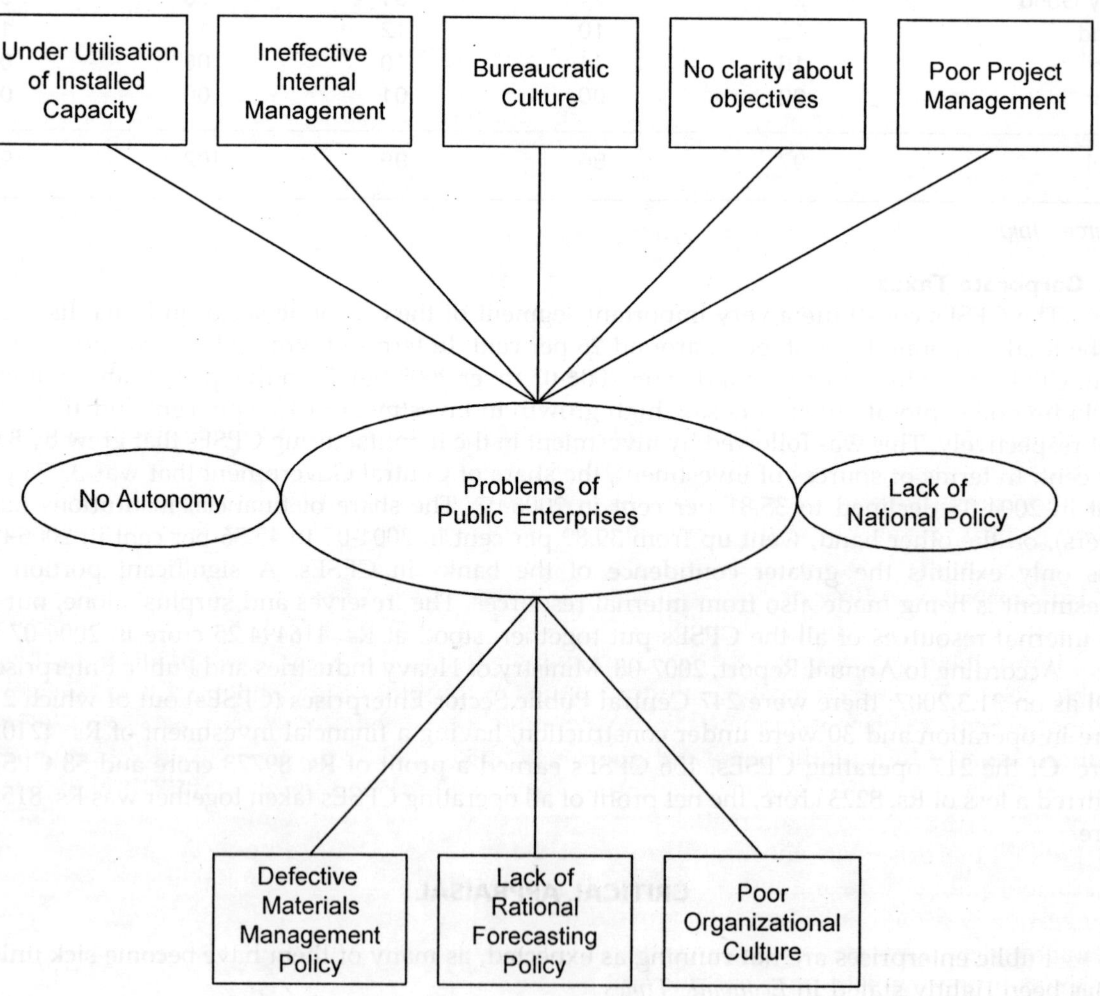

Let us discuss the problems facing Public Enterprises:

1. Sway of Bureaucratic Culture

It has been observed that the bureaucracy directly and constantly interferes in the functioning of public enterprises. It always claims a superior status over all other services. Progress in the direction of introducing professionalism and industrial management culture in the public sector industry has been sabotaged over the years by the civil bureaucracy by every available means. Indeed, a reverse trend has been introduced in the recent years in the management structures of public sector undertakings. This is evident from the fact that deputationists from the civil bureaucracy are getting back into top management positions in public sector enterprises.

More marked, however, has been the induction of representative of the civil bureaucracy into the management boards of the public sector undertakings as the preponderant element even if a professional or a technocrat may be holding the office of the chief executive.

Under these arrangements, the civil bureaucracy is able to bring into play its powers fully both at the secretariat and the Management board levels to hold the professional-technocratic element in the public sector undertakings in tight leash.[4]

2. Public Enterprises Selection Board—A Myth

A close study of the functioning of the selection Board gives an impression that the public enterprises have not reposed their confidence in its ability in the fair, unbiased, and proper selections for key posts. One of the criticisms against the Board is that it has lately started giving preference to the induction of persons from the private sector in utter regard to the promotion of experienced and more dedicated personnel from within. Besides, the recommendations of the Board being 'advisory', the administrative ministries have the prerogative to reject them on extraneous grounds. One of the critics has even remarked that it is the Prime Minister's secretariat which acts as the final authority in selections and appointments. This is evident from the fact that one of the circulars has recently specifically called for a report from the administrative ministries on the filling of vacancies in public enterprises.[5] It would be in the fitness of things if the Board like the UPSC is given complete autonomy and discretion in the matter of personnel—an asset to the organisation and key to development.

3. Lack of National Policy

In recent years, the role of public enterprises in the growth strategy is being diluted due to the shift in the policy adopted by the Government. It is for the first time in the planning era that public sector has been relegated to the second position in matter of financial allocation in the proposed Seventh Plan as compared to private sector. The opening up of areas for private ventures hitherto reserved for public sector in the name of efficiency and because of paucity of resources for investment is casting its own shadow on the performance of public enterprises.

It was during the Janata regime that a group of so called consultants engaged by the Bureau of Public Enterprise was encouraged to moot the suggestion that some of the loss-making and inefficient public sector undertakings should be closed down or sold to the private sector. This suggestion was then talked and the move did not make any headway. But the same idea is now being convassed more effectively in Government quarters. It is even frankly said by leading lights in the ruling administration that outright denationalisation may be politically inexpedient but what is called privatisation on the pattern of the U.K. under Mrs. Thatcher's leadership needs, to be, actively considered, and is being vigorously pursued inside the Government.

The widening of business opportunities for the private sector (including foreign capital), the dilution of M.R.T.P. restrictions on big business houses (including trans-national corporations) and the relaxation of licensing procedures (together with fiscal and financial concessions and incentives) testify this position.

These trends have been most marked in the case of high-technical areas, especially electronics and telecommunications. It would appear that the ground is being prepared for the revision of the present industrial policy on a more generalised and broad basis in the future.

Once the role of public sector enterprise in development plans is 'Suitably pruned, the way will be cleared not only for enlarging the scope of private enterprise—both Indian and foreign—in the economic growth process with all its implications but also for what is called the privatisation of the existing public sector enterprise in industry and commerce.[6]

Thus, the joint sector is being tipped as more potent instrument of public sector which remains to be tested and may not prove conducive to the good morale of management.[7]

4. Autonomy Versus Accountability

One of the most important factors effecting the performance of the public sector undertakings is their accountability. It has been the considered opinion of all concerned that the public enterprises do not show an inkling of initiative, innovation and taking risks which is so vital for their efficient and effective functioning. In fact, more we talk about autonomy, the greater is the Political interference in the public sector without any corresponding accountability. In our country, the political executives have often called for "political push" to get results from the public enterprises, but in vain. On the contrary, it has further eroded their autonomy and has perverted the concept of accountability to man day-to-day supervision and conduct of public sector executives.

In this context, it would be worthwhile to quote the Jha Panel Report which has strongly advocated for free public sector units.[8] The Jha Commission on Reform of Economic Administration bas stressed the need to free public enterprises from excessive centralisation and bureaucratic control which cripple the initiative and enterprise of their managers.

In its report on "the autonomy and accountability of public enterprises" submitted to the Government, the Commission said that if this was not done these units would continue to be a drag on the economy of the nation. At present every major decision of executives of the State-owned enterprises had to be cleared by the Government. Unless the managers had sufficient freedom to exercise their own judgement and even take calculated risks, their accountability to the public would suffer.

As such, the existing system of accountability should be improved in such a way as to leave no room for any organization to evade responsibility. Secondly, these organizations should be made free from the unnecessary encroachments of the politicians and ministries in their day-to-day working.[9] A considerable degree of autonomy should be given to the management in operational matters if it is to be made financially accountable and to yield desired objectives. "Autonomy must co-exist with accountability."[10]

5. Defective Personnel Policy

The personnel policies of these enterprises have also been found to be faulty. The appointment of retired and super-annuated government officials has particularly been criticised. Over-staffing and lack of regular scheme of "executive development", absence of reward for excellence in work, inefficiency and indiscipline among the workers further lower productivity.

Labour unrest and constant pressure by trade unions to raise wages also affects productivity adversely. At present, salaries and perks of the public sector executives are comparatively low as compared to their counter-parts in the private sector. It is said that the salary of the administrative secretary sets a ceiling on the remuneration of Chief Executives of public sector enterprises which is not a healthy trend. The over-all result is that talent from the private sector cannot be attracted at all. Hence a good food for thought on the Personnel policies is required on the part of the government for imparting dynamism and efficiency to the management of commercial and industrial enterprises. Since ultimate progress of public enterprises depends upon the perception, ethos and attitudes of personnel in public enterprises, therefore, there is need to pay special attention to the various aspects of personnel administration. He said that in France and some other countries, the management and the workers entered into a contract every year for achieving a higher target and remarked, "we should not hesitate to experiment if conventional methods fail to yield results."[11] Let us hope that management of public enterprises would certainly ponder over such issues and implement concrete proposals for improvement.

6. Ineffective Internal Management

The single most important issue in the performance of the public sector units is the quality of internal management. The efforts for improvement have to be persistent and not sporadic spurts of remedial measures if the gains of good performance are to be consolidated and further improved upon. The factors which are within the control and competence of public sector management themselves are such as recruitment of proper personnel in keeping with the job description; avoiding over-staffing; rationalisation and review of procedures and decentralisation of powers; evolution of an effective and workable system of two-way flow of Corporate decision-making information; imparting stimulus to participative management; career development and training of managerial personnel and other employees; cost reduction; standardisation; scientific cost management; inventory control; maximisation of capacity utilisation; maintenance and upkeep of the plant and machinery; control over expansion activity keeping the cost and quality consideration in constant view; co-ordination with other sister concerns in the public sector in regard to purchase and supply of inputs and outputs; developing a sense of competition of the market place; development, and innovation of new technology and above all preparation of corporate plans for further development. This list is long, but proper functioning of any enterprise, public or private, has to take care of these factors. For uniformity and continuity of efforts, it is desirable that the top executives of the public sector enterprises should not be frequently shifted.

7. No Clarity about Rationale and Objectives of Public Enterprises

In the developing countries like ours, the public enterprises is "the most important invention of 20th century in the sphere of government institutions",[12] and expected to provide "a combination of public ownership, public accountability and business management for public ends"[13] have failed to deliver the goods and services because of their overall as well as specific objectives have not been stated with clarity. In fact, rationale of public enterprises is varied and multi-dimensional. There are primary as well as secondary objectives. The relative emphasis on the objectives may also change with the passage of time. Besides, some objectives are general to all (economic growth and social justice) and some are specific for a particular enterprise (e.g. augmenting revenue for state, competing private sector, conserving foreign exchange, achieving socialistic pattern of society, generating employment, enhancing production of essential goods and the like.) Sometimes it so happens that the objectives of an organisation become mutually inconsistent, causing a havoc to its performance. For instance, Indian public undertaking has been set-up not only for public utilities, but also in other areas for promoting industrialisation, removal of regional disparities, helping depressed communities, and running hotels, selling liquors or cigarettes and what not. Thus depending upon the nature of an enterprise, the balance between social and economic dimensions vary too much. In this context, the Committee on Public Undertakings has rightly observed: "a clear definition of the objectives with which an undertaking is set-up is a *sine qua non* for its success."[14]

The A.R.C. (1967) too recommended that the Government should make a comprehensive and clear statement on the objectives and obligations of public undertakings.

Inspite of all this, it has been observed that the government generally feels shy of declaring their intentions and expectations which in turn act as a stumbling block in the performance evaluation of the public enterprises. To quote the Committee on Public Undertakings, "the performance of public undertakings continues to be judged by a variety of vague objectives and considerations which afford scope for uninformed criticism and makes for dilution of managerial accountability."[15]

It has once again strongly advocated for laying down clearly the economic, social and financial objectives of each enterprise.[16] Let us hope that something concrete would be done in this direction for the optimum performance of public undertakings.

8. Under-utilisation of Installed Capacity

Most of these undertakings are working below capacity. This has been due to the faulty planning with respect to the projections of demand for their products, managerial inefficiency, lack of proper working techniques and the failure to install complementary equipment. Due to under-utilisation, their costs of production are not at their minimum. This naturally affects their efficiency adversely. Emphasising the importance of capacity utilisation, our late Prime Minister recently remarked that "profit must come through better utilisation of plant capacity and resources, by greater efficiency and productivity using better co-operation of labour."

9. Poor Project Management and Indigenisation

One of the major problems in the public sector has been the inordinate delay in implementing a project. It is quite common that by the time a project is completed, the actual cost becomes 100%-200% more than the original estimate leading to a situation which makes a viable proposition uneconomic. One of the major reasons for this delay is due to endeavours towards maximum indigenisation. Since the equipment/parts are to come from different agencies which vary in their supply capabilities, often, supplies are inordinately delayed and difficult to coordinate. While self-reliance has to continue and indigenous industry has to be supported there has to be a balance between timely supply of capital goods and equipment for projects and maximum indigenisation.[17]

10. Defective Materials Management Policy

Most of the public enterprises have not given due attention in evolving a Suitable materials management policy. Inventory of stocks—a sub system of materials management, all the more, requires special consideration. Inventory management implies right amount of stock at the right place and at right time. Though Inventories cost a good deal by way of interest charges, cost of storage and handling, deterioration and obsolescence costs, it also acts as a boon especially in an inflationary situation. The Indian experience of handling inventory, management gives a dismal picture because inventory/turn-over ratio continues to be very high. This is Clear from the fact that as on March 1983, whereas the total turnover was Rs. 41,984 crores, the inventories constituted a sum of Rs. 10,286 crores. It has been estimated that if the inventories can be brought down by 10%, the country can save more than Rs. 300 crores per year.

As such, targets must be set and monitored in the area of inventory management on the area of fixing targets for production sales, profits, etc. The following measures can further facilitate in improving a better inventory management for the public enterprises:

1. Fixing achievable inventory targets and inter-firm comparison in setting targets.
2. Standardisation and rationalisation of products/processes, both in-company and at national level.
3. Strong and efficient material planning/purchase department with clear cut procurement policies; including vendor development and vendor rating and ancillarisation.
4. Aggressive import substitution and indigenization.
5. Computerisation of inventory management;
6. Modernisation and replacement of plants.
7. Power conservation and setting up of captive power generation plants.
8. Annual planned holidays.
9. Aggressive marketing strategies.
10. Effective Preventive Maintenance.
11. Better communication and customer relations.
12. Disposal of redundant and slow moving items.

11. Lack of Rational Pricing Policy

It has been generally observed that Government has adopted a very inconsistent pricing policy for the public enterprises resulting in recurrent losses. The people, including the poorest of the poor, who pay excise and sales tax on the articles of daily use, subsidise the inefficiency of public undertakings and. also suffer because of ever increasing cost of living. For instance, coal India's losses of over Rs.1000 crores, and its high priced but low-quality coal are pushing up prices of electricity and cloth and the cost structure of the entire economy.

Since one of the primary obligation of the public enterprises is to generate resources for the economy, it should be the endeavour of the government to be more vigilant and considerate in the matter of pricing policy, however, keeping in view the cardinal principal of Social Justice and economic growth.

The United Nations have evolved the following guidelines which must be taken care of:

1. Prices should cover the necessary operating costs and the replacement of assets plus a contribution to the cost of public services and to the expansion of the Public Enterprise Sector.
2. They should be so set that surplus generation is maximum in respect of amenity goods and lowest in respect of basic consumer goods and key investment inputs.
3. Prices are part of a price system and not individual items. Intervention in respect of price levels and relationship should be systematic and not piecemeal.
4. To procure the resources for the public sector and the government through appropriate price policy the whole sector's requirements including the relationship between prices, taxes and domestic borrowing must be thoroughly explored.

5. Cross subsidisation between high and low surplus generating product should be organised in such a way as to minimise distortions in production and investment and also undesired shifts in consumption.
6. Exceptions from the general sectoral guidelines for some enterprises or products may be made as necessary. But these should be kept simple and coherent and the exceptions should not swamp the guidelines.
7. Financial targets in respect of each sector must be set-up in order to plan pricing guidelines and to estimate in advance the effect of price charges and evaluate in retrospect the results of such changes.
8. Detailed financial analysis should be made of the claims of Public Enterprises for the imposed prices in accordance with broad national goals.
9. Taxation is not a public enterprises function. Sale or excise taxes should be substituted for the fiscal monopoly element in the prices. This will rationalise fiscal policy and allow a more rigorous examination of an enterprise's productive or trading efficiency.[18]

Even the Jha Panel has strongly recommended that the public enterprises should have the right to increase prices when warranted due to rise in the cost of operation. It adds, the situation has often been allowed to drift and the government has been bringing about large price increases suddenly, thereby giving a jolt to the public.[19]

12. No Proper Surveys

Efficient planning requires careful analysis of the availability of inputs such as raw material, power, fuel, credit position, skilled and unskilled labour and proper survey of the product market. The former, i.e. analysis of the availability of resources, would when the plant stay operating, reduce to a minimum the resource bottlenecks and enable the production process to work smoothly whereas the latter, the analysis of the market of the commodity to be produced will ensure that the amount produced, finds a ready market. Studies conducted by various experts have shown that in the case of many of these enterprises, proper analysis was not done.

13. Unsatisfactory Location

Most of the public enterprises are located at such places where these may not be able to enjoy maximum benefits. In fact, location of the plants are decided more on political considerations than taking into consideration the best sites and also to lessen the regional disparities of industrial development. This results in increased cost of production and reduces the chances of profitability.

The only via media is that the project site should be selected on the basis of techno-economic surveys. In this context, the Bureau of Public enterprises has also recently issued new guidelines. According to the Bureau, a decision on the location of units in various States will be taken by the Government on techno-economic considerations.

While selecting a site, the availability of necessary infrastructural facilities and raw materials should be kept in view, the guidelines say:

In the initial stages, a systematic techno-economic study should be undertaken by a high-level committee. The Ministry concerned should approach the State Government before setting up projects for suggesting suitable sites. The guidelines suggest that a site selection committee, including representatives of agencies involved in the provision of the infrastructure, should examine and evaluate alternative sites. A time-limit should be fixed for the committee to submit its report. The Government should select a project site only on the basis of the committee's report, the guidelines add.[20]

14. Recent/Latest Developments

Since independence, there has been an extensive expansion in growth and operations of Public Enterprises. But these organisations have failed to deliver the expected goods and services. In this context, the 2nd Conference of Chief Executives of the Public Sector Enterprises which met at Delhi (May 30-31, 1984) pondered over a large number of issues. In his welcome address, the Director General, Bureau of Public Enterprises, raised the issue with regard to improvement of the quality of performance of public sector. The Finance Minister in his inaugural address emphasised that economic viability must be cardinal test for the survival of an organisation. In the valedictory address, the Planning Minister stressed the need for greater attention to inventory reduction (1% reduction in inventories can increase profitability by about Rs. 20 crores), higher capacity utilisation, and improving productivity. Similarly, one of the experts from the Planning Commission advocated for timely completion of projects to minimise cost over-runs and to increased productivity.

SUGGESTIONS TO IMPROVES PERFORMANCE

Some of the important recommendations made by the conference for improving the overall performance of public enterprise are given below:

Organisational Culture

1. Organisational excellence is a result of harmonious- effort of Management and Labour. It is a collective endeavour in which both the Management and Workers have their respective roles to play. Effort towards excellence does not necessarily involve getting the best out of men, but it is more of an innovative approach to improve the quality of the existing manpower and getting the best out of them through training and motivation. The Public Sector companies should strive to bring about a psychological ethos and inculcate in the employees of all levels, a sense of *espirit de corps* dedication and belonging. Attitudinal changes should flow down from the top.
2. Organisational excellence can be predicated when there is greater awareness of action to be initiated within organisation.
3. A total sense of loyalty to the Enterprise and commitment to the cause of Public Sector is necessary if excellence is to be achieved. Team spirit at the top is of prime importance.
4. The continuity and consistency of the top management philosophy is an essential pre-requisite for organisational excellence and for this longer tenures for the Chief Executives and other top management executives is vital.
5. For ensuring a truly business culture in the Public Enterprises, the present fragmentary approach should be eschewed and replaced by a systems approach.
6. A long-term corporate management development and career plan is essential for the employees to perceive their own growth with the growth of the organisation.
7. The experiment of bringing about organisational excellence through a concrete

Production and Profit Improvement Management System (PPIMS) deserves consideration.

8. For efficient performance, it is necessary that delegation of powers should be such as to obviate repeated back and forth reference to Government and procedural delays in operational matters, if any, should be reviewed.
9. A major constraint faced by several Enterprises is existence of surplus staff and labour. Concerted efforts are called for to put such surplus manpower to productive use.

Conceptual Review of Public Enterprises

10. Massive investments have been made and continue to be made in the Public Sector, which is truly the people's sector. Sufficient returns to the economy must come out of the investments made. Economic viability must be the principal test for the survival of an Enterprise.
11. An omnibus set of criteria cannot be applied indiscriminately for purposes of performance evaluation. The criteria for such evaluation should be evolved with reference to the objectives of the Enterprises and the type of activities they are engaged in.
12. The concept of social profitability also deserves consideration in the performance evaluation.
13. Public Sector Enterprises should strive for greater self-reliance. Dependence on subsidies, Governmental protection and preferences should be phased out.
14. Though there has been ample justification for according price preferences to Public Sector Enterprises, it is realised that it often leads to over-capitalisation. as well as unintended cost imposed on the buyer Enterprises. In the fitness of things therefore, such price preference should be extended to Selected Enterprises for a limited period of time till they become competitive. A working group may be constituted for examining the question of continued price preference to certain public Enterprises and the term thereof.
15. Now that several Public Sector Enterprises have been in existence for more than 5 decades, some of them might have outlived their original business purpose and a thorough review of their objectives is called for. Diversification based on the internal strength and external opportunities will be in order.

System of Project Approval and Execution—Investment Strategy and Priority

16. An integrated Public Sector plan co-terminus and dovetailed with the National Plan is desirable. It will facilitate clearance of inter-linked projects as a package rather than separate clearance of individual projects with a possibility of imbalance in the inter-link projects. As a first step towards this objective, the inter-meshing of the Corporate Plans of major Sectors like Steel, Coal, Heavy Engineering, Fertilisers and Transport could be attempted.
17. A system of two stage clearance of New Projects appears to have many advantages viz;
    (a) It gives the needed time and funding to the organisation for detailed investigation and preparation of a detailed project report.

(b) The major parameters having been determined in the first stage conceptual clearance, it becomes possible for the inter-linked Sectors to participate in the preparation of detailed project report and also to plan their own respective activities for supply of equipment, construction and fabrication jobs involved in such projects.

(c) The identification of import needs and procurement of capital equipment can be done before the investment decision is taken. DGTD would also be associated in this. It will, thus facilitate the long cherished objective of a single window clearance obviating. separate references to the Government for importing individual items.

(d) The estimates. of projects become more reliable and chances of cost over-runs are reduced.

18. Problem of project delays and cost over-runs could be tackled successfully at the site, if the Management is alert to the need for completion of the Project on schedule.

Industrial Relations

19. Any guideline to public sector enterprises on wage/salary matters should leave sufficient scope to the public sector managements to negotiate.
20. However there is need to establish a linkage of wage revisions with production and productivity norms.
21, There is need to examine the housing problem of public sector employees in cities. Abolition of the system of leasing of houses by the Companies would create enormous difficulties for the executives.
22. Leadership style should be oriented towards participation in management. It should permeate the entire organisation and help in the evolution of a culture of a participative management.
23. Surplus labour is eating into the, profitability and existence of some public sector enterprises particularly construction units. Retrenchment and transfer policies need to be reviewed.
24. The present workers' education programme is lacking in effectiveness and coverage. The Government and Public Sector Enterprises should take active steps in making these programmes of value to workers, trade unions and the industry.
25. Alienation of officers at junior and middle management levels on account of reduced differential in wages *vis-a-vis* workers is having an adverse impact on sustaining capacity utilisation drives on continuing basis from year to year. Necessary monetary as well as non-monetary incentives along with social motivational programme need to be evolved to arrest this trend.

Inventory Management

26. Inventory Management is an import aspect of the total: management of an enterprise and hence inventory targets should be set and monitored at the highest level as in the case of targets for production, sales and profit. Separate targets may be fixed for each product/profit division of the company. Interfirm comparisons would be useful in setting these targets.

27. Efforts should be made to reduce the inventory levels and the enterprises should aim at a reduction of five per cent in inventory sales ratio over the previous year.
28. There should be in-company standardisation, oriented towards company's products, processes and equipment.
29. There should be a strong and efficient material planning/purchase department staffed with qualified personnel and with clear-cut procurement policies.
30. Aggressive marketing strategies by the enterprises would help in reduction of finished goods inventory.
31. There should be aggressive import substitution and indigenisation efforts by the companies.

Capacity Utilisation

32. Efforts should be made by all public enterprises to improve the capacity utilisation by atleast 5%.
33. Adequate protection in selected areas is required to be given to select public enterprises against unfair competition from overseas suppliers especially dumping practices.
34. There is an urgent need for replacement of the out-dated technology and introduction of the latest technology (as per market requirement) without which some of the public sector enterprises will not be able to survive.
35. In case of Public Sector Enterprises where the business is shrinking, expeditious diversification proposals should be supported.
36. High capacity ulilisation *per-se* need not be the overriding company objective especially when there are marketing constraints. Simultaneous attention also needs to be given by managements to profitability, salebility as well as productivity while improving the capacity utilisation.
37. To improve the utilisation of the installed capacity within the public sector, the purchases by Government as well as the public sector units should be made as far as possible from public enterprises as in the case of textiles.
38. Special efforts need to be made to look into the problems of joint sector enterprises where both State and Central Governments have made investments; remedial measures to improve capacity utilisation in such enterprises is also considered necessary.
39. Taking over of terminally sick units from private sector should' not be encouraged.

It may also be pointed out here that the recommendations already made by Sh. L.K. Jha, Chairman of the Economic Administration Reforms, on the subjects entitled: "Top Management and the Boards Autonomy and Accountability, and Government Clearancés and Approvals, are already under" the active consideration of the Government.

The Government of India, has also set-up a committee of the Secretaries under the Chairmanship of Dr. Arjun Sen Gupta, Special Secretary to the Prime Minister, solely with a view to analyse the performance of public enterprises, identify constraints and to 'Suggest measures to improve their functioning. The term of reference of the Committee are as under':

1. To review the role of public enterprises in the context of the economic structure and overall planning;
2. to analyse the performance of public enterprises in different sectors of the economy so as to identify the critical problems and constraints on their operation;
3. to select a set of performance evaluation criteria for different groups and sectors of public enterprises;
4. to review the present system and institutions of Government controls and monitoring for public enterprises, accountability of the management to the Government and Parliament;
5. to examine alternative organisational structures and suggest appropriate changes so as to impart greater autonomy and responsibility to the management of public enterprises; and
6. to suggest an appropriate policy framework and simplified procedures for investment decisions, technological upgradation incentives and productivity increase, cost and pricing, labour relations, wage structure including wage negotiations, employment and personnel policy, closure of non-viable units, etc. with the objective of improving the performance of public Sector units.

The Committee is likely to submit its report by the year-end. Let us hope that with the implementation of the recommendations made Jha Commission, the Conference of Chief Executives, and the Committee of Secretaries, the image and credibility of the public enterprises in terms of performance and quality would be enhanced.

Thus, there is a great need of improving the performance of public enterprises in order to achieve economic and social purposes. Performance need not be measured in terms of profit. It ought to be measured in terms of production functions at the lowest costs, job satisfaction, fairness in the organisation and the government should feel that the organisation is achieving its developmental, social and economic goals.

According to Eleventh Plan PSEs have made a notable contribution to the economic growth of the country, particularly by creating a diversified industrial base. After the introduction of economic reforms in 1991-92, a policy of disinvestments and privatization was adopted and upto 2001-02 equity had been sold in 123 enterprises and receipt of Rs. 26012 crore realized. During the first two years of the Tenth Five Year Plan, the process intensified and a sum of Rs. 18895 crore was realized from disinvestments. In 2004-05, there was a policy shift and the United Progressive Alliance , (UPA) government, while expressing a commitment toward a strong and effective public sector, decided that 'generally profit making companies will not be privatized'. Residual disinvestments made in the last three years of the Plan brought in receipts of Rs. 4335 crore.

RECENT DEVELOPMENTS

Performance of Central Public Sector Undertakings

Despite the privatization accomplished upto the middle of the Tenth Five Year Plan, when the policy changed, the role of PSEs and their contribution to the GDP has not diminished. In fact, the GDP from non-departmental enterprises (NDEs) registered an increase during the first two years of the Tenth Five Year Plan as shown in the Table 12.9

In 2004-05, the share of CPSEs in the GDP was 6.82% out of 11.85% for NDEs. The number

TABLE 12.9

Contribution of Non-Departmental Enterprises to GDP at Factor Cost (Current Price)

Year	*GDP from NDE's (Rs.Crore)*	*GDP at Factor Cost (Rs. Crore)*	*Share (%)*
1996-97	141710	1260710	11.24
2001-02	244345	2100187	11.63
2002-03	282518	2265304	12.47
2003-04	312364	2549118	12.24
2004-05	338352	2855933	11.85

Source: National Accounts Statistics 2007 for 2001-02 onwards; for 1996-97 based on "back series" information provided by CSO.

of operational CPSEs has decreased from 231 in 2001-02, the last year of the Ninth Five Year Plan, to 225 in 2005-06. What is significant is that the number of profit-making CPSEs has gone up from 120 to 157 and the number of loss-making CPSEs has decreased from 109 to 58. The profits of profit-making CPSEs have increased from Rs. 36432 crore to Rs. 76240 crore and the losses of loss-making ones has come down from Rs. 10454 crore to Rs. 5752 crore during the same period.

The net profits made by the CPSEs has led to the accumulation of large reserves which totaled as much as Rs. 353641.62 crore for 157 profit-making enterprises at the end of the financial year 2006-07. Between 2002-03 and 2005-06, the cash and bank balances of all CPSEs rose from Rs. 53,453 crore to Rs. 150,680 crore. Thus, CPSEs have accumulated large amounts of investible funds, which are not being put to productive use.

The top 10 profit-making CPSEs made a net profit of Rs. 47371 crore in 2005-06. The ONGC (Rs. 14431 crore), Bharat Sanchar Nigam Ltd. (BSNL) (Rs. 8940 crore), National Thermal Power Corporation (NTPC) (Rs. 5820 crore) were the top three profit-making CPSEs. The top 10 loss-making CPSEs accounted for a net loss of Rs. 4552 crore, the top three loss-making units being the Fertilizer Corporation of India, Food Craft Institute (FCI) (Rs. 1294 crore), Hindustan Fertilizer Corporation Limited, HFC (Rs. 965 crore), and Hindustan Photo Films Co. Ltd. (Rs. 561 crore). While the top 10 profit-making enterprises are diversified, the top 10 loss-making enterprises largely concentrated in manufacturing.

Mid-year review (April-September 2006 against April-September 2005) showed that the turn-over of 202 CPSEs (out of 225) for which data was available increased by 24.07% and the net profit increased by 18.18%.

Policies toward CPSEs and their Implementation

In accordance with the mandate in the NCMP the two main elements of the GOI policy have been devolution of full managerial and commercial autonomy to successful, profit-making companies and modernization and restructuring of sick PSUs (as well as sell-off or closure of chronically sick CPSEs).

Pursuant to the recommendations of an *ad hoc* group of experts under the chairmanship of Arjun Sengupta, the government introduced a series of measures for enhancement of financial delegation to *Navratnas, Miniratnas,* and profit-making CPSEs. These include measures for creation of and disinvestment in subsidiaries, transfer of assets to such subsidiaries, and floating of fresh equity.

Under the provisions of Sick Industrial Companies (Special Provisions) Act, 1985, 62 CPSEs had already been referred to the BIFR earlier and during the Tenth Five Year Plan 12 more were referred to them for considering revival/restructuring/closure. A total of 28 of these had been recommended for winding up. Because of the delays inherent in the process of BIFR, the government has already sought to replace it by the National Company Law Tribunal (NCLT) but the creation of NCLT has been under dispute in the Honourable Supreme Court. Hearing in the special leave petition is already over and the final judgment has been reserved.

According to Annual Report, 2007-08, Ministry of Heavy Industries and Public Enterprises, GOI as on 31.3.2007, there were 247 Central Public Sector Enterprises (CPSEs) out of which 217 were in operation and 30 were under construction, having a financial investment of Rs. 421089 crore. Of the 217 operating CPSEs, 156 CPSEs earned a profit of Rs. 89773 crore and 58 CPSEs incurred a loss of Rs. 8223 crore, the net profit of all operating CPSEs taken together was Rs. 81550 crore. The cognate group-wise profit of profit-making CPSEs and loss of loss making CPSEs are indicated in Chart 1 and Chart 2 respectively.

The government constituted a Board for Reconstruction of Public Sector Enterprises (BRPSE) in December 2004, as a part time advisory body to address the task of strengthening, modernization, revival, and restructuring of CPSEs. Until February 2007, the 3RPSE had considered cases of 46 CPSEs received from 14 administrative ministries/departments and made recommendations in respect of 40 CPSEs. On he basis of the recommendations of BRPSE, the government has also approved the winding up of one CPSE, namely, Bharat Opthalmic Glass Limited. It has approved revival schemes in respect of 25 CPSEs, envisaging assistance of Rs. 1951.30 crore in cash by way of equity/loan/grant and Rs. 5709 crore by way of waiver of interest/loan/guarantee fees. Out of the 20 CPSEs for which the budgetary support has been sanctioned for revival, 13 had posted profits after tax in 2005-06 while the remaining have continued to incur losses. The data for 2006-07 that have been made available in respect of some CPSEs show that while some like the Cement Corporation of India, Heavy Engineering Corporation, Mineral Exploration Corporation Ltd. (MECL), Bharat Compressors Ltd. have shown better financial performance than projected in the revival proposal, others such as Hindustan Antibiotics Ltd and Andrew Yule & Company Ltd. have been below the projected levels. Thus rehabilitation proposals have been effective in about 50% of the cases. However, it must be observed here that the improvement in market situation and hand-holding by the government in terms of price preference, placing of orders on nomination basis have also contributed to the success of the revival efforts of the government.[21]

CONCLUSION

The Approach to the 11th Five Year Plan notes: "Public Sector Enterprises have made a major contribution to the economic growth of the country by creating a diversified industrial base. They have been major providers of organized sector (CPSES) have had strong financial results over many years and recently some more have turned the corners." In 2005-06, the number of profit making CPSEs increased to 157 from 119 in 2002-03 and aggregate profit rose to Rs. 76,240 croress from Rs. 43,316 crores. The number of loss-making enterprise declined from 105 in 2002-03 to 58 in 2005-06. Moreover, the total loss of loss making enterprises declined sharply from Rs. 10,972 crores in 2002-03 to Rs. 5,952 crores in 2005-06. Indicating the new directions of policy, the Approach mentions: "The necessary conditions for further improvements in the performance of the PSEs are ensuring autonomy, delegation of more powers to PSE Boards, Freedom from informal levers of control excercised by the administrative Ministries and a clear statement on future ownership. If these conditions are met, CPSEs do not need to the supported by measures such as administered prices, or price or purchase preference in government purchases or any type of *de jure* or *de facts* favourable treatment *vis-à-vis* the private sector.[22]

Notes and References

1. A.H. Hanson, "Public Enterprise and Economic Development", 2nd ed. (London, Routledge and Kegan Paul, 1972, p. 23.
2. Development Administration, *op. cit.*, p. 167.
3. Prem Shankar Jha, "Public Sector Losses: An Accountant's Illusion", *The Economic Times*, New Delhi, March 23, 1979.
4. *The Tribune*, June 18, 1984.
5. *The Tribune*, August 14, 1984.
6. *The Tribune*, Oct. 9, 1984.
7. *The Tribune*, August 14, 1984.
8. *The Tribune*, August 3, 1984.
9. The Committee on Public Undertakings (1978-79) in *its* fourteenth report on Jute Corporation of India organisational matters—recommended that in regard to "the amount of autonomy, actually enjoyed by the Corporation, in the functioning of the Corporation in its day-to-day working. matter should be sorted out through free and frank discussions, supported by concrete cases of undue interference, between the Managing Director of the Corporation and some officers of an appropriate status in the Ministry, in order to pin-point the lacuna in the existing relationship between the Corporation and the Government so as to ensure that day-to-day affairs of the Corporation are managed by its affairs without any unauthorised interferences from the Ministry," (C.P.U. No. 346, *op. cit.*, p. 10).
10. J.R.D. Tata,"Autonomy and Framework of Controls", in *Lok Udyog*, Vol. IV, No. 7, (October, 1970), p. 785.
11. *The Tribune*, June 9, 1984.
12. W.A. Robson, National Industry and Public Ownership, Allen and Unwin, London, 1960.
13. Herbet Morison; Sociolization and Transport, London, 1933.
14. Committee on Public Undertakings, "Management & Administration of Public Undertakings", 3rd Lok Sabha, 13th Report, *1965*.
15. C.P.U., "Role and Achievements of Public Sector Undertakings, 40th Report, 8th Lok Sabha, 1973.
16. C.P.U., 49th Report, 7th Lok Sabha, April, 1982.
17. Key note address, Chairman, Steel Authority of India Ltd. at the Conference of Chief Executives of Public Enterprises, May 1984, *Lok Udyog*, XVIII, No. 4, July 1984.
18. U.N.: Financing of Public Enterprises in Developing Countries, New York, 1976, pp. 7-8.
19. *The Tribune* August 3, 1984.
20. *The Tribune*, Oct. 22, 1984.
21. Eleventh Five Year Plan 2007-12, Volume III, Planning Commission, GOI, New Delhi, pp. 153-55.
22. Planning Commission (2006), An Approach to the 10th Five Year Plan, p. 37.

APPENDIX 12.1

NTPC

National Thermal Power Corporation: A Case Study

1. Company Profile

NTPC was incorporated on 7.11.1975 under the Companies Act 1956 with an objective to develop and provide reliable power, related products and services at competitive prices, integrating multiple energy sources with innovative and eco-friendly technologies and contribute to society. It is a schedule "A"/Navratna CPSE in Power Sector under the administrative control of M/o Power with 89.50% shareholding by the Government of India. Its Registered and Corporate offices are at New Delhi.

2. Industrial/Business Activities

NTPC is engaged in an integrated and efficient development of Thermal/Hydro power and power through Non-Conventional/Renewable energy sources in India and abroad including planning, construction, generation, operation, maintenance, transmission, distribution, etc. in accordance with national economic policies and objectives. The company diversified across the power value chain in India by considering backward and forward integration into areas such as power trading, transmission, distribution, coal mining, coal beneficiation, etc.

NTPC has 26 stations/projects consisting of 15 coal based power plants (3 projects) and 7 gas/liquid gas fuel based power plants (one joint venture) at Delhi, U.P., Rajasthan, Haryana, Gujarat, Kerala, Himachal Pradesh, Chhattisgarh, Uttaranchal, Andhra Pradesh, Orissa, Madhya Pradesh, Bihar and West Bengal.

It has five wholly owned subsidiaries namely Pipavav Power Development Co. Ltd., NTPC Electric Supply Co. Ltd., NTPC Vidyut Vyapar Nigam Ltd., NTPC Hydro Ltd. and Vaishali Power Generating Company Ltd. The company *also* has 7 joint venture projects with a share holding of 50% in 5 JVs and 8% and 28.33% respectively in two JVs.

3. Production/Operational Profile

The service range of the company comprises of generation and supply of coal and Gas based power. The Average Capacity Utilization for coal-based power plants was 89.43% and Gas based 71.90% during 2006-07. The performance details of electricity generation by the company are as follows:

Major Products/ Units Services	*Production during (% capacity Utilization)@*			*Average of three years*
	2006-07	*2005-06*	*2004-05*	
Generation of electricity/MW	188674 (89.43)	170880 (87.54)	159110 (87.51)	172888 (88.16)

4. Major Financial Highlights

(Rs. In crores)

Particulars	*Performance during*			*% change over previous year*
	2006-07	*2005-06*	*2004-05*	
Turnover	32595	26905	22565	21
Cost of Production	26484	22658	19478	17
Net Profit/Loss(-)	6865	5820	5807	18
Dividend declared (as % of PBT	30	34	33	-12
Net worth	49253	45399	41776	8
Paid up capital	8245	8245	8245	0
Share of Central Government	7380	7380	7380	0

5. Key Performance Factors

The increase in turnover and profitability is attributed to addition of new generation capacity, increase in revenue due to revision of tariff for NTPC stations, increase in other income (from banks and others) and impact of prior period adjustments.

Tariff for sale of power from NTPC's stations is regulated and determined by Central Electricity Regulatory Commission (CERC). Turnover of the company depends on the tariff as well as total generation of electricity.

NTPC contributes more than one-fourth of India's total power generation with around one-fifth capacity Projects in NTPC implemented at optimum cost and time, run with desired quality through Integrated Project Management and Control System. With 20% share of total installed capacity of the nation, NTPC contributed 28.5% of the electricity generation in the country during 2006-07.

The company has availed of a cumulative Government Guarantee of Rs. 3097.02 crore as on 31.3.2007. The Earning Per Share of the company during 200607 was Rs. 8.33. The share price of the company ranged between Rs. 85.1 to Rs.157.9 during the year 2006-07 as compared to Rs. 80.10 to Rs. 142 in 2005-06. The average share price during the year was Rs. 121.5. Company scored 'Very Good' MOU rating during the year 2006-07.

6. Human Resource Development (HRD)

The enterprise employed 24,122 regular employees (executives 12,285 and non-executives 11,837) as on 31.3.2007 as against 24,044 employees as on 31.3.2006. About 29.71% of the employees were having professional qualifications. Around 25% employees come under the age bracket of 51 and above years.

The retirement age in the company is 60 years. It is following IDA 1997 pattern of remuneration. A total of 222 employees retired during the year. In addition, 460 skilled and 20 unskilled employees also left the company in attrition. However, 822 new skilled and 11 un-skilled employees joined during the year.

During the year, 4 employees availed of VRS and an amount of Rs. 0.11 crore was spent in this regard. Since the introduction of VRS a total of 1104 employees have retired under the scheme.

The total number of Directors in the company, as on 31.3.2007 was 13 out of which 4 were part time Non-official Directors/professionals, 7 full time Functional Directors and 2 Government/official Directors. As per listing agreement, 9 Non-official Directors/professionals are required.

7. Strategic Issues

For the XIth Five Year Plan period (2007-12), the target for power is 21,941 MW for which 8 projects are on-going with a total capacity of 7840 MW and planning for 15 new projects is under way with a combined capacity of 14,101 MW.

Availability of fuel at an affordable price is a major challenge for which company is planning to adopt a strategy of backward and forward integration and is entering into coal mining, LNG value chain, power trading, distribution, etc.

8. Project Implementation

During 2006-07, 2415 MW of capacity was added which included 1000 MW at Vindhyachal III, 210 MW at Unchahar III, 500 MW at Kahalgaon II and 705 MW taken over at Badarpur TPS.

Presently NTPC is implementing power projects with a capacity of 13,360 MW (including 3000 MW in various JVs). During the year company has initiated steps to form one more N and one more subsidiary namely Aravali Power Company Ltd. with 50% shareholding and Vaishali Power Generating Company Ltd. with 51% shareholding.

9. Research and Development (R&D)

NTPC established a R&D centre way back in 1980-81. A new R&D center was set-up in Noida during 1993 at a cost of Rs.28 crore. R&D center in association with agencies like BARC, CPRI, IIT Kharagpur, etc. also undertakes various generic and specific problems of power stations. In future R&D will switch over to high-end scientific services. To carry out these in a structured manner Indian Institute of Science, Bangalore has been appointed as consultants for up-gradation of R&D center. However, the R&D expenditure of the company constituted only 0.02% of its turnover.

10. Environmental Initiatives

The environment initiatives taken by the company during 2006-07 are related to use of ash, Glacier study, introduction of Biomethanation process, adaptation of small punch technique for health assessment, etc. During the year, about 20.80 million tones of ash (53.21% of ash generated) has been utilized for various road embankments, mine filling, Ash Dyke raising, land development, brick manufacturing and in cement and asbestos industry. Further, under Clean Development Mechanism (CDM) the company has identified five projects.

Source: Public Enterprises Survey, 2006-07, Vol. II, Annual Report on the performance of Central Sector Undertakings, GOI, Ministry of Heavy Industries and Public Enterprises, New Delhi, pp. 19-21.

CHAPTER

13

Regulatory Administration: Industrial Policy Resolutions

(Chart 13.1)

Industrial Policy of a country is like economic constitution, which contains all aspects of future industrial development. It contains the policy regarding industrial location; policy regarding foreign capital, amount of protection to be provided to the domestic industries, policy regarding regional development and many other policy statements regarding other aspects of industrial development. Industrial policy in India as in other countries, has been concerned as an instrument for bringing about a rapid economic transformation of the country through the process of industrialisation.[1]

The Industrial Policy has evolved since independence and is still developing. It covers all aspects of industries, principles, rules and regulations, labour policy, public and private sector allocation, etc.

INDUSTRIAL POLICY, 1948

Immediately after independence, it was realised by our policy-makers and decision-makers that industrialisation plays a vital role in accelerating the economy of the country. Accordingly, the Government came forward with the First Industrial Policy Resolution on April 6, 1948. The resolution envisaged a mixed type of economy and an urgent need for a planned and rapid development. In other words, both the public sector and private sector were assigned specific activities by classifying the industry into 4 major categories. For instance, some industries exclusively the monopoly of the state; e.g. manufacture of Arms and Ammunition, Atomic energy, Railways, etc. industries reserved with state's initiative e.g. coal, agro and steel, ship-building, telegraph and iron, etc. industries earmarked for private sector which were to be subject to

CHART 13.1

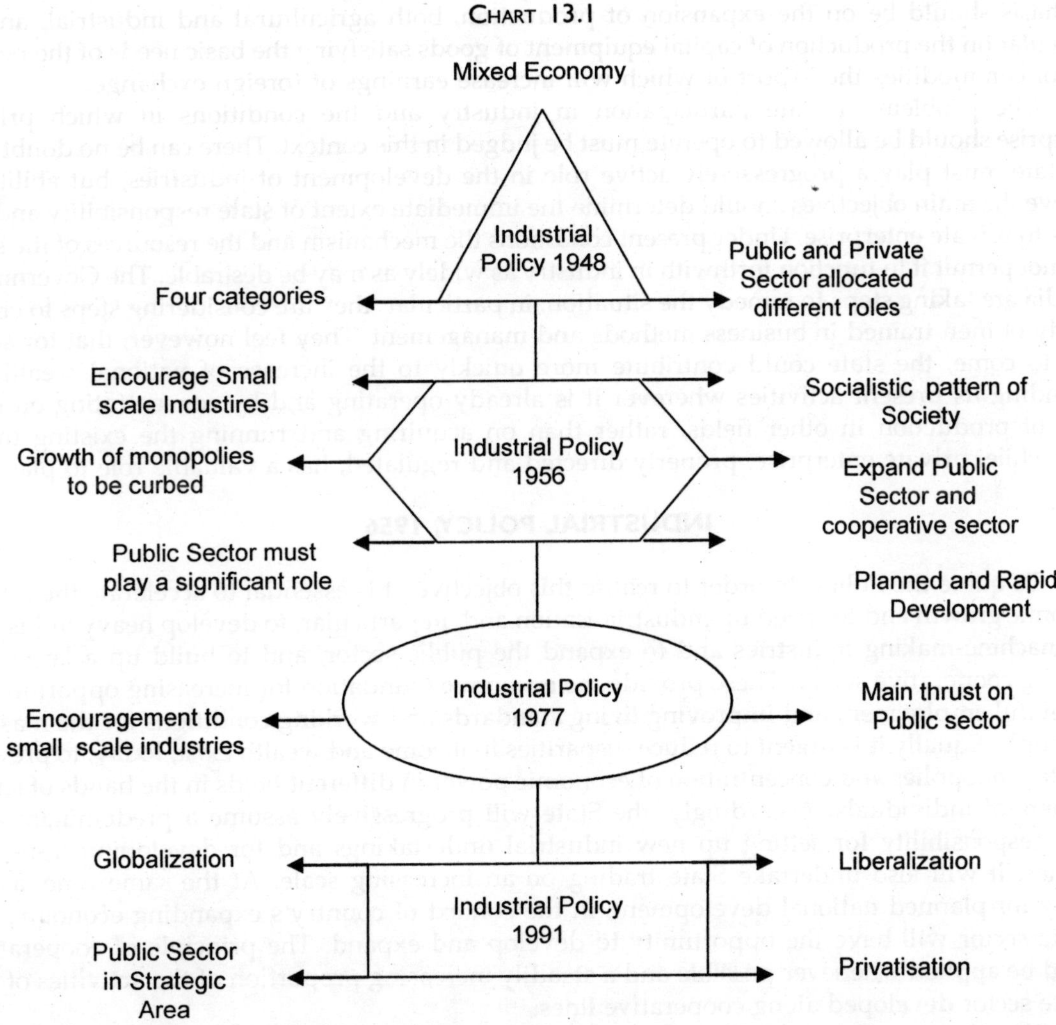

governmental control and regulation. A fourth category comprising the remainder of the industrial field left upon to private enterprises and co-operatives. It also assigned an important role to Cottage and Small Scale Industries in the national economy. Besides, in order to foster the pace of industrialization, it recognised need for participation of foreign capital ultimately leading to progressive indianisation of foreign concerns. In the meanwhile, the Nehru Government was determined to establish a Socialistic Pattern of Society where the principal means of production were to be under social ownership and control.[2]

To quote the Policy Resolution 1948: Any improvement in the economic conditions of the country postulates an increase in national wealth, a mere redistribution of existing wealth would make no essential difference to the people and would merely mean the distribution of poverty. A dynamic national policy must, therefore be directed to a continuous increase in production by all possible means, side by side with measures to secure its equitable distribution. In the present state of the nation's economy, when the mass of the people are below the subsistence level, the emphasis should be on the expansion of production, both agricultural and industrial, and in particular on the production of capital equipment of goods satisfying the basic needs of the people and of commodities the export of which will increase earnings of foreign exchange.

The problem of state participation in industry and the conditions in which private enterprise should be allowed to operate must be judged in this context. There can be no doubt that the state must play a progressively active role in the development of industries, but ability to achieve the main objectives should determine the immediate extent of state responsibility and the limits to private enterprise. Under present conditions the mechanism and the resources of the state may not permit it to function forthwith in industry as widely as may be desirable. The Government of India are taking steps to remedy the situation; in particular, they are considering steps to create a body of men trained in business methods and management. They feel however, that for some time to come, the state could contribute more quickly to the increase of national wealth by expanding its present activities wherever it is already operating and by concentrating on new units of production in other fields, rather than on acquiring and running the existing units. Meanwhile, private enterprise, properly directed and regulated, has a valuable role to play.

INDUSTRIAL POLICY, 1956

To quote the Policy: In order to realise this objective, it is essential to accelerate the rate of economic growth and to speed up industrialisation and, in particular, to develop heavy industries and machine-making industries and to expand the public sector, and to build up a large and growing cooperative sector. These provide the economic foundation for increasing opportunities for gainful employment and improving living standards and working conditions for the mass of the people. Equally it is urgent to reduce disparities in income and wealth exist, today, to prevent private monopolies and concentration of economic power in different fields in the hands of small numbers of individuals. Accordingly, the State will progressively assume a predominant and direct responsibility for setting up new industrial undertakings and for developing transport facilities. It will also undertake State trading on an increasing scale. At the same time, as an agency for planned national development, in the context of country's expanding economy, the private sector will have the opportunity to develop and expand. The principle of cooperation should be applied whenever possible and a steadily increasing proportion of the activities of the private sector developed along cooperative lines.

The adoption of the socialist pattern of society as the national objective, as well as the need for planned and rapid development, require that all industries of basic and strategic importance, or in the nature of public utility services, should be in the public sector. Other industries which are essential and require investment on a scale which only the State, in present circumstances, could provide have also to be in the public sector. The State has, therefore, to assume direct responsibility for the future development of industries over a wide area. Nevertheless, there are limiting factors which make it necessary at this stage for the State to define the field in which it will undertake sole responsibility for further development, and to make a selection of industries in the development of which it will play a dominant role. After considering all aspects of the problem in consultation with the Planning Commission, the Government of India have decided to classify industries into three categories, having regard to the part which the State would play in each of them. These categories will inevitably overlap to some extent and too great a rigidity might defeat the purpose in view. But the basic principles and objectives have always to be kept in view and the general directions hereafter referred to be followed. It should also be remembered that it is always open to the State to undertake any type of industrial production.

To quote A.H. Hanson, "whatever the ultimate perspectives may be, the country anxious to develop economically has no alternatives but to use public enterprise on a considerable scale, at the very least in order to get things going."[3]

According to President Roosevelt, any Business organisation clothed with power of government, can be called as a public enterprise. A very comprehensive definition has been given in a United Nations publication. It is referred to as "economic undertaking, especially industrial, agricultural or commercial concerns, which are owned (wholly or in part) and controlled by the State. It includes those mixed enterprises, which are controlled by the State. A mixed enterprise is one jointly owned by the State and by private persons. If the State contributes over half of its capital, it automatically has a controlling interest. In some cases, the State even has control over a mixed enterprise for which it provides less than half of its capital."[4]

Thus on a general understanding, a public enterprise can be termed as under:[5]

> "An enterprise is public when the state on any other national. regional or local authority holds at least 51% of its capital; it is under state control and reports to the state; and its objectives are of a public or multi-dimensional nature. This multi-dimensional aspect presupposes financial investments, marketing of products and services, financial returns, a system of business accounts and a social return which the enterprise must account for."

It was increasingly being felt that industrial development in our country was beyond the capacity and capability of the 'private sector and it required a positive state action. As a result, the Second Industrial Policy Resolution passed by the Government on April 30, 1956. Henceforth, the industries were categorized under three headings: industries which are the exclusive responsibility of the State (Railways, Defence); progressively state-owned industries where private sector was expected to play a supplementary and complementary role (transport, fertilizers); and those industries which were exclusively within the domain of private sector. In spite of the grouping of industries under 3 categories, enough provision was made for flexibility depending upon exigencies of time. In other words, there was no waterlight compartmentalisation of industries as such.

The policy statement assigned a pre-eminent role to the public sector as compared to private sector. To quote, "There will be an expanding role of the public sector in several fields. Not only will it be the producer of important and strategic goods of basic nature, but, it will also be used as a stabilizing force for maintaining essential supplies for the consumer." The policy resolution unlike 1948 resolution affirmed that private sector would be given a fair and non-discriminatory treatment in such situations where there exists public and private units in the same field. Some of the other salient features of this policy were as under:

- active participation by Government in industrial development,
- growth of monopolies to be curbed,
- reduction in social and economic regional disparities,
- Encouragement to village and small scale industries,
- development of a large co-operative sector,
- channelisation of skills and expertise,
- expansion of employment avenues, and
- nationalisation of industries not necessary.

The Government failed to establish a suitable machinery for public sectors planning and execution. As such, there was lack of co-ordination between various ministries and the planning commission often resulting in administrative conflicts. Consequently, the rate of growth of industrial output has often fallen short of planned targets and we have also seen two phases of recession in the economy.

This industrial policy, despite some desirable, achievements had resulted in some problems viz. "Unemployment has increased, rural-urban disparities have widened and the rate of real investment has stagnated. The growth of industrial output has been on more than three to four per cent per annum on the average. The incidence of industrial sickness has become widespread and some of the major industries are worst affected."

INDUSTRIAL POLICY, 1973

The two policy resolutions though reaffirmed that public and private sector would play equal role, it was increasingly being felt that due to progressive nationalisation and expansion of public sector, private sector was being given a secondary importance resulting in slow growth of industrial development. That is why, the Central Government modified its industrial policy on February 2, 1973. Henceforth, large houses were given liberalisations in grant of licences in all such areas except for those reserved for production in public sector or small sector. The foreign concerns were invited to participate in such industries. The policy stressed for development of co-operatives, small and medium industries for the production of mass consumption goods alongwith public sector. Above all, joint sector was to be developed as a promotional instrument especially in priority areas.

INDUSTRIAL POLICY, 1977

For the past 20 years, the Government Policy in the sphere of Industry had been governed by Industrial Policy Resolution of 1956. The policy has not been a success in its objectives.

Until 1977, the main thrust of the Government was to make public sector really dominant *vis-a-vis* the private sector.[6] It was, however, with the change in the political set-up at the Central Government in 1977, the Janata Government framed its own industrial policy. It was laid before Parliament by the then Industries Minister on December 23, 1977.

The Policy States:

In the 1977 Policy Statement it was noted that though some elements of the Industrial Policy Resolution of 1956 still remained valid, certain structural distortions had crept in the system. The new policies were hence directed towards removing these distortions. It provided for a closer interaction between the agricultural and industrial sectors, accorded the highest priority to the generation and transmission of power and an exhaustive analysis of industrial products was made to identify products which are capable of being produced in the small scale sector. The list of industries exclusively reserved for the small scale sector was expanded from 180 items to more than 500 items. It provided for an annual review of this list in view of new products and new processes of manufacture that emerge. Within the small scale sector, a tiny sector was also defined with investment in machinery and equipment upto Rs. 1 lakh and situated in towns with a population of less than 50,000 according to 1971 census figures, and in villages. Special legislation to protect cottage and household industries was also proposed to be introduced.

The Policy Categorically Mentioned

The Emphasis on industrial policy so far has been mainly on large industries, neglecting cottage industries completely and relegating small industries to a minor role.... The main thrust of the new industrial policy will be on effective promotion of cottage and small industries widely dispersed in rural areas and small town. It is the policy of the government that whatever can be produced by small and cottage industries must not be so produced.

The industrial policy Statement stated in unequivocal terms: "The growth of Large Houses has been disproportionate to the size of their internally generated resources and has been largely based on borrowed funds from public financial institutions and banks. This process must be reversed." To ensure that no unit of business group acquired a dominant or monopolistic position in the market, large industrial houses would have to rely on their own internally generated resources for financing new projects or expansion of the existing ones. The funds of the public sector financial institutions would be largely available for the small sector. Further, even in the case of capital-intensive field where these large industrial houses were dominant, preference would be given to medium entrepreneurs and the public sector corporations so that further concentration of economic power might be restricted.

"In areas where foreign technological know-how is not needed, existing collaborations will not be renewed. The policy statement further elucidated: "As a rule, majority interest in ownership and effective control should be in Indian hands though the Government may make exceptions in highly export-oriented and/or sophisticated technology areas. In hundred per cent export-oriented technology the Government may consider even a fully owned foreign company.

The Policy Statement suggested approach on the question of sick units. It mentioned: "While the Government cannot ignore the necessity of protecting existing employment the cost of maintaining such employment has also to be taken into account. In many cases, very large amounts of public funds have been pumped into the sick units which have been taken over but they continue to make losses which have to be financed by the public exchequer. This process cannot continue indefinitely.

This policy too did not make major departure from all this although the complementary role of the private sector was also emphasized by the then Finance Minister.[7]

Some of the important features of the policy were as under:

- Setting up of cottage and small scale industries in all parts of the country.
- Number of industrial products that can be produced in the small sector increased from 180 to 807.
- The concept of "tiny sector" was widely elaborated where under a unit with investment up to Rs. 1 lakh in town with a population of less than 50,000 was to constitute a unit in tiny sector.
- In order to deal with all the problems of small scale sector under one single roof, District Industries Centre at every district headquarter was to be set-up.
- The Khadi and Village Industries Commission was assigned a much bigger role to play for development of village industries.
- Public sector was to encourage development of a wide range of ancillary industries and contributing to growth of decentralised production by making available its expertise in technology and management to small scale and cottage industry sectors.
- The large business houses were relegated to a second position in matter of finances and their diversification plans.

- The process of sickness in industry was not allowed to continue indefinitely.
- Indigenous technology to be developed and foreign technical know-how used sparingly except in national interest.
- Encouraging workers' participation in decision-making processes and also in the equity of industrial units at all levels.
- Support to be provided by the Government and its public sector organisations in marketing the products of small scale sector on priority basis.

Really speaking, Industrial Policy Statement 1977 was an extension of Industrial Policy resolution of 1956 with some differences in detail. The thrust on small scale and cottage Industries was a welcome step, but was a big blow to large industrial houses.

INDUSTRIAL POLICY, 1980

Since the Janata Government's stay at the Central Government was a temporary phase, the new Congress Government again announced its industrial policy on July 23, 1980.

The Congress government announced its industrial policy in July 1980. Outlining the philosophy behind the Industrial Policy of 1980, the Minister for Industry Stated: "The Industrial policy announcement of 1956 in fact reflects the value system of our country and has shown conclusively the merit of constructive flexibility. In terms of this resolution, the task of raising the pillars of economic infrastructure in the country was entrusted to the public sector for reasons of its greater reliability, for the large investments required and the longer gestation period of the projects crucial for economic development. The 1956 resolution, therefore, forms the basis of this statement." It, therefore, suggested the following measures:

(i) Effective operational management of the Public sector.
(ii) Integrating industrial development in the private sector by promoting the concept of economic federalism.
(iii) Redefining of small units.
(iv) Regularization of unauthorized excess capacity installed in the private sector.
(v) Automatic expansion.
(vi) Industrial sickness.

The policy reiterated efforts for rapid and balanced industrialization with the twin objective of benefiting the common man. The policy aimed at promotion of small scale sector which would ultimately help in generating employment, increasing income, and ensuring easy availability of goods at reasonable prices.

It will be government's endeavour to reverse the trends of the last three years towards creating artificial divisions between small and large-scale industry under the misconception that these interests are essentially conflicting. While making all efforts towards integrated industrial development, it proposed to promote the concept of economic federalism with setting up of a few nucleus plants in each district, identified as industrially backward, to generate as many ancillaries and small and cottage units as possible."

Industrial Policy July 24, 1991: The Policy statement observes:

A. Industrial Licensing Policy

(i) Industrial Licensing will be abolished for all projects except for a short list of industries related to security and strategic concerns, social reasons, hazardous chemicals and overriding environmental reasons, and items of elitist consumption. Industries for the small scale sector will continue to be so reserved.

(ii) Areas where security and strategic concerns predominate, will continue to be reserved for the public sector.

(iii) In projects where imported capital goods are required, automatic clearance will be given:

(a) in cases where foreign exchange availability is ensured through foreign equity,

or

(b) if the CIF value of imported capital goods required is less than 25% of total value (net of taxes) of plant and equipment, upto a maximum value of Rs. 2 crore. In view of the current difficult foreign exchange situation, this scheme (i.e. (iii) b) will come into force from April, 1992.

In other cases, imports of capital goods will require clearance from the Secretariat of Industrial Approvals (SIA) in the Department of Industrial Development according to availability of foreign exchange resources.

(iv) In locations other than cities of more than 1 million population, there will be no requirement of obtaining industrial approvals from the Central Government except for industries subject to compulsory licensing. In respect of cities with population greater than 1 million, industries other than those of a non-polluting nature such as electronics computer software and printing will be located outside 25 kms. of the periphery, except in prior designated industrial areas. A flexible location policy would be adopted in respect of such cities (with population greater than 1 million) which require industrial regeneration.

Zoning and Land Use Regulation and Environmental Legislation will continue to regulate industrial locations. Appropriate incentives and the design of investments in infrastructure development will be used to promote the dispersal of industry particularly to rural and backward areas and to reduce congestion in cities.

(v) The system of phased manufacturing programmes run on an administrative case by case basis will not be applicable to new projects. Existing projects with such programmes will continue to be governed by them.

(vi) Existing units will be provided a new broad banding facility to enable them to produce any article without additional investment.

(vii) The exemption from licensing will apply to all substantial expansions of existing units.

(viii) The mandatory convertibility clause will no longer be applicable for term loans from the financial institutions for new projects Procedural consequences.

(ix) All existing registration schemes (Delicenced Registration, Exempted Industrial Registration, DGTD registration) will be abolished.

(x) Entrepreneurs will henceforth only be required to file an information memorandum on new projects and substantial expansions.

B. Foreign Investment

(i) Approval will be given for direct foreign investment upto 51 per cent foreign equity in high priority industries. There shall be no bottlenecks of any kind in this process. Such clearance will be available for foreign equity covers the foreign exchange requirement for imported capital goods, consequential amendments to the Foreign Exchange Regulation Act (1973) shall be carried out.

(ii) While the import of components, raw materials and intermediate goods, and payment of know-how fees and royalties will be governed by the general policy applicable to other domestic units, the payment of dividends would be monitored through the Reserve Bank of India so as to ensure that outflows on account of dividend payments are balanced by export earnings over a period of time.

(iii) Other foreign equity proposals including proposals involving 51% foreign equity which do not meet the criteria under (i) above, will continue to need prior clearance. Foreign equity proposals need not necessarily be accompanied by foreign technology agreements.

(iv) To provide access to international markets, majority foreign equity holding upto 51% equity will be allowed for trading companies primarily engaged in export activities. While the thrust would be on export activities, such trading houses shall be at par with domestic trading and export houses in accordance with Import Export Policy.

(v) A Special Empowered Board would be constituted to negotiate with a number of large international firms and approve direct foreign investment in select areas. This would by a special programme to attract a substantial investment that would provide access to high technology and world markets. The investment programmes of such firms would be considered in totality free from pre-determined parameters or procedures.

C. Foreign Technology Agreements

(i) Automatic permission will be given for foreign technology agreements in high priority industries upto a lumpsum payment of Rs. 1 crore, 5% royalty for domestic sales and 8% for exports, subject to total payments of 8% of sales over a 10 year period from date of agreement or 7 years from commencement of production. The prescribed royalty rates are net of taxes and will be calculated according to standard procedures.

(ii) In respect of industries other than those in automatic permission will be given subject to the same guidelines as above if no free foreign exchange is required for any payments.

(iii) All other proposals will need specific approval under the general procedures in force.

(iv) No permission will be necessary for hiring of foreign technicians, foreign testing of indigenously developed technologies. Payment may be made from blanket permits or free foreign exchange according to RBI guidelines.

D. Public Sector

(i) Portfolio of public sector investments will be reviewed with a view to focus the public sector on strategic, high tech and essential infrastructure. Whereas some reservation for the public sector is being retained there would be no bar for areas of exclusivity to be opened up to the private sector selectively. Similarly, the public sector will also be allowed entry in areas not reserved for it.

(ii) Public enterprises which are chronically sick and which are unlikely to be turned around will for the formulation of revival rehabilitation schemes, be referred to the Board for Industrial and Financial Reconstruction (BIFR), or other similar high level institutions created for the purpose. A social security mechanism will be created to protect the interests of workers likely to be affected by such rehabilitation packages.

(iii) In order to raise resources and encourage wider public participation a part of the government's shareholding in the public sector would be offered to mutual funds, financial institutions, general public and workers.

(iv) Boards of public sector companies would be made more professional and given greater powers.

(v) There will be greater thrust on performance improvement through the Memoranda of Understanding (MOU) system through which managements would be granted greater autonomy , and will be held accountable. Technical expertise on the part of the Government would be upgraded to make the MOU negotiations and implementation more effective.

(vi) To facilitate a fuller discussion on performance, the MOU signed between Government and the public enterprise would be placed in Parliament. While focusing on major management issues, this would also help place matters on day-to-day operations of public enterprises in their correct perspective.

E. MRTP Act

(i) The MRTP Act will be amended to remove the threshold limits of assets in respect of MRTP companies and dominant undertakings. This eliminates the requirement of prior approval of Central government for establishment of new undertakings, expansion of undertakings, merger, amalgamation and takeover and appointment of directors under certain circumstances.

(ii) Emphasis will be placed on controlling and regulating monopolistic restrictive and unfair trade practices. Simultaneously the newly empowered MRTP Commission will be authorized to initiate investigation *suo moto* or on complaints received from individual consumers or classes of consumers in regard to monopolistic, restrictive and unfair trade practices.

(iii) Necessary comprehensive amendments will be made in the MRTP Act in this regard for enabling the MRTP Commission to exercise punitive and compensatory powers.

In the supplementary industrial policy, which dealt with small and tiny units and which was announced on 6th Aug., 1991, the Government raised the investment limit for tiny enterprises to Rs. 5 lakh from the present Rs. 2 lakh. The Government, also announced an increase in the investment unit in plant and machinery of small scale industry to Rs. 60 lakh and ancillary and export-oriented industry to Rs. 75 lakh each.

The SSI policy envisages a package under which the following items are specially stressed:

(a) A single window loan scheme will cover projects upto Rs. 20 lakh;
(b) Special Monetary Agency will be set-up for meeting the credit needs of small scale industries;
(c) A Technology Development Cell will be set-up;
(d) An Export Development Centre will also be established;
(e) Mass Consumption items will be marketed under common brand name;
(f) Greater incentives are to be given to handloom and handicraft sectors; and
(g) Participation (upto 30% investment) by large and medium sized industrial undertaking will be allowed in the small scale sector. This last point deserves comment. With 30% investment being permitted by larger industrial undertaking in small industries, larger and more powerful companies will control and dominate over the small scale units.

As a result, parent ancillary relationship will be further strengthened. In fact, the ancillary type of small scale industries will develop faster than the independent type of small units and the newly started ones by technically qualified entrepreneurs.

To sum up, the NIP whose three main building blocks, are deregulation, competitive efficiency and globalisation, should convince the captains of our industry, both in the public and private sectors that quality and productivity are the key elements for surviving in competitive domestic and international markets.[8]

The Government took a decision in April 1993 to remove three more items, i.e. motor cars, white goods (Air conditioners, Refrigerators; Washing Machines and raw hides and skins and patent leather from the list of 18 industries reserved for licensing in the 1991 Industrial Policy. The purpose was to increase investment in these areas to benefit middle class people.

In December 1996, the government took a decision for 16 industries where foreign investments equivalent to 51 percent equity participation was possible. These 16 industries were in the area metallurgical, entertainment, electronics, capital goods, food processing and export potential.

The Government also approved a list of 9 industries for which automatic approval upto 74 percent equity existed e.g. mining services, basic metals and alloy industries, etc. The purpose was to facilitate direct foreign investment in infrastructure sector, core and priority sectors, etc.

Dr. Manmohan Singh, the then Finance Minister, and architect of the new policy, asserted that India should not be unnecessarily afraid of foreign capital inflow as an attack on Indian sovereignty. Actually India had very little foreign investment amount to $ 425 million in 1989, while small countries like Indonesia ($735 million), Argentina ($1,028 million), Thailand ($1,650 million), Malaysia ($1,846 million), Mexico ($2,241) had a much bigger quantum of foreign investment. Even China had foreign investment of the order of $1,400 million.

It may be stated that the new Industrial Policy may be able to attrack foreign investment and give a boost to domestic investment, but whether it will lead to more employment along with higher output growth is doubtful. Besides, excessive freedom to foreign capital may ultimately, affect our economic sovereignty and as also push the country a debt trap further. These are gloomy forebodings, but the recent East Asian economic crisis as well as the happenings in Russia and South American countries point out to the dangers of too much dependence on market mechanism, uncontrolled liberalization and globalization and unfettered freedom to import foreign capital.[9]

Since 1991 the role of Indian state in licensing and other related economic activities has been on he decline. The state has wide latitude in areas of sovereign functioning like public order, crime control, justice administration, crime investigation and related matters, in the absence of effective institutional checks against abuse of authority. No matter how much we limit the role of state, these are vital areas which will always be within the state sphere and when conditions for good governance are not fulfilled, abuse of power in these areas become the norm.

Over the past several years there is mounting evidence of such a phenomenon resulting in increased criminalisation of politics, greater politicisation of crime investigation, and increasing nexus between political class, state agencies and organised criminal gangs and operators. In effect such abuse of power in the critical areas of state functioning leads to complete lawlessness and undermines the firm foundations of our society and civilisation. A rogue state whose legitimacy is in question, whose appetite for ill-gotten funds is uncontrollable, and whose actions are not accountable to the people will continue to use the limited economic decision-making power under its control for private gain and personal ends at the cost of public good and economic growth.

In fact, it is this failure that explains in a large measure the limited success of economic reforms. In the absence of good governance, economic reform in itself will lead to modest growth at best for some period and the fruits of reform will be transient and self-limiting. Inadequate human development and the failure of our delivery systems have led to appallingly low levels of literacy and skills, poor health coverage and hopelessly inadequate infrastructure. The vast majority of Indians are thus left outside the pale of the productive process of the nation. Besides, even with economic liberalisation the state will continue to play an important role to ensure fair competition.

Therefore mere economic liberalisation in itself is not a panacea to resolve our governance crisis. There is no substitute to good governance characterised by liberty to all citizens, self-governing institutions, empowerment of people and stakeholders, rule of law and institutional safeguards against abuse of authority.[10]

O.P. Dwivedi,[11] observes that by the end of the 1990s a worldwide change occurred with a process of globalization, expressed in an increased mobility of elites, circulation of communications and capital across national boundaries conveying and strengthening that image. Nevertheless, when we talk about the globalisation, we are referring to a relatively small portion of humanity: the affluent, the powerful, and the informed, the privileged who really possess a translational character while the bulk of the world's population, though affected by the planetary character of communications, production, distribution, and accumulation, does not partake in the benefits of a new social regime.

A resurgent India requires cooperation from all political parties and interest groups, including civil society, business community, the public at large, as well as the NRIs. Notwithstanding its growing population, India is poised to become a great world power with less poverty, better and affordable healthcare facilities, world class education for all, and improved environmental quality; and thus, on the long-term basis, by moving towards sustainability in every field, India may aspire to achieve a good balance of human and environmental well-being; such a step will not only benefit its people, both rich and poor, but also will make a contribution regionally and internationally by reducing pollution that spreads beyond its borders.

Globalization indicating a growing integration of economies and societies around the world is a complex process. This process has influences on individual and institutions of the countries. With the process of opening up and integration with the outside world, the domestic institutions responsible for development need lot of reorientation for meeting with the challenges. India has embarked on the path of planned economic development in the overall framework of mixed economy where both public and private sector have freedom to operate side by side.[12]

Notes and References

1. Bachcha Pathak, Industrial Policy of India: Changing Facts, Deep & Deep, New Delhi, 2007, p. 21.
2. Avadi Resolution passed by All India Congress (January, 1955).
3. A.H. Hanson, "Public Enterprise and Economic Development", 2nd ed. (London, Routledge and Kegan Paul, 1972), p. 23.
4. Development Administration; Current Approaches and Trends in Public Administration for National Development (United Nations Publication Sales No. E-76, II. H I), p. 66.
5. Dietrich-Carsten Burning, "Public Enterprises in France and Germany", State Enterprises, Vol. II, No. 2 (New Delhi, Standing Conference of Public Enterprises, April-June 1983), p. 147.
6. Ashok Mehtra, "India Today", Delhi, S. Chand and Co., 1974, p. 51.
7. H.M. Patel, "Public Enterprises in Indian Economy: Problems of Management', *Lok Udyog*, XI, No. 11, February 1978, p. 6.
8. Bachcha Pathak, Industrial Policy of India: Changing Facets, Deep & Deep, New Delhi, 2007, pp. 102-06, 57-58.
9. Ruddar Datt, K.P.M. Sundaram, Indian Economy, S. Chand & Company Ltd., 2006.
10. Furquan Ahmad and Akhtar Ali, "Globalization, Governance and the State", *IJPA*, Vol. LIV, No. 2, April-June 2008, pp. 365-66.
11. O.P. Dwivedi, India in a Globalized World: Transforming Bureaucracy for the Well-being and Prosperity of All" in *IJPA*, Oct.-Dec. 2007, pp. 724, 740.
12. Biswajit Chatterjee and Dalip Kumar Ghosh, Globalization and Decentralized Governments—Reflections of Panchayats in India, in *IJPA*, April-June 2003.

CHAPTER

14

Capacity Building for Development Administration and Management

(See Chart 14.1)

Today, in India, Public Administration is passing through a serious crisis of confidence, credibility and achievement of the objectives of development administration. How can we expect from the civil services at all levels the success of the development administration mentioned in clear cut terms in the constitution and all important documents? Administration is supposed to serve the people and ensure their satisfaction. What has gone wrong with the civil services. Civil servants have created mess of public administration which is instrument for making development administration, i.e. welfare of all a success but the things did not occur and the mess is multiplying with no solutions. The civil servants lack capacity to develop and administer development administration. The role of Civil Servants has changed from mere interpretation of rules and regulations to ensure actual delivery of services. However, in practice, this has remained only on paper and civil servants never try to implement it in their own interest, i.e. to make themselves unnecessarily authoritative, irresponsive and arrogant causing a gulf between civil services and the citizens. The state of poor affairs of administration has been voiced by all. Commission and committees and most of the people at the helm of affairs. Second Administrative Reforms Commission quoted the views of former Prime Minister Mrs. Indira Gandhi which are reproduced below as these reflect in clear terms the status of administration in India.

Prime Minister Indira Gandhi was even more critical. Replying to the debate on the President's address in the Parliament in March 1966, she said, "what India needed today, was a 'revolution in the administrative system' without which no enduring change could be brought about in any field." In an interview she gave to a news agency on completing 100 days in office, she observed:

"The problem of administration has added to the difficulties of the country. All along the line, administration has deteriorated—at the Centre, in the States, and even in the lower rungs of the governmental set-up. Toning up would have to be done, new procedures might have to be evolved, and even fresh recruitment at all levels would have to be considered."

In her convocation address to the University of Roorkee in November 1967, she noted that, "Administrators sometimes lag behind the situations they are supposed to administer. If a large proportion of the investment we have made under the plans remains unutilised, the cause is to be found in administrative shortcomings."

There is nothing wrong with the principles of development administration as such provided those who are to work with these principles are given rigorous training in capacity building and attune them to adjust themselves to the needs of the socio-economic development of the country. Paul H. Appleby in his report "Public Administration in a Welfare State" (1966) mentioned the attributes of a Good administrator which may be developed in our Civil Services through capacity building

Paul H. Appleby in his book, "Public Administration for Welfare State", 1998, mentions the following attributes of a Good Administrator:

(a) Willingness to assume responsibility.
(b) A steadily enlarging ability to deal with more problems.
(c) A strong bent towards action.
(d) A good listener.
(e) Effective with people.
(f) Capacity to build his own strength by building the competence of his organization.
(g) Capacity to use his institutional resources.
(h) Avoiding using power or authority for their own sake.
(i) Welcoming reports of troublesome things.
(j) A good team-worker.
(k) A good initiator.

In the Human Development Report, 1997, the United Nations Development Program (UNDP) has summed up elements of good governance thus: "People's participation, rule of law, transparency, responsiveness, consensus orientation in decision-making, equity, effectiveness and efficiency, accountability and strategic vision. These characteristics have to be built into a corruption free administration to provide good governance to the people."

Stogdill suggested the following qualities:

1. Capacity (Intelligence, alterness, verbal facility, originality, judgement).
2. Achievement (scholarship, knowledge, athletic accomplishments).
3. Responsibility, dependability, initiative, persistence, aggressiveness, self-confidence, desire to excel).
4. Participation capacity, sociability, cooperation, adaptability, humour.
5. Status (socio-economic position, popularity).
6. Situation mental level, status, skill needs and interests of followers, objectives to be achieved, etc.

The author feels the following qualities among Civil Services:

- Intelligence
- Emotional stability
- Energy and enthusiasm
- Accommodation and adaptability
- Human Engineering
- Co-existence with subordinates
- Objectivity
- Willingness to make personal sacrifices to assist subordinates
- Developing team spirit
- Insight into human behaviour
- Ability to plan, organize and direct efforts of others
- Decision-making ability on a practical and realistic basis
- Ability to co-ordinate the efforts of others
- Keep the environment of work place stimulating
- Citizen centric and citizen responsive.

For all this qualities, we have to give capacity building training to civil servants at intervals to keep them motivated. We have not been able to fulfil the aspirations mentioned in the First Five Year Plan. To quote the Plan: "The central objective of planning in India is to raise the standard of living of the people to open to them opportunities for a richer and more varied life. Planning must, therefore, aim both at utilizing more effectively the resources.... And also at reducing inequalities of income, wealth and opportunity.

Capacity Building connotes that the trainers can influence the performance of the trainees. The influence takes the form of knowledge, attitude and action. The ultimate success of the training depends upon the change in behaviour of the trainees, who in turn can inject efficiency and effectiveness in their services. Action training is aimed at creating a situation in which employees can act optimally. Morton R. Davies rightly mentions the need of Action Training. To quote him, "Action training is training designed to achieve explicit, predetermined results which will enhance attainment of an objective of an enterprise in a recognizable, preferably quantifiable way. Action Training is designed to solve a problem, to effect change, to implement a policy or to arrive at other observable and predictable results."[1]

One of the key factors in the effort of the government to accomplish its development goals is to enhance its administrative capability for development at all levels of administrative hierarchy, which is very much a part of the development process. Such complex problems call for a multi-disciplinary solution, to which concerned people at all levels must apply their technical skills, general knowledge and understanding. The education and training of all responsible staff engaged in economic and social development are absolutely essential, if worthwhile results are to be obtained. This is true whether they are politicians, administrators, executives, technical people or clerical personnel. But, our experience during the last three decades has demonstrated that the development plans have not been satisfactorily implemented, because of inadequate administrative performance. The reasons for the low level of administrative performance include: organisational defects, lack of coordination, complex and cumbersome administrative and financial procedures, etc. These defects and deficiencies need to be corrected in order to bring about a sharp reduction in the administrative obstacles to development and bridge the gap

CHART 14.1

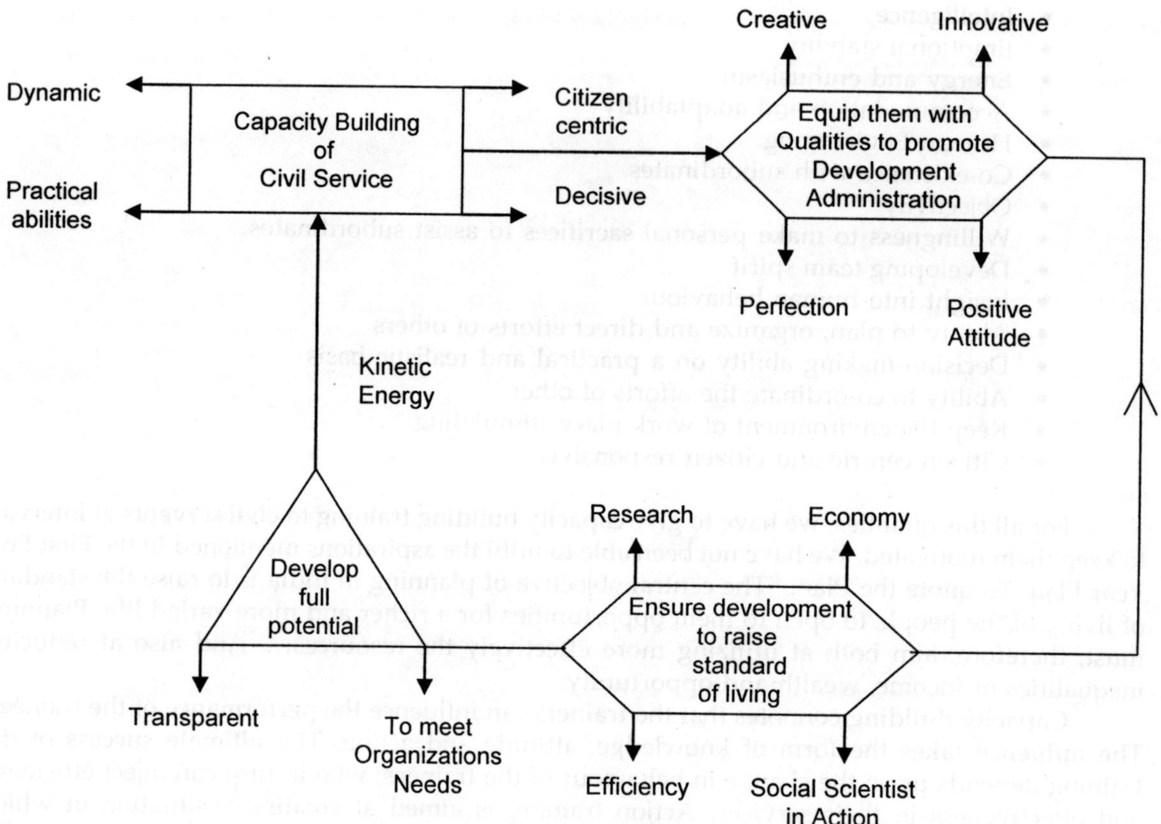

between aspirations and performance. Simultaneously, the level of competence of public service personnel directly involved in the execution of projects and implementation of development plans can be raised by training them in modern concepts and techniques of development administration and management. This category of personnel at the senior or intermediate level, comprising both technocrats and generalists, is constantly called upon to discharge increasingly heavy administrative and managerial responsibilities. In order to equip these personnel with the required expertise, skill, methodology and aptitude, there is a need to train such personnel. In fact, the then Prime Minister, while addressing the Chief Executives of the Public Sector Enterprises on May 29, 1985 stated, "There was need for imparting training to the management cadres of public enterprises. The percentage of Executives who have undergone training at present was low and the situation must be changed." In this context, one of the International Cooperative Alliance's Seminars on Cooperative leadership held in New Delhi in 1960, rightly declared in the first sentence of its recommendations that "cooperative education and training should be organized in appropriate forms at all levels and in every branch of the movement's activity."[2] All agree that right training is the first priority for developing countries. The most fruitful investments are not in material supplies, but in efforts undertaken to train men and women who, through their own development and initiative, can in turn be catalytic in transforming people's outlook and change their attitudes, perception and behaviour in favour of a better life style.

Mr. Nicol (Executive Director, UNITAR) has rightly said in this context, "It was generally accepted that professional training in the field of public administration was a necessity. Many countries which had introduced training schemes with an emphasis on an up-to-date approach to the day-to-day problems had achieved impressive improvements in efficiency. There was little doubt that the need for adequate training in modern Public Administration techniques was even greater in the United Nations System where the officials came from diverse backgrounds and had acquired different administrative habits during their formative years. It is true that sending an official on a training course meant a loss of working time. That had to be balanced, against the gain from increased. efficiency on return to work. Experience around the world had shown that the long-term benefits of carefully planned training far outweighed the short-term loss."[3]

It is now generally accepted that administrators are not born; they are trained. The experience in industry and other fields has shown that people can be trained in managerial skills so as to make them better managers as well as workers. It is a continuous process lasting through the career of the service of an employee. Mr. Joung Whang has rightly said that "Training is: (a) an action process, (b) by which capabilities of the personnel can be improved, (c) to meet the organisational needs in terms of their knowledge, skills, and atiitudes required in performing organisational tasks and functions, and (d) within relatively short period of time."

C.R. Dooley, has rightly observed that, "training is not something that is done once to new employees—it is used continuously in every well run establishment. Every time you get someone to do work the way you want it to be done, you are training. Every time you give directions or discuss a procedure, you are training."[4]

As such, training is the fastest growing segment of personnel activities.[5] It is an essential feature of a career service and should become a constant pre-occupation for any organization. One aspect is job security; the other, and more important, is retention and development of staff in order to improve their efficiency and utilize them effectively. Training enables the employees to improve their knowledge, skills, sensitivity and creativity, and also enables them to adjust to the social-political environment, thereby contributing to the improvement and relationship of such environment.

Training is well articulated effort to promote competence in the public services by imparting professional knowledge, by broadening of vision and adoption of correct patterns of behaviour among the employees regarding their existing functional responsibilities. It also enables the employees to equip themselves for senior administrative positions in future. Stressing the same view, Willoughby said: "No matter how well grounded an employee may be in the general subjects to which his work relates, there is much for him to learn in respect of particular duties of his position."[6]

The Standing Committee on Common Grading Standards established by the UN Consultative Committee on administrative questions also found that the benefits of systematic recruitment at the entrance grade of candidates with good potentialities would be lost if adequate training was not given to the staff after recruitment. It is beyond doubt that effective staff training is a sound investment and the use of untrained staff is expensive in more ways than one.[7]

Mr. Nazimuddin Ahmed in his Article on "Speaking of Executive Development" in *Business India*, January 26 to February 8, 1987 has rightly said that an organization with a future cannot wait for executives to rise from the ranks by chance. It must be actively engaged in a continuous talent hunt and grooming the selected candidates for future executive positions. All top executives must participate in identifying future leaders and help them reach their fullest potential through systematic development in a challenging organisational climate. There must be planned job progression, job rotation, coaching on the job and continuous need-based formal training; self-development activities in a supportive environment; identification at an early stage of individual potential; participation in University programmes and outside courses; service in professional and civic and social organizations.

OBJECTIVES OF TRAINING

T.V. Rao in his article on "Human Resources Development" in Business India, January 13-26, 1986 has rightly mentioned that:

> "Human Resource development aims at creating mechanisms and processes in organizations to continuously develop the qualities of employees so that they can perform their present jobs well, become better equipped to perform the future roles of the changing organizations may demand and thus contribute to organization vitality and growth."

The objective of the training is to provide an individual with the knowledge of the environment or ecology under which he is to function; the knowledge of administrative management to achieve optimum performance and cultivation of necessary attitudes. Let us discuss these in detail.

(a) Environmental or Ecological Understanding

An employee must understood the legal framework under which he is to operate. He must be provided with the basic knowledge of social sciences to understand the existing literature critically. With the knowledge of social sciences, he can react with the environment favourably. A.R. Tyagi has justified it from three different points:

(i) Administration is a human process largely depending upon first hand experience drawn from actual administrative situation in all its facets and on weighing each and every problem in all its pros and cons.

(ii) The role of public servant in a welfare state is that of a social scientist in action. In order to be able to act properly and effectively, he must have a scientific acumen which he can develop only by a systematic and sustained education in the theory and practice of social science.

(iii) The need of a basic training in the fundamentals of social sciences becomes all the more necessary in the context of our public recruitment being based on lower age limit; which limits the advanced research students from entrance to the public service.[8]

(b) Improving Administrative Capability

There is a great need to enhance the Administrative capability of public services, so that they can achieve the objectives of the Government in the shortest time possible. Administrative capability is an important means of converting or processing programme inputs into outputs such as goods and services. Kantz says: "Administrative Capability for development involves the ability to mobilize, allocate and combine the actions that are technically needed to achieve development objective."[9] It is felt that the scope of experimentation is a costly and slow process.

As such, we need to learn from the experience of others and use their results to help achieve our goals. In this context, Ernest Dale and L.C. Machelon observe that, "Today's Managers lives in a world of rapid change, yet, the rate of change is likely to increase in the years ahead. Unless he can keep up with this change, he is likely to find himself obsolete—perhaps unpromotable or even unemployable."[10] Despite all the efforts of governments through their internal resources, despite the spectacular scientific and technical progress, despite the efforts of the governments through external resources, through bilateral and multi-lateral agencies, the poverty is still a naked fact, which is forcing millions of people to lead a very poor life with poor standards of living. In the words of Joseph Klatzmann, Professor at the National Institute of Agronomy in Paris: It is really easier to go and collect pebbles from the surface of the moon than to feed the hungry masses of Bombay and Calcutta. In order to overcome these grave problems, it is necessary that the capacities and capabilities of existing systems should be upgraded and their human resources optimized so that they will be self-sufficient technically, financially and institutionally.

(c) Cultivating Genuine Attitudes

Administration is manned by and meant for human beings. Administration is an art of conducting human affairs. Training must also aim to cultivate a new attitude and behaviour in human personality. In the public services, this is more important than the other two objectives. Most of the projects run by the Government failed as the personnel responsible for the management of these projects lacked the art of the human relations aspects of cross cultural services. H.M. Mathur in his article on "Social Aspects of Administering Technical Aid Programme" stated that it is the human factor and not the technological one that is more important in the implementation of the technical assistance programmes. In fact, the technical assistance in operation is often bedevilled by problems of a sort that have nothing to do with anything technological." [11] Marshell suggests the development of the following ingredients to promote right and rational attitude.[12]

(i) development of rational thinking,
(ii) development of objective thinking,
(iii) development of social understanding,
(iv) development of aesthetic responsiveness,
(v) development of practical abilities, and
(vi) development and placement of memory in action.

Krishna Mohan Mathur, in his Article on Human Resources Development in Administration, in *The Indian Journal of Public Administration*, April-June 1987, Vol. XXXIII, No. 2, pp. 213-12; has mentioned the following objectives:

1. To equip the civil servant with precision and clarity in transaction of business;
2. To attune the civil servant to new tasks which he will be called upon to perform in a changing world;
3. To develop resistance to the danger of becoming mechanized by visualizing what he is doing in a wider setting and by preserving with his own educational development;
4. To develop his capacity for higher work and greater responsibility;
5. To develop and maintain staff morale particularly because large number of people have to deal with tasks of a routine nature;

6. To indicate right attitude towards the public, never forgetting that the civil servant is the servant and not the master of the community; and
7. To sustain the human touch not only in direct personal contacts with the public but also in handling correspondence which demands a proper sense of urgency and due consideration of the "man at the other end.[13]

We can conclude the needs and objectives of the training in the public services with the observations of the UN Special Committee on Public Administration: "No administrative system can be better than the men and women who conduct, indeed, it might be said who personify it."[14] That is why, it has been stated that human rather than capital is the key to development. "Thus, the breakthrough in administrative development can be attained through the continuous and cumulative effect of individual training and development." [15]

Training is essential for building confidence, commitment and competence. Mahabir Singh Kasana, rightly observes, "Training is very important component of Human Resource Development. It is, perhaps the most cost effective method of improving competencies amongst the manpower of any organisation. Training has been defined as a planned process to impart knowledge, develop skills and modify attitude of the work force through learning processes to achieve the effective performance in any activity or range of activities. The right mix of knowledge, skills and attitudinal components in a training course or a training programme is essential for performance improvement. Performance calls for upgrading confidence, competence and commitment of the persons to enable them to handle the situation and show the results on the ground. Whereas, increase in knowledge, arguability imparts confidence, the skills contribute to enhancement of competency of individuals. The attitude primarily leads to commitment to job. Possessing of the right attitude, combined with appropriate knowledge and skills is required to be assured through training efforts. It is, therefore, necessary that a systematic approach to training linking it with performance is necessary. Developing confidence, competence and commitments require enriching learning experience consisting of Tell, Show, Do, Check and Act through systematic approach to training."[16]

There is also a need to process training for entrepreneurial development. Lakshmi Narasaiah rightly says that, "Ravitalistion of the management training infrastructure in order to establish and restore quality seems to be one of the main elements. In the process of adjustment of training institutions, there is certainly a need for some selective expansion of training programmes. If the focus is shifted from training exclusively directed towards the public sector to training likewise for the entrepreneurial sector, some expansion is needed.

What is drastically needed is a re-conceptualisation of management training, expanding the concept to include a large variety and multiplicity of learning activties outside of formal classroom training sessions. There are a wide variety of management training approaches and methods available for enhancing managerial talent such as on the job training, action training and non-formal training."[17]

Second Administrative Reforms Commission, in its Tenth Report on "Refurbishing of Personnel Administration—Scaling New Heights" observed that reforms in these countries have recognized that in order to sustain high levels of productivity and to be compatible with the changing structure of government and the changing policy environment, the civil service will increasingly required skilled recruits and structured learning and development strategies for all employees. It is also recognized that the skills needed for coordinated policy work and flexible policy implementation are different from those required of civil servants when they were the sole suppliers of advice to governments and administered service monopolies. In the changed circumstances the civil service requires strong technical skills, especially in contract management, financial and risk management, information technology and communications in view of the community demands and expectations of improved access to governmental services through user-friendly e-government and e-business.

(d) Training Contents (Chart 14.2)

The training courses generally include the following aspects:

(a) *Job Aspects*: The particular job that has to be supervised such as the knowledge of the job, planning procedures, work analysis, methods of work, organization and coordination and costs analysis of the service

(b) *Human Aspect*: Skills to improve motivation to increase the productivity of personnel working in the organization.

(c) *Organization Aspects*: Such as the knowledge of the organization, the use of records, communication skills and ways of raising the morale of the employees.

CHART 14.2

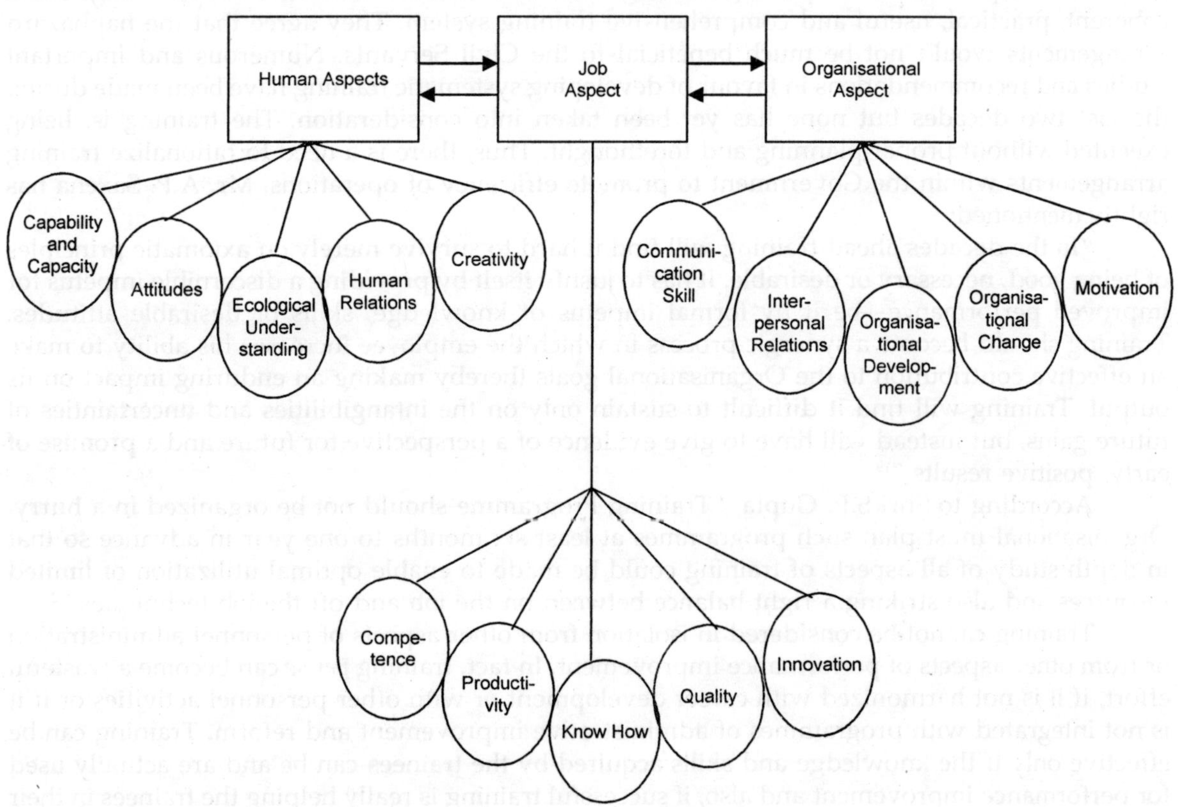

Mr. Rose C. Horner has given seven steps required to plan, design and direct a training programme. These include:

(a) Determination of specific skills and abilities required for the desired performance in the job for which training may be required now and for the foreseeable future;
(b) Assessing the abilities possessed by employees or potential employees as related to the job or organization;
(c) From the information obtained in the previous steps—determining precise training requirement for individual and groups;
(d) Assessing the available training resources;
(e) Planning of detailed programme to develop the required skill;
(f) Directing and evaluating the training programme in operation; and
(g) Evaluation of the results of the training through measurement of post-training job performance.[18]

We can briefly say that training must be suited to the needs of the organization, potentialities of the employees and requirement of the job. Besides, the training must fit the employees in the ecology of the organization and lead to emotional integration.

We have discussed above the essentials to promote ideal training arrangements. Moreover, even those responsible for imparting training are fully convinced of the vital need to organize a coherent, practical, useful and comprehensive training system. They agree that the haphazard arrangements would not be much beneficial to the Civil Servants. Numerous and important studies and recommendations in favour of developing systematic training have been made during the last two decades but none has yet been taken into consideration. The training is. being executed without proper planning and forethought. Thus, there is a need to rationalize training arrangements within the Government to promote efficiency of operations. Mr. A.P. Saxena has rightly mentioned:

"In the decades ahead training will find it hard to survive merely on axiomatic principles of being good, necessary or desirable. It has to justify itself by providing a discernible impetus for improved performance—be it by formal impetus of knowledge, skills or desirable attitudes. Training should become a synergic process in which the employee increases his ability to make an effective contribution to the Organisational goals thereby making an enduring impact on its output. Training will find it difficult to sustain only on the intangibilities and uncertainties of future gains, but instead will have to give evidence of a perspective for future and a promise of early, positive results."[19]

According to Shri S.P. Gupta, "Training Programme should not be organized in a hurry. Organisational must plan such programmes at least six months to one year in advance so that in depth study of all aspects of training could be made to enable optimal utilization of limited resources and also striking a right balance between on the job and off-the-job techniques."[20]

Training cannot be considered in isolation from other aspects of personnel administration or from other aspects of performance improvement. In fact, training *per se* can become a wasteful effort, if it is not harmonized with career development or with other personnel activities or if it is not integrated with programmes of administrative improvement and reform. Training can be effective only if the knowledge and skills acquired by the trainees can be and are actually used for performance improvement and also, if successful training is really helping the trainees in their career development. It is high time that a few lessons are drawn by the management from the experience gained so far and necessary steps, as suggested above, are taken to design the training facilities. A well designed training programme can be a real weapon to accommodate the philosophy and tools of organisational change, to achieve optimum performance.

The factors which contribute to training success may thus be summarized as follows:

- Top management support and commitment, preferably direct involvement;
- The encouragement of team work, i.e. work achievement by cooperative effort towards defined goals;
- High standards of professionalism; a sound knowledge of training principles and methods and an intimate knowledge of the organization how it operates; a reputation establishment by a good track record in identifying and satisfying needs;
- Skill in recognizing the necessity for change and being able to handle it efficiently;
- Adaptability in responding to varying individual and group characteristics;
- Evaluation procedures which enable training activities to be monitored and if necessary modified; and
- Recognition that training should be cost effective.[21]

According to Morton R. Davies following suggestions can yield good results.

1. Training should be delivered as close an approximation to the work situation as possible, and that which is intended to achieve the implementation of specified tasks or procedures should be whenever possible, carried out in the work place itself.
2. For most operatives, especially junior or relatively low level staff, the most influential trainer is the immediate supervisor, even though much of this training is provided sub-consciously or unconsciously. The immediate organisational superior has a considerable influences on the working of the group and his or her behaviour can effect the normative structure of the work group. The supervisor's behaviour is as powerful a training tool as any overt verbal message about the execution of work, etc.
3. A priority within many training programmes should be given to the managers who are in important respects the real trainers within organizations. They need to be made aware of the significance of their own behaviour, and to that extent taught how to train.
4. If it is accepted that the training function should be kept as close to the work situation as possible, it follows that ideally the training organization should have a decentralized structure. Responsibility for training also involves responsibility for action. For example, if a work group is required to tend and maintain municipal gardens, the persons in the best positions to train workers in "how to do it" are their supervisors. To become good trainers, however, such person need to know not only the technical requirements of the job but also the best methods of imparting on the job training. This is merely of particular application of the general principle that the delegation of any function achieves the best results when the delegate has both the knowledge and skill required to perform the functions that have been delegated.
5. Action training, as conceived above, may be designed to solve particular problems, to effect change or to implement new policies or procedures. These cannot be achieved simply by training in the immediate work situation, there has to be, in addition, some overarching or coordinating activity at higher levels in the organization. Without this,

there is little chance of training *per se* contributing very much to the achievement of organisational or national goals.

6. Training is more often than not about the introduction of new ideas or new technology and these are conceived for the most part in institutions of advanced learning and research organizations.
7. Top managers need training whether or not they are aware of the need on receptive of the idea. The immediate question that arises is "Who should/can train these senior managers? Only rarely could subordinates be successful in such an endeavor.
8. In order to secure to cooperation and participation of senior managers in the training function, it is imperative to gain the active support at the highest level in the organization or the government.
9. The support of chief executives or ministers/prime ministers is likely to be forthcoming only if they can be convinced of its use as a strategy for implementing policies and decisions, and that the training is compatible with the values of the society or community in which the training takes places. Such top officials are unlikely to appreciate the normative/re-educative strategies involved in the training, but are likely to give their support because they see training as a means of accomplishing administrative goals.
10. When training is provided as a framework of action, the overall training process is likely to take the form of a series of projects specifically aimed at implementing new programmes, policies or procedures. One of the major advantages of a project-based training programme is the possibility it affords to identify specific goals and objectives to each element of the programme.[22]

EVALUATION OF TRAINING PROGRAMMES

Introduction

With rapid developments in technology and changing nature of today's business, the role of training has assumed increased importance. The amount spent by organizations on formal training is estimated to be 60 billion dollars in the United State alone. Hence, business is demanding not only accountability but also greater articulation of how training programs benefit organizations.[23] Evaluating training programs is a very difficult task and several issues need to be considered, which include employee development, performance improvement and employee retention.

We begin with a description of the different approaches to evaluate training programs. This is followed by the issues in evaluating training programs and a critical analysis on the relevant literature related to this topic.

Organization conduct evaluation programs for three specific reasons:[24]

- o To justify the existence of the training department and how it contributes to the organisational goals and objectives.
- o To evaluate the cost effectiveness of value of training programs.
- o To gain information on employee needs and ongoing requirements to improve future training programs.

In addition, what has been the role of training in making development administration to success.

There are many approaches to evaluating training programmes but the most popular was published by Donald Krikpatrick. His model has 4 levels of evaluating training programmes. (See Char 14.3)

CHART 14.3

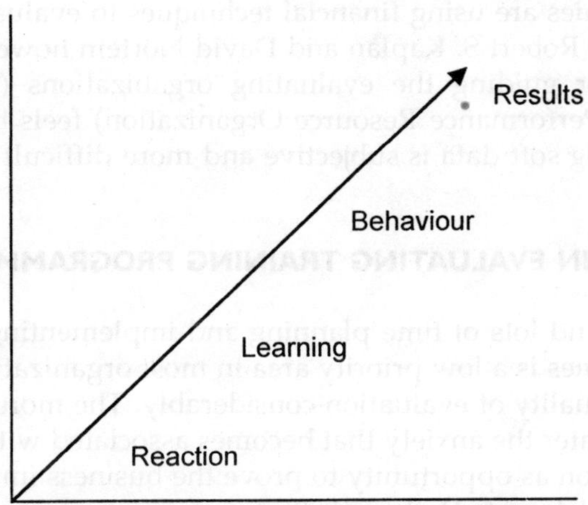

Krikpatrick's Evaluation Model

Reaction

Evaluation on this level measures the reaction of the participants. This is also known as "Happiness Sheet or Smile Sheet" evaluation. Measuring reaction is important as it gives valuable feedback, which could be incorporated in future programs to improve organisational performance. Though this is used in many countries, it is extensively used in countries in the Asian region and in the Middle East.

Learning

Learning can be defined as the extent to which participants change attitudes, improve knowledge, and improve their skills as a result of attending the program (Krikpatrick, 1998). Performance tests are an important mechanism to evaluate training at this level.

Behaviour

Behaviour is the change in the participant as a result of the training program. Evaluating behaviour is difficult because trainees cannot change their behaviour unless they have an opportunity to do so. Surveys and periodical questionnaires are a good way of evaluating changes in behaviour. Companies in the US with particular reference to Anderson Consulting and IBM are using the behavioural approach extensively in evaluating their training programs with particular reference to measuring the soft skills. [25]

Results

Evaluating results is the most difficult and cumbersome of the evaluation procedure. The final results include increased production, decreased costs, which might be the reason for having these training programs (Krikpatrick, 1998). Evaluating results is a difficult task because trainers find it difficult to measure the results and compare them with the cost of the program. This is especially true when measuring soft skills, as they are difficult to quantify.

Apart from Krikpatricks' 4 stage evaluation model, there are several other theories of evaluation. Evaluating training programs through Return on Investment ROD is another approach to measure the value of training investments in financial terms. With the integration of the European Union, companies are using financial techniques to evaluate the value of training programs (O'Connor, 1992).[26] Robert S. Kaplan and David Nortem however argue that financial measures are inadequate for guiding the evaluating organizations (Abernathy, 1999). Jack Phillips, founder of P.R.O. (Performance Resource Organization) feels that though it is easy to measure hard data, measuring soft data is subjective and more difficult to transfer of monetary values (Wholey, 1999).[27]

ISSUES IN EVALUATING TRAINING PROGRAMMES

Though companies spend lots of time planning and implementing training programmes, evaluating training programmes is a low priority area in most organizations. The attitude of the organization influences the quality of evaluation considerably. The more insecure people feel in a particular situation, the greater the anxiety that becomes associated with evaluation. Employee trainers should treat evaluation as opportunity to prove the business impact of training, instead of looking at it as a threat (Nelson & Dailey, 1999).[28]

Another issue is the design of a suitable evaluation programme. Training in many ways is an intangible asset and the measurement of soft skills can prove to be a difficult task for an organization. Even today "smile sheets" are the most popular form of evaluating training programs even though they are at Level 1 of the evaluation process, many organizations are thinking further but have not been successful due to lack of evaluation knowledge and also because of lack of pressure from management (Krikpatrick, 1998).[29]

With the growing tendency of organizations to resort to flatter structures, managers cannot spend a lot of time and effort on evaluating programs as they have other responsibilities too. Evaluation also becomes a problem when there is more than one stake holder. There is another issue as to who should be evaluating the programmes in these circumstances.

An in-depth analysis of the vast literature on evaluating training programmes, one comes to an understanding that even though companies spend thousands of dollars on training programmes, there is little effort to measure its effectiveness. Managers at higher levels are worried only about profits, stock prices and other areas of concern for top management. They pay little attention to training programmes unless they hear something negative about it (O'Connor, 1992). With the importance of training programmes increasing significantly, it has become easier to convince top management about the benefits of training. Hence organizations today believe in investing more money in training than on detailed evaluation. These include having training programmes in exotic locations with all the available luxuries, instead of focusing on delivering a high quality training programme. There is also a tendency among trainers to conduct costly research projects to determine the value and effect of training. This makes the process of evaluation tedious, cumbersome and hence, ineffective.

Though it is difficult to put a dollar value on the effect of training programmes, through continuous evaluation, companies can actually measure the returns on training programmes. Companies like General Electric have used evaluation to improve the effectiveness of their training programmes. A good approach could be to get line managers involved in evaluation so that it is more interactive and participative. Also evaluation should be conducted on an ongoing basis rather than being a one time affair.

Suggestions given by Second Administrative Reforms Commission in its Tenth Report "Refurbishing of Personal Administration—Scaling New Heights".

Capacity Building

(a) Every government servant should undergo a mandatory training at the induction stage and also periodically during his/her career. Successful completion of these trainings should be a minimum necessary condition for confirmation in service and subsequent promotions. Mandatory induction trainings should be prescribed for Group D staff also before they are assigned postings.

(b) A monitoring mechanism should be set-up for overseeing the implementation of the National Training Policy (1996).

(c) The practice of having a 'Common Foundation Course' for all Group 'A Services—generalist, specialized and technical, should continue. For Group 'B' and 'C' Services, the Institute of Secretarial Training and Management (ISTM) may be developed as the nodal agency for design and delivery of common Foundation Courses.

(d) All civil servants should undergo mandatory training before each promotion and each officer/official should be evaluated after each training programme. Successful completion of the training programmes should be made mandatory for promotions.

(e) The objective of mid-career training should be to develop domain knowledge and competence required for the changing job profile of the officer. To this end, mid-career learning opportunities relevant to specific domains or specializations should be made available for officers.

(f) Public servants should be encouraged to obtain higher academic qualifications and to write papers for reputed and authoritative journals.

(g) A strong network of training institutions at the Union and State levels needs to be built up to cater to the training requirements of civil servants. However, instead of spreading resources over a large number of institutions, a few institutions should be identified for capacity building and upgradation.

(h) The composition of governing bodies of the national training institutions such as the LBSNAA, SVPNPA, IGNFA and also the State Administrative Training Institutes should be broadened by inducting eminent experts. The governing bodies should be adequately empowered to enable them to discharge their functions efficiently.

(i) A national institute of good governance may be set-up by upgrading one of the existing national/state institutes. This institute would identify, document, and disseminate best practices and also conduct training programmes.

CONCLUSION

Training programmes are an integral part of most organizations across the globe. To maintain competitive advantage, it has become imperative for organizations to provide ongoing training and development to its employees. As a result of huge amounts being spent on training programmes, evaluating training programmes has gained increased importance. Positive evaluation ensures that organizations conduct training programmes that improve performance standards of both the employee and organisation. Evaluators should conduct a thorough study of the organization before designing an evaluation programme and should strive to keep evaluation as simple as possible.

Notes and References

1. Morton R. Davies, Organising For Training, *IJPA*, January-March, 1992.
2. ICA: The Role of Co-operation in Social and Economic Development (edited), Asia Publishing House, New Delhi, 1966, p. 159.
3. UN: Ale. 51/SR-1492-1559; New York; 1974, p. 470.
4. C.R. Dooley in *International Labour Review*, Vol. 154, Nos. 3-4, Sept-October, 1966, p. 161.
5. Ernest Dale: Management: Theory and Practice, International Student Edition, (3rd Ed.), McGraw Hill, Kogakusha Ltd., Tokyo, 1973, p. 375.
6. W.E. Willioughby: Principles of Public Administration, (Indian Edition, Allahabad), p. 202.
7. UN: ICSAB/IX/5, CO-ORD/CC/80/136, New York, June 1966, p. 5.
8. A.R. Tyagi: "Administrative Training: A Theoretical Postulate", *International Review of Administrative Science*, Vol. XI, No.2, 1974, p. 157.
9. M. Kantz, Saul: Methodological notes on appraising Administrative Capability for Development, UN Publication (Sales No. E-69-1I-4.2), p. 8.
10. Ernest Dale and I.O. Michelon: Modern Management Techniques", Penguin Books, 1974,
11. H.M. Mathur 'Social Aspects of Administering Technical Aid Programme', *The Indian Journal of Public Administration*, Vol. XVII, No. 2, April-June, 1972, pp. 243-53.
12. James I. Marshell, Development Teaching, (New York: 1949), pp. 190-306.
13. Asheton Committee Report on the Training of Civil Servants, 1944. Quoted in Training of Civil Servants in the United Kingdom, Training Monograph No. 12, Training Division, 1972, p. 1.
14. UN: Standards and Techniques of Public Administrations, New York, 1951, pp. 20-54.
15. Habib Mohammad Zafarullah, "Perspective in Administrative Training," The Dacca University Studies, Vol. XXXVI, Part A, June, 1977, p. 106.
16. Mahabir Singh Kasana, "Systematic Approach to Training for Rural Industrialization" in Management in Government, January-March 2000, pp. 56-57.
17. M. Lakshmi Narasiaiah, Management Training in India, in Management in Government, January-March 2000, pp. 52-53.
18. C. Rose: The Development and Supervision of Training Programme, (London: 1964), p. 76.
19. A.P. Saxena, Training in the Decade Ahead; Some Design Consideration in *IJPA*, Vol. XXVI, No.3, July-Sept. 1980.
20. S.P. Gupta, *Indian Journal on Training and Development*, October, 1986, p. 216.
21. S.K. Bhatia and Nirmal Singh, Principles and Techniques of Personnel Management/Human Resource Management, Deep & Deep, New Delhi, p. 380.
22. Morton R. Davies, Organizing for Training. Some Observations and Functions of a National Training Organization in *IJPA*, January-March, 1993, 1117-19.
23. L.N. Long (1999), ROI: Capturing of Big Picture (Industry trend or event), *Technical Training*, Vol. 1016, p. 31.
24. D. Krikpatrick (1998), Evaluating Training Programs, Berrett- Koehler Publisher Inc.
25. D.J. Abernathy, (1999), Thinking Outside the Evaluation Box., *Training and Development*, Vol. 53 12, p. 18(6).
26. R. O'Connar (1992). New Approaches for Europe' 93, *Personnel Journal*, Vol. 71, n. 5, p. 96.
27. S.J. (1990) Performance Based Management, *Public Productivity and Management Review*, San Francisco
28. B.Nelson & P. Daily, (1999), Four steps of evaluating recognition programmes, *Workforce Journal*.
29. D. Krikpatrick (1996) Great Ideas Revisited: Evaluation of Employees Training Programmes, *Training and Development*, Vol. 50, n. 1., p. 54.

CHAPTER

15

Environment Policy and Sustainable Development

Over the years, together with a spreading of environmental consciousness, there has been a change in the traditionally-held perception that there is a trade-off between environmental quality and economic growth as people have come to believe that the two are necessarily complementary. The current focus on environment is not new-environmental considerations have been an integral part of the Indian culture. The need for conservation and sustainable use of natural resources has been expressed in Indian scriptures, more than three thousand years old and is reflected in the constitutional, legislative and policy framework as also in the international commitments of the country.

—T.R. Baalu
Union Minister for Environment and Forests

The whole universe together with its creatures, belongs to the Lord (Nature) Implicit in this thought is that no creature is superior to any other and that a human being should not have absolute power over Nature. Let no one species encroach over the rights and privileges of the other species. One can enjoy the bounties of nature by giving up greed.

—Isho-Upanishad

Modern Man is not protecting but exploiting the environment making it more miserable and not a fit place to live in. Environment is the sum total of all factors conditions, and ingredients that are essential for the life on earth. Vinish Kathuria and Haripriya Gundimeda have stated in their article on "Industrial pollution control: Need for Flexibility." All economic activities either impinge on or are affected by nature and environmental resources. Activities such as extraction, processing, manufacturing, transport, consumption and disposal not only change the stock of natural resources, but also add stress to the environmental system besides introducing wastes to it. The productivity of an economic system depends in part on the supply and quality of natural and environmental resources. Furthermore, todays economic activities affect the stock of natural resources available for the future and thus affect the welfare of future generations.

Development is essential for socio economic development especially in the developing countries like India to tackle the problems of poverty, unemployment, squalor, diseases and illiteracy. We have been engaged on development without examining its repercussions on environment and thus we could not be successful in our mission. Man's ambition for limitless comforts has put him on collision course with environment. The proper environmental management requires that society and man's demands should be so regulated that natural environment is able to sustain the need for development.

Development without regard to environmental consequences cannot be sustained and defeats the very purpose of development by aggravating poverty and unemployment. Environment is not just a matter of aesthetic concern or saving some white legged mouse from going extinct as in a popular cartoon serial without lampoons environmentalists. Environmental concern arises essentially on two grounds. First, a reckless use of resources to maximize short run gain can lead to depletion which would adversely affect development in future, which may not be a very distant future. It is not in the interests of sustainable development. Second is that one does not have to wait for future generations to feel the adverse impact on environment. Livelihoods are lost, sources of drinking water are made unusable, and victims are subjected to agonizing misery (sometimes irreversibly) due to negative externalities (environment) of so called development projects. While a few already better of sections may become still better off, many others become worse off. The former cannot offset the latter's effect.

Rapidly growing population, urbanization, changing agricultural, industrial and water resource management, increasing use of pesticides and fossil fuels have all resulted in a perceptible deterioration in the quality of environment and attendant adverse health consequences. Environment pollution due to developmental activities are increasingly becoming the focus of concern. The interactive interdependence of health, environment and sustainable development was accepted as the fulcrum of action under Agenda 21 at the Earth Summit in Brazil in 1992. In the case of India, against an economic growth of 163 percent in the past 20 years, the pollution load has increased by more than 475 percent. During the period from 1975 to 1995 industrial pollution grew by 247 percent, whereas the vehicular pollution load shot up phenomenally by 650 percent. Environmental health in its broader perspective would have to address the detection, prevention and management of:

(i) existing deficiencies or excesses of certain elements in natural environment.
(ii) Macro environmental contamination of air, land, water and food; and
(iii) Disaster management.

This ordering of priorities has brought our civilization to the brink of ruin. We know we must find a way out, a way back to values and priorities that represent the real, whole nature of man. But all the ways that were once intended to help us from our authentic well-being and our authentic responsibility are themselves deeply stained by the money question.

K. Ramamurthy, in his Article, "Environment and Development some issues in G.S. Monga rightly states, "Excessive technological growth has created an environment in which life has become physically and mentally unhealthy. Polluted air, irritating noise, traffic congestion, chemical containments, radiation hazards and many other sources of physical and psychological stress have become part of everyday life for most of us. These manifold health hazards are not just incidental by products of technological progress, they are integral features of an economic system obsessed with growth and expansion, continuing to intensify its high technology in an attempt to increase productivity." This passage from best seller "The Turning Point by Fritj of Capra" admirably sums up the effects of so called 'development' of the Western countries. Development without regard for ethics and environment has produced many harmful effects. The last hundred years have seen whole families of previously unknown diseases: new infections, genetic disorders that frustrate any attempts at prevention, endocrine disorders, allergies, toxic diseases, including the radiation and toxic allergic sickness gaining momentum with the growing mass of synthetic materials totally alien to natural human environment; the notorious AIDS is but the latest addition to the list. Further, the development has the effect of making the developed countries richer and developing countries poorer, besides the mindless exploitation of valuable natural resources.

"The World Chapter for Nature" adopted on October 29, 1982 declared that "Mankind is a part of nature and life depends on the uninterrupted functioning of natural system which ensures the supply of energy and nutrients; that civilization is rooted in nature, which has shaped human culture and influenced all artistic and scientific achievement and living in harmony with nature gives man the best opportunities for the development of his creativity, leisure and recreation.

The situation pertaining to environmental sanitation is horrifying at the global, regional and national levels. It has been admitted by various agencies responsible for it at all levels. Attainment of the global target of the UN Second Development Decade (DD2) and UN Millennium Development Goals had not been feasible in most countries of the region. The Regional Director of the World Health Organization South East Asia Region office, Delhi in his Annual Report has warned:

"In spite of the continuing efforts of governments and international and bilateral agencies, only the fringe of the problem has been tackled ... there is an urgent need to mobilize further support from all available sources to solve this difficult problem. Investment in this field will be amply rewarded not only in terms of reduction of incidence of communicable diseases, but also by substantially contributing towards an improvement in the standard of living."

Dr. Abel Wolman, one of the "father figures" of environmental health and Professor Emeritus of Sanitary Engineering at the Johns Hopkins School of Engineering, Baltimore, USA says while talking of the world health situation: "It always leads great conferences to pass resolutions to do something about providing water to impoverished people. Resolutions become opiate because they are gratifying substitutes for action." He warns the policy-makers and administrators against complacence and says, "Viewed on a global basis, we have little to be sanguine about. The disease consequences of poor and insufficient water, of living with human excreta, and of unhygienic personal habits, are disastrous—they have been familiar for so long a time that they no longer excite even the statistician or epidemiologist. People accept their devastation, as they so often abjectly bear their real and spiritual poverty. We speak of the toll of deaths, due to environmental deficiencies in a casual way, even though the figures mount to hundreds of millions. The communicable diseases, often the sequels of poor sanitation are maiming and killing men, women and children—not computer data." It is beyond doubt that a lasting solution to many of the existing and future problems of how to provide sanitary facilities to hundreds of millions of people still without even minimum sanitary facilities? How to tackle such programmes? How to find the resources required for these programmes? What are the responsibilities of planners and policy-makers to ensure integrated approach? We shall discuss the facts and suggestions to provide good environment for the healthy growth of the people essential requirement of development administration.

The answers to all the questions relating to the protection of environment are very clearly detailed in our ancient Sanskrit literature. Bhagavad Gita has provided guidance in mutual cooperation and interdependence as key to preserve environment in its pure form. Yajurveda, Artharveda, Kautilyas Arthashastra, Vedas have propounded sermons and methodology to keep environment pure and soothing. Dr. Biswaanaryan Shastri in his paper, "Environment in Sanskrit literature" in world Sanskrit conference 2001 held in New Delhi has desired to follow the teaching of Sanskrit literature to maintain environmental equilibrium. To quote him:

"With the passage of time and the development of science and technology, trade and industry, the total economic growth have caused a sea change in the living pattern of the people of today with those of yore. In short the economic growth and the environment are moving in two directions and hence science and technology seem to be the enemy of nature and the question of environment arises. On the other hand in this scientific age nobody could think of stepping opposite progress of science and technology. The natural environment is the ideal of humanity, and that is why the Vedic and puranic literatures sing the glory of nature and environment. Today the situation caused by the man to fulfil his greed is bent upon to destroy nature in the name of advancement of material civilization, which eats at its root. The greed surpasses the need and it becomes a global problem. To maintain the purity of air and water as a remedial measure one may look into the Sanskrit literature to find an answer for living with nature and may prove that green is good? Sanskrit has the inherent capacity to find a solution in the face of aggression by the modern technology to save not only the human beings but the inanimate beings too, the ecology."

Vineet Ghildial mentioned that one of the most serious problems faced by human beings today is the environmental problem. The solutions of these problems can be traced in Sanskrit works staring from the Rgveda down to classical times. Early man was a successful practicing ecologist. He survived in a rich and competitive biotic community and his relationship to this community was continually intimate. He was by no means the strongest, the swiftest, nor the hardiest, but he possessed several distinct advantages—effective social organization, manipulative ability and an emerging intelligence. The present contribution encompasses the ecological knowledge of man since the hunting and gathering society of Paleolithic period to pastoral and agro society of Neolithic period. Man's attitude towards his environment during the present industrial and technological revolution has been changed drastically. The consequences of these changes resulted in terms of several environmental problems—excessive deforestation, wildlife depletion, global warming, air and water quality deterioration. The environmental conservation ethics as revealed in the vast Sanskrit literature provides a guideline for the solution of all the current environmental problems faced by human species.

We can thus conclude that the present approach of UN system, developed countries and developing countries to solve environmental problem independently is superfluous with no lasting solution. The Ancient Sanskrit literature clearly brings out the following points:

1. Unity of Environment

Environment cannot be split into developed and developing countries—it is one and inter dependent and inter-connected. President Roosevelt has rightly said that poverty anywhere is a danger to prosperity everywhere.

2. Integrated Approach

The approach should be unified one as diseases know no boundaries. We cannot isolate environment into compartments. Disease in one part of the world is a danger to the entire world.

3. Creative use of Science and Technology

Developed countries have to exert discipline and make use of science and technology not for destruction but for the betterment of life. Otherwise, this process would recoil on the developed world itself.

4. Benefits of Development Need be Shared by All Countries

Large part of the wealth in possession of few people in developed countries is a cause of concern for environment as their greed has no limit. Such a situation is politically unstable morally untenable and psychologically unsound.

5. Practice of Ethical and Spiritual Life

Environment would automatically be protected through ethical and spiritual life of the people and not through laws.

6. Need of Change in Lifestyle

Life style should be changed to avoid over use of science and technology and make use of human energy and not mechanical, electrical and nuclear energy only.

7. Need of Environmental Education

Unfortunately, knowledge of environment hygiene, awareness of pollution hazards are seriously lacking amongst even our enlightened citizens. The Stockholm conference of Human Environment in June 1972, heralded the efforts, both national and international to "Establish programmes of environment education, interdisciplinary in approach, in school and out of school en-compassing all levels of education and directed towards the general public in particular the ordinary citizens living in rural and urban area, youth and adult alike, with a view to educating him as to simple steps he might take, within his means to manage and control his environment."

8. Human Factor

Man's capability to transform his surroundings can bring to one and all the benefits of development and also an opportunity to enhance the quality of life. Wrongly or heedlessly applied, the same power can do incalculable harm to human beings and to human environment. Unfortunately, there exists a growing evidence of man-made harm in many regions of the earth: dangerous levels of pollution in water, air, earth and living beings; major and undesirable disturbances in the ecological balance of biosphere; destruction and depletion of irreplaceable resources; and gross deficiencies harmful to physical, mental and social health of man.

The term environment in Sanskrit literature encompasses broader areas than the definitions given in the context of various commissions and conferences in India, abroad and United Nations System. Most of these definitions are limited to deal with the problems of developed countries and even their solutions pertain to them. In developing countries like India, Environment includes all and its boundary is unlimited. Sanskrit literature reveals that our ancestors never looked upon forests as well as domestic and wild life animals and human beings and Environment, as just a cluster, but they deemed it as a total Biological live landscape with perfect rhythm and harmony.

Eminent scientist like Einstein strongly believed in nature's inherent harmony. His concern throughout was to find a unified foundation of physics. According to our Seers and Sages as well as Einstein's observations were that "nature is like a vibrating Veena" with perfect rhythum with live waves. They were also aware of the vital functions of non-living entities such as clouds which move and break down, rivers grow, air gains strengths and speed, etc.[1] We cannot forsee a situation where environment can be seen in the context of individual countries . It has to be seen globally and solutions for it are to be seen globally. Even president Roosevelt dwelt upon this idea when he remarked that poverty anywhere is a danger to prosperity. (See Chart 15.1)

Sanskrit literature has always been perceiving the problem in toto and its solution also in toto. To quote Sanskrit verse:

सर्वे भवन्तु सुखिनः सर्वे सन्तु निरामयाः ।
सर्वे भद्राणि पश्यन्तु मा कश्चित् दुःख भाग्भवेत् ।।
(Vedic Benediction)
(May All Humanity Be Happy
May all be without disease
May all witness auspicious sights
May none have to undergo suffering)

Man is a discovering specie. Economic man has always had to be concerned with his environment. Until recently, environment was seen as a boundless cornucopia, to be enjoyed, plundered and rearranged for profit. Today, many thoughtful people see it as a limited resource. The relationship between modern man and his environment is a major and a growing problem. The very survival of man as a specie depends upon intelligent and moral human action with respect to these problems.[2]

ENVIRONMENT AND SUSTAINABLE DEVELOPMENT

Environment and development are closely inter-linked. Development cannot subsist on a deteriorating environmental base. Implicit in this is that development cannot take place without exploiting the environment, but harmony between the two is a pre-requisite for the safeguard and preservation of all life on Earth. Development in the absence of emphasis on effective environment, ironically has resulted into pollution of air, water and soil, which in turn has invited the resurgence of a number of life threatening diseases like Cancer, Asthma, Jaundice, Malaria, Dengue, Gastroenteritis, Plague, Tuberculosis, Respiratory illness, Mental disorder, etc. This situation is arising perhaps due to our orientation in deep seated ideologies of production and consumption.[3]

According to the UN Report, "Sustainability means meeting the needs of present generation without compromising the abilities and opportunities of future generation. It thus, implies both inter-generational and intra-generational equity. Sustainability is an important dimension of human development. Human development is a process of enlarging peoples choices. But such enhancement must be for both present and future generations without sacrificing one for the other." Thus, sustainable development is a technique of eating the portion of bread and butter by the present generation in such a way that it must last long so as to enable the future generations to enjoy over it.[4]

CHART 15.1

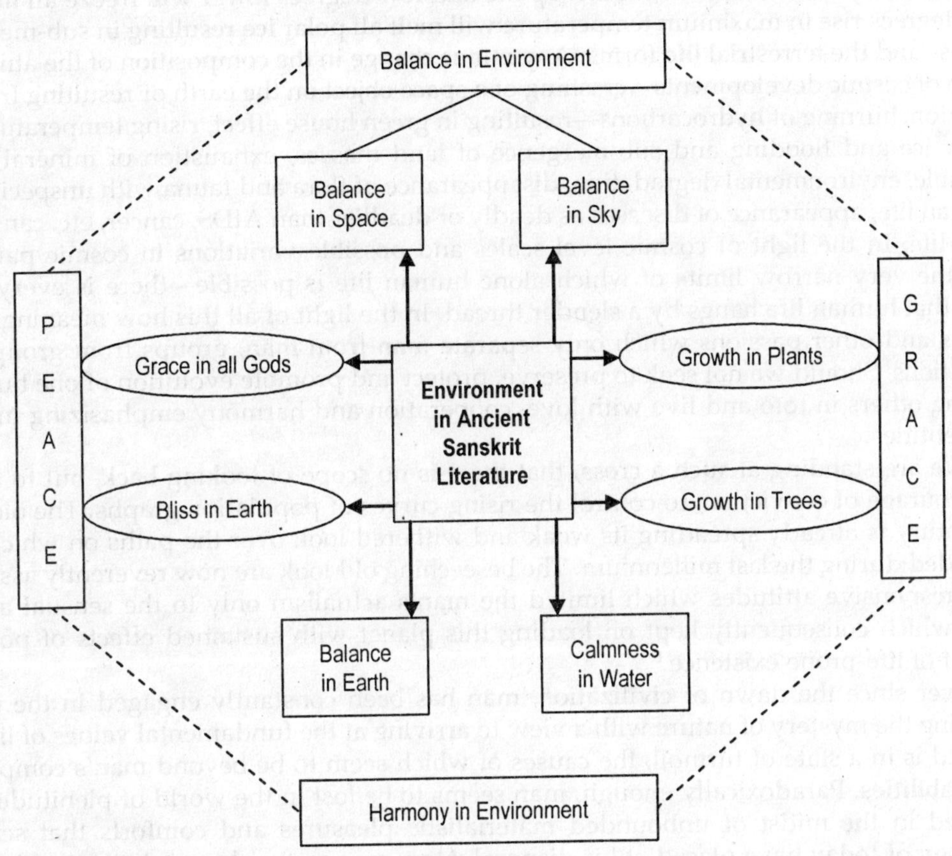

Bahuguna follows the way and is showing it to all of us. The way is R'ta. Our saints discovered it through communion with nature. The native people can teach us R'ta through their reverence for nature.[5]

Our earth is an infinitely insignificant part of the cosmos. Life is only a recent and insignificant development on earth. Man is only one amongst millions of species—plants as well as animals, past and present, confined to only the outer surface of the earth of a few inches out of 8,000 miles of earth's interior and a few feet above in the atmosphere. We are exposed to space hazards. Some 65 millions years ago a heavenly body crashed down on our planet leading to extinction of many life species including Dinosaurs. In 1908 a comet or a meteor with a mass between 1,00,000 to 10,00,000 tonnes exploded over central Siberia. The impact was 1500 times more powerful than the bomb dropped in Hiroshima and destroyed an area of woodland 40 kms. by 50 kms large.

Dangers of Environmental Pollution

Man is also, like-wise, participating in many social circles—concentric circles—family, village, block, district, state, country, continent and the global society at large. Life exists between a small temperature band. A few degree higher temperature resulting from changes in solar radiation or any other reason will burn up life and few degrees lower will freeze all life to death. A few degrees rise in maximum temperature will melt all polar ice resulting in sub-merging of all landmass and the terrestrial life forms. Any minor change in the composition of the atmosphere—because of cosmic developments—crashing of a space object on the earth or resulting from human civilization, burning of hydrocarbons—resulting in green house effect, rising temperature, melting of polar ice and flooding and sub-mergence of land masses, exhaustion of mineral resources, ozone hole, environmental degradation, disappearance of flora and fauna with unspecified effects on human life, appearance of diseases as deadly or deadlier than AIDS, cancer, etc. can extinguish human life. In the light of cosmic level scales and possible variations in cosmic parameters—within the very narrow limits of which alone human life is possible—there is every reason to believe that human life hangs by a slender thread. In the light of all this how meaningful are our religious and other passions which only separate man from man, groups from groups, nations from nations. Should we not seek to preserve, protect and promote evolution of one humanity by accepting others in toto and live with love, cooperation and harmony emphasizing unity rather than identities.

We are standing at such a cross, that there is no scope of looking back, but to act swiftly with a courage of conviction, to control the rising curves of population graphs. The old frame of 20th century is already spreading its weak and withered look over the paths on which the man has treaded during the last millennium. The beseeching old look are now reverently assessing our past unresponsive attitudes which limited the man's actualism only to the sensual and lustful desires which consequently kept on loading this planet with sustained effects of pollution on every bit of life-prone existence.[6]

Ever since the dawn of civilization, man has been constantly engaged in the pursuit of unraveling the mystery of nature with a view to arriving at the fundamental values of life. Today, the world is in a state of turmoil, the causes of which seem to be beyond man's comprehension and capabilities. Paradoxically enough, man seems to be lost in the world of plenitude. His soul is starved in the midst of unbounded materialistic pleasures and comforts that science and technology of today have placed at his disposal. Now man everywhere is bedeviled by complex and complicated moral, cultural and social issues. The harder he strives to extricate himself out of the web of these problems, the more he is caught and involved in it. Underneath the morass of conflicting values lies man's quest for the real meaning of life and the destiny to which it leads.

With all the scientific and technological revolutions that humanity has achieved so far, we have not risen above the level of satisfying the bare physical needs of man. Science does not help us to discuss the fundamental moral and spiritual values of life or how to live and here we see that the advancement of science hassled to mankind's lopsided growth and development.

R. Venkataram, former President of India, in his article, "Need for Ecological Balance" in *Bhavan's Journal* (April 15, 2002) states that Modern civilization has brought in its trail many ill-effects caused by our failure to respect and preserve the balance of ecological factors in the human environment. More often than not, we have in our decision-making allowed economic and material considerations to outweight human and spiritual ones much of this has happened in the developing nations because we have attempted to develop along western models forgetting that the west is already suffering from the consequences of indiscriminate use of modern technology. In the rural areas the very sources of livelihood of the people are being threatened. There is the pollution of lakes, of rivers and the sea .... In fact, man has not understood nature and its secrets and will realize it only after destroying its boundaries.

Gandhiji has clearly stated that "Nature produces enough for our wants and if every one took enough for himself and nothing more; there would be no pauperism and starvation in this world.

The reasons for this tragic situation lie in the lack of inner spiritual growth, the erosion of spiritual values and the failure of our religious and intellectual organizations to actively propagate the ideals of love, compassion, fellowship and harmony. The interfaith movement with which I am closely involved, has been making efforts through the last century to undertake such programmes, but it has achieved only limited success.[7]

Ecology works as the substratum in the patterning of human culture. Ecology is no doubt a complicated comprehension and it has been defined as the study of plants and animals (including man) in relation to each other and to their environment. The study of ecology increases our understanding of the world and its life. This is important because our survival and well-being depend on ecological relationship throughout the world. Even changes in distant parts of the world and its atmosphere affect us and our surroundings. The study of ecology is specifically characterized by the integrated mode of understanding of the surroundings, both biotic and abiotic. Man, in course of his daily life, interacts with these surroundings which result in the development of an integrated bio-cultural modes of behaviour in relation to the people concerned. Ecology can best be studied with a holistic, integrated and multidisciplinary approach. As human life and activities are governed by multifarious forces most of which are meant for putting effective adjustment with the surroundings so the ecological models in exploring human problems and need of diversified nature are seen to be very much effective.[8] The need of today is to find indigenous solutions to make pollution free environment and use restraint in exploiting the natural resources, i.e. change of mind set. We may follow the Sukla—in Yajurveda (36.17) which is a solution to all environmental problems.

Sunderlal Bahuguna in his article: "Environment Conservation for Survival" (*Indian Journal of Public Administration,* July to Sept, 1989) rightly states:

There are no two opinions on this that our "Planet is Dying." The threats are from our materialistic 'civilization', which has defined development as affluence. In order to achieve this, man has become the butcher of Nature. We, unlike our forefathers, live in a world, where trees are dying, rivers are drying and the top fertile soil is flowing down to the sea. The media comes with the stories of depletion of ozone layer, global warming, increase in Carbon-dioxide (CO_2) and so many other horrifying facts; but the modern man unmindful of all these continues to behave in a manner which accelerates the process of degradation. Now it is up to a small minority of sensitive people—the humanitarian scientists, social activists, and the compassionate literary men to come forward and launch crusade against destruction and for a society in which long lost harmonious relationship between "Man and Nature" is revived. [9]

Shri T.N. Chaturvedi in his Editorial to *IJPA,* July-Sept. 1989 (Special Number on Environment and Administration) rightly sees the intimate relationship between human beings and nature since times immemorial. To quote: "Man, since his origin, has lived in harmony with Nature through the ages, holding Nature in awe and reverence. The Vedas, folklore and scriptures of different religions, faiths and beliefs also speak of the need for harmony with the universe, which is the habitat not only of man but also of all animals, birds, insects, plants and vegetation. The mutually supportive role of all living things is often mentioned as a crucial factor for a balanced social and harmonious existence. The ecological balance is inherent in the very process of creation. Everywhere, the seers, poets and thinkers, through the ages, have referred to the need for living in harmony with environment. In fact, the Taitariyopanishad looks at the relationship between man and his environment in its totality and stresses complete harmony and interdependence between them in order to attain real prosperity."

Rajiv Agarwal and Praveen Pradeshi rightly say as has been in the teachings of ancient Sanskrit Literature.[10]

Reconciling of economic development with environmental preservation has become an unavoidable necessity though it is still an open question whether "development without destruction" is possible. However, if the environmental impact of each project is identified in advance and suitable safeguards implemented to mitigate the negative environmental impact, we may perhaps be able to minimize the damage to the environment.

Dr. Hiroshi Nakajima, former Director-General of World Health Organization, sounded a warning alarm about degradation of this planet in his Article, "A Wounded Planet."[11] He rightly visualises that it is now increasingly evident that more and more diseases stem from the degradation caused by man to his own environment. The potential harmful effects of industrial development on our global ecosystem are now better known. Ozone layer depletion, acid rain, climate change, chemical pollution are some examples of the man-made wounds to our planet.

We are at a turning point; warnings of the damage to our health and quality of life are growing louder. An increasing number of people are acting to stop the degradation of our environment. The degradation of our environment has to be arrested immediately otherwise it would have long-term impact on the quality of life of future generations ... We should also take this opportunity to educate our children regarding the importance of the preservation of our environment. Dr. Wilfried Kreisel[12] also elaborates the aspects of environment which affect health of mankind.

Environmental health refers to the ecological balance that must exist between man and his environment in order to ensure his well-being. The deterioration of the human environment through the population explosion, pollution of air and water, and other disruptions of the ecological balance pose a major international health hazard and a serious challenge. Professor J. Logan, in a paper published in *American journal of Tropical Medicine* was able to show that environmentally transmitted diseases were responsible for the sufferings of 500 million people every year particularly among infants and children.[13] The UN Secretary General's report on problem of the human environment sounds a similar ominous note: "If current trends continue, the failure of life on earth could be engendered and thus, it is urgent to focus world attention on these problems which threaten humanity in an environment that permits the realisation of the highest human aspirations.[14]

The close relationship that exists between an unhealthy environment and the economic condition of a community was pinpointed by a panel of experts which met in 1971 to discuss the environmental problems of the developing countries. "Poverty and the very lack of development", these experts said, "constitute an essential environmental problem in the developing countries. They recommended an attack on the problems of inadequate water supply, poor housing, sanitation, nutrition and widespread diseases as prime targets in an effort to improve the environment of millions of people, and to lay the groundwork for their economic betterment."[15]

Primitive tribal groups were very careful about environment as they attached importance to these as super-natural powers.

Rapidly growing population, urbanisation, changing agricultural, industrial and water resource management, increasing use of pesticides and fossil fuels have all resulted in a perceptible deterioration in the quality of environment and attendant adverse health consequences. Environment pollution due to developmental activities are increasingly becoming the focus of concern. The interactive interdependence of health, environment and sustainable development was accepted as the fulcrum of action under Agenda 21 at the Earth Summit in Brazil in 1992. Environmental health in its broader perspective would have to address the detection, prevention and management of:

(i) existing deficiencies or excesses of certain elements in natural environment;
(ii) macro-environmental contamination of air, land, water and food; and
(iii) disaster management.

Agenda 21, United Nations Conference on Environment and Development held in Rio de Saneiro, Brazil (June 3-14, 1992) states in its preamble:

Humanity stands at a defining moment in history. We are confronted with a perpetuation of disparities between and within nations, a worsening of poverty, hunger, ill-health and illiteracy, and the continuing deterioration of the ecosystems on which we depend for our well-being. However, integration of environment and development concerns and greater attention to them will lead to the fulfilment of basic needs, improved living standards for all, better protected and managed ecosystems and a safer, more prosperous future. No nation can achieve this on its own; but together we can—in a global partnership for sustainable development.

In order to meet the challenges of environment and development, States have decided to establish a new global partnership. This partnership commits all States to engage in a continuous and constructive dialogue, inspired by the need to achieve a more efficient and equitable world economy, keeping in view the increasing interdependence of the community of nations and that sustainable development should become a priority item on the agenda of the international community. It is recognized that, for the success of this new partnership. It is important to overcome confrontation and to foster a climate of genuine cooperation and solidarity. It is equally important to strengthen national and international policies and multinational cooperation to adapt to the new realities.

Ever since the United Nations Conference on Human Environment held at Stockholm in 1972 proclaimed the right of the people to a clean environment, the Government of India as well as the state governments have initiated a number of measures to control the various types of pollution. However, the disastrous consequences of a technological civilization which has disturbed the delicate balance of various ecological factors are yet to be fully realized by the humans. Until recently nature was able to absorb the pollutants added to it and again provide a clean environment on the planet. But today an advanced industrial society and greedy humanity is polluting the environment at a rate faster than the nature's capacity to remedy the same. The United Nations has given a timely call to halt the suicidal tendency of the humanity to destroy the very planet which has been sustaining its existence.[16]

Dr. Zbigniew Bankowski, spells out the code of ethics to protect the environment . It would be unrealistic, however, to suppose that the damage that has been done, and still continues to be done, can be arrested and undone in the short-term. Rather, long-term global policies must be envisaged and, if they are to be successful, they will require changes in our perceptions of man in nature. If our global physical environment is not to be further degraded, we must change our conceptual environment, our ways of thinking and behaving. Perhaps the worst environmental pollution is pollution of the mind, and the greatest need is for well thought out principles of environmental ethics.

All spheres of human conduct private and public, are subject to ethical principles or rules.

When governments or other corporate bodies despoil the environment in the name of development or political dominance or national security, when government adopt *laissez faire* policies that permit the exploitation of nature for narrow, short-term gains, they contravene the basic ethical principle of the greatest good for the greatest number of people. It is necessary to approach the problem in a holistic manner by linking sanitation with religion, culture, health, agriculture, environment and production of energy. The basic attitude that needs to be formed is to link it with Bhakti. It has to be stressed that cleanliness is godliness and unless cleanliness becomes a part of our lives, we cannot be true devotees of God.[17]

As early as in 1972, the United Nations Declaration on Human Environment warned:

We see around us growing evidence of man-made harm in many regions of the earth; dangerous levels of pollution in water, air, earth and living beings; major and undesirable disturbances to the ecological balance of the biosphere, destruction and depletion of irreplaceable resources; and gross deficiencies harmful to the physical, mental and social health of men, in the man-made environment, particularly in the living and working environment.

The Tribune editorial, Sept. 6, 2002, "Who cares for the earth" has rightly hit on the policies of the developed world. To quote: The environmental health of the planet did not improve after the path-breaking earth summit at Stockholm in 1972. It did not change in spite of the decibel level being raised at Rio in 1992 to a point that ensured the whispered reservations of the rich could be heard across the globe. The message from Johannesburg that hosted the latest round of the World Summit on Sustainable Development is not encouraging either. It is the same old story of the poor being allowed a forum from which they can share with the rest of the world their concerns about environment-related issues. However, in the end it is the will of the rich that prevails. The fact that former President George W. Bush did not deem it necessary to be present on the occasion conveyed in clear terms what the USA—the biggest polluter—thought about such summits. At Rio Ms. Meneka Gandhi had stolen the thunder by insisting that for a safe and fair world order it was necessary to adopt the principle that made the polluter pay for messing around with the fragile ecology of the planet. She received applause, but at the end of the day countries like the USA continued to add to the rising pollution levels without any sense of remorse. The Earth Summit 10 years ago at Rio de Janerio grandly resolved to save all nature, from the humblest algae to the majestic elephant. It agreed that the planets delicate climate urgently needed protection before global warming rises to dangerous levels. What has been the contribution of the developed community at Rio? They asked the smaller nations to comply with the strict provisions while they busied themselves in buying unused greenhouse emission permits from countries that in any case do not produce even a fraction of the permissible level.

In addition the multinational corporations are responsible for environmental degradation. The multinational corporations and their role in raising the pollution level is not a secret. Union Carbide was responsible for the Bhopal tragedy and the USA did not allow the law to get hold of the guilty for trial in India. In the UK a company by the name of British Nuclear Fuels Ltd. dumped approximately 182 kg of plutonium into the Irish sea over the past 50 years. Lobsters from the polluted region and near the Norwegian coast have tested positive of high levels of radioactive contamination. Should anyone be allowed to play in these waters? What about eating the contaminated seafood? World leaders need to do an honest introspection for saving the planet from certain disaster. They must realize that every living being shares the same earth. If the lungs develop cancer, the rest of the body cannot survive by removing the lungs.

Environment is common for all the countries as well as inter-connected as polluted environment can move freely through diffusion as already explained in the introduction. A global effort based on the wisdom contained in Sanskrit literature and new knowledge generated through science and technological research should be employed to combat the menace of environmental degradation. The developed world should not remain isolated as the impact of endangered environment would recoil on them. All the affluence of the developed world would be of no use if the total environment is not smoothing.

Churamani states that just as waves merge into sea and become one, so developed and developing countries should think of ocean, i.e. collective approach and not isolated approach. Life is nothing but a wave in the vast sea. Each wave is having a feeling of individuality and it does not consider itself the part and parcel of the sea or the sea itself but considers itself separate from the vast sea. The feeling of separation has caused its existence in the universe. The drama of action and reaction of wave motion always continues in the sea. None can judge how many water waves are taking birth and how many are dying. The waves are of different strengths and their existence is also of different time periods.[18]

Therefore, there is a need of redefining the environmental issues so that a peaceful solution can be found to make it fit for all the people of the world to live. We should also associate rural and urban Governments in protecting the environment as these institutions understand the problem and can provide operational solution. Today, we are thinking and tackling Physical environment but the major problem resides in the realm of mental, social, spiritual and astronomical objects. So a complete solution by all the countries is essential. We must consult Sanskrit Literature for solution beyond Physical environment, i.e. in the sphere of Metaphysical.

Bernard Lovell, and Al Gore also emphasize Ethical basis which is the core view of Ancient Indian Sanskrit Literature. "The vital question is whether the framework of society in which science is perused can develop the ethical basis and moral purpose necessary to ensure that in our future progress we overcome the forces leading to decay and destruction.[19]

Today, we need a communion, that our heart be wide enough so that no one is excluded as all of them have a well defined subtle role to build up ecological capital and to maintain the balance of nature.

In the 21st century the Deep Ecologists begin to feel a sense of oneness with nature and as a part of Natural order of life, the very same philosophy our ancestors practiced, propagated and insisted to adopt to maintain peace in the planet. They had respect to nature, which is the safest, cleanest and most refined level of inter-species communication and communion.

Protection of the environment has to be a central part of any sustainable inclusive growth strategy. This aspect of development is especially important in the Eleventh Plan when consciousness of the dangers of environment degradation has increased greatly. Population growth, urbanization, and anthropogenic development employing energy-intensive technologies have resulted in injecting a heavy load of pollutants into the environmental degradation has increased greatly. More recently, the issue assumed special importance because of the accumulation of evidence of global warming and the associated climate change that it is likely to bring.

CONCLUSION

Now the time is on action and not contemplation. We should follow the principles and prescriptions given in our Sanskrit Literature and improve the quality of Environment.

It is realized that industrialization is essential if an economy is to develop. But the transformation of natural resources for industrialization is accompanied by serious environmental degradation. When this transformation of nature by man, instead of showing a symbiotic relationship between man and nature, shows a man centric effort to conquer nature and ultimately overpower it, the economy that is aimed to be built by man to protect himself and prosper, is itself stressed. This gives the background of one's understanding on industrial ecology. If mankind is to live over generations, the eco-system, which feeds them, has to be sustained and there comes the question of controlling man's exercise of power over nature.[20]

Most of the environmental problems of the present day are essentially man made. The role of man is therefore important because it is his attitude and values which shape the environment. In developed countries mad race after materialism puts too much pressure on environment. The materialistic attitude of man multiplies the human needs and ultimately leads towards resources exploitation, without considering the future consequential disharmony with the environment. Man has to evolve a balanced way of thinking, acting and feeling towards the environment. So human ethics, attitude, values, decision-making analysis of ecological, economic, social and technical aspects come under the scope of environmental education. [21]

Education, including formal education, public awareness and training should be recognized as a process by which human beings and societies can reach their fullest potential. Education is critical for promoting sustainable development and improving the capacity of the people to address environment and development issues. While basic education provides the underpinning for any environmental and development education, the latter needs to be incorporated as an essential part of learning. Both formal and non-formal education are indispensable to changing people's attitudes so that they have the capacity to assess and address their sustainable development concerns. It is also critical for achieving environmental and ethical awareness, values and attitudes, skills and behaviour consisted with sustainable development and for effective public participation in decision-making. To be effective, environment and development education should deal with the dynamics of both the physical/biological and socio-economic environment and human (which may include spiritual) development, should be integrated in all disciplines, and should employ formal and non-formal methods and effective means of communication.

Sanskrit literature is full of techniques, methods, rationale and philosophy of saving human beings from the horrible impact of environment pollution. What is required is to educate the people in advanced and developing countries to stop exploiting nature for making palatial buildings, huge industries, nuclear plants, etc. All this is possible if we develop virtuous people as defined in Gita, Vedas, and other ancient Sanskrit scriptures.

The current environmental and development trends in the world are clear indication that the world is far from attaining the objectives enshrined in Agenda 21. Some will question even the rate of progress, which has been rather slow and uneven. One part of the reason for the unsatisfactory progress can be traced to the global system of allocation of resources and unredeemed promises while the other part remains the responsibility of national governments.

The main policies and programmes contained in Agenda 21 provide a major re-affirmation of a number of traditional values inherent in the Indian culture. It is also in conformity with all those values that are enshrined in the Indian constitution. The nation of 'sustainable development' is not a new one. The history of the country is replete with innumerable initiatives undertaken by people that demonstrate not just concern for environment, but also the awareness of the need to balance it with livelihood resources. This 'tradition' of care, conservation and preservation of environmental resources is also reflected in the spirit of the Constitution of India, which has acted as the guiding inspiration of the nation now for over half a century. The strength of the Indian Constitution lies in the fact that it does not advocate any new or imported principles, instead it builds on the deep-rooted and therefore, resilient, practices of sustainable development that have evolved over time in the country.

Environment provides bliss to people leading their life perfectly Rivers bliss us with sacred water and medicines—provide us health. Night, morning, vegetation. Sun bliss us with peaceful life. Our cows provide us sweet milk.

"A society or a Nation can be well and sustainable provided both its people and the Eco system are healthy. Human well-being and the health of Eco-system are closely linked because the eco-system surround people much in the same manner as the white of an egg surrounds and supports the Yolk."[22]

Any holistic model of sustainable development should take into account the three-fold transformation of human individual, human society and the cosmos. This should be the end-all and be-all of all planning and strategies of development at the global level. Then only it can be a total development which can be really sustainable and enduring.

Transformation and regeneration of human individual is the first and foremost requirement. It stands for development of all dimensions of human personality—physical, mental, intellectual, moral and spiritual. Mere physical or mental or intellectual development is lopsided and can never be sustainable. This requires a value-oriented scheme of education a blue-print of which could be prepared by a world body like UNESCO and which could be universally adopted by suitable modification according to the regional needs and aspirations and conditions. The ideal situation is to have a global planning and strategy. This is of course a utopian dream but given wisdom and will it is not unreleasable.

Social transformation is another foundation of sustainable development. It is establishment of a social order and organisation in a democratic form in which equality is seasoned with justice and freedom is tempered with discipline, where tolerance is a guide to mutual relations and cooperation is the law of interaction, where there is practice of *anekantavda* (a Jaina view of life consisting in perspectivism) in thought, words and deeds. But this again requires a proper type of education in social living.

Transformation of nature is the third pre-requisite of sustainable development. It consists of all such policy efforts which enable us to safeguard the natural capital stock of all five material elements (pancabhuta) of earth, water, fire, air and space, in such a manner that it does not get polluted and depleted. It means that in nature there should be no negative change, no environmental degradation, no agricultural clearance of forests, no housing on agricultural land, no extinction of forest flora and fauna and natural live stock, etc. On the contrary, there should be positive change by forest resource management, land, water, air and space resource management, etc. Simultaneously there should be supporting efforts like check in population growth, revival of traditional sustainable practices, etc. These days there is a growing awareness of all these policy measures. It is unfortunate that given the present human psychology all these policies and programmes mostly remain confined to papers only and nothing concrete and practical is being done though statistics may show otherwise.

Ashok Kosla "Technology and Environment: Role of Independent Sector in Sustainable Development", in *IJPA*, July-Sept. 1989, Vol. XXXV clearly observed that development that does not conserve over a sufficiently long period into the future the resource base on which it stands, cannot be sustained—and herein must lie the central thrust of future policy-making and planning. While addressing the issue of productivity, self-reliance, equity and other fundamental indices of development, development planning must now incorporate, integrally, also the need for conserving resources. But it is also becoming clear that further progress will require even broader commitment, not only at the policy and programmatic level, but also at the operational level of the field worker, and perhaps most important, the individual citizen. It can only be achieved if environmental concerns permeate the thinking of all those involved in promoting or implementing the development process, from the national policy-maker to the peasant farmer.

Checking Wasteful Overutilisation and Enhancing Access of the Poor

Wasteful overutilisation of natural resources provides one of the primary threats to the health of our environment. If development is to lead to sustainable benefits for mankind, affluent societies will undoubtedly have to change the way they use the planet's resources, and to learn to conserve these far more effectively than they have in the past. Much of the environmental degradation faced by Third World Countries is also caused by overutilisation of resources, but not so much by wasteful practices as by the conduct of day-to-day activities necessary for survival and subsistence. There exists common agreement that the solution to these environmental problems lies largely in rapid social and economic development—as long as it is an equitable and broad-based development.[23]

Environment

Protecting the Environment

While in the short-run there may seem to be a trade-off between environmental sustainability and economic growth, in the longer run, recourse is to be taken to the complementarities between environmental sustainability and human well-being. The development strategy therefore, has to be sensitive to these concerns and should ensure that threats and trade-offs are appropriately evaluated.

Notes and References

1. A.N. Yellappa, Role of Sanskrit in Preservation of Wild Life Bio-Diversity and Environment", Souvenir, World Sanskrit Conference 5-9 April, 2001, Ed., Prof. Vachaspati Upadhyaya, Shri Lal Bahadur Shastri Rashtriya Sanskrit Vidyapeeth, p. 183.
2. S. Murty, Economic Growth and Environment: Some issues in Environmental Challenges of the 21st century ed. (S. Radha and Amar Singh Sankhyan, New Delhi, Deep & Deep 2002, p. 44.
3. O.P. Monga, Ecology, Development and Society: Future Challenges, in *Ibid.*, p. 75.
4. Baidya Nath Prasad Singh, Environment and Sustainable Development: A suitable Strategy Needed for their Striking Balance, in *Ibid.*, p. 72.
5. Raghbir Singh Pirta, The Himalayas, Tehri and Bahuguna, *Ibid.*, p. 277.
6. Gurcharn Singh, Pollution to Purity of Environment, New Delhi, Deep & Deep, 2005, p. 113.
7. Dr. Karan Singh, Souvenir, World Congress on Global Vision and Strategies for Peace, Non-Violence and Harmony, ALIYAR, 2002.
8. R.M. Sarkar Culture, Ecology and Tradition—The Interactional Patterns in Shaping the Modes of Behaviour in a Primitive Behaviour, A Quarterly Journal of Anthropology, *Man in India*, Vol. 82, Nos. 1 & 2, Jan. to June 2002, p. 5.
9. Sunderlal Bahuguna, Environment conservation for Survival " In *Indian Journal of Public Administration*, July to Sept. 1989, New Delhi, p. 379.
10. Rajiv Agarwal and Praveen Pradeshi, Development without Destruction, in *IJPA*, July to Sept. 1989, p. 547.
11. Hiroshi Nakajima, "A Wounded Planet" in *World Health*, January-February, 1990, p. 3.

12. Dr. Wilfried, Kreisel, "Environmental Health in the 1990s" in *World Health*, January-February, 1990, p. 5.
13. WHO: *World Health*, May 1972, p. 29.
14. U. Thant quoted in Clellan, M.C. and S. Grant (ed.) Protecting our Environments (New York, 1970), p. 206.
15. WHO, *World Health*, May, 1972, p. 29.
16. S.P. Ranga Rao, and MS Prakasa Sastry, "Control of Water Pollution in Andhra Pradesh" in *IJPA*, July-Sept., 1990, p. 548.
17. Zbigniew Bankowski, "A code of Ethics" in *World Health*, January-Feb. 1990, p. 18.
18. Parmod Churamani, way to Mental Freedom, Chapter 5.
18A. Lean, Geoffrey, Rich World Poor World, p. 332.
19. S.S. Narata Rao and Pratibha Narata, Industrialization and Environment: Agenda for the 21st century in Environmental challenges of the 21st century, Editors S. Radha and Amar Singh Sankkyan, 2002, p. 124.
20. Maba Kumar Patnaik and P. Sasi Bhushan Rao, Environment Education for 21st century in Environment Management and Audit, Editors, P. Pasi Bhushan Rao and P. Mohana Rao, Deep & Deep, New Delhi; 2000, p. 206.
21. Agenda 21, UNCED, Rio de Janerio Brazil, June 3-14, 1992, Chapter 36.
22. Robert Prescott Allen, The Well-being of Nations: A Country-by-country Index of Quality of Life and the Environment, Washington, DC Island Press, 2001, p. 4
23. S.R. Bhatt, "Welfare State in Indian Classics" in M.M. Sankhdher and Sharda Jain (eds.) Social Security, Welfare and Polity, New Delhi, Deep and Deep, 2004, pp. 309-10.

CHAPTER

16

Population Policy and Development

The ultimate goal of the world's population policy must be to achieve an equilibrium based on low birth and death rates that can be sustained throughout a distant future for the world and its several parts.

—*F.W. Notestein*

The programme of family welfare and family planning is in the interest of peace and humanity in order to improve the quality of life for families in developing countries particularly in rural areas and in urban disadvantaged poor.

—*Tokyo Declaration of Parliamentarians*

INTRODUCTION

The problem of overpopulation especially in the developing world is one of the bottlenecks to socio-economic development. It was mentioned by the Secretary-General of the United Nations that current and potential world-wide population trends evidently cannot continue for as long as even one century without causing serious dislocations and crises in many areas.[1] India's population figure has crossed 100 million from 34.2 million in 1947. Ministry of Health and Family Welfare, Government of India has rightly sounded the grave concern about the trends in population explosion. To quote the report:

"The demographic situation in India is a matter of grave concern and has serious implications for overall socio-economic development. Ever-increasing numbers have shadowed the achievements that the nation has made on the economic front."[2]

The performance of the family planning programme to control population has not been adequate as compared to the resources put in the programme. The programme has been examined from different angles but very little effort has been made to examine the family planning programme from administrative angle. It was also reported in the UN document. To quote, "A principal obstacle every where to the development of successful official family planning lies in the area of organization and administration .... The challenge for planners and administrators is to work out effective means for delivery of this technology and service to the public."[3]

The Planning Commission's observations against the Union Ministry of Health and Family Welfare for its failure to implement various projects and initiatives for population control are alarming. In a paper, Yojna Bhavan has voiced concern on the increasing population growth and feared that the situation would worsen by 2015 if remedial steps were not taken. Clearly, the Union Ministry's lackadaisical attitude is deplorable because it is expected to play a leadership role in executing various birth control schemes. If it does not take the initiative, show dynamism and direction, how would it convince the states about the crucial need for population control?

Union Health Minister had drawn up a list of 150 districts in five states—Uttar Pradesh, Bihar, Jharkhand, Madhya Pradesh and Rajasthan—to carry out population control projects. Targeting the five states because of their "high fertility status" may seem justifiable, but the Ministry has a long way to go. According to the National Family Health Survey (1998-99), about 25 per cent of fertility cases in the country are unwanted due largely to unfulfilled needs of contraception. Surely, the Centre cannot abdicate its responsibility or policy.

India's population is increasing by about 50,000 a day. The country may not be able to manage the burgeoning population in view of the limited land, water and capital resources. Literacy and health care do help promote birth control. But on both these fronts, the picture is not encouraging. Most primary health centres (PHCs) in the countryside lack infrastructure, training and critical inputs. As a result, they carry out sterilizations only in occasional camps and not regularly. The government should encourage participation by Panchayats and local communities in villages to give a boost to the population control programme. Private hospitals could also be paid for services like contraception counselling, supplies, tubectomy and vasectomy operations, consultations, check ups and so on. The nation cannot afford to lose time in fight against the numbers.[4]

J.P. Singh has rightly warned that: If the country opts for a natural course of demographic transition, then it will have to pay a heavy price in the form of unmanageable unemployment, rampant poverty, political chaos leading to ethnic violence and even dismemberment of the country in the long-run. In fact, the whole South Asia would have to encounter similar experience and would take the shape of Africa or Europe in terms of number of independent nations fighting among themselves. Here the process have already set in, as the population bomb has already exploded. It is altogether different matter that some of us at the helm of affairs deliberately tend to camouflage the reality or do not want to recognize it. Some of them even ignore the description of dismal demographic scenario of India by branding it a pure academic exercise. Even many Indian social scientists seem blissfully unaware of how rising population of India threatens its future, while the population issues have already started dominating India's future. One simply wonders whether new advancements in science and technology will really do any magic to save India from impending disaster following population explosion.[5]

SOCIO-ECONOMIC IMPLICATIONS OF POPULATION EXPLOSION

The growth rate in population absorbs the national income and lowers the standard of living. The world population conference indicated in the population plans of action that population growth and population policy must be viewed not in isolation, but in the context of development.

Myrdal in his book Asian Drama gave a stem warning to the world in regard to population explosion when he said, "Demographers are of the view that if fertility does not decrease, a time will come when mortality will lose its relative independence of levels of living and being to rise again."[6]

Family planning programmes have led to a considerable decrease in average family size in developing countries: from 6.1 children per woman in the early 1960s to 3.9 today. Yet this is still far higher than the average of 2.1 children per woman at which level the population would stop growing. Actual numbers continue to increase. The population of developing countries has doubled in the same period, reaching 4100 million in 1990. It is predicted to rise to 5000 million by 2000, out of an optimistic forecast of a world total of 6300 million.

This poses enormous challenges in terms of providing the food, water, energy and services required to support such numbers, let alone improve their quality of life. For the health sector, the sheer numbers magnify the burden of disease. More training, facilities and funding will be needed for all services, including family planning.[7]

In view of this alarming situation, an urgent call was made by the representatives of the national academies of science throughout the world at an unprecedented "Science Summit" on World Population in New Delhi, India, on 24-27 October 1993. The participants, in a joint statement, asked for immediate action by governments and decision-makers to adopt an integrated policy on population and sustainable development on a global scale. They hoped that the Statement would reach the attention of governments and peoples of all countries and contribute to further discourse and appropriate policy decisions on these complex but critically important matters, and provide scientific input into preparations for the International Conference on Population and Development.

The Statement declared: "Humanity is approaching a crisis point with respect to the interlocking issues of population, environment, and development. Scientists today have the opportunity and responsibility to mount a concerted effort to confront our human predicament. But science and technology can only provide tools and blueprints for action and social change. It is the governments and international decision-makers, including those meeting in Cairo in September 1994 at the United Nations International Conference on Population and Development, who hold the key to our future.

"We urge them to take decisive action now and to adopt an integrated policy on population and sustainable development on a global scale. With each year's delay the problems become more acute. Let 1994 be remembered as the year when the people of the world decided to act together for the benefit of future generations."

Signed by representatives of 58 academies, the Statement reflects continued concern about the intertwined problems of rapid population growth, wasteful resource consumption, environmental degradation and poverty. The academies believe that ultimate success in dealing with global social, economic and environmental problems cannot be achieved without a stable world population. The Statement underscored the goal of reaching zero population growth within the lifetime of our children.

One of the main conclusions reached was that sustainability in natural world is everyone's responsibility, including individual communities, private institutions, governments, non-governmental organizations and the international community.

Among the major recommendations are:

- Equal opportunities for women and men in sexual, social and economic life so that they can make individual choice about family size;

- Universal access to convenient family planning and health services, and a wide variety of safe and affordable contraceptive options; and
- Encouragement of voluntary approaches to family planning, and elimination of unsafe and coercive practices.

The Statement ended by declaring: "Action is Needed Now." Thus, there is a great need of stabilizing population. According to Frank W. Notestein:

"The ultimate goal of the worlds population policy must be to achieve an equilibrium based on low birth and death rates that can be sustained throughout a distant future for the world and its several parts."[8]

As long as the birth rate is not restricted in these countries, it would not be possible to bring about improvements in the living standard of the people.

In a 'capital poor' and technologically backward country, growth of population diminished the rate of capital accumulation, increases the amount of disguised unemployment and lowers the standards of living of the people, i.e., resources go to the formation of population, not capital. According to Prof. A.W. Singir, population growth has a negative effect on the rate of economic development. According to him:

$D = SP - r$
where
D = rate of economic development,
S = rate of net savings,
P = productivity of new investment, and
r = rate of increase in population.

In the above equation, r appears as a negative factor with a minus sign.

"Population growth is an important variable determining the rate of improvement in per capita income."[9] P.B. Desai analysis this problem in its broader context. To quote him, "We must, however, emphasize that of rapid population increase is not limited to the enlargement of the denominator of the ratio of national product and national population. It is much more pervasive. It is quite plausible that its absence would have made a positive contribution to the growth of national product. Besides, creating the imperative of demographic investment required to prevent deterioration in the levels of living, it has served to increase the dependency load, tended to undermine the achievement of predetermined composition of the national product, hampered the path of changes in the structure of its economy warranted by development, and led in all probability, to accentuation of the imbalances in the regional as well as in the rural-urban distribution of population. Implications of rapid population growth should thus appear to be more serious.[10]

Let us examine the impact of population growth on the socio-economic development. (See Chart 16.1).

I. Offset Economic Growth

Thomas Mathur has rightly mentioned that population explosion offsets economic growth. To quote him:

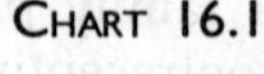

CHART 16.1

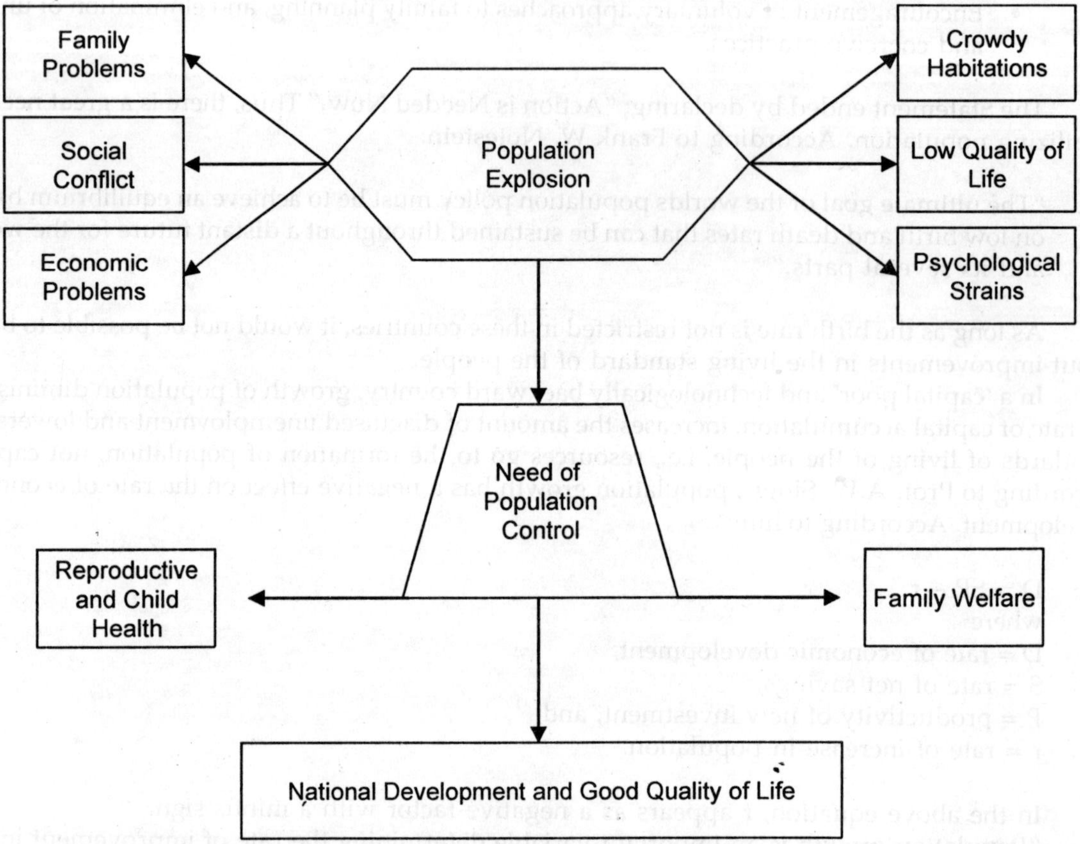

"The increasing population has been eating into the gains of economic growth. While the net national product at constant prices increased by 165 per cent, the per capita income went up by only 45 per cent. That this Yawning chasm between the growth of national product and per capita income is the direct result of the prolific increase in population needs no elaboration."[11]

The population growth requires more investment while the population rise reduces the capacity of the people to save. This creates a serious gap between investment requirements and the availability of investible funds resulting in the low rate of growth of an economy.

According to Coale and Hoover, "The significant feature of population as such is that a higher rate of population growth implies a higher level of needed investment to achieve a given per capita output; while there is nothing about faster growth that generates a great supply of investible resources."[12]

2. Reduction in the Rate of Capital Formation

The composition of the people in underdeveloped countries (40-50 percent of the population in unproductive age-group) is such that it reduces the capacity of the people to save which affects the rate of capital formation. According to Prof. Meier, "This high dependency requires the economy to divert a considerable part of its resources, that might otherwise go into capital formation, to the maintenance of high percentage of dependents who may never become producers or, if so, only for relatively short working life."[13] Recognizing this, the Third Plan states:

> "In an underdeveloped economy with very little capital per person, a high rate of population growth makes it even more difficult to step up the rate of saving which, in turn, largely determines the possibility of achieving higher productivity and incomes. Moreover, for a given investment, a larger proportion will need to be devoted to the reduction of essential consumer goods at the expense of investment goods industries thereby still further slowing down the potential rate of growth."[14]

3. Food Problem

Food is an essential item of consumption for human survival. The demand of food is rising faster than the production of food. In a study carried out by Food and Agricultural Organization, it was found that the failure of food production to keep up with population growth was especially pronounced in the case of the developing countries. Out of the total of 106 countries studied, 72 were classified as developing; but in 24 of these (or one-third) food production lagged behind the growth of population. In the more recent period, it was mentioned; the situation was even less favourable. In India, Food Production increased from 51 million tones to 151 million tones between 1950-51 and 1983-84 giving an increase of three times. During the same period, the population has doubled. However, per capita availability of food grains has not increased much.[15]

4. Unemployment and Underemployment

The result of more population would affect the employment situation as there is already a back-log of unemployment and underemployment in these countries. The growing unemployment of these countries is not only an economic but it is also a social evil.

5. Poor Health Standards

Population control through Family Planning and Health are intimately related. Family planning can promote women's health through the prevention of unwanted pregnancies, limiting number of births, and proper spacing, timing of births and foetal health. Family planning also promotes the health of the child through the reduction of child mortality, and promotion of the child development. Maryellen Fullam stresses the importance of family planning as instrument for the promotion of health. He says:

> "Uncontrolled fertility directly threatens the health of mothers and infants and may undermine the health of other family members. Today, no health programme can be considered complete unless it offers ready access to the appropriate family planning measures for all potential parents."[16]

Angile Petros-Barvazian in his Article, "Family Planning a preventive health measure" in *World Health*, June 1984 has rightly mentioned that the effects of unregulated fertility of births to women who are too young or too old, of closely spaced births and of high parity births make themselves felt very early in life, often even before birth, in high foetal and neonatal death rates. In many developing countries, deaths in the first mouths of life make up the major portion of infant mortality. The indirect effects of unregulated fertility—through infection and malnutrition—tend to make themselves felt later. Family Planning has an important contribution to make in reducing all the above mentioned risks .... Pregnancy makes heavy demands on a woman and too closely spaced pregnancies that do not allow enough time for her body to recover may lead to maternal depletion. This is particularly marked under conditions of deprivation and shows itself in fatigue, depression and a general lowering of health status which may result in higher reproductive risk. Many chronic hygaecological conditions which cause long-term ill-health and suffering increase with the number of pregnancies that the woman has. Debilitating conditions such as prolapsed uterus add to the burden of women with large families. Reductions in the number of high-risk pregnancies, brought about largely through family planning, have substantially lowered mortality in many countries compared with about 10 in the U.S. and U.K. Family Planning can prevent maternal mortality because it can help couples avoid high risk pregnancies.

Professor Fraser Brockington has rightly said that over-population affects the health of the community, physically and mentally. It undermines physical health by increasing the risks of infection and by the most subtle, but more powerful influence of malnutrition; by shortening life; by disrupting the family through deaths of its younger members; by damaging the health of the child bearing population through frequent pregnancies without corresponding gain; by denying the community many of the essentials of health. Mental health suffers because of the hopelessness of life in circumstances where there exist neither house-room, food, well-being, nor any of the essentials which make life of fulfilment and purpose possible."[17]

A UN report on World Population Trends, Vol. I (1983) has rightly concluded that in many developing countries, rapid population growth is considered to be a matter of great concern and programmes to reduce fertility have been given high priority. Furthermore, it is, now well documented that family planning can favourably influence the health, development and well-being of the family, particularly mothers and children.

In a Population Report, it has been rightly said that family planning is an effective way to prevent maternal and infant mortality because family planning can help couples avoid high risk pregnancies. Evidence from around the world shows that the risk of maternal or infant illness and death is highest in four specific types of pregnancy:

(a) Pregnancies before age 18,
(b) Pregnancies after age 35,
(c) Pregnancies after four births, and
(d) Pregnancies less than two years apart.

In developing countries, about 6.6 million infant deaths and 200,000 maternal deaths could be avoided if women choose to have their children within the safest years. This amount to about half of the estimated 10.5 million infant deaths and 450,000 maternal deaths now occurring.

6. Social and Psychological Tensions

Rapid population growth leads to social and psychological tensions, and breakdown of a distribution system. Civil amenities such as water and power supply, housing, transport and social utilities like schooling, educational, health and medical services fall much short of demand inspite of their constant expansion. Besides, it leads to political and social corruption and accentuates economic disparities. The frequency of communal riots or clashes has increased. There has always been a clash between landowning class and landless labourers resulting sometimes into armed struggle. Because of competition in urban life, people fall prey to many social risks like gambling, prostitution, etc.

Thus, we can say that the problem of growing population has reached such menacing proportions that it has become a real threat to the socio-economic stability of the country. The excessive growth in population does not affect the stability of the national economy alone, it disturbs the stability of the entire body politic. It poses a colossal threat to our social structure. In our fight against poverty, disease, hunger, malnutrition and unemployment, checking the rapid growth of population is as raising production in the farms and factories and provision of social services. Population control is one of the chief issues which the country has to resolve and accord top priority in its march towards social and economic development.

The programme of family planning is of vital importance for our country. It is a positive and constructive approach to the betterment of the quality of life of the community. Thus, it is evident that the key to India's economic future based on social justice lies in the immediate and effective implementation of a nation-wide population programme.

The experiences and lessons gained from Indian Planning suggests that effective population control, designed to restore the balance between vital rates by reducing the level of fertility, has a positive influence on the process of economic development and modernization. An eminent scholar has rightly mentioned that "A reduction in infertility would make the process of modernization more rapid and more certain. It would accelerate the growth of income, provide more rapidly the possibility of productive employment of all adults who need jobs, make the attainment of universal education easier and it would have the obvious and immediate effect of providing the women of low income countries some relief from constant pregnancy, parturition and infant care."[18]

L.R. Brown in his book on "Twenty-two Dimensions of the Population Problem", Washington D.C., 1976 has given Twenty-two dimensions of the population problem which underlines the need for the control of population growth. Important of them are:

- Hunger
- Housing
- Crowding
- Environmental Illness
- Income
- Urbanization
- Political Conflict
- Poor Health
- Lack of Water
- Unemployment
- Shortage of Energy
- No Individual Freedom
- Lack of Literacy
- Less Natural Recreation areas
- Pollution
- Inflation

With a population of about one billion, India has achieved many dubious distinctions. Now India is a country with largest number of unemployed youth, handicapped people, beggars, slum-dwellers and illiterate in the world. The population of illiterates in India is larger than the total population of any country in the world except for People's Republic of China. Every third illiterate in the world is an Indian. It is irony that in all these areas India, come what may, will lead the world for many more years to come. It is pity indeed that in near future we will be able to achieve a few more dubious demographic distinctions.[19]

What has happened elsewhere can happen in India too provided there is massive campaign to educate eligible couples, particularly in villages about the benefits of limiting the size of the family. This point has of course been emphasized innumerable times and at different places but it has never been sincerely implemented. Rural people, steeped in ignorance and obsolete religious belief, still do not know the harm that big family size brings to them and consider every child as a gift of God. This notion must be altered if family planning is to succeed. However, the education campaign must always be backed by easy availability of modern contraceptive measures that can enable people to plan their families. One of the reasons why family planning measures have not yielded the desired results is that it has not been honestly implemented. The unmet need for family planning has been reported to be quite high. According to the National Family Health Survey the current unmet need for family planning is 16 per cent and it is higher in rural areas than in urban areas.[20]

If the country opts for a natural course of demographic transition, then it will have to pay a heavy price in the form of unmanageable unemployment, rampant poverty, political chaos leading to ethnic violence and even dismemberment of the country in the long-run. In fact, the whole South Asia would have to encounter a similar experience and would take the shape of Africa or Europe in terms of number of independent nations fighting among themselves. Here the process have already set in, as the population bomb has already exploded. It is altogether a different matter that some of us at the helm of affairs deliberately tend to camouflage the reality or do not want to recognize it. Some of them even ignore the description of dismal demographic scenario of India by branding it a pure academic exercise. Even many Indian social scientists seem blissfully unaware of how rising population of India threatens its future, while the population issues have already started dominating India's future. One simply wonders whether new advancements in science and technology will really do any magic to save India from impending disaster following population explosion.[21]

NATIONAL POPULATION POLICY

Population Policy is a conscious, deliberate and explicit attempt of a government to influence the size, growth and composition of the population. However, population policies in the developing countries aim at the reduction of growth rate. However, we should not interpret that the population policies in the past have been directed towards increasing the growth rate and those of the present at decreasing the growth rate. In fact, population policies would differ as the need demands. For example, in early 1930's the Japanese Government encouraged increase in fertility but immediately after the Second World War Japan legalised abortions with a view to controlling its population growth. However, in a broad sense, population policy must be looked at not merely controlling the growth rate but all aspects of population to ensure quality of life to the people.

Former Prime Minister has rightly said on September 30, 1983, at New York, while receiving the United Nations Population Award:

It is said that prosperity is a good contraceptive. But the effects of development are submerged unless we bring about a low birth rate. Family Planning is an input for development, an indispensable exercise in human capital formation. Education, better capacity for producing and earning a higher rise in per capita income are possible only when population growth is curbed. A population policy based on realistic estimates and parameters can really generate the necessary momentum to ensure the slowing down of fertility and enriching the quality of life.

India adopted a comprehensive and holistic National Population Polity (NPP)-2000 with clearly articulated objectives, strategic themes and operational strategies. The Policy enumerates certain socio-demographic goals to be achieved by 2010, which will lead to achieving population stabilization by 2045. The Policy also prescribes an Action Plan for implementing the strategic themes listed in the Policy.

The National Population Policy, 2000 has identified the immediate objectives as meeting the unmet needs for contraception, health care infrastructure and trained health personnel and to provide integrated service delivery, with the following interventions: (i) Strengthen community health centres, primary health centres and sub-centres; (ii) Augment skills of health personnel and health care providers; (iii) Bring about convergence in the implementation of related social sector programme so that the Family Welfare Programme becomes a peoples' programme; (iv) Integrate package of essential services at village and household level through mobile clinics and counselling services; and (v) Explore the possibility of accrediting private medical practitioners and revive the system of licensed medical practitioners, who could provide specified clinical services.

National Population Policy (See Chart 16.2)

The National Population Policy, 2000 (NPP, 2000) affirms the commitment of Government towards voluntary and informed choice and consent of citizens while availing of reproductive health care services and continuation of the target free approach administering family planning services. The National Population Policy, 2000 provides a policy framework for advancing goals and prioritizing strategies during the next decade, to meet the reproductive and child health needs of the people of India, and to achieve net replacement levels of total fertility rate by 2010. It is based upon the need to simultaneously address issues of child survival, maternal health and contraception, while increasing outreach and coverage of a comprehensive package of reproductive and child health services with government, and industry and the voluntary non-government sector, working in partnership.

The immediate objective of the National Population Policy, 2000 is to address the unmet needs of contraception, health infrastructure, health personnel and to provide integrated service delivery for basic reproductive and child health care. The medium-term objective is to bring the total fertility rates to replacement level by 2010, through vigorous implementation of inter-sectoral operational strategies. The long-term objective is to achieve population stabilization by 2045, at a level consistent with the requirements of sustainable economic growth, social development and environment protection.

The 42th Constitutional Amendment has frozen the number of representatives in the Lok Sabha (on the basis of population) at 1971 Census levels. The freeze serves as an incentive for State Governments to fearlessly pursue the agenda for population sterilization. It has been extended until 2026.

National Commission on Population

The National Commission on Population, presided over by the Prime Minister, with the Chief Minister of all States and UTs, and the Central Ministers in-charge of concerned Central Ministries and Departments, reputed demographers, public health professionals and NGOs as

CHART 16.2

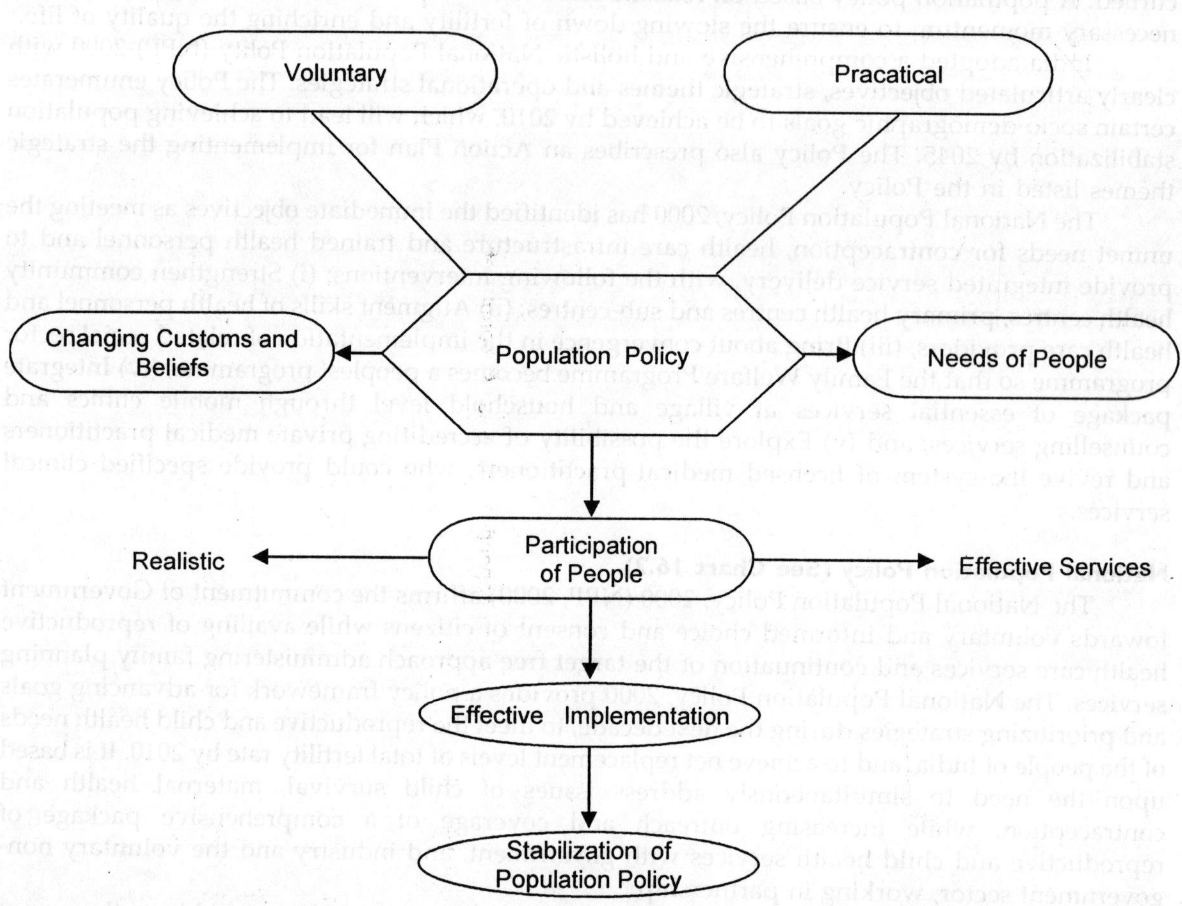

members, has already been constituted on 11th May, 2000. The Commission will oversee and review implementation of the National Population Policy.

State Population Commission

State Population Commissions have been constituted in Andhra Pradesh, Arunachal Pradesh, Assam, Haryana, Himachal Pradesh, J & K, Kerala, Madhya Pradesh, Maharashtra, Meghalaya, Mizoram, Punjab, Rajasthan, Sikkim, Tamil Nadu, A & N Island and Lakshadweep.

State Population Policies

Some State Governments have formulated their own State Population Policies with specific strategies, goals and programmes. These States are: Andhra Pradesh (1997), Rajasthan (December 1999), Madhya Pradesh (January 2000), Uttar Pradesh (July 2000), and Gujarat (March 2000). Some other States like Orissa and J & K have sent their draft population policies for eliciting comments of Government of India. Some States are offering: incentives and disincentives for promotion of two-child norms, as a measure for achieving population stabilization. The Government of India, does not support measures, which are in violation of the NPP, 2000, and has constituted a National Level Resources Committee to ensure that State Population Policies are in consonance with the letter and spirit of the NPP, 2000.[22]

Government of India has enunciated the new Population Policy in February, 2000. Commenting on the New Population Policy, *Business Standard Editorial*, "Sense on Population" dated February 17, 2000, remarked: The new national population policy, 2000, however may have a greater chance of acceptances it incorporates some of the lessons learnt from recent successes in curbing population growth. While the earlier attempts merely emphasized physical targets and ignored the vital aspects of health and education, especially that of the girl child, which are vitally linked to birth rates, the latest policy seeks to squarely address these issues. Besides, it also makes the right kind of noises about investment in social infrastructure as an essential prerequisite for promoting small family norms.

Success of the new policy will depend largely on the way it is implemented by the laggard states and the pace of socio-economic development (including in the field of health and education) that accompanies it. Measures like freezing the number of seats in the Lok Sabha at the current level are essentially facilitators, dispelling states' fears that population control will reduce their quota of MPs. There has to be an adequate political will to achieve the twin, veritably inseparable, objectives of reducing family size and improving the quality of life.

However, *The Tribune Editorial* "Gaps in Population Policy" dated February 17, 2000, suggested the gaps in new policy and stressed the need to make up these gaps. Increasing population packs a greater destructive power than what Pakistan can cause by hurling a few nuclear bomb-blasts. That is because it is concentrated at the bottom of the social and economic pyramid covering three-fourth of the population. The failure to control the exploding numbers is the most damaging, of all failures. What the country needed was a radical review of the old policies, alertness to deploy all available instruments and establish enduring contacts with the target segment in rural India. Sadly these are missing in the New National Population Policy unveiled. The document still pins its hopes on a few tired incentives and shapeless promises to rein in population growth. Such sops will be available only after the event—that is, after individuals or couples take themselves out of the reproduction cycle. Actually, the concentration should have been on goading people to enter the charmed circle.

STATUS IN INDIA

Demographic Scenario Status in India

The population of the country was 1027 million in March 2001 as per current census enumeration with 531 million males and 496 million females.[23]

India is following the demographic transition pattern of all developing countries from initial levels of "high birth rate-high death rate" to the intermediate transition stage of "high birth rate-low death rate."

The data from the Sample Registration System (SRS, 2000) indicate that the Crude Birth Rate (CBR) at the national level has gone down to 25.8 per 1000 population from a level of 29.5 in 1991. Within this, States exhibit-wide variation in the estimated Crude Birth Rates. Among major States, Uttar Pradesh (CBR 32.8), Rajasthan and Madhya Pradesh (CBR 31.2), Bihar (CBR 31.9), Haryana (CBR 26.9) and Assam (CBR 26.9) recorded higher crude birth rate than the national level of 25.8. Among smaller States and UTs and D&N Haveli (CBR 34.9), Meghalaya (CBR 28.5), Chhattisgarh

(CBR 26.7), Daman and Diu (CBR 27.3) and Jharkhand (CBR 26.5) recorded higher birth rate than the national average. The lowest birth rate was recorded in the State of Kerala (CBR 17.9) among major States. In smaller States and UTs, Goa (CBR 14.3) recorded the lowest birth rate during this year.

Crude Death Rate (SRS, 2000) at national level was estimated as 8.5. The States of Madhya Pradesh (CDR 10.2), Orissa (CDR 10.5), Uttar Pradesh (CDR 10.3), Assam (CDR 9.6) and Bihar (CDR 8.8) recorded excess from national average. Among the smaller States and UTs Chhattisgarh (CDR 9.6), Meghalaya (CDR 9.2) and Jharkhand (CDR 9.0) recorded higher Crude Death Rate than the national average.

The Infant Mortality Rate (IMR) 2000 was estimated to be 68 at national level. The States of Orissa (IMR 96), Madhya Pradesh (IMR 88), Uttar Pradesh (IMR 83), Rajasthan (IMR 79), and Assam (IMR 75), recorded higher IMR than the national average. As per SRS estimates, the Child Mortality Rate (CMR) (0-4) years has come down from 57.3 in 1972 to 26.5 in 1991 and 22.5 in 1998. The highest CMR has been recorded in Madhya Pradesh (32.6) followed by Uttar Pradesh (29.6) and Orissa (29.0) and the lowest in Kerala (3.6) per thousand children.

The natural growth rate, which is the difference between the birth rate and death rate, was estimated 1.73% in 2000 against 1.97% in 1991 and 1.91% in 1992.[24]

The current high population growth rate in some parts of the country is due to:

- The large size of population in the reproductive age group (estimated contribution 60%).
- Higher fertility due to unmet need for contraception (estimated contribution 20%).
- High wanted fertility due to prevailing high infant mortality rate (IMR) (estimated contribution about 20%).

A look at the census figures of the last four decades indicates a perceptible decline in recent years, in the growth rate of the country's population.

According to United Nations Population Division, World Population Prospects (the 1998 Revision):

Although, in terms of population USA ranks third in the world after India, there is a yawning gap of 746 million between the population of these two countries. India accounts for a meager 2.4 percent of the world surface area of 135.79 million square kms yet it supports and sustains a whopping 16.7 percent of the world population. In 1950, China with 22 percent share of the world population led the scene followed by India, which had a share of 14.2 percent. It is now estimated that by 2050, India will most likely overtake China to become the most populous country on the earth with 17.2 percent population living here.

The United Nations has estimated that the world population grew at an annual rate of 1.4 percent during 1990-2000. China registered a much lower annual growth rate of population (one percent) during 1990-2000, as compared to India (1.9 percent during 1991-2001). In fact, the growth rate of China is now very much comparable to that of the USA (0.9 percent).

Table 19.1 presents the population of India as recorded in each decadal census since 1901. Some other indicators of growth rate such as decadal growth rate, change in decadal growth, average annual exponential growth rate and progressive growth rate over 1901 during each decade have also been presented in this statement. Thus, the population of India, which at the turn of the twentieth century, was only around 238.4 million increased by more than four times in a period of hundred years to reach 1027 million at the dawn of the twenty first century.

Interestingly, the population of India grew by one and half times in the first half of the twentieth century, while in the later half it recorded almost a phenomenal three-fold increase. India's population growth during the twentieth century can be chartered and classified into four distinct phases as follows:

1901-1921: Stagnant population 1921-1951: Steady growth 1951-1981: Rapid high growth 1981-2001: High growth with definite signs of slowing down.

The story of population growth in India is fairly in tune with the classical theory of demographic transition. During most of the nineteenth century, India witnessed a fluctuating but ultimately more or less a stagnant growth of population, which drifted into the twentieth century until 1921. Thereafter, the country passed through successively all the phases of demographic transition and is now widely believed to have entered the fifth phase, usually characterized by rapidly declining fertility. The crucial question is—how long will this phase extend and when will India achieve a stable population? The National Population Policy (NPP), 2000, recently adopted by the Government of India states that 'the long-term objective is to achieve a stable population by 2045, at a level consistent with the requirements of sustainable economic growth, social development, and environment protection'. It has been assumed in the policy document that the medium-term objective of bringing down the Total Fertility Rate (TFR) to replacement level of 2.1 by 2010 will be achieved. It is envisaged that if the NPP is fully implemented, the population of India should be 1013 million by 2002 and 1107 million by 2010. However, in 2001 itself, India has already exceeded the estimated population for the year 2002 by about 14 million. It will no doubt require a Herculean effort on the part of the government and the people to achieve the much-cherished goal of a stable population.

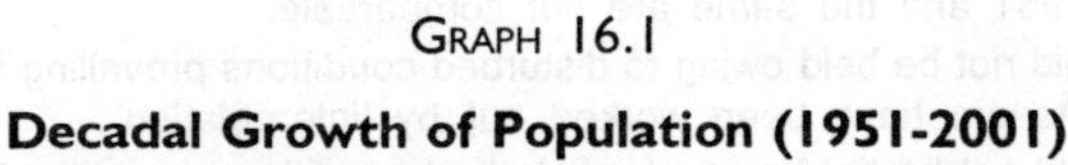
GRAPH 16.1

Decadal Growth of Population (1951-2001)

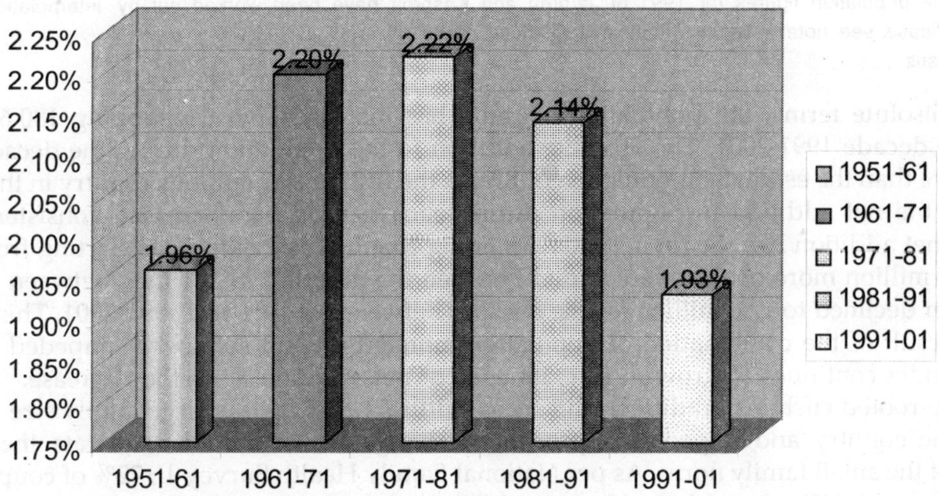

Source: Annual Report, 2002-03, Ministry of Health and Family Wekfare, GOI, New Delhi.

TABLE 16.1

Population and its Growth, India: 1901-2001

Census year	Population	Decadal Growth Absolute	Decadal Growth Percent	Change in decadal growth Absolute	Change in decadal growth Percent	Average annual exponential growth rate over 1901	Progr-essive growth rate (percent)
1901	238,396,327	—	—	—	—	—	—
1911	252,093,390	13,697,063	5.75	—	—	0.56	5.75
1921	251,321,231	-772,177	-031	-14,469,240	6.05	-0.03	543
1931	278,977,238	27,656,025	11.00	28,428,202	1.04	1.04	17.02
1941	318,660,580	39,683,342	14.22	12,027,317	1.33	1.33	33.67
1951	361,088,080	42,427,510	13.31	2,744,168	1.25	1.25	51.47
1961	439,234,771	78,146,681	21.64	35,719,171	1.96	1.96	84.25
1971	548,159,652	108,924,881	24.80	30,778,200	2.20	2.20	129.94
1981	683,329,097	135,169,445	24.66	26,244,564	3.16	2.22	186.64
1991	843,387,888	163,058,791	23.86	27,886,346	0.80	2.14	255.03
2001	1,027,015,247	180,627,359	21.35	17,568,568	-2.52	1.93	330.80

Note: 1. In working out 'Decadal Growth' and 'Percentage Decadal Growth' for India 1941-51 and 1951-61 the population of Tuensang district for 1951 (7,025) and the population of Tuensang (83,501) and Mon (5,774) districts for 1961 census of Nagaland state have not been taken into account as the areas were censuses for the first time in 1951 and the same are not comparable.

2. The 1981 Census could not be held owing to disturbed conditions prevailing in Assam. Hence the population figures for 1981 of Assam have been worked out by 'interpolation'.
3. The 1991 census could not be held owing to disturbed conditions prevailing in Jammu and Kashmir. Hence the population figures for 1991 of Jammu and Kashmir have been worked out by 'interpolation'.
4. Please see note 1 below graph at a Glance.

Source: Census

In absolute terms, the population of India has increased by a whopping 180.6 million during the decade 1991-2001. The absolute addition to the population during the decade 1991-2001 is more than the estimated population of Brazil, the fifth most populous country in the world. Although, the net addition in population during each decade has increased consistently, the change in net addition has shown a steady declining trend over the decades starting from 1961. While 27.9 million more people were added between the decade 1981-91 than between 1971-81, this number declined to 17.6 million for the decades between 1981-91 and 1991-2001. This implies that as a result of the combination of population momentum and somewhat impeded fertility, although India continues to grow in size, its pace of net addition is on the decrease.

Deep-rooted customs, traditions and socio-cultural belief favour large family size in many parts of the country and impede the process of change which would accelerate the willing adoption of the small family norm. As per National Family Health Survey-II, 72% of couples with two children and 84% of couples with three children are either sterilized or do not want more children. Socio-economic factors such as female literacy, age at marriage of girls, status of women, strong son preference and position of employment of women have a crucial bearing on the fertility behaviour of the people.[25]

As per Census-2001 Report, the growth in indices of GDP and food production has been more than the growth in population.

Initially, planners placed greater thrust on population control measure but later, the significance of addressing issues pertaining to Child and Mother Health was recognized. During the Sixth Five Year Plan (1980-85), Government of India adopted a National Health Policy with the aim of achieving "Health For all by year 2000" and undertook to develop a primary health care system as an integral part of this strategy. Universal Immunization Programme (UIP), Oral Rehydratiga Therapy (ORT) and safe motherhood programme were introduced nationwide during the Seventh Five Year Plan (1985-90). Under the Eighth Five Year Plan, achieving a slower rare of population growth was considered as one of the most important priorities facing the nation. During Ninth Five Year Plan, focus was on reduction in the population growth, mortality and achieving desired level of fertility. During Tenth Five Year Plan (2002-07), the main approach of the family welfare programme was to provide need-based, client centered and demand driven RCH care; to strengthen the infrastructure for service delivery and bridging the gap in essential infrastructure and manpower; providing additional assistance to poorly performing districts identified on the basis of the 1991 census and RCH Surveys and ensuring uninterrupted supply, of essential drugs and contraceptives; and promoting male participation in the planned Parenthood.

The Tenth Five Year Plan has identified the following monitorable targets relating to the Department of Family Welfare for the Plan (2002-07) and beyond: (See Table 16.2)

TABLE 16.2

Indicators	*Past Level*	*Current Level*
Crude Birth Rate (Per thousand population)	40.8 (1951)	25.8 (2000)
Crude Death Rate (per thousand population)	25.1 (1951)	8.5 (2000)
Infant Mortality Rate (per thousand live births)	146 (1951-61)	68 (2000)
Maternal Mortality Ratio	437 (1992-93)	407 (1998)
Total Fertility Rate (per woman)	6.0 (1951)	3.2(1999)
Couple Protection Rate (%)	10.4 (1970-71)	48.6
Life Expectancy at Birth (in years)	1951)	2001-06)
Male	37.1	63.67
Female	36.1	66.91
Immunization Status	1985-86	2001-02
For pregnant Woman		
TT	40	85.6
For Infants		
BCG	29	100.4
MEASLES	44	90.4
DPT	41	95.4
POLIO	36	96.0

Source: Ibid.

- Reduction in the decadal rate of population growth between 2001 and 2011 to 16.2%.
- Reduction in Infant Mortality Rate (IMR) to 45 per thousand live birth by 2007 and 28 by 2012.
- Reduction in Maternal Mortality Ratio (MMR) to 2 per thousand live births by 2007 and 1 by 2012.

The current Scenario in respect of these targets is as follows:

- The decadal growth rate of population has declined from 23.86% during 1981-91 to 21.34% during the decade 1991-2001.
- Infant Mortality Rate, which has been stagnant at a level of 70 during the 90's, has started showing a decline and currently it has been estimated to be 68 (SRS-2000).
- Maternal Mortality Ratio has been stagnant during the 90's and the current estimate of this indicator is 407 per 1,00,000 live births (SRS-1998).

As may be seen, the 10 States and Union Territories of Tamil Nadu, Kerala, Goa, Nagaland, Delhi, Pondicherry, A & N Islands, Chandigarh and Mizoram have already achieved replacement levels of fertility. The 11 States and Union Territories of Karnataka, Andhra Pradesh, West Bengal, Maharashtra, Punjab, Himachal Pradesh, Manipur, Arunachal Pradesh, Lakshadeep, Daman and Diu and Sikkim have Total Fertility Rate of more than 2.1 but less than 3.0. There are at least 12 states and Union Territories that have Total Fertility Rate of over 3. They are: Uttar Pradesh, Madhya Pradesh, Bihar, Rajasthan, Assam, Haryana, Gujarat, Tripura, Meghalya, Jammu & Kashmir, Dadar and Nagar Haveli. The 8 States of U.P., Madhya Pradesh, Uttaranchal, Chhattisgarh, Bihar, Jharkhand, Rajasthan and Orissa, which currently constitute nearly 44% of the total population of India, are projected to constitute 48% of the total population of India in 2016. In other words, these states alone will contribute an anticipated 55% increase during the period 1996-2016. Demographic outcomes in these states will determine the timing and size of population at which India achieves population stabilization.

The Eleventh Five Year Plan goal is to achieve a reduction of TFR to 2.1 by 2012. State specific goals have also been suggested. The Plan will ensure that all issues of demographic change, the population policies, and programmes to achieve population stabilization are addressed without violating the people's rights of decision-making and choices. Most importantly this should be done without adversely affecting the sex ratio.

Involvement of Civil Society and NGOs

As per the NFHS data, less than 10% of rural women report that they are visited by the ANMs during a year. On the other hand, there is a large pool of formally or informally qualified Rural Health Practitioners (RHPs) who meet the day-to-day health care needs of people in 6 lakh villages. In the Eleventh Five Year Plan, it is proposed to enlist their services for many tasks including the delivery of non-clinical methods of contraception and referring the clinical cases to the PHCs or FRUs. The successful experiment by a VO, Janmi, in Bihar may be studied and replicated.

There is an urgent need to increase the involvement of CSO, VOs and NGOs including private sector in the delivery of family planning services, especially in areas where the public sector is weak. Jansankhya Sthirata Kosh (JSK) (National Population Stabilization Fund) is a registered society of the MoHFW to accelerate population stabilization efforts. JSK is expected to work in close cooperation with the government, private, and voluntary sectors to promote small and healthy families. State governments, district officials, and other organizations will be encouraged to suggest innovations in enhancing family planning services which can be supported by JSK on a pilot scale. Expertise of the Population Foundation of India will be sought to scale up good pilots in the country. Centres of excellence can also play a vital role.

During the Eleventh Five Year Plan greater focus will be on the following for voluntary fertility reduction:

- Expanding the basket of contraceptive choices
- Improving social marketing
- Increasing male involvement
- Enhancing role of mass media for behavioural change
- Disseminating through satisfied users.[26]

POPULATION CONTROL—FAMILY PLANNING (See Chart 16.3)

Family planning programme makes a planned and scientific approach to the issues and problems of family life and attempts to solve them to make the family life happier, harmonious and fruitful. Family planning was thought of as a public health problem. It was stated in the First Five Year Plan:

It is apparent that population, "at a level consistent with the requirement of national economy should be stabilised." This can be secured only by the realisation of the need for family limitation on a wide scale by the people. The main appeal for planning is based on considerations of health and welfare of the family. Family limitation or spacing of the children is necessary and desirable in order to secure better health of the mothers, and better care and upbringing of children. The measures described to this end should, therefore, form part of the public health programme.

A distinction must be made between population control and family planning. Population control is influenced and determined by a government policy motivated by socio-economic considerations. Family planning, on the other hand, is a responsibility of the family. World Health Organization has given various definitions of family planning.

An Expert Committee (1991) of the WHO defined family planning as: "a way of thinking and living that is adopted voluntarily upon the basis of knowledge, attitudes and responsible decisions by individuals and couples, in order to promote the health and welfare of the family group and thus contribute effectively to the social development of the country."[27]

Another Expert Committee[28] defined and described family planning as follows: "Family Planning refers to practices that help individuals or couples to attain certain objectives:

(a) to avoid unwanted births;
(b) to bring about wanted births;
(c) to regulate the intervals between pregnancies;
(d) to control the time at which births occur in relation to the age of the parents; and
(e) to determine the number of children in the family."

A WHO Expert Committee (1970)[29] has stated that family planning includes in its purview: (1) the proper spacing and limitation of births, (2) advice on sterility, (3) education for parenthood

CHART 16.3

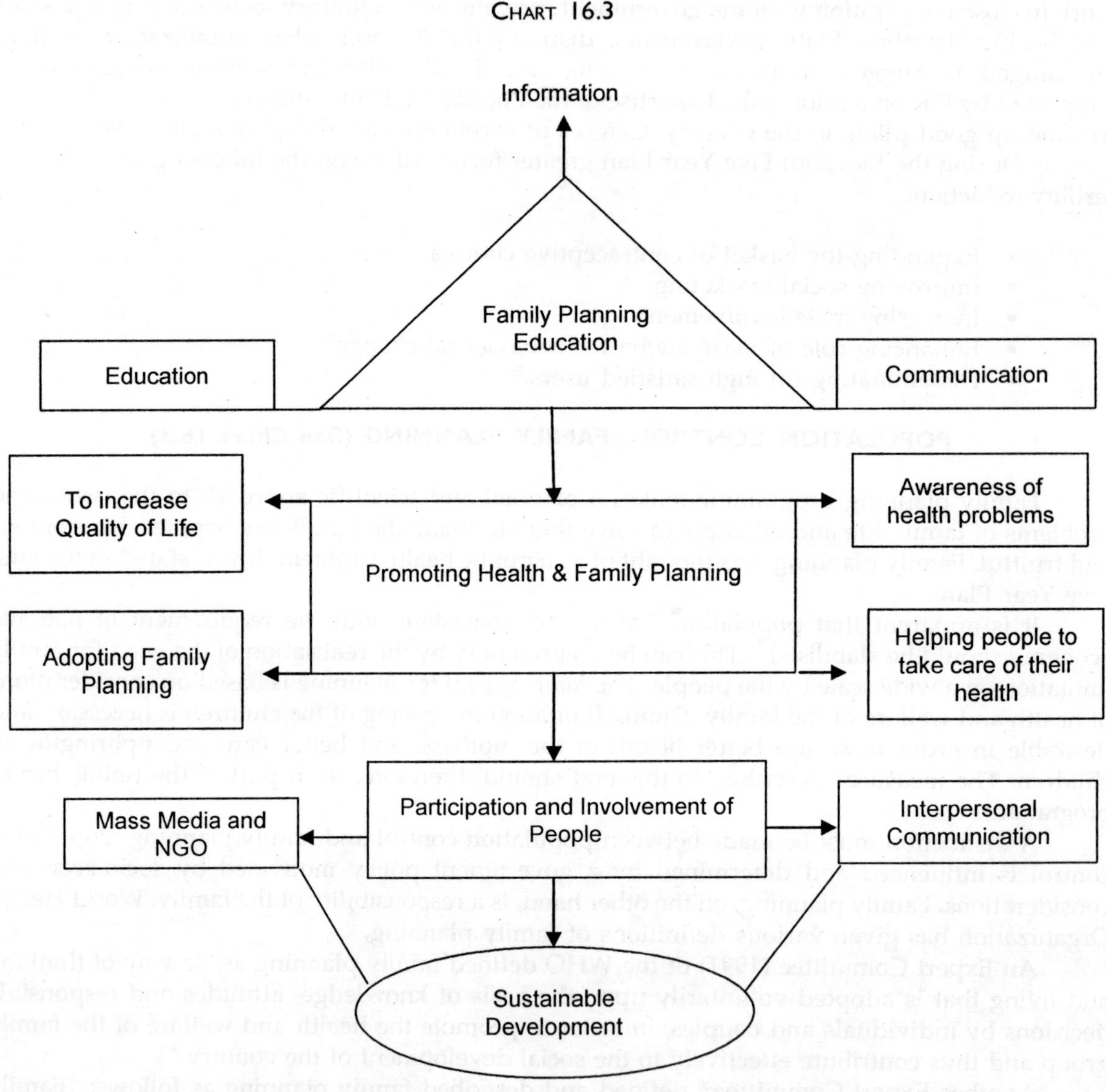

including pre-natal and post-natal care, (4) sex education, (5) screening for pathological conditions related to the reproductive system (e.g. cervical cancer), (6) genetic counseling, (7) pre-marital consultation and examination, (8) carrying out pregnancy tests, (9) marriage counselling, (10) the preparation of couples for the arrival of their first child, (11) providing services for unmarried mothers, (12) teaching home economics and nutrition, and (13) providing adoption services. These activities vary from country to country according to national objectives and policies with regard to family planning. This is the modern concept of family planning.

CRITICAL APPRAISAL

To quote J.P. Singh again, What has happened elsewhere can happen in India too provided there is a massive campaign to educate eligible couples, particularly in villages, about the benefits of limiting the size of the family. This point has of course been emphasised innumerable times and at different places but it has never been sincerely implemented. Rural people, steeped in ignorance and obsolete religious belief, still do not know the harm that big family size brings to them and consider every child as a gift of God. This notion must be altered if family planning is to succeed. However, the education campaign must always be backed by easy availability of modern contraceptive measures that can enable people to plan their families. One of the reasons why family planning measures have not yielded the desired results is that it has not been honestly implemented. The unmet need for family planning has been reported to be quite high. According to the National Family Health Survey 2, the current unmet need for family planning is 16 per cent and it is higher in rural areas than in urban areas.

Inspite of the existence of infrastructure and availability of technology to control the growth of population, we have not been achieving the desired results. K.B. Sahay[30] in his article, "Population: Time for Tough Measures", in the *Daily Tribune*, January 28, 2000, has rightly portrayed the present population scene which present a depressing picture. To quote him: "It is very well known that we are adding at least about 1.5 crore "additional" children every year to our population. Thus, the reality is that hardly 10 percent of the "additional" children accruing every year in India are getting (even) enrolment in primary schools and the rest 1.35 crore per year are being left to grow up without any school education. Thus, we need to open at least 60,000 new primary schools per year to meet the constitutional requirement whereas we have been opening only 6000 new primary schools per year. Thus, our "educational rate" is, in fact, declining about 1.4 per cent per year. It is feasible now for the country to open 60,000 new primary schools per year and provide free and compulsory primary education to all the children as required in the constitution without first controlling our population growth? And, again, it is possible to empower women without even primary school education?

It might be recalled that in 1970 Dr. Norman Borlaug, in his speech said that he gave on the occasion of receiving the Nobel Prize cautioned that whatever was being done by way of increasing food production would give us a breathing time of not more than 30 years which should be used to tame the population monster. We have now come to the end of that grace period but our population is still increasing by about 1.6 crore per year. Also, according to a recent study report, "Population, Food Production and Nutrition in India", published by UNFPA, India (Oct. 1999), "there is an urgent need to reduce population growth so that the demand for foodgrains can be reduced and effectively met."

The question arises as to what is the major problem? It may be mentioned that the main problem in the less developed world including India is that of inadequate and inefficient administration which directly or indirectly impinge on the implementation of family planning programmes. The success of family planning programmes can be ensured only through innovative, impartial, honest and efficient administration.

There is a need that Family Planning Administration must be modernized, i.e., recreated, renewed and revitalized to achieve the pre-designed changes and output. This needs a different trend and magnitude of administrative management, culture and capability especially in a challenging area of Family Planning.

CONCLUSION

Joung Wahang has identified some potential areas where administrative reforms and improvements can help in increasing operational efficiency, i.e.,

(a) To get F.P. methods (including instruments and services) identified and defined;
(b) To get sufficient amount and reliable quality of F.P. instruments and services available to the clients;
(c) To get F.P. instruments and services available to clients in the most appropriate places;
(d) To get F.P. instruments and services available to clients at the most reasonable prices and costs; and
(e) To get F.P. instruments and services available without any psychological embarrassment and disturbance to the privacy of clients.

We should not be pessimistic. We should hope that the present momentum built-up since the Sixth Plan would continue. We should not hesitate to bring about innovative changes to make the programme realistic. We cannot afford to allow the programme to go slow as the programme is a source of strength to all other schemes of socio-economic development, whatever may be their immediate goal. Prime Minister Indira Gandhi, has rightly said on September 30, 1983, at New York, while receiving the United Nations Population Award.

The enabling objectives during the Ninth Plan period, therefore, was to reduce the population growth rate by:

(a) meeting all the felt-needs for contraception, and
(b) reducing the infant and maternal morbidity and mortality so that there is a reduction in the desired level of fertility level and undertake area specific micro-planning, and
(c) To provide need-based, demand-driven high quality, integrated reproductive and child health care.
(d) Bridging the gaps in essential infrastructure and manpower through a flexible approach and improving operational efficiency through investment in social, behaviour and operational research.
(e) Providing additional assistance to poorly performing districts identified on the basis of the 1991 census to fill existing gaps in infrastructure and manpower.
(f) Ensuring uninterrupted supply of essential drugs, vaccines and contraceptives, adequate in quantity and appropriate in quality.
(g) Promoting male participation in the Planned Parenthood movement and increasing the level of acceptance of vasectomy.

Efforts will be intensified to enhance the quality and coverage of family welfare services through:

(a) Increasing participation of general medical practitioners working in voluntary, private, joint sectors and the active cooperation of practitioners of ISM and Homeopathy.
(b) Involvement of the Panchayat Raj Institutions for ensuring inter-sectoral coordination and community participation in planning, monitoring and management.

(c) Involvement of the industries, organised and unorganised sectors, agriculture workers and labour representatives.

It is said that prosperity is a good contraceptive. But the effects of development are submerged unless we bring about a low birth rate. Family Planning is an input for development, an indispensable exercise in human capital formation. Education, better capacity for producing and earning a higher rise in per capita income are possible only when population growth is curbed.

To quote J.P. Singh again, according to the provisional results of the 2001 Census, India's population stood 1,027 million on March 1, 2001, comprising 531 million males and 496 million females. From 361 million at the time of Independence the population reached one billion in 2001, registering an increase of nearly three times. All this had happened when the country is not in a position to guarantee adequate nutrition, healthcare and education to the burgeoning population. At the same time, it is also true that all this has happened because of mass poverty in the country. Indifferent governance is also partly responsible for the current demographic and health scenario. Every year about 18 million people were added to India's population during 1991-2001 as against 16 million annually during 1981-91. In other words, each year India's population increases by the equivalents of the number of inhabitants of Ghana, Australia, Mozambique or Saudi Arabia.

The creation of awareness is integral to the process of social development. The possibility for the power of communication to liberate the minds and potential of people to critical awareness is real in every field linked to human development, and the generation of public will hinges on effective communication of information and ideas that relate to people needs, aspirations and capacities for progress in thought and action. In this sense, getting the development process started is largely task of information, education and communication. (see Chart 16.3)

We may conclude with the words that as population plays a significant part in protecting the environment and attaining the cherished goal of sustainable development through fully integrating population into all aspects of policy-making and planning. Thus population and development are directly linked and hence this philosophy must be promoted.

NOTES AND REFERENCES

1. UN: F.E. 875, XIII, 7, p. 76.
2. GOI, Ministry of Health and Family Welfare, Annual Report, 1988-89.
3. UN: F.E. 875, XIII, 7, p. 76.
4. J.P. Singh, 'Problems of Population and Sustainable Development in India," *The Tribune*, Chandigarh, Thursday, July 15, 2004.
5. *Indian Journal of Public Administration*, Vol. XLIX, No. 1, January-March 2003, p. 94.
6. Gunnar Myrdal, Asian Drama: An Inquiry into the Poverty of Nations, Vol. III, London, 1968, p. 154.
7. WHO: Alexander Kessler, Family Planning and the role of WHO, *World Health*, May-June, 1994, p. 154
8. Frank Notestein, W., "Population Policy and Development, a summer View", *Population Debate*, Vol. I, Part Four, Para 4.
9. Government of India, Planning Commission, Fourth Five Year Plan, *op. cit.*, p. 31.
10. P.B. Desai, "Economic Development and Population Control", in "Aspects of Population Policy in India", Council for Social Development, New Delhi, 1969, p. 11.
11. Thomas Mathur: "India's Population: The Worsening Scenario", in *Yajna*, Vol. 30, No. 19, Oct. 16-31, 1986, p. 4.

12. Coale and Hoover, Population Growth and Economic Development in Low Income Countries, 1958, p. 19.
13. Geral Miere, Leading Issues in Economic Development, OUP, 1975, p. 591.
14. GOI, Planning Commission, Third Five Year Plan, p. 22.
15. FAO: Population, Food Supply and Agricultural Development, *Population Debate*, Vol. I, Part Four, Para 8.
16. Maryellen Fullen, "In People' a *Journal of International Planned Parenthood Federation*, Vol. 5, No. 4, 1978, p. 27.
17. P.F. Brockington: "The Health of the Development World", The Buh Guild Limited, Lewes, 1985, p. 94.
18. Ansley, J. Coale, "Population and Economic Development", in Phillip, M. Hauser (ed.): The Population Dilemma, p. 69.
19. J.P. Singh, 'Problems of Population and Sustainable Development in India", *Indian Journal of Public Administration*, Vol. XLIX, No. 1, January-March 2003, p. 88.
20. For detailed information on this issue see the findings of the National Family Health Surveys I & II India: Introductory Report, Mumbai, International Institute for Population Science, 1994 and 2000.
21. *Indian Journal of Public Administration*, Vol. XLIX, No. 1, January-March 2003, p. 94.
22. Annual Report, 2002-03, M/o Health and Family Welfare, GOI, pp. 145-52.
23. Family Welfare Programme in India, Year Book 2001, M/o Health and Family Welfare, GOI, New Delhi, p. 35.
24. *Ibid.*, pp. 35-36.
25. Family Welfare Programme in India, Year Book, 2001, M/o Health and Family Welfare, GOI, New Delhi, p. 35.
26. GOI, Planning Commission Eleventh Five Year Plan 2007-12, Vol. II, Social Sector, Planning Commission, GOI, p. 96
27. WHO (1971), Technical Report Series, 473.
28. WHO (1971), Technical Report Series, No. 483.
29. WHO Technical Report Series, No. 442.
30. *The Daily Tribune*, January 28, 2000.

CHAPTER

17

Policies and Programmes for Women Development and Empowerment

At the Union levels, Ministry of Women and Child Development, National Commission for Women, Central Social Welfare Board look after the welfare of women. At the state level, state agencies carry out women welfare activities. Voluntary organizations plays an important role.

WOMEN POPULATION

There has been a slight increase in the total female population of the country, from 407.1 million (48.1 percent of total population) in 1991 to 495.7 million (48.3 per cent) in 2001. While the percentage increase of 0.2 is very marginal, increase in term of absolute numbers was 88.6

TABLE 17.1

Sex Ratio (1981-2001)

Census	*Sex Ratio*
1981	934
1991	927
2001	933

Note: Sex Ratio: Females per thousand males.
Source: Census of India, 2001, Provisional Population.

million as against 77.1 million between 1981 and 1991. The grown rate of female population for the 1991-2001 decade was 21.79 percent, which was 0.86 percentage points higher than that of the total population. Yet, the demographic imbalances between women and men continue to exist till date. (Refer Table 17.1)

Expectation of Life

The life expectancy at birth among females has been steadily improving over the years from 23.3 in 1901 to 65.3 in 2001 and has surpassed that of men since the eighties. Male life expectancy in 2001 is 62.3 years. The urban female life expectancy is higher at 68. The rural-urban difference is the highest in Madhya Pradesh (8.6) and the lowest in Kerala (1.0). (Refer Table 17.2)

TABLE 17.2

Life Expectancy at Birth (1981-2001)

(In Years)

Year	*Females*	*Males*
1981-85	55.7	55.4
1989-93*	59.7	59.0
1996-2001	65.3	62.3

* Based on the Sample Registration System.
Source: *Ibid.* Estimates.

Maternal Mortality Rate

In India the Maternal Mortality Rate (MMR), which is calculated as the number of maternal deaths per 100,000 live births, is among the highest in the world and therefore a matter of great concern. It has come down from 468 in 1980 to 407 in 1988.

TABLE 17.3

Maternal Mortality Rate (1990-1998)

Per lakh live births

Year	*Maternal Mortality Rate*
1980	468
1993	437
1998	407

Source: *Ibid.*

There is wide range of variation in MMR across regions and States—from 28 in Gujarat to 707 in Uttar Pradesh.

Mean Age at Marriage

Similarly, the effective mean age at marriage for females has also increased from 18.3 years in 1981 to 19.5 years in 1997. The Child Marriage Restraint Act, 1976 which raised the age of marriage for girls from 15 to 18 years has no doubt, helped reduce child/early marriages and the consequent early pregnancies and birth of premature babies at the same time, education and employment of women/girls has also played a very important role in raising the age of marriage.

TABLE 17.4

Mean Age at Marriage (1981-1997)

(in years)

Year	*Females*	*Males*
1981	18.3	23.3
1991	19.5	23.9
1997	19.5	N.A.

Source: Sample Registration System Bulletins for respective years, Registrar-General and Census Commissioner, GOI, New Delhi.

While the Birth Rate has declined by 7.8 points from 33.9 in 1981 to 26.1 in 1999, the Death Rate has also declined by 3.8 points from 12.5 in 1981 to 8.7 in 1999. (Refer Table 17.4 and 17.5)

TABLE 17.5

Birth Rate (1981-1999)

(per thousand)

Year	*Birth Rate*
1981	33.9
1991	29.5
1999	26.1

Source: Ibid.

TABLE 17.6

Death Rate (1981-1999)

(per thousand)

Year	*Females*	*Males*	*Total*
1981	12.7	12.4	12.5
1991	9.7	10.0	9.8
1999	8.3	9.0	8.7

Source: Ibid.

To sum up, Table 17.7 presents the status of women including that of the girl child along with the progress made by them over a period of two development decades (1981-2001) as reflected in the 21 Selected Gender Development Indicators. (Table 17.7)

TABLE 17.7

The 21 Selected Gender Development Indicators: 1981 to 2001

Sr. No.	Indicators	Women	Men	Total	Women	Men	Total
(1)	(2)	(3)	(4)	(5)	(6)	(7)	(8)
	Demography and Vital Statistics						
1.	Population (in million in 1981-2001)	330.0	353.4	683.4	495.7	531.3	1027.0
2.	Decennial Growth (1981 and 2001)*	24.93	24.41	24.66	21.79	20.93	21.34
3.	Sex Ratio (1981 and 2001)**	934	-	-	933	-	-
4.	Life Expectancy at Birth in years in (1981-85 and 1996-01)	55.7	55.4	-	65.3	62.3	-
5.	Mean Age of Marriage in years in (1981 and 1991)	18.3	23.3	-	19.5	23.9	-
	Health and Family Welfare						
6.	Birth Rate (per thousand in 1981 and 1999)	—	-	33.9	-	-	26.1
7.	Death Rate (per thousand in 1981 and 1999)	12.7	12.4	12.5	8.3	9.0	8.7
8.	Infant Mortality Rate (per thousand live births in 1988 and 1999)	93.0	96.0	94.5	70.8	69.8	70.0
9.	Child Mortality Rate (per thousand live births under 5 years of age in 1985 and 1997)	40.4	36.6	-	24.5	21.8	-
10.	Maternal Mortality Rate (per one lakh live births in 1980 and 1998)	468	-	-	407	-	-
	Literacy and Education						
11.	Literacy Rates (1981 and 2001)*	29.76	56.38	43.57	54.16	75.85	65.38
12.	Gross Enrolment Ratio (1980-81 and 1999-2000)						
	—Classes I-V	64.1	95.8	80.5	85.2	104.1	94.9
	—Classes VI-VII	28.6	54.3	41.9	49.7	67.2	58.8
13.	Drop-out Rate (1980-81 and 1999-2000)						
	—Classes I-V	62.5	56.2	58.7	42.3	38.7	40.3
	—Classes VI-VIII	79.4	68.0	72.7	58.0	52.0	54.6

Work and Employment						
14. Work Participation Rate (1981 and 2001)*	19.7	52.6	36.7	25.7	51.9	39.3
15. Organised Sector (No. in million in 1981 and 1999)	2.80 (12.2%)	20.05	22.85	4.83 (17.2%)	23.28	28.11
16. Public Sector (No. in million in 1981 and 1999)	1.5 (9.7%)	14.0	15.5	2.8 (14.5%)	16.6	19.4
17. Government (No. in million in 1981 and 1997)	1.2 (11%)	9.7	10.9	1.6 (14.6%)	9.1	10.7
Decision-Making						
18. Administration (No. in IAS and IPS in 1987 and 2000)	360 (5.4%)	6262	6622	645 (7.6%)	7815	8460
19. PRIs (No. in thousand in 1995 and 2001)	318... (33.5%)	630...	948...	725 (26.6%)	1997	2722
20. Parliament (No. in 1998 and 2001)	594 (7.2%)	761	820	70 (8.5%)	750	820
21. Central Council of Ministers (No. in 1985 and 2001)	4 (10%)	36	40	8 (10.8%)	66	74

* Figures in per cent; ** Females per 1,000 males; *** Refers to 1995 in respect of some states, namely, Gujarat, Haryana, Karnataka, Kerala, Madhya Pradesh, Punjab, Rajasthan, Tripura and West Bengal.

Notes: (i) Figures in prentheses indicate the percentage to the total and year of the data in respective columns. Although, efforts were made to keep a common 'base and common comparable year', but the same could not be kept up because of the limitations in the availability of data and other practical problems; (ii) The years given in the parentheses refers to the year of the data in columns 3, 4, 5, 6, 7 and 8 respectively.

Source: Official Documents.

1. Census of India, 1991, Census of India, 2001: Provisional Population Totals; and SRS Bulletins for respective years, Registrar General and Census Cimmissioner, GOI, New Delhi; 2. Selected Educational Statistics for respective years, Dept. of Education, Ministry of HRD, New Delhi; 3. Annual Report, 1999-2000, Depts. of Elementary and Literacy and Secondary and Higher Education, Ministry of HRD, New Delhi; 4. Employment Exchange Statistics, DGE&T, Ministry of Labour, New Delhi, 5. Dept. of Personnel and Training, New Delhi; 6. Ministry of Rural Development, New Delhi; 7. Election Commission of India, New Delhi; 8. National Informatics Centre, Parliament House, New Delhi.

A quick review of the progress made by women has not only focused light on the gains but also brought forth to surface certain critical areas of concern relating to women by Draft Tenth Plan requiring attention of the Government during the Tenth Plan. They include: increasing burden of poverty; unequal access to primary health care, under/malnutrition, high rates of illiteracy and lack of training; lack of access and control on assets and resources; inequalities in sharing of power and decision-making; lack of access to information and media; increasing violence against women, adolescent and the girl child persisting discrimination against the girl child, etc. Keeping these Issues/Concerns in view.

The Constitution of India has guaranteed equality before law and equal protection of law (Art. 14) and prohibits discriminatory provisions for women and children (Art. 15). It has made provisions to prohibit traffic in human beings and provides for just and human conditions of work along with maternity relief (Art. 23 and Art. 42). It is a constitutional duty of every citizen to renounce practices derogatory to the dignity of women (Art. 51A).

The special attention given to the needs and problems of women to enable them to enjoy and exercise their Constitutional equality of status, along with other specific provisions relating to the hitherto suppressed sections of our society have led many scholars to describe the Indian Constitution as a 'social' document embodying the objectives of a social revolution. There is no doubt that the Constitution contemplates attainment of an entirely new social order by making deliberate departures in norms and institutions of democratic governance from the inherited social, political and economic systems. In doing so the Constitution assigns primacy to law as an instrument of directed social change. It thus demands of the legislature, the executive and the judiciary, continuous vigilance and responsiveness to the relationship between law and social transformation in contemporary India.

We believe: (See Chart 17.1)

1. that equality of women is necessary, not merely on the grounds of social justice, but as a basic condition for social, economic and political development of the nation;
2. that in order to release women from their dependent and unequal status, improvement of their employment opportunities and earning power has to be given the highest priority;
3. that society owes a special responsibility to women because of their child-bearing function. Safe bearing and rearing of children is an obligation that has to be shared by the mother, the father and society;
4. that the contribution made by an active housewife to the running and management of a family should be admitted as economically and socially productive and contributing to national savings and development;
5. that marriage and motherhood should not become a disability in women's fulfilling their full and proper role in the task of national development. Therefore, it is important that society, including women themselves, must accept their responsibility in this field;
6. that disabilities and inequalities imposed on women have to be seen in the total context of a society, where large sections of the population—male and female, adults and children—suffer under the oppression of an exploitative system. It is not possible to remove these inequalities for women only. Any policy or movement for the emancipation and development of women has to form a part of a total movement for removal of inequalities and oppressive social institutions, if the benefits and privileges

CHART 17.1

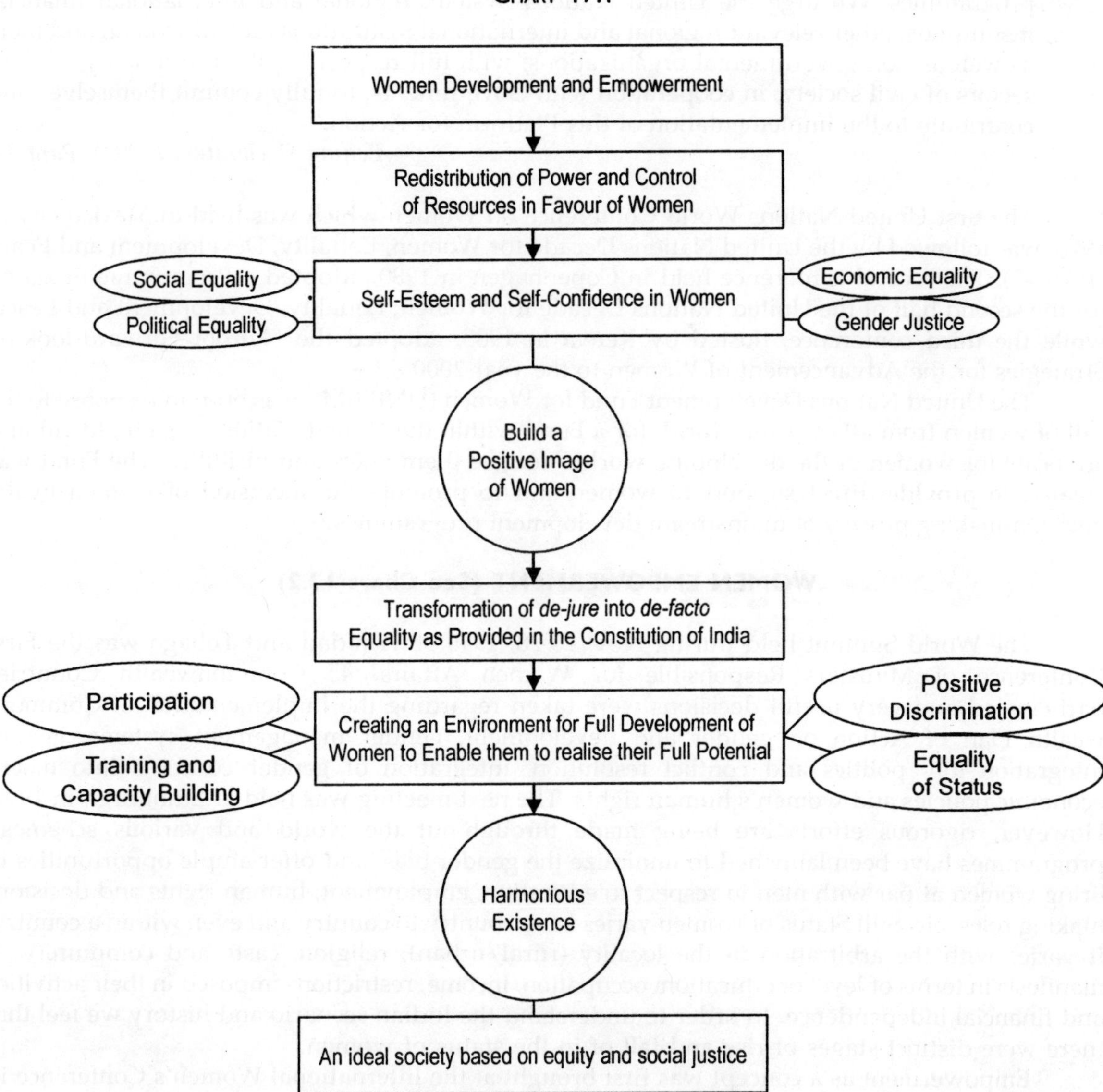

won by such action are to be shared by the entire women population and not be monopolized by a small minority; and

7. that if our society is to move in the direction of the goals set by the Constitution, then special temporary measures will be necessary, to transform *de-jure* into *de facto* equality.[1]

"We hereby adopt and commit ourselves as Governments to implement the following Platform for Action, ensuring that a gender perspective is reflected in all our policies and programmes. We urge the United Nations System, regional and international financial institutions, other relevant regional and international institutions and all women and men, as well as non-governmental organizations, with full respect for their autonomy, and all sectors of civil society, in cooperation with Governments, to fully commit themselves and contribute to the implementation of this Platform for Action."

—*Beijing Declaration (1995), Para 38.*

The first United Nations World Conference on Women which was held in Mexico city in 1975, was followed by the United Nations Decade for Women; Equality, Development and Peace (1976-85). The second conference held in Copenhagen in 1980, adopted a Programme of action for the second half of the United Nations Decade for Women; Equality, Development and Peace, while the third conference, hosted by Kenya in 1985, adopted the Nairobi Forward-looking Strategies for the Advancement of Women to the year 2000.

The United Nations Development Fund for Women (UNIFEM), was born in response to the call of women from all over the world, for a Fund within the United Nations system, to aid and advocate for women of the developing world—to give them voice and visibility. The Fund was created to provide direct support to women and to promote the inclusion of women in the decision-making process of mainstream development programmes.[2]

WOMEN EMPOWERMENT (See Chart 17.2)

The World Summit held during Nov. 25-28, 1996 at Trinidad and Tobago was the First Conference of Ministers Responsible for Women Affairs. 45 Commonwealth Countries participated and very useful decisions were taken regarding the implementation of Commonwealth Plan of Action on gender and development, gender management systems, gender integration into politics and conflict resolution, integration of gender concerns into macro economic policies and women's human rights. The next meeting was held at Edinburgh in 1997. However, rigorous efforts are being made through-out the world and various schemes/programmes have been launched to minimize the gender bias, and offer ample opportunities to bring women at par with men in respect to education, employment, human rights and decision-making roles, etc. Still Status of women varies from country to country and even within a country. It varies with the arbitration in the locality (rural/urban), religion, caste and community. It manifests in terms of level of education, occupation, income, restrictions imposed in their activities and financial independence. In order to understand the Indian scenario and history we feel that there were distinct stages of rise and fall of in the status of women.[3]

Empowerment as a concept was first brought at the International Women's Conference in 1985 at Nairobi. The conference concluded that empowerment is a redistribution of power and control of resources in favour of women through positive intervention.

The Programme of Action 1992 has comprehensively given the below mentioned parameters of empowerment of women:

- Enhance self-esteem and self-confidence in women.
- Build a positive image of women by recognizing their contribution to the society, polity and economy.
- Develop in them an ability to think critically.
- Foster decision-making and action through collective process.

- Enable women to make informed choices in areas like education, employment and health especially reproductive health.
- Ensure equal participation in the developmental process.
- Provide information, knowledge and skill for economic independence.
- Enhance access to legal literacy and information related to their rights and entitlements in the society with a view to enhance their participation on an equal footing in all areas.

CHART 17.2

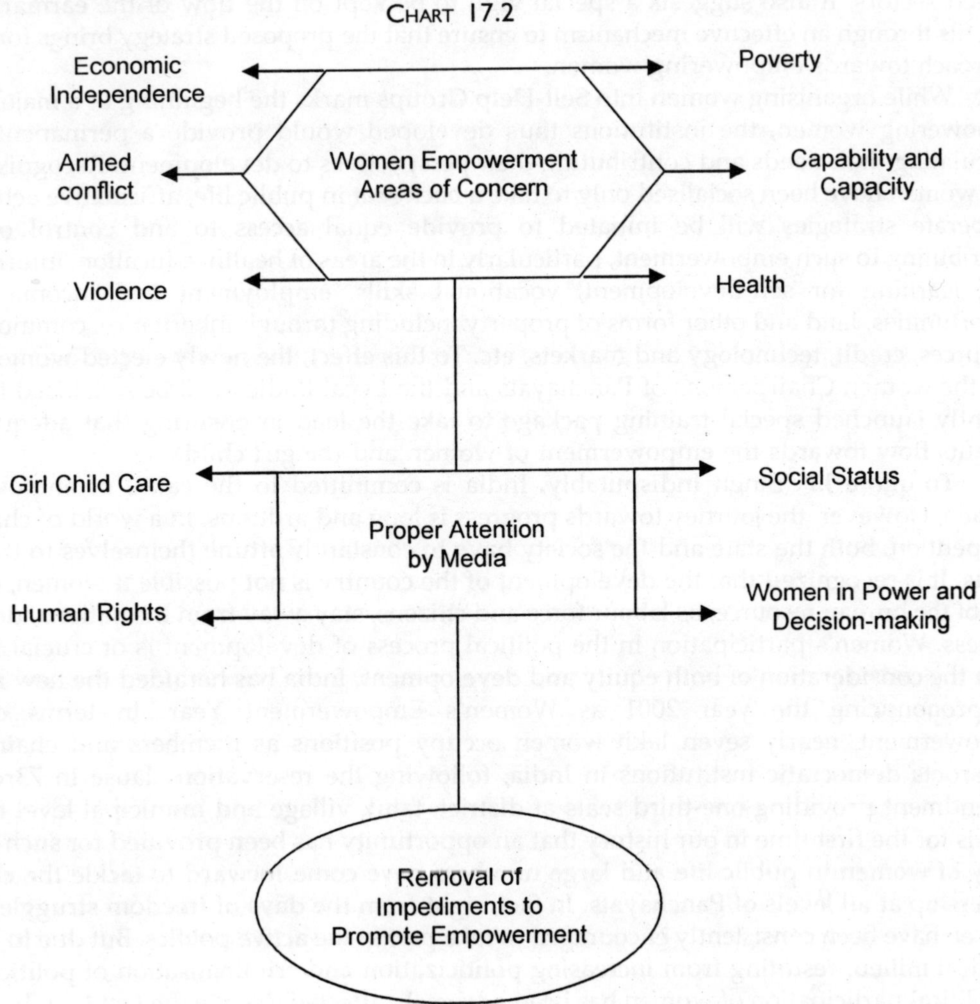

Empowerment of women' being one of the nine primary objectives of the Ninth Plan, every effort will be made to create an enabling environment where women can freely exercise their rights both within and outside home, as equal partners along with men. This will be realized through early finalization and adoption of the 'National Policy for Empowerment of Women' which laid down definite goals, targets and policy prescriptions along with a well defined Gender Development Index to monitor the impact of its implementation in raising the status of women from time to time.

An integrated approach will be adopted towards empowering women through convergence of existing services, resources, infrastructure and manpower available in both women-specific and women-related sectors with the ultimate objective of achieving the set goal. To this effect, the Ninth Plan directs both the Centre and the States to adopt a special strategy of 'Women's Component Plan' through which, not less than 30 per cent of funds/benefits are earmarked in all the women-related sectors. It also suggests a special vigil to be kept on the flow of the earmarked funds/ benefits through an effective mechanism to ensure that the proposed strategy brings forth a holistic approach towards empowering women.

While organising women into Self-Help Groups marks the beginning of a major process of empowering women, the institutions thus developed would provide a permanent forum for articulating their needs and contributing their perspectives to development. Recognising the fact that women have been socialised only to take a back seat in public life, affirmative action through deliberate strategies will be initiated to provide equal access to and control over factors contributing to such empowerment, particularly in the areas of health, education, information, life-long learning for self-development, vocational skills, employment and income generating opportunities, land and other forms of property including through inheritance, common property, resources, credit, technology and markets, etc. To this effect, the newly elected women members and the women Chairpersons of Panchayats and the Local Bodies will be sensitised through the recently launched special training package to take the lead in ensuring that adequate funds/ benefits flow towards the empowerment of women and the girl child.

To quote J.P. Singh Indisputably, India is committed to the cause of empowerment of women, However, the journey towards progress is long and arduous. In a world of challenge and competition, both the state and the society have to constantly attune themselves to the changing needs. It is recognized that the development of the country is not possible if women, comprising half of the human resource, as labour force and citizens, stay away from the national development process. Women's participation in the political process of development is of crucial importance from the consideration of both equity and development. India has heralded the new millennium by pronouncing the year 2001 as Women's Empowerment Year. In terms of political empowerment, nearly seven lakh women occupy positions as members and chairpersons of grassroots democratic institutions in India, following the reservation clause in 73rd and 74th Amendment providing one-third seats at district, taluk village and municipal level for women. This is for the first time in our history that an opportunity has been provided for such substantial entry of women in public life and large numbers have come forward to tackle the challenge of leadership at all levels of Panchayats. In fact, right from the days of freedom struggle the Indian women have been consistently encouraged to take part in the active politics. But due to the vitiated political milieu, resulting from increasing politicization and criminalisation of politics, the level of political participation of women has been adversely affected despite the fact that there has been a marked increase in the level of literacy and political awareness of women.[4]

It is recognized that the goals of poverty alleviation are difficult to achieve without the full and active participation of women, who constitute a large section of the workforce in the country. Women's empowerment is critical to the process of development of the community and, therefore, bringing them into the mainstream of development has been a major concern of the Government.

Towards this end and in order to empower women, an enabling environment, with requisite policies and programmes, institutional mechanisms at various levels and adequate financial resources has been created. The Ministry of Rural Development has special components for women in its programmes and funds are earmarked as 'Women's Component' to ensure flow of adequate resources for their development.[5]

The 73rd and 74th Amendments to the Constitution passed by the Parliament in 1992 and ratified in 1993 provide for 33 per cent reservation among elected representatives to the local governments. This has been hailed as a watershed achievement in empowerment of women, as over one million rural women have joined village panchayat posts as sarpanch or adhyaksha or members of community administration.

Policy for the Empowerment of Women

In order to address the concerns of women in society, the Government of India has established the Department of Women and Child Development within the Ministry of Human Resource Development which has been redesigned as independent Ministry of Women and Child Development. A National Policy for the Empowerment of Women, 2001, provides the framework for addressing women's issues. The objectives of the policy are as follows:

- Creating an environment through positive economic and social policies for full development of women to enable them to realize their full potential.
- The *de-jure* and *de-facto* enjoyment of all human rights and fundamental freedom by women on equal basis with men in all spheres-political, economic, social, cultural and civil.
- Equal access to participation and decision-making of women in social, political and economic life of the nation.
- Equal access to women to health care, quality education at all levels, career and vocational guidance, employment, equal remuneration, occupational health and safety, social security and public office, etc.
- Strengthening legal systems aimed at elimination of all forms of discrimination against women.
- Changing societal attitudes and community practices by active participation and involvement of both men and women.
- Mainstreaming a gender perspective in the development process.
- .Elimination of discrimination and all forms of violence against women and the girl child.
- Building and strengthening partnerships with civil society, particularly women's organizations.

Poornima Advani in her Preface to Year of Endeavour, 2002 rightly states that the last century has been witness to several revolutions, economic and political, with various 'isms' e.g. socialism, capitalism, fascism, etc. wrestling for primacy. They sought to redefine the relations between classes and masses, and between man and man. But the social revolution which promises to transform society even more fundamentally has just begun. This is the movement for women's rights, which affects every home, every factory and every office. Concerning, as it does, half the population of the globe, that is, all womankind, this issue will be centre stage in the political discourse of the coming decades world-wide.

The winds of change have been blowing furously here at home also. The Constitutional mandate of equality for all citizens, the myraid law and rulings designed to protect this equality and the numerous schemes introduced by the Government to strengthen women's status have erected a framework for protecting and promoting the rights and conditions of women in our country.

However, true equality and dignity are still a far cry for women. Social degradation, economic inequality and criminal wrongs are commonly heard of even today. There is thus a huge shadow that falls between the promise and the reality.

POLICIES AND PROGRAMMES IN FIVE YEAR PLANS: A REVIEW (See Chart 17.3)

Development of women has been receiving attention of the government right from the very First Plan (1951-56). But, the same has been treated as a subject of 'welfare' and clubbed together with the welfare of the disadvantaged groups like destitute, disabled, aged, etc. The Central Social Welfare Board (CSWB), set-up in 1953, acts as an Apex Body at national level to promote voluntary action at various levels, especially at the grassroots, to take up welfare-related activities for women and children. The Second to Fifth Plans (1956-79) continued to reflect the very same welfare approach, besides giving priority to women's education, and launching measures to improve maternal and child health services, supplementary feeding for children and expectant and nursing mothers.

The shift in the approach from 'welfare' to 'development' of women could take place only in the Sixth Plan (1980-85). Accordingly, the Sixth Plan adopted a multi-disciplinary approach with a special thrust on the three core sectors of health, education and employment. In the Seventh Plan (1985-90), the developmental programmes continued with the major objective of raising their economic and social status and bringing them into the mainstream of national development. A significant step in this direction was to identity/promote the 'Beneficiary-Oriented Schemes' (BOS) in various developmental sectors which extended direct benefits to women. The thrust on generation of both skilled and unskilled employment through proper education and vocational training continued. The Eight Plan (1992-97), with human development as its major focus, played a very important role in the development of women. It promised to ensure that benefits of development from different sectors do not by-pass women, implement special programmes and to monitor the flow of benefits to women from other development sectors and enable women to function as equal partners and participants in the development process.

The Ninth Plan (1997-2002) made two significant changes in the conceptual strategy of planning for women. Firstly, 'Empowerment of Women' became one of the nine primary objectives of the Ninth Plan. To this effect, the Approach of the Plan was to create an enabling environment where women could freely exercise their rights both within and outside home, as equal partners along with men. Secondly, the Plan attempted 'convergence of existing service' available in both women-specific and women-related sectors. To this effect, it directed both the center and the states to adopt a special strategy of 'Women's Component Plan' (WCP) through which not less than 30 per cent of funds/benefits flow to women from all the general development sectors. It also suggested that a special vigil be kept on the flow of the earmarked funds/benefits through an effective mechanism to ensure that the proposed strategy brings forth a holistic approach towards empowering women.

To ensure that other general developmental sectors do not by-pass women and benefits from these sectors continue to flow to them, a special mechanism of monitoring the 27 BOS for women was put into action in 1986, at the instance of the Prime Minister's Office (PMO). The same continues to be an effective instrument till today.

CHART 17.3

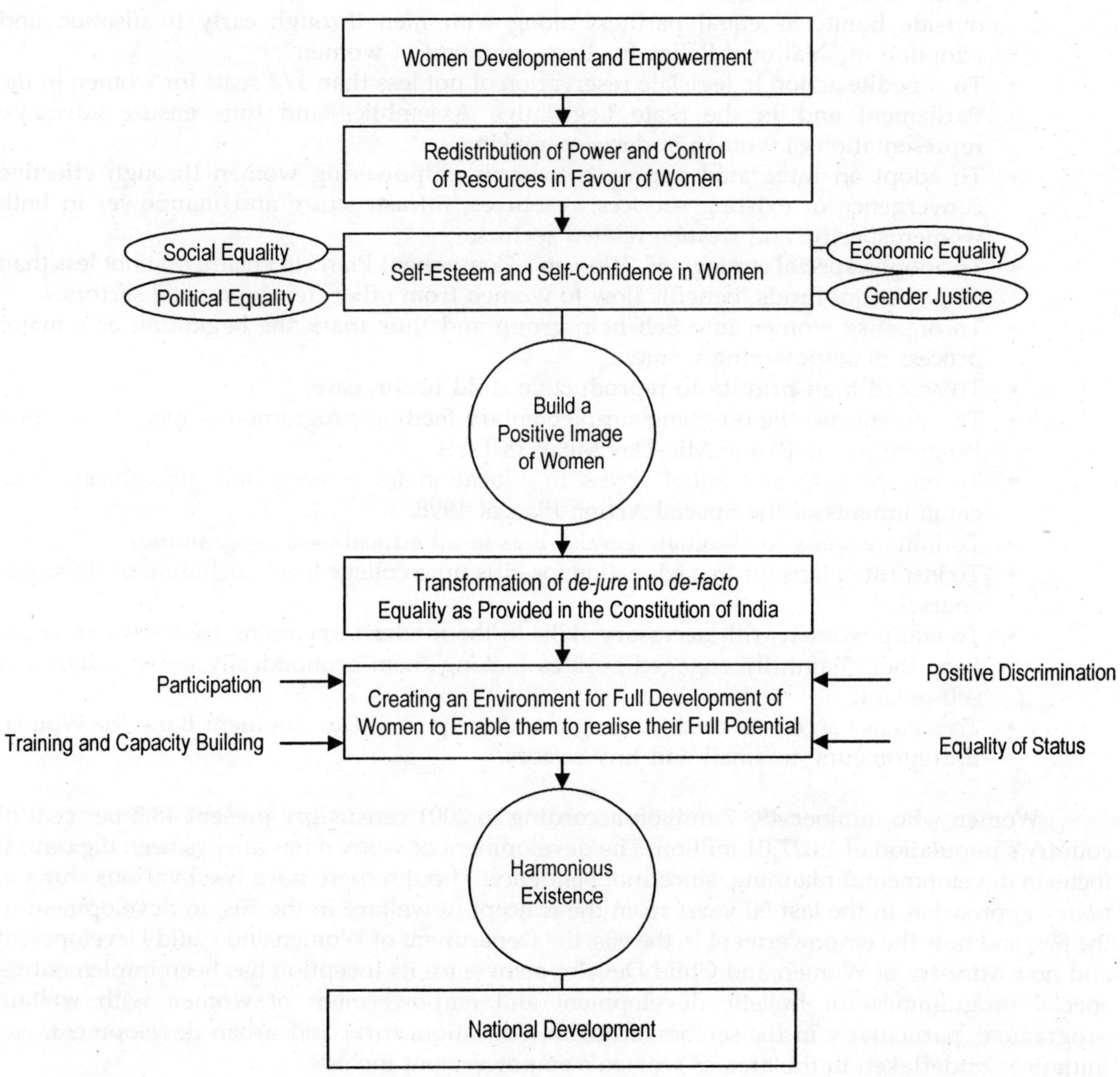

COMMITMENTS OF THE NINTH PLAN (1997-2002)

Objective

- Empowering Women As The Agents Of Social Change And Development

Strategies

- To create an enabling environment for women to exercise their rights, both within and outside home, as equal partners along with men through early finalisation and adoption of "National Policy for Empowerment of women".
- To expedite action to legislate reservation of not less than 1/3 seats for women in the Parliament and in the State Legislative Assemblies and thus ensure adequate representation of women in decision-making.
- To adopt an integrated approach towards empowering women through effective convergence of existing services, resources, infrastructure and manpower in both women specific and women related sectors.
- To adopt a special strategy of "Women's Component Plan" to ensure that not less than 30 percent of funds/benefits flow to women from other developmental sectors.
- To organise women into Self help group and thus mark the beginning of a major process of empowering women.
- To accord high priority to reproductive child health care.
- To universalise the on-going supplementary feeding programme—Special Nutrition Programme (SNP) and Mid-Day Meals (MDM).
- To ensure easy and equal access to education for women and girls through the commitments of the Special Action Plan of 1998.
- To initiate steps to eliminate gender bias in all educational programmes.
- To institute plans for free education for girls upto college level, including professional courses.
- To equip women with necessary skills in the modern upcoming trades which could keep them gainfully engaged besides making them economically independent and self-reliant.
- To increase access to credit through setting up of a 'Development Bank for Women Entrepreneurs' in small and tiny sectors.[6]

Women who number 498.7 million according to 2001 census pre-present 48.2 per cent of country's population of 1,027.01 million. The development of women has always been the central focus in developmental planning, since Independence. Though there have been various shifts in policy approaches in the last 50 years from the concept of welfare in the 70s, to development in the 80s, and now the empowerment in the 90s, the Department of Women and Child Development and now Ministry of Women and Child Development since its inception has been implementing special programmes for holistic development and empowerment of women with welfare programme, particularly in the sectors of health, education, rural and urban development, etc. Initiatives undertaken in the area of women's empowerment include:[7]

- Welfare and Support Services
- Employment and Training
- Socio-economic Programme
- Swayamsiddha
- Swa-shakti Project
- Balika Samriddhi Yojna
- Plan of Action to combat Sexual Exploitation of Women and Children

- Declaring 2001 as Women's Empowerment year
- Instituting National Commission for Women
- Rashtriya Mahila Kosh
- National Institute of Public Cooperation and Child Development
- Central Social Welfare Board
- Food and Nutrition Board
- Information and Mass Education

COMMITMENTS OF THE TENTH PLAN TO EMPOWER WOMEN

The Approach

To continue with the major strategy of 'Empowering Women' as Agents of Social Change and Development.

Strategies

To adopt a Sector-specific 3-Fold Strategy for empowering women, based on the prescriptions of the National Policy for Empowerment of Women. They include:

- **Social Empowerment**—to create an enabling environment through various affirmative developmental policies and programmes for development of women besides providing them easy and equal access to all the basic minimum services so as to enable them to realize their full potentials;
- **Economic Empowerment**—to ensure provision of training, employment and income-generation activities with both 'forward' and 'backward' linkages with the ultimate objective of making all potential women economically independent and self-reliant; and
- **Gender justice**—to eliminate all forms of gender discrimination and thus, allow women to enjoy not only the *de-jure* but *de-facto* rights and fundamental freedom on par with men in all spheres, viz. political, economic, social, civil, cultural, etc.

Social Empowerment

Create an enabling environment through adopting various affirmative development policies and programmes for development of women, besides providing them easy and equal access to all the basic minimum services so as to enable them to realize their full potential through—

- Providing easy and equal access to ensure basic minimum service of primary health care and family welfare with a special focus on the under-served and under-privileged segments of population through universalizing Reproductive and Child Health (RCH) services.
- Achieving the goals set by the National Population Policy (2000) with regard to reducing infant mortality Rate (IMR) to 30 per thousand and Maternal Mortality Rate (MMR) to 100 per lakh live births by 2010.
- Supplementing health care and nutrition services through the Pardhan Mantri Gramodaya Yojana (PMGY) to fill the critical gaps in the existing primary health care infrastructure and nutrition services.

- Taking both macro and micro-nutrient deficiencies through nutrition, supplementary feeding and nutrition education and nutrition awareness, etc.
- Consolidating the progress made under female education and carrying it forward for achieving the set goal of 'Education for Women's Equality' as advocated by the National Policy on Education, 1986 (revised in 1992).
- Providing easy and equal access to and free education for women and girls at all levels and in the field of technical and vocational education and training in up-coming and job-oriented trades.
- Increasing enrolment/retention rates and reducing drop-out rates by expanding the support service through mid-day meals, hostels and incentives like free supply of uniforms, textbook, transport charges, etc.
- Extending the existing network of regional vocational training centres to all the states and Women's Industrial Training Institutes and Women's Wings with General Industrial Training Institutes with residential facilities in all districts and sub-districts and provision of training in marketable trades.
- Encouraging the media to project positive images of women and the Girl Child: change the mind-set of the people and thus promote the balanced portrayals of women and men.
- Gender sensitizing both the administrative and enforcement machinery and ensuring that the right and interests of women are taken care of, besides involving them in planning, implementation and monitoring of processes.

Economic Empowerment

Ensure provision of training, employment and income generation activities with both 'forward' and 'backward' linkages with the ultimate objective of making all women economically independent and self-reliant through—

- Organising women into Self-Help Group under various poverty alleviation programmes, viz. Swarnajayanti Gram Swarozgar Yojana (SGSY), Swaranjayanti Shahari Rozgar Yojana (SJSRY), Rashtriya Mahila Kosh (RMK), Support of Training and Employment Programme (STEP), Training-*cum*-Production Centers for Women (NORAD), etc. and offering them a range of economic option along with necessary support measures to enhance their capabilities and earning capacities with an ultimate objective of making them economically independent and self-reliant.
- Ensuring that women in the informal Sector who account for more than 90 per cent are given special attention with regard to improve their working conditions as the same continued to be very precarious without even minimum or equal wages, leave aside other legislative safeguards.
- Making concerted efforts to ensure that the benefits of training and extension in agriculture and its allied activities of horticulture, small animal husbandry, poultry, fisheries, etc. reach women in proportion to their numbers; and also issue of Joint Pattas for husband and wife under the Social Forestry and Joint Forest Management programmes.
- Ensuring that the employers fulfil their legal obligations towards their women workers in extending child care facilities, maternity benefits, special leave, protection from occupational hazards, allowing formation of women workers, associations/unions, legal protection/aid, etc.

- Re-training/upgrading the skills of women displaced from traditional sectors due to advancement of technology so that they can take up jobs in the new and expanding areas of employment and formulating appropriate policies and programmes to promote alternative opportunities for wage/self-employment in traditional sectors like khadi and village industries, handicraft handlooms, sericulture, small scale and cottage industries.
- initiating affirmative action to ensure at least 30 per cent of reservation for women in services in the Public Sector as their representation in 1999 was only 14.5 per cent, along with required provisions for upward mobility.
- Increasing access to credit for women either through the establishment of new micro-credit mechanisms or micro-financial institutions catering to women or strengthening existing arrangements in these areas along with an expansion of the limited coverage of RMK.

Gender Justice

Eliminate all forms of gender discrimination and, thus, enable women to enjoy not only *de-jure* but also *de facto* rights and fundamental freedom on par with men in all spheres, viz. political, economic, social, civil, cultural, etc. through—

- Complete eradication of female foeticide and female infanticide through effective enforcement of both the Indian Penal Code, 1860 and the Pre-Natal Diagnostic Technique (Regulation and Prevention of Misuse) Act, 1994 with most stringent measures of punishment so that a very harsh path is set for the illegal practitioners.
- Adopting measures that take into account the reproductive rights of women to enable them to exercise their reproductive choices.
- Working out strategies, in close collaboration with the Ministry of Labour, to ensure extension of employment opportunities and thus, remove inequalities in employment —both in work and accessibility.
- Initiating interventions at the macro-economic level to amend existing legislations to improve women's access to productive assets and resources.
- Ensuring that the value added by women in the Informal Sector as workers and producers is recognized through redefinition/re-interpretation of conventional concepts of work and preparation of Satellite and National Accounts.
- Defining the Women's Component Plan (WCP) clearly and identifying the schemes/programmes/projects under each Ministry/Department which should be covered under WCP and ensuring the adoption of women-related mechanisms through which funds/benefits flow to women from these sectors.
- Initiating action for enacting new women-specific legislations; amending the existing women-related legislation, if necessary, based on the review made and recommendations already available to ensure gender justice, besides, reviewing all the subordinate legislations to eliminate all gender discriminatory references.
- Expediting action to legislate reservation of not less than 1/3 seats for women in the Parliament and in the State Legislative Assemblies and thus ensure women in proportion to their numbers reach decision-making bodies so that their voices are heard.

- Arresting the ever-increasing violence against women and the Girl Child including the Adolescent girls on top priority with the strength and support of a well-planned Programme of Action prepared in consultation with all the concerned, especially the enforcement authorities; implementing effectively with the strength of the Law and Order Authorities both at the centre and state levels and assessing the situation.
- Expediting standardisation of a Gender Development Index based on which the gender segregated the data will collected at national, state and district levels; compiled/collated and analysed to assess the progress made in improving the status of women at regular intervals with an ultimate objective of achieving equality on par with men.
- Initiating/accelerating the process of societal reorientation towards creating a Gender-Just Society.[8]

The Eleventh Plan 2007-12 roadmap for the Eleventh Five Year Plan can be clubbed under a five-fold agenda—

(i) Ensuring economic empowerment.
(ii) Engineering social empowerment.
(iii) Enabling political empowerment.
(iv) Effective implementation of women-related legislations.
(v) Creating institutional mechanisms for gender mainstreaming and strengthening delivery mechanisms.

The gender perspectives incorporated in the plan are the outcome of extensive consultations with different stakeholders, including a Group of Feminist Economists. In the Eleventh Plan , for the first time, women are recognized not just as equal citizens but as agents of economic and social growth. The approach to gender equality is based on the recognition that intervention in favour of women must be multi-pronged and they are: (i) provide women with basic entitlements, (ii) address the reality of globalization and its impact on women by prioritizing economic empowerment, (iii) ensure an environment free from all forms of violence against women (VAW—physical, economic, social, psychological, etc., (iv) ensure the participation and adequate representation of women at the highest policy levels, particularly in Parliament and State Assemblies, and (v) strengthen existing institutional mechanisms and create new ones for gender main-stream and effective policy-implementation.

NATIONAL POLICY FOR EMPOWERMENT OF WOMEN

One of the landmark achievements of the year 2001 was the approval of the first ever National Policy for the Empowerment of Women. The main objective of this Policy is to bring about the advancement, development and empowerment of women and to eliminate all forms of discrimination against women and to ensure their active participation in all spheres of life and activities.

The policy prescribes affirmative action in areas such as Legal System, Decision-making Structure, Mainstreaming of Gender Perspective in Development Process, Economic Empowerment through increased access to resources like micro-credit, better resource allocation through Women's component Plan, Gender Budget exercises and development of Gender Development

Indices and Social Empowerment of Women through, *inter-alia*, universalisation of education, adoption of holistic approach to women's health, etc. The policy commits to making compulsory the registration of marriages and to eliminate child marriage by 2010. The Policy takes into account the new developments initiated by the process of economic reforms and the impact of globalization and liberalization on women, particularly in the informal sector. The policy further prescribes that the provisions of various legislation including personal laws, which are discriminatory against women shall be reviewed and amended with the support and initiatives of concerned communities. Review of women-oriented legislations will be completed by 2003.

The Policy envisages setting up of a Council at the National level to oversee the implementation of the Policy. The National Council will be headed by the Prime Minister. Similar Councils will also be set-up at the State levels to be headed by the concerned Chief Ministers. All Central and State Ministries/Departments would be required to draw up Action the Ministry of Women and Child Development, which was designated as the Nodal machinery for the development and empowerment of women, is playing crucial role in the formulation and monitoring of women's component Plan which was devised as an operational strategy in the Ninth Plan to ensure that not less than 30 percent of funds/benefits earmarked for women in all the women-related sectors.

The Ministry has advised all the concerned Ministries/Departments for inclusion of an identifiable Women Component Plan in their programmes right from the planning process and implementation and monitoring of their programmes to ensure that the benefits reach the women. The Department has further requested all the Ministries/Departments to set-up Advisory Committees for women in each sector to help in the preparation, monitoring and implementation of Women's Component Plan, set-up a women's cell and to include a Chapter on Women's Component Plan in their Annual Report.

On the instruction of Prime Minister's Office (PMO), the Department has also been monitoring 27 Beneficiaries Oriented Schemes or Women implemented by Central Government. It has been decided to extend the scope of the monitoring to include the entire gamut of the women's Component Plan.

The review of the disabilities and constraints on women, which stem from socio-cultural institutions, indicates that the majority of women are still very far from enjoying the rights and opportunities guaranteed to them by the Constitution. Society has not yet succeeded in achieving the required norms or institutions to enable women to fulfil the multiple roles that they are expected to play in India today. On the other hand, the increasing incidence of practices like dowry indicate a further lowering of the status of women. They also indicate a process of regression from some of the norms developed during the Freedom Movement. We have been perturbed by the findings of the content analysis of periodicals in the regional languages, that concern for women and their problems, which received an impetus during the Freedom Movement, has suffered a decline in the last two decades. The social laws that sought to mitigate the problems of women in their family life have remained unknown to a large mass of women in this country, who are as ignorant of their legal rights today as they were before independence.

Changes in social attitudes and institutions cannot be brought about very rapidly. It is, however, necessary to accelerate this process of change by deliberate and planned efforts. Responsibility for this acceleration has to be shared by the State and the community, particularly that section of the community which believes in the equality of women. We, therefore, urge that community organizations, particularly women's organizations, should mobilize public opinion and strengthen social efforts against oppressive institutions like polygamy, dowry, ostentatious expenditure on weddings and "Child" marriage, and mount a campaign for the dissemination of information about the legal rights of women to increase their awareness. This is a joint responsibility, which has to be shared by community organizations, legislators, who have helped to frame these laws and the Government which is responsible for implementing them.

Women of India have a background of history and tradition behind them, which is inspiring, but they have suffered much from various kinds of suppression and all these have to go so that they can play their full part in the life of the nation.[9]

SUGGESTIONS TO STRENGTHEN WOMEN EMPOWERMENT (See Chart 17.4)

Women empowerment is not something which can be handed over to women. This is a process which involves sincerity, earnestness and capacity and capability on the part of both men and women. It is a challenging task in village India as even today, if a woman is to travel to her parents house or go somewhere, she must be accompanied by some male members of the family. She cannot take an independent decision. She feels even subordinate to her son. Let us discuss ways and means to improve the process of women empowerment.

1. Low status: Need of Upgradation

Most of the women in a family feel inferior to male members of the family. From olden times, women act as workers and do not take part in decision-making. This attitude needs change to make women as part and parcel of the family by carving out an important place for her. Swami Vivekananda repeatedly stressed the need for cultivating the faith in one self: "The ideal of faith in ourselves is of the greatest help to us. If faith in ourselves had been more extensively taught and practised. I am sure a very large portion of the evils and miseries that we have would have vanished. Throughout the history of mankind, if any motive power has been more potent than another in the lives of all great men and women, it is that of faith in themselves. Born with the consciousness, that they were to be great they come great. Prof. V.C. Kulandaiswamy, Former Vice-Chancellor, Indira Gandhi National Open University, New Delhi, delivered the convocation address at the Eleventh Convocation of the Avinashilingam Institute for Home Science and Higher Education for Women (Deemed University), Coimbatore. He said, "Women's studies should (therefore) concentrate on the nature of opportunities that now emerge for women to prepare themselves for playing an equal role—not necessarily identical role—with men in the affairs of the society. The research studies should consider the areas of disability, the handicaps, the impediments and the prejudices that women face and devise ways of educating and enabling men and women to remove them."[10]

2. Low Morale: Need of Creating Positive Attitude (See Chart 17.4)

At present women posses low morale which is a depressing situation where she does not get a sense of belongingness. We must develop positive attitude in her by enlightening her about her creative potential for contributing to the overall development of self, family and society. Dr. (Miss) A.S. Desai, former Chairperson, University Grants Commission, delivered the Convocation Address at the annual convocation on the S.N.D.T. Women's University, Mumbai. She said, "While education for women is a necessary condition for social development, it has to be accompanied by increasing levels of awareness with respect to the place of women in a patriarchal society, the means to change their position and role, as also to assure that women's rights are seen as an important and major component of human rights.

CHART 17.4

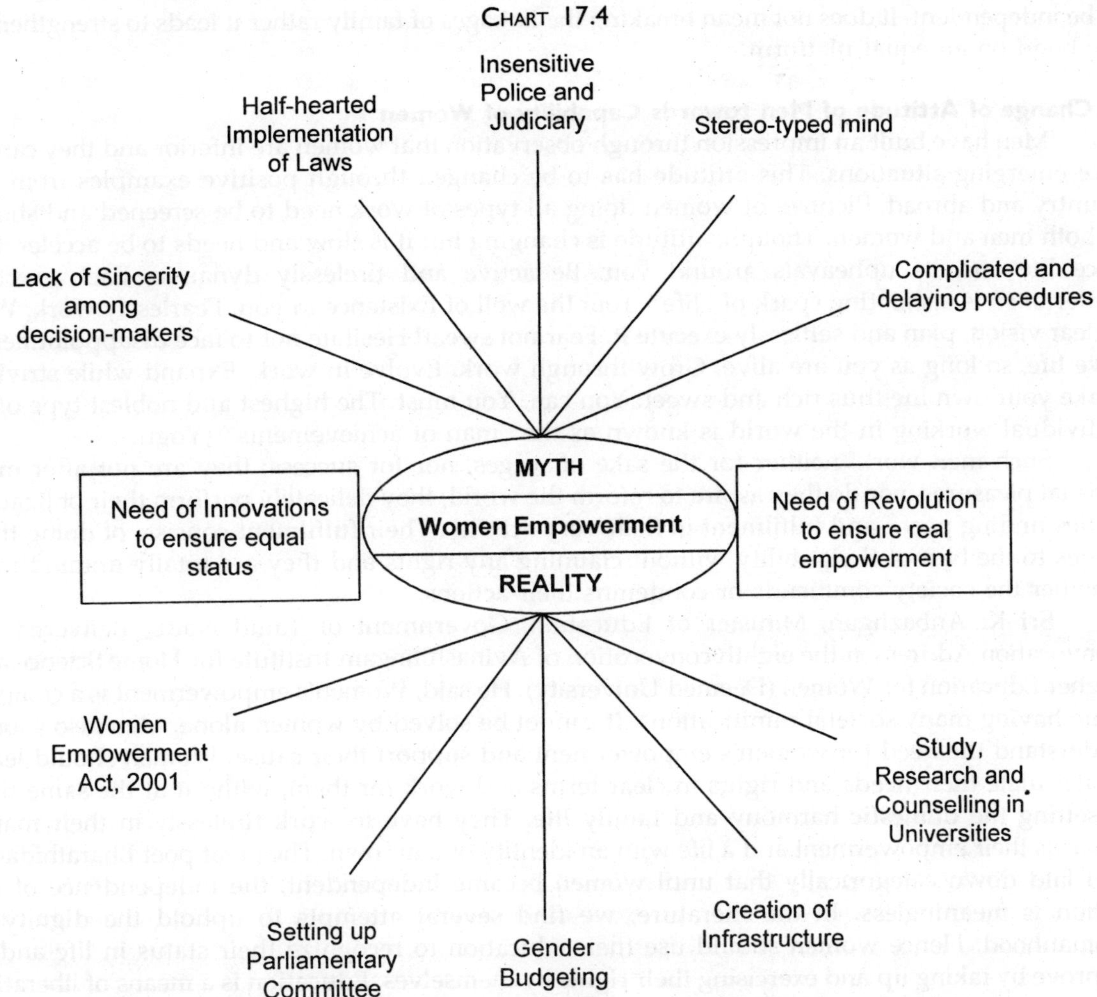

All this leads us to consider the importance of empowerment of women achieved through both education and greater social awareness. No one, ever in history, has achieved rights without a struggle. Women have to unite across caste, class, ethnicity and religion, if change has to be brought. Political empowerments is now made possible for women at the local levels through the 73rd and 74th Amendments to the Constitution. It has brought a million women opportunity to participate in decision-making and policies at the village, block and district levels as also in the urban municipal corporations. Educated women have a major social obligation to participate in this great experiment, uniquely launched in our country by reserving one-third of the seats at this level. Expanding women's education will serve no purpose if women do not participate in policy and decision-making.[11]

3. Dependence upon Men since Childhood: Need of Independence from Early Stages

In Indian villages, girls remain dependent upon father, brother or cousin and this very feeling continue in their married life. We must give capacity building training to girls in schools to be independent. It does not mean breaking the linkages of family rather it leads to strengthening the bond on an equal platform.

4. Change of Attitude of Men towards Capability of Women

Men have built an impression through observation that women are inferior and they cannot face emerging situations. This attitude has to be changed through positive examples from our country and abroad. Pictures of women doing all types of work need to be screened and shown to both men and women. Though, attitude is changing but it is slow and needs to be accelerated. Face life and its upheavals around you. Be active and tirelessly dynamic. Each exertion undertaken is a shooting spark of "life" from the well of Existence in you. Fearlessly work. With a clear vision, plan and selflessly execute it. Fear not sweat! Hesitate not to face disappointments. Live life, so long as you are alive. Grow through work. Evolve in work. Expand while striving. Make your own life thus rich and sweet. You can. You must. The highest and noblest type of an individual working in the world is known as the "man of achievements" (Yogi).

Such men work, neither for the sake of wages, nor for success; they are not after mere sensual pleasures, nor do they aspire to reform the world; they delicately perform their obligatory duties finding peace and fulfilment in their very activity. Their fulfilment consists of doing their duties to the best of their ability without claiming any rights and they are totally unmindful of whether the society commends or condemns their actions.

Sri K. Anbazhgan, Minister of Education, Government of Tamil Nadu, delivered the Convocation Address at the eighth convocation of Avinashilingam Institute for Home Science and Higher Education for Women (Deemed University). He said, Women's empowerment is a complex issue having many societal ramifications. It cannot be solved by women alone. Men also should understand the need for women's empowerment and support their cause. Women should learn to articulate their needs and rights in clear terms and work for them, without at the same time upsetting the domestic harmony and family life. They have to work tirelessly in their march towards their empowerment and a life with an identity of their own. The great poet Bharathidasan had laid down categorically that until women became independent, the independence of the nation is meaningless. In the literature, we find several attempts to uphold the dignity of womanhood. Hence women should use their education to recognize their status in life and to improve by taking up and exercising their rights by themselves. Education is a means of liberation for everyone. But it is more so for women.[12]

5. Women Elected Representatives of PRIs give Way to their Men Folk: Need of taking Independent Decisions

Women representatives in PRIs must be trained in the art and science of decision-making so that they are not influenced by extraneous factors. They should discuss among other women and take their opinion. They must develop leadership qualities. K.D. Gangrade in his Article, "Gandhi and Empowerment of Women—Miles to Go", Smt. Savita Singh (International Centre of Gandhian Studies and Research, Gandhi Samiti and Darshan Samiti, New Delhi, "The 74th and 73rd Constitutional Amendments on Panchayati Raj and Nagarpalika with 33 per cent reservation for women has created political space for women. But in most cases they exercise "proxy" power on behalf of men. In reality women have never been able to get more than ten-percent seats in Parliament or other bodies of decision-making. It is hoped that 81st Constitutional Amendment when passed will give 33 per cent reservation of seats in Parliament and State legislatures. This will go a long way to have their say. We should be ashamed of ourselves that

after more than half a century of freedom we have neither been able to clothe our women nor able to provide them something as basic as secure and adequate number of toilets and shelter even in the capital city of Delhi."

6. Lack of Interest and Enthusiasm: Need of Enthusiasm

Women lack interest in PRI on account of luke warm attitude to PRIs by state and Union Government. To make life worthwhile and fruitful, they must generate enthusiasm within themselves. Generation of enthusiasm will take place when they discover for themselves a goal and attach themselves to the Altar with a spirit of dedication, reverence and love. Once they have surrendered themselves to it, the ideal itself will provide them with the inspiration and strength. Then nothing can hinder the progress of women's march towards that Goal and the ideal. The love for the ideal will overcome and vanquish all the hurdles from the ideal, and if it comes to that, life itself will be cast off with a smile, a dedication at that Altar. That was how Bhagat Singh could walk to the gallows with a smile on his face. What is important is that one should choose the right ideal an ideal worthwhile even it comes to sacrificing one's own life in the endeavour. The ideal should be inspiring, it should arouse the spring of activity in us. Thus, the discovering of the ideal is the secret of generating in ourselves, dynamism and vitality in its fullness.

Dr. Ela R. Bhatt, Founder, Self-Employed Women's Association (SEWA) Ahmedabad delivered convocation address at the Ninth Convocation of Sri Padmavati Mahila Visvavidyalayam, Tirupati on Monday, the 8th March, 1999 (Women's Day). She said, "Over a period of time, we realized that the right to vote was not enough for the poor and women. They wanted a voice and visibility. It took still more years for us to realize that this was not possible without access to and ownership of economic resources by these poor women. Coming out of their state of exploitation by men, society, and the State, the poor women wanted to enjoy what I now call second Freedom: Doosri Azadi." Exerpts.[13]

7. No Forum to Exchange Ideas: Need for All Women Forum

Elected representatives of three tiers should meet once in three months. At present elected representatives rarely meet at one platform to form opinion upon different activities being carried out at various levels. There is a need to have a quarterly meeting of all the elected representatives to exchange their view points. In this way, the would be more participative while deliberating on important issues.

8. Women MLA's MPs do not take Interest in them: Need for Change

Women MLAs and MP's by their own examples should visit frequently the elected representatives of PRIs to solve the problems faced by women members and encourage them in their efforts of socio-economic development.

9. Women do not Struggle for Empowerment

Need to acquire empowerment Sarojini Vardappan in her Article, "The challenge of the 21st and Role of Indian Women" observed that —"The emphasis now is empowerment. Empowerment is now active process. Power is not a commodity to be transacted. Power cannot be given away as alms. Power has to be acquired, once acquired it needs to be exercised, sustained and preserved. Women have to empower themselves. It is a multidimensional process which should enable individuals or group and individuals to realise their full identity and power in all spheres of life. It consists of greater access to knowledge and resources, greater autonomy in decision-making to enable them to have greater ability to plan their lives or have greater control over the circumstances that influence their lives and freedom from shackles imposed on them by customs, belief and practice. Discrimination of women from womb to tomb is well known, age long traditions and worn out customs are handicaps, woman have to struggle on their way up."

One of India's greatest poets, Rabindranath Tagore, felt a pain and inequity of the situation more than half a century ago, thus:

"O Lord Why have you not given
woman the right to conquer her destiny?
Why does she have to wait head bowed,
By the roadside,
Waiting with tired patience, I
Hoping for a miracle in the morrow

10. Mere Legislations do not Help "Women": Need of Action

Every new legislation has only worsened the position of women. And now her right to property granted by law in a recent judgment by the Supreme Court poses a new threat to her life.

Let us mention the Important Legislations in support for Women

Women-Specific Legislations

- The Immortal Traffic (Prevention) Act, 1956
- The Dowry Prohibition Act, 1961 (28 of 1961)
- The Indecent Representation of Women (Prohibition) Act, 1986
- The Commission of Sati (Prevention) Act, 1987 (3 of 1988)
- Domestic Violence Act, 2005
- Hindus succession Amendment Act, 2005.

Women-Related Legislations

- The Guardians and Wards Act, 1960
- Indian Penal Code, 1860
- The Christian Marriage Act, 1872 (15 of 1872)
- The Indian Evidence Act, 1872 (yet to be reviewed)
- The Marriage Women's Property Act, 1874 (2 of 1874)
- The Workmen's Compensation Act, 1923
- The Legal Practitioners (Women) Act, 1823
- The Indian Succession Act, 1925 (39 of 1925)
- The Child Marriage Restraint Act, 1929 (9 of 1929)
- The Payments of Wages Act, 1936
- The Muslim Personal Law (Shariat) Application Act, 1937
- The Factories Act, 1948
- The Employees State Insurance Act, 1948
- The Plantation Labour Act, 1951
- The Cinematograph Act, 1952
- The Speical Marriage Act, 1954

- *The Hindu* Marriage Act, 1955 (28 of 1989)
- *The Hindu* Adoption and Maintenance Act, 1956
- The Hindi Minority & Guardianship Act, 1956
- *The Hindu* Succession Act, 1956
- The Maternity Benefit Act, 1961 (53 of 1961)
- The Beedi and Cigar Workers (Conditions of Employment Act, 1966)
- The Foreign Marriage Act, 1969 (33 of 1969)
- The Indian Divorce Act, 1969 (4 of 1969)
- The Medical Termination of Pregnancy Act, 1971 (34 of 1971)
- Code of Criminal Procedure, 1973
- The Bonded Labour System (Abolition) Act, 1976
- The Equal Remuneration Act, 1976
- The Contract Labour (Regulation & Abolition) Act, 1979
- The Inter-State Migrant Workmen (Regulation of Employment and Conditions of Service) Act, 1979
- The Family Court Act, 1984
- Juvenile Justice Act, 1986
- The Child Labour (Prohibition & Regulation) Act, 1986.
- National Commission for Women Act, 1990 (20 of 1990)
- The infant Milk Substitutes, Feeding Bottles and Infant Foods (Regulation of Production, Supply and Distribution Act, 1992)
- The Pre-Natal Diagnostic Technique (Regulation and Prevention of Misuse) Act, 1994.

These developments only reinforce the belief that laws alone do not lead to social transformation, unless followed by resolute action and societal awareness of the wrong from time immemorial. And as the eminent jurist V.R. Krishna Iyer rightly says, "The Constitutional provisions are weapons, not victories. Law has to be activated." In short, the struggle for justice -social, economic and political remains to be fought and won. In this scenario, all talk of women Empowerment is nothing more than empty jargon. The situation demands a revolution of consciousness in the minds of women in the ways they think about themselves. Women must realize that gender deprivation is inconsistent with their basic human rights. They must realize that they have Constitutional rights to quality health care, economic security, access to education, employment opportunities, equity and political power.[14]

The Eleventh Plan will foster women's access to legal services through a range of measures. Women will be exempted from paying fees to fight cases of human rights violations. Funds for legal assistance will be provided to poor women seeking legal redress. Legal awareness programmes will be carried out in all States in collaboration with NGOs working at the grassroots level. Legal Aid Cells consisting of committed and gender-sensitive lawyers will be set-up at the Panchayat level to provide information and support to rural women, especially poor women. *Lok Adalats* will be organized to encourage alternate dispute settlement mechanisms for efficacious settlement of cases. The Plan will also work towards increasing the percentage of women in police and judicial services. Training on use of gender specific laws will be provided to all Members and Authorities involved in providing legal services. Concept of *fan Sunwaiye* will be adopted to listen to people's voices.

11. Group Discussions are not Sufficient: Need of Positive Mass Media

Arun K. Gupta and Nisha Jain in their article Gender, Mass Media and Social Change: A case study of T.V. Commercials in *Universal News* (August 11, 1997) observe that T.V. commercial also place heavy emphasis on the sexuality of women. In fact, the modernized version of commercials has resulted in a greater emphasis on woman's body and beauty. In the process, woman is reduced to her sexual personality's Whatever else maybe the basis of projection of women, the sexual stereotyping of women continues.

A strong awareness requires to be inculcated among leaders of industry, business and corporate sectors, advertising executives and media directors and personnel to exhibit realistic but emancipated attitude with respect to women. Such an outlook should be in tune with the requirement of increasing consciousness among both men and women about women. As commercials have mass appeal, these can and should be used for generating gender friendly consciousness and for reducing bias against women.

Report on the Status of Women rightly mentions that development in its wider perspective covers all aspects of community life. The accepted goals of national development such as maximum production, full employment, and attainment of economic equality and social justice apply equally to men and women. Their realization in an egalitarian society is not, however, possible, unless special efforts are made to assist the underprivileged groups. Our constitution therefore stresses the urgent need for promoting the educational and economic interests of the weaker sections of the people; and as women are handicapped by social customs and traditions, they need special attention to help them to play their full and proper role in a national life.[15]

"The great occupation of women should be to beautify life; to cultivate, for her own sake and that of those who surround her, all her faculties of mind, soul, and body; all her powers of enjoyment, and powers of giving enjoyment; and to diffuse beauty, elegance, and grace, everywhere. If in addition to this the activity of her nature demands more energetic and definite employment, there is never any lack of it in the world; If she loves, here natural impulse will be to associate her existence with him she loves, and to share his occupations; in which, if he loves her (with that affection of equality which along deserves to be called love) she will naturally take as strong an interest, and be as thoroughly conversant, as the most perfect confidence on his side can make her.[16]

Dr. (Miss) Mira Seth, the then Member, Planning Commission, Government of India, delivered the convocation address at the annual convocation of the Banasthali Vidyapeeth (Deemed University). She said that the Parliament legislation has been an instruments of giving equality and status to women in our country and this has taken the place of the ancient Vedic, Paurnaic, Shastra and Smriti injunctions. Our Parliament has enacted sixteen laws from *the Hindu* Marriage Act, 1955 to the Commission of Sati (Prevention) Act, 1987 for giving legal sanction to this principle of equality.

In the development processes and the Five Year Plans of our country, they give emphasis to the instrument of education as one of the major tools for empowering women. The focus on educational planning for women has shifted from their traditional role as housewives and mothers to non-traditional roles as producers, partners and partakers in the national development.[17]

Ms. Terjani Vakil, Former Chairman & Managing Director, Export-Import Bank of India, delivered the Convocation address at the Banasthali Vidyapith, Banasthali (Rajasthan). She said, "Keep a space for yourself as a person. Think about what you are, what you want to be, what is your personal raison de etre for living. What interests you, what pleases you, do that. Keep a time and space for yourself in your life. For you are an individual, a human being and not just someone's wife, mother, daughter. I would want you to think about this."[18]

Indian National Council for Women suggested the following to bridge the gap between theory and practice:

- Empowerment should be viewed as a two-fold process. Constructive activities to reorganize women's role system have to be accompanied by effective interventions leading to the community internalizing the idea of women's empowerment for its better future.
- Providing economic and political strength to women through collective activities, should be given the necessary focus. Clubbing of women's issues should be avoided.
- The need for women to have social space like "Sakhi Sabha", "Mahila Mandal", etc. within the community set-up through panchayat Samities should be given due recognition. Formalization of women NGOs network to play a catalytic role in the social transformation should be given due attention. Development of leadership among women for advancement of the community is also necessary.
- Communication within the women's organizations and the community at large has to be fostered.[19]

CONCLUSION

Women empowerment should ensure harmonious existence. Dr. Farncis_ Soundaraj, Principal, Kodaikanal Christian College, Kodaikanal, delivered the Convocation Address at the annual convocation of the Fatima College (Autonomous), Maduari. He said, "Education has empowered women: they compete better, perform more efficiently and secure values and traditions more carefully than their male counterparts. Are these not reasons and justifications enough for educated women to shake off pessimism and rise up to meet the challenges which none else but they alone can meet?"

God created human race male and female. He made neither of them superior to the other; on the other hand, he created them for a harmonious existence together. Therefore, the challenges that lie ahead of you cannot be met unless they are approached with a sense of humility and with a sense of togetherness with men. While some of them can be met exclusively by women, they can achieve more by pooling the resources of all.

Gender equality is an issue of primary importance to the welfare and progress of all nations. It is fundamental to achieving people-centered development. What humanity needs is a world that is free, fair and equal; a world that will have no discrimination, violence, or exploitation, a world where opportunity and prosperity are shared by all. So, why is violence against Women and discrimination so widespread all over the world? It is because discrimination begins in the minds of people, where gender-bias becomes a habit in thought and action. These have over centuries developed deep-rooted cultural traditions which regard women as subservient, the girl-child as a liability, and discrimination as normal. The root of all prejudice is ignorance. Education, greater awareness, public policy and the media can play an important role in eradicating such prejudices. Recent work has brought out very clearly that women's literacy and informed participation in decisions within and outside family strongly influence the relative respect and regard for women's well-being which in turn is a sure step for National Development.

The Vision of Eleventh Five Year Plan is to end the multifaceted exclusions and discrimination faced by women to ensure that every woman in the country is able to develop her full potential and share the benefits of economic growth and prosperity. Success will depend upon our ability to adopt a participatory approach and empowers woman and makes them partners in their own development. The road map has already been laid in the national policy women 2001.

Notes and References

1. GOI, Deptt. of Social Welfare, Ministry of Education and Social Welfare, Towards Equality, Report on the Committee on the Status of Women in India, 1974, pp. 3-8.
2. Annual Reprot, 2001-02, Deptt. Of Women and Child Development, Ministry of HRD, GOI, New Delhi, pp. 163-64.
3. Beena Shah, Women and Empowerment in India—The Educational Dimension in *University News*, Augst, 31, 2000.
4. J.P. Singh Indian Democracy and Empowerment of Women, in *IJPA*, Oct.-Dec., 2000.
5. GOI, Ministry of Rural Development, Annual Report, 1999-2000, p. 66.
6. GOI, Planning Commission, Ninth Five Year Plan, 1997-2002, Vol. II, p. 322.
7. India, 2002, Ministry of Information and Broadcasting, GOI, New Delhi, p. 230.
8. GOI, Planning Commission, Xth Five Year Plan, New Delhi, 2002-07, pp. 202, 249.
9. GOI, Deptt. of Social Welfare, Ministry of Education and Social Welfare, Towards Equality, Report of the Committee on the Status of Women in India, New Delhi, Dec. 1974, p. 101.
10. *University News*, Dec. 6, 1999, p. 27.
11. *University News*, April 6, 1999.
12. *University News*, January 13, 1997.
13. *University News*, January 26, 1999.
14. Aruna Goel, Organization and Structure of Women Development and Empowerment, New Delhi, Deep & Deep, 2004, p. 85.
15. ICCSR, Status of Women in India, *op. cit.*, p. 116.
16. John Stuart Mill and H.T. Mill, Early Essays on Marriage and Divorce, Alice and Rossi (ed.) Essays on Sexual Equality, p. 225.
17. AIU, *University News*, July 22, pp. 18-19.
18. AIU, *University News*, April 13, 1990, p. 12.
19. NCW-1990-2000, New Delhi, p. 135.

APPENDIX 17.1

SELF HELP GROUPS (SHGs)

Empowering Strategies

The erstwhile programme of Indira Mahila Yojana launched in 1995, was recast as Swayamsidha in 2001 to empower women by generating awareness and helping them to achieve economic strength through micro-level income-generation activities and facilitate easy convergence of various services such as literacy, health, non-formal education, rural development, water supply, entrepreneurship, etc. Out of Ninth Plan outlay of Rs. 165 crore, no expenditure was incurred during the first three years of the Plan as the scheme was being recast. The expenditure during 2000-01 and 2001-02 was Rs. 8.95 crore to expand the existing 238 blocks in 1999-2000 to 650 blocks in 2001-02 to form 53,100 Women's SHGs covering 9.3 lakh women beneficiaries. Another empowering intervention refers to 'Swa-Shakti project, sanctioned in 1998 for a five-year period till 2003 with assistance from the International Development Association and International Fund for Agricultural Development. Swa-Shakti has been in action in 57 districts of 9 states of Bihar, Chhattisgarh, Gujarat, Haryana, Jharkhand, Karnataka, Madhya Pradesh, Uttaranchal and Uttar Pradesh. Its major objective is to create an enabling environment for empowerment of women through setting up of self-reliant women's SHGs and developing linkages between SHGs and lending institutions in order to ensure women's continued access to credit facilities for income generation activities. Of the Ninth Plan outlay of Rs. 102.94 crore, the expenditure was Rs. 36 crore to set-up around 9,735 SHGs through 118 NGOs (till October 2001).[1]

Swayamsidha is an integrated scheme for women's empowerment through formation of women into Self-Help Group (SHGs) The scheme was launched in February 2001 across the States and Union Territories of the country with a total budget outlay of Rs. 116.30 crore. But subsequently discontinued from Goa, Daman & Diu, Dadar & Nagar Haveli and Chandigarh due to lack of interest among the UTs. The scheme is expected to culminate in March 2008. The long-term objective of the programme is holistic empowerment of women though a sustained process of mobilization and convergence of all the on-going sectoral programmes by improving access of women to micro credit, economic resources, etc. The programme is being implemented in 650 blocks in the country including 238 Indira Mahila Yojana (IMY) blocks, covering 335 districts. Each block consists of 100 Self Help Groups. The programme is being implemented in many States through ICDS infrastructure; while in some States, the scheme is implemented through State Women's Development Corporations. In addition to monitoring the scheme through normal means such as Quarterly Progress Report (QPR) and field visits, a system of Quarterly Review Meetings of State Nodal Officers has been put in place.

The most important component of the programme is the formation, implementation and monitoring of blocks specific composite project for 4-5 years incorporating the following four elements:

- Group formation/mobilisation activities;
- Community-oriented innovative interventions;
- Convergence with specific schemes of MWCD, namely STEP, SEP and AGP along with other schemes, if there is a felt need for the same; and
- Schemes of other Ministries, whether converged under Government of India's directions or State Government initiative.

Achievements under Swayamsidha

- 69,690 SHGs have been formed against the target of 65,000 SHGs
- 10.03 lakh women are covered under the scheme
- 579 block level federations of SHGs have been formed.
- Rs. 143.64 crores have been saved by SHGs under the scheme
- 63,714 SHGs (98%) have Bank Accounts
- Rs. 100.55 crores have been deposited by the SHGs in Banks
- Rs. 154.34 crores loan has been taken from Banks by SHGs
- 51,208 SHGs (79%) involving over 5.98 lakhs women are engaged in Income Generation Activities (IGA)
- 45,060 SHGs (69%) are given Skill Development Trainings
- 41,365 SHGs (64%) are benefiting from convergence with other Government schemes
- Many States have created Community Assets and the process is going on. Till now, 4322 Community Assets have been created

Trainings on ten basic topics (Concept of Swayamsidha, SHG Concept, Savings and credit, Group Rules, Group Dynamics, Confidence building, Conflict resolution, Book Keeping and cash management, Opening bank account and Leadership development) have been imparted to SHGs.

Financial achievements under Swayamsidha

Against the BE of Rs. 27.90 Crores for 2007-08 under Swayamsidha, an expenditure of Rs. 11.52 crores (as on 31.1.2008) has been incurred. State-wise funds released during 2006-07 and 2007-08 (as on 18.3.2008), number of districts covered, blocks allocated and SHGs. (See Table 17.1 and 17.2)

Review Meetings for Officers of Swayamsidha

The Ministry has organized three exposure-*cum*-review meetings of Nodal Officers implementing Swayamisidha, the details of which are as given below:

Date	*Venue*	*Participant*
16 July 2007	Delhi	31
25-27 September 2007	Kovalam, Kerala	29
3-4 January 2008	Delhi	22

The review meeting and exposure meets served as a platform to discuss the achievements made in the previous quarter with focus on training, convergence, bank linkage, income generation/micro-enterprise activities and community assets created under the project. Expenditure and utilization of funds, problems and issues relating to implementation, etc. were also discussed. Technical guidance was also given to the States. The Nodal Officers were taken to field to study base practices adopted in the States during exposure visits.

Evaluation of the Scheme of Swayamsidha

The Scheme was evaluated by an external agency, IIPO, New Delhi in 2005. The major findings of the evaluation are as under:

Formation of Self Help Groups (SHGs)

Under Swayamsidha, group formation target was 65,000 SHGs for 650 blocks. So far, 67,971 SHGs have been formed. Most of the States achieved their targets and some States formed more SHGs than the target set for them. The analysis of data reveals that in most cases, the number of SHG members fall between 10-20 against the target of 15-20 members per SHG. The total number of SHG members is 9.89 lakhs against the target of 11.37 lakhs. Registers and cash boxes were provided to most of the groups as soon as these were formed. All groups have formulated their by-laws and followed them. Attendance is 100% in nearly all sample blocks except a few cases where revenue villages are scattered over several kilometers. The low rate of savings is usually in areas where group members are extremely poor and are not able to save regularly. Otherwise savings and inter-loaning is the backbone of these SHGs. Most of the groups received all basic training and are receiving training on income generation activities. Nearly all groups have their bank accounts. So far as the Community Asset Creation is concerned, in some States, it is completed or work is in advanced stage. In other States the SHGs have already planned the type of community assets to be created. Thus, Swayamsidha has benefited women in several ways by increasing income, awareness level, decision-making process, participation in political and social processes, knowledge of legal rights, health issues, etc.

Economic Empowerment

Economic status of women has definitely improved after joining the SHGs. The Swayamsidha group members have been able to further strengthen their own economic activities as individuals and as groups by taking loans from their own kitty and from the banks and other credit institutions. This has generated enthusiasm and self confidence in women in the Swayamsidha SHGs who become role models for other women in the village to emulate. The result is that once one or two groups get formed, there is a chain reaction and other groups come up. These women handle their own money, keep their own accounts, maintain group registers and individual pass books as also are proud of their Group's account in the banks with photographs of their office bearers. The Scheme has helped in poverty alleviation and income increase has definitely taken place from moderate to high level among the SHG members. Lakhs of rupees have been pooled to start income generation activities that reflect the local needs. With a few exceptions, all SHG members are involved in individual or group income generating activities—some with loan from their groups and others with Bank loans. 50-60% of nutritious meals in ICDS centers are supplied by the SHG members. There are good number of success stories that speak of their economic empowerment and augmentation of family income.

Social Empowerment

Awareness on various social issues has also been created among women. Under the convergence component of the scheme, they are now being made familiar with various developmental schemes of several Departments which benefit women. Women now always enjoy relatively more freedom and there are no restriction on their movement outside home for social or business purpose. Being part of the Swayamsidha group has given them enhanced status. After joining SHGs, the women members are increasingly participating in family decision-making, demanding their rights from family, community and government. They have developed the ability to interact with others and have developed negotiation skills. In conclusion, women in Swayamsidha Blocks have strengthened their social standing in society. Awareness of social evils like alcoholism, dowry and female foeticide has shown that sex ratio in Villages has improved.

A strong bond has been established between group members. They have attachment for each other. Being members of the group, gives them a feeling of security.

Political Empowerment

Politically women are active. Thus whoever gets time participates in Gram Sabha activities. The participation of women in local self-government has increased. The percentage of women's voting has gone up considerably. The members are now more sensitive about political issues and their impact on their lives. Participation of women at Panchayat levels has increased and some of them have been elected to the Panchayats and urban local bodes. Most of the members of Panchayati Raj Institutions (PRIs) are elected from the SHGs. Almost all the members participate in election/political process.

Bank Linkages

The scheme helped to establish close linkage between SHGs and banks/credit societies. The bank officials were sensitized about SHG concept. The Animators and Programme Implementing Agencies (PIAs) were quite helpful to SHGs in opening bank accounts and monetary transactions. Initially all the SHGs faced some problems with regard to opening bank accounts. With the intervention of District Collector and PIAs soon these were resolved. Banks that extended help and co-operation are Nationalised banks as well as private banks. Banks were made aware of the guidelines issued by the Reserve Bank of India (RBI) for opening accounts of SHGs. Banks that participated in SHG stabilization activities are lead bank officers and rural bank officers. Women are involved in micro-credit operations and are interacting with different financial institutions like the nationalized banks, private banks, cooperatives, rural banks, etc. In most places, the banks are providing all the cooperation to SHGs in their activities. Some bank officials try to reach out to SHG women personally and have relaxed their timings so that the SHGs can operate their bank accounts comfortably. Some banks organized Loan Mela for SHG group members. The overall experience with the Credit institutions was found positive.

Legal Rights

The SHG members have begun to know their legal rights through the awareness generation programmes organized under the scheme. All women members are now aware of their legal rights and laws forbidding child marriage, child labour, equal wages for equal work, among others. They have awareness on dowry laws; age of marriage, and state that they do not discriminate between sons and daughters. They are opposed to sex selective abortions but admit that this practice is going on and women actually do not have much control over it.

Health Issues

Swayamsidha Awareness Camps and Basic Training programmes created awareness among SHG members on issues such as Family planning health and nutrition of pregnant women, child care, issues of adolescents, need for immunization of children, problems of HIV/AIDS, to name a few. They know the importance of a clean environment, keeping the house and surrounding neat and clean; importance of health care (family health, reproductive health), etc. Some groups participated in Pulse Polio, Immunization, and, Awareness programmes.

Community Asset Creation

The scheme of Swayamsidha has provision for creation of community assets as per felt needs of the women SHG members. The cost of community assets could be up to Rs. 10 lakhs per block out of which Rs. 6 lakhs would be GOI share and the remaining amount would be State share. The evaluation report indicates that in some States creation of community assets has been completed or in advanced stage. The other States have already planned the form of community asset to be created. The community assets are being created after consulting the SHGs and to meet their requirements. There is delay in the initiation of community assets in some States due to non-availability of 40% community share. The sources identified by the states for the 40% state share are State Rural Development Department, concerned Deputy Commissioners, Block Development Officers, MPIMLA Grants, other donors, etc. Only some states have been able to raise this share for Swayamsiddha Blocks.[1]

Conclusion

In conclusion, women In Swayamsidha Blocks have strengthened their social standing in society. Awareness of social evils like alcoholism, dowry and female feticide is visible. Economic status of women has definitely improved after joining the SHGs. Number of women members in Panchayat levels has increased and some of them have been elected to local bodies.

Women across the board have as asked a pertinent question, "Why did it take Sarkari to bring in this scheme 50 long years." At places, they are willing to sustain the movement with or without support. Groups are fairly stable although at different stages of evolution. Swayamsidha is a movement and a dynamic process. This programme has unleashed woman power and one comes across some very vibrant, confident women who understand the concepts of savings and investment and the need to equip themselves with sound economic skills. On the technical front, more work is needed but the programme is moving towards the broad goals of social, economic and political empowerment of women. The scheme needs to run for another five years for stabilization/growth, sustainability and self-reliance.[2]

While strengthening SHG initiatives, policies and schemes the Eleventh Plan will simultaneously increase women's awareness, bargaining power, literacy, health, vocational, and entrepreneurial skills. It will prioritize training, capacity-building inputs, and the creation of backward-forward linkages, which are essential to generate sustainable livelihood opportunities. Given the scale of the phenomenon, there is a need to review the SHG interventions and ground realities to determine how SHGs may better serve the interests of poor women, and suggest changes required in overall SHG policy frameworks. The Eleventh Plan recognizes the importance of this issue and proposes a HLC to conduct a review of SHG-related policies and programmes.[3]

Given the fact that SHGs are the preferred anti-poverty strategy for women, it can be concluded that the strategy has met with some success since groups have reduced poverty, reached out to very poor women and raised their awareness levels quite significantly. An important caveat is that the programmes have not reached the poorest women who are not in a position to save and who are poor credit risks. What Stree Shakti must now do is to focus on the poorest women (BPL) who are not getting credit for various reasons and ensure their needs are met by linking them with local rural wage employment programmes to build a sustainable base for micro-credit. A second set of actions must focus on strengthening/diversifying the vocational base and developing marketing linkages. Ensuring that services are provided in time and efficiently speaks of the need for better governance. Gender sensitisation, literacy, health and nutrition awareness would be the third set of actions. All actions must be complementary, not sequential.[3]

1. Annual Report, 2007-08, GOI, Ministry of Women and Child Development, New Delhi.
2. GOI, Planning Commission, Xth Five Year Plan, p. 223.
3. GOI, Planning Commission, XIth Five Year Plan, Vol. II, p. 193.

TABLE 17.1

State-wise Funds Released, Number of Districts, Blocks Covered and SHGs Formed under Swayamsidha during 2006-07

(as on 31.3.2007)

S.No.	*States*	*Release of funds during 2006-07 (Rs. In lakhs)*	*No. of districts*	*No. of blocks covered*	*No. of SHGs formed (As on 31.3.2007)*
1	*2*	*3*	*4*	*5*	*6*
1.	Andhra Pradesh	231.84	23	38	3874
2.	Aurnachal Pradesh	0	6	6	600
3.	Assam	100	20	24	2400
4.	Bihar	270.00	19	63	6340
5.	Chattisgarh	25.00	16	17	1708
6.	Gujarat	299.40	20	27	2772
7.	Himachal Pradesh	34.39	7	8	800
8.	Haryana	0	3	13	1300
9.	Jammu & Kashmir	36.85	13	13	1250
10.	Jharkhand	50.00	11	24	2427
11.	Karnataka	26.05	12	20	2992
12.	Kerala	52.60	7	18	2451
13.	Madhya Pradesh	100.00	13	36	3667
14.	Maharashtra	100.00	20	36	3939
15.	Manipur	14.49	3	3	300
16.	Meghalaya	30.89	5	5	530
17.	Mizoram	0.33	3	3	300
18.	Nagaland	0	5	6	600
19.	Orissa	100	9	36	3600
20.	Punjab	71.76	8	15	1937
21.	Rajasthan	200.00	26	30	3000
22.	Sikkim	39.44	4	5	572
23.	Tamil Nadu	150.01	5	44	5452
24.	Tripura	0	3	3	327
25.	Uttar Pradesh	485.35	54	94	9268
26.	Uttaranchal	37.79	5	11	1100
27.	West Bengal	327.75	4	39	1184
28.	A&N Islands	0	3	3	196
29.	Delhi	10	3	4	256
30.	Lakshadweep	0	1	3	226
31.	Pondicherry	14.80	1	3	300
	Other Expenses	11.35	0	0	0
	Total	2820.49	335	650	69669

Source: Ministry of Women and Child Development, Annual Report, 2007-08, p. 214.

TABLE 17.2

State-wise Funds Released, Number of Districts, Blocks Covered and SHGs Formed under Swayamsidha during 2006-07

(as on 31.3.2007)

S.No.	*States*	*Release of funds during 2007-08 (As on 18.3.2008)*	*No. of districts*	*No. of blocks covered*	*No. of SHGs formed (As on 30.6.2007)*
1	*2*	*3*	*4*	*5*	*6*
1.	Andhra Pradesh	0	23	38	3874
2.	Aurnachal Pradesh	9.35	6	6	600
3.	Assam	110.12	20	24	2400
4.	Bihar	492.45	19	63	6340
5.	Chattisgarh	57.63	16	17	1620
6.	Gujarat	48.36	20	27	2772
7.	Himachal Pradesh	0	7	8	800
8.	Haryana	0	6	13	1300
9.	Jammu & Kashmir	36.85	13	13	2424
10.	Jharkhand	127.47	11	24	2992
11.	Karnataka	0	12	20	2442
12.	Kerala	0	7	18	3667
13.	Madhya Pradesh	115.40	13	36	3923
14.	Maharashtra	36.04	20	36	300
15.	Manipur	0	3	3	524
16.	Meghalaya	0	5	5	300
17.	Mizoram	0	3	3	600
18.	Nagaland	0	5	6	3600
19.	Orissa	105.93	9	36	1960
20.	Punjab	99.96	8	15	3000
21.	Rajasthan	3.23	26	30	573
22.	Sikkim	0	4	5	5452
23.	Tamil Nadu	0	5	44	327
24.	Tripura	19.75	3	3	9268
25.	Uttar Pradesh	14.96	54	94	1100
26.	Uttaranchal	0	5	11	5148
27.	West Bengal	0	4	39	196
28.	A&N Islands	0	3	3	276
29.	Delhi	0	3	4	273
30.	Lakshadweep	0	1	3	—
31.	Pondicherry	0	1	0	300
	Other Expenses	366.43	0	—	0
	Total	1643.62	335	650	69669

Source: Ministry of Women and Child Development, Annual Report, 2007-08, p. 214.

CHAPTER

18

Peoples' Participation in Development

Public Participation is one of the most significant contribution for the efficiency and effective Governance. Time has come for a strong message to be conveyed that administration is for the people and not for the local bureaucracy. There has to be a change of attitudes, and Public servants should realise that efficiency will be measured not in terms of what the services purport to offer, but in terms of public satisfaction. Simultaneously, there has also to be a cleansing of the services and codification of ethics, values systems and the interface with the politicians.

M. Ariz Ahamed, has strongly advocated as follows: "Transparency and people participation in regulatory and development administration is very crucial not only in bridging the gap between the administration and the public but also in nation-building by way of reducing the corruption and complaints against the system. Further, it helps the people to understand the limitation of the administration at different levels."[1]

Ministry of Environment and Forests in its report "Empowering People for Sustainable Development" (2002) observes that Panchayati Raj Institutions represent virtually the last step in the system of representative democracy. This process of empowering people is being further strengthened by serious experimentation with participatory democratic processes in managing the livelihood resources. Joint Forest management (JFM), Participatory Irrigation Management (PIM), Participatory Watershed Management, etc. are some of the examples of participatory development.

In an article, "Public Pressure for Change" in *Hindustan Times*, Oct. 30, 2006, Preeti Singh Saksena observes: One of Yawning gaps in governance is the lack of meaningful citizen-government interface from one election to another. But the growth of organized voluntary activity is enabling concerned citizens to channelise private initiative to meet public goals.

Indian democracy is moving to another level, with its citizens demanding their own space in an increasingly DIY (do it yourself) world. Two impulses have contributed to deliver on its promises and the other is its inability to meet its development goals in certain spheres. It is here that civil society groups have stepped in to enhance the democratic potential of the state, leading to new and innovative models of citizen participation.

Broadly speaking, goodness of governance emerges from positive developmental roles of functionaries, underpinned with a summation of positive values—including morality, ethics, accountability, transparency, etc.—in a Weberian model of public administration operating in a democratic context. A true democracy visualizes decentralization and delegation of political power to realize true people's participation, who are the ultimate beneficiaries of all administrative activities relating to law and order development, social welfare, etc. Assertion of this angle is clearly visible behind the demand for enforcement of people's charter. In the twenty first century, let the people themselves decide what they want, when, how and where and in what proportion and let public administration restrict itself to a mere enabling role and not guiding them or leading them in their onward march to realise their socio-economic and development goals.[2]

According to Dennis E. Populin,[3] a community is "a unit of social and territorial organisation in which people live, work, attend school, and carry on many other activities which are a part of daily living. Indeed, communities are unique in that all of a person's needs can potentially be met within them."

Murray G. Ross, defines community as "a process by which a community identifies its needs or objectives, gives priority to them, develops the confidence and will to work at them, finds resources (internal and external) to deal with them, and in doing so, extends and develops co-operative and collaborative attitudes and practices within the community."[4]

Though the 8th Plan recognised the importance of people's initiatives and participation, the Ninth Plan has gone further in unambiguously putting people's participation at the fore-front of the development process:

> "The principal task of the Ninth and Tenth Plans have been to usher in a new era of people-oriented planning, in which not only the governments at the Centre and States, but the people at large, particularly the poor, can fully participate. A participatory planning process is an essential precondition for ensuring equity as well as accelerating the rate of growth of the economy."

Good Governance and citizens are intimately related to each other as the existence of one without the other is not possible in a civilized society. The harmonious relationship depends upon the sincerity, earnestness and co-operation between the two. To quote Robson, "The achievement of good relations between the government and the public is a matter which does not by any means depend solely on the conduct of civil servants and politicians. It depends equally on the attitude of citizens, groups, corporations, associations of all kinds and, indeed, of all unofficial bodies to public authorities. If we want public servants to behave well towards us, we must behave well towards them. Moreover, we must normally assume that they for their part will behave well. ..if politicians and civil servants are held in low esteem, if their work is decried, if abuse and invective is poured on them continuously, if loose and unsubstantial allegations are made about their incompetence, dishonesty, laziness and indifference to the public interests, it is unlikely that officials will develop or display qualities of integrity, industry and public spirit."[5]

Administration based on good governance is never something apart from people and their needs, rather it is the means by which these needs are met and the administrator who thinks of his organisation as something apart from the community will fail to recognise significant problems of the citizens and the administration and will not be in a position to deliver the goods.

ARC has also observed in this very connection: "If, in the prosperity of the people, lies the strength of a government, it is in their contentment that lies the security and stability of democracy."[6]

Some of the principles of successful community participation through Good governance are:

(a) deal with problems which the community recognizes as its problems;
(b) provide for community self-determination;
(c) engage the community in an active way in the solution of the problems;
(d) move at a pace that is comfortable for the community;
(e) encourage growth in the community through solving of problems; and
(f) encourage community self-understanding and integration. The main principle of community organization is to involve people in formulating and solving their own problems.

According to Lisk, F.A.N., "with regard to rural development.... Participation includes people's involvement in decision-making processes, in implementing programme.... their sharing in the benefits of development programmes, and their involvement in efforts to evaluate such programme."

T.K. Moulik says, "Participation in development process implies stimulating individuals to take the initiative and mobilizing people to work for overall societal development."

According to Koenroad Verhagen, "Participation is generally presented as the active involvement of target groups in the planning, implementation and control programmes and projects and not merely their passive acquiescence in performing predetermined task, not merely their exploitation in order to reduce the labour cost. Participation, it is argued, guarantees that the beneficiaries own interests are taken into account.

P.K. Bajpai, has rightly said that Government must understand that conscientisation of the people and their active participation in the development process, on one hand, and asserting their rights, on the other, does not weaken the authority of the State but is the symptom of true and mature democracy.[7]

Development is a multi-dimensional phenomenon, which cannot be achieved unless the community itself is involved. Resources available with any government are limited especially in the developing countries like India. Communities, according to their capacity, need to mobilise human, financial and material resources to supplement the resources provided by the national government and other extra-community sources in order to effectively carry out local improvement efforts. Substantial, financial and human resources can be mobilised from the community, some which may otherwise remain unused, such as the enthusiasm and energy of youth and women for community action. Thus, the community participation is most widely seen as a way to mobilise resources for that would otherwise not be available. A local body promoting to meet the diverse needs of the people may be faced with expenditure it could not meet if the entire effort had to be financed out of the public purse. So, in order to cut costs, the intended beneficiaries themselves contribute to the extension of community activities.

Community participation involves members of communities in planning, implementing and monitoring of activities. Thus, community is wholly involved in the programme rather than being asked to either contribute or to take advantage of the services offered under it. Community participation is the process in which individual families assume responsibility in their own programme. They come to know their own situation better and are motivated to solve their

common problems. This enables them to become agents of their own development instead of passive beneficiaries of development aid. They, therefore, need to realize that they are not obliged to accept conventional solutions that are not suitable. They have to acquire the capacity to appraise a situation, weigh the various possibilities and estimate what their own contribution can be. They must join hands with the Government on equal footing to promote good governance and make development administration successful.

PURPOSES

Based upon our earlier observations, let us mention the important purposes that can be served by encouraging people's participation for making development administration successful.: (Chart 18.1)

(i) Creating will and determination among the members of the community for improvement in their present and future life;
(ii) Identification and development of the local resources, thereby generating self-reliance among the community;
(iii) Achieving integrated area co-ordination among various agencies interested in community welfare;
(iv) Mobilising the available manpower for productive and useful activities;
(v) Keeping the members of the community constantly informed about the developments in the area;
(vi) Arranging functional literacy programmes which can help them in understanding new technology;
(vii) Organising various clubs of youth, women to serve as centres of discussion and development;
(viii) Providing an open forum for the community to discuss its problems and find indigenous solutions, which may be efficient and economical;
(ix) To develop local leaders who can further educate and mobilise the people in the area;
(x) Encouraging the people to adopt modren changes, which can accelerate their socio-economic development;
(xi) Arranging extra-curricular activities to generate social awareness through well designed publicity;
(xii) Encouraging the people to develop themselves rather than depend upon the Government for all activities and thus become self-reliant, which is the key to development.
(xiii) To ensure that the Government is running administration based on good governance.

Though people's participation is a pre-condition for success of development programmes and there must be an in- built mechanism to involve people in their conceptualisation, planning, implementation, monitoring and management of resources (funds). This may increase the efficacy and acceptance of the programme on the one hand and reduce the operational and administrative costs on the other. Yet government and voluntary organizations have not been successful in evolving a precise method of involving the people and, therefore, many programmes launched with laudable objectives and great expectations start loosing their momentum sooner or later.

Marsen considers[8] that meaningful participation is concerned with achieving power, i.e.,

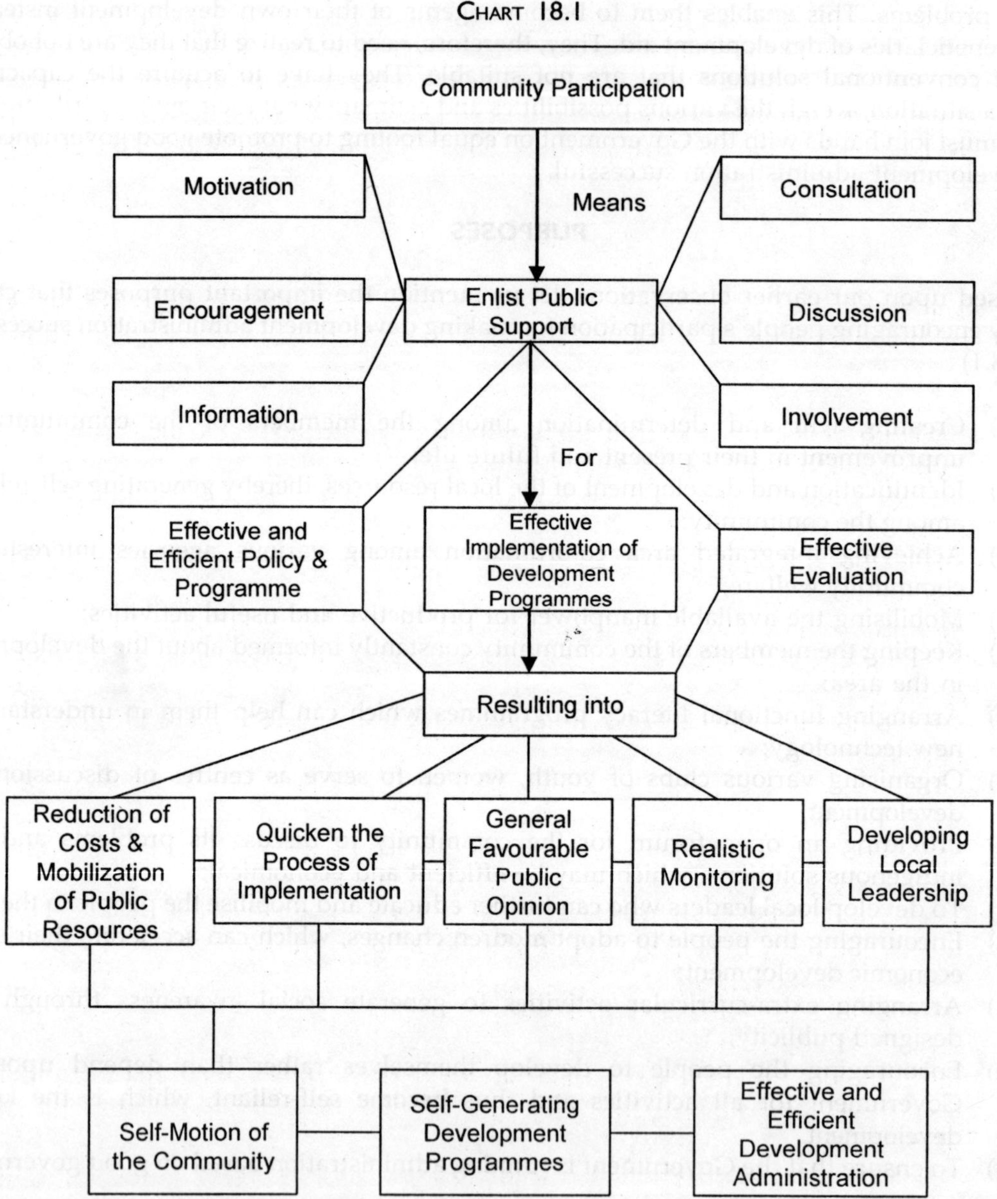

the power to influence the decision that affects one's. livelihood. So power is the key variable to influence decision- making and lack of it not only causes but also perpetuates the ill-being of the poor. Thus, participation, power and well-being are inter-linked. Indian experience has been altogether different as policies and programmes meant for development of poor have rendered only intoxicating impact and have genuinely not been concerned with sharing power.

The people's participation in development process has been elusive. This has been caused by two factors: (l) Lack of honesty on the part of NGOs and government or traders of development;

and/or; (2) People's apathy owing to many reasons who more often than not, are either deviated or resisted to join the moves seeking their participation.[9]

For democracy to be successful at the national level, the grass root organisations have to be strong and must be run on good governance. The local authorities have to respond to the felt needs of the people. The citizens have to have faith in the efficacy of the administrative system so that the distance between people and the government is reduced. The administration, for good governance has to be accessible. In developing countries, it is the government, which initiates and implements development programmes. It must gain support of the people in the discharge of these programmes, particularly at the cutting-edge. Such support would strengthen democracy as well as a positive response of the community to developmental programme, which should be the ultimate goal of good governance.[10]

TECHNIQUES OF PEOPLE'S PARTICIPATION (See Chart 18.2)

1. Strengthening Public Relations through Mass Media

The creation of awareness is integral to social and economic development. The possibility for the power of communication to liberate the minds and potential of people to critical awareness is real in every field linked to human development and the generation of public will hinges on effective communication of information and ideas that relate to people's needs, aspirations and capacities for progress in thought and action. In this sense, getting development process started is largely the task of information, education and communication through public relations.

Public relations is the establishment of a climate of understanding. It means interpreting the programme of an organisation to the public and *vice versa.* According to J.L. Mccany: "Public relations in government is the composite of all the primary and secondary contacts between the bureaucracy and the citizens and all the interaction of influences and attitudes established in these contacts."

According to Harwood: "Public relations may be defined as those aspects of our personal and corporate behaviour, which have a social rather than private and personal significance."[11]

The purpose of public relations is not only to supply information, but also to encourage an understanding and co- operation between the citizens and the public servants. The objectives of public relations should be to increase prestige and goodwill and to protect the life of the organisation by safeguarding it against unwarranted attacks as well as to remove the genuine complaints and grievances of the people. All this would depend upon the Government which only through good governance can win the confidence of the people.

2. Understanding Public Needs and Values of the Community

The first important step in public relations is to understand the community. Every community is different and there are differences between each local community in the same country in terms of their work culture and living standards, family life, social structure, population structure and attitudes. Besides, values, beliefs and customs, religious practices, etc. differ in different areas. There is a need to understand the need of the people based upon this diversity before launching any field operations. How to learn about the people and the community? Some of the important methods are:

(i) Discussion with People

Discussion can be both formal and informal. Discussion can be held with formal groups

CHART 18.2

Process of Participation Management

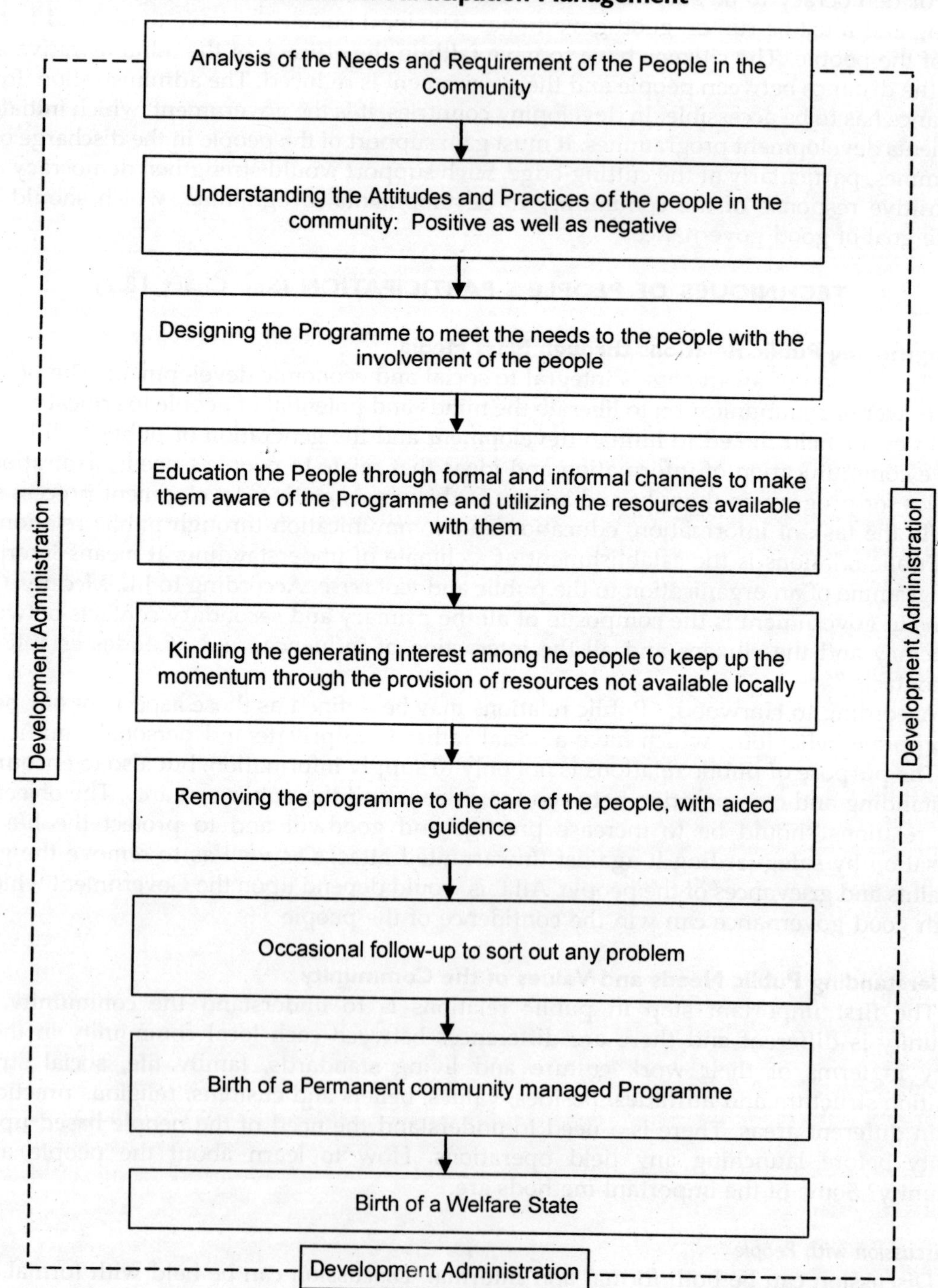

of the people. However, informal discussions with people in the markets and common places will throw light as to what concerns people most. In ascertaining the health needs of the people, CNA (Community Needs Assessment) surveys are carried out before introducing facilities in the area. Mahatma Gandhi had to tour the country to understand the problems of the country. Jawaharlal Nehru advised bureaucracy not to retire in their cells after work but should mix with all kinds of people, which would provide them with material that is not in their files.

(ii) Study of Newspapers. Magazines and Other Published Literature

A public relations department needs to study the published material wherein people express their needs and mention their likes and dislikes. This is a rich source of information.

(iii) Complaint and Suggestion Boxes

Most of the departments have put complaint and suggestion boxes. The analysis of complaints and suggestions can help the organisation in understanding the needs of the people.

(iv) Surveys

A well designed survey, opinion poll, or census can help us to know the reactions of the people about organisations. Researchers generally use such surveys to understand the problems.

Thus, the understanding of the people is vital for public relations to be effective. Hiroshi Nakajima, Former Director-General of the World Health Organisation, has rightly stressed the need of understanding the people. To quote him:

"People are the true measure of the success of policies and programmes. At the same time, people are the determinants of success. Experience teaches us that, whether in the most sophisticated cities or in the most remote villages, when people act with determination and understanding in pursuit of goals they deem essential, they achieve success. Previously insoluble problems are solved and resources are mobilised. Miracles happen."[12] The people's energy and its use are the pillars of Good Governance.

3. Informing People and the Community

Public relations departments/sections need to make the people aware about the people's benefit programmes they want to undertake for the people's benefit or the benefit of the country/area. This would aim at educating the people about the schemes in operation-their objectives, services, eligibility criteria, agencies and functionaries for the delivery of services. A good public relations exercise would provide the information in a way as to generate community's conviction about the efficacy and usefulness of the services. It would also lead to community's clear understanding of its participation and contribution. Knowledgeable citizens can ensure good governance through their active participation.

4. Creating Satisfactory Climate

For any public relation campaign to be effective, it is important to create an environment of goodwill based on equity. People must be given their due status and must be taken into confidence based on trust. Satisfactory relations between administration and people are necessary conditions for good governance.

5. Advising People

The government may advise the people to act in a way, which may be beneficial to them and to the government/agency concerned. Public relations through its various channels need to inject the desired changes to generate development, dynamism and modernization. Thus, the advice to be effective should be preceded by extensive planning of the public relations strategies to be followed.

Prem Kumar has rightly stressed the right to participate in the affairs of the country is meaningless unless the citizens are well informed on all sides of the issues, in respect of which they are called upon to express their views. One-sided information, disinformation, misinformation and non-information—all equally create an uninformed citizenry, which makes democracy a farce when medium of information is monopolised either by a partisan central authority or by a private individual. This is particularly so in a country like ours where about 48 per cent of the population is illiterate and hardly 6.5 per cent of the population has access to the print media, which is not subject to pre-censorship. When, therefore, the electronic media is controlled by one Central agency or a few private agencies of the rich, there is a need to have a Central agency, as stated earlier, representing all sections of the society. Hence, to have a representative central agency to ensure viewer's right to be informed adequately and truthfully is a part of the right of the viewers under Article 19(1)(a) of the Constitution of India.[13]

6. Creating Independent and Attractive Mass Media

The media of any society are among the most important institutions. Democracy without free media is a contradiction in terms. Mass media should be the watchdog of democracy, and not the poodle of the establishment. The media has a greater responsibility today than they ever had to guide the nation and make every citizen conscious of his fundamental duties enshrined in the Constitution. Public relations is carried out through many ways. Let us discuss some of the important ones.

(a) Press

Press is a very important channel of public relations, especially in metropolitan cities where literacy rate is very high. However, it has its limitations because of low literacy in developing countries like India. Besides, the press in developing countries does not co-operate with the Government in creating positive atmosphere, which is ideal for development. Rather, the press generally concentrates on negative aspects of the government resulting in alienation between the Government and the people. Besides press release, the Government publishes useful books to highlight Government programmes and projects. Besides, Directorate of Advertisement and Visual Publicity (DAVP) publicises the policies, programmes and performance of the Government of India through advertisements in the press, posters, brochures, folders, cinema slides, etc. These are not done regularly and on a continuous basis, but intermittently to deal with particular situations.

(b) Radio and Television

Radio and Television also play an effective role in public relations. Television has become very popular and its visual impact is high. However, the programmes aiming at development are not presented in a way as can influence the minds of the people, besides, the time devoted for development activities is very less.

(c) Films

Public relations departments make films in the areas of health, education, family planning, literacy, grow more food, agriculture, etc. which are quite useful. These films are screened with the films shown in theatres as well as screened in villages by mobile units. However, the contents of these films are not attractive to motivate the people to attend.

(d) Songs and Dramas

Public relations departments arrange folk, songs, drama, dances to make the people understand the problems. For example, songs and dramas are used for depicting population problems. Public relations in the Government of India at the Union and State levels have not been effective in meeting the needs of the country. Public relations is quite effective in the private sector but the government sector needs improvement. Let us discuss some of the problems and suggest remedies.

I. Wrong Presumptions about the Homogeneity of the Population

Population differs in different areas in terms of their knowledge, values and attitudes. It is, therefore, important for the Government to understand these variations and divide the population into homogeneous units through segmentation and direct its public relation activities accordingly to be productivity useful and usher an era of good governance.

2 Public Relations Directed to Promote Vested Interest

Public relations in government is done to promote the Interest of the ruling party as well as to project the personalities of key persons, which is nothing but propaganda. This type of public relations creates misgivings and misunderstandings among the masses in general and affected interests in particular. There is a need to adopt impartiality and scientific attitude in public relations to ensure its fruitful results. Morton R. Davies rightly mentions: "Politicians must resist the temptation to use the information services for party/political advantage; administrators must equally resist the tendency to acquiesce in the demands of their political master, and be constantly vigilant of the limitations that should be imposed on their role."[14] For good governance the administration must take care of the poorest.

3. Public Relations Mainly Directed to Urban Areas

Most of the formal public relations aim at influencing the public opinion of urban population as they are the vocal and influential segments of the society. It is quite discouraging that 70 per cent of the population living in villages and other backward areas is not covered through the desired programmes of public relations. According to F.C. Gera, "It is not enough for mass media to be blaring forth statement of Government's policies and programmes. There must be deliberate and organised attempts also to assess the needs of people, to listen to their grievances and to redress them. And the people, particularly the uneducated people, must be treated with courtesy instead of being shouted at and compelled to shell out bribes."[15]

4. Very Little Research in Public Relations

Most of the research in public relations are elementary and urban-based and have been adopted from foreign models. It is suggested that indigenous models may be developed which can serve a developing country like India. This is succinctly stated by Ross when he said, "As public relations field has grown in sophistication, this no longer means simply advertising as news report, nor even highly polished receptionist and telephone-answering service, but careful study (again often using social scientists) of employees, consumers, and the community at large, so that there is awareness within the organisation of the strength and weakness of its own position in the community."[16]

Public relations programmes need to be fair, honest, truthful, impartial, open, authoritative and responsive. They must be conducted in the public interest. It should attempt at lubricating Government and public relationship based on trust and confidence. All these would help in the promotion of good governance.

As media is both under Government controlled and in private sector, there is all the more need to formulate a comprehensive media policy. There has to be a close co-ordination with the concerned local body and other institutions responsible for programme implementation. The vast potential of the mass media has to be utilised for making different sections of the society conscious of their constitutional responsibilities and fundamental duties while integrating entertainment with socially relevant and useful message in the entertainment programmes themselves.[17]

7. Personnel Communication

The art of developing common understanding about people is vital to bring about change of attitudes and behaviour among bureaucracy. Sociologists have classified the diffusion process, which leads to a widespread acceptance of the development programme into five stages:

1. Awareness (the individual's first introduction to a new idea or practices);
2. Interest (the stage at which he actually seeks further information and background data);
3. Evaluation (the stage of assessment on theoretical grounds);
4. Trial (a limited phase of experiment), and finally
5. Acceptance or adoption.

Naturally, the duration of the process depends upon personality factors which differ with individuals. Mass media helps in creating awareness. in providing stimulation and motivation and in giving ready access to information. But at the specific stage of evaluation, trial and adoption, inter-personal, face to face, communication counts for much more and the inability of the mass media to maintain a two-way dialogue with regular feedback restricts their utility.[18] Therefore, no medium of communication is as effective as one human being talking to another. The UNESCO has rightly stated:

> "The process of social and economic development is a process of human development, for people are the targets as well as the essential variable in development. Communication being a two-way process. provides for participation at whatever stage of enlightenment of the individuals composing a society find themselves. Change agents are key factors in the communication development process since they are instruments for getting facts to the people upon which decisions can be based."[19]

There has been heavy, and perhaps unwarranted, reliance on mass media. be it printed, projected or broadcast. There is a need to re-examine the methods, materials and mass communication media currently in use and to determine what methods and materials are appropriate to achieve a proper mix between the individual, group and mass communication.

Thus, the impersonal methods are relatively simpler and even less time consuming. The radio, TV, newspapers, posters, and pamphlets can also help in improving public relations. Experience with personal and impersonal methods of public relations has revealed that if both the methods are used simultaneously, one can obtain better results than simply using one or the other method. Alastair Metheson, Deputy Director of UNICEF's division, remarks on the basis of his research that "to get people to act in ways that conform to new values almost always requires that mass communications be reinforced by personal influence."[20]

8. Need of Empowering the People, Especially the Disadvantaged Sections of the Society to Promote Good Governance

Participation has goals and objectives, which the community commonly shares. This common sharing makes the members of the community come together to take collective action to achieve the common goal. The goal sets the parameters and defines, in different situations, who the participants are? The roles different participants perform depend upon their capacity and capability like skills, technical knowledge, formal position, education, control over funds, connection with those in power, etc.

The hierarchy makes the powerful participants active and others passive. This affects participation in favour of those who have the power to make decisions for others.

The poorer groups, who are generally the most affected of the development process, are the least endowed and least powerful. The poor are automatically excluded from the participation process. Decision-making is the first step in the development process. Therefore, a key objective of participation is to find out ways to include the hitherto neglected groups, who are directly affected by the negative impacts of development, in the decision-making process.

Participation is a process of giving weightage to the poorer groups in the development process so that they may have say and control over decisions, which affect their lives; participation is a process of empowering the poorest. The indicator of genuine participation is the extent the poorer groups have power over decision-making and over resource management.

Panchayat Raj Act has taken a bold step in providing reservations to the weaker sections of the society. As a result, majority representation has been provided to them to undo the socio-economic handicaps thrust on them, in the traditionally exploitative society. These weaker sections of the society have also been given an opportunity to get elected to the posts of Adhyakshas and Upadhyakshas. If this provision was not made in the Act, the disadvantaged groups would have been reduced to mere numbers, having no great say in the decision-making process. Due to their illiteracy, ignorance and social backwardness, they could not have mustered enough courage to stand up to the cause of their communities. Thus, for the first time the local governments have been transformed into a system of people's governance of themselves. They can also mobilise the prospective beneficiaries to participate in the process of planning as well as execution. They can, therefore, effectively initiate a process of bottoms-up approach to development.

There should not be mere participation but empowerment should be entrusted to poor people. Arvind K. Sharma rightly mentions:

> "This reappraisal attributed poverty not just to a violently iniquitous distribution of wealth and resources but equally to an oppressive system of governance in which power was unequally distributed. This, it was asserted, prevented the majority from participating in the political processes; and, therefore, this majority has no opportunity to influence the decisions, which affect them. The silent majority remains an object of development, not its agent." The recognition of the inadequacies of the traditional capital-centred development, and the re-examination, which such recogniztion triggered, has led to emergence of a new perspective, referred to as ,'alternative development'. It is also identified by such other labels as people-centred development, participatory development, bottom up development, and so on.[21]

9. Attitudinal Changes among Personnel Responsible for Services

A democratic reorientation of the attitudes of the officials towards the citizens has become very much necessary for both the prevention of the citizen's complaints and their prompt redress. Local Bodies should pay great attention to the opinions of the people. Reorientation of the attitudes of the officials towards the citizens is a very difficult task. It will require thinking on several fronts such as in service training, recruitment from a wider social base, special assignments in rural areas and the like. The officials of local bodies of today should not only possess traditional service virtues like efficiency, integrity and loyalty but should also shake off all the feelings of exclusiveness and superiority. There should be a desire to establish contacts with the citizens to understand their problems. Unless the change in the attitudes of civil servants as a whole is brought about, all other measures to deal with the citizen's grievances will be of limited use.

C.N. Ray has rightly felt that the Government of India has been concerned about the frustration and dissatisfaction among the people, especially the vulnerable groups of the civil society regarding deterioration in the performance of agencies meant for delivery of public services. Despite recognition of the critical role of responsive State, public administration and civil services at all levels, in terms of eroded credibility and effectiveness of the civil services, public perception of an unholy nexus between politicians, civil servants and criminals (as illustrated in the Vohra Committee Report), has been growing with an increasing criticism of low levels of honesty, transparency and accessibility of the democratic elements in-charge of administration. In order to restore the faith of the people in the fairness and capacity of the administration, the Prime Minister had inaugurated a Conference of the Chief Secretaries in November 1996 on "an agenda for an effective and responsive administration." The objective of the conference was to make public service more efficient, clean, accountable and citizen-friendly by evolving a concrete action plan. The adoption and implementation of the proposed action plan would require strong political will and commitment from the Central and State Governments.[22]

It is of utmost national importance that the civil servants are honest and upright in the discharge of their public duties, particularly at a time when clouds of political uncertainty and instability are hovering over our national life. It is at this time that the civil servants should serve the nation honestly by giving a sense of continuity. If they fail, the future of the nation may be dark.[23]

Former Prime Minister, Atal Bihari Vajpayee, rightly stressed: "My greatest concern today is in the area of implementation. The National Agenda for governance has clearly spelt out our priorities. In the light of these priorities, a large number of good policies, programmes, and schemes have been worked out of course. We have also inherited a large number of good policies, programmes, and schemes from the previous governments. Where we fumble, however, is in implementing them in a manner that satisfies the people. I have said it before, and I say it again, that I cannot accept delays and slippages in implementation. I cannot, because the people cannot. The people want to see action, and not just hear words of promise repeated again and again. I want to see the entire administrative machinery, from top to bottom, work with a sense of mission and result-oriented approach. I want to see them work with their hearts and minds fully in the administrative responsibility they hold. I want to see them work faster and work better. I want to see them work with a sense of mission and accountability. In doing so, I want to see them work without any fear or favour."[24]

10. Strengthening of NGO's/Voluntary Agencies and Ensuring their Accountability

Voluntary agencies have a long history of active involvement in the promotion of human welfare and well-being. Lord Beveridge called them "a private enterprise for social progress." Voluntary agencies come into existence spontaneously, voluntarily and without any compulsion or control to fulfil the particular needs of some groups of people. These agencies are flexible and possess the virtues of human services with dedication. Voluntary action is the soul of democracy as this medium secures the active involvement of the people from policy-making to implementation. It is the life and blood of democracy.

A voluntary agency may be defined as: "An organisation that is administered by an autonomous board which holds meeting, collects funds for the support, chiefly from private sources, and expends money, whether with or without paid workers, in conducting a programme."

According. to Dharma Vira: "Work of voluntary organisations and citizen participation are two sides of the same coin. Citizens work in organisations but on their work depends the quality of the service the organisations render. Voluntary Organisations provide a frame for citizen participation. Without effective citizen participation, the organisation would only be empty forums."[25]

It is very difficult to provide all the services to the people through the Government, as it is very costly. The voluntary agency can exploit the unused energies of the people for the development of the country. Energy of the people, if unused, cannot be preserved. This unused energy "like the unused vast water resources flowing down in Himalayas is not only wasted like those rivers, but also, like the river waters that take with them the top soil of the Himalayan region causing permanent losses in social erosion, cause permanent damage to the human spirit and will in a community through dependence and frustration born out of ever-increasing level of abject poverty over the generations.[26]

Voluntary agencies can help in the programme implementation, collaboration and co-ordination with other activities. They can contribute to social welfare development in many ways through programme implementation. They can:[27]

(1) Provide assistance to develop and/or strengthen local NGO capabilities and activities with particular attention to local community development groups.

(2) Conduct reviews and assessment of existing development programmes and assist communities in the exercise of their own role in such reviews. A greater emphasis on evaluative techniques will render all new programmes more accountable to real community needs.

(3) Develop innovative programmes in the context of comprehensive human development.

(4) Ensure that their existing programmes and new initiatives promote full participation by individuals and communities in the planning, implementation and control of these programmes.

(5) Expand their training efforts to respond to the needs of programmes, e.g., training of health workers, supervisors, administrators, planners and various agricultural and development workers.

(6) Extend their efforts to develop locally sustainable and appropriate technologies and use of resources, with particular attention to energy, water, agriculture, sanitation and medical care.

(7) Contribute to the creation of new and effective methods of education, which enable

both individuals and communities to assume greater responsibility for their own health.

(8) Recognise the essential roles of women in the promotion and in the full range of community development concerns.

(9) Further extend their capacity to work with poor, disadvantaged and remote populations enabling them to break the cycle of deprivation, and in this way contribute to the search for greater social justice.

N.V. Lalitha & Mathu Kohli have given the following points to enhance performance of voluntary sector:

(i) The government should spell out clearly the policy towards voluntary organizations indicating the relative role of the government and the voluntary sector, entitlement to funds, etc. This is very necessary in view of the fact that social welfare programme suffer from ad-hocism and uncertainty which come in the way of promoting voluntary efforts.

(ii) There is an urgent need to make a serious review of the working of voluntary organisations in terms of assets, financial soundness, service conditions of staff, quality of service, etc. Such a review would help identify the genuine agencies and give them all the support they need financial and technical because voluntary agencies can do excellent work and bring in better results. The government should also have certain controls in terms of audit, submission of accounts, work report, etc.

(iii) The Directorates of Social Welfare should equip themselves with facts and figures regarding voluntary organisations, their specialised areas of work, problems faced by them in their day-to-day functioning, etc., so that they can deal with them better. The inadequate and scanty information available at present create considerable difficulties both for the government and the voluntary organisations.

(iv) The government should insist on certain rules and procedures of recruitment, salary scales and working/service conditions so that voluntary organisations would get properly qualified persons to man their programmes.

(v) Grants should not be released as a matter of routine. The government should see that the organisations qualify for grants.[28]

These associations can perform the following functions:

(a) Provision of information and advice to the citizens in the making of applications and complaints.

(b) Educating the citizens in regard to their duties to the State and advising them about what should not be expected from administration.

(c) Lending support to the citizen's genuine demand and complaints.

(d) Bringing to bear influence on the Government departments and agencies for improvement of policies, programmes and procedures in the interest of the citizen's welfare and satisfaction.

(e) Promotion of high standards of public morality for good governance.

The women's voluntary organisation in the form of Mother's Club in the Republic of South

Korea have been quite useful in raising the status of women. By mid-2005, nearly 90,000 such clubs had been organised. The clubs provide opportunities for village women to get-together to talk about health, education of children and improvement of environment. The club helps in family planning, vaccination and treatment of emergency cases. The mothers' clubs are a genuinely grass-root community network which owes little to outside administrators or planners. I.C. Abcede, in his article on "Women-Power in Korea" observes that mother's clubs are helping to change age-old social attitudes towards women. He says, "The growth of women's clubs in Korea has coincided with considerable changes in social attitudes towards women.

The trend is towards greater recognition of womens' contribution to the Community, better communication between husband and wife, and more open discussion of family planning matters . . . it seems clear that the enhanced status of women and the growth of mothers' clubs have gone hand-in-hand and are contributing significantly to the development of rural communities in Korea."[29]

Such clubs should be set-up in other countries as well. These would help mobilise voluntary resources lying idle and if not used can be a source of destruction. In the developing countries like India, voluntary organisations are urban-based and serve the urban area. These organisations must create a strong base by setting up such clubs in rural and uncovered areas and diffuse information to them to be passed among the members of the community. This would bring about a socio-economic revolution and contribute substantially to modernisation and development.

However, NGO's should aim at making people self-reliant and not dependent on them. Touching upon the critical role to be played by the NGOs, the former Primer Minister Shri P. V. Narasimha Rao, while addressing the NGOs on March 7, 1994 at Vigyan Bhavan said:

In all this, we have to remember that the people must occupy the centre stage. At all times, they should be the focus of all that we aim to do. Therefore, when I talk of a participatory approach to development, I have in mind an approach where the people would be helped to help themselves. In other words, we should envisage a situation in our country, where people would deal with their problems on their own in the not too distant a future, without having to depend upon outside agencies. In the ultimate analysis, the people should not merely change their masters; people should be their own masters. That is what people-centred development is all about. Therefore, if a particular area is taken up by a NGO, it is not expected that it would function there for all times to come. A time should come when the people would have been fully mobilised and made aware of and empowered to deal with their own problems. In other words, the NGOs should withdraw after the task is done and shift to other areas, where their services are needed.

11. Administrative Reforms to Simplify Procedures to Ensure People's Participation

Increased productivity in the developing countries depends to a great extent on the executive branch, which should pursue efficiency with greater determination. The executive branch can pursue its objectives, provided the prevailing administrative system is conducive to socio-economic progress. The design of an administrative system is a basic aid to the achievement of its primary objectives; if the design is unsound, the achievement of objectives is likely to fall short of expectations. The administration can provide the means whereby the most effective use can be made of the knowledge and skills of the personnel engaged in different activities. The benefits of modern science and technology can reach the people only if such services are properly planned and effectively implemented. There are no two different opinions on this issue. All agree that without consistent and persistent efforts to achieve perfection of administration, progress in increasing efficiency/productivity is impossible. A scientific approach and determination are important factors in raising administrative efficiency. Simplification of the procedures should take place into matters like:

(a) Regard for public comfort and convenience.
(b) Speed in disposal of applications.
(c) Minimum inter-departmental/office references.
(d) Reduction in the number of levels required to examine cases.
(e) Reduction in the number of agencies with which the citizen has to deal with.
(f) Supply of detailed information to the citizen as to how is he to go about to receive a certain benefit or approval from administration.

12. Well Equipped Machinery to Handle Citizens' Complaints

A democratic reorientation of the attitude of the officials towards the citizens has become very much necessary for both the prevention of the citizens complaints and their prompt redress. Administrators should pay great attention to the opinions of the people. Reorientation of the attitude of the official towards the citizens is a very difficult task. It will require assault on several fronts such as service training, recruitment from a wider social base, special assignments in rural areas and the like. The public servant of today should not only be equipped with traditional service virtues like efficiency, integrity and loyalty but should also shake-off all the feelings of exclusiveness and superiority.

13. Transparency

Mr. K.R. Venugopal, retired Secretary to GOI, argued that "Transparency of governance and right to information should be fundamental rights of all people." These are the basic guarantees for human and social development. A similar critique and plea is evident in an analysis of most evaluation studies of the anti-poverty programmes. One can thus safely argue that official thinking on poverty alleviation and sustainable human development is increasingly veering towards a framework that recognizes the inherent limitations of a centralized, top-down hierarchic approach to poverty alleviation. This approach recognizes the importance of NGOs/CBOs in activating institutions of civil society, mobilizing and organizing the people, strengthening the institutions of local governance, ensuring accountability of official structures and schemes, and facilitating the development of expertise for local development.

SUGGESTIONS TO PROMOTE PEOPLE'S PARTICIPATIONS (See Chart 18.3)

1. Harmonious Relationship

The success of the development administration depends, to a great extent, upon the harmonious relationships between the citizens and administration. Local Government should not function as a machinery but in a humane and purposeful way. The people in Local Body should have a sense of dedication, responsibility, be responsive and alert to the aspirations of the citizens. Citizens, on the other hand, should also provide meaningful cooperation to Local Bodies. Under such an atmosphere, it would be very easy to implement the developmental tasks, to bring about social change and modernisation in the country. The strengthening of democracy in its social and economic aspect has to be attained through the participation on the part of the people. A similar shift is evident in international thinking.

CHART 18.3

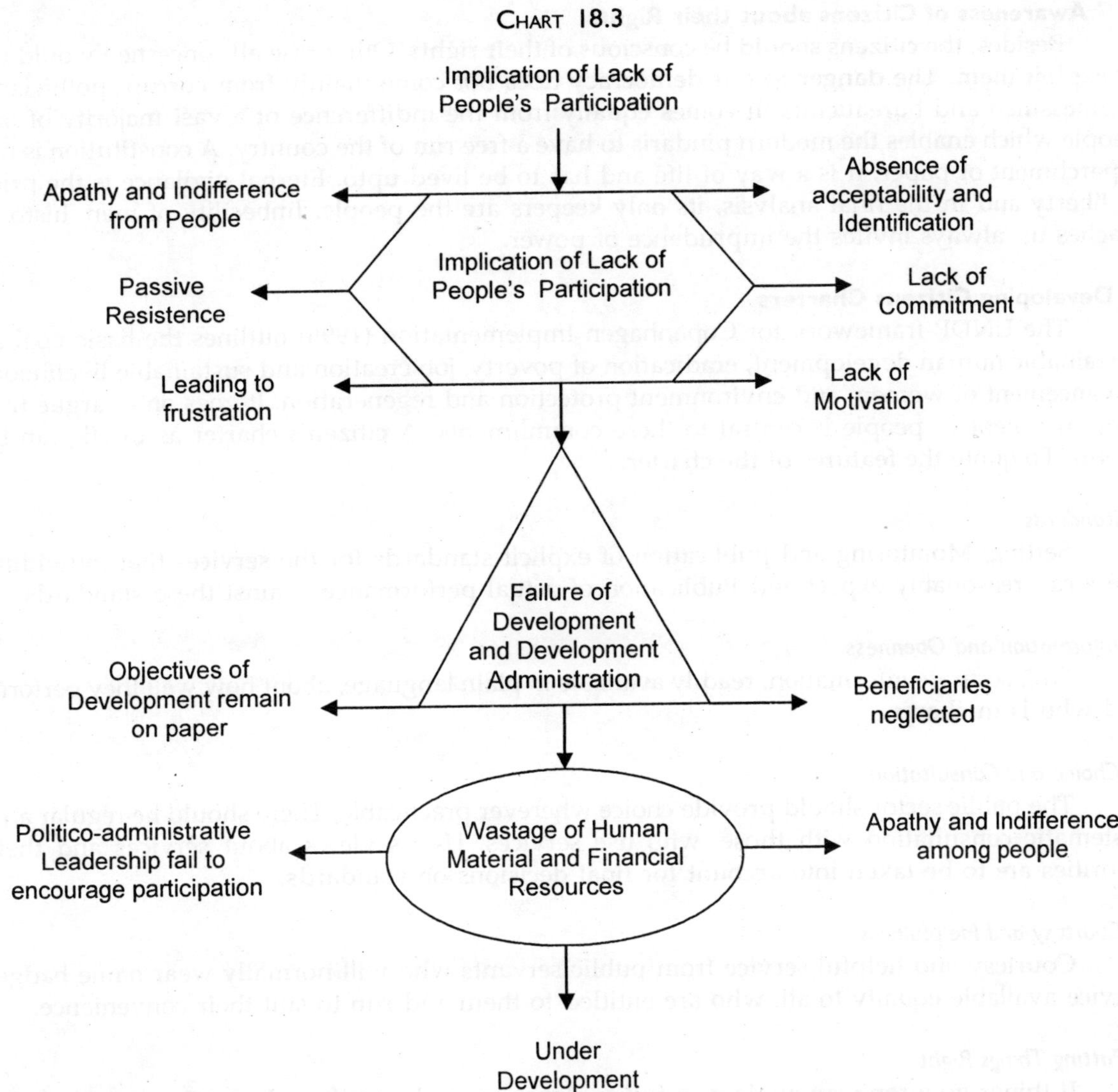

2. Avoids Unrest and Tensions

If the citizens' grievances are allowed to mount up, the dissatisfaction with the administration may add to any existing social unrest and tensions. The phenomenon of growing social discontent which erupts into frequent acts of violence finds substance in the citizen's frustration with the administration, it is, therefore, necessary that the citizen's faith in the Government of which the administration is the chief executive agency should not be allowed to deteriorate but should be reinforced adequately. This is important both for political stability and preservation of the social fabric. The dissatisfaction of the citizens with the administrative machinery has grown in recent years. There has been general agreement that the administration has not been able to provide efficient and timely service.

3. Awareness of Citizens about their Rights

Besides, the citizens should be conscious of their rights. Otherwise all concerned would try to exploit them. The danger to our democracy does not come mainly from corrupt politicians, businessmen and bureaucrats. It comes equally from the indifference of a vast majority of our people which enables the modern pindaris to have a free run of the country. A constitution is not a parchment of paper, it is a way of life and has to be lived upto. Eternal vigilance is the price of liberty and in the final analysis, its only keepers are the people. Imbecility of men, history, teaches us, always invites the imprudence of power.

4. Developing Citizens Charters

The UNDP framework for Copenhagen Implementation (1996) outlines the basic goal as sustainable human development, eradication of poverty, job creation and sustainable livelihood, advancement of women, and environment protection and regeneration. It goes on to argue that Empowerment of people is central to these commitments. A citizen's charter as in UK can be useful. To quote the features of the charter:

I. Standards

Setting, Monitoring and publication of explicit standards for the services that individual users can reasonably expect and Publication of actual performance against these standards.

2. Information and Openness

Full, accurate information, readily available in plain language, about how well they perform and who is in charge.

3. Choice and Consultation

The public sector should provide choice wherever practicable. There should be regular and systematic consultation with those, who use services. User's views about services and their priorities are to be taken into account for final decisions on standards.

4. Courtesy and Helpfulness

Courtesy and helpful service from public servants who will normally wear name badge. Service available equally to all, who are entitled to them and run to suit their convenience.

5. Putting Things Right

If things go wrong, an apology, a full explanation, and a swift and effective remedy to be offered. Well published and easy to use complaint procedures with independent reviews, wherever possible to be introduced and maintained.

6. Value for Money

Efficient and economical delivery of public services within the resources, the nation can afford and independent validation of performance against standards.

5. Promotes Development Administration

Thus, the people are key to good governance both as beneficiary and as agents. Public participation promotes maximum development at minimum cost. Public participation enhances the prestige dignity and role of individuals in development administration. People become part and parcel of development administration.

6. Citizen-Centric and Citizen-Friendly

B.B . Tandon in his article, "Quality in Government in Management in Government rightly suggests that we are now on the threshold of the twenty first century. In the new millennium, above all, the government would need to re-invent itself to become citizen-centric and citizen-friendly. It would need to limit its role to core functions such as security, law and order, social services, creation of infrastructure and macro economic management. Greater delegation and decentralization of authority and responsibilities would need to be introduced at all levels. A combination of Citizens' Charters and the Right to Information would ensure greater accountability and would need to be introduced at all levels. At the same time, good citizenry would also need to be emphasized for all round development of the society. Besides enjoying their rights, the citizens would need to behave responsibly and perform their duties to the state. Clearly defined ethical standards would also need to be adopted by the civil servants as well as politicians. In order to achieve all this, innovative use of information technology would be critical."

In short we can say:

(a) People's Participation is sine-quo-non for development and good development administration..
(b) People's Participation provides kinetic energy for development and good governance.
(c) People's Participation strengthens the values of Democracy and development administration.
(d) People's Participation avoids social unrest, tensions, violence and other social upheavals which do not allow good governance to flourish.

C.H. Bala Ranules righthly observes:[30]

The concept of participation is not something new and there is close relationship between participation and development ever since the evolution of the society. The best state is one where there is broad participation with no class dominating others. Possible ways of involving people in development activities are: (i) convincing the people about the importance of the programme; (ii) need for better planning with people; (iii) need to consult the local organisations before launching the programmes; (iv) inviting the villagers for discussion before introducing the programmes; (v) taking into consideration the felt needs of the people; (vi) respect for the ideas of the local people; (vii) informing the benefits that the local people/individual likely to get out of the programmes; (viii) local control over the amount, quality and distribution of benefits; (ix) voluntary commitment of the individuals, groups, organisations; and (x) commitment of the political parties, particularly the party in power to take up the programmes and encouraging the people to participate in them, etc. All these factors make the people to pool their energies, resources, ideas, together and work for attainment of the objectives of any project/programme they set for government.

Therefore, the sustainable development calls for multi-faceted and comprehensive interventions to address wide varieties of problems of the people. The people, for whom the development programmes are meant, must take part in planning and execution. Further strengthening of people's institutions at the grassroots level by providing autonomy in designing the projects, integrating their activities under the umbrella of PRIs, providing adequate financial resources and imparting training to the local leadership, 'development of human resources, proper utilisation of both indigenous and modern technology, etc., are imperative for participatory development in the state/country'.

Right to Information made people's Participation meaningful. To quote Sound Administration Reforms Commission: Without good governance, no amount of developmental schemes can bring improvements in the quality of life of the citizens. Good governance has four elements-transparency, accountability, predictability and participation. Transparency refers to availability of information to the general public and clarity about functioning of governmental institutions. Right to information opens up government's records to public scrutiny, thereby arming citizens with a vital tool to inform them about what the government does and how effectively, thus making the government more accountable. Transparency in government organisations makes them function more objectively thereby enhancing predictability. Information about functioning of government also enables citizens to participate in the governance process effectively. In a fundamental sense, right to information is a basic necessity of good governance.[31]

Thus fuller participation is important both as a means of tapping the practical and intellectual resources of all the people for the benefits of the success of development programmes. Such participation would be meaningful both to Government implementing the development programmes and the people.

7. Obstacles to Participation

Participation of people in development programme though theoretically available in one form or the other is pratically non-existent. Most of the people during discussion in large number of research projects reveals that the government functionaries at all levels provide superficial participation which serves as an eye-wash

Dynamism in development administration cannot be declared by fiat, nor can it be generated by the artificial insemination of imposed systems, procedures and job demands. The participation of people is an effective corollary of effective development administration. Without it, the whole management effort of development administration becomes a kind of drudgery never moving beyond a mechanical process. Thus, we can say that the people's participation will be conducive to the success of development administration. In such a situation the energy and initiative among the people would be self-generating. In addition, all their potential energy would be changed into kinetic energy which can be used for the success of development administration.

1. Politicians never want people's participation in reality

Politicians do not encourage participation of the people in development administration programmes in right earnest. They do it only superficially to get the support of the people. Elected MPs, MLAs, do not visit frequently their constituencies and give the people only a lip service. People's participation they fear, would expose their corrupt practices in which they indulge in collaboration with bureaucracy.

2. Bureaucracy mind set do not encourage participation

Development administration is run by bureaucracy alone without participation of the people. Bureaucrats think that they are a nuisance and hurdles in the implementation of development administration programmes. People may be associated for ceremonial purposes and not for real development programmes.

3. People themselves do not exert their rights

People have also become apathetic as they do not find that their passive association can be meaningful. Therefore, there is a need to motivate people through making them aware of development programmes being implemented. In actual practice there is a dichotomy between people and bureaucracy without any meeting point.

4. Vested Interests are roadblocks in the path of Development and development administration

Agents or vested interests of politicians and bureaucracy are patronized to help them to siphon money and keep the people away from reality.

5. Lack of Popular acceptance and involvement of people

Let us discuss it in the context of health administration

Merle Fainsod remarks: "The most favourable setting for progress in development administration exists where politically influential and dynamic modernizing elite strongly desires development and can successfully project this attitude into both the bureaucracy and the population at large."[32] .

Many well-intentioned and technically sound programmes aimed at solving health problems have been frustrated by a lack of popular acceptance and community participation. "It has been observed that such programmes are either not actively associated or passively ignored because they do not 'belong' to the population they are designed to help; they are rather seen by the population as imposed external programmes that belong to the government and consequently deserve and require little, if any, of the population's attention, action, or other response."[33] We must be clear that health cannot be imposed; it can only be acquired. This requires participation based on enlightenment of the beneficiaries.

Dr Madiou Toure; Director Hygiene and Health Protection, Ministry of Public Health, Republic of Senegal, in his article. "The Health Revolution", in *World Health* (November, 1979) has rightly said: "The medicine of tomorrow will be shaped by the people for the people, because the people themselves will determine their own condition, their own destiny."

6. Lack of Administrative Capability and Competence

Administrative capability is *sine qua non* for the success of any programme. It is a major and crucial factor in the success or failure of development programmes. It is the scarcest of all resources in the developing world. The general administrator is fit only for the maintenance of law and order and he is not suitably equipped to deal with the problems of development and welfare economics.

According to K.N. Rao: "Unlike advanced countries there is no pool of experienced and well informed leaders of thought available as potential leaders for ministerial positions which greatly handicaps their assuming policy-making and decision-making responsibilities in the Government. This results in over-dependence on the Secretaries who are non-technical general administrators."[34]

7. Deep-rooted corrupt practices

Development projects do not achieve their targets because of corrupt practice. Recently implemented Rural Employment Guarantee programme is not achieving success because of inherent corrupt practices. This prevents the people from participation in development project. O.P. Dwivedi feels that it is useful to draw on lessons from other countries in order to avoid making the same mistakes: (1) full political support is required to the cause at the designing stage of administrative reform; (2) the reform agenda should be concise, clear and achievable; (3) once reform agenda has been put in place, a regular monitoring and feedback system should be put in place so that mid-course correction can be made or a change in original expectations can be modified; (4) time-frame should not be underestimated because any reform takes time to take effect and get nurtured, thus judging the effect within two three years will be too early; (5) reformers should be ready to encounter and overcome resistance from the middle management, and hurdles from the unions, therefore, a strategy of cooperation and cooptation should be considered; and (6) there are cultural nuances and values inherent in any paradigm or a model transported from the outside; transplanting such a system requires cultural and attitudinal changes (for example, when work days were changed from six days to five days a week with concomitant changes in working hours, there was no appreciable change in the working habits of office employees.)

8. Bureaucracy unable to implement women-related programmes efficiently

We inherited from the British an elaborate administrative system with in-built, organic continuum from a village-level Patwari to the Prime Minister. For obvious historical reasons, it was designed as an instrument of regulatory administration. But being a nation in a hurry, we decided to use it as a delivery system for economic growth and social change also. Inevitably, the developmental tasks which required to be performed by the people's participation and initiative, were assigned to bureaucracy for implementation. Thus, a unique opportunity for harnessing the titanic energies of our masses in the cause of national development through participatory democracy was lost .... An Editorial in *The Hindustan Times* noted as follows: Whatever be the arrangement, the effort should be to ensure people's participation in the planning process from the Gram Sabha to the Zila Parishad level.[35]

CONCLUSION

People's participation is thus sine quo non for development and development administration. The government should facilitates the process and methods of people's participation earnestly. It is an active process in which people influences the direction and execution of development projects rather than merely receiving a share of project benefits.

Community Based Health Partnership is the key to sustaining health action even with limited resources. This can take many forms, through the PRIs, community-based and NGOs, and of people participating at all levels of health interventions. This cannot be achieved only by giving financial and administrative powers to the Panchayats, it needs active participation of the people for local action. Partnership with community groups (through youth, mahila mandals, SHGs, and Gram Sabhas) is necessary for local solutions to local problems In this regard, successful communitization of health services in Nagaland should be studied and replicated.

The NRHM envisages community participation such as described above. Under the framework for implementation, the Mission tries to ensure that more than 70% of the resources are spent through bodies that are managed by peoples' organizations and at least 10% of the resources are spent through grants-in-aids to NGOs. The mechanism of untied funds at the local level is meant to give them a little flexibility. During the Eleventh Five Year Plan, efforts will be made to promote various community-based initiatives.

NOTES AND REFERENCES

1. M. Aziz Ahamed, "Good Governance Through Transparency", in Management in Government, Dec. 1999.
2. M.K. Gaur, Political Stability and Good Governance, in T.N. Chaturvedi (ed.), New Delhi, IIPA, 1999.

3. Dennis E. Populin, Communities: A Survey of Theories and Methods of Research, McMillan, 1972.
4. Murray G. Ross and B.W. Happin, Community Organisation: Theory, Principles and Practice, Harper and Row, N.Y., Second Edition.
5. William A. Robson (Ed.), The Civil Services in Britain and France. Hogarth Press, 1956, p. 13.
6. ARC: Interim Reports of ARC on Problem of Redress of Citizens' Grievances, p. 17.
7. P.K. Bajpai, People's Participation in Development in *IJPA*, Oct.-Dec., 1998, p. 823.
8. D. Marsden and P. Oakley, "Radical Community Development in the Third World", in M.G. Graig. *et. al.* (eds.) 1982, pp. 153-56.
9. P.K. Bajpai, *op. cit.*, p. 817.
10. A.P. Barnabas, Good Governance at Local Levels, in *IJPA*, July-Sept., 1998, p. 453 (Special Number on Towards Good Governance).
11. Harwood, Childs L., An Introduction to Public Opinions. *op. cit.*, p. 2.
12. WHO, *World Health*, May-June, 1992, p. 3.
13. Prem Kumar, Fundamental Duties and Media in *IJPA*, Oct.-Dec., 1999, pp. 698-730.
14. Mortun, R Davies, 'Government and Administrative Responsiveness in Britain' in *IJPA*, Vol. XXXIII, No. 2 (April-June. 1987), p. 209.
15. F.C Gera. 'Need for Public Relations in Administration' in *IJPA*, Vol. XXI, July-Sept. 1975, pp. 545-46.
16. Marray, G. Ross, Community Organisation. New York. Harper and Row, 1967, p. 25.
17. Prem Kumar, *op. cit.*, p. 718
18. UNESCO, Communication in Media, Family Planning and Development. No. 1, Paris, p. 1975.
19. UNESCO, Communication in Support of Population. Family Planning and Development, E/F/S/75, XIII, 5, p. 482.
20. UNICEF, UNICEF News. 'Communication: A Tool for Development', Issue, 84/1975/2, p. 18.
21. Arvind K Sharma, People's Empowerment in *IJPA*, July-Sept. 1996, p. 236.
22. C.N. Ray, Citizens' Charter in India: An Overview. in *IJPA*, Oct.-Dec., 1998, p. 236.
23. R.P. Dubhdshi, Administrative Autonomy, in *IJPA*. Oct.-Dec. 1998. p. 102.
24. Atal Behari Vajpayee, Indian Administration Today, In *IJPA*, Jan. to March 1999, p. 4.
25. Dharam Vir, Citizen Participation in Encyclopedia of Social Work, Vol. I, p. 102.
26. Malhotra, R.C., *op. cit.*, p. 11.
27. World Federation of Public Health Association, *op. cit.*, pp. 45-46.
28. N.V. Lalitha and Madhu Kohli, Status of Voluntary Effort in Social Welfare, *Ibid*, pp. 124-25.
29. WHO: *World Health*, May 1979, p. 19.
30. Ch. Bala Ramulu, "Participation Development: The Experience of Andhra Pradesh", *IJPA*, Vol. XLVIII, No. 4, Oct.-Dec. 2002, pp. 667-68.
31. Government of India, Second Administrative Reforms Commission, First Report on Right to Information: Master Key to Good Governance, June 2006, para 1.1.1, p. 1.
32. Melre Fainsod, "The Structure of Development Administration", in Irving Swerdlow (ed.) Development Administration: Concepts and Problems, (Syracuse, N.Y. Syracuse University Press, 1963, p.1.
33. WHO: *Chronicle*, 30 (1976), pp. 177-78.
34. R.N. Rao, Some Challenges in Health Administration", Background document to Xth Staff College course at NIHFW, Mimeorgraphy.
35. "Planning from Below", *The Hindustan Times*, New Delhi, August 25, 1988, p. 11.

CHAPTER 19

Administrative Reforms

Dr. Manmohan Singh, Former Union Finance Minister and presently Prime Minister of India said that overall, the country faces a crisis of governance and there is an urgent need to modernize the Indian state at all levels to make it more effective and more caring about the welfare of our people. Fortunately, recent advances in modern science and technology, particularly advances in information, communication and bio technologies make it possible, as never before in human history, to leapfrog in the race for the social and economic change." If you keep track of the results—you can dispense with a lot of red tape.

The Second Administrative Reforms Commission very emphatically remarked that there is a growing realization that many agencies of government are functioning sub-optimally, and government programmes have not always yielded the desired results. While the achievements of the public services are praiseworthy in dealing with the vast expanded responsibilities since Independence and especially during difficult periods of crisis, they are often deficient in crucial areas such as productivity, responsiveness, accountability and integrity. Authority frequently appears to be divorced from accountability, leading to a system of realistic and plausible alibis for non-performance. Inefficiency, corruption and delays have become, in public perception, the hallmarks of public administration in India.[1]

Administration should be reformed to bring about improved transparency, greater accountability and streamlining of the structure of government, based on decentralization, civil services reform, an open and responsive government, rule of law, fiscal and environmental sustainability and elimination of all forms of corruption. There is need to restructure our governance institutions and rejuvenate our administrative system so that it can respond to the growing challenges of governance. The State needs to reorient its focus on the core functions of government such as maintaining peace and stability in the country and the task of social investment and provision of public goods through investment in the social sectors like health and education, as these are critical to lifting people out of abject need, preventing inter-generational transmission of poverty, long-term development of human capital, achievement of full human potential and promotion of rapid, sustainable and equitable economic growth. (See Chart 19.1)

CHART 19.1

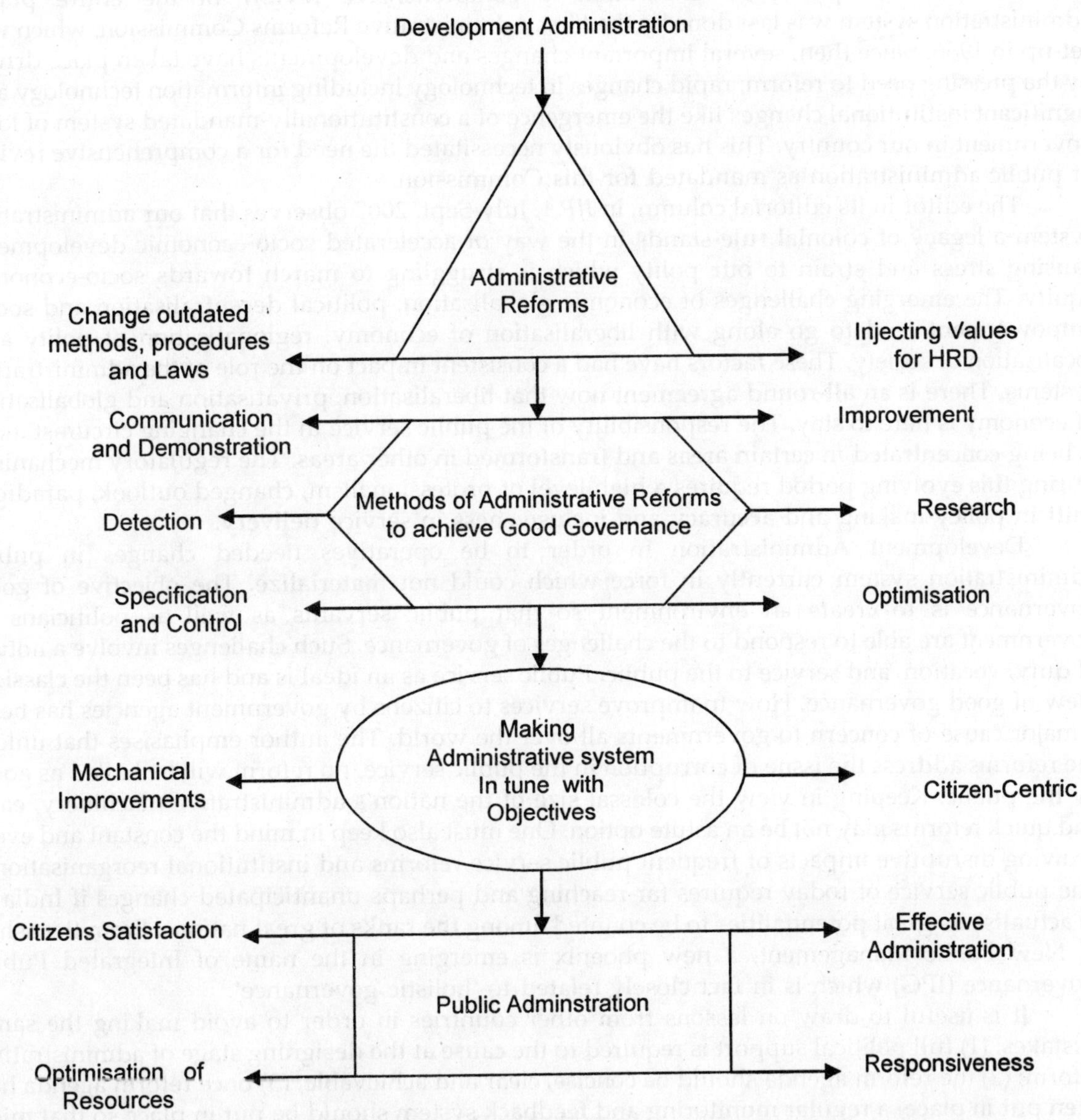

Administration must become far more accountable and effective in delivering results with the same expenditure. In order to accomplish these goals, there should be conscious efforts to establish the links and fuse authority with accountability. While compliance with processes is important to ensure objectivity and fairness, the processes themselves need to be simplified and changed from time to time. Priority needs to be given to ensuring that the intended outcomes benefit society. There is need to redesign our delivery mechanisms in an innovative manner based on past experience and best practices and deploy the nation's finest talent for this purpose.

Although several Commissions and Committees have been set-up in the past to examine various aspects of public administration, a comprehensive review of the entire public administration system was last done by the First Administrative Reforms Commission, which was set-up in 1966. Since then, several important changes and developments have taken place driven by the pressing need to reform, rapid changes in technology including information technology and significant institutional changes like the emergence of a constitutionally-mandated system of local government in our country. This has obviously necessitated the need for a comprehensive review of public administration as mandated for this Commission.

The editor in its editorial column, in *IJPA*, July-Sept. 2007 observes that our administrative system-a legacy of colonial rule-stands in the way of accelerated socio-economic development, causing stress and strain to our polity which is struggling to march towards socio-economic equity. The emerging challenges of economic globalisation, political decentralisation and social empowerment tend to go along with liberalisation of economy, regionalisation of polity and localisation of society. These factors have had a consistent impact on the role of the administrative systems. There is an all-round agreement now that liberalisation, privatisation and globalisation of economy is here to stay. The responsibility of the public service in the changing circumstances is being concentrated in certain areas and transformed in other areas. The regulatory mechanism during this evolving period requires a high level of professionalism, changed outlook, paradigm shift in policy-making and accuracy and inclusiveness in service delivery.

Development Administration in order to be operatives needed changes in public administration system currently in force which could not materialize. The objective of good governance is to create an environment so that public servants as well as politicians in government are able to respond to the challenges of governance. Such challenges involve a notion of duty, vocation, and service to the public. Public service as an ideal is and has been the classical view of good governance. How to improve services to citizens by government agencies has been a major cause of concern to governments all over the world. The author emphasises that unless the reforms address the issue of corruption in the public service, no reform will be hailed as good by the public. Keeping in view the colossal size of the nation's administrative machinery, easy and quick reforms may not be an astute option. One must also keep in mind the constant and ever-growing disruptive impacts of frequent public service reforms and institutional reorganisations. The public service of today requires far-reaching and perhaps unanticipated changes if India is to actualise its great potentialities to be counted among the ranks of great nations. From the ashes of New Public Management, a new phoenix is emerging in the name of Integrated Public Governance (IPG) which is in fact closely related to 'holistic governance'.[2]

It is useful to draw on lessons from other countries in order to avoid making the same mistakes: (1) full political support is required to the cause at the designing stage of administrative reform; (2) the reform agenda should be concise, clear and achievable; (3) once reform agenda has been put in place, a regular monitoring and feedback system should be put in place so that mid-course correction can be made or a change in original expectations can be modified; (4) time-frame should not be underestimated because any reform takes time to take effect and get nurtured, thus judging the effect within two three years will be too early; (5) reformers should be ready to encounter and overcome resistance from the middle management, and hurdles from the unions, therefore, a strategy of cooperation and co-optation should be considered; and (6) there are cultural nuances and values inherent in any paradigm or a model transported from the outside; transplanting such a system requires cultural and attitudinal changes (for example, when work days were changed from six days to five days a week with concomitant changes in working hours, there was no appreciable change in the working habits of office employees).[3]

Most of the significant recommendations on civil service reforms in the past failed to yield desired result because the mindest of civil servants implementing these recommendations did not change. As a result most of the civil servants are looked down upon as a predatory group of power brokers. With such an unsavoury public perception, civil servants can handly be relied upon as trustworthy facilitators in the context of globalization and liberalizations. The best reform that any Commission can usher will be to make the bureaucracy duty conscious and service-oriented.

Without good governance, no amount of developmental schemes can bring improvements in the quality of life of the citizens. Good governance has four elements—transparency, accountability, predictability and participation. Transparency refers to availability of information to the general public and clarity about functioning of governmental institutions. Right to information opens up government's records to public scrutiny, thereby arming citizens with a vital tool to inform them about what the government does and how effectively, thus making the government more accountable. Transparency in government organisations makes them function more objectively thereby enhancing predictability. Information about functioning of government also enables citizens to participate in the governance process effectively. In a fundamental sense, right to information is a basic necessity of good governance.[4]

Administrative Reforms in industrial sector is known as work study. Work study aims at the elimination of inefficiency in the functioning of management and administration through ensuring optimum utilization of resources—men, money and material. It is probably the most well known and widely publicised analytical technique used in works management. Lord Mountbatten, in a message to the Defence Institute of Work Study, said, "Work Study is a really effective service in management. It will pay dividends which are handsome, speedy and beyond expectations. But, it must have, for its success, the unstinted support of management."

Pandit Nehru said, "work Study, almost a new idea, has now come to us in order to improve our administrative methods, to streamline them, and make them more efficient and effective."

To quote R.M. Currie, "It is essentially a ruthlessly analytical and inquisitive approach to the use of manpower, materials and equipment coupled with a desire to apply the facts from such inquiry to improve existing methods by the elimination of waste in every form."

Many of the ills of public administration today stem from rigidity of attitudes, absence of review techniques, and inadequate appreciation of the factors that motivate men. Generally, it is not realized that the nascent productivity sciences play a vital role in promoting productivity. Work study, in particular, can reduce the wastes arising from undue delay in decision-making, and in communication; from underutilization of skills; and from inadequate use of resources—time, equipment, men, money, material and space.

Today, the nation is being geared for a better allround performance and the country is called upon to meet various challenges. With the growing emphasis on increasing productivity in public services, in nationalized banks, in public sector undertakings, and in the 'sick' industries committed to the care of public agencies—Administrative Reforms which is work study in office systems.[5]

The quote Sir Edward Smith, "Whatever thinking may have been in the past, we have found the impact of works study prevailing steadily away from the shop floor to the Board room. We now regard it as symbolizing the analytical and progressive attitude of mind which is mainly concerned with making management manage better, rather than getting the worker into work harder."

"Work Study is a generic term for those techniques, particularly method study and work measurement, which are used in the examination of human work in all its contexts, and which lead systematically to the investigation of all the factors which affect the efficiency and economy of the situation being reviewed in order to effect improvement."[6]

Other reasons for use of Work Study are summarized as under:

1. It is a means of raising the productive efficiency (productivity) of a factory of operating unit by the reorganization of work, a method which normally involves little or no capital expenditure on plant and equipment.
2. It is systematic. This ensures that no factor affecting the efficiency of an operation is overlooked, whether in analysing the original practices or in developing the new, and that all the facts about that operation are available.
3. It is the most accurate means yet evolved of setting standards of performance, on which the effective planning and control of production depends.
4. The savings resulting from properly applied works study start at once and continue as long as the operation continues in the improved form.
5. It is a tool which can be applied everywhere. It can be used with success wherever manual work is done or plant is operated, not only in manufacturing shops, but in offices, stores, laboratries and service industries such as wholesale and retail distribution and restaurants, and on farms.
6. It is one of the most penetrating tools of investigation available to management. This makes in an excellent weapon for starting an attack on inefficiency in any organization, since, in investigating one set of problems, the weakness of all other functions affecting them will gradually be laid bare.

This techniques has been used widely in the developed countries with great success, e.g., in Imperial Chemical Industries, 1500 work study specialists are working (1 per 50 employees) to ensure optimum performance. After the Second World War, many firms have engaged the services of works study specialists to improve their performance. Besides, many institutes, like National Productivity Council (Established in 1958), Defence Institute of Work Study (Mussoorie), Institution of Work Study and the National Institute for Training in Industrial Engineering, are doing useful work in this direction. The Secretariat Training School, Ministry of Home Affairs, Government of India is imparting training in Work Study/O&M Techniques.

FUNCTIONS OF A WORK DEPARTMENTAL SECTION

The range of activities which a well established work study department may be called upon to undertake will depend to a large extent on what other technical staff/departments or sections there are in the Organization. In most instances, the work study department will be expected to carry out the following:

(a) Method studies of existing jobs and operations, leading to the installation of improved methods.
(b) Work measurement and the determination of time standards.
(c) Examination of proposed changes affecting the work of the operative, and in particular the preparation of plant and machine layout schemes for any extensions of reorganizations.

(d) The routine compilation of control statements for supervision and for management, insofar as these are concerned with the use of worker's time and the output produced.
(e) Design and installation of incentive schemes for workers.

O & M (ORGANISATION AND METHODS—ADMINISTRATIVE REFORMS IN GOVERNMENT)

Work Study in government is generally known as O&M in Indian and other Common Wealth Countries, the two alphabets stand for organization and methods. In U.S.A., it signifies Organization and Management. The latter sense includes the entire process of management, viz., Planning, organization, coordination, directing, staging and controlling. As such O&M are used in the wider sense. When two alphabets are read together, it is known as OM. OM stands for God or perfection. It means to ensure the perfection of instruments of Public Administration or weeding out unwanted organizations and methods. Management improvement is a challenge that must be faced by all developing countries including India. The gap between the developed and developing countries is sometimes thought to be a gap in managerial development; but whether this gap is the cause of underdevelopment of the result or not is a question that has still to be answered. The primary concern, however, is that the gap must be bridged.

The O&M aims at making the surgical operation to ensure simplification and improvement of office methods and procedures. In the words of S.B. Bapat, the founder of O&M in India: "In simple terms it means paying intelligent and critical attention not only to what is done but also to how it is done and at what cost, in what time, labour and money; paying attention to the design of the machine and its working processes and not merely to its end product."

In the words of the British Select Committee on Estimates (1947), "The purpose of O&M in the Civil Service is to secure maximum efficiency in the operation of the Government's executive machinery, by the expert application of scientific methods of organization, to reduce cost and labour."

OBJECTIVES

In the words of Milward, "the usual functions of O&M are the examination of the structure of the organization under review and the studying of administrative and clerical procedures and methods, office mechanization and equipment, office layout and working conditions. Work study deals with systematic activities concerned with the investigation, recording, measurement and improvement of the following work factors: what the operator does; the machine and equipment used and the materials and the working conditions. Operations Research is the scientific approach to, and analysis of problems in an organization to provide management with information for obtaining its most effective overall operation."[7]

The objectives of O&M entail all aspects which can help in making organization and system of public administration scientific. We may mention some of the important objectives which must be ensured through O&M.

1. Administrative reform must ensure the adjustment of the administrative structure to socio-economic changes.
2. Administrative services must be studied continuously in the search for greater efficiency and economy of public expenditure.

3. To restructure the administrative system in a way that would permit a well coordinated development effort.
4. To suggest means for increasing the efficiency, economy and capability of the administrative machinery at different levels.
5. To suggest means for effective coordination among various units and making them more capable.
6. To suggest means for brining about better coordination among existing training programmes and for making them more useful and effective.
7. To suggest means whereby the people might obtain redress for grievances against the public administration.
8. To eliminate an institutionalized corruption from each substratum.
9. To facilitate easy, standardized access to the 'window of administration', for the general public, when they come in contact with the public authorities.
10. Development of better administrative laws and regulations to replace laws based on outmoded ideas and concepts.
11. Improvement of organisational plans to clarify objectives, improve structures and define responsibilities and relationships.
12. Simplification of procedures and work methods.
13. Development of improved investigative and disciplinary practices to check abuses of public laws, misuse of government resources and violation of government ethics.
14. Formulating proposals for office accommodation and their proper layout.
15. To install methods, systems and procedures in an organization that will not only increase efficiency but also reduce costs at all levels.
16. To adopt a programme of work simplification at all levels within an organization.
17. To enhance vitality of an organization and increase its capacity to face challenges posed by external forces.

Management improvement is a continuous process, and it cannot be achieved overnight. The main responsibility for effecting improvements in administration lies with the administrators themselves; but as administrators are over burdened with day to day routine work and have less time to study operations, some kind of agency is needed to supplement and strengthen them in improvement work. To quote Milward again: "It exists not only as a management tool—as an agent of the top management—but also as for service of managers, auditors or others who need it because they have not themselves the time or the necessary expertise. This dual purpose of agent and service makes the position difficult. In some companies it is all agent, in others all service, but somehow both roles need to be combined. There are widely differing views not only about the content of O&M, but also concerning its relationships with other techniques concerned with improving effectiveness and efficiency.[8]

T.N. Chaturvedi in his editorial, in *IJPA*, July to Sept. 1998, has rightly stressed that Good Governance, however, is not a finished product. It is a dynamic concept ... The search for good governance has to be a continuing exercise.

FUNCTIONS

Let us discuss the important functions of Administrative Reforms:

1. Training

To provide practical and academic training for government officials in order to raise the standard of administration, prepare officials for more responsible tasks and stimulate efficiency and economy in government. This is achieved by means of in service training, both full time and part time, through the media of classroom lecture and discussion sessions, field-work conferences, workshops, projects or administrative management and programmes for executive development.

2. Research

It is the primary function of O&M to conduct studies on current and emerging administrative problems in public administration for the purpose of administrative improvement.

3. Consultation

To produce manuals and other documents on administrative operations required for in service training; to issue publications on administrative problems, to hold professional conferences, roundtable discussions, etc., to promote the exchange of information on significant development in public administration in India and abroad; to maintain a library of technical information, up to date literature on public administration for the purpose of reference and research.

4. Investigation

It is the function of O&M department to carry out investigation either at its own initiative or on the invitation of other departments or offices.

FUNCTIONS OF THE CENTRAL ADMINISTRATIVE REFORMS DEPARTMENT

The central management analysis unit should be engaged preferably in activities that have a multiplier effect on the entire service and refrain, as much as possible, for activities that could be carried out successfully by individual units in the agencies. In fact, the basic role of the central unit in relation to the departmental unit should be to provide functional authority and to stimulate sound development.

The assessment by the Public Administration Section of E.C.A. revealed the following situation pertaining to African countries which are true in the context of Asian countries as well including India.

"Many administrative problems face the developing countries of Africa, but there are at least four aspects of the administration which need to be put on sound lines before planning and plan implementation, as well as the other business of government can be assured of any measure of success. Budget, accounting and other financial procedures must be regulated to ensure that government money is applied effectively to end foreseen in well conceived budgets; with a minimum of waste, leakage and misapplication. Recruitment practices must be reformed, personnel administration must be improved and adequate programmes of training must be designed and implemented to ensure that suitable persons, adequately trained, are available when needed and utilized when available. Purchasing and stores procedures must be designed and improved to ensure maximum value to the country for every dollar spent on equipment and supplies. The machinery of government, organisational structure of ministries and practices and procedures on all aspects of government work must be designed as to maximize the effectiveness of the administration. These are some of the urgent tasks of which the governments of the region are to address themselves, if the other vital development resources are to be applied at the right points and with the maximum impact."[9]

The functions of Administrative Reforms within the Management Services Unit are the following:

(a) Organisational and Management Analysis

Analysis and review of organisational structure, including defining of responsibilities and inter relationship; and improvement of administrative and management procedures and practices;

(b) Staff Utilization and Job Analysis

Staff utilization reviews, including staff complement and grading, job analysis and evaluation, review of personnel function in ministries, and administration of staff schemes.

(c) Office Services and Procedural Analysis

Simplification of work systems, procedures and methods; systems analysis and mechanization studies of electrical work, including work and method study and performance standards; utilization and standardization of office equipment and furniture, office layout and office space standards; control and design of forms, etc.

Appelby envisaged a broad role of the O&M unit. He said that "I recommend that the Government of India give consideration to the establishment of a central office charged with responsibility for giving both extensive and intensive leadership in respect of structure, management and procedures. At one level of highly technical and scientific sort, it would give attention to work management, work flow, office management, filling system, space arrangements and the like; at another level it would be charged with general governmental studies and proposals. I should hope that at his level also it would have character of responsibility for the enhancement of democratic manner and method, within the bureaucracy and between the bureaucracy and the public."

ESSENTIALS OF ADMINISTRATIVE REFORMS

If an Administrative Reforms department is to play an effective role, its organization should have the following features:

1. Top management must not only be convinced of the need of the programme but must be actively associated with it. They must initiate it and must lend active continuing support so that managers at departmental and lower levels feel enthusiastic about it.
2. Outside Administrative Reforms consultants may be employed initially to make a broader survey to identify problems and suggest guidelines. Afterwards the managers should be involved in its implementation and further development.
3. An organization and methods expert should possess the following characteristics.
   (a) He must possess an analytical, creative and inquisitive mind.
   (b) He must be specially trained in the tools and techniques of work simplification.
   (c) He should possess a pleasant personality and be able to persuade people.
   (d) He must possess common sense, imagination, enthusiasm, objectivity and sense of humour.
   (e) He must be ready to face resistance to his ideas and dispel it with fact, patience and consideration. The aim should be to develop acceptance through cooperation.

An ILO Publication on Work study mentions the following essential qualities in Administrative Reforms analysis:

- *Sincerity and honesty*—The work study man must be sincere and honest, only in this way will he gain the confidence and respect of those with whom he has to deal.
- *Enthusiasm*—He must be really keen on his job, believe in the importance of what he is doing and be able to transmit his enthusiasm to the people around him. Interest in and sympathy with the people.
- *Tact*—Tact in dealing with the people comes from understanding people and not wishing to hurt their feelings by unkind or thoughtless words, even when these may be justified. Without tact, no work study man is going to get very far.
- *Good Appearance*—He must be neat and tidy and look efficient. This will inspire confidence in him among the people with whom he has to work.
- *Self-Confidence*—This can come with good training and experience of applying work study successfully. The work study man must be able to stand upo top management, foremen, trade union officials or workers in defence of his opinions and findings, and do so in such a way that he will win respect and not give offence.

O AND M IN INDIA

The importance of creating a permanent organization to improve the functioning of administration was emphasized by Mr. A.D. Gorwala in 1947, the late Mr. N. Gopalaswamy Ayyangar in 1949, the Economy Committee in 1949, the Manpower Shortage Committee in 1943, and many other Commissions appointed from time to time. Paul Appelby conducted a survey of the Public Administration in India in 1953. Most of these Committees and Survey recommended the creation of some machinery (O and M) to ensure dynamic administration to suit the changing conditions. The Central O and M Division in India was created in March 1954 and it was located in Cabinet Secretariat. But each Ministry/Department set-up their internal O and M cells. A decade's existence of O and M Division could not make much impact as its top leadership (Director) went on changing frequently. Besides, this Division has not been able to coordinate its activities with similar functional agencies, e.g., the special Reorganzation Unit in the Finance Ministry and the Committee on Plan Projects in the Planning Commission.

A Department of Administrative Reforms was set-up on March 25, 1964 in the Ministry of Home Affairs to which was transferred the O and M Division located earlier in the Department of Cabinet Affairs. The immediate task which this Department undertook was to appoint the Administrative Reform Commission in January 1966 to "give consideration to the need for ensuring the highest standards of efficiency and integrity in the Public Services and for making Public Administration a fit instrument for carrying out social and economic policies of the Government and achieving social and economic goals of development, as also one which is responsible to the people." The Commission submitted the reports on the following aspects which provided valuable insights into the working of the administrative machinery at all levels and concerning major fields:

(a) The machinery of the Government of India and its procedures of work;
(b) The machinery for planning at all levels;
(c) Centre-State Relationships;

(d) Financial Administration;
(e) Personnel Administration;
(f) Economic Administration;
(g) Administration at the State Level;
(h) District Administration;
(i) Agricultural Administration; and
(j) Problems of redness of citizens grievances.

The Commission submitted 20 Reports in all, as per the details given below, before winding up in Mid-1970.

S.No.	*Name of the Report*	*Date of Presentation to Government*
1.	Problems of Redress of Citizens' Grievances (Interim)	20.10.1966
2.	Machinery for Planning (Interim)	29.4.1967
3.	Public Sector Undertakings	17.10.1967
4.	Finance, Accounts & Audit	13.1.1968
5.	Machinery for Planning (Final)	14.3.1968
6.	Economic Administration	20.7.1968
7.	The Machinery of GOI and its procedures of work	16.9.1968
8.	Life Insurance Administration	10-12-1968
9.	Central Direct Taxes Administration	6-1-1969
10.	Administration of UTs & NEFA	28-11-1969
11.	Personnel Administration	18-4-1969
12.	Delegation of Financial & Administrative Powers	12-6-1969
13.	Centre-State Relationships	19-6-1969
14.	State Administration	4-11-1969
15.	Small Scale Sector	24-12-1969
16.	Railways	30-1-1970
17.	Treasuries	27 -2-1970
18.	Reserve Bank of India	11-3-1970
19.	Posts & Telegraph	15-5-1970
20.	Scientific Departments	1970

Those 20 reports contained 537 major recommendations. Based on the inputs received from various administrative ministries a report indicating the implementation position was placed in Parliament in November, 1977.

In 1970, the Department was transferred to the newly created Department of Personnel and Administrative Reforms in the Ministry of Home Affairs. It had its two wings—Personnel and Administrative Reforms. Later on independent Ministry, i.e. Ministry of Personnel, Public grievances and pensions was set-up. The Administrative Reforms Department is responsible for suggesting improvements in administration with a view to increase work satisfaction and suggest measures for the improvement in the quality of working in every field of administration.

The ministry is under the overall charge of the Prime Minister assisted by two Ministers of State—one for the Department of Personnel and Training and Department of Pension and Pensioners Welfare and the other for the Department of Administration Reforms and Public Grievances. All the three Departments of the Ministry have been functioning under the charge of Secretary (Personnel) who is presently assisted by four Additional Secretaries, three joint Secretaries and other supporting offices and staff.

The Department of Administrative Reforms and Public Grievances is the nodal agency of the Government of India for administrative reforms as well as redress of public grievances relating to the State in general and grievances pertaining to Central Government agencies in particular. The Department disseminates information on important activities of the Government relating to administrative reforms and public grievances redress through Management Publications and Documentation. This Department also acts as the nodal agency in regard to Organisation and Methods activities and offers advice to the Ministries/Departments. It also undertakes activities in the field of international co-operation and exchanges to promote public service reforms.

The Department is also the apex body of government in the field of administrative reforms. Its main functions in this area are:

(i) Advising the government on policy matters concerning administrative reforms;
(ii) Providing management consultancy services to the organizations of the central government, the state governments, public sector and local bodies;
(iii) Promotion and development of the management efforts in the government; and
(iv) Imparting management education and disseminating information on administrative practices and modern management techniques.

For discharging these functions the department carriers on a continuous dialogue with the various ministries at the centre and also with the state administrations to identify new areas of reforms and to keep in touch with the progress of the steps already taken in this direction. It also works as a clearing house regarding reforms measures both at the Centre and in the States.

The Administrative Reforms Department is headed by an Additional Secretary. The methods of work relating to administrative reforms are study and research-oriented. Personnel for this work are selected from different services/departments for their diverse administrative experience and academic/professional qualifications as also their aptitude for study and research work.

The Department carriers out the following types of activities:

(a) Management Studies;
(b) Measures for Achieving Administrative Improvements;
(c) Management Services;
(d) Management Education;
(e) Management in Government;
(f) Research and Administrative Intelligence;
(g) Other activities, e.g. Appointment of Commission, Study Groups, Task Force, etc.
(h) Efficiency Unit;
(i) Award Scheme; and
(j) Records Management.

Let us understand the role of Administrative Reforms and Public grievances with the help of latest development in the area of Review of Laws, Regulations and Procedure as reported in the Annual Report of the Ministry of Personnel, Public grievances and pensions of the year 1999-2000.

The Commission on Review of Administrative Laws which was set-up in May 1998, *inter alia*, recommended repeal of 1382 Central Acts. The Commission also recommend amendment to various Central Acts, rules, regulations, etc.

A Bill for repealing 315 Amendment Acts has been introduced in Rajya Sabha in December 1999. The question of repeal of 700 Appropriation Acts was referred to the Attorney General of India for advice, which has been recently received and is being examined by the Ministry of Finance. 114 Central Acts relating to State Laws have been referred to the concerned State Governments for repeal.

Action to repeal or otherwise of the remaining Acts is at various stages of processing. Most of the Ministries/Departments have also initiated action to bring about suitable amendments in the Acts and laws being administered by them with a view to improve service delivery and transparency in the functioning of the Government.

A Plan Scheme was introduced in 1987-88 to help the Ministries/Department to improve their work environment through adoption of functional layout, creation of open offices to facilitate better supervision, better service to the public, more efficient management of data through reduction in paper work by sung modern aids as well as cost and space effective records management. The scheme helps to set-up model units in Ministries/Departments which are expected to induce all round modernization of all the units of the Ministries/Departments over a period of time.

The Department coordinates the efforts to formulate and operationalise citizens/Users Charters by the Central Government Ministries/Departments and their PSUs/automonous/ statutory bodies in areas in which they provide services to the members of the public. These charters publicise the commitment of the organization, the expected standards of service delivery, time frame, grievance redress mechanism and laying their performance open to public scrutiny. 61 Central Ministries/Departments/Organisations have framed their charters.

The Department also coordinates the effort of formulating and operationslising Citizens charter in various states/UTs. As a result, 133 charters have been prepared by various states/UTs.

The concept of quality has been widely applied in private sector to improve the performance of organizations and to endow them with a competitive edge. The watchword is continuous improvement. The relevance of TQM in Government organizations has been highlighted by increasing focus on citizen friendly, transparent and accountable Government.

Computerised information and Facilitation Counters (IFCs) have been set-up to provide information and assistance to the public regarding the schemes and procedures of the concerned organization as well as acknowledgement and status report of individual applications and grievances.

Government of India, Ministry of Personnel, Public Grievances & Pensions, Department of Administrative Reforms and Public Grievances in its Resolution in New Delhi dated 31st August 2005 vide No. K-11022/9/2004-RC set-up a Commission of Inquiry to be called the Second Administrative Reforms Commission (ARC) to prepare a detailed blueprint for revamping the public administration system.

The Commission will, *inter alia*, consider the following:

(i) Organisational structure of the Government of India
(ii) Ethics in governance
(iii) Refurbishing of Personnel Administration
(iv) Strengthening of Financial Management Systems
(v) Steps to ensure effective administration at the state level
(vi) Steps to ensure effective district administration
(vii) Local Self-Government/Panchayati Raj Institution
(viii) Social Capital, Trust and Participative Public service delivery
(ix) Citizen-centric administration
(x) Promoting e-governance
(xi) Issues of Federal Polity
(xii) Crisis Management
(xiii) Public Order

The Commission consists of the following:

(i) Shri Veerappa Moily—Chairperson
(ii) Shri V. Ramachandran—Member
(iii) Dr. A.P. Mukherjee—Member
(iv) Dr. A.H. Kalro—Member
(v) Dr. Jayaprakash Narayana—Member
(vi) Smt. Vineeta Rai—Member-Secretary

The Commission will suggest measures to achieve a proactive, responsive, accountable, sustainable and efficient administration for the country at all levels of the government.

Second Administrative Reforms Commission submitted Eleventh Reports which are as follows: (Feb. 2009)

1. Right to Information
2. Unchecking Human Capital
3. Crisis Management
4. Ethics in Government
5. Public orders
6. Local Governance
7. Capacity Building for Conflict Resolution
8. Combating Terrorism
9. Social Capital
10. Refreshing of Personnel Administrative Scaling New Height
11. Promoting E-governance

CRITICAL APPRAISAL

We have not been able to improve our administrative set-up even after fifty years of independence. Let us examine some factors which stand in the way of effective functioning of Administrative Reforms department.

1. Lack of Appreciation of Administrative Reforms among Civil Servants

The Line Managers and Supervisors are usually suspicious of the activities of the Administrative Reforms analyst. Their perception of the Administrative Reforms analyst is one who has come there to load them with more work and reduce their wage rate. Naturally, they are likely to oppose him. Modern organizations must adapt themselves continuously to changing situations. Such transformations can be gradual and almost constant provided the organization's officials who, from direct experience, are aware of the need of change, are permitted to introduce innovations on their own initiative or persuade the competent authorities to do so.

The Staff Survey Project described by Arthur Naftalin, Minnesota's Commissioner of Administration and Director of Self Survey experiment is very illuminating: "Instead of summoning, 'outside experts'.... We have put our administrators, technicians, employees and legislators to work (without additional pay) on what is intended to be a top to bottom analysis of all aspects of general management, personnel operating procedures, and long-term—needs and outlook." The underlying idea behind 'Do it Yourself' is that every member of an organization should look to his work critically and creatively so as to make efforts at improvements.

Successful change, in general, appear to be those which operate as follows:

(a) Spread throughout the organization to include and affect many people;
(b) Produce positive changes in staff attitudes;
(c) Prompt people to behave more effectively in solving problems;
(d) Result in improved performance by the organization;
(e) Encourage the whole range of disciplines among workers to interact positively; and
(f) Oblige top decision makers systematically to focus on the important, as distinct from the trivial.

2. Lack of Personnel Specialized in Administrative Reforms Work

We have very few specialists trained in the art and science of Administrative Reforms. most of the trained personnel are half baked. They understand only theoretical principles but fail to apply them or modify them according to the needs of a given situation.

3. Budgetary Limitations

Budgetary limitations directly affect both the physical and human integration within Administrative Reforms units. The government must give priority to this activity and allocate sufficient resources to ensure better results.

4. Absence of Rationalization of the Aims of Government

The governments must define its objectives in concrete terms. The Administrative Reforms units can help in advising the restructuring of the machinery of government to pursue those objectives. If objectives are not clear, the functioning of Administrative Reforms would be like groping in the dark.

It would seem that the ineffectiveness of administration reform measures in Latin America has, from the beginning, been largely due to the tendency to substitute the means for the ends. It is the ends, however, that deserve priority, among ... other things as a prerequisite for rationalizing the means. The same is true of all developing countries.

As one author points out:

"Development administration is not administrative development. It is that aspect of Public Administration which focuses on government influenced change towards progressive political, economic and social objectives.... Development administration thus encompasses the organization of new agencies such as planning organizations and development corporations; the reorientation of established agencies such as departments of agricultures; the delegation of administration powers to development agencies; and the creation of a cadre of administrators who can provide leadership in stimulating and supporting programmes of social and economic improvement. It has the purpose of making change attractive and possible ..."

5. Restricted Coverage

The activities of Administrative Reforms are restricted only to the headquarters of the Union and State Governments. These must percolate to the field to ensure optimization of results. The efficiency of administrative machinery depends upon the good service provided by its field officers.

6. Absence of Humanistic Approach in Public Administration

No doubt, perfection of procedures is very important but it is only a mechanical approach to administration. What is, therefore, needed is a reform in the human attitudes and behaviours of those who administer. The officials whether in the higher or lower ladder of administration should develop a sense of responsibility and moral conscientiousness and "the capacity to move with millions." Pt Nehru, once remarked:

".... Administration, like most things is, in the final analysis, a human problem, to deal with human beings, not with some statistical data. statistical data help in understanding. But, there is a danger that pure administrators at the top—not so much at the bottom, because they come into contact with human beings—may come to regard human beings a mere abstraction. There is that danger at times in both types of society, whether it is what might be called Capitalist Society or Communist Society ... The administrator may think in abstract of the people he deals with, come to conclusions which are justifiable apparently, but which miss the human element. After all, whatever department of government you deal with, it is ultimately a problem of human beings, and the moment we forget them, we are driven away from reality. Administration is meant to achieve something and not to exit in some kind of an ivory tower, following certain rules of procedure, and looking Narcissus like, looking on itself with complete satisfaction. The test after all is the human beings and their welfare."[11]

7. Lack of Exchange of Information

Inspite of the existence of a separate Ministry of Personnel and Administration Reforms, we have not gone far to ensure exchange of information between the Union and States inter se. The remarks made by Prof. A. Avasthi in 1963 hold good even today. "Attention may also be drawn to the fact that at present there is no forum for exchange of Administrative Reforms experience among different states. There are all India Conferences of high officers of almost all departments. But so far Administrative Reforms officers from different states have not met in such a conference no their exists any other institutional arrangement for the purpose. Such a conference would help in the pooling of experience and exchange of ideas in the field of Administrative Reforms.[12]

8. Lack of Professionalization

The results tend to be better when the staff is more 'professional' (joint qualities of board knowledge and experience) as opposed to technical. The structure of Administrative Reforms units should be person-oriented rather than system-oriented in order to provide for the innovative capacity needed for management analysis.

9. Lack of Regards for Public Sentiments and Urgency

Administration is manned by and meant for human beings. Therefore, there is a need to instil basic human concepts among civil servants besides mechanical efficiency so that they may treat the people cordially and equitably.

"The administrator, whether he is low down or high up in the scale, must give the impression, even if that impression is not cent per cent correct, that he is working through the public will and carrying it out. Of course, this cannot always be done; the administrator cannot carry out every body's will, but he must give the broad impression that he is functioning in accordance with the public will, always thinking of public grievances trying to remedy them and consulting the people.[13]

10. Use of Jargons

Sometimes Administrative Reforms analysts are often limited in perspective, and may go over board on the most modern technology without due consideration of how they may influence overall effectiveness and economy.

There are semantic barriers which increases resistance. The terminology used by Administrative Reforms analysts is generally beyond the comprehension of the people within an organization. Since line manager and supervisors do not understand it, they become passive towards it. We must use simple and intelligence vocabulary.

11. Lack of Decentralization

Yogendra Narain in his article "Government Functioning in the Centre—An Agenda for Reform" stated that functioning of ministers in the governments, both at the state as well as the centre, has been severely criticized. Decision-making is said to be unduly delayed, replies are not received in time and the whole machinery is getting bogged down with files and references. On the other hand, the government servants at the middle and senior levels are being thrust with greater responsibility and a greater level of accountability has crept in. however, with these heavier workloads, each government servant at his level is finding that he is doing more routing work, rather than making any positive contribution to the system. The politician, whether he is in the ruling party or outside, tends to criticize the 'bureauractic' procedures of the functionary. From the Secretary downwards, everybody becomes the 'whipping boy' for the government in power. Everybody has the same complaint. Why so much centralization? Why don't we delegate more powers to the officers in field? And yet if one mistake is committed in the field, the politician feels that all such decisions should be taken only at the higher level of the government. The bureaucracy in the Ministry also tends to toe the line with the result that inspite of all declarations of 'decentralization' what has actually happened is that centralization has become more acute than before.[14]

Machiavellie Sydney has very beautifully said there is no thing more difficult to take in hand, more perilous to conduct, more uncertain in its success than to take the lead in the introduction of a new order of things.

No administrative system can ever be absolutely perfect and in order to achieve some sort of perfection, it has to engage itself with the help of Administrative Reforms cells in devising ways and means for improvement which have to be adopted in the light of a nation's basic policies and programmes. We may keep the above mentioned factors which impede the growth of the efforts of Administrative Reforms to inject the required changes in the organization, process and the philosophy of administration. The ultimate success of the measures suggested by Administrative Reforms cells depends to a great extent upon the effective implementation of the measure suggested. The Third Five Year Plan has rightly commented:

"Nevertheless, without a concerted attempt to make the administration much more action-oriented than at present, these may not yield enough results.[15]

S.S. Singh in his article "Administrative Lawlessness: Concept and Concern" stated that the culture and climate of justice in a society often necessitate strong governance through a powerful and progressive administration. It is so because justice without power is impotency and power without justice is tyranny. Indeed, creation of strong, powerful and extensive state machinery and its sub systems are justified by an appeal to the need to errect a powerful state which alone can attend to the tasks of justice. It is a political truism that administrative apparatus is a repository of public power and administrative system is a combination of centres of power. The various centres of administration are created and power have been conferred on these with the authority of law to discharge their duties in accordance with the law. They are required to manifest in their actions and performance that they are functioning for public interest, public good and public purpose with sense of accountability and responsibility and not in public detriment. Deviant behaviour and detrimental actions of administration certainly effect the very legitimacy of the administrative system.

It should be remembered by persons in power that law is not only a command of the sovereign/administration but also command to them. It is trite but true that howsoever high and might, one may be, the law is always above him and not the vice versa. Finally, it should also be remembered that the legitimacy and credibility of administrative system is deeply rooted in the confidence of the people which depends on the degree of justness, fairness and reasonableness manifested in the actions and behaviour of the administration. Thus, existence of authority without accountability to the sustenance of its credibility is nugatory.[16]

It is suggested that the Need of Reforms at All Levels and Cover all Aspects

Under the Article 154 of the Constitution, the State Government is represented by the Governor, Council of Ministers headed by Chief Minister and the officers of the government. The permanent executive of the government carries out the affairs of the government according to the decisions of the political executive. In this process, the permanent executive will also be guided by the law of the land and bound by the Constitution. The accepted norms of the government developed over the years, usually codified in the form of rules, procedures, etc. guide the permanent executive in discharge of its responsibilities. Any change in these procedures involves lengthy and cumbersome processes and many obstacles are to be overcome. Therefore, the civil service becomes inflexible and rigid even if some procedures have outlived their utility.

- Any reforms in governance/government, therefore, will have to cover all levels of the government, both bureaucratic and political.
- Reforms will have to cover the change in attitudes of all functionaries involved at all levels of the government. Reforms would also mean a close look and change of the Government processes and procedures.

- Therefore, the scope of the reforms should to a large extent cover the higher echelons of the government and necessarily have to start from the way ministers and secretaries to government function.

The components of governance reforms would constitute reform in the following major areas:

- Delegation of powers between the Ministers and Secretaries
- Civil Service reform
- An anti-corruption strategy
- An Effective Grievance Redressal Mechanism
- Amalgamation of schemes
- E-Governance

Civil Service Reforms would comprise of:

(a) Accountability of the civil service
(b) Redefining functional goals
(c) Improving systems and work methods
(d) Rationalization of the civil service
(e) Review of performance appraisal system
(f) Human resource development

An Anti-Corruption strategy would include:

(g) Transparency and the Right to Information
(h) Meritocratic recruitment
(i) Legislation on transfers
(j) Strengthen anti-corruption mechanisms
(k) Simplification of disciplinary procedures

Amalgamation of Schemes

- Schemes with nominal budget provisions to be merged.
- Schemes which are continuing for the purpose of providing salaries to employees to be abolished.
- Similar schemes to be merged.
- Schemes with less than Rs. 5.00 lakh allocation to be merged/discontinued.
- Agriculture Department need not set-up Entomological/Pathological Laboratories: or even Bio-Fertilizer Laboratories. This work could be entrusted to Agricultural Universities.
- All the training schemes in the departments should be merged under one head of account.
- It is not possible to carry out State Horticultural Census with the provision of Rs. 1.0 lakhs. The Horticulture Department may examine the relevance of such scheme.

- Schemes which have outlived their utility should be abolished. (e.g. Cashew nut and Matchwood Plantation Schemes in Forest Department).
- The head of account for Lalbagh Botanical Garden and Vidhana Soudha GardenS shown under Forest Department should be shifted to Horticulture Department.

CONCLUSION

Administrative reforms or work study is an essential ingredient of the process of development. Many of our development programmes have not yielded expected results because of out dated administrative machinery. Therefore, it is essential to pay equal attention to the machinery of government whether it is fit to deliver goods and services to the people? If not, what reforms can be injected to make it fit? Upon the answers to these questions would depend the quality of reforms and ultimate socio-economic development. There is widespread agreement now that without improvements in governance, development will prove to be neither equitable nor sustainable. Good governance is based on the observance of certain principles such as accountability of government leaders, transparency in the use of public funds, responsiveness of government to popular aspirations and room for people to participate in all spheres of social and economic life to produce, to organize their mutual assistance, and to express their views on development decisions affecting their existence.[17]

One may suggest here that the Administrative Reforms Commission should be made a permanent statutory body to suggest administrative reforms and review their implementation. In the process of implementation it may be impressed upon various ministries and departments of Government of India that the suggested reforms are the outcome of an absorbing intellectual exercise which need to be implemented in all earnestness. The existence of the above recommended permanent Administrative Reforms Commission will be a constant reminder of government's genuine quest for good governance. This will also help in saving the current and future recommendations from meeting the same fate that haunt the hitherto unimplemented recommendations of the first Administrative Reforms Commission (1966-68).

NOTES AND REFERENCES

1. *University News,* July 10, 2000.
2. O.P. Dwivedi, On Administrative Reforms—Missings, *IJPA,* July-Sept. 2007, p. 346.
3. P.C. Hota, "Administrative Reforms in the Era of Liberalisation and Globalization: Need for Changing of Mind set of Civil Servants, *IJPA,* July-Sept., 2007, p. 336.
4. GOI, Second Administrative Reforms Commission, First Report on Right to Information: Master Key to Good Governance, June 2006, para 1.1.1., p. 1.
5. R.L. Malhotra Work study and public administration in *IJPA,* Oct-Dec, 1976, p. 633.
6. The definition given here is that adopted in the British Standard Glossary of Terms in Work Study, ILO: Introduction to Work Study, (Revised Edition, Geneva, 1974, p. 35).
7. G.E. Milward, (ed.). Organization and Methods, London, Macmillan, p. 253.
8. *Ibid.,* p. 252.
9. ECA: Summary of Public Administration Activities in ECA, 1966-70.
10. Geral E. Caiden, "Development System" paper prepared for the United Nations Economic Commission for Latin America for the Meeting of Experts on Administrative Capability for Development, held in November, 1970.
11. *Indian Journal of Public Administration,* Jan-March, 1955.

12. A. Avasthi, Article on O & M—The States, *IJPA*, July-Sept., 1963.
13. Jawaharlal Nehru quoted in "Glorious Thoughts of Nehru" by N.B. Sen.
14. Yogendra Narain, *IJPA*, October-December, 1990, p. 840.
15. GOI: Planning Commission:Third Five Year Plan, "Administration and Plan Implementation", New Delhi, pp. 271-73.
16. S.S. Singh, Administrative Lawlessness, in *IJPA*, April-June 1994, p. 134.
17. M. Lakshmi Narasaiah, Management Training in India, in Management of Government, Jan.-March, 2000, p. 54.

CHAPTER

20

Right to Information

Development administration in order to be fruitful requires transparency, accountability and responsiveness of government implementing development programme. RTI can help us in making development administration a success.

Secrecy in government is the most important cause of corruption, inefficiency and irresponsiveness and an enemy to Good Governance. In addition to other measure made available to people Right to Information Act, 2005 is a landmark achievement as through this corrupt politicians and bureaucracy would be exposed and there is a hope to develop a clean public life an essential ingredient of development administration. RTI Act, 2005 will strengthen democracy and would usher an era of socialistic pattern of society as enunciated by Late Pt. Jawahar Lal Nehru. Since Independence Government of India and State Governments have been entrusted by the Legislature on behalf of the people of India, Billions of crores of rupees for various schemes for the welfare and development of the people so that the disadvantaged group of people can enjoy the fruits of freedom. Mahatma Gandhi, the father of the nation, wanted complete Swaraj—Social, political, economic so that the tall man is also provided the decent life. However, under cover of secrecy, top personnel, whether in legislature, or judiciary or executive or Defence or NGOs left no chance to grab the money meant for poor people. There are large number of institutions set-up from time to time to support and help the poor and unprivileged people but vested interests made them non-functional or non-operative rather made them also dens of corruption. One feels pained to read newspapers, see T.V. and other Magazines which are full of scandals. The ideals of socialistic pattern of society enshrined in the constitution have crumbled in the hands of politico—Administrative Leadership. Right to Information is a right step to strengthen development administration.

Indra Jeet Mistry[1] very emphatically observes that the main thrust of the law is to change the culture of secrecy and aloofness that has long plagued India's monolithic and opaque bureaucracy. The RTI Act promises to reverse this culture of secrecy and unaccountability by recognizing that the government only holds information on behalf of its owners—the citizens. It requires public authorities to disclose all information about their activities proactively and

CHART 20.1

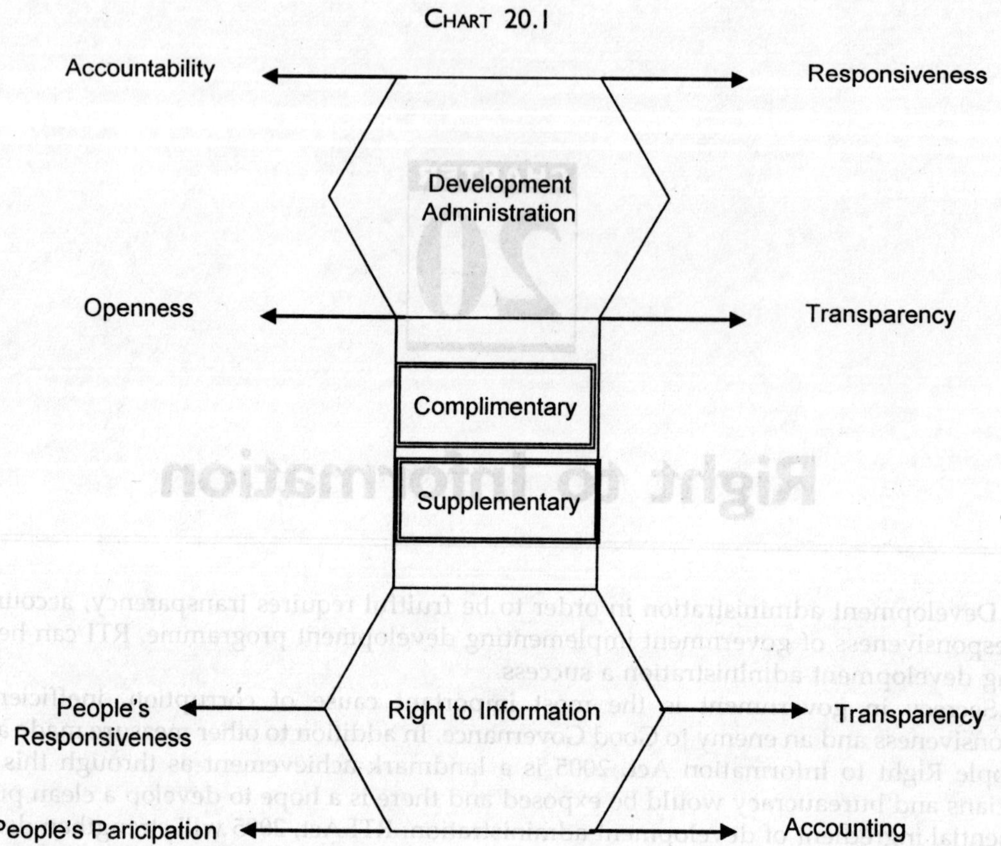

maintain all information they keep in a manner that facilitates the people's right to information. Indeed, by breaking down this culture of secrecy, the law will also open channels of communication between the citizen and the government. Currently, communication between the government and people is one-way traffic, where citizens are susceptible to government manipulation of information which is often used to suit government interest. Without access to reliable information on government activities—rather than, propaganda—it is difficult for citizens to make, political informed choices in the ballot box. However, the RTI Act can provide citizens with a vital tool to inform themselves about a government's record in office. In this way, it can empower ordinary people to make more informed electoral decisions, giving them an opportunity to participate more effectively in governance and policy formulation which are basis of development administration.

The Act has the potential to crack down on corruption on a nationwide basis. Indeed, Section 21 specifically notes that though certain bodies are exempted from the Act, they are still obliged to release information if it pertains to corruption or human rights issues.

Prof. Manmohan Singh, the Prime Minister accordingly emphasized this crucial aspect in his speech on 15th August, 2005 from the Red Fort: "I would like to say that the biggest challenge in running a Government is to ensure that development programmes are implemented in an effective manner. We will ensure that our outlays of expenditure are visible to citizens as outcomes

CHART 20.2

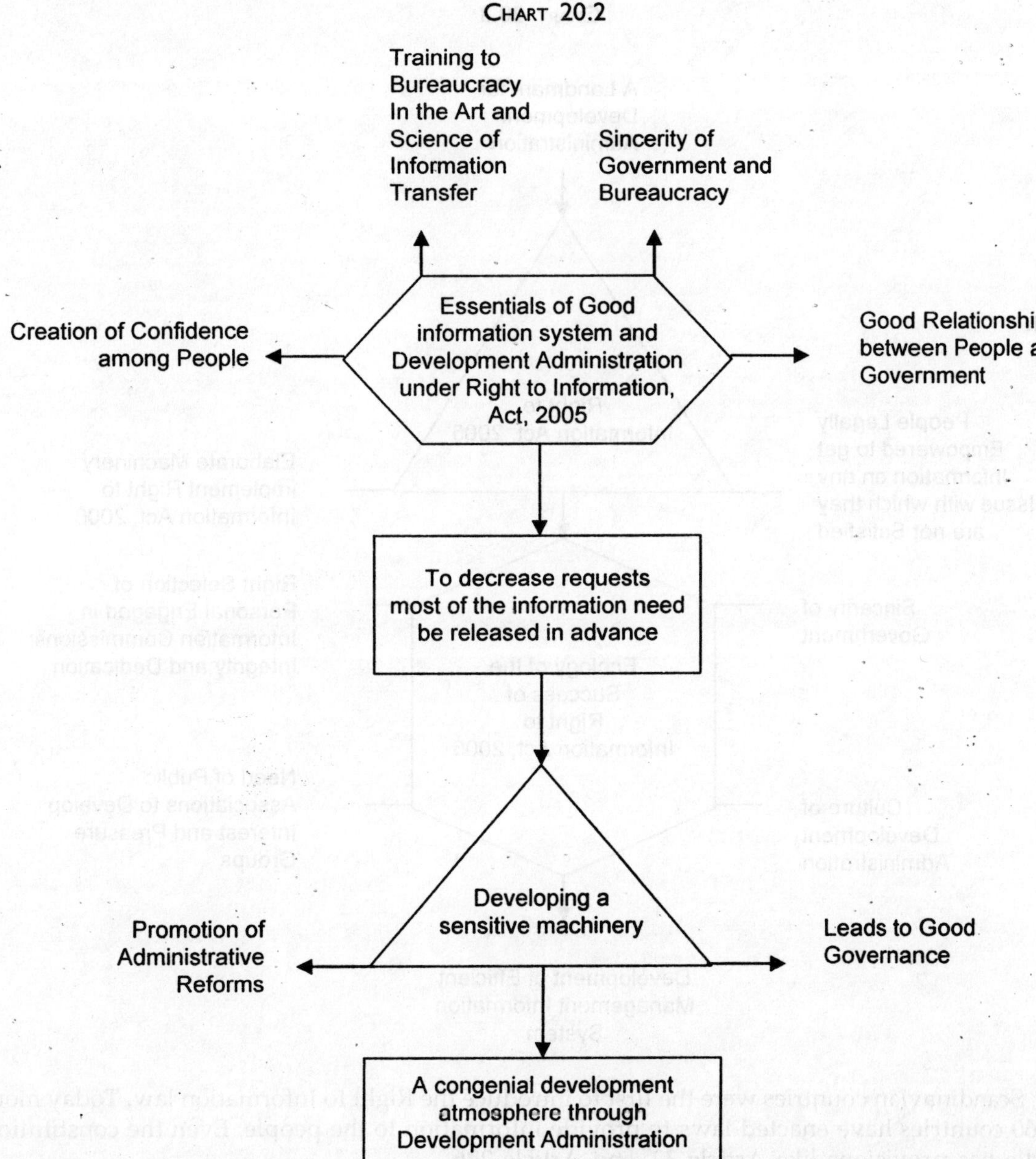

of progress. The Central Government, State Governments and Panchayats have to work together so that the expectations of people are fulfilled. If we have to achieve results, there is need to change the manner in which, governments function. There is no space in our government or in our society for corruption and arbitrary action. We are not prepared to tolerate this at any cost. Government servants must work with a sense of public service and they should be held accountable to the people. Governments will have to be made more transparent and accountable. The recently passed Right to Information Act is a landmark step in this direction." (See Chart 20.2)

CHART 20.3

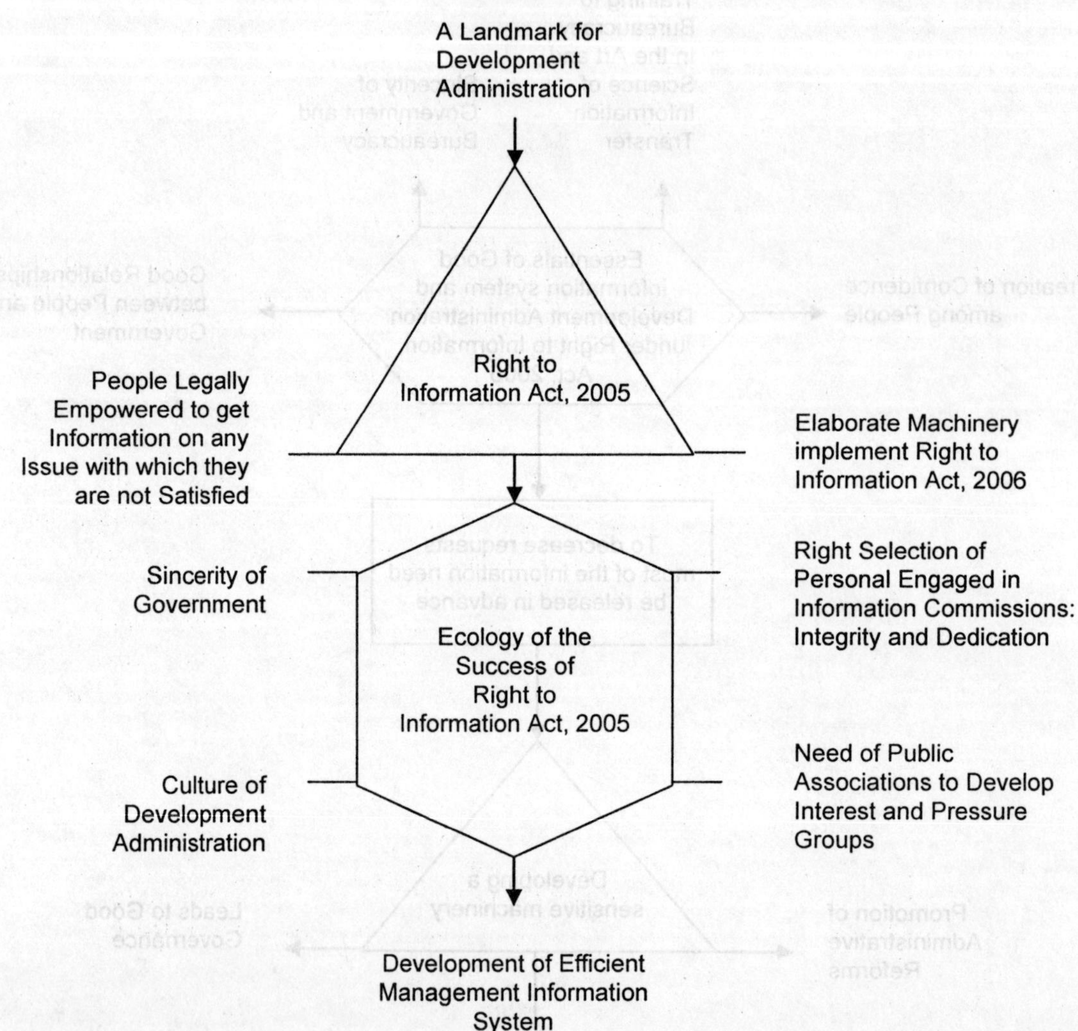

Scandinavian countries were the first to introduce the Right to Information law. Today more than 60 countries have enacted laws to provide information to the people. Even the constitution of India has provisions like Article 32, and Article 226.

The RTI Bill introduced in Parliament was referred to a Parliamentary Standing Committee whose recommendation with certain changes were introduced in the Lok Sabha on March 21, 2005.

The Minister of state in the Ministry of Personnel, Public Grievances and Pensions and Minister of state in the ministry of Parliamentary Affairs moving the motion for consideration of the bill said that this Bill promises to make this right to information more progressive, participatory and meaningful, ... Our endeavor has all along been to make the Right to information as potent as possible, and the number of amendments that we have accepted are ample evidence of it. It was the dream of our leader, Late Shri Rajiv Gandhi, that the common citizens of India must enthusiastically participate in the whole process of governance.

We wanted this to be known emphatically, that the citizen of India is not only free to ask for information from the Government, but also had a right to get it. The scope of this Bill extends to all authorities and bodies under the Constitution or any other law, and *inter alia* includes all authorities under the Central Government, State Governments and local bodies The non-Governmental organizations substantially funded, directly or indirectly, by the public funds also fall within the ambit of this Bill. A duty has been cast, in clause 4 of the Bill, on every public authority to *suo motu* provide to the public with the information as prescribed therein, so that the public has to take minimum recourse to the use of this legislation for obtaining information. The procedure for securing information as provided in clause 6 of this Bill prescribes a procedure which intentionally has been kept very simple. A citizen has to merely make a request to the concerned Public Information Officer or Assistant Public Information Officer specifying the information sought by him. The fee payable shall be reasonable. We have provided that information shall be provided free of cost to citizens living below the poverty line.

To assure that the information sought is provided quickly, clause 7 of the Bill makes it mandatory for the Public Information Officer to provide the information within 30 days if the information requested concerns the life or liberty of a person, it has been made mandatory to provide it within 48 hours of the receipt of the request. The Government is fully conscious of the fact that even the most ambitious legislation often remains confined to the law books for want of an effective regime to implement and enforce their provisions. In order to avoid such a fate, the Bill provides for penalities in case of failure to provide information in time, or for refusing to accept application for information, or for giving incorrect, incomplete or misleading information, or destroying information and so on. In addition, the Commission has also been empowered to recommend disciplinary action against the Government servant. The Bill establishes a two-tier mechanism for appeal. The first appeal lies to an officer within the organization who is senior in rank to Public Information Officer. The second appeal lies to the Information Commission. The jurisdiction of the lower courts is barred under clause 20 of the Bill. The categories of information exempted from disclosure in this Bill are kept to a bare minimum.

Even these exemption are not absolute if disclosure of the information outweighs the harm to the public authorities. Such disclosure has been permitted, even if it is in conflict with the provisions of the Official Secrets Act, 1923 Barring three categories that relate to disclosure of information or the information, relating to Cabinet papers, etc., or to Parliamentary privileges, etc., other categories of exempted information could be disclosed after twenty years.

Even in the case of security and intelligence agencies and organizations which are exempted from the provisions of this Bill, if there are cases of allegation of corruption and human rights violation, such exemption would not be available. In cases of allegations of violation of human rights, information would be made available after the approval of the information commission.

The Prime Minister while speaking on the Bill of Right to Information on May 11, 2005 said, "efficient and effective institutions are the key to rapid economic and social development, institutions which can translate promises into policies and actionable programmes with the least possible cost and with the maximum possible efficiency; institutions which can deliver on the promises made and convert, as the hon. Finance Minister pointed out a few days ago while presenting the Budget, "outlays into outcomes." For institutions to be efficient and effective, they must function in a transparent, responsive and accountable manner. This is dependent not only on processes internal to the institutions but also on the ability of citizens and external agents to enforce their rights, *vis-à-vis* these very institutions. The Right to Information Bill, will bring into force another right which will empower the citizen in this regard and ensure that our institutions and their functionaries discharge their duties in the desired manner. It will bring into effect a critical right for enforcing other rights and fill a vital gap in a citizen's framework of rights. This is an innovative bill, where there will be scope to review its functioning as we gain experience. Therefore, this is a piece of legislation, whose working will be kept under constant reviews. We will need to have a sustained effort to establish institutions and systems envisaged under the Bill, to build the capacity of our civil servants to discharge their obligations and above all, inform our citizens about the new rights conferred on them.

The RTI Bill was passed on 11th May in Lok Sabha and 12th May in Rajya Sabha with 146th amendments. On 15th June, 2005, President of India gave his consent to the RTI Act 2005. It came into force on 21st June 2005 after notification in the Gazattee of India.

H.K. Misra observes that the Right to Information Act, 2005 has come into force in India. With its legislation, it is said that Indian citizen has now the right to "demand information" if desired and every public authority is liable to share information. This right to information act is perhaps originating from Article 21 of right to life and liberty. It recognizes the importance of informed citizenry, maintenance of transparency of information which are vital to its functioning and to hold government and their instrumentalities accountable to the governed. In other words, it is meant for putting systems in place; operationalise these to bring transparency in governance systems.

It is hoped that Right to Information Act, 2005, would make the citizens active, participative and articulate to make democratic processes and development administration a reality. In addition, Right to Information Act, 2005 would develop deep roots and join other Acts e.g. Consumers Protection Act, 1986, Democratic Decentralization through 73rd and 74th Amendments, Human Rights Act, 1993, etc. to make Democracy a reality and functional.

MEANING

The Act defines information in sec. 2 (t) as any material in any form, including the records, documents, memos, e-mails, opinions, advices, press releases, circulars, orders, log books, contracts, reports, papers, samples, models, data material held in any electronic form and information relating to any private body which can be accessed by a public authority under any law for the time being in force. Sec. 2(i) defines the word 'record' as including (a) any document, manuscript and file, (b) any microfilm, microfiche and facsimile copy of documents, (c) any reproduction of image or images embodied in such microfilm, and (d) any other material produced by a computer or any other device.

The "right to information" is defined in sec. 2 (j) as a right to information accessible under the Act which is held by or under the control of any public authority and includes a right to (i) inspection of work, documents, records, (ii) taking notes, extracts or certified copies of documents or records, (iii) taking separate samples of material, (iv) obtaining information in the form of diskettes, floppies, tapes, video cassettes or in any other electronic mode or through print outs where such information is stored in a computer or in any other device.

Shekhar Singh and Misha Singh observe that the RTI Act, 2005 covers all central, state and local government bodies and, in addition to the executive, it also applies to the judiciary and the legislature. It covers all bodies owned, controlled or substantially financed, either directly or indirectly by the government, and non-government organizations and other private bodies substantially funded, directly or indirectly, by the government. This would seem to include private schools, hospitals and other commercial institutions that have got subsidies in the form of land at concessional rates or tax concessions, among others.[2]

Apart from these, the law, interestingly, also covers the private sectors as it provides the citizens access to all information that the government can itself access through any other law currently in force.

The RTI Act, if effectively implemented, could change the nature of governance in India. It could start a process of transparent and inclusive governance that could gradually shift the Indian democracy from being almost totally a representative one to a vigorously participatory one essential for the success of development administration. It could bring a sense of empowerment to the citizens of this country, empowerment that is necessary to check the rapid downward slide of government performance and standards, and the concurrent trend of declining public expectations. The people would see for themselves that it is not that the government has no money to spend on their welfare, but that much of this money gets illegally diverted.

Ajit Bhatta Charian observes that the key to the change in approach is reflected in the title. 'Freedom of Information' suggested an act of dispensation by authority; 'Right to Information' an inalienable right of every citizen—a truly revolutionary change from the era of secrecy. But the battle is not over. Without continuing mass pressure, implementation will be tardy and errant officials continue to evade punishment. And unless efforts are made to ensure that information about procedures to secure information reaches Nevathi Bai, (people) the act's far-reaching objectives will remain on paper.[3]

Prakash Kardaley, in an article, "A New Era", in Seminar, 551, July 2005 observes that DASSERA, the India festival of transition to a better tomorrow, will this year herald a new era of empowerment for the common man in India? By the present countdown, the national Right to Information Act should be operationalised by around Dassera, thus enabling a faceless citizen to demand to know from the high and mighty in the government details of every action they take, professedly on behalf of the people. For the first time in 55 years, the brown sahib will be obliged by law to offer himself to public scrutiny.[4]

India has a real chance to break the shackles of poor governance that have hindered its development since Independence and left the majority of its population disillusioned with successive government's promises to lift them out of poverty. Development administration would be the successful in such atmosphere. In this respect, the government must now wake up and realize the extent to which its resistance to the Act is placing India's development future at stake.

Though the passage of RTI Act was a legal watershed, without the government's full backing for the law's full and effective implementation, fulfilling the right to information for Indian citizens can never happen.

SCOPE

Section 4 of the Act prescribes the scope

(1) Every public authority shall:

(a) maintain all its records duly catalogued and indexed in a manner and the form which facilitates the right to information under this Act and ensure that all records that are appropriate to be computerized are, within a reasonable time and subject to availability of resources, computerized and connected through a net-work all over the country on different systems so that access to such records is facilitated;

(b) publish within one hundred and twenty days from the enactment of this Act—
   (i) the particulars of its organization, functions and duties;
   (ii) the powers and duties of its officers and employees;
   (iii) the procedure followed in the decision-making process, including channels of supervision and accountability;
   (iv) the norms set by it for the discharge of its functions;
   (v) the rules, regulations, instructions, manuals and records, held by it or under its control, or used by its employees for discharging its functions;
   (vi) a statement of the categories of documents that are held by it or under its control;
   (vii) the particulars of any arrangement that exists for consultation with or representation by, the members of the public in relation to the formulation of its policy or implementation thereof;
   (viii) a statement of the Boards, Councils, Committees and other bodies consisting of two or more persons constituted as its part or for the purpose of its advice, and as to whether meetings of those Boards, Councils, Committees and other bodies are open to the public, or the minutes of such meetings are accessible for public;
   (ix) a directory of its officers and employees;
   (x) the monthly remuneration received by each of its officers and employees, including the system of compensation as provided in its regulations;
   (xi) the budget allocated to each of its agency, indicating the particulars of all plans, proposed expenditures and reports on disbursements made;
   (xii) the manner of execution of subsidy programmes, including the amounts allocated and the details of beneficiaries of such programmes;
   (xiii) particulars of recipients of concessions, permits or authorizations granted by it;
   (xiv) details in respect of the information, available to or held by it, reduced in an electronic form;
   (xv) the particulars of facilities available to citizens for obtaining information, including the working hours of a library or reading room, if maintained for public use;
   (xvi) the names, designations and other particulars of the Public Information Officers;
   (xvii) such other information as may be prescribed, and thereafter update these publications every year;

(c) publish all relevant facts while formulating important policies or announcing the decisions which affect public;

(d) provide reasons for its administrative or quasi-judicial decisions to affected persons.

(2) It shall be a constant endeavour of every public authority to take steps in accordance with the requirements of clause (b) of sub-section (1) to provide as much information *suo motu* to the public at regular intervals through various means of communications, including internet, so that the public have minimum resort to the use of this Act to obtain information.

(3) For the purposes of sub-section (1), every information shall be disseminated widely and in such form and manner which is easily accessible to the public.

(4) All materials shall be disseminated taking into consideration the cost effectiveness, local language and the most effective method of communication in that local area and the information should be easily accessible, to the extent possible in electronic format with the Central Public Information Officer or State Public Information Officer, as the case may be, available free or at such cost of the medium or the print cost price as may be prescribed.

Sowmya Sivakumar and Eric Kerbart in their article, "Changing Discourse", observe that three aspects stand out while scanning the extensive Right to Information (RTI) literature in India. First, there is significant and marked shift in the entire discourse from the mid-'90s onwards. The phrase 'right to information' has earned a new meaning and interpretation in the Indian context, spawning a literature distinct from its western counterpart around 'freedom of expression'. Second and more recently, 'right to information' has found growing mention in connection with a vast spectrum of topics—from public distribution systems to elections, dams and disappearances. The documentation also points to an increasing recognition of its practical relevance across all classes of society.

Finally, it is striking that there is little 'anti'-literature on the subject it is apparent that the 'adversaries' of the right to information have consistently maintained a staunch façade of silence behind their actions. It is telling that while concrete battles are being fought against them day after day and stories of resistance abound, not a single bureaucrat or politician appears to have directly or openly penned their resentment against this powerful concept and tool.

LIMITATIONS

Section 8 deals with exemptions from disclosure of information.

Exemption from disclosure of information—(1) Notwithstanding anything contained in this Act, there shall be no obligation to give any citizen:

(a) information, disclosure of which would prejudicially affect the sovereignty and integrity of India, the security, strategic, scientific or economic interests of the State, relation with foreign State or lead to incitement of an offence;
(b) information which has been expressly forbidden to be published by any Court of law or Tribunal or the disclosure of which may constitute contempt of Court;
(c) information, the disclosure of which would cause a breach of privilege of Parliament or the State Legislature;
(d) information including commercial confidence, trade secrets or intellectual property, the disclosure of which would harm the competitive position of a third party, unless the Competent Authority is satisfied that larger public interest warrants the disclosure of such information;
(e) information available to a person in his fiduciary relationship, unless the Competent Authority is satisfied that the larger public interest warrants the disclosure of such information;
(f) information received in confidence from foreign Government;
(g) information, the disclosure of which would endanger the life or physical safety of any person or identify the source of information or assistance given in confidence for law enforcement or security purposes;
(h) information which would impede the process of investigation or apprehension or prosecution of offenders;

(i) cabinet papers including records of deliberations of the Council of Ministers, Secretaries and other officers:

Provided that the decisions of Council of Ministers, the reasons thereof, and the material on the basis of which the decisions were taken shall be made public after the decision has been taken, and the matter is complete, or over:

Provided further that those matters which come under the exemptions specified in this section shall not be disclosed: information which relates to personal information the disclosure of which has no relationship to any public activity or interest, or which would cause unwarranted invasion of the privacy of the individual unless the Central Public Information Officer or the State Public Information Officer or the Appellate Authority, as the case may be, is satisfied that the larger public interest justifies the disclosure of such information:

Provided that the information which cannot be denied to the Parliament or a State Legislature shall not be denied to any person.

(2) Notwithstanding anything in the Official Secrets Act, 1923 (19 of 1923) nor any of the exemptions permissible in accordance with sub-section (1), a public authority may allow access to information, if public interest in disclosure outweighs the harm to the protected interests.

(3) Subject to the provisions of clauses (a), (c) and (i) of sub-section (1), any information relating to any occurrence, event or matter which has taken place, occurred or happened twenty years before the date on which any request is made under Section 6 shall be provided to any person making a request under that section:

Provided that where any question arises as to the date from which the said period of twenty years has to be computed, the decision of the Central Government shall be final, subject to the usual appeals provided for in this Act.

To conclude in the words of Dr. N.R. Madhava Menon, Director National Judicial Academy, Co-ordinator, National Collogquium on RTA (2nd Jan. 2006) observes that enactment of the Right to Information Act, 2005 is indeed one of outstanding legislative accomplishment in the democratic evolution of the Indian Republic. Yet, the transition is not going to be either smooth or simple. An entrenched mindset of denial of information on the part of the bureaucracy coupled with justifiable apprehension of the consequences of which disclosure might tend to distort procedures and delay full implementation of the provisions of the Act. The capacity of the common man to access the information is today very limited because of socio-economic and historical reasons. Therefore, there is no possibility of a discernible change in the quality of governance in the immediate future. Nevertheless, the mandate of the law and the commitment on the part of a section of the intelligentsia to make common cause with the people who for long have been at the receiving end of maladministration and corruption, might increasingly create a climate for transparency and intelligence a change in the desired direction. In that process of change, the National colloquium at NJA sponsored by the Administrative Reforms Commission is a small, yet important step.[5]

A. ORGANISATIONAL SET-UP AT UNION LEVEL

Section 12 of the Act prescribes the Constitution of Central Information Commission.—

(1) The Central Government has, by notification in the Official Gazette, constituted a body to be known as the Central Information Commission to exercise the powers conferred on, and to perform the functions assigned to it, under this Act.

(2) The Central Information Commission consists of—

(a) the Chief Information Commissioner, and such number of Central Information Commissioners, not exceeding ten, as may be deemed necessary.

Appointment[6]

Section 12 (3) suggests that:

(3) The Chief Information Commissioner and Information Commissioners are appointed by the President on the recommendation of a committee consisting of:

(i) the Prime Minister, who is the Chairperson of the Committee;

(ii) the Leader of Opposition in the Lok Sabha; and

(iii) a Union Cabinet Minister to be nominated by the Prime Minister.

Explanation

For the purposes of removal of doubts, it is hereby declared that where the Leader of Opposition in the House of the People has not been recognized as such, the Leader of the single largest group in opposition of the Government in the House of the People shall be deemed to be the Leader of Opposition.

Functions

Section 12 (4, 5, 6 and 7) prescribes the functions of Central Information Commission:

(4) The general superintendence, direction and management of the affairs of the Central Information Commission vests in the Chief Information Commissioner who is assisted by the Information Commissioners and may exercise all such powers and do all such acts and things which may be exercised or done by the Central Information Commissions autonomously without being subjected to directions by any other authority under this Act.

(5) The Chief Information Commissioner and Information Commissioners shall be persons of eminence in public life with wide knowledge and experience in law, science and technology, social service, management, journalism, mass media or administration and governance.

(6) The Chief Information Commissioner or an Information Commissioner shall not be a Member of Parliament or Member of the Legislature of any State or Union Territory, as the case may be, or hold any other office of profit or connected with any political party or carrying on any business or pursuing any profession.

(7) the headquarters of the Central Information Commission shall be at Delhi and the Central Information Commission may, with the previous approval of the Central government, establish offices at other places in India.

Terms of Office and Conditions of Service

Section 13 (Section 1-6) specifies the conditions of service:

(1) The Chief Information Commissioner shall hold office for a term of five years from the date on which he enters upon his office and shall not be eligible for reappointment. Provided that no Chief Information Commissioner shall hold office as such after he has attained the age of sixty-five years.

(2) Every Information Commissioner shall hold office for a term of five years from the date on which he enters upon his office or till he attains the age of sixty-five years, whichever is earlier, and shall not be eligible for reappointment as such Information Commissioner:

Provided that every Information commissioner shall, on vacating his office under this sub-section be eligible for appointment as the Chief Information Commissioner in the manner specified in sub-section (3) of Section 12:

Provided further that where the Information Commissioner is appointed as the Chief Information Commissioner, his term of office shall not be more than five years in aggregate as the Information Commissioner and the Chief Information Commissioner.

(3) The Chief Information Commissioner or an Information Commissioner shall before he enters upon his office make and subscribe before the President or some other person appointed by him in that behalf, an oath or affirmation according to the form set out for the purpose in the First Schedule.

(4) The Chief Information Commissioner or an Information Commissioner may, at any time, by writing under his hand addressed to the President, resign from his office. Provided that the Chief Information commissioner or an Information Commissioner may be removed in the manner specified under Section 14.

(5) The salaries and allowances payable to and other terms and conditions of service of—

(a) the Chief Information Commissioner shall be the same as that of the Chief Election Commissioner; and

(b) an Information Commissioner shall be the same as that of an Election Commissioner:

Provided that if the Chief Information Commissioner or an Information Commissioner at the time of his appointment is, in receipt of a pension, other than a disability or wound pension, in respect of any previous service under the Government of India or under the Government of a State, his salary in respect of the service as the Chief Information Commissioner or an Information Commissioner shall be reduced by the amount of that pension including any portion of pension which was commuted and pension equivalent of other forms of retirement benefits excluding pension equivalent of retirement gratuity:

Provided further that if the Chief Information Commissioner or an Information commissioner if, at the time of his appointment is, in receipt of retirement benefits in respect of any previous service rendered in a Corporation established by or under any Central Act or State Act or a government company owned or controlled by the Central Government or the State Government, his salary in respect of the service as the Chief Information Commissioner or an Information Commissioner shall be reduced by the amount of pension equivalent to the retirement benefits:

Provided also that the salaries, allowances and other conditions of service of the Chief Information Commissioner and the Information commissioners shall not be varied to their disadvantage after their appointment.

(6) The Central Government shall provide the Chief Information Commissioner and the Information Commissioners with such officers and employees as may be necessary for the efficient performance of their functions under this Act, and the salaries and allowances payable to and the terms and conditions of service of the officers and other employees appointed for the purpose of this Act shall be such as may be prescribed.

Section 14 (1-4) describes Removal of Chief Information Commissioner or Information Commissioner.

(1) Subject to the provisions of sub-section (3), the Chief Information Commissioner or any Information Commissioner shall be removed from his office only by order of the President on the

ground of proved misbehaviour or incapacity after the Supreme Court, on a reference made to it by the President, has, on inquiry, reported that the Chief Information Commissioner or any Information Commissioner, as the case may be, ought on such ground be removed.

(2) The President may suspend from office, and if deems necessary prohibit also from attending the office during inquiry, the Chief Information Commissioner or Information Commissioner in respect of whom a reference has been made to the Supreme Court under sub-section (1) until the President has passed orders on receipt of the report of the Supreme Court on such reference.

(3) Notwithstanding anything contained in sub-section (1), the President may by order remove from office the Chief Information commissioner or any Information Commissioner if the Chief Information Commissioner or a Information Commissioner, as the case may be—

(a) is adjudged an insolvent; or
(b) has been convicted of an offence which, in the opinion of the President, involves moral turpitude; or
(c) engages during his term of office in any paid employment outside the duties of his office; or
(d) is, in the opinion of the President, unfit to continue in office by reason of infirmity of mind or body; or
(e) has acquired such financial or other interest as is likely to affect prejudicially his functions as the Chief Information Commissioner or a Information Commissioner.

(4) If the Chief Information Commissioner or a Information commissioner in any way, concerned or interested in any contract or agreement made by or on behalf of the Government of India or participates in any way in the profit thereof or in any benefit or emolument arising there from otherwise than as a member and in common with the other members of an incorporated company, he shall, for the purposes of sub-section (1), be deemed to be guilty of misbehaviour.

B. STATE INFORMATION COMMISSION

Chapter 15, Section 15 (1 & 2) prescribe the Structure of the Constitution of State Information commission—

(1) Every State Government shall, by notification in the Official Gazette, constitute a body to be known as the … (name of the State) Information Commission to exercise the powers conferred on, and to perform the functions assigned to, it under this Act.

(2) The State Information Commission shall consist of—

(a) the State Chief Information Commissioner; and
(b) such number of State Information Commissioners, not exceeding ten, as may be deemed necessary.

Appointment

Section 15 (3-7 Defines the process of Appointment)

The State Chief Information Commissioner and the State Information commissioners shall be appointed by the Governor on the recommendation of a committee consisting of

(i) the Chief Minister, who shall be Chairperson of the Committee;
(ii) the Leader of Opposition in the Legislative Assembly; and
(iii) a Cabinet Minister to be nominated by the Chief Minister.

Explanation

For the purpose of removal of doubts, it is hereby declared that where the Leader of Opposition in the Legislative Assembly has not been recognized as such, the Leader of the single largest group in opposition of the government in the Legislative assembly shall be deemed to be the Leader of Opposition.

Functions

(4) The general superintendence, direction and management of the affairs of the State Information commission shall vest in the State Chief Information commissioner who shall be assisted by the State Information Commissioners and may exercise all such powers and do all such acts and things which may be exercised or done by the State Information commission autonomously without being subjected to directions by any other authority under this Act.

(5) The State Chief Information Commissioner and the State Information Commissioners shall be persons of eminence in public life with wide knowledge and experience in law, science and technology, social service, management, journalism, mass media or administration and governance.

(6) The State Chief Information Commissioner or a State Information Commissioner shall not be a Member of Parliament or Member of the Legislature of any State or Union Territory, as the case may be, or hold any other office of profit or connected with any political party or carrying on any business or pursuing any profession.

(7) The headquarters of the State Information Commission shall be at such place in the State as the State Government may, by notification in the Official Gazette, specify and the State Information Commission may, with the previous approval of the State Government, establish offices at other places in the State.

Terms of Office & Conditions of Service—Section 16 (1-6) describes this:

(1) The State Chief Information Commissioner shall hold office for a term of five years from the date on which he enters upon his office and shall not be eligible for reappointment:

Provided that no State Chief Information Commissioner shall hold office as such after he has attained the age of sixty-five years.

(2) Every State Information Commissioner shall hold office for a term of five years from the date on which he enters upon his office or till he attains the age of sixty-five years, whichever is earlier, and shall not be eligible for reappointment as such State Information Commissioner:

Provided that every State Information commissioner shall, on vacating his office under this sub-section, be eligible for appointment as the State chief Information Commissioner in the manner specified in sub-section (3) of Section 15.

Provided further that where the State Information Commissioner is appointed as the State Chief Information Commissioner, his term of office shall not be more than five years in aggregate as the State Information commissioner and the State Chief Information Commissioner.

(3) The State Chief Information commissioner or a State Information Commissioner, shall before he enters upon his office make and subscribe before the Governor or some other person appointed by him in that behalf, an oath or affirmation according to the form set out for the purpose in the First Schedule.

(4) The State Chief Information Commissioner or a State Information Commissioner may, at any time, by writing under his hand addressed to the Governor, resign from his office.

Provided that the State Chief Information Commissioner or a State Information Commissioner may be removed in the manner specified under Section 17.

(5) The salaries and allowances payable to and other terms and conditions of service of—

(a) the State Chief Information Commissioner shall be the same as that of an Election Commissioner; and

(b) the State Information commissioner shall be the same as that of the Chief Secretary to the State Government:

Provided that if the State Chief Information Commissioner or a State Information Commissioner, at the time of his appointment is , in receipt of a pension, other than a disability or wound pension, in respect of any previous service under the Government of India or under the Government of a State, his salary in respect of the service as the State Chief Information Commissioner or a State Information Commissioner shall be reduced by the amount of that pension including any portion of pension which was commuted and pension equivalent of other forms of retirement benefits excluding pension equivalent of retirement gratuity.

Provided further that where the State Chief Information Commissioner or a State Information Commissioner if, at the time of his appointment is, in receipt of retirement benefits in respect of any previous service rendered in a Corporation established by or under any Central Act or State Act or a Government Company owned or controlled by the Central Government or the State government, his salary in respect of the service as the State Chief Information Commissioner or the State Information Commissioner shall be reduced by the amount of pension equivalent to the retirement benefits:

Provided also that the salaries, allowances and other conditions of service of the State Chief Information Commissioner and the State Information Commissioners shall not be varied to their disadvantage after their appointment.

(6) The State Government shall provide the State Chief Information Commissioner and the State Information Commissioners with such officers and employees as may be necessary for the efficient performance of their functions under this Act, and the salaries and allowances payable to and the terms and conditions of service of the officers and other employees appointed for the purpose of this Act shall be such as may be prescribed.

Removal

Section 17 (1-4) discusses Removal of State Chief Information Commissioner or State Information Commissioner (1) Subject to the provisions of sub-section Commissioner shall be removed from his office only by order of the Governor on the ground of proved misbehaviour or incapacity after the Supreme Court, on a reference made to it by the Governor, has on inquiry, reported that the State Chief Information Commissioner or a State Information Commissioner, as the case may be, ought on such ground be removed.

(2) The Governor may suspend from office, and if deem necessary prohibit also from attending the office during inquiry, the State Chief Information Commissioner or a State Information Commissioner in respect of whom a reference has been made to the Supreme Court under sub-section (1) until the Governor has passed order on receipt of the report of the Supreme Court on such reference.

(3) Notwithstanding anything contained in sub-section (1), the Governor may by order remove from office of the State Chief Information Commissioner or a State Information Commissioner, if the State Chief Information Commissioner or a State Information Commissioner, as the case may be—

(a) is adjudged an insolvent; or
(b) has been convicted of an offence which, in the opinion of the Governor, involves moral turpitude; or
(c) engages during his term of office in any paid employment outside the duties of his office; or
(d) is, in the opinion of the Governor, unfit to continue in office by reason of infirmity of mind or body.

(4) If the State Chief Commissioner or a State Information Commissioner in any way, concerned or interested in any contract or agreement made by or on behalf of the Government of the State or participants in any way in the profit thereof or in any benefit or emoluments arising therefrom otherwise than as a member and in common with the other members of an incorporated company, he shall, for the purposes of sub-section (1) be deemed to be guilty of misbehaviour.

Designation of Public Information Officers

(1) Every public authority shall, within one hundred days of the enactment of this Act, designate as many officers as the Central Public Information Officers or State Public Information Officers, as the case may be, in all administrative units or offices under it as may be necessary to provide information to persons requesting for the information under this Act.

(2) Without prejudice to the provisions of sub-section (1), every public authority shall designate an officer, within one hundred days of the enactment of this Act, at each sub-divisional level or other sub-district level as a Central assistant Public Information Officer or a State Assistant Public Information Officer, as the case may be, to receive the applications for information or appeals under this Act for forwarding the same forthwith to the Central Public Information Officer or the State Public Information Officer or Senior Officer specified under sub-section (1) of Section 19 or the Central Information Commission or the State Information Commission, as the case may be:

Provided that where an application for information or appeal is given to a Central Assistant Public Information Officer or a State Assistant Public Information Officer, as the case may be, a period of five days shall be added in computing the period for response specified under sub-section (1) of Section 7.

(3) Every Central Public Information Officer or State Public Information Officer, as the case may be, shall deal with requests from persons seeking information and render reasonable assistance to the persons seeking such information.

(4) The Central Public Information Officer or State Public Information Officer, as the case may be, may seek the assistance of any other officer as he or she considers it necessary for the proper discharge of his or her duties.

(5) Any officer, whose assistance has been sought under sub-section (4), shall render all assistance to the Central Public Information Officer or State Public Information Officer, as the case may be, seeking his or her assistance and for the purposes of any contravention of the provisions

of this Act, such other officer shall be treated as a Central Public Information Officer or State Public Information Officer, as the case may be.

Procedure Request for obtaining Information

(1) A person, who desires to obtain any information under this Act, shall make a request in writing or through electronic means in English or Hindi or in the official language of the area in which the application is being made accompanying such fee as may be prescribed, to—

(a) the Central Public Information Officer or State Public Information Officer, as the case may be, of the concerned public authority; and

(b) the Central Assistant Public Information Officer or State Assistant Public Information Officer, as the case may be, specifying the particulars of the information sought by him or her.

Provided that where such request cannot be made in writing, the Central Public Information Officer or State Public Information Officer, as the case may be, shall render all reasonable assistance to the person making the request orally to reduce the same in writing.

(2) An applicant making request for information shall not be required to give any reason for requesting the information or any other personal details except those that may be necessary for contacting him.

(3) Where an application is made to a public authority requesting for an information—

(i) which is held by another public authority; or

(ii) the subject-matter of which is more closely connected with the functions of another public authority,

the public authority, to which such application is made, shall transfer the application or such part of it as may be appropriate to that other public authority and inform the applicant immediately about such transfer:

Provided that the transfer of an application pursuant to this sub-section shall be made as soon as practicable but in no case later than five days from the date of receipt of the application.

Disposal of Request

(1) Subject to the proviso to sub-section (2) of Section 5 or the proviso to sub-section (3) of Section 6, the Central Public Information Officer or State Public Information Officer, as the case may be, on receipt of a request under Section 6 shall, as expeditiously as possible, and in any case within thirty days of the receipt of the request, either provide the information on payment of such fee as may be prescribed or reject the request for any of the reasons specified in Sections 8 and 9.

Provided that where the information sought for concerns for life or liberty of a person, the same shall be provided within forty-eight hours of the receipt of the request.

(3) Where a decision is taken to provide the information on payment of any further fee, representing the cost of providing the information, the Central Public Information Officer or State Public Information Officer, as the case may be, shall send an intimation to the person making the request, giving—

(a) the details of further fees representing the cost of providing the information as determined by him, together with the calculations made to arrive at the amount in accordance with fee prescribed under sub-section (1), requesting him to deposit that fees, and the period intervening between the dispatch of the said intimation and payment of fees shall be excluded for the purpose for calculating the period of thirty days referred to in that sub-section;

(b) information concerning his or her right with respect to review the decision as to the amount of fees charged or the form of access provided, including the particulars of the Appellate Authority, time-limit process and any other forms.

(4) Where access to the record or a part thereof is required to be provided under this Act and the person to whom access is to be provided is seriously disabled, the Central Public Information Officer or State Public Information Officer, as the case may be, shall provide assistance to enable access to the information, including providing such assistance as may be appropriate for the inspection.

(5) Where access to information is to be provided in the printed or in any electronic format, the applicant shall, subject to the provisions of sub—section (6), pay such fee as may be prescribed.

Provided that the fee prescribed under sub-section (1) of Section 6 and sub-sections (1) and (5) of Section 7 shall be reasonable and no such fee shall be charged from the persons who are of below poverty line as may be determined by the appropriate Government.

(6) Notwithstanding anything contained in sub-section (5), the person making request for the information shall be provided the information free of charge where a public authority fails to comply with the time-limits specified in sub-section (1).

(7) Before taking any decision under sub-section (1), the Central Public Information Officer or State Public Information Officer, as the case may be, shall take into consideration the representation made by a third party under Section 11.

(8) Where a request has been rejected under sub-section (1), the Central Public Information Officer or State Public Information Officer, as the case may be, shall communicate to the person making the request:

(i) the reasons for such rejection;

(ii) the period within which an appeal against such rejection may be preferred; and

(iii) the particulars of the Appellate Authority.

(9) An information shall ordinarily be provided in the form in which it is sought unless it would disproportionately divert the resources of the public authority or would be detrimental to the safety or preservation of the record in question.[7]

Powers and Functions of Information Commissions, Appeal and Penalties

Section 18 deals with the powers and functions of Information Commissions:(1) subject to the provisions of this Act, it shall be the duty of the Central Information Commission or State Information Commission, as the case may be, to receive and inquire into a complaint from any person—

(a) who has been unable to submit a request to a Central Public Information Officer or

State Public Information Officer, as the case may be, either by reason that no such officer has been appointed under this Act, or because the Central Assistant Public Information Officer or State Assistant Public Information Officer, as the case may be, has refused to accept his or her application for information or appeal under this Act for forwarding the same to the Central Public Information Officer or State Public Information Officer or Senior Officer specified in sub-section (1) of Section 19 or the Central Information Commission or the State Information Commission, as the case may be;

(b) who has been refused access to any information requested under this Act;
(c) who has not been given a response to a request for information or access to information within the time-limit specified under this Act;
(d) who has been required to pay an amount of fee which he or she considers unreasonable;
(e) who believes that he or she has been given incomplete, misleading or false information under this Act; and
(f) in respect of any other matter relating to requesting or obtaining access to records under this Act.

(2) Where the Central Information Commission or State Information Commission, as the case may be, is satisfied that there are reasonable grounds to inquire into the matter, it may initiate an inquiry in respect thereof.

(3) The Central Information Commission or State Information Commission, as the case may be, shall, while inquiring into any matter under this section, have the same powers as are vested in a Civil Court while trying a suit under the Code of Civil Procedure, 1908 (5 of 1908), in respect of the following matters, namely—

(a) summoning and enforcing the attendance of persons and compel them to give oral or written evidence on oath and to produce the documents or things;
(b) requiring the discovery and inspection of documents;
(c) receiving evidence on affidavit;
(d) requisitioning any public record or copies thereof from any Court or office;
(e) issuing summons for examination of witnesses or documents; and
(f) any other matter which may be prescribed.

(4) Notwithstanding anything inconsistent contained in any other Act of Parliament or State Legislature, as the case may be, the Central Information Commission or the State Information Commission, as the case may be, may, during the inquiry of any complaint under this Act, examine any record to which this Act applies which is under the control of public authority, and no such record may be withheld from it on any grounds.

Hindustan Times Editorial dated November 7, 2006 under the heading "An Opening Chapter" observes the success of RTI Act. To quote: The Central Information Commission's decision to allow right to information activist Arvind Kejriwal to inspect all cabinet files and notings of FDI in brand retailing is a landmark decision. This is for the first time that cabinet papers have been accessed under the Right to Information Act, 2005. By over ruling the objections raised by the central public information officer on the issue, the CIC has sent across the right signal to the pubic and to private servants. One of the many impediments before the implementation of the RTI—in spirit, and not just in letter—has been the attitude of the bureaucracy. While corrupt officials have a stake in trying to keep potentiality damaging information secret, many honest officials also resent having to divulge information due to an ingrained culture of secrecy that views answering the public's questions as an attack on their personal power and esteem. While the system allows public access to even cabinet decisions, little is being done to open information relating to the past, or provide reasonable access to information on critical areas like national security.

Appeal

Section 19 deals with the Appeal.—(1) Any person who, does not receive a decision within the time specified in sub-section (1) or clause (a) of sub-section (3) of Section 7, or is aggrieved by a decision of the Central Public Information Officer or State Public Information Officer, as the case may be, may within thirty days from the expiry of such period or from the receipt of such a decision prefer an appeal to such officer who is senior in rank to the Central Public Information Officer or State Public Information Officer as the case may be, in each public authority:

Provided that such officer may admit the appeal after the expiry of the period of thirty days if he or she is satisfied that the appellant was prevented by sufficient cause from filing the appeal in time.

(2) Where an appeal is preferred against an order made by a Central Public Information Officer or a State Public Information Officer, as the case may be, under Section 11 to disclose third party information, the appeal by the concerned Third party shall be made within 30 days from the date of the order.

(3) A second appeal against the decision under sub-section (1) shall lie within ninety days from the date on which the decision should have been made or was actually received, with the Central Information Commission or the State Information Commission:

Provided that the Central Information Commission or the State Information Commission, as the case may be, may admit the appeal after the expiry of the period of ninety days if it is satisfied that the appellant was prevented by sufficient cause from filing the appeal in time.

(4) If the decision of the Central Public Information Officer or State Public Information Officer, as the case may be, against which an appeal is preferred relates to information of a third party, the Central Information Commission or State Information Commission, as the case may be, shall give a reasonable opportunity of being heard to that third party.

(5) In any appeal proceedings, the onus to prove that a denial of a request was justified shall be on the Central Public Information Officer or State Public Information Officer, as the case may be, who denied the request.

(6) An appeal under sub-section (1) or sub-section (2) shall be disposed of within thirty days of the receipt of the appeal or within such extended period not exceeding a total of forty-five days from the date of filing thereof, as the case may be, for reasons to be recorded in writing.

(7) The decision of the Central Information Commission or State Information Commission, as the case may be, shall be binding.

(8) In its decision, Central Information Commission or State Information Commission, as the case may be, has the powers to:

(a) require the pubic authority to take any such steps as may be necessary to secure compliance with the provisions of this Act, including—

(i) by providing access to information, if so requested, in a particular form;

(ii) by appointing a Central Public Information Officer or State Public Information Officer; as the case may be;
(iii) by publishing certain information or categories of information;
(iv) by making necessary changes to its practices in relation to the maintenance, management and destruction of records;
(v) by enhancing the provision of training on the right to information for its officials;
(vi) by providing it with an annual report in compliance with clause (b) of sub-section (1) of Section 4;

(b) require the public authority to compensate the complainant for any loss or other detriment suffered;
(c) impose any of the penalties provided under this Act; and
(d) reject the application.

(9) The Central Information Commission or State Information Commission, as the case may be, shall give notice of its decision, including any right of appeal, to the complainant and the public authority.

(10) The Central Information Commission or State Information Commission, as the case may be, shall decide the appeal in accordance with such procedure as may be prescribed.

Penalties

Section 20 of the Act discusses about penalties: (1) Where the Central Information Commission or State Information Commission, as the case may be, at the time of deciding any complaint or appeal is of the opinion that the Central Public Information Officer or the State Public Information Officer, as the case may be has, without any reasonable cause, refused to receive an application for information or has not furnished information within the time specified under sub-section (1) of Section 7 or malafidely denied the request for information or knowingly given incorrect, incomplete or misleading information or destroyed information which was the subject of the request or obstructed in any manner in furnishing the information, it shall impose a penalty of two hundred and fifty rupees each day till application is received or information is furnished, so however, the total amount of such penalty shall not exceed twenty-five thousand rupees:

Provided that the Central Public Information Officer or the State Public Information Officer, as the case may be, shall be given a reasonable opportunity of being heard before any penalty is imposed on him:

Provided further that the burden of proving that he acted reasonably and diligently shall be on the Central Public Information Officer or the State Public Information Officer, as the case may be.

(2) Where the Central Information Commission or State Information Commission, as the case may be, at the time of deciding any complaint or appeal is of the opinion that the Central Public Information Officer or the State Public Information Officer, as the case may be, has, without any reasonable cause and persistently, failed to receive an application for information or has not furnished information within the time specified under sub-section (1) of Section 7 or malafidely denied the request for information or knowingly given incorrect, incomplete or misleading information or destroyed information which was the subject of the request or obstructed in any manner in furnishing the information, it shall recommend for disciplinary action against the Central Public Information Officer or the State Public Information Officer, as the case may be, under the service rules applicable to him.[8]

Monitoring and Reporting

(1) The Central Information Commission or State Information Commission, as the case may be, shall, as soon as practicable after the end of each year, prepare a report on the implementation of the provisions of this Act during that year and forward a copy thereof to the appropriate Government.

(2) Each Ministry or Department shall, in relation to the public authorities within their jurisdiction, collect and provide such information to the Central Information Commission or State Information Commission, as the case may be, as is required to prepare the report under this section and comply with the requirements concerning the furnishing of that information and keeping of records for the purposes of this section.

(3) Each report shall state in respect of the year to which the report relates—

(a) the number of requests made to each public authority;
(b) the number of decisions where applicants were not entitled to access to the documents pursuant to the requests, the provisions of this Act which theses decisions were made and the number of times such provisions were invoked;
(c) the number of appeals referred to the Central Information Commission or State Information Commission, as the case may be, for review, the nature of the appeals and the outcome of the appeals;
(d) particulars of any disciplinary action taken against any officer in respect of the administration of this Act;
(e) the amount of charges collected by each public authority under this Act;
(f) any facts which indicate an effort by the public authorities to administer and implement the spirit and intention of this Act; and
(g) recommendations for reform, including recommendations in respect of the particular public authorities, for the development, improvement, modernization, reform or amendment to this Act or other legislation or common law or any other matter relevant for operationalising the right to access information.

(4) The Central Government or the State Government, as the case may be, may, as soon as practicable after the end of each year, cause a copy of the report of the Central Information Commission or the State Information Commission, as the case may be, referred to in sub-section (1) to be laid before each House of Parliament or, as the case may be, before each House of the State Legislature, where there are two Houses, and where there is one House of the State Legislature before that House.

(5) If it appears to the Central Information Commission or State Information Commission, as the case may be, that the practice of a public authority in relation to the exercise of its functions under this act does not conform with the provisions or spirit of this Act, it may give to the authority a recommendation specifying the steps which ought in its opinion to be taken for promoting such conformity.

Section 26 discusses about Appropriate Government to prepare programmes.—(1) The appropriate Government may, to the extent of availability of financial and other resources—

(a) develop and organize educational programmes to advance the understanding of the public, in particular of disadvantaged communities as to how to exercise the rights contemplated under this Act;

(b) encourage public authorities to participate in the development and organization of programmes referred to in clause (a) and to undertake such programmes themselves;

(c) promote timely and effective dissemination of accurate information by public authorities about their activities; and

(d) train Central Public Information Officer or State Public Information Officers, as the case may be, of public authorities and produce relevant materials for use by the public authorities themselves.

(2) The appropriate Government shall, within eighteen months from the commencement of this Act, compile in its official language a guide containing such information, in easily comprehensible form and manner, as may reasonably be required by a person who wishes to exercise any right specified in this Act.

(3) The appropriate Government shall, if necessary, update and publish the guidelines referred to in sub-section (2) at regular intervals which shall, in particular and without prejudice to the generality of sub-section (2), include—

(a) the objects of this Act;

(b) the postal and street address, the phone and fax number and, if available electronic mail address of the Central Public Information Officer or State Public Information Officer, as the case may be, of every public authority appointed under sub-section (1) of Section 5;

(c) the manner and the form in which request for access to an information shall be made to a Central Public Information Officer or State Public Information Officer, as the case may be;

(d) the assistance available from and the duties of the Central Public Information Officer or State Public Information Officer, as the case may be, of a public authority under this Act;

(e) the assistance available from the Central Information Commission or State Information Commission, as the case may be;

(f) all remedies in law available regarding an act or failure to act in respect of a right or duty conferred or imposed by this Act including the manner of filing an appeal to the Commission;

(g) the provisions providing for the voluntary disclosure of categories of records in accordance with Section 4;

(h) the notices regarding fees to be paid in relation to request for access to an information; and

(i) any additional regulations or circulars made or issued in relation to obtaining access to an information in accordance with this Act.

(4) The appropriate Government must, if necessary, update and publish the guidelines at regular intervals.

Power to make Rules by Appropriate Government

Section 27 explains (1) The appropriate Government may, by notification in the Official Gazette, make rules to carry out the provisions of this Act.

(2) In particular, and without prejudice to the generality of the foregoing power, such rules

may provide for all or any of the following matters, namely—

(a) the cost of the medium or print cost price of the materials to be disseminated under sub-section (4) of Section 4;
(b) the fee payable under sub-section (1) of Section 6;
(c) the fee payable under sub-sections (1) and (5) of Section 7;
(d) the salaries and allowances payable to and the terms and conditions of service of the officers and other employees under sub-section (6) of Section 13 and sub-section (6) of Section 16;
(e) the procedure to be adopted by the Central Information Commission or State Information Commission, as the case may be, in deciding the appeals under sub-section (10) of Section 19; and
(f) any other matter which is required to be, or may be, prescribed.

Power to make Rules by Competent Authority

Section 28 explains (1) The Competent Authority may, by notification in the Official Gazette, make rules to carry out the provisions of this Act.

(2) In particular, and without prejudice to the generality of the foregoing power, such rules may provide for all or any of the following matters, namely—

(i) the cost of the medium or print cost price of the materials to be disseminated under sub-section (4) of Section 4;
(ii) the fee payable under sub-section (1) of Section 6;
(iii) the fee payable under-section (1) of Section 7; and
(iv) any other matter which is required to be, or may be, prescribed.

Power to make Procedure of laying of Rules

Section 29 provides about that (1) Every rule made by the Central Government under this Act shall be laid, as soon as may be after it is made, before each House of Parliament, while it is in session, for a total period of thirty days which may be comprised in one session or in two or more successive sessions, and if, before the expiry of the session immediately following the session of the successive sessions aforesaid, both Houses agree in making any modification in the rule or both Houses agree that the rule should not be made, the rules shall thereafter have effect only in such modified form or be of no effect, as the case may be, so, however, that any such modification or annulment shall be without prejudice to the validity of anything previously done under that rule.

(2) Every rule made under this Act by a State government shall be laid, as son as may be after it is notified, before the State Legislature.

Power to Remove Difficulties

Section 30 deals with (1) If any difficulty arises in giving effect to the provisions of this Act, the Central government may, by order published in the Official Gazette, make such provisions not inconsistent with the provisions of this Act as appear to it to be necessary or expedient for removal of the difficulty:

Provided that no such order shall be made after the expiry of a period of two years from the date of the commencement of this Act.

(2) Every order made under this session shall, as soon as may be after it is made, be laid before each House of Parliament.

The Freedom of Information Act, 2002 (5 of 2003) is hereby repealed (Section 34)

Amendment of the Act

The Government initiated a move to amend the RTI Act in July 2006 with seven amendments in a very short span of time of the enactment of the Act. UPA Government in their manifesto promised clean and responsive administration but one cannot understand the compulsion and necessities which went into the thinking of amending the Act. It appears that the Vested interests including politicians, bureaucrats sensing problems for them from this act, thought to put pressure on the Govt to amend the Act. This is not fair and undermines the credibility of the Government.

1. The amendment would thwart the efforts to remove corruption—a cancer to Indian Democracy.
2. The amendment would encourage bureaucrats to forget the people and only think of obliging the politicians and vested interests.
3. The amendment would take the soul out of the Act and leave it with mere skelton.
4. The amendment would undermine transparency, accountability and responsiveness.
5. The amendment would give unlimited powers to the departments as they would be selective in imparting with information, i.e. Information desired would be made confidential and information not desired would be given resulting into wastage of money, time and energy.
6. The Amendment would loose credibility—an essence of Democracy.
7. Amendment would serve no purpose. This shows that the Government is not serious and simply want to enact to make public opinion. This has rather created a poor opinion about the Government among the people.

The proposed amendments seek to restrict access to 'file notings' and allow access to only "substantial notings relating to social and developmental issues." That would not only alter the letter of the Act, but violate its spirit as well. The RTI law is a constitutional guarantee that is subject to restrictions, under Article 19(2) ,only when it undermines and/or endangers "the sovereignty and integrity of India, the security of the state, friendly relations with foreign states, public order, decency or morality"; or when it amounts "to contempt of court, defamation and incitement to an offence." Section 8 of the Act already refers to that. What needs legislation, therefore, is specified heads that must be exempt from the RTI Act. To that extent, the government's contention that the current amendments constitute a progressive step is patently disingenuous and ham-handed.[9]

The United Progressive Alliance Government has decided not to bring in the proposed controversial amendments to the Right to Information Act, at least in the current session of Parliament. Congress president Sonia Gandhi and Prime Minister Manmohan Singh received many representations against the proposed amendments aimed at deleting 'file notings' from the new transparency regime.

Ms. Sonia Gandhi is believed to have advised the Government that there should be wider consultations among the stakeholders before the controversy over the file noting provisions got sorted out.

CONCLUSION

In the words of second Administrative Reforms Commission:

The Right to Information law of 2005 signals a radical shift in our governance culture and permanently impacts all agencies of state. The effective implementation of this law depends on three fundamental shifts: from the prevailing culture of secrecy to a new culture of openness; from personalized despotism to authority coupled with accountability; and from unilateral decision-making to participative governance. Obviously one single law cannot change everything. But this fine legislation is an important beginning. Its effective application depends largely on the institutions created, early traditions and practices, attendant changes in laws and procedures, and adequate participation of people and the public servants. The Commission, therefore, focused on two broad categories of issues.

The first set of issues relates to changes in other laws and practices involving state secrets civil service conduct rules and classification of documents. The Commission firmly believes that the Official Secrets Act, 1923 in the current form is antiquated and unsuitable for emerging needs. The second set of issues relates to implementation of the RTI Act itself, particular process engineering, record keeping, disclosures, access and monitoring. In respect of the second category of issues, the Commission's recommendations are largely within the framework of the present law.

It is well recognized that right to information is necessary, but not sufficient, to improve governance. A lot more needs to be done to usher in accountability in governance, including protection of whistle blowers, decentralization of power and fusion of authority with accountability at all levels. Nevertheless, this law provides us a priceless opportunity to redesign the processes of governance, particularly at the grass roots level where the citizen interface is maximum. Now that the romance of the struggle for transparency is over, the tedious process of system-building has to take over. It is in this spirit that the Commission made specific recommendations and attempted to provide a road map for their time-bound implementation.[10]

In the words of Dr. N.R. Madhava Menon, Director National Judicial Academy, Co-ordinator, National Collogquium on RTA (2nd Jan. 2006) the enactment of the Right to Information Act, 2005 is indeed one of outstanding legislative accomplishment in the democratic evolution of the Indian Republic. Yet, the transition is not going to be either smooth or simple. An entrenched mindset of denial of information on the part of the bureaucracy coupled with justifiable apprehension of the consequences of which disclosure might tend to distort procedures and delay full implementation of the provisions of the Act. The capacity of the common man to access the information is today very limited because of socio-economic and historical reasons. Therefore, there is no possibility of a discernible change in the quality of governance in the immediate future. Nevertheless, the mandate of the law and the commitment on the part of a section of the intelligentsia to make common cause with the people who for long have been at the receiving end of maladministration and corruption, might increasingly create a climate for transparency and influences a change in the desired direction. In that process of change, the National colloquium at NJA sponsored by the Administrative Reforms Commission is a small, yet important step.[11]

Prime Minister, Manmohan Singh rightly remarked that the implementation of Right to Informatiion Act, is, therefore, an important milestone in our Quest for building an enlightened and at the same time, a prosperous society. Therefore, the exercise of the Right to Information cannot be the privilege of the few.

Development administration can be a great success provided all citizens take interest in development activities. Whenever they feel that money allocated to development activities like health, education, social welfare is not being used properly they can expose such authorities through RTI. Eternal Vigilence is the safeguard of achieving the goals of development administration.

Notes and References

1. Indra Jeet Mistry, RTI will Improve Governance, *The Daily Tribune*, dated 1.10.2006.
2. Shekhar Singh and Misha Singh, "Changing Governance for ever", in *Yojna*, New Delhi, January, 2006.
3. Ajit Bhatta Charian, "From Freedom to Right", *Yojna*, January 2006.
4. Prakash Kardaley, "A New Era", in Seminar SSI, July, 2005.
5. Second Administrative Report Commission, Report 1, p. 94
6. Right to Information Act, 2005, (Central Act No. 22 of 2005), pp. 15-16
7. The Right to Information Act, 2005, (Central Act, No. 22 of 2005), *Karnataka Law Journal Publication*, Bangalore, pp. 10-12.
8. The Right to Information Act, 2005, (Central Act, No. 22 of 2005), *Karnataka Law Jouranl Publication*, Bangalore, pp. 22-25.
9. *Economics Times*, dated 15th August
10. M. Veeranppan Moily, Second Administrative Reforms Commission, 1st Report, GOI, New Delhi, p. 56.
11. *Ibid.*, p. 94.

CHAPTER

21

Administrative Ethics

We are passing through critical times when the environment all around is unethical which stand in the way of Development Administration and good governance. K.R. Narayanan, Former President of India, while delivering his address, on the eve of Independence Day, on 14th August, 2000, was critical of the nexus between politicians and criminals, who are, in the process polluting the environment of the country. The malpractices in every sphere have become cancerous and are engulfing the entire system geared to provide good standard of living to people. T.N. Chaturvedi in his Editorial on the Special Number on Ethics in Public life of *the Indian Journal of Public Administration* (July-Sept., 1995) has rightly remarked.[1] (See Chart 21.1)

The potential damage and threat to the political fabric of a system is not dependent on the character of government, i.e. whether it is an activist or limited in scope. History shows that neither a capitalist nor a socialist nor a welfare state is immune to the corrosive evil of corruption. The standards of conduct and behaviour of people in political authority have their malignant influence in other walks of life in society. The ethical dimensions of how influential and powerful people conduct themselves in private life and the public domain set a precedent for the lesser human beings and groups in society to follow or to seek justification for their own self-seeking or even scandalous conduct. The perniciousness ripple-effect encompasses all segments of society. It is not only the public systems that are under attack. The people harbour grievances against trade, industry, business, academia, medical and other professional groups and organisations. The evil within and outside the government circle, is thus, not limited to any narrow confines. Similarly, the influence of ethical conduct in positive terms is also not contained or concerned with only some specific sections and select groups but is relevant to the entirety of society and its wider network of relationships. As is often said, the moral basis for the unity and stability of society demands that ethical restraints must operate not only in respect of individuals but also organised groups —be they industrial, business and trade associations, labour unions, political parties, military and civil services, judiciary, non-governmental organisations, academic or professional associations, agriculturists organisations, etc.—apart from government itself. The all-pervading and inter-locking nature of ethics in public life is to be comprehended in all its

manifestations and dimensions. This is borne out by history in different times and ages and also by the prowess of civilisation today.

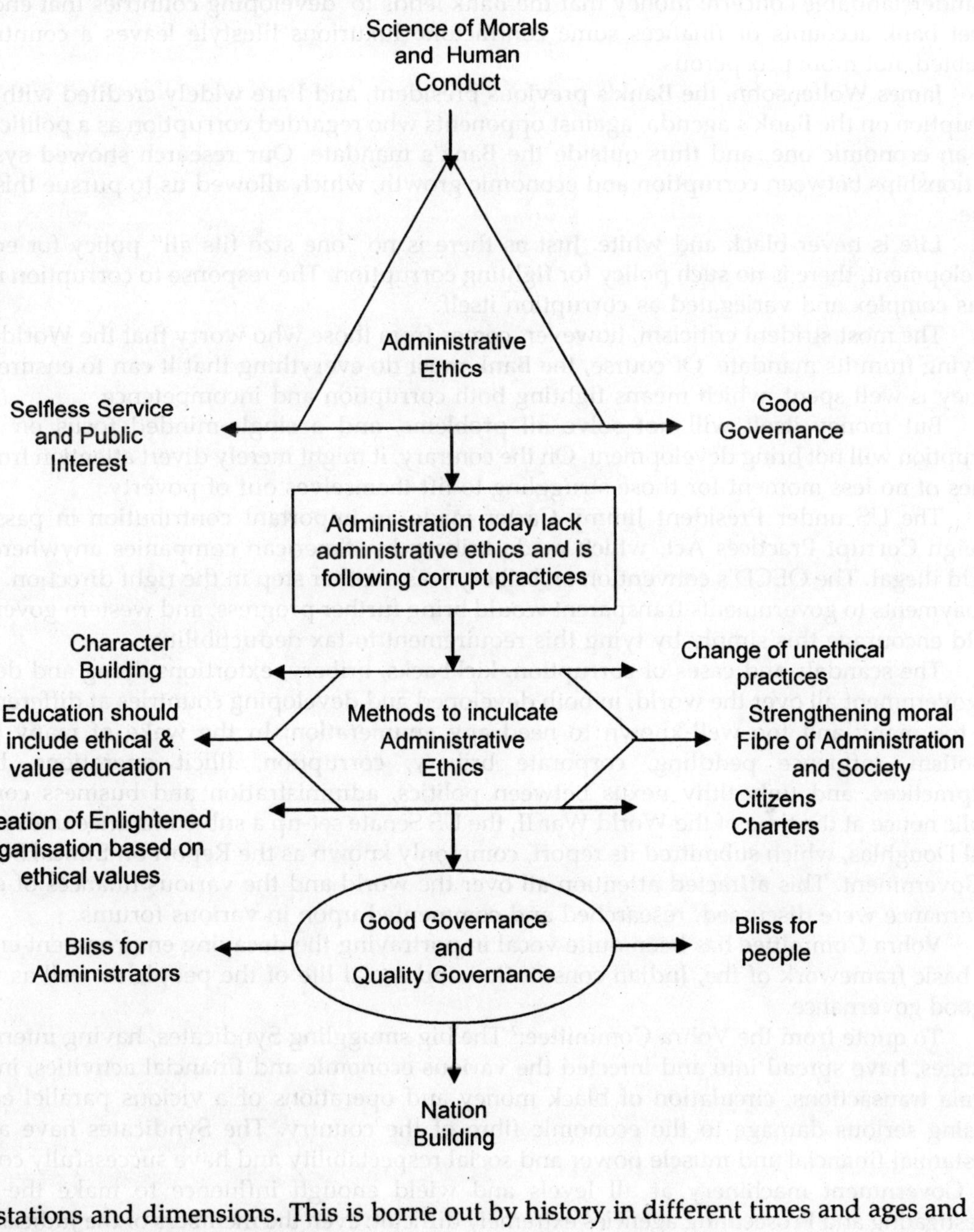

Jospeph E. Stiglitz, a Noble laureate in Economic and a Professor of Economics in Columbia University in *Economic Times*, Oct. 20, 2006 in an article "Corrupting fight against corruption" observes that—

At its recent annual meeting, World Bank officials spoke extensively about corruption. It is an understandable concern: money that the Bank lends to 'developing countries that ends up in secret bank accounts or finances some contractors' luxurious lifestyle leaves a country more indebted, not more prosperous.

James Wolfensohn, the Bank's previous president, and I are widely credited with putting corruption on the Bank's agenda, against opponents who regarded corruption as a political issue, not an economic one, and thus outside the Bank's mandate. Our research showed systematic relationships between corruption and economic growth, which allowed us to pursue this critical issue.

Life is never black and white. Just as there is no "one size fits all" policy for economic development, there is no such policy for fighting corruption. The response to corruption needs to be as complex and variegated as corruption itself.

The most strident criticism, however, comes from those who worry that the World Bank is straying from its mandate. Of course, the Bank must do everything that it can to ensure that its money is well spent, which means fighting both corruption and incompetence.

But money itself will not solve all problems, and a single-minded focus on fighting corruption will not bring development. On the contrary, it might merely divert attention from other issues of no less moment for those struggling to lift themselves out of poverty.

The US under President Jimmy Carter made an important contribution in passing the Foreign Corrupt Practices Act, which made bribery by American companies anywhere in the world illegal. The OECD's convention on bribery was another step in the right direction. Making all payments to governments transparent would bring further progress, and western governments could encourage this simply by tying this requirement to tax deductibility.

The scandals and cases of corruption, kickbacks, bribery, extortions, lying and deception by government all over the world, in both developed and developing countries at different times, are too many and too well-known to need any enumeration. In the wake of many cases of nepotism, influence peddling, corporate bribery, corruption, illicit operations, business malpractices, and unhealthy nexus between politics, administration and business coming of public notice at the time of the World War II, the US Senate set-up a sub-committee under Senator Paul Doughlas, which submitted its report, commonly known as the Report on Ethical Standards in Government. This attracted attention all over the world and the various nuances of ethics in governance were discussed, researched and commented upon in various forums.

Vohra Committee has been quite vocal in portraying the decaying environment engulfing the basic framework of the, Indian constitution and social life of the people as well as inimical to good governance.

To quote from the Vohra Committee:[2] The big smuggling Syndicates, having international linkages, have spread into and infected the various economic and financial activities, including havala transactions, circulation of black money and operations of a vicious parallel economy causing serious damage to the economic fibre of the country. The Syndicates have acquired substantial financial and muscle power and social respectability and have successfully corrupted the Government machinery at all levels and wield enough influence to make the task of Investigating and Prosecuting agencies extremely difficult; even the members of the Judicial system have not escaped the embrace of the Mafia. How can we think of good governance under such a polluting environment.

Developing respect for law and thereby strengthening the foundation of Rule of Law, as a part of promoting the culture of good governance, should be achieved. The respect for individual dignity and human rights should also be promoted. For all public officials—ministers, elected representatives, public servants, and others—it must be obligatory to act as trustees of public interest. For this purpose, ethical obligations should be created through the Public Service Ethics Act. The Advisory Panel on Public Service Ethics should also be created on public-private partnership basis as a part of the Public Service Ethics Act for supervision, review and further reform in this area. Suggested reforms, will no doubt, enhance the culture of good governance.[3]

Justice V.R. Krishna Iyer has even blamed the elite clan for joining the criminals and make the nation stink by their frivolous activities. To quote him:[4]

Lawyer, Doctors, Company Secretaries, Chartered Accountants, Engineers and Scientists, not to speak of the talented bureaucrats, are all slowly selling their souls for a mess of pottage. Even the leaders in the professions have let us down. To quote Browning's verse:

Just for a handful of silver he left us,
Just for a riband to stick in his coat.
We that had loved him so, followed him, honored him,
Lived in his mild and magnificent eye,
Learned his great language, caught his clear accents,
Made him our pattern to live and to die.

MEANING AND NATURE OF ETHICS

Let us now understand the meaning and contents of ethics which need to be ingrained into the Politico Administrative machinery of the Government to promote good governance.

The word "Ethics" is defined by the Concise Oxford Dictionary as "the science of morals in human conduct: moral philosophy: moral principles: rules of conduct."[5] The utility of ethics rests on the fact that it requires one to reason, to analyse and to search for morally correct position while taking a decision. Ethics in the area of public services is called administrative ethics. Chester Bernard has described moral behaviour as "governed by beliefs or feelings of what is right or wrong regardless of self-interest or immediate consequences of a decision to do or not to do specific things under particular conditions." S.K. Chakraborty has suggested work ethics where everybody is motivated by the ethical and moral values and works with the doctrine of Nishkam-karma. The salient features of Nishkam-karma have been identified as under: (a) Psychological energy conservation, (b) Reactionless steady action, (c) Perfection (as the aim), (d) Inner autonomy, (e) Freedom (Swaadheen), (f) Socio-Economically appropriate, (g) Work Commitment, (h) Work as Worship for excellence, (i) Mind-Enrichment, and (j) Leads to yoga with the transcendent/higher Self. Nishkam-karma will bring holistic transformation in work and will culminate in the following results: (1) a stress-free mind at work, (2) a feeling for works as acts of consecration, (3) a pure, transparent mind, (4) an abiding instinct for ethical rectitude, (5) an inner sanctuary of fullness, and (6) an all-embracing, other-related mind. All these factors can promote good governance, development and dynamism.

Manoj Pandey in his article, "Assessing Moral Values. For Higher Civil Services Selections in India" in *IJPA*, April-June, 2000 (p. 219) rightly defines that moral values, in simple terms, are the values that tell us what is the right, proper and acceptable way of behaving. Moral values are indispensable for good governance. An efficient and technologically sound administrative machinery, unless it stands on high moral pedestal, does not serve the public, but it serves a self-perpetuating and exploitative system.

Unfortunately, the Indian Government sector cannot boast of high moral standards. Superior courts have made highly critical comments on the conduct of bureaucrats, and the media is full of reports of high-handedness, corruption and other forms of inappropriate conduct of the bureaucrats. Honest and upright civil servants themselves are concerned about the low morality of the bureaucracy and have been voicing concern at various fora." How civil servants occupying high positions can provide leadership and good governance? They can do it through belief and practice in administrative Ethics.

According to Annual Report, 2005-06, Ministry of Personnel Public Grievances and Pensions, GOI, A day-long Conference of Chief Secretaries held on 2-11-2004 under the Chairmanship of Cabinet Secretary focusing on good governance, administrative reforms and related issues had agreed to have a Model Code of Governance which would enshrine the fundamental principles and benchmarks of good governance and would look at governance from the point of view of the citizen and outline the framework for good governance, based on identifiable benchmarks for comparison and evaluation, which can be a model for States to follow. Accordingly, a Model Code of Governance, which is in the form of a road-map for the administration was finalized and sent to all Chief Secretaries of States/UTs on 14-4-2005. The main components of the Model Code cover action points under the heads (i) Improving Service Delivery, (ii) Development of Programmes for Weaker Sections and Backward Areas. (iii) Technology and System Improvement, (iv) Financial Management and Budget Sanctity, (v) Accountability and Transparency, (vi) Public Service Morale and Anti-Corruption Measures, and (vii) Incentivising Reforms.

TECHNIQUES TO INCULCATE ADMINISTRATIVE ETHICS

I. Change Environmental Factors, which Tactily Permit Unethical Practices and are Inimical to Good Governance

Bata K. Dey, has sounded an alarming bell to save the nation from the onslaughts of unethical values dominating all walks of life and spoiling. the entire fabric of the society. To quote him: "Public life is in a desperate state today, with vice-regal regalia dominating it with its fierce ferocity and crushing criminality, sounding the death-knell of ethicality, morality, and value-system. There is dire need to save it. Public men at—whatever station of life they function—must be 'men' for the public; leaders must lead; and, most importantly, politicians must stop 'politicking'. Public opinion—which is often branded as meaning neither public nor opinion—must be built up against acceptance and tolerance of unethical behaviour and action by anybody, howsoever high and mighty he may be. Crisis of confidence which admittedly is a function of culture—must be restored in public life; otherwise; the ancient civilisation that we boast of will be no more; there will remain no public, no life, worth living, without ethics.[6]

Prashant Bhushan feels that the prevailing environment is full of corrupt practices at all levels. "Corruption has steeped into every pore of this country's public life. From top to bottom, Prime Minister to a peon, cutting across almost every office or organisation of all Governments, Central, State or local, the vast majority of public officials in this country has become corrupt."[7]

S.R. Maheshwari suggests immediate measures to root out this growing menace of unethical practices to save the nation. To quote him:[8]

Low ethics, today, is no doubt a world-wide phenomenon but its effects are most prenicious in developing countries, like India, characterised as these are by vulnerable economies. The country's policy-makers must realise that its economic and social costs are virtually devastating:

it demoralises the civil service and adversely affects its performance. It must be fought. Otherwise, the society will be forced to resort to extraordinary measures, like violence, to deal with the evil.

An analysis of above statements by eminent scholars, experts and administrators reveal that there cannot be any development until and unless, we can inject morality in the Government machinery. The writing on the wall is clear that the nation. is going to follow the dictates of criminals giving rise to violence, unrest and explosive situations. The recent Supreme Court judgement in Veerapan case against Karantaka Government is a pointer in this very direction. Supreme Court held in a very clearcut verdict that if Government cannot tackle such criminal menace, they must leave.

Dwivedi, an eminent scholar, suggests the need of moral base for the Government to save the country from further degradation. To quote him:[9]

No country is immune from the moral disarray which we have seen recently. Even in the People's Republic of China, which was hailed as a paragon of public virtue and morality by some cases of public service unethical activities and corruption have been reported. In many nations, a widespread sense of moral disarray exists, neither industrial nor Third World countries are exempt from this disarray. Everywhere, instances are on the rise detailing the collapse of standard and quality of service. This has contributed to the public cynicism; but at the same time, public is clamouring for a new set of bases for public morality and decent moral standards. Because, if we don't wish to be swallowed by the sea of amorality and self-centered hedonism, there will have to be some agreement (or consensus) about the behaviour of individuals, particularly those holding public offices.

The vacuum created because of traditional and 'old fashioned' values drawn from religious sources and based on common sense being discarded in favour of materialism and selfish individualism, clearly, points to the need for a code of ethics. As a matter of fact, no specific, standards were left sacred against which the conduct of public offices (as well as business people) could be measured. And as clergy and religious leaders were told to keep out of the state affairs, the protection layer of public morality was left exposed to 'the onslaught of corruption, dishonesty, sleaziness, deception and selfish individualism', protective layer in the body politic is needed back. For no nation or society, irrespective of its political and religious orientation, can live in a moral vacuum. There have to be some articles of faith (drawn from societal culture, traditions, and religions) governing our lives, which must be resurrected and strengthened. We already know that one cannot legislate honesty and good behaviour these have to come from within?

For that, one has to look to our religions where such attributes are considered sacred. But, one does not acquire such attributes by thinking alone; these have to be drilled in the thinking process of the officials. But that could be possible if their moral consciousness is raised so that they are able to fight against the forces of corruption, favouritism, and malpractice. Otherwise, they will continue to be adrift in the sea of a moralism, of which the prevailing administrative culture has come to symbolise. It is to prevent further decay that they ought to think in terms of drawing on their priceless spiritual and cultural heritage. Thus, there is a need within the secular domain of the administrative culture to seek the spiritual guidance. Only by demonstrating high standards of personal integrity, fairness, justice, and by regarding their work as Dharma, public officials may be able to arrest those insidious forces which have penetrated the foundation as well as the structure of India's administration. Such is the requisite of a moral government.[10]

Moral values, in simple terms, are the values that tell us what is the right, proper and acceptable way of behaving. Moral values are indispensable for good governance. An efficient and technologically sound administrative machinery, unless it stands on high moral pedestal, does not serve the public, but it services a self-perpetuating and exploitative system.

Unfortunately, the Indian Government sector cannot boast of high moral standards. Superior courts have made highly critical comments on the conduct of bureaucrats, and the media is full of reports of high handedness, corruption and other forms of inappropriate conduct of the bureaucrats. Honest and upright civil servants themselves are concerned about the low morality of the bureaucracy and have been voicing concern at various fora.[11]

2. Understand Religious Foundations of Administrative Culture (Ethics) which can Promote Good Governance

The Scripture of many world religions contain pearls of wisdom about how one should behave in the public office, or what is expected of those who govern people. When scriptures were written, the world was ruled by kings; hence advice is rendered for the king and his servants. Hindu religion is no exception to this pattern; except that unlike some other religions, edicts and codes are not handed down by the rulers. The religious foundation of the duties and conduct of public officials as described in some scriptures of *the Hindu* religion is examined here. Let us begin by quoting Krishna in Gita:

One ought to understand what is duty
and what is forbidden in the regulations laid down
by the scriptures (Shastras).
Knowing such rules and regulations, one should behave accordingly.
(Gita, Chapter XVI, Verse 24)
Lord Krishna further says:
O Partha ! that understanding by
which one knows what ought to be done
and what ought not to be done,
what is to be feared and what is not,
what is obligatory and what is permitted,
leads to the righteous path.

That righteous path in Hindu religion is called Dharma. How does one know the righteous path for specific functions or duties, Hindu scriptures (Shastras) provide guidelines. These guidelines or rules of Dharma have been prescribed by great many seers, each according to his or her wisdom.

3. Practices Ethics in Management to Inject Good Governance

Col. D.S. Cheema in his article, "Ethics in Management: The Indian Scene"[12] in *The Tribune*, dated 11.9.2000 stated that since a manager is expected to get desired and specified results from and through people, the focus of attention of management and that of the managers is on results. There is no doubt that the manager should be result-oriented, yet it appears that almost exclusive emphasis is laid on results and results alone. Many a management thinkers believe that the solution to the problems of managerial obsession with results and its undesirable effects lies in our heritage, traditions and ethos. It is relevant to mention here the concept of "Karmayoga" and "Sthitha Pragnya" as propounded in the Bhagwad Gita. It is well known that 'Karmayoga' calls for action without expecting the results and 'Sthitha Pragnya' denotes equanimity whether the results are achieved or not. A manager should aim at professional commitment when it is action and emotional detachment when it is the results.

Pursuing material and spiritual happiness and the welfare of mankind can lead any organisation confidently into the future. The essence of all this is 'management from the heart' and it is much closer to our way of life than anybody else.

'Kamala Prasad has beautifully defined the concept of Ethics and morality which needs to be understood and practiced to usher in a moral Government.'[13]

This will call for defining morality for governance. Morality signifies pursuit of ethical conduct and performance of duties assigned in such a manner that the declared purpose is realised. In the Greek tradition, it implied the development of the latent capabilities of an individual for the full flowering of his/her personality to deliver public good. To this end, there was rigorous training and preparation for the holders of public office so that the aims of public office were served. Dharma, in the Indian tradition, commands morality in the sense of righteous conduct. As propagated by Emperor Ashok, it further implied inculcation and practice of virtue in the performance of assigned duties. To an extent, the normative morality would subjugate personal interests to community interests and particular aims to general aims of the society. Mahatma Gandhi has raised Dharma to a higher pedestal, signifying a quality through which we know "our duty in human life and our relation with other selves." Thus, ethics in public life is important to understand our place in society and the duties we owe to the society by virtue of what society gives us. The common people may not articulate it in as many words but this is built into their thinking process when they make an assessment of the conduct pattern of their representatives and leaders and the system over which the representatives have command.

All modern governments suffer from the persistent preoccupation with procedures and functional rationality to the exclusion of ethical values and standards. It is not surprising, then, to see that public servants view their domain as a rational, objective, and value-free, where expediency and technical considerations dominate the policy decisions of vital socio-economic consequences. Ethical dilemmas faced by a public servant include many issues of contention, for example, if there is a conflict between an individual's privately held convictions and publicly held obligations, as determined by his organisation, what should he do? Should he interpret government policies and programmes according to his personal sense of right and wrong? Or, when a public servant feels that there is a clear-cut conflict between what he is required (by his senior officials or by the political leadership) to do and what he really thinks is right, where should his loyalty lie? Is a public servant committed to keeping information secret that might be embarrassing to the government of the day? What should an employee do when he finds certain indications of deliberate inefficiency, protection of incompetence, extravagant and unreasonable use of public funds, use of government equipment and machinery for personal use or subjective criteria used in recruitment or in the award of government grants or favours?

To what extent, should a public servant support the political ideology practised by the current political leadership of the government? Or, when a person accepts public service employment, how much should he subordinate or abdicate his claims to private life, property and values?[13] Obviously, neither the traditional concept of 'bureaucratic neutrality' nor a 'code of bureaucratic conduct' can cover all such situations or resolve such dilemmas. In addition to certain code of public ethics (determined in accordance with the prevailing socio-cultural political norms in the society), a public servant needs to develop an inner sense of professional responsibility, refined by the considerations of 'humanism', 'responsiveness' and 'public good'. As Dwivedi has so emphatically put it, "public responsibility" is multi-dimensional in nature, it flows upward and downward as well as outward and inward. Such a complex notion is bound to create dilemmas; consequently a responsible administrator would be well advised to be on guard against forces which might attempt to influence him to act otherwise."[14]

It has been noted by many observers that Singapore has succeeded in developing a Public Service ethos which emphasises merit, equity, probity, integrity, and ethical conduct, apart from leadership, quality and productivity. In Malaysia, the Government has always insisted on the highest levels of discipline in its employees, discipline meaning adherence or conformance to set work ethics and value systems.

It is clear that the existing legal provisions as well as the elaborate rules, regulations, standing instructions, etc. have not been able to prevent large scale administrative corruption in India. There are some objective and impartial observers who are of the view that in the last two decades, administrative corruption has increased in tandem with growing corruption among elected officials in India. They feel that without tackling political corruption, administrative corruption cannot be contained in India. While, in theory, one has to admit that political corruption on a large scale will have repercussions on the administrative set-up, the two need not necessarily go hand in hand, as the Japanese example illustrates. But it is certain that if political corruption is negligible and there is strong political determination, administrative transparency is insisted upon and norms of political as well as administrative behaviour are well publicised, making them known to the general public including the Press, there is a good chance that corruption can be contained if not eliminated.

4. Practice Ethical and Moral Values to Ensure Quality Governance

According to revered Chinmaya, be a noble person in life. The tides of circumstances and the tussle of happenings may toss us hither and thither, may buffet us up and downs, but stay noble in your thoughts and actions—you will be ever safe.

Let us discuss the various aspects of it.

(a) Serving the Government as per the Constitution

Public service must be committed to the philosophy and programmes of the present government. They should tender their unbiased advice and implement the policies of the Government sincerely.

(b) Serving the People

Public Servants should serve the people efficiently and effectively. Almost by definition, a democracy demands a responsive administration accountable to the people. It means that administration must be sensitive to the needs of the people, it must ensure its credibility and prestige.

(c) Integrity

Integrity is essential in dealing with administrative activities. The importance of character, dedication and sense of service are the important attributes of integrity.

(d) Transparency

Since the civil services in India is the major instrument of the Government for the implementation of policies for economic growth and the delivery of services, the restructuring of the civil service and the reorientation of its attitudes and value systems are essential components of a responsive administration. While there are striking examples of officials with demonstrated excellence, motivation and commitment to the cause of the under-privileged, these have been perceived by the public as out-numbered by inaccessibility, indifference to the public, undue emphasis on procedures and regulations, lack of quality and promptitude, proneness to corruption, and the lack of accountability for results. The associations of civil servants, on the other hand, complain about demoralisation, political interference and lack of motivation. The assumption of an executive role by the judiciary in recent years is seen as arising from the failure of the civil service in different levels of Government in the proper and responsive performance of assigned functions and in conforming to the code of conduct. The need is to function in the above framework of Ethics to usher in an Era of citizen-friendly administration.

(e) Taking Active Interest and not be Indifferent and Apathetic

Shekhar Singh in his article, "Ethics and Administration" rightly mentions that there is also a class of apathetic officers who, though they refuse to participate in or condone corruption, are not willing to fight it. Very often such officers are erstwhile fighters who have been beaten down or have become cynical. They withdraw into themselves and are often marginalised within the system. They sometimes take to other, non-administrative, pursuits, and try to revive their sagging spirits and sense of self-worth by excelling in the arts, or as intellectuals or sports persons.

Their immorality lies in the fact that they continue to be public servants without serving the public. They don't directly seek any benefits from their office except their salaries, their legitimate perks, and the freedom to do their own thing. But even in doing so, they take their due from the public, without in return giving the public its due.[15]

(f) Creating Climate to Promote Ethical Values

B. Rattan Reddy opines that there is no doubt that Indian Administration needs a strong core of dynamic values to transform its ethos at all levels. Laws can be enacted and rules framed to this end. Enforcement agencies can prosecute and the system can punish. This will have an impact. Nonetheless, enforcement of morality through law will largely remains an external process that can at best delineate a framework for public behaviour that should not be transgressed. But beyond that, laws or rules have inherent limitations in addressing the question of societal and individual change. As such, lasting public morality and ethics cannot be forced from outside. These must take roots and grow within the system itself. People have to understand and accept it so that change becomes organic.

(g) Code of Ethics for the Public Services in India

The document prepared by Deptt. of Administrative Reforms and Public Grievances has chalked out a Code of Ethics which need implementation. The objective of Code is to prescribe standards of integrity and conduct that are to apply in the public services. The principles stated below underlie and supplement the rules and laws to regulate the public and private conduct of various public services.

Selflessness: Holders of public office should take decisions solely in terms of the public interest. They should not do so in order to gain financial or other material benefits for themselves, their family, or their friend.

Integrity: Holders of public office should not place themselves under any financial or other obligation to outside individuals or organisations that might influence them in the performance of their official duties.

Objective: In carrying out public business, including making public appointments, awarding contracts, or recommending individuals for rewards and benefits, holders of public office should make choice on merit.

Accountability: Holders of public office are accountable for their decisions and actions to the public and must submit themselves to whatever scrutiny is appropriate to their office.

Openness: Holders of public office should be as open as possible about all the decisions and fictions that they take. They should give reasons for their decisions and restrict information only when the wider public interest clearly demands.

Honesty: Holders of public office have a duty to declare any private interest relating to their public duties and to take steps to resolve any conflicts arising in a way that protects the public interest.

Leadership: Holders of public office should promote and support these principles by leadership and example.

These principles apply to all aspects of public life. The Committee has set them out here for the benefits of all who serve the public in any way. Even the chambers of commerce has formulated a Code of Ethics and the important features of the Code of Ethics promulgated by the PHD chamber read as follows:

- Business must maintain highest standards of behaviour so that their actions and decisions result in the benefits for industry, employees, customers, shareholders and society.
- Goods and service must conform to the commitment promised to customers. Business must be realistic and truthful in stating claims.
- Customers must be given best possible service and treated with respect and fairness.
- Best way of promoting high standards of business practices is through self-regulation. The Code has been designed as an instrument of self-regulation to serve as voluntary guideline towards better quality of life and higher standards of business practices.

(i) Obligation to Government and the Constitution

The Constitutional and administrative role of the Public services is to assist the duly constituted Government, of whatever political colour, in formulating and implementing policies of the Government and in administering the public services under the Central Government in the most effective and efficient manner, within the framework of the Indian Constitution.

It is the obligation of every employee in the public services to uphold the Rule of Law and respect for human rights, and to act solely in the public interest while making recommendations or exercising administrative authority. He or she must maintain the highest standards of probity and integrity.

In relation to the general public, employees in the public services should conduct themselves in such a manner that the public feels that the decisions taken or the recommendations made by them are objective and transparent, and are not calculated to promote improper gains for the political party in power, for themselves or for any third party.

Employees in the public services should not seek to frustrate or undermine the policies, decisions and actions taken in the public interest by a duly constituted Government by declining or abstaining from action which flows from ministerial decision or statutory obligations. Where, following the instruction of the superior authority implementation of such decisions or action would appear to conflict with the exercise of impartial professional judgment, or affect the efficient administration of the department or undertaking, the employee should set out the points of disagreement clearly and courteously in writing to the superior authority, and seek explicit written instruction thereon.

Where an employee in public services has reasonable grounds to believe that he or she is being required by the superior authority to act in a manner which is illegal or against prescribed rules and regulations, or if any legal infringement comes to his or her notice, he or she should decline to implement the instruction. He or she would also have a right to bring the facts to the notice of the Head of Department or the Chief Secretary (Cabinet Secretary in the Central Government) or the Minister. It shall be incumbent on the Chief Secretary (Cabinet Secretary in the case of Central Government) to examine the issue carefully and advise the Chief Minister (Prime Minister in the case of Central Government) appropriately.

(ii) Right of Public Comment

Generally, employees in public services have the same rights of free speech and independence in the conduct of their private affairs as other members of the public. However, they also have a duty not to compromise the Government by public criticism of, or comment on, policies. They should, therefore, ensure that their contribution to any public debate or discussion on such matters maintains the discretion appropriate to the position they hold, and is compatible with the need to maintain a politically neutral Public Service.

(iii) Conflict of Interest and Peer Pressure

Employees in public services should refrain from decision in respect of which they have reason to believe that they are calculated to benefit any particular person or party at the expense of the public interest.

Every employee in the public services shall disclose any clash of interest when there is conflict between public interest and private interest, or he or she is likely to benefit from any act of omission or commission while discharging his or her functions.

Employees in public services should be alert to analytical or potential conflict of interest, financial or otherwise, and should disclose this to their superiors, whether the conflict covers them or their family members.

Employees in public services should maintain their independence, dignity and impartiality by not approaching politicians and outsiders in respect of service matters or private benefit, and exercise peer pressure to dissuade those within their own cadre who do so, and to set in motion disciplinary proceedings against such persons. Any such approach on his or her behalf in such matters would be deemed to be at the instance of the employee.

(iv) Accountability and Responsiveness to the Public

Consistent with accountability to the superior officers and the Ministers in accordance with Constitutional provisions, employees in the public services should be accessible to the people and practice accountability to them in terms of quality of service, timeliness, courtesy, people orientation, and readiness to encourage participation of, and form partnerships with, citizen groups, for responsive Government.

Employees in the public services should be consistent, equitable and honest in their treatment of the members of the public, with particular care for the weaker sections of society, and should not ever be, or appear to be, unfair or discriminatory. Decisions in pursuit of discretionary powers should be justifiable on the basis of non-arbitrary and objective criteria. Employees in the public services should accept the obligation to recognize and enforce the citizen's right for speedy redressal of grievances and commit themselves to provide service of declared quality and standards to the citizens. Employees in public services should respect the right of the public to information on all Government activities and transactions except where they are debarred from releasing information by provisions of law or valid instructions.

(v) Concern for the Value of Public Assets and Funds

Employees in public services should avoid wastage and extravagance, ensure effective and efficient use of public money within their control, and endeavour that the benefits of schemes for disadvantaged and poor sections of society are not wasted or diverted for the benefit of others. They should avoid ostentation and set examples of austerity for others.

(vi) Non-Abuse of Official Position

Since employees in public services have a responsibility to take decisions on merits, and they are in a position of trust, they must not use their official position to influence any person to enter into financial or other arrangements with them, or with anyone else. They must not abuse official position to obtain a benefit for themselves or for someone else, in financial or other forms.

(vii) Safeguards in Release of Information

Employees in the public services should not unauthorisedly release information which is not permitted by law, or compromise private or business interests, or the privacy of an individual when such information has been received in confidence. They should not take improper advantage of official information acquired in the course of their work, for unwarranted gain for themselves or others.

(viii) Integrative Role

Every employee in public services should recognize the integrative role of public services in national development, and resist internal and external attempts to fragment public services and society on caste, communal or religious lines. He or she should cultivate national outlook to rise above sectarian, service, cadre or departmental loyalties.

(ix) Continuous Improvement Through Professionalism and Teamwork

Every employee in the public services should continuously upgrade his or her skills and knowledge, strive for creativity and innovation and nurture values of team working and harmony. All employees in public services should promote and exhibit public and private conduct in keeping with the appropriate behaviour and standards of excellence and integrity. They should support the juniors in the latter's efforts to resist wrong or illegal directives and in abiding by the Code of Ethics. At the same time, they should reward good work and punish any dereliction of duty or obligations, based on objective and transparent criteria.

The government at the union and state levels should pursue ethical and moral values to develop the country on a permanent footing. The government must stop the rot crept into public life and improve the moral and ethical fibre of the society.[16]

(x) Practice of Ethical Values at Top Level

O.P. Dwivedi, a doyen on moral and ethical work, suggests the need of selfless service by the people in government. To quote him:[17] Holding of a public office requires that its incumbent is willing not only to acknowledge the moral responsibility for his/her actions but also to accept the accountability for such actions. Deflecting responsibility does not make action and its consequences disappear. Nothing is more damaging to public trust than justifying fraud and deception in the name of national security, government needs/or nation-building. Problems are more pervasive at the top simply because it is there where more is to be gained. That is why moral leadership had to come from people at the top. The absence of such leadership breeds cynicism and generates tolerance of hypocrisy, greed, and self-indulgence. The State (and finally society at large) becomes the victim of those individuals holding public offices who are unable to put the public business above their selfish leanings.

Enlightened Citizens believing in Ethical values. Without the co-operation of citizens, nothing can be achieved. They have to be vigilant and enlightened. T.N. Chaturvedi in his Editorial has cautioned that moral and ethical fibre of society can be upgraded only with the co-operation of the citizens. To quote him:[18] The need for organisation, activation, articulation and assertion of public opinion and enlightened citizenship is the life-breath of any vibrant democratic system. Public apathy leads to moral decay. Public vigilance and public awareness of its role and responsibilities provides a safeguard to the sustenance of ethical conduct of public affairs. It is well to recall here what the then United States Secretary of the Interior Harold lacks said during the hearings of the Ethics Committee: "Within my knowledge, no public officer has bribed himself," and he went on to emphasise the fact that official mortality is more than a political problem. "By all means let us consider how to assist in the establishment of higher moral standards in the official conduct of the Government, but at the same time let us realise that we cannot hope to assist the Government in this regard unless we are willing to assist ourselves and each other in the establishment of higher moral standards as between man and man in private life. Politics is an important part, an integral part, but only a part of the whole pattern of life" (George A. Graham, Morality in American Politics).

5. Create Enlightened Organisations based on Ethical Values which would Automatically Impart Good Governance and Satisfaction to the People

The ultimate purpose of all these reforms would be to set-up spiritual or enlightened organization as narrated by Jaideep Singh. To quote him:[19]

The Enlightened Organisation would be intensely imbued with a. sense of spiritual mission. Take the case of a company producing, say, shoes. It would experience itself not merely in the business of manufacturing and selling shoes, but, simultaneously, in the spiritual mission of protecting and taking care of human feet. The degree to which members of the organisation feel themselves involved in a spiritual mission will bring to them the deep psychic experience of living a worthwhile, meaningful life and will be reflected directly in their level of motivation and cooperation. This is so because the deeper biological layers of man, as Professor Abraham Maslow has identified in his Theory of the Hierarchy of Human Needs, are Self-Actualisation. Being Needs, i.e., the needs for Truth, Goodness, Beauty; Justice, Perfection, Completeness, Unity, Uniqueness, Meaningfulness, etc., and it is precisely these propulsion that we have traditionally called the spiritual thirst of man.

6. Develop Ethical Traditions and Practices to keep Balance and Concentrate on Good Governance

Justice R.S. Pathak has rightly sensed the traditions. To quote him: A code of ethical principal related to each public office, but in general there are applicable to all public offices. Those principles enumeration, they are well known and undisputed, continuing traditions indicate the identity and scope of and determine the ethos controlling the exercise of all I when I refer to traditions, I refer to traditions, classically evolved as most appropriate for the exercise. It is for that reason that it becomes necessary to educate ethical traditions of their office.

It is important to remember that when state power is channelised through a network of public institutions and public offices, it is intended to create a functioning system held in organic balance and unity, a system which in its holistic operation gives to the nation the intended opportunities for development and secures to the citizen high dignity and worth and the possibility of personal growth. It is vital that the constitutional system be kept in equilibrium. It may lose that organic balance and unity if its channels are clogged in consequences of the misuse or abuse or non-use of power in one or more of its constituent offices. The higher and more significant the office in the hierarchy within the system, the greater the potential for damage to the system.[20]

7. Universities can Act as Nodal Centres for Generating Ethical Values which can Impel Civil Service to Impart Quality Governance

Universities can play great role in imparted value education. L.P. Singh in a Document, "Morality in Public Affairs" has rightly stressed the role of universities in this direction. To quote him: A university has the unique opportunity of imparting its values and disciplines to the youth, who are potentially the most creative part of a society, and who are at the stage when the mind is most capable of imbuing the right ideas and principles. The number of boys and girls passing out of our universities every year runs into several lakhs, and it is from these that our ministers and most of our legislators (compared to legislature of many democratic countries the Lok Sabha has a higher percentage of members who are graduates or have higher degrees) are drawn. It is from the annually enlarging pool of educated youth that our civil services, learned professions, and business and industries at the higher levels, are manned. And what is of immense importance, it is graduates of universities who, in vast numbers, become teachers in schools, where they can start the process of moulding the minds and character of our adolescents. The universities have been and can again become radiating centres not only of knowledge, but also values. They can provide to our talented scholars an environment in which they can realise creative potentialities; they now do so in most cases only when they go out to work in foreign universities where they earn great distinction. A high standard of creative work can help our universities to regain their soul.

Our universities can, over a period, make a decisive contribution to the enlightenment of the public mind, and restoration of ethical standards. I believe that if we succeed in taking care of standards and values in our universities, the moral problems of the rest of society will take care of themselves. You members of the universities community have great challenge before you, and it is for you to respond to it.

Summary of Recommendations—Second Administrative Reforms Commission in its Fourth Report—"Ethics in Government" recommendations the following to promote ethics in governance:

Fourth Report: Ethics in Governance

1. Reforms of Political Funding
2. Tightening of Anti-Defection Law

3. Disqualification—Section 8 of the Representation of the People Act, 1951 needs to be amended to disqualify all persons facing charges related to grave and heinous and corruption, with the modification suggested by the Election Commission.
4. Coalition and Ethics
5. Appointment of the Chief Election Commissioner/Commissioners
6. Expediting Disposal of Election Petitions
7. Grounds of Disqualification for Membership
8. Ethical Framework for Ministers
9. Enforcement of ethical norms in Legislatures
10. Office of Profit
11. Code of Ethics for Civil Servants
12. Code of Ethics for Regulators
13. Ethical Framework for the Judiciary
14. Defining Corruption
15. Collusive Bribery (Loss to State or public interest)
16. Sanction for Prosecution
17. Liability of Corrupt Public Servants to Pay Damages
18. Speeding up Trials under the Prevention of Corruption Act.
19. Corruption Involving the Private sector
20. Confiscation of Properties Illegally Acquired by Corrupt Means
21. Prohibition of 'Benami' Transaction
22. Protection of Whisleblowers
23. ANG Serious Economic Offences
24. Prior concurrence for Registration of Cases: Section 6A of the Delhi Special Police Establishment Act, 1946
25. Immunity Enjoyed by Legislators
26. Constitutional Protection to Civil Servants—Article 311.
27. The Lokpal
28. The Lokayukta
29. Ombudsman at the Local Levels
30. Strengthening Investigation and Prosecution
31. Citizens' initiatives
32. False Claims Act
33. Role of Media
34. Social Audit
35. Promoting Competition
36. Simplifying Transactions
37. Using Information Technology
38. Integrity Pacts
39. Reducing Discretion
40. Supervision
41. Ensuring Accessibility and Responsiveness
42. Monitoring Complaints
43. Risk Management for preventive Vigilance
44. Audit
45. Proactive vigilance on corruption

46. Intelligence gathering
47. Vigilance network
48. Protecting the Honest Civil Servant

CONCLUSION

Administrative Ethics and development administration based on Good Governance support each other. Persons with ethical values can never deviate from their assigned duties as well as perform their duties with decency and interest. Such people are sure to pave the way for good governance. Ethics is the moving spirit of a welfare state. All the problems emanating today in a family or a society or Government are the product of ignoring ethics for selfish motives. Ethical government may appear to be harsh for temporary period, but this is the only alternative for a permanent beneficial government. One could argue that ethical behaviour should in itself be rewarding. However, there are tangible benefits as well. Business is built on relationships with the suppliers, customers, employees, and other groups.

The administrative Vigilance Division of the Department of Personnel & Training is the nodal agency in the field of Vigilance and Anti-corruption. Its main tasks, *inter alia*, are to oversee and provide necessary directions to the Government's programme of maintenance of discipline and eradication of corruption from the public services. In order to step up efforts towards containment of corruption, the three-pronged strategy of prevention, survelliance and detection as well as deterrent and punitive action adopted during the preceding years, was followed during the current year too. Towards this end, the implementation of the Anti-corruption action plan of each Ministry/Department has been monitored through quarterly reports. Emphasis was laid on preventive/procedures in selected areas. Apart from this, other anti-corruption measures, such as strengthening of the departmental vigilance and recourse to the powers of premature retirement of Government servants under appropriate rules as well as the monitoring of vigilance work of various Ministries/Departments, were also implemented.

The strength of these relationships is largely a function of the amount of trust the parties have in each other . . . "Studies have shown that the firms which maintain ethical standards perform much better than others due to the good relationships they have with their suppliers, customers, employees and general public. Thus, ethics are cornerstone of business success."[21]

We get a good governance by creating those conditions within which a moral government can operate. This is done by making it possible for officials to acquire the necessary traits and by the practice of the same. An exemplary public servants, to be specific, is not simply one who obeys the laws and behaves within the confines of law but is also one who strives for a moral government. Such is the duty of those who wish to be involved in the difficult and complex world of governance. This is the essence and basis of a moral state.[22]

Public life is in a desperate state today, with vice-regal regalia dominating it with its fierce ferocity and crushing criminality, sounding the death-knell of ethicality, morality, and value-system. There is dire need to save it. Public men—at whatever station of life they function-must be men for the public; leaders must lead; and, most importantly, politicians must stop 'politiking'. Public opinion— which is often branded as meaning neither public nor opinion—must be built up against acceptance and tolerance of unethical behaviour and action by anybody, howsoever high and mighty he may be. Crisis ('If confidence—which admittedly is a function of culture—must be restored in public life; otherwise, the ancient civilisation that we boast of will be no more; there will remain no public, no life, worth living, without ethics.[23]

We must remember that it is the top men in each department who set the tone of the administration. It is they who set the example for those under them to emulate. When the acts of those at the top become tainted, when their reputation becomes shady, they will not be able to enforce high standards of integrity in those below them. It is, therefore, imperative that men at the top should observe the highest standards of personal integrity, probity and rectitude. As Sir Ivor Jennings observed, the most elementary qualification demanded of a minister is honesty and incorruptibility. It is, in addition, necessary not only that he should possess this qualification but also that he should appear to possess it.[24]

An action is noble because of the ideal which one strives, in itself an action is neither good nor bad. It is the motive in the heart of man that makes an act either good or bad. Once we are careful to choose for ourselves the right type of motive to inspire our activities, the achievement is not only spectacular, but the entire effort becomes rewarding in terms of the feeling of peace and sense of fulfilment that floods the bosom. When we work joyously to gain a great ideal or goal. Our efficiency increases—Chinmaya.

If Administrators work with ethics in their heart and soul, we are sure to make India a heaven on this earth where people from other parts of the world would seek spiritual, ethical and moral pleasure atmosphere of development administration based on good governance every where.

Notes and References

1. T.N. Chaturvedi, Editorial, *IJPA*, July-Sept. 1995, pp. ix-x.
2. India, Report of Vohra Committee (Chairman N.N. Vohra), para 6.2.
3. S.S. Singh, Distilling Contributions of Administrative Law in Promoting the Culture of Good Governance in T.N. Chaturvedi (ed.) Towards Good Governance, New Delhi, *IJPA*, 1999, p. 132.
4. Justice V.P. Krishna Iyer, Ethical Entropy in Public Life, in *IJPA*, July to Sept, 1995, p. 350.
5. S.K. Chakraborty, Ethics in Management, Delhi, Oxford, 1996, (A book review by Krishan Mohan Mathur), in *IJPA*, Jan.-March, 1997, p. 102.
6. Bata K. Dey, Ethics—Maladies and Remedies, in *lJPA*, July-Sept., 1995, p. 461
7. Prashant Bhushan, Stemming the Tide of Corruption in *IJPA*, July-Sept., 1995, p. 472.
8. S.R. Maheshwari, Ethics for Civil Service in India, in *IJPA*, July-Sept., 1995, p. 505.
9. O.P. Dwivedi, Administrative Theology, in *IJPA*, July-Sept. 1990, pp. 418-19.
10. Swami Ranganathananda, A Charter of Ethics, Reading Material for Trainees (Some abstracts).
11. O.P. Dwivedi, Administration Theology in *IJPA*, July-Sept., 1990, pp. 408-09.
12. Col. D.S. Chama, The Ethics in Management: The Indian Scene, *The Daily Tribune*, 12th Sept. 2000.
13. Kamla Prasad, "India's Pursuit of Public Good and the Democratic Dilemma", in *IJPA*, July-Sept., 1995.
14. See O.P. Dwivedi and R.B. Jain, India's Administrative State, New Delhi, Gitanjali Publishing House, 1985, p. 257.
15. Shekhar Singh, Ethics and Administration, in *IJPA*, July-Sept., 1997, p. 334.
16. L.P. Singh: Morality in Public Affairs in *IJPA*, July-Sept., 1995, p. 633. O.P. Dwivedi, Reflection on Moral Government, in *IJPA*, July-Sept., 1995, p. 30.
17. O.P. Diwvedi, Reflection on Moral Government, *IJPA*, July-Sept., 1997, p. 324.
18. T.N. Chaturvedi, *op. cit.*, pp. xvii and xviii.
19. Jaideep Singh, The Enlightened Organisation, in *IJPA*, April-June, 1979, p. 44
20. Ministry of Personnel, Public Grievances and Pensions, New Delhi, Nov. 1997, p. 15.
21. Atul Dhingra and M.R.P. Singh, "Ethics is making all the Difference" in *Indian Management*, July, 2000.
22. O.P. Dwivedi, "Conclusion: A Comparative Analysis of Ethics, Public and Public Service", James S. Bowman and E.A. Elliston (eds.) Ethics, Government and Public Policy, New York, Greenwood Press, 1988, p. 318.
23. Bata K. Dey, Ethics—Maladies and Remedies, in *IJPA*, July-Sept. 1995, p. 461.
24. H.R. Khanna, Ethics in Public Life, Issues and Remedy, in *IJPA*, July-Sept. 1995, p. 357.

CHAPTER 22

Tackling Corruption

Corruption today is the greatest enemy of developing administration and causing harm to democracy and development. People in India must bow their heads in shame as they are living in a country where every organ, activity and function are conducted with corrupt practices. How can we think of developing administration? Whatever the number of institutions we create, they themselves become other dens of corruption. Good governance and corruption cannot co-exist.

Corruption in the civil service has become a common phenomenon in every developing country and India is not an exception to it. Bureaucratic corruption cannot be studied separately from political corruption, since the two phases are closely associated and, at a certain point, are cause-and-effect to each other.[1]

P. Chakrabory in his article, "Cancer of Corruption and the Numbering Millennium" clearly said: "I see in the near future a crisis approaching, that unnerves me and causes me to tremble for my country ... an era of corruption in high places will follow and the money-power of the country will endeavour to prolong its reign by working on the prejudices of the people until the wealth is aggravated in a few hands and the Republic is destroyed."

Former Prime Minister A.B. Vajpayee, while addressing the Sixth Conference of Lokayuktas and Upalokayuktas in New Delhi on 22nd January, 2001, emphatically remarked that corruption is the biggest hurdle in the path of development. The worst victims of corruption in administration and governance are the common people. Over the years, successive Governments at the Center and in the States have spent tens of thousands of crores of rupees on various programs and schemes. Had these resources been spent properly and without leakage at various levels, we would have long solved many of our problems in education, healthcare, housing and other areas of social development. We would have also removed many bottlenecks in our infrastructure, which are today exacting a heavy price on our economy. Above all, we would have been able to make a deeper dent in poverty and unemployment, which have robbed millions of our countrymen of their right to a decent life.

Corruption is not only an enemy of development and good governance. It is also a foe of democracy. The absence of transparency and accountability in governance and administration

CHART 22.I

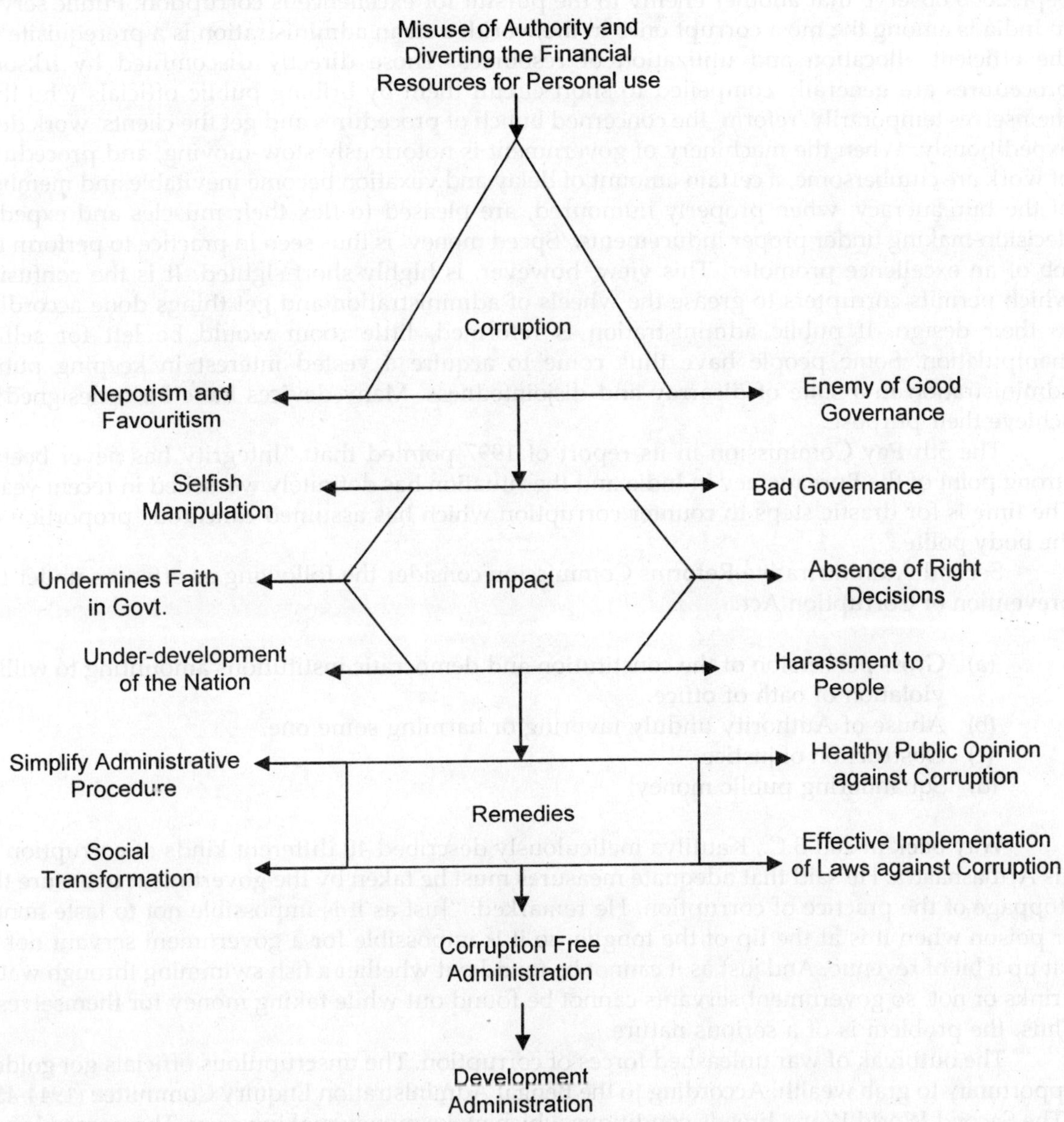

and our people's sense of helplessness, weakens our democratic process. A mature democracy must have effective checks and balances against abuse of power by public servants for self-enrichment. Over the past few decades, rampant corruption has bred contempt for the law. The failure of the law to catch the corrupt and then to deliver deterrent punishment to them has led to widespread cynicism among the people. It has also resulted in a decline in moral values throughout society.[2]

S.R. Maheswari[3] in his article, "Towards Excellence in Public Service of India" in *IJPA*, July-Sept. 2006 observe that another enemy to the pursuit for excellence is corruption. Public service in India is among the most corrupt ones in the world; a clean administration is a prerequisite for the efficient allocation and utilization of resources. Those directly discomfited by irksome procedures are generally compelled to short-circuit them by bribing public officials who then themselves temporarily 'reform' the concerned bunch of procedures and get the clients' work done expeditiously. When the machinery of government is notoriously slow-moving, and procedures of work are cumbersome, a certain amount of delay and vexation become inevitable and members of the bureaucracy, when properly humoured, are pleased to flex their muscles and expedite decision-making under proper inducements. 'Speed money' is thus seen in practice to perform the job of an excellence promoter. This view, however, is highly short-sighted. It is the confusion which permits corrupters to grease the wheels of administration and get things done according to their design. If public administration is reformed, little room would be left for selfish manipulation. Some people have thus come to acquire a vested interest in keeping public administration in a state of disarray and disjointedness. Many devices have been designed to achieve their purpose.

The 5th Pay Commission in its report of 1997 pointed that: "Integrity has never been a strong point of the Bureaucracy in India and the situation has definitely worsened in recent years. The time is for drastic steps to counter corruption which has assumed cancerous proportion on the body polite."

Second Administrative Reforms Commission consider the following as offences under the prevention of Corruption Act.

(a) Gross perversion of the constitution and democratic institutions amounting to willful violation of oath of office.
(b) Abuse of Authority unduly favoring or harming some one.
(c) Obstruction of justice.
(d) Squandering public money.

Way back in 200 B.C., Kautilya meticulously described 40 different kinds of corruption in his Arthashastra. He said that adequate measures must be taken by the government to ensure the stoppage of the practice of corruption. He remarked: "Just as it is impossible not to taste honey or poison when it is at the tip of the tongue, so it is impossible for a government servant not to eat up a bit of revenue. And just as it cannot be found out whether a fish swimming through water drinks or not, so government servants cannot be found out while taking money for themselves." Thus, the problem is of a serious nature.

The outbreak of war unleashed forces of corruption. The unscrupulous officials got golden opportunity to grab wealth. According to the Bengal Administration Enquiry Committee (1944-45), "The Second World War. ..breeds conditions which make money making easy. The possession of a license became a thing of high value and dishonest and unscrupulous persons did not hesitate to offer bribes in order to secure the license to trade in the commodities effected. War conditions, thus, provided the opportunity, and it cannot be denied that it became all too easy for dishonest men to seize the opportunity of illicit gain by reason of two things, namely, (a) ill-advised administrative action; (b) defects in the Law which make detection of offences difficult and which provide inadequate penalties for convicted offenders."[4]

After independence and especially in the last three decades, there is not a day, when you find a newspaper without any news of corruption—big or small. Mention may be made of Supreme Court judge, who was found guilty of corrupt deeds by a High Power Judicial Committee, HDW Deal, 1981, Air-Bus A 320 Deal (April 1990), Bofors Pay Off (1987-still pending), Harshad Mehta Suit Case Episode (1993), JMM bribery case, Fodder Scam by Bihar Chief Minister (1999-2000), the Jain Hawala case, urea scam, sugar import scam, the Telecom scandal, UTI 64 scandal, several frauds in Nationalised Banks and Tehlka.com Defence Gate Scam, 2001, Matto Murder Case, Jassica Lal Murder Case, etc. Besides, individual cases of corruption are unlimited.

Everyone is accusing the other persons/parties of corruption, but without any solution or result. The corruption has become one of the ills of inefficiency, demonstration and an enemy of good governance in the country. Just to illustrate *The Tribune* editorial dated Nov. 21, 2006 'Tackling the Big Fish: The System has failed to do" observed that the Prime Minister Manmohan Singh call to the CBI and state anti-corruption bureau officers to pursue cases of corruption in high places vigorously is timely. Addressing the 16th biennial conference of CBI officers in New Delhi, he said that they must take a "broader view" of individual cases and pursue them to their logical conclusion. The Prime Minister's remarks are well-intentioned but the problem is that the system has failed to produce a verdict in all high-level corruption cases mainly because of political pressure. This has eroded the people's faith that the system is incapable of brining to book those who misuse public funds. Consider the Telgi fake stamp paper case. It is a massive scam spread over many states and functionaries of many parties. Yet, the politicians and other bosses involved in the scam are still at large. The Taj corridor case and the disproportionate assets case involving Ms Mayawati are two more examples. The UPA governments, like the NDA, is not interested in taking action against her. The reason: both want her support.

CBI Director Vijay Shankar has blamed the courts for the delays. This may be true to some extent, but what has the CBI itself done to expedite high profile cases? It either does not finalise them or files charge-sheets very late without bothering about follow-up. Its dilatory tactics and prevarication imply that the sharpness of its anti-corruption drive is lost on the public. One does not know when the Bihar fodder scam case involving Mr. Laloo Prasad Yadav and Ms. Jayalalitha's disproportionate assets case would see the light of the day.

In another editorial on the same day "Weight of Corruption: The end of a Bridge in Himachal Pradesh" in *The Tribune* strongly observes that the collapse of a new bridge undergoing a load test before it is opened to traffic at Tashigang in Poh subdivision of Kinnaur district is a sad commentary on the state of affairs in the state Public Works Department. That three people, including a junior engineer of the PWD were drowned adds to the enormity of the lapse. The reason for the disaster is not far to seek. The private construction company, which has been building it is certainly at fault. Even guiltier are the engineers in the PWD, who had approved of the faculty designs and had turned a blind eye on the use of sub-standards material and other kinds of cheating. An inquiry has been ordered and by the time its report comes, the corrupt engineers and officers would have covered up everything. For the sake of punishment, one or two low-level officials would be put under suspension, only to be revoked sooner than later. How is it that dozens of pre-independence bridges in Himachal Pradesh continue to be used while new bridge like the one at Tashigang collapses? The answer is obvious: Rampant corruption in the PWD.

The conference of Chief Secretaries, held on November 20, 1996, all of a sudden woke up to the realisation that there was a crisis of good governance in Indian administration. It was necessary to take corrective steps to arrest the present drift before it becomes too late. In the agenda note entitled "For An Effective and Responsive Administration in India", it was admitted that,

"The public administration and the civil service at all levels are passing through difficult times in terms of eroded credibility and effectiveness of the civil service, growing public perception of an unholy nexus between certain elements among politicians and civil servants and criminals (as elaborated in the Vohra Committee Report), and increasing criticism of the low level of honesty, transparency and accessibility to the political and bureaucratic elements in charge of administration." Thus the good governance has touched a low level.

The imperative need was for governments at all levels to reinvent themselves and redefine their roles and responsibilities to usher in good governance and bring about reforms in all areas, which have an impact on the lives of the people.[5] Corruption cannot be tackled simply by creating institutions or amending; constitution, but only by people who have to take pledge to root out this evil. A constitution is not a shade better than the men and women who are called upon to interact with it. B.R. Ambedkar made the most suitable observation in the Constituent Assembly of India, which deserves to be mentioned; "I feel, however good a constitution may be, it is sure to turn out bad because those who are called to work, happen to be a bad lot. The working of the constitution does not depend wholly upon the nature of the constitution. The constitution can provide only the organs of state such as the legislature, the executive and the judiciary. The factors on which the working of those organs of the state depend are the people and the political parties, they will set-up as their instruments to carry out their wishes and their politics. Who can say how the people of India and their parties will behave?"[6] However, those who were responsible for execution of constitutional provisions wrecked it from within resulting into ever increasing corrupt practices.

The governments, both at the center and the state, share the concern for good governance that is ensuring responsive, accountable, transparent, decentralised and people-friendly administration at all levels. There is, however, considerable frustration and dissatisfaction amongst the people, especially the weaker sections of society, about the apathy, irresponsiveness and lack of accountability of public servants, even as the expenditure on administration continues to increase. There is increasing anxiety about growing instances of corruption and criminalisation in public life and administration. The people, particularly the vulnerable groups, are also greatly concerned about the deterioration in the performance of agencies concerned with law and order and the investigation of offences. Their faith in the registration of offences, their timely investigation and the delivery of prompt justice has been eroded. These are clear cut signs of deteriorating governance. Time has come for a strong message to be conveyed that administration is for the people and not for the public servants themselves. There has to be a change of attitude and public servants should realize that efficiency would be measured not in terms of what the services purport to offer, but in terms of public satisfaction. Simultaneously, thère has also to be a cleansing of the services and codification of the ethics, value systems and the interface with the politician.[7]

People feel concerned only when they are individually going to be affected by the action of the officials. Hence, the Railway Corruption Enquiry Committee rightly observed, "... citizens of a free country have the right, nay the duty to insist that public servants render due service for which they are paid from public coffers. ..citizens themselves will have to be vigilant and they must insist upon their rights. They should also be prepared to pay, if necessary, the price of such insistence with some temporary loss or inconvenience to themselves. A strong public opinion must therefore be created and a determined effort made to withhold payment of illegal gratification and should struggle to ensure good governance."[8]

Corruption is a multi-faceted problem having legal, political, economic, psychological and administrative dimensions. Epidemic corruption seems too malevolent in its nature and implications, which has equally encompassed the capitalistic and socialistic societies in the world. In the developing countries (i.e. Third World), corruption has attained exorbitant ascendancy. In a country like India, this malignant trouble has sufficiently punctured and extremely hampered the process of healthy economic growth and development. Starting from the political bosses to the lowest level of bureaucratic functionary, none seems to be either an exception or immune from its evil effects. Such an assertion does not denote that everyone is corrupt but simply highlights the said prevalent plight of affairs. Even a sacrosanct person finds himself sufficiently circumscribed to yield under its vociferous pressure and tastes the bitter bite of this panic in divergent walks of life.[9] Corruption has spread its tentacles in a way as to usurp every aspect of good governance.

O.P. Dwivedi and D.S. Mishra[10] in their article, "A Good Governance model for India: Search from Within" in *IJPA*, Vol. II, Oct.-Dec. 2005 clearly observe that corruption at the cutting edge level is most harmful for the common public. Their day to day activities like seeking basic services or amenities are adversely affected. There is often an under-hand deal between official who have the authority to do a job and the touts who take services charge from ordinary men and women to get their job done. It must be noted that the service charge is usually not for a favour but for a legitimate piece of work and is undertaken on a turnkey basis. Unfortunately this has become a way of life, often unquestioned. Whether dealing with Development Authorities, Transport Offices, Passport Offices, Police Department or Banks—it is the same story for the all places. False billing or depriving the government of revenue by collusive sharing of the dues is also common practice. Blackmailing and harassment of the guilty, and sometimes even the innocent by the media or press is another form of corruption. Like cancer, the disease of corruption has spread all over the body of governance.

Governance involves mechanisms, processes and institutions, through which people articulate their interests, exercise their rights, meet their obligations and mediate their differences. The characteristics of good governance include core values of rule of law fairness, equity, participation, transparency, responsiveness, consensus, economy, efficiency and effectiveness, and above all impeachable accountability. As people are the source of all power in a democracy, accountability to people is the hallmark of democratic governance.

IMPACT OF CORRUPTION

In developing countries like India, corruption is spreading like a cancer, engulfing the entire social fabric. That is why, people are not getting the benefits of development. In 1964, a political party made serious indictment on the state of the Nigerian nation, which is true of India as well. It observed that, "There was systematic frustration of the lofty aspirations of the masses. Money and material wealth has since become the supreme value in our society and the goal of all social action. This has given rise to corruption, selfishness, malingering and a general lack of patriotism and social responsibility. The country abounds in..... Ministers who do not scruple to play false with the nation for personal gain."[11]

It is deplorable that people who have the opportunity to serve the nation in high capacities should use it to line their own pockets and indulge in ostentatious living thus causing a great harm to budding democracy through bad governance. While we are crying for foreign capital, some, including ministers, invest their wealth overseas. Far from setting the much needed good example, some politicians take the lead in activities that are not to the best interest of the nation.[12]

Prof. Smith notes that for development of Nigerian industry, agriculture, communications, etc., large scale complicated plans were devised. But, when we get down to putting these plans into operation, we find that the implementation of the great development programs rapidly creates facilities not so much for the development intended but for social corruption of all sorts.[13]

MEANING OF CORRUPTION

Corruption has a variety of meanings. According to David H. Bailey: Corruption is a general term covering misuse of authority as a result of considerations of personal gain, which need not be monetary.[14] In the view of Jacob Van Kalveren: Corruption means that a civil servant abuses his authority in order to obtain an extra income from the public.[15] As defined by Robert C. Brooks, corruption is the intentional mis-performance or neglect of a recognised duty, or the unwarranted advantage more or less directly personal.[16]

We may say that corruption means to perform one's duty with some ulterior motive and not for the duty sake. These may include:

(a) Misappropriation of Public Money and equipment.
(b) Showing favours to people who offer gratification.
(c) Acceptance of gifts.
(d) Claiming false TA, house rent, LTC, etc.
(e) Abuse of official position/powers.
(f) Under assessment of taxes.
(g) Allotment of land at cheap rates.

Section 5 of the Prevention of Corruption Act (I) defines the scope of corruption with regard to public servant. According to this Act, five kinds of acts constitute criminal misconduct, i.e. (i) habitual acceptance of gratification; (ii) the obtaining of any valuable thing without consideration; (iii) misappropriation; (iv) the abuse of position to obtain pecuniary advantage; and (v) the possession of pecuniary resources or property in excess to one's sources of income.

Indian penal code has 11 sections, which also prescribes corrupt practices. Section 161, the first of this set of section together with two more sections 165 and 165-A are cross-connected with provisions in the Prevention of Corruption Act. Section 161 defines the offence of corruption or illegal gratification. Section 165 defines another aspect of the offence of corruption with reference to "any valuable thing." The main provisions of other sections which are not so cross linked with the provisions of prevention of Corruption Act, 1947 are:

(1) Taking gratification by corrupt or legal means in order to influence public servant (section 162).
(2) Section 163 deals with taking gratification or exercise of personal influence by public servant.
(3) Section 164 pertains to punishment for abetment by public servant.
(4) Section 166 relates to public servants disobeying law with intent to cause injury to any person.
(5) Section 167 is concerning public servants who frame incorrect documents with intent to cause injury.
(6) Section 168 relates to public servants unlawfully engaging in trade.

(7) Section 169 is meant for public servants unlawfully buying or bidding for property.
(8) Section 170 and Section 171 relate to personating to public servants and wearing or carrying token used by public servant with fraudulent intent respectively.

EXTENT

Corruption has become a way of life. G.L. Nanda, the then Home Minister, openly admitted in the Lok Sabha on December 18, 1963 that corruption in administration was "on a fairly large scale. It has been found that every department of Government has become a den of corruption."[17] Further, "The whole country in every sphere and department of life is plunged in the stagnant ocean of corruption."[18] It is a widespread impression that lack of integrity is not common among ministers and that some ministers have enriched them illegitimately.[19]

Corruption is one of the most common as well as the most dangerous forms of ethical failure. In one form or another, it has existed in all societies at all times of history. But in recent years in India, it has assumed frightening proportions. It has not only spread to every part of the governmental machinery, but has had a more rapid growth amongst the professional politicians as well as the party men, both at state and central levels. The worst thing about it is that people have started accepting it as a fact of life and have adjusted with it. It has given credence to Voltaire's notion that corruption is an evil that grows respectable with age in India, although it has become our past time to talk about corruption hardly any genuine effort has been made to eradicate it.

Corruption is rooted in our acquisitive society where greatness of individuals and nobility of their family is judged by what they possess rather than by what they are. The acquisition of wealth has become *sine qua non* of life. People indulge in acquiring wealth without caring for the means they adopt. All these factors are responsible for bad governance.

FORMS OF CORRUPTION

The report of the Santhanam Committee on Prevention of Corruption stated that while it is true that accruing some kind of pecuniary or other material advantage directly or indirectly for oneself or family, relatives or friends, constitutes the most common form of corruption, other forms are coming into existence as society becomes more and more complex. The committee further pointed out that the roots and ramifications of corruption were spread throughout the society.

One of the most widespread forms of corruption is "speed money." Another form noted by the Santhanam Committee is peculiar to the highest level of the industrial and mercantile elite. This form is embodied in the liaison or contact man. These contact men are maintained at metropolitan centers to cultivate close social relations with high government officials and thereby influence them with money and undue favours.

In its widest connotation, corruption includes improper or selfish exercise of power and influence attached to a public office or to a special position one occupies in public life. Viewing the problem in this light means that an appraisal of the entire system of moral values and the socio-economic structure of society is needed. How can we expect good governance when politico-Administrative leaderships is entrenched in corrupt practices?

HARMFUL EFFECTS OF CORRUPTION: BAD GOVERNANCE

1. Within the bureaucracy, corruption may cause widespread cynicism and social disunity and thus reduce the willingness to make sacrifices for the society's economic development.[20]
2. Bureaucratic corruption undercuts popular faith in government. People become alienated from the government. [21]
3. Corruption, especially in the form of bribery, causes decisions to be weighed in terms of money, not in terms of human need. In other words, the wheels of the bureaucratic machine must be oiled with money.[22]
4. Corruption causes a rise in the price of administration. People who have already paid the tax are forced to bribe in order to get government service. All these factors indicate that soil for good governance is non-existence. The soil has been spoiled by top level people in government.

CAUSES OF CORRUPTION

The prevalence of corruption in our system can be attributed to a variety of reasons. These can be discussed under the following headings:

I. Historical Causes

In India, corruption has its roots in the colonial rule of the past. British administration was not interested in the overall development of the country. All superior and important positions were filled in by British people and they were paid handsomely. Lower posts were offered to Indians. Salaries to these posts were very low. So they indulged in corrupt practices.

After World War II, scarcities led to many types of controls. It gave added opportunities to these low paid employees to resort to corrupt practices. Then it became habitual. It was during World War II that corruption reached the highest mark in India. The climate for integrity, which had been rendered unhealthy by wartime controls and scarcities was further aggravated by the post-war flush of money and the consequent inflation. Development programs, which the government has launched over the years, also constitute another fertile area of corruption. Since large funds are available for disbursement as grants, subsidies and loans, influential legislators and other politicians browbeat the civil servants in cornering to themselves a lion's share. More often than not, the politicians and the civil servants get hand in glove with each other to divert these funds either to themselves or to their favourities and relatives.

2. Environmental Causes

The second important cause of corruption in Public service is fast urbanisation and industrialisation, where material possessions, position and economic power determine the status and prestige of a person in the society. Since salaries are low and inflation is unabated, poor civil servants fall prey to corrupt practices in order to keep status in the society. A Political Party in Nigeria (United Progressive Grand Alliance) observed, "there was systematic frustration of the lofty aspirations of the masses. ….Money and material wealth has since become the supreme value in our society and the goal of all social action. This has given rise to corruption, selfishness malingering and a general lack of patriotism and social responsibility."[23]

Corruption and the forces which give rise to corruption, are not always to be located in the administrative, political and economic institutions and processes. There are several aspects of our society and several shortcomings of our social structure, attitudes and value systems, which provide an impetus to corruption, political pitfalls, economic failures and administrative loopholes have only worsened the situation.

3. Economic Causes

Inadequate remuneration of salary scales and the rising cost of living are important causes of corruption. In recent years, the fast rising cost of living has brought down the real income of various sections cf the community, particularly the salaried classes. Though this cannot be pleaded as an extenuation of the fall in the standard of integrity, the fact remains that economic necessity has encouraged those who had the opportunities to succumb to temptations.

4. Lack of Strong Public Opinion against the Evils of Corruption

People do not report to the government against corrupt officials. Instead they offer bribes to get their illegitimate claims accepted. People must take up the cudgels against corruption and build a strong public opinion against it.

5. Inadequate Laws to deal with Corruption

The Indian Panel Code and other laws, which deal with corruption cases, are outmoded and provide insufficient penalties. It takes too much time to get a corrupt official punished under the laws. Summary trials and stricter punishments should be awarded to end corruption. Laws will have to be changed accordingly.

6. Collusion of Vested Interests

Big businessmen, dishonest merchants, suppliers and contractors grease the palms of civil servants, in order to get undue favours from them. Sometimes they share a portion of their ill-earned profit with the government servants. Pressure groups like the Indian Chamber of Commerce, Trade Associations, State Chambers of Commerce, are said to help in breeding corruption through their activities of getting favours for their communities. They influence the ruling elite through dinners, parties, luncheons, etc.

7. Diminishing Faith in the Judicial System

Today, the judicial system, especially at the lower levels, is not functioning efficiently, resulting in delays and corrupt practices. Rahul Pathak[24] has rightly said that, "The System is growing under its own weight. There are far too many cases, too many unnecessary adjournments and often pointless appeals. Cost of litigation is exorbitant, the process tedious and the quality of justice, given the appalling lack of talent, is suspect."

P.N. Bhagwati, former Chief Justice of India has observed that, "If the Supreme Court exists only for the rich, what is the use of its existence? I have known judges who have sat on judgments for two years."

What will happen to good governance when people have lost faith in the judicial system as well which was considered as a lighting lamp to keep democracy and good governance shining.

8. Political Causes

Member of the political elite are also responsible for corrupt practices. The recent security scam clearly indicates the involvement of politicians and administrators in a big way. Kuldip Nayar, in his article, "Politics of Corruption" has rightly said that corruption by itself is bad enough. But it becomes worse when mixed with politics. The Punjab Administrative Reforms Commission (1956), has mentioned the following causes of corruption:

1. Lack of proper education and training of civil servants.
2. Low salaries
3. Inadequate and inefficient supervision
4. Political patronage of officials.
5. Complicated and dilatory procedures
6. Collection of funds through officials.
7. Poor public opinion
8. Lack of examples from above.
9. Unwillingness of the people to complain against corrupt officials due to lack of education or a genuine desire on the part of better placed people to eliminate corruption.
10. Ineffective action against corrupt officials.
11. Double standards of conduct, one for the officials and another for the politicians.
12. Tedious and ineffective machinery to bring corrupt officials to book.
13. The tortuous and costly judicial procedure.

P.S. Ramamohan Rao, Former Governor of Tamil Nadu strongly feels that bureaucratic corruption emanates from political corruption. To quote him: 'What should we do? Where do we start' a vast apparatus to combat corruption has indeed been erected both in the States and at the Centre. But it is targeted and focused mainly on the permanent bureaucracy. Arrangements to deal with corruption and malfeascence at the political level had been, at best, tentative and half-hearted. It is necessary to appreciate, in this context, that eradication of the evil of corruption has to be a top down process and not bottom up. If the political leadership of Government is dishonest there is no way that the bureaucracy can be insulated from corruption. Transparent and simple procedures combined with the use of the latest technology at such conduct may not provide the ingredients of a criminal case even while constituting enough basis for exit from government employment. Thus, while it may be difficult to establish direct culpability, an irrebuttable inference of constructive responsibility could be drawn.[25]

9. Lack of Integrity and Impartiality among Top Level Politicians and Bureaucracy

It has been rightly said in Geeta that the character of the people is shaped by leaders. As is the king, so are the subjects—our high ups in both politics and bureaucracy are highly corrupt. According to Narayan Hazare, "Corruption owes its origin to important political causes. Though at the top people preach integrity, more often than not they lack the virtue of example. Ministers are permitted to live in glaring extravagance while they make impassioned appeals for popular sacrifice. Socialism in a Rolls Royce may be eloquent but it seldom conveys an impression of sincerity. Thus, corruption, like sacrifice, starts at the top and, percolating down, colors the whole society.[26]

The one-party rule for nearly the last three decades has also encouraged corruption in our public life. Officials, businessmen, contractors, if they establish rapport with the top people in the party have nothing to fear. Big magnates of industry and trade, after donating liberally to the party in power, go on indulging in all sorts of malpractices, from adulteration to income-tax evasion. Had there been the likelihood of any other party coming into power in the near future, such things would not have happened.

10. Cumbersome Administrative Procedures Causing Delay and Harassment

It is alleged that the working of certain government departments like the Customs and Central Excise, Imports and Exports, Railways, Supplies and Disposals, Police, Income Tax, , etc. is complicated, cumbersome and dilatory. This has encouraged the growth of dishonest practices like the system of 'speed money'.

Cumbersome administrative procedures and delays also breed corruption. Frequently, delay is deliberately contrived to obtain some kind of illicit gratification. To avoid delay, the bribe given persuades the officials through speed money to get the work done speedily. This custom of speed money has become one of the most serious causes of delay and inefficiency. The *London Times* wrote about speed money and delay thus: "Speed money actually has the role of a brake on administration, slowing it down even further. Delay will deliberately be caused in order to invite the payment of a bribe to accelerate it again."[27]

Moreover, the administrative power and growth of discretion vested in the officials provide opportunities and scope for harassment, malpractices and corruption.[28] These need to be corrected to promote good governance.

11. Security of Services under Article 311 Breeds Complacency

Article 311 of the Indian Constitution, which provides protection to civil servants, as interpreted by our courts, made it difficult to deal effectively with corrupt public servants. Reluctance of higher officials to take disciplinary action against corrupt officials, who are in collusion with them in actual practice, has further aggravated the situation.

Article 311 of the Indian Constitution, as interpreted by the Courts has made it very difficult to deal effectively with corrupt officials. Many heads of organisations are themselves corrupt, therefore, they can never combat corruption in their organisations for fear of exposure by their subordinates. Moreover, too much security of tenure is assured to the bureaucracy. No public servant "shall be dismissed or removed by an authority subordinate to that by which he was appointed", and, further, "No such person shall be dismissed or removed or reduced in rank until he has been given a reasonable opportunity of showing cause against the action proposed to be taken in regard to him." This clearly indicates that a public servant has been provided with enough security of tenure.

The prevailing laws dealing with corruption are inadequate to take action against the inefficient and corrupt public servants. For instance, in our country, Indian Penal Code and other laws have become out-moded and provide insufficient penalties. Too much time is consumed in punishing the guilty official under the laws. Similarly, as per existing legal provisions, both the giver and receiver of bribes are held guilty. But the plight of the situation is that the departmental heads find it difficult to obtain formal proof of corrupt practices. Moreover, Article 311 of the Indian Constitution provides protection to the civil servants. The interpretations by the court of this provision have made it very difficult to deal effectively with corrupt public servants. Reluctant attitude adopted by the top officials to take disciplinary action against the corrupt elements within the organization has aggravated the situation in our country. The legal system must be reformed to promote good governance.

12. No Safety Mechanisms and Recognition for Honest Officials

An honest and sincere official, performing his job efficiently and loath to converge with the corrupt channels, is swiftly shifted and replaced by a convenient official in the guise of public interest. Over-temptation, too much greediness and craze for material possessions has degenerated the individual to fall prey to corrupt practices. Instead of abhorring, rejecting and condemning the ill-earned possessions, the established societal norms have accorded full recognition to such illegal gratification of the individuals. Consequently, corruption seems to have been unequivocally legitimised in the societal norms. In the context of eroding ethical standards of public life, minor innovations will render no help and a total transformation and complete overhauling is essentially called for to save the individual/society from his/its present degeneration.[29]

Sukraniti V-5-14-151: This Sloka mentions five causes, which give rise to the charge of corruption. These are: (a) Raga (Affection in favour of a party); (b) Lobha (greed); (c) Bhaya (fear); (d) Dvesha (ill-will against a party); and (e) Secret pact with personal gains.

Katyayana-33-340 mentions that "The King (Court) should not delay in examining the witnesses. A serious defect, namely, miscarriage of justice, would result owing to delay in examination of witnesses. Delay is the mother of Corruption."

REMEDIES FOR CORRUPTION

David H. Bayley proposes three strategies that can be employed in the transitional situation to reduce corrupt practices. First, policy may be adopted for containing the grosser forms of corruption, while waiting for changed circumstances to remove the functional utility of such practices. This strategy is essentially a passive one and may be fatally flawed by the implicit assumption that corruption will not exert such harmful consequences as to jeopardize progress to a less unstable level. Secondly, corruption may be rooted out without hesitancy or remorse, counting upon the power of the state to contain repercussions. Coercion is used to offset the discontinuity in social accommodation which the removal of corruption may occasion. Third, the climate of opinion may be generated so that the temptation to corruption on the part of both the briber and the bribed is substantially reduced.

1. Make Service Conditions Attractive

Government officials, particularly at lower level, are forced by poverty to regard office holding as a source of income, which they would seek to maximize. Services tend to be bad and slow if no bribe is given. Raising of pay, consequently, is a basic means to wipe out the widespread bribery in the civil service. The salary structure should be fair, so that employees can meet their basic needs without resorting to corrupt practices.

2. Simplify Working of Government Machinery

The root cause of proliferation of corruption seems to be the complicated procedures of government offices. These procedures need to be evaluated and simplified. Delays must be prevented and officials made fully responsive to the needs of all the people.

3. Create Healthy Public Opinion against Corruption

Corruption will flourish until the general mass of people resists it with determination and strength. Most of all, the elimination of corruption requires widespread and steadfast opposition to it, coupled with the courage to act against it. There can be no doubt that the people of India can get rid of corruption and enjoy good governance provided they become active in reporting corrupt practices.

4. Ensure High Standard of Conduct by the Top Personnel

High officials having considerable discretionary powers must be thoroughly disciplined to refuse costly gifts, invitations and other favours. S. Nil Àheleh Mensah remarked: What makes official corruption really harmful for economic environment, and therefore for growth, is its tendency to promote general corruption. The Italian proverb, "when a fish rots, it starts at the head" sums up the process. Though the perpetration of official corruption is secretive, it usually involves a large number of people—apart from the corrupt officials, there may be intermediaries, local and/or foreign entrepreneurs, local and/or foreign institutions, etc. The locals cronies of corrupt officials, who become involved, may also involve subordinates for various , cover-up practices; and the list continues downward, giving corruption a kind of multiplier effect, which makes it erode the legitimacy and authority of the officials up the corruption ladder. A kind of demonstration effect fuels the corruption multiplier process and soon public servants charge the public for services they are hired to render.

5. Social Transformation

There is a need to change social values to ensure social discipline to promote a society based on Social Service. To quote S.C. Dubey, "The vitiated social ethos stands in need of a transformation so that society may undergo a major shift from the ethic of power and self-gratification to the ethic of service and self-imposed authority."

6. Integrative Approach

Corruption is a multi-dimensional problem having legal, political, economic, psychological and administrative dimensions. Therefore, unless we develop an integrative perspective, corruption cannot be properly cornered. This needs an effective linkage between the nature of polity and its aims. George Bush, in his inaugural address in 1988, said that, "America is never wholly herself unless she is engaged in a high moral principle. We as a people have a purpose today. It is to make kinder the face of the nation and gentler the face of the world."

What are the root causes of the pervasive, penetrating corruption involving even the highest levels—political, judicial, administrative and the phenomenon of the network alliance amongst the business, the politician and corrupt bureaucrats? Though this crime has been experienced from various perspectives: constitutional, i.e. the nature of polity; the political processes, in particular the election system; sociological; economic; cultural; administrative; role of education and the collusive alliance between the business, the politician is developed, corruption cannot be effectively cornered. Such a perspective is feasible by relating the nature of polity and its aims.[30]

7. Need of Radical Steps

We may sum up with the observations so aptly made by the Punjab Administrative Reforms Commission that mere wishful thinking or injunctions to officials to be honest or even the fear of retribution, will not achieve the necessary reformation of corrupt officials (Para 9.7.2). Instead, "The problem calls for certain radical steps and that unless these steps are taken no tangible results are to be expected." (Para 9.29) The Government will have to appoint men of highest integrity in responsible positions and give them powers to deal with corrupt subordinates if it is really serious about putting a stop of this galloping evil. [31]

8. Effective Implementation of Conduct Rules

The following are the sets of conduct rules for Government Servants:

(a) All India Services (Conduct) Rules, 1954.
(b) Central Civil Services (Conduct) Rules, 1955.
(c) Railway Services (Conduct) Rules, 1956, etc.

Apart from these there are several rules and instructions dealing with public servants. Regarding rules of conduct, Justice H.R. Khanna has observed: "The present condition of rules of conduct or declaration of assets cannot assure rectitude among Ministers and other members in the public life. What is needed is a climate of strong public opinion wherein none may dare to deviate from the path of rectitude. The ramparts of a clean and healthy administration are within the hearts of people; laws can only punish occasional lapses."[32]

9. Overhaul Vigilance Machinery

In its crucial role for maintenance of integrity in public services, the Department of Personnel and Training determines policy on the subject and coordinates the work of various Ministries/Departments for maintenance of discipline and eradication of corruption in their respective operational areas. The Department also handles all policy and administrative matters pertaining to the Central Vigilance Commission and the Central Bureau of Investigation. It also deals with the complaints of corruption against the Chief Ministers of States and the Union Ministers.

The Department is responsible for the examination of and decision on vigilance and disciplinary cases against members of the Indian Administrative Service and the Central Secretariat Service officers (Grade I and above).

The three-pronged strategy for prevention, surveillance and detection as well as deterrent and punitive action adopted, during the preceding years, was also followed during the year 2005-06. Based on the last year's experience, a detailed action Plan on Vigilance and Anti-Corruption measures was formulated for the benefit of all the Ministries/Departments. Accordingly, a calendar of vigilance action was also drawn up specifying the dates by which the administrative authorities were to complete action on each item. The Ministries/Departments and public sector undertakings under them were asked to implement certain specific measures in accordance with this Plan. Emphasis was laid on preventive vigilance that might involve appropriate changes in the existing rules/regulations/procedures in selected areas/Departments as well as review of the staffing policies in functional areas. Apart from this, the other measures undertaken included strengthening of the departmental vigilance and anti-corruption machinery, expeditious disposal of disciplinary cases and recourse to the powers for premature retirement of Government servants under FR 56(1) as well as the monitoring of vigilance work of various Ministries/Departments and that of the CBI.[33]

10. Strengthen CBI and Make It Impartial

Central Bureau of Investigation (CBI) was established in 1963. Its functioning is regulated in accordance with the provisions of the Delhi Special Police Establishment Act, 1946. Initially its main object was to look into anti-corruption cases. Over the years, it has evolved into a premier investigating agency of Government of India to investigate complex and important cases. It is also responsible for prosecution of accused persons for offences in respect of various specified acts. CBI has its offices all over the country. CBI Academy started functioning at Gaziabad w.e.f. 1.10.1996. It has the following divisions:

(i) Investigation and Anti-Corruption Division;
(ii) Technical Division;
(iii) Crime Records and Statistics Division;
(iv) Research Division;
(v) Legal and General Division; and
(vi) Administrative Division.

The Bureau is headed by a Director who is supported by three Additional/Special Directors and fifteen Joint Directors and other officers besides a Legal Adviser and supporting staff."[34] In addition, there are 5891 sanctioned posts.

11. Create Institutions of Lok Pal and Lokayuktas

Former Prime Minister A.B. Vajpayee while addressing the 6th Conference of Lokayuktas and Up-Lokayuktas in Delhi on 22nd January, 2001 stated: "As regards the setting up of a Lokpal at the Center, several attempts were made in the past to enact an enabling legislation. These did not yield desired results as most of the earlier Lokpal Bills lapsed consequent upon the dissolution of the respective Lok Sabhas. Our Government had committed to the people in the National Agenda for Governance, that we would enact the Lokpal Bill with adequate powers to deal with charges of corruption against anyone, including the Prime Minister. We stand committed to this promise. A group of Ministers has been working on a new draft of the Lokpal Bill. This will be introduced in Parliament soon. To ensure that free flow of information is available to the public, the Government has already introduced the Freedom of Information Bill, 2000 in the Lok Sabha. This has been referred to a Select Committee. When enacted, it will go a long way in bringing in greater transparency in governance.

Today, only about fifteen States have a Lokayukta. I understand that in some of them, the Chief Minister falls within the ambit of the Lokayukta. In others, the Chief Minister is outside its purview. Similarly, there is lack of uniformity in the jurisdiction of the Lokayuktas over members of the State Legislature. I think that the Lokayukta legislation should be uniform on all such aspects. I would like this Conference to consider this matter and initiate necessary action in this direction. Right to Information Act has been passed in 2005 and is in operation for more than a year.

12. Provide Statutory Status and Wider Powers to Vigilance Commission

The Center has taken many steps to strengthen the institutional mechanism to check corruption and to ensure probity in public life. The Central Vigilance Commission Bill was introduced in the Lok Sabha on December 20, 1999. This provided for the constitution of a Central Vigilance Commission to inquire, or cause inquiries to be conducted into, offenses alleged to have been committed under the Prevention of Corruption Act, 1988 by certain categories of public servants. A Joint Committee of Parliament has already deliberated on various provisions of the Bill and has submitted its report. The Government is examining the recommendations of this Committee. A statutory status has been given to vigilance commission.

13. Ensure Openness and Accountability

Shri Atal Behari, Former Prime Minister of India has again rightly cautioned that the purpose of economic liberalisation, besides accelerating our economic growth, has also been to create more openness and accountability in the system. The license-permit-quota Raj had created excessive controls and discretionary powers. Besides causing inefficiency, these had bred many corrupt practices. While economic reforms have significantly changed this situation, there is still an urgent need to create a hassle-free environment for our businesses, especially small businesses. Experience has shown that our efforts to strengthen probity in civil service and the polity cannot yield desired results: without extending the norms of accountability in the judiciary. The inability of our judicial system to deliver speedy justice has itself become the source of much injustice. It has also eroded the credibility of our judiciary in the eyes of the public.

14. Empower People

To quote former Prime Minister A.B. Vajpayee again, unfortunately, information about many such developmental schemes, be they of the Center or the States, does not always reach the common people, especially in rural and remote areas. When people have no information, they can hardly participate in their implementation or monitor their progress. In the absence of people's participation, such programs are invariably implemented in the usual bureaucratic manner. This breeds corruption, inefficiency, and lack of accountability. As a result, common people become cynical about governmental programs and schemes. I have often heard complaints from even MPs and MLAs that they too are not involved in the implementation process. If such is the complaint of our MPs and MLAs, one can imagine how members of Panchayati Raj institutions must be feeling."

We cannot leave the fate of our policies and programs, in which we spend thousands of crores of rupees each year, to the care of the bureaucracy alone. The active participation of the people, and of people's elected representatives is a must for the success of all our developmental endeavours. The Ministries of Information at the center and in States have a vital role in correcting this imbalance.

15. Electoral Reforms

Former Prime Minister, Atal Behari Vajpayee, while addressing on the occasion of Golden Jubilee celebration of the Election Commission of India on 17th January, 2001, at New Delhi, rightly remarked that when elections become more contentious and confrontational, it is also natural for criminal and anti-social elements to find a foothold in the electoral process. This erodes people's confidence in free and fair elections which are the heart of a democracy. It is, therefore, high time that all political parties evolved a consensus on how to check and reverse the malignant trend of corruption and criminalization in our electoral process.

16. United Nations Convention against Corruption

Administrative Vigilance division has been actively involved in formulating Government's stand in the United Nations Convention against Corruption. Government of India has been represented by an inter-Ministerial Delegation in the negotiations held at Vienna, Austria. The negotiations have been successfully completed after Seven Sessions and led to finalization of the United Nations Convention against corruption.

The Convention prescribes a series of measures for preventing corruption, which include formulating and implementing effective anti-corruption policies and practices; constituting preventive anti-corruption bodies; adopting transparent system for recruitment, promotion, etc. of civil servants; establishing criteria of candidature for election to public office and ensuring transparency in the funding of candidature for elected public office/political parties; establishing Code of Conduct for public officials; establishing systems based on transparency, competition and objective criteria in public procurement and management of public finances; public access to information; preventing opportunities of corruption among members of judiciary; enhancing transparency and proper conduct of business in the private sector; active participation of community-based organizations in fighting against corruption and instituting regulatory and supervisory regime for financial institution in order to deter and detect money laundering. India has signed the Convention on 9th December, 2005.

17. Methods to Control Corruption in Ancient Literature

In this regard Atrismriti (28) laid down thus:

> "To punish the wicked, to honour (protect) the good, to enrich the treasury (exchequer) by just methods, to be impartial towards litigants and to protect the kingdom. There are the five Yajnas (selfless duties) to be performed by a King."

The same idealism was incorporated by Kautilya in his Arthasastra while summing up the objects and purpose of the exercise of sovereign power by the King. He stated thus: "In the happiness of his subjects lies the happiness of the King. In their welfare, his welfare, he shall not do what pleases him. He shall do what pleases his subjects."

18. Eternal Vigilance to Check Corruption

Former Central Vigilance Commissioner N. Vittal, while delivering a talk on "Impact of Corruption on the security and stability of our nation" at Panjab University on Sept. 1, 2001, likened corruption to white ants nibbling away at the life of plants. Our country is corrupt and corruption flourishes because there are people in power who benefit from the present system. Unfortunately, those who benefit from the power are also those who have to initiate the change and check corruption. Corruption has weakened the fabric of democracy in the country. Out of 91 countries in the world India stands at 71st position in terms of being the most corrupt. Bangladesh (91) tops the list with Finland (1) being the least corrupt. If the corruption level of our country comes down to that of Finland, there would be an additional growth of 1.5 percent in GDP, he added. The CVC during his visit to Bangkok in 1994 was told that there was corruption both in Thailand and India and that corruption in Thailand was honest corruption and in India there was dishonest corruption. A Thai explained that in Thailand, there was bribe to be paid for every activity and once the bribe was paid, the work was done. If the work was not done, the bribe would be returned.

On the other hand, in India, once you pay the bribe, the work may not be done and worse, the bribe is not returned. Needless to say, corruption among public servants, in fact, in the case of holders of any public office, should be considered as a social crime and should be more severely dealt with than any ordinary crime. The problem of corruption, is indeed, very grave and calls for urgent remedial action on all fronts. Both short-term and long-term measures in dealing with the preventive, detective and punitive in our administration are required. One must recognize that power corrupts and absolute power corrupts absolutely and, therefore, eternal vigilance on the conduct of all public men and officials exercising any state power through any of its organs, is essential to keep them on the right path.

Corruption has become constitutionalised and is ruining the very basis of the polity built with abounding faith and sincerity by Gandhi and Nehru. The average citizen finds himself helpless and is swept along with the tide. An atmosphere in which countless public servants even at senior levels, think that they must not miss any opportunity to make money because everyone else does, is a sorry reflection on those who rule the country. Corruption is now one of the major threats to Indian democracy and it is rapidly eroding the social structure. J. Dobel has rightly said in this connection that, "Once corruption becomes widespread, there is very little possibility of successful, significant reform of injustice in the State (and) even a successful violent revolution becomes almost an impossibility. ...Any significant legal, political or even economic changes will be quite irrelevant since the citizens will either frustrate the goals or use the new arrangements for their own radically self-interested benefit. Without the consensual loyalty and trust of the citizenry, the new reforms will simply be shams to rationalize the continuation of corrupt practices."

The Eleventh Plan observed that Corruption not only undermines the moral fibre of the society but can have serious irreversible practical consequences for politics, economic development and governance. In an overwhelmingly corrupt society, value-based politics loses its meaning. The legitimacy of government based on impartial application of the rule of law no longer holds. Resources which ought to be available to the exchequer for welfare and development are diverted into the private coffers of certain individuals. Honest public servants are demoralized while the corrupt are rewarded. Corruption is a major factor in the wastefulness, inefficiency and inequities we find in public administration today. It particularly affects the poor who cannot afford to pay. The burden of corruption saddles the private sector, and ultimately the consumer, with high costs and an inefficient infrastructure. Many more ramifications of corruption can be identified, but what is important to appreciate is that as corruption intensifies and accelerates, it tends to perpetuate itself in even widening and deeper forms. No time can, therefore, be lost in efforts to arrest and roll back this pernicious process.

Some suggestions which need to be seriously worked upon are:

- The Prevention of Corruption Act, 1988 and other related laws need to be reviewed with an effective role assured for the Central and State Vigilance Commissions. They should have wide powers with independent budgets and staff so as to be able to initiate and pursue investigations on their own.
- Strengthening the 'watch dog' role of the Comptroller and Auditor-General of India and his establishment in order to ensure probity, transparency and accountability in all public financial transactions. This will involve, inter-alia: (i) wider powers for audit, (ii) prompt publication and discussion of audit reports, (iii) follow-up by the vigilance machinery of financial irregularities brought to light by audit, and (iv) provision for audit based on references from citizens and investigative reports in the media.
- Tackling corruption in public utilities and in municipal and other services provided by the State and its agencies. This will involve (i) the adoption or Clear and verifiable standards for performance, (ii) institution of transparent practices and systems and (iii) adequate mechanisms such as Ombudsman-for the redressal of public complaints and grievances.
- A thorough and systematic review of all legislations, rules and executive orders which involve discretionary decisions, thereby creating financial stakes and inducements for

the giving and taking of bribes. The objectives will be to eliminate, or considerably reduce the role for discretion in governmental actions, discipline the exercise of discretion, where inescapable, through objective and transparent guidelines, and provide public access to information relating to discretionary decisions having direct or indirect financial implications.

- Formulation and enforcement of a code of conduct to regulate relations between government and private enterprises, domestic and multi-national. Enterprises which violate the code of conduct should be blacklisted with due publicity.
- Appropriate self-policing arrangements should be developed by independent authorities and professions such as the judiciary, lawyers, doctors, media persons, chartered accountants, architects and contractors.

N. Vittal in his article, "In the arms bazaar"—thanks to politicians, there's corruption in defence deals" observes that in his very perceptive article (*The Tribune*, Feb. 7) one of our leading strategic thinkers, K. Subrahmanyam, has highlighted three important aspects of defence procurement, including the aspect of procurement, a world-wide phenomenon. Secondly, it is the politicians, and not the procedures, which are to be blamed in the case of corruption in defence procurement. Thirdly, "our politicians are yet to realize that corruption allows terrorists to penetrate our borders, explosive to be landed on our shores, leads to mis-governance, slows down our development and economic growth and delays weapon and equipment procurement vitally needed for our national security. Political corruption is as big a threat to our nation as jihadi terrorism."

In a recent byelection in Tamil Nadu, for instance, there were allegations that enourmous amounts of money were paid to the voters directly even to the extent of Rs. 7000 per vote.

An idea about the gargantuan levels of black money and money stashed abroad was highlighted in the Swiss banking Association report of 2006. According to report, the five countries nationals who top the deposits held in banks in the territory of Switzerland are:

India—$1,456 billion
Russia—$470 billion
UK—$390 billion
Ukraine—$100 billion
China—$96 billion

In other words, India with $1,456 billion or $1.4 trillion has more money in Swiss banks than the rest of the world put together. Simply put, these are monies—doubtless of questionable origin—that are meant to and continue to remain outside public knowledge and reach.

Systematic efforts to reduce the presence of black money in our system are, therefore, a national priority to safeguard our country. The political class benefiting from the present system will not take the lead. This will have to come from the people. NGOs and institutions like the judiciary, the Election Commission and the CVC.

Ruchika M. Khanna in his article, "Corruption at full throttle" in *The Sunday Tribune* dated January 22, 2009 observed that how much should a jeep cost, if its parts have been bought from a scrap dealer and assembled? Certainly not more than what it costs to buy a new jeep. But in Haryana, flush with funds, nobody minds when a second-hand vehicle is bought by a government department for almost double the cost of a new vehicle!

The vehicle, a tacky jeep assembled by a local mechanic, had the seller laughing all the way to the bank with Rs. 6.48 lakh in his pocket for a piece of junk. But the story does not end here.

The same government department, Industrial Training and Vocational Education, also spent Rs. 9.83 lakh on buying a second-hand Tata 407 truck from a scrap dealer as against a tender of Rs. 5,15,381 lakh submitted by Tata Motors for supply a brand new jeep. The case came to light after a complaint of these financial irregularities was received by the Lokayukta, Haryana, Justice J.K. Sud. After the Lokayukta initiated an inquiry against the department, senior officials in the department agreed to conduct an inquiry against the accused officials.

However, after an initial probe, these six officials of the department were charge-sheeted a few months ago. Since then, no further action has been initiated against them. Though the Lokayukta has been looking into the aspect of misappropriation of money used for purchase of the second-hand vehicle, the department has issued charge sheets to the six accused officials for charges of only irregularly in making purchases, without following the correct procedure.

Interestingly, these irregularities in purchase of vehicles came to light during another inquiry initiated against officials of Industrial training and Vocational Education, wherein misappropriation of funds for purchase of study material and irregularity in appointment of instructors was being probed. It was then decided to make these allegations of irregularity in purchase of vehicles, a part of the initial inquiry.

The Tribune Editorial dated Feb. 24, 2009 observes that those found guilty of corruption should be given exemplary punishment to act as a deterrent. If corruption in high places is on the rise today, it is because of the lack of the fear of the law among the public servants, especially ministers and bureaucrats. One does not know when will the big fish involved in the fodder scam, The Taj corridor scandal, the Telgi scam and allegations about excessive wealth against Mr. Mulayam Singh Yadav will be taken to their logical conclusion. Unfortunately, our criminal prosecution system is slow and it often comes under the influence of the politicians. The best way to tackle corruption in high places is by expediting all the pending cases, preferably on fast track.

CONCLUSION

Development administration cannot function and achieve results unless and until the Government itself is firmly committed to the task of the weeding out dishonest and corrupt officials, irrespective of rank and status. All government employees, irrespective of rank, whose integrity and honesty are even slightly in doubt, should be dealt with severely. Punishment for corruption should be exemplary, the least being dismissal from service. The Government should also ensure that anti-corruption agencies are manned by personnel whose integrity and spirit of dedication can never be questioned.[35]

The real remedy for the evil of corrupt practices lies in creating a clean and healthy atmosphere in which every person holding a prominent position in the political, social, religious and even educational spheres shall follow a certain standard of conduct, a life of austerity and simplicity, and imbibe the good values of our country.[36]

So far there do not seem to be strong social, and governmental enforcement mechanism against corruption in Nigeria. The nation seems to exist at the mercy of this social evil. Her leaders and citizens have to choose between accepting corruption and living with it or taking bold measures to save the nation and its people from it. Same is true about India. On these considerations, the nation should accept the following submission of J. Patrick Dobels, "No social or political system will ever transform human beings into spontaneously altruistic and caring individuals with sufficient strength to transcend the temptation of selfishness and arrogance. That once corruption becomes widespread in a polity, the success of significant reforms towards arresting the trend remains doubtful."[37]

Yawning inequality between classes of people creates room for corruption for those who would have shun the evil practice. India must wage war against corruption. For, to take corruption seriously is to take civic virtue seriously; to take civic virtue seriously is to demand not just moral education but to demand substantive participation, and economic and political equality.[38]

Eternal vigilance is required on the part of people who are the ultimate beneficiary of a corruption free polity and administration. The rulers also should know that people understand what is what and that the nation is still vibrant. They would be inviting their doom only unless they follow ethical standards of behaviour and stop defrauding the nation. In the words of our former Prime Minister Atal Behari Vajpayee, "It is the consistent endeavour of our Government to provide clean, efficient, and transparent administration. The drive against corruption in public life has to be a continuing process.

We have pledged to give the people a stable, honest, and corruption-free Government, capable of delivering all-round development. We have further committed that the principle of 'Zero Tolerance' would apply while dealing with corruption. The independent institutions of the Lokpal at the Center and the Lokayukta at the States were envisaged to deal with this problem. They were visualised to be non-political, with their status comparable to the highest judicial functionaries in the country. These institutions were to provide an independent forum, where the people could take their allegations of corruption and administrative excesses, and seek quick and effective redressal."

However, this mechanism of redressal has not lived up to the people's expectations, although I must hasten to add that, this is not the fault of the Lokayuktas. For example, only yesterday, I read in the newspapers about the findings of an Administrative Reforms Commission in Karnataka, which presented some startling figures. Between 1986 and 2000, the Lokayukta in the State ordered investigation in 2,840 cases. Of these, 1,677 were charge-sheeted. However, only six per cent of these cases resulted in conviction. As many as 1,118 cases are still pending trial.[39]

Public morality has touched a new low. Accepted norms have collapsed all round. Appearances were once sought to be maintained, at least outwardly. Even the pretence is now shed. Conscience is no longer troubled in doing something wrong. There is no sense of shame in being found out. Lies are told brazenly and hawked as truth even in the country's highest temple of democracy. Good administration is provided by the virtue, public spirit, honour and sense of justice of its civil servants. Administration stinks when the courageous among its civil servants are banished from the mainstream because they dare to be honest and the profligates are rewarded because they flatter the power brokers only to betray the people.

The top-level functionaries, both political and administrative, must discharge their duties in consonance with the Articles laid down in the constitution and laws enacted by Parliament to usher in an era of good governance. This would help in eradicating corruption from all walks of life.

In a editorial page in the Financial Express dated Oct. 20, 2006 under the heading "Integrity in India—CII's initiative on graft is welcome" but tackling corruption in any meaningful way will need far more than just good intentions. What we need is a sustained, multi-pronged approach that includes electoral and judicial reform, tighter surveillance and prosecution mechanisms, improved civil service pay and a rational tax regime. More important, we need a groundswell of public outrage against graft at all levels of civil society, backed by unswerving political will to root out corruption at local, state and central administrations. To be sure, the question that we, the citizens of India, must ask ourselves is what kind of society do we want to bequeath future generations: one that is emasculated by enticement and cynical by scandal or one that is strengthened by systems and lauded for laws that work. If the CII initiative goes some way towards helping us find the answer to that vital question, then its efforts would not have been in vain. Right to Information can help a great deal in this good cause of eradicating corruption and promoting good governance.

The launch yesterday in Bangalore of the Integrity India Campaign against corruption by the Confederation of Indian Industry (CII) is a welcome, albeit small, step in the right direction. Clearly a response to recent bold press, the initiative assumes significance as it is spearheaded by a highly respected industry association and presided over by India Inc's statesman-in-residence, N.R. Narayana Murthy. Corruption in India has assumed gargantuan proportions, contributing significantly to the guesstimated $ 50-100 billion growth of the parallel economy each year of everyday life. According to a study by transparency International (which recently gave India the dubious distinction of being the most corrupt exporting nation in the world), more than Rs. 21,000 crore is paid in bribes by ordinary citizens every year. However, as we all know, political corruption-often in connivance with industry-is probably the most insidious of all. So, it comes as no surprise that the CII initiative, lasting three years, will focus on corporate behaviour and good governance by showcasing success stories and model codes of conduct.

A corruption free environment is bound to improve the quality of governance. Checking or controlling corruption is an effective means of better governance. The rights, guaranteed under the Constitution, lose all their relevance especially, if a citizen cannot have good governance. Corruption gives a slant to the working and favours those, who become a party to talk of good governance and ensuring the enjoyment of fundamental human rights can be relevant if the citizens can be ensured corruption free service.

Prime Minister Manmohan Singh on the concluding day of the 16th biennial conference on anti-corruption organized by the CBI called for a comprehensive strategy to reduce the scope for corruption and an integrated approach to deal with it. "The anti-corruption machinery in the country should create deterrence against corruption by aggressively pursuing cases of high-level corruption to their logical end. Rapid, fair and accurate investigation of allegations of corruption against public servants at all levels should remain a priority." "We must recognize the need for an integrated approach to deal with corruption. Agencies like your's cannot operate in isolation. You must have the resources to take a broader view of individual cases and be able to make a distinction between a 'bona fide mistake' Not only must the guilty be brought to book more speedily, but the innocent must be spared the trauma of delayed justice.

CBI Director Vijay Shankar said that it is highly desirable that adequate number of special courts are set-up to deal exclusively with anti-corruption cases. The Central Government is financing setting up of such courts in the sates but much more needs to be done. "Judicial process is marred by long delays and poor conviction rates. We complete investigations in over 90 percent of our cases within a year or two. But it takes the courts 10,15 or even over 20 years to complete the trails."

Notes and References

1. David H. Bayle. "The Effects of Corruption in Developing Nations" ed. By Arnold S. Heidenheimer. New York, Holt, Rinehart and Winston. Inc.. 1970. p. 523
2. The Directorate of Advertising and Visual Publicity. Ministry of Information & Broadcasting. Govt of India, New Delhi, March 2001.
3. S.R. Maheswari, Towards Excellence in Public Services, in *IJPA*, July-Sept. 2006.
4. Report of the Bengal Administration Enquiry Committee. 1945. Paras 223-24
5. Quoted in Mohit Bhattacharya. "Conceptualizing Good Governance" in *IJPA*, July-Sept.. 1998. p. 289.
6. Constituent Assembly Debates. Vol XI, No 11, November 25, 1949, p. 975.
7. Action Plan for an Effective and Responsive Government. Document. Prepared by Administrative Reforms and Public Grievances, New Delhi, GOI.
8. Santhanam Committee Report, pp. 117-18.
9. S.K. Sharma, Corruption In Policy Formulation and Implementation: The Question of Land Reforms in India, in ed S. Bhatnagar and S.K. Sharma. Corruption in Indian Politics and Bureaucracy. ESS ESS Publications. New Delhi. 1991. p. 123.
10. O.P. Dwivedi and D.S. Mishra, A Good Governance Model for India: Search From Within, in *IJPA*, Oct.-Dec., 2003.
11. Statement by UGPA. Cited in West Africa. Nov. 28. 1964. p. 1331.
12. West Africa. January 27. 1962. p. 98.
13. Abdul Smith. "Development of Corruption" (First Ed.).
14. Jacob Van Klaveren. "The Concept of Corruption" in Political Corruption. ed. By Arlond. J. Heidenheimer. New York. Holt. Rinehart and Winston. Inc.. 1970. p. 38).
15. *Ibid.*
16. *Ibid.*
17. *The Hindustan Times,*. Nov. 4. 1972.
18. Report of the Committee on Prevention of Corruption. New Delhi. GOl. Ministry of Home Affairs. 1964. Para 216.
19. *Ibid.*, Para 11.2.
20. Nathaniel H. Leff. Economic Development Through Bureaucratic Corruption in Political Corruption ed. By Arnold J. Heidenheimer. New York. Holt. Rinehart, and Winston, Inc. 1970, p. 517.
21. Bayley. p. 627.
22. *Ibid.*, p. 528.
23. West Africa. November 28, 1964, p. 1331.
24. In *India Today*, June 30, 1992.
25. P.S. Rammohan Rao, Probity in Public Life, Whither Standards, in IIPA, Occasional Papers, IIPA, New Delhi, 2006, p. 10.
26. P.S. Mathur, Indian Administration. Organization and Working, IPSA. Patiala. 1966. pp. 94-97.
27. *London Times*, Aug. 5. 1964
28. Report of the Committee on Prevention of Corruption, Para 6.63.
29. S.K. Sharma, *op. cit.*, p. 123.
30. P.C. Suri, Corruption: A Diagnosis (Integrative): A Search for Relevant Management Strategies in Bhatnagar & S.K. Sharma, *op. cit.*, p. 58.
31. Singh, Uppal, 'The Galloping Evil of Corruption', Public Administration (Kanpur), Vol. 10, No. 1, January 1, p. 19.
32. See Report of Khanna Commission, Published by Home Deptt. of Government of Orissa.
33. Annual Report, 1999-2000, Ministry of Personnel, Public Grievances and Pensions, GOI, p. 37.

34. *Ibid.*, p. 39.
35. A. Rai and S.P. Singh, Current Ideas and Issues In Indian Administration, New Delhi, Uppal, 1979, p. 209.
36. C.N. Bhalerao (Ed), Administration, Politics and Development In India, *op. cit.*, pp. 227-28.
37. E.A. Ikolwak, Public Officials and Corruption in Nigeria, 1960-79, in *IJPA*, January-March 1987, p. 71.
38. Quoted in *Ibid.* (J. Patrick Dobets, *op. cit.*, p. 972)
39. Address of Prime Minister to the Sixth Conference of Lokayukta and Upa-Lokayuktas, 22 January, 2001, New Delhi.

CHAPTER

23

Consumers' Protection Machinery

(Consumers' Protection Act, 1986 as amended up-to-date)

INTRODUCTION

United Nations Organ, i.e. Economic and Social Council urged the need of Protecting the Consumers in 1976's. As a result, the United Nations came out with Guidelines for Consumers' Protection by Consensus" on 9th April 1985. In USA, there is already a powerful institution. "The Consumer Product Safety Commission." Same is the case with other European countries. The thrust of all these experiences made the developing countries realize the need of some institutions to protect the consumers.

Good Governance is the most important and essential to protect the consumers in the age of globalization, liberalization and privatization. Consumers are always at the mercy of producers and distributors. They are cheated. Though there are many remedies available but due to lack of good governance, these agencies are not yielding desired results. Citizens have always been exploited by agencies and institutions, both in private and public sectors as they are not organised formally to take remedial action. Such complaints are more in public utility services like Electricity, Water, Gas, Railways, and Transport because of their monopolistic nature. Besides, the legal machinery is beyond the purview of a common citizen. Rosy Kumar in his article, 'The Consumers' Protection Act *vis-a-vis* the Monopolies and Restrictive Trade Practices Act: A Comparative Approach rightly observes, "In the past the consumer was considered supreme and occupied a central position in the economy. However, with the advance of the economy, increasing liberalisation and technological advancement, the focus of corporate philosophy has gradually shifted from the consumer to profit at any cost, reducing the concept of consumer sovereignty to a mere myth than reality."[1]

Foregoing discussion on the contributions of a Consumer Protection Law and its operations in relation to the accountability of services providers to their consumers reveal that through

CHART 23.1

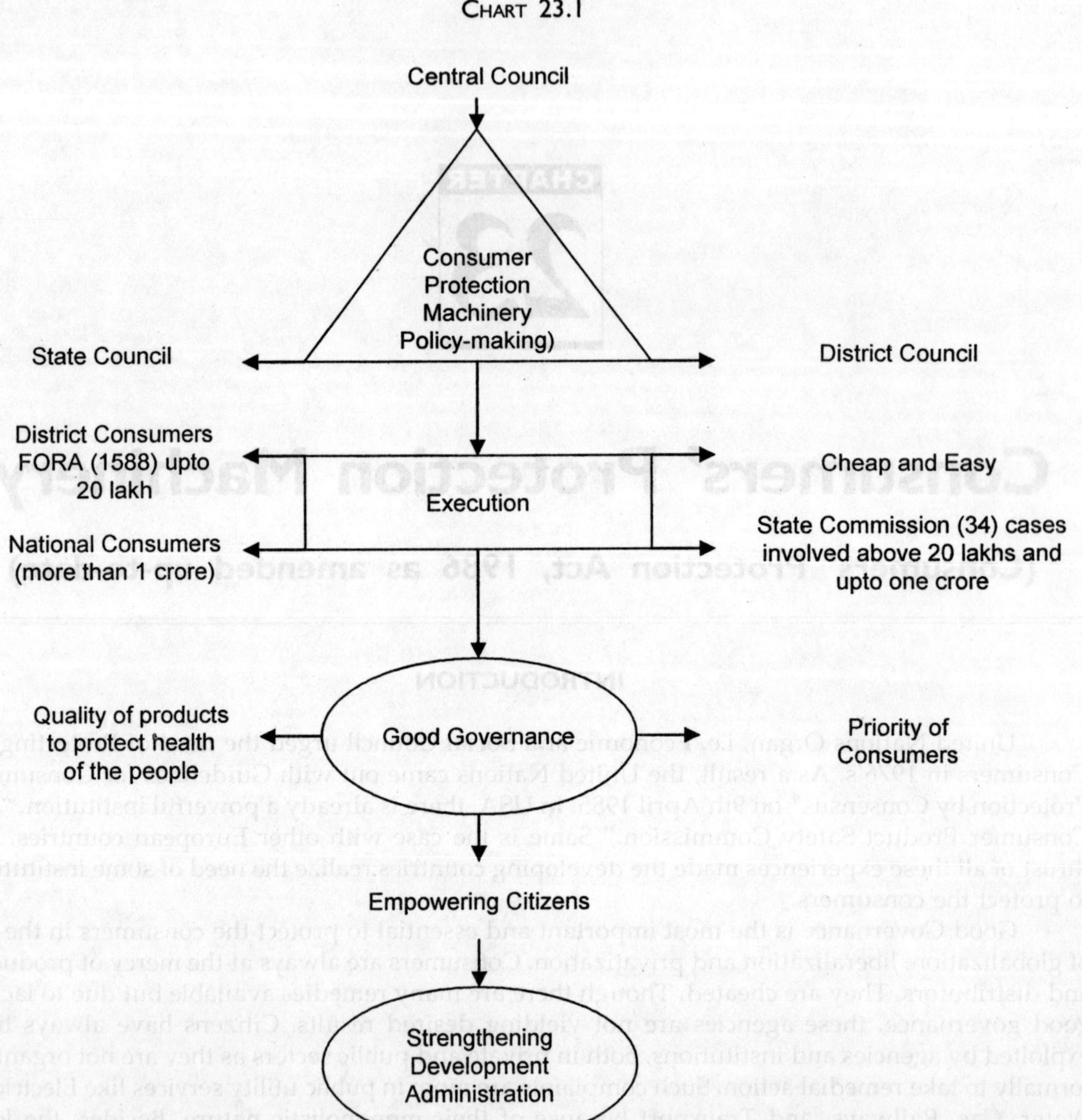

efficient and effective implementation of the consumer law the quality of services affecting the consumers' rights and interests may be improved to a considerable extent. In this way, the concern of the good governance movement in enhancing the accountability of public services providers can be guaranteed. It is true that the improvement in service delivery sector will no doubt have direct impact on the quality of better life. This may in turn result in emergence of the better society for tomorrow. A society which is responsible, caring and accountable will certainly be considered a better place to live in. therefore, the need of accountability of service providers, be they in public sector, private sector or co- operative sector, should not be over emphasised. One may like to add finally that the accountability, inter-alia, is the soul of good governance and the absence of it is the sign of bad governance.

Twelfth Report on Standing Committee on Food Civil Supplies and Public Distribution 2001 (13th Lok Sabha), Section 3 of Consumer Protection Act, 1986 stresses the need of the Act in the following words:

One of the most important milestones in the consumer movements in the country has been the enactment of the Consumer Protection Act, 1986 for enabling people to secure speedy and inexpensive redressal of their grievances. This Act was necessitated because the well organized sectors or manufactures, traders and service providers, armed with knowledge of the market and manipulative skills, often attempt to exploit the consumers, despite the existence of provisions in different laws protecting their interests. Moreover, various factors including increase in the population resulted in enormous pendency and delay in disposal of cases in the Civil Courts. Consumers cannot be asked to wait for years for settlement of even small claims. Hence, the Consumer Protection Act, 1986 was enacted to better protect the interest of the consumers. It is one of the most progressive and comprehensive pieces of legislation and it is an umbrella legislation covering all goods and services, The Act provides for a separate three-tier quasi-judicial consumer disputer redressal machinery at the National, State and District levels and is intended to provide simple, speedy and inexpensive redressal for consumer's grievances.

The Consumer Protection Act, 1986 which provides for the setting up of a three-tier quasi-judicial machinery at the National, State and District levels to deal with consumer complaints against defective or hazardous goods, deficient services, unfair trade practices, etc. and also provides for the setting up of Consumer Protection Councils at the Central, State and District level which are Advisory Bodies to promote and protect the rights of consumers. The Act was amended in 1991 and 1993 in the light of the experience gained during the implementation of the provisions of the Act.

Although effective use of the redressal agencies has been made by consumers, a number of practical difficulties have been brought to the notice of the Central Government including the pronouncements of Consumer Redressal Forums, High Court and the Supreme Court which has bearing on the working of the redressal agencies. On the recommendation of the Central Consumer Protection Council, a Working Group was constituted by Government in June, 1994, under the Chairmanship of Shri Naren De, Minister of Food and Civil Supplies, Government of West Bengal, to examine the need for further changes in the Consumer Protection Act, 1986. Suggestions were also invited from the State Government, members of the Central Consumer Protection Council, Presidents of the State Commissions and District Forums and Voluntary Consumers' Organizations. All these suggestions were considered by the working group which submitted its report in May 1995.

Proposals for amendment of the Consumer Protection Act, 1986 were formulated on the basis of the recommendations of the Working Group and also those of an Expert Group set-up in July 1997. Extensive consultations were held with representatives of consumer interests, President of the National Commissions and State Commissions and all the concerned Ministers of the Central Government. The Amendment Bill was finally introduced in the Rajya Sabha on 26.4.2001.

In exercise of the powers conferred by sub-section (2) of section 1 of the Consumer Protection (Amendment) Act, 2002, (62 of 2002), the Central Government hereby appoints the 15th Day of March 2003 as the date on which all the provisions of the said Act shall come into force.

Realising the increasing problems of citizens discontentment, the Government of India enacted the Consumers Protection Act in 1986 amended from time to time which provided for the creation of quasi-legislative machinery in the form of consumer councils. The Act applies equally to all' goods and services irrespective of whether the same are produced and marketed by public, cooperative or private sectors. However, a service rendered free of charges is outside the purview of the Act. The citizens can now move the consumers' protection machinery to get redressal in areas like Railways, Electricity Boards, Banks, LIC., Post and Telegraph, , etc., which were earlier very difficult to approach. [2] Before we discuss the Consumer Protection Machinery, let us define the consumer as per the Act.

WHO IS A CONSUMER?

The Act gives the definition of a consumer and only those, who fall into this definition, can take benefits of the Act. This definition is somewhat different than dictionary/literal meaning. It also specifically excludes some kind of consumers from its purview.

The definition of consumer is given in two parts:

1. Consumer of Goods
2. Consumer of Services

- The goods or services must not be free. Some consideration (price) should be paid for them. It includes purchase on credit or part payment or in installments.
- It clearly states that any person who uses goods or services with the consent of purchaser or is beneficiary is also a consumer. For instance, if the son uses a telephone connection, which is in the name of his father, he is also a consumer.
- It excludes commercial dealings or goods purchased for resale from the definition of consumer with exception of goods and services purchased for self-employment. For instance, if a commercial concern purchases a car for the use of its own staff, it does not use it as a taxi or hiring to others. Such a use cannot be termed as commercial. The purchaser of such a car, though a commercial concern, is a consumer here because the vehicle is not used for commercial purpose.

MACHINERY: POLICY-MAKING

The Act provides for the creation of policy-making agencies at the Union, State and District levels in the form of Central Consumer Protection Council, State Consumer Protection Councils and District Consumer Protection Council.

I. Central Consumer Protection Council

The Central Council consists of the following members, namely:

(a) the Minister in charge of the (consumer affair) in the Central Government, who shall be its Chairman, and

(b) such number of the other official or non-official members representing such interests as may be prescribed.

Composition of Central Council

The Central Government shall, by notification establish a council to be known as the Central Consumer Protection Council. This council shall consist of a chairman and with such other official or non-official members as may be prescribed. The minister in-charge of the consumer affairs in the Central Government shall be Chairman.

Rule 3 of the Consumer Protection Rules, 1987 provides:

The Constitution of the Central Consumer Protection Council and the Working Groups—

1. The Central Government shall, by notification in the Official Gazette constitute the Central Consumer Protection Council (hereinafter referred to as the Central Council) which shall consist of [the following members, not exceeding 150, namely—

(a) [the Minister-in-charge of Consumer Affairs in the Central Government) who shall be the Chairman of the Central Council;
(b) the Minister of State (where he is not holding independent charge) or Deputy Minister [in-charge of Consumer Affairs in the Central Government] who shall be the Vice-Chairman of the Central Council;
(c) the [...] Minister in-charge of Consumer Affairs in States;
(d) eight Members of Parliament—five from the Lok Sabha and three from the Rajya Sabha;
[(e) the Secretary of the National Commission for Scheduled Castes and Scheduled Tribes);
(f) representatives of the Central Government Departments and autonomous organisations concerned with consumer interest—not exceeding twenty;
(g) representatives of the Consumer Organisations or consumers—not less than thirty-five;
(h) representatives of women—not less than ten;
(i) representatives of farmers, trade and industries—not exceeding twenty;
(j) persons capable of representing consumer interest not specified above—not exceeding fifteen; and
(k) the [Secretary in-charge of Consumer Affairs in the Central Government) shall be the member-secretary of the Central Council.

2. The term of the Council shall be three years.

3. Any member may, by writing under his hand to the Chairman of the Central Council, resign from the Council. The vacancies, so caused or otherwise, shall be filled from the same category by the Central Government and such person shall hold office so long as the member whose place he fills would have been entitled to hold office, if the vacancy had not occurred.

4. For the purpose of monitoring the implementation of the recommendations of the Central Council and to suggest the working of the Council, the Central Government may constitute from amongst the members of the Council, a Standing Working Group, under the chairmanship of the Member Secretary of the Council. The Standing Working Group shall consist of not exceeding 30 members and shall meet as and when considered necessary by the Central Government.[3]

Meeting

(1) The Central Council shall meet as and when necessary , but (at least one meeting) of the council shall be held every year.
(2) The Central Council shall meet at such time and place as the Chairman may think fit and shall observe such procedure in regard to the transaction of its business as may be prescribed.

Objects of the Central Council

(1) The objects of the Central Council is to promote and protect the rights of the consumers.

(a) the right to be protected against the marketing of goods which are hazardous to life and property;
(b) The right to be informed about the quality, quantity, potency, purity, standard and price of goods so as to protect the consumer against unfair trade practices;
(c) The right to be assured, wherever possible, access to a variety of goods at competitive prices;
(d) The right to be heard and to be assured that consumers interests will receive due consideration at appropriate forums;
(e) The right to seek redressal against unfair trade practices or unscrupulous exploitation of consumers; and
(f) The right to consumer education.

2. State Consumer Protection Council

Composition

(2) The State Council shall consist of the following members, namely:

(a) the Minister incharge of consumer affairs in the State Government who shall be its Chairman;
(b) such number of other official or non-official members representing such interests as may be prescribed by the State Government; and
(c) such number of other official or non-official members, not exceeding ten, as may be nominated by the Central Government.

Meetings

(3) The State Council shall meet as and when necessary but not less than two meetings shall be held every year.

(4) The State Council shall meet at such time and place as the Chairman may think fit and shall observe such procedure in regard to the transaction of its business as may be prescribed by the state government.

Objects of the State Council

The objects of every State Council shall be to promote and protect within the state rights of the consumers laid down as in Central Council.

3. The District Consumer Protection Council

(1) The State government shall establish for every district, by notification, a council to be known as the District Consumer Protection Council.

Composition

2. The District Consumer Protection Council shall consist of the following members; namely—

(a) the collector of the district who shall be its Chairman; and
(b) such number of other official and non-official members representing such interests as may be prescribed by the State Government.

Meetings

(3) The District Council shall meet as and when necessary but not less than two meetings shall be held every year.

(4) The District Council shall meet at such time and place within the district as the Chairman may think fit and shall observe such procedure in regard to the transaction of its business as may be prescribed by the State Government.

CONSUMER DISPUTES REDRESSAL AGENCIES

Establishment of Consumer Disputes Redressal Agencies: The following agencies have been established for the purposes of this act:

(a) a Consumer Disputes Redressal Forum to be known as the "District Forum" established by the State Government in each district of the state by notification. State if it deems necessary can establish more than one forum.
(b) A Consumer Disputes Redressal Commission to be known as the "State Commission" established by the State Government in the state by notification; and
(c) A National Consumer Disputes Redressal Commission established by the Central Government by notification.

At present, there are 34 State commissions, one for Union Territories of 'Daman & Diu' and 'Dadra & Nagar Haveli' and one in each of the remaining States/UTs and 588 District Fora besides the National Commission. The state governments are responsible to set-up the District Fora and State Commissions. States have been empowered to establish additional District forums and additional benches in the State commissions and also to hold circuit benches. The Central government set-up the National commission in 1988 at New Delhi. It has been empowered by the act to appoint additional Members to facilitate creation of more benches and holding of circuit benches by the National Commission. The third bench of the Commission has started functioning from 13 July 2004.

Composition of the District Forum: Each district forum consists of:

(a) President: a person who is, or has been, or is qualified to be a District Judge.
(b) Two other members, who are persons of ability, integrity and standing, and have adequate knowledge or experience of, or have shown capacity in dealing with, problems relating to economics, law, commerce, accountancy, industry, public affairs or administration, one of whom must be a woman.

Selection

All appointments at the District forum are made by the State Government on the recommendation of a selection committee consisting of the following namely,

(i) The President of the State Commission —Chairman
(ii) Secretary, Law Department of the State —Member

(iii) Secretary, in-charge of the Department dealing —Member with consumer affairs in the state

Provided that where the President of the State Commission is, by reason of absence or otherwise, unable to act a Chairman of the Selection Committee, the State Government may refer the matter to the Chief Justice of the High Court for nomination of a sitting Judge of that High Court to act as Chairman.

Tenure

Every member of the District Forum holds the office for a term of five years extendable for another terms of 5 years or up to the age of 65 years, whichever is earlier.

Provided that a member may resign his office in writing under his hand—ddressed to the State Government and on such resignation being accepted, his office shall become vacant and may be filled by the appointment of a person possessing any of the qualifications mentioned earlier in relation to the category of the member who has resigned.

Qualification

(a) a person who is, or has been, or is qualified to be a District Judge, who shall be its President;

[b) two other members, one of whom shall be a woman, who shall have the following qualifications, namely:

(i) be not less than thirty-five years of age,

(ii) possess a bachelor's degree from a recognized university,

(iii) be persons of ability, integrity and standing, and have adequate knowledge and experience of at least ten years in dealing with problems relating to economics, law, commerce, accountancy, industry, public affairs or administration:

Provided that a person shall be disqualified for appointment as member, if he—

(a) has been convicted and sentenced to imprisonment for an offence which, in the opinion of the State Government, involves moral turpitude; or

(b) is an undischarged insolvent; or

(c) is of unsound mind and stands so declared by a competent Court; or

(d) has been removed or dismissed from the service of the Government or a body corporate owned or controlled by the Government; or

(e) has, in he opinion of the State Government, such financial or other interest as is likely to affect prejudicially the discharge by him of his functions as a member; or

(f) has such other disqualifications as may be prescribed by the State Government.]

The salary or honorarium and other allowances payable to, and the other terms and conditions of service of the members of the District Forum are such as may be prescribed by the State Government.

JURISDICTION OF THE DISTRICT FORUM

(1) Subject to the other provisions of this act, the District Forum shall have jurisdiction to entertain complaints where the value of the goods or services and the compensation, if any, claimed does not exceed rupees 20 lakhs.

(2) A complaint shall be instituted in a District forum within the local limits of whose jurisdiction,

(a) the opposite party or each of the opposite parties, where there are more than one, at the time of the institution of the complaint, actually and voluntarily resides or personally works for gain, or

(b) any of the opposite parties, where there are more than one, at the time of the institution of the complaint, actually and voluntarily resides, or personally works for gain, provides that in such case either the permission of the District Forum is given, or the opposite parties who do not reside or personally work for gain, as the case may be, acquiesce in such institution; or

(c) the cause of action, wholly or in part, arises.

Procedure of Receipt of Complaint

A complaint in relation to any goods sold or delivered or agreed to be sold or delivered or any service provided or agreed to be provided may be filed with a district forum by:

(a) the consumer to whom such goods are sold or delivered or agreed to be sold or delivered or such service provided or agreed to be provided.

(b) any recognized consumer association whether the consumer to whom the goods sold or delivered or agreed to be sold or delivered or service provided or agreed to be provided is a member of such association or not;

(c) one or more consumers, where there are numerous consumers having the same interest, with the permission of the District Forum, on behalf of, or for the benefit of, all consumers so interested, or

(d) the central or the state government as the case may be, either in its individuals capacity or as a representation of interests of the consumers in general.

(2) Every complaint filled under sub-section (1) shall be accompanied with such amount of fee and payable in such manner as may be prescribed

(3) On receipt of a complaint made under sub-section (1), the District Forum may, by order, allow the complaint to be proceeded with or rejected:

Provided that a complaint shall not be rejected under this sub-section unless an opportunity of being heard has been given to the complainant:

Provided further that the admissibility of the compliant shall ordinarily be decided within twenty-one days from the date on which the complaint was received.

(4) Where a complaint is allowed to be proceeded with under sub-section (3), the District Forum may proceed with the complaint in the manner provided under this Act.

Provided that where a complaint has been admitted by the District forum, it shall not be transferred to any other court or tribunal or any authority set-up by or under any other law for the time being in force.

(1) The District Forum shall, on receipt of a complaint, if it relates to any goods,

(a) refer a copy of the complaint to the opposite party mentioned in the complaint directing him to give his version of the case within a period of thirty days or such extended period not exceeding fifteen days as may be granted by the District Forum;
(b) where the opposite party on receipt of a complaint referred to him under clause (a) denies or disputes the allegations contained in the complaint, or omits or fails to take any action to represent his case within the time given by the District Forum, the District Forum shall proceed to settle the consumer dispute in the manner specified in clauses (c) to (g);
(c) where the complaint alleges a defect in the goods which cannot be determined without proper analysis or test of the goods, the District Forum shall obtain a sample of the goods from the complainant, seal it and authenticate it in the manner prescribed and refer the sample so sealed to the appropriate laboratory along with a direction that such laboratory make an analysis or test, whichever may be necessary, with a view to finding out whether such goods suffer from any defect alleged in the complaint or from any other defect and to report its findings thereon to the District Forum within a period of forty-five days of the receipt of the reference or within such extended period as may be granted by the District Forum;
(d) before any sample of the goods is referred to any appropriate laboratory under clause (c), the District Forum may require the complainant to deposit to the credit of the Forum such fees as may be specified, for payment to the appropriate laboratory for carrying out the necessary analysis or test in relation to the goods in question;
(e) the District Forum shall remit the amount deposited to its credit under clause (d) to the appropriate laboratory to enable to carry out the analysis or test mentioned in clause (c) and on receipt of the report from the appropriate laboratory, the District Forum shall forward a copy of the report along with such remarks as the District Forum may feel appropriate to the opposite party;
(f) if any of the parties disputes the correctness of the findings of the appropriate laboratory, or disputes the correctness of the methods of analysis or test adopted by the appropriate laboratory, the District Forum shall require the opposite party or the complainant to submit in writing his objections in regard to the report made by the appropriate laboratory;
(g) the District Forum shall thereafter give a reasonable opportunity to the complainant as well as the opposite party of being heard as to the correctness or otherwise of the report made by the appropriate laboratory and also as the objection made in relation thereto under clause (f) and issue an appropriate order under section 14.

(2) The District Forum shall, if the complaint received by it under section 12 relates to goods in respect of which the procedure specified in sub-section (1) cannot be followed, or if the complaint relates to any services—

(a) refer a copy of such complaint to the opposite party directing him to give his version of the case within a period of thirty days or such extended period not exceeding fifteen days as may be granted by the District Forum;
(b) where the opposite party, on receipt of a copy of the complaint, referred to him under

clause (a) denies or disputes the allegations contained in the complaint, or omits or fails to take any action to represent his case within the time given by the District Forum, the District Forum shall proceed to settle the consumer dispute –

(i) on the basis of evidence brought to its notice by the complainant and the opposite party, where the opposite party denies or disputes the allegations contained in the complaint, or

(ii) ex-parte on the basis of evidence brought to its notice by the complainant where the opposite party omits or fails to take any action to represent his case within the time given by the Forum.

(3) No proceedings complying with the procedure laid down in sub-sections (1) and (2) shall be called in question in any court on the ground that the principles of natural justice have not been complied with.

(4) For the purposes of this section, the District Forum shall have the same powers as are vested in a civil court under Code of the Civil Procedure, 1908 while trying a suit in respect of the following matters, namely:

(i) the summoning and enforcing the attendance of any defendant or witness and examining the witness on oath,

(ii) the discovery and production of any document or other material object producible as evidence,.

(iii) the reception of evidence on affidavits;

(iv) the requisitioning of the report of the concerned analysis or test from the appropriate laboratory or from any other relevant source;

(v) issuing of any commission for the examination of any witness; and

(vi) any other matter which may be prescribed.

(5) Every proceeding before the district Forum shall be deemed to be a judicial proceeding within the meaning of sections 193 and 228 of the Indian Penal Code (45 of 1960) and the District Forum shall be deemed to be a civil court for the purpose of section 195, and Chapter XXVI of the Code of Criminal Procedure, 1973 (2 of 1974).

(6) Where the complainant is a consumer referred to in sub-clause (iv) of clause (b) of sub-section (1) of section 2, the provisions of rule 8 of Order 1 of the First Schedule to the Code of Civil Procedure, 1908 (5 of 1908) shall apply subject to the modification that every reference therein to a suit or decree shall be construed as a reference to a complaint or the order of the District Forum thereon.

Finding of the District Forum

(1) If, after the proceeding conducted under section 13, the District Forum is satisfied that the goods complained against suffer from any of the defects specified in the complaint or that any of the allegations contained in the complaint about the services are proved, it shall issue an order to the opposite party directing him to do one or more of the following things, namely:

(a) to remove the defect pointed out by the appropriate laboratory from the goods in question;

(b) to replace the goods with new goods of similar description which shall be free from any defect;

(c) to return to the complainant the price, or as the case may be, the charges paid by the complainant;
(d) to pay such amount as may be awarded by it as compensation to the consumer for any loss or injury suffered by the consumer due to negligence of the opposite party;
(e) to remove the defects or deficiencies in the services in question;
(f) to discontinue the unfair trade practice or the restrictive trade practice or not to repeat them;
(g) not to offer the hazardous goods for sale;
(h) to withdraw the hazardous goods from being offered for sale; and
(i) to provide for adequate costs to parties.

Appeal

Any person aggrieved by an order made by the District Forum may prefer an appeal against such order to the State Commission within a period of thirty days from the date of the order, in such form and manner as may be prescribed. The power of the District Forum has been increased to cases Worth 20 Lakhs

COMPOSITION OF THE STATE COMMISSION

(1) Each State Commission consists of—

(a) a person who is or has been a Judge of a High Court, appointed by the State Government, who shall be its president: Provided that no appointment under this clause shall be made except after consultation with the Chief Justice of the High Court. Two other members, who shall be persons of ability, integrity and standing and have adequate knowledge or experience of, or have shown capacity in dealing with, problems relating to economics, law, commerce, accountancy, industry, public affairs or administration, one of whom shall be a woman. Provided further that a person shall be disqualified for appointment as a member if he—
(b) has been convicted and sentenced to imprisonment for an offence which, in the opinion of the Sate Government, involves moral turpitude; or
(c) is an undischarged insolvent; or
(d) is of unsound mind and stands so declared by a complaint Court; or
(e) has been removed or dismissed from the service of the Government of a body corporate owned or controlled by the Government; or
(f) has, in the opinion of the State Government, such financial or other interest, as is likely to effect prejudicially the discharge by him of his functions as member; or
(g) has such other disqualifications as may be prescribed by the State Government.]
(h) Provided that every appointment under this clause shall be made by the state government on the recommendation of a selection committee consisting of the following, namely—
  (i) President of the State Commission — Chairman
  (ii) Secretary of the Law Department of the State — Member
  (iii) Secretary, incharge of Department dealing with consumer affairs in the state — Member

Provided that where the President of the State Commission is, by reason of absence or otherwise, unable to act as Chairman of the Selection Committee, the State Government may refer the matter to the Chief Justice of the High Court for nominating a sitting Judge of that High Court to act as Chairman.

(2) The salary or honorarium and other allowances payable to, and the other terms and conditions of service of, the members of the State Commissions shall be such as may be prescribed by the State Government.

(3) Every member of the State Commission shall hold office for a term of five years extendable to another terms of 5 years or up to age of sixty-seven years whichever is earlier.

(4) Notwithstanding anything contained in sub-section (3), a person appointed as a President or as a member before the commencement of the Consumer Protection (Amendment) Act, 1993, shall continue to hold office as President or member, as the case may be, till the completion of his term.

Jurisdiction of the State Commission

Subject to the other provisions of this Act, the State Commission shall have jurisdiction to entertain—

(i) complaints where the value of the goods or services and compensation, if any, claimed exceeds, 20 lakhs but not more than one crores rupees

(ii) appeals against the orders of any District Forum within the State; and

(iii) to call for the records and pass appropriate orders in any consumer dispute which is pending before or has been decided by any District Forum within the State, where it appears to the State Commission that such District Forum has exercised a jurisdiction not vested in it by law, or has failed to exercise a jurisdiction so vested or has acted in exercise of its jurisdiction illegally or with material irregularity.

A complaint shall be instituted in a State Commission within the limits of whose jurisdiction—

(a) the opposite party or each of the opposite parties, where there are more than one, at the time of the institution of the complaint, actually and voluntarily resides or carries on business or has a branch office or personally works for gain; or

(b) any of the opposite parties, where there are more than one, at the time of the institution of the complaint, actually and voluntarily resides, or carries on business or has a branch office or personally works for gain, provided that in such case either the permission of the State Commission is given or the opposite parties who do not reside or carry on business or have a branch office or personally works for gain, as the case may be, acquiesce in such institution; or

(c) the cause of action, wholly or in part, arises.]

[Provided further that no appeal by a person who is required to pay any amount in terms of an order of the State Commission, shall be entertained by the National Commission unless the appellant deposited in the prescribed manner fifty percent. Of the amount or rupees thirty-five thousand, whichever is less.]

Transfer of Cases

On the application of the complainant or of its own motion, the State Government may, at any stage of the proceedings, transfer within the State if the interest of justice so requires.

Circuit Benches

The State Commission shall ordinarily function in the State Capital but may perform its functions at such other place as the State Government may, in consultation with the State Commission, notify in the Official Gazette, from time to time.

Procedure applicable to State Commissions—The provisions of Sections 12, 13 and 14 and the rules made there under for the disposal of complaints by the Disposal of disputes by the State Commission.

Appeals

Any person aggrieved by an order made by the State Commission in exercise of its powers conferred by sub-clause (i) of clause (a) of section 17 may prefer an appeal against such order to the National Commission within a period of thirty days from the date of the order in such form and manner as may be prescribed.

Provided that the National Commission may entertain an appeal after the expiry of the said period of thirty days if it is satisfied that there was sufficient cause for not filing it within that period.

Hearing of Appeal

An appeal filed before the State Government or the National Commission shall be heard as expeditiously as possible and an endeavor shall be made to finally dispose of the appeal within a period of ninety days from the date of its admissions:

Provided that no adjournment shall be ordinarily granted by the State Commission or the National Commission, as the case may be unless sufficient cause is shown and the reasons for grant of adjournment have been recorded in writing by such Commission

Provided further that the State Commission or the National Commission, as the case may be, shall make such orders as to the costs occasioned by the adjournment as may be provided in the regulations made under this Act:

Provided also that in the event of an appeal being disposed of after the period so specified, the State Commission or, the National Commission, as the case may be, shall record in writing the reasons for the same at the time of disposing of the said appeal.

APPOINTMENT OF NATIONAL COMMISSION

Provided that every appointment under this clause shall be made by the Central Government on the recommendation of a selection committee consisting of the following, namely:-

(a) a person who is a Judge of the Supreme Court, to be nominated by the Chief Justice of India —Chairman

(b) the Secretary in the Department of Legal Affairs in the Government of India —Member

(c) Secretary of the Department dealing with Consumer affairs in the Government of India —Member

Composition of the National Commission

(1) the National Commission shall consist of:

(a) a person who is or has been a Judge of the Supreme Court, to be appointed by the Central government, who shall be its President:
(Provided that no appointment under this clause shall be made except after consultation with the Chief Justice of India;)

(b) Not less than four, and not more than such number of members, as may be prescribed, and one of whom shall be a woman, who shall have the following qualifications, namely:
  (i) be not less than thirty-five years of age;
  (ii) possess a bachelor's degree from a recognized university; and
  (iii) be persons of ability, integrity and standing and have adequate knowledge and experience of at least ten years in dealing with problems relating to economics, law, commerce, accountancy, industry, public affairs or administration:

Provided that not more than fifty per cent of the members shall be from amongst the persons having a judicial background.

[(1-A) (i) The jurisdiction, powers and authority of the National Commission may be exercised by Benches thereof.

(ii) A Bench may be constituted by the President with one or more members as the President may deem fit.

The jurisdiction , powers and authority of the National Commissions may be exercised by Benches thereof.

(2) The salary or honorarium and other allowances payable to and the other terms and conditions of service 2[***] of the members of the National commission shall be such as may be prescribed by the Central Government.

(3) Every member of the National Commission shall hold office for a term of five years extendable for another term of 5 years or up to the age of seventy years, whichever is earlier and shall not be eligible for reappointment.

(4) Notwithstanding anything contained in sub-section (3) a person appointed as a President or as a member before the commencement of the Consumer Protection (Amendment) Act, 1993, shall continue to hold such office as President or member, as the case may be, till the completion of his term].

Jurisdiction of the National Commission

Subject to the other provisions of this Act, the National Commission shall have jurisdiction to entertain—

(i) complaints where the value of the goods or services and compensation, if any, claimed exceeds rupees one Crore, and

(ii) appeals against the orders of any State Commission; and

(b) to call for the record and pass appropriate orders in any consumer dispute which is pending before or has been decided by any State Commission where it appears to the

National Commission that such State Commission has exercised a jurisdiction not vested in it by law, or has failed to exercise a jurisdiction so vested, or has acted in the exercise of its jurisdiction illegally or with material irregularly.

Power and procedure applicable to the National Commission

(1) The provisions of sections 12, 13 and 14 and the rules made there under for the disposal of complaints by the District Forum shall, with such modification as may be considered necessary by the Commissions, be applicable to the disposal of disputes by the National Commissions.

(2) Without prejudice to the provision contained in sub-section (1) the National Commission shall have the power to review any order made by it, when there is an error apparent on the face of record.

22-A. Power to set aside ex-parte orders.—Where an order is passed by the National Commission ex-parte against the opposite party or a complainant, as the case may be, the aggrieved party may apply to the Commission to set aside the said order in the interest of justice.

22-B. Transfer of cases—On the application of the complainant or of its own motion, the National Commission may, at any stage of the proceeding, in the interest of justice, transfer any complaint pending before the District Forum of one State to a District Forum of another State or before one State Commission to another State Commission.

22-C Circuit Benches—The National Commission shall ordinarily function at New Delhi and perform its function at such other place as the Central Government may, in consultation with the National Commission, notify in the Official Gazette, from time to time.

22-D. Vacancy in the office of President—When the office of President of a District Forum, State Commission, or of the National Commission, as the case may be vacant or a person occupying such office is , by reason of absence or otherwise, unable to perform the duties of his office, these shall be performed by the senior most member of the District Forum, the State Commission or of the National Commission, as the case may be:

Provided that where a retired Judge of a High Court is a member of the National Commission, such member or where the number of such member is more than one, the senior most person among such members shall preside over the National Commission in the absence of President of that Commission.

Appeal

Any person, aggrieved by an order made by the National Commission in exercise of its powers conferred by sub-clause (i) of clause (a) of Section 21, may prefer an appeal against such order to the Supreme Court within a period of thirty days from the date of the order.

Provided that the Supreme Court may entertain an appeal after the expiry of the said period of thirty days if it is satisfied that there was sufficient cause for not filling it within that period. Provided further that no appeal by a person who is required to pay any amount in terms of an order of the National Commission shall be entertained by the Supreme Court unless that person has deposited in the prescribed manner fifty per cent. Of the amount or rupees fifty thousand, whichever is less.

Finality of order: Every order of a District Forum, the State Commission or the National Commission shall, if no appeal has been preferred against such order under the provisions of this act, be final.

[24-A. Limitation period.—(1) The District Forum, the State Commission or the National Commission shall not admit a complaint unless it is filed within two years from the date on which the cause of action has arisen.

(2) Notwithstanding anything contained in sub-section (1), a complaint may be entertained after the period specified in sub-section (1), if the complainant satisfies the District Forum, the State Commission or the National Commission, as the case may be, that he had sufficient cause for not filing the complaint within such period.

Provided that no such complaint shall be entertained unless the National Commissions, the State Commission or the District Forum, as the case may be, records its reasons for condoning such delay.

Administrative Control: (1) The National Commission shall have administrative control over all the State Commissions in the following matters, namely:

(i) calling for periodical return regarding the institution, disposal, pendency of cases;

(ii) issuance of instructions regarding adoption of uniform procedure in the hearing of matters, prior service of copies of documents produced by one party to the opposite parties, furnishing of English translation of judgements written in any language, speedy grant of copies of documents; and

(iii) generally overseeing the functioning of the State Commissions or the District Forum to ensure that the objects and purposes of the Act are best served without in any way interfering with their quasi-judicial freedom.

(2) The State Commission shall have administrative control over all the District Forum within its jurisdiction in all matters referred to in sub-section (1).

Enforcement of orders of the District Forum, the State Commission or the National Commission.—(1) Where an interim order made under this act, is not complied with, the District Forum or the State Commission or the National Commission as the case may be, may order the property of the person, not complying with such order to be attached.

(2) No attachment made under sub-section (1) shall remain in force for more than three months at the end of which, if the non-compliance continues, the property attached may be sold and out of the proceeds thereof, the District Forum or the State Commission or the National Commission may award such damages as it thinks fit to the complainant and shall pay the balance, if any to the party entitled thereto.

(3) Where any amount is due from any person under an order made by a District Forum, State Commission or the National Commission, as the case may be, the person entitled to the amount may make an application to the District Forum, the State Commission or the National Commission as the case may be, and such District Forum or the State Commission or the National Commission may issue a certificate for the said amount to the Collector of the district (by whatever name called) and the Collector shall proceed to recover the amount in the same manner as arrears of land revenue.]

Dismissal of frivolous or vexatious complaints: Where a complaint instituted before District Forum, the State Commission or, as the case may be, the National Commission is found to be frivolous or vexatious, it shall, for reasons to be recorded in writing, dismiss the complaint and make an order that the complainant shall pay to the opposite party such cost, not exceeding ten thousand rupees, as may be specified in the order.

Working

Since enactment, Consumer Protection Machinery is doing a good work.

Since its inception and up to December 2004, 36,856 cases were filed out of which 28,820 cases were disposed of in the National Commission: Similarly, out of 3,34,524 cases filed, 2,24,282 were disposed of by the State Commissions and out of 19,61,133 cases field before District Forums

17,36,716 cases were disposed of. Overall 19,89,818 cases have been disposed of out of 23,32,513 cases field with a remarkable disposal rate of 83.32 per cent.[4]

The Supreme Court had in a judgement in the case of Charan Singh v/s Healing Touch Hospital warned "The consumer forums must take expeditious steps to deal with the complaints filed before them and not keep them pending for years. It would defeat the object of the Act, if the forums at the district, state and national levels do not dispose of summary trials, expeditiously. Steps in this regard are required to be taken right in earnest." The observation of the Supreme Court also reflects the concern of the consumers and its desire to bring in efficiency and effectiveness in disposal of cases.

Consumers Education (Consumer Clubs)

1. In order to encourage Consumer Education Consumer Clubs have been set-up to the tune of 3957 till the end of March, 2005 with the start of in 2002. These are set-up in schools and a grant of Rs. 10,000 is given to each club to educate its members.

2. Promoting involvement of Research Institutions/Universities/Colleges, etc., in consumer protection and welfare: This scheme has been launched with a view to sponsor research and evaluation studies in the field of consumer welfare to provide solution to the practical problems being faced by the consumers, to sponsor seminars/workshops/conferences on the consumer related topics, and to have necessary inputs for the formulation of policy/programme/scheme for the protection and welfare of the consumers. The Indian Institution of public Administration, New Delhi, has been identified as the nodal organization to administer the scheme. Till March 2005, 247 applications were received and 55 proposals have been recommended for sanction of grant.

3. National Consumer Helpline: A National Consumer Helpline project has been established in coordination with Delhi University, Department of Commerce. Consumers form all over the country can dial toll-free number 1600-11-4000 and seek telephonic counseling for problems that they face as consumers. At the time of inception the Help line intends to deal with problems related to telecom, courier, banking, insurance, financial services, etc. The Helpline has been formally launched on 15 March 2005, i.e., World Consumer Right Day.

4. Consumer Online Research and Empowerment (Core) Centre: A Consumer Online Research and Empowerment (Core) Centre has been set-up in collaboration with Consumer Coordination Council (CCC). The CORE Centre is intended to provided the most scientific and effective system of collection and dissemination of consumer related information to generate consumer awareness and empowerment of all the society. It also provides e-counselling and mediation for consumer problems. The CORE project was formally launched on 15 March 2005.

CRITICAL APPRAISAL

It is a matter of great credit to Governments at the Union and State levels to promote Consumer Protection efficiently. It is a matter of greater appreciation that Government of India is also encouraging the education, training and research in the area of Consumers awareness. In addition, the Government of India has involved all types of agencies—schools, universities, NOG's to support the Consumers' movement. Inspite of such impressive performance, we suggest the following:

I. Real Success of the Consumers' forums at National, State and Local levels

It depend upon the perception, ethos and interest of the persons working for these forums.

It has become a standard practice that retired personnel are generally appointed in the forums causing apathy indifference and lack of dynamism. They do not remain active. What is the problem if we appoint fresh people on deputation to promote vitality and dynamism among these forums.

2. Lack of Infrastructure Facilities

Consumer forum lack infrastructure—lack of basic facilities like drinking water, lavatories, and sitting facilities for consumers is a matter of great concern. In addition, the consumer forums lack secretarial and other facilities which stand in the way of good governance.

3. Attitude of persons on the forums is not sympathetic as they have imported the old attitudes

The retired people who are put on these forums do not understand the difference between their old jobs and new jobs. There is a need of training to change their behaviour to be soft with consumers.

4. Lawyers fleecing the consumers

The scheme of consumers forums was designed to make it cheap and easy. If one visits the District forum, we would find that all consumers' have handed over their cases to lawyers with huge fees. The members of the consumers forums must create a culture where the consumers' themselves can present their own cases. This is the basic spirit of such forums.

5. Lack of Education to consumers as well as the Owners of Firms

The real purpose of consumers' forums is to educate the consumers and owners of firms to educate them to develop harmonious relationships as one cannot exist without the other. Consumers have to purchase while the supplier has to supply. Such education would create an amicable atmosphere—the most essential role of consumer forums.

6. Lack of speedy disposal

It has been experienced based upon personal experience of the author that it takes too much time to get justice. Owners can put pressure as they can make friendship with the persons on the forums. Poor consumers are given less attention while the forums have been set-up for them.

7. Soft Approach with Owners responsible for fraud

Forums adopt soft approach with persons responsible for fraud. These trends make the defaulters fearless. There is a need to be strict with the defaulters.

8. Lack of decent consumers' protection policy

The consumer protection policy suggests that should creates an environment whereby the clients, customers, and consumers receive satisfaction from the delivery of goods and services needed by them. Good governance requires efficiency, effectiveness, empowerment, rationality, impartiality and participation of citizens. The concern of consumer protection is to ensure fair trade practices; quality of goods and efficient services with information to the consumer with regard to quality, quantity, potency, composition and price for their choice of purchase. Thus, proper and effective implementation of consumer protection law promotes good governance.

9. Lack of Specific Standards of good

Setting standards is not enough for assuring the consumer of quality. For this, governments needs to establish the full quality infrastructure, embracing standardization conformity assessment and enforcement. The constituents of quality infrastructure are:

Standardization

- Standard development
- Standard information
- Metrology
- Quality assurance/conformity assessment
- Testing
- Inspection
- Product certification
- Management systems of Certification (ISO 9000/14000/2200/2700/OHSMS, etc.
- Regulation and enforcement
- Accreditation

10. Lack of National Competition Policy

The broad objectives of the NCP should be: (i) to preserve the competitive process and to encourage competition in the domestic market so as to optimize efficiency, (ii) promote innovation and maximize consumer welfare, (iii) to promote, build and sustain strong competition culture within the country; (iv) to achieve harmonization in policies, laws and procedures regarding competition dimensions at all levels of governance, (v) to ensure competition in regulated sectors and to establish an institutional mechanism for synergized relationship between the Competition Commission and sectoral Regulators, and (vi) to strive for a single national market. The NCP should be based on the following principles: (i) there should be effective control on anti-competitive conduct which undermines competition in markets in India; (ii) there should be competitive neutrality or a level playing field among all players, whether these be private enterprises, PSEs or government departments engaged in non-sovereign commercial activity; (iii) the procedures should be rule bound, transparent, fair and non-discriminatory; (iv) there should be institutional separation between policy-making, operations and regulation; (v) where a separate regulatory arrangement is set-up, it should be consistent with the principles of competition; (vi) third party access to essential facilities on fair terms should be available; (vii) any deviation from the principles of competition should be only to meet desirable social, environmental, developmental or other national objectives which are clearly defined, transparent, non-discriminatory, rule-based and having the least competition restricting effect. The above principles of competition should be applicable across all sectors of the economy and be incorporated in policies, which govern them.[5]

CONCLUSION

We may key the following rights of consumer in mind:

- Right to choose from variety of goods and services
- Right to seek redressal against unfair trade practices

- Right to be protected against the marketing of goods and services, which are hazardous to life and property.
- Right to be informed about the quality, quantity, potency, purity, standards and price of goods.
- Right to acquire the knowledge and skill to be an informed consumer
- Right to be heard.

Good Governance of District Forums, State and National Commissions is *sine-qua non* for the protection of Consumers. For this purpose, we must ensure that excellent people are put on such sensitive institutions. They must develop credibility, sensitivity and earnestness to solve the problems of the aggrieved persons. We can conclude with the remarks that consumer forum are not only for settling disputes only but also spread consumer education which can check defaulters and thus reduce the rush of complaints.

In *Laxmi Engineering Works* v. *P.S.G. Industrial Institute* (A.I.R. 1995 S.C. 1428), it was held: "The idea was to provide an additional forum providing inexpensive and Speedy resolution of disputes arising between consumers and suppliers of goods and service. The Forum so created is uninhibited by the requirement of court fee or formal procedure of a court. Any consumer may go and file a complaint. Complaint need not necessarily be filed by the complainant himself, any recognized consumers' association can espouse his cause. Even the Central or state government can act on his/their behalf. The idea was to help the consumers get justice and fair treatment in the matter of goods and services purchased and availed by them in the market dominated by large trading and manufacturing bodies. Indeed the entire act revolves round the consumer and is designed to protect his interest. The Act provides for business to consumers' disputes and not for "business to business" disputes.

NOTES AND REFERENCES

1. Rosy Kumar: "The Consumer Protection Act *vis-à-vis* the Monopolies and Restrictive Trade Practice Act: A Comparative Study", in *Consumer Protection and Trade Practice Journal*, New Delhi, 1993, p. 9.
2. Section 2(1) of the Act.
3. R.N.P. Chaudhary, "Consumer Protection Law—Provision and Procedure", pp. 47-48.
4. India, 2006, A Reference Annual Public Division, Ministry of Information and Broadcasting, GOI, New Delhi.
5. GOI, Planning Commission, Eleventh Five Year Plan, pp. 247-51.

CHAPTER 24

Human Rights and Duties

Prof. Mohammad Mujtaba Khan *observes that Human Rights, are, indeed a sine qua non for the development of human personality and an indispensable ingredient for the physical strength and mental fortification of humanity. As a matter of fact, human rights are an expression of dignity, freedom of conscience and a civilized means of subsistence. The genesis of the concept is to be found in the classical liberal traditions reinforced by renaissance that made a passionate defense of the principles of competitive individualism and rule of law aimed at the realization of individual dignity, liberty and freedom.*

"O my Lord of Light and Love, fill my heart with light and love;
O my Lord of Bliss and Joy, fill my heart with bliss and joy;
O my Lord of Truth and Peace, fill my heart with truth and peace;
O my Lord of Transcendental Virtues, fill my heart with those virtues"

—*R.P. Dhokalia*

Human Rights and Development Administration are intimately related. Development Administration promotes human Rights while human rights are a source of Development administration. The basic purpose of Development Administration is to promote the human dignity and status. The Supreme Court in a judgement observed that whenever human dignity is wounded-civilisation takes a step backward. The flag of humanity on each occasion must fly half-mast. Good Governance can be a great success provided Government ensures the fulfilment of human rights which one gets with birth and are recognized by the state. For example, recently implemented Domestic Violence Act, 2005 can usher an era of peace, love and affection among all members of the family provided every one in the house respects the Human Rights provisions of Act sincerely, honestly and in letter and spirit. Family life would be a heaven for its inmates.

INTRODUCTION (See Chart 24.1)

All human beings are born free and equal in dignity and rights. The inherent dignity of all

CHART 24.I

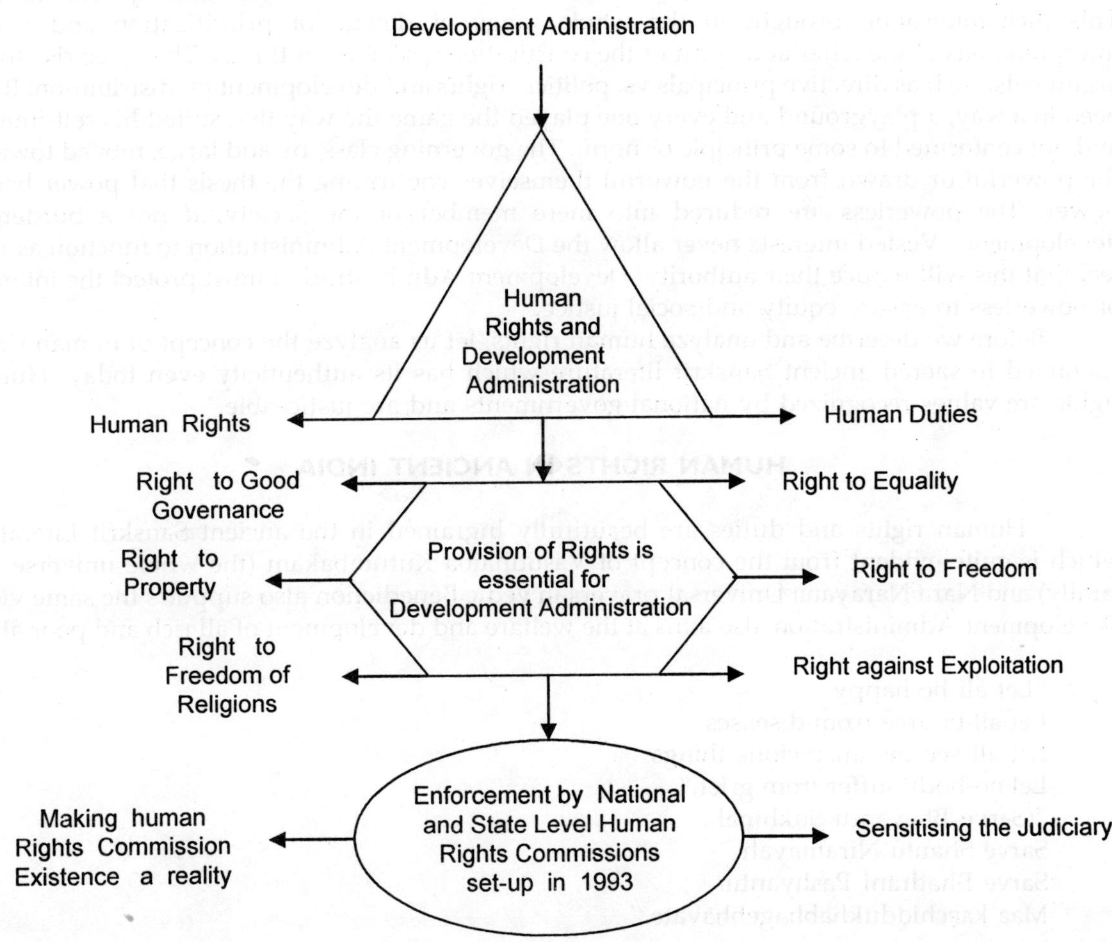

members of the human family is the foundation of freedom and justice and peace in the world as given in the Universal declaration of human rights in its preamble. Human rights are the moral claims, which are inalienable and inherent in all human individuals by virtue of their humanity alone. These are the rights of all human beings, because they are born in human family. The concept of human rights and the human rights movement is getting more and more impetus in today's social and political background because it is now universally accepted need that human rights are essential in human lives and hence they must be protected.[1] Without ensuring the guarantee of human rights, Development Administration would remain only on paper.

Development Administration must ensure that Human Rights are made available to all to enjoy decent life. Development would be of no use until and unless, Development Administration creates conditions under which human beings can enjoy the inherent Human Rights.

The overall evidence suggests that while there are some gains to the poorer sections of the society, the Development Administration in general moved in a direction that is helpful to the powerful classes. They used all the organs of the State to their advantage, whenever it was permissible and against the poor whenever it was necessary. In the process, the guarantees given to the poor both in the Part III and Part IV of the Indian Constitution started getting dichotomized. This dichotomisation brought in the whole range of debate of prioritization and varied interpretations of the letter and spirit of the constitutional scheme of things. This gave rise to the arguments, such as directive principals vs. political rights and development *vs.* distribution. It has been in a way, a playground and every one played the game the way that suited his self-interest and not conformed to some principle or norm. The governing class, by and large, moved towards the powerful or drawn from the powerful themselves confirming the thesis that power begets power. The powerless are reduced into mere member of the society, if not a burden to development.[2] Vested interests never allow the Development Administration to function as they feel that this will reduce their authority. Development Administration must protect the interests of powerless to ensure equity and social justice.

Before we describe and analyze human rights, let us analyze the concept of human rights contained in sacred ancient Sanskrit literature which has its authenticity even today. Human rights are values recognized by national governments and are justiceable.

HUMAN RIGHTS IN ANCIENT INDIA

Human rights and duties are beautifully Ingrained in the ancient Sanskrit Literature which is quite evident from the concept of Vasudhaiba Kutumbakam (the whole universe is a family) and Nara Narayana Universal prayers in vedic Benediction also supports the same view. Development Administration also aims at the welfare and development of all rich and poor alike.

"Let all be happy
Let all be free from diseases
Let all see the auspicious things
Let no-body suffer from grief."
"(Sarve Bhavantu Sukhinah,
Sarve Shantu Niramayah
Sarve Bhadrani Pashyantu
Maa kaschiddukhabhagebhavate."

Similarly a prayer in Shiksha Vali of the Taittiriya Upanishad also stress the same

"May He (God) protect us both together
May He nourish us both together
May we work jointly with great energy
May our study be vigorous and effective
May we not hate anyone
Let there be Peace, Peace and Peace."

In the Rig Veda, it has been rightly said, "No one is superior or inferior. All are brothers and all should strive for the interest of all and progress collectively." Similarly in Atharva Veda, it has been pointed out, "All have equal rights in articles of food and water." Yoke of the chariot of life is placed equally on the shoulders of all. All should live together with harmony supporting one another like the spokes of the chariot connecting the rim and the hub.

The same idealism was incorporated by Kautilaya in his Arthasastra while summing up the objects and purpose of the exercise of Sovereign power by the King. He stated thus. In the happiness of his subjects lies his happiness; in their welfare, his welfare; whatever pleases him (personally) he shall not consider as good, but whatever makes his subjects happy, he shall consider good. (Arthasastra Chapter IXXX 39).

An analysis of ancient literature would reveal the duties out weigh rights and that is why there were no exploitation. The voice about human rights in various parts of the world were voiced through full freedom functions when rights are balanced with responsibilities and choice is balanced with conscience.

There cannot be the experience, individually or collectively, if attention and effort are focused only on rights and choice. When rights and choice are misunderstood or misused, debts are incurred—mentally, physically, spiritually, socially, economically, politically and so on. A responsible person fulfils the assigned duty by staying true to the aim. Duties are carried out with integrity and sense of purpose.

It was only recently that human movements got active in various countries of the world e.g. Magna Carta in Britain in 1215 AD, Petition of Rights in 1628 AD, Habeas Corpus Act, 1628 AD, Bill of Rights in 1689 AD, American Declaration of Independence in 1676 AD and Declaration of Rights of men in France during 1789 AD and subsequently and more recently, in the Delcaration of Universal Human Rights by UN in 1948.

R.P. Dhokalia feels that today humanity binds us together because the global society has created oneness of mankind. Human rights and their co-relative human duties are founded on eternal and universal human values and ideals transcending all man-made boundaries-civilization, cultural or geographic. In our times of social, political and economic globalization, additional values are being questioned and challenged and so education as a social institution is confronted with new challenges in respect to the view of man, one's perception of knowledge and the educational aims and the vision of good life and values and its substantive features. The goal of elevation of man's awareness and consciousness, and of enlightenment of his soul with a view of making a new harmonious multi-cultural world order and a more humane civilization requires a synthesis of varieties of cultural and religious diversities of materialism with spiritualism and of the values, ideals and the spirit of all major religions of the world. This further underlines harnessing of every branch of knowledge and the union of moral and secular values with constitutional and legal norms. Revival of the duty-oriented society, a spiritual basis and balancing of human rights and duties as co-relatives and spiritual regeneration of the entire human life through education in a wider sense, can pave the way for a harmonious, just and peaceful global order. Moral and spiritual source of rights and duties enjoins tenacious pursuit of worthy ideals and human values.[1] Development Administration can take roots in such congenial human rights based on well-being of all members of humanity.

The term 'human rights' is commonly used to denote rights which every human being is entitled to enjoy by virtue of being a human being, and for no other reason. All cultures and societies throughout their history have been evolving conceptions of rights which they held sacrosanct. Various states in their legal systems and constitutions have incorporated rights which are inviolable. While the contemporary conceptualization of human rights which the Universal Declaration of Human Rights and its accompanying Convenants embody has drawn on the rich legacy of the past, it is distinguished by its universality, by the fundamental principle that all human rights are meant to be enjoyed by all human beings, anywhere in the world.

'Human rights' have, in practice, been redefined to encompass every aspect of dignified human existence and to make every human being an equal member of the human family. The goal is still very far, but the road to it has been marked. Mahatma Gandhi has said: "It has always been a mystery to me how men can feel themselves honoured by the humiliation of their fellow beings."

National Human Rights Commission highlighted the responsibility of Governments at the Union and State levels in the following words: "It is the primary and inescapable responsibility of the State to protect the right to life, liberty, equality and dignity of all of those who constitute it. It is also the responsibility of the State to ensure that such rights are not violated either through overt acts, or through abetment or negligence. It is a clear and emerging principle of human rights jurisprudence that the State is responsible not only for the acts of its own agent, but also for the acts of non-State players acting within its jurisdiction. The State is, in addition, responsible for any inaction that may cause or facilitate the violation of human rights."

The United Nations Charter, in its Preamble, reaffirms 'faith in fundamental human rights, in the dignity and worth of the human person, in the equal rights of men and women and of nations large and small'. Article 1 of the Charter laid down the purposes of the United Nations which included 'promoting and encouraging respect for human rights and for fundamental freedoms for all without distinctions as to race, sex, language or religion'. All the Member states also pledged themselves 'to take..... action for the achievement' of 'universal respect for, and observance of, human rights and fundamental freedoms'. The Charter did not define, in precise terms, the meaning of 'human rights and fundamental freedoms'. It authorized the Economic and Social Council, one of the principal organs of the United Nations, to make recommendations for the purpose of promoting respect for, and observance of human rights and fundamental freedoms for all.

The United Nations sponsored human rights movement and their enshrinement in national constitutions have brought about a great revolution in human thoughts, relations and institutions. Abuse and misuse of human rights in the form of recurrent strikes, demonstration, rallies and animosities on the basis of status, class, castes, tribes and rural-urban divide have created social, political and economic chaos and convulsions in human affairs. On the other hand, breaches and violations of human rights in varying degrees almost everywhere and poignant gulf between law and practice have generated great disillusionment and pervasive frustration. The UN Human Rights Declaration and the two Conventions enumerate only human rights and these are spoken of as ideal standards to be achieved and as rights to be duly protected bylaw and pursued in the courts of law under the constitutions of all countries. By ignoring the imperativeness of the co-relationship of rights and duties, generally law has not placed equal emphasis on duties of man. Both rights and duties essentially have moral and spiritual basis of which law provides only an external formulation for an effective implementation. Development Administration aims at socio-economic development so that all human beings irrespective of class, caste or region can enjoy, political, economic and social rights to make life meaningful and fruitful.

The Universal Declaration of Human Rights stirred the moral consciousness as well as the political assertiveness of the people in the countries. Another impact of the Declaration was that the various countries adopted these rights in their national constitutions and laws. But the Declaration lacked the binding force of a law over the members, like Conventions and Covenants. The UN got success after 20 years of continuous negotiations, compromises and debates and ultimately in December 1966 the General Assembly promulgated International Covenants comprising three instruments:

1. International Covenants on Economic, Social and Cultural Rights;
2. International Covenants on Civil and Political Rights; and
3. Optional Protocol (on individual petition) to the Covenants on Civil and Political Rights.

The Covenants have assumed a prime place in international law as the instruments that influence and that at the same time judge the disregard of states. It is through Covenants that the conditions of individual rights in particular countries are to be assessed. India signed the Instrument of Accession to the Human Rights Covenants on 27th March 1979. By 1994, already 130 countries had become the party to the two covenants.

Human Rights are basically the claims of the individuals throughout the world, for such conditions which are essential for the development of personality and realization of the innate characteristics without which nobody can seek to be himself at his best. These rights are inherent and inalienable to human beings and are necessary to ensure survival, dignity and personality development of the individual irrespective of race, colour, religion, sex, language, political or other opinion, national or social origin, property, birth or other status. The Human Rights represent what was agreed upon, by the international community, as the minimum of those rights and fundamental freedom which are inherent and inalienable to all human beings and which must be available to all the people. [4]

However, one must be clear in mind that all claims of individuals are not Human Rights. Only those claims are Human Rights which are recognised by the United Nations as the essential conditions for the development of one's human personality. The United Nations has also fixed *Duties* along with Human Rights and the *Article 29(1)* of the Universal Declaration reiterates that *"everyone has duties to the community in which alone the free and full development of his personality is possible."* On the other hand, reasonable restrictions can be imposed on the individual. *Article* 29 (2) of UDHR says that "In the exercise of his rights and freedoms, everyone shall be subject only to such limitations as are determined by law solely for the purpose of securing due recognition and respect for the rights and freedoms of others and meeting the just requirements of morality, public order and the general welfare in a democratic society. Similarly, these rights and freedoms may in no case be exercised contrary to the purposes and principles of the United Nations [Art. 29 (3) of UDHR]. [5]

HUMAN RIGHTS IN INDIAN CONSTITUTIONS

Let us now discuss about human rights as enshrined in the constitution of India.

Preamble

The Preamble to the Constitution of India which outlines the objectives of the Constitution states:

> "We the people of India, having solemnly resolved to constitute India into a Sovereign, Socialist, Secular, Democratic Republic and to secure to all its citizens; Justice, social economic and political; Liberty of thoughts, expression, belief, faith and worship; Equality of status and of opportunity; and to promote among them all Fraternity assuring the dignity of the individual and the unity and integrity of the nation."

The Constitution of India has provided a detailed list of human rights and incorporated them in the form of Fundamental Rights (Part III) and the Directive Principles (Part IV).

FUNDAMENTAL RIGHTS

1. Right to Equality

Articles 14-18 of the Constitution of India deal with the right to equality.

(i) Equality before law and equal protection of law to all persons within the territory of India—(Article 14)
(ii) State cannot discriminate on grounds of religion, race, castes, sex or place of birth. It also provides public places for all without discrimination—(Article 15).
(iii) Equality of opportunity in matters of public appointment or public services—(Article 16).
(iv) Abolition of untouchability—(Article 17).
(v) Abolition of titles (other than military and academic)—(Article 18).

These provisions (Articles 14-18) clearly establish that all citizens have been guaranteed political and social equality. The constitution protects also the citizens against discriminatory treatment and provide them equal opportunity in social and public life.

2. Right to Freedom

Articles 19 to 22 cover the right to freedom.

(i) Six fundamental freedoms—(Art. 19)

(a) Freedom of speech and expression.
(b) Freedom to assemble peacefully and without arms.
(c) Freedom to form associations and unions.
(d) Freedom to move freely throughout the territory of India.
(e) Freedom to reside and settle in any part of India.
(f) Freedom to practice any profession, or to carry on any occupation, trade or business.

(ii) Protection in respect of Conviction for Offences (Art. 20)

This provides that no person shall be convicted of any offence except for violation of law in force at the time of the commission of the act. Nobody should be subjected to the penalty or punishment greater than that provided under law at the time of an offence. This also prohibited punishment on double jeopardy and *ex-post facto* laws.

(iii) Protection of Life and Personal Liberty—(Art. 21)

The Constitution of India provides that "no person shall be deprived of his life or personal liberty except according to the procedure established by law." The right to life and personal liberty (Art. 21) is the most fundamental of all fundamental rights and it can never be suspended (along with Art. 20), not even during emergency.

(iv) Protection Against Arrest and Detention in Certain cases—(Art. 22)

(a) It lays down that no person who has been arrested shall be detained in custody without being informed, as soon as may be, on the ground for such arrest.

(b) Arrested person shall not be denied the right to consult and to be defended by a legal practitioner of his choice.

(c) Each arrested/detained person has to be produced before the nearest magistrate within twenty four hours of such arrest and cannot be kept in custody beyond twenty-four hours without the authority of the magistrate.

(d) The Constitution, however, provides for arrest in Preventive Detention Act of a person committing anti-national activities. In such a case the initial detention may be for two months (or as fixed by the Parliament) and the further detention can only be on the recommendation of an Advisory Board under the chairmanship of a Judge of High Court also having two other High Court Judges as members.

3. Right Against Exploitation

(a) prohibition of traffic in human beings, beggar and forced labour—(Art. 23).

(b) Prohibition of employment of children below the age of fourteen years in factories, mines or other hazardous jobs—(Art. 24).

4. Right to Freedom of Religion

The Constitution of India provides freedom of religion under Articles 25 to 28 to all persons—

(a) Freedom of conscience and right to profess, practice and propagate any religion (subject to public order, morality and health)—(Art. 25).

(b) Freedom to manage religious affairs, to own and acquire moveable and immovable property and to administer such property—(Art. 26).

(c) No person shall be compelled to pay any taxes for the promotion or maintenance of any particular religion—(Art. 27).

(d) No religious instructions can be provided in an educational institution wholly maintained out of State funds or receiving aid from the state—(Art. 28). Similarly, there is freedom to attend religious instructions or religious worship in certain educational institutions and No body shall be forced or compelled to attend any religious instructions or functions.

5. Cultural and Educational Rights

(a) Protection of the interests of minorities and to enable them to conserve their language, script or culture—(Art. 29).

(b) Right of minorities to establish and administer educational institutions of their choice—(Art. 30).

6. Right to Property

The original Constitution provided the right to property as a fundamental right to all the citizens (Art. 31). This included the right to acquire, hold and dispose off property. But this right was omitted from the list of Fundamental Rights by the Forty-Fourth Amendment carried out in 1978. However, right to property is still a constitutional and legal right as the 44th Amendment had added a new Article, Article 300 A in Part XII of the constitution which provided that "No person shall be deprived of his property save by authority of law."

7. Right to Constitutional Remedies

Article 32 grants the right to move the Supreme Court by appropriate proceedings for the enforcement of the rights conferred by the Constitution. The Supreme Court has been vested with the authority to issue writs, orders or directions. The writs in the nature of *Habeas Corpus*, Mandamus, Prohibition, Quo-Warranto and Certiorari whichever may be appropriate for the enforcement of rights, can be issued by the Supreme Court. Under Article 226, the people can even move to High Courts for the enforcement of Fundamental Rights.

Similarly, the directive Principles of State Policy which have been provided in Part IV of the Constitution (Arts. 38 to 51) aiming at realizing the high ideals of justice, liberty, equality and fraternity as outlined in the Preamble to the Constitution. The framers of the Constitution borrowed this feature from the Constitution of Irish Republic.

DIRECTIVE PRINCIPLES OF STATE POLICY

Some of these Directive Principles which show resemblance with Human Rights are:

Art. 38(1)

The state shall strive to promote the welfare of the people by securing and protecting a social order in which justice, social, economic and political, shall inform all the institutions of national life.

Art. 38(2)

Inserted by 44th Amendment Act 1978)—The state shall, in particular, strive to minimize the inequalities in income, and endeavour to eliminate inequalities in status, facilities and opportunities, not only amongst individuals but also amongst groups of people residing in different areas or engaged in different vocations.

(a) to provide the right to an adequate means of livelihood for all—(Art. 39a).
(b) the ownership and control of the material resources of the community to be so distributed as to secure the common goal—(Art. 39b).
(c) Prevention of concentration of wealth and means of production—(Art. 39c).
(d) Equal pay for work to both men and women—(Art. 39d).
(e) Protection of the health of workers—(Art. 39e).
(f) Protection of children against exploitation –(Art. 39f).
(g) Provision for securing right to work, to education and to public assistance in case of unemployment, old age, sickness and disablement—(Art. 41).
(h) Provision for securing just and humane conditions of work and maternity relief—(Art. 42).
(i) To secure to all workers a living wage, better conditions of work and decent standard of life—(Art. 43).
(j) to secure a uniform civil code—(Art. 44).

(k) Free and compulsory education to all children upto14 years of age—(Art. 45).
(l) Protection of educational and economic interests of weaker sections, particularly Scheduled Castes and Scheduled Tribes—(Art. 46).
(m) To provide adequate standard of living and raise level of nutrition and public health—(Art. 47).

DUTIES OF THE CITIZENS

The fundamental Duties are ten in number, incorporated in Art. 51A (Part IV A) which has been inserted by the 42nd Amendment Act, 1976. Under this article, it shall be the duty of every citizens of India —

I. to abide by the Constitution and respect the National Flag and the National Anthem;
II. to cherish and follow the noble ideals which inspired our national struggle for freedom;
III. to protect the sovereignty, unity and integrity of India;
IV. to defend the country;
V. to promote the spirit of common brotherhood amongst all the people of India;
VI. to preserve the rich heritage of our composite culture;
VII. to protect and improve the natural environment;
VIII. to develop the scientific temper and spirit of inquiry;
IX. to safeguard public property;
X. to strive towards excellence in all spheres of individual and collective activity.

Steep rise in violence is noticeable in every sphere of life. India has reasons to be proud of its democracy, but what is happening in the name of democracy in various parts of the country should shame every Indian. In the face of mounting violence and crime, police performance is bound to come under public scrutiny. The police image has generally suffered, but in some states like Bihar, it is much worse than in other states. Police image, never very bright, has darkened even further. Instead of an instrument to enforce the Rule of Law, it is increasingly seen in public eye as a willing tool in the hands of unscrupulous politicians.[6]

NATIONAL HUMAN RIGHTS COMMISSION: MACHINERY FOR OVERSEEING, IMPLEMENTATION OF HUMAN RIGHTS

For better protection of human rights, the parliament of India passed the protection of Human Rights Act on 12 Oct., 1993 under the Human Rights Ordinance of 28th September, 1993 which was soon after enacted as the Protection of Human Rights Act, 1993 (NOIO of 1994). In terms of section 2 of the Act, Human Rights means the Rights relating to life, liberty, equality and dignity of the individual guaranteed.

In his speech in Chandigarh on 29th September 2003, the President of India Dr. A.P.J. Abdul Kalam observed:

> "It is necessary to work towards a Unity of Minds. It is the citizen's responsibility to do everything possible to protect the rights of every individual, without stamping out their individual characteristics and basic identity."

The Commission is deeply appreciative of this fervent call by the President to respect human rights. It is indeed the responsibility of all citizens, and the constitutional duty of the Central and State Governments, to honour this call.

The National Human Rights commission (NHRC), established under this Act, functions from New Delhi with jurisdiction all over India. Since its establishment the National Human Rights Commission has been engaged in protecting the human rights by investigating human rights abuses, forwarding cases to courts for trials and recommending necessary measures to the government in concerned cases.

ORGANIZATION

The NHRC consists of a Chairperson, four full time members and three ex-officio members. The tenure of the chairperson and members is of five years or till the age of 70 years, whichever is earlier.

The Chairperson of the Commission is appointed out of those who has served as a Chief Justice of the Supreme Court. One Member is appointed who is, or has been a Judge of the Supreme Court and one Member is a person who is, or has been the Chief Justice of a High Court. The remaining two members are appointed from amongst persons having knowledge of, or practical experience in matters relating to human rights. The three Ex-Officio Members are: (I) the Chairperson of National Commission of Minorities, (II) the Chairperson of National Commission for Scheduled Castes and Tribes, and (III) The Chairperson of the National Commission for women. There is also the provisiosn of a Secretary General who is the Chief Executive Officer of the Commission and exercises such powers and discharges such functions as it may be delegated to him.

Methods Appointment and Removal

The method of appointment designed in the Act is that it is made by the President on the recommendations of a high-powered Committee consisting of the following:

(a) The Prime Minister —Chairperson
(b) Speaker of the House of the People —Member
(c) Minister in-charge of the Ministry of Home Affairs in the Government of India —Member
(d) Leader of the Opposition in the House of the People —Member
(e) Leader of the Opposition in the Council of States —Member
(f) Deputy Chairman of the Council of States —Member

However, no sitting Judge of the Supreme Court or a sitting Chief Justice of a High Court shall be appointed without prior consultation with the Chief Justice of India. The Chairperson or any other Member of the Commission can only be removed from his office by an order of the President on the ground of proved misbehaviour or incapacity after the Supreme Court has, on an inquiry held in this behalf recommended such removal. All these provisions have been made to keep the working of Human Rights Commission independent and impartial.

The Officers and others staff of the commission

The Act provides that in addition to the Secretary-General, the Central Government shall ensure the availability to the Commission an officer not below the rank of Director-General of Police and such other officers and staff as may be necessary for the efficient performance of the functions of the Commission. The Commission may appoint other administrative, technical and scientific staff considered necessary in conformity with the Rules made by the Central Government in this behalf.

Functions

State Human Rights Commission have also the same functions.

The Commission shall perform all or any of the following functions, namely:

1. Inquire, suo motu or on a petition presented to it by a victim or any person on his behalf, into complaint of—
   (a) violation of human rights or abetment thereof;
   (b) negligence in the prevention of such violation, by a public servant;
2. Intervene in any proceeding involving any allegation of violation of human rights pending before a court with the approval of such court;
3. Visit, under intimation to the State Government, any jail or any other institution under the control of the State government, where persons are detained or lodged for purposes of treatment, reformation or protection, to study the living conditions of the inmates and make recommendations thereon;
4. Review the safeguards provided by or under the Constitution or any law for the time being in force for the protection of human rights and recommend measures for their effective implementation;
5. Review the factors, including acts of terrorism, that inhibit the enjoyment of human rights and recommend appropriate remedial measures;
6. Study treaties and other international instruments on human rights and make recommendations for their effective implementation;
7. Undertake and promote research in the field of human rights;
8. Spread human rights literacy among various sections of society and promote awareness of the safeguards available for the protection of these rights through publications, the media, seminars and other available means;
9. Encourage the efforts of non-government organsations and institutions working in the field of human rights; and
10. Such other functions as it may consider necessary for the promotion of human rights.

Powers Relating to Inquiries

(I) The commission shall, while inquiring into complaints have all the powers of a civil court trying it under the Code of Civil Procedure, 1908 and in particular in respect of the following matters, namely:
   (a) summoning and enforcing the attendance of witnesses and examining them on oath;
   (b) discovery and production of any document;
   (c) receiving evidence on affidavits;
   (d) requisitioning any public record or copy thereof from any court or office;
   (e) issuing summons for the examination of witnesses or documents; and
   (f) any other matter which may be prescribed.

(II) The Commission while inquiring into the complaints of violations of human rights may call for information or report from the Central Government or any State Government or any other authority or organization subordinate there to within such time as any be specified by it. If the Commission is not satisfied with the report, it may initiate its own inquiry. In case the commission does not receive the asked report on time, in such case also, it may proceed to inquire into the complaint on its own.

(III) The commission shall have power to require any person, subject to any privilege which may be claimed by that person under any law for the time being in force, to furnish information on such points or matters as, in the opinion of the Commission, may be useful for, or relevant to, the subject matter of the inquiry and any person so required shall be deemed to be legally bound to furnish such information within the meaning of Section 176 and Section 177 of the Indian Penal Code.

(IV) The Commission or any Gazetted Officer, specially authorized in this behalf by the Commission may enter any building or place where the Commission has reason to believe that any document relating to the subject matter of the inquiry may be found, and may seize any such document or take extracts or copies there from subject to the provisions of Section 100s of the Code of Criminal Procedure, 1973, in so far as it may be applicable.

(V) The commission shall be deemed to be a Civil Court and when any offence as is described in Section 175, Section 178, Section 179, 180 or 228 of the Indian Penal Code is committed in view or presence of the Commission, the Commission may, after recording the facts constituting the offence and the statement of the accused as provided for in the Code of Criminal Procedure, 1973, forward the case to a Magistrate having jurisdiction to try the same. The Magistrate to whom any such case is forwarded shall proceed to hear the complaint against the accused as if the case has been forwarded to him under Section 346 of the Code of Criminal Procedure, 1973.

(VI) Every proceeding before the Commission shall be deemed to be a judicial proceeding within the meaning of Sections 193 and 228, and for the purposes of Section 196, of the Indian Penal code, and the Commission shall be deemed to be a Civil Court for all the purposes of Section 195 and Chapter XXVI of the Code of Criminal Procedure, 1973.

Powers Relating to Investigation

(I) The commission may, for the purpose of conducting any investigation pertaining to the inquiry, utilize the services of any officer or investigation agency of the Central government or the State Government with the concurrence of the Central government or the State Government, as the case may be.

(II) For the purpose of investigating into any matter pertaining to the inquiry, any officer or agency whose services are utilized, (subject to the direction and control of the Commission)—

(a) summon and enforce the attendance of any person and examine him;
(b) require the discovery and production of any document; and
(c) requisition any public record or copy there of from any office.

(III) The Officer or agency whose services are utilized by the Commission, shall investigate into any matter pertaining to the inquiry and submit a report thereon to the Commission within such period as may be specified by the Commission in this behalf.

(IV) The Commission shall satisfy itself about the correctness of the facts stated and the conclusion, if any, arrived at in the report submitted to it and for this purpose the Commission may make inquiry (including the examination of the person or persons who conducted or assisted in the investigation).

Action based on Inquiry

The Commission may take any of the following steps upon the completion of an inquiry:

1. where the inquiry discloses the Commission of violation of human rights or negligence in the prevention of violation of human rights by a public servant, it may recommend to the concerned Government or authority the initiation of proceedings for prosecution or such other action as the Commission may deem fit against the concerned person or persons;
2. approach the Supreme Court or the High Court concerned for such directions, orders or writs as that Court may deem necessary;
3. recommend to the concerned Government or authority for the grant of such immediate interim relief to the victim or the members of his family as the Commission may consider necessary;
4. subject to the provisions of (5) below, provide a copy of the inquiry report to the petitioner or his representative;
5. the Commission shall send a copy of its inquiry report together with its recommendations to the concerned Government or authority and the concerned Government or authority shall, within a period of one month or such further time as the Commission allow, may forward its comments on the report, including the action taken or proposed to be taken thereon, to the Commission; and
6. the Commission shall publish its inquiry report together with the comments of the concerned Government or authority, if any, and the action taken or proposed to be taken by the concerned Government or authority on the recommendations of the Commission.

The Commission is statutorily required to submit an Annual Report to the Central Government as well as the State Government concerned. Besides, the Commission may at any time submit. Special Reports on any matter which, in its opinion, is of such urgency or importance that it should not be deferred till submission of the Annual Report.

It is enjoined on the Central Government as well as the concerned State Government to lay before each House of Parliament or the State Legislatures respectively the Annual and Special Reports of the Commission along with a memorandum of action taken or proposed to be taken on the recommendations of the Commission and the reasons for non-acceptance of the recommendations, if any.

ASSESSMENT OF NATIONAL HUMAN RIGHTS COMMISSION

Commenting on its work a year after it was established, the commission observed:

"The commission cannot begin to assert that its efforts have transformed the human rights ethos in the country or that it has as yet adequately developed a capacity to defend the least powerful of the citizens of India. But it can assert that its efforts have begun to strengthen the hands of the just and the compassionate, of whom there are legion in this country, in all States and in all walks of life."

Mindful of this challenge, the Commission was determined from its Inception—to examine and to exercise the powers conferred upon it by the Act to the fullest extent possible. It was no less determined to discharge the vast and varied functions entrusted to it under Section 12 of the Act as methodically as it could. It resolved to confront with Independence and transparency the most difficult human rights problems facing the country. Above all, the Commission set as its objective giving the people of India a greater sense of confidence in the apparatus of this country?[7]

The protection of human rights required an altogether different perspective and approach, which had to be proactive. The Commission had to look into the reasons for police violence, the nature of training, conditions of service and the need for reform; it was also necessary to examine procedures and practices, including the manner in which investigations and post-mortems were conducted, and the adequacy of the existing laws, the conditions of jails, sub-jails, and lock-ups had to be corrected, and this led to the drafting of an altogether new and revised Indian prisons law to replace that of 1894.[8]

State Governments have to set-up their own Human Rights Commission enacted by State Legislature. We mention here the states and their Chairpersons who have set-up Human Rights Commissions. It is strange that it has not been possible to cover all the States so far.

State Human Rights Commissions

15 states have set-up Human Rights commission so far.

State	*Chairperson's name*
Andhra Pradesh	Justice Shri B. Subhashan Reddy
Assam	Justice Shri Jailendu Nath Phukan
Himachal Pradesh	Vacant
Jammu and Kashmir	Justice Shri Ali Mohammad Mir
Kerala	Justice V.P. Mohan Kumar
Madhya Pradesh	Justice Shri D.M. Dharmadhikari
Maharasthra	Justice Shri A.D. Mane
Manipur	Mr. Justice W.A. Shishak
Orissa	Justice Shri D.P. Mohapatra
Punjab	Shri Justice R.L. Anand
Rajasthan	Shri Justice N.K. Jain
Tamil Nadu	Justice Thiru S. Thangaraj
Uttar Pradesh	Justice Shri A.P. Mishra
West Bengal	Justice Shymal Kumar Sen
Chhatisgarh	Shri Lal Jayaditya Singh

The State Commission shall consist of:

(a) A Chairperson who has been a Chief Justice of a High Court.
(b) One Member who is, or has been, a Judge of a High Court.
(c) One Member who is, or has been, a District Judge in that state;

(d) Two Members to be appointed from amongst persons having knowledge or practical experience in, matters relating to Human Rights.

The Headquarters of the State Commission shall be at such place as the State Government, by notification specify. Terms and other conditions are the same as of The National Human Rights Commission.

Appointment and Removal

The Chairperson and other Members of the Commission shall be appointed by the Government after obtaining the recommendation of Committee consisting of:

(a) The Chief Minister — Chairperson
(b) Speaker of the Legislative Assembly — Member
(c) Minister-in-charge of the Department of Home in the state — Member
(d) Leader of the Opposition in the Legislative Assembly — Member

Where there is a Legislative Council in a state, the Chairman of that Council and the Leader of the Opposition in that Council shall also be members of the Committee. No sitting Judge of a High Court or a sitting District Judge shall be appointed except after consultation with the Chief Justice of the High Court of the concerned state.

The Chairperson or any other Member of a State Commission can only be removed from his office by an order of the President in accordance with the procedure envisaged for the National Commission.

Officers and Staff of the State Commission

The concerned State Government shall make available to the State Commission an officer not below the rank of a Secretary to the State Government who shall be the Secretary of the State Commission alongwith such police and investigative staff under an officer not below the rank of an Inspector-General of Police and such other officers and staff as may be necessary for the efficient discharge of the functions of the State Commission. The State Commission may appoint such other administrative, technical and scientific staff as it may consider necessary.

Functions of the State Commission

A State Commission may inquire into violations of human rights only in respect of matters relating to any of the entries, enumerated in List II and List III in the Seventh Schedule of the Constitution. However, if any such matter is already being inquired into by the National Commission or any other Statutory Commission, the State Commission shall not inquire into the said matter. Subject to this, the powers, the procedure of investigation, inquiry and steps to be taken thereafter are the same as those of the National Commission.

The Act envisages that for the purpose of providing speedy trial to offences arising out of violation of human rights, State Government may with the concurrence of the Chief Justice of the concerned High Court specify for each District Court of Sessions to be a Human Rights Court to try such offences. For every Human Rights Court, the State Government shall Specify a public prosecutor appoint an advocate of at least seven years standing as a Special Public Prosecutor for the purpose of conducting cases in that Court.

The State Commission shall submit Annual Report to the respective State Government and may, at any time, submit Special Reports on any matter which in their opinion is of urgency or importance. It is enjoined on the state government to cause to lay on the Table of the respective State Legislature the Annual and Special Reports of the State Human Rights Commission.

CRITICAL EVALUATION: WE MENTION NOW SOME FACTS AND SUGGESTIONS

The Human Rights Commission has done a good work. We should all be proud of the Indian Judiciary role in the protection of human rights. Members of state human rights commissions in the country have to keep close to their hearts and minds, the judiciary's proactive approach to scrupulosity and overzealously guard the rights fundamental for human existence. Their orders and directions should secure the enlarged scope of the right to life to include within it the right to live with dignity, healthy environment, humane conditions of work, right to education, shelter and social security, right to know, adequate nutrition and clothing, pollution-free water, air and many other such rights. All these can be achieved through the machinery of efficient development administration.

1. Creating a Culture and Ethos of Human Rights—Realisation among People the Presence of Feeling of Human Rights

The Commission cannot begin to assert that its efforts have transformed the human rights ethos in the country or that it has as yet adequately developed a capacity to defend the least powerful of the citizens of India. But it can assert that its efforts have begun to strengthen the hands of the just and the compassionate, of whom there are legion in this country, in all States and in all walks of life.

2. Created awakening in Government to Fulfil Human Rights and Compensate for Human Rights Violations

To quote Justice Verma former Chairman, National Human Rights Commission: That statement remains substantially true even today. But in the course of the past decade, despite its inadequacies of which it is acutely aware, the Commission has—in the public estimation—evolved from being a body that was initially viewed with unconcealed skepticism to one that is widely viewed as an instrument of good governance, on which increasing reliance can and is being placed by the citizens of India to ensure the defence of their rights and the verities of the Constitution of their Republic.

3. Protection of Human Rights in Situation of Terrorism and Insurgency

The manner in which a State acts to exercise this right and to perform this duty can, however, have the most profound effect on the character of a society and the manner in which it treats issues of human rights and human dignity. Thus, the Supreme Court has observed in DK Basu vs. State of West Bengal that the "Challenge of terrorism must be met with innovative ideas and approach. State terrorism is no answer to combat terrorism. State terrorism would only provide legitimacy to terrorism: that would be bad for the State, the community and above all for the rule of law. The State must, therefore ensure that the various agencies deployed by it for combating terrorism act within the bounds of law and not become law unto themselves."

4. Suggesting Systematic Police Reforms to Protect Human Rights and Inject Good Governance

With every passing year, the evidence before the Commission mounts that there must be major police reforms in the country if the human rights situation is to improve, if the investigation work of the police is to be insulated from 'extraneous influences', and if the police is to regain the public trust that is essential for the proper discharge of its duties as a key element of the criminal justice system of the country.

Experience of the year 2002-03 confirms the earlier assessment of the Commission. The failure to investigate with integrity has, too often, resulted in a failure to provide justice. The Commission has, thus, continued to receive numerous complaints of police complicity in wrong-doing. No country can afford to let its criminal justice system slide downward in public trust and esteem. Institutions that function with integrity are the hallmark of a democratic society no less than are free and fair elections. It therefore becomes critically important that the basic reforms that are required for the greater good of the country must be implemented without prevarication or procrastination, setting aside considerations of political or other expediency.

The Commission therefore urges, once again, that the police reforms in respect of which it has made specific recommendations—and that are outlined in detail in its earlier annual reports and in its submissions before the Supreme Court in the case Prakash Singh *vs.* Union of India—be acted upon without further delay. The Commission earnestly requests that this matter be taken up at the highest political level in the country, in a non-partisan spirit, so that the over-arching need to act in furtherance of the Constitution and the Rule of Law is the sole guide in the consideration and implementation of the needed reforms.

5. Need of Human Rights Training for Civil Servants to Promote Good

Governance In July 2002, a meeting was held in the Commission, with the selected resource persons, to further discuss the modalities of the preparation of the manual and, thereafter, a suitable template was designed. The objectives of the manual are to:

- Sensitize District Magistrates/District Collectors/Deputy Commissioners on human rights issues;
- Sharpen their professional knowledge and skills and strengthen human rights values;
- Foster and promote a culture of human rights at all levels in district Administration;
- Provide a legal framework for enhanced respect for and protection of Human Rights at the district level; and
- Enable the District Magistrates/District Collectors/Deputy Commissioners to effectively meet the challenges of socio-political change and economic development in so far as these relate to the domain of their public duties.

ESSENTIALS

I. Rights and duties must be pursued simultaneously

Human rights education must include also the component of obligations towards others. Mahatma Gandhi, in a letter to Julien Huxley in 1947, had said:

> "I learned from my illiterate but wise mother that all rights to be deserved and preserved come from duty well done. Thus, the very right to live accrues to us when we do the duty of citizenship of the world. From this one fundamental statement, perhaps it is easy enough to define duties of man and woman and correlate every right to some corresponding duty to be first performed...."

2. Need of Genuine Leadership to Support Rights of Common Men

Common man in developing countries cannot enjoy the human rights as leaders both political and bureaucratic usurp all powers.

The objective knowledge, which has up till now been discovered by the man through scientific adventures is only said to be limited one. Our visionaries have given us in our religious books, that the knowledge measurable by the dimensional parameters, can be transferred and passed on from one generation to the other. Even its factual results can be verified and changed by the future scientist, but the subjective knowledge is not transferable and hence remains the prized possession of the vision and insight.

The man must remain with the essential limits for the existence of his family. The acquisition of wealth, by scams, and scandals, would ultimately take our people to mental pollution and the nation as a whole will be put to degradation, for which only the people in authorities would be responsible. It is a fact, in absolutism, that tendencies to give name and fame to money launderers, on political scenario of our country, should be discouraged in all compartments. At least we should not allow such persons to pull the strings, to unfurl the national flag, who so ever it may be. There are already under currents in our people that the battery of sycophants and jugglery of words, on such occasions, make such person enjoy the epithet of leaders or Netajee. As we see now that there is not dearth of leaders these days, while the Sewadar is none. We must see reason to discard such crooks, conferred with leadership, by their relatives. Otherwise fear that the list of essentials for their existence, would not limit to the foreign bank accounts only, but they would now be aspiring for transmission channel for their entertainments in the orbital trajectories of other planets in the family of sun.

With the change of times now, the imprints of elevated consciousness and covetous preciousness of our national mind, had been camouflaged with so many question marks, on our future citadels which have now come under the control of a vertical and greedy leadership. As all the cybernetics of our prospective developments, and all the struts and columns which are supporting our system to eliminate our people from drudgery and ignorance, to boost up the spirit and esteem of the Indian mind, have now come under pressure and are exposed to rust and cracks, by the so called leaders, whose patriotism has now mostly become a salable commodity, impregnated with diplomatic jugglery and a rank hypocracy. The common man is totally confused in the populous slogans of opportune politics which is taking the people to degeneration and denigration from the real focus.[9]

3. Need of Sensitizing Police Personnel through Education and Training

The commission has given high priority to the training and re-training of police personnel in human rights observance, so that they would reduce the violation of human rights by themselves and become better protector of human rights of others. On Commission's urge, with adequate governmental support the Sardar patel National Police Academy in Hyderabad has been emphasizing on human rights education. It is a major training center for I.P.S. officers. The Commission discussed with the Director Generals of Police of the States and Union Territories and the efforts have been successful that a three-tier model syllabus has been prepared for Constables, sub-Inspectors/Inspector, Deputy Superintendents of Police and other senior officers. This model syllabus has been circulated to all States and Union Territories with recommendation that they adopt it for training of police personnel.[10]

4. Need of Inculcating Ethical and Moral Values

The Modern world is marked by a widespread explosion of knowledge and tremendous achievements in Science and Technology, coupled with a general decline and reversal of human values as well as an alarming deterioration of moral and mental health both of individuals and societies. The recent spate of crimes, violence, terrorism and drug abuse make us aware of the significance of human values, without which human life losses all meaning. It is also evident that a mere economic prosperity and material wealth cannot result in a lasting well-being of mankind. The inner strength of mankind springs from within, which seems ill-nourished now.[11]

5. Emphasis on Human Rights Education in Universities

Education is an important human activity. It was born with the birth of the human race and shall continue to function as long as the human race exists. The importance of education can be specified by the saying "MAN" becomes "MAN" through education. It has been rightly said that without education, man is a splendid slave, a reasoning savage. Education fashions and models man for society. It signifies man's supreme position in societies. It teaches what man lives and struggles for. Aristotle says "Educated men are as much superior to uneducated as the living are to the dead." Epithets says Education is an essential concomitant of all human societies.

Education makes man rational, reliant, selfless, self-conscious, civilized, sociable and harmonious creature. It inculcates good habits in man and makes his life systematic, develops aspirations, ambitions and desires in him, makes him powerful and paves way for his development. In other words education opens a new world before the human beings.[12]

Colleges and Universities are supposed to provide extension services to the society as well as advice to the Government/agencies engaged in human rights. Universities are the bridges between the government and the community. What are the ways through which colleges and Universities can play an important role in protecting the violation of Human Right? There are many methods through which colleges and universities can play this role effectively. Let us analyze them.

We may suggest the following approach to make educational programmes practical and useful for protection of Human Rights:

(a) The existing educational institutions and programmes need to be consolidated and put to optimum use to serve the goals of development in the community as a whole including awareness about human rights.

(b) Provision of suitable educational facilities in backward areas and for the deprived groups and promotion of non-formal and Distance Education programmes at all levels in a systematic way are important to promote awareness about Human Rights.

(c) It is vital to transform the system of education qualitatively in terms of value content, standards and relevance to life. The role of education to promote humanistic outlook sense of brotherhood and a commitment to cultural human rights principles and ethical values need to be re-emphasized.

(d) The importance of human rights has to be adequately provided for developing young men and women for promotion of peace and development.

6. Research and documentation in Human Rights

The higher education system in India can take up research projects in different aspects of human rights and their violation in their catchments area. Their findings can be documented by one cell set-up specially for this purpose These documentation can be regularly sent to policy-making, planning and decision-making agencies quarterly. This would help in analyzing the

Human Rights Issues purely on the basis of facts and can bring forth solutions based on analysis of Data. In addition, case studies can be undertaken to throw lights on atrocities on Dalits, violence against women, and general violence of human rights in depth and true perspective.

7. Introducing Topics of Human Rights in Undergraduate and Post-graduate Education

To make the youth aware of Human Rights. The UGC must ensure that some topics of human rights suiting different areas of study should be incorporated by Universities and colleges in their syllabi of Human Rights Syllabus for practical orientation and not merely understanding theory.

8. Introducing Independent Teaching on Human Rights

In Disciplines like political science, sociology, public administration Human Rights papers can be introduced or set-up independent departments of Human rights to award M.A. Degree in Human Rights. At present many universities in India have set-up independent diploma, degree and post-degree courses for Human Rights.

Both the approaches are being implemented by many universities but their number is small. We have to introduce human rights programme in a big way especially in colleges and universities located in rural areas, tribal areas, urban slums and backward areas where they can observe actual situations of Human Rights in India.

9. Arranging Seminar on Different Areas of Human Rights through Experts from Different Disciplines by Engaging Interdisciplinary Approach

UGC, ICSSR, Nation and State Commissions for women should finance such Seminars liberally. These seminars must be focused and not simply a discussion house. The seminar must come out with definite suggestions which can be useful for agencies engaged in the implementation of Human rights. We must consolidate the reports of these seminars in Human Rights cell.

10. Lectures to Disseminate the Current Provisions of Human Rights

To Agencies like Judiciary, Police engaged in its implementation and the procedure to deal with human rights issues. It would be of great interest if the copy of the lectures is circulated among the audience. These lectures may be later on broadcasted for the benefit of general public through radio and Television.

11. Discussion with Opinion Leaders in Cities and Villages

Like Panches, Sarpanches, Chairmen Panchayat Samitis, Chairmen Zila Parishads (Both men and women), Municipal Commissioners, etc. The Universities and colleges can divide the catchment area and allocate to different/institutions the work of educating the masses about the scope and limitation of human rights. In addition, they can also bring to the notice of the executive agencies responsible for implementation of these human rights, the cases which have been ignored or action has not been taken. These may also be released to the press for wider use. These would create a movement wherein violation of Human Rights would be difficult.

12. Involvement of Students

Students team can be constituted after training in theory and practice of Human Rights which can go to different areas of cities and villages and impart education in Human Rights by discussion or lecture or informal methods. Students can be encouraged through:

(a) awarding some extra marks,
(b) giving some certificates which can help them in employment, and
(c) preference in admissions to higher education institutes.

Youth once motivated can create a momentum and people can get real education. Women faculty members and women students can mobilize public opinion and educate women about their rights/privileges. They can help the women in PRI system to prove their worth. Women studies centers wherever located can do a lot for women human rights. The need is to stress extension of education to the community.

PROBLEMS

Lack of Functional Autonomy and Independence

The National Human Rights Commissions generally do not possess any independence in their functioning, as there are several restrictions that are imposed by the statute itself or by the government in discharging their responsibilities. This casts doubts on the ability of the NHRC to conduct an impartial inquiry into charges of human rights violations against the government officials and departments.

Lack of Financial Autonomy

The NHRCs do not have finances and hence, are dependent upon the government for their funding. They are faced with severe financial crunch and hence it becomes difficult to sustain an institution of this stature.

Improper Selection of Members

The members who are selected are close to the government and hence, feel obliged to be soft with the government which has not only appointed them, but also exercises a good deal of power and authority to control their functions. This can also be done by appointing as members or other officials of the NHRC, from the former civil servants who have been loyal to government.[13]

Lack of Enforcement Powers

The NHRCs lack any enforcement powers that are needed to fulfill the direction they make to the government. In fact, the directions of the NHRCs are generally called recommendations, as their mandates do not give any more powers than making recommendation to the government.

However, G.Parmanand Singh feels that the presence of NHRC has at least made human right violation more visible and has enhanced public awareness about human values. It has also been taking all possible steps to promote a culture of human rights through media publicity, human rights seminars and human rights education for police, para-military and armed personnel and in the system of general education. At times, it has drawn commissions attention of concerned State governments to be accountable to human rights and bring human right violators to the book.[14]

Lack of Knowledge and Implications of Human Rights

Most of the people in India lack knowledge and an awareness about Human rights. This makes them tolerate the excesses of other people and government. This is more true with people living in villages, women, dalits, illiterates.

Machinery designed to ensure the protection of Human Rights is not adequate to tackle large number of personnel and People who are unaware of the structure and functions of such machinery—Human rights commissions at union and state levels are not so active as most of the persons appointed on these bodies are retired person. We must engage people in service and not people after retirement so as to provide dynamism as well as provide employment to new people.

There is centralization: Need of Decentralization—It is very difficult for people to come at headquarters to file their complaints for human right violations. The machinery dealing with Human rights need decentralization.

Universities, colleges and other institutions not involved in the education of Human Rights—Universities and colleges numbering about 12000, can bring a revolution if educational system is used of for the benefit of common man. Universities are dealing only with theoretical concepts and not providing extension services. Universities can do a lot provided the thrust is changed.

Politicians of whatever political parties they belong do not adhere to Human Rights and duties—They rather create fear and exploit the people for their interest. Politicians maybe made to understand that they should not indulge in Human Rights Violations rather they should maintain its dignity.

Facts:

(1) Violation of human rights is a regular features by persons in power or persons belonging to the under-world.
(2) Police violation of human rights is a recurring phenomenon.
(3) Judiciary takes a long time in deciding the cases of Human rights violations.
(4) Women and children are abused at every place.
(5) Minorities human rights are violated on one pretext or the other.
(6) Moral and ethical values to promote human rights are existing in name only. No practices of values are done.
(7) Materialism is mostly causing the violation of human rights.
(8) Human rights commission are slow and their composition is detrimental to human rights. Instead of appointing retired people, fresh persons may be appointed to inject dynamism.
(9) Even Government at the union and state levels are engaged in violation of human rights purely to continue in power.
(10) Enforcement machinery is dilatory and lack the desired powers.
(11) Punishment for human rights violation is very less causing encouragement to human rights violators.
(12) Rights and duties must be pursued simultaneously.

In interacting with the National Human Rights Commission, certain of the State Human Rights Commissions have expressed their unhappiness over the difficulties they are experiencing in terms of lack of support, both financial and otherwise. The Protection of Human Rights Act, 1993, envisaged a network of Commissions, at the National and State levels, working in complementarily with each other for the better protection of human rights in the country. Under the Act as it is at present, the National Human Rights Commission is not in a position to make any recommendations regarding issues before the State Human Rights Commissions. It was in light of this that an amendment to the Act was proposed by the National Human Rights

Commission with the aim of developing a mechanism that would govern inter-institutional relationships between the National Human Rights Commission and the State Commissions, including the grant of powers of superintendence to the former, similar to those under Article 136 of the Constitution. Strong Commissions reinforce each other, and add substantially to the creation of better governance and a more human society. It is therefore of great interest to the country as a whole that full support is extended by the Central and State Governments to the Commissions, in order to ensure that the scheme of the Act is respected and its objectives are achieved. The Commission should be viewed as instruments that contribute to the better protection of human rights, supplementing the work of Governments, it being an obligation of the State to protect the human rights of its people. The commission urges both the Central and the State Governments to keep this goal constantly in mind.

R.S. Kalha in his article, "Human Rights a victim of Global Politics" in *The Tribune* dated Oct. 14, 2006 mentioned that there is no single definition that would probably satisfy everyone. However, it is generally accepted that all human beings are born equal in dignity and rights. These are moral claims that are inalienable and inherent in every human being. It is these claims that when translated and articulated in various international in various international documents that form the core of our rights. It is possible that such a definition, when it assumes legal sanction, also becomes universally acceptable, but it should always be remembered that there is still a long distance between legal documentation and actual practice.

It was for such experiences, besides others, that the NHRC in its Annual Report for 2003-2004 recorded its regret over the delay on the state governments part in setting up or "providing necessary staff and infrastructure support" for the smooth functioning of the state commissions. It impressed upon the state governments the vital need to realize that it was "insufficient merely to designate or establish" the state human rights commission.

It is absolutely indispensable that their "quality must be ensured, both in terms of personnel and financial autonomy" and "they must be extended the support that they need if they are to fulfil the purpose envisaged for them" under the law.

The Tribune, dated Nov. 9, 2006 under the heading, "Rights panel member quits stated that: Mr. I.D. Bali, a senior advocate resigned in Nov. 2006, as member of the State Human Rights Commission in protest against the failure of the government to make the institutional functional. The resignation was handed over by him to the Governor, Mr. V.S. Kokje, at Raj Bhawan. Mr. Bali said the commission had virtually become defunct with no chairman, no staff and other infrastructure and no regular office. Meetings of the commission to take up complaints could not be held in the absence of chairperson and the government also did not appoint any acting chairperson after the exit of Justice N.K. Jain. As a result hundreds of complaints had piled up."

He said he had been a member of the commission for more than three years but during this period it properly functioned hardly for about four months. There was no point in continuing as a member of a defunct institution.

The previous BJP government had, in fact, scrapped the commission and it was reconstituted by the present government on the directions of the state High Court on a public interests litigation.

Though the UP Human Rights Commission has handled a large number of complaints, some resulting in directions in the nature of award of compensation or recommendation for disciplinary action against the errant public servants, the mounting deficit is a matter of concern. In the coming years, the state commissions' areas of interest and focus will not be confined to the traditional subjects of custodial deaths, custodial rapes, encounter deaths, rights of arrestees, human rights and prisons and women's rights.

Given the direction in which human rights law is heading, and for which policy the NHRC is also to be given credit, they would shoulder the responsibility in the areas as varied as right to healthcare, right to gainful employment, right to corruption-free governance, right to relief in times of man-made or natural disasters, right to food and potable water, right against sexual harassment or abuse, rights against child labour and child marriage, etc.

The growth and development of mankind depends on how well the human societies regulate their internal affairs and how they work for common welfare and the dignity of each individual.

The theory of natural law of existence depends largely upon the concept of inalienable and innate rights of man, commonly known as human rights. It is primarily for this reason that human rights are generally rooted in the cultural and political ethos of each free modern state in the present times.[15]

The Protection of Human Rights Act, 1993 is premised on the mutually reinforcing character of the efforts that are to be made by the Commission and by the Governments, both at the Centre and in the States. A 'Unity of Minds' is indeed required to ensure the better protection of human rights in the country.

Mere knowledge about human rights is not sufficient. An understanding as to how human rights can easily become vulnerable to abuse of various structures and processes of power is crucial. It may be added that understanding of abuse and misuse of power alone serves no purpose unless people in general and professionals in particular are imparted skills for protection and enforcement of these rights.

Thus, it becomes incumbent on the Union and State Governments to provide human rights to every citizen especially the under-privileged, Scheduled Caste, Scheduled Tribe, Women, etc. through good governance. The provisions of these rights to all would be the litmus test for good governance.

CONCLUSION

Human Rights are essential for the human beings for their survivals, development and dignity. The existing public administration has failed to provide the basic human rights inspite of UN declaration and the provisions in the Indian Constitution framed on 26th January 1950. What is the way to come out of this apathy and indifference of Indian administration. It was thought that Development Administration with its dynamic and creative qualities would change the existing deficiencies of Public Administration. But, development administration also could not provide basic rights to people. What is needed is to make development administration practical through administrative improvements and reforms so that this New Development Administration can do miracles so that people can get their due even after 61 years of Indian independence.

NOTES AND REFERENCES

1. Snehal Fadnoval Impact of Women Rights Movement on the Development of Human Rights Movements in South Asian Countries in the Institute of *Journal of Human Right*, Vol. III, No. 1, Nagpur.
2. G. Hargopal, "Good Governance: Human Rights Perspective", in T.N. Chaturvedi, Towards Good Governance, New Delhi, 1999, p. 51.
3. R.P. Dhokalia, External Human Values and World Religious, New Delhi, NCERT, 2001, p. 10.
4. Arjun Dev (ed.), A Handbook of Human Rights", Creative Learning Series, NBT, New Delhi, 2003, p. VII.

5. Sabira Khan, "Human Rights in India (Protection and Violence), New Delhi, Devika Publication, 2004, pp. 12-13.
6. Ved Marwah, Police and Good Governance: Promotion of Human Rights in T.N. Chaturvedi (ed.) Towards Good Governance, New Delhi, IIPA, 1999, p. 226.
7. NHRC, Annual Report, 1995-96, pp. 1-6
8. NHRC, *op. cit.*, p. 4.
9. Gurcharan Singh, Pollution of Purity of Environment, New Delhi, Deep & Deept, 2000.
10. R.P. Dhokalka, *op. cit.*, pp. 109-10.
11. *Ibid.*, Forewords, p. viii.
12. Vijaya Kumar and K.V. Rama Lakshmi, Protection of Social Sciences Education to Save Human Rights, *University News*, No. 15, 1999, p. 3
13. UNIFEM, Support Services to Counter Violence Against Women, 2002, West Bengal, New Delhi, pp. 7-11. (Sanhita)
14. Quoted in R.P. Dhokalia, *op. cit.*, pp. 109-10.
15. Justice Y.K. Sabharwal, "Human Rights—State Commission need teeth", in *The Sunday Tribune*, dated August 13, 2006.

CHAPTER 25

Organisational Development (OD) for Development Administration

Development Administration aims at strengthening organisational development through which all development activities are carried out. Thus organisational development in its structure, functions, personnel is *sine-qua-non* for the success of development programmes and development administration.

Even the best machine gets rusty without timely maintenance. Many aspects of the working of an Organization have to be examined, to evolve a modified design for an on-going organization, in order to ensure their efficiency. Development in information technology requires further dramatic organisational restructuring through organisational analysis. National competitiveness will increasingly depend on flexibility requiring fast responses from a government that is enabling rather than providing the directions for change.

Thus to keep organization efficient and economical through Organisational development is essential to make the development administration successful and achieve its objectives. "Organizations exists to enable ordinary people to do extraordinary things." Development Administration can strengthen organizations.

There have been continuous efforts on the part of successive Governments to mould the organisations to make them more responsive to the needs of the people and to make them more efficient. Ironically, these reforms have failed to inject necessary changes in organisational structures and processes. Organisational development is an important instrument to resolve these organisational issues and ensure success of development administration.

Organisational Development (popularly known as OD) is a systematic and educative approach to improve the organisational efficiency and effectiveness. It is a dynamic and continuous process to ensure insulation of organisation from being static.

Organisation Development is a new and dynamic approach, based on behavioural science knowledge to introduce planned change in the total organisation, with the objective of improving

CHART 25.1

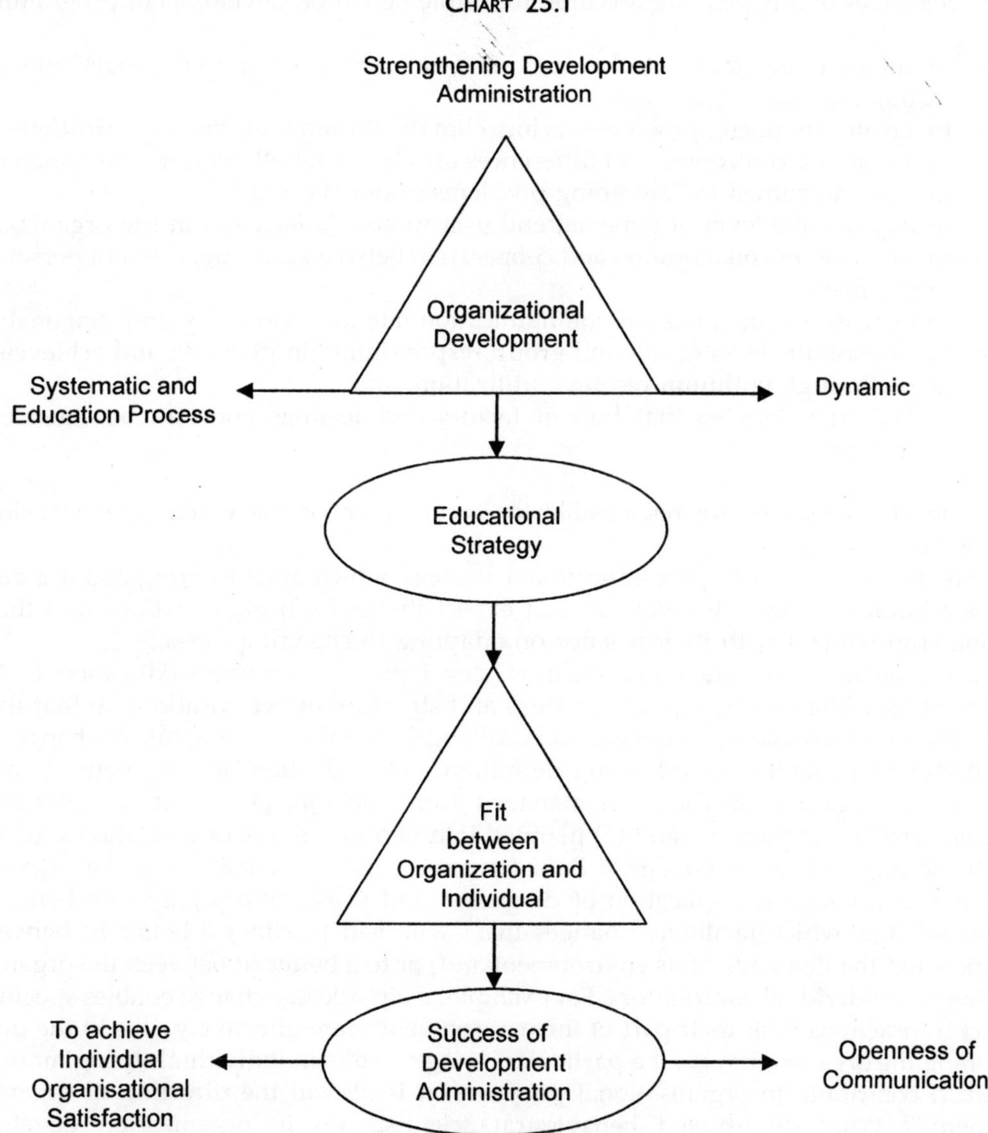

its health and effectiveness. It is based primarily on the action-research model, in which data is gathered, fed back to relevant teams, leading to joint diagnosis and action planning. The unit of change is not only individual, but mainly the teams and their relationships with other inter-dependent teams. Planned interventions are made in the process system, structure and goals of organisation. OD effort has to be related to the mission of the organisation and it must be oriented to bring about change in the culture and other relevant aspects of the total organisation. OD work is based on system theory, is a long-range effort, and is successful only when the top management is committed to it. To ensure success of OD interventions, it is necessary that there is an ongoing monitoring and review of plans and outputs.

The objectives of a typical organisation for implementation development programme are:

(i) to increase the level of the trust and support among individuals and groups throughout the organization;
(ii) to create an open, problem-solving climate throughout the organization—where problems are confronted and differences are clarified, both within group and between groups in contrast to "sweeping problems under the rug."
(iii) to increase the level of personal enthusiasm and satisfaction in the organization;
(iv) to attain better collaboration and cooperation between inter-department persons and/or groups;
(v) to increase the openness of communication laterally, vertically and diagonally;
(vi) to increase the level of self and group responsibility in planning and achievement of goals through optimum resource utilization; and
(vii) a shift in values so that human factors and feelings come to be considered as legitimate.[1]

All the above factors are responsible for acceleration of the working of Development administration.

OD is defined as a "complex educational strategy which aims to bring about a better fit between the human beings who work in and expect things from organizations and the busy, unrelenting environment with its insistence on adapting to changing times."[2]

Warren Bennis has called organization development "complex educational strategy intended to change the beliefs, attitudes, values and structure of organisations so that they can better adapt to new technologies, markets, and challenges, and the dizzying rate of change itself."[3] Richard Bechhard provides the following definition, "Organization development is an effort: (1) planned, (2) organization-wide, (3) managed from the top, (4) to increase organization effectiveness and health through, and (5) planned interventions in the organization's 'processes' using behavioural-science knowledge."[4] Paul Lawrence and Jay Lorsch describe organization development as a complex application of diagnoses and prescriptions based on behavioural-science knowledge, which facilitates changes that "will lead to either a better fit between the organization and the demands of its environment and/or to a better fit between the organization and the needs of individual contributors. For example, if a particular change enables specific units to conduct transactions with their part of the environment more effectively, it is in the direction of developing the organization . . . If a particular change results in individuals being more highly motivated to contribute to organisational purposes, it is also in the direction of organization development."[5] What do applied behavioural scientists do in organization development programmes? Lawrence and Lorsch emphasize the use of behavioural-science concepts and methods for gathering data and making diagnoses: "How differentiated is the organization? Where are problems occurring in achieving integration? How are members managing conflict? Where are the sources of individual satisfaction and dissatisfaction? Where do member feel the individual contribution contract is inadequate?"[6] Beckhard discusses four kinds of activities in organization development: "(1) working with teams on team development; (2) working on planning and goal-setting processes for individuals, teams and larger systems; and (3) working on educational activities for upgrading the knowledge, skills, and abilities of key personnel at all levels."[7]

Hyman K. Randall[8] has defined this concept as "Organization Development is a reorientation of man's thinking and behaviour toward his Work Organizations. It applies the scientific method and its underlying values of open investigation and experimentation to individual and work group behaviours as they are directed toward the solution of work problem. It views both man and change optimistically. It applies a humanistic value system to work behaviours. It assumes people have the capability and motivation to grow through learning how to improve their own work climate, work processes and their resulting products."

Alexander Winn defines the concept as a normative, re-education strategy intended to affect systems of beliefs, values, and attitudes within the organization, so that it can adapt better to the accelerated rate of change in technology, in our industrial environment and society in general. It also includes formal organisational restructuring, which is frequently initiated, facilitated and reinforced by the normative and behavioural changes.

OD depends, upon the purely internal initiative of the employees of an organization. The present emphasis in administration is only on structural changes, but structural changes without personnel dedication and capabilities would be of no avail. It is high time that we must introduce OD in all our big institutions to ward off the bureaucratic attitudes which result in low output and stagnation. We have the other techniques to achieve this objective, e.g. Management by Objectives, Participative Management. We must try to integrate all these techniques for optimising the efficiency of personnel in an organization.

The most important task of Personnel Department must be to give abundant evidence of its belief that personnel in an organization are key to development. This requires proper motivation of the employees. Motivation is of utmost importance as it constitutes the base for the management functions of planning and organizing. It has been noticed that the performance of the personnel either as individuals or members of a group is less as compared to their capabilities in terms of skills, abilities, and capacities. Finer, for example, states that demonstrated performance generally never exceeds more than fifty per cent of the individuals ability to perform.[9] Most individuals tend to balance their efforts around an assessment of relative costs (time and energy) and benefits.[10] A climate of creativity must be developed and maintained by management. Maiser and Hayes say that "the optimal climate for creativity ... is whatever human conditions optimal for individual freedom and self-expression in social setting.[11] It is the duty of the officers of such units to make the employees feel that their work and their association with a given organization represent a vehicle which will accelerate the achievement of personal goals as well as achievement of goals of the organization.

Henry B. Schacht, commenting on the changing trend in Organisational design and the use of human resources, has stressed that managers must learn to handle both the under-privileged and the bright young people, especially those who were calling for change. He states:[12]

> "What this means is shorter, flatter Organizations; it means responsive management; it means a true willingness to allow people to participate in setting their own destiny; it means that militaristically-oriented hierarchy that has characterized societies and most business enterprises is a thing of the past, and the quicker we recognize it the better ... all organizations will have to think of their key assets in terms of people and knowledge. People can be the most flexible of all assets; knowledge is the one thing that will give us insight into change and the consequences of change."

The success of this technique depends upon its proper implementation by the top executive. He has to use the information generated for the good of the organization. The emphasis in all OD programmes is on changing the attitudes, values and beliefs of employees, so that the employees themselves can visualise and implement organisational changes to promote efficiency.

In 1970's, Chris Argyris (Management and Organisation Development, New York, McGraw Hill, 1971), Partin J. Jennings (Current Perspectives in Organisation Development Readings, Mass, Addison Wesley, 1973), Noel Ticky Demix, Absorption or Renewal for the Future of the Organisation Development, Chapter 6 in W. Warner Burke (Ed.) and others came to the conclusion that OD includes Organisational improvements including interpersonal relationships. In 1980's, G. Thoman Cummings (Systems Theory for Organisation Development, Chichester, John Whiley, 1980 (ed.), W. Warner Burke, Trends and Issues in Organisation Development: Current Theory and Practices, Leo Jolla, Calif, University Associates, 1980, and others concentrated upon the system theory approach, rather than dealing merely with one of the components.

GOALS OF OD

The goal of OD is to ensure dynamic organisation to accommodate existing and potential problems so that the organisation remains action-oriented. The personnel working in these organisations would feel satisfied and are encouraged to make use of creative ideas with dedications. The OD builds trust and confidence among employees and there is no dichotomy between organisational goals and individual's goals. OD promotes both individual and organisational efficiency.

Organisation Development is one of the few recent educational programmes on all aspects of organisation as well as managerial responsibility. It has the potential to create an institution capable enough of coping with turbulent future. Probably the organisational sciences owe their rescue from classical malaise to especially the OD movement.[13]

Strengths of OD

1. It borrows freely from the proven procedures for improving functioning of individuals, groups and organisations.
2. Adoption of action research model, and a change strategy that focuses on the culture of work teams and the organisation make OD more powerful and relevant than most change strategies.[14]

Weaknesses of OD

1. Its over preoccupation with human and social dynamics of an organisation, to the detriment of attending to the task, technical and structural aspects, and their interdependencies;
2. Conceptual foundation underlying OD strategies have limitations, as most of their models were built on collaborative approach rather than on power, coercion and competition; and
3. OD has no quick remedies, and no shortcuts to total organisational improvement.[15]

CONCLUSION

In India, the Machinery of Development Administration has failed to live upto the expectations of the people and have not been able to optimise resources because the top management in India never find time for OD, rather remain busy with petty things, which can be done by other people. Most of the organisations in India have become dead woods and unproductive. In order to vitalise and rejuvinate them, we must plan OD to give fresh life to Indian administration and management. All the top administrators in India should be given training in Organisation Building and Development, so that they can make use of this training in maintaining the Organisational health, through consistent and persistent efforts. This would require the restructuring of the administrative apparatus, so that the top managers are really managers and not managers by virtue of merely sitting at the top. The managers must create the desired climate where the achievements of results become the main concern—both quantitatively and qualitatively. Development administration is bound to succeed in a soil where OD has been in existence and properly implemented.

Notes and References

1. S.K. Bhatia and Nirmal Singh, Principles and Techniques of Personnel Management/Human Resource Management, Deep & Deep, New Delhi, (2nd Ed., 2000), p. 106.
2. Wendell, L. French and Cecil, H. Bell, "Definition and History of Organization, Developments: Some Comments", Organisational Behaviour: A Book of Reading, ed., Keith Davis, Reading No. 38, McGraw-Hill Book Co., New York, 1977, pp. 247-55.
3. Warren G. Bennis: Organization Development: Its Nature, Origins and Prospects (Reading, Mass, Addison-Wesley Publishing Co., 1969).
4. Richard Bechkard: Organization Development: Strategies and Models (Reading, Mass: Addison-Wesley Publishing Co., 1969.
5. Paul R. Lawrence and Jay W. Lorsch: Developing Organizations: Diagnosis and Action (Reading, Mass, Addison-Wesley Publishing Co., 1969).
6. *Ibid.*
7. Bechard, *op. cit.*, p. 35.
8. Hyman K. Randhall, A Practical Approach to Organization Development through MBO, Ed. by Back and Hillmach, Wesley, 1972, p. 4.
9. H. Finer: Theory and Practice of Modern Government, p. 106.
10. Eli Ginzberg: "Perspective on Work Motivation", *Personnel*, Vol. 31, No. (July), 1959, pp. 48-49.
11. Maier Bennis, Organization Development: Its Nature, Origins and Prospectus, Reading, Mass: Addison-Wesley, 1969.
12. Henry B. Sachacht, Business Horizens, August, 1970, pp. 29-34.
13. R. Anuradha, Organization Development As a Theme of Seventies and Eighties, in *IJPA*, Oct.-Dec, 1988, p. 985.
14. R. Anuradha, Organisation Development as a Theme of Seventies and Eighties, in *IJPA*, Oct.-Dec., 1988, p. 982.
15. *Ibid.*

CHAPTER 26

Role of Management Techniques in Development Administration

In a liberalized economy and a knowledge society, the archaic, structure of Government has to necessarily undergo a change for Development Administration. The organisations have to become lean and thin. The staff has to become responsive and accountable. The institutions have to justify their existence by being result-oriented, customer-centric and transparent in approach. Words like cost cutting, downsizing or disinvestment, etc. are catching up but with lot of resentment and hostility arising within the affected organization. These negative responses take the process of change, two steps backward. Hence, there is a need for internalization of progressive goals of each organization by each member and fulfilment of these objectives with cost and time over runs to ensure efficient Development Administration. It has been rightly said that India does not suffer from resource problem in order to overcome its socio-economic ills, instead it is the management of the available resources which is the crux of the issue.

Training, motivation and ethical grounding of the personnel is a major challenge before development administration today. The top leadership has to take interest in developing its human resource capital by equipping them with technical and managerial skills. Problem-solving, creative thinking and ethical behaviour need to be encouraged systematically among public servants. No amount of tutoring can generate these miracles. Only self-driven desire to continuously improve upon one's achievements and abilities can change the destiny of an institution, a society and the country.

The author has rightly mentioned, "The Public expects services to meet their demands in terms of quality, accuracy, timeless and user-friendliness. People can no longer tolerate delays, bureaucratic mistakes or excessively time consuming and difficult procedures after waiting for more than six decades since India's independence. There is a need to make use of Management Techniques through Development Administration.

It is generally agreed by all concerned that the new policies of economic reforms, liberalization, privatization and globalization would require massive changes in the functioning of Government and its methodology to cope with the changed environment.

A large number of people in the developing countries including India continue to live in extreme poverty. They are still deprived of adequate food, clean water, and other basic necessities of life despite the massive administrative structure created to spearhead national development programmes.

The various centres of administration are created and powers have been conferred with the authority of law to discharge their duties in accordance with the law. They are required to manifest in their actions and performance that they are functioning for serving public interest, public good and public purpose with a sense of accountability and responsibility and not at public detriment. These are the features of Development Administration.

H.C. Saxena in his article, "Administration and the People: Higher Bureaucracy Needs Radical Reforms" in *MIG*, Oct.-Dec., 2000 mentions the following problems of administrative system:

- Too large and slow.
- Extremely rigid and mechanical.
- Consequently not flexible and adaptive to cope with change.
- Not innovative and enterprising.
- Low motivation and low morale.
- Low Accountability.
- Undemocratic.
- Lack of expertise.

The question arises as to how the developing countries can translate their aims and objectives enshrined in their constitution to change the lives of teeming millions suffering from abject poverty, disease, squalor, hunger, unemployment, and other socio-economic ailments. This is possible only if these countries are administered and managed efficiently through development administration. It requires an overhaul of the old administrative structure creating a new administrative set-up required for socio-economic development called development administration. Organizations are not mere structures but action systems. Action system is a structured device through which resources are mobilised and transformed by the use of certain skills and technology to produce pre-designed output. Increased productivity in the work of the developing countries depends to a great extent on the executive branch. The Executive Branch can pursue its objectives provided the prevailing administrative system is conducive to the socio-economic system. The design of an administrative system is a basic aid to the achievement of its primary objectives; if the design is unsound, the achievement of objectives is likely to fall short of expectation. Developed Administration can provide the means whereby the most effective use cart be made of the knowledge and skills of the personnel engaged in different activities. The benefits of modern science and technology can reach the people only if such services are properly planned and effectively implemented through development administration. An increase in the scientific nature of determination is an important factor in raising its efficiency.

The prevailing administrative set-up in the developing countries is in a state of crisis. Its design and methods are inadequate and outworn. There is a need to design an integrated management system which may cover the planning of work programmes, budget preparation, resource programming, reviewing and evaluating results and definitions of programmes and aims. Besides, obsolete methods of work must be improved or replaced. Our experience during the last three decades has demonstrated that the development plans have not been satisfactorily implemented because of inadequate administrative performance resulting from out-dated administrative system entailing organisational defects, lack of co-ordination, complex and cumbersome administrative and financial procedures, etc. These defects and deficiencies need to be corrected in order to bring about a sharp reduction in the administrative obstacles to development to bridge the gap between aspirations and performance through the use of development administration.

David Osborne and Tech Gabler have suggested the following responsibilities of development administration to fulfil its role:[1]

1. Crusading reformer, intent on transforming some aspect of community life according to preconceived notions of the ideal society;
2. Proactive policy formulator, ready with possible strategies to meet the unknown;
3. Social change-agent, ready to accept new ideals and push others into accepting them also;
4. Crisis manager, slow to burn out but quick to react and brilliant at immediate improvisation;
5. Dynamic programme manager, able to show new courses and adapts on-going arrangements;
6. Humanitarian employer, treating staff with respect and meeting out even-handed justice;
7. Political campaigner, responsive to public needs and champion of public causes;
8. Competent administrator, ensuring effective performance with minimum political embarrassment;
9. Interest broker, choosing among competing interests and reconciling all parties to the outcome;
10. Public relations expert, adept at building up support, showing his area to advantage;
11. Speedy decision-maker, oriented to assume responsibility and clear instructions;
12. Constructive thinker, not easily led astray by others who would want to make up his mind for him; and
13. Optimistic leader, not easily discouraged in adversity, but able to command attention and stimulate subordinates.

Thus, there is a need to introduce development administration to ensure social change and modernization.

NEED FOR MANAGEMENT TECHNIQUES FOR DEVELOPMENT ADMINISTRATION

Emphasizing the need for management techniques in improving the system of development administration. Mr. Mohan Kanda, Vice-Chairman and Managing Director, Andhra Pradesh Fisheries Corporation, Hyderabad, rightly says: "Government activity in our country is so pervasive and vast, in terms of the range of functions, the number of functionaries, and the areas of operation, that it would be risky to fail to appreciate the need for rationalisation of the process both of decision-making and of implementation of policies. To resist, mindlessly, the need to import scientific techniques to meet this need is to resign ourselves to chaos."

CHART 26.1

Management Technique in Development Administration

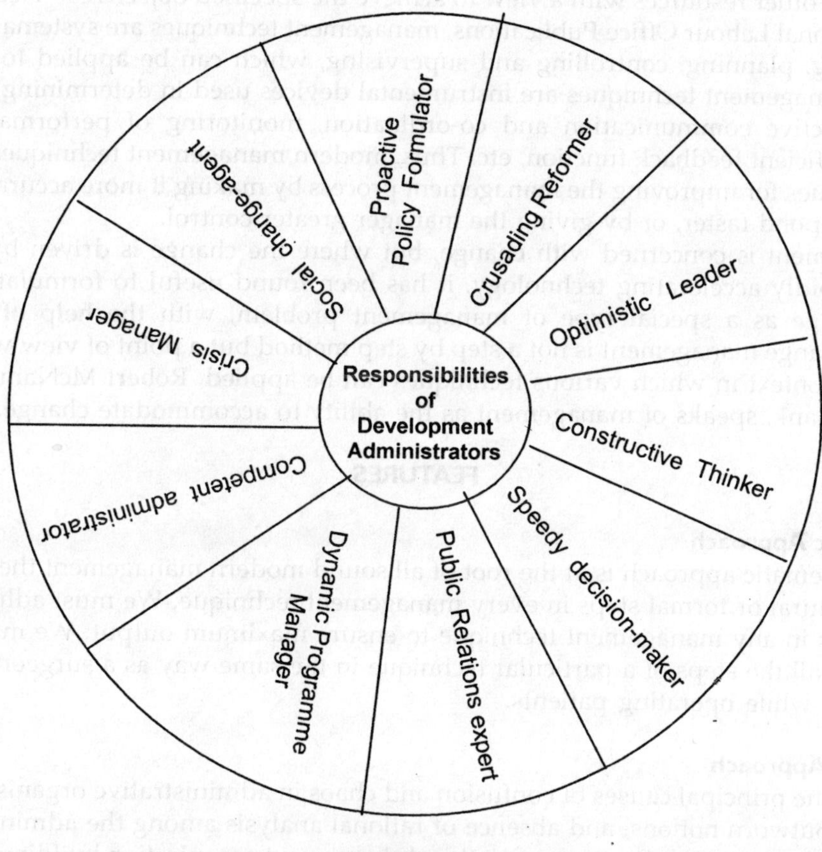

MEANING

In order to understand the meaning of 'management techniques', we must be clear about the two concepts, namely, 'management' and 'techniques'. There are many definitions of Management, and some of the important ones are quoted here:

"Management may be defined as the art of securing maximum results with a minimum of efforts so as to secure maximum prosperity and happiness for both employer and employee and give the public the best possible service."[2]

Peter F. Drucker has rightly pointed out that "Management is the crucial factor in economic and social development. It was obvious that the economists' traditional view of development as a function of savings and capital investment do not produce management and economic development. On the contrary, management produces economic and social development and with its savings and capital investment. It becomes apparent that the developing countries are not underdeveloped, they are under managed.[3]

Now, let us define 'Techniques'. Techniques are methods of accomplishing a desired aim or goal or purpose. It is the ability to solve technical details.

Thus, we can say that management technique is a set of procedural steps which may be loosely stated as embodying a multiple idea content and which are either concerned with decision-making in general or with decisions relating to planning, organising or controlling of human and/or other resources with a view to achieve the specified objectives.[4] According to one of the International Labour Office Publications, management techniques are systematic procedures of investigating, planning, controlling and supervising, which can be applied to management problems.[5] Management techniques are instrumental devices used in determining goals and for providing effective communication and co-ordination, monitoring of performance, effective supervision, efficient feedback function, etc. Thus, modern management techniques, in actuality, are the techniques for improving the management process by making it more accurate, by making the process respond faster, or by giving the manager greater control.

Management is concerned with change, but where the change is driven by government policy and rapidly accelerating technology, it has been found useful to formulate and control desirable change as a special type of management problem, with the help of management techniques. Change management is not a step by step method but a point of view which is useful to clarify the context in which various techniques can be applied. Robert McNamara, President of the World Bank, speaks of management as the ability to accommodate change.

FEATURES

1. Systematic Approach

The systematic approach is at the root of all sound modern management theory. There are a set of procedural or formal steps in every management technique. We must adhere rigorously to all the steps in any management technique to ensure maximum output. We must ensure the application of all the steps of a particular technique in the same way as a surgeon makes use of his techniques while operating patients.

2. Scientific Approach

One of the principal causes of confusion and chaos in administrative organisations is blind adherence to outworn notions, and absence of rational analysis among the administrators. Such an atmosphere is not conducive to organisational change and organisation building. Management techniques transplant the scientific method in theory and practice of management. In a wide sense, any method of investigation by which a systematic knowledge is acquired is called a scientific method. Therefore, the management techniques introduce the scientific approach in management through careful and accurate classification of facts and observation of their correlation and sequence.

3. Ecological Approach

Public Administration affects and is affected by the macro, intermediate and immediate environment. Therefore, the management techniques have to be adapted to suit the ecology of a particular organisation. These techniques should not be adopted but adapted to suit the organisational environment to attain maximum output/efficiency/productivity.

"Productivity improvement strategies developed in the United States may not be applicable in Asia because they do not take into consideration differences in the number of constraints, the nature of the constraints and the length of time required for implementation."[6]

CHART 26.2

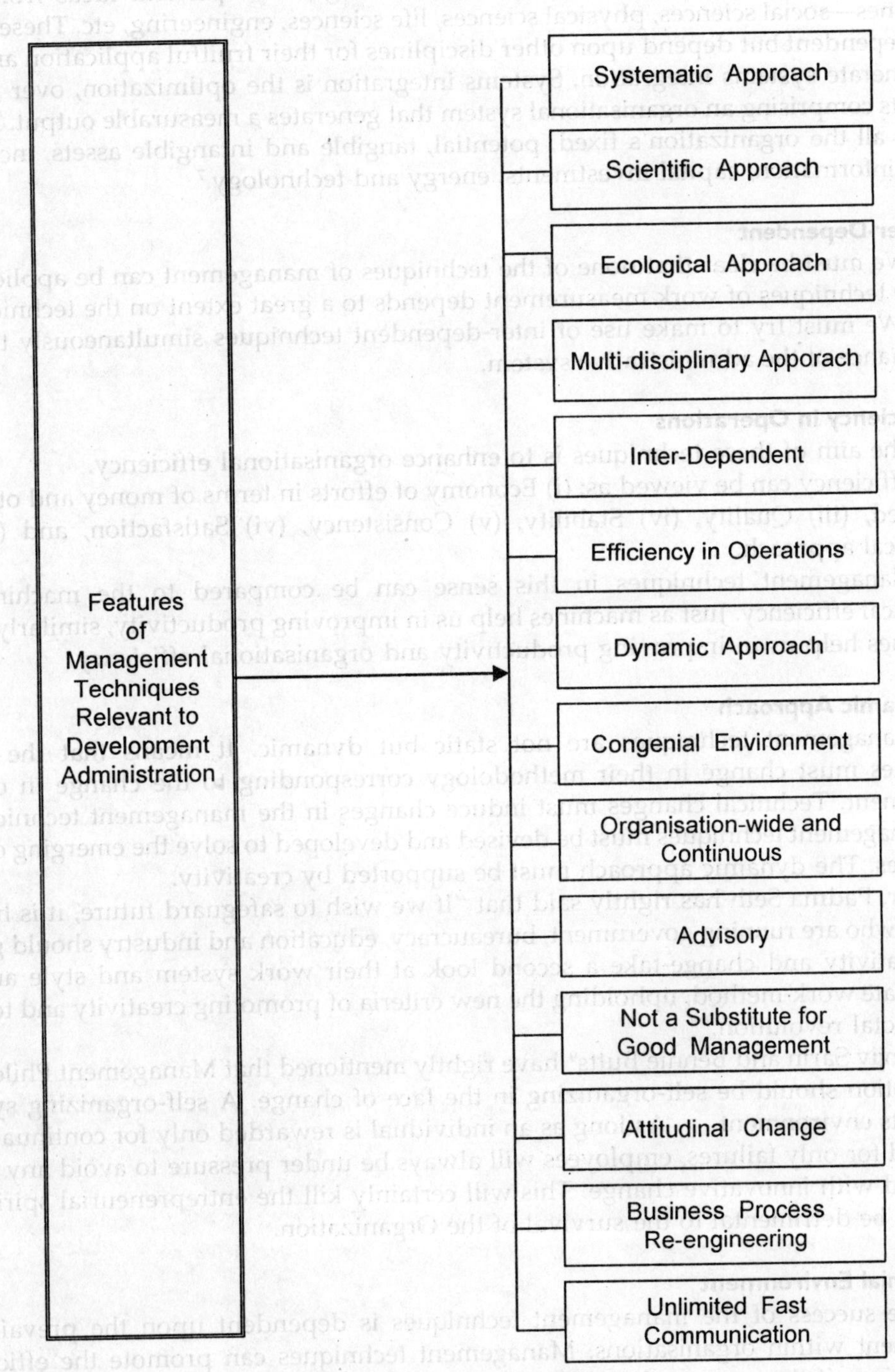
Features
of
Management
Techniques
Relevant to
Development
Administration
Systematic Approach
Scientific Approach
Ecological Approach
Multi-disciplinary Apporach
Inter-Dependent
Efficiency in Operations
Dynamic Approach
Congenial Environment
Organisation-wide and
Continuous
Advisory
Not a Substitute for
Good Management
Attitudinal Change
Business Process
Re-engineering
Unlimited Fast
Communication

4. Multi-disciplinary Approach

Management techniques employ the knowledge, concepts and ideas from a number of disciplines—social sciences, physical sciences, life sciences, engineering, etc. These techniques are not independent but depend upon other disciplines for their fruitful application and results. This will generate systems integration. Systems integration is the optimization, over time, of all the elements comprising an organisational system that generates a measurable output. These elements include all the organization's fixed, potential, tangible and intangible assets, including people, money information, capital investments, energy and technology.[7]

5. Inter-Dependent

We must be clear that none of the techniques of management can be applied in isolation, e.g., the techniques of work measurement depends to a great extent on the technique of method study. We must try to make use of inter-dependent techniques simultaneously to improve the performance of the administrative system.

6. Efficiency in Operations

The aim of these techniques is to enhance organisational efficiency.

Efficiency can be viewed as: (i) Economy of efforts in terms of money and other resources, (ii) Speed, (iii) Quality, (iv) Stability, (v) Consistency, (vi) Satisfaction, and (vii) Aesthetic rhythmical approach.

Management techniques in this sense can be compared to the machines and their mechanical efficiency. Just as machines help us in improving productivity, similarly management techniques help us in improving productivity and organisational efficiency.

7. Dynamic Approach

Management techniques are not static but dynamic. It means that the management techniques must change in their methodology corresponding to the change in organisational environment. Technical changes must induce changes in the management techniques. Besides, new management techniques must be devised and developed to solve the emerging organisational challenges. The dynamic approach must be supported by creativity.

Mr. Padma Seth has rightly said that "If we wish to safeguard future, it is high time that all those who are running government, bureaucracy, education and industry should get concerned with creativity and change-take a second look at their work system and style and evolve an appropriate work-method, upholding the new criteria of promoting creativity and total change—if not a total revolution."[8]

Sanjiv Sarin and Bennie Butts[9] have rightly mentioned that Management Philosophy of the Organization should be self-organizing in the face of change. A self-organizing system adapts itself to its environment . . . As long as an individual is rewarded only for continual success and penalized for only failures, employees will always be under pressure to avoid any risks usually associated with innovative change. This will certainly kill the entrepreneurial spirit and, in the long-run, be detrimental to the survival of the Organization.

8. Congenial Environment

The success of the management techniques is dependent upon the prevailing internal environment within organisations. Management techniques can promote the efficiency of the Organisations if the personnel at all levels are keen and willing to improve the efficiency. The benefits of the management techniques can come if there is earnestness and sincerity in their application by the upper echelons in administration.

9. Orsanization-wide and Continuous

Management techniques must be used in improving the operations of entire organisation involving a spectrum of different types and levels of activities in a systematic way. Besides, concentrating on their internal performance, we may also examine the impact of distant environmental factors which promote or limit the performance of the organisation. Management techniques must take into consideration environment factors before suggesting organisational changes. It should not be understood that piece-meal measures for reform may not be adopted, but such measures should be in consistency with the vision of larger reforms and should be incorporated, at a later stage in a more comprehensive plan. The ultimate objective should be in favour of institution building rather than case work.

10. Advisory

The Management technique experts must function in advisory capacity. They must help the management with the implementation of improvements. They should not have direct responsibility in executive operations. Management experts cannot take executive decisions. They merely make recommendations for consideration by the management.

11. Not a Substitute for Good Management

Management techniques can serve the management through the various techniques which can help the development administrators in effective planning, implementation and evaluation. These should not be taken as panacea for all the management crisis. These techniques do not provide a magic wand. Techniques cannot create morale and motivation among the employees of an organisation.

12. Attitudinal Change

Management techniques require that the staff should have a positive attitude towards change. Mr. Krish Pennathur has rightly said that "Productivity is primarily an attitude of mind; an attitude of welcoming a change for the better; an attitude of looking at things afresh so as to explore the scope for improvement; an attitude of making the optimum use of available resources towards the achievement of a specified aim. Only after the proper climate has been created through the right attitude of mind can the concepts and techniques of productivity be applied to functional areas."

The radical reorientation in the concepts, ethos, perception and attitude of the employees would make the effective ground ready for the physical application of these techniques.

13. Business Process Re-Engineering (BPR)

Hammer and Champy, the early proponents of BPR concept, define reengineering as: "The fundamental rethinking and radical redesign of business process to achieve dramatic improvements in critical, contemporary measures of performance such as cost, quality, service and speed."[10]

14. Unlimited Fast Communication

With the introduction of internet, and information technology communication has surpassed distance.

CLASSIFICAITON

Management techniques can be classified in different ways. For example, they can be grouped according to the outlet and the department in which they are applied as, for example, marketing techniques, production techniques and purchasing techniques. This does not, however, cover all techniques. For example, where would we place the techniques of brain-storming or critical examination? An alternative can be classification according to parent discipline.

Clay gives a classification based on the objective of the technique, i.e., what does the technique hope to achieve? He mentions the following eight objectives which various management techniques attempt to achieve.[11]

(a) Detection

To find out or discovering something, e.g., what is happening or what is wrong? We can include here techniques of Input-Output Analysis, Attitude Survey, Production Study, Activity Sampling, Critical Path Examination, Break Even Analysis.

(b) Evaluation

To measure or estimate the value of an item—We can include here techniques of Evaluation, Work Measurement, Work Estimation, Performance Appraisal, Cost-Benefit Analysis.

(c) Improvement

To improve performance—We can include here techniques of Management by Objectives, Method Study, Value Analysis, etc.

(d) Optimisation

To optimise performance—We can include here techniques like Linear Programming, Operations Research, etc.

(e) Specification

To specify a desired value or situation or action—We can include here techniques of Strategic Planning, Office and Plan Layout, Designing, etc.

(f) Control

We can include here such techniques as Cost Control, Credit Control, Labour Control, Budget Control, etc.

(g) Communication

To communicate information—We can include here such techniques as Incentive Schemes, Visual Aids, Suggestion Schemes, Report Writing, Communication Theory, Information Theory, Management Information, etc.

(h) Demonstration

To physically show something—We can include here such techniques as Programmed Learning, Job Instruction, Management Development and Training, etc.

This achievement criteria tells us that these techniques can help us in finding something in evaluating the performance, in improving the performance, in optimising the performance in specifying a desire value of a situation, in controlling a variable, in communication or in demonstration.

The management techniques can also be classified in terms of the various resources of any organisation, viz., human, material, machinery and equipment, money and time. As such, some of the techniques which can be applied to bring about increased managerial capability, efficiency, effectiveness and productivity can be depicted as shown in Chart 26.1

The Chart 26.2 would show that a technique is applied in one form or the other at all the three levels of management. Because the lowest level has to perform operational functions, management techniques like Work Study, Network Analysis, Capacity Utilisation Studies are adopted. At the middle level, where the policy is executed, some more important techniques like Manpower Planning, Cost-Benefit Analysis, Statistics and Forecasting, etc., are applied to effect improvements. The top management uses more strategic techniques like Technological Forecasting, Performance Budgeting, Operational Research Studies, etc.

P.R. Dubhashi suggests the following to inject administrative reforms:[12]

1. The civil servant should be allowed to function in their allotted field without any interference and according to the Rule of Law. This is the concept of the independence of the civil service similar to the concept of independence of the judiciary.
2. Transparency in administration by making information about administrative decisions available to the citizens. Information Act, 2005 suggests that Administration should be open and accessible.
3. Tightening of the machinery of administrative vigilance.
4. Changing administrative orientation-making administrators, facilitators rather than controllers.
5. Simplifying administrative procedures and making them citizen-friendly.
6. Abolition of obsolete laws and legal provisions.
7. Reforms in the judiciary to eliminate delay in disposal of cases and huge tendencies.
8. Greater decentralization of administration in every sphere and at all levels.

CHART 26.3

Different techniques used in Management of Resources

1. Human resources	1. Organisational analysis 2. Job evaluation 3. Training 4. Incentive schemes 5. Suggestion schemes 6. Method study 7. Work Measurement
2. Material	1. Inventory control 2. Value analysis

	3. Standardisation
	4. Material Handling
	5. ABC Analysis
3. Machinery and equipment	1. Method study
	2. Value analysis
4. Space and building	1. Layout planning
	2. method study
5. Money	1. Cost-benefit analysis
	2. Budgetary Control
	3. Performance budgeting
6. Time	1. Method Study
	2. Work Measurement
	3. Net work analysis (PERT/CPM)

Source: Management Techniques, S.L. Goel and Shailini Rajneesh.

CHART 26.4

Management Techniques and Various Levels

Levels of Management	Activities of Management
Passive Regulatory Lower	Service-providing
Passive Regulatory	Network analysis
Functioning	Work study
Short-term	Simulation studies
	Capacity Utilization studies
	Behavioural science
	Information systems and record linkage
Middle:	
Structural Medium-term	Statistics and forecasting
	Manpower Planning
	Demand Models
	Cost-benefit analysis
	Simulation studies
	Allocation Models
	Systems Analysis
Higher: Organization Long-term	Technological Forecasting
	Systems Analysis
	Strategic Studies
	Programme Budgeting
	Cost-benefit analysis
	Manpower Planning
	Statistical Trends

Source: WHO: Public Health Paper, (55) Modern Management Methods and the Organization of Health Services, Geneva, 1977, pp.15-16.

Dr. K. Kasturirangan, Chairman, Indian Space Research Organisation/Secretary, Department of Space, Government of India, has rightly said that "There are no short cuts or magic in the nation-building task through development administration. We have to learn to work effectively in a network, extending mutual faith and goodwill and achieve excellence as a team. In the knowledge-based society of the future, success comes to those who can organize networks of multi-function and multi-disciplinary systems which can deliver complex products or services, with increasing efficiency and productivity."[13]

Let us discuss some of the important management techniques:

A. PERT/CPM

"Basically PERT and CPM are techniques of project management to ensure effective planning, scheduling and control. These techniques can be used for any project, where the start and the finish of the project can be identified, e.g. installation of plant and equipment, construction of a building, town planning, etc."

There are a number of techniques which can help us in ensuring implementation of Plan, Programmes and Projects. PERT/CPM are important techniques dealing with the development of Integrated Planning, Scheduling and Control System of Programmes and Projects. These help the management in getting the projects completed in time. It also helps in early completion, through rescheduling or deploying additional resources. These techniques have been developed from Gantt Charts designed by Henry Gantt around 1900 and Milestone Charts.

PERT methodology is scientific in character as can be judged from the systematic, logical, and mathematical basis behind it. It Provides a means for bringing about a common understanding of what is to be done, by whom, when and for what purpose, amongst all personnel associated directly or indirectly with the programme/project.

Basically, PERT and CPM are techniques of project management to ensure effective planning, scheduling and control. These techniques can be used for any project, where the start and the finish of the project can be identified, e.g. installation of plant and equipment, construction of a building, town planning, etc.

PERT, an acronym for "Programme Evaluation and Review Technique" was designed as a means to plan and accelerate the development of the Polaris Ballistic Missile Project of the USA Navy. This technique was developed with the help of management consulting firm 'Booz Allen and Hamilton'. The Navy claimed a reduction of 30 per cent in project's execution time.

Closely akin to PERT, but developed independently, is the technique known as the Critical Path Method (CPM). This technique was first developed by James E. Kelley of Remington Rand and Morgan Walker of the Du Pont in 1957 for Planning and Scheduling of construction projects of the E.I. Du Pont de Numerous Company.

Initially, the two techniques had many differences. Today, these differences have narrowed down and we can say that these techniques are complementary to each other. Today, the terms PERT and CPM are used almost synonymously as Network Techniques. With minor modifications both have given rise to several other programmes such as PEP (Programme Evaluation Procedure), LCES (Least Cost Estimating and Scheduling) and SCANS (Scheduling and Control by Automated Network Techniques) is a managerial device which can satisfy a variety of needs, such as systems design, planning and control. The network is a composite refinement of a number of charting techniques, dating back at least as far as the use of the Gantt Chart, but made more frequently useful today because of the use of computer capabilities in applying the technique. The network and related techniques are particularly effective control devices for complex projects, especially in large development and construction projects. Since older scheduling techniques have never enjoyed much success in connection with these kinds of project management.

Let us now mention the main difference between the two, i.e. PERT and CPM.

(a) PERT is event-oriented while CPM is activity-oriented.
(b) In CPM, times are related to costs, while in PERT, this is not done.
(c) PERT is used where the emphasis is on shortening and controlling projects execution time without considering the cost implications. CPM is used were the emphasis is on obtaining the trade-off between cost and completion date for large projects.
(d) Only one time estimate is given in CPM for each set of activities leading to a given event, while in PERT three time estimates-most likely, most pessimistic and most optimistic times are given.
(e) CPM assumes previous experience with the work necessary for the completion of each event. This is not necessary in PERT.

Advantages

- These techniques help the management to ensure effective planning, implementation and review of projects. It provides a visual and, therefore, more easily grasped record of the logical progression of activities involved in a project.
- The network diagrams are intelligible and depict the complex interrelationships of activities which comprise a project.
- Network techniques focus our attention on those activities which need our top priority to accomplish results.
- CPM helps the executives to estimate the cost of projects realistically.
- These techniques ensure the timely completion of the projects.
- These techniques can help us in locating the factors responsible for the slow progress of the project. A timely action can help the executives to ensure timely completion.
- These techniques help the executives to make rational decisions.

Conclusion

Like other techniques, networking has both strengths and weaknesses. The strengths include simplicity, by bringing simple order out of a mass of detailed data, which could be confusing; universality of project coverage, especially for one time projects; a good basis for decision analysis; an increased reliability of data for purposes of forecasting; the charts are relatively easy to update and flexibility is evident in that portion of a network which can easily be changed to reflect programme changes. Some of the weaknesses of networking are that accuracy is only as valid as the time estimates; the reliability of the time estimates; sometimes the concept of slack and network families is difficult for all levels of management to grasp; and since a large project requires a considerable amount of data, the element of cost may be significant one.

The present expansion of major new development programmes, particularly those associated with family planning, food and agriculture, provide unusual opportunities for the innovative application of networking techniques. At major policy levels, the techniques can be used to analyse and test the feasibility of all major operational aspects of broad plans and programmes. After approval of programmes, the techniques can provide administrative controls at the highest national, regional and sectoral levels. At project levels, their effective application can provide the basis for realistic, current activity control. The use of these techniques has grown explosively on a world-wide basis in recent years. The potential for even more extensive applications is almost unlimited

(B) MANAGEMENT INFORMATION SYSTEM (MIS)

Significance

In the present era of information technology dominated environment, the need for acquisition, processing, storage, retrieval and dissemination of information is gaining utmost importance. With the advent of revolutionary means of electronic communication, the world-wide web, the shape and method of rendering information and sharing of the same are undergoing a revolutionary change. This has its great potentialities as well as dangers.

There is more than a subtle semantic difference between data "information and intelligence." Data consists of isolated or independent observations of attributes or events that carry little meaning when considered alone. The aggregation of data over time, space and populations, and in the context of decisions that can or should be made, constitute information for the planner, manager and evaluation. It is the transformation of information through integration with experience and perceptions based on social and political values as well as on constraints that produce intelligence, an aggregation of internalized knowledge, that provides the context in which policy-makers, politicians and decision-makers act. Unless data is refined and expressed as information, that in turn can be used as a basis for intelligence, it is unlikely to influence choices; and unless in choices, the potential value of indigenously acquired viable data is recognised the choices are unlikely to reflect accurately the functional and practical relationships between needs, resources and use.

Modern technology has been able to make a major contribution towards improved management practices, with respect to information systems. The contribution is possible because of two factors: firstly, the generally increased sophistication of management theory and practice, permitting the identification of information needs and uses; and secondly, the development of electronic data processing permitting the analysis of huge quantity of data in a short time to permit use.

The significance of information can be seen from the Nepoleonic Phrase—an army marches on its stomach and the administration marches on information. Information is the life blood of an organization. Information is .the data transmitted before or after processing. Management is the planning, implementation and control of the use of a set of resources to achieve objectives. A system is a set of sub-systems having independence so as to form a complex unity. Management Information System is thus a system in which required data are collected, analysed and transmitted to help the managers at various levels in the process of planning, implementation and evaluation. According to R.R. Duersch: "It is a system which provides management with the information it requires to monitor progress, measure performance, detect trends, evaluate alternatives, make decisions and to take corrective action."[14]

Information is the planner's raw material, forming the basis for the diagnosis, structuring his objectives and permitting him to evaluate the programme efficiency and effectiveness. Information is the coin of the management realm being the essential link between means and ends. It can be studied, analysed, organized, stored for future reference, summarised and/or displayed. Information is substantially different from mere data in that data is raw information, while information is the aggregate of facts or data organized into knowledge or intelligence. One of the roles of management must be to sift out the information found within the data, and even before, to ensure that the data collected will in fact furnish information needed. Peter Drucker has rightly said that the manager has a specific tool information.[15] It has been rightly mentioned that "Information is now recognized as a valuable resource and has been termed as one of the 8 m's-men, materials, machine, money, methods, markets; moments and messages—a term used for information." Information is a relative term. To quote Harper Marion: "Information may involve anything from the most minute and finite to the Universal. Processing information today calls not only for distinguishing the forest from the trees but distinguishing leaves and chlorophyll—while still not losing sight of forest."[16] The degree to which a planner can be successful in terms of the provision of services will depend upon the degree to which he is able to obtain information about them, which is valid and reliable. The term system has been defined as a coherent, integrated whole, being a combination of number of entities or elements. Similarly, in the information area, there are a number of elements which have to be considered in an integrated manner, as components of one system, so that they are viewed in totality as means of providing administrator with required information in the appropriate form and at an appropriate time.

As the universe is saturated with information, administration must select the pertinent information for their programmes, otherwise rational policy or decision may not be possible. This technique is tailored to provide such information to the decision-makers, which is most relevant, accurate, complete, concise, timely, economic, reliable and efficient. A good information system provides data for monitoring and evaluating the programmes and gives the requisite feedback to the administrators and planners at all levels.

Meaning

"A management Information System is a combination of planned procedures, processes, suitably designed forms, an appropriate organization structure and managers who are capable of utilising the facts which are produced in a suitable form."

According to G. Murdich, "MIS is a system that collects, stores, processess data and provides information to managers for planning, controlling and decision-making."[17]

Prof. Murdich has rightly said that MIS would ensure in:

(a) Providing to managers information on the impact of men, money, materials, equipment and facilities on the various systems and the business as a whole.
(b) Maintaining Central Data banks and model banks for integrated planning, control and decision-making.
(c) Sensing, through designated communication channels, the effectiveness of systems operations.
(d) Providing timely feedback to managers on performance of all systems by means of summary, key elements and exception reports.
(e) Scanning the environment by formal intelligence operations to keep managers informed of environmental changes impinging the various systems of the business.[18]

A Management Information System (MIS) has been defined as "the combination of human and computer-based capital resources which result in the collection, storage, retrieval, communication and use of data for the purpose of efficient management of operations."[19] During September-December 1962, the Advanced Systems Development Division of IBM conducted a survey to determine the scope and goals of an Advanced Management Information System. The major information problems were found to fall into seven categories:

1. Complexities in the information flow cause major communication problems and inhibit responsiveness and growth.
2. *Duplication of effort*: Identical reports are generated, data files are created and maintained at several locations.
3. *Variations in field processing*: At the present time field locations vary the processing of similar information and vary information flows.
4. *Inaccessibility of data*: Useful and necessary data are available, but often in a form or location that makes them uneconomical and unfeasible to retrieve.
5. *Time lapse*: Data are simply not being moved fast enough. Time lags are caused by mail, multiple audit points and varying closing periods. In many cases the data are no longer of value when they are made available.
6. *Inaccurate sources data*: The sheer volume of data makes it humanly impossible to be consistently accurate and efficient.
7. *Limited information support*: The relation between the creation of information and the servicing of all those who could benefit from it is poor?[20]

Gordon B. Davis and Margrethe H. Olson define MIS as an integrated, user-machine system for providing information to support operations, management and decision-making functions in an organization. The system utilises computer hardware and software, manual procedures, models for analysis, planning, control and decision-making, and a database.

Management Information System helps in integration of organisational information processing to avoid inconsistent and incompatible data from multiple information system. The MIS concept is now a federation of sub-systems within the overall plan, standards and procedures.

The development of suitable techniques for a good information system would improve the capacity of administrators to take appropriate policy decisions. The information system may not serve the purpose if the administrators are not committed to use the information constructively. The administrators should use the available information sensibly and logically, than to construct complex information systems, which may not finally be used. A fully integrated management information system is a system of obtaining, classifying, storing and analysing data to enable the management to define objectives, to plan to meet these objectives and to complete the cycle by evaluating progress and redefine the objectives, if there is a change in the internal or external ecological factors of management. The MIS is to control the functioning of an organization in the same manner as is done by the nervous system in the human body.

It is very difficult for a complex organization to keep track of the costs of the activities that lead to the accomplishment of a goal. Keeping track of the costs and pay-offs for each activity ensures an organization's continued health and guards against financial disaster. An organization may be successful in some areas and failing in others. Without mechanism for monitoring performance, management is unable to act quickly to minimize, damage and prevent further financial loss. Mechanism that provides information about the organization's performance serves as an early warning system that prevents little problems from becoming catastrophes.

MIS has become necessary for organizations to meet the following emerging developments:

(a) Increased complexity of organizations.

(b) Development of technological revolution.
(c) Emphasis on research and development.
(d) Diversification of functions and activities.
(e) Information explosion.
(f) Complex management issues.
(g) Development of computer, Internet, E-commerce and E-Governance.

The combined result of all these developments is the need of designing the management Information systems.

The purpose of an MIS is to raise managing from the level of piecemeal spotty information, intuitive guesswork and isolated problem-solving to the level of systems insights, systems information, sophisticated data processing and systems problem-solving. Managers have always had 'sources' of information; the MIS provides a system of information. It is thus a powerful method for aiding managers in solving problems and making decisions.

Advantages

The following advantages can accrue from a good information system:

(a) Timely availability of information develops a high degree of confidence between top executives and the members of the management.
(b) The management need not resort to frequent meetings to sort out various issues.
(c) The executive time can be saved and devoted to critical issues.
(d) It helps in reviewing actual performance and enables taking corrective action.
(e) It helps in reviewing strength and weakness of an organization, knowledge of which is most essential in formulating future plans and strategies.

C. INFORMATION TECHNOLOGY

IT increases knowledge and knowledge is like light-weightless and intangible. It can easily travel across the world enlightening the lives of the people everywhere.[21]

Digital Technology has influenced all sectors—Business, Government utility services and personal life. Information explosion is taking place at a very fast rate. Even an educated person cannot cope with this terrific increase in availability, accessibility and indispensability of knowledge. What can be done? Information Technology can help in coping with the information explosion. In the new millennium, information is being treated as the most important resource, besides men, money, machine, material and time.

In the history of civilization, no work of science has so comprehensively impacted on the course of human development as Information Technology (IT). Undoubtedly, IT has been the greatest change agent of this country and promises to play this role even more dramatically in the coming decades. IT is changing every aspect of human life-communications, trade, manufacturing, services, culture, entertainment, education, research, national defence and global security. It is breaking old barriers and building new interconnections in the emerging Global Village. IT has also become the chief determinant of the progress of nations, communities and individuals.

For India, the rise of Information Technology is an opportunity to overcome historical disabilities and once again become the master of one's own national destiny. IT is a tool that will enable India to achieve the goal of becoming a strong, prosperous and self-confident nation. In doing so, IT promises to compress the time it would otherwise take for India to advance rapidly in the march of development and occupy a position of honour and pride in the comity of nations.

The Government of India has recognized the potential of Information Technology for rapid and all-round national development. The National Agenda for Governance, which is the Government's Policy blueprint, has taken due note of the Information and Communication Revolution that is sweeping the globe. Accordingly, it has mandated the Government to take necessary policy and programmatic initiatives that would facilitate India's emergence as an Information Technology Superpower in the shortest possible time.

This commitment to Information and Communication Technology in the National Agenda for Governance has been forcefully articulated by former Prime Minister Shri Atal Bihari Vajpayee on a number of occasions. In his first televised address to the Nation on March 25, the Prime Minister declared that promotion of Information Technology would be one of his Government's five top priorities.

In his speech at the CII Annual Session on April 28, 1998, the Prime Minister said: "This is one area where India can quickly establish global dominance. India can be fully competitive in this area with tremendous pay-offs in terms of wealth creation and generation of high quality employment."[22] However, information should be correct and authentic, otherwise wrong information can upset the whole process of planning, implementation and evaluation. So to avoid wrong decisions, information should be used properly.

UNESCO defines Information Technology (IT) as "scientific, technological, engineering disciplines and the management techniques used in information handling and processing, their application, computers and their interaction with men and machines, and associated social, economical and cultural matters."

OECD (1987) treats Information Technology as "a term-covering technologies used in the collection, processing and transmission of information. It includes micro-electronic and info-electronic-based technologies incorporated in many products and production processes and increasingly affecting the service sector. It covers *inter alia* computers, electronic office equipment, telecommunication, industrial robots and computer controlled machine, electronic components and software products."

Gujarat Information Technology Policy has given definitions of various concepts used in IT. IT software means any representation or instructions, data sound of image including source code, object code recorded in a machine readable form and capable of being manipulated or providing inter-connectivity to user by means of automatic data processing machine falling under head "IT Products."

IT Services is defined as any service which results from the use of any IT software over a system of IT products for realizing value addition. IT products would include computer, digital data communication and digital data broadcasting products as notified by the Ministry of Finance, Government of India or Central Board of Excise and Custom. IT industry would include development of production and services related to IT products, IT software and IT services.[23]

Broadly speaking, IT deals with information systems, data storage, access, retrieval, analysis and intelligent decision-making for enhancing organisational effectiveness. IT is the technology of the present and of the future too. Convergence of telephone, computer and television technologies have become a reality in the twentieth century, the next century should conceive of and achieve something more novel and exciting. High speed networks, also referred to as information superhighways convey material that is at once rich and varied. These have enormous potential for education, business and other sectors of society.

Information Technology has been accepted world over as a tool that improves productivity, ensures learning ability and allows connectivity to the whole world. Information technology is being used to increase the quality, reduce costs and improve overall efficiency and effectiveness in various fields of life. Information technology is not an end in itself, but a means to provide better quality of life to the citizens of the State.

Having realized that IT is a valuable tool with which tremendous progress can be achieved in various fields of human activity, nations of the world are addressing themselves to the mechanism by which the benefit of the IT revolution can reach the common man. This is becoming a particularly significant point for deep consideration by developing countries which are keen to take advantage of the new scenario.[24]

The coming new century is widely referred to as the "Knowledge Century." The Knowledge Century will provide opportunities for unending learning and education. However, it will help to make life rich and meaningful only if we use knowledge to build a country where every child, woman and man has an opportunity for a productive and healthy life. Thanks to the modern information technology and world-wide web, we can monitor from our rooms global progress in every area of human endeavour arts, culture, science, agriculture, industry and politics. Information explosion also necessitates that we must develop our capacity to analyse them and to separate grain from chaff.

Advantages of Information Technology

Let us now discuss the advantages which can flow from the use of Information Technology:

1. Speed and Accuracy

It is highly useful in situations calling for massive memory, repetitive calculations and quick feedback of information. The speed is high and the column of output is also high.

2. Economy

To process a great volume of data, we will have to employ electrical or data processing staff resulting in more expenditure. A Digital information system, fully and properly used, not only saves money for its user, but can also make more money.

3. Flexibility

The digital computer can be put to a large number of uses not possible with other methods, such as time sharing, multi-programming and remote batch processing, etc.

4. Choice of Configuration

The various types of input, storage and output available, allow a choice of configuration according to the needs of the organization.

5. Information for Management

The great volume of output and the speed and accuracy of performance of the digital technology ensure that management is fed with accurate up-to-date information, which is so essential for effective planning, implementation, control and evaluation. For example, computers can provide the following information services: (i) locating a particular resolution, (ii) determining the progressive utilization of any account head under the budget, or the amount drawn by disbursing officer, (iii) collating the departmental requirements for the annual budget, (iv) testing alternative proposal for inclusion in the plan, (v) monitoring district-wise achievements in different fields, and (vi) maintenance of personnel records for transfer, promotion, etc.

6. Promotes Organisational Change and Development

Effective management can be obtained through electronic data processing. An EDP system appears to be pervasive device whose very existence acts to cause significant organisational change. A major reason for this effective change may be the capacity of the computer to absorb large quantities of data which have not previously been analysed. The availability of new information and new analysis often seems to demand action. The speed of the machines in making this information available produces a dynamic organisational climate which was not by book-keepers, clerks and manual systems of information. Such a dynamic climate places certain disciplinary demands on management which would not have existed under a manual system.

D. INFORMATION TECHNOLOGY AND E-GOVERNANCE

As information technology gradually permeates the working of the Central Government a minimum agenda for e-governance has been drawn up with the assistance of the IT Managers, designated in various Ministries and Departments on the lines of the Grievance Officers, Vigilance Officers, etc. This minimum agenda *inter alia* ensures provision of a basic minimum infrastructure as well as certain Government to Government and Government to Citizen transactions.

The crux of e-governance, however, is in its citizen interface. The Department of Telecommunications has set-up Customer Service Centres. The Central Passport Organization of the Ministry of External Affairs proposes to set-up franchisee centers for collection of applications. A project is being prepared for setting up of multi-utility centers of Central and State Governments to provide certain value-added services to the citizens through one-stop nonstop shops (OSNSs). As regards the Central Government, the services such as payment of telephone bills, making application for telephone connections, filing income tax returns, submitting passport applications, making airlines and railway booking, availing of postal services, applying for school, college and university admissions, etc. could be provided through the OSNSs. As far as the States are concerned, the services such as payment of electricity bills, supply of ration card, registration of vehicles, issue of driving licenses, filing of First Information Report (FIR), obtaining of birth and caste certificates, issue of land-holding certificate, etc. could be provided by these centers. A pilot center of this type (TWINS) has been set-up in Hyderabad, by the Government of Andhra Pradesh. The Central Government proposes to support similar initiatives on a pilot basis in selected States. If possible, the Central and State multi-service centers could be integrated or at least located at the same venue.

As part of the recommendations of the Task Force on Information Technology, the Ministry of Personnel, Public Grievances and Pensions has been entrusted with the task of setting up of a National Institute of Smart Government. The Institute would attempt to raise societal awareness of and capability in smart governance by promoting policies and practices which reinforce 'hassle free' environment for the citizens. It would develop high impact e-governance applications of delivery of citizen services for the central and state governments. It would be the focal referral site for any information on solutions, benchmarks and best practices within the country and abroad. It would have a physical as well as virtual existence, moving gradually more towards the latter with the passage of time.

The role of IT in improving the governance is manifolds, as follows:

1. It helps in improving the management of public resources.
2. It supports development and maintenance of a transparent and stable economic and regulatory environment, conducive to efficient private sector activities (for example, price systems, exchange and trade regimes and banking systems and their related regulations).
3. It helps in institutional reforms of treasury, budget preparation and approval procedures, tax administration, accounting and audit mechanisms, central bank operations, and official statistical functions.
4. It provides assistance in the regulatory and legal areas with focus on taxation, banking sector laws and regulations, establishment of free and fair market (for: instance, tax codes, commercial and central bank laws, etc.).
5. It injects efficiency and transparency into the entire economic reform programme presently being implemented in many countries, including India.[25]

In the context of administration, IT has to be used as an 'enabling technology' to achieve the broader goal of good governance. But to have an idea of how to go about it, let us take a look at the following agenda items of good governance:

- Enhancing effective and efficient administration;
- Improving quality of life of citizens;
- Establishing legitimacy and credibility of institutions;
- Making administration responsive, citizen-friendly, and citizen caring; Ensuring accountability;
- Securing freedom of information and expression;
- Reducing cost of governance;
- Making every department result-oriented;
- Improving quality of public services;
- Improving productivity of employees;
- Eradication of corruption to re-establish credibility of government by ensuring integrity of individuals;
- Removal of arbitrariness in exercise of authority; and
- Use of IT-based services to de-mystify procedures and improve the citizen government interface.[26]

CONCLUSION

Development administration can be more effective and efficient if it makes use of management techniques which are more scientific and provide the tools for effective policy-making, planning, decision-making and implementation of developed programmes. These techniques can provide energy and vision to development administrators in their endeavour to provide development activities which are citizen centric, transparent and responsive to the urges and feelings of people. Management techniques can help development administration in promoting efficiency, effectiveness, economy and timely completion of development projects.

Notes and References

1. Dr. T. Adeoye Lanbo, (Deputy Director General, World Health, Organization), Towards Justice in Health, The Magazine of the WHO, July 1979, p. 3-4.
2. John F. Mee, Managmeent Thought in A Dynamic Economy, New York, 1963.
3. Peter F. Drucker, *op. cit.*, pp. 13-14.
4. T.N. Rastogi, Changing Scenario of Management Discipline" in *IJPA*, Jan.-March, 2000, p. 15
5. ILO, "Introduction of Works Study", Geneva, 1969, p. 26.
6. Ruth Greenwald, Industrial Engineering, May 1986, p. 16.
7. *Ibid.*, p. 65.
8. Padma Seth, Creativity, Change and Future, Indian Council of Management, 1980, No. 3, p. v.
9. Sanjiv Sarin and Bennil Butts, "The Industrial Engineer as Entrepreneural Individual for Managing Innovation", Industrial Engineering, July 1986.
10. M. Hanner and J. Champy, Re-eingineering the Corporation: A Manifesto for Business Revolution, New York, Harper Collins, 1993, p. 32.
11. M.J. Clay, "General Theory of Management Techniques—Part-I, in Work Study and Management Service, London.
12. P.R. Dubhashi, Restructuring Reform of Indian System, in *IJPA*, July-Sept. 1997, p. 367.
13. AIU, *University News*, New Delhi, Aug. 21, 2000.
14. Raymond, J. Coleman and M.J. Rilley (ed.) Management Dimensions, Holden-Day WC 500, Samesone Street, San Franciso, California, p. 15.
15. James, J.O., Brien, P.E.: "Management and Information System", Van Nostrann, New York, 1970, pp. 2-3.
16. Harper Marion, "A New Profession to Aid Mangement", Charles Coolidge Parlin Memorial Lecture, p. 13.
17. Robert G. Murdick, "MIS for MBO", *Journal of Systems Management*, March 1977.
18. *Ibid.*
19. W.C. Churchil, *et al.*, "Proposed Research on MIS", Management Science Research Report, No. 54, p. 2.
20. IBA Corporation Office Products Division, Preliminary System Design for Project OMNI, NY, 1965, pp. 10-11.
21. World Bank, "Knowledge for Development", World Development Report, Oxford, Oxford University Press, 1999.
22. Ministry of Information and Technology, GOI, March 14, 2000; Document, Information Technology, Action Plan, Preamble.
23. Based on Gujarat Government Information Technology Policy.
24. K. Aludipillai, Towards an Information Technology (IT) Literate Society, in *University News*, Dec. 7, 1998, AIU, New Delhi.
25. Mohd. Muzammil, IT, Government and Economic Development, in *IJPA*, July-Sept. 2000, pp. 358-59.
26. Jagdish C. Kapur, IT and Good Governance, in *IJPA*, July-Sept., 2000, p. 389.

CHAPTER

27

Public-Private Partnership (PPP)

In a liberalized economy and a knowledge society, the archaic structure of Government has to necessarily undergo a change for the better. The organisations have to become lean and mean. The staff has to become responsive and accountable. The institutions have to justify their existence by being result-oriented, customer-centric and transparent in approach. Words like cost cutting, downsizing or disinvestment, etc. are catching up but with lot of resentment and hostility arising within the affected organization. These negative responses take the process of change, two steps backward. Hence, there is a need for internalization of progressive goals of each organization by each member and fulfilment of these objectives with cost and time over runs.

It has been rightly said that India does not suffer from resource problem in order to overcome its socio-economic ills, instead it is the management of the available resources which is the crux of the issue.

"The Public expects services to meet their demands in terms of quality, accuracy, timeliness, user formalism people can no longer tolerate delays, bureaucratic mistakes or excessively time consuming and difficult procedures after waiting for more than half a century since India's independence."

It is generally agreed by all the concerned that the new policies of economic reforms, liberalization, privatization and globalization would require massive changes in the functioning of government and its methodology to cope with the changed environment.

The prevailing administrative set-up in the developing countries is in a state of crisis. Its design and methods are inadequate and outworn. There is a need to design an integrated management system which may cover the planning of work programmes, budget preparation, resource programming, reviewing and evaluating results and definitions of programmes and aims. Besides, obsolete methods of work must be improved or replaced. Our experience during the last three decades has demonstrated that—the development plans have not been satisfactorily implemented because of inadequate administrative performance resulting from out-dated administrative system entailing organisational defects, lack of co-ordination, complex and cumbersome administrative and financial procedures, etc. These defects and deficiencies need to

CHART 27.1

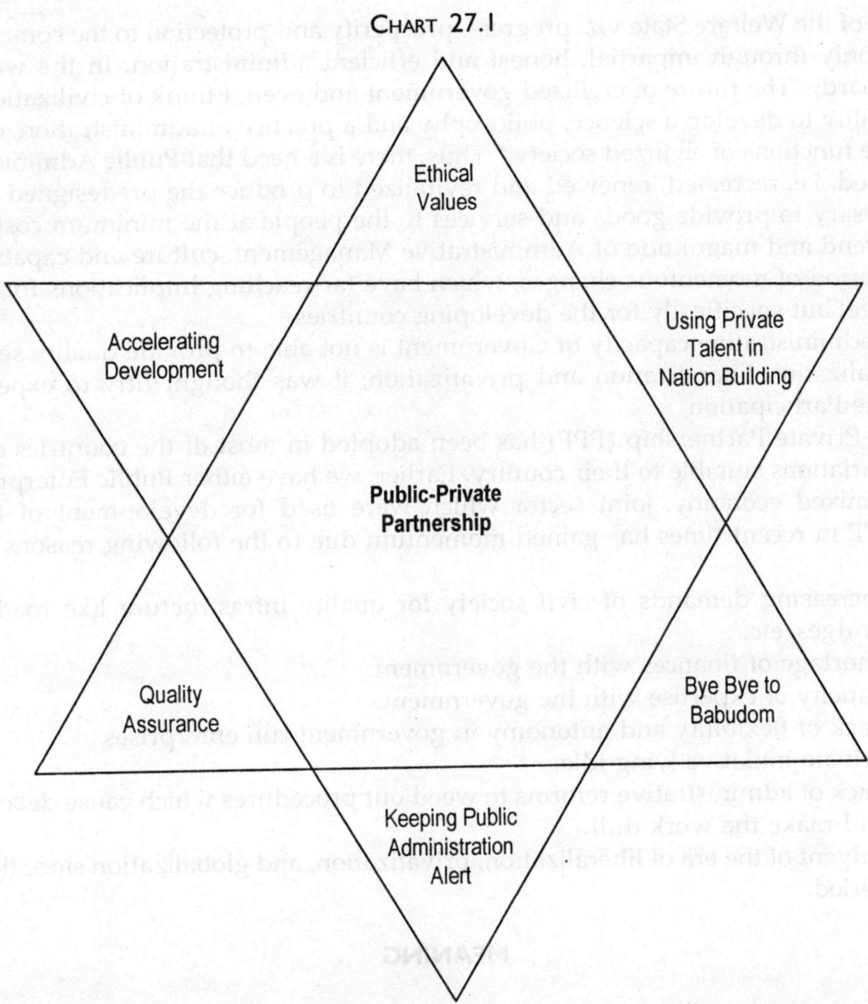

be corrected in order to bring about a sharp reduction in the administrative obstacles to development to bridge the gap between aspirations and performance.

Andrew Mariadoss Packajraj in his article "Administration that Delights the People" in MIG, July to Sept. 2000, rightly mentioned that People in India now expect the Governments in India to PEFORM. They are disenchanted with hollow promises, speeches, rhetorics and eloquent repertoires. They don't just desire effective and responsive Governments but they demand a Government that meets their aspirations. "It is for the Government to be effective and responsive in their (Govt.'s) own interest, otherwise they will be thrown out for falling short of people's expectations.

The three most vital players in the arena are the Elected Ruling Government, the Appointed Administrative Machinery and the Demanding Public. While the ultimate responsibility and answerability/accountability rests with the first component, the actual job of delivering results rests on the administrative machinery. It is, in the ultimate analysis a joint team effort of the three but any weak link can jeopardise the outcome and efforts of any other.

Ideals of the Welfare State viz. progress, prosperity and protection to the common man, can be secured only through impartial, honest and efficient administration. In the words of Prof. Charles Bernard, "The future of civilized government and even, I think of civilization itself rests upon our ability to develop a science, philosophy and a practice of administration, competent to discharge the functions of civilized society." Thus, there is a need that Public Administration must be modernized, i.e. recreated, renewed and revitalized to produce the predesigned changes and output necessary to provide goods and services to the people at the minimum cost. This needs a different trend and magnitude of Administrative Management, culture and capability. We are living in a period of momentous changes, which have far-reaching Implications for not only the world-at-large, but specifically for the developing countries.

Since administrative capacity of Government is not able to provide quality services in the area of globalization liberalization and privatization; it was thought fifty to experiment with Public-Private Participation

Public-Private Partnership (PPP) has been adopted in most of the countries of the world with some variations suitable to their country. Earlier, we have either Public Enterprises, private enterprises, mixed economy, joint sector which were used for development of the country. However, PPP in recent times has gained momentum due to the following reasons

1. Increasing demands of civil society for quality infrastructure like roads, railways, bridges, etc.
2. Shortage of finances with the government.
3. Paucity of expertise with the government.
4. Lack of flexibility and autonomy in government run enterprises.
5. Private initiative lying idle.
6. Lack of administrative reforms to weed out procedures which cause delays, irritation and make the work dull.
7. Advent of the era of liberalization, privatization, and globalization since the post-1991 period.

MEANING

PPP is a mode of implementing government pogarmmes or schemes in partnership with private sector. It is essentially a cooperative endeavour between public and private sectors to restructure the provision of public services for making them more efficient. It is a legal contractual arrangement in which the public and private sectors share equity, investment, finance, risk, responsibility and profits in the venture.[1]

With the advent of Public Choice Theory, the criteria of efficiency and economy, decentralisation and participation requires the monolithic state to shed non-sovereign and non-strategic activities to non-state agencies. PPP can be seen as a broad spectrum of cooperation between public and private sectors with varying percentages of participation with one end being government monopoly and other end outright privatisation.[2]

PPP has been widely recognized as the institutional innovation mechanism to facilitate the private sector's efficiencies in public services and government-run programmes. It enables a win-win situation for all stakeholders and blends public objectives with marketability and profitability. The advantage that PPP projects have is that they can incorporate a social focus without affecting the economic viability and efficiency of the project. PPPs have been successfully structured and applied in the last decade, to the infrastructure sector and have typically followed the B-O-T (Build-Operate-Transfer) model and its variants. The lessons learnt from these successes have set the foundation for the adaptation and application of the PPP model to other sectors.[3]

To make PPP model viable and sustainable, the government will have to continue to safeguard public interest and monitor the performance of private sector generally and privatized undertakings in particular. The determination and commitment of Government will have to be match readiness and cooperation from the private sector. "The interaction between Government and the private sector will have to be transformed into "smart partnership" of co-operation and complementarily that emphasises with situations· The drive towards diversified growth must be led by the private sector, which is expected to display the qualities of good corporate citizenship including the promotion of citizen empowerment. The public sector will have to progressively diminish its role in the provision of marketable goods and services and will rather seek to facilitate and, where necessary, regulate the operation of business by the private sector."

The government must ensure that privatisation should not lead government to curtail any of its core responsibilities which include good governance, safety and welfare of its citizens. The process must be carried out with a human face and efforts be made to safeguard national interests. It is hoped that a healthy public-private partnership shall foster inclusive growth and social empowerment besides contributing to improved service delivery and good governance.[4]

Experiences with reforms have unmistakably revealed that market failures do exist along with government failures, especially in the provision of public services. The reform programme witnessed a paradigm shift in the role of the state. For the first time in the history of post-colonial India, there was a conscious retreat of the state based on the acknowledgement of its apparent economic and development failure, also of the fact that it was not doing its business well and that there were other ways of doing business. In this context, the reforms were at crucial juncture in India's economic trajectory of the changes that were to follow, both in what were to be the economic goals of the post reform state, and how these goals were to be achieved. Public-Private Partnership (PPP) could be a way to utilise the best of both worlds, while overcoming the specific weaknesses of each. So the new public management becomes a factor to reckon with and it is now an accepted principle throughout the world. Of the essential characteristics of PPP, one is making Government functions more ready-to-face market tests, such as contracting out in an attempt towards reducing government functions through privatisation and other forms of contracting. In theory the proposed changes will result in a consumer-employed, competitive and market-oriented government that will reduce regulations, create revenue through fees and charges and concentrate on the decentralisation of authority, the privatisation of management and improvement of quality of public services.

Public-Private Partnership (PPP) is essentially a collaboration between the government and the private sector to create a structure in which improved value for money can be achieved through the involvement of private sector. So, it does not undermine the governments' overall responsibility to the taxpayer for the quality of the services provided to·them. But, it emphasizes on the role of government from direct service provider to management and coordination of services on the pattern suggested by the new public management (NPM) theory. So PPP is a system in which a government service or private business venture is funded and operated through a partnership of government and one or more private sector companies. It is important to mention the difference between PPP and privatisation. The responsibility for providing services rests under PPP with the government but in privatisation responsibility for delivery and funding a particular service rests with the private sector. In case of ownership rights public sector is the legal owner of PPP projects but in privatisation the private sector is the owner of associated benefits and costs as well. The nature and scope of service is contractually determined between the two parties in PPP but it is determined by the private provider in privatisation. The risks and rewards are shared between the public and the private sector under PPP but in privatisation all the risks and rewards involved in the business rest with the private sector.[5]

For the economy to grow at 9% per annum over the Eleventh Plan period, it is targeted to increase the GCF in the infrastructure from 5% of GDP at the start of the Tenth Plan to around 9% at the end of the Eleventh Plan. For this to be achieved, private sector participation in a big way is imperative. The areas identified for private sector participation include new manufacturing units, multi-modal logistics parks, construction of high-speed passenger corridors, induction of privately owned rolling stock of container operators, commercial development of land and air spaces, port connectivity works of the private ports, ore lines for steel plants, upgradation of major freight and passenger terminals, construction of road over bridges (ROBs), and railway OFC network.[6]

INITIATIVES TAKEN TO FACILITATE PRIVATE SECTOR INVESTMENT

- In order to maximize the volume of investments in the road sector, given the limited availability of public resources or the need to use them for development of roads in backward/remote areas, it has been decided that all the sub-projects in NHDP phase III to Phase VII would be taken up on the basis of PPP on BOT mode.
- The government has announced several incentives such as tax exemptions and duty-free import of road-building equipment and machinery to encourage private sector participation.
- The MCA for NHs, which was approved by CoI in 2005, has now been adopted for implementation of PPP projects by Ministry of Shipping, Road Transport, and Highways (MoSRTH)/NHAI; the MCA for SHs has been published by the Planning Commission.
- A review of tolling policy in respect of NHs has been concluded and the report, once finalized, would serve to impart greater certainty in revenue projections for concessionaires.
- Manuals of Standards and Specifications for four-Ianing and six-laning of NHs through PPPs are Under finalization by DoRTH. Adoption of these manuals would reduce project preparation time as project specific manuals would no longer be needed.
- The substantial completion of NHDP Phase I, that is GQ, has called for a shift in emphasis to corridor management so as to deliver maximum throughput in terms of speed and traffic volume, while minimizing operational cost and enhancing road safety. In this regard, an MCA for O&M of Highways has been published by the Planning Commission.[7]

Almost all State Governments have facilitated entry of private sector in providing passenger transport services to ease pressure on the public sector. As on 31 March 2004, the share of private buses was 85%. Private bus operators have, however, exhibited deplorable quality of service, with disregard to traffic rules, unsafe driving practices, unscheduled operation, and usage of irrational cost cutting measures and tax evasion. The private sector has also adversely affected the performance of public sector by resorting to unfair competition.

A prerequisite is, therefore, to strictly enforce rules, for which specially designated regulatory bodies need to be set-up, with powers to lay down minimum basic service standards, impose heavy fines, suspend or even cancel licenses, and launch and pursue prosecutions for accidents vigorously.[8]

The government has put in place a scheme for private participation in major ports mainly in container terminals, specialized cargo berths, warehousing/storage facilities, etc. on BOT basis with a concession period not exceeding 30 years. The scheme also includes formation of joint venture by the ports with the private operators selected on the basis of competitive bidding. The scheme did not take off as expected during the Tenth Plan. Necessary policy initiatives in respect of management control, etc., are required to be evolved for facilitating the formation of joint ventures. In case of non-major ports, the VGP scheme of the GOI will have to be made compatible with the requirements and the operational imperatives of the sector so as to enable the non-major ports to access these funds. During the Tenth Plan period, private sector schemes costing Rs. 11,257 crore were identified, eight schemes costing Rs. 2435 crore have been completed with incremental capacity addition of 44.40 million mt, another six schemes costing Rs. 3818 crore have already been awarded to private operators which are expected to create an additional capacity of 45.50 million mt.[9]

It may be mentioned that PPP does not reduce responsibility and accountability of the government. The government remains accountable for service, quality, price certainty and cost-effectiveness; in fact the role of government gets redefined as one of facilitator, and enabler, while private sector plays the role of financier, builder and operator of service. Under PPP approach, the skills, expertise and experience of both public and private sector get combined to deliver higher standard service to the consumers. The public sector contributes assurance in terms of stable governance, citizens' support, financing and also assumes social, environmental and political risks. The private sector brings along operational efficiencies, innovative technologies, managerial effectiveness, access to additional finances, and bears construction, commercial and operational risk of the project. In fact PPP approach is not new, it was followed a few centuries ago in different countries for development of infrastructure and social services.

ESSENTIALS FOR THE SUCCESS OF PUBLIC-PRIVATE PARTNERSHIP (PPP)

1. Sincerity of the Private Sector

Private sector has been generally interested in profit making without having any consideration to quality and needs of the people. The profit motive makes the private sector use inferior quality of material and low wages to the persons employed causing great risks to the citizens of the country. The first and foremost criteria on which PPP model can work is the sincere and right attitude of private sector. They must be sincere to their work while earning a reasonable profit.

2. Honesty and Integrity of Government Officials entrusting projects to private sector

It has been generally seen that politicians and bureaucrats indulge in corrupt practices and ask the private sector to pay them under the table amount mutually agreed upon. From where the private sector would compensate this money. The only solution is to decrease quality at the cost of corrupt practices endangering life of the citizens. Good governance demands transparency, integrity and citizen 'centric approach'.

T.N. Chaturvedi in his Editorial on the Special Number on Ethics in Public life of *the Indian*

Journal of Public Administration (July-Sept., 1995) has rightly remarked: "The potential damage and threat to the political fabric of a system is not dependent on the character of government, i.e. whether it is an activist or limited in scope. History shows that neither a capitalist nor a socialist nor a welfare state is immune to the corrosive evil of corruption. The standards of conduct and behaviour of people in political authority have their malignant influence in other walks of life in society. The ethical dimensions of how influential and powerful people conduct themselves in private life and the public domain set a precedent for the lesser human beings and groups in society to follow or to seek justification for their own self-seeking or even scandalous conduct. The perniciousness ripple-effect encompasses all segments of society. It is not only the public systems that are under attack. The people harbour grievances against trade, industry, business, academia, medical and other professional groups and organizations. The evil within and outside the government circle, is thus, not limited to any narrow confines. Similarly, the influence of ethical conduct in positive terms is also not contained or concerned with only some specific sections and select groups but is relevant to the entirety of society and its wider network of relationships. As is often said, the moral basis for the unity and stability of society demands that ethical restraints must operate not only in respect of individuals but also organized groups—be they industrial, business and trade associations, labour unions, political parties, military and civil services, judiciary, non-governmental organizations, academic or professional associations, agriculturists organisations, etc.—apart from government itself. The all-pervading and inter-locking nature of ethics in public life is to be comprehended in all its manifestations and dimensions. This is borne out by history in different times and ages and also by the prowess of civilization today.

The scandals and cases of corruption, kickbacks, bribery, extortions, lying and deception by government all over the world, in both developed and developing countries at different times, are too many and too well-known to need any enumeration. In the wake of many cases of nepotism, influence peddling, corporate bribery, corruption, illicit Operations, business malpractices, and unhealthy nexus between politics, administration and business coming of public notice at the time of the World War II, the US Senate set-up a sub-committee under Senator Paul Doughlas, which submitted its report, commonly known as the Report on Ethical Standards in Government. This attracted attention all over the world and the various naunces of ethics in governance were discussed, researched and commented upon in various forums.

Moral values, in simple terms, are the values that tell us what is the right, proper and acceptable way of behaving. Moral values are indispensable for good governance. An efficient and technologically sound administrative machinery, unless it stands on high moral pedestal, does not serve the public, but it services a self-perpetuating and exploitative system.

Hon'ble Supreme Court of India in its judgment in the case of *Vineet Narain* vs. *Union of India* (AIR 1998 SC 889), stated that:

> "These principles of public life are of general application in every democracy. And one is expected to bear them in mind while scrutinizing conduct of every holder of a public office. It is trite that the holder of the public offices are entrusted with certain powers to be exercised in public interest alone and, therefore, the office is held by them in trust for the people. Any deviation from the path of rectitude by any of them amounts to a breach of trust and must be severely dealt with instead of being pushed under the carpet. If the conduct amounts to an offence, it must be promptly investigated and the offender against whom a *prima facie* case is made out should be prosecuted expeditiously so that the majesty of law is upheld and the rule of law vindicated. the adverse impact of lack of probity in public

life leading to a high degree of corruption is manifold. It also has adverse effect on foreign investment and funding from the International Monetary Fund and the World Bank who have warned that future aid to under-developed countries may be subject to the requisite steps being taken to eradicate corruption, which prevents international aid from reaching those for whom it is meant."

In the case of *State of Assam* vs. *P.C. Mishra* (AIR 1966 SC 430) the Supreme Court stated that "It is incumbent for each occupant of every high office to be constantly aware that the power invested in the high office he holds is meant to be exercised in public interest and only for public good, and that it is not meant to be used for personal benefit or merely to elevate the personal status of the current holder of that office. Constant awareness of the nature of this power and the purpose for which it is meant would prevent situations leading to clash of egos and the resultant fall out detrimental to public interest."

His Excellency the Governor of Karnataka on the Republic Day, 26th January 2007, address said, "Corruption is not merely a dirty word. It describes a dirty act. We need to have a policy of zero tolerance towards all acts of corruption. We need to assert that there is no difference between a small act of corruption and major instances of malfeasance. There is no such thing as petty corruption—there is corruption. *per se*. It is necessary to strike at the very roots of corruption, for if we allow its tentacles to grow we will be firmly in its grip, with no way out. This is a very real danger. Corruption in any walk of life can corrode, decay and annihilate our democratic system. We can ignore or minimize its evil effects at our own risk. Corruption and un-refuted allegations of misuse of power for self and pelf do shake the faith of ordinary citizens in our democratic system."

Lord Nolan has mentioned that public officials must possess selflessness, integrity, accountability openness, honesty and leadership to serve public.

3. Providing Facilities to Private Sector

All the facilities as agreed upon must be supplied to the private sector so that the work can be completed in time. It has been seen that government creates delays and harassment to private sector affecting the completion of projects.

4. Fair Practices by Private Sector

- Business must maintain highest standards of behaviour so that their actions and decisions result in the benefits for industry, employees, customers, shareholders and society.
- Good and Service must conform to the commitment promised to customers. Business must be realistic and truthful in stating claims.
- Customers must be given best possible service and treated with respect and fairness.
- Best way of promoting high standards of business practices is through self-regulation. The Code has been designed as an instrument of self-regulation to serve as voluntary guidelines towards better quality of life and higher standards of business practices.

5. Mutual Trust

For the success of PPPs, conducive and workable environment is required. It also requires improved attitudes and mutual trust; transparent and accountable management and financial systems; structural adjustment to ensure quality; effective coordination among the partners and other institutions/agencies; requisite legal support; strong political and administrative commitments; strict adherence to prescribed and agreed norms and standards; appropriate policy for capacity building; and mechanisms of regular and effective monitoring and evaluation. If necessary changes are made to expedite the on-going process of PPPs, the desired results can be achieved within specified time frame.[10]

6. Accountability

Public or private sector cannot manage funds in investment without having strong accountability mechanisms in place. People need to know that they are getting value for their money and that their taxes/fees/duties are being administered with probity and distributed fairly. One of the priorities of the national policy/planning and each committee is to ensure that regular audit takes place for any partnership between public and private sector. A private contractor/ organisation/institution that hopes to succeed and establish a reputation for effective delivery of service must be accountable to its public sector partner(s) and to the public at large. It is accepted that "retaining the publicness of a PPP is essential in order to provide democratic steering and societal accountability for its delivery of public policy goals." Accountability holds the key to successful involvement of citizens and the private sector.[11]

7. Strategic Planning by Government

Strategic planning and management by government is essential to that PPPs can succeed and they should be managed by expert teams. Governments also need to use technical and financial advisors, where needed, to match the advantages of the private sector, particularly in large-scale programme. Project development needs to be done by government, and it needs to invest in it by creating dedicated funds.[12]

LIMITATIONS AND ACTIONS

Government of India has introduced several innovative Schemes aimed at promoting PPPs. Whereas to attract the private sector, commercially viable projects should be on offer and to inculcate the discipline of 'user pay principle' and provision of these services should be based on payment of tariff, Government must also fulfil its commitment towards inclusive growth which makes it obligatory to fix the tariffs based on the capacity of the common man to pay. Due diligence is also essential given the substantial contingent liability that could devolve on the State in such projects.

While encouraging PPPs, six constraints have been identified:

(i) Policy and regulatory gaps, specially relating to specific sector policies and regulations;

(ii) Inadequate availability of long-term finance (10 year plus tenor)—both equity and debt;

(iii) Inadequate capacity in public institutions and public officials to manage PPP processes;

(iv) Inadequate capacity in the private sector—both in the form of developer/investor and technical manpower;

(v) Inadequate shelf of bankable infrastructure projects that can be bid out to the private sector, and

(vi) Inadequate advocacy to create greater acceptance of PPPs by the public.

To address these constraints, several initiatives have been taken by Government of India to create an enabling framework for PPPs by addressing issues relating to policy and regulatory environment. Progressively more sectors have been opened to private and foreign investment, levy of user charges is being promoted, regulatory institutions are being set-up and strengthened, fiscal incentives are given to infrastructure projects, standardised contractual documents including the Model Concession Agreement are being notified, approval mechanism for PPPs in the Central sector has been streamlined through setting up of PPPAC and a website exclusively devoted to PPPs has been launched to serve as a virtual market place for PPP projects.

SUGGESTIONS: REGULAR MONITORING

(1) There is a need of regular monitoring of physical, financial and quality measures by government during the process of implementation and completion to ensure high quality performance.

(2) Ensuring quantity and quanltiy of materials—Private business entrepreneurs generally indulge in unethical practices causing a great harm to development progrmme. This is evident from daily newspapers exposing scandals by private business man in collaboration with government functionaries.

(3) Choice of private businessmen—Private businessmen must be selected on the basis of his reputation, previous record and reliability.

(4) Strict Action against corrupt officials—Strict action against government functionaries indulging in collusion with private businessmen. Exemplary punishment must be given to government functionaries who were entrusted the task of supervision, who instead indulged in corrupt practices.

(5) Heavy penalities need be imposed for any malpractices—Government must provide for heavy penalities in the contract for any development work if they violate any of the clause of the contract affecting the quality of development programme.

(6) Strict observance of administrative ethics—Politicians and bureaucrats must follow the conduct rules in letter and spirit to ensure the success of developing programmes.

Inspite of Public-Private Participation, the government have to keep its administrative system in perfect order to take full benefits of Public-Private Partnership otherwise private people may not give the desired results.

David Osborne and Tech Gabler have suggested the following responsibilities of Public Administration to fulfil its role:[6]

1. Crusading reformer, intent on transforming some aspect of community life according to preconceived notions of the ideal society;
2. Proactive policy formulator, ready with possible strategies to meet the unknown;
3. Social change-agent, ready to accept new ideals and push others into accepting them also;

4. Crisis manager, slow to burn out but quick to react and brilliant at immediate improvisation;
5. Dynamic programme manager, able to show new courses and adapts on-going arrangements;
6. Humanitarian employer, treating staff with respect and meeting out even-handed justice;
7. Political campaigner, responsive to public needs and champion of public causes;
8. Competent administrator, ensuring effective performance with minimum political embarrassment;
9. Interest broker, choosing among competing interests and reconciling all parties to the outcome;
10. Public relations expert, adept at building up support, showing his area to advantage;
11. Speedy decision-maker, oriented to assume responsibility and clear instructions;
12. Constructive thinker, rot easily led astray by others who would want to make up his mind for him; and
13. Optimistic leader, not easily discouraged in adversity, but able to command attention and stimulate subordinates.

Thus, there is a need to introduce desired improvements and reforms in administration to ensure social change and modernization.

We must keep an eye on the outcome of Public-Private Partnership to take care of the following aspects.

We need to take care of the following aspects to promote Public-Private Partnerhsip:

1. A closer focus on results in terms of efficiency and effectiveness, and service quality;
2. The replacement of highly centralised hierarchical organisational structures with decentralised management environments, where decisions on resource allocation and service delivery are taken closer to the point of delivery, and which provide scope for feedback from clients and other interest groups;
3. Flexibility to explore alternatives to direct public provision, which might provide more cost-effective policy outcomes;
4. New personnel management policies to provide greater flexibility in the deployment of staff (e.g., through multiskilling);
5. The use of mechanisms to improve performance such as performance contracting and the creation of competitive market environment within and among public sector organisations;
6. Incentives to improve performance (or at least removing disincentives) through enabling organisations to retain a portion of savings from improved performance;
7. The strengthening of strategic capacities at the centre to "steer" government to respond to external changes and diverse interests quickly, flexibly and at least cost; and
8. Greater accountability and transparency through requirements to report on results.[13]

Peter F. Drucker has rightly pointed out that "Management is the crucial factor in economic and social development. It was obvious that the economists traditional view of development as a function of savings and capital investment do not produce management and economic development. On the contrary, management produces economic and social development and with its savings and capital investment. It becomes apparent that the developing countries are not underdeveloped, they are under managed."[14]

CONCLUSION

Public-Private Partnership seems attractive and valuable for the development of the country. The purpose of this is to tap the potential energy of the private sector in national development and accelerate the process of development.

However, in practice, we have to exercise supervision, monitoring and evaluation as private sector is likely to indulge in making money through foul means which defeats the purpose of their participation. We have to be cautious and not make it another den of corruption. These private people can also pollute government machinery through speed money to get their project approved.

Notes and References

1. Seminar Report, Public-Private Partnership, IAS Professional Course, Phase, I, 2005, Batch, LBSNAA, Mussoorie, 2005.
2. *Idem.*
3. Deepak Sharma, Public-Private Partnership in Indian Government Sector: An illustrative Analysis, *IJPA*, July-Sept., 2008, pp. 618-19.
4. Sushma Yadav, Governance in India and Public-Private Partnership: A Paradigm Shift, *IJPA*, July-Sept., 2008, p. 652.
5. R.K. Kunder and S.S. Chahar, Public-Private Partnership: A Social Sector Review, *IJPA*, July-Sept. 2008, pp. 522-23.
6. GOI, Planning Commission, XIth Five Year Plan, Vol. III, p. 289.
7. *Ibid.*, p. 296.
8. *Ibid.*, p. 305.
9. *Ibid.*, pp. 315-16.
10. Mohinder Singh: Public-Private Partnership in India, *IJPA*, July-Sept, 2008, p. 571.
11. Inderjeet Singh Sodhi, Public-Private Partnership in India, *IJPA*, July-Sept., 2008, p. 682.
12. R. Thandavan and Kalachelvi Sivaranam, Public-Private Partnership within Policy Framework, *IJPA*, July-Sept. 2008, p. 475.
13. David Shand, New Public Management, Challenge and Issues in an International Perspective, in *IJPA*, July-Sept. 1998, pp. 717-18.
14. Peter F. Drucker, *op. cit.*, pp. 13-14.

CHAPTER 28

Participative Management

Absolute authority, though having the legal right to command, fails to create interest among employees. The trend today is to make use of authority in collaboration with colleagues or developing teamwork. Teamwork would encourage participation, leading to following benefits:

(a) Participation yields personal commitment and involvement of employees toward organisational goals;
(b) Participation produces the free flow of communications for an informal workforce and atmosphere;
(c) Control systems are primarily for self-monitoring and guidance and not needed for external control;
(d) It produces high degree of mutual respect and trust among organisational members;
(e) Through participation, employees are likely to obtain stronger motivation towards an objective. Even those who disagree will feel compelled to loyalty by the sheer weight of the group opinion; and
(f) A high degree of confidence is shown in subordinates, which facilitates interpersonal process.

An employee's participation would build his morale and ultimately his efficiency. An ILO document mentions that the "individual worker is not just a cog in the very big wheel, but that his personal effort is essential for the achievement of the overall production plan."[1]

The research theory in social organisational psychology has also suggested that participation in group decision-making enhances satisfaction among members and remove tensions. Micheal R. Cooper and Micheal T. Wood have shown that satisfaction is affected by the participation. Satisfaction was greater where participation was complete than where it was partial.[2]

Authority in an organisation means the power to take decisions, communicating them to the subordinates for implementation and thus influencing their behavioural pattern. How far authority is accepted and obeyed depends on the capacity and judgment of the superior and subordinates. He has to take his subordinates with him. He has to create his own image in the minds of the subordinates, so that there exists identification of purpose in the members of the organisation. Authority is exercised to achieve the purposes of the organisation. This is not possible unless the person accepting authority is able to understand as to what is expected of him. The exercise of authority will be smooth if the person exercising it is able to inspire confidence among other members of the organisation. Subordinates should dream as the superiors do.

AUTHORITY COMMENSURATE WITH RESPONSIBILITY

Another very important fact is that for the successful functioning of an organisation, authority must be commensurate with responsibility. Adequate authority should be delegated to realize the purposes of the organisation. An individual should have all the authority at his disposal to achieve the objectives for which he has been made responsible. Whether he can achieve those objectives or not depends upon his intelligence, capacity and capability for hard work, but he should not be handicapped in the performance of his responsibilities for the lack of desired authority. One should have authority to take action in order to meet a particular situation. Further, one who exercises authority is also held responsible for the results of the exercise of that authority. But one cannot be held accountable, if his powers are less than what the occasion demands. Authority and responsibility must be co-terminus, equal and defined. Senior people should keep this in mind.

Let us mention the views of some eminent thinkers on participative management.

1. Rensis Likert

Likert claims to present "a newer theory of organization based on the management principles and practices of the mangers who are achieving the best results in American business and government." He suggests the setting up of foundations for the art of management. He says, "Of all the tasks of management, management of human component is the central and most important task, because all else depends on how well it is done." All now agree that human rather than capital is the key to development.

Likert treats the organization as a complex system based on the principle of supporting relationships, in which decision-making, leadership, motivation, communication and control move together.[3] For achieving orgnanisational objectives; he emphasizes participation in such a fashion that "a satisfactory integration of the needs and desires of all members of the organization and of persons are functionally related to it."

The most important contribution of Rensis Likert lies in developing different systems of management along a continuum. He devised a four-level model of organization effectiveness incorporating the basic categories of task orientation and people-orientation. Likert feels that personnel are the precious assets and therefore must be treated and managed carefully. Likert classifies management philosophies into four convenient systems. 1. Exploitative authoritative, 2. Benevolent authoritative, 3. Consultative, and 4. Participative.

In first approach, authority is centralised at the top and the subordinates are asked merely to obey under the threats of punishment. In system two, the leader is benevolent and autocratic. He allows the people to express themselves, but by and large, he behaves like a dictator. These managers have "Condescending Confidence" in employees. The system three refers to consultative management, wherein managers have substantial, but not complete confidence in employees abilities. The leader invites suggestions and ideas, shows his willingness to listen to his subordinates and may consider their views. He may, however keep control over decisions. In system four, "Participative" the manager runs the administration with the full consent and co-operation of the employees. Decision-making is highly decentralized and the subordinates are delegated authority to a great extent. Likert's conclusion is that most efficient organizations have system-4 characteristics and therefore organizations should move to system-4. Since the employees feel belongingness to the organization in system-4, it can yield positive results. After considerable study, Likert proposed that in contemporary society, System-4, organizations utilize human and technical resources more fully than System-1. The System-4 design emphasizes the importance of decentralized authority and non-directive, participative management behaviour. Relatively wide spans and control and heterogeneous departments facilitate the interaction of multiple and diverse points of view. Consequently, as circumstances and technology change, the organization is able to respond because of the diverse perspectives that can be brought to bear on any issue or problem that it confronts. Thus, advocates of System-4 organization design believe that it is universally applicable. But more important, they believe that it is the best way to organize in modern society. Likert argues that all managers should strive toward a system 4 participative style if they wish to maximize the quantity and quality of performance from employees. System-4 which is seen as the superior alternative in comparison to Systems-1, 2 and 3.[4]

He stressed on the importance of individuals in an organization. Consistently, in study after study, the data show that treating people as 'human beings' rather than as 'cogs in a machine' is a variable related to the attitudes and motivation of the subordinate at every level in the organization."[5]

To conclude this portrayal of Professor Likert's model, in his own words:

> "The performance and output of any enterprise depends entirely upon the quality of the human organization and its capacity to function as a tightly knit, highly motivated, technically competent entity, i.e. as a highly effective interaction influence system. High productivity, high quality products, high earnings and successful use of research and development are not accomplished by inter-personal equipment or computers. These goals are achieved by human beings. Successful organizations are those making the best use of competent personnel to perform well and efficient all the tasks required by the enterprise."[6]

Likert ideas if practiced in true spirit can generate, dynamisms and development in all organizations through his system-4 approach.

An individual human being is marvel of God's creation. He is unique in more than one sense. He is endowed with infinite potentialities, most of which remains untapped and unutilized. If these potentialities are harnessed and actualized properly, they are capable of bringing wonders. Human beings are like atoms containing tremendous energies. The physical law of 'fission' and 'fusion' operates on them also. If positively motivated they can bring prosperity to the humanity but if motivated negatively they can spell disaster.

Likert has tried to suggest such leadership based on participation. Likert system-4 organisation should be used in our present day malfunctioning organizations. Every member of the organization has high performance aspirations and by means of group interaction process, the precise goals that are set represent an optimum integration of the needs and desires of the organization members the financiers, the customers, the suppliers, others who are interested in the enterprises and the members of the citizenary substantively affect by its operatives. In order to remove dead wood from Indian Administrative System, we must inject in them System 4 management through Systems-2 and 3. The research for future leadership also supports Likerts ideas.

TABLE 28.1

Likert's System of Management Leadership

Organisational Variable	*System-1 Exploitative*	*System-2 Benevolent*	*System-3 Consultative*	*System-4 Participative*
1. Extent to which superiors have confidence and trust in subordinates	Have no trust and confidence in subordinates	Have condence-ding confidence and trust such as master has to servant	Substantial but not complete confidence and trust, still wishes to keep control of decisions.	Complete confidence and trust in all matters
2. Extent to which superiors behave so that subordinates feel free to discuss important things about their jobs with their immediate superiors	Subordinates do not feel free at all to discuss things about the job with their superiors	Subordinates do not feel very free to discuss things about the job with their superiors	Subordinates feel rather free to discuss things about the job with their superiors.	Subordinate feel completely free to discuss things about the job with their superiors.
3. Extent to which immediate superior in solving job pro-blems generally tries to get sub-ordinates ideas and makes constructive use of them	Seldom gets ideas and opinions of subordinates in solving job problems	Sometimes gets ideas and opinions of subordinates in solving job problems	Usually gets ideas and opinions and usually tries to make constructive use of them.	Always gets ideas and opinions and always tries to make constructive use of them

Source: Renis Likert: The Human Organizations, McGraw Hill Book Company, New York, 1967, p. 4.

2. Chris Argyris

This process of participation is based on the combined benefits of individuals and organization

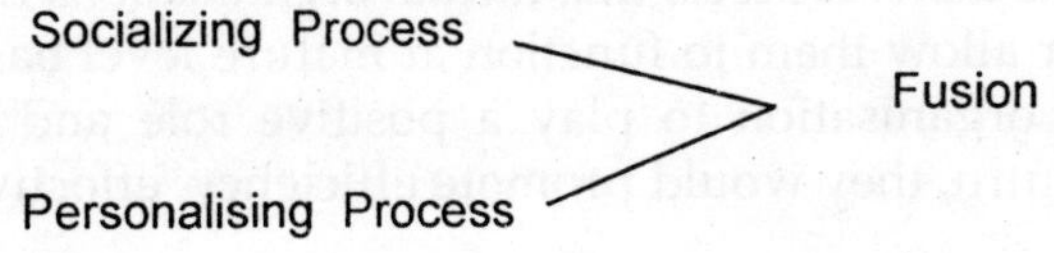

In socializing process, organisation encourages individuals to develop fully and make use of the energies of individual while in Personalising process, individuals are encouraged to contribute to the development of the organisation. The process is both formal and informal and the resultant process of fusion takes out of the individual potentialities to ensure organisational effectiveness to promote creative and innovative organizations.

The fusion process was developed over a period of more than twenty years of intensive research in different types of organizations by Argyres.

Professor Argyris later tested this theory. He undertook to study the operation of a bank. The results of this study were published in 1954. This study is significant, as for the first time the functioning of an organisation was examined in a systematic way.

The organisation, in order to be successful, should strive to meet its own needs as well as the needs of the individuals serving within the organisation. Argyris' fusion model depicts the real situation in the organisation.

The personality factors which were taken into account for the personalizing process are: Passive, Recluse, self-responsible variety seeking, mathematically minded, security conscious, directive, sociable, upward mobile, Challenge Accepting or rejecting, industrious, mechanical minded, detail minded and short hour minded.

Organisational factors taken into account were passive work, isolated work, self guided work, varied work, low wage work, security, directive works, diplomatic employee work, increasingly responsible work, continuous work, Free time Advantages work, Blind Alley work, Multi-Detailed work, Diplomatic customer work, accurate work, hostility accepting work. Based upon these factors fusion model was listed which gave interesting results.

He helped in designing creative and innovative organizations based upon his research. It is easy to understand that all problems would be solved automatically in an enlightened organization based on creativity and innovation.

The Immaturity-Maturity model of Personality—The Immaturity-Maturity model is considered to be a great contribution of Chris Argyris

The following table shows the immaturity-maturity continuum developed by Argyris:

Immaturity	*Activity*
Passivity	Maturity
Dependence	Independence
Few ways of behaving	Diverse behaviour
Shallow interest	Deep interest
Short-term perspective	Long-term perspective
Subordinate position	Superordinate position
Lack of self-awareness	Self-awareness and control

Source: Adapted from Chris Argyris, Personality and Organisation, Harper & Bros., New York, 1957, p. 50.

Argyris feels that all persons reach the maturity end of the continuous and they do not move as per the stages given in the table. He feels that formal organizations treat individuals as passive, dependence, etc. and never allow them to function at mature level based on self-awareness and control. He wants formal organisation to play a positive role and encourage individuals to develop maturity and in return, they would promote efficiency, effectiveness and productivity. It will also create formal organizations which are enlightened. He wanted formal organizations to create an healthy environment in which individuals can achieve maturity.

Inter-Personal Relations

Organizations consist of individuals, who work in relation to one another in different capacities, to produce results. Only a coordinated effort among individuals can sustain the efficiency of an organization. Else a major effort would be wasted in misunderstandings, jealousies, etc. Today, most of the organiations are plagued by poor interpersonal relations, resulting in lack of interactions, team work, harmony and resultant low output. Only effective interpersonal relations can lay the foundation of a sound organization, otherwise it would lead to desperate elements working in different directions, causing great harm to the efficiency of the organization.

Managers of today need to be trained in understanding the inter-personal relationships and their management to insulate the organization from internal behavioural disturbances. There are three inter-personal needs, (i) inclusion need for interaction and association, (ii) control—the need for authority and power, and (iii) affection—the need for being loved and cared. Developing a successful inter-personal relation, conducive to achievement of organisational goals, is a challenging task and a slow process. It requires a deep psychological understanding of oneself as well as of others, with whom one comes in contact in various organisational capacities.

Argyris is a strong advocate of Inter-Personal relationship for which he lays down three conditions:

1. *Self-acceptance*: This refers to the degree to which the person values himself in a positive fashion.
2. *Confirmation*: By confirmation, Argyris means the reality-testing of one's own self-image.
3. *Essentiality*: This third condition for interpersonal competence is defined by Argyris as one's opportunity to 'utilise the central abilities and express his central needs'.

Argyis based upon his research mentioned four types of behaviour which can help in increasing competence of organizations:

1. Owning upto, or accepting responsibility for one's ideas and feelings.
2. Being open to ideas and feelings of others and those from within one's self.
3. Experimenting with new ideas and feelings.
4. Helping others to owe upto, be open to, and to experiment with their ideas and feelings.[7]

Agryris research findings on inter-personnel relations if applied can save the organization from a large number of problems occurring at informal as well as formal level. Team work is essential to avoid wastage on conflicts.

According to Chris Argyris organizations very often keep their members passive and thus stunt their psychological growth. He stressed that individuals and organizations must adapt to the need of each other.

He suggests the following:

The objectives of a typical organization development programmes are:

(i) to increase the level of the trust and support among individuals and groups throughout the organizations;
(ii) to create an open, problem-solving climate throughout the organization—where problems are confronted and differences are clarified, both within group and between groups in contrast to "sweeping problems under the rug";
(iii) to increase the level of personal enthusiasm and satisfaction in the organizations;
(iv) to attain better collaboration and cooperation between inter-department persons and/ or groups;
(v) to increase the openness of communication laterally, vertically and diagonally;
(vi) to increase the level of self and group responsibility in planning and achievements of goals through optimum resource utilization; and
(vii) a shift in values so that human factors and feelings come to be considered as legitimate.[8]

3. McGregor

He propounded two contrasting theories—One is negative called Theory X and another positive called Theory Y.

Theory X:

In his own words these assumptions are as follows:

(i) Management is responsible for organizing the elements of productive enterprises—money, materials, equipment, people—in the interest of economic ends.
(ii) With respect to people, this is a process of directing their efforts, motivating them, controlling their actions, modifying their behaviour to fit the needs of the organization.
(iii) Without this active intervention by management, people would be passive—even resistant—to organisational needs. They must be persuaded, rewarded, punished, controlled, and their activities must be directed. This is management's task. We often sum it up by saying that management consists of getting things done through other people.
(iv) The average man is by nature indolent—he works as little as possible.
(v) He lacks ambition, dislikes responsibility, prefers to be led.
(vi) He is inherently self-centred, indifferent to organisational needs.
(vii) He is, by nature, resistant to change.
(viii) He is gullible, not very bright, the ready dupe of charlatan and the demagogue.

Executives believing in above mentioned characteristics of human nature believe in control, close supervision of their employees.

Theory Y:

McGregor, however, points out that man's motivation is far too complex and varied to be explained away wholly by the aforementioned assumptions. In line with other thinkers of social psychology school, McGregor describes his alternative model of motivation as theory Y. The assumptions of theory Y are described by McGragor's in the following words:

(i) The expenditure of physical and mental effort in work is natural as play or rest. The average human being does not inherently dislike work. Depending upon controllable conditions, work may be a source of satisfaction or a source of punishment.

(ii) External control and the threat of punishment are not the only means for bringing about effort towards organisational objectives. Man will exercise self-direction and self-control in the service of objectives to which he is committed.

(iii) Commitment to objectives is a function of the reward associated with their achievement. The most significant of such awards, e.g. the satisfaction of ego and self-actualisation needs, can be direct product of effort directed towards organisational objectives.

(iv) The average human being learns under proper conditions not only to accept, but to seek responsibility. Avoidance of responsibility, lack of ambition, an emphasis on security are generally consequences of experiences, not inherent human characteristics.

(v) The capacity to exercise a relatively high degree of imagination, ingenuity, and creativity in the solution of organisational problems is widely, not narrowly, distributed in the population.

(vi) Under the conditions of modern industrial life, the intellectual potentialities of the average human being are only partially utilized.

McGregor's assumptions in theory Y roughly correspond to what Maslow and Argyris have stated about human motivation. The running theme of all these thinkers has been to show that adequate attention has not been paid, so far, to the actual potentialities, creativity and responsible behaviour with which the ordinary man is endowed. That way, McGreger has successfully discarded the assumptions of classical school of thoughts. Douglas McGreger has rightly given his preference for theory Y, which helps in true organisational building and development. He states:

"Theory X leads naturally to an emphasis on the tactics of control procedures and techniques for telling people what they need to do, for determining whether they are doing it, and for administering rewards and punishments. Since an underlying assumption is that people must be made to do what is necessary for the success of the enterprise, attention is naturally directed to the techniques of direction and control. Theory Y, on the other hand, leads to a pre-occupation with the nature of relationships, with creating an environment which will encourage commitment to organisational objectives and which will provide opportunities for the maximum exercise of initiative, ingenuity, and self-direction in achieving them."[9]

A so-called human resources model is often associated with Douglas McGregor. McGregor and other theorists criticized the human relations model as simply a more sophisticated approach to the manipulation of employees. They also charged that, like the traditional model, the human relations model oversimplified motivation by focusing on just one factor, such as money or social relations.

McGregor identified two different sets of assumptions about employees. The traditional view, known as Theory X, holds that people have an inherent dislike of work. Although workers may view it as a necessity, they will avoid it whenever possible. In this view, most people prefer to be directed and to avoid responsibility. As a result, the work is of secondary importance, and managers must push employees to work.

Theory Y is more optimistic. It assumes that work is as natural as play or rest. In Theory Y, People want to and can derive a great deal of satisfaction from work. In this view, people have the capacity to accept—even seek—responsibility and to apply imagination, ingenuity, and creativity to organisational problems.[10]

Another important research finding according to McGregor is that leadership is a relationship. "It means that leadership is not a property of the individual, but a complex relationship" among the variables relating to the characteristics of the leaders, the followers, the organization and the social economic and political milieu. It means functioning according to Theory Y, but also that supervisors should create the essential conditions in their individual ways and with due regard for their own particular situations.

Notes and References

1. ILO, International Labour Conference, 33rd Session, Provisional Records, p. 34.
2. Micheal, Cooper, R. and Micheal, Wood T., "Member participation and commitment in group decision-making on influence satisfaction and decision riskness", *Journal of Applied Psychology*, Vol. 59, No. 2, April 1974.
3. Rensis Libert, New Patterns of Management, 1961.
4. *Ibid.*, p. 337.
5. Dalton, E. McFarland, Management, Principles and Practices, 1970, pp. 551-52.
6. Rensis Likert, *op. cit.*, p. 134.
7. Chris Argyris, Interventions Theory and Method, A Behavioural Science View, Reading (men) Addison-Wesley, 1970, p. 40.
8. S.K. Bhatia and Nirmal Singh, Principles and Techniques of Personnel Management/Human Resource Management, Deep and Deep, New Delhi, (2nd ed. 2000), p. 106.
9. Douglas, *op. cit.*, p. 132.
10. Landy and Becku, Motivation theory Reconsidered, pp. 7-8. These processes are commonly called congnitive processes.

CHAPTER

29

Techniques of Cost Benefit Analysis

(With Special Reference to Social Cost and Social Benefit)

The techniques of cost benefit analysis can be grouped into two categories. We must combine the two while determining the true cost benefit ratios.

I. TECHNIQUES DEALING WITH COMMERCIAL PROFITABILITY

We shall discuss here the following techniques in brief:

(a) Pay-Back Period,
(b) Internal Rate of Return, and
(c) Discounted Cash Flow Technique.

(a) Pay-Back Period

It is the period just enough for recovering the initial capital cost of any project. It involves calculation of the cash flows which would arise from the investment in each year of the life of the project. These cash flows are accumulated, year by year, till the time they equal the amount of the original investment made in the project. The length of time it takes to obtain the necessary cash flows equal to the original investment determines the pay-back period for the project. It is not a good criterion for project evaluation as it concentrates its attention on the profitability of the project in the beginning. It ignores the returns obtained in the later life of the project.

(b) Internal Rate of Return

The internal rate of return is defined in terms of expected profit as a percentage of the investment made. In this technique,

Present Value of Investment = Cost

(Discounted)
Or PVI = 2

$$\text{Or } C = \frac{R_1}{1 + r} + \frac{R_2}{(1+r)^2} + \ldots\ldots + \frac{R_n + S_n}{(1+3)^n}$$

where, r is known as the Value of Internet Rate Return. That project should be selected where we find r greater than the rate of return R. Both these techniques have their limitations in that they do not take into consideration the timing of cash flows and the value of the residue or scrap value.

(c) Discounted Cash Flow Technique

The technique of discounted cash flow (DCF) is based on the recognition of time value of money. In big projects, we notice that the gestation period is too long. Such projects required heavy capital costs in the initial stages and the yield from the project comes very late. Future profits as per the present valuation would be less, since the value of money in terms of its power will decline. Even the Banks get Rs. 30 or so today and pay Rs. 100 after 11 years, which means that if we think for getting a profit of Rs. 100 after 11 years, it is worth Rs. 30 today (if the rate of interest is about 10%).

Since every project would involve a different profile of costs and returns over its life-time, it becomes essential to reduce the streams of costs and benefits for each project to a common point of time for relating the total costs of a project to its benefits and also for making comparison between the projects. A discounting procedure is applied for the purpose of finding the present value at the point of calculating the benefits and costs associated with each project. A rate of interest is determined for us in the discounting process.

Let us consider a project which required capital cost of Rs. C and yields return R_1, R_2 ..... R_n, where N is the life of the project. Let S_n be the scrap value of the project at the end of its life. Then the Present Value of investment in the project (PVI) can be deduced with the help of the following formula:

$$PVI = \frac{R_1}{1 + r} + \frac{R_2}{(1+r)^2} + \ldots\ldots + \frac{R_n}{(1+r)^n} + S_n$$

where r is the opportunity cost of money available in the market.

Thus, the profitability of the Project can be deduced as:

The Net Present Value of Investment in the Project minus cost or NPVI = PVI–C. Discounted Cash Flow technique takes into account the timing of cash flows and the internal rate of return.

2. SOCIAL COST AND SOCIAL BENEFIT

Socially profitable projects are those projects where discounted social benefits are greater than discounted social costs. In private profitability calculations the earnings equal the actual output produced multiplied by their market price, and costs equal the amount of inputs actually used multiplied by their market price. Social cost-benefit analysis rejects this notion of projects. Social cost benefit analysis measures the benefits in terms of the positive effects of the project and costs in terms of the negative effects of the project.

(a) Social Price

The prices of various inputs and outputs in terms of their social values are called Social Prices. Market prices do not reflect the true valuation of goods and services. The value of the input and output is not calculated in terms of actual market price, but in terms of what is known as shadow or accounting price. If unemployment is regarded as a bad thing *per se*, the shadow price of labour in this case would in fact be negative, i.e. instead of the employment of labour being a cost it would be a benefit. Shadow pricing might also be relevant to the saving or earning of foreign exchange at a time when in the economy of any case the Shadow price of foreign exchange would be higher than the normal exchange rate. For many benefits which do not have market prices, valuation is often attempted by indirect means. The value of health benefits is sometimes estimated in terms of the avoidance of loss of earnings through ill-health although this obviously ignores the intrinsic worth of good health to the individual.

Let us now review some studies which have analyzed the loss resulting from poor health or diseases. Sinton (1936) made an assessment of the financial loss due to Malaria to the individual and the family alone at not less than Rs. 11,000 lakhs annually. In this conservative estimate of the annual financial loss to the country due to malaria, Sinton arrived at the figures of Rs. 1000 crores. He stated: "It constitutes one of the most important causes of economic misfortune engendering poverty, diminishing the quantity and quality of food supply, lowering the physical and intellectual standards of the nation and hampering increased prosperity and economic progress in every way."[1]

Tuberculosis is a widespread and contagious disease. A study was carried out by Dr. A.S. Sen and Dr. R.N. Basu, Consultants and Senior Research Officer, Planning Commission, Government of India, to measure the cost of tuberculosis in India.[2] They found that the total asses from mortality, morbidity and the direct cost[3] of the disease amounted to Rs. 420.4 crores and Rs. 29.68 crores respectively. The value of the production loss due to mortality and morbidity from tuberculosis is very large. As compared to these losses, the amount of direct expenditure which is being incurred on the control programme is very small. The annual direct cost for a population of about six million works out to Rs. 0.49 person per annum. Hence, the eradication of tuberculosis is not only a social welfare activity but an ultimate economic gain.

Because of this inter-relationship, economic development cannot be isolated from the social context. Health Programmes cannot be related unilaterally to either the economic or the social spheres, as they influence both and are influenced by both.

(b) Social Rate of Discount (SRD)

It is the marginal rate of substitution between consumption. at consecutive points of time and is used to link the costs and benefits occurring in different time periods. The rate of discount in cost benefit analysis is social rate of discount. It is generally lower than the private rate of discount, particularly for a developing economy. It may be mentioned that since social rate of discount is less than private rate of discount, a project that private sector may consider unprofitable position, public sector may consider profitable. It has been found to be one of the most difficult parameters to estimates so far. It has not been possible to give a nation-wide uniform marginal rate of substitution and therefore, there is no SRD expressly stated.

The above brief analysis suggests that the application of cost benefit analysis in the public sector is limited. It is very difficult to quantify the innumerable variables impinging upon the project. R. Parkash in his Article on Workable Tool for Social Cost Benefit Anaysis has rightly concluded that "Evaluation of investment proposals from the social point of view with the conventional methodology has revealed a wide gap between theory and practice of project evaluation. The theory of assigning weight to social parameters, assessing social prices, applying social rate of discount and then developing decision criteria in the form of net present value or internal rate of return or benefit cost ratio is academically sound and sophisticated but the limited validity in practice to aid those responsible for investment decisions."[4]

3. COST BENEFIT ANALYSIS—SOCIAL PERSPECTIVE

A benefit or a loss to one part of the economy—to one or more persons or groups—does not necessarily count as a benefit or loss to the economy as a whole. And in cost-benefit analysis we are concerned with the economy as a whole, with the welfare of a defined society, and not any smaller part of it. Economic analysis goes beyond the application of cost-benefit criteria. Political decisions to help the less fortunate members of society do not always entail direct cash transfers. The available cash can be used instead to promote economic opportunity among such groups. Financing education or medical services, recreational facilities, the building of dams or irrigation works, the provision of tools, technical equipment and advice, and the establishing of industries or information centers, are all ways in which the state may help others to help themselves. None of these ways in which the state may help others to help themselves. None of these ways might meet a strict cost-benefit criterion. Yet all of them might be regarded as superior to direct cash transfers. The economist can contribute to such decisions to the extent of selecting—within the limits of a number of seemingly equally appropriate ways of helping these groups—those opportunities which yield the maximum social benefit per dollar transferred to such groups. Clearly, the discounted present value of the maximum benefit per dollar invested in these socially approved ways may turn out to be less than a dollar. But such 'investment' have the merit of encouraging people to help themselves.[5]

Interest in social cost-benefit analysis for assessing the overall impact of a project on society as a whole has significantly increased in recent year; in the developing countries. The Fifth Five Year Plan of India had emphasized the need for exercising utmost care in choosing the investment projects and increasing the use of the tool of cost-benefit analysis in the process of project formulation and selection.

However, it has been very difficult to devise universal criteria for social cost benefit analysis. World Bank assigned weights to social objectives, assessing social prices, applying social rate of discount and developing decision criterion through the universally accepted procedure of working out net present value or internal rate of return or benefit-cost ratio. Logically, the theory is quite elegant and sophisticated but when put to operation it reveals a wide gap between the theory and practice of project evaluation.[6]

In practice, therefore, a relatively simple method tailored to economic realities is needed. The operational methodology which could assess the soundness of a project with tolerable degree of precision is the value-added approach. The value-added approach coupled with additional indices relating to different national plan objectives does not assign numerical weights. Though this approach may not appear to be elegant from a theoretical point of view, yet it is more realistic and workable. It permits use of one set of data in both commercial and social profitability analysis.[7]

We must be clear that analysis of commercial and social profitability is complementary and not substitutable. The first ensures operational efficiency while the second helps in efficient allocation of national resources. Hence, the removal of poverty and allocation of resources to poverty alleviation programmes would be beneficial to individual and community in the long-run.

Governments are changing their policies in favour of poor for long-term benefits, though there may be losses in short-term. Private sector may not venture into it. Government must eradicate poverty even forgetting temporary benefits. President Roosevelt of USA has rightly said that poverty any where is a danger to prosperity.

Recent Development

In the past, we have been examining cost-benefit analysis in a narrow sense. We have been making programmes which have not benefited poor people resulting into great losses in terms of poor manpower resources. There is a thinking now that-all projects must be made to benefit poor people to sustain overall development. Cost benefit analysis must be interpreted in a wider sense and devote more resources for social priorities which would lay the solid foundation of economic benefits. To quote World Development, 2000-2001 (Attacking Poverty) by world Bank: In nearly every country the public sector often pursues activities that are not socially justified and, in some cases, that generate rents for the elite. During the past two decades, as societies and their governments have become aware of this problem, they have launched public sector reforms to focus public action and programs on social priorities and increase the capacity of the state to reduce poverty.

Public sector reform and modernization have great potential to reduce poverty; if they are at the core of a development strategy that establishes clear priorities for public action. The functional and organisational structure of the public sector needs to be rationalized to improve resource allocation for programme that are social priorities and have greater capacity to reduce poverty. Most important is to streamline and "rightsize" public administrative entries and privatize public enterprises and other operational public programmes.

Beyond rationalizing the structure of the public sector there is a need to improve public management systems to make public programs more efficient and accountable. Involving civil society in planning, monitoring, and evaluating public programs and policies is also crucial to ensure steady progress towards a fully responsive and accountable state.

This would be possible only if—

- Public administrations implement policies efficiently and are accountable and responsive to users, corruption and harassment are curbed, and the power of the state is used to redistribute resources for actions benefiting poor people.
- Legal systems promote legal equity and are accessible to poor people.
- Central and local govenments create decentalized mechanisms for broad participation in the delivery of public services and minimize the scope for capture by local elites.
- Governments generate political support for public action against poverty by creating a climate favourable to pro-poor actions and coalitions, facilitating the growth of poor people's associations, and coalitions, and increasing the political capacity of poor people.
- Political regimes honour the rule of law, allow the expression of political voice, and encourage the participation of poor people in political processes.

Any strategy to overcome these inequalities will undoubtedly want to accord highest priority to overall poverty alleviation broad-based social and economic development.

Thus, there is a need to perfect our tools to carry out social cost benefit analysis. Noel J. Kavanagh has rightly said that though the problems of measuring benefits is a serious limitation but we cannot leave it as we cannot avoid the cost benefit analysis approach in our world today to select and administer projects which can raise the standards of the people and help the millions of people suffering from abject poverty, disease, hunger, squalor and unemployment. In spite of the inherent limitations, we must make use of this technique to ensure effective policy-making, planning and decision-making for the welfare of masses. H.G, Walsh and Alan Willians in their Article on current issues in the Cost Benefit Analysis have rightly said that the advantages of cost benefit analysis lie not in ensuring that decision-making is simpler, but in the possibilities for the systematic examination of each part of a problem in hand, for putting diverse decisions on a par; and for following the logical consequences of a synoptic view. In short, it is a means of organizing thought, not a means of avoiding it.[8] We must make use of all the techniques—commercial profitability, cost effectiveness and social cost benefit analysis to choose the project for public welfare.

Notes and References

1. A.Wailliams, Output Budget in C.A.S. Occasional Paper No. 4 (London), H.M. Stationery Office, April 1967.
2. J.A. Sinton, What Malaria Costs in India Nationally, Soically and Economically, condensed and reprinted in *Health Bulletin* in 1951, No. 26, Government of India Press, p. 125.
3. A.S. Sen and B.N. Basu, Economic of Health—The Cost of Tuberculosis, Planning Commission, Government of India, Health Division, 1968, pp. 1-36.
4. Direct Cost means expenditure on hospitals, clinics, drugs, research, training BCG Vaccinations, etc.
5. R. Prakash, Workable Tool for Social Cost Benefit Analysis, Managment in Government (ed.) by B.S. Mathur, *et. al.*, Ministry of Information and broadcasting, Government of India, New Delhi, 1979, p. 370.
6. E.J. Mishan, *op. cit.*, pp. 11-24.
7. R. Prakash, Workable Tool for Social Cost Benefit Analysis, in MIG, B.C. Mathur, *et. al.* (ed.) *op. cit.*, p. 36.
8. Cost Occasional Paper, 11, H.M.S.O.

CHAPTER 30

Problems of Administration in Coalition Regime

Coalition has become a fact and reality and not merely a matter for theoretical discussion. Regional parties are playing an important role in elections. Coalition government is being run in centre as well as in states. What are its implications on administration? What problems are being faced by administration? How can we maintain the basic and necessary ingredients of effective administration, i.e. citizen centric, responsive and efficient? How can civil services maintain harmony with the coalition partners. We give here some of the problems and suggestions which can help to make coalition administration a success.

I. Lack of clear-cut policy formulation: Need of detailed policy formulation to avoid confusion

It is hard enough to design public policies and programs that look good on paper. It s harder still to formulate them in words and slogans that resonate pleasingly in the ears of political leaders and the constituencies to which they are responsive. And it is excruciatingly hard to implement them in a way that pleases anyone at all, including the supposed beneficiaries or clients."

The first and the foremost essential ingredient of the process of development is to formulate policy in all areas, like industrial policy, monetary policy, food policy, health policy, education policy, etc. Policy formulation is both a science and art and if rightly used, can help us in making most of the problems solved.

However in coalition policies are not clear as there are minimum agreed programme on which administration is to function: Even when it comes to conflict, the coalition partner whom the policy does not suit would raise objections. Therefore, there is need to make a detailed policy where there is no scope of any misinterpretation.

According to Koontz and O'Donnell, a detailed written policy is preferable, as:

"It builds on proved decisions of the past conserving executive energy for new decisions: it creates an atmosphere in which individual actions may be taken with confidence; it speeds administration by reducing repetition to routine; it supports consistency of endeavour across a large group through the years; it stabilizes the enterprises; it frees the top management so that more creative considerations can be given to the problem of today and the new programme of tomorrow."

Machiavelli said in a famous remark: "There is nothing more difficult to take in hand, more perilous to conduct, more uncertain in its success than to take the lead in the introduction of a new order of things." Therefore, the policies of coalition government must be made to suit the ideology of all partners.

2. Civil services do not appreciate the coalition government and show apathy in implementing the policy in right earnest causing coalition Government to disreputation

"The performance and output of any enterprise depend upon the quality of the human organization and its capacity to functions as a tightly knit, highly motivated, technically competent entity, i.e. as a highly effective interaction-influence system. High productivity, high quality products, high earnings and successful use of research and development are not accomplished by impersonal equipment or computers. These goals are achieved by human beings. Successful organizations are those making the best use of competent personnel to perform efficiently all the tasks required by the enterprise."

Civil services need be trained in the art and science of coalition government as they were used to administer policies of a single party leadership.

3. Difficult to take rational decisions as interests of coalition clash—Need of creativity

The decision-making process involves a problem to be solved, a number of conflicting objective to be reconciled, a number of possible alternative course of action from which the 'best' has to be chosen and some way of measuring the value or pay off of alternative courses of action.

For example, it becomes difficult for government to disinvest public enterprises as the views vary of different partners of coalition. However, intelligent bureaucracy can help the coalition government in taking rational decisions.

New problems demand new solutions and the Civil Services who can come out from the routine are highly prized. This requires creativity in the sphere of decision-making. Newmann has indicated five distinct stages which can help the Civil Services in this process.

1. *Saturation*: to be familiar with the problem.
2. *Deliberation*: to consider alternative solutions and to rearrange them.
3. *Incubation*: to let the sub-conscious mind work on the problems.
4. *Illustration*: to get a new ideas and sensing that it may work.
5. *Accommodation*: to work out the new ideas so that it is practical solution to the problem.

Thus the civil services must find out the solutions which are highly appreciated by all the partners of the coalition.

4. Co-ordination of the view points of all coalition partners becomes difficult and arduous task—Need of caution and sensitive

According to Gulick, some of the difficulties arise from (a) the uncertainty of the future as to the behaviour of individuals and of people; (b) the lack of knowledge, experience, wisdom and character among leaders and their confused and conflicting ideas and objectives; (c) the lack of administrative skill and techniques; (d) the vast number of variables involved and the incompleteness of human knowledge, particularly with regard to man and life; and (e) the lack of orderly methods of developing, considering, perfecting and adopting new ideas and programmes.[1] To these are added four more by Seckler-Hudson. These are the "*size* and complexity, personalities and political factors, the lack of leaders with wisdom and knowledge pertaining to public administration and the accelerated expansion of public administration to international dimensions."[2]

Coordination is becoming complex as the quantitative operations of the organisations are increasing at a very fast rate without making changes in the administration structure and procedures responsible for coordination. Therefore, there is a need of advance planning and decision-making to achieve effective coordination. There is also need to create administrative structures like Cabinet Secretariat, Staff Agency, etc. to help in coordination. It is a continuous process. Coordination is not a simple process but is directly linked with the total management. Until and unless all the principles of the organisation like planning, objectives, span of control, unity of command, authority and responsibility, etc. are well defined, coordination becomes impossible and impracticable. A good organisation leads to prompt and good coordination and *vice-versa*.

Civil Services need to ascertain the view points of coalition partners and then merged them in a way suitable to all to a large extent.

5. Lack of effective Leadership to keep coalition intact—Need of location of impartial leadership

To keep the coalition united for the whole duration of the term requires honest, dedicated and clear-cut ideology and leadership. Leader may belong to one party but when dealing with coalition issues, leader must detach himself/herself from the interest of his/her party. It is highly difficult but not impossible. Therefore, such leader should be located who can be treated and who can keep coalition intact.

Kanwalpreet in her article, "Leading the leadership race" in *The Tribune* dated November 10, 2002 opines that successful leaders are like ants who never wave even if a lot is placed as an obstacle in their way. They have a knack of springing up after every failure. When Michealangelo was asked as to why he spends so much time in trying to perfect every piece of art, he replied, "Trifles make up perfection and perfection is no trifle." Dr. Rashmi Diwan, in her article, "Self-Development must for Transformational Leadership" feels that Transformational leadership would call for drastic changes in the behaviour of self before it could be applied to the organization. Good managers can be transformed into successful leaders but through real world leadership training.

The leader of coalition should be participative and democratic whose qualities should be:

- Share information with participants;
- Prevent dominant personalities from having disproportionate influence;
- Solicit opinions, facts, and feelings from participants;
- Assist participants in communication with one another;

- Minimize blame-oriented statements;
- Redirect in focused discussion back to the problem at hand;
- Encourage the generation of alternative solutions;
- Delay evaluation of alternatives until all have been presented; and
- Guide the process of screening alternatives and selecting the solution.

6. Crisis Management in Coalition

In coalition government, there is no time when crisis can pick up and there is a danger to government to come to minority. The whole administration becomes shaky.

Anurag Goel suggests that leaders must know the methods to deal with a crisis situation which has become essential to keep coalition intact:

The requisites of crisis management can be summed up as under:

(i) Identify the problems that could lead to a crisis and learn when and how to intervene most effectively;
(ii) Know how to carry out the difficult planning and coordination activities associated with preparing for, and managing, a crisis;
(iii) Develop special negotiating and communication skills required to reduce conflict or ensure cooperation in a crisis situation; and
(iv) Develop special knowledge and expertise in the field.

7. Frequent Eruption of Conflicts within Coalition Partners—Need of Conflict Resolution

Administration and management have to struggle to achieve productivity and effectiveness. Effectiveness could be defined as the degree to which organization realizes its goals.[3] It can be judged in terms of survival of the organization.[4] Organisational effectiveness is the extent to which an organization, given certain resources and means, achieves its objectives without placing undue strain on its members.[5] It is the ability of an organization to mobilize its centres of power for action-production and adaptation.[6]

However, effectiveness of Organizations is often marred by conflict, which slowly damages the performance and even become a threat to survival. Conflict may be defined as a disagreement between two or more members or groups within an Organization, emanating from formal and informal relationships. Such disagreements take place in every Organization and thus conflict is an inevitable dimension of Organisational Climate.

Most of the executives spend a great deal of their time in resolving conflict, whether the conflict may be between individuals, individual and a group, between groups, or between organizations. According to Newman, "Life is not a grand harmony, conflict exists."[7] Scholars have viewed conflict differently at different times. We can classify them into traditional, behavioural and interactionist view. We must not allow the conflict to sustain which can be harmful to the existence of coalition government.

8. Leaders of the coalition do not encourage participation of all partners of coalition resulting into explosive situation: Need of involvement of all members of coalition government through MBO approach

Peter Drucker defines the Philosophy of MBO thus: "What the Business enterprise needs is a principle of management that will give full scope to individual strength and responsibility, and at the same time give common direction of vision and effort, establish teamwork and harmonize the goal of the individual with the common weal ... The only principle that can do this is management by objectives and self-control. It makes the common weal the aim of every manager. It substitutes control from outside by control from within. It motivates the manager to action, not because somebody tells him to do something or takes him into doing it, but because the objective needs of his task demand it. He acts not because somebody wants to but because he himself decides that he has to—he acts, in other words, as a free man."[8]

According to George Odiorne, "MBO (Management By Objectives) is a system wherein the superior and the subordinate managers of an organization jointly define its common goals, define each individual's major areas of responsibility in terms of the results expected of him and use these measures as guides for operating the unit and assessing the contribution of each of its members"[9]

Reddin says that MBO is "the establishment of effectiveness areas and effectiveness standards for managerial positions and the periodic conversion of the measurable time bound objectives linked vertically and horizontally with future planning."[10]

From these definitions, it is clear that MBO is an approach which can help us in coinciding the objectives of the organization and the individuals working in it and their ultimate achievement. It brings commitment on the part of personnel resulting in ultimate organisational efficiently.

Ingredients of MBO

We mention here some essential ingredients required for the success of MBO in coalition government:

(a) Active participation and involvement of all constituents in Planning, implementation and evaluation of Programme of Government.
(b) Emphasis on team spirit and team approach.
(c) Open Communication among the members of the coalition irrespective of their status.
(d) Increased skill in inter-personal communication.
(e) Personal counseling and guidance.

9. Coalition is not based on administrative ethics—Need of ethics in all partners of coalition

We are passing through critical times when the environment all around is unethical K.R. Narayanan, Former President of India, while delivering his address, on the eve of Independence on 14th August, 2000, was critical of the nexus between politicians and criminals, who are, the process polluting the environment of the country. The malpractices in every sphere has become cancerous and are engulfing the entire system geared to provide good standard of life to people. T.N. Chaturvedi in his Editorial on the Special Number on Ethics in Public life of *Indian Journal of Public Administration* (July-Sept., 1995) has rightly remarked.[11]

The potential damage and threat to the political fabric of a system is not dependent on the character of government, i.e whether it is an activist or limited in scope. History shows that neither a capitalist nor a socialist nor a welfare state is immune to the corrosive evil of corruption. The standards of conduct and behaviour of people in political authority have their malignant influence in other walks of life in society. The ethical dimensions of how influential and powerful people conduct themselves in private life and the public domain set a precedent for the lesser human beings and groups in society to follow or to seek justification for their own self-seeking or even scandalous conduct. The perniciousness ripple-effect encompasses all segments of society.

It is not only the public systems that are under attack. The people harbour grievances against trade, industry, business, academia, medical and other professional groups and organizations. The evil within and outside the government circle, is thus, not limited to any narrow confines. Similarly, the influence of ethical conduct in positive terms is also not contained or concerned with only some specific sections and select groups but is relevant to the entirety of society and its wider network of relationships. As is often said, the moral basis for the unity and stability of society demands that ethical restraints must operate not only in respect of individuals but also organized groups—be they industrial, business and trade associations, labour unions, political parties, military and civil services, judiciary, non-governmental organizations, academic or professional associations, agriculturists organisations, etc.— apart from government itself. The all-pervading and inter-locking nature of ethics in public life is to be comprehended in all its manifestations and dimensions. This is borne out by history in different times and ages and also by the prowess of civilization today.

O.P. Dwivedi, an eminent scholar, suggests the need of moral base for the Government to save the country from further degradation. To quote him:[12]

No country is immune from the moral disarray which we have seen recently. Even in the People's Republic of China, which was hailed as a paragon of public virtue and morality by some cases of public service unethical activities and corruption have been reported. In many nations, a widespread sense of moral disarray exists, neither industrial nor Third World countries are exempt from this disarray. Everywhere, instances are on the rise detailing the collapse of standard and quality of service. This has contributed to the public cynicism; but at the same time, public is clamouring for a new set of bases for public morality and decent moral standards. Because, if we don't wish to be swallowed by the sea of amorality and self-centered hedonism, there will have to be some agreement (or consensus) about the behaviour of individuals, particularly those holding public offices.

The vacuum created because of traditional and 'old-fashioned' values drawn from religious sources and based on common sense being discarded in favour of materialism and selfish individualism, clearly points to the need for a code of ethics. As a matter of fact, no specific standards were left sacred against which the conduct of public officials (as well as business people) could be measured. And as clergy and religious leaders were told to keep out of the state affairs, the protective layer of public morality was left exposed to the onslaught of corruption, dishonesty, sleaziness, deception and selfish individualism. That protective layer in the body politic is needed back. For no nation or a society, irrespective of its political and religious orientation, can live in a moral vacuum. There have to be some articles of faith (drawn from the societal culture, traditions, and religions) governing our lives, which must be resurrected and strengthened. We already know that one cannot legislate honesty and good behaviour; these have to come from within. For that, one has to look to our religions where such attributes are considered sacred. But, one does not acquire such attributes by thinking alone; these have to be drilled in the thinking process of the officials. But that could be possible if their moral consciousness is raised so that they are able to fight against the forces of corruption, favoritism, and malpractice. Otherwise, they will continue to be adrift in the sea of anomalism, of which the prevailing administrative culture has come to symbolise. It is to prevent further decay that they ought to think in terms of drawing on their priceless spiritual and cultural heritage. Thus, there is a need within the secular domain of the administrative culture to seek the spiritual guidance. Only by demonstrating high standards of personal integrity, fairness, justice, and by regarding their work as Dharma, public officials may be able to arrest those insidious forces which have penetrated the foundation as well as the structure of India's administration. Such is the requisite of a moral government.[13]

Moral values, in simple terms, are the values that tell us what is the right, proper and acceptable way of behaving. Moral values are indispensable for good governance. An efficient and technologically sound administrative machinery, unless it stands on high moral pedestal, does not serve the public, but it services a self-perpetuating and exploitative system.

Unfortunately, the Indian Government sector cannot boast of high moral standards. Superior courts have made highly critical comments on the conduct of bureaucrats, and the media is full of reports of high-handedness, corruption and other forms of inappropriate conduct of the bureaucrats. Honest and upright civil servants themselves are concerned about the low morality of the bureaucracy and have been voicing concern at various fora.

Coalition partners are not based on any ethical principle and that is why coalition has failed many times in Union and State Governments. In order to ensure good governance through coalition government, we must ensure that all partners of coalition work on ethical basis.

10. Administrative personnel do not exhibit neutrality and impartiality causing irritants

Administrative personnel must be loyal to all partners of coalition—The prestige and reputation of the civil service depends to a great extent upon the ethos, attitudes and perception of its members. As Prof. Inis Claude has commented:

In a very significant senses, the identity of every organization ... is logged in its professional staff. Members, stockholders or citizens may control the organization but they cannot do it; the staff is the organization.[14]

In this context, the foremost characteristics required among civil servants are impartiality and consistency in the transaction of public business. Civil servants are required to be completely impartial to avoid corruption and favouritism; civil servants must maintain the dignity and authority of the public office. They must meticulously implement the policies and programmes as laid down in the laws, regulations and rules.

In developing countries, including India, it is observed that civil servants are interpreting the laws and enforcing them to safeguard the interests of the influential individuals and groups and that is why they are always under attack from most quarters. All the commissions of enquiry appointed from time to time to investigate the charges of corruption and favouritism against ministers and civil servants are a testimony to it. We can cite examples of irregularities in all the fields of administration, i.e. allotment of land, admission to an academic institution, disbursement of loans, treatment in a hospital, etc. There is a need to develop good administrative traditions which may impel civil servants to perform their activities impartially to keep the administration above board. The civil servants at higher levels of administration must set standards of independence and impartiality through constant practice. Such standards would be imbibed consciously or unconsciously by the personnel in the lower echelons of administration. At critical times or situations, some civil servants may be under pressure to favour a course of action which are against the established laws, rules and moral standards. They must have the capacity to resist impending challenges to impartiality rather than succumbing to it. By such actions the image of the administration will become brighter. Each official on his appointment swears solemnly to perform, in all loyalty, discretion and conscience, the functions entrusted to him and to discharge these functions and regulate his conduct with the interest of the organisation alone in view. The practice of these principles must be inculcated through the development of professional standards.

An allied requirement of promoting impartiality is the necessity of developing and maintaining a national outlook. It involves on the part of the civil service a willingness to try to understand and be tolerant of different points of view, different cultural patterns, and different work habits. It also entails willingness to work without prejudice or bias with persons of all regions, religions and cultures. It involves conduct of the highest type and exercise of judgement and restraint in all expressions of view whether public or private; any expressions which could be construed as biased or intolerant, particularly in respect of regional interests or political issues with which the organisation is confronted, must be scrupulously avoided.

We can thus conclude by saying that loyalty and impartiality requires a positive attitude, i.e., to act with dedication divorced from emotions and prejudices. The Roman Emperor, Marcus Aurelius wrote about his duties in memorable words which are quoted below and must be imbibed by civil servants in the present day:

Do what comes to hand with correct and natural dignity and with humanity, independence and justice, and allow your mind freedom from all other considerations.

Neutrality

Political neutrality is an essential ingredient of civil service in a democratic set-up for integrity and efficiency in administration. It means that the civil service should give free and frank advice to the government impartially and without any political consideration. It also means the implementation of the decisions of the government by the civil service faithfully whether such decisions were in consonance with their advice or not. P.C. Sethi in his article, "New Challenges in Administration" in *The Indian Journal of Public Administration* (April-June, 1975) says that the concept of neutrality should be emphasized to generate:

(a) public confidence in the administrators against political influences;
(b) trust among the ministers that their orders would be faithfully carried out irrespective of their ideology; and
(c) keeping of an atmosphere of appraisals and promotions in the civil service which would be free from political influence.

He further adds that administrators should manifest complete commitment to the goals of their organisations and maintain the necessary non-partisanship and impartiality in taking decisions in individual cases to prevent discrimination merely on grounds of political affiliation. Let us now analyse the practice followed in the USA, UK and India. One of the important aspects of political neutrality is the limitation on the political rights of the civil servants to ensure their impartiality. On the other hand, there is a need for association of the elite in the political affairs of the country.

The Masterman Committee in its report on the political activities in civil servants (H.M.S.O., C.M.O. 7,718) assesses this problem: (i) "In a democratic society it is desirable for all citizens to have a voice in the affairs of the State and for as many as possible to play an active part in public life, and (ii) the public interest demands the maintenance of political impartiality in the civil service and of confidence in that impartiality as an essential part of the structure of Government. Let us now examine the practice in different countries.

CONCLUSION

Coalition has been in existence for long in India and civil servants have exhibited their caliber to work with the coalition partners. There is a need of training to civil servants to make them understand as to how to make coalition government a success, otherwise repeated elections would cost a lost to state exchequer. Coalition partners must also be sincere, clear and honest in their dealings within the coalitions government as upon their attitudes, perception and ethos depend the success of coalition government. The coalition partners as well as civil services must keep in mind that the basic characteristics of governance—citizen-centric, citizen-friendly, responsiveness, transparent and corruption-free. For people, it hardly matters as to who is in power, they want that their welfare must be the first priority within the government whether one party government or coalition government.

Notes and References

1. Gulick, L. and Urwick, L. Papers on the Science of Administration, p. 40.
2. Seckler-Hudon, *op. cit.*, p. 53.
3. Amitai Etizioni, Modern Organization, Englewood, Cliffs, NJ, Printice-Hall, 1964, p. 8.
4. John Kimberly, "Issues in the Criterion of Organization, Initiation, Innovation and Instrumentalization', Academy of Management Journal, Sept., 1979, p. 17.
5. Basil Geogopolous and Arnold S. Tannenbaum, 'A study of Organisational Effectiveness", *American Sociological Review*, 22, 1957, pp. 535-36.
6. Paul E. Mott, Characteristics of Effective Organizations, New York, Harper, 1972, p. 17.
7. W.H. Newman and E.K. Warren, The Process of Management, New Delhi, Prentice-Hall, 1979, p. 14.
8. Peter Drucker, Practice of Management, 1954, pp. 135-36.
9. George S. Odorine: Management by Objectives, New York, Pitman, 1965, p. 55.
10. W.J. Reddin, Effective Management by Objectives, New York, McGraw Hill, 1970.
11. T.N. Chaturvedi, Editorial, *IJPA*, July-Sept. 1995, pp. ix-x.
12. O.P. Dwivedi, Administrative Theology, *IJPA*, July-Sept. 1990, pp. 418-19.
13. N.R. Ranganathan, A Charter of Ethics, Reading material for Trainees (Some abstracts).
14. Inis Claude, "Swords into Plowshares, 3rd ed., New York: Random House, 1964, p. 174.

CHAPTER 31

Nature, Scope and Role of NGOs

Non-government Organizations are the pivot and the means to primate development administration as the NGOs are engaged in all areas in which Development Administration is interested. NGOs supplement and support Development Administration.

Poonam Sharma in her editorial "A Question of Trust" (Social Welfare, January 2009) observes that Pt. Jawahar Lal Nehru had called the voluntary sector the 'heart of the welfare state'. It has also been described as the fifth and central pillar of democracy. Envisioned by the architects of the Indian democracy and shaped by the leading lights of the freedom movement, the voluntary sector in India is a vibrant alternative support system for the common man. In recent years, there has been a mushrooming of voluntary organizations all over the country. The question before many of them is one of trust. Voluntary organizations in India occupy a special place in the minds and hearts of the people. They are the hope of the helpless and the saviour of the needy. The voluntary sector cannot afford to lose the trust of the people and it is imperative that it maintains its reputation of service and honesty.

Non-Government Organizations (NGOs) also called Voluntary agencies have a long history of active involvement in the promotion of human welfare and well-being. Our literature is replete with examples, where the tendency to help a poor, weak, old, sick, disabled, helpless, hungry, thirsty—existed from ancient times. This tendency of helping other(s) or doing good to others by an individual or a group of benevolent people has been considered a service to the God (Nar Sewa-Narayan Sewa or never forget Darider-Narayan) and a path to Moksha. Religion and charity always co-exited in our set-up. Lord Beveridge called them "a private enterprise for social progress." NGOs come into existence spontaneously, voluntarily and without any compulsion or control to fulfil the particular needs of some groups of people. These agencies are flexible and possess the virtues of human service with dedication. Voluntary action is the soul of democracy as this medium secures the active involvement of the people from policy-making to implementation of social services.

NGOs today are involved in all areas, e.g. health, education, agriculture, rural development, poverty alleviation programmes, adult education, environment awareness and development, women empowerment, old age homes and other areas of benefit to old people, family planning, drug addiction, rehabilitation, etc.

It is the life and blood of democracy. Their programmes cover a diverse range of functions embracing human welfare. The NGOs include the strictly professional, specialised and technical organisations: broadly-based associations of persons or groups organised for a particular purpose, e.g. information and service activities, educational institutions and associations, social welfare organisations, religious groups, women's organisations, youth groups, children councils, trade unions, family planning associations, etc. Many NGOs at national level are linked with international federations or associations. There are many which though not directly involved in social welfare, indirectly influence the promotion of the programmes of social welfare as human development cannot be fragmented. Social and economic sectors are closely allied and interdependent, e.g. it is useless to promote a health insurance scheme if employment opportunities are so limited that participation is beyond the reach of most. Provision of a source of clean water to a community will have impact on waterborne diseases only in so far as the community is educated in its use and management. The programme of other NGOs, which are of great and direct relevance to social welfare administration include projects to improve nutrition, food production, housing, potable water, promote literacy, provide educational and instructional material, enhance community development, improve environmental sanitation, child and women welfare, etc. Thus, they are helping to create conditions to the protection, promotion and maintenance of health and the prevention of illness. In a sector as important as social welfare, there is a great scope for voluntary effort which government is promoting and assisting. NGOs can take up action-oriented programmes based on areas of priority. They should be allowed to work with dirty, responsibility and partnership so as to take the form of a national movement. To perform their role effectively, greater representation and encouragement has to be given to them and they have to be considered as equal partners in tasks of national concern. Their deep involvement can pay rich dividends as they enjoy many advantages over the official machinery. At the same time, if voluntary organisations are to assume greater responsibility for social welfare schemes, it is necessary that they also conduct their work on scientific lines and have access to specialists and experts for necessary advice and guidance.

Voluntary action, no one will dispute, is a measure of the health and strength of democratic-society. Voluntary action would flourish in a society which is buoyant and vibrant and decline in that which is subdued and dependent. However, voluntary action has to be viewed as a canvas much more expansive than what is encompassed by the term voluntary organisation. Normatively when primary institutions of society are strong and well-equipped with security dispensation mechanisms, there should be little scope for externally designed NGOs. This was the state of affairs in India before 'industrialised' modernisation made inroads into our society. NGOs and the welfare state appeared on the scene only when these primary institutions of our society got dissipated under the impact of new technological developments and were no longer fully capable of looking after their weak and the needy members. The welfare role of government as also that of NGOs should, therefore, be viewed only as a historical imperative and not as categorical imperative. In fact, both these agencies should find their self-fulfilment in their self-cancellation when their enabling role has succeeded in generating the capacity for self-management among the people.

The progressive replacement of extraneous voluntary organisations by indigenous community organisations should, therefore, not be construed as a measure of decline in voluntary action, rather, it should be viewed as a positive development and legitimate desideratum. In the ultimate analysis the authentic indicator of the health of voluntary action would be the conspicuous absence from the welfare scene of voluntary agencies rather than their flamboyant presence.[2]

MEANING AND DEFINITIONS OF VOLUNTARY AGENCIES

An NGO is an independent, flexible, democratic, secular, nonprofit people's organization working for and/or assisting in the empowerment of economically and socially, marginalized groups. CBO: Community Based Organization; NGO: Non-Government Organization; NGDO: Non-Government Development Organization; POO: Private Development Organization; PSO: Public Service Organization; VO: Voluntary Organization.

(a) Folder on Keywords and Concepts Associated with NGOs?

With the UN and the world bank recognizing the key roles played by NGOs (in the broader sense of the term)—at the grass-roots, intermediary and decision-making levels, a considerable body of literature has emerged, expanding on and highlighting the issues involved. The list is a compilation of terms, phrases and cliches (!) found in the literature.

Criteria used in defining NGOs and related concepts

Size, organisational structure, operational programme areas, geographical specificity, founding sources, membership structures, position on the project cycle.

Some of the terms used to define NGOs based on its organisational format

Non-governmental organization, non-profit organization, private voluntary organization, non-governmental development organization, government-organized NGO [GONGO), donor-organized NGO [DONGO], social movements, civil society, community-based organization, people's organization, grass-roots organization.

(b) Operational Areas, Tools and Strategies

Some of the operational areas within which NGOs have worked independently and in collaboration with other organizations.

Organization of the community, democracy, education, enterprise development, environment, health, housing, human rights, infrastructure, political franchise, poverty alleviation.

Intervening tools and strategies adopted by NGOs in their projects community organizing, decision support, information dissemination, leadership development, participation, training and development, workshops.

(c) Membership Structures, Catch-phrases and Cliches

Membership structure of NGOs can consist of: professionals, women, youth, community, religion, volunteers, students. Catch-phrases and cliches used in NGO literature, with tongue firmly placed in the cheek bottoms-up, disadvantaged, charity, civil society, empowerment, grass-roots, independence, morality, social capital, sustainability, top-down.

SOME DEFINITIONS OF NGO

- A non-profit making, voluntary, service-oriented/development-oriented organization, either for the fit of members (a grass-roots organization) or of other members of the population (an agency).
- It is an organization of private individuals who believe in certain basic social principles and who structure their activities to bring about development to communities that they are servicing.
- Social development organization assisting in empowerment of people.
- An organization or group of people working independent of any external control with specific objective and aims to fulfil tasks that are oriented to bring about desirable change in a given community or area or situation.
- An independent, democratic, non-sectarian peoples' organization working for the empowerment of economic and/or socially marginalized groups.
- An organization not affiliated to political parties, generally engaged in working for aid, development and welfare of the community.
- Organization committed to the root causes of the problems trying to better the quality of life specially for the poor, the oppressed, the marginalized in urban and rural areas.
- Organizations established by and for the community without or with little intervention from the government: they are not only a charity organization, but work on socio-economic-cultural activities.
- An organization that is flexible and democratic in its organization and attempts to serve the people without profit for itself.

NGO's ADVANTAGES AND DISADVANTAGES

Advantages

- They have the ability to experiment freely with innovative approaches and, if necessary, to take risks.
- They are flexible in adapting to local situations and responding to local needs and therefore able to develop integrated projects, a well as sectoral projects.
- They enjoy good rapport with people and can render micro-assistance to very poor people as they can identify those who are most in need and tailor assistance to their needs.
- They have the ability to communicate at all levels, from the neighbourhood to the top levels of government.
- They are able to recruit both experts and highly motivated staff with fewer restrictions than the government.

Disadvantages

- Paternalistic attitudes restrict the degree of participation in programme/project design.
- Restricted/constrained ways of approach to a problem or area.
- Reduced replicability of an idea, due to non-representativeness of the project or

CHART 31.1

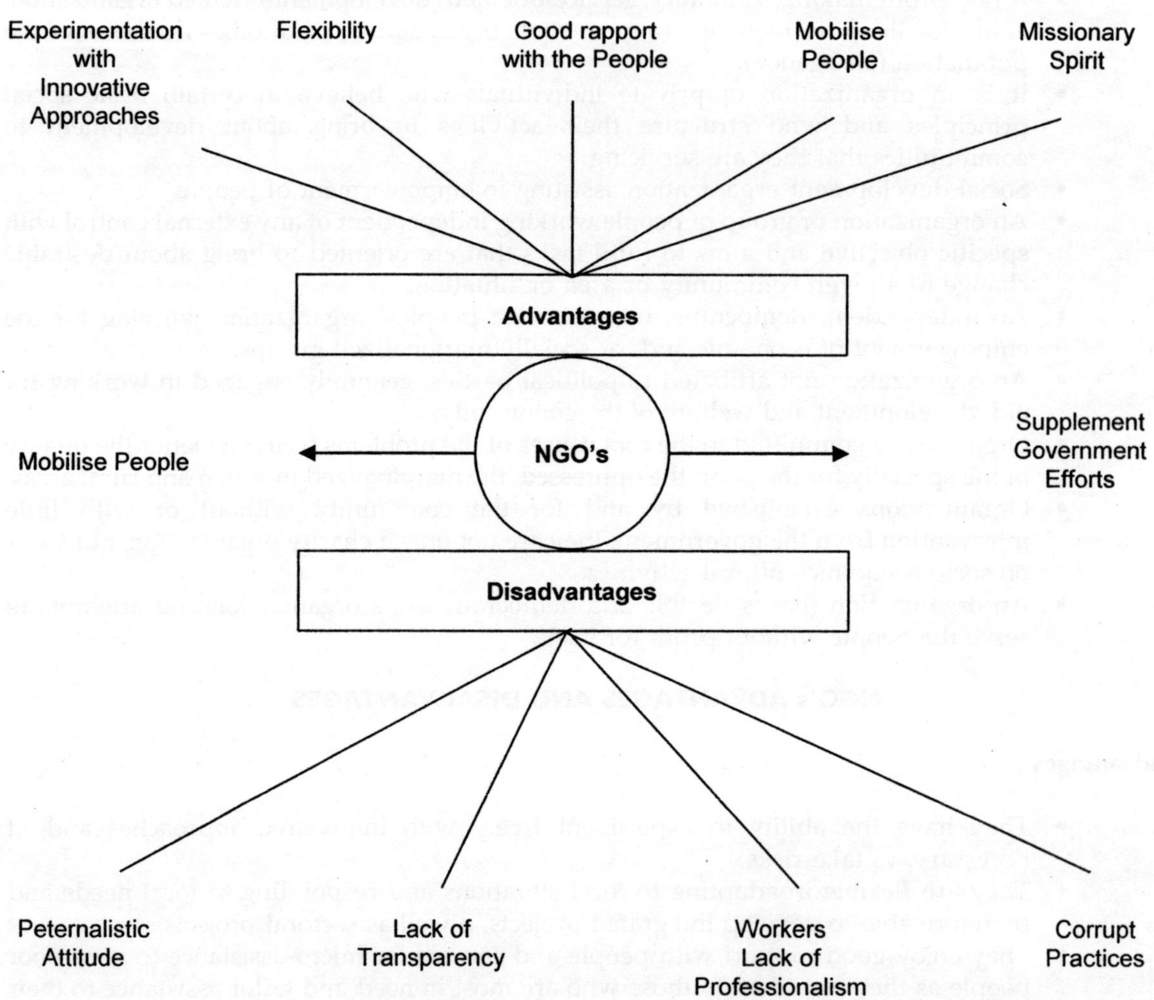

selected area, relatively small project coverage, dependence on outside financial resources, etc.

- Territorial possessiveness of an area or project reduces cooperation between agencies, seen as threatening or competitive.

The diversity of NGOs strains any simple definition. They include many groups and institutions that are entirely or largely independent of government and that have primarily humanitarian or cooperative rather than commercial objectives. They are private agencies in industrial countries that support international development: indigenous groups organized regionally or nationally, and member-groups in villages. NGOs include charitable and religious associations that mobilize private funds for development, distribute food and family planning services and promote community organization. They also include independent cooperatives, community associations, water-user societies, women's group and pastoral associations. Citizen Groups that raise awareness and influence policy are also NGOs.

TYPES OF NGOs BY ORIENTATION AND LEVEL OF OPERATIONS

NGO type can be understood by their orientation and level of cooperation:

NGO Types of Orientation

- Charitable Orientation often involves a top-down paternalistic effort with little participation by the "beneficiaries." It includes NGOs with activities directed toward meeting the needs of the poor—distribution of food, clothing or medicine; provision of housing, transport, schools, etc. Such NGOs may also undertaken relief activities during a natural or man-made disaster.
- Service Orientation includes NGOs with activities such as the provision of health, family planning or education service in which the programme is designed by the NGO and people are expected to participate in its implementation and in receiving the service.
- Participatory Orientation is characterized by self-help projects where local people are involved particularly in the implementation of project by contributing cash, tools, land, materials, labour, etc. In the classical community development project, participation begins with the need definition and continues into the planning and implementation stages. Cooperation often have a participatory orientation.
- Empowering Orientation is where the aim is to help poor people develop a clearer understanding of the social, political and economic factors affecting their lives, and to strengthen their awareness of their own potential power to control their lives. Sometimes, these groups develop spontaneously around a problem or an issue, at other times outside workers from NGOs play a facilitating role in their development. In any case, there is maximum involvement of the people with NGOs acting as facilitators

NGO Types by Level of Operation

- Community-based Organisations (CBOs) arise out of people's own initiatives. These can include sports clubs, women's C organizations, neighbourhood organizations, religious or educational organizations.
- There are a large variety of these, some supported by NGOs, national or international NGOs, or bilateral or international agencies, and other independent of outside help. Some are devoted to rising the consciousness of the urban poor or helping them to understand their right in gaining access to needed services while others are involved in providing such services.
- City-wide Organization include organizations such as the Rotary or lion's Club, chambers of commerce and industry, coalitions of business, ethnic or educational groups and associations of community organizations. Some exist for other purposes,

and become involved in helping the poor as one of many activities, while others are created for the specific purpose of helping the poor.

- National NGOs include organizations such as the Red Cross, YMCAs/YWCAs, professional organizations, etc. Some of these have state and cuts branches and assist local NGOs.
- International NGOs range from secular agencies such as Redda Barna and Save the Children Organizations, OXF AM, CARE, Ford and Rockefeller Foundations to religiously motivated groups. Their activities vary from mainly funding local NGOs, institutions and projects, to implementing the projects themselves.

A voluntary agency may be defined as: "An organisation that is administered by an autonomous board which holds meetings, collects funds for its support, chiefly from private sources, and expends money, whether with or without paid workers, in conducting a programme directed primarily to furthering the public welfare by providing services or education or by advancing research or legislation or by a combination of these activities.[3]

"A voluntary agency is a group of persons who have organized themselves as a legal corporate body to render social services or rural development through organized programmes. It is accountable to the community that it serves and from which it has supported. It is controlled and administered by an association of citizens, rather than by the government, although primarily financed by contribution from the community."[4]

David Sills, a sociologist, writes that definitions of the term "voluntary association" differ widely but that they generally contain three elements.[5] A voluntary association is an organized group of persons:

(a) that is formed in order to further some common interest of its members;
(b) in which membership is voluntary in the sense that it is neither mandatory nor acquired through birth; and
(c) that it exists independently of the state.

David Sills defines NGO as "a group of persons organized on the basis of voluntary membership without state control, for the furtherance of some common interests of its members."
Sills excluded three types of similar associations:

(i) making a living association (like business firms, trade associations, etc.);
(ii) religious organizations; and
(iii) political parties.

Attempting a comprehensive definition of voluntary organization, N.R. Inamdar observes: "A voluntary organization in development to be of durable use to the community has to nurse a strong desire and impulse for community development among its members, to be economically viable to possess dedicated and hard working leadership and command resources of expertise in the functions undertaken."[6]

An organization formed of free will, with a choice to leave, of workers who pursue a goal generally related to the search of man-in-community to his economic problems and social oppressions.

World Bank defines it as: "The diversity of NGOs strains any simple definition. They include many groups and institutions that are entirely or largely independent of government and that have primarily humanitarian or cooperative rather than commercial objectives. They are private agencies in industrial countries that support international development: indigenous groups organized regionally or nationally; and member-groups in villages. NGOs include charitable and religious associations that mobilize private funds for development, distribute food and family planning services and promote community organization. They also include independent cooperatives, community associations, water-user societies, women's groups and pastoral associations. Citizen Groups that raise awareness and influence policy are also NGOs."

NGO is an organization that is flexible and democratic in its organization and attempts to serve the people without profit for itself. The wide variety of roles that NGOs can play, the following six can be identified as important, at the risk of generalization: (See Chart 31.2)

I. Development of Infrastructure

Community-based organizations and cooperatives can acquire, sub-divide and develop land, construct housing, provide infrastructure and operate and maintain infrastructure such as walls or public toilets and solid waste collection services. They can also develop building material supply centres and other community-based economic enterprises. In many cases, they will need technical assistance or advice from governmental agencies or higher-level NGOs.

2. Supporting Innovation, Demonstration and Pilot Projects

NGO have the advantage of selecting particular places for innovative projects and specify in advance the length of time which they will be supporting the project-overcoming some of the shortcomings that governments face in this respect. NGOs an also be pilots for larger government projects by virtue of their ability to act more quickly than the government bureaucracy.

3. Facilitating Communication

NGOs use interpersonal methods of communication, and study the right entry points whereby they gain the trust of the community they seek to benefit. They would also have a good idea of the feasibility of the projects they take up. The significance of this role to the government is that NGOs can communicate to the policy-making levels of government, information about the lives, capabilities, attitudes and cultural characteristics of people at the local level. NGOs can facilitate communication upward from people to the government and downward from the government to the people. Communication upward involves informing government about what local people are thinking, doing and feeling while communication downward involves informing local people about what the government is planning and doing. NGOs are also in a unique position to share information horizontally, networking between other organizations doing similar work.

4. Technical Assistance and Training

Training institutions and NGOs can develop a technical assistance and training capacity and use this to assist both CBOs and governments.

5. Research, Monitoring and Evaluation

Innovative activities need to be carefully documented and shared-effective participatory monitoring would permit the sharing of results with the people themselves as well as with the project staff.

CHART 31.2

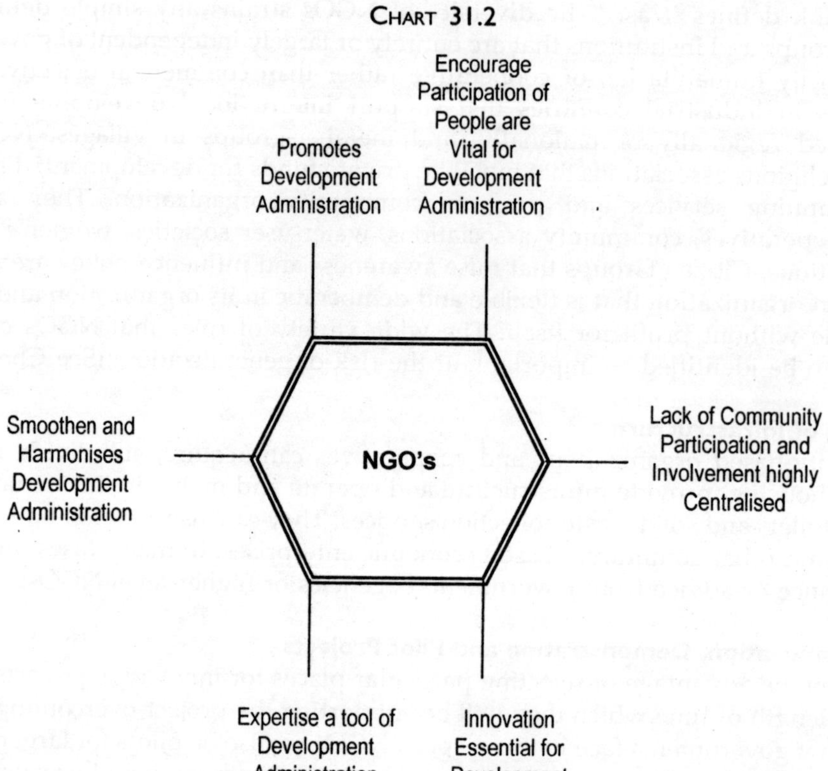

6. Advocacy for and with the Poor

In some cases, NGOs become spokepersons or ombudsmen for the poor and attempt to influence government policies and programmes on their behalf. This may be done through a variety of means ranging from demonstration and pilot projects to participation in public forums and the formulation of government policy and plans, to publicizing research results and case studies of the poor. Thus, NGOs play roles from advocates for the poor to implementors of government programmes; from agitators and critics to partners and advisors; from sponsors of pilot projects to mediators.

CHARACTERISTICS OF AN NGO

Voluntary organizations have certain features and characteristics which distinguish them from other organizations. Following are the few characteristics of a voluntary organization:[8]

1. It is registered under an appropriate Act to give a corporate status to a group of individuals, so that they get a legal personality, and an individual liability may give place to group liability.
2. It has an administrative structure, and a duly constituted managing/executive committee.

3. It has definite aims and objects, and programmes in fulfilment of these.
4. It is an organization initiated and governed by its own members on democratic principles without any external control.

D. Paul Chowdhary has given the following characteristics of an NGO:[9]

1. It is the result of the voluntary effort, which though motivated by different factors, is spontaneous in nature.
2. It is an organization initiated and governed by its own members on democratic principles without any external control.
3. It is registered under an appropriate Act to give a corporate status to a group of individuals so that they get a legal personality and individual liability may give place to group liability.
4. It has a general body and a regularly constituted managing committee, representing all interest, men, women, professionals, public men, etc.
5. It has definite aims and objects and a programme in socio-economic development of these objectives.
6. It is known and accepted by the community in which it is formed.
7. It has considerable autonomy and flexible planning and management of its programmes and services.
8. It has a sense of commitment to human development/welfare.
9. It undertakes people's needs and help to solve their socio-economic problems.
10. It plans and implements its own programmes through its own voluntary and paid workers.
11. It raises its funds from the community.
12. It maintains its accounts and is accountable to people and the government so far as it receives grant.

In Seventh Five Year Plan, greater stress has been laid for the involvement of Voluntary Organisations/NGOs in the implementation of development programmes. More specifically, the voluntary organisations are asked to perform the role in the following directions. These continue future plans as well:

1. To supplement government efforts so as to offer the rural people: choices and alternatives;
2. To be the eyes and ears of the people at village level;
3. To set an example; it should be possible for the voluntary organisations to adopt simple, innovative, flexible and inexpensive means with its limited resources to reach a larger number with less overheads and with greater community participation;
4. To activate the delivery system and to make it effective at the village level to respond to the felt needs of the poorest of the poor;
5. To disseminate information;
6. To make communities as self-reliant as possible;
7. To show how village support and inadequate resources could be used as well as how human resources, rural skills and local knowledge grossly unutilised at present could be used for their own development.

8. To domestify technology and bring it in simpler forms to the rural poor;
9. To train a cadre of grass-root workers who believe in professionalising volunteerism;
10. To mobilize financial resources from within the community with a view to making communities stand at their own feet; and
11. To mobilise and organise the poor and generate awareness to demand quality services and impose a community system of accountability on the performance of village level government functionaries.

Lobtha and Kohli has stressed that:

"Voluntary Organisations/(NGOs) in the country have played a pioneering role in the provision of welfare services for the vulnerable sections especially for women, children and the handicapped. The decade that followed India's Independence marked a phenomenal increase in the number of voluntary agencies in the country. They expanded their activities to cover practically every field of social welfare. They not only undertook programmes with their own resources but also implemented projects sponsored by the State.[10]
The major objectives of NGOs in Kerala are mentioned below.

- providing physical education and organising competitions,
- giving training to the youth,
- initiating self-employment ventures (for men and women),
- organising leadership/personality development programmes,
- propagating Gandhian ideology and literature,
- creating awareness,
- conducting de-addiction programmes,
- forming self-help groups,
- doing research and surveys,
- working for social justice,
- offering legal advice,
- organising mother and child care programmes,
- protecting the interests of consumers,
- organising value-based education sessions,
- working for prohibition, and
- assisting in housing.[11]

Let us illustrate in the context of Nagaland. The post-independent era in Nagaland, more so the last two decades, witnessed the formation of nearly twenty-two voluntary associations. These functions in the spheres of: (1) public help in general, (2) development and welfare of tribal people, (3) highlighting of problems and prospects of planning and development, (4) bringing peace and political settlement, (5) providing services to socially and physically handicapped children, (6) religious ideology, (7) providing elementary medical services to the people, and (8) providing humanitarian and cultural services to people, fostering talent and the like.[12]

To see a list of a large number of NGOs engaged majority in education sector, See appendix.[13]

Various NGOs cover the following areas:

- awareness programmes,
- marketing,
- training for employment,
- education,
- environmental protection,
- survey and research,
- agriculture and related programmes,
- networking and consultancy,
- information technology,
- distribution of funds, and
- housing.[14]

CLASSIFICATION

Voluntary agencies are functioning in almost all the countries of the world. In some countries, voluntary services have played an important role in stimulating and initiating the development of social services while in other countries they have given leadership in promoting the establishment and progressive extension of Government responsibilities. In some countries these agencies carry the major responsibilities and may provide the only social services available to the people. For example, the voluntary services in India have played a significant role as the problems are so large that it is not possible for the Government alone to tackle it. The main object of planned development is to mobilise the total, known as well as hidden material and human resources in such a way as to improve the socio-economic living conditions of the people to the maximum at a given time. They have been supplementing the efforts of the government from ancient times to this date. Thus, we find that "such agencies and the Services they provide differ widely in terms of auspices and objectives, types of services, methods of operation, extent of coverage, standards maintained, source of financing and relationship to Government and to other non-governmental agencies."[15] The voluntary organisations are different from the non-official organisations, because non-official organisations are an instance of inducted volunteerism by the state which mayor may not secure popular support.

Voluntary Organisation falls in two groups, viz.,

I. Non-Profit and Non-Partisam Organisations

Non-profit and non-partisam organisations are those voluntary organisations which have legal entity. It should have broad-based objectives serving the social and economic needs of the community as a whole and mainly the weaker sections. It should not work for profit but on "no profit and no loss bases." Its activities should be open to all citizens of India irrespective of religion, caste, creed, sex or race. It should have the necessary flexibility, professional competence and organisational skills to implement programmes.

Its office-bearers and organisational skills help in implementing programmes. Its office-bearers should not be elected members of any political party. It declares that it adopt constitutional and non-violent means for development. It is constituted on the basis of secular and democratic concepts and methods of functioning.

2. Conventional Voluntary Organisations

As pointed out earlier, Conventional Voluntary Organisations are those which have their own constitution, elected office-bearers with defined division of responsibility of the office-bearers, etc.

J.B. Singh classified them:[16]

(1) *Charity*: Giving food, clothing, medicine, alms, in cash and in kind, land, building, etc.
(2) *Welfare*: Providing facilities for education, health, drinking water, roads, communication, etc.
(3) *Relief*: Responding to call of duties during natural calamities like floods, drought, earthquakes, and man-made calamities like refugee influx, ravages of war, etc. See appendix for NGO involvement in development and disaster reduction.
(4) *Rehabilitation*: Continuing and follow-up of the work in areas struck by calamities and starting activities that are durable in nature.
(5) *Services*: Building up infrastructure in depressed backward areas.
(6) Development of socio-economic environment around human beings.
(7) *Development of Human Beings*: Conscious raising, awakening, raising conscience, organizing, recording of priorities to suit social justice: redeeming the past and opening doors for opportunities to the oppressed and the exploited.

Asian Development Bank, Manila classified them through their orientation and level of operation.[17]

NGO types by orientation viz. Charitable Orientation with little participation by the "beneficiaries." Service orientation with activities such as the provision of health, family planning or education services. Participatory orientation where local people are involved particularly in the implementation of a project. Empowering Orientation, where the aim is to help people develop understanding and awareness of their own. Potential power to control their lives. Develop spontaneously around a problem or an issue.

NGO Types by level of operation include: Community-based Organizations (CBOs) arise out of people's own initiatives, e.g. sports clubs, women's organizations, religious or educational organizations: supported by NGOs, national or international NGOs, or bilateral or international agencies, and others independent of outside help; Citywide Organizations such as the Rotary or Lion's Club; National NGOs include organizations such as the Red Cross, YMCAs/YWCAs, professional organizations, etc.

Non-Government Organizations (NGOs) are playing increasingly important role in the development process in less developed countries (LDCs). They are supposed to perform a very distinct function of filling the gaps ignored or bypassed by other agencies, both in private as well as public sectors. These gaps are often caused by the development process itself and, at times, are the results of activities of institutions in the two sectors. NGOs are found operating in what is sometimes labelled as the 'third or voluntary sector' to distinguish it from public (State) and private (market) sectors. Although the NGOs are part of the so-called 'third sector', yet it is important to note that they are among many other types of organizations covered by this particular sector. For example, all kinds of charities, people, community and grass-roots organizations, cultural and religious bodies, cooperatives and numerous other types of voluntary bodies are also part of the same sector and are non-profit seeking private organizations too. The distinguishing features of NGOs are: their objectives underscoring social welfare through participation, non-bureaucratic structures, and commitment to development and change. They are also different in terms of their approach to development issues as they combine the dual strategy of poverty alleviation with development with grass-roots approach. This makes these NGOs very distinct (almost unique) as other forms of organisations are not very successful in combining the two features in such an explicit manner. State and its agencies are supposed to achieve this but have not always been very successful due to well-known reasons.

The importance of NGOs is also growing because of the shift in the focus from the traditional approach to economic growth and to human development. Recent literature in that area coupled with deliberate attempts by international agencies like the UN, World Bank, ILO and others, make it inevitable that more and more attention is turned to the activities of NGOs as the real resources to aid development are also being channelled through them. The attempts to roll back frontiers of State and the general tendencies leading to privatisation and globalisation are creating serious poverty gaps that cannot be filled by other types of organisations and is further contributing in enhancing the role of NGOs in the development process in LDCs. Due to their success in tackling some serious issues, there is also a growing argument for "scaling up" of NGOs function in the existing as well as new areas too.

We have tried to define NGOs but an analysis of various definitions would reveal that there is no exact definition of NGO which is possible as the area, contents and ecology are different. Hence, there is no need of any attempt for a universal concept of NGO. However, NGOs are existing in one form or another throughout the world.

IMPORTANT FEATURES OF NGOs

(a) Participation of Beneficiaries

NGOs are nearer to the people and get better response from them in the implementation of programmes than official agencies and thus they are in a better position to render effective service. By and large, they have a better knack of communicating with the beneficiaries members of official agencies. This of course, is a natural manifestation of the ancient civilization of India, which has attached the greatest importance to the participation of the people in decision-making. The mobilisation of the energies and resources of the beneficiaries themselves is the key factor in increasing their welfare and self-reliance. People's participation through NGOs in the promotion of social welfare means involvement of the people in the process of social welfare voluntarily and willingly. Such participation cannot be forced. People's involvement can be assured through the participation of the beneficiaries in the decision-making, implementation, monitoring and evaluation of programmes carried out by the voluntary agencies. This will lay the solid foundation in the prevention and promotion of social services and the people would become self-reliant rather than depend on the help from the Government. According to Dharma Vira: "Work of voluntary organisations and citizen participation are two sides of the same coin. Citizens work in organisations but on their work depends the quality of the service the organisations render. Voluntary Organisations provide a frame for citizen participation. Without effective citizen participation, the organisation would only be empty forms."[18]

(b) Creating a Sense of Responsibility through Direct Involvement

Programme results are more successful and meaningful if the potential beneficiaries take part in their design and implementation through the forum of voluntary organisations. For example, if uncollected garbage draws flies, or drains become dogged and overflow or if dirty pathways become ankle-deep mud sloughs in the rainy season, they will like to do something to remedy the situation from complaining to the Health Department to dredging canals and filling in muddy pathways themselves.

The more important role of voluntary agencies is to stimulate active citizen participation in matters that concern them and their community. How can this role be effectively played? It has been pointed out in the introductory chapter that the religious and philanthrophic auspices of most agencies had resulted in creating a climate of apathy, resignation and fatalism. Today, it is generally accepted that social and economic development cannot take place unless these forms of traditional inertia are broken so that the masses can be imbued with confidence in their capacity to solve their own problems.

There is a noticeable absence of any visible mechanism to assess and evaluate the performance of NGOs, particularly by the beneficiaries (target groups/communities). Let us argue for the development of a transparent and easy-to-operate mechanism built into the organisational structure of NGOs to allow beneficiaries to express their views. It is important to assess the realisation of the most important stated objectives of 'Empowerment/participation' by the beneficiaries (target groups and communities) with regards to the operation of NGOs, which distinguishes them from other forms of organisations. This is all the more important if the mistakes and disillusionment of the past, associated particularly with the role of the State and its agencies, is to be avoided. Let us suggest adoption of 'project specific' approach in this regard.

Donor agencies carry special responsibilities and can use their influence to help and encourage NGOs to develop such a mechanism and also to oversee its use. Such an attempt will strengthen the role of these organisations and generate more confidence among those directly affected. It should also help donors, who monitor use of resources by the recipient NGOs any way. Monitoring will become more meaningful by involving the beneficiaries too.[19]

(c) Rectification of Planner's Mis-conception

It is very difficult for people to let their views be known individually. And planners find it difficult to appreciate their needs. People's participation through voluntary agencies can rectify planning errors by making it possible for clients to point out to planners, policy-makers and administrators, what will work and what will not. For example, if the rural people participate through various voluntary agencies in the process of planning, the disparity between the urban and rural care can be removed. If things are left only to the specialists, they would ignore the demands of the masses. The higher status experts thus set the framework of discussion and carry it through in categories meaningful to themselves but often incomprehensible to the ordinary, poor and lowly educated laymen.

(d) Greater Understanding and Positive Attitudes among the Beneficiaries (Formation of Public Opinion)

The involvement of the beneficiaries in the socio-economic development or national reconstruction is dependent to a great extent upon their enlightenment. This can take place when voluntary agencies interpret and explain the issues and problems of administration to the public, e.g., Family Planning Association of India with its branches in all the States has been quite active in the population education programme of the public. The voluntary agencies are also trying to help by creating in the people an urge, an attitude to adopt new methods of social welfare by arranging for the people services and opportunities to acquire new knowledge and techniques and by acting as a mediator between the people and the official machinery to interpret the problems and needs of the one to the other in order to develop better appreciation of each other.

(e) Effective Policy Formation Through Interpretation of Public Opinion

The voluntary agencies can present the real needs of the social welfare and development of the people to the various decision-making bodies. They can also interpret social welfare plans based on their contacts with bilateral and multi-lateral agencies. Information is the policy-makers' raw material, forming the basis for his diagnosis, strengthening his projections and permitting him to evaluate the programmes which have been planned. The degree to which a social planner will be able to plan in terms of social needs will depend on the degree to which he is able to obtain information about them which is valid and reliable. The information supplied by voluntary agencies can be reliable, as it is based on the outcome of their intimate contacts with the population.

(f) Flexibility and Experimentation

The NGOs are autonomous in their functioning. They are not bound by well defined laws and regulations which are difficult to change. This gives the voluntary agencies an opportunity to experiment with a given programme and adjust it according to the environmental conditions. The programme must develop environmental linkages in order to be of lasting value and benefit to the people. The autonomous character of the voluntary agencies provide them flexibility to adopt their programme according to the needs and aspirations of the people. We know that the best structure can come up only in a congenial soil. The health problems of the people differ from area to area and hence, it is difficult to solve the problems for all the areas with the same solution. The NGOs can experiment with different models in different areas and adopt and develop the best for the area for a given time dimension as the models of development are bound to change with the time dimension.

(g) Initiative and Leadership

Voluntary agencies involve the people in the policy formulation and implementation of the programmes. This encourages the local potential leaders to develop as agents of socio-economic change. The people are not dependent on the initiative of the Government alone. They take the initiative and believe in self-help rather than help from outside.

(h) Channelise Human Resources

It is very difficult to provide all the social services to the people through the Government as it is very costly. The voluntary agency can exploit the unused energies of the people for the development of the country. Energy of the people, if unused, cannot be preserved. This unused energy like the unused vast water resources flowing down the Himalayas is not only wasted like those rivers, but also, like the river waters that take with them the soil of the Himalayan region causing permanent erosion, cause permanent damage to the human spirit and will in a community through dependence and frustration born out of ever-increasing level of abject poverty over the generations.[20]

We can explain this in the context of the provision of Primary Health Care Services. Voluntary health agencies can train the educated and willing workers in the art of elementary health care and health education. Such trained and motivated people in turn would be able to provide primary health care to the people. This would be cheaper and efficient as can be seen from the Chinese experience.

(i) Advancing Social Legislation

In a welfare state, social welfare laws are as essential as security laws. These come under the purview of social legislation. It is the tool with which the social administrator is able to help the community from hazards. The social legislation need radical changes to cover all the people. Voluntary agencies can mobilise public opinion in support of such legislations. These agencies can prepare the people to act as a pressure group to motivate the Government to enact legislations for the welfare of the masses. A political system remains in equilibrium only if it channelises the demands of the people into policies, and decisions are beneficial to the people.

(j) Supplement the Efforts of Government

The problems of development are so vast and stupendous that it is difficult to solve these problems with the efforts of the Government machinery alone. There is a need to share this responsibility and the voluntary sector which possess immense potential to take up this burden. During the last three decades, the governments have been trying to bring about socio-economic revolution but the progress has been halted because of the non-availability of needed resources. Thus, there is a need of a voluntary sector to supplement the efforts of the Government. The working group appointed by the Planning Commission remarked that the country's social and economic problems are so vast and multifarious that the Government's administrative machinery alone cannot tackle them. The establishment of a self-reliant society implies progressive curtailment, of people's dependence on the Government. From time immemorial voluntary agencies in our country have played a significant part promoting people's welfare.[21] Government has to assume the major responsibility, not only for preventive and developmental programmes but also in providing leadership and resources for NGOs to continue their work. This partnership or complimentary relationship now needed eventually be lessened to a point where it can be possible to have demarcation of roles.

(k) Help in Efficient Programme Implementation

Voluntary agencies can help in the programme implementation, collaboration and co-ordination with other activities. They can contribute to social welfare development in many ways through programme implementation.[22] They can:

(1) Provide assistance to develop and/or strengthen local NGO capabilities and activities with particular attention to local community development groups.
(2) Conduct reviews and assessment of existing development; programmes and assist communities in the exercise of their own role in such reviews. A greater emphasis on evaluative techniques will render all new programmes more accountable to real community needs.
(3) Develop innovative programmes in the context of comprehensive human development.
(4) Ensure that their existing programmes and new initiatives promote full participation by individuals and communities in the planning, implementation and control of these programmes.
(5) Expand their training efforts to respond to the needs of programmes, e.g., training workers, supervisors, administrators, planners and various agricultural.
(6) Extend their efforts to develop locally sustainable and appropriate technologies and use of resources, with particular attention to energy, water, agriculture, sanitation and medical care.
(7) Contribute to the creation of new and effective methods of education which enable both individuals and communities to assume greater responsibility for their own welfare.

(8) Recognise the essential roles of women in development and in the full range of community development concerns.
(9) Further extend their capacity to work with poor, disadvantaged and remote populations enabling them to break the cycle of deprivation, and in this way contribute to the search for greater social justice.

In the past, persons associated with NGOs were sincere and dedicated to the cause of humanity and they were keen to serve through their personal efforts-money, time and human resources. They were motivated by the teachings of Great men like Swami Vivekananda, Swami Dayananda, Guru Nanak Dev, Christ, Sri Sai Baba, etc. However, in the present day, persons associated with Voluntary Organizations are those who want to exploit the people, i.e. getting money from different sources but not spending the same for the purpose—for which the money has been allocated. Influential persons from NGOs get it registered and get huge grants from Government, UN system and foreign sources for making money, thus exploiting both the people and the donor agencies. They remain ornamental and remain busy in liaison with donor agencies rather than serving the people. In the 21st Century, we have to ensure the following to make NGOs successful:

(a) Verification of the persons associated with NGOs in terms of their Social Service background and interest in social welfare activities.
(b) Clarity of purpose of the NGOs.
(c) Dedication and a spirit of Social Service.
(d) Contacts with the beneficiaries.
(e) Previous achievements.
(f) Previous record of Social Service.

For NGOs to be successful and fruitful in new millennium, we suggest the following:

(1) Registration of NGOs after verifying the credentials of the persons associated with NGOs after giving a public notice giving the names, objectives, etc. in some dailies.
(2) Mandatory association of beneficiaries in the running of NGOs.
(3) Provision of special audit by Accountant General or his designatory in case of any doubt of misappropriation.
(4) Appointment of auditors should be done by sponsoring organization.
(5) In the governing body, there should be some representatives from local bodies.
(6) There should be transparency in the functioning of NGOs.
(7) An outside evaluation should be got done of the report submitted by NGOs.
(8) If an NGO is found fraudulent, persons associated with such an NGO should not be allowed to form another NGO or if already a member of an NGO, it should be withdrawn.

Thus, there is a need of overhauling the structure, functioning and financial audit in the 21st century if we really want to associate NGOs with the process of development. Rajkumar Siwach in his article, "Prospective Role of VOs in Tenth Plan" in *Social Welfare*, February, 2003 states—

The policy measures of the government reveal that the VOs have a zig-zag path to tread towards their destination. The common masses and bureaucracy, however, still perceive them as crooked and dishonest. Their credibility, owing to numerous inexplicable reasons, is at stake. The government, as well as, NGO people should take keen and genuine interest to promote voluntarism with devotion. The NGO sector should ex-communicate those fraudulent organizations who have been giving a bad name to the fraternity and, the government, on the other hand should stick to 'carrot and stick' approach to encourage committed and punish suspicious VOs. Keeping everything in consideration, the policy-makers and planners in the government circles should devise ways and means to improve the performance of the VOs. They should, at least, pay sincere attention towards some developments happening in the VO field.

- Ensuring good governance among VOs working.
- Realising and analysing the prospects and pitfalls of Corporate Social Responsibility.
- Introducing Non-Profit Management Education courses in Indian Universities and Colleges for making Third Sector a viable professional livelihood.
- Galvanising the languishing spirit of voluntarism.

Voluntary organizations are mostly in the control of vested interests who are not interested in the uplift of downtrodden but act as middle men to siphon Government or donor's money for the benefit of vested interests. The question here is as to what is the need of Voluntary Sector when we have developed rural and urban infrastructure under 73rd and 74th amendments which can cater to the welfare of all the needy persons. All the grants whether from Union, State or other donor agencies must be made to local bodies which should plan and execute for various programmes.

This would streamline the process of development and would check misuse of money by NGOs. NGOs should get financial resources from local bodies and be responsible to them. At present, accountability of NGO cannot be ascertained because there is big distance between financial agencies and local bodies.

APPRAISAL OF THE FUNCTIONING OF THE NGOs

The examination is based on the writer's discussions with the officials, non-officials and beneficiaries of the voluntary organisations. The writers got the opportunity to examine the functioning of some of the organisations in depth. Some of the observations and comments in this analysis are born out of this study.

Lack of Effective Collaboration among the NGOs themselves

Co-ordination implies the prevention of both duplication and overlapping so as to avoid administrative wastes of efforts, manpower and resources and pool resources and experiences in dealing with problems and in achieving common objectives. Co-ordination—a means to an end and not an end itself—must be considered in relation to its practical purpose which is to facilitate better performance and greater administrative efficiency in the system. To ensure efficient and economical functioning of an organisation, co-ordination is not only desirable but even essential. For the same reason, inter-organisation coordination is advisable, especially when the activities of the various organisations concerned are of a complementary nature.

Apart from the continuing need to avoid overlapping and inconsistencies, co-ordination is more and more conceived in a positive and dynamic sense aimed at providing an agreed direction and a framework for action and at ensuring not only that activities dovetail into one another but there is also full measure of forethought and harmony in carrying out our responsibilities.

Co-ordination is distinct from the hierarchical process of authority, command and control. It requires collection of information about other organisations whose operations have identical objectives.

Co-ordination may lead to one organisation performing services or attacking a problem on behalf of all organisations in the system. It may also lead to one or more parties, on the basis of information and consultation, to refrain entirely from the participation in a given activity so as to avoid duplication of efforts. Co-ordination under such circumstances is accomplished by a decision to work in concert. According to H.K.D. Tondon,

"The experience of social work and social welfare institutions in different countries has revealed that the resources of voluntary agencies can be utilised more fruitfully and voluntary efforts could be mobilised more effectively if there is proper co-ordination between the NGOs."[23]

There is little co-ordination among the NGOs to achieve the intended goals. Uncoordinated activities can be wasteful and may even have a damaging effect on the beneficiaries. It was mentioned by a non-official in one of the voluntary health agencies: "It does seem to me that one of the defects that should be remedied in the work of the voluntary health agencies that concern more than one agency is the absence of a greater degree of collaboration in many matters. So far as I am aware, there is not at the present moment sufficient machinery to deal with this problem. I think, steps might be considered for greater collaboration and consultation on problems that are common to more than one agency, which would make the work much more useful."[24]

According to M.R. Malkhani, "The need for co-ordination and cooperation among voluntary organisations and the state agencies is very urgent but remains unfulfilled." It was also mentioned as one of the handicaps of voluntary effort in the National Plan of Action for women. It was stated that, "Most of the NGOs have been operating independently of each other. They have, therefore, not been able to fully benefit the community. The role of existing organisations should be determined and measures should be initiated to co-ordinate the efforts of various organisations at each district level."[25] Some NGOs like rotary dubs, have succeeded in setting-up such projects,[26] where government proved inadequate. Rotary Project Rosemary (2.4 crores) at Bilaspur, solved a 100 year old flood problem, that used to plague the residential colonies of the city, by storm water inundation. The component of government grant, in the whole project was small, but the contribution of rotary foundation was substantial.

Similarly, on January 26, 2001 when Gujarat was struck with a devastating earthquake affecting lakh of people, Rotary Gujarat Earthquake Rebuild Trust, Bhuj came forward to help homeless people, by providing low cost shelters and construct schools. Many other NGOs joined hands to help the unfortunate people.

The Blood Resource Centre, Chandigarh is a living example of a 'good work' done by Rotary International (See appendix for the details of the project) with Sh. D.C. Mahendru as the Project Director.

It is suggested that the following steps may be taken to improve inter-agency relationships:

(i) representation at each other's meetings on all appropriate occasions;
(ii) early consultation when one organisation felt that the other might be interested, or involved in an activity;

(iii) creation of standing or *ad hoc* joint committees whenever circumstances warrant;
(iv) full and continuous personal contacts among the officials of allied voluntary agencies;
(v) housing all the offices at various levels in the same building; and
(vi) exchanging information on a regular basis.

Control Measures Inadequate

Governments provide financial assistance and technical guidance. In some places, financial assistance may be provided in the form of grants-in-aid which help in establishments, extension or improvement of services by the voluntary agencies. Voluntary agencies have to fulfil certain criteria to be eligible for grants-in-aid. As stated in a UN publication, "The objective of such controls should be to facilitate the provision of social services in keeping with national social policy and plans; to safeguard the interest of all the people, to ensure at least minimum standards of services and efficiency, to avoid duplication of effort and to ensure the most effective use of available resources."

This necessitates the cordial relations between the Government and the voluntary agencies The Government has a right to supervise the functioning of the voluntary sector to ensure its efficient functioning and to help it improve the standards of service. The officials of the voluntary agencies, however, complain of excessive control by their respective departments and bureaucratic machinery of the Government. Their autonomy is thus vitiated resulting in inefficiency and poor standards of service. But this appears to be one sided approach. There is a need to find out the methods which can help in the synthesis of control and autonomy. In a document, presenting a draft resolution on social policy for the consideration of the governments, the Council of Social Development has described the relationship between Government and voluntary organisations as:

> "The nature of relationship between the government and voluntary organisations reflects the nexus between the state and the society, representing two approaches, namely, the legal and the non-legal to the tackling of social problems and meeting of social needs. A co-partnership between governmental and non-governmental organisations and sharing responsibilities for the information and execution of social policies between them is in keeping with the spirit of true democracy and genuine welfare-state."

In order to create mutual trust and understanding between the Government and voluntary agencies from higher level to village level, Seventh Plan has stressed the need of establishing consultative groups of voluntary agencies in all the states and give operational responsibilities and this group is to be registered under the Societies Registration Act as people's action for development (PAD). This forum can provide consultancy as well. Besides training, code of conduct have also to be developed by the voluntary organisations to achieve intended goals. The objectives of the programmes are to be to organise women in socio-economic activity groups with the dual objective of providing self-employment opportunities and social strength to them. In the process, voluntary agencies and peoples' action group are to be involved to the maximum extent.

Lack of Competence to Develop Integrated Area Plans

Who should be responsible for the socio-economic planning in a particular sector and area—say Block level—in India? The present situation of voluntary organistioans is that there is no clear-cut demarcation of objectives, functions, and activities between this sector and the Government on the one hand and among the voluntary agencies themselves on the other. In such a situation, we cannot entrust the task of planning in a particular sector or area to anyone of the voluntary agencies howsoever competent it may be. Besides, "most of the voluntary agencies lack planning competence. However, the Government must seek the active co-operation, guidance and advice of the voluntary agencies while planning in a sector in which these agencies have developed competence and expertise. The working group appointed by the Planning Commission to initiate Block level planning recommended:

> "The responsibility for preparing an integrated area planning cannot be handed over to a voluntary agency, however, competent. This responsibility must be squarely borne by the government. The Planning team at the district level should consult and actively seek the assistance of the voluntary agencies in their area while preparing the plan and selectively entrust to them the implementation of some sectoral plans in which they may have requisite expertise and experience. It can even be joint venture but the ultimate responsibility will be that of the Planning team."[27]

Lack of Identity with the Programmes among the Personnel of the Voluntary Agencies

Most of the persons working in various capacities in the voluntary agencies are not committed to the ideals and philosophy of these agencies. They have not developed identity and faith with the task environment. Mrs. Gresst pointed out in an interview to the *World Health* the secret of success of the eradication of the small-pox from the world. This secret must be adopted by all personnel concerned with the execution of a programme. She says:

> "A good programme needs only a few highly experienced and qualified people at the top level. We had these: out of the hundreds recruited by WHO, many had no past experience in small-pox eradication, when they first arrived. The qualities they needed rather than past experience, were faith in their work, courage, perseverance, adaptability to any situation, imagination, efficiency, capacity to take on responsibility yet flexibility to work easily as part of a team, but not least, willingness to work hard."[28]

She equates good people with a good programme. It is better to have a post vacant than have it filled with a wrong person. The ideal solution is worthless if it cannot be implemented. Efficiency in every aspect is more important than hypothesis or long reports. Workers at all levels must spend more time working in the fields than in the offices. Besides, the effective supervision from the highest to the lowest level is essential for getting the job done.

The personnel engaged in these voluntary organisations must be ready to accept hardships. Because of neglect, the people have become apathetic to taking a hand in matters beyond their immediate family domain. Voluntary workers must keep in mind this apathy of the people generated after years of powerlessness and neglect. Their ambition and enthusiasm should not be dampened by local conditions which may not provide them with the necessary facilities. This should, rather, motivate them to exert more and find innovative ways to bring them out of this morass. Unfortunately, the sense of dedication has been the greatest casualty of the prevailing atmosphere of cynicism bred by increasing propensity towards expediency with no linkages with salary structure. We should try to train the workers of these agencies so that they can develop identity with the programme and have faith in them. Faith is as contagious as any infectious disease and is perhaps the most important factor for the successful implementation of the objective of these agencies. The personnel need adequate salary structure.

Non-involvement of Community/People

The governing bodies of the voluntary agencies formulate policies and supervise their implementation. Policy-making is an art and depends upon the sound knowledge of sodal work in the country. The nomination of the members on these governing bodies is normally not done on the basis of skill, interest and aptitude. It is suggested that the chairman and the members of these bodies be appointed on the basis of their interest in by the community skill, interest and aptitude, etc.

Poor Linkages with the Beneficiaries

The present relationship between the beneficiaries and the voluntary agencies is not cordial and harmonious. The success of the voluntary agencies depends on their response to the social milieu and to the ideas, beliefs, expectations and values of the people. These agencies must try to solve the problems without disrupting people's customs or straining their emotional susceptibilities to the point of social recoil or disintegration. This clearly means that the objectives of these agencies must be understood and accepted by the people. They must render the services through the personal human touch and sympathy rather than through an impersonal bureaucratic machinery. The programmes of these agencies can be effectively implemented only through a favourable environment for co-operation between various co-operative agencies, governmental and non-governmental, and the community. These agencies must be given freedom to administer, to execute, to change and adapt, to find their own solutions for the problems which may arise from day-today management within each community. It is suggested that women may be involved actively in the work of social welfare as many of them have spare time which is wasted in idle pursuits. Today, developing countries are not utilising more than 15 per cent of the potential capacity of human beings.[13] This calls for an active participation of women on a bigger scale in the task of development, national reconstruction and social change. As Helvi Sipila, a Finish lawyer, UN Deputy Secretary General for Social Development asserted: "We cannot hope to solve the increasing international problems of economic and social development and improve the quality of human life while leaving aside half the resources of humanity."

We can involve the women in this stupendous task through the institutions of mothers' club. This experiment has been a great success in the Democratic Republic of Korea. Family Planning Association of India (Haryana Branch) experimented with this idea at three places with success. The details of the mothers' club were published by PEN, an issue of FPAI (Haryana Branch) in their issue of May, 1977. The important ideas about the club are reproduced below.[29]

The basic requirement of such clubs is that the voluntary agencies and the Government must plan in advance as to what information is necessary to enlighten the people which is a prerequisite for their involvement in socio-economic development. This information in a coordinated fashion must reach the members of the mothers' club who would diffuse such information to the beneficiaries. Once the beneficiaries get functional literacy, political consciousness and the understanding of their responsibility for socio-economic development, the process of national development would be accelerated.

A mothers' club implies a group of 25-40 women depending upon the size and population of the village or city. Those who have skills to spare, and those who have the will to do something for others by using their time and energy, can be provided with an organisational framework whereby their contribution could be made more meaningful and satisfying to themselves. The problem lies in providing the organisational framework. These women must be married and sufficiently influential. The other women of the village or city must have confidence in them. It is the task of sociologists to locate such women from all the mohallas/wards through sociometry, etc. It would be better if the women from all the mohallas/wards are represented on it. As the work progress, more mothers can join the club if the village or city is vast; then two or more mothers' clubs can be constituted. So, we must find out women who possess the following qualities to carry out the challenging task of social change and modernisation-missionary zeal, the capacity to communicate with others, the ability to get along with colleagues and the people, cultural adaptability, the capacity to organise and manage, the capacity to instill confidence in others, patience and dignity. Besides, they must have faith in the ideas of the programme. They should be willing to accept hardships and be prepared to work in the spirit of service.

The mothers' club to start with, may have limited objectives, e.g., the promotion of the child welfare programmes, the programme for Child Nutrition, the Education programme (especially functional literacy), programme against disease and dirt, or even prohibition. As the work progresses, these clubs can extend their activities to the whole cultural, social and economic (small-scale industries) aspects of the village/city life. This would also have the positive effect of utilising their energy for constructive purposes. Most of the women interviewed by the authors revealed that "half of their working time is spent for uninteresting problems, which are born because the women are idle."

Voluntary Agencies not Objectives-oriented

There is a haphazard growth of the voluntary agencies. Even the social welfare department is not aware of the number of such agencies operating in a State. Such agencies are set-up on *ad hoc* basis to deal with a particular and pressing problem but such agencies continue even though their functioning have become obsolete. It is high time that we must scrutinise the existence of all the voluntary agencies. We must examine their utility in terms of. their objectives and performance. A new technique called 'sunset' has been devised to weed out ineffective voluntary agencies. It means that we should apply this and other techniques to make the operation of these agencies worthwhile and objective-oriented. This would strengthen the agencies which are already doing useful work. The State should patronise agencies which are really contributing to socio-economic development of the country. Thus, in order to develop a good image of these agencies, the Government has to think in terms of appointing a committee to go into the performance of these agencies and recommend the winding-up of such agencies which are not serving the objectives for which these were set-up and extend help to such agencies which are doing commendable work.

Not Properly Equipped and Staffed

It is perhaps not unfair to say that voluntary organisations by and large are not properly equipped and are understaffed. Competent and qualified persons do not usually remain with these agencies for long due to the uncertain circumstances of voluntary organisations. A study carried out by the Central Institute of Research and Training in Public Co-operation identified some important gaps in the field of voluntary action. It mentioned that voluntary work has been on the decline since independence. Voluntary workers now tend to feel that the State should assume greater responsibility for various welfare programmes. Voluntary agencies are also in need of workers who are committed and remain with these agencies for longer assignments. Voluntary workers, often, have been unable to fulfil their commitments to the agencies due to rising transportation cost and lack of long-term incentives. This study recommended that a bureau be set-up to enlist the services of workers and to place them appropriately with the agencies.

Voluntary workers will have to be trained for short period so that they can better appreciate the requirements and expectation of the beneficiaries as well as those of the agencies. This training would be broadly in the areas of organisation of services, administration and account keeping and developmental services with an emphasis on the rural reconstruction. Since, most of the agencies surveyed did not have adequate financial and organisational support to undertake such programmes, the study recommends that this could be done through the Central Social Welfare Boards own infrastructure, the existing schools of social work and other professional organizaions. The universities can play a great role in this direction. The rapport between the voluntary workers and the agencies would depend to a large extent on the mutual perceptions of their problems and common causes.[30]

Absence of Systems Mechanism to Co-ordinate the Functioning of Allied Agencies in a Geographically Functional Area

Human development cannot be fragmented. In same area many voluntary agencies are working without any co-ordinating mechanism, e.g., in the field of child welfare there were more than 558 voluntary agencies rendering welfare services for children. Of these, 152 organisations provided education for children, 98 offered nutrition services, 95 rendered welfare services for socially handicapped children, 89 provided recreational and cultural programmes, 76 promoted medical and health facilities, 23 organised maternity and child welfare services, 29 undertook research work and another 10 provided facilities for psychological services. It is suggested that in a particular area, e.g., State headquarters or at the district level, some organisations may be entrusted to function as a co-ordinating agency as has been done in the UN system. United Nations Development Programme has been designated by the UN system to serve as the co-ordinating agency at the national level on behalf of all the agencies of the UN system. In the same way, we may entrust this function to the Central Social Welfare Board and its branches in the State to serve as co-ordinating agency for the welfare services provided in every State. The CSWB is the main spokesman of voluntary organisations.

Lack of Interest among the Intellectual Elite

The universities and colleges as in the German Democratic Republic can really serve as the bridges between government and community. At the moment, intellectual elite in India—teachers in the universities, colleges, schools and training institutions have not much perception of their responsibility to the community. The intellectual elite can help these agencies in improving their functioning with their innovative ideas based on basic and applied researches. It is suggested that these voluntary agencies must involve the teachers from these institutions to help them grow and live up to the expectations of the beneficiaries.

Non-utilisation of Funds

There is a general feeling among the beneficiaries that the funds of these voluntary organisations are not utilised properly. A report of the Study Team on social Welfare on "Economic and Efficient Utilisation of Resources" has stated that there is a "chaotic situation in which the grants are given in an haphazard manner without any well-defined criteria to go by and there are no means of ensuring that they contribute to a proper and balanced growth of the institutions."

The funds are spent in arranging activities in the urban areas. In this way, the real purpose of these organisations is defeated. It is suggested that an efficiency audit may be conducted of the operations of these organisations by a committee of the people or legislators belonging both to the ruling and the opposition parties. These efficiency audit, reports may be published in the daily newspapers for the enlightenment of the people. This will give help to good organisations and a retreat to bad organisations. For the misdeeds of a few, the voluntary sector as a whole will not suffer because mistrust and misdeed of a few.

Absence of Sound Administrative Set-up to deal with Social Work

Administration is the vehicle through which the objectives of voluntary agencies can reach the beneficiaries. The administrative structure, processes and procedures of these agencies are not conducive to the functioning of such agencies. The ability to assume new tasks, to cope with complexity, to solve novel problems, to mobilise resources, depends upon the administrative capacity based on increased professionalisation and administrative talent. According to Tara Ali Baig, "What is increasingly clear, however, is that the improved management principles, geared to the worker potential of the country could greatly increase the positive contribution to progress that we seek in community activity and more efficient techniques in social welfare services."[31]

We have to examine the existing structure and process of these agencies so that they can be fit instruments to cope with the existing functions and future development. One of the officials in these agencies mentioned that: "Administration of these agencies is bureaucratic and is more legalistic than result-oriented."

The administrative culture of these agencies is unsuitable for the tasks imposed on them. The administrative system cannot function properly and administrators lack the necessary skills and environment for adequate performance. To achieve pre-conceived plans over a period of time, these two agencies should develop common working rules, right policy-formulation, proper inspection and review of work, high quality decision-making, decentralised operations, monitoring of information, managerial planning, cost accounting, immediate error-correction mechanism, committed workers' professionalisation, improved administrative techniques and administrative adaptability including organisational research and the built-in administrative mechanism to gain the confidence, loyalty and participation of the beneficiaries.

Lack of Indigenous Community Organisations

Many voluntary organisations, old and new, set themselves to provide non-residential and non-institutional services making community at large as their locale. Even those running residential institutions tended to utilise the existing community resources rather than organising services on their own within their precincts. This approach was not only economical but also instrumental in drawing the institutions closer to the community. However, most of them switched over to a model of services organised direct within the community for specific groups like income generating activities for poor and destitute women, pre-school education for children hailing from low-income families, health and nutrition programmes for women and children from poorer sections and educational and training programmes for the disabled. These services being technically better designed also carried some preventive strain in their problem-solving endeavour. They continued to be philanthropic in character, planned and implemented for the community rather than with or by the community. Whether organised independently or within the policy framework of Government these services sought to involve the community mainly as consumers.[32] More and more Mahila Mandals of the villages be registered as voluntary organisation and be encouraged to take up more and more social welfare programmes. Our discussions with the village women folk has revealed, that this experience has proved very successful as well as rewarding.

The Seventh Five Year Plan states some of the significant issues in the context of Voluntary Organisations:

- The financial allocations and physical targets under the programmes are determined on a uniform basis per state without regard to the incidence of poverty or even the size of population,
- Wrong identification of the voluntary organisations,
- Non-involvement of the voluntary organisations in the survey and selection of programme and lack of awareness among the beneficiaries,
- Absence of backward and forward linkages and infrastructural support structures for the promotion of voluntary organisations,
- Absence of expertise to man the projects and programmes,
- Absence of vertical and horizontal co-ordination and integration between different departments, and
- Sporadic and uneven growth of voluntary organisations leading thereby to regional imbalances.

B. Chatterjee has mentioned some of the areas in which voluntary agencies have to give greater attention in the last quarter of the present century. These are as follows:

(a) Voluntary organisations need to develop a reasonable personnel policy to attract qualified and stable personnel to implement their programmes.
(b) They need to evaluate their programmes and performance so as to improve the quality of services.
(c) They need to develop a sound accounting system which not only meets their demands but also the demands of the government and the community.
(d) Voluntary agencies should play an increasing supportive role to Government programmes and complement the Government's efforts.
(e) Voluntary organisations at present are too much programme-oriented, they should develop a broader perspective of the field in which they are working and enlarge the scope of their activity to meet the problems faced by the majority of the population.
(f) There is a need for them to work in the area of social action and thereby facilitate social change.
(g) The majority of voluntary agencies are concentrated in urban areas and there is an urgent need to expand their work in rural area where the majority of India's population lives."[33]

The Government may therefore define in clear terms the role of voluntary organisations *vis-a-vis* the support of Government for social welfare and development. Statutory functions and non-statutory functions have to be clearly demarcated. N.V. Lalitha and Madhu Kohli have given the following points to enhance performance of voluntary sector:

(i) The government should spell out clearly the policy towards voluntary organisations indicating the relative role of the government and the voluntary sector, entitlement to funds, etc. This is very necessary in view of the fact that social welfare programme suffer from *ad-hocism* and uncertainty which come in the way of promoting voluntary efforts.[34]

(ii) There is an urgent need to make a serious review of the working of voluntary organisations in terms of assets, financial soundness, service conditions of staff, quality of service, etc. Such a review would help identify the genuine agencies and give them all the support they need, i.e. financial and technical, because voluntary agencies can do excellent work and bring in better results. The government should also have certain controls in terms of audit, submission of accounts, work report, etc.

(iii) The Directorates of Social Welfare should equip themselves with facts and figures regarding voluntary organisations, their specialised areas of work, problems faced by them in their day-to-day functioning, etc., so that they can deal with them better. The inadequate and scanty information available at present create considerable difficulties both for the government and the voluntary organisations.

(iv) The government should insist on certain rules and procedures of recruitment, salary scales and working/service conditions so that voluntary organisations would get properly qualified persons to man their programmes.

(v) Grants should not be released as a matter of routine. The government should see that the organisations qualify for grants.[35]

Prof. Jacob Thudipara in an article, "Credibility a Challenge before NGOs" in *Social Welfare*, January 2009 gave suggestions to improve NGO's.

A number of strategies can be seen being used by NGOs to build their credibility (Srinivas, 2000).

- Use of academics and experts to evaluate NGO projects and activities.
- Associating with national or regional associations, alliances, or forums.
- Obtaining UN accreditation.
- Finding credible spokespeople
- Speaking and publishing regularly.
- Seeking awards and prizes as recognition for the work done.
- Partnering with key community, governmental and industry entities.
- Writing case studies that tell compelling stories from people and communities they serve.
- Getting some good press stories.
- Keeping a significant presence online—both web and email.
- Generating a good image through newsletters, bulletins, press, etc.

Credibility Alliance

Credibility Alliance is an Indian consortium of voluntary organizations committed towards enhancing accountability and transparency in the voluntary sector through good governance. The initiative emerged as an independent non-profit organization after an extensive two-year consultative process involving thousands of voluntary organizations all over India. Credibility Alliance aims to build trust among all the stakeholders through improving governance and accountability in the voluntary sector. The organization sets norms or standards of governance, which operate on the principle of self-regulation. In the development of suitable norms, credibility alliance relies on participatory and voluntary processes among its members. In addition, Credibility Alliances is developing an Accreditation System based on the norms to strengthen and enhance the legitimacy and the credibility of individual organizations in the sector. Capacity building initiatives required to equip voluntary organizations to meet the norms shall also be promoted.

In India the Government also imposes levels of control, over the registration, management and funding of civil society organizations. Some view it as means of public accountability while others interpret it as mechanism for interference of the government in the functioning of the voluntary sector.

Another major enabling factor that could bring about credibility in the NGO sector is the enactment of the Right to Information act (RTI) by the Government of India in the year 2005. Under this act any person can ask for the details of any aspect of an organization, which should be provided by the chief information officer of the organization concerned within a period of 30 days. It is binding on all organizations that receive substantial funds from the Government to abide by the provisions in this act.

In India, much of the pre-occupation with credibility of NGOs has been about accountability of NGOs for the funds received by them; accountability in not only in the sense of financial integrity but in the broader sense of achievement of objectives for which the funds were given.

Less attention has been paid, and certainly hardly at all at the academic level, to the other aspect of credibility, viz. whether the organization is working in the public interest or is merely self-serving, and whether it is true to the vision and mission of the organization, irrespective of monetary or other considerations which might work to the contrary.

CONCLUSION

In the past, persons associated with NGOs were sincere and dedicated to the cause of humanity and they were keen to serve though their personal efforts—money, time and human resources. They were motivated by the teachings of Great men like Swami Vivekananda, Swami Dayananda, Guru Nanak Dev, Christ, Sri Sai Baba, etc. However, in the present day, persons associated with Voluntary Organizations are those who want to exploit the people, i.e. getting money from different sources but not spending the same for the purpose for which the money has been allocated. Influential persons from NGOs get it registered and get huge grants from Government, UN system and foreign sources for making money, thus exploiting both the people and the donor agencies. They remain ornamental and remain busy in liaison with donor agencies rather than serving the people. In the 21st Century, we have to ensure the following to make NGOs successful:

(a) Verification of the persons associated with NGOs in terms of their Social Service background and interest in social welfare activities.
(b) Clarity of purpose of the NGOs.
(c) Dedication and a spirit of Social Service.
(d) Contacts with the beneficiaries.
(e) Previous achievements.
(f) Previous record of Social Service.

For NGOs to be successful and fruitful in new millennium, we suggest the following:

(1) Registration of NGOs after verifying the credentials of the persons associated with NGOs after giving a public notice giving the names, objectives, etc. in some dailies.
(2) Mandatory association of beneficiaries in the running of NGOs.
(3) Provision of special audit by Accountant General or his designatory in case of any doubt of misappropriation.

(4) Appointment of auditors should be done by sponsoring organization.
(5) In the governing body, there should be some representatives from local bodies.
(6) There should be transparency in the functioning of NGOs.
(7) An outside evaluation should be got done of the report submitted by NGOs.
(8) If an NGO is found fraudulent, persons associated with such an NGO should not be allowed to form another NGO or if already a member of an NGO, it should be withdrawn.

Thus, there is a need of overhauling the structure, functioning and financial audit in the 21st century if we really want to associate NGOs with the process of development

Rajkumar Siwach in his article, "Prospective Role of VOs in Tenth Plan" in *Social Welfare*, February, 2003 states—

> The policy measures of the government reveal that the VOs have a zig-zag path to tread towards their destination. The common masses and bureaucracy, however, still perceive them as crooked and dishonest Their credibility, owing to numerous inexplicable reasons, is at stake. The government, as well as, NGO people should take keen and genuine interest to promote voluntarism with devotion. The NGO sector should ex-communicate those fraudulent organizations who have been giving a bad name to the fraternity and, the government, on the other hand should stick to 'carrot and stick' approach to encourage committed and punish suspicious VOs. Keeping everything in consideration, the policy-makers and planners in the government circles should devise ways and means to improve the performance of the VOs. They should, at least, pay sincere attention towards some developments happening in the VO field.
>
> - Ensuring good governance among VOs working.
> - Realising and analysing the prospects and pitfalls of Corporate Social Responsibility.
> - Introducing Non-Profit Management Education courses in Indian Universities and Colleges for making Third Sector a viable professional livelihood.
> - Galvanising the languishing spirit of voluntarism.

Voluntary organizations are mostly in the control of vested interests who are not interested in the uplift of downtrodden but act as middle men to siphon Government or donor's money for the benefit of vested interests. The question here is as to what is the need of Voluntary Sector when we have developed rural and urban infrastructure under 73rd and 74th amendments which can cater to the welfare of all the needy persons. All the grants whether from Union, State or other donor agencies must be made to local bodies which should plan and execute for various programmes.

This would streamline the process of development and would check misuse of money by NGOs. NGOs should get financial resources from local bodies and be responsible to them. At present, accountability of NGO cannot be ascertained because there is big distance between financial agencies and local bodies.

Notes and References

1. N.V. Lalitha and Madhu Kohli, Status of Voluntary Effort in Social Welfare, National Institute of Public Co-operation and Child Development, New Delhi, pp. 187-88.
2. *Ibid.*
3. Abstracted from—Cousins William, "Non-Governmental Initiatives" in ADB, "The Urban Poor and Basic Infrastructure Services in Asia and the Pacific", Asian Development Bank, Manila 1991.
4. Escap as quoted in Voluntary Efforts in Social Welfare and Development by D. Paul Chowdhary, 1990, p. 31.
5. Skill, D.L., Voluntary Associations: Sociological Aspects in International Encyclopedia of Social Sciences, Vol. 16, Collier-McMillan, 1968, pp. 363-67.
6. Inamdar, N.R., 'Role of Volunteerism in Development' as quoted in Social Welfare Administration by D.R. Sachdev, Kitab Mahal, Allahabad, p. 2003.
7. Gonsalves, G.J., "Development and Voluntary Agencies", *Voluntary Action*, Vol. XVII, No. 3, March, 1975, pp. 58-59.
8. Gangrade, K.D., Encyclopaedia of Social Work in India, Ministry of Information and Broadcasting, Government of India, New Delhi, 1987, pp. 220-21.
9. Choudhry, D. Paul, Voluntary Efforts in Social Welfare and Development, Sidhartha Publishers, New Delhi, 1990, pp. 32-33.
10. Sublime Grace: An *Economic Times* presentation, Sept. 2003.
11. R. Soory Amoorthy, The NGO Sector: Lessons from Kerala, in *IJPA*, April-June, 2002, p. 171.
12. Nalini Natrajan, Role of Voluntary Organisations in the Development of Backward Areas: Nagaland in *IJPA*, July-Sept., 1977, pp. 561-62.
13. Annual Report, 2001-02, Deptt. of Secondary and Higher Education, Ministry of HRD, Government of India, pp. 223, 302.
14. R. Soory Amoorthy, *op. cit.*, p. 172.
15. U.N. Report on the Organisation and Administration of Social Services, New York, 1962, p. 19, Sf/SOA/44/E/CN5/360/Rev. 1.
16. Singh, J.P.: *Yojna*, November, 1984, p. 46.
17. Regional workshop on networking and collaboration among NGOs of Asian Countries in disaster reduction and response, Feb. 20-22, 2002.
18. Dharma Vira, "Citizen Participation" in Encyclopedia of Social Work, Vol. I, p. 102.
19. Barkat Alam, *op. cit.*, p. 49.
20. Malhotra, R.C., *op. cit.*, p. 11.
21. GOI, Planning Commission, Report of the Working Group on Block Level Planning, 1978, pp. 139-40.
22. World Federation of Public Health Associations, *op. cit.*, pp. 45-46.
23. Tandon, H.K.D., "Public Co-operation" in Encyclopaedia" in Encyclopedia of Social Work in India, Vol. 2, p. 132.
24. Malkani, M.R., "Voluntary Agencies and Social Welfare" in Encyclopaedia of Social Work, Vol. II, p. 409.
25. Government of India, Department of Social Welfare, Blueprint of Action and National Plant of Action for Women, New Delhi, 1977, p. 23.
26. *Rotary News*, October, 2003, p. 3.
27. Government of India, Planning Commission, Report of the Working Group on Block Level Planning, 1978, p. 140.
28. WHO, World Health Organization, Nov. 1975.
29. UNDP, 12th Session of UNDP Governing Council, 7-23, June 1971, pp. 112-14.
30. For details refer to PEN, an issue of Family Planning Association of India, Haryana Branch, May 1977.
31. National Institute of Public Cooperation and Child Development, Study of the Young Child in India: Case Study, New Delhi, 1976, pp. 64-65.
32. Tara Ali Baig, "Social Administration in Voluntary Social Welfare Agencies" in Encyclopaedia of Social Work in India, Vol. II, p. 245.
33. N.V. Lalitha and Madhu Kohli, Status of Voluntary Effort in Social Welfare, *Ibid.*, pp. 165-66.
34. B. Chatterjee, "Voluntary Agencies for Social Welfare", in Social Development, Edited by B.N. Ganguli, Sterling Publishers Ltd. New Delhi, 1977, pp. 258-59.
35. N.V. Lalitha and Madhu Kohli, Status of Voluntary Effort in Social Welfare, *Ibid.*, pp. 124-25.

CHAPTER 32

Disaster Administration: Meaning, Scope and Impact

INTRODUCTION

Disaster whether natural or man-made are causing a great loss to all sorts of life—human beings, animals, plants and resources—buildings, infrastructure and above all cause psychological problems. Disasters are increasing with the move to material civilization, urbanization and industrialization. With this new cult, even natural disasters are occurring because of the disturbances in natural equilibrium caused by the greed and lust of human beings to exploit natural resources to get rich quickly. World Bank in India (January 2007) in its Article, "Two Years after the Tsunami, South Asia Prepares against Future Disasters", observes that across the world, natural disasters are growing in number and destructiveness, and their human toll is escalating. In the past 20 years alone, more than 4 billion people have been affected by natural catastrophes from floods, cyclones, and tsunami, earthquakes, landslides, and volcanic eruptions.

Apart from the suffering, the loss of human life, and the destruction of livelihoods, the economic costs of major disasters are huge: countries worldwide are estimated to have lost an average of 2-5 percent of their GDP from natural calamities in the recent past.

A recent World Bank study has shown that developing countries are often the disaster hotspots of the world. The South Asia region with its drought or deluge pattern of monsoon rainfall, long and cyclone-prone coastline, and periodically seismically active Himalyan belt, is one of these.

SIGNIFICANCE

Disaster cause huge losses in terms of death, of human and animal lives, many persons become living dead, with attendant socio-economic losses in developing countries because of lack of good administration for disaster management. These can be seen from millions of people suffering one or other type of disasters in developing countries. We shall discuss the losses from different disasters in India in subsequent chapters. If we examine in the context of developed countries, we find that the loss from disasters is negligible because of good, prompt and efficient administration. Let us take the example of recent Tsunami in Japan on 13th January, 2006.

The quake struck in the early afternoon near the Kuril Trench, about 500 km east of the Etorofu island, the largest of a disputed four-island chain known as the Northern Territories in Japan and the Kuril islands in Russia. The Japanese agency initially estimated the magnitude as 8.3 but later reduced that to 8.2, the same strength recorded by the US Geological Survey. The quake struck 30 km below the seabed.

More than three hours after the quake, the largest wave, at 40 centimetres, hit Chichijima, an island of 2,000 people. Small tidal swells were observed elsewhere. No injuries or damage were immediately reported from the offshore quake.

A powerful magnitude 8.2 earthquake off northern Japan triggered tsunami warnings, sending thousands fleeing to higher ground but causing no reported injuries or damage. Japan's Meteorological Agency immediately issued tsunami warnings, prompting an evacuation order for many coastal residents on the main northern island of Hokkaido. The agency cancelled all tsunami advisories about nine hours after the temblor occurred. Hokkaido lifted evacuation orders for 85,000 coastal residents in 22 towns as the fear of killer waves subsided.

On the other hand in South Asia builds back: over 200,000 people died in the December 2004 tsunami, more than 1.5 million people lost their homes and livelihoods and losses were estimated at more than US $57 billion.

Ten months later, the Pakistan earthquake rocked the region, killing more than 74,000 people and injuring over 106,000. Again, the poor were the most affected.

THE DAMAGES DUE TO NATURAL DISASTERS

Sharad Pawar rightly remarked that Disaster Management is an all-comprehensive area where every one has a duty to perform. The eternal preparedeness has to start at individual, family, community, district, state, national and regional level. The challenges before us today are to have effective response in the speediest possible way to save lives and the properties. The knowledge of science and technology and people's wisdom should be incorporated in mitigating the impact of disasters. Safety culture should be taken up in a mission mode. Adequate and relevant literature has to be prepared, made available and right information and awareness creation has to be created at all levels especially in the vulnerable areas. (See Table 32.1)

MEANING

Disaster Management Act, 2005 defines Disaster as: "Disaster" means a catastrophe, mishap, calamity or grave occurrence in any area, arising from natural or man-made causes, or by accident or negligence which results in substantial loss of life or human suffering or damage to, and destruction of, property, or damage to, or degradation of, environment, and is of such a nature or magnitude as to be beyond the coping capacity of the community of the affected area;

"disaster management" means a continuous and integrated process of planning, organising, coordinating and implementing measures which are necessary or expedient for—

TABLE 32.1

Damage due to Natural Disaster in India

Year	*People affected (in lakhs)*	*Houses and Buildings, partially or totally damaged*	*Amount of property damages/loss (Crores)*
1965	595.5	2449.878	40.06
1966	550.0	2049.277	30.74
1967	483.4	2919.380	20.57
1968	101.5	242.553	40.63
1990	90.1	782.343	20.41
1991	31.7	1019.930	10.71
1992	342.7	570.696	10.90
1993	190.9	1529.916	20.05
1994	626.5	1051.223	50.80
1995	235.3	355	10.83
1996	549.9	2376.693	40.73
1997	443.8	1103.549	50.43
1998	521.7	1563.405	NA
1999	501.7	3104.054	1020.97
2000	594.34	2736.355	800.00
2001	788.19	864.878	12000.00

Source: Annual Report, NDM Division, Ministry of Agriculture.

(i) prevention of danger or threat of any disaster;
(ii) mitigation or reduction of risk of any disaster or its severity or consequences;
(iii) capacity-building;
(iv) preparedness to deal with any disaster;
(v) prompt response to any threatening disaster situation or disaster;
(vi) assessing the severity or magnitude of effects of any disaster;
(vii) evacuation, rescue and relief; and
(viii) rehabilitation and reconstruction.

The term 'Disaster' owes its origin to the French word 'Desastre' which is the combination of two terms 'des' meaning bad or evil and 'astre' meaning 'star'. The combined expression is 'Bad or Evil Star'. In earlier days a disaster was considered to be the loss due to some unfavourable star.

Disaster is associated with following features:

(1) Disruption to normal pattern of life. Such disruption is usually severe and may also be sudden, unexpected and widespread and thus human beings remain in shock for a long period.
(2) Human effects such as loss of life, livelihood and property, injury, hardship and adverse affects on health—physical as well as mental.

(3) Effects on social structure such as destruction of or damage to infrastructure buildings, communication and other essential services leading to disruption of life and the resources become scarce.

(4) Community needs such as shelter, food, clothing, medical assistance and social care.

A complete definition of disaster may be "an event, concentrated in time and space, which threatens a society or a relatively self-sufficient sub-division of a society with major unwanted consequences as a result of the collapse of precautions which had hitherto been culturally accepted as inadequate" (Turner, 1976).

The world bank operational directive OD 8.50 Emergency Assistance Work system DC, 1989 regards disaster as an extra-ordinary event of limited, duration or strictly speaking a natural event causing serious disruption of countries economy.

Fredic Krimgold in his article: "Overview of the priority area natural disaster" (UN, 1976) regards that a native tendency is to equate natural hazards with natural disasters, the correct notion emerges only when natural disaster and or hazards are considered in the context of what are caused vulnerabilities.

According to G.F. White, "Disaster is an interaction between people and the nature governed by the co-existent state of adjustment in the human use system and the state of nature and the natural event system."

Luzzari Stefarno in a WHO document defines a disaster as any occurrence causing damage, ecological disruption, loss of human lives, deterioration of health and health services on a scale sufficient to warrant any extra-ordinary intervention from outside the affected community. D.K. Smith in a WMO document defines natural disaster as "catastrophic consequence of natural phenomena or a combination of phenomena resulting in injury, loss of life or input in a relatively large-scale and some disruption to human activities."[1]

Anthony, R. Michaelis has sought to define a natural disaster on the basis of casualties suffered by the people involved: if thousand to one million people be dead or be in immediate danger or death, he would call the event a natural disaster.[2]

Haroid D. Foster has put forward the most comprehensive notion of natural disaster, his scale being built around a social stress rating, derived from individual's loss or a change subsequent to his being involved in a disaster, his is one of few definitions, formally making allowance for the difference between the developed and developing countries so as to arrive at the total stress caused during a disaster.[3] WHO has often considered another phase before the pre-disaster phase and it has been labeled as non-disaster phase; the very titles speak of their import.

Thomas E. Drabek drawing upon extant studies on human responses to disasters, has proposed a rich inventory and this has enabled him to put forward a distinct classification system by disaster phase and system level of response. The disaster phases are preparedness—(1) Planning; (2) Warning, response; (3) Evacuation; (4) Emergency, recovery; (5) Restoration; (6) Reconstruction and mitigation; (7) Hazards perception; and (8) Adjustment. The system levels range from the individual to the international.[4]

The United Nations defines disasters as "The Occurrence of a sudden or major misfortune which disrupts the basic fabric and normal functioning of a society or community."

The Webster's Dictionary, defines disaster as "any event that overwhelms existing resources to deal with the event." According to Ministry of Environment and Forest, GOI, "A disaster is a Catastrophic consequence of Natural Phenomena or a combination of Phenomena resulting in injury, loss of life or input in a relatively large scale and some disruption to human activities." Prof. Dilip Kumar Sinha in his Presidential Address to Indian Science Congress, "Coping with Natural disasters: An integrated approach" at Indore in 1991 feels that—In an Indian setting, natural disasters whatever be the kind, are seldom found to be stingy in respect of their impact and aftermath, Ravages wrought by them are invariably pervasive; populations whatever be the nature become victims; settlements, human and other, are disrupted; buildings and structures are dismantled, often razed to the ground; mental frame is found reeling heavily; environment in its entirety becomes thus terribly degraded. As mitigation and alleviation of miseries stand out to be necessary tasks in the wake of natural disasters, attention to medical care and needs often come as third in order of priority, food and shelter having obviously higher precedence.[5]

Disaster is defined as: ". . . a serious disruption of the functioning of a society, causing widespread human, material, or environment losses which exceed the ability of the affected society to cope using its own resource." A disaster is the product of a hazard such as earthquake, flood or windstorm coinciding with a vulnerable situation which might include communities, cities or villages. There are two main components in this definition: hazard and vulnerability. Without vulnerability or hazard there is no disaster. A disaster occurs when hazards and vulnerability meet.[6]

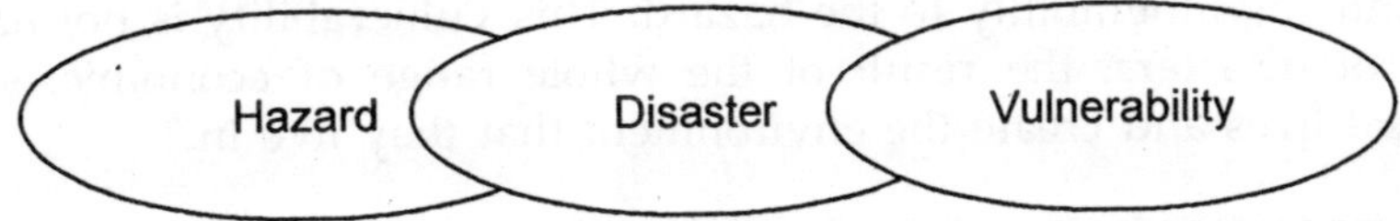

A natural disaster is an event of the nature, which causes sudden disruption to the normal life of a society and causes damage to property and lives, to such an extent, that normal social and economic mechanisms, available to the society, are inadequate to restore normalcy. Viewed in this perspective, a host of natural phenomena constitutes disasters to a society, whether they are related to an occurrence in a micro-environment or not. In macro-terms, the disasters, which cause widespread damage and disruption in India, are drought, flood, cyclone, and earthquakes.

Response to natural disasters have evolved over time the world over. From a purely humanitarian urge to offer succour to the victims, the response to the challenge of natural disasters has come to address itself to preparedness to mitigate their impact and reduce their occurrences to sustain the developmental effort. India is not an exception to this changing scenario. The philanthropy and the munificence of the rich is still evident in offering humanitarian assistance. But this is a small part of the total relief effort. The dynamics of voluntary action does contribute to the building up of the resilience of the disaster-prone societies but these efforts are isolated, and still the major part of this task rests on the governmental interventions. It is, in this context, that there is a need to closely appraise the existing response mechanisms and relief delivery so as to realize the objectives of the natural disaster reduction in this International Decade of Natural Disaster Reduction (IDNDR).[7]

DISTINCTION BETWEEN HAZARD AND DISASTER

Hazard and disaster are closely related. ". . . A hazard is a natural event while the disaster is its consequence. A hazard is a perceived natural event which threatens both life and property . . . a disaster is the realization of this hazard. . ." (John Whittow, Disaster, 1980). Pan American

Health Organization in its Scientific Publication No. 575 in 2000 describes the difference very clearly. To quote:

The term "disaster" usually refers to the natural event (e.g., a hurricane or earthquake) in combination with its damaging effects (e.g., the loss of life or destruction of buildings). "Hazard" refers to the natural event, and "vulnerability" to the susceptibility of a population or system (e.g., a hospital, water supply and sewage system, or aspects of infrastructure) to the effects of the hazard. The probability that a particular system or population will be affected by hazards is known as the "risk." Hence, risk is a function of the vulnerability and the hazard, and is expressed as follows:

$$\text{Risk} = \text{Vulnerability} \times \text{Hazard}$$

Twigg, J. 2001 extracted from Living with Risk, A global review of disaster reduction initiatives 2004 version States, "Strictly speaking, there is no such thing as a natural disaster, but there are natural hazards, such as cyclones and earthquakes. The difference between a hazard and a disaster is an important one. A disaster takes place when a community is affected by a hazard (usually defined as an event and even psychological factors that shape people's that overwhelms the community's capacity to cope). In other words, the impact of the disaster is determined by the extent of a community's vulnerability to the hazard. This vulnerability is not natural. It is the human dimension of disasters, the result of the whole range of economic, social, cultural, institutional, political lives and create the environment that they live in."

DEFINITION OF TERMINOLOGY USED IN DISASTER MANAGEMENT (See Chart 32.1)

Culture of Prevention

A culture of prevention, it was felt needs to be installed in all communities and amongst disaster managers. This requires active involvement of all groups of society, national, international organizations, governments and private organizations. Early warnings and conscious developmental programming are the key elements of preventive planning. The new culture that is permeating the disaster management in the present times is based on the premise that hazards both natural and human-induced are inevitable, but the disasters that follow can be handled effectively through adequate preventive measures.

At the conference, Ajay Chibber, Director of the Bank's Independent Evaluation Group (IEG) and Ron Parker, Lead Evaluator presented Hazards of Nature, Risks to Development, an evaluation of the past two decades of Bank assistance for natural disasters. Chibber pointed out that poorly planned development can turn a recurring natural phenomenon into a human and economic disaster. "While hazards are created by nature, disasters are largely made-made," he said. Parker noted that "although the incidence of disasters is rising, their costs escalating, and suffering they inflict mounting, disasters are also more foreseeable and preventable." There is, therefore, much that can be done to prevent their devastation on communities and economies.

Preparedness

The United Nations Disaster Relief Office (UNDRO) defines Disaster Preparedness as "(a series of) measures designed to organize and facilitate timely and effective rescue, relief and rehabilitation operations in cases of disaster. Measures of preparedness include among others, setting up disaster relief machinery, formulation of emergency relief plans, training of specific

CHART 32.1

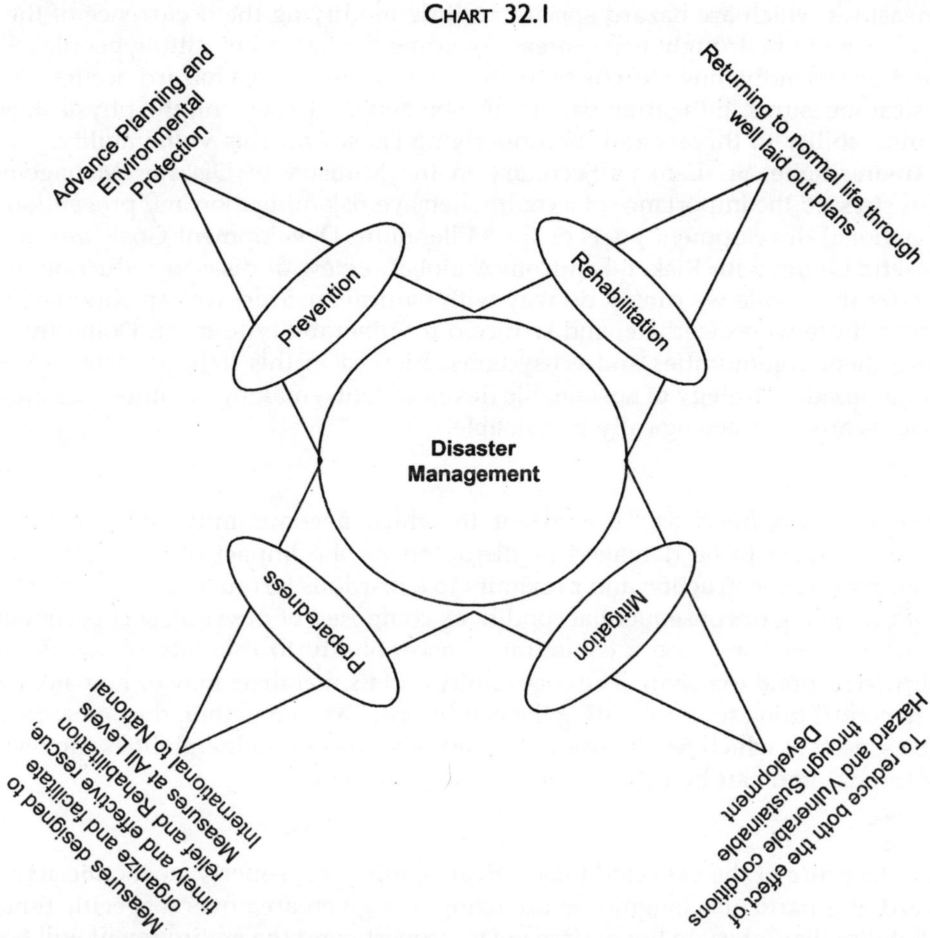

groups (and vulnerable communities) to undertake rescue and relief, stock piling supplies and earmarking funds for relief operations."

This protective process embraces measures which enable governments, communities and individuals to respond rapidly to disaster situations to cope with them effectively. Preparedness includes the formulation of viable emergency plans, the development of warning systems, the maintenance of inventories and the training of personnel. It may also embrace search and rescue measures as well as evacuation plans for areas that may be at risk from a recurring disaster.

Preparedness therefore encompasses those measures taken before a disaster event which are aimed at minimizing loss of life, disruption of critical services, and damage when the disaster occurs. All preparedness planning needs to be supported by appropriate legislation with clear allocation of responsibilities and budgetary provisions.

Mitigation

Mitigation embraces all measures taken to reduce both the effect of the hazard itself and the vulnerable conditions to it in order to reduce the scale of a future disaster. Therefore, mitigation activities can be focused on the hazard itself or the elements exposed to the threat. Examples of mitigation measures which are hazard specific include modifying the occurrence of the hazard, e.g. water management in drought prone areas, avoiding the hazard by sitting people away from the hazard and by strengthening structures to reduce damage when a hazard occurs. In addition to these physical measures, mitigation should also be aimed at reducing the physical, economic and social vulnerability to threats and the underlying causes for this vulnerability.

P.D. Amarasinghe, Sri Lanka's Secretary in the Ministry of Disaster Management and Human Rights stressed the importance of a comprehensive risk mitigation and prevention strategy if countries' national development goals or the Millennium Development Goals are to be met.

Abravovtiz Living with Risk, taken from A global review of disaster reduction initiatives, ISDR, 2004 states that while we cannot do way with natural hazards, we can eliminate those we cause, minimize those we exacerbate, and reduce our vulnerability to most. Doing this requires healthy and resilient communities and ecosystems. Viewed in this light, disaster mitigation is clearly part of a broader strategy of sustainable development—making communities and nations socially, economically and ecologically sustainable.

Vulnerability

Vulnerability is defined as "The extent to which a community, structure, service or geographic area is likely to be damaged or disrupted by the impact of particular hazard, on account of their nature, construction and proximity to hazardous terrain or a disaster prone area."

A set of prevailing or consequential conditions composed of physical, socio-economic and/ or political factors which increase a community susceptibility to calamity or which adversely affect its ability to respond to events. The community and its members may or may not be willing participants in contributing to or tolerating the conditions. Taken together, they create a dynamic mix of variables, each of which results from a continuous process. Vulnerabilities can be physical, social, or attitudinal and can be primary or secondary in nature.

Risk

Risk is a measure of the expected losses (deaths, injuries, property, economic activity, etc.) due to a hazard of a particular magnitude occurring in a given area over a specific time period.

A probability that injury to life or damage to property and the environment will occur. The extent to which risk is either increased or diminished is the result of the interaction of a multitude of causation chains of events.

Rehabilitation

Settling people in a way that they return to their normal life as far as possible through well laid out plans. In Pakistan, the Earthquake Reconstruction program has also achieved some impressive milestone: Construction has begun in more than 150,000 homes and over 80,000 workers have been trained in seismic resistant construction. A total of 490,000 beneficiaries have received the first two instalments of the housing reconstruction grant to rebuild their homes.

Hazard

An event or occurrence that has the potential for causing injury to life or damage to property or the environment. The magnitude of the phenomenon, the probability of its occurrence and the extent and severity of the impact can vary. In many cases, these effects can be anticipated and estimated.

Response to natural disasters have evolved over time the world over. From a purely humanitarian urge to offer succour to the victims, the response to the challenge of natural disasters has come to address itself to preparedness, to mitigate their impact and reduce their occurrences to sustain the developmental effort. India is not an exception to this changing scenario. The philanthropy and the munificence of the rich is still evident in offering humanitarian assistance. But this is a small part of the total relief effort. The dynamics of voluntary action does contribute to the building up of the resilience of the disaster-prone societies but these efforts are isolated, and still the major part of this task rests on the governmental interventions. It is, in this context, that there is a need to closely appraise the existing response mechanisms and relief delivery so as to realize the objectives of the natural disaster reduction in this International Decade of Natural Disaster Reduction (IDNDR).

The tsunami and the subsequent earthquake in Pakistan have proved to be a turning point for the region. Countries are increasingly working towards adopting a proactive rather than a reactive approach and preventing losses from future disasters—human, economic or otherwise.

Given the region's high exposure to hazards, the World Bank's South Asia region has developed a Hazard Risk Management Program that was launched at a Regional Conference held in New Delhi.

The program aims at increasing the resilience of countries to disasters while decreasing underlying risk factors and vulnerabilities. The preparation of a regional hazard risk management strategy, knowledge sharing and dissemination activities, and internal training and capacity building, are some of the many activities involved in the program.

In the World Conference on Natural Disaster Reduction, Yokohama, 1994 the following suggestions were discussed:

- Risk assessment is a required step for the adoption of adequate and successful disaster reduction policies and measures.
- Disaster prevention and preparedness are of primary importance in reducing the need for disaster relief.
- Disaster prevention and preparedness should be considered integral aspects of development policy and planning at national, regional, bilateral, multilateral and international levels.
- The development and strengthening of capacities to prevent, reduce and mitigate disasters is a top priority area to be addressed so as to provide a strong basis for follow-up activities by IDNDR.
- Early warnings of impending disasters and their effective dissemination are key factors to successful disaster prevention and preparedness.
- Preventive measures are most effective when they involve participation at all levels from the local community through the national government to the regional and international level.
- Vulnerability can be reduced by the application of proper design and patterns of development focused on target groups by appropriate education and training of the whole community.
- The international community accepts the need to share the necessary technology to prevent, reduce and mitigate disaster.
- Environmental protection as a component of sustainable development consistent with poverty alleviation is imperative in the prevention and mitigation of natural disasters.

Each country bears the primary responsibility for protecting its people, infrastructure, and other national assets from the impact of natural disasters. The international community should demonstrate strong political determination required to make efficient use of existing resources, including financial, scientific and technologies means, in the field of natural disaster reduction, bearing in mind the needs of the developing countries, particularly the least developed countries.

DISASTER POTENTIAL OF INDIA

India covers an area of 32,87,263 sq. km. extending from snow covered Himalayan heights in the North to the tropical rain forest of the South. In the North, the territory is bounded by the Great Himalayas and stretches southwards tapering off into the Indian ocean between the Bay of Bengal and the Arabian Sea. The main land extends between latitude 8″4′ and 37″6′ North and longitudes 68.7 and 97.25 East, measuring about 32,000 km from North to South and West to East. The vast land frontier of 15,200 km and coastline of 7,500 km. also has group of islands located both in the Bay of Bengal and the Arabian Sea. Hardly any other country has such a large land mass with such a diverse range of geo-agro-climatic zones. The main land of India comprises of four regions, namely, the Great Mountain Zone, Plains of the Indus, Ganges and the Brahmaputra the Desert Region, and the Southern Peninsula. The Himalayan range comprises three almost parallel ranges interspread with large plateaus and valleys. The mountain wall extends over a distance of 24,000 km. with a varying width of 240 to 320 km. The plain about 2,400 km. long, are formed by basins of three distinct river systems, viz. the Indus, the Ganges and the Brahmaputra. The desert region is clearly delineated in two parts—Sindh Frontier while the little desert extends between Jaisalmer and Jodhpur upto Punjab. The desert region is inhabited by local communities which have developed their own coping and recovery mechanisms. Between the two deserts is a zone of absolute sterile region, consisting of rocky land cut up by limestones ridges."

India has been traditionally vulnerable to natural disasters on account of its unique geo-climatic conditions. Floods, droughts, cyclones, earthquakes and landslides have been a recurrent phenomena. About 60% of the landmass is prone to earthquakes of various intensities; over 40 million hectares is prone to floods; about 8% of the total area is prone to cyclones and 68% of the area is susceptible to drought. In the decade 1990-2000, an average of about 4344 people lost their lives and about 30 million people were affected by disasters every year. The loss in terms of private, community and public assets has been astronomical.

According to 2001 census, India had a population of 1027 million with 195.02 million housing units. The literacy rate as per 2001 census was 65.38 percent, 75.85 percent for male and 54.16 percent for female. To protect such a large population with low levels of education from the fury of natural hazards is not an easy task. However, local initiatives and the government efforts combined over the years, have tried to reduce risks and build community capacity to deal with emergencies.

At the global level, there has been considerable concern over natural disasters. Even as substantial scientific and material progress is made, the loss of lives and property due to disasters has not decreased. In fact, the human toll and economic losses have mounted. It was in this background that the United Nations General Assembly, in 1989, declared. The decade 1990-2000 as the International Decade for Natural Disaster Reduction with the objective to reduce loss of lives and property and restrict socio-economic damage through concerted international action, specially in developing countries.

Because of the large geographical size of the country, India often faces natural hazards like floods, cyclones and drought occurring frequently in different parts of the country. At times, some area normally subjected to drought situation have got flooded in certain years. Hazards like earthquakes, hailstorms avalanches, landslides, etc. occur quite suddenly but they are restricted in their impact in terms of time. The extent of the impact of an earthquake depends on its magnitude, season and time of occurrence.

Indeed, as Kofi Annan, former Secretary General of United Nations, stated at the Programme Forum of the International Decade for Natural Disaster Reduction (IDNDR) held in Geneva, "The humanitarian community does a remarkable job in responding to disaster. But the most important task in the medium and long-term is to strengthen and broaden programmes which reduce the number and cost of disasters in the first place." While we should continue to improve and strengthen our response capacity, we need to engage in working together to build a "global culture of prevention." This means greater efforts to reduce vulnerability to natural hazards in the first place.

The recent occurrence of massive Tsunami on 26.12.2004 has worsened the situation. Though complete prevention of natural disasters is beyond human capabilities, the adverse impact of any disaster on human lives and their livelihoods can be minimized by taking adequate early warning, preparedness and mitigation measures.[8]

TYPES OF DISASTERS (See Chart 32.2)

These can be divided into two types (i) Natural, and (ii) Man-made disaster.

Natural Disasters

(i) Wind-related-Storm, cyclone, tornado, Huricane, Storm surge, Tidal waves.

(ii) Water-related-Food, Cloud Burst, Flash flood, Excessive rains, Drought, Communicable diseases..

(iii) Earth-related-Earthquake, Tsunamis, Avalanches, Landslides, Volcanic eruptions.

Man-made Disasters

(i) War/battle/hostile enemy actions.

(ii) Arson/sabotage/internal disturbance/riots.

(iii) Accidents of vehicles/trains/aircraft/ships.

(iv) Industrial accidents/explosion of boilers/gas cylinder or gas chambers/gas leaks.

(v) Fire and Forest fires.

(vi) Nuclear explosion/accidents/radioactive leakages.

(vii) Ecological disasters like deforestation/soil erosion/air/water pollution.

(viii) HIV/AIDS, Life Style diseases.

(ix) Violence.

A High Powered Committee (HPC) of the Government of India, in its report, submitted to Government of India in October 2001 mentions the following types of disasters:

CHART 32.2

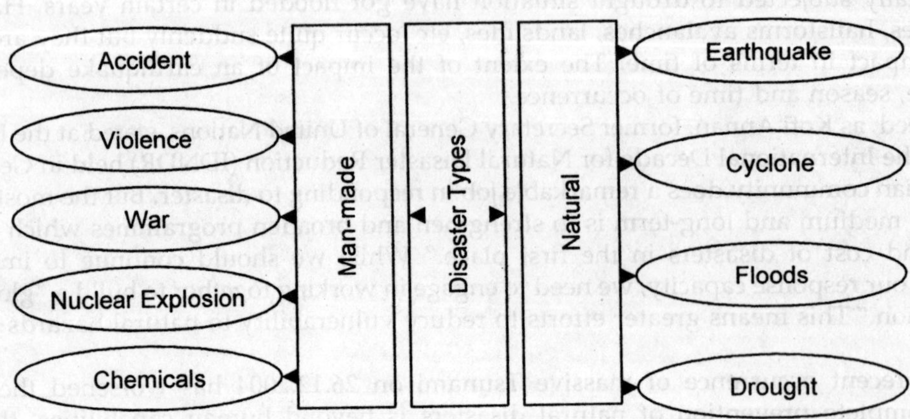

I. Water and Climate-related Disasters

1. Floods and Drainage Management
2. Cyclones
3. Tornadoes and Hurricanes
4. Hailstorm
5. Cloud Burst
6. Heat Wave and cold Wave
7. Snow Avalanches
8. Droughts
9. Sea Erosion
10. Thunder and Lighting

II. Geologically-related Disasters

1. Landslides and Mudflows
2. Earthquakes
3. Dam Failures/Dam Bursts
4. Mine Fires

III. Chemical, Industrial and Nuclear-related Disasters

1. Chemical and Industrial Disasters
2. Nuclear Disasters

IV. Accident-related Disasters

1. Forest Fires
2. Urban Fires
3. Mine Flooding

4. Oil Spill
5. Major Building Collapse
6. Serial Bomb Blasts
7. Festival Disasters and Fires
8. Electrical Disasters and Fires
9. Air, Road and Rail Accidents
10. Boat Capsizing
11. Village Fire

V. *Biologically-related Disasters*

1. Biological Disaster and Epidemics
2. Pest Attacks
3. Cattle Epidemics
4. Food Poisoning

Different natural calamities can be distinguished from each other in terms of their nature and extent of their impact. Calamities like earthquakes, hailstorms, avalanches, landslides, etc. occur quite suddenly but they are restricted in their impact in terms of time and space. Similarly, though floods and cyclones occur with some element of warning yet their occurrence is confined in duration. Drought, on the other hand, spans over a much longer time-frame and its adverse impact on the economic activities and life of an area is of a more lasting nature. The measures required to meet the threats posed by different calamities, therefore, differ considerably in terms of disaster preparedness and amelioration of the economic and social life of the affected people.

Natural calamities may be broadly grouped into major and minor types depending upon their potential to cause damage to human life and property. While natural calamities like earthquakes, droughts, floods and cyclones could be regarded as major, hailstorms, avalanches, landslides, fire accidents, etc. whose impact is localised and intensity of the damage is much less can be categorised as minor calamities.

Minor calamities like hailstorms, avalanches, landslides and fires also occur without any appreciable degree of forewarning and cause damage to properties and lives. However, areas prone to such disasters also could be identified and certain precautionary measures taken in the context of potential threat requiring general awareness and an ability to relate to a predefined system of appropriate responses on the part of the local administration

IMPACT OF DISASTERS (See Chart 32.3)

Today it is a proven fact that Natural Disasters can happen at any place irrespective of the developed, developing or the least developed status of a country. It can cause massive destruction to the lives and livelihoods of large population and hence, to the national economies. It is experienced that the least developed and developing countries are impacted more severely by large scale natural disasters.

The impact of natural disasters in term of human and economic losses has risen in recent years, and society in general has become more vulnerable to natural disasters. Those usually most affected by natural and other disasters are the poor and socially disadvantaged groups in developing countries as they are least equipped to cope with them.

CHART 32.3

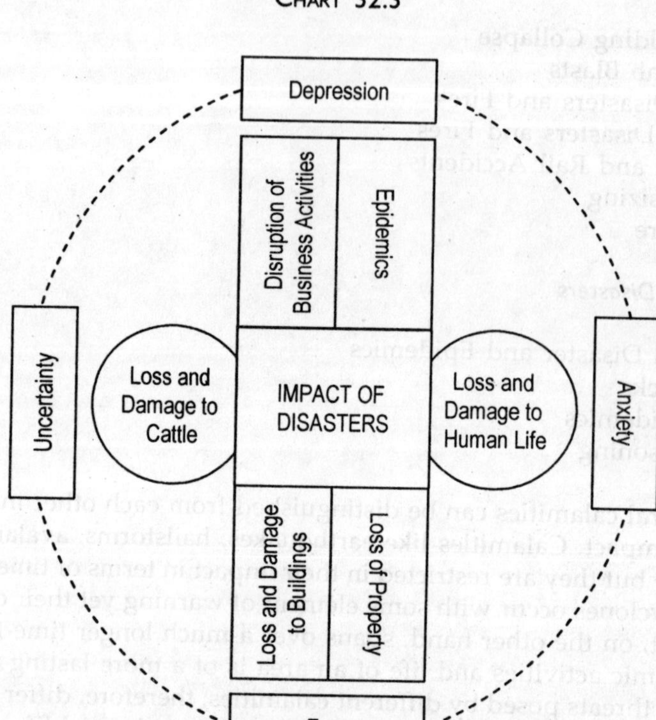

Though all disasters are unique in that they affect areas with different levels of vulnerability and with distinct social, health, and economic conditions, there are still similarities between disasters. If recognized, these common factors can be used to optimize the management of health and humanitarian assistance and use of resources (see Table 32.2). The following points should be noted:

"In a matter of minutes an entire country can see its infrastructure destroyed, its economy smashed and its people even deprived of their livelihood. Mankind has been stricken by earthquakes, cyclones, floods, drought and epidemic diseases throughout recorded history. Man's own folly too leaves endless suffering in its wake, and Spaceship Earth carries a menacing burden as it whirls its human crew through time and space. Nuclear weapons, the population explosion and the yawning gulf between rich and poor still trouble our planet until the question arises whether we are not fast approaching the day of some vast and final catastrophe."[9]

Whether disasters are of natural origin or man-made, their effects in a country's life can be detected for months, and sometimes even years. It is therefore essential that any support operation be designed and implemented with a long-term perspective.[10]

The struggle against disasters is still a matter of development. As with all other misfortunes that plague humanity, such as disease and ignorance, disasters strike hardest at those who most lack any defence. But as in other fields it is on these same people that we can most rely. Just as we have observed communities actively interesting themselves in their own development ever since international aid movements have learnt to see problems through the eyes of the

TABLE 32.2

Short-term Effects of Major Disasters

Effects	*Earth-quakes*	*High Winds (without flooding)*	*Tidal waves/ flash floods*	*Slow-onset floods*	*Landslides*	*Volcanoes/ Lahars*
Deaths*	Many	Few	Many	Few	Many	Many
Severe injuries requiring extensive treatment	Many	Moderate	Few	Few	Few	Few
Increased risk of communicable disease	Potential risk following all major disasters (Probability rising with overcrowding and deteriorating sanitation)					
Damage to health facilities	Severe (structure and equipment)	Severe	Severe but Localized	Severe (equipment only)	Severe but localized	Severe (structure and equipment)
Damage to water systems	Severe	Light	Severe	Light	Severe but localized	Severe
Food Shortage	Rare	Common	Common	Common	Rare	Rare
Major Population Movements	(may occur due to economic and logistic factors) Rare may occur in heavily damaged urban areas)		Common (generally limited)			

* Potential lethal impact in absence of preventive measure.

underdeveloped themselves, so the strangers who first arrive on the scene of a disaster invariably find the victims, not sitting passively by and waiting for help, but already busily engaged in making sure that daily life goes on. It is among these reserves of goodwill and community spirit that we may perhaps find the greatest fund of human resources for reconstruction.[11]

Natural disasters strike countries, both developed and developing, all over the world. Every year, more than twenty natural disasters occur throughout the globe. In last two decades, disasters have claimed more than three billion lives and affected about one billion people. The frequency of natural disasters is many times more in Asia and pacific region. India, like many other developing countries, is affected by different types of disasters every year, such as earthquakes, floods, droughts, cyclones, snowstorms, hailstorms, etc. These disasters hinder many developmental projects as huge amounts have to be diverted for relief and recovery.[12]

A natural hazard is an event of nature, which causes sudden disruption to the normal life of a society and causes damage to life and property, to such an extent that normal, social and economic mechanisms available to the society are inadequate to restore normalcy. Viewed in this manner, a host of natural phenomena causes disasters to a society, whether they are related to an occurrence in micro-environment or not. In macro-terms, the hazards, which cause widespread damage and disruption in India, are floods, cyclones, earthquakes and landslides.

The past decade has witnessed an extraordinary increase in the number and extent of natural disasters. As Kofi Annan, Secretary General of the United Nations, pointed out, "The facts are startling. The costs of weather-related disasters in 1998 exceeded the costs of all such disasters in the decade of the 1980s. In the Caribbean, the hurricanes designated George and Mitch Miued more than 13,000 people, with Mitch being the deadliest atlantic storm in 200 years. Major floods hit India, Nepal, Bangaldesh and much of East Asia, with thousands killed. Two-thirds of Bangladesh was inundated for months, leaving millions homeless. There were three times as many great natural hazards in the 1990s as in the 1960s, while disaster costs increased more than nine-fold in the same period.[13]

"The humanitarian community does a remarkable job in responding to disasters. But the most important task in the medium and long-term is to strengthen and broaden programmes which reduce the number and cost of disasters in the first place." While we should continue to improve and strengthen our response capacity, we need to engage in working together to build a "global culture of prevention." This means greater efforts to reduce vulnerability to natural hazards in the first place.

As we approach the beginning of a new millennium, the IDNDR is proved to have contributed with all its partners world-wide to fostering a "global culture of prevention" for the 21st Century. To build on the progress achieved during the IDNDR, we have to act decisively, so that disaster reduction becomes an essential element of government policies. Recalling the Geneva Mandate adopted at the IDNDR Programme Forum, we have to adopt and implement policy measures at the international, regional, national and local levels aimed at reducing the vulnerability of our societies to natural disasters. These measures should have as main objectives the establishment of hazard resistant communities, the protection of people from the threat of disasters, and the safeguarding of our natural and economic resources and of our social well-being.[14]

K. Rajan, suggests the following adversities which befall on people and the area:

- Loss of crops and availability of essentials like food and agricultural commodities;
- Loss of employment opportunities in the area where natural Disaster occurs and particularly on rural employment;
- Problems of health and diseases arising both from insufficient availability of the basic necessities causing malnourishment, hunger, etc. or on the availability of good and hygienic drinking water;
- Financial distress caused to the farming community and those dependent on land which affect their ability to withstand hard conditions immediately following the occurrence of the natural disaster but also importantly, their ability to recover well enough before the next cropping season and take full advantage of normal conditions which may prevail;

- Impact on industrial sector due to loss of production of raw materials, reduce generation of power, etc.; and
- Lastly, the impact of the disaster on the cattle wealth.[15]

V. Suresh rightly feels that Natural disasters, which damage national economies and produce hardships for large sections of the population, are one of the single largest concerns for most nations. Human settlements are frequently affected by natural disasters—earthquake, floods, hurricanes, cyclones, landslides, sea erosions—which take a heavy toll on human lives, destroy buildings and infrastructure and have far reaching economic and social consequences for communities.[16]

Ashok Pahwa has rightly said, "Natural hazards are not new to the earth system. Like natural resources, they have been, and are, a part of biosphere and eco-systems. It is the human interventions, its endeavours towards development, that these hazards turn into disasters, causing enormous devastation to the life and property of the nations. The extent and frequency of damage, that is being caused by these extreme events, has raised concerns all over the world resulting into declaration of present decade (1990s) as international Decade for Natural Disaster reduction."[17]

Bhagat Singh has suggested the ways to reduce its serious effects while Occurrence of these natural disasters cannot be prevented altogether, their adverse impact can be reduced substantially—by undertaking various preparedness and mitigation measures by community involvement. Minimizing the loss of precious human life is the first priority in disaster management. Significant achievement has been made in designing of disaster resistant houses and inventing quality building materials to withstand the fury of natural disasters. It is gratifying to note that HUDCO has given a lead by taking a number of initiatives to propagate these designs as well as materials among the vulnerable community besides imparting training to the artisans and masons through their building centers.[18]

Earthquakes, floods, draught, cyclones, accidents, AIDS are major Types of disaster phenomenon occurred in the South-East Asia Region, India is a large country and has had more than its share of major natural hazards like drought, floods, earthquakes and cyclones throughout its history of civilization." Naturally, the country developed its own practices and strategies for coping with the various natural calamities. Since independence in 1947, India has developed a nationwide relief administration where a lead role of the State Governments is envisaged.[19]

V. Thiruppugazh and Sudhir Kumar in their article, "E-Governance And Disaster Management" in the Silver symposium of Institute of Rural Management, Anand (Gujarat) rightly stated that in recent years, link between disaster and development is being established by the development community as disasters not only claim lives and destroy social networks but also eat away the development result and pushes back the society and country by several months or years. Hence amalgamation of the Disaster Management with Development Plan/interventions is the key for stable, equitable and sustainable growth and hence poverty reduction. Development should be such that it saves from disaster. "Development should not be such that it itself becomes disaster."

Shivraj Patil, Minister of Home Affairs has rightly said that the increasing incidents of disasters have been hampering poverty reduction, environmental protection and sustainable development. Disasters wipe out years of development and consumer resources that could have been used for development and social welfare of the people. Disasters and poverty compound each other in vicious cycle.

The following can be the impact of disasters:

1. People, loss of life.
2. Personal health, injury or disease
3. Damage, destruction of property
4. Damage, destruction of infrastructure, public service systems.
5. Damage, destruction of environment.
6. Damage, destruction of crops.
7. Disruption, loss of production.
8. Disruption, loss of essential services.
9. Disruption, loss of national infrastructure.
10. Disruption to governmental process systems.
11. Loss to national, local economies.
12. Disruption, loss of community or lifestyle.
13. Sociological and psychological consequences.

Disasters when occur, have a severe impact on all sections of the society. But globally, it is observed that it is certain sections who are more susceptible. These vulnerable sections lack resources and are deprived of basic necessities, that expose them to the adverse effects. Preparedness activity, is to be holistic that takes into consideration, the hazards the vulnerable are exposed to, existing resources, capacities and capabilities and attempt to harness their potentials. They need to be integrated in the overall disaster management process. The general tendency is to overlook the contribution of vulnerable groups and consider them more as victims.

Natural Disaster arrest the process of economic development and often set it back by many years. Restorations and repair of the fractured infrastructure, particularly, roads, communications, power, irrigation are undoubtedly a daunting task. It also requires substantial resources. The desirability of integrating restoration work in the development plans of the State must be examined. The Planning Commission and the successive Finance Commissions have also emphasized this aspect. A disaster management programme which will address itself to mitigating disasters such as cyclone, floods, landslides and earthquake along the lines of the Drought Prone Area Programme would facilitate the process of integration of restoration work in the Plan. Such a programme may include preventive precautionary measures and specific projects schemes for Earthquake and Cyclone-prone area.

Disaster Management has to be a multi-disciplinary and pro-active approach. Besides various measures for putting in place institutional and policy framework, disaster prevention, mitigation and preparedness enunciated earlier and initiatives being taken by the Central and state Governments, the community, civil society organisations and Media also have a key role to play in achieving our goal of moving together, towards a safer India. The message being put across is that, in order to move towards safer and sustainable national development, development projects should be sensitive towards disaster mitigation.

Our mission is vulnerability reduction to all types of hazards, be it natural or man-made. This is not an easy task to achieve, keeping in view the vast population, and the multiple natural hazards to which this country is exposed. However, if we are firm in our conviction and resolve that the Government and the people of this country are not prepared to pay the price in terms of massive casualties and economic losses, the task, though difficult, is achievable and we shall achieve.

We have taken the first few but significant steps towards vulnerability reduction, putting in place prevention and mitigation measures and preparedness for a rapid and professional response. With a massive awareness generation campaign and building up of capabilities as well as institutionalization of the entire mechanism through a techno-legal and techno-financial framework, we are gradually moving in the direction of sustainable development.

Our vision 2020 is to build a safer and secure India through sustained collective effort, synergy of national capacities and people's participation. What looks a dream today will be transformed into reality in the next two decades. This is our goal and we shall strive to achieve this goal with a missionary zeal. The path ahead, which looks difficult today, will become a lot easier as we move along together.

Community awareness forms the basic crux of present day disaster management. The prime objective is to raise the awareness levels, knowledge base of the community to make them alert, self-reliant and cope with the consequences. People have coping strategies that they derive from the past experience. The communities possess the capacity and strength arising out of previous experiences in facing emergencies. This needs to be harnessed. The awareness is required to enable the community understand the impact of disaster, efforts they need to put to reduce its impact and save their lives and property.

TRAINING FOR DISASTER MANAGEMENT

The HT special correspondent in the issue of January 4, 2007 clearly observed that the disasters remained with us but we can lessen the damage to lives and property if only we are technically sound and prepared for the calamities. This is possible only through a well-established system of training. A masters course in disaster management builds trained manpower in the areas of emergency planning, risk assessment, community development, humanitarian aid, capacity building and also enhances the skills of professionals in the field.

For planning for disasters and emergency preparedness training, government has created a few institutes that offer short-term courses. Notable amongst them being the National Centre for Disaster Management (NCDM) set-up by the Indian Institute of Public Administration and the Centre for Disaster Management set-up by Y.S. Chavan Academy of Development Administration conduct workshops and seminars for civil servants and government officials. Similarly, the Disaster Management Institute, Bhopal set-up after the gas tragedy conducts awareness programmes for NGOs and the public at large.

Let us mention some other training arrangements:

- Guru Gobind Singh Indraprastha University, Delhi.
- Centre for Disaster Management, Pune.
- PRT Institute of Post-graduate Environmental Education, Bhopal.
- National Civil Defence College, Nagpur.
- Sikkim Manipal University of Health, Medical and Technological.
- The Indira Gandhi National Open University (IGNOU) was the first to offer a six month certificate course in disaster management for Plus two students. A Diploma Course in Disaster Management has also been started. The programme is offered through distance mode.

- IGNOU also offers a comprehensive programme on community awareness in disaster preparedness.
- Himachal Pradesh University offer Diploma in Disaster Management.

NATIONAL INSTITUTE OF DISASTER MANAGEMENT

NIDM set-up by Ministry of Home Affairs, Government of India, is a centre for excellence and learning in the field of disaster management. It is a premier resource institution for human resource development, training, capacity building, applied research, implementation and dissemination of information and knowledge for holistic disaster mitigation, preparedness, response and recovery, towards sustainable development.

NIDM Objectives

Applying critical assessment methods to disaster events, NIDM seeks to create a well-established network of people and institutions with outstanding expertise in the field by:

- Professionalizing disaster risk management in India and the region by developing an independent cadre of trained emergency and mitigation managers.
- Building disaster-resilient communities by promoting public awareness to instill a culture of preparedness.
- Filling knowledge gaps by providing a common platform for collation and sharing of information and experiences with practitioners of disaster management.
- Providing policy assistance to facilitate multi-disciplinary and sectoral support for prevention strategies, technical assistance, implementation techniques and know-how dissemination with respect to natural and man-made disasters.
- Networking and building partnerships with governments, institutions of learning and training, the corporate sector, international agencies, NGOs and civil society organizations, to synergize disaster mitigation efforts.
- Developing mechanisms for risk financing, risk transfer and insurance for effective disaster management.
- Mainstreaming disaster risk management into development planning.
- Working as a resource institution for the national and state governments for policy, planning and capacity building.

Researching and documenting disaster events to draw lessons and best practices.

Without prejudice to the generality of the provisions contained in sub-section (8), the National Institute, for the discharge of its functions, may:

(a) develop training modules, undertake research and documentation in disaster management and organise training programmes;

(b) formulate and implement a comprehensive human resource development plan covering all aspects of disaster management;

(c) provide assistance in national level policy formulation;

(d) provide required assistance to the training and research institutes for development of training and research programmes for stakeholders including Government functionaries and undertake training of faculty members of the State-level training institutes;

(e) provide assistance to the State Governments and State training institutes in the formulation of State level policies, strategies, disaster management framework and any other assistance as may be required by the State Governments or State training institutes for capacity-building of stakeholders, Government including its functionaries, civil society members, corporate sector and people's elected representatives;

(f) develop educational materials for disaster management including academic and professional courses;

(g) promote awareness among stakeholders including college or school teachers and students, technical personnel and others associated with multi-hazard mitigation, preparedness and response measures;

(h) undertake, organise and facilitate study courses, conferences, lectures, seminars within and outside the country to promote the aforesaid objects;

(i) undertake and provide for publication of journals, research papers and books and establish and maintain libraries in furtherance of the aforesaid objects;

(j) do all such other lawful things as are conducive or incidental to the attainment of the above objects; and

(k) undertake any other function as may be assigned to it by the Central Government.

Mobilizing HRD Resources

NIDM's efforts at human resources development in key areas of disaster risk training have been initiated and include:

- Nation-wide Training Need Analysis for the National Human Resource Plan.
- National Human Resource Development Plan on Disaster Management.
- Development of Capacity-building Framework for Disaster Management Centres at State-level institutions.
- Partnerships with National and International Training Institutes.
- Professional Course on Disaster Management.

Looking Ahead

NIDM has identified the following key areas for intervention and expansion:

- disaster management policy, planning and techno-legal regime.
- Framework for NGOs and civil society capacity building.
- Framework and training modules for reconstruction and rehabilitation of disaster affected areas.
- Socio-psychological issues in disaster management.
- Gender issues in disaster management.
- Urban risk mitigation.
- Launching a mass awareness campaign.
- Focusing on school awareness and safety programmes.
- Programmes addressing special needs of vulnerable groups.
- Risk financing and cost-benefit analysis of disaster mitigation schemes.
- Strengthening the national GIS laboratory.
- Knowledge management and dissemination at the national level.

- Establishing a disaster management laboratory for simulation.
- Setting up a model emergency operations center for training.
- Mainstreaming disaster management into the education sector.
- Developing a national-level dynamic database of trained human resource personnel in the field of disaster management.

NIDM Partners

NIDM works in close association with the following national and international organizations:

- Ministries of the government of India.
- State Governments.
- Centre for Disaster Management (CDM)/State Administrative Training Institutes (ATIs).
- State Institute of Rural Development (SIRDs).
- Indian Space Research Organization (ISRO).
- National Remote Sensing Agency (NRSA).
- Central Board of Secondary Education (CBSE).
- National Council for Education, Research and Training (NCERT).
- Indian Institute of Technology (Pawai, Kharagpur, Roorkee).
- Council for Scientific and Industrial Research (CSIR) Laboratories, Structural Engineering Research Centre (SERC) Chennai.
- Institute of Insurance and Risk Management (IIRM), Hyderabad.
- All India Institute of Local Self-Government, Pune.
- Federation of Indian Chambers of Commerce and Industry (FICCI).
- Financial Institutions.
- The World Bank Institute, Washington, DC.
- United Nations Development Program (UNDP), India.
- United Nations Children's Fund, India.
- United States Agency for International Development (USAID).
- Federal Emergency Management Agency (FEMA), USA.
- India Meteorological Department (IMD).

Officers and other Employees of the National Institute

The Central Government shall provide the National Institute of Disaster Management with such officers, consultants and other employees, as it considers necessary, for carrying out its functions.

Training in the Incident Command System is done by Lal Bahadur Shastri National Academy of Administration.

SUGGESTIONS

1. Need of Training in Theory and Practice of Disaster Management

One of the key factors in the effort of the government to accomplish its development goals in the area of disaster management is to enhance its administrative capability for development at all levels of administrative hierarchy, which is very much a part of the development process. Such complex problems call for a multi-disciplinary solution, to which concerned people at all levels must apply their technical skills, general knowledge and understanding. The education and training of all responsible staff engaged in disaster management are absolutely essential, if worthwhile results are to be obtained. This is true whether they are politicians, administrators, executives, technical people or clerical personnel. But, our experience during the last three decades has demonstrated that the development plans have not been satisfactorily implemented, because of inadequate administrative performance.

The reasons for the low level of administrative performance include: organisational defects, lack of coordination, complex and cumbersome administrative and financial procedures, etc. These defects and deficiencies need to be corrected in order to bring about a sharp reduction in the administrative obstacles to disaster management and bridge the gap between aspirations and performance. Simultaneously, the level of competence of public service personnel directly involved in the execution of projects and implementation of development plans can be raised by training them in modern concepts and techniques of disaster administration and management. This category of personnel at the senior or intermediate level, comprising both technocrats and generalists, is constantly called upon to discharge increasingly heavy administrative and managerial responsibilities. In order to equip these personnel with the required expertise, skill, methodology and aptitude, there is a need to train such personnel.

Training is essential for building confidence, commitment and competence. Mahabir Singh Kasana, rightly observes, "Training is very important component of Human Resource Development. It is, perhaps the most cost effective method of improving competencies amongst the manpower of any organization. The right mix of knowledge, skills and attitudinal components in a training course or a training programme is essential for performance improvement. Performance calls for upgrading confidence, competence and commitment of the persons to enable them to handle the situation and show the results on the grounds. The attitude primarily leads to commitment of job. Possessing of the right attitude, combined with appropriate knowledge and skill is required to be assured through training efforts. It is, therefore, necessary that a systematic approach to training linking it with performance is necessary. Developing confidence, competence and commitments require enriching learning experience consisting to Tell, Show, Do, Check, and Act through systematic approach to training.

2. Need of Designing the Culture of Preparedness

The increasing awareness about the consequences of disasters is raising issues about the massive costs of disasters, relevance of disaster reduction, and eliciting participation from different stakeholders. There is a paradigm shift from disaster emergency response to prevention. This has been the result of several significant measures taken globally and by each country during 1990s.

In 1989 the United Nations General Assembly through its resolution, launched the International Decade for Natural Disaster Reduction (IDNDR, 1990-2000). The Decade, it was envisaged, would enable governments to focus on hazard vulnerability and risk assessment, disaster prevention, sustainable development, effective early warning systems, sharing of knowledge and transfer of technology. It emphasized on concerted international action, particularly in developing countries, to handle loss of life, property damage, social and economic disruption caused by natural disasters. This had laid the basis for the shifting of focus from rescue and relief to preparedness and mitigation. The IDNDR envisaged that by the year 2000, all the countries would have had achieved:

- Comprehensive national assessment of risks from natural hazards with these assessments taking into account their impact on developmental plans;
- Mitigation plans at the national and or local levels, involving long-term prevention, preparedness and community awareness; and
- Ready access to global, regional, national and local warning systems and widespread dissemination of such warnings.

In May 1994, a major Conference of the IDNDR programme was held which brought out a plan of action for disaster reduction called the Yokohama Strategy. It made a case for an accelerated implementation of a Plan of Action with development of a global culture of prevention as a key component of the integrated approach to disaster reduction. The strategy emphasized on the need to increase awareness on the importance of disaster reduction policies, support of states from the international community and evolving an integrated approach to disaster management in all spheres.

The Yokohama Strategy and Plan for Action for a Safer World vehemently propagated a comprehensive prevention, mitigation and preparedness strategy along with developing a culture of prevention, formulating and maintaining preparedness and response plans at the national, state and district levels, adopting a policy of self-reliance in each vulnerable area, and enhancing the capabilities of those involved at all levels through education and training. The International Strategy for Disaster Risk Reduction (ISDR) formulated by the United Nations in 2000 aims to provide a global framework to foster the resilience of communities to the effects of natural hazards through the implementation of risk management, hazard mitigation and sustainable development.

(1) Risk assessment is a required step for the adoption of adequate and successful disaster reduction policies.
(2) Disaster prevention and preparedness are of primary importance in reducing the need for disaster relief.
(3) Disaster prevention and preparedness should be considered an integral part of the development policy and planning at the national, regional, bilateral, multilateral and international levels.
(4) Early warning of impending disasters and their effective dissemination using telecommunication are the key factors to successful prevention and preparedness.
(5) Prevention measures are most effective when they involve participation at all levels, from the local, community, national to the regional and international levels.
(6) Vulnerability can be reduced by the application of proper design and patterns of development focused on target groups through appropriate education and training.
(7) The international community accepts the need to share necessary technology to prevent, reduce and mitigate disasters, which should be made freely available and done in a timely manner as an integral part of technical cooperation.
(8) Each country bears the primary responsibility of protecting its people, infrastructure and other national assets from the impact of natural disasters. The international community should demonstrate strong political determination required to mobilize and make efficient use of existing resources, including financial, scientific and technological means (High Powered Committee Report, 2001).

Disaster Prevention requires various measures, which any country needs to adopt. These include:

(1) Integrating disaster prevention with national development plans: The culture of disaster prevention needs to be a part of development plans and projects. Measures directed at reducing the occurrence of floods through construction of embankments, etc., promoting earthquake resistant structures, watershed management, rainwater harvesting, alternative cropping patterns, etc., to manage situations of drought are efforts towards disaster prevention.
(2) Formulating a disaster management policy for the whole country, providing for a legal framework for the management of all types of disasters in a comprehensive manner. This facilitates the proper implementation of preventive measures at all levels by the concerned organizations.
(3) Making the community aware, educated and their capacities built to manage disasters. A community leadership is to be built, to make them self-reliant and resilient to cope with disasters.
(4) Involving educational, training institutions, corporate sectors, and non-governmental organizations (NGOs) in eliciting public participation, generating awareness amongst all concerned stakeholders.
(5) Strengthening of existing infrastructure such as building, communication system, water supply, sanitation facilities, etc.

The High Powered Committee (2001) has outlined the following proactive measures to bring in the culture of prevention. Some of them include:

(i) Proactive measures for disaster preparedness and mitigation should be administrative, financial, legislative and techno-legal.
(ii) Capacity building in disaster management has to be at policy, institutional and individual level.
(iii) Raising and recruitment of professionals to build up expertise for mitigation and management.
(iv) Enforcement of protection and prevention measures.
(v) Generating a proper understanding of risk among different stakeholders, training and confidence building among professionals and masons with appropriate development planning strategies.
(vi) Rehabilitation to be viewed as a long-term phased activity. Mid-term rehabilitation vision is focused on reconstruction of infrastructure and livelihoods, while long-term programmes are geared towards addressing the issues of prevention, mitigation and preparedness.

The Tenth Five Year Plan (2002-07) outlined the need for preventive planning, which is intrinsically linked to disaster prevention. Some of the steps in the regard are:

(a) Introduction of a comprehensive process of vulnerability analysis and objective risk assessment.
(b) Building a robust and sound information database which is comprehensive including land use, demography, and infrastructure developed at the national, state and local

levels along with current information on climate, weather and man-made structures. In addition, resource inventories of governmental and non-governmental systems including personnel and equipment help in efficient mobilization and optimization of resources.

(c) Creating state-of-the art infrastructure is important. The entire disaster mitigation game plan must necessarily be anchored to frontline research and developed in a holistic mode.

(d) Establishing linkages between all knowledge-based institutions is vital. A National Disaster Knowledge Network tuned to the felt needs of a multitude of users like disaster managers, decision-makers, community, etc., must be developed as the network of networks to over natural, man-made and biological disasters in all their varied dimensions.

3. Need for Effective, Transparent and Accountable Administration (See Chart 32.4)

Administration is the heart of development. Any systematic effort towards disaster management must be preceded by, or coupled with efforts, to make the functioning of governmental machinery more effective. Administration is essential both for developed and developing countries. No system of government can survive without a good system of administration. It can be found in the poetic couplet: "For forms of government, let fools contest, whatever administered best, is the beast."

CHART 32.4

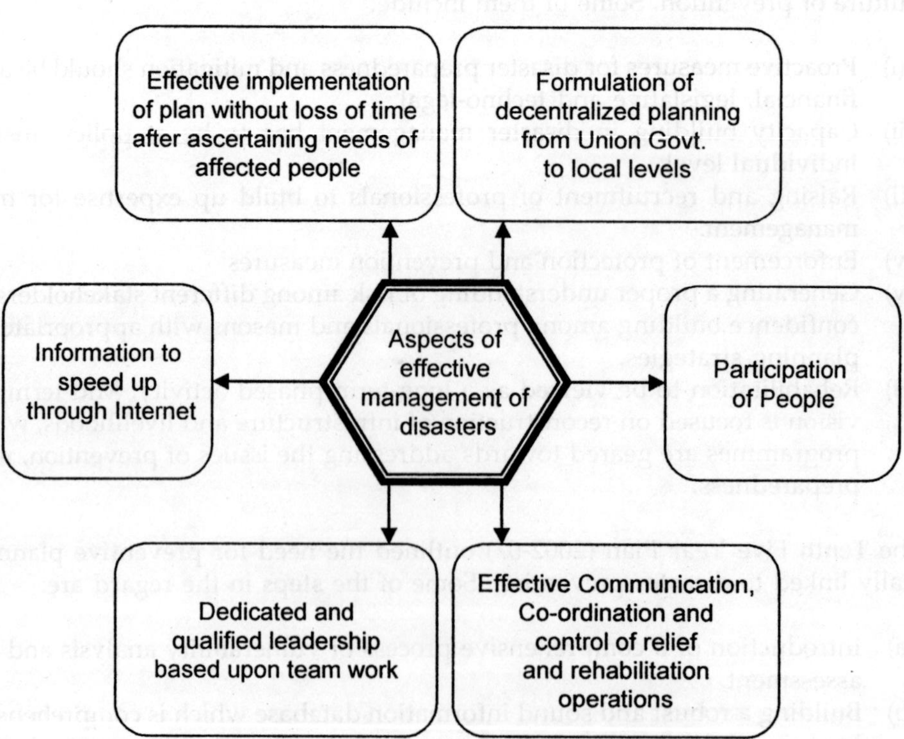

Meticulous Preparedness by Streamlining Administration

Ghose (2001) suggests that "we cannot stop such disasters, what is needed is to learn from failures and make the administrative system perfect for future to take care of all mistakes and faults in advance." He has pointed out that "we will continue to live in shadow of peril, and we will never know when it will come, whether it will come at all, and if it does, what shape it will take. But life must continue; shops must open, business and offices must engage in whatever activity they are there to do, trains must run, power units function (in the manner in which they're used to). In short, it has to be business as usual. Even in Gujarat, when there have been devastation, the business of living will come to some kind of terms with grief and devastation, the business of living will continue. What we would call everyday living will, of necessity, be resumed, as time passes."

Prompt and Effective Administration for Effective Preparedness

There will always be damage, deaths, grief and terror. That no one can prevent. But it can be minimized, to the extent that an effective government can, with a system that responds quickly, has access to what is needed, gets it there, mobilizes personnel and—very importantly—make as much information available as possible. In addition, there is a need for effective communication, coordination, control as well as effective leadership. (See Chart 32.5)

CHART 32.5

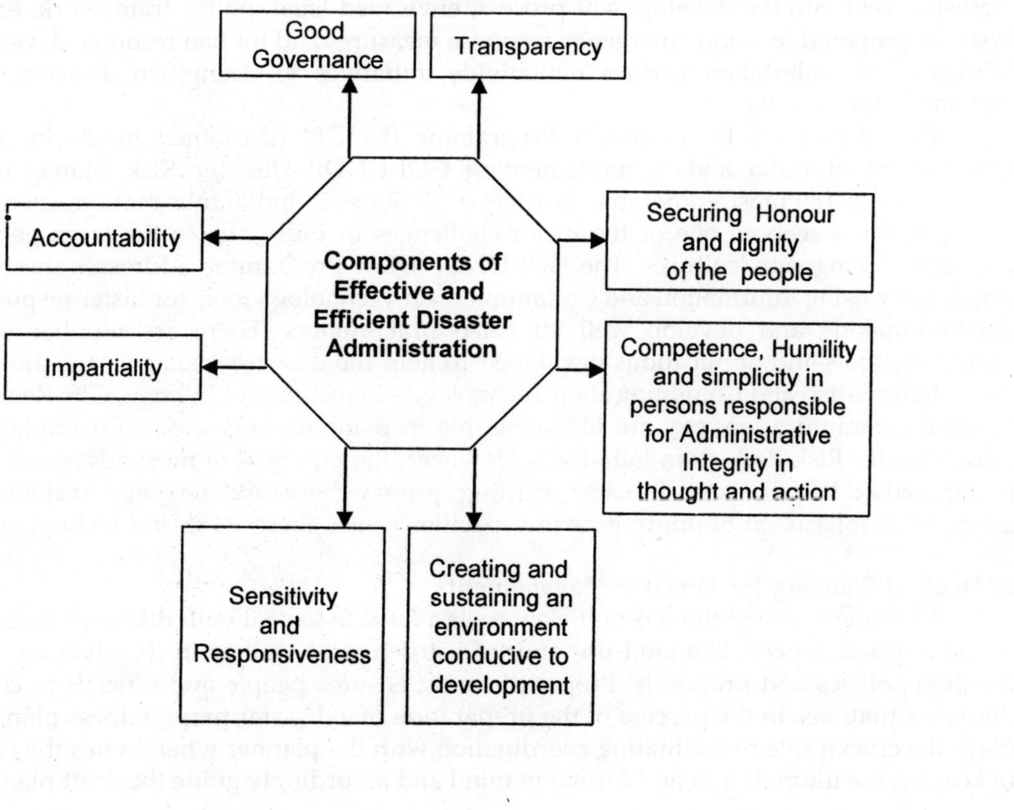

Components of Effective and Efficient Disaster Administration

- Good Governance
- Transparency
- Accountability
- Impartiality
- Securing Honour and dignity of the people
- Competence, Humility and simplicity in persons responsible for Administrative Integrity in thought and action
- Sensitivity and Responsiveness
- Creating and sustaining an environment conducive to development

4. Need of use of Modern Information and Communicative Technology

ICT in Disaster Risk Reduction

With advancement in Information and Communication Technology in the form of Internet, GIS, Remote Sensing, satellite-based communication links; ICT can help a great deal in planning and implementation of disaster risk reduction measures. These technologies have been playing a major role in designing early warning systems, catalyzing the process of preparedness, response and mitigation. ICT tools are also being widely used to build knowledge warehouses using internet and data warehousing techniques. These knowledge warehouses can facilitate planning and policy decisions for preparedness, response, recovery and mitigation at all levels. Similarly, GIS-based systems improve the quality of analysis of hazard vulnerability and capacity assessments, guide development planning and assist planners in the selection of mitigation measures. Communication systems have also become indispensable for providing emergency communication and timely relief and response measures.

The Indian Experience

In order to reduce the risk and vulnerabilities in India the Ministry of Home Affairs, being the Nodal Ministry for Disaster Management, is taking lead on disaster management and mitigation in the country. The Ministry has drawn up a National Disaster Management Framework for the country. This National Framework covers the prime sectors such as institutional mechanism at all administrative levels, disaster mitigation/prevention to be mainstreamed into the development process, envisaged legal/policy framework, early warning systems, preparedness and emergency response measures and human resource development. The Ministry has undertaken various nationwide initiatives to strengthen disaster management systems in the country.

United Nations Development Programme (UNDP) has joined hands in this effort of Government of India and is implementing GOI-UNDP Disaster Risk Management (DRM) programme in 169 most vulnerable Districts of 17 States in India. Information, coordination and management is seen as one of the major challenges in India due to the large geography and diversity of language/cultures. The GOI-UNDP DRM Programme addresses these issues very carefully by using information and Communication Technology tools for faster response, effective decision-making and develop well informed practitioners. There are number of ICT-based initiatives, tools and applications developed to help the disaster managers function efficiently.

Information and Communication Technologies in the form of Internet, GIS, Remote, Sensing, Satellite communication, etc. are indispensable in planning and successful implementation of most Disaster Risk Reduction initiatives. However, the potential of most advanced technologies is required to be harnessed in early warning, preparedness and response systems along with adequate emphasis on building human capacities to use these tools and technologies.[20]

5. Need of Planning for Disaster Management

Planning is one of the most efficient tools available to deal with disasters. It can be applied in the physical aspects like land-use and infrastructure as well as in its advocacy form, which involves policies and proposals. Proper planning ensures people and officials to cope better in disaster situations. In the process of the preparation of a disaster preparedness plan, the planner plays the crucial role of facilitating coordination with the planner wherein lies the responsibility of keeping the ultimate aim and format in mind and accordingly guide the draft plan preparation process. A judicious combination of long-term and short-term planning measures is the best possible way to achieve the mitigation of disasters. Long-term and short-term planning techniques should ideally be applied after a sensible cost-benefit ratio has been arrived at. Long-term measures are sometimes not given their due importance as disaster management is often not of a high priority in the national development agenda.

A Disaster Preparedness Plan made at any level:

- Provides for hazard identification and risk analysis.
- Indicates basic information about the resources, demography, existing organisational set-up, administrative facilities at that level, be it state, district and local levels.
- Lists preparedness and mitigation measures and response mechanisms.
- Defines specific roles and responsibilities for various actors at various levels.
- Ensures networking/coordination with media, NGOs, international agencies and other stakeholders.

6. Building Disaster Resilient Houses and Infrastructure to cope with Disasters

Post-disaster studies of some of the devastating earthquakes like Uttarkashi Earthquake (M-6.6) in October 1991, Killari earthquake (M-6.3), 1993, Chamoli Earthquake (M-6.8) in March 1999, and Kutch Earthquake (M-6.9) in January 2001 showed the need for planning and engineering intervention in development plan, design and construction of buildings to make them strong enough to withstand the impact of natural hazards and to impose restrictions on land use so that the exposure of the society to the hazards situation is avoided or minimized. Due to lack of adequate or no land use restrictions in the hazard prone areas in the town and country planning laws, Master Plan rules or bye laws, cities tend to expand in all directions, occupying even most vulnerable areas resulting in vulnerability of more and more areas getting threatened by natural hazards. Realizing this an urgent need was felt for establishing a proper techno-legal regime through appropriate provisions for safety against natural hazards.

The Expert Committee constituted by the Ministry of Home Affairs, studied the existing guidelines, Acts, Regulations, Development Control Rules and Bye-laws and prepared a Model Building Regulations to enable the states in Seismic Zones III, IV and V to adopt them for safety against natural hazards.

Prior to seismic strengthening/retrofitting of any existing structure, evaluation of the existing structure as regarded structural vulnerability in the specified wind/seismic hazard zone shall be carried out by a Registered Structural Engineer (RSE)/Registered Structural Design Agency (RSDA). If as per the evaluation of the RSE/RSDA the seismic resistance is assessed to be less than the specified minimum seismic resistance in the note below, action will be initiated to carry out the upgrading of the seismic resistance of the building as per applicable standard guidelines.

A.S. Arya (2005) opines that unless states including Delhi, take steps to make buildings structurally sound, it might prove too late when disaster strikes again. Though nodal building bye-laws were framed in September 2004, no state has incorporated them so far. Multi-storied buildings have come up in flagrant violation of norms. People living in single-storey houses have added three story's using walls that are only half-brick thick. These vertical extensions are most likely to collapse in an earthquake. Trained structural engineers are not used by builders. As a result, most of the buildings do not have seismic bands and lack proper reinforcement. Awareness is crucial and people should enquire about the safety aspects in the building, the structural engineers involved and steps taken to ensure that the building is safe.

7. Integrating Disaster Management Programmes in Development Planning

The Secretary General of the United Nations in his statement on International Decade for Natural Disaster Reduction has rightly remarked that 'natural disaster arrests the process of economic development and often set it back by many years'. There is a need of integrating Disaster Management in Development Planning.

8. Need of Cultivating Public Awareness

The first important task must be promotion of public awareness in disaster-prone countries of the potential for disaster reduction. This must be pursued even when we are not faced with a natural disaster, and must also be linked with the development of effective systems of early warning. Scientific and technological advances now make it possible to provide effective protection against all types of hazards. Even for disasters which are physically impossible to control, there are now ways of reducing their catastrophic effects. And in the face of disasters, public awareness must continue after the first phase of relief effort so as to help enable all sectors of society mitigate the consequences.

Information, Education and Communication (IEC) are of vital significance for disaster preparedness, prevention and mitigation. It promotes an alert community which is *sine qua non* for any successful activity. IEC are the essential constituents of any programme especially in a disaster-related scenario. IEC requires the administrative machinery, Non-Governmental Organisations (NGOs), Community-based Organisations (CBOs), other agencies and the community to be prompt, active and well informed to carry out the activities confidently. Hence IEC should be given top priority in any disaster management programme.

9. Mobilisation and Utilization of Financial Resources (See Chart 32.6)

Finance is the fuel of administration. Finance is required to provide relief and rehabilitation to the victims of earthquakes. We can tap the financial resources from the various sources such as, Union Government, State Governments, Industrialists, NGOs, People in general, Philanthropists, Bilateral and Multilateral Agencies, private Institutions, etc. While mobilizing financial resources, we may keep some of the following essentials in view.

The most serious problem in India is not as much of resource mobilization as that of resource utilization, In the case of Gujarat, there was no dearth of resources yet the desired impact was not produced. Let us discuss the views of some authorities on the subject. In this connection, J.L. Iboko has remarked that: "It is accepted that the inability to manage efficiently or utilize effectively the available and potential resources is the common ill of the all less developed countries. It follows that the successful development demands a sound programme for managerial improvement."[21] It has also been pointed out by an Asian administrator, Y.P. Pant, that it is only after a country is prepared for the possible process of change that international relations or foreign aid would do much to help its onward March.[22]

Let us understand the nature of these problems which impede and bedevil the effective functioning of the machinery dealing with disaster administration—

(a) Lack of concrete definition of terms, policy and decisions required to mitigate the sufferings of disaster victims and their rehabilitation.

(b) Lack of clear demarcation of authority and responsibilities of personnel engaged in disaster to avoid duplication of efforts.

CHART 32.6

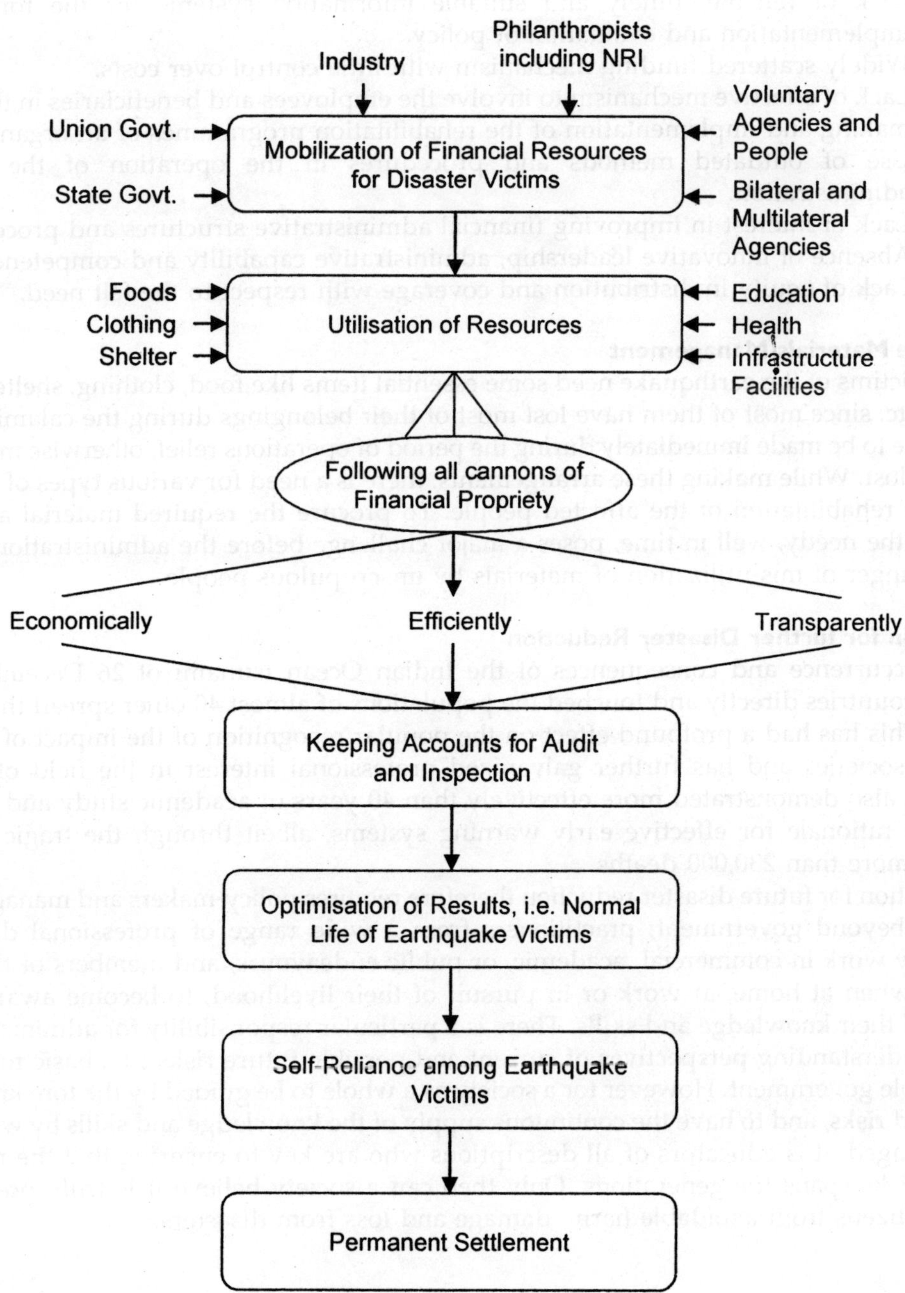
Industry
Philanthropists including NRI
Union Govt.
State Govt.
Mobilization of Financial Resources for Disaster Victims
Voluntary Agencies and People
Bilateral and Multilateral Agencies
Foods
Clothing
Shelter
Utilisation of Resources
Education
Health
Infrastructure
Facilities
Following all cannons of Financial Propriety
Economically
Efficiently
Transparently
Keeping Accounts for Audit and Inspection
Optimisation of Results, i.e. Normal Life of Earthquake Victims
Self-Reliance among Earthquake Victims
Permanent Settlement

(c) Lack of coordination among the allied agencies and within the units of a department, resulting in duplication and wastage of financial resources.
(d) Lack of reliable, timely and suitable information systems for the formulation, implementation and evaluation of policy.
(e) Widely scattered funding mechanism with little control over costs.
(f) Lack of effective mechanism to involve the employees and beneficiaries in the policy-making and implementation of the rehabilitation programmes of an organization.
(g) Use of outdated methods and procedures in the operation of the financial administration.
(h) Lack of interest in improving financial administrative structures and procedures.
(i) Absence of innovative leadership, administrative capability and competence.
(j) Lack of equity in distribution and coverage with respect to the felt need.

10. Effective Materials Management

The victims of the earthquake need some essential items like food, clothing, shelter, health, sanitation, etc. since most of them have lost most of their belongings during the calamity. These supplies have to be made immediately during the period of operations relief, otherwise many more lives can be lost. While making these arrangements, there is a need for various types of materials required for rehabilitation of the affected people. To procure the required material and made available to the needy, well in time, poses a major challenge before the administration as there is a great danger of mis-utilization of materials by unscrupulous people.

11. Education for further Disaster Reduction

The occurrence and consequences of the Indian Ocean tsunami of 26 December, 2004 affected 12 countries directly and touched the populations of almost 40 other spread throughout the world. This has had a profound effect on the popular recognition of the impact of disasters on modern societies and has further galvanized professional interest in the field of disaster reduction. It also demonstrated more effectively than 40 years of academic study and technical abilities, the rationale for effective early warning systems, albeit through the tragic negative example of more than 230,000 deaths.

Education for future disaster reduction therefore requires policy-makers and managers, both within and beyond government; practitioners from a wide range of professional disciplines whether they work in commercial, academic, or public endeavours, and members of the public themselves when at home, at work or in pursuit of their livelihood, to become aware and to contribute of their knowledge and skills. There is a particular responsibility for administrators to relate the understanding perspectives of current and possible future risks as a basic foundation for responsible government. However for a society as a whole to be guided by the fore knowledge of anticipated risks, and to have the continuous supply of the knowledge and skills by which they may be managed, it is educators of all descriptions who are key to ensuring that the reduction of disaster risks spans the generations. Only then can a society believe it is truly prepared to protect its citizens from avoidable harm, damage and loss from disasters.[23]

Education

UGC can start disaster management courses and research in allied departments of the universities on a priority basis. Such experiences can be pooled and shared. J.C. Pant in his keynote address at the opening session of the Workshop on Disaster prevention, held at NIRD,

Hyderabad on 19th-20th December, 2000 remarked: coming back to the main theme of disaster management, I would like to highlight the role of the elite and intellectual segments of our society. Every disaster is a unique event and every kind of data emerging out of it needs to be meticulously recorded for posterity. The scientific community, the technologists, the social scientists and other branches of knowledge need to be mobilized at short notice to record data and carry out necessary studies whenever a disaster strikes. This gives rise to a need for laying out a structure for initiating the learning exercise, at short notice, which can be used to collect data whenever a disaster strikes, in order to generate knowledge which may prevent future disasters as well as prepare people to face them in a better manner whenever they recur. This learning process has to be traced backward to know about the causes of various kinds of disasters, which is only possible through a process of networking of such knowledge as is available throughout the world today. We have decided to broadly network knowledge in three groups:

(i) Knowledge relating to natural disasters;
(ii) Knowledge relating to non-natural disasters; and
(iii) Knowledge relating to biological disasters.

This will also involve identifying centers of excellence in different fields of knowledge and technology, which would need to collaborate to develop the required networks of knowledge. A small task force of eminent persons in the field of science and technology is working in this area and we hope to give concrete shape to this concept in the near future. This would help the country to prevent and reduce the occurrence of disasters and mitigate their impact whenever they strike. This exercise of harnessing science and technology in aid of disaster management promises to be an exciting venture which would hopefully usher in a comparatively safer world in the near future. In the rapidly changing scenario, the real wealth will lie in knowledge, innovation and speedy action.

Universities, colleges, schools possess vast potentiality and with some training to students, a lot of rehabilitation work can be done after disaster with the help of students. National service scheme and NCC students can be used for such work. They would do such work with great pleasure.

The existing mechanism of continuing education, adult education or even mass education can be effectively used as instruments for imparting disaster education and training. Educational studies on natural disasters are interwomen with environmental education. UNESCO thinks that the goals for IDNDR are nothing short of extensions of Environmental Education (EE) which, over the decades, reflect inter-disciplinary, problem-solving and community participation in environmental decisions. UNESCO's perspectives for integrating the two categories of education will help each to share each other's developments in respect of education and training. What has been achieved under IEEP of UNESCO either through formal or non-formal channels for various targets groups may perhaps be appropriated so as to facilitate attainments of the goals of IDNDR and presumably beyond them.

12. Building Capacities and Capabilities of the Community

V. Suresh and Taranjot K. Gadhok in their article "Disaster to Development", (*Shelter*, Oct. 13, 1999) rightly suggest that it is high time that the thinking process is brought to a turn around from "actions to precaution." It requires strong political will to put knowledge base to work, to use the forces of legislation, education, public awareness and policy-making on development and relief to make disaster reduction measures part of our everyday consciousness and planning activities. Whenever disasters strike, they do not discriminate or differentiate between men and nations, poor or rich, young or old. They do not negotiate or and they do not wait, they simply come, kill and destroy, irreparable losses which are irrecoverable. And when these hazards strike, it is the communalities who are first to react, it is the communities irrespective of their profession, status, cast or culture who need to react. Therefore, it is important that capacities of communities are built to observe, understand and prepare themselves for worst impact. It is important to allow transparency of actions of the nodal agencies working towards mitigation measures to encourage countries to get involved, so that at the time of occurrence of disasters, they do not wait for help they can stand on their own feet and mobilize self-help, before rescue and relief reaches them. This may require coordination with NGOs, which are trained to handle such situation. In the rapidly changing scenario, the real wealth will lie knowledge, innovation and speedy action. It would mean discarding the bureaucratic apparels and getting into the space suit of the 21st century. The road ahead is bumpy, but exciting being totally in an uncharted territory. It is up to us to use our intellectual prowess and negotiate the road with bold imagination, and deep urge to succeed.[24]

13. Need of Reforms

In a country of contrasting vulnerability and regular disaster occurrences, the system of managing disasters requires a comprehensive strategy, planning and action at various levels. Strangely enough, this realization has gained ground globally during the last decade. It is heartening that once the movement for a comprehensive strategy has begun, the momentum has not demised with time, rather picked up, with remarkable initiatives being taken the world over. The recently adopted Hyogo Framework for Action (HFA) and subsequent intellectual churning on its components have been manifested in a complete paradigm shift in disaster management in many countries.[25]

Second Administration Reforms Commission under the Chairmanship of Shri Veerappa Moily has asked the National Institute of Disaster Management to carry out a study about various aspects of natural and made-made disasters and give its analysis, findings and recommendations on the following six elements:

(1) Identification of areas prone to the crisis,
(2) Preventive and preparedness measures,
(3) Early warning systems,
(4) Mitigation measures,
(5) Emergency response systems, and
(6) Relief and rehabilitation measures.

The Institute has prepared a Concept Paper and a Questionnaire for eliciting views, comments, suggestions, perspectives and opinions from Institutions, organizations and individuals on the subject. The Concept Paper was discussed with concerned Ministries, Departments and organizations of Government of India in a National Consultation Workshop at New Delhi. Based on the deliberations, a Base Paper was prepared for discussion at three: Brainstorming Regional Workshops at Jammu, Chennai and Mumbai. Each Workshop focused on specified themes and considered case studies of how disaster situations were dealt with at state and district levels. The Institute expects to complete its study by the end of March 2006.[26]

CONCLUSION

Focusing on the way forward, Christoph Pusch, South Asia Regional Hazard Risk Management Coordinator, elaborated on the four areas for strategic action:

- Emergency Preparedness including building public awareness;
- Risk Mitigation Investments such as gathering data, mapping risk, ensuring effective land use planning, and putting in place warning and monitoring system;
- Institutional Capacity Building including decentralizing emergency management systems, emphasizing community participation, training and knowledge sharing, and international co-operations.

Notes and References

1. Quoted in Indian Science Congress Association, Presidential Addresses by Prof. Dilip Kumar Sinha, 1991, The Shaping of Indian Science, Indian Science Congress Association, Presidential Address, 2003, Vol. III, 1982-2003; p. 1729.
2. *Ibid.*
3. *Ibid.*
4. *Ibid.*
5. *Ibid.*, pp. 1730-31.
6. GOI, Ministry of Home Affairs, National Disaster Management Division: A Primer For Parliamentarians, Version 1.0 p. New Delhi, pp. 5-6.
7. NIDM, Disaster Development, Vol. I, Number 1, Nov. 2006, p. 112.
8. ICT for Disaster Risk Reduction—Ministry of Home Affairs, National Disaster Management Division, GOI, p. 1.
9. Christane Viedma, Disaster Alert, *World Health*, June 1978, p. 14.
10. J. Oetio Espiniza, Responding to Disasters, in *World Health*, Nov.-Dec. 1991, p. 28.
11. Christiane Videma, *op. cit.*, p. 17.
12. M. Wadhwani, Director, Indian Institute of Public Administration, Foreward, quoted in Vinod K. Sharma, Disaster Management, New Delhi, IIPA, 1999.
13. R.K. Celley and T.N. Gupta, Dimensions of Natural Disaster Management in India, *Shelter*, Oct. 12, 1992.
14. Phillips, and Boulle, Message, in *Shelter*, Dec. 13, 1999.
15. K. Rajan, Natural Disaster Management in National Development—An Indian Perspective quoted in Vinod K. Sharma, Disaster Management, IIPA, New Delhi, 1999, p. 26.
16. V. Suresh, Message Towards a Safer Millennium in *Shelter*, Dec. 13, 1999.
17. Ashok Pahava, *Ibid.*
18. Bhagat Singh, *Ibid.*
19. IDNDR, Indian Experiences and Initiative, p. 3.
20. ICT for Disaster Risk Reduction, Ministry of Home Affairs, National Disaster Management Division, GOI, pp. 1-2.
21. J.I. Ibokes: Developing the Administration in a Developing Country, International Review of Administration Sciences, Vol. XXVIII, No. 2, 1972, p. 293.
22. Y.P. Pant, Economic Development of Nepal (Allahabad, 1965, p. 24).
23. Terry Jeggle, "Public Recognition and Professional Responsibilities: Education for future disaster risk reduction," in *Disaster Development*, Vol. 1, Number 1, Nov. 2006, p. 140.
24. V. Suresh and Taranjot K. Gadhok, *Shelter*, Dec. 13, 1999, p. 110.
25. NIDM, Executive Director, P.G. Dhar Chakraborte, Tidings, *NIDM Newsletter*, Vol. I, No. 7, 2006.
26. *Ibid.*

CHAPTER

33

Good Governance: A Pre-requisite for Development Administration

Development Administration in order to be successful in any given situation must sustain good governance as of paramount importance. Good governance would enhance the capacity and capability of development administration to achieve the intended results.

Good governance is about providing an efficient and effective administration that is committed to improving the quality of life of the people. It is about what people expect from the administration, and the willingness and capacity of the administration to fulfil their expectations. The main tenets of good governance can be enumerated as (i) improved delivery systems for services, (ii) increasing simplicity and accessibility of systems and procedures, (iii) increased fiscal responsibility and efficiency of expenditures through sound financial management, (iv) higher levels of accountability and transparency in governance, and (v) stringent anti-corruption measures. Good governance enables a citizen-friendly, citizen-caring and responsive administration, and in the process, results in the exercise of public authority for the common good.[1] (See Chart 33.1)

Good Governance is an essential ingredient for socio-economic development of the country. The Government of India and State Governments come out with new ideas and approaches but these do not succeed when put to action because of lack of good governance. Good Governance is of paramount importance in these times of far reaching changes. In this backdrop of major changes, we need to re-orient ourselves to deliver ways and means to promote, good governance. No government of course can hope to survive without a strong and effective good governance nor can an administrative system exist without the support of those it was established to serve.

S.G. Barve feels that Good Governance is more an art than a science and there can be very few esoteric principles about it. It is a question of performance rather than theory or action. There are no sensational short cuts to good governance. There are no spectacular solutions. What is wanted is a long and patient siege? Another outstanding deficiency is failure to locate definite

CHART 33.1

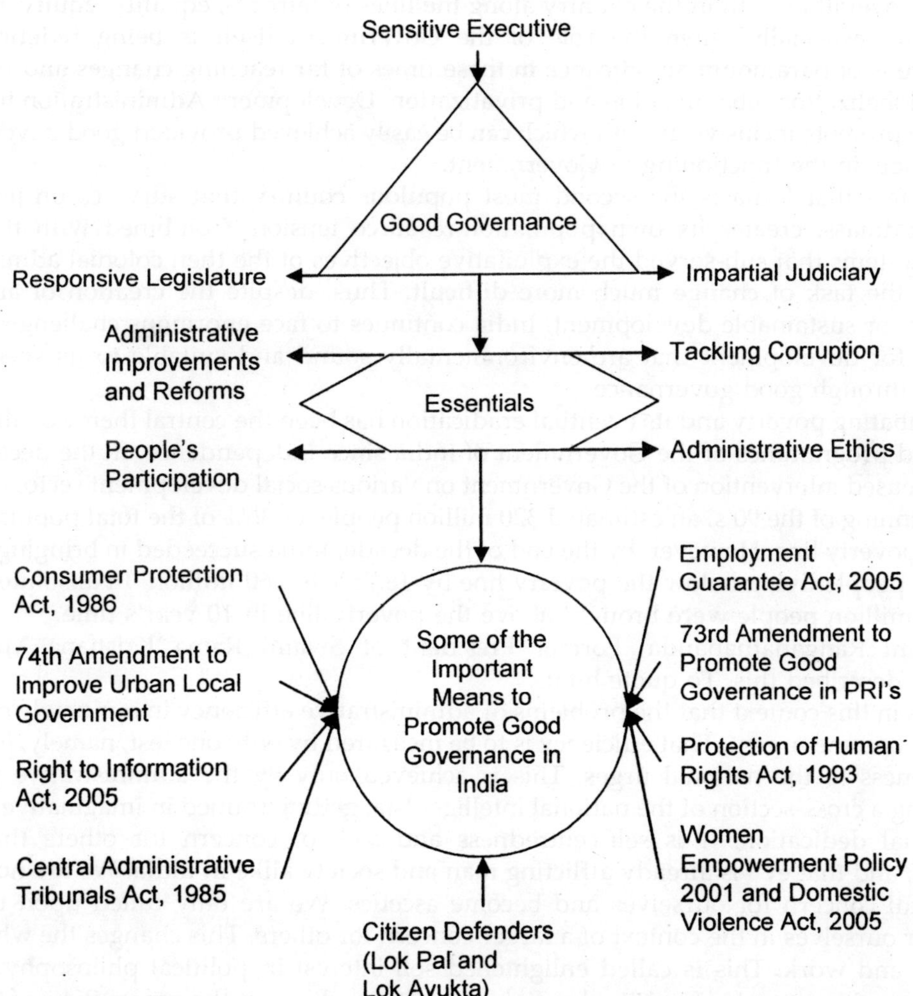

responsibility at different points and levels of the administrative hierarchy. This location of responsibility has to be finally carried down to the level of the individual functionary.

The issue of good governance has, in recent times, emerged at the forefront of the agenda for sustainable human development. It is imperative that this process while being sustainable in terms of resources over generations and across space, recognizes the legitimate claim of each person in a society to be an active and a productive participant. Empowering people for meaningful participation in this development process is one of the key interventions of the government of India in its attempt to usher in sustainable development.

Good governance implies utmost concern for people's welfare wherein the government and its bureaucracy follow policies and discharge their duties with a deep sense of commitment; respecting the rule of law in a manner which is transparent, ensuring human rights and dignity, probity and public accountability.

In the new millennium, the greatest challenge before the largest democracy of the world, is to steer the overall growth in the country along the lines of fairness, equality, equity, justice and sustainability especially when the role of the Government itself is being redefined. Good Governance is of paramount significance in these times of far reaching changes and ushering in an era of globalization, liberalization and privatization. Development Administration has also the objective to promote inclusive growth which can be easily achieved provided good governance has taken its roots in the functioning of Government.

The fact that India is the second most populous country that survives on just 2.4% of world's landmass, creates its own population-resource tension. Combined with the colonial legacy of systems that sub-served the exploitative objectives of the then colonial administration, was made the task of change much more difficult. Thus, despite the creation of an enabling framework for sustainable development, India continues to face enormous challenges in search of options for development that are environmentally sound and suitable to its specific social conditions through good governance.

Combating poverty and its eventual eradication has been the central theme of all the major policies and programmes of the Government of India since Independence. In the decades of the 90's, the focused intervention of the Government on various social development sectors bore fruit. At the beginning of the 90's, an estimated 320 million people, or 36% of the total population, were below the poverty line. However, by the end of the decade, India succeeded in bringing down the number of people living below the poverty line by 18.75% to 260 million. In absolute numbers, a huge 60 million people were brought above the poverty line in 10 year's time.

Swami Ranganathananda, Former President of Swami Rama Krishana Mission has beautifully described this. To quote him:

"It is in this context that the problems of administrative efficiency in our newly established democracy become urgent. That efficiency is to be measured by only one test, namely, its dynamic responsiveness to the national urges. This is achieved only by the administrative personnel, representing a cross-section of the national intelligentsia, getting trained in imaginative sympathy and national dedication. It is self-centredness and lack of concern for others that lead to corruption; and that evil is already afflicting man and society alike in India. We are not required to forego all concern for ourselves and become ascetics. We are only called upon to put this concern for ourselves in the context of a larger concern for others. This changes the whole aspect of our life and work. This is called enlightened self-interest in political philosophy. It is self-interest, but with a touch of spiritual enlightenment, resulting in the recognition of mutuality, inter-dependence and the spirit of service, as the truth of all healthy social processes."

India today is at the cross roads. We are in a curious predicament. The obverse of the coin is bright, the reverse grim. We are heirs to a glorious civilization whose mighty stream has been flowing uninterruptedly down the millennia, enriching and ennobling all on its path. Sixty one years back we have also recovered our political independence from the largest empire the world has seen, and that without firing a single shot—something unique in history. Yet chaos stalks the land. Things are falling apart. Values cherished over the centuries are getting eroded. In a country of rich natural resources the poverty of the masses is abysmal. The haves exploit the have-nots in a hundred ingenious ways. Women and the weaker sections of society reel under injustice and handicaps. Corruption is rampant. Mindless violence mains and destroys the precious lives of the innocent. The sensitive citizen finds himself asking, "Whither India?."[2] The prices of land and the impact of Globalisation, Privatisation and Liberalization would lead India to a capitalist country with no hope for poor people to enjoy the fruits of development. Development Administration and Good Governance can help in solving these problems.

The Governments, both at the Center and the State, share the Concern for ensuring responsive, accountable, transparent, decentralized and people-friendly administration at all levels. There is, however, considerable frustration and dissatisfaction amongst the people, especially the weaker sections of society, about the apathy, irresponsiveness and lack of accountability of public servants, even as the expenditure on staff continues to increase. There is increasing anxiety about growing instances of corruption and criminalisation in public life and administration. The people particularly the vulnerable groups, are also greatly concerned about the deterioration in the performance of agencies concerned with law and order and the investigation of offences. Their faith in the registration of offences, their timely investigation and the delivery of prompt justice has been eroded. At the local level inspite of 73rd and 74th Amendments, people cannot get any of their work sanctioned, complaints redressed under the very eyes of elected representatives. For example, experience of building of a house is nothing short of getting experiences of bad governance. Government talks big but people do not achieve even little. This gap is so wide that at the present speed, it may take a century to dream of good governance. That is why development administration has failed because of bad governance.

M. Aziz Ahammed in his article, "Good Governance through Transparency" in Management in Government, Oct.-Dec. 1999, clearly mentioned that over the years governance has become more and more decentralised. However, still the distance between the decision-makers and the subjects is very large enough. Thus, it continues to distort the very objectives of Government both in regulatory and developmental process at grass root level by way of corruption and apathy over the peoples' problems. In this regard a question arises, just as decision/policy-makers have an impact on every village so their policies must be monitored by the people, they affect. Here comes the importance of right to information in bridging the gap. Precisely in this sphere, good governance demands transparent administration by letting both not only decision-making criterion and the programmes drawn up open to the public but also by involving them. Further the right to information, rather transparent administration with people's participation, becomes a need of the hour as corruption and malpractices have become an undeniable fact in the administration.[3]

We are now on the threshold of the twenty-first century. In the new Millennium, above all, the government would need to reinvent itself to become 'citizen-centric' and 'citizen-friendly'. It would need to limit its role to core functions of infrastructure and macro-economic management. Greater delegation and decentralization of authority and responsibilities would need to be introduced at all levels. A combination of Citizens' Charters and the Right to Information would ensure greater accountability in the administrative system. The process of consultation with the participation of citizens in decision-making would gradually become more pronounced in order to ensure accountability. At the same time, good citizenry would also need to be emphasized for all round development of the society. Besides enjoying their rights, the citizens would need to behave responsibly and perform their duties towards the state. Clearly defined ethical standards would also need to be adopted by the civil servants as well as politicians. In order to achieve all this, innovative use of information technology would be critical.[4] All these if followed in practice would promote good governance. All the above concepts appear easy to be implemented but their implementation would remain a dream. Such popular concepts like citizen-centric are good to make lecture interesting or a talk by top persons in Government in Vigyan Bhawan, Delhi appreciated but in reality, they never come in practice even in the offices of persons who write or speak about them. This has lost the credibility of government of every party as they harp only on the promises when in power. The practical life of people in facing the government is worse than beggars. The government if serious, must pursue the individual cases of Public harassment sincerely so as to cultivate the culture of good governance. We have so far not felt the fringe of good governance. Government has to struggle hard before taking any credit for Good governance.

Good governance can be a reality provided every organ of the Government, i.e. legislature, executive and judiciary does its work meticulously, and with integrity. This reality would multiply manifolds through the active support and participation of the people in all the tasks of Government, i.e. policy-making, planning, implementation and monitoring. The Government has to create conditions and encourage people to participate in Governance to make the people participation—a reality. This would promote democratic administration which is *sine-qua-non* for good governance.

For a democratic administration which is another term for good governance wide belief in the virtues of democracy on the part of the people and the administrators is an essential requisite. One of the assumptions of democracy is that the 'people are organized to serve themselves'. Naturally, therefore, democratic administration should offer adequate opportunities to the mass of people to participate in its operations. Three important features of democratic administration are: "(i) it functions in the interest of the people and not of a class or section of the people; (ii) it is susceptible to public opinion and respects civil and political liberties; and (iii) it is subordinate to the control of ministers responsible to the legislature." To add further, "the two pillars of democracy are liberty and equity, so the two ends to be served by democratic administration should be the furtherance of both liberty and equality."[5]

INDICATORS OF GOOD GOVERNANCE (See Chart 33.2)

There are no standard indicators for good governance. International agencies have developed indicators for human development, but these alone cannot be taken as indicators for good governance. Reduction in infant mortality, improvement in literacy rates or reduction in poverty levels may reflect the success of a government in its policies or implementation procedures. However, while these measures are indicators of the effective implementation of programmes, they do not completely capture the qualitative aspects of good governance. If, for example, family planning targets are achieved through coercion rather than awareness building, then the qualitative aspect is missing. Transparency International Corruption Perception Index is possibly the best known governance indicators. However, this is a very broad indicator and cannot really help the government in initiating specific public sector reforms. The problem is that such an indicator implicates many institutions and policies at the same time and there is no suggestion of a solution.[6] Essentials of Good Governance which can promote Development Administration.

Need to Narrow the Gap between Theory and Practice

In theory, the Government at the Union and State level have promised to provide them all essentials of life through constitutional provisions, enactments and administrative orders but in practice, there is hardly much achievement. Kusum Nair feels that by merely shifting around responsibilities within the central bureaucracy and thus giving false sense of devolution of decision-making powers to lower levels of governments, would further strengthen local elite who have nothing to do with the participation of the poor. Local elite, local governments and the other actors operating on the local scene such as political parties and even some NGO's have often been proved to co-opt popular movements in order to further their own agendas. Moreover, the delivery

CHART 33.2

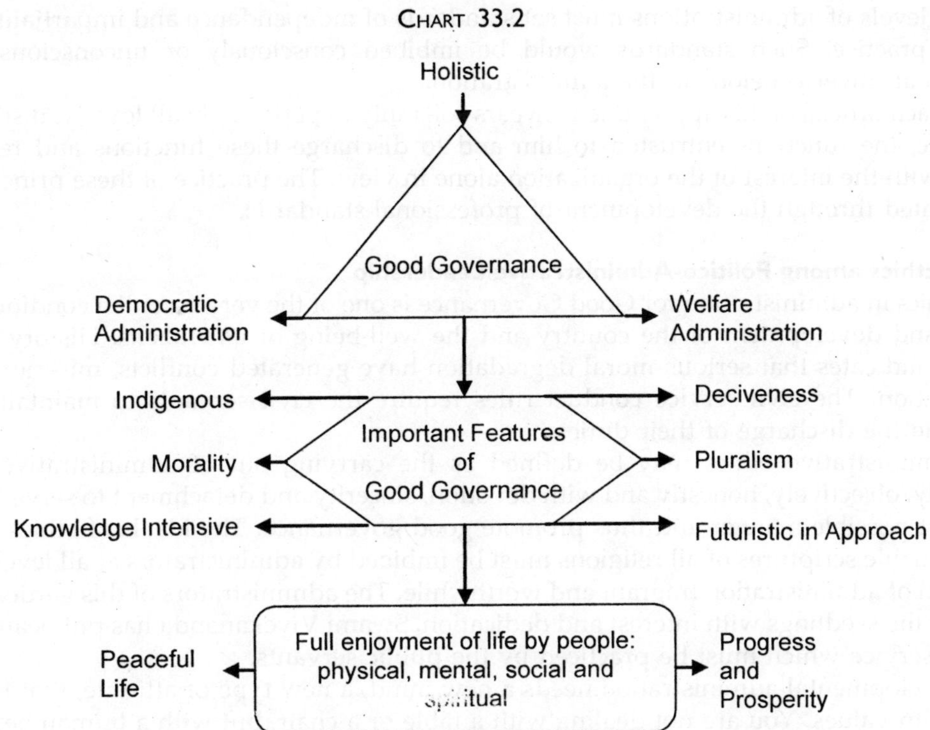

system has many loop holes. Even the adequate money, which is earmarked does not actually reach the targeted section. A coterie of touts and brokers have mushroomed everywhere and therefore while implementing projects for the rural development, they along with the local politicians, village and block level officials, contractors and the like, manipulate the execution of plans and in such a way that a very meager portion of funds is left for target beneficiaries. This is true more of backward states of Northern and Western zones.[7]

Dr. K. Venkatasubramanium, Member, Planning Commission at India-Brazil, Ministerial Meeting on Sustainable Development—Perspectives and Possibilities about the inefficient administrative machinery said that " the major reason why the poor have been unable to overcome their conditions of poverty is not so much the lack of initiative or knowledge on their part but rather the existence of institutionalized obstacles to effective action. Overcoming these systematic obstacles requires both releasing the creative energies of the poor themselves as well as lead role for the state."

Need of Impartiality among Politico-Administrative Leadership

For Good Governance foremost characteristics required among the civil servants are impartially and consistency in the transaction of public business. Civil servants are required to be completely impartial to avoid corruption and favouritism; civil servants must maintain the dignity and authority of the public office. They must meticulously implement the policies and programmes as laid down in laws, regulations and rules.

There is a need to develop good administrative traditions which may impel civil servants to perform their activities impartially to keep the administration above aboard. The civil servants at higher levels of administrations must set standards of independence and impartiality through constant practice. Such standards would be imbibed consciously or unconsciously by the personnel at lower echelons in the administration.

Each official on his appointment swears solemnly to perform, in all loyalty, discretion and conscience, the functions entrusted to him and to discharge these functions and regulate his conduct with the interest of the organization alone in view. The practice of these principles must be inculcated through the development of professional standards.

Need of Ethics among Politico-Administrative Leadership

Ethics in administration for Good Governance is one of the very essential conditions for the stability and development of the country and the well-being of its citizens. History of several countries indicates that serious moral degradation have generated conflicts, miseries and even disintegration. The civil service conduct rules require the civil servants to maintain absolute integrity in the discharge of their duties.

Administrative ethics may be defined as the carrying out of administrative activities impartially, objectively, honestly and with devotion, sincerity and detachment to serve the people in the best possible manner and thus promote good governance. The ideals of ethics enshrined in our valuable scriptures of all religions must be imbibed by administrators at all levels to make the garden of administration fragrant and worthwhile. The administrators of this garden will take care of all the seedlings with interest and dedication. Swami Vivekananda has put beautifully the ideals of service which must be practiced by the public servants.

Developmental administration needs a new mind, a new type of attitude, that is suffused with human values. You are not dealing with a table or a chair, but with a human being. He or she has problems. You are there to solve them. That chair of authority on which you sit is not a chair of comfort. It is a chair with a heavy human responsibility on your head. Rise to the level of the responsibility that chair signifies. Our mental awareness must rise to that level.

Our people are hungering for development. Government servants are the instruments of that developmental administration. These instruments must become more humanized, more concerned with human development. Then something great will happen. Things will march faster and faster. Whatever achievements we have made so far have not been due to steady purposeful progress, but are the product of our mostly wobbly movements. Some good has come, but the real progress will come when this human value becomes embedded in every part of the administration so that his or her work becomes dynamic. Everything will become dynamic and the tendency to corruption and value erosion will become correspondingly less. Take away the human value element, corruption and evil must fill the administration and public life. Put human value within and to that extent they will be reduced thereby. We have increased evils in society only because we took away the one central inspiring principle, 'the concern for the next individual'. I was at a big dam site a few months ago. We have spent crores and crores of rupees to build the dam with a view to bringing succor to the people—better agriculture, more income for the people. Now all the money that has been spent there can be upset by the people who handle the irrigation channels. If I do not open the channel and let out water to the field, all the money spent on the dam becomes wasted. That person who controls the channels must have a human sense in him or her and must open the channel so that the farmer gets his water; but if he is corrupt and says, give me 100 rupees then only will I open this channel for you, how tragic it will be. All over India this is going on every day. What is the trouble then? Our men and women have not become humanized. He or she is not a free citizen of India, but only a job-hunter, and job-holder. We have yet to develop the attitude that this is my country and these are my fellow citizens. If this attitude is not there, all this money will be simply waste, as we are seeing every day. Crores and crores of rupees are wasted. The fruits of the crores become very much reduced by the time it reaches the people concerned. It is here that human values come in to correct the situation.[8]

When this value is liberated in the hearts of increasing sections of our vast population, we shall witness a tremendous phenomenon of human integration in about a seventh of the human race. It will convert India into a national grid of awakened humanity, just as we are taking all steps to achieve a national electrical grid for the industrial unification and development of our country. This is enduring nation-building through man making. And the clarion call that can inspire us today is what Vivekananda has given to us from the Katha Upanisad: 'Arise, Awake, and stop not till the goal is reached.'[9]

B.B. Tandon rightly says, that this change in attitude of the bureaucracy, however, cannot be brought about by merely amending conduct rules or issuing of circulars. The need for it has to be realized by each and everyone of us and the urge for change has to come from within. With a view to clarify and focus on the centrality of the civil service values which emphasize adherence to Rule of Law, human values and the Constitution of India, customer friendliness, accountability and transparency, besides objectivity and political neutrality, a Code of Ethics has been drafted with a view to promote sensitivity within the civil service to core values. The draft code of ethics is already under the consideration of the Government and the proposed code will be in addition to the Civil Services conduct rules. While it is true that any voluntary code is effective only when majority of persons in a cadre observe most of norms for most of time, the fact remains that due to constant change in the value framework in recent years and public perception of deterioration of the values within the civil service, there is a need to re-emphasize and clarify such values.[10]

Need of Protecting the Interests of the People

Good Governance can help in accelerating welfare of the people provided it is run in the interest of the people. The contents of Development Administration for Good Governance are:

(i) Openness in the sense of having wide contact with the people administered;
(ii) A sense of justice, fair play and impartiality in dealing with men and matters;
(iii) Sensitivity and responsiveness to the urges, feelings and aspirations of the common people;
(iv) Securing the honour and dignity of the human being, however humble he or she might be;
(v) Humility and simplicity in the persons manning the administrative machinery and their easy accessibility;
(vi) Creating and sustaining an atmosphere conducive to development, growth and social change; and
(vii) Honesty and integrity in thought and action.

D.K. Oza in his Article based upon his experience as an ICS officer suggested the following to ensure good governance.[11]

Decisions must be taken in the public interest. This phrase, 'public interest,' must be understood properly. No decision should be taken under any kind of pressure. Every decision should be such as benefits the whole community. The decision must be able to stand close scrutiny. This was the first lesson we learnt from those who trained us in the Civil Service in the early years. I think nowadays this is totally ignored.

Time has come for a strong message to be conveyed that administration is for the people and not for the public servants themselves. There has to be a change of attitudes, and public servants should realize that efficiency will be measured not in terms of what the services purport to offer, but in terms of public satisfaction. Simultaneously, there has also to be a cleansing of the services and codification of the ethics, value systems and interface with the politicians.[12]

Need to Promote and Follow Rule of Law

Good governance means that we must follow the rule of law. The concept of rule of law means that the society must be governed by law or Dharma and not according to the whims and fancies of a Ruler or by powerful individuals. This has been evolved in this country from most ancient times. The necessity of scruples practice of Dharma is forcefully expressed by Manu: "Dharma protects those who protect it. Those who destroy Dharma get destroyed. Therefore, Dharma should not be destroyed, so that we may not be destroyed as a consequence thereof. (Manu VIII-15).[13] The people in government should take decisions on the basis of reason which can make the life of people happy. They should protect the interests of the people and see that their development is promoted based on Dharma. The people in government should cultivate the mind and keep peaceful, calm and quiet so that people can enjoy their glowing actions with truth, sincerity and reason. Whatever misery, anxiety and intolerable difficulty (may overtake a man) they are lost in the tranquil mind like darkness in the sun.

Need to Follow Transparency and Public Interest

Administration must be transparent. Nothing should be done in secret. Secrecy breeds evil. The reasons for taking a decision must be recorded for all to see. This will also help to eliminate the almost universal corruption in politics and administration today.

Civil servants should leave behind their caste, community, religion, and language in their own homes. They should not carry these labels with them when they go to work. At the work place a civil servant is just a public servant acting in the public interest, trying to serve the public.

Need to Develop Good Character of Persons in Government

For good governance character of those who are entrusted with public functions must be above board. When we do not have enough character, in society there will be more quarrel and fight, agitation and unrest, corruption and nepotism than peace and harmony, control and happiness, honesty and uprightness. When we do not have enough character, we will corrupt the taste of people, nay, of our own children in order to make money by selling goods which would pamper their low and vulgar tastes. When we do not have enough character, religion will be reduced to soulless ritualism, ethical code will be perverted into sophistry, altruism will become self-aggrandizing social work, our spirituality will be reduced to secularity, secularity to hedonism, hedonism to ruination, surer than death.[14]

"In life to handle yourself, use your head but to handle others, use your heart. Be strict and intelligently critical about yourself and your own weakness and follies. But to manage others, be critical, but cushion your words and attitudes with love. Love is the greatest persuasive power we know in life."

Action Plan for an effective and Responsive Government rightly stresses the need of good governance. Necessary corrective steps must be taken to arrest the personal drift in Government and public services, and take urgent measures to restore the faith of the people in the fairness and capacity of administration.[15]

Need to Inject Improvements and Reform in Administrative System

We need to take care of the following aspects to promote administrative reforms:

1. A closer focus on results in terms of efficiency and effectiveness, and service quality;
2. The replacement of highly centralized hierarchical organisational structures with decentralized management environments, where decisions on resource allocation and service delivery are taken closer to the point of delivery, and which provide scope for feedback from clients and other interest groups;
3. Flexibility to explore alternatives to direct public provision, which might provide more cost-effective policy outcomes;
4. New personnel management policies to provide greater flexibility in the deployment of staff (e.g., through multi-skilling);
5. The use of mechanisms to improve performance such as performance contracting and the creation of competitive market environment within and among public sector organizations;
6. Incentives to improve performance (or at least removing disincentives) through enabling organizations to retain a portion of savings from improved performance;
7. The strengthening of strategic capacities at the centre to "Steer" government to respond to external changes and diverse interests quickly, flexibly and at least cost; and
8. Greater accountability and transparency through requirements to report on results.

World Bank has identified the following characteristics of good governance as: political accountability; availability of freedom; law abiding citizens and people in power; bureaucratic accountability; transparency; availability of information; effectiveness; efficiency; and cooperation between government and society.

Hari Jaisingh in his article, "A Question of Judicial Dharma" in the daily Tribune dated Sept. 11,2002 has warned about consequences of bad governance. A serious crisis of credibility has gripped the instruments of governance, including the administration of justice, amidst scams, scandals, cover-up operations and communication gaps at all levels.

V.K. Kapoor in his Article, "Problems of governance and suggestions" in *The Tribune* dated September 22, 2002, clearly mentions: We have too much government and too little governance, too many public servants and, too little public service, too many laws and too little justice, too many controls and too little justice, too much talk and too little action. We have a large manpower without will power and short of effective skill power. Our people inherently dislike work. The national actual working average can be liberally reckoned as three hours a day. The scale on which corruption damages the work ethos of the country is evidenced by poor productivity and growth rate.

People avoid responsibility. Why should anybody take responsibility if the pay is guaranteed for presence and promotion is secured by seniority and reservation? Indians prefer to be directed and coerced into making the effort. We have to accept that fear and insecurity have a tonic role to play in creating a healthy motivational climate. The key to quality products and services is a quality person. And the key to personal quality is character and competence. The quality and standard of human resource defines a country's cutting edge. The good qualities of rulers/political leaders can promote good governance. The reverse is also true, i.e. their bad qualities can ruin them.

Good Governance is not a fill-in-the blank rhetoric. This has to be article of faith on the part of all those who have anything to do with the instruments of governance, the judiciary included. Herein lies the big challenge before the custodians of power and justice. Will they rise to the occasion and do justice? Will they learn from the mistakes of the past and apply the correctives so that the citizens can breathe more freely in a comparatively less corrupt and hush-hush atmosphere than that prevailing today? This can be done only if each power-holder plays his or her legitimate role sincerely, honestly and in a responsible manner.

The expectations of the people are high and their patience is running out. As I have said earlier in these columns, we all are under watch; the administration, the judiciary, the Bar and even the media. Each organ has to conduct itself with determination, dignity and sobriety not only for the sake of survival today but also for the legacy it leaves for the youth who are the future of the country and the flag-bearers of its rich conversational values and traditions. There are no easy escape routes. What has to be kept in mind, as enshrined in the holy books and scriptures, is that there is a divine court above which also expects transparency in justice and the enforcement of judicial ethics and accountability.

Good governance and effective management is the only panacea for all the evils, ills and stumbling blocks plaguing us. Transformation of the country is possible only when the necessary transformations are brought about. We need a revolution of a different kind led by the right thinking and right acting leaders, who should not only prepare, but implement blue print for future development in a fixed time schedule.[16]

Mahatma Gandhi put it beautifully: I shall work for an India in which the poorest shall feel that it is their country in whose making they have an effective voice, an India in which there shall be no high class and low class of people, an India in which all communities shall live in perfect harmony.

In short Good Governance would mean:

(a) Making administration responsive
(b) Making administration citizen-friendly
(c) Making administration transparent
(d) Making administration ethical
(e) Making Public services excellent

Good Governance is difficult to establish because the issues attached to it are complex and involve many players: public sector, private sector and civil society organisations, including non-government organisations. The following are suggestions on how to establish good governance:

1. Good governance can engage in big solutions to small problems and in decision-making and implementation. Big solutions need strong political will with longer time-frame with massive support from various stakeholders. Small innovative solutions with greater impact at small cost will readily help facilitate improvements in human development and democratisation.
2. Enactment of appropriate rules and laws and establishment of appropriate mechanisms that positively effect investment climate, promote growth, equity and justice and reduce poverty are to be looked into. Safeguarding the disadvantaged and vulnerable groups and promoting women's status are also very important.
3. To minimise and ultimately eradicate corruption, the establishment and strengthening

of: (i) electoral system that is free and fair and regular elections; (ii) partnership with public, private sectors and civil society; and (iii) watchdog organisations that are essential.

4. To improve the quality of leadership across fields and at all levels through: capacity development; defined core values; and clear vision and mission that are important.

Need of Implementing the Tecommendations of Committees and Commissions Appointed by Government from time to time and the Need of Truth to Prevail over Dishonesty and Falsehood

A plethora of reports of committees and commissions appointed by Government have been thrown in dust without any action on their recommendations. Why do we appoint such commissions costing crores of rupees to the State exchequer? The answer is simple that is befool the people and keep the present Government above Board. How can we ever think of Good governance under these circumstances. To quote Shah Commission Final Report (tabled in Parliament on August 31, 1978.) The commission owes it to the citizen of India to emphasize that appointments of Commissions by themselves are not enough if the Governments concerned do not follow up and implement at least such of the recommendations as are avowedly accepted by the Government Unless the Government is prepared to apply the corrective principles in the Minister-Civil-Servant relationship effectively and with a determination to produce the desired results at different levels and within the several components of the Government The agonizing impact of this unfortunate malaise would be felt by the common man in the streets, in the villages, in the factories and in the far distant corners of this vast country.

As borne out by the records of the Government and the depositions of several responsible Government servants, dishonesty and falsehood became almost a way of official life during the emergency. As Robert Frost said, "most of the change we think we see in life is due to truth being in or out of favour." If administrative machinery in our country is to be rendered safe for our children, the Services must give a better account of themselves by standing up for the basic values of an honest and efficient administration. That alone can resurrect the people's lost faith once again in our services. If a democratic heritage is to be left for future generations, we should want the truth again to be enshrined in its legitimate place in the socio, economic and political scheme of things in our country. There is nothing unattainable or profound in this. It is a simple human message.

The Preamble of Public Service Bill, 2006 is to provide a statutory basis for the regulation of the Public Services in India, to review and lay down the fundamental values of Public Services, the Public Services Code of Ethics, Public Service Management Code, Protection of Whistleblowers and the Recruitment Code governing the Public Services, to establish Public Services Authority for facilitating review and proper development of public services and for matters connected therewith or incidental thereto, with the overarching objective of developing public services as a professional, politically neutral, merit-based, and accountable instrument for promoting good governance and better delivery of services to the citizens.

Recognizing and affirming:

- that good governance is an inalienable right of the citizens in a democracy,
- that good governance should be participatory, transparent. accountable, governed by the rule of law and be informed by equity and inclusiveness in governance and effectiveness and efficiency in service, and
- that a politically neutral, professional, accountable and efficient public service need be available.

The OECD uses the World Bank definition of governance with following links; legitimacy of the government (the degree of democratization), accountability of political and official elements of government (media freedom, transparent decision-making, accountability mechanisms), competence of governments to formulate policies and deliver services, and respect for human rights and rule of law for individual and group rights and security, framework for economic and social activity, and participation.[17]

B. Sudhakar Rao feels that Good Governance is being emphasized as a prerequisite for solving many problems in the developing world. In spite of abundant resources, manpower, institutions, etc., the major objective of economic growth and human development is not taking place in some countries because of improper distribution, civil strife and absence of the provision of basic services essential for human welfare. The issue of good governance not only aims at simplifying rules and regulations but also refers to the involvement of a large number of people, institutions and civil society organizations in decision-making, in making choices and in implementing the projects and programmes.[18]

The tests of good governance lie in the goals and objectives of a government, in its policies and programmes, in the manner of their execution, in the results achieved and above all, in the general perception of the people about the quality of functioning of its various agencies, their attitudes and behaviour towards the public, their sincerity, honesty, and commitments towards public duties. It is also important to see that there is no undue concentration of power.

It is recommended that the following measures should be initiated:

- Set-up a Task Force in governance reforms;
- Bring out an annual governance strategy and action plan;
- Have a governance strategy and action plan for each district. This would also help to focus on reducing regional disparities;
- Bring out an e-governance action plan for every government department;
- Give greater publicity to the Right to Information Act and also improve documentation, archives of documents;
- Continue to take action to rationalise government activities and schemes;
- Extend the success of the Sachivalaya Vahini to districts, beginning initially with the offices of the Deputy Commissioners and Chief Executive Officers of the zilla panchayats;
- Strengthen the public-private partnership, especially in the areas of infrastructure development so that government investments are reduced and the private sector also gets encouraging returns on its investments; and
- Have grievance adalats at the district, taluk and gram panchayat levels to address issues pertaining to land, food security, housing, health, education, public works, drinking water, sanitation, power, agriculture, with special emphasis on areas pertaining to law, order and crime, and especially crimes against women.[19]

The Eleventh Plan vision of inclusive growth, reducing poverty and bridging the various divides that continue to fragment our society can only be achieved if there is a significant improvement in the quality of governance. There are many different definitions of good governance but it is generally agreed that good governance must be broadly defined to cover all aspects of the interface between individuals and businesses on the one hand and government on the other.

The Eleventh Plan must build on the initiatives already taken and seek to achieve a decisive improvement in governance in the Plan period. Some of the major challenges are:

- The Plan accords priority to providing access to quality health care and education, particularly in the rural areas and for girls, minorities, SCs and STs, backward classes and BPL families. It also emphasizes programmes of employment under the Rural Employment Guarantee Programme. Access to clean and good quality water, sanitation, housing and electricity are also critical. These services are delivered at the local level and this calls for both empowerment and accountability of the relevant authorities and effective monitoring of service delivery, particularly for low income groups.
- Effective administration of the rule of law resulting in efficient criminal and civil justice system delivering swift decisions and, particularly, ensuring access to the poor is of extreme importance. An effective security and policing system is required for Naxalite affected and communally sensitive areas.
- The Plan relies heavily on a dynamic private sector to expand investment and create new employment opportunities. This requires developing a business-friendly environment, enabling setting up and exiting of business and promoting efficiency, matching world standards.
- Space must be provided to VOs for developing citizen initiatives, acting as a watchdog on government systems and strengthening group initiatives. This can only be done if full transparency is assured.
- Finally, it is necessary to tackle the problem of corruption which is widely perceived as being all pervasive and is a major source of complaint about the quality of governance.[20]

CONCLUSION

Development administration can be made successful only through good governance as it is engaged in activities like health, education, agriculture, social welfare, etc. which are quite challenging. The modern State cannot carry out development activities without Good governance. Thus, Good Governance, and Development Administration are intimately related. HE President Pratibha Patil rightly observe (Social Welfare Board, Feb.-March 2008), that today, our nation is working for inclusive growth, which means development of social sectors to complement our economic growth with a view to have a sustainable and equitable path of growth. What do we need to do for achieving inclusive growth? In my view it entails four essential steps—the identification of those sections of the population who have got left behind, followed by the formulation of a framework of policies and programmes for their benefit. In these two first steps, we have made considerable progress. The next two steps are implementation and a monitoring system for the proper implementation of programmes and policies designed for the upliftment of the weaker sections of society. The effectiveness of any development programme can be assessed by the actual impact it has on the lives of the beneficiaries and society at large. If a large segment of the population remains beyond the purview of the 'safety net' of socio-economic programmes because of the failure of the implementation machinery, then their purpose is entirely defeated. Implementation and monitoring remain the principal challenges we face. This can only be done with the collective effort of the Government, civil society organizations and the people themselves. Popular participation, in fact, holds the key to the success of any programme of socio-economic change.

Notes and References

1. Government of Karnataka, Karnataka Human Development Report, 2005, Investing in Human Development, 2006.
2. Swami Ranganathananda, "Democratic Administration in the light of practical Vedanta, Madras, Sri Ramakrishna Mission, 2003,
3. M. Aziz Ahamed, Good Governance Through Transparency in *Management in Gvernment*, Oct.-Dec., 1999.
4. B.B. Dandon, Quality in Government, in *Management in Government*, Jan.-March, 2002, pp. 8-9.
5. Parmatma Sharan, Public Administration in India, Meenakshi Prakashan, Meerut, 2000, p. 14
6. Karnataka Human Development Report, 2005, *op. cit.*, p. 274.
7. Kusum, Nair, Blossoms in the Dust, Gerah Duck Worth & Co., London, 1961, p. 14.
8. Swami Ranganathananda, *op. cit.*, pp. 123-24.
9. *Ibid.*, p. 240.
10. B.B. Tandon, "Quality in Government" in *Management in Government*, Jan.-March, 2002, p. 14.
11. D.K. Oza, Values in Administration, in Values, The Key to a Meaningful Life, Shir Ramakrishna Math, Madras, 1996, pp. 103-104.
12. Department of Administrative Reforms and Public Grievances, Ministry of Personnel Public Grivances, New Delhi, GOI, Document I, Action Plan for an Effective and Responsive Government, in *IJPA*, July to Sept, 1998, p. 628.
13. M. Rama Jois, *op. cit.*, pp. 11-12.
14. Swami Budhananda, How to Build Character, Advaita Ashrama, Kolkata, 1983, pp. 19-20, 51-52.
15. Department of Administrative Reforms and Public Grievances, Ministry of Personnel Public Grievances, New Delhi, GOI, Document I, Action Plan for an Effective and Responsive Government, in *IJPA*, July to Sept. 1998, p. 628.
16. Joginder Singh, Good Governance, Delhi, Indian Publishers Distributors, 2002, p. 13.
17. World Bank, Governance, The World Banks' Experience, Washington, World Bank, 1994, p. XIV.
18. B. Sudhakar Rao, Guideline for Good Governance, The Common Wealth Secretariat, p. 1.
19. Karnataka Human Development Report, 2005, p. 276.
20. GOI, Planning Commission, Eleventh Five Year Plan (2001-12), Vol. I, Inclusive Growth, New Delhi, 2008, pp. 223-24.

APPENDIX 33.1

The main components of good governance are:

1. Improving Service Delivery

- To provide services to the people in accordance with specified standards, devoid of harassment or corruption, minimizing waiting time or inconvenience to the members of the public;
- To ensure cost effectiveness in the provision of services by adopting the most appropriate system;
- To adopt participatory mechanism in public service delivery, involving the people, people's institutions civil society groups, community-based organizations, and self-help groups;
- To develop the appropriate cost, time and quality benchmarks for service delivery outcomes;
- To develop, implement and monitor performance measurement and management systems by developing performance indicators for service delivery;
- To promote decentralization and strengthen rural and urban local bodies in order to deliver services by empowering them with devolution of functions, finances and functionaries, and undertaking capacity building programmes; and
- To undertake objective assessments of programmes and obtain feedback in order to improve policy contents and implementation mechanisms.

2. System Improvement

- To take steps to simplify government procedures, reduce costs and improve interface with citizens;
- To improve systems in order to improve transparency, cut red tape and ensure better performance management;
- To modify complicated and rigid government processes so as to reduce and eliminate delay, duplication and redundancy, and improve the speed and quality of public service; and
- To reform processes dealing with citizens and those which breed corruption, such as procurement and tenders.

3. Financial Management

- To ensure fiscal responsibility and sanctity of the budget process;
- To move away from expenditure targets to performance-related measures and milestones which can be defined and are measurable; and
- To institute effective budget formulation, execution, monitoring, reporting and asset management in order to ensure that public money is made available quickly and without delay for the purpose for which it is meant and utilised properly for the benefit of the people.

4. Accountability and Transparency

- To develop and implement Citizens' Charters and Service Charters so as to obtain feedback on implementation and take corrective action with the involvement of citizens;
- To develop and implement a grievances monitoring and redressal mechanism to ensure sensitivity of the administration to the problems faced by the citizens;
- To end secrecy and opacity in administration and bring about transparency so that the administration is seen as just and fair, especially in matters relating to public procurement;
- To ensure that citizens have maximum access to governmental information, by making transparency the rule and official secrecy the exception; and
- To establish citizen evaluation mechanisms such as citizen report cards, social audit, user groups monitoring and independent evaluation by professional agencies.

5. Anti-corruption Measures

- To declare zero tolerance for corruption, strengthen vigilance and anti-corruption machinery, eliminate duplication in enforcement functions and to promote measures to prevent and combat corruption more effectively and efficiently.

Source: Government of Karnataka, Karnataka Human Development Report, 2005, Investing in Human Development, 2006, p. 270.

CHAPTER

34

Welfare State and Development Administration

(See Chart 34.1)

The main objective of development administration is to promote a welfare state wherein all individuals irrespective caste, creed, colour, sex enjoy the benefits of development as well as participate in the process of development. Even after 62 years of independence, schedules castes, scheduled tribes, backward classes, minorities, women, children, elderly people have to face the impact of chronic poverty. Development administration must promote the welfare of these classes and help them in falling in line with mainstream of the country and enjoy decent life. Thus, development administration must work for making India a Welfare State as enshrined in our constitution in preamble, directive principles of state policy and fundamental rights.

IMPLICATIONS OF A WELFARE STATE

No effort is made to discover as to what is the nature and meaning of welfare state. Often, welfare state is equated with welfare society. The two are by no means synonymous. The ideas underlying the welfare state are derived from many different sources. The French Revolution (based on the ideas of liberty; equality and fraternity), utilitarian philosophy of Bentham (greatest happiness of the greatest number), Bismarck Beveridge (concepts of social insurance and social security), the Fabian socialists (Principle of public ownership of basic industries and essential services), John M. Keynes (doctrines of controlling the trade cycle and avoiding mass unemployment), Webbes (championing the cause of the poorest and cleaning up the base of society), Leonard Hobhouse (concept of welfare) and writers like Dicken, Ruskin, J.S. Mill and others placed an emphasis on the welfare of human beings. There is however, no positive or comprehensive philosophy, no ideology that underlies the many policies and programmes that

CHART 34.1

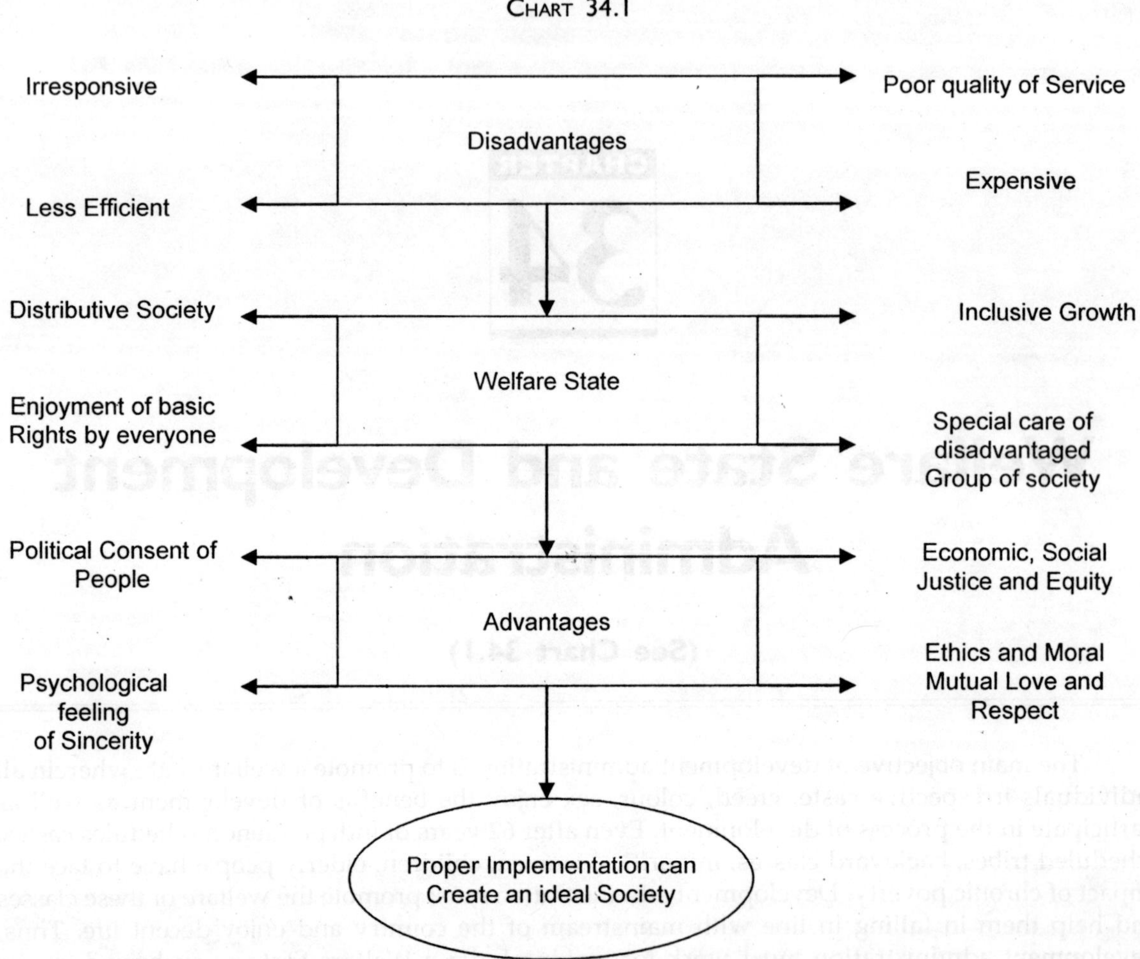

are supposed to form part of the Welfare State. Different scholars have given different views on the concept of Welfare State.

To quote G.D.H. Cole, "The Welfare State is a society in which an assured minimum standard of living and opportunity becomes the possession of every citizen."[1]

According to Professor Marshall, the essential characteristics of the welfare state are its intense, individualism and its collectivism. The former confers on the individual an absolute right to receive welfare, the latter imposes a duty on the state to promote and safeguard the whole community, which may transcend the aggregation of individuals claims.[2] He considers that the welfare state has not rejected the capitalist economy but gives it only qualified approval since there are some elements in civilized life of greater importance which can be attained only by restricting or supplanting the market. The result is "a kind of capitalism softened by an injection of socialism and many socialists disliked or mistrusted the mixture."[3]

The welfare state which exists to promote the welfare of its people aims at making the distribution of welfare more egalitarian or fair through the implementation of various social policies than without such policies. The immediate goal of redistributive policies is equality in the distribution of available goods and unavoidable burdens.

The goals of equality can be given either a weak or a strong interpretation. In the former it implies a guaranteed minimum standard to all members of society, including economic security in the case of inability to earn one's own income. In the latter the redistributive goal refers to the entire "structure of inequality" such as to distribution of income, purchasing power, or consumption, the general standard of education, and other social services and the degree to which different socio-economic income groups have the same opportunities to access to service of the same quality. In the first case, the ambition is to eliminate destitution and individual misery, in the second case to eliminate in addition, social cleavages which might cause conflict and tension in society.[4]

There is no dearth of social security and welfare legislations in India. But the effective and efficient enforcement of these legal measures is far from satisfactory. The chief obstacles in the way of the full blossoming of the welfare state in India are: lack of welfare society, lack of will power, resources, and participation of people, corruption and inefficiency in social, political, administrative systems, the new economic policy of the Government, poverty, low position of women and workers in the unorganised sectors, failure of the family planning programme to arrest the population explosion and illiteracy.

In his famous 'Tryst with Destiny' speech made on the eve of Independence of India in August 1947, its first Prime Minister, Nehru, pledged to get millions of its poor rid of their sufferings by ending poverty, ignorance, disease and inequality of opportunity. This objective of ensuring welfare of the people was to be achieved within a democratic framework of polity with a mixed-economy model of development in which the state and a large infrastructural public sector was to participate as the key actor not only in regulating, protecting and promoting certain specific economic and social activities but also in production and distribution in some sectors of economy. A welfare ethos was reflected in various constitutional provisions, such as, in the Directive Principles of State Policy, Fundamental Rights with arrangements for 'protective discrimination in favor of certain marginalised and vulnerable sections of society and in various policy interventions made from time to time by different branches of government at central and state level. In short, economic growth with social justice was the most pronounced objective that was supposed to translate the promise for a better future into practice.

The Welfare State is organized to ensure the well-being of its citizens and use their resources to that end.[5]

Cormack speaks of the Welfare State as characterized by the provision of a basic minimum —the essentials of life for those who cannot provide for themselves and of a basic optimum—the best standard of life that the community can afford for its citizens without distinction of caste or class. [6]

Hobman has described the Welfare State as a compromise between the two extremes of communism on the one hand and unbridled individualism on the other and as such inspite of all its imperfections, setting a pattern for any humane and progressive society. It guarantees a minimum standard of subsistence without removing incentives to personal enterprise and brings about a limited re-distribution of income without pretending to establish economic equality among its citizens. It assures adequate help to all in need, giving assistance as of right not as charity and not with the stigma of pauperism.[7] Welfare State is a compromise between communism on the one side and unbridled individualism on the other.

PRINCIPLES OF WELFARE STATE

According to Ebenstein,[8] "the main principles of the welfare state are relatively simple: first, the recognition that every member of the community is entitled, solely, because he is a human being, to a minimum standard of living. Second, the welfare state is committed to a policy of economic stability and progress, seeking to eliminate the cycles of violent booms and busts in the economy by public policies whenever private enterprise is unable to prevent by itself the threat of economic instability or decline. Third, the welfare state is committee to full employment as one of the top priorities of public policy Adherents of the welfare state believe that free enterprise can be preserved and strengthened by full employment policies without going to the extreme of nationalization. Taxation properly adjusted to periods of prosperity and depression, interest rates determined by governmental decisions according to current and prospective economic needs and conditions, fiscal policies designed to redistribute purchasing power in—harmony with the best interests of the nation, investment incentives to private business in times of slack, public works for direct unemployment relief, government credits to builders or buyers of homes—these are but a few of the measures the government can adopt in stabilizing the economy without changing its foundations." In the field of social-security, the welfare state aims at protection against want, sickness and old age.

Man is not satisfied only with bare living, but good life. The vision of good life is at the root of the welfare state. Thus the welfare state is no longer the police state of the nineteenth century. It undertakes the responsibility of bringing about the material welfare of the people. It takes steps to remove illiteracy, poverty and unemployment. It upholds the rights of all without any discrimination of caste, colour, creed and sex. It respects the dignity of the human personality and assures justice to all. It does not leave the poor and the weak to their own fate, it goes to their rescue and tries to provide them with adequate and equal opportunities to develop themselves. It regulates economic and other activities of the people in the larger interests of society and does not allow a particular class to exploit the other classes.

POTENTIAL ADVANTAGES AND DISADVANTAGES OF A WELFARE STATE

(i) Advantages

(a) *Economic Advantages*: The welfare state provides security against poverty, old age, illness, hunger, disease, etc. The modern welfare state ensures a palladium against socio-economic injustice and inequality.

(b) *Political Advantages*: Welfare State is based on the consent of the people and hence is permanent in nature.

(c) *Ethical and Moral Advantages*: It is based on mutual love and trust and not on force. In this way it establishes the ties of love among the members of the community.

(ii) Disadvantages

Welfare state is criticised for being too expensive. Financing the services has become a gigantic burden. The cost has to be borne by the middle and the upper middle classes through the instrument of progressive taxation. Tax evasion has proliferated. Consequently, the weaker sections have to share the burden of taxation. Though the standards of living have increased but they have increased unequally among the wealthy and the lower strata.

It is feared that the welfare state would shrivel to what it once was, a publically financed, low level system with poor quality of service. The alternative future could be assured by making use of new technology and encouraging people in maintaining their own health, teaching themselves and looking after each other. New techniques imply a decentralised, flexible, participating welfare state in which professionals are called upon, where needed, for advice or help, but are no longer allowed to form the front line of the welfare state? All this requires leaving the welfare activities to the individuals themselves instead of professional bureaucrats. In this way, we can hope for a responsive and accountable welfare state offering people wider choices. If the opportunity is not grasped, the traditional welfare state will wither away leaving millions of the deprived people to suffer.

The future prospects of welfare state must take into account not only the financial statistics but also the attitudes towards social programmes and spending. Over bureaucratization and lack of responsiveness may have little to do with the size of the budget. It may be due to conflicting expectations. On the one hand we expect the welfare state to be both paternalistic and equitable in providing the needs defined by professionals and flexible and accommodating in responding to demands defined by consumer preference.

The fact that the welfare state, in its institutionalized form, has failed to provide social justice or egalitarian society in advanced liberal democracies, does not negate the case for public enterprises and social services. The purpose of welfare state in these societies was to guarantee certain minimum rights and not an egalitarian society.

In social services are privatized, only those who can afford them will be benefited. Further, there is no guarantee that the private sector will provide the same quality of service as was provided by the public sector. Under privatization, the social costs and disadvantages do not disappear. Rather, they fall on the individual and the families. For instance, if there is a cut in the resources for the care of elderly people, the loss will have to be borne by the individual himself or his family members.[9]

(a) Economic Disadvantages

(1) The modern welfare state is a danger to incentive.

(2) There is a serious danger that public provision of social services may undermine responsibility, self-reliance and self-respect.

(3) Its ideology that people should depend on the state for everything has a demoralising and corrupting influence on the society.

(4) It tends to diminish the encouragement to save and invest.

(b) Political Disadvantages

(1) It poses grave threat to freedom, individual independence, initiative and freedom must not be bartered.

(2) The Welfare State costs a heavy burden and strain on the governmental machine.

(3) In attempt to secure an increase in the standard of living beyond the capacity of the productive system will inevitably lead to disappointment, resentment, frustration, and even revolution.

(c) Moral Disadvantages

(1) The modern welfare state tends to discourage all initiatives and enterprise.
(2) It encourages a spirit of despondency.
(3) *Bureaucratization*: It is said that a welfare state in practice means too much of bureaucracy and too much of departmentalization. Even the American jurist Pound argues that a 'super-service state' must develop a vast bureaucracy, and ultimately it may lead to a totalitarian State with maximum communism and political communism in its pedigree."[10]

In brief, we can say that Welfare programmes should be undertaken very cautiously and we must keep in mind the warning given by the great American economist Pigou that the "welfare state holds in itself a cumulative threat to productivity which is also a threat to its own survival. That threat should be continually and carefully watched. We must not advance too far or too fast."[11] It must move but slowly, firmly and cautiously for the welfare of all.

Welfare State in India. Before we discuss about India, let us discuss the origin and development of the concept in other countries of the world. There is no doubt that almost all states take pride today in calling themselves welfare states. By the end of nineteenth century nearly all the states followed the policy of *laissez-faire*. The promotion of welfare was left entirely to individuals and groups of individuals. The movement from *laissez-faire* to welfare had its origin in England. It was in the days of Queen Elizabeth I that the first Poor Law Act was passed. In France too, Napolean III, in the fifties of the last century. initiated a large number of reforms which could rightly be called the necessary features of a welfare state. Bismarck in Germany made the first great welfare experiment by introducing social insurance against sickness, accident, old-age and disability. This programme was further taken over and expanded by social democrats after 1900. In U.S.A., though there is lot of opposition to the welfare state concept which was described by Hoover, a former president, as the back road to collectivism, there has been a gradual formulation of a number of social and economic 'reforms' which have practically turned America into a welfare state. Denmark, Norway and Sweden are the other welfare states of Europe. Even totalitarian states are, welfare states in an indirect way. The only difference is that in totalitarian states more attention is paid to material welfare than to moral and spiritual welfare and welfare is planned and executed from above. Thus the welfare state concept has now become a universal concept.

According to Ebenstein,[12] the forces behind the movement of classical western liberalism for *laissez-faire* to the welfare state were economic, political and psychological." The miseries caused by the growth of industrialism with the policy, of *laissez-faire* left man with no other option but to look towards the state as the instrument which could help the individual in bettering his lot. According to Ebenstein, the purpose of the welfare state[13] "is to lessen the harmful effects of economic dependence and helplessness which necessarily threaten the individual in the economy of today." On the political level the universal suffrage has enabled the voters to discover that right to vote entailed, not only the political power to elect members of the legislature or the executive but also vast social and economic powers. Now people feel both in advanced and under-developed countries that misery and poverty do not result from unchangeable decrees of nature but from changeable institutions of society. All this has resulted in making the state a welfare state.

The Colonial rule in India till August, 1947 was not congenial to the growth of welfare state. Although a unified and well-knit administration prevailed for about a century and a half the primary task of the British in India was one of maintaining law and order. Not much was done to improve the lot of the common man.

After independence, the immediate task before the political leaders and the constitution framers had been to bring about considerable socio-economic improvements. The prime aim was to improve economic conditions of the masses by utilising, mobilising and consolidating the meagre under-developed resources available with the country in the best manner. India committed herself to the idea of a Welfare State. It can be ascertained from the following sources:

I. Constitutional Provisions:
   (a) Preamble.
   (b) The Directive Principles of State Policy.
   (c) Fundamental Rights.
II. Commentaries by Eminent jurists.
III. Five Year Plans.
IV. Manifestos of Political Parties.
V. Social Legislation.
VI. Allocation of Resources.
VII. Greater Importance attached to groups belonging to deprived sections of society by UN System

I. Constitutional Provisions

(a) Preamble

The Preamble to the constitution stated: "We the people of India, having solemnly resolved to constitute India into a Sovereign Democratic Republic, and to secure to all its citizens; justice, social, economic and political."[14]

The cardinal concept, of justice, social, economic and political, embodied in the Objective Resolution and the Preamble to the Constitution of India quoted above was the foundation stone of the edifice of the modern democratic Welfare State in India.

(b) The Directive Principles of State Policy

The ideal of socio-economic justice which is the sheet anchor of a modern democratic Welfare State is spelled out in specific terms in 'The Directive Principles of State Policy', embodied in Part IV of our Constitution. Among the economic rights and principles of social policy contained in the directive principles are:

(i) adequate means of livelihood (Art. 39);
(ii) equal pay for equal work for both men and women (Art. 39);
(iii) distribution of the material resources of the country so as best to sub-serve the common good (Art. 39);
(iv) protection of child and adults labour (Art. 39);
(v) right to work, to education and to public assistance in cases of unemployment, old age, sickness and disablement and in other cases of undeserved want (Art. 41);
(vi) provision for just and humane conditions of work and for maternity relief (Art. 42);
(vii) a living wage to all workers (Art. 43);
(viii) conditions of work ensuring a decent standard of life and full enjoyment of leisure and social and cultural opportunities (Art. 43);

(ix) provision for just and compulsory education of children upto the age of 14 (Art. 45);
(x) promotion of educational and economic interests of scheduled castes, scheduled tribes and other weaker sections of the people (Art. 46); and
(xi) raising the level of nutrition and standard of living of the people and improvement of public health (Art. 47).

Taken together the above provisions are a manifesto for the ideal of the Welfare State. India is committed to the creation of a socialist Welfare State and these are guidelines for the achievement of this ideal.

(c) Fundamental Rights

Part III of the Constitution embodies Fundamental Rights. "The whole object of Part III of the Constitution is to provide protection for the freedoms and rights mentioned therein against arbitrary invasion by the State."[15] Like the English Magna Carta the Indian Bill of Rights protects fundamental liberties.

Art. 14 lays down that the State shall not deny to any person equality before the law or the equal protection of the law. The guiding principle of this Article is that all persons and things similarly circumstanced shall be treated alike both in privileges conferred and liabilities imposed.

Article 15(1) prohibits the State from discriminating against citizens on the grounds only of religion, sex, caste, place of birth or any of them. This in fact is a specific application of the general principle of equality embodied in Article 14. Clauses (3) and (4) of this Article empower the State to make special provision in favour of women, children and any socially and educationally backward classes of citizens or for the Scheduled Castes and the Scheduled Tribes.

Article 32 provides the right to move the Supreme Court or High Court by appropriate proceedings for the enforcement of fundamental rights. So there is Constitutional guarantee.

II. Commentaries by Eminent Jurists

Most of the judges have also indicated that India is committed to a Socialistic Welfare State. Mr. P.B. Gajendragadkar, former Chief Justice of India said, "The Indian Constitution makers were fully alive to the problems posed by the ideal of the Welfare State and so the Constitution has guaranteed to its citizens justice—social, economic and political."[16]

Mr. Hidyatullah, former Chief Justice of India stated that our Constitution is an instrument admirably suited for the establishment of a liberal and socialistic democracy "in which the rival claims of individual and society can be completely reconciled and through which the election of a Welfare State is rendered practical."[17]

III. Five Year Plans

In March, 1950, the Planning Commission was set-up by a Resolution of the Government of India to formulate a Plan for the most effective and balanced utilization of the country's resource. The First Five Year Plan document stated clearly, "The goals of social and economic policy are prescribed in the Directive Principles of the Constitution." The First Five Year Plan represents the first attempt to translate these principles into a national program to ensure the building of a welfare state.[18]

The Second Five Year Plan document explained that the accent of the socialist pattern is on the attainment of positive goals. The raising of living standards, the enlargement of opportunities for all, the promotion of enterprise among the disadvantaged classes and the creation of a sense of partnership among all sections of the community. The directive principles of State policy in the Constitution had indicated the approach in broad terms, the socialist pattern of society is a more concretized expression of this approach.[19]

The Third Five Year Plan stated: "The basic objective of India's development must necessarily be to provide the masses of Indian people the opportunity to lead a good ltfe."[20] The Fourth and Fifth Five Year Plans also placed a great deal of stress upon removal of poverty and unemployment. The Sixth Five Year Plan (1980-85) laid stress on "improving the quality of life of the people in general with special reference to the economically and socially. handicapped population." The objective of national planning in India is not only to raise the national income or the per capita income but also to ensure that the benefit is evenly distributed, that disparities in income and living are not widened but in fact narrowed, and that the process of economic development does not lead to social tensions endangering the fabric of the democratic society. Thus the objective of Planning, has been to ensure socialistic Welfare State.

This very philosophy continued in 7th to 10th plan. In his forward to XIth Five Year Plan Prime Minister observed India's commitment to planned economic development is a reflection of our society's determination to improve the economic conditions of our people and an affirmation of the role of the government in bringing about this outcome through a variety of social, economic, and institutional means. The Eleventh Five Year Plan, which was approved by the National Development Council on 19 December 2007 reaffirms this commitment. It provides a comprehensive strategy for inclusive development, building on the growing strength of the economy, while also addressing weaknesses that have surfaced.

The strength of the economy is evident from the remarkable transition to a high growth path, which has been achieved in recent years. The Tenth Plan period (2002-03 to 2006-07) began modestly, but then saw the economy accelerating steadily to achieve an average growth rate of 7.7%, for the Plan period as a whole, which is the highest ever achieved in any Plan period. In the last four years the growth rate has averaged 8.9% making India one of the fastest growing economies in the world. The transition to high growth is an impressive achievement, but we must not forget that growth is not the only measure of development. Our ultimate objective is to achieve broad based improvement in the living standards of all our people. Rapid growth is essential for this outcome because it provides the basis for expanding incomes and employment and also provides the resources needed to finance programmes for social uplift. However, it is not by itself sufficient. We also need to ensure that growth is widely spread so that its benefits, in terms of income and employment, are adequately shared by the poor and weaker sections of our society, especially the Scheduled Castes (SCs) and the Scheduled Tribes (STs), Other Backward Classes (OBCs) and minorities. For this to happen, the growth must be inclusive in the broadest sense. It must occur not just in our major cities but also in our villages and small towns. It must be spread across all states and not just limited to some. It must generate sufficient volumes of high quality employment to provide the means for uplift of large numbers of our population from the low income low quality occupations in which too many of them have been traditionally locked.

Deputy Chairman in his preface mentioned that the Eleventh Plan began in very favourable circumstances with the economy having grown at the rate of 7.7% per year in the Tenth Plan period. However, far too many of our people still lack the basic requirements for a decent living in terms of nutrition standards, access to education and basic health, and also to other public services such as water supply and sewerage. Disadvantaged groups, especially the Scheduled Castes and Scheduled Tribes and the minorities have benefited less than they should have. Regional imbalances have emerged across and even within states.

The Eleventh Plan seeks to remedy these deficiencies by seeking to accelerate the pace of growth while also making it more inclusive. The growth objective is to achieve an average growth rate of 9% per annum for the Plan period. The objective of inclusiveness is reflected in the adoption of 26 other monitorable targets at the national level relating to (i) income and poverty, (ii) education, (iii) health, (iv) women and children, (v) infrastructure, and (vi) environment. Some of these national targets have also been disaggregated into 13 state-level targets and it is expected that the state governments design policies and programmes to achieve them.

IV. Manifestos of Political Parties

Most of the political parties, have indicated in their manifestos that these are wedded to the ideals of a socialistic Welfare State. The strategy to achieve the Welfare State may differ from party to party but the aim is the same.

V. Social Legislation

In order to tackle various problems associated with social defence, the Central and State Governments have enacted several legislations in the past in the field of juvenile delinquency, crime, probation, prostitution, etc. to provide the necessary statutory frame-work for correctional and rehabilitation services.

VI. Allocation of Resources

In plans and Annual budgets, more resources are being allocated for the social welfare of children, women, old people and depressed classes. The programmes relating to children, women and depressed classes find prominent place in the revised 20 Point Economic Programme of the Prime Minister.

VII. Greater importance attached to these groups by the U.N. System

The U.N. System is doing a lot for the welfare of children and women and old people to promote welfare of the groups. The U.N. also gives assistance to the member States. India being a member of the agencies of the U.N. System takes advantage of their technical assistance for the promotion of social welfare.

SOCIALISTIC STATE

A State cannot be a welfare state if the aims of removal of poverty and substantial rise in the level of employment are not accompanied by social justice. Today, in India, very few people are controlling a substantial amount of wealth in the country. This is not conducive to good development. As the ultimate purpose of development is to provide increasing opportunities to people for a better life, it is essential to bring about a more equitable distribution of income and wealth for promoting both social justice and efficiency of production, to raise substantially the level of employment, to achieve greater degree of income security, to expand improved facilities for education, health, nutrition, housing and social welfare and to safeguard the environment. Thus qualitative and structural changes in the society must go hand in hand with rapid economic growth, and the existing disparities—regional, sectoral and social—should be substantially reduced.

The objective of social justice as articulated in the plans has two major dimensions. The first dimension is an improvement in the living standards of the poorest groups in society and second is a reduction in inequalities in asset distribution. In 1954, the Parliament declared that the broad objective of economic policy should be to achieve a socialistic pattern of society, under which the basic criteria for determining the lines of advance would be social gain and greater equality in income and wealth and not private profit. The Second Five Year Plan (1956-57 to 1961-62), therefore, sought to promote a pattern of development which would ultimately lead to the establishment of a socialistic pattern of society in India. In particular, it stressed that the benefits of economic development should accrue more to the relatively less privileged sections of society and there should be a progressive reduction in the concentration of incomes, wealth and economic power.

One of the objectives of the Third Five Year Plan was also to establish progressively greater equality of opportunity and bring about reduction in disparities of income and wealth and a more even distribution of economic power. The Fourth Five Year Plan (1969-70 to 1973-74) aimed at raising the standard of living of the people through programmes which at the same time were designed to promote equality and social justice. The Plan laid particular emphasis on improving the condition of the less privilege and weaker sections of the society especially through the provision of employment and education. Efforts were also directed towards reduction of concentration and a wider diffusion of wealth, income and economic power.

In the Fourth Plan the broad objectives of planning has been defined as. rapid economic development accompanied by continuous progress towards equality and justice and establishment of a social and economic democracy. Fifth plan emphasized the minimum needs programme to ensure the welfare of the weaker sections Sixth plan also aimed at the development of the weaker sections of the society.

For about six decades, Government of India and State Governments are using a variety of instruments ranging from direct attacks on poverty and asset inequality to more indirect fiscal measures, have been used to pursue these ends. However, there has not been much visible and perceptible impact on the people. The gulf between the haves and have-not has not narrowed down. The implementation of' the programmes intended to establish socialistic-society are not effective resulting in *status quo*. Therefore, we must provide greater degree of redistributive bias into our development effort to ensure the growth of socialistic society.

A plethora of Institution is in existence like Ministry of Social Justice and Employment to look after Scheduled Tribes, other backward classes, economically weaker sections, older people, Ministry of Tribal Affairs, Ministry of Women and Child Welfare and Statutory Commissions for Scheduled Castes, Scheduled Tribes, Other backward classes, Minority Commission, etc. have been set-up to help the deprived sections of community.

ASSESSMENT OF WELFARE STATE IN INDIA

India has achieved good progress to promote welfare of the masses suffering from abject poverty. In the Chapter on Social Welfare Administration in India, we shall discuss the progress made in all the areas. Besides, there has been good improvements in the provision of Social Services. On examining critically, we find that we lag behind in many ways. Position of women and children is not satisfactory. Besides, Scheduled castes, scheduled tribes, backward classes, weaker sections, etc. have not developed as expected. What are the reasons for it? Why have we not been able to meet the aspirations of the people enshrined in our sacred documents? It is a pity that a country with such an intellectual heritage had failed to grapple these problems. At present, India is not a Welfare State in reality. It is only in theory and not in practice. India is struggling for a Welfare State and thus we can say that Welfare State is emerging in India. We suggest some methods to ensure Welfare State in India:

(I) Need of a Clear and Definite Policy

The objectives of social welfare must be spelt out in clear terms. Besides, social welfare must be linked with broader objectives of social policy and socio-economic development to achieve an integrated national Social Welfare Programme.

Social Welfare programmes should be closely coordinated with economic development to achieve an integrated national social welfare programme. Adequate coordination is required among all the governmental bodies concerned with social welfare and related social programmes, such as education, health, housing, justice and labour at the central level and all other levels of government, among the central authorities responsible for social services and their field offices or the responsible agencies at subordinate levels of government; among governmental, semi-governmental and non-governmental organisations. The planning and coordinating machinery should also facilitate communication and the continues exchange of general and specific information, as well as ensure effective collaboration at the operational level. According to J.E. Bulsara:

> "Social and economic development are complementary and social welfare are essential for a balanced and healthy growth of the society, whether it be technologically advanced or economically underdeveloped. Social Welfare contribute substantially to economic productivity by creating amongst the people a healthy psychological atmosphere and a sense of belonging in being cared for through an appropriate provision of badly needed social and welfare services." In developing countries, the objectives of social welfare are not spelt out clearly. This results in low priority being given to these services.

(2) Need of the Development of Scientific Social Planning

All round social planning should be based on scientifically collected and pertinent factual data. Such planning is not being done in the developing world because of the non-availability of reliable data of sufficient quantity and right quality. In the absence of such data, it becomes difficult to convince the planners resulting in the poor allocations to social welfare.

(3) Need of Active Participation of the Beneficiaries

We should encourage the active participation of citizens in the planning and implementation of social welfare programmes. Public Co-operation is an active and living element in a dynamic democracy. The resources in the developing world are limited and we can serve more people in an efficient manner through their active involvement.

(4) Need of Decentralisation to Ensure Speedy and Efficient Implementation

Responsibility for the administration of social welfare should be decentralised to a great extent to ensure close relationship with the beneficiaries and the communities to be served. This would also help in getting the feedback from the people which would be useful in the planning and evaluation of social welfare. Besides, we must provide these welfare services in the rural areas, urban slums and tribal areas.

Government should make special efforts to extend social welfare to neglected rural areas on an adequate basis, taking into account the particular needs of rural areas. These services must be provided in these areas according to the needs of the areas.

(5) Need of Developing Technical Standards

Technical standards for social welfare programmes should be developed by the Government with the help of institutions engaged in the education and training of social workers. These standards should be adapted according to different situations to ensure implementation of the overall social policy. Technical standards should be simple and; clear so that they are really understandable to all concerned with social welfare and to the general public.

(6) Strengthening of Voluntary Organisations

In many countries, voluntary organisations have traditionally played and continue to play an important role in providing social welfare. Governments should encourage and assist such organisations by providing finances, technical consultation and supervision to help them maintain standards and improve their effectiveness. The care may be taken that the voluntary organisations may not be reduced to bureaucratic organisations.

(7) Need of Developing Administrative Competence in the Field of Social Welfare

There is a shortage of qualified people to manage this sector. Administrators in key positions of responsibility for social welfare programmes at policy-making, planning and operational levels should be selected on the basis of administrative, ability and technical qualifications in the field of social welfare. The general administrators should not be deputed to plan and implement the social welfare.

(8) Well-defined Procedures to Assess the Functioning of Social Welfare

Clearly defined administrative procedures should be developed for handling all complaints regarding the functioning of social welfare activities. The procedure should be simple and intelligible so that beneficiaries and general public can make use of it. This will help in assessing the impact of these services on the people.

Good relationship with the general public are of crucial importance to the development and administration of social programmes. Suitable provisions should therefore be made for public relations activities to be carried out by the bodies responsible for social welfare. Such activities should be designed to provide interpretation and wider understanding of the programmes, stimulate interest and support of social welfare and to create a favourable climate of public opinion. The public relations activities relevant to social welfare programmes should be coordinated and conducted in close cooperation with those of such other central or local authorities responsible for general public relations activities of the Government on an overall basis.

(9) Globalization, Liberalization and Privatisation

Since 1990's Globalization, Privatization and Liberalization (GLP) has been in operation causing many hardships and problems to social sector. There is need to take care of social welfare alongwith economic development. A second aspect of the changed role of government in the Eleventh Plan is that the public sector will increasingly concentrate in areas that lie in the domain of the state governments, and within the states in the domain of panchayati raj institutions. This is especially true of elementary education, health, rural drinking water, rural sanitation, child nutrition, housing for the poor, the national employment guarantee, and schemes for watershed management. Programmes in these areas are implemented at the local level and often depend critically upon local level authorities and the system of governance and accountability should therefore be at the local level. The 73rd and 74th Amendments to the constitution were landmark steps in empowering the Panchayats and urban local bodies and to give full effect to these amendments it is necessary to transfer functions, functionaries, and funds to the PRIs. While the functions to be transferred have been clearly identified, the actual progress made in transferring the functionaries and funds remain limited. It is also necessary to build capacity at the local level. NGOs can play an important role in building capacity or in encouraging empowerment or participation or ways should be found of engaging the NGO community more actively in local level programmes.

The government has so far being shouldering primary responsibility for social sector development with varying degree of success given the resource and implementation constraints. The changed scenario in wake of liberalisation and privatisation requires that the state should not only monitor enforcement of the rules of fair play in key privatised sector but also ensure adequate allocations for social sector. Liberalisation may mean erosion and sometimes elimination of state institutions in social sector. This could be perilous for a nation that has pushed equity and social justice as equally important a goal as economic growth. Such a social damage could itself frustrate economic objectives.[21]

(10) Absence of 'Cutting Edge' of Administration

The State Government is implementing these welfare policies through their civil administration which is meant for strengthening the revenue and the law and order machinery. However, they have not reorganised the local-level administration for delivering social services. They are also not professional people with proper training and sensitivity to handle these problems. In a corner of the District Collectorate, one finds the Social Welfare Department. The space in the district administration is very limited for welfare activities. That explains the commitment of the Government for implementing the welfare policies. Decentralisation of Political power after 73rd and 74th Amendments of the Indian Constitution has brought Local administration in shambles. It is not yet reorganised the need to deliver the social services. The Panchayati Raj System has not been given the power to deliver these social services.

The social administration needs proper administrative structures manned by the professional people with proper budgetary support which does not exist today in any State. After 60 years, our economy has grown from strength to strength which has the capacity to sustain a proper social security system. But there is no political will on the part of the political elite to frame those policies. Once the Social administration is organised, it would help depoliticisation of bureaucracy. Discretionary power for the bureaucrats and the politicians would be very little. Social Administration would bring better relationship between the State and citizen mediated by the local administration their day-to-day problems need to be satisfied with the help of the local administration. The Welfare State would run with the help of an efficient and honest local administration which would create better legitimacy for the democratic system.[22]

Welfare may be vague and vast, but it need not be wooly and wobbling. When welfare becomes a function of considerable magnitude, under Governments at different levels, it should be developed as a definite programme of action, subject to all aspects of administrative efficiency and accountability. A clear formulation of policy and its follow-by concretizing the operational exercises in its implementation would be a great help in the delineation of Union-State administrative relations in the welfare field.

On both the points, the Second Five Year Plan observed:

"In the administration of development programmes, care is to be taken to ensure that schemes are so formulated that the weaker sections of the population are aided in the largest possible manner .... The special provisions made in favour of backward classes should be so utilized as to enable them to derive the maximum advantage from the general development programmes and to make up, as speedily as possible, for retarded progress in the past."[23]

According to Prof. Peter Drucker, "Development is largely a matter of the dynamics of individuals and of a local community. These can be supplied only by generating local, responsible initiative and multiplying human energies."

CONCLUSION

There has been a great concern for disadvantaged and deprived sections of society which is visible through the allocation of massive funds to social sector. Lack of precise planning, poor implementation, corrupt practices, bureaucratic wranglies have been responsible for the present poor conditions of disadvantaged and deprived classes. There is a need of strong awareness among the members of disadvantaged and deprived sections towards their rights as well as active participation in their own welfare.

NOTES AND REFERENCES

1. Quoted in Herbert L. Marx, (Ed.), The Welfare State, 1950, p. 9.
2. T.H. Marshal, Sociology at the Crossroads, London, Heinemann, 1963, p. 246.
3. *Ibid.*, p. 284.
4. Stein Ringen, *op. cit.*, p. 8.
5. Bruce Marshall, The Coming of the Welfare State, London, 1951, p. 293.
6. Cormack, U., The Welfare State, Lock Memorial Lecture, 1951 Family Welfare Association.
7. Hobman D.C., The Welfare State, John Murray, 1952.
8. Ebenstein, W., Great Political thinkers, pp. 811-12.
9. Asha Gupta, "Welfare State and Privatisation in Canada", *IJPA*, Oct.-Dec. 1990, Vol. XXXVI, No. 4, pp. 877-78.
10. Ebenstein, W. Great Political Thinkers, 3rd Ed., pp. 816-17.
11. *Ibid.*, p. 818.
12. Ebenstein, W., Great Political Thinkers, 3rd ed., p. 809.
13. *Ibid.*, p. 810.
14. Shukla, V.N., The Constitution of India (4th ed.) Lucknow, 1964, p. 1.
15. A.I.R. 1954 SCR 587.
16. Law, Liberty and Social Justice, Bombay, 1965 p. 82.
17. Mr. Hidayatullah, Justice, S.C. of India, Democracy in India and the Judicial Process, Bombay, 1966, p. 62.
18. GOI: First Five Year Plan, p. 115.
19. GOI: Second Five Year Plan, p. 24.
20. The Third Five Year Plan, p. 1.
21. J.C. Mohanty, Social Sector at Crossroads, *IJPA*, July-Sept. 2005, Vol. LI, No. 3, p. 531.
22. R.K. Barik, "Welfare Administration in India: A critical Evaluation" Fifty Years of Indian Administration—Retrospect and Prospects, Edited by: T.N.Chaturvedi, IIPA, New Delhi, 1998, p. 497.
23. Second Five Year plan, 1956, Planning Commission, GOI, New Delhi, pp. 588-89.

Appendix 34.1

Tryst with Destiny

Long years ago, we made a tryst with destiny, and now the time comes when we shall redeem our pledge, not wholly or in full measure, but very substantially. At the stroke of the midnight hour, when the world sleeps, India will awake to life and freedom. A moment comes, which comes but rarely in history, when we step out from the old to the new, when an age ends, and when the soul of a nation, long suppressed, finds utterance. It is fitting that at this solemn moment we take the pledge of dedication to the service of India and her people and to the still larger cause of humanity.

At the dawn of history India started on her unending quest, the trackless centuries are filled with her striving and the grandeur of her successes and her failures. Through good and ill fortune alike she has never lost sight of that quest or forgotten the ideals which gave her strength. We end today a period of ill fortune and India discovers herself again. The achievement we celebrate today is but a step, an opening of opportunity, to the greater triumphs and achievements that await us. Are we brave enough and wise enough to grasp this opportunity and accept the challenge of the future?

Freedom and power bring responsibility. The responsibility rests upon this Assembly, a sovereign body representing the sovereign people of India. Before the birth of freedom, we have endured all the pains of labour and our hearts are heavy with the memory of this sorrow. Some of those pains continue even now. Nevertheless, the past is over and it is the future that beckons to us now. That future is not one of ease or resting but of incessant striving so that we might fulfil the pledges we have so often taken and the one we shall take today. The service of India means the service of the millions who suffer. It means the ending of poverty and ignorance and disease and inequality of opportunity. The ambition of the greatest man of our generation has been to wipe every tear from every eye. That may be beyond us but as long as there are tears and suffering, so long our work will not be over.

And so we have to labour and to work and work hard to give reality to our dreams are for India, but they are also for the world, for all the nations and peoples are too closely knit together today for anyone of them to imagine that it can live apart.

Peace has been said to be indivisible; so is freedom, so is prosperity now, and so also is disaster in this one world that can no longer be split into isolated fragments. To the people of India, whose representatives we are, we appeal to join us with faith and confidence in this great adventure. This is not time for petty and destructive no time for ill-will or blaming others. We have to build the noble mansion of free India where all her children may dwell.

—Pt. Jawahar Lal Nehru

Appendix 34.2

Social Welfare in India

Durgbabai Deshmukh

First Former Chairman, Central Social Welfare Board

India's declared objective is the attainment of a Welfare State. That means that we shall steadily strive to work to bring about conditions of life that will assure every citizen freedom from want and fair share of the necessities of life. In other words, each individual will be assured a reasonable living standard, and full opportunities to lead a complete life will be every citizen's birthright.

This great sub-continent has awakened from the long deep slumber of centuries and it is again regaining slowly and consistently something of its own initiative, strength, vitality and power. Let it not be forgotten however, that New India has to be built on the foundation of an immediate past which has left deep scars.

The social structure in India is product of long historical evolution. Evolved over several thousand years it has felt the impact of other cultures and civilizations. For centuries, social reformers have tried to deal with social evils, and these efforts have been some join aided and accelerated by social legislation But social reform and legislation by themselves are not adequate because of the organised resistance of vested interests and orthodoxy. What is now required is a dynamic approach, harnessing public consciousness to this effort and at the same time educating the public and creating in them an awareness of the need to tackle social evils relating of social inequalities, social health, social defence, vulnerable groups and so on. A dynamic approach is required to bring about a changed outlook and philosophy to deal with these social problems and to work for common welfare. This approach should be based on a proper determination of objectives to be achieved speedily with a devotion to high purpose, discipline and efficiency, and concerted action towards planned progress.

India's First Five Year Plan, which is also the first attempt towards planned economy for the country, having recognised the importance of social services in general and social welfare in particular, has rightly given the lead to all agencies, at Central, State, local and voluntary levels, in the vital .spheres relating to the welfare of women and children, family welfare, community organization and youth welfare, as also in combating social vice, delinquency and crime with measures of social defence and correctional administration. In the past, welfare services have been the special field of private agencies and recent investigations have revealed the existence of more than 10,000 known institutions with different programmes of social welfare. Combining the best talent, intention, and effort they have far served. a very real need in their respective fields. But it must be admitted that most of the institutions are unorganised and are often unable to carry on their activities efficiently faced as they are with the complexity of factors peculiar to modern society. The situation called for careful analysis and two important factors emerged.

Firstly, the goal is the attainment of a Welfare State. The State, at the Central, regional and local level, has to bear the burden of undertaking; major tasks of social welfare, either because they are of a specialised nature or because these services have to benefit a large section of the community. Barring such fields, however, social welfare services must be sponsored and actively, worked by voluntary organizations and private individuals must come forward with their cooperation. While this was one way of drawing in the voluntary worker and making him realise his responsibility to the community, it was also the chief means of promoting private charity and philanthropy and encouraging a spirit of services and sacrifice.

Secondly, while accepting the above, it was at the same time necessary to realise that these voluntary agencies must be given guidance and assistance. These are two-fold: one was to help them to better organise programmes and activities in the light of the recommendation contained in the Five Year Plan, provide for supervision and training and set-up, better standards and techniques. The second way in which assistance was to be given was to make available financial aid. This was necessary since the sources of many large private incomes have virtually dried up with the social and economic changes that have, to late, taken place in the country or are still taking place.

Bearing in mind the above two factors, the Five Year Plan provides plenty of opportunities for public partnership. Indeed, the Prime Minister of India has repeatedly emphasized the need of an imaginative and objective approach to the problems of the welfare of the people so as to make them realise that they are partners in a tremendous undertaking, in a great adventure. This is true particularly in the field of social welfare private sectors have been informed that social welfare services are their major responsibility: that deserving institutions will be given financial assistance for which provision of Rs. 40 million has been made in the Plan. Definite standards have been set-up for these organizations to reorientate and improve their programmes and activities; the need for registration and licensing have been brought home to them; facilities are being made for research and investigation in the several fields of social welfare. Voluntary organisations could in future, so plan their programmes and see that each institution meets a felt need of the area of the community, and that, far from overlapping, these agencies work in perfect harmony bringing about maximum integration and coordination.

As an immediate step in the implementation of the recommendation of the Five Year Plan the Union Government of India has set-up a Central Social Welfare Board, (with a view to providing assistance, guidance and help to voluntary social welfare organisation in the country which stand in need of such assistance or help). This is an autonomous body with eminent social workers on its Board. The functions of the Central Social Welfare Board include a survey and assessment of the needs and requirements of social welfare organisation in the country, evaluation of their programmes and coordination of assistance under the Ministries of the Central and State Governments. The Board will call for applications from the voluntary agencies in the country, and examine them in the light of the rules laid down for this purpose by the Board. The Board has also Advisory Panels which again consist of tried social workers in their respective fields. There are at present four Panels and they have already made their reports:

1. Child Welfare
2. Women's Welfare
3. Panel dealing with the physically handicapped, juvenile delinquents, and Correctional Administration.
4. Family Welfare Panel.

It follows from what has been already stated that the role of voluntary agencies in implementing the welfare programmes so urgently needed in the country is of considerable significance and consequently several facilities are being provided to enable them to actively participate in this effort.

One novel way of brining about this participation is to persuade the welfare agencies to take up an authorized agency for the sale of small saving certificates. The organisation in its corporate capacity become the authorized agent and voluntary workers will use their influence and tap the small income groups. The results of this scheme in its wider perspective are of considerable importance. In the first place, voluntary welfare organisations help the country in: implementing the Five Year Plan by obtaining finance through Small Savings. Secondly, by purchasing Small Saving Certificates even the common person is made to understand what the Five Year Plan means, for the country, and for himself, and how he can join in this grand national enterprise. By purchasing a Small Saving Certificate he or she gets the sensation of partnership with the rest in the building of India's future. Lastly, the welfare organization earn their commission by these sales and this will go to finance their welfare programmes enlarge their scope and increase the tempo of their activities.

Finally, there are special programmes from a definite section of population in the country, namely, the Backward Classes. They constitute nearly 70 millions and they have been neglected so far. The Constitution again provides these groups special guarantees and, in conformity with these, definite programmes for their cultural, economic and educational advancement have been formulated and put into execution in the several States. As much as Rs. 440 millions have been provided for the Welfare of Backward Classes for the Plan period of 1951-56.

Our Social Welfare Programmes will naturally be influenced by the culture, tradition, financial and human resources in the country. Naturally too our patterns and methods of social work will grow and develop out of the social and psychological milieu of the land in which we live. We stand, in effect, at the beginning of a new period of planned and co-ordinate national development.

CHAPTER

35

Time Management and Development Administration

Public administration in developing countries is not utilizing the time for priority activities resulting in delays in execution of development projects and programmes. Lack of punctuality and large number of holidays result in loss of valuable time. Development administration must make the personnel to understand the role of time management in the process of development. People n Government do not understand the role of time in promoting dynamism and development in administration.

Development administration has to accelerates the tempo of inclusive growth, i.e. welfare of all disadvantages groups like Scheduled Castes, Schedules Tribes, Backward Classes, Minorities, Women, Children, Senior citizens. How can it be possible when we find that those who re engaged in development administration are wasting time on one pretext or the other. They orget that time is inelastic. We have already failed to deliver goods in the past for more than six ecades. Development administration must ensure timely completion of development programme n the areas of health, education and social welfare. Development administration must ingrain the alue of time in the minds of administrators engaged in development administration.

In this chapter, we would discuss the techniques of time management which must be nderstood and put in practice for making development administration a success, as the rural unctionaries like doctors, teachers, development functionaries either absent themselves or reach te. They do not understand as to huge loss they are doing to the nation.

As the village functionaries do not devote time for village development, how can evelopment administration become a success in promoting rural development. Development lministration need fast action with sincerity and devotion. Another problem faced by evelopment administration is that the functionaries are devoting time to activities which are not eir concern. Development administration expects the use of time purposefully and efficiently.

Time is not thought of as a resource. However, it is the most important and crucial factor time is inelastic and non-renewable. An event cannot take place unless there is a time for it.

CHART 35.1

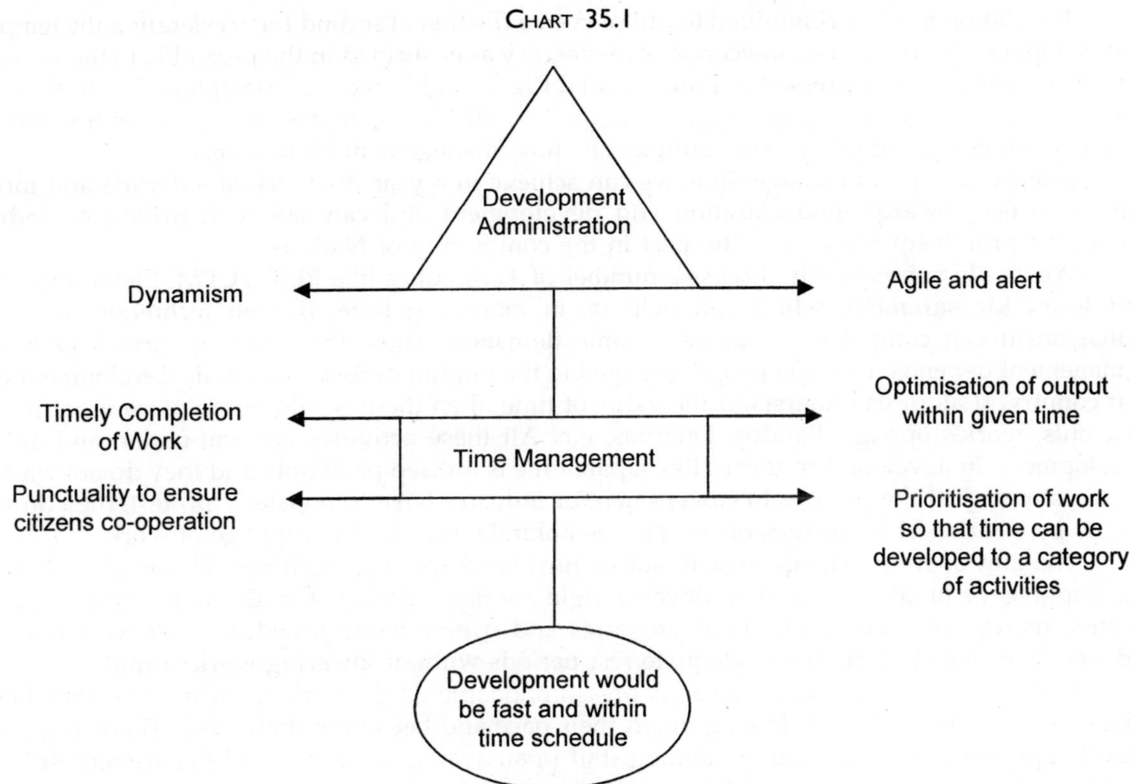

Time and tide wait for none. We may keep in mind that time is neutral, i.e. it is neither good nor bad by itself. Therefore, to blame the time for any inaptitude for failure will be quite unfair. The Statement that "Time is money" sums up the significance of time management. Though most people in Government, Public Enterprises and Private Sector understand the implications of time management, but in actual practice, we find that time is wasted and its importance is undermined. Most of the executives in administration complain that they are too busy but still they while away a lot of their time in unnecessary activities. All other resources can be increased whenever required but not time as it is inelastic and therefore, we must make the best use of time. Just to illustrate the importance of time, many studies conducted revealed that persons in administration hardly devote 30 to 40 per cent of their time for the activities they have been engaged for. It means that if proper use is made of time, we can provide services with the existing infrastructure two to three times more and thus the process of development can be accelerated.

Thus, if all the services make the best use of time, we can accelerate the process of development and help the people of the country suffering from abject poverty, ill-health, illiteracy, unemployment, in leading a good standard of life. In developed countries, the most precious resource is time and that is why they are developed, but in developing countries, time is unconsciously and consciously wasted in useless activities, resulting in underdevelopment and backwardness. Time has a value like currency and like the financial management, it can be organised to get more with less. Time once lost is lost forever. Therefore, we should not waste even a single second.

The Nation must be committed to utilise even a fraction of second for accelerating the tempo of development to usher in socio-economic democracy as enshrined in the preamble to the Indian constitution and further stressed in Fundamental Rights and Directive Principles of State Policy. How to go about it? How to ensure optimization of time? How to make the best use of time? The answers to these questions are very simple, i.e., time management at all levels.

If our country can manage time, we can achieve in a year the work of a decade and thus can move fast towards modernisation and development and can say with pride that India occupies a prominent place as in the past in the community of Nations.

We would subsequently discuss a number of Techniques like PERT/CPM, Method Study and Work Measurement, which can help us in managing time, but no technique of time management can compel us to move as time demands. Thus, the ultimate success of time management depends upon the people engaged in the pursuit of socio-economic development of that country. If all of us understand the value of time, then there would be no place for strikes, lock outs, work-stoppage, Bandhs, Dharnas, etc. All these activities are anti-nation and anti-development. In developed countries like Japan, time is utilised profitably and they do not waste time in any way. If the persons in Government or industry have to register a protest, they do so simply by wearing black badges or present memoranda, but not by stoppage of work.

The aim of time management is not to turn workers into machines who work without interruptions or breaks, nor is it to develop rigid routines. Rather, the aim is to organise and arrange the use of time so that time pressures and overcrowded schedules and wastages as reduced, and that staff can have adequate rest periods without lowering work output.

If forced to work under continuous pressure, people devise various means of escape like taking days off for illness or slowing down their pace and becoming inefficient. These ways of relieving pressure may be observed among staff in an average overcrowded department. It has been repeatedly shown in industry that regular breaks increase work efficiency and work output.

TIME MANAGEMENT TECHNIQUES (See Chart 35.2)

Laurenr Jaung and Susank Jones in their book, "Time Management for Executives" (Charlo Scriknero Songs, New York, 1981) have said that the happiest people are busy people. But, there are two kinds of busy persons—harried or disorganised busy and calm effective busy. You can improve your "effectiveness quotient" and become an enlightened consumer of time, if you master the basic time-management skill.

It is very difficult to enlist all the techniques of time-management as these are many and range from simple commonsense approach to sophisticated techniques of PERT/CPM, OR, Method Study, Work measurement, etc. We discuss here the techniques not discussed in other chapters.

I. Assessment of Time Use for Activities that are not Related to Work

In this technique, write down in columns all the activities that are not related to work and that might take place during the course of a working day (e.g., relaxing in staff room or canteen, personal telephone calls, going out to shop, reading a newspaper, tea or coffee breaks, arriving late, leaving early, interruptions by other staff).

Give copies of the papers to staff members who have volunteered to take part in this exercise. Ask them to record the number of minutes spent on each activity not related to work over a period of one or more days. Collect the records and add up the minutes spent on non-working activities each day by each staff member.

CHART 35.2

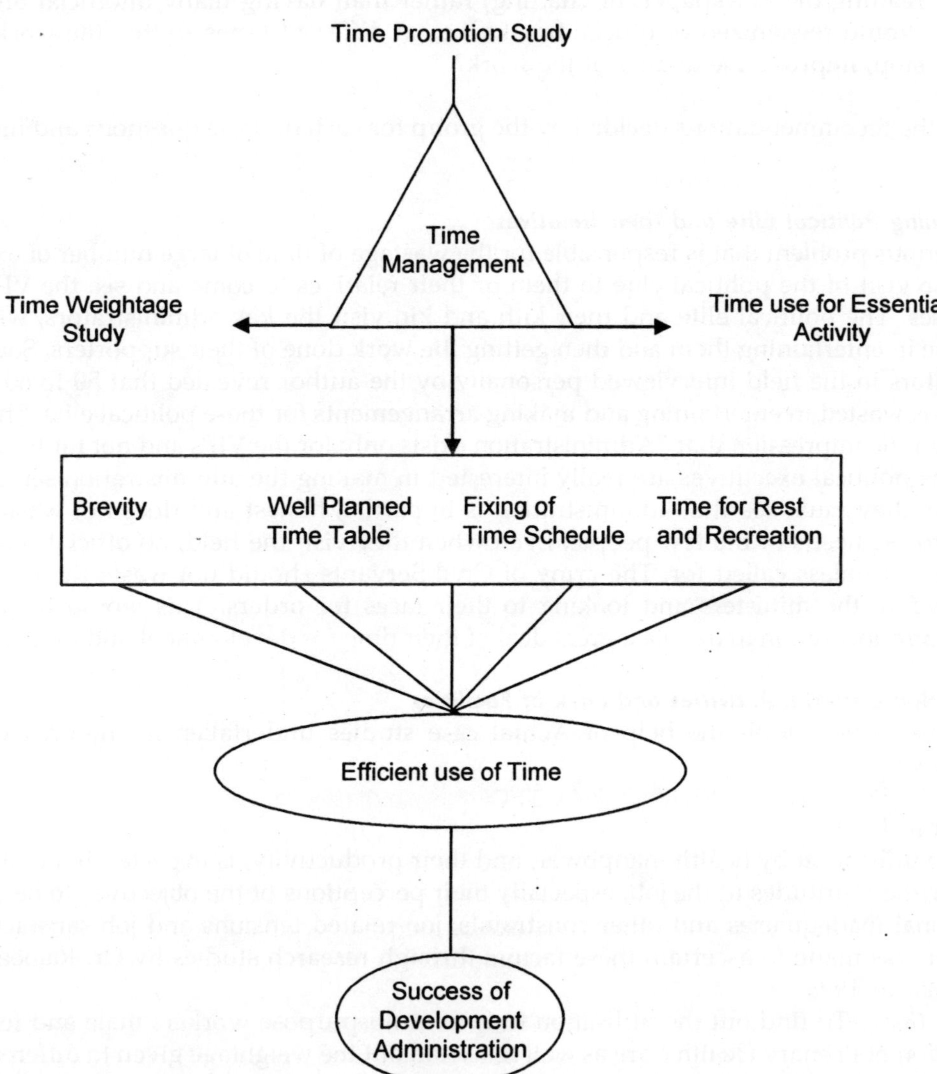

Request all staff members who have agreed to record their non-work activities to meet together to discuss the results or some team of outside experts may be deputed to collect this data. Give the group the totals from above without revealing the identity of the staff members who provided the data.

Discuss the following questions with the groups:

(a) Is the amount of time spent in non-working activities reasonable, too much, or not enough?

(b) Would it be better to have recognized time breaks (e.g., 30 minutes for tea, shopping, reading the newspaper, or chatting) rather than having many unofficial breaks?

(c) Would recognized or official breaks, i.e., at different times so that the work did not stop, improve the quality of the work?

List the recommendations decided by the group for each of these questions and implement them.

1. Entertaining Political Elite and their Relatives

A serious problem that is responsible for the wastage of time of large number of executives is either the visit of the political elite to them or their relatives to come and see the VIPs in the guest houses. The political elite and their kith and kin visit the key administrators, who waste a lot of time in entertaining them and then getting the work done of their supporters. Some of the administrators in the field interviewed personally by the author revealed that 50 to 60 per cent of the time is wasted in entertaining and making arrangements for these political elite. The people have formed the impression that "Administration exists only for the VIPs and not for the common man." If the political executives are really interested in making the administration sensitive and responsible, they must see that administration is impartial, honest and does not waste time in attending to the needs of the few people. Even when they visit the field, no official should visit them until and unless called for. The army of Civil Servants should not waste the time simply standing before the ministers and looking to their faces for orders. This would help the key officials in administration to devote a great deal of their time for development and modernization.

2. Busy in Non-essential Activities and Lack of Facilities

Let us explain with the help of Actual case studies undertaken in the area of health administration.

Case Study No. 1

Time utilization by health manpower, and their productivity, is expected to be influenced *inter alia* by their attitudes to the job, especially their perceptions of the objectives to be pursued; organisational inadequacies and other constraints; job-related tensions and job satisfaction, etc. An attempt was made to ascertain these factors through research studies by Dr. Rajneesh Goel, in Karnataka in 1998.

Objectives—To find out the utilisation time of multi-purpose workers male and female for the promotion of Primary Health Care as well as to find out the weightage given to different health activities out of the utilised time. The emphasis of the study is to locate the factors which consume time on non-productive activities and also to find the weightage given *vis-a-vis* the priority of the Primary Health Care.

Research Methodology—He prepared activity schedules both for male and female workers as per their job description and made arrangements to fill the form continuously for four days for each worker. 5 males and 5 females, one for each worker (male for male and female for female) were briefed about observation technique and filling the forms for five days for each worker. This was done in March 1998 from 9 AM to 5 PM. Continuous observation was made from the time they started the work till completion during the day except the lunch break. It is presumed that workers should devote 8 hours leaving aside 1 hour for lunch break.

The Study suggests the following pattern of time utilisation:

S. No.	Activity	Time spent by male workers	Time spent by Female worker
1.	Movement	3 hrs	3 hrs
2.	Personal Work	1 hrs	1 ½ hrs
3.	Late arrivals and early departure	1 hrs	1 ½ hrs
	Total	5 hrs	3 hrs

It is presumed that workers should devote 8 hours leaving aside 1 hour for lunch break. An analysis of above record indicates that multipurpose workers, both male and female, spend 62.5 percent of their time in unproductive activities, i.e. only 37.5 percent of the time is used productively. It may be added that out of utilised time, 50 percent is spent on record keeping to maintain their image and reputation on paper. This record is not accurate, causing complications for policy-makers and planners.

Inferences

We draw the following inferences from this study:

(a) We may provide vehicle facility to the workers to reduce time spent in visiting different places.
(b) We may reduce time spent on record keeping by systematizing records management. We may even think of providing computers to ensure the supply of right information with less time consumption with ready made software.
(c) There is a need to ensure quality supervision by PHC Staff, especially Health Assistants, to ensure punctuality.
(d) There is a need for training to make the workers responsive and dedicated.
(e) There is a need to provide residential accommodation to workers with all facilities in the village to encourage them to stay near the sub-centre and improve rapport with the people.
(f) People may be motivated to move to the sub-centre rather than waiting for the workers' visit at their door-steps, after initial meetings.
(g) Advance schedule for a month and its wide circulation can optimise time resource utilisation.

After clubbing various activities carried out during utilised time, he has exhibited them in Tables 35.1 and 35.2, the weightage given by 5 male and 5 female workers for different health activities.

An analysis of the time utilization by service components showed that most of their service time was devoted to family planning activities (percent of service time devoted ranged from 33-49%) followed by MCH services (22-27%), and immunization (5-15%).

Thus all MPWS (male and female) were found to devote most of their service time on family planning activities. This could well be attributed to the government's emphasis on target achievement in the family planning programme. Since these workers are given a set target to achieve family planning, they are forced to spend more time on this activity, and thus neglect other

TABLE 35.1

Percent of Time Utilization for Various Activities (MPW—Male)

Sl. No.	*Activity/Service*	*Percent of time utilised Health worker No.*				
1.	Malaria eradication	27.01	22.6	32.1	23.6	32.2
2.	Control of communicable diseases	2.1	11.1	12.6	11.6	12.5
3.	Environmental sanitation	1.1	4.4	1.2	3.4	2.2
4.	Immunization	2.8	6.2	4.6	6.4	3.6
5.	Family planning	41.8	31.6	31.7	32.0	31.8
6.	MCH services	3.1	4.6	0.2	.2	0.1
7.	Vital statistics collection	3.3	3.7	3.6	2.6	3.6
8.	Nutrition	5.1	7.7	2.1	4.6	2.1
9.	Primary medical care	3.3	3.3	4.8	5.4	4.8
10.	Team activities	2.1	1.8	1.4	1.2	1.4
11.	Record maintenance	7.7	3.0	5.0	7.0	5.0
12.	Work at PHC	-	-	-	-	-
13.	Interaction with community health volunteers/Dais	0.6	-	0.7	2.0	.7
	Total	100.0	100.0	100.0	100.0	100

TABLE 35.2

Percent of Time Utilization for Various Activities (MPW—Female)

Sl. No.	*Activity/Service*	*Percent of time utilised Health worker No.*				
1.	MCH	26.9	22.4	23.5	21.6	24.7
2.	Family Planning	48.5	34.8	42.3	49.3	33.2
3.	Nutrition	2.1	6.0	0.1	0.7	11.7
4.	Immunization	5.4	16.2	15.4	5.5	9.8
5.	Vital statistics collection	2.8	3.8	0.2	2.3	5.0
6.	Control of communicable diseases	5.9	6.0	6.2	7.2	6.2
7.	Primary medical care	4.6	3.7	5.0	8.3	4.3
8.	Team activity	3.6	5.8	7.3	2.5	2.8
9.	Record maintenance	—	0.8	—	2.0	2.1
10.	Preparation (for immunization)	—	0.4	—	—	—
11.	Interaction with CHV/Dais	—	—	—	0.6	0.5
12.	Cleaning	—	—	—	—	0.3
13.	Group meeting	0.2	0.1	—	—	—
	Total	100	100	100	100	100

important activities. However, the target approach has been abolished and its impact is yet to be felt.

The main purpose of the scheme was to devote more time on health education, nutrition, inter-sectoral co-ordination, people's participation, which could not be attended to. There is a need to impart training to these workers to make them realise their true role. Only such understanding on their part can change health scene of rural India, otherwise, it would prove to be another institution with liabilities. The main function of MPW is to make people participate in Primary Health Care activities and get most of the functions performed by them. Besides, they never devoted much time for Inter-Sectoral Co-ordination, an essential Component of Primary Health Care.

2. Assessment of Time Use for Activities that can be done at Lower Levels

Most of the senior persons in the organisation perform the work, which can be done at lower levels or that does not require the competence of the level where it is being done. If such work is delegated to the lower levels, the time spent by the busy people at the higher level can be saved. This would also be economical, since the salary scales are higher at upper levels. Let us understand this with the help of a Case Study from Thailand, reported in Public Health Development and Administration by Dr. K. Klinoubol (New Delhi, Deep & Deep Publications, 1989, pp. 336-44).

Acceptance of female sterilization in Thailand has increased considerably, but because of the shortage of doctors, especially in rural areas, long delays occurring before surgery are common. Women are discharged from hospital within 24 to 48 hours of delivery and although many wish to have post-partum sterilization, they often find it inconvenient to return to hospital for tubal ligation. Besides, it is very costly.

The Thai Ministry of Public Health decided to introduce the performance of post-partum tubal ligation by trained nurse-midwives, since this could alleviate the shortage of doctors and so reduce waiting times and free doctors for more skilled tasks. This reduces costs as well.

In 1979, a pilot study was conducted by the Ministry of Public Health in which five nurse-midwives with operating-room experience were trained to perform post-partum tubal ligation, by a minilaparotomy incision under local anaesthesia. The performance of the trained nurse-midwives was compared with that of doctors in a controlled, randomized clinical trial. The results suggested that trained nurse-midwives can safely perform the procedure. [1]

In the subsequent study, an expanded field trial of the nurse training programme was carried out by the Ministry of Public Health to evaluate the replicability of the training programme in provincial settings.

The results of the field Trial of the nurse-training programme are similar to those of the pilot study which further demonstrate,[2] that trained nurse-midwives with operating-room experience can safely perform post-partrum tubal ligation under local anaesthesia in provincial settings. The nurse-midwives gained both surgical experience and self-confidence in a relatively short period. The average operating time of the nurse after 12 months (15 minutes) compared favourably with that of the doctors in the previous study (12 minutes).

The acceptability of the service, as perceived by the patients, was clearly impressive. The attitude of doctors toward the use of trained nurse-midwives in their hospitals to perform tubal ligation was very positive. As a result of this study, the Ministry of Public Health was advised that an expanded programme be planned and implemented. Secondly, it was suggested that as medical procedures become accepted and routine, doctors should delegate these tasks to nursing and other personnel.[3] Delegation does not undermine the professional role; it enhances it. The more the doctor delegates, the more is the time available for those tasks he cannot delegate and the more his work becomes confined to problems that staff with less training have failed to solve. In addition, more of his time can be devoted to supervising the work he has delegated and to providing continuing education to the personnel engaged locally in activities to improve health.

But delegation is also a matter of economics. The ratio between the remuneration of the doctor and the average worker tends to be much higher in developing countries than in the more developed countries. Auxiliaries can also be trained at much lower cost than can higher grades of professional staff. Thus, it is much more important to ensure that the doctor's time is used only for tasks that require his skill and knowledge. The same is true of other highly trained health professionals—dentist, pharmacists, health inspectors, nurses, sanitary engineers and many others. There is a strong case for every highly trained professional grade to be matched by a corresponding auxiliary grade. Furthermore, as their training is shorter, auxiliary staff can be working in the field much earlier than more highly trained personnel.

To quote Allan Rosenfield:

> "I firmly believe that personnel other than physicians can and should be trained in the techniques of vasectomy, post-partum and interval tubal ligation, provision of injectable normal contraceptives and where legally and culturally acceptable, the carrying out of menstrual regulation or early first trimester abortion procedures."[4]

The author as a professor at a training Institute conducted a survey with three senior groups of civil servants and found that 40 per cent of their time is being spent on activities which can easily be done at the lower levels and thus through proper planning, we can save their time. In the University, there are generally three levels of teachers. Lecturers, Readers and Professors. Generally the nature of work performed by all of them is the same. The professors, who are supposed to build the tempo of research and guide the faculty, are busy in routine teaching as others are doing, resulting in the wastage of scarce resources. The analysis suggests the need for careful planning of work to save time and money. We may make use of the techniques like ABC Analysis, Management By Exception, etc. to plan the work at a particular level.

Time Proportion Study to give Weightage to Priority Areas

The executives should plan their work according to the priority, so that more attention can be paid to the important activities. Here the executive may analyse the activities done during the day and the time devoted on each activity. The author has carried out this exercise on many executives. The analysis of the results of such exercise suggests that the executives spend more time on activities that are less significant and spend less time on activities that are very important. It means that the executives never devote time in proportion to the intensity of the activity, resulting in many wrong decisions and affecting the performance of the organisation. For example, the Universities, Apex institutions in all areas at the National level are created to do research, which can help in policy-making and planning in different areas, but on examination, they are found to be engaged in routine activities. An opening of a department of a subject like Public Administration, Sociology, etc. in a University and a College is done with different objectives: that is why staffing at two levels is entirely different. The University Department is supposed to engage itself in Research, Consultancy, and teaching while a college department is mostly meant for teaching. A careful analysis in practices would indicate that both are engaged merely in teaching and that is why we generally hear that the Universities have become white elephant on the State exchequer. Administrative Reforms Commission examined the problem of administration and it has observed that in most cases the top administration only okays the proposal initiated at lower levels. This means that the high level administration finds no time to think of real issues meant for them like Organisational Development, Management of Change, Conflict Management, etc.

Time-Proportion Study on Meetings

In today's administration, top level executives/experts attend a number of meetings, which are not well planned and well focused, resulting in the wastage of time of executives/experts. Whenever you go to the Secretariat of any Government or Corporation, you will find that most of the key people are busy in one meeting or the other. The analysis of the agenda and outcome of the meetings would indicate that there is too much wastage of time and that is why the key officials find no time to listen to the grievances of the people and develop a climate of understanding. Let me quote here the study conducted in the context of International Administration by the author (International Administration by Dr. S.L. Goel, New Delhi, Sterling, 1977, pp. 153-54).

The technical staff of the South East Asia Regional Office of World Health Organisation, Delhi has to spend a lot of time in attending meetings of other regional agencies for liaison purpose. Besides, they have to prep'are a large number of documents to exchange information with other regional organizations. These activities have been increasing over the years, largely because the increasing number of organizations tend to complicate the process of co-ordination, This was also pointed out by the UN Secretary-General who wrote:

I detect a sense of concern in many quarters at the growth in the number of bodies and programmes which have been established primarily for co-ordination purpose or in which coordination activities play an important and increasing role, in the time and the documentation required to service them, and in the complexities and even the duplications which they involve.[5]

The meetings and the documentation service dealing with co-ordination should be reduced to a level essential for programme achievement. This can save a lot of the specialists' time which would be utilized for other fruitful activities.

It is strange that even in Universities, most of the time of the key officials is spent on meetings like Senate, Syndicate Finance Board and Plethora of Sub-Committees and it is very difficult to meet them and discuss important issues. The key officials who must find time to ensure academic excellence in the University get no time for it as they are exhausted in the meetings, dealing with matters of relatively lesser importance. It is, therefore, suggested that the time spent on these meetings may be reduced to be utilised for areas of greater significance.[6]

Concentration of Time on Solving Symptoms and not the Real Problems

It has been generally seen that most of the executives do not find time to decide a case thoroughly from all angles, but rather deal with the symptoms and thus deal with it temporarily. In this way, the issue lingers on and continues in this way for long, resulting in the wastage of time and resources not only of the management but also of the beneficiaries, as well as creating bitterness between the two. It has been seen that the cases which could be dealt with in a week's time continue for years.

An analysis of the decided cases by various courts in the country would show that the key officials in the administration initiate action against the employees on disciplinary grounds hurriedly, and without following due procedure, resulting in wastage of resources and time of the administration in attending courts. All these litigations can be avoided if the key personnel take interest and work thoroughly rather than doing it half-heartedly. Key officials, by attending to real problems, can save a lot of time in the long-run and make the administration efficient and responsible.

Well Planned Time Table for Field Visits

Many of the key personnel have to control a wide-network of offices. A part of it can be controlled through telephone, or reporting. But, there is a need of personal discussion among the headquarter and the field staff, which involves the use of time in travelling and discussion. It is suggested that field/headquarter visits must be well planned so that the discussion can be pertinent and all the issues are discussed to avoid meetings off and on. The headquarter personnel must carry with them a well prepared schedule to guide them in the field, while the field people must also come prepared with full information to clarify the vague points.

Fixing of Time Schedule to Devote Time to Work

It has been observed that in most of the offices, the time for the visitors is fixed, so that they may not be visiting throughout the day and waste the time of the personnel. At the Scheduled time, the aggrieved petitioners visit the offices. It is suggested that the Personal Assistants, before sending any person to visit the officials, must listen to him and keep his file ready, so that action can be taken immediately and the person concerned need not visit again and again. A brief training to staff and especially the Personal Assistants can help in quick disposal of public cases and thus avoid their recurrent visits.

Providing Regular Times for Rest and Recreation to Avoid Fatigue

Executives are human beings and thus cannot work beyond their capacity. It is, therefore, suggested that they may observe regular rest periods to feel fresh. However, these rest periods may not be done at will, but must be already notified to avoid difficulty to the staff and the people, until and unless there are compelling reasons for it.

Brevity

Besides, the executives must learn to be brief and to the point and discourage relatives/ friends to visit them in offices. Telephonic discussions must also be brief.

CONCLUSION

Time management would not only be beneficial to the executives but would also provide more opportunities to the people to share their ideas and views with the administration and thus we would be able to lay the solid foundation for People's Participation, Development and Modernisation.

Prabhat Kumar in his Article, "A Responsive and Effective Government" rightly suggests that "we forget that time is our most valuable resource, the only one that is absolutely nonrenewable. No one has the right to waste it, every one should control his own time. It can be given but never should be taken away by another. Unfortunately, lateness is the rule in Government and waiting is a national past time."

The development and modernization of developing countries can be accelerated by an efficient time management. It has been observed that Personnel in Administration are not utilising their time for the assigned job. They are wasting a lot of time in unnecessary and trivial activities which are non-productive. We must manage our time purposefully to build Modern India, otherwise we would remain an under-developed country as time and tide waits for none.

The management requires a high degree of self-discipline. The habit of entertaining casual visitors during office hours must be shunned ruthlessly. Designate a prime time, may be an hour or so, during the working hours, which is strictly your own time and distractions should never be permitted to interfere. It is the man who should manage time and not the other way round.

Development administration must find out ways and means which can conserve time and accelerate the process of development which can promote national development and modernization. We can learn the lesson from developed countries where development activities are planned in advance with time schedule and completed within that time schedule. Time constraint in all development activities is managed in such a way that no extraneous reasons can delay the completion of any development activity. Take the case of Japan. The secret of development of Japan in a short period of time is the use of time in the best possible way.

Notes and References

1. N. Dusitsin, *et. al.*, "Post-partum-tuballigation by nurse-midwives and doctors in Thailand," The Lancet 1, No. 8169, 22 March, 1980, pp. 638-39.
2. N. Dusitsin, *et. al.*, cited in note 2.
3. WHO: Poverty Development and Health Policy, PHP 69, Geneva, 1978, p. 103.
4. Allan Rosenfield, The Ethics of Supervising Family Planning in Developing Nations, Hasting Centre Report, February 1977, pp. 25-29.
5. 23rd Annual Report of the Secretary-General to the Central Assembly (1968), paras 80 and 82.
6. Prabhat Kumar, "A Responsive and Effective Government", in *Management in Government*, January-March, 2000, p. 3.

CHAPTER

36

Employees Health and Development Administration

Development administration is a challenging task which requires balance of mind to take rational decisions for the development of the country. Executives involved in development administration get frustrated which lead to stress for a number of reasons like—

(a) Lack of Co-operation from the colleagues
(b) Shortage of resources
(c) Resistance to change
(d) Lack of motivation
(e) Absence of proper organisational climate

Executive under stress cannot handle development tasks causing delays, higher costs and lower output. What can be done to make developmental tasks successful? What can be done to complete developmental tasks complete in time? How can the executives can be kept full of energy and enthusiasm? (See Chart 36.1)

The answer to all these questions is to make executive stress free. In this chapter we would discuss that until and unless, employees especially executives are not healthy, they cannot concentrate on development activity. It means that until and unless employees are healthy—Physically, mentally, socially and spiritually, they cannot execute development programmes sincerely, earnestly and timely. Therefore, organizations engaged in development activities; can deliver results provided its employees are healthy. It has been nicely said in the proverb "Health is Wealth"

Good health can promote high labour morale and productivity, i.e., a healthy worker can work full-time and has a greater productivity potential. According to Benjamin, in countries "where health conditions are worst, relatively simple and low cost health programmes can produce dramatic lessening of the disability of the labour force."[1]

CHART 36.1

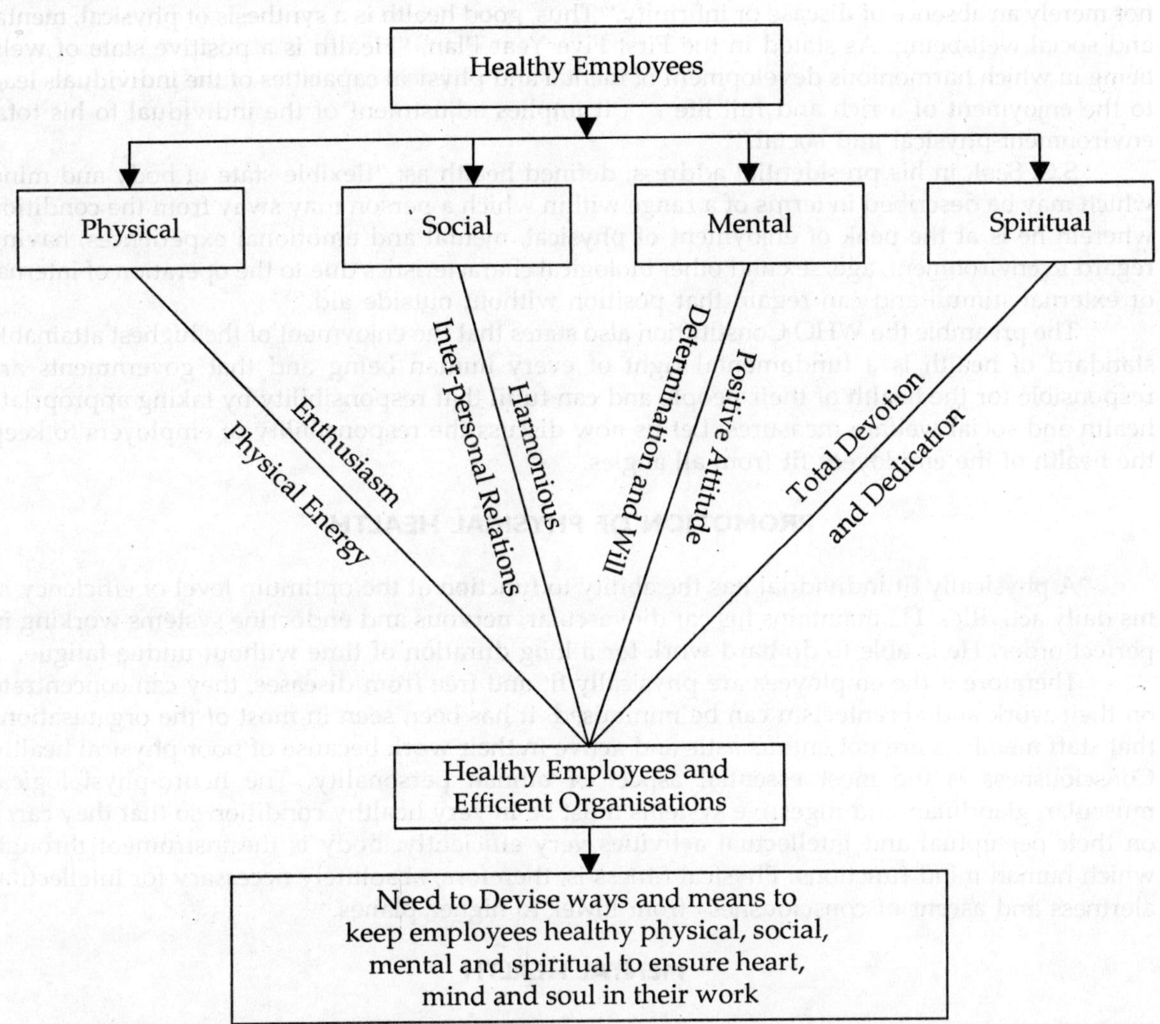

Better health is generally associated with better capability and leadership. In a study by ILO on qualitative difference in the labour force, health was found to be the factor most clearly related to difference in economic growth.[6] According to Myrdal: "The required personal qualities are certainly multiple and probably have a synergistic action. However, there can be no doubt that health plays an essential part."[2]

Better health induces positive attitudes, conducive to economic growth and modernization. The individuals become better citizens as they hope for future betterment and work hard to make the future more pleasant and enjoyable. Improved health may drive people to increase productivity and reduce family size.[3] The people with good health are generally enthusiastic and try to achieve higher and higher goals in life.

Health is viewed differently by different people all over the world. The World Health Organisation defined health as "a state of complete physical, mental, and social well-being and not merely an absence of disease or infirmity." Thus, good health is a synthesis of physical, mental and social well-being. As stated in the First Five Year Plan, "Health is a positive state of well-being in which harmonious development of mental and physical capacities of the individuals lead to the enjoyment of a rich and full life . . . It implies adjustment of the individual to his total environment-physical and social."[4]

S.C. Seal, in his presidential address, defined health as: "flexible state of body and mind which may be described in terms of a range within which a person may sway from the condition wherein he is at the peak of enjoyment of physical, mental and emotional experiences, having regard to environment, age, sex and other biological characteristics due to the operation of internal or external stimuli and can regain that position without outside aid."[5]

The preamble the WHO Constitution also states that the enjoyment of the highest attainable standard of health is a fundamental right of every human being and that governments are responsible for the health of their people and can fulfil that responsibility by taking appropriate health and social welfare measures. Let us now discuss the responsibility of employers to keep the health of the employees fit from all angles.

PROMOTION OF PHYSICAL HEALTH

A physically fit individual has the ability to function at the optimum level of efficiency in his daily activities. He maintains his car diovascular, nervous and endocrine systems working in perfect order. He is able to do hard work for a long duration of time without undue fatigue.

Therefore if the employees are physically fit and free from diseases, they can concentrate on their work and absenteeism can be minimised. It has been seen in most of the organisations that staff members are not enthusiastic and active in their work because of poor physical health. Consciousness is the most essential aspect of human personality. The neuro-physiological muscular, glandular, and digestive systems must be in very healthy condition so that they carry on their perceptual and intellectual activities very efficiently. Body is the instrument through which human mind functions. Physical fitness is, therefore, absolutely necessary for intellectual alertness and ascent of consciousness from lower to higher planes.

MENTAL HEALTH

There is very close relationship between mental equanimity, peace and happiness of an individual and his physical health and efficiency. A mentally tense, anxious and sick person has a tendency to develop various symptoms of organic disorders. Thus, other conditions remaining equal a normally serene and cheerful person may be expected to have various pathological symptoms in his body.[6]

Consciousness shrinks in a mentally abnormal person, and his shrunken consciousness finds expression through his pathological organic disorders. The consciousness of a diseased person has a trend towards continuous contraction. The domain of consciousness of a mentally and organically sick person becomes narrow, clouded and depressed. The ancient Indian seers used the conception of 'mental equanimity' instead of the concept of 'mental health'. Sri Aurobindo used the concept of mental serenity in the same sense as the concept of 'mental equanimity' of ancient Indian seers. The concept of 'mental equanimity' is more satisfactory than the concept of mental health because the former alone can produce spiritual development in an individual.[7]

Mind is the most powerful part of the human system. It is a Super Computer. Staff members in the organisation don't realise its potential or devise ways and means to harness this most important source. Organisations can achieve excellence provided they know the secret of tapping human mind. We generally notice that most of the employees are not mentally positive as one or the other problem concerning their employment continuously bogs them down. Many of them become mental wretches and a liability on the organisation. The Organisations instead of solving their problems, cause further deterioration. 25 percent of employees in even, organisation are a liability and the other 75 percent are not contributing as per their potential. Employers should try to create positive mental attitudes among the employees. Positive mental attitude is a state of mind that reflects the strength of employee's belief in what they do. It generates inner and voluntary emotions which enhances motivation, resulting in positive thoughts. Positive thinking is the key to development and is result-oriented.

Ethical behaviour in the public service is considered as a blend of moral qualities and mental attitudes. The requisite moral qualities include not only the willingness to serve the public but also the willingness to behave competently, efficiently, honestly, responsibly, objectively, fairly, and accountably. Mental attitudes include awareness of moral dilemmas inherent in policies and conflicting claims on the substantive and procedural aspects of policy, an empathy for divergent views held not only by some members of the public but also by professional colleagues, and a sensitivity to paradoxes of rules that may lead to frustrating and unkind actions. Thus, an appropriate blend of moral qualities and mental attitudes become an essential ingredient for moral government and administration. Such a mixture strengthens the basis of legitimate and effective government which is founded on public trust and confidence.

We get a moral government by creating those conditions within which a moral government can operate. This is done by making it possible for officials to acquire the necessary traits and by practicing the same. An exemplary public servant, is not simply the one who obeys and behaves within the confines of law but is also one who strives for a moral government. Such is the duty of those who wish to be involved in the difficult and complex world of government. This is the essence and basis of a moral State.[8]

Public life is in a desperate state today, with vice-regal regalia dominating it with its fierce ferocity and crushing criminality, sounding the death-knell of ethics, morality, and value-system. There is a dire need to save it. Public men, at whatever station of life they function—must be 'men' for the public; leaders must lead; and, most importantly, politicians must stop 'politicking'. Public opinion—which is often branded as meaning neither public nor opinion—must be built up against acceptance and tolerance of unethical behaviour and action by anybody, howsoever high and mighty he may be. Crisis of confidence—which admittedly is a function of culture—must be restored in public life; otherwise, the ancient civilisation that we boast of, will be no more; there will remain no public, no life, worth living, without ethics.[9]

The ancient Indian philosophers laid stress on mental equanimity for the general well-being of individuals. The mind of an ordinary person is usually very restless. Myriads of desires produce upheavals in the mind of an individual. Over and above this, the mind of an ordinary person is afflicted by several tensions.

The ancient Indian philosophers maintained that if the mind of an individual usually remains in a disturbed state, he is very likely to develop pathological symptoms. An individual with pathological mental symptoms quite often develop certain pathological organic symptoms because there is very close relationship between the body and the mind of an individual. The mind of an individual becomes free from anxiety and miseries, if there is peace in his mind.[10]

Let us mention the methods to maintain the mental health of the employees.

1. Ensuring all Facilities to Employees in Time, to Avoid Tensions and Diversion of Mind

Most of the employees in an organisation waste about 25 percent to 50 percent of their time in getting their due benefits, e.g. arrears of salary, leave salary, duty leave, sanction for various allowances, due to the unsympathetic attitude of establishment sections/employers. Such situations create frustration, indolence and indifference, leading to lack of interest and enthusiasm. Thus, there should be a specialised cell responsible for timely disposal of cases. The progress should be regularly reviewed by the head of department. These are simple acts but can promote greater efficiency, if acted upon.

2. Prompt Decision-making Concerning the Cases of the Employees

Many differences crop up between administration and employees on account of issues arising out of their daily work. For example, a wrong promotion can cause mental tension and the employee loose all interest in his work. In such situations, employees approach the court of law with vengeance. They give up their loyalty to the organisation and even most efficient employees can become dead wood or hardliners. Their minds become deranged and they start behaving negatively. It is therefore, suggested that the administration should be prompt and judicious so that employees are relieved of their mental agony. Even if the decision does not favour them, still they would feel satisfied with timely and fair decision.

3. Ensuring Transparency in Administration to Develop Confidence and Commitment among Employees

Personnel in administration at top level are secretive and some times use their discretion wrongfully to oblige those who are otherwise ineligible. Such instances demoralise those who work hard with all sincerity. For example, a Vice-Chancellor appointed 23 persons during last days of his tenure, causing heart burn and jealousy down the line. In the absence of explicit criteria and indicators, there is lack of transparency in operations. Genuine efforts to make the system transparent would develop commitment among employees and they would work to their full mental capabilities and capacities.

4. Encouraging Honest and Hardworking Employees to Create Mental Happiness

Most of the persons who achieve excellence and self-actualization are ignored or not given enough recognition. They develop a negative attitude as they feel that there is no purpose in what they're doing. As a result, they slip into the category of mediocres and below averages. It is thus the duty of the employers to encourage honest and hardworking employees through various means, e.g. sending a letter of appreciation, getting the news published in the paper, getting the item noted in the governing body and so on. This would accelerate the development of the organisation and may stimulate even the dead woods.[15] Psychologists have proved the motivational value of non-monetary factors, as mentioned above. Such motivation to self-actualise would lead to mental happiness.

Lawyers, Doctors, Company Secretaries, chartered Accountants, Engineers and Scientists, not to speak of the talented bureaucrats, are all slowly selling their souls for a mess of pottage. Even the leaders in the professions have let us down.[11]

In such other areas of governance, as professional services, like teaching, medical, legal accountancy and engineering, ethics is perhaps the ultimate principle which can keep them on the right track. No amount of laws and rules, and threats of punishment can proverbially bring the horse to water but cannot force it to drink. Unless the experts and professionals are guided by a sense of accountability and ethics, it is almost impossible to receive good service from these people. As Harold Laski pointed out, political-legal rights must have a moral basis. Men must learn to subordinate their self-interest to the common welfare. This is the only definition of morality.[12] As Swami Vivekananda said: "That which is selfish is immoral, and that which is unselfish is moral." Unless this kind of moral basis of government could be created, it would be impossible to build up a democratic, social-welfare state.

5. Locating Shirkers and Providing Counselling to them

There are many employees who lose interest in work and become a liability. Their existence dampens the enthusiasm of good workers. Their lethargy becomes contagious and we discover in the long-run that indiscipline spreads, causing short fall in output and poor quality of services. The employers should follow the proverb "Nip the Evil in the Bud." The employers should not ignore them but should try to sublimate their mental energies in a purposeful direction. This may require counselling in the initial stages. However, if it does not work, such employees may be dealt with sternly by conducting disciplinary proceedings and awarding minor/major penalties. In this way, the mental health of the organisation would be protected.

6. Inculcation of Ethical Values

The ethical degradation and moral decline within the bureaucracy in Bangladesh is almost similar, if not worse, to that in other developing countries: They don't believe that they are serving anyone else but themselves and exploit their positions for personal gain. They generally arrive at work late and leave early. They take extra long lunch recesses. They steal public property. They accept bribes for the performance of duties that are contractually part of their responsibilities. When they do work they work very slowly. They stymie the public by losing the files: through excessive review of the issue at hand or by simply pretending that they have not heard of the matter before. For all of this, they acknowledge now wrong doing, for they do not believe that what they are doing is wrong.[13]

This situation is rampant in third World countries and calls for defining morality in governance. Morality signifies pursuit of ethical conduct and performance of duties assigned in such a manner that the declared purpose is realised. In the Greek tradition, it implied the development of the latent capabilities of an individual for the full flowering of his/her personality to deliver public good. To this end, there was rigorous training and preparation for the holders of public office so that the aims of public office were served. Dharma, in the Indian tradition, commands morality in terms of righteous conduct. As propagated by Emperor Ashok, it further implied inculcation and practice of virtue in the performance of assigned duties. To an extent, the normative morality would subjugate personal interests to community interests and particular aims to general aims of the society. Mahatma Gandhi has raised Dharma to a higher pedestal, signifying a quality through which we know "our duty in human life and our relation with other selves." Thus, ethics in public life is important to understand our place in society and the duties we owe to the society by virtue of what society gives us. Employees should be given regular inputs in different forms in order to inculcate ethical values in work situation.[14]

7. Stimulating Leadership to Create Qualities of Head and Heart among Employees and Removing Mental Tensions/Fears

Employees look for standards from the top. As is the king, so are the subjects. Leaders should possess mental agility which they can percolate among employees. Thus, the organisation should be careful in selecting their top personnel as they are rare birds.

We must remember that it is the top men in each department who set the tone of the administration. It is they who set the example for those under them to emulate. When the acts of those at the top become tainted, when their reputation becomes shady, they will not be able to enforce high standards of integrity in those below them. It is, therefore, imperative that men at the top should personify the highest standards of personal integrity, probity and rectitude. As Sir Ivor Jennings observed, the most elementary qualification demanded of a minister is honesty and incorruptibility. It is, in addition, necessary not only that he should possess this qualification but also that he should appear to possess it.

Dr. Narendra N. Wig, WHO consultant in his article "Mental Health and Work" in *The Tribune*, dated Sept. 27, 2000 has made the following observations:

> "It is important that the place of work should be made conducive to mental health. Unfortunately, very little attention is being paid to this aspect in our offices and factories. In view of the rising cost of mental illness because of stress at work, it is high time the senior management in offices and industry paid attention to this aspect. The following are some of the suggestions for de-stressing the modern workplace:
>
> 1. Modify the pressure placed on the working people by creating a healthy environment and sound management policies and practices.
> 2. Keep the mental health of the workers as an integral part of the business agenda and regularly briefing the senior management about it.
> 3. Improve interpersonal communication at all levels.
> 4. Provide recreational facilities for workers.
> 5. Arrange regular sessions to teach workers how to reduce stress by techniques like yoga, relaxation exercises, etc.
> 6. Organise professional help by counsellors and such other persons for the vulnerable members of the staff at an early stage."[15]

SOCIAL HEALTH

Another dimension of health is social health, i.e. how an individual can have healthy relations with persons with whom he comes in contact. We find that there are many persons who sit in isolation and they get socially marginalised. Such persons get sick as socialising with others is essential aspect of human nature. Aristotle has rightly spelt out that man is a social animal. In an organisation, the colleagues with whom one is working should be friendly and one could share with them about his personal and official problems. One should have good relationships with superiors and subordinates. Social health is a buffer stock to avoid physical and mental breakdowns. Let us examine as to what the employers can do to provide a decent social environment and social health to his employees. I.M. Somi in his article, "Spreading Sunshine with a Smile" in *The Tribune*, dated August 20, 2000 rightly exhorts to set out with the intention of cheering others when they are depressed, and lifting their depression with a witty remark. It is the sharing of a gift that gives its value. This is equally true to spreading sunshine in other's life. Make a daily reflection and you will find your attitude gradually changing in practice. The benefit, in health and happiness, that such a change of attitude can bring is well worth the effort required to achieve it.

SPIRITUAL HEALTH

In sum, individuals can have perfect health only when they are able to ascend from the lower to the higher states of consciousness, and remain perfectly poised in the higher plane of consciousness for a considerable duration of time. Perfect health is a comprehensive concept which includes mental equanimity, physical fitness and spiritual development of an individual.

The most crucial problem with which mankind is faced at present is the problem of health in its comprehensive sense. Health in its comprehensive sense means perfect physical fitness, mental serenity and vivid comprehension of the higher planes of consciousness in an individual. Healing means restoration of an individual to his normal state of physical efficiency, mental equanimity and clear comprehension of the higher planes of consciousness.

Health has its base in spiritual powers. Organisation can arrange different lectures on spirituality which can keep the health of the employees in good shape as well move them to positive actions. J.L. Gupta in his article, "Power of Prayer" in *The Daily Tribune*, dated August 31, 2000 stated that, "Today, we care for what we eat, but not for what is eating us. We worry about what we wear, not what is wearing us out. We build houses and furnish them at considerable cost to make them comfortable. Then we look for the fastest cars to get away from our homes. We get every place air-conditioned so that we do not sweat-at work or on the road of life. Then we spend more—we buy a treadmill or join a gym, even to go to a health club—all to be able to sweat out."

Such indeed is the dichotomy in our lifestyle. In the new millennium we are moving fast, at a rather rapid pace, but we are not aware of the direction. We are rudderless. No wonder, we have problems—of body and mind. All tension and lot of stress. There is not a moment of peace and rest. No time to stand and stare. Resultantly, the medicos claim a substantial share of our earnings regularly.

Shirish Joshi rightly stresses the need of spiritual health. To quote that the notion that religious faith can promote physical well-being is now new. Most of us have heard of cases in which someone, seemingly by sheer faith and will, has miraculously recovered from a terminal illness or survived far longer than doctors thought possible. What is new is that such rewards of religion are becoming the subject of study by scientists.[16]

In the final analysis, the physical, social, mental and spiritual balance is the most desirable for holistic health. Unless a person is physically fit and active; he cannot perform at his best level. On the other hand, it is the mind which accounts for 80 percent of physical and social problems. These are called psychosomatic diseases. Lastly, it is the spirit which ultimately directs the mind and through it to the body. The employers should devise ways and means to ensure synergy of the physical, social, mental and spiritual capabilities, which would release the infinite potential powers of the employees and generate efficiency and happiness in the organisation.

Efficiency is the freedom in us to step up willfully our own inherent abilities and capacities, which we exhibit in the fields of our actions. The efficient and the inefficient ones are ever there among those who strive in the endless developments of human activities. And nowhere is the efficiency measured by the quantity of work done, nor it is estimated by the texture and quality of the work turned out. In fact, efficiency of a man is found expressed in the dynamism of his actions, in his cheerfulness at his work. In the glow of the very work turned out, we glimpse the efficiency of the workers. It is the shine, the aura, the secret sparkle, in the work done that we detect the efficiency of the worker. He who has this secret power in him, to him is all success and achievement. In fact, an efficient man's work really endures and continues yielding a growing dividend of joy and cheer to himself, and brings an unrolling of light, grace and blessings to the society."[17]

Notes and References

1. B. Benjamin, "Social and Economic Factors Affecting Mortality" in Confluence: Surveys of Research in the Social Services, Vol. V, (Hague, Mauton and Co.), pp. 1-5.
2. G. Myrdal, Asian Drama—An Inquiry into the Poverty of Nations, New York, Pantheon, 1968.
3. M. Perlman, "On Health, Population Change, and Economic Development", in M. Perlman and other (eds.), Spatial, Regional and Population Economics, Essays in Honour of Edgar M. Hoover (New York and Breach, 1972), pp. 293-310.
4. Government of India, First Five Year Plan, p. 488.
5. S.C. Seal, (1963), Presidential Address, 50th Science Congress, Delhi.
6. WHO, Public Health Papers, No. 49, 1973, p. 9.
7. A.K. Sinha, Science and Tantra Yoga, 1993, p. 91
8. O.P. Dwivedi, Reflections on Moral Government and Public Service as a Vocation, in *IJPA*, July to Sept., 1995, p. 297.
9. O.P. Dwivedi, "Conclusion: A Comparative Analysis of Ethics, Public and the Public Service", James S. Bowman and F.A. Elliston (eds.), Ethics, Government and Public Policy, New York, Greenwood Press, 1988, p. 318.
10. Bata K. Dey, Ethics Maladies and Remedies, in *IJPA*, July-Sept., 1995, p. 461.
11. A.K. Sinha, *op. cit.*, pp. 70-71.
12. Justice V.R. Krishna Iyer, Ethical Entropy in Public Life, in *IJPA*, July-Sept. 1995, p. 350.
13. Ashok Mukhopadhyay, Ethics in Governance, in *IJPA*, July-Sept., 1995, p. 399.
14. Mohammad Mohabat Khan, Politics of Administrative Reform, the Case of Bangladesh, New Delhi, Ashish, 1999.
15 Kamla Prasad, Pursuit of Public Government in *IJPA*, July-Sept., 1995, p. 430.
16. *The Sunday Tribune*, Shirish Joshi, August 19, 2000.
17. Chinmaya International Foundation, Sanskrit Research and Modern Challenges, ADI, Sankara Nilayam, Veliyanadu, Ernakulam, April 1997, p. 143.

CHAPTER

37

Gender Budgeting for Women Empowerment

INTRODUCTION

Development administration in order to be effective must utilize the potential of women power for development. Development Administration on the one hand promotes women development and empowerment and on the other hand would promote development of the country through women power. Hence, development administration must address itself to gender, human development and gender budgeting to promote inclusive development for women so that they can lead a dignified life and contribute to the society.

There is a need to examine, scientifically, objectively and in a systematic manner the issues and problems concerning women leading to concrete suggestions to provide them the benefits of development to make this universe vibrant with peace and bliss.

Gender equality is an issue of primary importance to the welfare and progress of all nations. It is fundamental to achieving people-centered development. What humanity needs is a world that is free, fair and equal; a world that will have no discrimination, violence, or exploitation, a world where opportunity and prosperity are shared by all. So, why is violence against women and discrimination so widespread all over the world? It is because discrimination begins in the minds of people, where gender-bias becomes a habit in thought and action. These have over centuries developed deep-rooted cultural traditions which regard women as subservient, the girl-child as a liability, and discrimination as normal. The root of all prejudice is ignorance. Education, greater awareness, public policy and the media can play an important role in eradicating such prejudices. Recent work has brought out very clearly that women's literacy and educated participation of women in decisions within and outside family strongly influence the relative respect and regard for women's well-being.

* See Appendices 37.1, 37.2, 37.3 and 37.4.

CHART 37.1

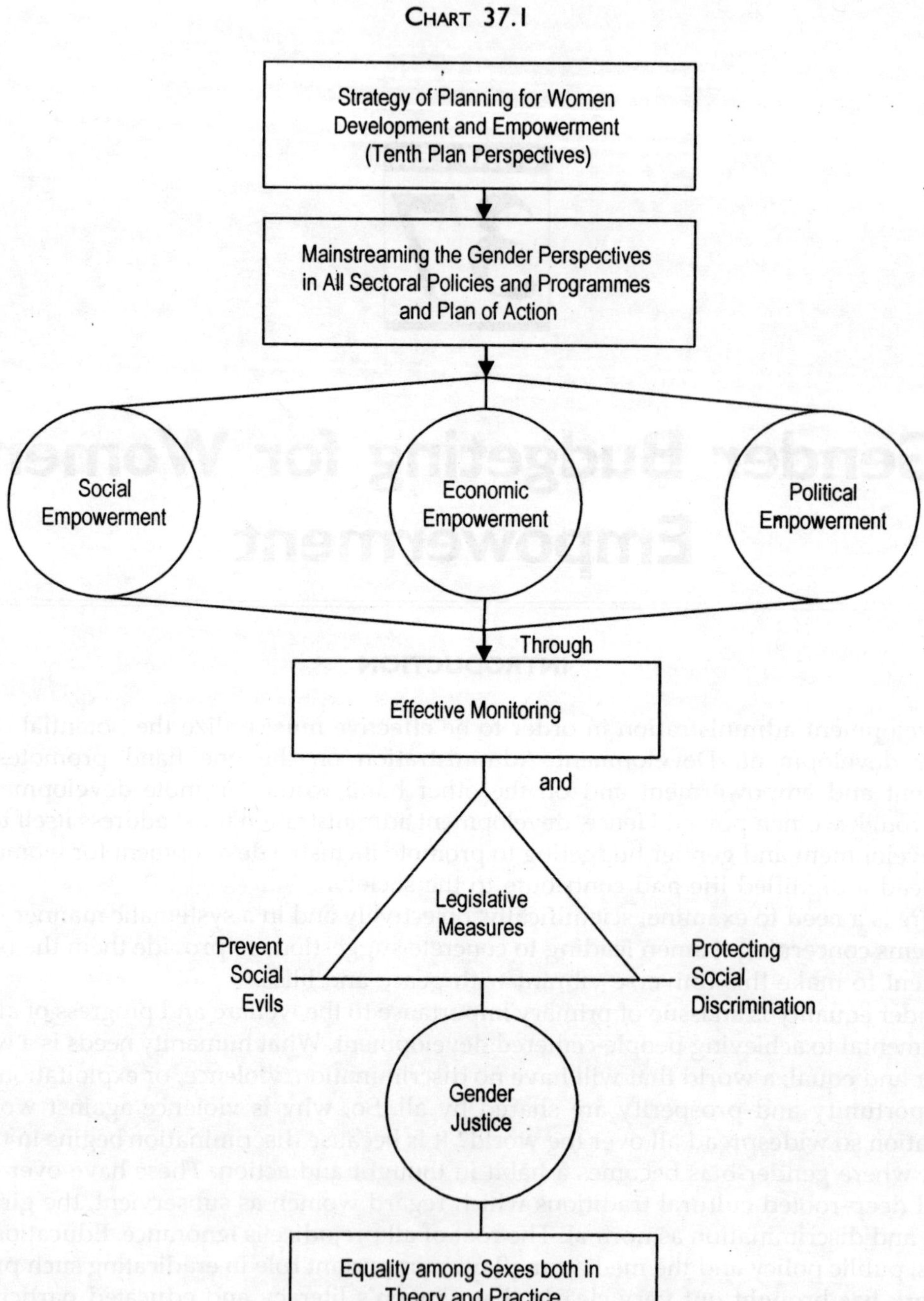

I. Gender Mainstreaming

Mainstreaming a gender perspective into all areas of societal development was established as a global strategy for promoting gender equality in the Platform for Action. Mainstreaming involves ensuring that attention to gender equality is a central part of all interventions—analyses, policy development, advocacy, legislation, research and the planning, implementation, monitoring and evaluation of projects and programmes.

The strategy of mainstreaming was further defined in Economic and Social Council agreed conclusions 1997/2 of 18 July 1997 (sect. LA.): "It is a strategy for making women's as well as men's concerns and experiences in integral dimension of the design, implementation, monitoring and evaluation of policies and programmes in all political, economic and societal spheres so that women and men benefit equally and inequality is not perpetuated. The ultimate goal is to achieve gender equality.

2. Life-Cycle Approach

The life-cycle approach considers life as a continuum embodying phases within the life course and their distinct realities and needs. The life-cycle approach is used in the Platform for Action to capture the prevalence and incidence of discriminatory practices that affect women at different stages of life, and it has been widely applied in the areas of health and education.

The life-cycle approach provides a powerful analytical tool for capturing: (a) the common conditions that surround women's lives at a specific stage of life and, in this regard, the girl-child has been included in the Platform for Action among the critical areas of concern requiring special attention; (b) the transformations in the conditions and attributes of various stages of life as a result of changes in values, life-styles, technology and so forth; for example, technological advances in bioengineering have had great impact on women's fertility patterns and medical advances have reversed adverse health conditions in all age groups and have increased life expectancy across the globe; and (c) emerging new areas associated with specific life stage that may have been previously neglected or overlooked.

3. Partnership between Women and Men

The attention to men in the Platform for Action is an indication of the important shift from an exclusive focus on women to a gender approach that focuses on both women and men and the relationships between them. A gender perspective is consistently utilized to compare the position and situation of women and men and the differences and disparities between them. The relationships between women and men are given specific attention, particularly in relation to sexuality and reproduction. Efforts to reduce negative gender stereotyping of women and men are encouraged and the Platform for Action calls for promotion of public debate on the new roles of women and men.

The need to ensure equal rights and opportunities for both women and men is a key focus in the Platform for Action. Particular emphasis is given to the sharing of family responsibilities by men. The Platform for Action calls on Governments to "...promote the equal sharing of responsibilities for the family by men and women, including through appropriate legislation, incentives and/or encouragement ..." (PfA, para 179)

The development of goals to eradicate poverty is closely connected with the advancement of women and gender equality. Low levels of education, high levels of illiteracy, and the poor health and nutritional status that prevail among women, as well as their limited access to productive resources and remunerative employment, negatively affect the well-being of a large number of women throughout the world, and impede efforts to eradicate poverty. The Platform for Action therefore recommends that poverty eradication strategies should be comprehensive and should address the multi-dimensional nature of poverty which includes both income poverty and such factors as autonomy, dignity and lack of violence.

In this regard, the following objectives are of particular importance for future actions and initiatives: To promote and strengthen the practical implementation of mainstreaming a gender perspective into all developmental policies and programmes; to enhance the development of gender analysis tools and methodologies; to expand gender training and this in its turn will require an improvement in the collection of sex-disaggregated data and national accounting that should include unremunerated labour;

To create a favourable political and macro-economic environment, including efforts to relieve foreign debt and to mobile human and financial resources;

To promote women's political and economic empowerment and participation in decision-making. It is important to address women's deprivation in basic capabilities such as education and health as well as in their entitlements such as access to capital and productive resources, including access and ownership of land; and

To set the concrete national, regional and international targets for the eradication of poverty among women and establish monitoring procedures and mechanisms.

Special efforts were to be made during the Millennium, UN Assembly in September 2000 has endorsed a gender-sensitive global poverty eradication strategies.

4. Human Development and Gender Dimensions

As has happened with many other concepts, 'empowerment' has been so overused and misused that it has lost its core meaning. One often finds a programme being described as a programme for women's empowerment without any clarity as to how it will actually change existing power relations. Rescuing the concept of empowerment so that it can have more analytical content for policies requires us to examine whether there has, in actual fact, been a change in mindsets, i.e. a paradigm shift away from the old 'welfare' approach and whether there has been a corresponding change in policies and institutions supported by a key ingredient of systemic change, namely investment or is it 'business as usual', with some tinkering of some of these issues.

5. Human development: Gender Dimensions and Differentials

For any patriarchal society to move towards greater gender equality, as part of a process of human development, requires change at many levels—in values and norms, in structures and institutions, and in behaviour and practices. This can happen if women are empowered in economic, political and socio-cultural terms. They need more access to resources, greater political voice and social transformations that lead to their exercising great agency and autonomy in the decisions that affect their own lives and society in general. However, focusing on women alone cannot make such changes happen. Such transformations in consciousness take time and require open public debate and discussion, and efforts through the educational system, and through communications and the media. Men must change their entrenched patriarchal discourse in favour of one that is inclusive and gender-friendly.

The role of the state lies in preventing harm and protecting girls and women on the one hand, and promoting women's empowerment, gender equality and male transformation on the other. In order to play this role effectively, the state must do at least four things: support changes in social norms and practices; promote key legal/political changes; create strong institutions at multiple levels from the village to the highest levels; and provide resources and make investments. How the state brings about changes in gender relations, and with what strategic vision during a period of significant socio-economic change brought on by economic liberalisation, will provide the touchstone for whether any real movement towards gender equality will occur in the coming decade.

Females are generally ignored in their efforts of development consciously and unconsciously. This has affected the health, education, employment and overall growth of female. Females do more work but get lesser share in government spending both at the Union and State levels. Ignoring women mean mortgaging the future as the children would be affected physically, psychologically and materially. In this way future becomes grim. These facts compelled to think seriously about allocating more resources for females through gender budgeting, i.e. allocating maximum resources for women development for the bright future of country. The idea took a concrete shape during Tenth Plan.

The Late Dr. Mahbub ul Haq, who launched the UNDPs Human Development Reports, used to say that "If development is not engendered it would be endangered."

Raising the status of women is not just a right issue, but also a strategic one. Economic liberalization creates new opportunities. Unless women, who constitute—half the population, are able to gain from such opportunities, development will continue to be lopsided. The extent of empowerment of woman is determined largely by three factors—her economic, social and political identity. These factors are intertwined and interlinked with many cross cutting linkages which imply that if efforts in even one dimension remain absent or weak, .outcomes and momentum generated by the other components cannot be sustained as they will not be able to weather any changes or upheavals. It is only when all three factors are simultaneously addressed and made compatible with each other, can the woman be truly empowered. Therefore for holistic empowerment of women, social, economic and political aspects impacting their lives must converge effectively.[1]

Difference between Gender and Sex

Gender is the culturally and socially constructed roles, responsibilities, privileges, relations and expectations of women and men, boys and girls and changes with time and from place to place. Sex refers to biological differences between the male and female of the species. It remains unchanged.[2]

Dimensions of Gender Budgeting: Empowerment which has to be

- Holistic (Political, Social and Economic)
- Universal (equal opportunity and level playing field)
- Participative and Inclusive

"Gender" is used to describe those characteristics of men and women which are socially constructed and therefore can change, in contrast to those that are biologically determined and therefore cannot change. Gender is thus a dynamic concept which looks at the social divisions and the interrelations between men and women.

A "gender approach to health" is based on an analysis of how differences and disparities between women and men determine their differential exposure to risk, their access to technology and health care, their rights and responsibilities, and their control over their own lives.

Why Gender Budgeting?

- Women represent 48 percent of the total population in the country.
- They face disparities in access to control over services and resources.

- Bulk of Public Expenditure and policy concerns are in "gender neutral" sectors—Powers, Defence, Petroleum, Transport, etc.
- Implications on women in the above sectors are not recognized or identified.
- Gender budgeting statement in Union Budget, 2007-08 indicates Rs. 31,178 crores covering 33 demand of grants of 27 Ministries which is only 4.9% of the total Public Sector Outlay.[3]

Definition of Gender Budgeting

- Gender Budgeting is a process that entails incorporating a gender perspective at various stages—planning/policy/programme formulation, assessment of needs of target groups, allocation of resources, implementation, impact assessment, reprioritization of resources.
- Gender Responsive Budget and Gender Mainstreaming are outcomes of Gender budgeting.

What is a Gender Budgeting—A Definition

Gender Budgeting is understood as a dissection of the Government budget to establish its gender-differential impacts and to translate gender commitments into budgetary commitments. Thus Gender Budgeting:

- Looks at Government budget from a gender perspective to assess how it addresses the needs of women in all sectors.
- It does not seek to create a separate budget but to provide affirmative action to address the specific needs of women.
- Gender responsive budgeting initiatives provides a way for assessing the impact of government revenue and expenditure on women.[4]

Gender Budgeting lends itself to strengthening administrative processes and actions to achieve the targets for improvements in the position of women. It not only entails a look at allocation of resources for women but goes beyond to cover tracking the utilization of allocated resources, impact analysis and beneficiary incidence analysis of public expenditure and policy from a gender perspective.

Hence gender budgeting is not an accounting exercise as commonly perceived and understood. It encompasses incorporating a gender perspective and sensitiveness at all levels and stages of the developmental planning, programs, scheme, processes and implementation. An important outcomes of the application of Gender Budgeting is that it paves the way for gender mainstreaming in the developmental process and in understanding how the needs of women can be addressed in not only "traditional" areas like agriculture, health, education but also in so called 'gender neutral' sectors like Power, Defence, Chemicals, Bio-technology, commerce, information technology, etc. where in the first instance, the gender implications do not seem apparent.

PROCESS OF GENDER BUDGETING

Gender Analysis

What is Gender Analysis?

Status of Women in Canada observes that 'Sex' identifies the biological differences between women and men. 'Gender' is the culturally specific set of characteristics that identifies the social behaviour of women and men and the relationship between them. Gender, therefore, refers not simply to women or men, but to the relationship between them, and the way it is socially constructed. Because it is a relational term, gender must include women and men. Like the concepts of class, race and ethnicity, gender is an analytical tool for undemanding social processes.

Gender analysis is a process that assesses the differential impact of proposed and/or existing policies, programmes and legislation on women and men. It makes it possible for policy to be undertaken with an appreciation of gender differences, of the nature of relationships between women and men and of their different social realities, life expectations and economics circumstances. It is a tool for understanding social processes and for responding with informed and equitable options.

It compares how and why women and men are affected by policy issues. Gender analysis challenges the assumption that everyone is affected by policies, programmes and legislation in the same way regardless of gender, a notion often referred to as 'gender-neutral policy'.

The place of gender analysis in policies and programmes that are intended to balance the pressures for economic growth with the needs of human development has been recognized, almost from the inception of the UN Human Development Reports. The development of specific indices such as the gender development index (GDI) and the gender empowerment measures (GEM) marks this recognition. It is well known that a high HDI ranking may not always be matched by a correspondingly high GDI ranking. However, low performance on gender indicators almost always goes hand in hand with poor human development indicators overall. Unequal gender relations, exacerbated by disparities to a lowering of the overall HDI, simply because women constitute almost half the population. Systemic gender biases mean that, where human development is poor, the burdens fall disproportionately on women.

'Empowerment' has emerged as a key concept in policy discussions on gender over the last decade and a half. The concept, in recent times, has become so elastic that it has lost the dimensions, which originally gave it strength and shape. Empowerment, conceptually, has certain key components: (i) it radically shifted from the old top-down 'welfare' approach of treating women as a disadvantaged group in need of handouts, towards a recognition of the structural roots of gender bias; (ii) it addressed the issue of power and powerlessness that goes with gender and other forms of inequality; (iii) most significant is the recognition that a change in power relations requires not only a change in control over external resources such as land and income but also a change in the person's sense of self-worth and confidence; (iv) it emphasized the importance of group processes and solidarity as a way of breaking the cycle of hopelessness and helplessness that unequal gender relations perpetuate.

Initiatives of the Ministry for Gender Budgeting

Setting up Gender Budgeting Cells (GBCs)

The Ministry has been continuously and actively pursuing with Ministries for setting up of Gender Budgeting (GB) cell. So far, 52 ministries/departments have set-up these cells. The role envisaged for these cells includes:

- Act as a nodal agency for all gender responsive budgeting initiatives.
- Pilot action on gender sensitive review of public expenditure and policies (expenditure/revenue/policies/legislation, etc.)
- Guide and undertake collection of gender disaggregated data for target group of beneficiaries covered under expenditure, revenue raising/policy/legislation.
- Guide Gender Budgeting initiatives within Departments as well as in field units responsible for implementing government programmes.
- Conduct gender-based impact analysis, beneficiary needs assessment and beneficiary incidence analysis to:
    - o Establish effectiveness of public expenditure.
    - o Identify scope for re-prioritization of public expenditure.
    - o Improve implementation, etc.
    - o Collate and promote best practices on participative budgeting for and implementation on schemes.

Apart from workshops, follow up discussions and one of the one interactions with several Ministries/departments were pursued to ensure that gender concerns are incorporated in all sectors. Several departments evinced interest and requested the Ministry to give detailed insight on Gender Budgeting for their officers and divisions.[5]

MWCD's Mission Statement "Budgeting for Gender Equity"

The approach of MWCD to Gender Budgeting

- In Gender Budgeting, "Gender" means women and her empowerment.
- It is not an accounting exercise.
- An ongoing process of keeping gender perspective in policy/programme formulation, implementation and review.
- To extend the process to all levels of governance—centre, state, district, town and village and also to Public Sector Units and Autonomous Bodies.
- Also extend it to Civil Society and Corporate Sector

Illustrative Lists of Responsibilities of MWCD

- 52 Ministries have set-up GBCs.
- Training of GBCs and Capacity Building through workshops and one-to-one Ministerial meetings.
- Regional workshops with state Governments.
- Workshops for Training Institutes to develop a core group of Trainers.

- Development of GB strategy framework and tools and their continuous upgradation.
- Formulation of Gender Budgeting Manual.
- Gender Impact Assessment (proposed).
- Network with National and International agencies.
- Dissemination of Best Practices.
- Constant Advocacy to set-up Gender Budget Cells (GBCs) in Ministries.
- Research and Surveys.

Gender Impact Assessment (GIA)

- Being proposed on the lines of Environment Impact Assessment.
- The objective of the GIA is to foresee the potential gender impact that would arise out of a proposed developmental project and address them in the planning and design stage. Post-project evaluation undertaken if required.
- Any development project above a certain cut-off investment will have to undertake GIA, before giving EFC/PIB.
- The GIA process will include screening; consideration of alternatives; data mechanisms; impact prediction, etc. Public hearing in some cases may even be necessary.
- GIA will assess socio-economic impacts on gender including demographic/ displacement impact; socio-economic status; access to resources, etc.
- GIA will comprise of a clearing Committee comprising of MWCD, relevant Ministry, sectoral and gender experts.

Components of Training for GB Cells

To serve as a focal points for coordinating gender budgeting initiatives within their Ministries/Departments through—

- Pilot action on gender sensitive review of their budgetary allocations.
- Guide their Ministries in review of policies and programme for gender content.
- Review whether the implementation mechanism is gender-friendly or sensitive.
- Have gender-based impact analysis, beneficiary needs assessment and incidence conducted.
- Ensure that the programme and implementing mechanism has in-built provision for gender disaggregated data collection and compilation.
- Identify gaps/constraints/shortcomings in existing programmes/budget heads which stand in the way of smooth flow of funds/benefits to women.
- Reprioritize budgetary allocation to address these gaps.[6]

Five Year Plan and Gender Budgeting

While taking note of the efforts initiated during the Ninth Plan towards ensuring a gender-just/gender sensitive budget, the Tenth Plan will continue the process of dissecting the Government budget to establish its gender-differential impact and to translate gender commitments into budgetary commitments. As the process of Gender Budgeting has its own limitations in terms of being a *post-facto* effort to dissect/analyse and thus offset any undesirable gender specific consequences of the previous budget, this cannot be an effective measure to ensure adequate flow of funds and benefits to ensure adequate flow of funds and benefits for women. Therefore, the Tenth Plan will initiate immediate action in trying up these two effective concepts of WCP and Gender Budgeting to play a complementary role to each other, and thus ensure both preventive and *post-facto* action in enabling women to receive their rightful share from all the women-related general development sectors. More than the quantum or percentage of outlays, what is more important for empowering women in ensuring that the funds from various developmental sectors are effectively converged, properly utilized and monitored. This can be done through a systematic process of identifying the existing gaps in services and facilities being provided and ensure reaching adequate resources to fill those gaps as these very gaps are standing as major obstacles in the process of empowering women. In this context, the Tenth Plan also takes note of the over riding priority given to the programmes of child development and the resultant intra-budgetary imbalances that exist today within the budget of the nodal Department of Women and Child Development and suggests to rectify the same through a much more balanced distribution of resources between 'Empowerment of Women' and 'Development of Children'—the two major responsibilities entrusted to it.[7]

Gender Budgeting and Gender Outcome assessment will be encouraged in all ministries/ departments at Central and State levels. Gender Budgeting helps assess the gender differential impact of the budget and takes forward the translation of gender commitments to budgetary allocations. During the Eleventh Plan efforts will continue to create Gender Budgeting cells in all ministries and departments. Data from these cells will be collated on a regular basis and made available in the public domain.

Gender outcome assessment of fund flows has been made a mandatory part of the outcome budget prepared by every ministry/department as part of their budget documents. In 2005-06, this exercise covered 10 departments and the total magnitude of the Gender Budget (that is, women specific allocations) was recorded at 4.8% of total Union Government expenditure. In 2006-07, 24 departments of the Union Government were included and the magnitude of the Gender Budget was 3.8% of total budget estimates. It was found that schemes, which do not have a 100% women's component, also found a mention as women specific schemes. The Eleventh Plan will therefore ensure that each ministry/department of both Centre and State should put in place a systematic and comprehensive monitoring and auditing mechanism for outcome assessment. In addition, the Ministry of WCD, Ministry of Finance, and Planning Commission will facilitate national level gender outcome assessments through spatial mapping of gender gaps and resource gaps. They will undertake gender audits of public expenditure, programmes, and policies, and ensure the collection of standardized, gender disaggregated data (including data disaggregated for SC/ST and minority women) at national, State, and district levels.

In the Eleventh Plan period, the existing system of gender-based planning will be extended to other ministries and departments and not confined only to those that have historically been perceived as 'women-related'. Ministries and departments, such as Education, Health and Family Welfare, Agriculture, Rural Development, Labour, Tribal Affairs, Social Justice, and Empowerment, which have the potential to exceed the 30% WCP requirement, will be encouraged to administer more women-related programmes. During the Eleventh Plan, efforts will be made to extend the concept of gender-based plan component to PRIs and to the 29 subjects transferred to them under the 73rd constitutional amendment. Recognizing that some women suffer greater deprivation and discrimination than others, the Eleventh Plan will refine the norms of WCP to prioritize the most vulnerable as beneficiaries, particularly SC, ST women, Muslim women, single women, differently able, and HIV-positive women, among others.

The Eleventh Plan period will seek to make all national policies and programmes gender sensitive right from their inception and formulation stages. The MoWCD is the nodal Ministry for Gender Budgeting and the coordination mechanism for gender budgeting will ensure that all policies including fiscal and monetary policies, agricultural policies, non-farm sector, information and technology policies, public policy on migration, health insurance schemes, disaster management policies, media policy, and the legal regime among others are relevant from a gender perspective and are thoroughly examined. It will ensure that all legislations before they are presented to Parliament for enactment are cleared by the Parliamentary Committee on Women's Empowerment.[8]

Experience of Government of Karnataka

The Government of Karnataka has taken up the theme of women's empowerment as one of the strategies to tackle the socio-economic poverty.

As a pioneer in gender budgeting of public expenditure, the state undertook resources for women in most sectors. Karnataka has achieved a high degree of progress in gender-related indicators on literacy, health, employment, etc. through introduction of several successful gender-related programmes (especially through the SHG movement).

Given the multitude of schemes and programmes for women, spread across various Departments and Ministries of the Government, one approach towards empowerment of women is seeking convergence of these interventions, mostly through SHGs or women cooperatives.

Government of Karnataka in the year 2007-08 has categorised budget allocations as A and B. Category A has 100 per cent budget allocations for women, whereas Category B has more than 30 per cent allocations.

Particulars 2007-08 BE (in crore)

	P	*NP*	*T*
Category A%	394.457.5	291.042.5	685.4100.0
Category B%	1869.361.2	1187.138.8	3056.4100.0

This budgetary allocation is monitored by Women and Child Development Department through a scheme called Karnataka Mahila Abhivrudhi Yojana. Under this scheme, Women and Child Development Department steers the implementation of 33 per cent reservation of funds in 25 departments of the Government. The gender specific benefit which can be given by each department is identified. Various departments which are implementing gender budgeting are agriculture, water shed, sericulture, industries and commerce, handloom, textiles, forest, youth services and sports, welfare of disabled and senior citizens, backward classes welfare, Social Welfare Department, Backward Classes Development Corporation, Minorities Development Corporation, Scheduled Tribes Welfare Development Corporation, animal husbandry, horticulture, etc.

Engendering Public Spending: Gender Budget and Audit

The main aim of gender budgets and gender audits is not a separate budget for women, but better analysis of the incidence of the expenditures and tax measures, as well as overall impact of a budget, improved targeting of public spending, and a clearer financial basis for counteracting any potential negative consequences of the budget. For the purposes of this discussion, we use the terms 'gender audit' and 'gender budget' interchangeably.

The first systematic audit of a government budget for its impact on girls and women was done in Australia in 1984. Since then, 'gender budget exercises', as they are called, have been undertaken in a number of countries, chief among them being South Africa, Fiji, St. Kitts and Nevis, Barbados, Sri Lanka, Canada, UK, Mozambique, Tanzania and Uganda. This growing acceptance of gender budgeting as a tool for engendering macroeconomics gained momentum after the Fourth World Conference on Women at Beijing in 1995, and after the Commonwealth Women's Affairs Ministerial meeting in New Delhi in 2000.

To be complete, gender budgets require good quality data. In practice, of course, a number of gender audits have yet to reach sophisticated levels of analysis, not having access to the data needed to incorporate many of the elements. Many existing audits include gender-aware policy appraisal and beneficiary assessment, but other elements require either a level of sensitisation of officials (for example, budget statements) or the kind of capacity for analysis (for example, tax incidence) that are not yet available in women's development departments or ministries. However, even just beneficiary incidence is a good place to begin, and a number of insights into the gender impact of development can be obtained through this process.

EVOLUTION OF GENDER AUDITS IN INDIA

The Ninth Five Year Plan (1997-2002) first proposed a Women's Component Plan under which both Central and state governments were asked to ensure that at least 30 per cent of funds and benefits were earmarked in all the women related sectors, and that a holistic approach to empowering women should be followed. After 2000, when a major conference on South Asia, was held, the National Institute of Public Finance and Policy (NIPFP) was commissioned to carry out research on a project on Gender Related Economic Policy Issues. Following this, a State Budgets Workshop was held in 2001, which led to gender audit projects in different states, but results have not yet been collated.

The NIPFP Report Classified Public Expenditure into Three Classes

1. Allocations under schemes and programmes specifically targeted to women and girls;
2. Pro-women allocations as part of the composite expenditure of schemes with a component for women, e.g. in social sector ministries like health, family welfare, education, rural development, etc. where women may benefit, both from targeted schemes and also from a share in the composite expenditure; and
3. Pro-women allocations in specific composite schemes in other ministries where there is typically no or very little women's component as such.

A look at most budgets will show that allocations under (1) above are a small fraction of the budget, while the relative size of (2) may vary, based on the priority given to the social sectors and to pro-women allocations within them. The bulk of public expenditure, however, is likely to fall under ministries/departments where there is not only little gender sensitivity, but which also include many public goods whose benefits cannot be specifically gender-attributed. In these latter ministries, one cannot assume that the impacts of expenditures will be gender neutral or provide equal benefits to women and men. Even seemingly neutral measures can be seen to have unequal benefits when viewed through a gender lens of differential use by women and men: for instance, road construction that leads to places where men rather than women work. Some measures may also actually be inimical to women: an example is expenditure on converting a street market where vendors (both women and men) hawk their wares, into a built set of stalls requiring leasing by small shop owners (mostly men because women often do not have access to the money needed to obtain a lease). Alternatively, by consuming the bulk of public expenditures, these sectors may crowd out other spending that more directly benefits women, e.g. the crowding out of social sector spending by other 'neutral' sectors.

Undertaking a Gender Budget Initiative

Undertaking a gender budget initiative can include some or all of the following:

- Gender-aware policy appraisal—Designed to analyse policies and programmes from a gender perspective, and identify the ways in which these policies and the resources allocated to them are likely to reduce or increase existing gender inequalities;
- Gender disaggregated beneficiary assessment—Implemented to evaluate the extent to which programmes or services are meeting the needs of actual or potential beneficiaries, as identified and expressed by themselves;
- Gender disaggregated public expenditure benefit incidence analysis—Used to evaluate the distribution of budget resources among women and men, girls and boys by estimating the unit costs of a certain service and calculating the extent to which this service is being used by each of the groups;
- Gender disaggregated analysis of the impact of the budget on time use—To establish a link between budget allocations, the services provided through them and the way in which different members within a household spend their time;
- Gender-aware medium-term economic policy framework—Designed to incorporate a gender perspective into the medium-term frameworks of policy development, planning and budgetary allocations, by disaggregating variables by gender. A gender aware budget statement refers to reports generated by government agencies on the implications of their expenditure on gender equity objectives;
- Disaggregated tax incidence analysis—Used to assess the differential impacts of taxation on women and men, as well as to evaluate the level of revenue raised in relation to the needs and demands for public expenditure.
- The state must start on the process of institutionalising a gender audit unit, either in WCD department or in the Planning Department. This would mean identification of objectives, developing a gender disaggregated database for analysis and putting monitoring mechanisms in place.
- KMAY should be independently evaluated to assess the extent to which women have benefited from this initiative.
- The current monitoring system focuses almost entirely on financial and physical numbers. This may have been necessary when KMAY was first put in place, but it is now time to start looking at the quality of outcomes.
- There is little evidence to suggest that KMAY seriously looks at indicators that reflect women's socio-economic status (e.g. work participation rate, MMR and IMR, female literacy, girls' enrolment and retention in schools, women in Panchayat institutions or the specific problems of women from the minorities or SC and ST women). As the nodal department for a gender responsive administration, WCD must periodically review women's status in all sectors and motivate departments to either step up their interventions or devise new programmes to address issues that have now surfaced.[9]

CRITICAL APPROACH

1. Limiting the budget to 30 percent for women development defeats the purpose of Gender Budgeting

Whatever is being done in the area of women, budgeting is more on paper than in reality. All the efforts of Government must be directed to empower women through Gender budgeting. For this, we should not provide 30 percent or more budget for women welfare but also ensure through performance audit the use of money actually. We have to find out ways and means to ensure more and more budgeting for women empowerment to ensure a bright future of the country. We should make use of development administration which is innovative and result-oriented to ensure the success of Gender budgeting.

2. Restricted Coverage

Thus, it is not adequate to restrict the gender budgeting exercise to a few sectors of the economy which are traditionally considered as women related. The analysis has to cover every rupee of public expenditure. It has to cover the way schemes are conceptualised and how women-friendly they are in implementation and targeting of beneficiaries. It has to embrace a gender sensitive analysis of monetary policies, covering impact of indicators like inflation, interest rates etc. and fiscal policies covering taxation, excise, etc. Thus gender budgeting analysis has to go hand-in-hand with gender main streaming for meaningful empowerment of women. A direct spin off of this would be immediate expansion in access of women to public resources and would help strengthen their economic identity.

3. Gender budgeting must also depict the role of women in productivity and development and not only beneficiary journal

While planning for women's empowerment, the outlook has been one of looking at women as a beneficiary segment rather than as equal participants in the development process. As a consequence, the gender budgeting exercise has mostly focused on provision of resources and programmes for women in the social sector. Sectors like education, health, nutrition, employment, etc. are no doubt critical in the empowering paradigm, but it is necessary that we look beyond. Women must be recognised as equal players in the economy whether they participate directly as workers or indirectly as members of the care economy. It has to be accepted that every policy of the Government—fiscal, monetary or trade, has an impact on the well-being of women and that in many cases there would be a gender differential in the impact.[10]

4. Outcome are very less as compared to allocation

Further, the ministry says—"The challenge of gender budgeting lies in translating stated policy commitments in to budgeting allocations and outcomes. The commitment towards women are reflected in our constitution, policies, legislation and five year plan documents. Gender budgeting lends itself to realizing the goals outlines therein." Gender budgeting is a dissection of the government budget to establish its gender differential impacts and to translate gender commitments in to budgetary commitments. In other words gender budgeting looks at the government budget from a gender perspective to assess how it addresses the needs of women in the core areas like health, education and employment, etc. It does not seek to create as separate budget but seeks affirmative action to address specific needs of women. Such type of responsive budgeting initiatives provides a way of assessing the impact of government revenue and expenditure on women. Every government shows his commitment and strategy towards socio-economic development.[11]

5. Need of correlating gender commitments into budgetary commitments

The Tenth Plan will continue the process of dissecting the government budget to establish its gender differential impact and to translate gender differential impact and to translate gender commitments into budgetary commitments .... The Tenth Plan will initiate immediate action in tying up these two effective concepts of women components plan and gender budgeting to play a complementary role to each other, and thus ensure both preventive and *post-facto* action in enabling women to receive their rightful share from all the women related gender development sectors."[12]

6. Need of Participative Budgeting

Involvement of women in decision-making is seen as a key to success of all gender budgeting initiatives. Women have to be treated as equal partners in decision-making and implementation rather than as beneficiaries. Thus Gender Budgeting advocates capacity-building of elected women representatives, women self-help groups, etc. and their active involvement in decision-making and budgeting at the field level.[13]

7. Creation of Gender Budget Bureau

At present the Ministry has no dedicated staff for Gender Budgeting. A Scheme for Gender Budgeting has been included in 11th Plan with an Outlay of Rs. 3 crore in the Annual Plan 2007-08. The Scheme comprises of two components: (1) A staff component for handling Gender Budgeting work, and (2) Training, workshops, Research and Surveys. The SFC for the Scheme is under consideration.[14]

8. Spatial mapping

Macro-level planning for micro level needs (See Chart 37.2) Women empowerment is a holistic concept which entails adequate resource allocation in all areas including health, education, water sanitation and nutrition, sustained employment, access to credit and asset ownership, skills, research and design technology and political participation. Further, regional imbalances have to be corrected. For this, it is necessary to focus on specific needs of women residing in villages and towns. Spatial mapping of social infrastructure and access to employment opportunities for women, would clearly highlight resources available, overall gaps, resource allocation required based on size of population and yardsticks for availability of facilities, etc. so that universalisation of basic socio-economic infrastructure is achieved progressively, and allocations and interventions are more focused. These spatial maps would then form the basis for concomitant regional plans and projection on funds for gender requirements, with maximum local participation. This would also enable taking into account regional imbalances within States and districts. The importance of Gender Budgeting (GB) has been emphasized in the Indian Budgets. The Finance Minister, Government of India in his budget speech of 2004-05 perceived the need for budget data to be presented in a manner that brought out the gender sensitiveness of the budgetary allocations and had mandated the setting up of Gender Budgeting Cells (GBC) in all Ministries/Departments for this purpose. In the Budget Speech of 2007-08 it was recognized that there is growing awareness of gender sensitivities of budgetary allocations. A Gender Budget Charter delineating the responsibilities of GBCs has also been circulated by the Ministry of Finance.[15]

CHART 37.2

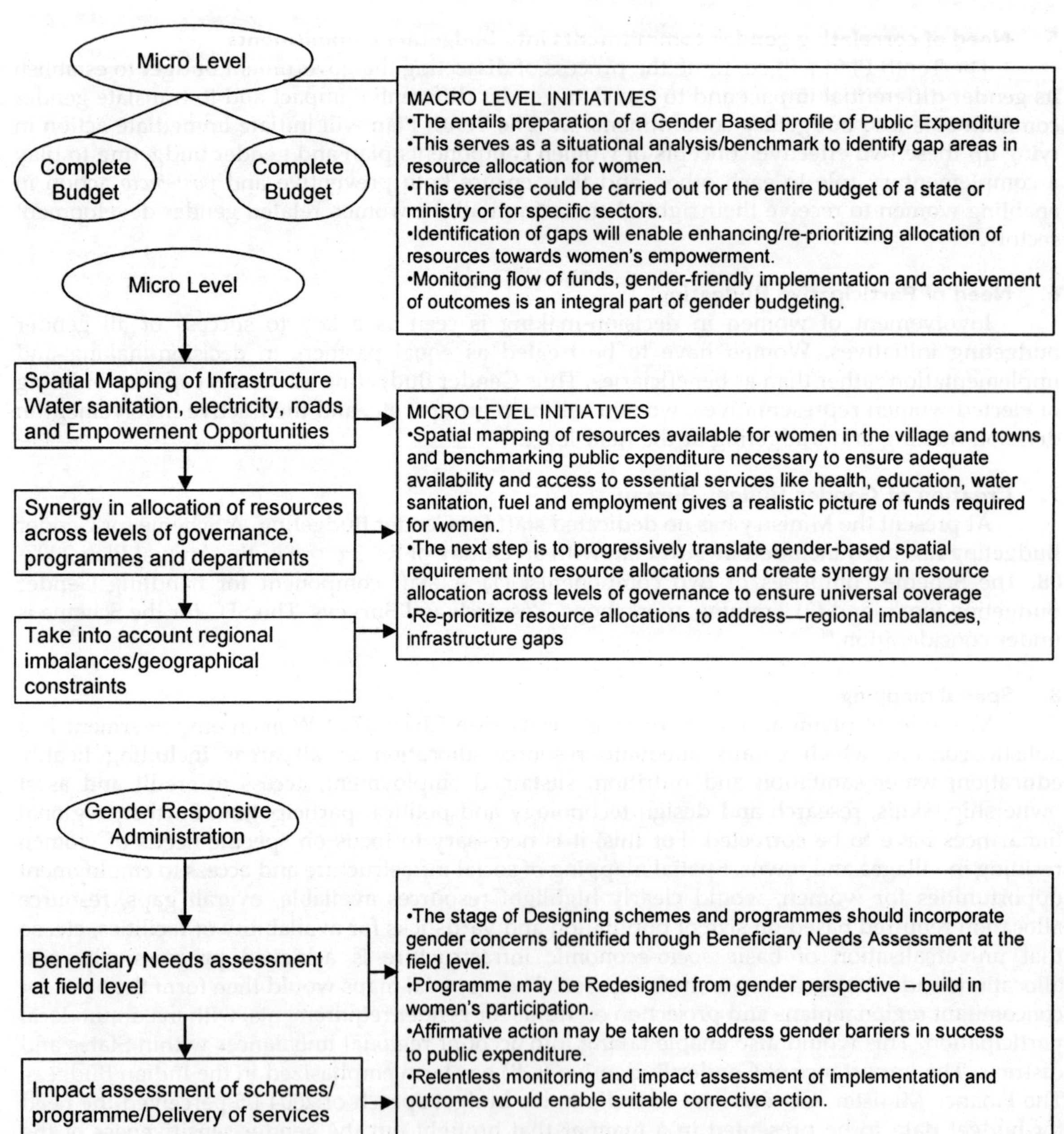

Source: Annual Report, 2007-08, Ministry of Women and Child Development, p. 113.

9. Impact Analysis through monitoring, evaluation and field level surveys

Establishing actual impact of public expenditure and policies from gender perspective, through monitoring, evaluation and field level surveys. This would include tracking flow of intended benefits. Results of impact analysis of programmes from a gender perspective help identify barriers in access to public services/expenditure by women, enable gender sensitive review of policy and programme design, change in quantum of allocation and implementation guidelines, etc.[16]

CONCLUSION

The Operational strategy, directs all the Central Ministries and State Departments to draw up Time-Bound Action Plans for Women for translating the Policy into a set of concrete actions through a participatory processes of consultations with all the concerned, both in the governmental and non-governmental sectors. Accordingly, the first step in this direction is to prepare a 'National Plan of Action' for implementation of the Policy by the nodal events of Women and Child Development through identifying its partners; specifying Action Points in all the women-related to development sectors; developing an in-built mechanism for effective coordinates and monitoring of the implementation of the Policy; besides evaluating/assessing the impact of the implementation of Policy in improving the status of women, based on a Gender Development Index.

The Plans of Action thus prepared need to clearly specify: (i) the measurable goals to be achieved alongwith the time targets, preferably in consonance with the time frames set by the other women-related national policies; (ii) commitment of resources; (iii) earmarking of the benefits under Women Component Plan (WCP); (iv) fixing of responsibilities for implementation of the Action Points; and (v) identification of structures and mechanisms to ensure effective review, monitoring, and impact assessment of all the related policies, Plans of Action and programmes in raising, the status of women, adolescent girls and girl children at par with their counterparts.

Another major strategy that has been identified is the strengthening of the institutional mechanism and capacity building for mainstreaming of the gender perspective in all policies and programmes. The 'National Policy' on Empowerment of Women, which was drafted after wide ranging consultations, is an important step in this direction. The Policy outlines the legal, institutional, and programmatic response of the State to the problems of gender discrimination.

NOTES AND REFERENCES

1. Address by Honorable Minister of Women and Child Development for the 2nd East Asia Gender Equality, Ministerial Meeting, *Social Welfare*, January 2008.
2. S.K. Kataria, Gender Budgetary: Need of the Hour, *Social Welfare*, July 2007, p. 10.
3. *Ibid.*
4. Annual Reports, 2007-08, Ministry of Women and Child Development, pp. 103-06
5. *Ibid.*, pp. 114-16.
6. Snap shots, Ministry of Women and Child Development, *Social Welfare*, November 2007, pp. 34-35.
7. GOI, Planning Commission, Xth Plan, pp. 252-53.
8. GOI, Planning Commission, Eleventh Five Year Plan, 2007-2012, Vol. II, pp. 200-01.
9. Karnataka Human Development Report, 2005, pp. 66, 68, 72.
10. Shalini Rajneesh, "Gender Budgeting to Gender Mainstreaming", *IJPA*, Oct.-Dec.. 2008, p. 907.

11. S.K. Kataria, Gender Budgeting: Need of the Hour, *Social Welfare*, July 2007, p. 10.
12. Dr. S.K. Kataria, "Gender Budgeting: Need of the Hour", *Social Welfare*, July 2007, pp. 10-11.
13. Annual Report, 2007-08, Ministry of Women and Child Development, p. 112.
14. *Ibid.*, p. 121.
15. *Ibid.*, pp. 112-14.
16. *Ibid.*, p. 112.

Appendix 37.1

Charter of Gender Budget Cells

Composition of Gender Budget Cells

The Gender Budget Cell should comprise a cohesive group of senior/middle level officers from the Plan, Policy, Coordination, Budget and Accounts Division of the Ministry concerned. This group should be headed by an officer not below the rank of Joint Secretary. The functions and working of the GRB may be reviewed at least once a quarter at the level of Secretary/ Additional Secretary of the Department.

Functions of Gender Budget Cells

The GBC may set for itself, specific quarterly/half yearly/annual targets to be achieved in terms of the following suggested areas of work.

(1) Identification of a minimum of 3 and maximum of 6 largest programmes (in terms of budget allocation) implementation by the Ministry and the major Sub-Programmes there under, with a view to conducting an analysis of the gender issues addressed by them.

- This is to be facilitated by describing the current situation with respect to the Sub-Programme (using disaggregated data in terms of beneficiaries as much as possible) and describing the activities for achieving the given output.
- Output indicators may be identified for measurement against performance in the coming year.
- Activities targeted at improving the situation of women under these programmes may be highlighted. In this regard, an assessment may be made of the extent to which sectoral policies address the situation of women, whether budget allocation are adequate to implement the gender responsive policy; monitoring whether the money was actually spent as planned, what was delivered and to whom; and whether the policy as implemented changed the situation described, in the direction of promoting/ achieving greater gender equality.
- Results of this analysis may be included as an annex titled "Gender Responsive Budgeting Initiative" in the Ministry's Outcome/Performance Budget for the year.
- GBCs of such Ministries/Departments which have identified programmes where 100% of the budgetary allocation for the scheme is earmarked to benefit women, may undertake a similar analysis as described above. Results of this analysis may also be included in the Ministry's Department's Outcome/Performance budget for the year.

(2) Conducting/Commissioning Performance audit (at the field level wherever possible) for reviewing the actual physical/financial targets of the programme, the constraints if any, in implementation, the need for strengthening delivery systems, infrastructure/ capacity building, etc.

(3) Organizing meetings/discussions. Consultations with GBCs of related departments within the Ministry, field level organization/civil society groups/NGOs working in the sector for exchanging ideas and getting feedback on the efficacy of sectoral policies and programmes.

(4) Suggesting further policy interventions based on findings of the above.

(5) Participating in an organizing Training/Sensitization/Capacity Building workshops for officials, concerned with formulation of policy/programme implementation & budget and accounts at the Ministerial level and also in the implementing agencies/ attached/subordinate offices and organizations under the administrative control of the Ministry.

(6) Apparently "gender neutral" programmes are not necessarily gender neutral in the impact they have, when seen through gender lens. Hence, in sectors like Defence, Power, Telecom, Communications, Transport and Industry, etc. GBCs may undertake an exercise to identify the possibility of undertaking initiatives/special measures to facilitate/improve access to services for women and their active participation in the decision-making process at various levels.

(7) Disseminate best practices followed by those Divisions of the Department/Ministry implementing schemes, which have done good work in analyzing the schemes/ programmes from gender perspective which have brought about changes in policy/ operational guidelines.

(8) Prepare a Chapter on Gender perspective related to the Sector/Service covered by the Ministry and the impact of the existing policies/programmes and resources employed in meeting the specific needs of women for reflection in the Ministry's Outcome/ Performance Budget.

Source: Annual Report 2007-08, Ministry of Women and Child Development, p. 107.

APPENDIX 37.2

Mission Statement—"Budgeting for Gender Equity"

Broad Framework of Activities

- Quantification of allocation of resources for women in the Union, States and Local Administration budgets and expenditure thereof.
  - # Refining and standardizing methodology and development of tools.
  - # Trend analysis of change in pattern, shift in priorities in allocation across clusters of services, etc.
  - # Variations in allocation of resources and actual expenditure.
  - # Adherence to physical targets.
  - Gender Audit of policies of the Government—monetary, fiscal, trade, etc. at the Centre and State level,
  - # Research and micro studies to guide macro-policies like credit policy, taxes, etc., Identification of gender impact of policies/interventions viewed as gender neutral.
  - # Micro-studies to identify need for affirmative action in favour of women towards correcting gender imbalances.
- Impact assessment of various schemes in the Union and State budgets.
- Micro-studies on incidence of benefits.
- Analysis of cost of delivery of services Analyzing programme, strategies, interventions and policy initiatives from the perspective of their impact on status of women as reflected in important Macro-Indicators like literacy, MMR, participation in work force.
  - # E.g.—analysis of substance and content of various interventions directed at health of women and correlate the same with indicator like MMR to establish need for corrective action in formulation of scheme/approach.
- Institutionalizing the generation and collection of gender dis-aggregated data.
  - # Developing MIS for feed-back from implementing agencies.
  - # Inclusion of new parameters in data collection in Census and surveys by NSO, CSO, etc., Consultation and Capacity building.
  - # Collation of research and exchange of best practices.
  - # Developing methodologies and tools for dissemination.
  - # Forums and Partnerships amongst experts and stakeholders.
- Reviewing of decision-making processes to establish gender equity in participation—review of extent participation of women in decision-making processes and to establish processes and models aimed at gender equity in decision-making and greater participation of women.
- Formulation and reflection of satellite accounts to capture the contribution of women to the economy by way of their activities in areas that go unreported like care economy, unpaid work in rearing domestic animals, etc.

Source: Ibid., p. 108.

Appendix 37.3

Checklist I for Gender Specific Expenditure

Conventionally, gender budget analysis, by way of isolation of women related expenditure, has been carried out for Ministries/Departments like Health and Family Welfare, Rural Development, Human Resource Development, Urban Employment and Poverty Alleviation, Youth and Sports Affairs, Labour, Social Justice and Empowerment, Tribal Affairs, Drinking Water, Small Scale Industries and Agro and Rural Industries, Science and Technology, Non-Conventional Energy Sources, Textiles and Agriculture.

Suggested steps that may be undertaken by these various Ministries/Departments who are running programmes/schemes of a gender specific nature, i.e. where the targeted beneficiaries are primarily women are as follows:

Planning and Budgeting

i. List of schemes and programmes which are gender specific.
ii. Briefly indicating activities undertaken under the programme for women.
iii. Indicating expected output indicator like number of women beneficiaries, increase in employment of women, post project increase in resources/income/skills, etc.
iv. Quantifying allocation of resources in annual budget and physical targets thereof.
v. Assessing adequacy of resources allocation in terms of population of targeted beneficiaries that need the concerned schematic intervention, the trend of past expenditure, etc.

Performance Audit

vi. Reviewing actual performance—physical and financial *vis-a-vis* the annual targets and identifying constraints in achieving targets (like need for strengthening delivery infrastructure, etc.
vii. Carrying out reality check—Evaluation of programme intervention, incidence of benefit, identifying impact indicators like comparative status of women before and after the programme, etc.
viii. Compiling a trend analysis of expenditure and output indicators and impact indicators.

Future Planning and Corrective Action

ix. Addressing constraints identified from step (vi) above.
x. Establishing requirement of Resources in terms of population of targeted beneficiaries/magnitude of perceived problems like IR, MMR, literacy ratio, etc.
xi. Reviewing adequacy of resources available-financial and physical like trained manpower, etc.
xii. Planning for modification in policies and/or programmes/schemes based on results of review.

Source: *Ibid*., p. 110.

APPENDIX 37.4

Checklist II for Mainstream Sectors

Mainstream sectors like Defence, Power, Telecom, Communication, Transport, Industry, Commerce, etc. may consider adopting the following checklist to determine the gender impact of their expenditure.

i. List of all programmes entailing public expenditure with a brief description of activities entailed.
ii. Identifying target group of beneficiaries/users.
iii. Establishing whether users/beneficiaries are being categorized by sex (male/female) at present and, if not so, what extent would it be feasible.
iv. Identify possibility of undertaking special measures to facilitate access of services for women—either through affirmative action like quotas, priority lists, etc. or through expansion of services that women specific like all women police stations, women's special buses, etc.
v. Analysing the empoloyment pattern in rendering of these services/programmes from the gender perspective and examining avenues to enhance women's recruitment.
vi. Focus on special initiatives to promote participation of women either in employment force or as users.
vii. Indicating within the sector and in the organizations and initiating action to correct gender biases and imbalances.

These exercises can be commenced by each Ministry/Department of the Government, to start with, for a few select programmes/schemes which may be selected either in terms of their perceived gender impact, or the selection can be based on considerations of heaviest budget allocation. Based on the result of carrying out the above steps, the gender budgeting exercise may be institutionalized in the manner detailed in checklist I.

Source: Ibid., p. 111.

CHAPTER

38

Method Study and Work Measurement

Development Administration in order to be successful must develop a scientific method study and Work Measurement techniques to run the development programme systematically, successfully and efficiently.

A large number of chief executives desire that the organizations they are heading should be models of efficiency, accountability, imaginative innovativeness and transparency, evoking confidence amongst all those who have to deal with them. However, many of them becomes inefficient because of their structural inadequacies, obsolescence and unresponsiveness to opportunities and challenges. Experience has indicated that even in normal times, the very best organizations require a reappraisal from time to time in terms of their methods, procedures and practices to keep the organisation in perfect equilibrium.

MEANING

Method study is one of the techniques of work study to improve on 'How' of doing work. It is a technique to improve method of work, with a view to increase efficiency and effectiveness of resources—men, money and material. In common parlance, 'Method' stands for the means of accomplishing an end while study means application of mind to a problem or an exercise. Method study, then traces the cases responsible for poor administrative performances so that appropriate remedial action may be taken. In broad terms, it may be said that the Method Study approach can help in successfully grappling with a view to find solutions to all problems which face the working of an organization. In sum, we can say that the Method Study is like an autopsy interested in eliminating the disease rather than the symptoms of ailment which is the purpose of Development Administration.

CHART 38.I

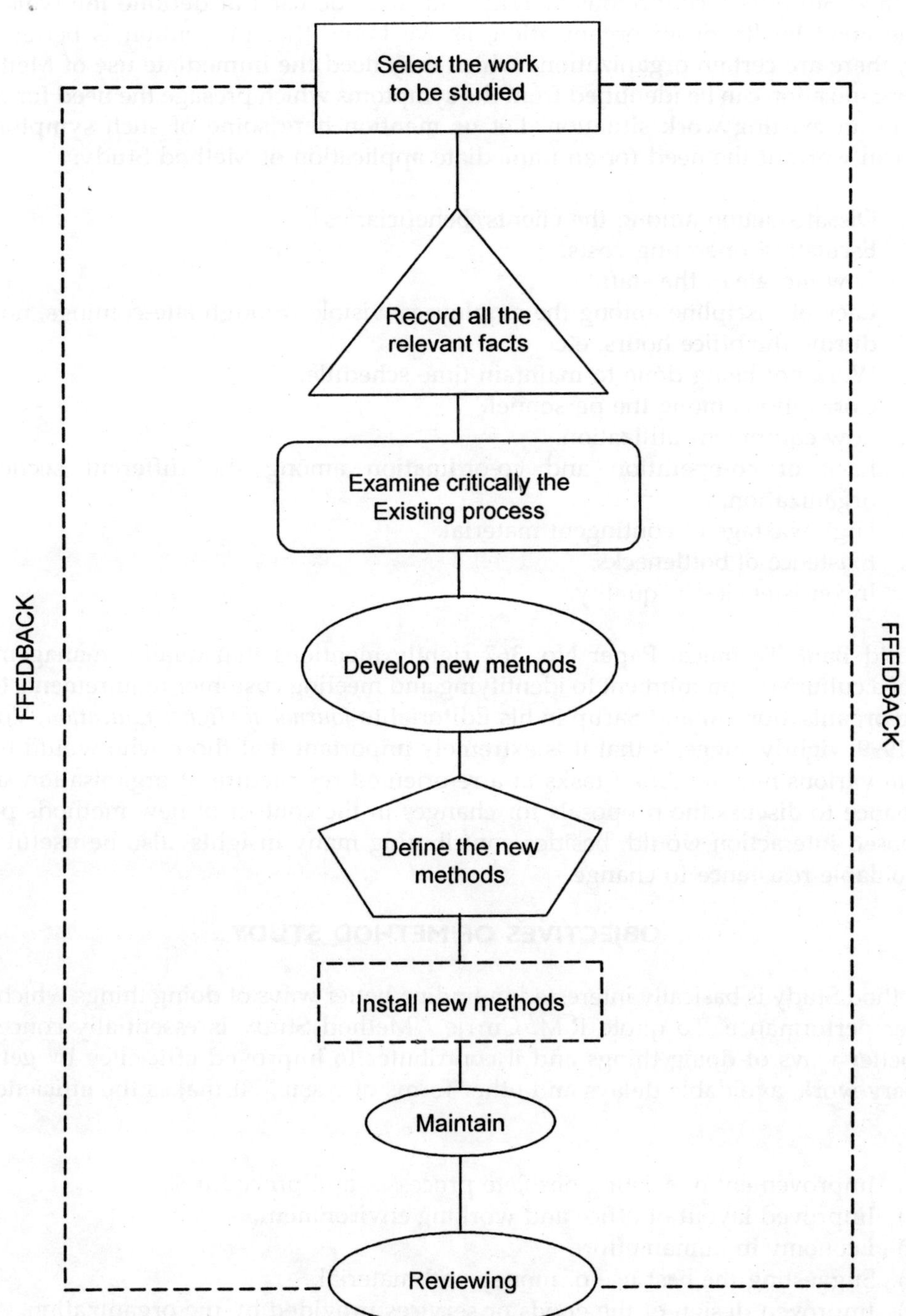
Select the work to be studied
Record all the relevant facts
Examine critically the Existing process
Develop new methods
Define the new methods
Install new methods
Maintain
Reviewing
FFEDBACK
FFEDBACK

NEED OF METHOD STUDY

Method Study is a continuous activity and must be used at definite intervals of time to ensure the good health of an organization, as we know that prevention is better than cure. However, there are certain organizations which may need the immediate use of Method Study. The sick organization can be identified from the symptoms which presage the need for the method of study in an existing work situation. Let us mention here some of such symptoms, whose presence can warrant the need for an immediate application of Method Study:

1. Dissatisfaction among the clients/beneficiaries.
2. Escalating operating costs.
3. Low morale of the staff.
4. Lack of discipline among the employees, visible through late-comings, not available during the office hours, etc.
5. Work not being done to maintain time schedule.
6. Corruption among the personnel.
7. Low equipment utilization.
8. Lack of co-operation and co-ordination among the different sections of an organization.
9. High wastage of contingent material.
10. Existence of bottlenecks.
11. Inconsistencies in quality.

World Bank Technical Paper No. 367 rightly mentions that quality management is the creation of a culture of commitment to identifying and meeting customer requirements throughout the whole organisation. Anand Sarup in his Editorial to *Journal of Higher Education*, Vol. 22, No.1 (Spring, 1999) rightly suggests that it is extremely important that those who would be required to perform various new modified tasks in a re-oriented restructure of organisation should also have a chance to discuss the proposals for changes in the context of new methods procedures. The proposed interaction would, besides contributing many insights, also be useful for toning down avoidable resistance to change.

OBJECTIVES OF METHOD STUDY

Method Study is basically interested in finding better ways of doing things which can result in a better performance. To quote R.M. Currie, "Method Study is essentially concerned with finding better ways of doing things and it contributes to improved efficiency by getting rid of unnecessary work, avoidable delays and other forms of waste." It makes the efficiency possible through:

(a) Improvement of existing obsolete processes and procedures.
(b) Improved layout of office and working environment.
(c) Economy in human effort.
(d) Suggesting the best use of money and material.
(e) Improved design of the goods or services provided by the organization.
(f) Improved quality. Quality is contagious.

(g) Job satisfaction.
(h) Improved flow of work.
(i) Standardisation of processes and products.

In brief the Method Study aims at optimization of resources which are:

Manpower

Brain, skill, morale and effort. Materials: Inventory, Quality, Standards. Equipment: Design and Operation.

Services

Communication and Information systems. Space and Building: Availability, design, utilisation.

ESSENTIALS OF METHOD STUDY

We must always keep in mind that Method Study is only an aid to better methods. Its success pre-supposes a number of essential elements. Let us mention some of them:

(a) An urge and desire on the part of the personnel in the organization and the Method Study Team to find better methods.
(b) Requisite skill, attitudes and ability in the persons engaged in Method Study.
(c) Proper rapport between the Method Study team and the key personnel in the organization.
(d) Involvement of the personnel of the organization being studied to get a lot of unwritten information and for understanding the dynamics of the organization.
(e) Need of suggesting the introduction of only such methods which can be implemented by the organization without much cost and resistance. Besides, the need of technical considerations may also be kept in mind.
(f) Making all the employees in the organization to understand the implications of new methods through seminars, lectures or any other method to thwart the potential fears amongst the employees of the proposed changes.

Joseph Prokopenko in his Article, "Management Approaches to Productivity Improvement" in *Management in Government*, April-June, 1995 suggests the following essentials based upon experiences in developed and developing countries.

Highly successful productivity programmes have been carried out at national, regional and local levels in many countries (i.e., Singapore, Japan, Hong Kong, Philippines, South Korea, some European countries, United States and Canada). Experience suggests that productivity promotion in public services at the micro-level typically follows certain directions. For example:

- changes in managerial styles and practices;
- awareness raising, management training and development;
- action-oriented productivity improvement;
- group activity and participation of various types;
- introduction of productivity incentive schemes; and

- development and strengthening of productivity improvement institutions, including international networking activities.

PROCEDURE OF METHOD STUDY (See Chart 38.1)

A Method Study investigation involves generally all the steps of a scientific method. There are seven essential steps in the application of a Method Study. Strict adherence to other sequence, as well as to their content, is essential for the success of an investigation. They are shown as below:

SELECT	: The work to be studied.
RECORD	: All the relevant facts about the present method by direct observation.
EXAMINE	: Those facts critically and in ordered sequence, using the techniques best suited to the purpose.
DEVELOPMENT	: The most practical, economic and effective method, having due regard to all contingent circumstances.
DEFINE	: The new method so that it can always be identified.
INSTALL	: That methods as standard practice.
MAINTAIN	: That standards practice by regular routine checks.
REVIEWING	: Locate discrepancies between the authorized procedures and current practice.

CONCLUSION

We may conclude as follows:

Karnataka Administrative Reforms Commission in its interim Report has suggested the need of improving systems and work methods.

The primary aim of improving systems and work methods should be to create a new work culture and introduce openness, transparency and accountability into the system. All work must be purposeful and must aim to provide the public greater satisfaction. In addition, improved systems and work methods would also enhance productivity of the civil service.

Therefore, it is suggested that:

- The paper work in government offices should be reduced by abolishing all unnecessary reports and returns, reducing number of circulars and with the increased use of computers.
- The existing system of file movement needs to be thoroughly revamped. Gradually files may have to be replaced by floppies. Until such time, file movement can be done on computers.
- The introduction of desk officer system, must be done at the earliest. This would be the first and the most important step to improving systems and work methods in the secretariat.
- All field offices should also follow a similar pattern and reduce file movements to only three or maximum of four levels.
- The number of meetings both at the secretariat and at the field-levels must be reduced.
- This would give more time to officers to go on tour and make inspection where necessary.

CHART 38.2

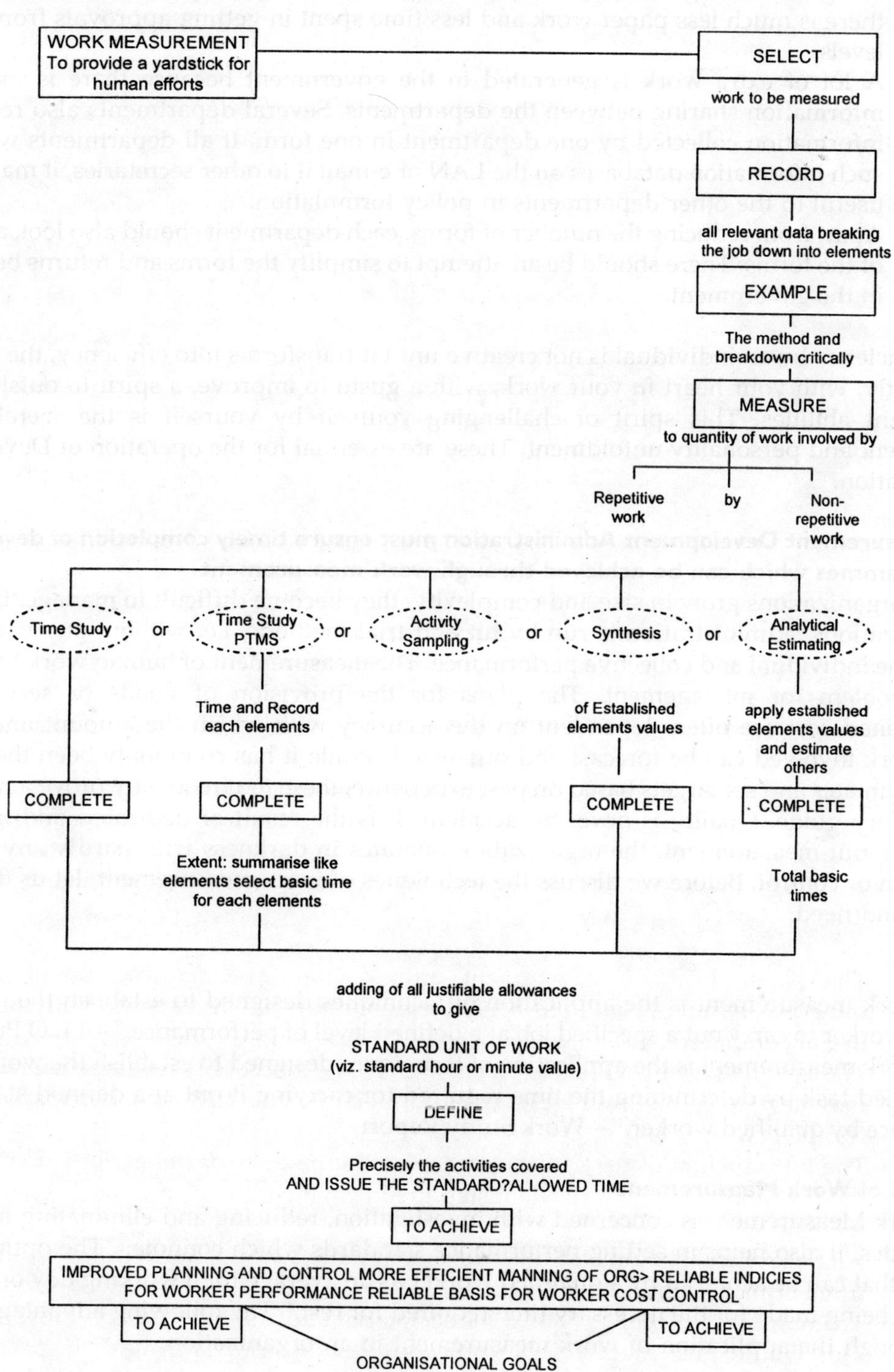
WORK MEASUREMENT
To provide a yardstick for human efforts
SELECT
work to be measured
RECORD
all relevant data breaking the job down into elements
EXAMPLE
The method and breakdown critically
MEASURE
to quantity of work involved by
Repetitive work
by
Non-repetitive work
Time Study
or
Time Study PTMS
or
Activity Sampling
or
Synthesis
or
Analytical Estimating
Time and Record each elements
of Established elements values
apply established elements values and estimate others
COMPLETE
COMPLETE
COMPLETE
COMPLETE
Extent: summarise like elements select basic time for each elements
Total basic times
adding of all justifiable allowances to give
STANDARD UNIT OF WORK
(viz. standard hour or minute value)
DEFINE
Precisely the activities covered
AND ISSUE THE STANDARD?ALLOWED TIME
TO ACHIEVE
IMPROVED PLANNING AND CONTROL MORE EFFICIENT MANNING OF ORG> RELIABLE INDICIES
FOR WORKER PERFORMANCE RELIABLE BASIS FOR WORKER COST CONTROL
TO ACHIEVE
TO ACHIEVE
ORGANISATIONAL GOALS

- The greater delegation of powers and exercise of delegated powers would ensure that there is much less paper work and less time spent in getting approvals from various levels.
- A lot of extra work is generated in the government because there is inadequate information sharing between the departments. Several departments also require the information collected by one department in one form. If all departments would put such information databases on the LAN or e-mail it to other secretaries, it may be very useful to the other departments in policy formulation.
- Apart from reducing the number of forms, each department should also look at the size of the forms. There should be an attempt to simplify the forms and returns being used in the government.

Proficiency by an individual is not creative until it transforms into efficiency, the means to act diligently, with your heart in your work, with a gusto to improve, a spirit to outshine your own present abilities. This spirit of challenging yourself by yourself is the secret of self-improvement and personality unfoldment. These are essential for the operation of Development Administration.

Work Measurement Development Administration must ensure timely completion of development programmes which can be achieved through work measurement

As organizations grow in size and complexity, they become difficult to manage. In most of the organizations, administration is run by hit and trial methods, i.e. without any yardstick to measure the individual and collective performance. The measurement of human work has always been a problem for management. The plans for the provision of goods or services at a predetermined cost are often dependent on the accuracy with which the amount and type of human work involved can be forecast and organized. While it has commonly been the practice to make estimates and set targets based on past experience, these too frequently prove a rough and unsatisfactory guide. Quality is never an accident. It is the result of dedicated and intelligent efforts. Without measurement, the organization operates in darkness with hardly any basis for comparison or control. Before we discuss the techniques of work measurement, let us discuss its meaning and need.

Meaning

"Work measurement is the application of techniques designed to establish the time for a qualified worker to carry out a specified job at a defined level of performance."—I.L.O Publication

"Work measurement is the application of techniques designed to establish the work content of a specified task by determining the time required for carrying it out at a defined standard of performance by qualified worker."—Work Study Report

Objectives of Work Measurement

Work Measurement is concerned with investigation, reducing and eliminating ineffective time. Besides, it also helps in setting performance standards which connote: "The optimum rate of output that can be achieved by a qualified worker as an average for a working day or shift due allowance being made for the necessary time required for rest." The following advantages would result through the application of work measurement in an organization:

1. Comparing Alternative Methods

There are generally many methods to perform a given job. Where two alternative methods seem equally good and suitable, the one which consumes less time for completion will be better. The techniques of Work Measurement offer the best means of making this choice.

2. Correct Manning of Work

Staffing is an important area of management. Work Measurement can help us in making the public offices staffed by persons in right quantity and quality. Most of the Committees and Commissions have reported that government offices are over-staffed to a great extent but they have not offered any method by which to assess and curtail the staff.

3. Perfect Planning and Estimation

Effective Planning and Scheduling of Operations require the exact estimation and availability of resources—men, money and material. All these can be made possible through the technique of Work Measurement as the information generated by this technique forms a reliable basis for planning and forward loading the men and material for the administrators to utilize them to their best advantage. The main cause of the failure of the planning in India has been the lack of any accurate measurement of work. Unless the work has been measured, it cannot be planned and scheduled with any assurance that a promised operation can be met.

4. Effective Means of Control

Once the operations have been planned, they are to be implemented. At the stage of implementation, management is interested to know how closely this is followed in practice. There is a need of control by the management to ensure the pre-designed output. Maintenance of proper records for all types of activities, plus a knowledge of the performance, which is maintained while work is being done, forms a reliable basis for control.

5. Helpful in Cost Estimation

Standards are helpful in determining the cost of the work performed. This is helpful to management in preparing budgets and in measuring the effectiveness of forecasts. By knowing what the cost should be and comparing them with budget figures, it is possible to ascertain the reasons for the difference. This may mean that there is a need for devising more efficient procedures and setting new standards to conform to them. Thus, standards help in reducing costs.

6. Better Staff Morale

It creates better morale among staff through their perception of what is expected of them in terms of quantity and quality. The efficient workers can be separated from the poor workers and thus the work of efficient workers can be recognized. This is also helpful in installing incentive wage system.

7. Measure of Efficiency

Standards serve as a basis for measuring the effectiveness of any organisation by indicating the achievement as compared with the standards.

8. Better Management

On the basis of the standards, managerial functions can be predicted and discharged more effectively.

9. Direction to Future Research

Standards give clue to the problem areas where research may be carried out to Solve the problem.

10. Improving Quality

Quality is magical. Quality passion has magical effect on our thinking patterns. We start seeking "Q" in every object.

Basic Procedure and Techniques (See Chart 38.2)

As enunciated earlier, there are fundamentally eight basic steps in performing a complete work study. Some of these are relevant for work measurement. Isolating those steps which are necessary for Work Measurement, the basic procedure could easily be formulated. Depending on the ultimate use for which the Work Measurement is to be put will determine as to whether all the eight steps are necessary. The essence of work measurement, would depend on selecting the requisite unit of measurement. A standard unit of measurement should be comparable, exact and stable. The measurement of all work done in an organization could be carried out through measuring by any of the three ways—measuring individual output, measuring groups routine work and groups on special work.

Basic Steps

Select	The work to be studied.
Record	All the relevant data relating to the circumstances in which the work is being done the methods and the elements of activity in them.
Measure	Each element in terms of TIME over a sufficient number of cycles of activity ensure that a representative picture has been obtained.
Examine	The recorded data and element times CRITICALLY to ensure that unproductive random elements are separated from productive elements; the recorded times each element and determine a representative time for each.
Compile	A time for the operation which will provide a realistic standard of performance and include time allowances to cover suitable rest, personal needs, contingencies, etc.
Define	Precisely the series of activities and method of operation for which the time has been allowed and issue the time as standard for the activities and methods specified

Scientific methods for Work Measurement

1. Time study
2. Pre-determined Motion Time Systems (PMTS)
3. Activity Sampling
4. Analytical Sampling
5. Synthesis

Development Administration can be a great success through the application of Method Study and Work Measurement as they keep the administrative system under constant review, analysis and perfection. Thus, methods study and work measurement are the important tools of Development Administration.

Bibliography

Ahmad, Shehzad, Social Justice., New Delhi: Anmol, 2007.

Ayres, R.L.: Banking on the Poor: The World Bank and World Poverty (London, MIT Press, 1983).

Berman, B.: "Structure and Process in the Bureaucratic States of Colonial Africa", *Development and Change*, Vol. 15, No.2, April 1984.

Braibanti, Ralph (ed.): Political and Administrative Development (Qurham, Duke University Press, 1969).

Brandt, W.: "North-South: A Programme for Survival", The Report of the Independent Commission on International Development Issues (London, Penguin, 1980).

Bryant, C. and White, L.G.: Managing Development in the Third World (Colorado, Westview, 1982).

Bryant, Coralie: "Development Administration: Where, should we go from here?", in Sharma, S.K. (ed.) Dynamics of Development: An International Perspective (Delhi, Concept, 1978), Vol. 2.

Caiden, Gerald E.: "International Consultants and Development Administration", *International Review of Administrative Sciences*, Vol. XLII, No. 1, 1976.

Chambers, R.: Putting the Last First (London, Longman, 1983).

Chaudhary, Sunil, Welfare Policy and Social Development, New Delhi: Global Vision, 2006.

Cheema, G.S. and Rondinelli, D.A.: Decentralization and Development: Policy Implementation in Developing Countries (Beverly Hills, Sage Publications, 1993).

Conyers, D.: "Decentralization and Development: A Review of the Literature", *Public Administration and Development*, Vol. 4. April-June 1984.

Conyers, D.: "Decentralization and Development: The Latest Fashion in Development Administration", *Public Administration and Development*, Vol. 3, April-June 1983.

Deaton, Angus, Guidelines for Constructing Consumption Aggregates for Welfare Analysis—Washington, D.C.: World Bank, 2002.

Dwivedi, O.P. and Nef, J.: "Crises and Continuities in Development Theory and Administration: First and Third World Perspectives", *Public Administration and Development*, Vol. 2, January-March 1982.

Eaman, M.J.: "Development Administration and Constituency Organisation", *Public Administration Review*, March-April 1978.

Fitzpatrick, Tony, Welfare Theory: An Introduction, New York: Palgrave, 2001.

Gant, G.F.: Development Administration: Concepts, Goals, Methods (Madison, University of Wisconsin Press, 1979).

Geoghegan, Luke, ICT for Social Welfare: A Toolkit for Managers, Bristol: Policy Press, 2004.

George, *Vic*, Globalization and Human Welfare, Houndmills: Palgrave, 2002.

Grindle, M.S. (ed.): Politics and Policy Implementation in the Third World (Princeton, Princeton University Press, 1980).

Honadle, G.: "Development Administration in the Eighties: New Agendas or Old Perspectives", *Public Administration Review*, March-April 1982.

Honadle, G. and Klauss, R.: International Development Administration: Implementation Analysis for Development Projects (New York, Praeger, 1979).

Hoogvelt, A.: The Third World in Global Development (New York, Macmillan, 1983).

Hope, K.R.: The Dynamics of Development and Development Administration (Westport, Greenwood Press, 1984).

Household risk management and social protection in Chile, Washington, D.C.: World Bank, 2005.

Hyden, G.: No Short Cuts to Progress: African Development Management in Perspective (Berkeley, University of California Press, 1983).

International Labour Organization: Meeting Basic Needs: Strategies for Eradicating Mass Poverty and Unemployment (Geneva, I.L.O. 1971).

International Social Policy: Welfare Regimes in the Developed World, New York: Palgrave, 2001. Kernaghan, Kenneth

Kannappan, P., Scheduled Caste Welfare, New Delhi: APH, 2008.

Karlson, Nils, The State of State: Invisible Hands in Politics and Civil Society, New Brunswick: Transaction, 2002

Karten, D.C. and Alphonso, F.B. (ed.): Bureaucracy and the Poor: Closing the Gap (West Hartford, Kumarian Press, 1981).

Kennett, Patricia, Comparative Social Policy: Theory and Research, Buckingham: Open Univ. Press, 2001.

Kernaghan, Kenneth, Rediscovering Public Service: Recognizing the Value of an Essential Institution, Toronto: Institute of Public Administration of Canada, 2001.

Korten, D.C. and Klauss, R. (ed.): People-Centred Development (West Hartford, Kumarian Press, 1983).

Kriesberg, M. (ed.): Public Administration in Developing Countries (Washington, The Brookings Institution, 1965).

Lewis, W.A.: Development Planning (London, Allen and Unwin, 1966).

Lund, Brian, Understanding State Welfare: Social Justice or Social exclusion?, London: Sage, 2002.

Montgomery, John and Siffin, William (eds.): Approaches to Development: Politics, Administration and Change (New York, McGraw-Hill, 1966).

Murray, D.J.: "The World Bank's Perspective on How to Improve Administration", *Public Administration and Development*, Vol. 3, October-December 1983.

Myrdal, G.: Asian Drama: An Inquiry into the Poverty of Nations (New York, Twentieth Century Fund, 1968).

Nef, J. and Dwivedi, O.P.: "Development Theory and Administration; A Fence Around an Empty Lot?", *Indian Journal of Public Administration*, Vol. 27, No. I, 1981.

New Social Policy Agendas for Europe and Asia: Challenges, Experience, and Lessons, Washington, D.C.: The World Bank, 2003.

Pai, Panandikar, V.A. (ed.): Development Administration in India (New Delhi, Macmillan, 1974).

Pearson, L.B.; Partners in Development (New York, Praeger, 1~69) .

Public Administration Review; "A Symposium; Comparative and Development Administration", November-December 1976.

Public Administration Review; "From the Professional Stream" (Articles on the Failure of Development Administration in Iran), September-October 1980.

Rashid, Mansoora, Household Welfare, the Labor Market, and Social Programs in Albania.—Washington, D.C.: World Bank, 2001.

Riggs, F. (ed.); Frontiers of Development Administration (Durham, Duke University Press, 1970).

Riggs, F.: Administration in Development Countries: The Theory of Prismatic Society (Boston, Houghton Miffin, 1964).

Rondinelli, D.A.: "Projects as Instruments of Development Administration: A Qualified Defence and Suggestions for Improvement", *Public Administration and Development*, Vol. 3, October-December 1983.

Rondinelli, D.A.: "The Dilemma of Development Administration: Complexity and Uncertainty in Control-oriented Bureaucracies", World Politics, Vol. 34, No.1, 1982.

Samanthakamani, Akkaraju, Durgabai Deshmukh—A Study in the Case of Freedom, Constitution Framing, Women and Social Welfare, Hyderabad: Andhra Mahila Sabha, 2002.

Sapru, R.K.: "American Approach to Development in Developing Countries Through the Mechanism of Public Administration", *Social Sciences Research Journal*, Vol. III, No.2, July 1978.

Sapru, R.K.: "Development Administration: An Approach to the Administrative Capability for Development", *Administrative Science Review*, Vol. IX, No. 3, September 1979.

Sapru, R.K.: "Nature, Needs and Strategy of Development in Developing Countries: A Review", *The Indian Journal of Economics*, Vol. LX, No. 238, January 1980.

Sapru, R.K.: "Organization Development: An Inticipated Issue", *Administrative Science Review*, Vol. XIII, No. 3, September 1983.

Sapru, R.K.: Public Administration for Development (Jalandhar, (International Book Co., 1983).

Sapru, R.K.; "Comparative Administration: Retrospect 'and Prospect", *Indian Journal of Political Science*, Vol 40, No. 3, September 1979.

Sapru, R.K.; "Development Administration: An Overview",

Sapru, R.K.; Civil Service Administration in India (New Delhi, Deep and Deep Publications, 1985)..

Sapru, R.K.; Development and Development Administration (Chandigarh, Mohindra, 1977).

Schaffer, B.B.: "Administrative Legacies and Links in the Post Colonial State: Preparation, Training and Administrative Reform", *Development and Change*, Vol. 9, No. 2, April 1978.

Schaffer, B.B.: "Deadlock in Development Administration", in Leys, C. (ed.), Politics and Change in Developing Countries (New York, Cambridge University Press, 1969).

Schaffer, B.B.: The Administrative Factor: Papers in Organisation, Politics and Development (London, Frank Cass, 1973).

Shielding the Poor: Social Protection in the Developing World, Washington, D.C.: Brookings Institution Press, 2001.

Singh, Dolly, Child Rights and Social Wrongs: An Analysis of Contemporary Realities, New Delhi: Kanishka, 2001.

Siwach, Raj Kumar, Voluntary Organisations and Social Welfare, Delhi: Shankar, 2004.

Streeten, P. *et. al.*: First Things First: Meeting Basic Need till Developing Countries (New York, Oxford University Press, 1982).

Swerdlow, I. (ed.): Development Administration: Concepts and Problems (Syracuse, N.Y., Syracuse University Press, 1963).

Swerdlow, I.: The Public Administration of Economic Development (New York, Praeger, 1975).

Targeting Social Benefits: International Perspectives and Trends, New Brunswick: Transaction, 2001.

The Changing Face of Welfare: Consequences and Outcomes from a Citizenship Perspective, Bristol: The Policy Press, 2005.

The Politics of Post-Industrial Welfare States: Adapting Post-war Social Policies to New Social Risks, London: Routledge, 2006.

United Nations: Development Administration: Current Approaches and Trends in Public Administration for National Development (New York, U.N. Publication, 1976).

Verma, S.P. and Sharma, S.K. (eds.): Development Administration (New Delhi, Indian Institute of Public Administration, 1984).

Waldo, Dwight (ed.): Temporal Dimensions of Development Administration (Durham, Duke University Press, 1970).

Weidner, Edward W.: Development Administration in Asia (Durham, Duke University Press, 1970).

Welfare, New Delhi: Viva Books, 2002.

Index